Excel® 2013

BIBLE

Excel® 2013 BIBLE

John Walkenbach

John Wiley & Sons, Inc.

Excel® 2013 Bible

Published by
John Wiley & Sons, Inc.
10475 Crosspoint Boulevard
Indianapolis, IN 46256
www.wiley.com

Published simultaneously in Canada

ISBN 978-1-118-49036-5 (pbk); ISBN 978-1-118-49030-3 (ebk); ISBN 978-1-118-49170-6 (ebk);
ISBN 978-1-118-49172-0 (ebk)

Manufactured in the United States of America

10 9 8 7 6 5

For general information on our other products and services or to obtain technical support, please contact our Customer Care Department within the U.S. at (877) 762-2974, outside the U.S. at (317) 572-3993 or fax (317) 572-4002.

Library of Congress Control Number: 2012956404

Wiley publishes in a variety of print and electronic formats and by print-on-demand. Some material included with standard print versions of this book may not be included in e-books or in print-on-demand. If this book refers to media such as a CD or DVD that is not included in the version you purchased, you may download this material at http://booksupport.wiley.com. For more information about Wiley products, visit www.wiley.com.

Credits

Sr. Acquisitions Editor
Katie Mohr

Project Editor
Elizabeth Kuball

Technical Editor
Niek Otten

Copy Editor
Elizabeth Kuball

Editorial Manager
Jodi Jensen

Editorial Director
Mary Corder

Vice President and Executive Group Publisher
Richard Swadley

Vice President and Publisher
Andy Cummings

Project Coordinator
Sheree Montgomery

Graphics and Production Specialists
Jennifer Creasey
Jennifer Mayberry

Quality Control Technicians
Jessica Kramer
Lauren Mandelbaum

Proofreading and Indexing
BIM Indexing & Proofreading Services

Vertical Websites Project Manager and Producer
Rich Graves

About the Author

John Walkenbach is a bestselling Excel author who has published more than 50 spreadsheet books. He lives amid the saguaros, javelinas, rattlesnakes, bobcats, and gila monsters in Southern Arizona — but the critters are mostly scared away by his clawhammer banjo playing. For more information, Google him.

Acknowledgments

Thanks again to everyone who bought the previous editions of this book. Your suggestions have helped make this edition the best one yet.

And a special thanks to two behind-the-scenes folks who helped considerably: Elizabeth Kuball (who made it more readable) and Niek Otten (who made it more accurate).

Contents

Introduction

Thank you for purchasing *Excel 2013 Bible.* If you're just starting with Excel, you'll be glad to know that Excel 2013 is the easiest version ever.

My goal in writing this book is to share with you some of what I know about Excel and, in the process, make you more efficient on the job. The book contains everything that you need to know to learn the basics of Excel and then move on to more advanced topics at your own pace. You'll find many useful examples and lots of tips and tricks that I've accumulated over the years.

Is This Book for You?

The *Bible* series from John Wiley & Sons, Inc., is designed for beginning, intermediate, and advanced users. This book covers all the essential components of Excel and provides clear and practical examples that you can adapt to your own needs.

In this book, I've tried to maintain a good balance between the basics that every Excel user needs to know and the more complex topics that will appeal to power users. I've used Excel for more than 20 years, and I realize that almost everyone still has something to learn (including myself). My goal is to make that learning an enjoyable process.

Software Versions

This book was written for Excel 2013 for Windows. Much of the information also applies to Excel 2007 and Excel 2010, but if you're using an older version of Excel, I suggest that you put down this book immediately and find a book that's appropriate for your version of Excel. The user interface changes introduced in Excel 2007 are so extensive that this book will be very confusing if you use an earlier version.

Also, please note that this book is not applicable to Excel for Mac.

Office 2013 is available in several versions, including a web version, and a version for tablets and phones. This book covers only the standard desktop version of Excel 2013.

Conventions Used in This Book

Take a minute to scan this section to learn some of the typographical and organizational conventions that this book uses.

Excel commands

Excel 2013 (like the two previous versions) features a "menu-less" user interface. In place of a menu system, Excel uses a context-sensitive Ribbon system. The words along the top (such as File, Insert, Page Layout, and so on) are known as *tabs*. Click a tab, and the Ribbon displays the commands for the selected tab. Each command has a name, which is (usually) displayed next to or below the icon. The commands are arranged in groups, and the group name appears at the bottom of the Ribbon.

The convention I use is to indicate the tab name, followed by the group name, followed by the command name. So, the command used to toggle word wrap within a cell is indicated as

Home ➪ Alignment ➪ Wrap Text

You'll learn more about the Ribbon user interface in Chapter 1.

Filenames, named ranges, and your input

Anything you're supposed to type using the keyboard appears in **bold**. Named ranges appear in a `monofont`. Lengthy input usually appears on a separate line. For example, I may instruct you to enter a formula such as the following:

```
="Part Name: " &VLOOKUP(PartNumber,PartList,2)
```

Key names

Names of the keys on your keyboard appear in normal type. When two keys should be pressed simultaneously, they're connected with a plus sign, like this: "Press Ctrl+C to copy the selected cells."

The four "arrow" keys are collectively known as the *navigation keys.*

Functions

Excel built-in worksheet functions appear in uppercase monofont, like this: "Note the `SUM` formula in cell C20."

Mouse conventions

You'll come across some of the following mouse-related terms, all standard fare:

- **Mouse pointer:** The small graphic figure that moves onscreen when you move your mouse. The mouse pointer is usually an arrow, but it changes shape when you move to certain areas of the screen or when you're performing certain actions.
- **Point:** Move the mouse so that the mouse pointer is on a specific item: for example, "Point to the Save button on the toolbar."
- **Click:** Press the left mouse button once and release it immediately.
- **Right-click:** Press the right mouse button once and release it immediately. The right mouse button is used in Excel to pop up shortcut menus that are appropriate for whatever is currently selected.
- **Double-click:** Press the left mouse button twice in rapid succession.
- **Drag:** Press the left mouse button and keep it pressed while you move the mouse. Dragging is often used to select a range of cells or to change the size of an object.

For Tablet Users

Excel 2013 is also available for mobile devices such as tablets and smartphones. If you happen to be using one of these devices, you probably already know the basic touch gestures.

This book doesn't cover specific touchscreen gestures, but these three guidelines should work most of the time:

- When you read "click," you should tap. Quickly touching and releasing your finger on a button is the same as clicking it with a mouse.
- When you read "double-click," tap twice. Touching twice in rapid succession is equivalent to double-clicking.
- When you read "right-click," press and hold your finger on the item until a menu appears. Tap an item on the pop-up menu to execute the command.

Make sure you enable Touch mode from the Quick Access toolbar. Touch mode increases the spacing between the Ribbon commands, making it less likely that you'll touch the wrong command. If the Touch mode command is not in your Quick Access toolbar, touch the rightmost control and select Touch Mode. This command toggles between normal mode and Touch mode.

How This Book Is Organized

Notice that the book is divided into six main parts, followed by three appendixes.

- **Part I: Getting Started with Excel:** This part consists of nine chapters that provide background about Excel. These chapters are considered required reading for Excel newcomers, but even experienced users will probably find some new information here.
- **Part II: Working with Formulas and Functions:** The chapters in Part II cover everything that you need to know to become proficient with performing calculations in Excel.
- **Part III: Creating Charts and Graphics:** The chapters in Part III describe how to create effective charts. In addition, you'll find chapters on the conditional formatting visualization features, Sparkline graphics, and a chapter with lots of tips on integrating graphics into your worksheet.
- **Part IV: Using Advanced Excel Features:** This part consists of eight chapters that deal with topics that are sometimes considered advanced. However, many beginning and intermediate users may find this information useful as well.
- **Part V: Analyzing Data with Excel:** Data analysis is the focus of the chapters in Part V. Users of all levels will find some of these chapters of interest.
- **Part VI: Programming Excel with VBA:** Part VI is for those who want to customize Excel for their own use or who are designing workbooks or add-ins that are to be used by others. It starts with an introduction to recording macros and VBA programming and then provides coverage of UserForms, add-ins, and events.
- **Part VII: Appendixes:** This book has two appendixes that cover Excel worksheet functions and Excel shortcut keys.

How to Use This Book

Although you're certainly free to do so, I didn't write this book with the intention that you would read it cover to cover. Instead, it's a reference book that you can consult when

- You're stuck while trying to do something.
- You need to do something that you've never done before.
- You have some time on your hands, and you're interested in learning something new about Excel.

The index is comprehensive, and each chapter typically focuses on a single broad topic. If you're just starting out with Excel, I recommend that you read the first few chapters to gain a basic understanding of the product and then do some experimenting on your own. After you become familiar with Excel's environment, you can refer to the chapters that interest you most. Some readers, however, may prefer to follow the chapters in order.

Don't be discouraged if some of the material is over your head. Most users get by just fine by using only a small subset of Excel's total capabilities. In fact, the 80/20 rule applies here: 80% of Excel users use only 20% of its features. However, using only 20% of Excel's features still gives you *lots* of power at your fingertips.

What's on the Website

This book contains many examples, and you can download the workbooks for those examples from the web. The files are arranged in directories that correspond to the chapters.

The URL is `www.wiley.com/go/excel2013bible`.

Part I

Getting Started with Excel

The chapters in this part are intended to provide essential background information for working with Excel. Here, you'll see how to make use of the basic features that are required for every Excel user. If you've used Excel (or even a different spreadsheet program) in the past, much of this information may seem like review. Even so, it's likely that you'll find quite a few tricks and techniques.

IN THIS PART

CHAPTER

1

Introducing Excel

IN THIS CHAPTER

Understanding what Excel is used for

Looking at what's new in Excel 2013

Learning the parts of an Excel window

Introducing the Ribbon, shortcut menus, dialog boxes, and task panes

Navigating Excel worksheets

Introducing Excel with a step-by-step hands-on session

This chapter is an introductory overview of Excel 2013. If you're already familiar with a previous version of Excel, reading (or at least skimming) this chapter is still a good idea.

Identifying What Excel Is Good For

Excel, as you probably know, is the world's most widely used spreadsheet software and part of the Microsoft Office suite. Other spreadsheet software is available, but Excel is by far the most popular and has been the world standard for many years.

Much of the appeal of Excel is due to the fact that it's so versatile. Excel's forte, of course, is performing numerical calculations, but Excel is also very useful for non-numeric applications. Here are just a few of the uses for Excel:

- **Number crunching:** Create budgets, tabulate expenses, analyze survey results, and perform just about any type of financial analysis you can think of.
- **Creating charts:** Create a wide variety of highly customizable charts.
- **Organizing lists:** Use the row-and-column layout to store lists efficiently.
- **Text manipulation:** Clean up and standardize text-based data.
- **Accessing other data:** Import data from a wide variety of sources.

- **Creating graphical dashboards:** Summarize a large amount of business information in a concise format.
- **Creating graphics and diagrams:** Use Shapes and SmartArt to create professional-looking diagrams.
- **Automating complex tasks:** Perform a tedious task with a single mouse click with Excel's macro capabilities.

Seeing What's New in Excel 2013

When a new version of Microsoft Office is released, sometimes Excel gets lots of new features and other times it gets very few new features. In the case of Office 2013, Excel got quite a few new features.

Here's a quick summary of what's new in Excel 2013, relative to Excel 2010:

- **Cloud storage:** Excel is tightly integrated with Microsoft's SkyDrive web-based storage.
- **Support for other devices:** Excel is available for other devices, including touch-sensitive devices such as Windows RT tablets and Windows phones.
- **New aesthetics:** Excel has a new "flat" look and displays an (optional) graphic in the title bar. The default color scheme is white, but you can choose from two other color schemes (light gray and dark gray) in the General tab of the Excel Options dialog box.
- **Single document interface:** Excel no longer supports the option to display multiple workbooks in a single window. Each workbook has its own top-level Excel window and Ribbon.
- **New types of assistance:** Excel provides recommended pivot tables and recommended charts.
- **Fill Flash:** Fill Flash is a new way to extract (by example) relevant data from text strings. You can also use this feature to combine data in multiple columns.
- **Support for Apps for Office:** You can download or purchase apps that can be embedded in a workbook file.
- **The Data Model:** Create pivot tables from multiple data tables, combined in a relational manner.
- **New Slicer option:** The Slicer feature, introduced in Excel 2010 for use with pivot tables, has been expanded and now works with tables.

- **Timeline filtering:** Similar to the Slicer, the Timeline makes it easy to filter data by dates.
- **Quick Analysis:** Quick Analysis provides single click access to various data analysis tools.
- **Enhanced chart formatting:** Modifying charts is significantly easier.
- **New worksheet functions:** Excel 2013 supports dozens of new worksheet functions.
- **Backstage:** The Backstage screen has been reorganized and is easier to use.
- **New add-ins:** Three new add-ins are included (for Office Professional Plus only): PowerPivot, Power View, and Inquire.

Understanding Workbooks and Worksheets

The work you do in Excel is performed in a workbook file. You can have as many workbooks open as you need, and each one appears in its own window. By default, Excel workbooks use an `.xlsx` file extension.

Note

In previous versions of Excel, users could work with multiple workbooks in a single window. That is no longer an option in Excel 2013. Every workbook that you open has its own window.

Each workbook contains one or more worksheets, and each worksheet is made up of individual cells. Each cell can contain a value, a formula, or text. A worksheet also has an invisible *draw layer,* which holds charts, images, and diagrams. Each worksheet in a workbook is accessible by clicking the tab at the bottom of the workbook window. In addition, a workbook can store chart sheets; a *chart sheet* displays a single chart and is also accessible by clicking a tab.

Newcomers to Excel are often intimidated by all the different elements that appear within Excel's window. After you become familiar with the various parts, it all starts to make sense, and you'll feel right at home.

Figure 1.1 shows you the more important bits and pieces of Excel. As you look at the figure, refer to Table 1.1 for a brief explanation of the items shown in the figure.

FIGURE 1.1

The Excel screen has many useful elements that you will use often.

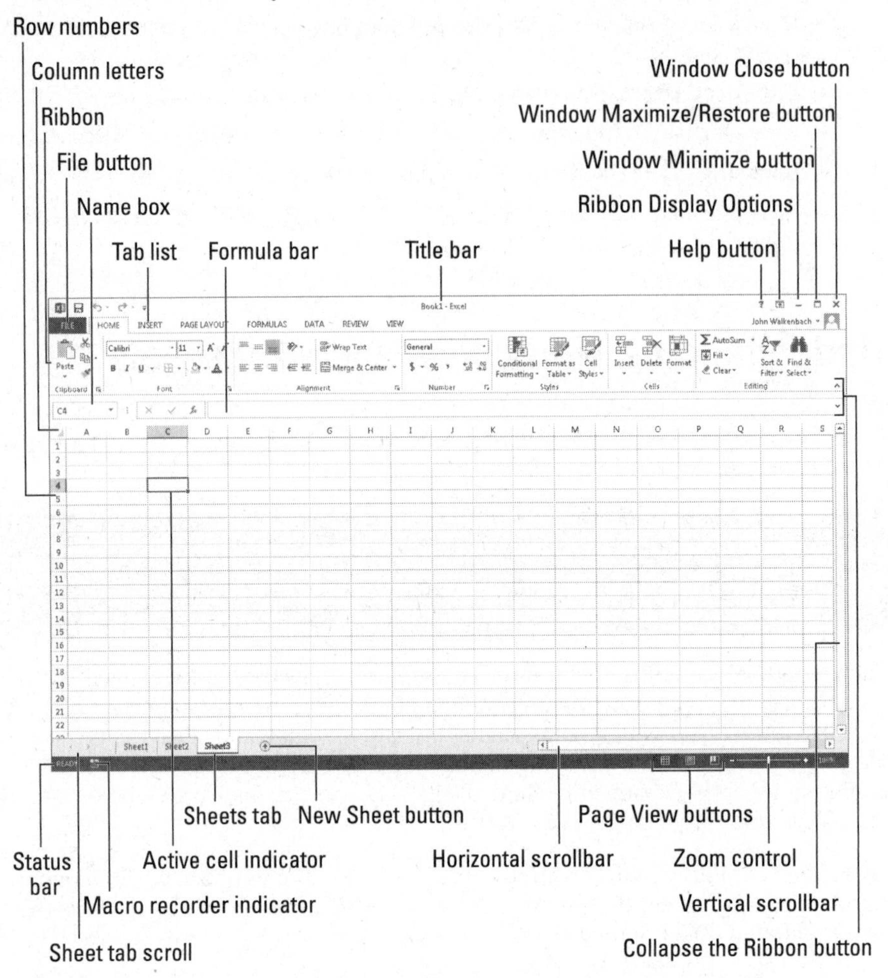

TABLE 1.1 Parts of the Excel Screen That You Need to Know

Name	Description
Active cell indicator	This dark outline indicates the currently active cell (one of the 17,179,869,184 cells on each worksheet).
Collapse the Ribbon button	Click this button to temporarily hide the Ribbon. Click it again to make the Ribbon remain visible.
Column letters	Letters range from A to XFD — one for each of the 16,384 columns in the worksheet. You can click a column heading to select an entire column of cells or drag a column border to change its width.
File button	Click this button to open Backstage view, which contains many options for working with your document (including printing) and setting Excel options.

Name	Description
Formula bar	When you enter information or formulas into a cell, it appears in this bar.
Help button	Click this button to display the Excel Help system window.
Horizontal scrollbar	Use this tool to scroll the sheet horizontally.
Macro recorder indicator	Click to start recording a VBA macro. The icon changes while your actions are being recorded. Click again to stop recording.
Name box	This box displays the active cell address or the name of the selected cell, range, or object.
New Sheet button	Add a new worksheet by clicking the New Sheet button (which is displayed after the last sheet tab).
Page View buttons	Click these buttons to change the way the worksheet is displayed.
Quick Access toolbar	This customizable toolbar holds commonly used commands. The Quick Access toolbar is always visible, regardless of which tab is selected.
Ribbon	This is the main location for Excel commands. Clicking an item in the tab list changes the Ribbon that is displayed.
Ribbon Display Options	A drop-down control that offers three options related to displaying the Ribbon.
Row numbers	Numbers range from 1 to 1,048,576 — one for each row in the worksheet. You can click a row number to select an entire row of cells.
Sheet tabs	Each of these notebook-like tabs represents a different sheet in the workbook. A workbook can have any number of sheets, and each sheet has its name displayed in a sheet tab.
Sheet tab scroll buttons	Use these buttons to scroll the sheet tabs to display tabs that aren't visible. You can also right-click to get a list of sheets.
Status bar	This bar displays various messages, as well as the status of the Num Lock, Caps Lock, and Scroll Lock keys on your keyboard. It also shows summary information about the range of cells selected. Right-click the status bar to change the information displayed.
Tab list	Use these commands to display a different Ribbon, similar to a menu.
Title bar	This displays the name of the program and the name of the current workbook. It also holds the Quick Access toolbar (on the left) and some control buttons that you can use to modify the window (on the right).
Vertical scrollbar	Use this to scroll the sheet vertically.
Window Close button	Click this button to close the active workbook window.
Window Maximize/Restore button	Click this button to increase the workbook window's size to fill the entire screen. If the window is already maximized, clicking this button "unmaximizes" Excel's window so that it no longer fills the entire screen.
Window Minimize button	Click this button to minimize the workbook window. The window displays as an icon in the Windows taskbar.
Zoom control	Use this to zoom your worksheet in and out.

Moving Around a Worksheet

This section describes various ways to navigate the cells in a worksheet.

Every worksheet consists of rows (numbered 1 through 1,048,576) and columns (labeled A through XFD). Column labeling works like this: After column Z comes column AA, which is followed by AB, AC, and so on. After column AZ comes BA, BB, and so on. After column ZZ is AAA, AAB, and so on.

The intersection of a row and a column is a single cell, and each cell has a unique address made up of its column letter and row number. For example, the address of the upper-left cell is A1. The address of the cell at the lower right of a worksheet is XFD1048576.

At any given time, one cell is the *active cell.* The active cell is the cell that accepts keyboard input, and its contents can be edited. You can identify the active cell by its darker border, as shown in Figure 1.2. Its address appears in the Name box. Depending on the technique that you use to navigate through a workbook, you may or may not change the active cell when you navigate.

FIGURE 1.2

The active cell is the cell with the dark border — in this case, cell C8.

	A	B	C	D	E	F
1		Last Year	This Year			
2	January	78	98			
3	February	77	102			
4	March	75	109			
5	April	82	112			
6	May	89	115			
7	June	88	115			
8						
9						
10						
11						
12						

Sheet1 Sheet2 Sheet3

Notice that the row and column headings of the active cell appear in a different color to make it easier to identify the row and column of the active cell.

NOTE

Excel 2013 is also available for devices such as tablets and phones. These devices use a touch interface. This book assumes the reader has a traditional keyboard and mouse — it doesn't cover the touch-related commands.

Navigating with your keyboard

Not surprisingly, you can use the standard navigational keys on your keyboard to move around a worksheet. These keys work just as you'd expect: The down arrow moves the active cell down one row, the right arrow moves it one column to the right, and so on.

PgUp and PgDn move the active cell up or down one full window. (The actual number of rows moved depends on the number of rows displayed in the window.)

TIP

You can use the keyboard to scroll through the worksheet without changing the active cell by turning on Scroll Lock, which is useful if you need to view another area of your worksheet and then quickly return to your original location. Just press Scroll Lock and use the navigation keys to scroll through the worksheet. When you want to return to the original position (the active cell), press Ctrl+Backspace. Then, press Scroll Lock again to turn it off. When Scroll Lock is turned on, Excel displays `Scroll Lock` in the status bar at the bottom of the window.

The Num Lock key on your keyboard controls how the keys on the numeric keypad behave. When Num Lock is on, the keys on your numeric keypad generate numbers. Many keyboards have a separate set of navigation (arrow) keys located to the left of the numeric keypad. The state of the Num Lock key doesn't affect these keys.

Table 1.2 summarizes all the worksheet movement keys available in Excel.

TABLE 1.2 Excel Worksheet Movement Keys

Key	Action
Up arrow (↑)	Moves the active cell up one row
Down arrow (↓)	Moves the active cell down one row
Left arrow (←) or Shift+Tab	Moves the active cell one column to the left
Right arrow (→) or Tab	Moves the active cell one column to the right
PgUp	Moves the active cell up one screen
PgDn	Moves the active cell down one screen
Alt+PgDn	Moves the active cell right one screen
Alt+PgUp	Moves the active cell left one screen
Ctrl+Backspace	Scrolls the screen so that the active cell is visible
↑*	Scrolls the screen up one row (active cell does not change)
↓*	Scrolls the screen down one row (active cell does not change)
←*	Scrolls the screen left one column (active cell does not change)
→*	Scrolls the screen right one column (active cell does not change)

* With Scroll Lock on

Navigating with your mouse

To change the active cell by using the mouse, just click another cell, and it becomes the active cell. If the cell that you want to activate isn't visible in the workbook window, you can use the scrollbars to scroll the window in any direction. To scroll one cell, click either of the arrows on the scrollbar. To scroll by a complete screen, click either side of the scrollbar's scroll box. You can also drag the scroll box for faster scrolling.

TIP

If your mouse has a wheel, you can use the mouse wheel to scroll vertically. Also, if you click the wheel and move the mouse in any direction, the worksheet scrolls automatically in that direction. The more you move the mouse, the faster the scrolling.

Press Ctrl while you use the mouse wheel to zoom the worksheet. If you prefer to use the mouse wheel to zoom the worksheet without pressing Ctrl, choose File⇨Options and select the Advanced section. Place a check mark next to the Zoom on Roll with IntelliMouse check box.

Using the scrollbars or scrolling with your mouse doesn't change the active cell. It simply scrolls the worksheet. To change the active cell, you must click a new cell after scrolling.

Using the Ribbon

In Office 2007, Microsoft made a dramatic change to the user interface. Traditional menus and toolbars were replaced with the Ribbon, a collection of icons at the top of the screen. The words above the icons are known as tabs: the Home tab, the Insert tab, and so on. Most users find that the Ribbon is easier to use than the old menu system; it can also be customized to make it even easier to use (see Chapter 24).

The Ribbon can either be hidden or visible (it's your choice). To toggle the Ribbon's visibility, press Ctrl+F1 (or double-click a tab at the top). If the Ribbon is hidden, it temporarily appears when you click a tab and hides itself when you click in the worksheet. The title bar has a control named Ribbon Display Options (next to the Help button). Click the control and choose one of three Ribbon options: Auto-hide, Show Tabs, or Show Tabs and Commands.

Ribbon tabs

The commands available in the Ribbon vary, depending upon which tab is selected. The Ribbon is arranged into groups of related commands. Here's a quick overview of Excel's tabs:

- **Home:** You'll probably spend most of your time with the Home tab selected. This tab contains the basic Clipboard commands, formatting commands, style commands, commands to insert and delete rows or columns, plus an assortment of worksheet editing commands.
- **Insert:** Select this tab when you need to insert something in a worksheet — a table, a diagram, a chart, a symbol, and so on.
- **Page Layout:** This tab contains commands that affect the overall appearance of your worksheet, including some settings that deal with printing.
- **Formulas:** Use this tab to insert a formula, name a cell or a range, access the formula auditing tools, or control how Excel performs calculations.
- **Data:** Excel's data-related commands are on this tab, including data validation commands.

- **Review:** This tab contains tools to check spelling, translate words, add comments, or protect sheets.
- **View:** The View tab contains commands that control various aspects of how a sheet is viewed. Some commands on this tab are also available in the status bar.
- **Developer:** This tab isn't visible by default. It contains commands that are useful for programmers. To display the Developer tab, choose File➪Options and then select Customize Ribbon. In the Customize the Ribbon section on the right, make sure Main Tabs is selected in the drop-down control, and place a check mark next to Developer.
- **Add-Ins:** This tab is visible only if you loaded an older workbook or add-in that customizes the menu or toolbars. Because menus and toolbars are no longer available in Excel 2013, these user interface customizations appear on the Add-Ins tab.

The preceding list contains the standard Ribbon tabs. Excel may display additional Ribbon tabs, resulting from add-ins or macros.

NOTE

Although the File button shares space with the tabs, it's not actually a tab. Clicking the File button displays a different screen (known as Backstage view), where you perform actions with your documents. This screen has commands along the left side. To exit the Backstage view, click the back arrow button in the upper-left corner.

The appearance of the commands on the Ribbon varies, depending on the width of the Excel window. When the Excel window is too narrow to display everything, the commands adapt; some of them might seem to be missing, but the commands are still available. Figure 1.3 shows the Home tab of the Ribbon with all controls fully visible. Figure 1.4 shows the Ribbon when Excel's window is made more narrow. Notice that some of the descriptive text is gone, but the icons remain. Figure 1.5 shows the extreme case when the window is made very narrow. Some groups display a single icon; however, if you click the icon, all the group commands are available to you.

FIGURE 1.3

The Home tab of the Ribbon.

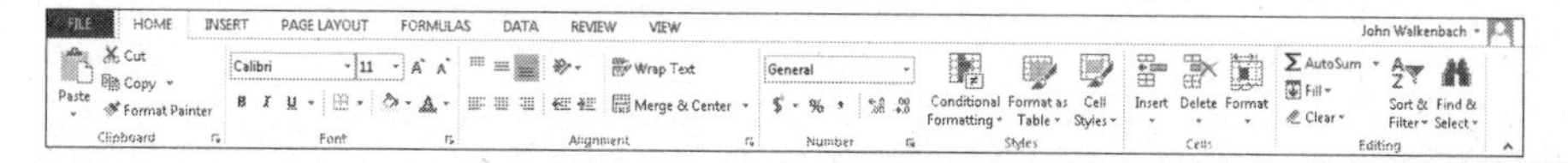

FIGURE 1.4

The Home tab when Excel's window is made narrower.

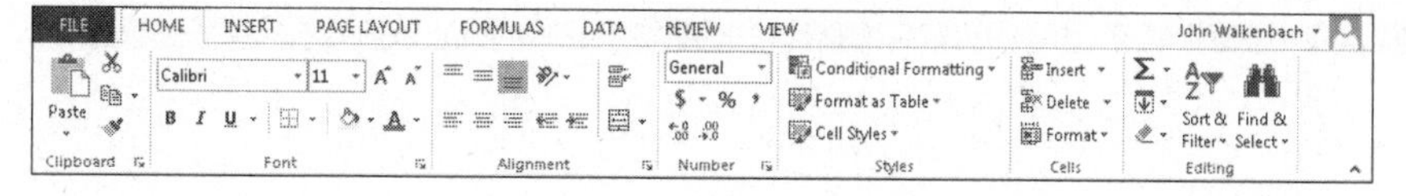

FIGURE 1.5

The Home tab when Excel's window is made very narrow.

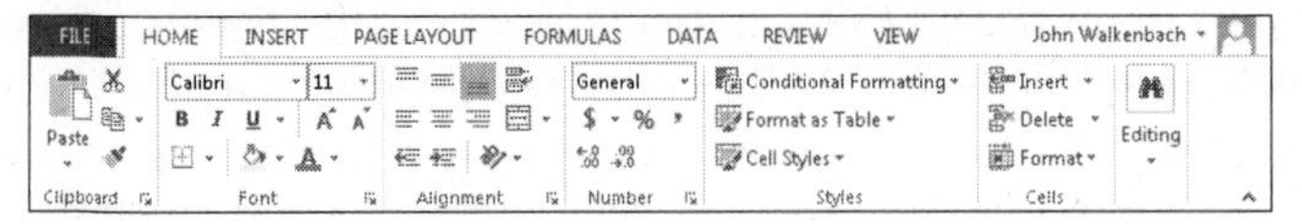

Contextual tabs

In addition to the standard tabs, Excel also includes *contextual tabs.* Whenever an object (such as a chart, a table, or a SmartArt diagram) is selected, specific tools for working with that object are made available in the Ribbon.

Figure 1.6 shows the contextual tabs that appear when a chart is selected. In this case, it has two contextual tabs: Design and Format. Notice that the contextual tabs contain a description (Chart Tools) in Excel's title bar. When contextual tabs appear, you can, of course, continue to use all the other tabs.

FIGURE 1.6

When you select an object, contextual tabs contain tools for working with that object.

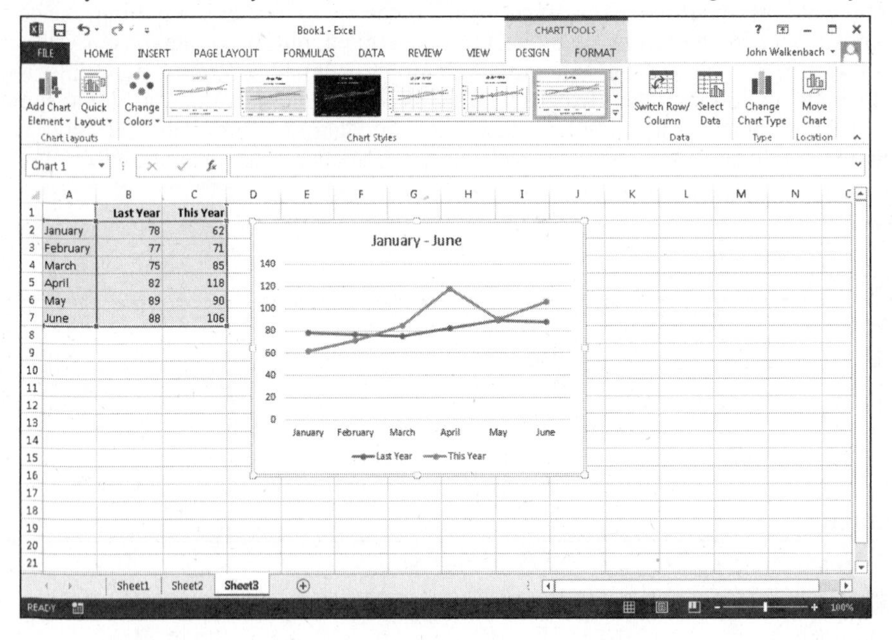

Types of commands on the Ribbon

When you hover your mouse pointer over a Ribbon command, you'll see a pop-up box that contains the command's name, as well as a brief description. For the most part, the commands in the Ribbon work just as you would expect them to. You'll find several different styles of commands on the Ribbon:

- **Simple buttons:** Click the button, and it does its thing. An example of a simple button is the Increase Font Size button in the Font group of the Home tab. Some buttons perform the action immediately; others display a dialog box so that you can enter additional information. Button controls may or may not be accompanied by a descriptive label.
- **Toggle buttons:** A toggle button is clickable and conveys some type of information by displaying two different colors. An example is the Bold button in the Font group of the Home tab. If the active cell isn't bold, the Bold button displays in its normal color. If the active cell is already bold, the Bold button displays a different background color. If you click the Bold button, it toggles the Bold attribute for the selection.
- **Simple drop-downs:** If the Ribbon command has a small down arrow, the command is a drop-down. Click it, and additional commands appear below it. An example of a simple drop-down is the Conditional Formatting command in the Styles group of the Home tab. When you click this control, you see several options related to conditional formatting.
- **Split buttons:** A *split button control* combines a one-click button with a drop-down. If you click the button part, the command is executed. If you click the drop-down part (a down arrow), you choose from a list of related commands. An example of a split button is the Merge & Center command in the Alignment group of the Home tab (see Figure 1.7). Clicking the left part of this control merges and centers text in the selected cells. If you click the arrow part of the control (on the right), you get a list of commands related to merging cells.

FIGURE 1.7

The Merge & Center command is a split button control.

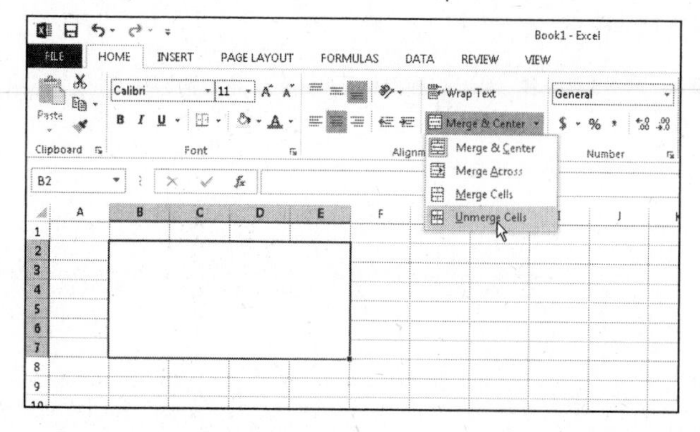

- **Check boxes:** A check box control turns something on or off. An example is the Gridlines control in the Show group of the View tab. When the Gridlines check box is checked, the sheet displays gridlines. When the control isn't checked, the gridlines don't appear.
- **Spinners:** Excel's Ribbon has only one spinner control: the Scale to Fit group of the Page Layout tab. Click the top part of the spinner to increase the value; click the bottom part of the spinner to decrease the value.

Some of the Ribbon groups contain a small icon in the bottom-right corner, known as a *dialog box launcher.* For example, if you examine the groups in the Home tab, you find dialog box launchers for the Clipboard, Font, Alignment, and Number groups — but not the Styles, Cells, and Editing groups. Click the icon, and Excel displays a dialog box. The dialog launchers often provide options that aren't available in the Ribbon.

Accessing the Ribbon by using your keyboard

At first glance, you may think that the Ribbon is completely mouse-centric. After all, the commands don't display the traditional underlined letter to indicate the Alt + keystrokes. But in fact, the Ribbon is *very* keyboard friendly. The trick is to press the Alt key to display the pop-up *keytips*. Each Ribbon control has a letter (or series of letters) that you type to issue the command.

TIP

You don't need to hold down the Alt key while you type keytip letters.

Figure 1.8 shows how the Home tab looks after I press the Alt key to display the keytips, and then the H key to display the keytips for the Home tab. If you press one of the keytips, the screen then displays more keytips. For example, to use the keyboard to align the cell contents to the left, press Alt, followed by H (for Home), and then AL (for Align Left).

FIGURE 1.8

Pressing Alt displays the keytips.

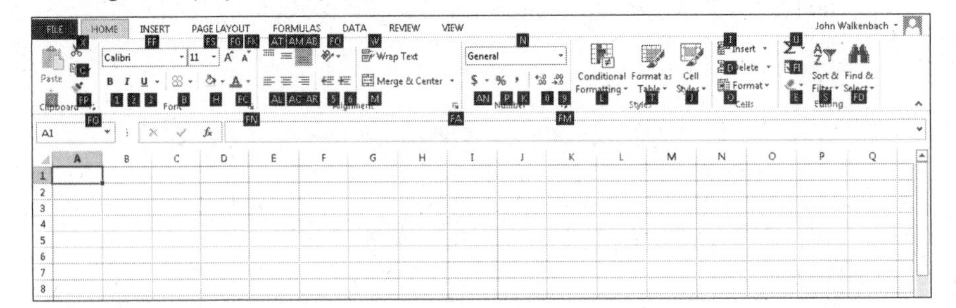

Nobody will memorize *all* these keys, but if you're a keyboard fan (like me), it takes just a few times before you memorize the keystrokes required for commands that you use frequently.

After you press Alt, you can also use the left- and right-arrow keys to scroll through the tabs. When you reach the proper tab, press the down arrow to enter the Ribbon. Then use left and right arrow keys to scroll through the Ribbon commands. When you reach the command you need, press Enter to execute it. This method isn't as efficient as using the keytips, but it's a quick way to take a look at the commands available.

TIP

Often, you'll want to repeat a particular command. Excel provides a way to simplify that. For example, if you applied a particular style to a cell (by choosing Home ➪ Styles ➪ Cell Styles), you can activate another cell and press Ctrl+Y (or F4) to repeat the command.

Using Shortcut Menus

In addition to the Ribbon, Excel features many shortcut menus, which you access by right-clicking just about anything within Excel. Shortcut menus don't contain every relevant command, just those that are most commonly used for whatever is selected.

As an example, Figure 1.9 shows the shortcut menu that appears when you right-click a cell. The shortcut menu appears at the mouse-pointer position, which makes selecting a command fast and efficient. The shortcut menu that appears depends on what you're doing at the time. For example, if you're working with a chart, the shortcut menu contains commands that are pertinent to the selected chart element.

The box above the shortcut menu — the Mini toolbar — contains commonly used tools from the Home tab. The Mini toolbar was designed to reduce the distance your mouse has to travel around the screen. Just right-click, and common formatting tools are within an inch of your mouse pointer. The Mini toolbar is particularly useful when a tab other than Home is displayed. If you use a tool on the Mini toolbar, the toolbar remains displayed in case you want to perform other formatting on the selection.

FIGURE 1.9

Click the right mouse button to display a shortcut menu of commands you're most likely to use.

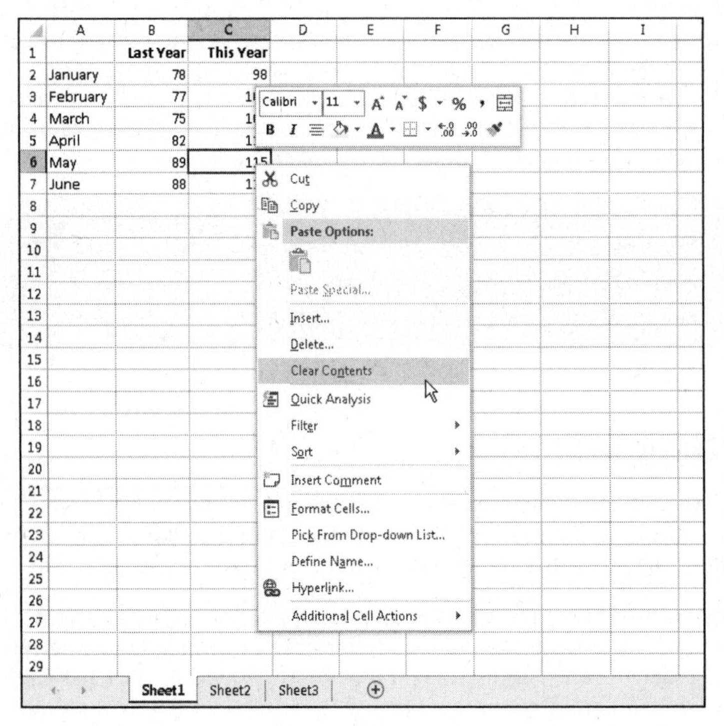

Customizing Your Quick Access Toolbar

The Ribbon is fairly efficient, but many users prefer to have some commands available at all times, without having to click a tab. The solution is to customize your Quick Access toolbar. Typically, the Quick Access toolbar appears on the left side of the title bar, above the Ribbon. Alternatively, you can display the Quick Access toolbar below the Ribbon; just right-click the Quick Access toolbar and choose Show Quick Access Toolbar below the Ribbon.

Displaying the Quick Access toolbar below the Ribbon provides a bit more room for icons, but it also means that you see one less row of your worksheet.

Changing Your Mind

You can reverse almost every action in Excel by using the Undo command, located on the Quick Access toolbar. Click Undo (or press Ctrl+Z) after issuing a command in error, and it's as if you never issued the command. You can reverse the effects of the past 100 actions that you performed by executing Undo more than once.

If you click the arrow on the right side of the Undo button, you see a list of the actions that you can reverse. Click an item in that list to undo that action and all the subsequent actions you performed.

Caution

You can't reverse every action, however. Generally, anything that you do using the File button can't be undone. For example, if you save a file and realize that you've overwritten a good copy with a bad one, Undo can't save the day. You're just out of luck unless you have a backup of the file. Also, changes made by a macro can't be undone. In fact, executing a macro that changes the workbook clears the Undo list.

The Redo button, also on the Quick Access toolbar, performs the opposite of the Undo button: Redo reissues commands that have been undone. If nothing has been undone, this command is not available.

By default, the Quick Access toolbar contains three tools: Save, Undo, and Redo. You can customize the Quick Access toolbar by adding other commands that you use often. To add a command from the Ribbon to your Quick Access toolbar, right-click the command and choose Add to Quick Access Toolbar. If you click the down arrow to the right of the Quick Access toolbar, you see a drop-down menu with some additional commands that you might want to place in your Quick Access toolbar.

Excel has quite a few commands (mostly obscure ones) that aren't available on the Ribbon. In most cases, the only way to access these commands is to add them to your Quick Access toolbar. Right-click the Quick Access toolbar and choose Customize the Quick Access Toolbar. You see the Excel Options dialog box, shown in Figure 1.10. This section of the Excel Options dialog box is your one-stop shop for Quick Access toolbar customization.

FIGURE 1.10

Add new icons to your Quick Access toolbar by using the Quick Access Toolbar section of the Excel Options dialog box.

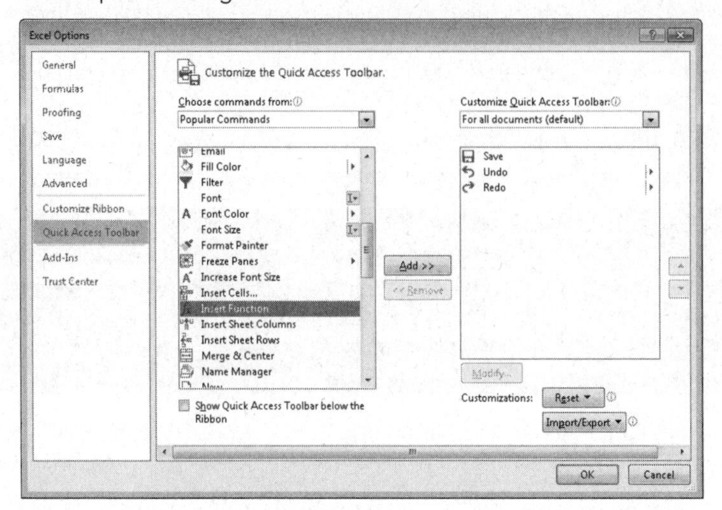

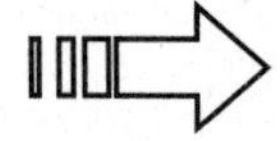

See Chapter 24 for more information about customizing your Quick Access toolbar.

Working with Dialog Boxes

Many Excel commands display a dialog box, which is simply a way of getting more information from you. For example, if you choose Review ➪ Changes ➪ Protect Sheet, Excel can't carry out the command until you tell it what parts of the sheet you want to protect. Therefore, it displays the Protect Sheet dialog box, shown in Figure 1.11.

FIGURE 1.11

Excel uses a dialog box to get additional information about a command.

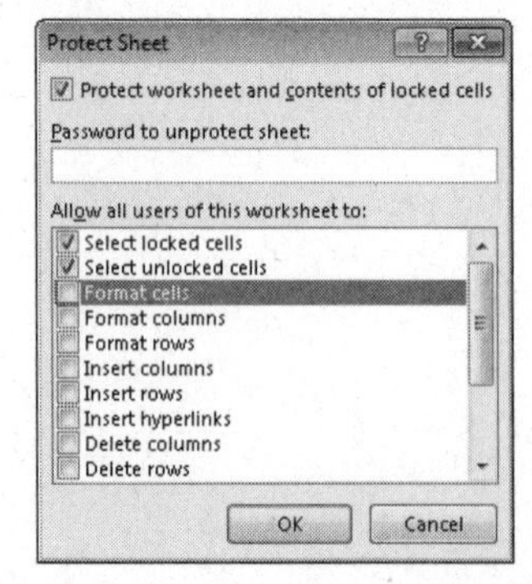

Excel dialog boxes vary in how they work. You'll find two types of dialog boxes:

- **Typical dialog box:** A *modal* dialog box takes the focus away from the spreadsheet. When this type of dialog box is displayed, you can't do anything in the worksheet until you dismiss the dialog box. Clicking OK performs the specified actions, and clicking Cancel (or pressing Esc) closes the dialog box without taking any action. Most Excel dialog boxes are this type.
- **Stay-on-top dialog box:** A *modeless* dialog box works in a manner similar to a toolbar. When a modeless dialog box is displayed, you can continue working in Excel, and the dialog box remains open. Changes made in a modeless dialog box take effect immediately. An example of a modeless dialog box is the Find and Replace dialog box. You can leave this dialog box open while you continue to use your worksheet. A modeless dialog box has a Close button but no OK button.

Most people find working with dialog boxes to be quite straightforward and natural. If you've used other programs, you'll feel right at home. You can manipulate the controls either with your mouse or directly from the keyboard.

Navigating dialog boxes

Navigating dialog boxes is generally very easy — you simply click the control you want to activate.

Although dialog boxes were designed with mouse users in mind, you can also use the keyboard. Every dialog box control has text associated with it, and this text always has one underlined letter (a *hot key* or an *accelerator key*). You can access the control from the keyboard by pressing Alt and then the underlined letter. You can also press Tab to cycle through all the controls on a dialog box. Pressing Shift+Tab cycles through the controls in reverse order.

TIP

When a control is selected, it appears with a dotted outline. You can use the spacebar to activate a selected control.

Using tabbed dialog boxes

Several Excel dialog boxes are "tabbed" dialog boxes: That is, they include notebook-like tabs, each of which is associated with a different panel.

When you select a tab, the dialog box changes to display a new panel containing a new set of controls. The Format Cells dialog box, shown in Figure 1.12, is a good example. It has six tabs, which makes it functionally equivalent to six different dialog boxes.

FIGURE 1.12

Use the dialog box tabs to select different functional areas of the dialog box.

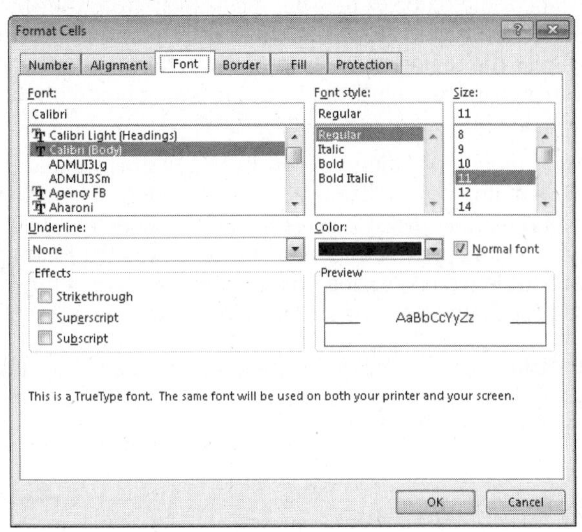

Tabbed dialog boxes are quite convenient because you can make several changes in a single dialog box. After you make all your setting changes, click OK or press Enter.

TIP

To select a tab by using the keyboard, press Ctrl+PgUp or Ctrl+PgDn, or simply press the first letter of the tab that you want to activate.

Using Task Panes

Yet another user interface element is the task pane. Task panes appear automatically in response to several commands. For example, to work with a picture, right-click the image and choose Format Picture. Excel responds by displaying the Format Picture task pane, shown in Figure 1.13. The task pane is similar to a dialog box except that you can keep it visible as long as you like.

NEW FEATURE

The role of task panes has increased dramatically in Excel 2013. For example, when working with a chart, you can access a task pane that has an extensive selection of commands for every element within the chart.

Many of the task panes are very complex. The Format Picture task pane has four icons along the top. Clicking an icon changes the command lists displayed below. Click an item in a command list and it expands to show the options.

There's no OK button in a task pane. When you're finished using a task pane, click the Close button (X) in the upper-right corner. If you prefer to use your keyboard to navigate task panes, make sure the task pane is displayed, and then press F6 to activate the task pane in keyboard mode. Then you can use the tab key, the arrow keys, the spacebar, and other keys that work in dialog boxes.

By default, the task pane is docked on the right side of the Excel window, but you can move it anywhere you like by clicking its title bar and dragging. Excel remembers the last position, so the next time you use that task pane, it will be right where you left it.

TIP

If you prefer to use your keyboard to work within a task pane, you may find that common dialog box keys such as Tab, Space, the arrow keys, and Alt key combinations don't seem to work. The trick is to press F6. After doing so, you'll find that the task pane works very well using only a keyboard. For example, use the Tab key to activate a section title, and then press Enter to expand the section.

FIGURE 1.13

The Format Picture task pane, docked on the right side of the window.

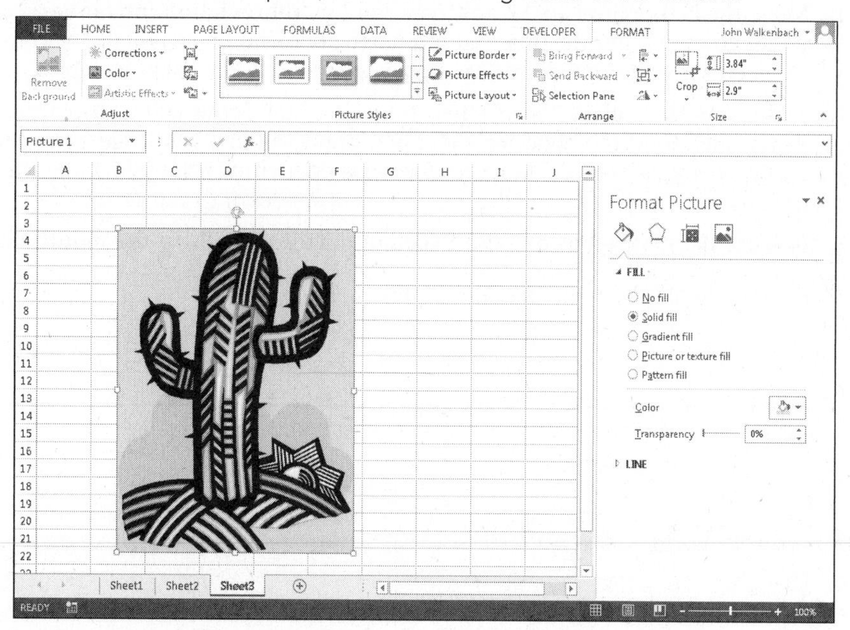

Creating Your First Excel Workbook

This section presents an introductory hands-on session with Excel. If you haven't used Excel, you may want to follow along on your computer to get a feel for how this software works.

In this example, you create a simple monthly sales projection table along with a chart.

Getting started on your worksheet

Start Excel and make sure that you have an empty workbook displayed. To create a new, blank workbook, press Ctrl + N (the shortcut key for File ⇨ New ⇨ Blank Workbook).

The sales projection will consist of two columns of information. Column A will contain the month names, and column B will store the projected sales numbers. You start by entering some descriptive titles into the worksheet. Here's how to begin:

1. **Move the cell pointer to cell A1 (the upper-left cell in the worksheet) by using the navigation (arrow) keys.** The Name box displays the cell's address.
2. **Type** Month **into cell A1 and press Enter.** Depending on your setup, either Excel moves the cell pointer to a different cell or the pointer remains in cell A1.
3. **Move the cell pointer to B1, type** Projected Sales, **and press Enter.** The text extends beyond the cell width, but don't worry about that for now.

Filling in the month names

In this step, you enter the month names in column A.

1. **Move the cell pointer to A2 and type** Jan **(an abbreviation for January).** At this point, you can enter the other month name abbreviations manually or you can let Excel do some of the work by taking advantage of the AutoFill feature.
2. **Make sure that cell A2 is selected.** Notice that the active cell is displayed with a heavy outline. At the bottom-right corner of the outline, you'll see a small square known as the *fill handle.* Move your mouse pointer over the fill handle, click, and drag down until you've highlighted from cell A2 down to cell A13.
3. **Release the mouse button, and Excel automatically fills in the month names.**

Your worksheet should resemble the one shown in Figure 1.14.

FIGURE 1.14

Your worksheet, after entering the column headings and month names.

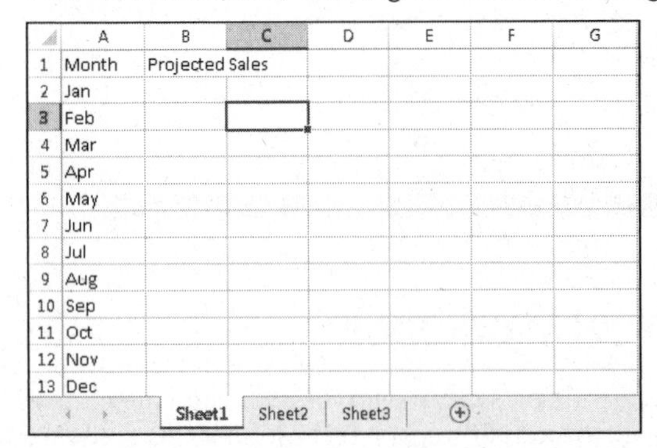

Entering the sales data

Next, you provide the sales projection numbers in column B. Assume that January's sales are projected to be $50,000, and that sales will increase by 3.5 percent in each subsequent month.

1. **Move the cell pointer to B2 and type** 50000**, the projected sales for January.** You could type a dollar sign and comma to make the number more legible, but you do the number formatting a bit later.
2. **To enter a formula to calculate the projected sales for February, move to cell B3 and type the following:** =B2*103.5%**.** When you press Enter, the cell displays 51750. The formula returns the contents of cell B2, multiplied by 103.5%. In other words, February sales are projected to be 103.5% of the January sales — a 3.5% increase.
3. **The projected sales for subsequent months use a similar formula, but rather than retype the formula for each cell in column B, take advantage of the AutoFill feature.** Make sure that cell B3 is selected. Click the cell's fill handle, drag down to cell B13, and release the mouse button.

At this point, your worksheet should resemble the one shown in Figure 1.15. Keep in mind that, except for cell B2, the values in column B are calculated *with formulas*. To demonstrate, try changing the projected sales value for the initial month, January (in cell B2). You'll find that the formulas recalculate and return different values. These formulas all depend on the initial value in cell B2, though.

FIGURE 1.15

Your worksheet, after creating the formulas.

	A	B	C	D	E	F	G	H
1	Month	Projected Sales						
2	Jan	50000						
3	Feb	51750						
4	Mar	53561.25						
5	Apr	55435.89						
6	May	57376.15						
7	Jun	59384.32						
8	Jul	61462.77						
9	Aug	63613.96						
10	Sep	65840.45						
11	Oct	68144.87						
12	Nov	70529.94						
13	Dec	72998.49						
14								
15								
16								

Sheet1 | Sheet2 | Sheet3

Formatting the numbers

The values in the worksheet are difficult to read because they aren't formatted. In this step, you apply a number format to make the numbers easier to read and more consistent in appearance:

1. **Select the numbers by clicking cell B2 and dragging down to cell B13.** Don't drag the fill handle this time, though, because you're selecting cells, not filling a range.
2. **Access the Ribbon and choose Home. In the Number group, click the drop-down Number Format control (it initially displays General), and select Currency from the list.** The numbers now display with a currency symbol and two decimal places. Much better, but the decimal places aren't necessary for this type of projection.
3. **Make sure the range B2:B13 is selected, choose Home ➪ Number, and click the Decrease Decimal button.** One of the decimal places disappears. Click that button a second time, and the values are displayed with no decimal places.

Making your worksheet look a bit fancier

At this point, you have a functional worksheet, but it could use some help in the appearance department. Converting this range to an "official" (and attractive) Excel table is a snap:

1. **Activate any cell within the range A1:B13.**
2. **Choose Insert ➪ Tables ➪ Table.** Excel displays the Create Table dialog box to make sure that it guessed the range properly.
3. **Click OK to close the Create Table dialog box.** Excel applies its default table formatting and displays its Table Tools ➪ Design contextual tab.

Your worksheet should look like Figure 1.16.

FIGURE 1.16

Your worksheet, after converting the range to a table.

	A	B	C	D	E
1	Month	Projected Sales			
2	Jan	$50,000			
3	Feb	$51,750			
4	Mar	$53,561			
5	Apr	$55,436			
6	May	$57,376			
7	Jun	$59,384			
8	Jul	$61,463			
9	Aug	$63,614			
10	Sep	$65,840			
11	Oct	$68,145			
12	Nov	$70,530			
13	Dec	$72,998			
14					
15					

Sheet1 Sheet2 Sheet3

If you don't like the default table style, just select another one from the Table Tools ➪ Design ➪ Table Styles group. Notice that you can get a preview of different table styles by moving your mouse over the Ribbon. When you find one you like, click it, and the style will be applied to your table.

Summing the values

The worksheet displays the monthly projected sales, but what about the total projected sales for the year? Because this range is a table, it's simple:

1. **Activate any cell in the table**
2. **Choose Table Tools ➪ Design ➪ Table Style Options ➪ Total Row.** Excel automatically adds a new row to the bottom of your table, including a formula that calculates the total of the Projected Sales column.
3. **If you'd prefer to see a different summary formula (for example, average), click cell B14 and choose a different summary formula from the drop-down list.**

Creating a chart

How about a chart that shows the projected sales for each month?

1. **Activate any cell in the table.**
2. **Choose Insert ➪ Charts ➪ Recommended Charts.** Excel displays some suggested chart type options.
3. **In the Insert Chart dialog box, click the second recommended chart (a column chart), and click OK.** Excel inserts the chart in the center of the window. To move the chart to another location, click its border and drag it.
4. **Click the chart and choose a style using the Chart Tools ➪ Design ➪ Chart Styles options.**

Figure 1.17 shows the worksheet with a column chart. Your chart may look different, depending on the chart style you selected.

ON THE WEB

This workbook is available on this book's website. The filename is `table and chart.xlsx`.

FIGURE 1.17

The table and chart.

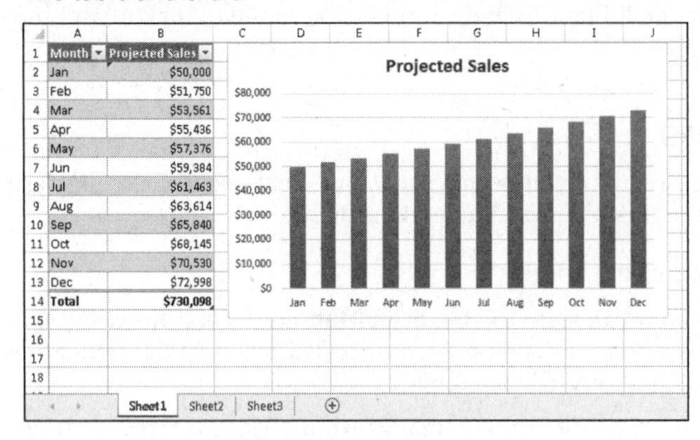

Printing your worksheet

Printing your worksheet is very easy (assuming that you have a printer attached and that it works properly).

1. **Make sure that the chart isn't selected.** If a chart is selected, the chart will print on a page by itself. To deselect the chart, just press Esc or click any cell.
2. **To make use of Excel's handy Page Layout view, click the Page Layout button on the right side of the status bar.** Excel displays the worksheet page-by-page so that you can easily see how your printed output will look. Figure 1.18 shows the worksheet zoomed out to show a complete page. In Page Layout view, you can tell immediately whether the chart is too wide to fit on one page. If the chart is too wide, click and drag a corner of the chart to resize it or just move the chart below the table of numbers.
3. **When you're ready to print, choose File⇨Print.** At this point, you can change some print settings. For example, you can choose to print in landscape rather than portrait orientation. Make the change, and you see the result in the preview window.
4. **When you're satisfied, click the Print button in the upper-left corner.** The page is printed, and you're returned to your workbook.

Saving your workbook

Until now, everything that you've done has occurred in your computer's memory. If the power should fail, all may be lost — unless Excel's AutoRecover feature happened to kick in. It's time to save your work to a file on your hard drive.

1. **Click the Save button on the Quick Access toolbar.** (This button looks like an old-fashioned floppy disk, popular in the previous century.) Because the workbook hasn't been saved yet and still has its default name, Excel responds with a Backstage screen that lets you choose the location for the workbook file. The Backstage screen lets you save the file to an online location or to your local computer.

FIGURE 1.18

Viewing the worksheet in Page Layout view.

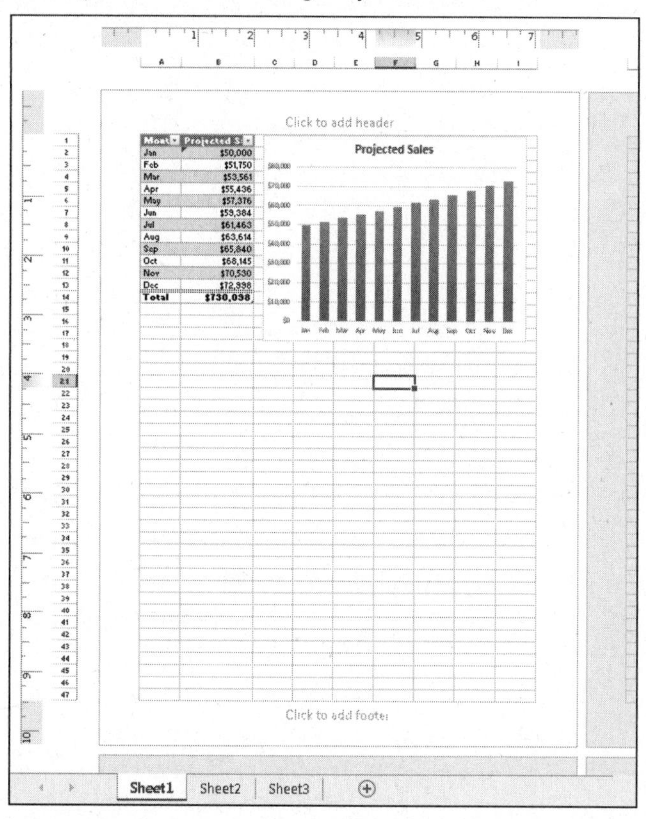

2. **Select Computer, and then click Browse.** Excel displays the Save As dialog box.
3. **In the File Name field, enter a name (such as Monthly Sales Projection), and then click Save or press Enter.** Excel saves the workbook as a file. The workbook remains open so that you can work with it some more.

Note

By default, Excel saves a backup copy of your work automatically every ten minutes. To adjust the AutoRecover setting (or turn if off), choose File ➪ Options, and click the Save tab of the Excel Options dialog box. However, you should never rely on Excel's AutoRecover feature. Saving your work frequently is a good idea.

If you've followed along, you may have realized that creating this workbook was not difficult. But, of course, you've barely scratched the surface of Excel. The remainder of this book covers these tasks (and many, many more) in much greater detail.

CHAPTER 2

Entering and Editing Worksheet Data

IN THIS CHAPTER

Understanding the types of data you can use

Entering text and values into your worksheets

Entering dates and times into your worksheets

Modifying and editing information

Using built-in number formats

This chapter describes what you need to know about entering and modifying data in your worksheets. As you see, Excel doesn't treat all data equally. Therefore, you need to learn about the various types of data that you can use in an Excel worksheet.

Exploring Data Types

An Excel workbook file can hold any number of worksheets, and each worksheet is made up of more than 17 billion cells. A cell can hold any of three basic types of data:

- A numeric value
- Text
- A formula

A worksheet can also hold charts, diagrams, pictures, buttons, and other objects. These objects aren't contained in cells. Instead, they reside on the worksheet's *draw layer,* which is an invisible layer on top of each worksheet.

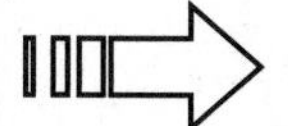

Chapter 23 discusses some of the items you can place on the draw layer.

Excel's Numeric Limitations

You may be curious about the types of values that Excel can handle. In other words, how large can a number be? And how accurate are large numbers?

Excel's numbers are precise up to 15 digits. For example, if you enter a large value, such as 123,456,789,123,456,789 (18 digits), Excel actually stores it with only 15 digits of precision. This 18-digit number displays as 123,456,789,123,456,000. This precision may seem quite limiting, but in practice, it rarely causes any problems.

One situation in which the 15-digit accuracy can cause a problem is when entering credit card numbers. Most credit card numbers are 16 digits, but Excel can handle only 15 digits, so it substitutes a zero for the last credit card digit. Even worse, you may not even realize that Excel made the card number invalid. The solution? Enter the credit card numbers as text. The easiest way is to preformat the cell as Text (choose Home⇨Number and choose Text from the Number Format drop-down list). Or you can precede the credit card number with an apostrophe. Either method prevents Excel from interpreting the entry as a number.

Here are some of Excel's other numeric limits:

- **Largest positive number:** 9.9E+307
- **Smallest negative number:** –9.9E+307
- **Smallest positive number:** 1E–307
- **Largest negative number:** –1E–307

These numbers are expressed in scientific notation. For example, the largest positive number is "9.9 times 10 to the 307th power" — in other words, 99 followed by 306 zeros. Keep in mind, though, that this number has only 15 digits of accuracy.

Numeric values

Numeric values represent a quantity of some type: sales amounts, number of employees, atomic weights, test scores, and so on. Values also can be dates (such as Feb-26-2013) or times (such as 3:24 a.m.).

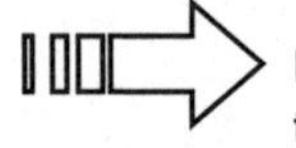

Excel can display values in many different formats. In the "Applying Number Formatting" section, later in this chapter, you see how different format options can affect the display of numeric values.

Text entries

Most worksheets also include text in some of the cells. Text can serve as data (for example, a list of employee names), labels for values, headings for columns, or instructions about the worksheet. Text is often used to clarify what the values in a worksheet mean or where the numbers came from.

Text that begins with a number is still considered text. For example, if you type **12 Employees** into a cell, Excel considers the entry to be text rather than a numeric value. Consequently, you can't use this cell for numeric calculations. If you need to indicate that the number 12 refers to employees, enter **12** into a cell and then type **Employees** into the cell to the right.

Formulas

Formulas are what make a spreadsheet a spreadsheet. Excel enables you to enter flexible formulas that use the values (or even text) in cells to calculate a result. When you enter a formula into a cell, the formula's result appears in the cell. If you change any of the cells used by a formula, the formula recalculates and shows the new result.

Formulas can be simple mathematical expressions, or they can use some of the powerful functions that are built into Excel. Figure 2.1 shows an Excel worksheet set up to calculate a monthly loan payment. The worksheet contains values, text, and formulas. The cells in column A contain text. Column B contains four values and two formulas. The formulas are in cells B6 and B10. Column D, for reference, shows the actual contents of the cells in column B.

FIGURE 2.1

You can use values, text, and formulas to create useful Excel worksheets.

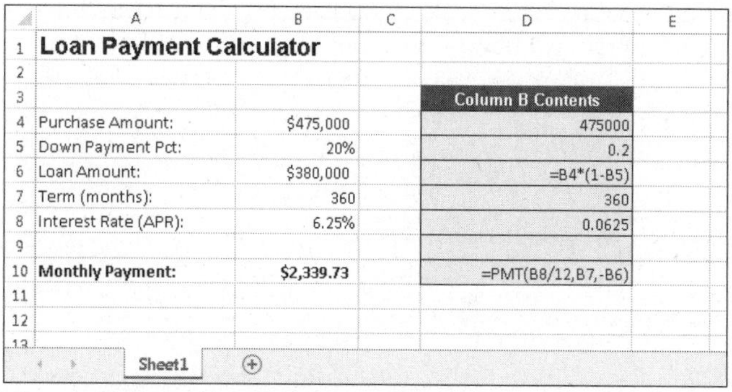

	A	B	C	D	E
1	**Loan Payment Calculator**				
2					
3				Column B Contents	
4	Purchase Amount:	$475,000		475000	
5	Down Payment Pct:	20%		0.2	
6	Loan Amount:	$380,000		=B4*(1-B5)	
7	Term (months):	360		360	
8	Interest Rate (APR):	6.25%		0.0625	
9					
10	**Monthly Payment:**	**$2,339.73**		=PMT(B8/12,B7,-B6)	
11					
12					

Sheet1

ON THE WEB

This workbook, named `loan payment calculator.xlsx`, is available on this book's website.

You can find out much more about formulas in Part II.

Entering Text and Values into Your Worksheets

To enter a numeric value into a cell, move the cell pointer to the appropriate cell, type the value, and then press Enter or one of the navigation keys. The value is displayed in the cell and also appears in the Formula bar when the cell is selected. You can include decimal points and currency symbols when entering values, along with plus signs, minus signs, and commas (to separate thousands). If you precede a value with a minus sign or enclose it in parentheses, Excel considers it to be a negative number.

Entering text into a cell is just as easy as entering a value: Activate the cell, type the text, and then press Enter or a navigation key. A cell can contain a maximum of about 32,000 characters — more than enough to hold a typical chapter in this book. Even though a cell can hold a huge number of characters, you'll find that it's not possible to actually display all these characters.

> **TIP**
>
> If you type an exceptionally long text entry into a cell, the Formula bar may not show all the text. To display more of the text in the Formula bar, click the bottom of the Formula bar and drag down to increase the height (see Figure 2.2). Also useful is the Ctrl+Shift+U keyboard shortcut. Pressing this key combination toggles the height of the formula bar to show either one row, or the previous size.

FIGURE 2.2

The Formula bar, expanded in height to show more information in the cell.

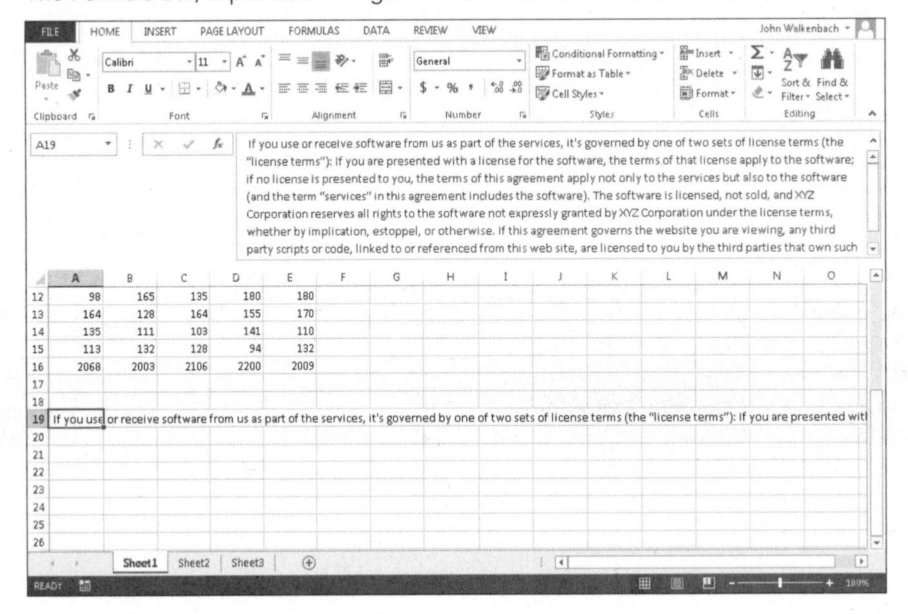

What happens when you enter text that's longer than its column's current width? If the cells to the immediate right are blank, Excel displays the text in its entirety, appearing to spill the entry into adjacent cells. If an adjacent cell isn't blank, Excel displays as much of the text as possible. (The full text is contained in the cell; it's just not displayed.) If you need to display a long text string in a cell that's adjacent to a nonblank cell, you have a few choices:

- Edit your text to make it shorter.
- Increase the width of the column (drag the border in the column letter display).
- Use a smaller font.
- Wrap the text within the cell so that it occupies more than one line. Choose Home ➪ Alignment ➪ Wrap Text to toggle wrapping on and off for the selected cell or range.

Entering Dates and Times into Your Worksheets

Excel treats dates and times as special types of numeric values. Dates and times are values that are formatted so that they *appear* as dates or times. If you work with dates and times, you need to understand Excel's date and time system.

Entering date values

Excel handles dates by using a serial number system. The earliest date that Excel understands is January 1, 1900. This date has a serial number of 1. January 2, 1900, has a serial number of 2, and so on. This system makes it easy to deal with dates in formulas. For example, you can enter a formula to calculate the number of days between two dates.

Most of the time, you don't have to be concerned with Excel's serial number date system. You can simply enter a date in a common date format, and Excel takes care of the details behind the scenes. For example, if you need to enter June 1, 2013, you can enter the date by typing **June 1, 2013** (or use any of several different date formats). Excel interprets your entry and stores the value 41426, which is the serial number for that date.

Note

The date examples in this book use the U.S. English system. Your Windows regional settings will affect how Excel interprets a date you've entered. For example, depending on your regional date settings, June 1, 2013 may be interpreted as text rather than a date. In such a case, you need to enter the date in a format that corresponds to your regional date settings — for example, 1 June, 2013.

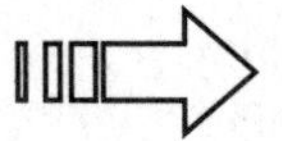
For more information about working with dates, see Chapter 12.

Entering time values

When you work with times, you extend Excel's date serial number system to include decimals. In other words, Excel works with times by using fractional days. For example, the date serial number for June 1, 2013, is 41426. Noon on June 1, 2013 (halfway through the day), is represented internally as 41426.5 because the time fraction is added to the date serial number to get the full date/time serial number.

Again, you normally don't have to be concerned with these serial numbers or fractional serial numbers for times. Just enter the time into a cell in a recognized format. In this case, type **June 1, 2013 12:00**.

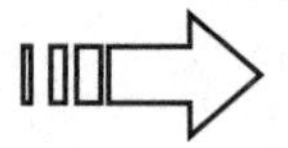
See Chapter 12 for more information about working with time values.

Modifying Cell Contents

After you enter a value or text into a cell, you can modify it in several ways:

- Delete the cell's contents.
- Replace the cell's contents with something else.
- Edit the cell's contents.

Note

You can also modify a cell by changing its formatting. However, formatting a cell affects only a cell's appearance. Formatting doesn't affect the cell's contents. Later sections in this chapter cover formatting.

Deleting the contents of a cell

To delete the contents of a cell, just click the cell and press the Delete key. To delete more than one cell, select all the cells that you want to delete and then press Delete. Pressing Delete removes the cell's contents but doesn't remove any formatting (such as bold, italic, or a different number format) that you may have applied to the cell.

For more control over what gets deleted, you can choose Home➪Editing➪Clear. This command's drop-down list has five choices:

- **Clear All:** Clears everything from the cell — its contents, its formatting, and its cell comment (if it has one).
- **Clear Formats:** Clears only the formatting and leaves the value, text, or formula.
- **Clear Contents:** Clears only the cell's contents and leaves the formatting.
- **Clear Comments:** Clears the comment (if one exists) attached to the cell.
- **Clear Hyperlinks:** Removes hyperlinks contained in the selected cells. The text remains, but the cell no longer functions as a clickable hyperlink.

NOTE
Clearing formats doesn't clear the background colors in a range that has been designated as a table unless you've replaced the table style background colors manually.

Replacing the contents of a cell

To replace the contents of a cell with something else, just activate the cell and type your new entry, which replaces the previous contents. Any formatting applied to the cell remains in place and is applied to the new content.

You can also replace cell contents by dragging and dropping or by pasting data from the Clipboard. In both cases, the cell formatting will be replaced by the format of the new data. To avoid pasting formatting, choose Home ➪ Clipboard ➪ Paste ➪ Values (V), or Hom e ➪ Clipboard ➪ Paste ➪ Formulas (F).

Editing the contents of a cell

If the cell contains only a few characters, replacing its contents by typing new data usually is easiest. However, if the cell contains lengthy text or a complex formula and you need to make only a slight modification, you probably want to edit the cell rather than re-enter information.

When you want to edit the contents of a cell, you can use one of the following ways to enter cell-edit mode:

- **Double-click the cell** to edit the cell contents directly in the cell.
- **Select the cell and press F2** to edit the cell contents directly in the cell.
- **Select the cell that you want to edit and then click inside the Formula bar** to edit the cell contents in the Formula bar.

You can use whichever method you prefer. Some people find editing directly in the cell easier; others prefer to use the Formula bar to edit a cell.

NOTE
The Advanced tab of the Excel Options dialog box contains a section called Editing Options. These settings affect how editing works. (To access this dialog box, choose File ➪ Options.) If the Allow Editing Directly in Cells option isn't enabled, you can't edit a cell by double-clicking. In addition, pressing F2 allows you to edit the cell in the Formula bar (not directly in the cell).

All these methods cause Excel to go into *edit mode.* (The word *Edit* appears at the left side of the status bar at the bottom of the screen.) When Excel is in edit mode, the Formula bar enables two icons: Cancel (the X) and Enter (the check mark). Figure 2.3 shows these two icons. Clicking the Cancel icon cancels editing without changing the cell's contents. (Pressing Esc has the same effect.) Clicking the Enter icon completes the editing and enters the modified contents into the cell. (Pressing Enter has the same effect.)

FIGURE 2.3

While editing a cell, the Formula bar enables two new icons: Cancel (X) and Enter (check mark).

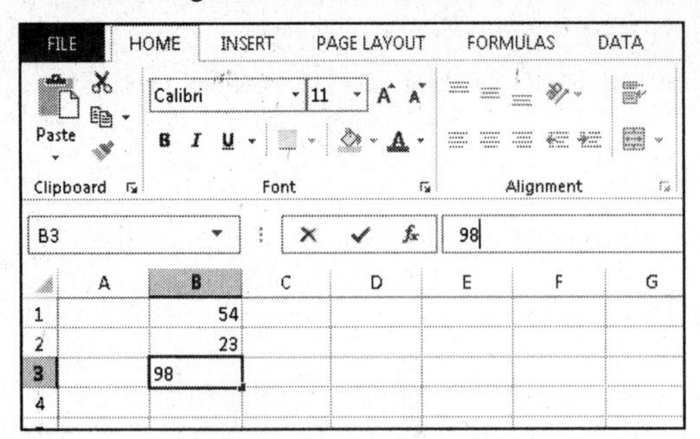

When you begin editing a cell, the insertion point appears as a vertical bar, and you can perform the following tasks:

- **Add new characters at the location of the insertion point.** Move the insertion point by
  - Using the navigation keys to move within the cell
  - Pressing Home to move the insertion point to the beginning of the cell
  - Pressing End to move the insertion point to the end of the cell
- **Select multiple characters.** Press Shift while you use the navigation keys.
- **Select characters while you're editing a cell.** Use the mouse. Just click and drag the mouse pointer over the characters that you want to select.

Learning some handy data-entry techniques

You can simplify the process of entering information into your Excel worksheets and make your work go quite a bit faster by using a number of useful tricks, described in the following sections.

Automatically moving the cell pointer after entering data

By default, Excel automatically moves the cell pointer to the next cell down when you press the Enter key after entering data into a cell. To change this setting, choose File ⇨ Options and click the Advanced tab (see Figure 2.4). The check box that controls this behavior is labeled After Pressing Enter, Move Selection. If you enable this option, you can choose the direction in which the cell pointer moves (down, left, up, or right).

Your choice is completely a matter of personal preference. I prefer to keep this option turned off. When entering data, I use the navigation keys rather than the Enter key (see the next section).

FIGURE 2.4

You can use the Advanced tab in Excel Options to select a number of helpful input option settings.

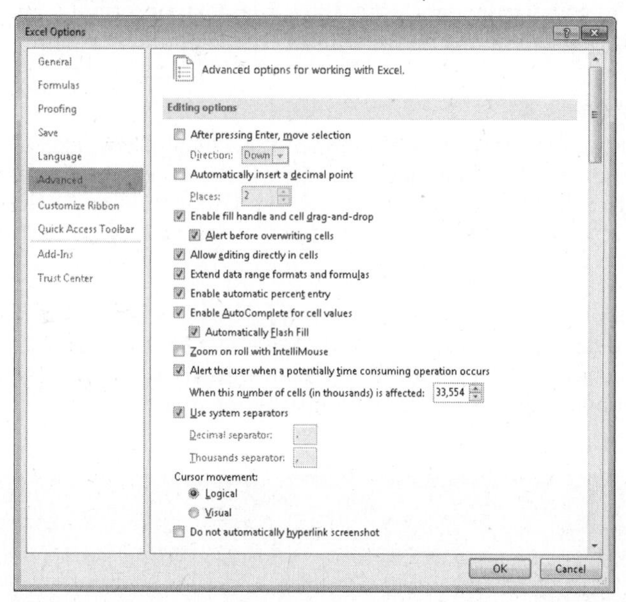

Using navigation keys instead of pressing Enter

Instead of pressing the Enter key when you're finished making a cell entry, you also can use any of the navigation keys to complete the entry. Not surprisingly, these navigation keys send you in the direction that you indicate. For example, if you're entering data in a row, press the right-arrow (→) key rather than Enter. The other arrow keys work as expected, and you can even use PgUp and PgDn.

Selecting a range of input cells before entering data

When a range of cells is selected, Excel automatically moves the cell pointer to the next cell in the range when you press Enter. If the selection consists of multiple rows, Excel moves down the column; when it reaches the end of the selection in the column, it moves to the first selected cell in the next column.

To skip a cell, just press Enter without entering anything. To go backward, press Shift + Enter. If you prefer to enter the data by rows rather than by columns, press Tab rather than Enter. Excel continues to cycle through the selected range until you select a cell outside of the range.

Using Ctrl+Enter to place information into multiple cells simultaneously

If you need to enter the same data into multiple cells, Excel offers a handy shortcut. Select all the cells that you want to contain the data, enter the value, text, or formula, and then press Ctrl + Enter. The same information is inserted into each cell in the selection.

Entering decimal points automatically

If you need to enter lots of numbers with a fixed number of decimal places, Excel has a useful tool that works like some old adding machines. Access the Excel Options dialog box and click the Advanced tab. Select the Automatically Insert a Decimal Point check box and make sure that the Places box is set for the correct number of decimal places for the data you need to enter.

When this option is set, Excel supplies the decimal points for you automatically. For example, if you specify two decimal places, entering **12345** into a cell is interpreted as 123.45. To restore things to normal, just clear the Automatically Insert a Decimal Point check box in the Excel Options dialog box. Changing this setting doesn't affect any values that you already entered.

Caution

The fixed decimal places option is a global setting and applies to all workbooks (not just the active workbook). If you forget that this option is turned on, you can easily end up entering incorrect values — or cause some major confusion if someone else uses your computer.

Using AutoFill to enter a series of values

The Excel AutoFill feature makes inserting a series of values or text items in a range of cells easy. It uses the AutoFill handle (the small box at the lower right of the active cell). You can drag the AutoFill handle to copy the cell or automatically complete a series.

Figure 2.5 shows an example. I entered **1** into cell A1 and **3** into cell A2. Then I selected both cells and dragged down the fill handle to create a linear series of odd numbers. The figure also shows an icon that, when clicked, displays some additional AutoFill options.

Tip

If you drag the AutoFill handle while you press and hold the right mouse button, Excel displays a shortcut menu with additional fill options.

Using AutoComplete to automate data entry

The Excel AutoComplete feature makes entering the same text into multiple cells easy. With AutoComplete, you type the first few letters of a text entry into a cell, and Excel automatically completes the entry based on other entries that you already made in the column. Besides reducing typing, this feature also ensures that your entries are spelled correctly and are consistent.

FIGURE 2.5

This series was created by using AutoFill.

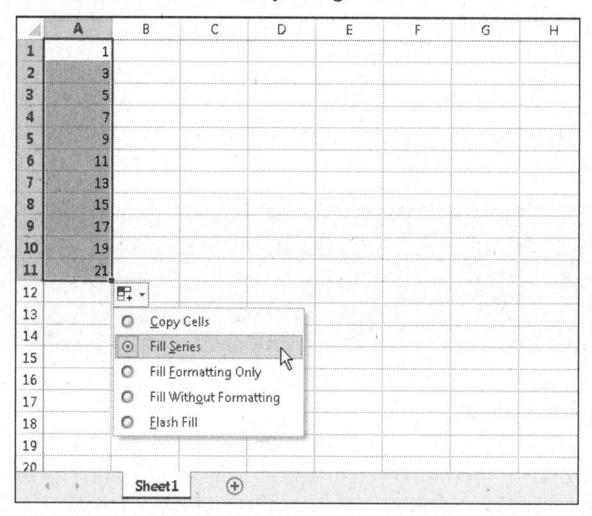

Here's how it works: Suppose that you're entering product information in a column. One of your products is named Widgets. The first time that you enter **Widgets** into a cell, Excel remembers it. Later, when you start typing **Widgets** in that same column, Excel recognizes it by the first few letters and finishes typing it for you. Just press Enter, and you're done. To override the suggestion, just keep typing.

AutoComplete also changes the case of letters for you automatically. If you start entering **widgets** (with a lowercase *w*) in the second entry, Excel makes the *w* uppercase to be consistent with the previous entry in the column.

TIP

You also can access a mouse-oriented version of AutoComplete by right-clicking the cell and choosing Pick from Drop-Down List from the shortcut menu. Excel then displays a drop-down box that has all the text entries in the current column, and you just click the one that you want.

Keep in mind that AutoComplete works only within a contiguous column of cells. If you have a blank row, for example, AutoComplete identifies only the cell contents below the blank row.

If you find the AutoComplete feature distracting, you can turn it off by using the Advanced tab of the Excel Options dialog box. Remove the check mark from the check box labeled Enable AutoComplete for Cell Values.

Forcing text to appear on a new line within a cell

If you have lengthy text in a cell, you can force Excel to display it in multiple lines within the cell: Press Alt+Enter to start a new line in a cell.

When you add a line break, Excel automatically changes the cell's format to Wrap Text. But unlike normal text wrap, your manual line break forces Excel to break the text at a specific place within the text, which gives you more precise control over the appearance of the text than if you rely on automatic text wrapping.

TIP

To remove a manual line break, edit the cell and press Delete when the insertion point is located at the end of the line that contains the manual line break. You won't see any symbol to indicate the position of the manual line break, but the text that follows it will move up when the line break is deleted.

Using AutoCorrect for shorthand data entry

You can use the AutoCorrect feature to create shortcuts for commonly used words or phrases. For example, if you work for a company named Consolidated Data Processing Corporation, you can create an AutoCorrect entry for an abbreviation, such as *cdp*. Then, whenever you type **cdp**, Excel automatically changes it to Consolidated Data Processing Corporation.

Excel includes quite a few built-in AutoCorrect terms (mostly to correct common misspellings), and you can add your own. To set up your custom AutoCorrect entries, access the Excel Options dialog box (choose File➪Options) and click the Proofing tab. Then click the AutoCorrect Options button to display the AutoCorrect dialog box. In the dialog box, click the AutoCorrect tab, check the option labeled Replace Text as You Type, and then enter your custom entries. (Figure 2.6 shows an example.) You can set up as many custom entries as you like. Just be careful not to use an abbreviation that might appear normally in your text.

TIP

Excel shares your AutoCorrect list with other Microsoft Office applications. For example, any AutoCorrect entries you created in Word also work in Excel.

Entering numbers with fractions

To enter a fractional value into a cell, leave a space between the whole number and the fraction. For example, to enter $6\frac{7}{8}$, enter **6 7/8** and then press Enter. When you select the cell, 6.875 appears in the Formula bar, and the cell entry appears as a fraction. If you have a fraction only (for example, $\frac{1}{8}$), you must enter a zero first, like this — **0 1/8** — or Excel will likely assume that you're entering a date. When you select the cell and look at the Formula bar, you see 0.125. In the cell, you see $\frac{1}{8}$.

FIGURE 2.6

AutoCorrect allows you to create shorthand abbreviations for text you enter often.

Using a form for data entry

Many people use Excel to manage lists in which the information is arranged in rows. Excel offers a simple way to work with this type of data through the use of a data entry form that Excel can create automatically. This data form works with either a normal range of data, or with a range that has been designated as a table (choose Insert➪Tables➪Table). Figure 2.7 shows an example.

FIGURE 2.7

Excel's built-in data form can simplify many data-entry tasks.

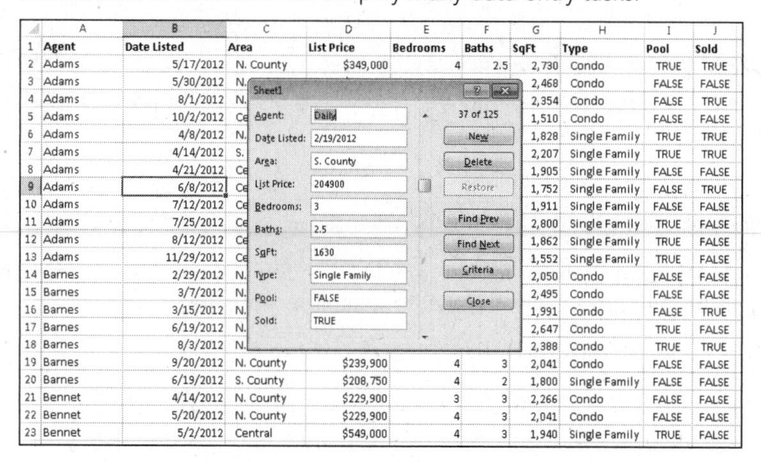

Unfortunately, the command to access the data form is not on the Ribbon. To use the data form, you must add it to your Quick Access toolbar or add it to the Ribbon. The following instructions describe how to add this command to your Quick Access toolbar:

1. **Right-click the Quick Access toolbar and choose Customize Quick Access Toolbar.** The Quick Access Toolbar panel of the Excel Options dialog box appears.
2. **In the Choose Commands From drop-down list, choose Commands Not in the Ribbon.**
3. **In the list box on the left, select Form.**
4. **Click the Add button to add the selected command to your Quick Access toolbar.**
5. **Click OK to close the Excel Options dialog box.**

After performing these steps, a new icon appears on your Quick Access toolbar.

To use a data entry form, follow these steps:

1. **Arrange your data so that Excel can recognize it as a table by entering headings for the columns in the first row of your data entry range.**
2. **Select any cell in the table and click the Form button on your Quick Access toolbar.** Excel displays a dialog box customized to your data (refer to Figure 2.7).
3. **Fill in the information.** Press Tab to move between the text boxes. If a cell contains a formula, the formula result appears as text (not as an edit box). In other words, you can't modify formulas using the data entry form.
4. **When you complete the data form, click the New button.** Excel enters the data into a row in the worksheet and clears the dialog box for the next row of data.

You can also use the form to edit existing data.

Entering the current date or time into a cell

If you need to date-stamp or time-stamp your worksheet, Excel provides two shortcut keys that do this task for you:

- **Current date:** Ctrl + ; (semicolon)
- **Current time:** Ctrl + Shift + ; (semicolon)

The date and time are from the system time in your computer. If the date or time isn't correct in Excel, use the Windows Control Panel to make the adjustment.

NOTE
When you use either of these shortcuts to enter a date or time into your worksheet, Excel enters a static value into the worksheet. In other words, the date or time entered doesn't change when the worksheet is recalculated. In most cases, this setup is probably what you want, but you should be aware of this limitation. If you want the date or time display to update, use one of these formulas:

```
=TODAY()
=NOW()
```


Applying Number Formatting

Number formatting refers to the process of changing the appearance of values contained in cells. Excel provides a wide variety of number formatting options. In the following sections, you see how to use many of Excel's formatting options to quickly improve the appearance of your worksheets.

TIP
The formatting that you apply works with the selected cell or cells. Therefore, you need to select the cell (or range of cells) before applying the formatting. Also remember that changing the number format does not affect the underlying value. Number formatting affects only the appearance.

Values that you enter into cells normally are unformatted. In other words, they simply consist of a string of numerals. Typically, you want to format the numbers so that they're easier to read or are more consistent in terms of the number of decimal places shown.

Figure 2.8 shows a worksheet that has two columns of values. The first column consists of unformatted values. The cells in the second column are formatted to make the values easier to read. The third column describes the type of formatting applied.

ON THE WEB
This workbook is available on this book's website. The file is named `number formatting.xlsx`.

TIP
If you move the cell pointer to a cell that has a formatted value, the Formula bar displays the value in its unformatted state because the formatting affects only how the value appears in the cell — not the actual value contained in the cell. There are a few exceptions, however. When you enter a date or a time, Excel always displays the value as a date or a time, even though it's stored internally as a value. Also, values that use the Percentage format display with a percent sign in the Formula bar.

FIGURE 2.8

Use numeric formatting to make it easier to understand what the values in the worksheet represent.

Unformatted	Formatted	Type
1200	$1,200.00	Currency
0.231	23.1%	Percentage
40942	2/3/2012	Short Date
40942	Friday, February 03, 2012	Long Date
123439832	123,439,832.00	Accounting
5559832	555-9832	Phone Number
434988723	434-98-8723	Social Security Number
0.552	1:14:53 PM	Time
0.25	1/4	Fraction
12332354090	1.23E+10	Scientific

Sheet1

Using automatic number formatting

Excel is smart enough to perform some formatting for you automatically. For example, if you enter **12.2%** into a cell, Excel knows that you want to use a percentage format and applies it for you automatically. If you use commas to separate thousands (such as 123,456), Excel applies comma formatting for you. And if you precede your value with a dollar sign, the cell is formatted for currency (assuming that the dollar sign is your system currency symbol).

TIP

A handy default feature in Excel makes entering percentage values into cells easier. If a cell is formatted to display as a percent, you can simply enter a normal value (for example, 12.5 for 12.5%). To enter values less than 1%, precede the value with a zero (for example, 0.52 for 0.52%). If this automatic percent entry feature isn't working (or if you prefer to enter the actual value for percents), access the Excel Options dialog box and click the Advanced tab. In the Editing Options section, locate the Enable Automatic Percent Entry check box and add or remove the check mark.

Formatting numbers by using the Ribbon

The Home ➪ Number group in the Ribbon contains controls that let you quickly apply common number formats (see Figure 2.9).

The Number Format drop-down list contains 11 common number formats. Additional options include an Accounting Number Format drop-down list (to select a currency format), a Percent Style button, and a Comma Style button. The group also contains a button to increase the number of decimal places, and another to decrease the number of decimal places.

FIGURE 2.9

You can find number formatting commands in the Number group of the Home tab.

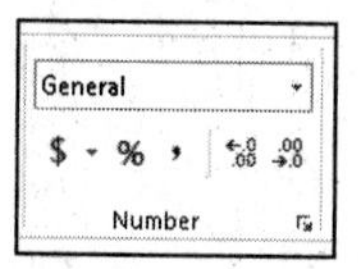

When you select one of these controls, the active cell takes on the specified number format. You also can select a range of cells (or even an entire row or column) before clicking these buttons. If you select more than one cell, Excel applies the number format to all the selected cells.

Using shortcut keys to format numbers

Another way to apply number formatting is to use shortcut keys. Table 2.1 summarizes the shortcut-key combinations that you can use to apply common number formatting to the selected cells or range. Notice that these Ctrl + Shift characters are all located together, in the upper left of your keyboard.

TABLE 2.1 Number Formatting Keyboard Shortcuts

Key Combination	Formatting Applied
Ctrl+Shift+~	General number format (that is, unformatted values)
Ctrl+Shift+$	Currency format with two decimal places (negative numbers appear in parentheses)
Ctrl+Shift+%	Percentage format, with no decimal places
Ctrl+Shift+^	Scientific notation number format, with two decimal places
Ctrl+Shift+#	Date format with the day, month, and year
Ctrl+Shift+@	Time format with the hour, minute, and AM or PM
Ctrl+Shift+!	Two decimal places, thousands separator, and a hyphen for negative values

Formatting numbers using the Format Cells dialog box

In most cases, the number formats that are accessible from the Number group on the Home tab are just fine. Sometimes, however, you want more control over how your values appear. Excel offers a great deal of control over number formats through the use of the Format Cells dialog box, shown in Figure 2.10. For formatting numbers, you need to use the Number tab.

FIGURE 2.10

When you need more control over number formats, use the Number tab of the Format Cells dialog box.

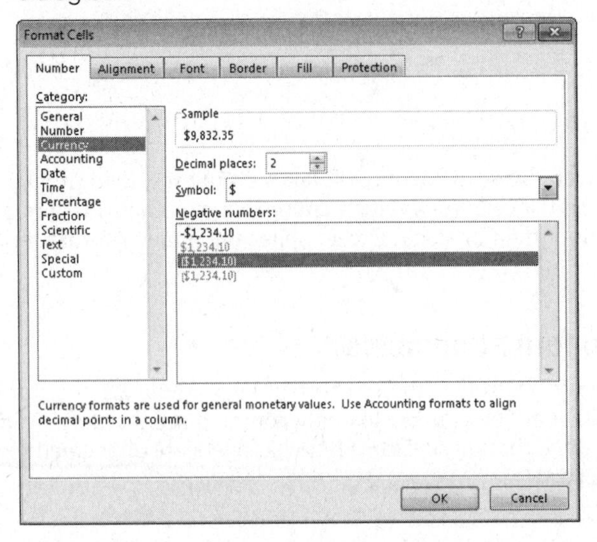

You can bring up the Format Cells dialog box in several ways. Start by selecting the cell or cells that you want to format and then do one of the following:

- Choose Home ⇨ Number and click the small dialog box launcher icon (in the lower-right corner of the Number group).
- Choose Home ⇨ Number, click the Number Format drop-down list, and choose More Number Formats from the drop-down list.
- Right-click the cell and choose Format Cells from the shortcut menu.
- Press Ctrl + 1.

The Number tab of the Format Cells dialog box displays 12 categories of number formats. When you select a category from the list box, the right side of the tab changes to display options appropriate to that category.

The Number category has three options that you can control: the number of decimal places displayed, whether to use a thousands separator, and how you want negative numbers displayed. Notice that the Negative Numbers list box has four choices (two of which display negative values in red), and the choices change depending on the number of decimal places and whether you choose to separate thousands.

The top of the tab displays a sample of how the active cell will appear with the selected number format (visible only if a cell with a value is selected). After you make your choices, click OK to apply the number format to all the selected cells.

When Numbers Appear to Add Incorrectly

Applying a number format to a cell doesn't change the value — it only changes how the value appears in the worksheet. For example, if a cell contains 0.874543, you may format it to appear as 87%. If that cell is used in a formula, the formula uses the full value (0.874543), not the displayed value (87%).

In some situations, formatting may cause Excel to display calculation results that appear incorrect, such as when totaling numbers with decimal places. For example, if values are formatted to display two decimal places, you may not see the actual numbers used in the calculations. But because Excel uses the full precision of the values in its formula, the sum of the two values may appear to be incorrect.

Several solutions to this problem are available. You can format the cells to display more decimal places. You can use the ROUND function on individual numbers and specify the number of decimal places Excel should round to. Or you can instruct Excel to change the worksheet values to match their displayed format. To do so, access the Excel Options dialog box and click the Advanced tab. Check the Set Precision as Displayed check box (located in the When Calculating This Workbook section).

Caution

Selecting the Precision as Displayed option changes the numbers in your worksheets to permanently match their appearance onscreen. This setting applies to all sheets in the active workbook. Most of the time, this option is not what you want. Make sure that you understand the consequences of using the Set Precision as Displayed option.

2

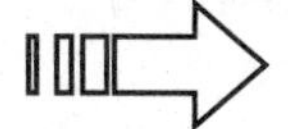

Chapter 10 discusses ROUND and other built-in functions.

The following are the number format categories, along with some general comments:

- **General:** The default format; it displays numbers as integers, as decimals, or in scientific notation if the value is too wide to fit in the cell.
- **Number:** Enables you to specify the number of decimal places, whether to use a comma to separate thousands, and how to display negative numbers (with a minus sign, in red, in parentheses, or in red and in parentheses).
- **Currency:** Enables you to specify the number of decimal places, choose a currency symbol, and how to display negative numbers (with a minus sign, in red, in parentheses, or in red and in parentheses). This format always uses a comma to separate thousands.
- **Accounting:** Differs from the Currency format in that the currency symbols always align vertically.
- **Date:** Enables you to choose from several different date formats.
- **Time:** Enables you to choose from several different time formats.
- **Percentage:** Enables you to choose the number of decimal places and always displays a percent sign.
- **Fraction:** Enables you to choose from among nine fraction formats.

- **Scientific:** Displays numbers in exponential notation (with an E): 2.00E+05 = 200,000; 2.05E+05 = 205,000. You can choose the number of decimal places to display to the left of E. The second example can be read as "2.05 times 10 to the fifth."
- **Text:** When applied to a value, causes Excel to treat the value as text (even if it looks like a number). This feature is useful for such items as part numbers and credit card numbers.
- **Special:** Contains additional number formats. In the U.S. version of Excel, the additional number formats are Zip Code, Zip Code +4, Phone Number, and Social Security Number.
- **Custom:** Enables you to define custom number formats that aren't included in any other category.

TIP

If a cell displays a series of hash marks (such as #########), it usually means that the column isn't wide enough to display the value in the number format that you selected. Either make the column wider or change the number format.

Adding your own custom number formats

Sometimes you may want to display numerical values in a format that isn't included in any of the other categories. If so, the answer is to create your own custom format.

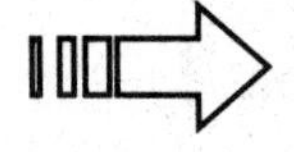

Excel provides you with a great deal of flexibility in creating number formats — so much so that I've devoted an entire chapter (Chapter 25) to this topic.

CHAPTER 3

Essential Worksheet Operations

IN THIS CHAPTER

Understanding Excel worksheet essentials

Controlling your views

Manipulating the rows and columns

This chapter covers some basic information regarding workbooks, worksheets, and windows. You'll discover tips and techniques to help you take control of your worksheets and help you work more efficiently.

Learning the Fundamentals of Excel Worksheets

In Excel, each file is called a *workbook,* and each workbook can contain one or more *worksheets.* You may find it helpful to think of an Excel workbook as a notebook and worksheets as pages in the notebook. As with a notebook, you can view a particular sheet, add new sheets, remove sheets, rearrange sheets, and copy sheets.

The following sections describe the operations that you can perform with worksheets.

Working with Excel windows

Each Excel workbook file that you open is displayed in a window. A workbook can hold any number of sheets, and these sheets can be either *worksheets* (sheets consisting of rows and columns) or *chart sheets* (sheets that hold a single chart). A worksheet is what people usually think of when they think of a spreadsheet. You can open as many Excel workbooks as necessary at the same time.

New Feature

In previous versions of Excel, you could open multiple workbooks and have them displayed in a single Excel window. With Excel 2013, you no longer have that option. An Excel 2013 window holds only one workbook. If you create or open a second workbook, it appears in a separate window.

Each Excel window has five buttons (which appear as icons) at the right side of its title bar. From left to right, they are Help, Full Screen Mode (or Exit Full Screen Mode), Minimize, Maximize (or Restore Down), and Close.

An Excel window can be in one of the following states:

- **Maximized:** Fills the entire screen. To maximize a window, click its Maximize button.
- **Minimized:** Hidden, but still open. To minimize a window, clicks its Minimize button.
- **Restored:** A nonmaximized size. To restore a maximized window, click its Restore Down button. To restore a minimized window, click its icon in the Windows taskbar. A window in this state can be resized and moved.

A nonminimized window can also be put into full-screen mode by clicking the Full Screen Mode button (which is a toggle). In full-screen mode, nonessential elements are hidden, providing the maximum amount of space for your workbook. You can toggle out of full-screen mode temporarily by clicking the top of the screen. To exit full-screen mode, click the top of the screen and then click the Full Screen Mode button again.

If you work with more than one workbook simultaneously (which is quite common), you need to know how to move, resize, and switch among the workbook windows.

Moving and resizing windows

To move or resize a window, make sure that it's not maximized (click the Restore Down button). Then click and drag its title bar with your mouse.

To resize a window, click and drag any of its borders until it's the size that you want it to be. When you position the mouse pointer on a window's border, the mouse pointer changes to a double arrow, which lets you know that you can now click and drag to resize the window. To resize a window horizontally and vertically at the same time, click and drag any of its corners.

If you want all your workbook windows to be visible (that is, not obscured by another window), you can move and resize the windows manually, or you can let Excel do it for you. Choosing View ➪ Window ➪ Arrange All displays the Arrange Windows dialog box, shown in Figure 3.1. This dialog box has four window arrangement options. Just select the one that you want and click OK. Windows that are minimized aren't affected by this command.

FIGURE 3.1

Use the Arrange Windows dialog box to quickly arrange all open nonminimized workbook windows.

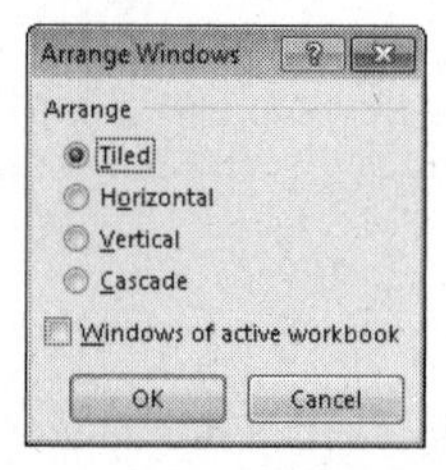

Switching among windows

At any given time, one (and only one) workbook window is the *active window*. The active window accepts your input and is the window on which your commands work. The active window appears at the top of the stack of windows. To work in a workbook in a different window, you need to make that window active. You can make a different window the active window in several ways:

- **Click another window, if it's visible.** The window you click moves to the top and becomes the active window. This method isn't possible if the current window is maximized.
- **Press Ctrl + F6 to cycle through all open windows until the window that you want to work with appears on top as the active window.** Pressing Shift + Ctrl + F6 cycles through the windows in the opposite direction.
- **Choose View ⇨ Window ⇨ Switch Windows and select the window that you want from the drop-down list (the active window has a check mark next to it).** This menu can display as many as nine windows. If you have more than nine workbook windows open, choose More Windows (which appears below the nine window names).
- **Click the Excel icon in the Windows taskbar.** You can then choose the window from the pop-up list.

Most people prefer to do most of their work with maximized workbook windows, which enables you to see more cells and eliminates the distraction of other workbook windows getting in the way. At times, however, viewing multiple windows is preferred. For example, displaying two windows is more efficient if you need to compare information in two workbooks or if you need to copy data from one workbook to another.

TIP

You also can display a single workbook in more than one window. For example, if you have a workbook with two worksheets, you may want to display each worksheet in a separate window to compare the two sheets. All the window manipulation procedures described previously still apply. Choose View ⇨ Window ⇨ New Window to open an additional window for the active workbook.

Closing windows

If you have multiple windows open, you may want to close those windows that you no longer need. Excel offers several ways to close the active window:

- Choose File⇨Close.
- Click the Close button (the X icon) on the workbook window's title bar.
- Press Alt + F4.
- Press Ctrl + W.

When you close a workbook window, Excel checks whether you made any changes since the last time you saved the file. If you have made changes, Excel prompts you to save the file before it closes the window. If not, the window closes without a prompt from Excel. Oddly, Excel provides no way to tell you if a workbook has been changed since it was last saved.

Activating a worksheet

At any given time, one workbook is the active workbook, and one sheet is the active sheet in the active workbook. To activate a different sheet, just click its sheet tab, located at the bottom of the workbook window. You also can use the following shortcut keys to activate a different sheet:

- **Ctrl + PgUp:** Activates the previous sheet, if one exists
- **Ctrl + PgDn:** Activates the next sheet, if one exists

If your workbook has many sheets, all its tabs may not be visible. Use the tab scrolling controls (see Figure 3.2) to scroll the sheet tabs. The sheet tabs share space with the worksheet's horizontal scrollbar. You also can drag the tab split control (to the left of the horizontal scrollbar) to display more or fewer tabs. Dragging the tab split control simultaneously changes the number of tabs and the size of the horizontal scrollbar.

FIGURE 3.2

Use the tab scrolling controls to activate a different worksheet or to see additional worksheet tabs.

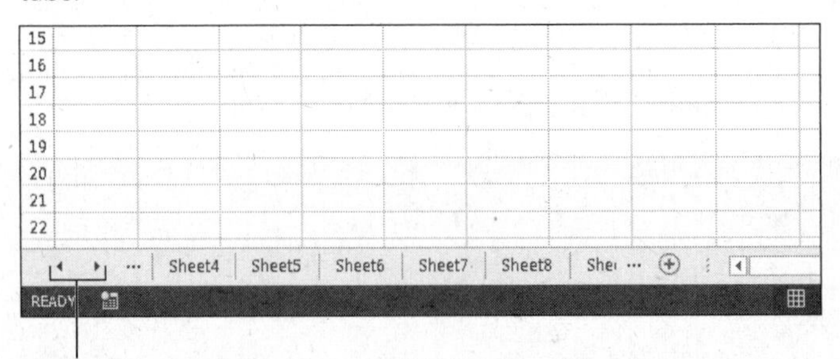

TIP

When you right-click any of the tab scrolling controls, Excel displays a list of all sheets in the workbook. You can quickly activate a sheet by selecting it from the list.

Adding a new worksheet to your workbook

Worksheets can be an excellent organizational tool. Instead of placing everything on a single worksheet, you can use additional worksheets in a workbook to separate various workbook elements logically. For example, if you have several products whose sales you track individually, you may want to assign each product to its own worksheet and then use another worksheet to consolidate your results.

Here are three ways to add a new worksheet to a workbook:

- Click the New Sheet control, which is the plus sign icon located to the right of the last sheet tab. A new sheet is added after the active sheet.
- Press Shift + F11. A new sheet is added before the active sheet.
- Right-click a sheet tab, choose Insert from the shortcut menu, and select the General tab of the Insert dialog box that appears. Then select the Worksheet icon and click OK. A new sheet is added before the active sheet.

3

Deleting a worksheet you no longer need

If you no longer need a worksheet, or if you want to get rid of an empty worksheet in a workbook, you can delete it in either of two ways:

- Right-click its sheet tab and choose Delete from the shortcut menu.
- Activate the unwanted worksheet and choose Home ➪ Cells ➪ Delete ➪ Delete Sheet.

If the worksheet contains any data, Excel asks you to confirm that you want to delete the sheet (see Figure 3.3). If you've never used the worksheet, Excel deletes it immediately without asking for confirmation.

FIGURE 3.3

Excel's gentle warning that you might be losing some data.

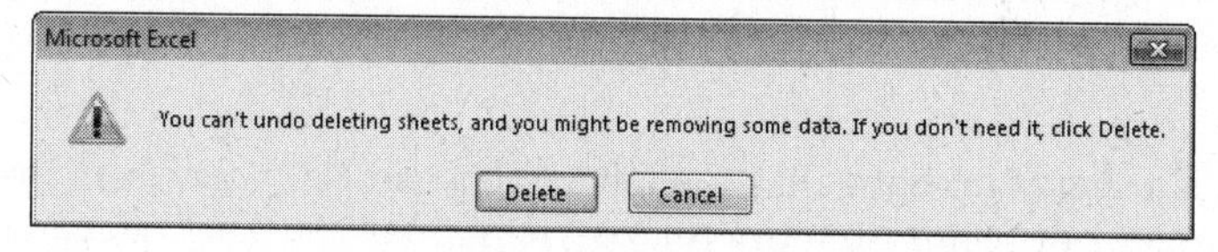

TIP

You can delete multiple sheets with a single command by selecting the sheets that you want to delete. To select multiple sheets, press Ctrl while you click the sheet tabs that you want to delete. To select a group of contiguous sheets, click the first sheet tab, press Shift, and then click the last sheet tab (Excel displays the selected sheet names bold and underlined). Then use either method to delete the selected sheets.

CAUTION

When you delete a worksheet, it's gone for good. Deleting a worksheet is one of the few operations in Excel that can't be undone.

Changing the name of a worksheet

The default names that Excel uses for worksheets — Sheet1, Sheet2, and so on — are generic and nondescriptive. To make it easier to locate data in a multisheet workbook, you'll want to make the sheet names more descriptive.

To change a sheet's name, double-click the sheet tab. Excel highlights the name on the sheet tab so that you can edit the name or replace it with a new name.

Sheet names can contain as many as 31 characters, and spaces are allowed. However, you can't use the following characters in sheet names:

- : colon
- / slash
- \ backslash
- [ ] square brackets
- ? question mark
- * asterisk

Keep in mind that a longer worksheet name results in a wider tab, which takes up more space onscreen. Therefore, if you use lengthy sheet names, you won't be able to see as many sheet tabs without scrolling the tab list.

Changing a sheet tab color

Excel allows you to change the background color of your worksheet tabs. For example, you may prefer to color-code the sheet tabs to make identifying the worksheet's contents easier.

To change the color of a sheet tab, right-click the tab and choose Tab Color from the shortcut menu. Then select the color from the color selector box. You can't change the text color, but Excel will choose a contrasting color to make the text visible. For example, if you make a sheet tab black, Excel will display white text.

Rearranging your worksheets

You may want to rearrange the order of worksheets in a workbook. If you have a separate worksheet for each sales region, for example, arranging the worksheets in alphabetical order might be helpful. You can also move a worksheet from one workbook to another and create copies of worksheets, either in the same workbook or in a different workbook.

You can move or copy a worksheet in the following ways:

- Right-click the sheet tab and choose Move or Copy to display the Move or Copy dialog box (see Figure 3.4). Use this dialog box to specify the operation and the location for the sheet.

FIGURE 3.4

Use the Move or Copy dialog box to move or copy worksheets in the same or another workbook.

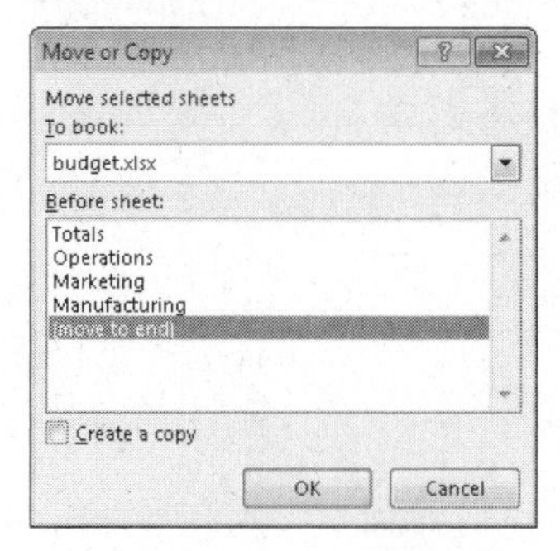

- To move a worksheet, click the worksheet tab and drag it to its desired location. When you drag, the mouse pointer changes to a small sheet, and a small arrow guides you. To move a worksheet to a different workbook, the second workbook must be open and not maximized.
- To copy a worksheet, click the worksheet tab, and press Ctrl while dragging the tab to its desired location. When you drag, the mouse pointer changes to a small sheet with a plus sign on it. To copy a worksheet to a different workbook, the second workbook must be open and not maximized.

TIP

You can move or copy multiple sheets simultaneously. First, select the sheets by clicking their sheet tabs while holding down the Ctrl key. Then you can move or copy the set of sheets by using the preceding methods.

Preventing Sheet Actions

To prevent others from unhiding hidden sheets, inserting new sheets, renaming sheets, copying sheets, or deleting sheets, protect the workbook's structure:

1. **Choose Review ➪ Changes ➪ Protect Workbook.**
2. **In the Protect Workbook dialog box, select the Structure option.**
3. **Provide a password (optional).**

After performing these steps, several commands will no longer be available when you right-click a sheet tab: Insert, Delete Sheet, Rename Sheet, Move or Copy Sheet, Tab Color, Hide Sheet, and Unhide Sheet. Be aware, however, that this is a very weak security measure. Cracking this particular protection feature is relatively easy.

You can also make a sheet "very hidden." A sheet that is very hidden doesn't appear in the Unhide dialog box. To make a sheet very hidden:

1. **Activate the worksheet.**
2. **Choose Developer ➪ Controls ➪ Properties.** The Properties dialog box, shown in the following figure, appears. (If the Developer tab isn't available, you can turn it on using the Customize Ribbon tab of the Excel Options dialog box.)
3. **In the Properties dialog box, select the Visible option and choose 2 – xlSheetVeryHidden.**

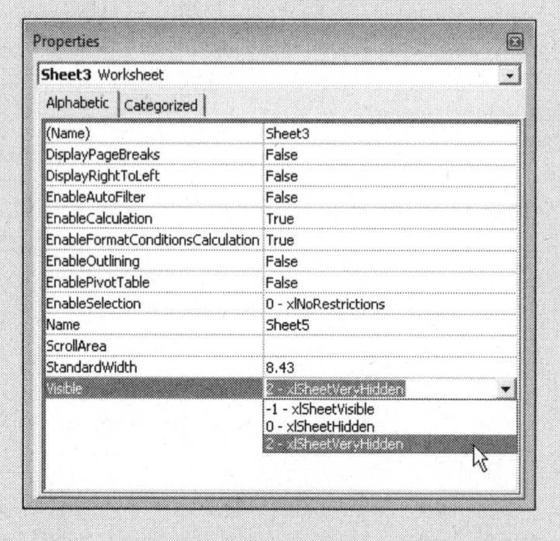

After performing these steps, the worksheet is hidden and doesn't appear in the Unhide dialog box.

CAUTION

Be careful! After you make a sheet very hidden, you can't use the Properties dialog box to unhide it because you aren't able to select the sheet! To unhide such a sheet, press Alt+F11 to activate the Visual Basic Editor. Locate the workbook in the Projects window and select the name of the sheet that is very hidden. Press F4 to display the Properties dialog box, in which you can change the Visible property back to –1 – xlSheetVisible.

If you move or copy a worksheet to a workbook that already has a sheet with the same name, Excel changes the name to make it unique. For example, Sheet1 becomes Sheet1 (2). You probably want to rename the copied sheet to give it a more meaningful name (see "Changing the name of a worksheet," earlier in this chapter).

NOTE

When you move or copy a worksheet to a different workbook, any defined names and custom formats also get copied to the new workbook.

Hiding and unhiding a worksheet

In some situations, you may want to hide one or more worksheets. Hiding a sheet may be useful if you don't want others to see it or if you just want to get it out of the way. When a sheet is hidden, its sheet tab is also hidden. You can't hide all the sheets in a workbook; at least one sheet must remain visible.

To hide a worksheet, right-click its sheet tab and choose Hide Sheet. The active worksheet (or selected worksheets) will be hidden from view.

To unhide a hidden worksheet, right-click any sheet tab and choose Unhide Sheet. Excel opens the Unhide dialog box, which lists all hidden sheets. Choose the sheet that you want to redisplay, and click OK. For reasons known only to a Microsoft programmer who is probably retired by now, you can't select multiple sheets from this dialog box, so you need to repeat the command for each sheet that you want to unhide. When you unhide a sheet, it appears in its previous position among the sheet tabs.

3

Controlling the Worksheet View

As you add more information to a worksheet, you may find that navigating and locating what you want gets more difficult. Excel includes a few options that enable you to view your sheet, and sometimes multiple sheets, more efficiently. This section discusses a few additional worksheet options at your disposal.

Zooming in or out for a better view

Normally, everything you see onscreen is displayed at 100%. You can change the *zoom percentage* from 10% (very tiny) to 400% (huge). Using a small zoom percentage can help you to get a bird's-eye view of your worksheet to see how it's laid out. Zooming in is useful if you have trouble deciphering tiny type. Zooming doesn't change the font size specified for the cells, so it has no effect on printed output.

Excel contains separate options for changing the size of your printed output. (Use the controls in the Page Layout ➪ Scale to Fit ribbon group.) See Chapter 9 for details.

Figure 3.5 shows a window zoomed to 10% and a window zoomed to 400%.

FIGURE 3.5

You can zoom in or out for a different view of your worksheets.

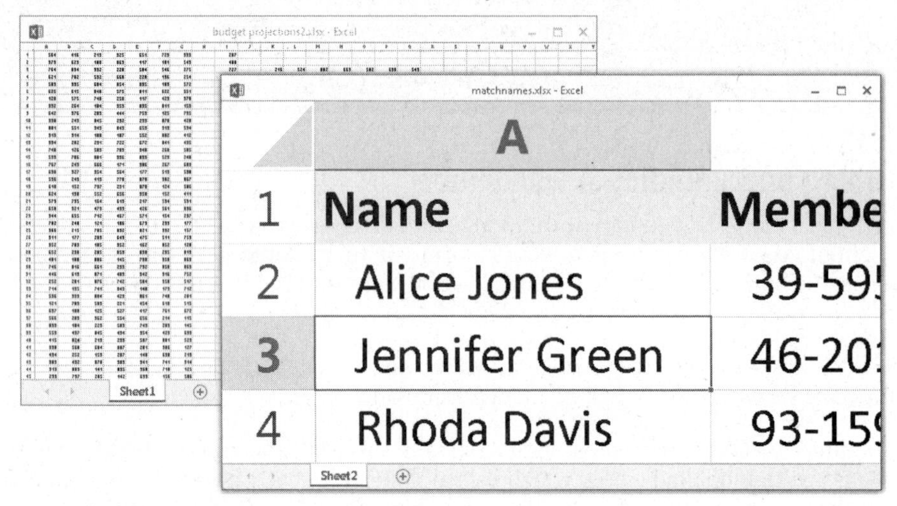

You can change the zoom factor of the active worksheet window by using any of three methods:

- Use the Zoom slider located on the right side of the status bar. Click and drag the slider, and your screen transforms instantly.
- Press Ctrl and use the wheel button on your mouse to zoom in or out.
- Choose View ➪ Zoom ➪ Zoom, which displays a dialog box with some zoom options.
- Select a range of cells, and choose View ➪ Zoom ➪ Zoom to Selection. The selected range will be enlarged so it fills the entire window.

TIP

Zooming affects only the active worksheet window, so you can use different zoom factors for different worksheets. Also, if you have a worksheet displayed in two different windows, you can set a different zoom factor for each of the windows.

If your worksheet uses named ranges (see Chapter 4), zooming your worksheet to 39% or less displays the name of the range overlaid on the cells. Viewing named ranges in this manner is useful for getting an overview of how a worksheet is laid out.

Viewing a worksheet in multiple windows

Sometimes, you may want to view two different parts of a worksheet simultaneously — perhaps to make referencing a distant cell in a formula easier. Or you may want to examine more than one sheet in the same workbook simultaneously. You can accomplish either of these actions by opening a new view to the workbook, using one or more additional windows.

To create and display a new view of the active workbook, choose View ➪ Window ➪ New Window.

Excel displays a new window for the active workbook, similar to the one shown in Figure 3.6. In this case, each window shows a different worksheet in the workbook. Notice the text in the windows' title bars: `climate data.xlsx:1` and `climate data.xlsx:2`. To help you keep track of the windows, Excel appends a colon and a number to each window.

FIGURE 3.6

Use multiple windows to view different sections of a workbook at the same time.

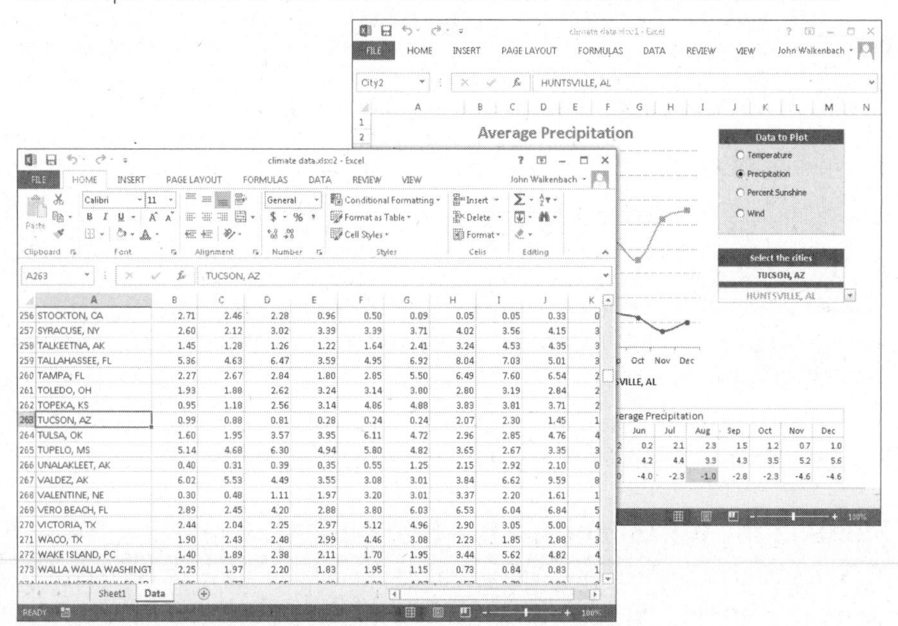

TIP

If the workbook is maximized when you create a new window, you may not even notice that Excel created the new window. If you look at the Excel title bar, though, you'll see that the workbook title now has `:2` appended to the name. Choose View ➪ Window ➪ Arrange All, and then choose one of the Arrange options in the Arrange Windows dialog box to display the open windows. If you select the Windows of Active Workbook check box, only the windows of the active workbook are arranged.

A single workbook can have as many views (that is, separate windows) as you want. Each window is independent. In other words, scrolling to a new location in one window doesn't cause scrolling in the other window(s). However, if you make changes to the worksheet shown in a particular window, those changes are also made in all views of that worksheet.

You can close these additional windows when you no longer need them. For example, clicking the Close button on the active window's title bar closes the active window but doesn't close the other windows for the workbook.

TIP

Multiple windows make copying or moving information from one worksheet to another easier. You can use Excel's drag-and-drop procedures to copy or move ranges.

Comparing sheets side by side

In some situations, you may want to compare two worksheets that are in different windows. The View Side by Side feature makes this task a bit easier.

First, make sure that the two sheets are displayed in separate windows. (The sheets can be in the same workbook or in different workbooks.) If you want to compare two sheets in the same workbook, choose View ⇨ Window ⇨ New Window to create a new window for the active workbook. Activate the first window; then choose View ⇨ Window ⇨ View Side by Side. If more than two windows are open, you see a dialog box that lets you select the window for the comparison. The two windows are tiled to fill the entire screen.

When using the Compare Side by Side feature, scrolling in one of the windows also scrolls the other window. If you don't want this simultaneous scrolling, choose View ⇨ Window ⇨ Synchronous Scrolling (which is a toggle). If you have rearranged or moved the windows, choose View ⇨ Window ⇨ Reset Window Position to restore the windows to the initial side-by-side arrangement. To turn off the side-by-side viewing, choose View ⇨ Window ⇨ View Side by Side again.

Keep in mind that this feature is for manual comparison only. Unfortunately, Excel doesn't provide a way to actually point out the differences between two sheets.

Splitting the worksheet window into panes

If you prefer not to clutter your screen with additional windows, Excel provides another option for viewing multiple parts of the same worksheet. Choosing View ⇨ Window ⇨ Split splits the active worksheet into two or four separate panes. The split occurs at the location of the cell pointer. If the cell pointer is in row 1 or column A, this command results in a two-pane split; otherwise, it gives you four panes. You can use the mouse to drag the individual panes to resize them.

Figure 3.7 shows a worksheet split into two panes. Notice that row numbers aren't continuous. The top pane shows rows 8 through 20, and the bottom pane shows rows 694 through 707. In other words, splitting panes enables you to display in a single window widely separated areas of a worksheet. To remove the split panes, choose View ➪ Window ➪ Split again.

FIGURE 3.7

You can split the worksheet window into two or four panes to view different areas of the worksheet at the same time.

	A	B	C	D	E	F	G	H	I	J	K	L	M
8	ABERDEEN, SD	0.48	0.48	1.34	1.83	2.69	3.49	2.92	2.42	1.81	1.63	0.75	0.38
9	ABILENE, TX	0.97	1.13	1.41	1.67	2.83	3.06	1.69	2.63	2.91	2.90	1.30	1.27
10	AKRON, OH	2.49	2.28	3.15	3.39	3.96	3.55	4.02	3.65	3.43	2.53	3.04	2.98
11	ALAMOSA, CO	0.25	0.21	0.46	0.54	0.70	0.59	0.94	1.19	0.89	0.67	0.48	0.33
12	ALBANY, NY	2.71	2.27	3.17	3.25	3.67	3.74	3.50	3.68	3.31	3.23	3.31	2.76
13	ALBUQUERQUE, NM	0.49	0.44	0.61	0.50	0.60	0.65	1.27	1.73	1.07	1.00	0.62	0.49
14	ALLENTOWN, PA	3.50	2.75	3.56	3.49	4.47	3.99	4.27	4.35	4.37	3.33	3.70	3.39
15	ALPENA, MI	1.76	1.35	2.13	2.31	2.61	2.53	3.17	3.50	2.80	2.33	2.08	1.83
16	AMARILLO, TX	0.63	0.55	1.13	1.33	2.50	3.28	2.68	2.94	1.88	1.50	0.68	0.61
17	ANCHORAGE, AK	0.68	0.74	0.65	0.52	0.69	1.06	1.70	2.93	2.87	2.08	1.09	1.05
18	ANNETTE, AK	9.67	8.05	7.96	7.37	5.73	4.72	4.26	6.12	9.49	13.86	12.21	11.39
19	APALACHICOLA, FL	4.87	3.76	4.95	3.00	2.62	4.30	7.31	7.29	7.10	4.18	3.62	3.51
20	ASHEVILLE, NC	4.06	3.83	4.59	3.50	4.41	4.38	3.87	4.30	3.72	3.17	3.82	3.39
694	ROCKFORD, IL	19.00	24.70	36.10	47.90	59.60	68.80	72.90	70.90	62.80	51.00	37.20	24.40
695	ROSWELL, NM	40.00	45.70	52.90	60.50	69.60	78.00	80.80	78.90	72.00	61.40	48.90	40.70
696	SACRAMENTO, CA	46.30	51.20	54.50	58.90	65.50	71.50	75.40	74.80	71.70	64.40	53.30	45.80
697	SAINT CLOUD, MN	8.80	16.10	28.40	43.60	56.60	65.10	69.80	67.20	57.40	45.30	28.80	14.40
698	SALEM, OR	40.30	43.00	46.50	50.00	55.60	61.20	66.80	67.00	62.20	52.90	45.20	40.20
699	SALT LAKE CITY, UT	29.20	34.50	43.10	50.00	58.80	69.00	77.00	75.60	65.00	52.50	39.60	30.20
700	SAN ANGELO, TX	44.90	49.70	57.20	65.00	73.10	79.20	82.40	81.30	74.80	65.40	54.00	46.40
701	SAN ANTONIO, TX	50.30	54.70	62.10	68.60	75.80	81.50	84.30	84.20	79.40	70.70	60.00	52.40
702	SAN DIEGO, CA	57.80	58.90	60.00	62.60	64.60	67.40	70.90	72.50	71.60	67.60	61.80	57.60
703	SAN FRANCISCO AP, CA	49.40	52.40	54.00	56.20	58.70	61.40	62.80	63.60	63.90	61.00	54.70	49.50
704	SAN FRANCISCO C.O., CA	52.30	55.00	55.90	57.30	58.40	60.50	61.30	62.40	63.70	62.50	57.50	52.70
705	SAN JUAN, PR	76.60	76.90	77.60	79.10	80.60	82.10	82.20	82.40	82.20	81.60	79.60	77.70
706	SANTA BARBARA, CA	53.10	55.20	56.70	58.90	60.90	64.20	67.00	68.60	67.40	63.50	57.50	53.20
707	SANTA MARIA, CA	51.60	53.10	53.80	55.50	57.80	60.90	63.50	64.20	63.90	61.10	55.50	51.60
708	SAULT STE. MARIE, MI	13.20	15.60	24.90	38.40	51.30	58.60	63.90	63.30	54.80	44.40	32.40	20.20

Sheet1 | Data

Keeping the titles in view by freezing panes

If you set up a worksheet with column headings or descriptive text in the first column, this identifying information won't be visible when you scroll down or to the right. Excel provides a handy solution to this problem: freezing panes. Freezing panes keeps the column or row headings visible while you're scrolling through the worksheet.

To freeze panes, start by moving the cell pointer to the cell below the row that you want to remain visible while you scroll vertically, and to the right of the column that you want to remain visible while you scroll horizontally. Then choose View ➪ Window ➪ Freeze Panes and select the Freeze Panes option from the drop-down list. Excel inserts dark lines to indicate the frozen rows and columns. The frozen row and column remain visible while you scroll throughout the worksheet. To remove the frozen panes, choose View ➪ Window ➪ Freeze Panes, and select the Unfreeze Panes option from the drop-down list.

Figure 3.8 shows a worksheet with frozen panes. In this case, rows 1:4 and column A are frozen in place. This technique allows you to scroll down and to the right to locate some information while keeping the column titles and the column A entries visible.

FIGURE 3.8

Freeze certain columns and rows to make them remain visible while you scroll the worksheet.

	A	D	E	F	G	H	I	J	K	L	M
1	**Normal Monthly Precipita**										
2	**NORMALS 1971-2000**										
3											
4	**City**	**MAR**	**APR**	**MAY**	**JUN**	**JUL**	**AUG**	**SEP**	**OCT**	**NOV**	**DEC**
131	JACKSONVILLE, FL	3.93	3.14	3.48	5.37	5.97	6.87	7.90	3.86	2.34	2.64
132	JOHNSTON ISLAND, PC	2.01	1.86	1.14	0.87	1.40	2.07	2.46	2.78	4.78	2.70
133	JUNEAU, AK	3.51	2.96	3.48	3.36	4.14	5.37	7.54	8.30	5.43	5.41
134	KAHULUI, HI	2.35	1.75	0.66	0.23	0.49	0.53	0.39	1.05	2.17	3.08
135	KALISPELL, MT	1.11	1.22	2.04	2.30	1.41	1.25	1.20	0.96	1.45	1.65
136	KANSAS CITY, MO	2.44	3.38	5.39	4.44	4.42	3.54	4.64	3.33	2.30	1.64
137	KEY WEST, FL	1.86	2.06	3.48	4.57	3.27	5.40	5.45	4.34	2.64	2.14
138	KING SALMON, AK	0.79	0.94	1.35	1.70	2.15	2.89	2.81	2.09	1.54	1.39
139	KNOXVILLE, TN	5.17	3.99	4.68	4.04	4.71	2.89	3.04	2.65	3.98	4.49
140	KODIAK, AK	5.22	5.48	6.31	5.38	4.12	4.48	7.84	8.36	6.63	7.64
141	KOROR, PC	8.79	9.45	11.27	17.54	16.99	14.47	11.65	13.41	11.62	12.33
142	KOTZEBUE, AK	0.38	0.41	0.33	0.57	1.43	2.00	1.70	0.95	0.71	0.60
143	KWAJALEIN, MARSHALL IS	3.82	7.63	8.62	8.86	10.24	10.42	11.82	11.46	10.74	7.94
144	LA CROSSE, WI	2.00	3.38	3.38	4.00	4.25	4.28	3.40	2.16	2.10	1.23
145	LAKE CHARLES, LA	3.54	3.64	6.06	6.07	5.12	4.85	5.95	3.94	4.61	4.60
146	LANDER, WY	1.24	2.07	2.38	1.15	0.84	0.57	1.14	1.37	0.99	0.61
147	LANSING, MI	2.33	3.09	2.71	3.60	2.68	3.46	3.48	2.29	2.66	2.17
148	LAS VEGAS, NV	0.59	0.15	0.24	0.08	0.44	0.45	0.31	0.24	0.31	0.40
149	LEWISTON, ID	1.12	1.30	1.56	1.16	0.72	0.75	0.80	0.96	1.21	1.05
150	LEXINGTON, KY	4.41	3.67	4.78	4.58	4.80	3.77	3.11	2.70	3.44	4.03
151	LIHUE, HI	3.58	3.00	2.87	1.82	2.12	1.91	2.69	4.25	4.70	4.78
152	LINCOLN, NE	2.21	2.90	4.23	3.51	3.54	3.35	2.92	1.94	1.58	0.86
153	LITTLE ROCK, AR	4.88	5.47	5.05	3.95	3.31	2.93	3.71	4.25	5.73	4.71
154	LONG BEACH, CA	2.43	0.60	0.23	0.08	0.02	0.10	0.24	0.40	1.12	1.76

Sheet1 | Data

Most of the time, you'll want to freeze either the first row or the first column. The View ➪ Window ➪ Freeze Panes drop-down list has two additional options: Freeze Top Row and Freeze First Column. Using these commands eliminates the need to position the cell pointer before freezing panes.

TIP

If you designated a range to be a table (by choosing Insert ➪ Tables ➪ Table), you may not even need to freeze panes. When you scroll down, Excel displays the table column headings in place of the column letters. Figure 3.9 shows an example. The table headings replace the column letters only when a cell within the table is selected.

Monitoring cells with a Watch Window

In some situations, you may want to monitor the value in a particular cell as you work. As you scroll throughout the worksheet, that cell may disappear from view. A feature known as Watch Window can help. A *Watch Window* displays the value of any number of cells in a handy window that's always visible.

FIGURE 3.9

When using a table, scrolling down displays the table headings where the column letters normally appear.

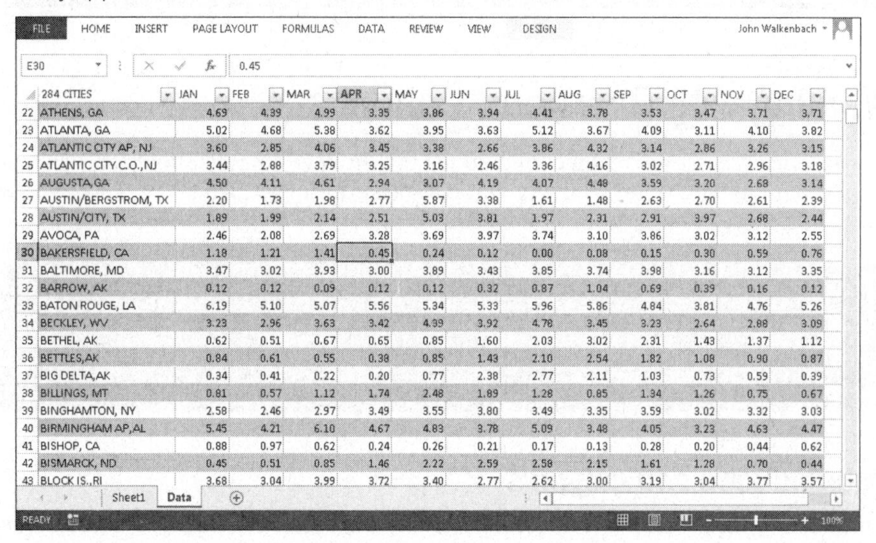

	284 CITIES	JAN	FEB	MAR	APR	MAY	JUN	JUL	AUG	SEP	OCT	NOV	DEC
22	ATHENS, GA	4.69	4.39	4.99	3.35	3.86	3.94	4.41	3.78	3.53	3.47	3.71	3.71
23	ATLANTA, GA	5.02	4.68	5.38	3.62	3.95	3.63	5.12	3.67	4.09	3.11	4.10	3.82
24	ATLANTIC CITY AP, NJ	3.60	2.85	4.06	3.45	3.38	2.66	3.86	4.32	3.14	2.86	3.26	3.15
25	ATLANTIC CITY C.O.,NJ	3.44	2.88	3.79	3.25	3.16	2.46	3.36	4.16	3.02	2.71	2.96	3.18
26	AUGUSTA,GA	4.50	4.11	4.61	2.94	3.07	4.19	4.07	4.48	3.59	3.20	2.68	3.14
27	AUSTIN/BERGSTROM, TX	2.20	1.73	1.98	2.77	5.87	3.38	1.61	1.48	2.63	2.70	2.61	2.39
28	AUSTIN/CITY, TX	1.89	1.99	2.14	2.51	5.03	3.81	1.97	2.31	2.91	3.97	2.68	2.44
29	AVOCA, PA	2.46	2.08	2.69	3.28	3.69	3.97	3.74	3.10	3.86	3.02	3.12	2.55
30	BAKERSFIELD, CA	1.18	1.21	1.41	0.45	0.24	0.12	0.00	0.08	0.15	0.30	0.59	0.76
31	BALTIMORE, MD	3.47	3.02	3.93	3.00	3.89	3.43	3.85	3.74	3.98	3.16	3.12	3.35
32	BARROW, AK	0.12	0.12	0.09	0.12	0.12	0.32	0.87	1.04	0.69	0.39	0.16	0.12
33	BATON ROUGE, LA	6.19	5.10	5.07	5.56	5.34	5.33	5.96	5.86	4.84	3.81	4.76	5.26
34	BECKLEY, WV	3.23	2.96	3.63	3.42	4.39	3.92	4.78	3.45	3.23	2.64	2.88	3.09
35	BETHEL, AK	0.62	0.51	0.67	0.65	0.85	1.60	2.03	3.02	2.31	1.43	1.37	1.12
36	BETTLES,AK	0.84	0.61	0.55	0.38	0.85	1.43	2.10	2.54	1.82	1.08	0.90	0.87
37	BIG DELTA,AK	0.34	0.41	0.22	0.20	0.77	2.38	2.77	2.11	1.03	0.73	0.59	0.39
38	BILLINGS, MT	0.81	0.57	1.12	1.74	2.48	1.89	1.28	0.85	1.34	1.26	0.75	0.67
39	BINGHAMTON, NY	2.58	2.46	2.97	3.49	3.55	3.80	3.49	3.35	3.59	3.02	3.32	3.03
40	BIRMINGHAM AP,AL	5.45	4.21	6.10	4.67	4.83	3.78	5.09	3.48	4.05	3.23	4.63	4.47
41	BISHOP, CA	0.88	0.97	0.62	0.24	0.26	0.21	0.17	0.13	0.28	0.20	0.44	0.62
42	BISMARCK, ND	0.45	0.51	0.85	1.46	2.22	2.59	2.58	2.15	1.61	1.28	0.70	0.44
43	BLOCK IS.,RI	3.68	3.04	3.99	3.72	3.40	2.77	2.62	3.00	3.19	3.04	3.77	3.57

To display the Watch Window, choose Formulas ➪ Formula Auditing ➪ Watch Window. The Watch Window is actually a task pane, and you can dock it to the side of the window or drag it and make it float over the worksheet.

To add a cell to watch, click Add Watch and specify the cell that you want to watch. The Watch Window displays the value in that cell. You can add any number of cells to the Watch Window. Figure 3.10 shows the Watch Window monitoring four cells.

FIGURE 3.10

Use the Watch Window to monitor the value in one or more cells.

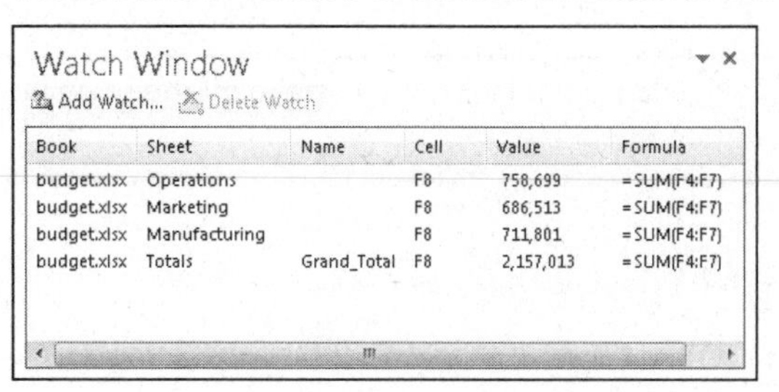

Watch Window

Add Watch... Delete Watch

Book	Sheet	Name	Cell	Value	Formula
budget.xlsx	Operations		F8	758,699	=SUM(F4:F7)
budget.xlsx	Marketing		F8	686,513	=SUM(F4:F7)
budget.xlsx	Manufacturing		F8	711,801	=SUM(F4:F7)
budget.xlsx	Totals	Grand_Total	F8	2,157,013	=SUM(F4:F7)

TIP

Double-click a cell in the Watch Window to immediately select that cell.

Working with Rows and Columns

This section discusses worksheet operations that involve complete rows and columns (rather than individual cells). Every worksheet has exactly 1,048,576 rows and 16,384 columns, and these values can't be changed.

NOTE

If you open a workbook that was created in a version of Excel prior to Excel 2007, the workbook is opened in Compatibility Mode. These workbooks have 65,536 rows and 256 columns. If you would like to increase the number of rows and columns, save the workbook as an Excel `.xlsx` or `.xlsm` file and then reopen it.

Inserting rows and columns

Although the number of rows and columns in a worksheet is fixed, you can still insert and delete rows and columns if you need to make room for additional information. These operations don't change the number of rows or columns. Instead, inserting a new row moves down the other rows to accommodate the new row. The last row is simply removed from the worksheet if it's empty. Inserting a new column shifts the columns to the right, and the last column is removed if it's empty.

NOTE

If the last row isn't empty, you can't insert a new row. Similarly, if the last column contains information, Excel doesn't let you insert a new column. In either case, attempting to add a row or column displays the dialog box shown in Figure 3.11.

FIGURE 3.11

You can't add a new row or column if it causes nonblank cells to move off the worksheet.

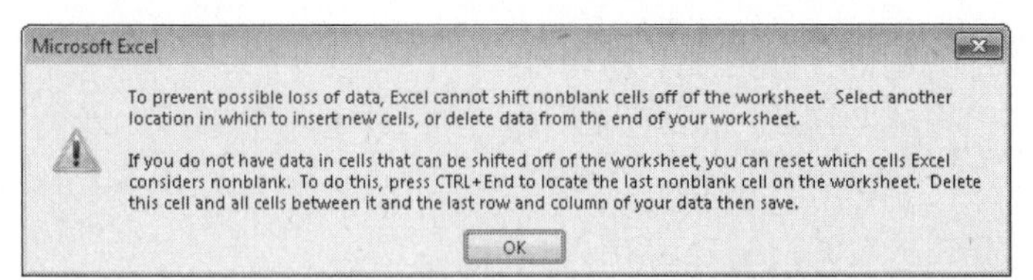

To insert a new row or rows, use either of these methods:

- Select an entire row or multiple rows by clicking the row numbers in the worksheet border. Right-click and choose Insert from the shortcut menu.
- Move the cell pointer to the row that you want to insert, and then choose Home ➪ Cells ➪ Insert ➪ Insert Sheet Rows. If you select multiple cells in the column, Excel inserts additional rows that correspond to the number of cells selected in the column and moves the rows below the insertion down.

To insert a new column or columns, use either of these methods:

- Select an entire column or columns by clicking the column letters in the worksheet border. Right-click and choose Insert from the shortcut menu.
- Move the cell pointer to the column that you want to insert, and then choose Home ➪ Cells ➪ Insert ➪ Insert Sheet Columns. If you select multiple cells in the row, Excel inserts additional columns that correspond to the number of cells selected in the row.

You can also insert cells, rather than just rows or columns. Select the range into which you want to add new cells and then choose Home ➪ Cells ➪ Insert ➪ Insert Cells (or right-click the selection and choose Insert). To insert cells, the existing cells must be shifted to the right or shifted down. Therefore, Excel displays the Insert dialog box shown in Figure 3.12 so that you can specify the direction in which you want to shift the cells. Notice that this dialog box also enables you to insert entire rows or columns.

FIGURE 3.12

You can insert partial rows or columns by using the Insert dialog box.

Deleting rows and columns

You may also want to delete rows or columns in a worksheet. For example, your sheet may contain old data that is no longer needed, or you may want to remove empty rows or columns.

To delete a row or rows, use either of these methods:

- Select an entire row or multiple rows by clicking the row numbers in the worksheet border. Right-click and choose Delete from the shortcut menu.

- Move the cell pointer to the row that you want to delete, and then choose Home ➪ Cells ➪ Delete Sheet Rows. If you select multiple cells in the column, Excel deletes all rows in the selection.

Deleting columns works in a similar way. If you discover that you accidentally deleted a row or column, select Undo from the Quick Access toolbar (or press Ctrl + Z) to undo the action.

Hiding rows and columns

In some cases, you may want to hide particular rows or columns. Hiding rows and columns may be useful if you don't want users to see particular information, or if you need to print a report that summarizes the information in the worksheet without showing all the details.

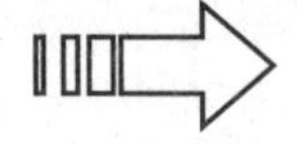

Chapter 27 discusses another way to summarize worksheet data without showing all the details — worksheet outlining.

To hide rows in your worksheet, select the row or rows that you want to hide by clicking in the row header on the left. Then right-click and choose Hide from the shortcut menu. Or you can use the commands on the Home ➪ Cells ➪ Format ➪ Hide & Unhide drop-down list.

To hide columns, use the same technique, but start by selecting columns rather than rows.

TIP

You can also drag the row or column's border to hide the row or column. You must drag the border in the row or column heading. Drag the bottom border of a row upward or the border of a column to the left.

A hidden row is actually a row with its height set to zero. Similarly, a hidden column has a column width of zero. When you use the navigation keys to move the cell pointer, cells in hidden rows or columns are skipped. In other words, you can't use the navigation keys to move to a cell in a hidden row or column.

Notice, however, that Excel displays a very narrow column heading for hidden columns and a very narrow row heading for hidden rows. You can click and drag the column heading to make the column wider — and make it visible again. For a hidden row, click and drag the small row heading to make the column visible.

Another way to unhide a row or column is to choose Home ➪ Find & Select ➪ Go To (or its F5 equivalent) to select a cell in a hidden row or column. For example, if column A is hidden, you can press F5 and specify cell A1 (or any other cell in column A) to move the cell pointer to the hidden column. Then you can choose Home ➪ Cells ➪ Format ➪ Hide & Unhide ➪ Unhide Columns.

Changing column widths and row heights

Often, you'll want to change the width of a column or the height of a row. For example, you can make columns narrower to show more information on a printed page. Or you may want to increase row height to create a "double-spaced" effect.

Excel provides several different ways to change the widths of columns and the height of rows.

Changing column widths

Column width is measured in terms of the number of characters of a *monospaced font* that will fit into the cell's width. By default, each column's width is 8.43 units, which equates to 64 pixels (px).

TIP
If hash symbols (#) fill a cell that contains a numerical value, the column isn't wide enough to accommodate the information in the cell. Widen the column to solve the problem.

Before you change the column width, you can select multiple columns so that the width will be the same for all selected columns. To select multiple columns, either click and drag in the column border or press Ctrl while you select individual columns. To select all columns, click the button where the row and column headers intersect. You can change columns widths by using any of the following techniques:

- Drag the right-column border with the mouse until the column is the desired width.
- Choose Home ➪ Cells ➪ Format ➪ Column Width and enter a value in the Column Width dialog box.
- Choose Home ➪ Cells ➪ Format ➪ AutoFit Column Width to adjust the width of the selected column so that the widest entry in the column fits. Instead of selecting an entire column, you can just select cells in the column, and the column is adjusted based on the widest entry in your selection.
- Double-click the right border of a column header to set the column width automatically to the widest entry in the column.

TIP
To change the default width of all columns, choose Home ➪ Cells ➪ Format ➪ Default Width. This command displays a dialog box into which you enter the new default column width. All columns that haven't been previously adjusted take on the new column width.

CAUTION
After you manually adjust a column's width, Excel will no longer automatically adjust the column to accommodate longer numerical entries. If you enter a long number that displays as hash symbols (#), you need to change the column width manually.

Changing row heights

Row height is measured in points (pt; a standard unit of measurement in the printing trade — 72 pt is equal to 1 inch). The default row height using the default font is 15 pt, or 20 px.

The default row height can vary, depending on the font defined in the Normal style. In addition, Excel automatically adjusts row heights to accommodate the tallest font in the row. So, if you change the font size of a cell to 20 pt, for example, Excel makes the row taller so that the entire text is visible.

You can set the row height manually, however, by using any of the following techniques. As with columns, you can select multiple rows.

- Drag the lower row border with the mouse until the row is the desired height.
- Choose Home ➪ Cells ➪ Format ➪ Row Height and enter a value (in points) in the Row Height dialog box.
- Double-click the bottom border of a row to set the row height automatically to the tallest entry in the row. You can also choose Home ➪ Cells ➪ Format ➪ Autofit Row Height for this task.

Changing the row height is useful for spacing out rows and is almost always preferable to inserting empty rows between lines of data.

CHAPTER 4

Working with Cells and Ranges

IN THIS CHAPTER

- Understanding Excel cells and ranges
- Selecting cells and ranges
- Copying or moving ranges
- Using names to work with ranges
- Adding comments to cells

Most of the work you do in Excel involves cells and ranges. Understanding how best to manipulate cells and ranges will save you time and effort. This chapter discusses a variety of techniques that are essential for Excel users.

Understanding Cells and Ranges

A *cell* is a single element in a worksheet that can hold a value, some text, or a formula. A cell is identified by its *address,* which consists of its column letter and row number. For example, cell D9 is the cell in the fourth column and the ninth row.

A group of cells is called a *range.* You designate a range address by specifying its upper-left cell address and its lower-right cell address, separated by a colon.

Here are some examples of range addresses:

C24	A range that consists of a single cell.
A1:B1	Two cells that occupy one row and two columns.
A1:A100	100 cells in column A.
A1:D4	16 cells (four rows by four columns).
C1:C1048576	An entire column of cells; this range also can be expressed as C:C.
A6:XFD6	An entire row of cells; this range also can be expressed as 6:6.
A1:XFD1048576	All cells in a worksheet. This range also can be expressed as either A:XFD or 1:1048576.

Selecting ranges

To perform an operation on a range of cells in a worksheet, you must first select the range. For example, if you want to make the text bold for a range of cells, you must select the range and then choose Home⇨Font⇨Bold (or press Ctrl + B).

When you select a range, the cells appear highlighted. The exception is the active cell, which remains its normal color. Figure 4.1 shows an example of a selected range (B5:C8) in a worksheet. Cell B5, the active cell, is selected but not highlighted.

FIGURE 4.1

When you select a range, it appears highlighted, but the active cell within the range is not highlighted.

	A	B	C	D	E	F	G	H
1	Date	Region	Sales					
2	1/2/2013	Eastern	10,909					
3	1/2/2013	Southern	8,098					
4	1/2/2013	Western	4,434					
5	1/3/2013	Eastern	11,126					
6	1/3/2013	Southern	8,079					
7	1/3/2013	Western	4,542					
8	1/4/2013	Eastern	11,224					
9	1/4/2013	Southern	8,131					
10	1/4/2013	Western	4,650					
11	1/5/2013	Eastern	11,299					
12	1/5/2013	Southern	8,161					
13	1/5/2013	Western	4,521					
14	1/6/2013	Eastern	11,265					
15	1/6/2013	Southern	8,071					
16	1/6/2013	Western	4,274					
17	1/9/2013	Eastern	11,328					
18	1/9/2013	Southern	8,082					
19	1/9/2013	Western	4,365					

Sheet1

You can select a range in several ways:

- Press the left mouse button and drag, highlighting the range. Then release the mouse button. If you drag to the end of the window, the worksheet will scroll.
- Press the Shift key while you use the navigation keys to select a range.
- Press F8 and then move the cell pointer with the navigation keys to highlight the range. Press F8 again to return the navigation keys to normal movement.
- Type the cell or range address into the Name box (located to the left of the Formula bar) and press Enter. Excel selects the cell or range that you specified.
- Choose Home⇨Editing⇨Find & Select⇨Go To (or press F5) and enter a range's address manually in the Go To dialog box. When you click OK, Excel selects the cells in the range that you specified.

Quick Analysis?

When you select a range of data, Excel may display a Quick Analysis icon at the lower right of your selection. Click the icon, and you'll see a list of analysis options that you can quickly apply to the selected data. You can add conditional formatting, create a chart, add formulas, create a pivot table, and generate Sparkline graphics. The exact options vary, depending on the data in the range.

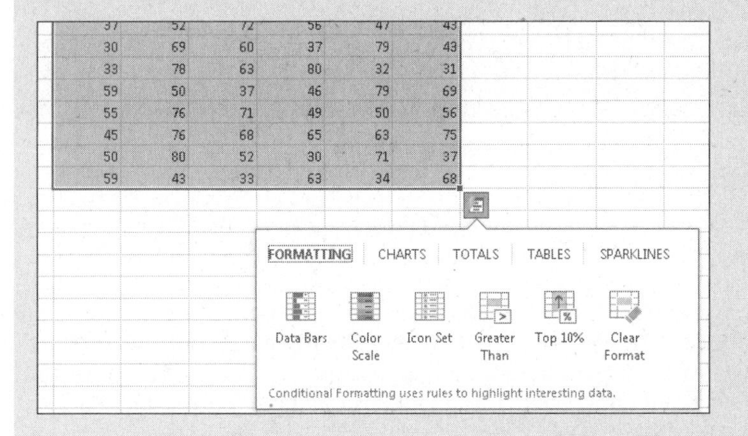

These options provide nothing that you can't do using standard commands, and all these options are discussed elsewhere in this book. If you find the Quick Analysis icon annoying, choose File ➪ Options to display the Excel Options dialog box, select the General tab, and deselect Show Quick Analysis Options on Selection.

TIP

While you're selecting a range, Excel displays the number of rows and columns in your selection in the Name box. As soon as you finish the selection, the Name box reverts to showing the address of the active cell.

Selecting complete rows and columns

Often, you'll need to select an entire row or column. For example, you may want to apply the same numeric format or the same alignment options to an entire row or column. You can select entire rows and columns in much the same manner as you select ranges:

- Click the row or column border to select a single row or column.
- To select multiple adjacent rows or columns, click a row or column border and drag to highlight additional rows or columns.
- To select multiple (nonadjacent) rows or columns, press Ctrl while you click the row or column borders that you want.

- Press Ctrl + spacebar to select a column. The column of the active cell (or columns of the selected cells) is highlighted.
- Press Shift + spacebar to select a row. The row of the active cell (or rows of the selected cells) is highlighted.

TIP

Press Ctrl+A to select all cells in the worksheet, which is the same as selecting all rows and all columns. If the active cell is within a table (created by choosing Insert ➪ Tables ➪ Table), you may need to press Ctrl+A two or even three times to select all cells in the worksheet. You can also click the area at the intersection of the row and column borders to select all cells.

Selecting noncontiguous ranges

Most of the time, the ranges that you select are *contiguous* — a single rectangle of cells. Excel also enables you to work with *noncontiguous ranges,* which consist of two or more ranges (or single cells) that aren't next to each other. Selecting noncontiguous ranges is also known as a *multiple selection.* If you want to apply the same formatting to cells in different areas of your worksheet, one approach is to make a multiple selection. When the appropriate cells or ranges are selected, the formatting that you select is applied to them all. Figure 4.2 shows a noncontiguous range selected in a worksheet. Three ranges are selected: A2:C3, A5:C5, and A9:C10.

FIGURE 4.2

Excel enables you to select noncontiguous ranges.

	A	B	C	D	E	F	G	H
1	**Product**	**Sold By**	**Month**					
2	Widget	Jones	Jan					
3	Widget	Walker	Jan					
4	Sprocket	Walker	Mar					
5	Widget	Smith	Mar					
6	Sprocket	Franklin	Jan					
7	Sprocket	Franklin	Mar					
8	Sprocket	Jones	Feb					
9	Widget	Franklin	Jan					
10	Widget	Walker	Jan					
11	Sprocket	Jones	Feb					
12	Sprocket	Jones	Feb					
13	Sprocket	Jones	Feb					
14	Widget	Walker	Jan					
15	Sprocket	Walker	Mar					
16	Widget	Jones	Mar					
17	Widget	Franklin	Mar					

Sheet1 | Sheet2

You can select a noncontiguous range in several ways:

- Select the first range (or cell). Then press and hold Ctrl as you click and drag the mouse to highlight additional cells or ranges.
- From the keyboard, select a range as described previously (using F8 or the Shift key). Then press Shift + F8 to select another range without canceling the previous range selections.
- Enter the range (or cell) address in the Name box and press Enter. Separate each range address with a comma.
- Choose Home ➪ Editing ➪ Find & Select ➪ Go To (or press F5) to display the Go To dialog box. Enter the range (or cell) address in the Reference box, and separate each range address with a comma. Click OK, and Excel selects the ranges.

NOTE

Noncontiguous ranges differ from contiguous ranges in several important ways. One obvious difference is that you can't use drag-and-drop methods (described later) to move or copy noncontiguous ranges.

Selecting multisheet ranges

In addition to two-dimensional ranges on a single worksheet, ranges can extend across multiple worksheets to be three-dimensional ranges.

Suppose that you have a workbook set up to track budgets. A common approach is to use a separate worksheet for each department, making it easy to organize the data. You can click a sheet tab to view the information for a particular department.

Figure 4.3 shows a simplified example. The workbook has four sheets: Totals, Operations, Marketing, and Manufacturing. The sheets are laid out identically. The only difference is the values. The Totals sheet contains formulas that compute the sum of the corresponding items in the three departmental worksheets.

FIGURE 4.3

The worksheets in this workbook are laid out identically.

budget.xlsx - Excel

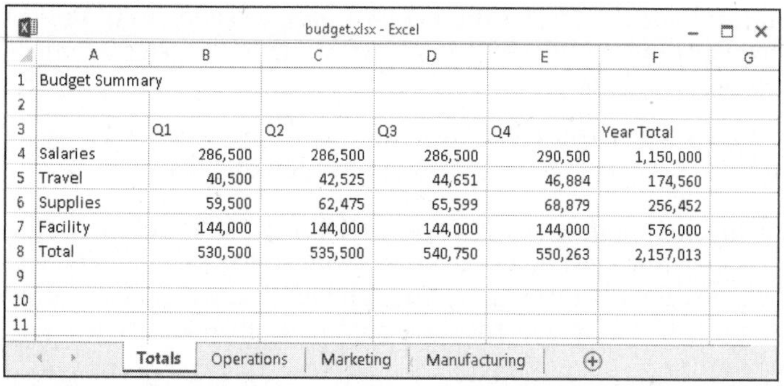

	A	B	C	D	E	F	G
1	Budget Summary						
2							
3		Q1	Q2	Q3	Q4	Year Total	
4	Salaries	286,500	286,500	286,500	290,500	1,150,000	
5	Travel	40,500	42,525	44,651	46,884	174,560	
6	Supplies	59,500	62,475	65,599	68,879	256,452	
7	Facility	144,000	144,000	144,000	144,000	576,000	
8	Total	530,500	535,500	540,750	550,263	2,157,013	
9							
10							
11							

Totals | Operations | Marketing | Manufacturing

ON THE WEB

This workbook, named `budget.xlsx`, is available on this book's website.

Assume that you want to apply formatting to the sheets — for example, make the column headings bold with background shading. One (albeit not-so-efficient) approach is to format the cells in each worksheet separately. A better technique is to select a multisheet range and format the cells in all the sheets simultaneously. The following is a step-by-step example of multisheet formatting, using the workbook shown in Figure 4.3.

1. **Activate the Totals worksheet by clicking its tab.**
2. **Select the range B3:F3.**
3. **Press Shift and click the Manufacturing sheet tab.** This step selects all worksheets between the active worksheet (Totals) and the sheet tab that you click — in essence, a three-dimensional range of cells (see Figure 4.4). Notice that the workbook window's title bar displays `[Group]` to remind you that you've selected a group of sheets and that you're in Group mode.

FIGURE 4.4

In Group mode, you can work with a three-dimensional range of cells that extend across multiple worksheets.

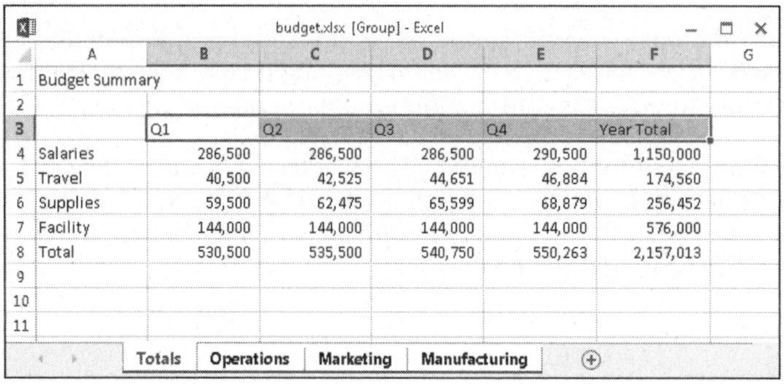

budget.xlsx [Group] - Excel

	A	B	C	D	E	F	G
1	Budget Summary						
2							
3		Q1	Q2	Q3	Q4	Year Total	
4	Salaries	286,500	286,500	286,500	290,500	1,150,000	
5	Travel	40,500	42,525	44,651	46,884	174,560	
6	Supplies	59,500	62,475	65,599	68,879	256,452	
7	Facility	144,000	144,000	144,000	144,000	576,000	
8	Total	530,500	535,500	540,750	550,263	2,157,013	
9							
10							
11							

Totals | Operations | Marketing | Manufacturing

4. **Choose Home ⇨ Font ⇨ Bold and then choose Home ⇨ Font ⇨ Fill Color to apply a colored background.** Excel applies the formatting to the selected range across the selected sheets.
5. **Click one of the other sheet tabs.** This step selects the sheet and also cancels Group mode; `[Group]` is no longer displayed in the title bar.

When a workbook is in Group mode, any changes that you make to cells in one worksheet also apply to the corresponding cells in all the other grouped worksheets. You can use this to your advantage when you want to set up a group of identical worksheets because any labels, data, formatting, or formulas you enter are automatically added to the same cells in all the grouped worksheets.

NOTE

When Excel is in Group mode, some commands are disabled and can't be used. For example, in the preceding example, you can't convert all these ranges to tables by choosing Insert ⇨ Tables ⇨ Table.

In general, selecting a multisheet range is a simple two-step process: Select the range in one sheet, and then select the worksheets to include in the range. To select a group of contiguous worksheets, you can press Shift and click the sheet tab of the last worksheet that you want to include in the selection. To select individual worksheets, press Ctrl and click the sheet tab of each worksheet that you want to select. If all the worksheets in a workbook aren't laid out the same, you can skip the sheets that you don't want to format. When you make the selection, the sheet tabs of the selected sheets display in bold with underlined text, and Excel displays `[Group]` in the title bar.

TIP

To select all sheets in a workbook, right-click any sheet tab and choose Select All Sheets from the shortcut menu.

Selecting special types of cells

As you use Excel, you may need to locate specific types of cells in your worksheets. For example, wouldn't it be handy to be able to locate every cell that contains a formula — or perhaps all the formula cells that depend on the active cell? Excel provides an easy way to locate these and many other special types of cells: Select a range, and choose Home ⇨ Editing ⇨ Find & Select ⇨ Go to Special to display the Go to Special dialog box, shown in Figure 4.5.

FIGURE 4.5

Use the Go to Special dialog box to select specific types of cells.

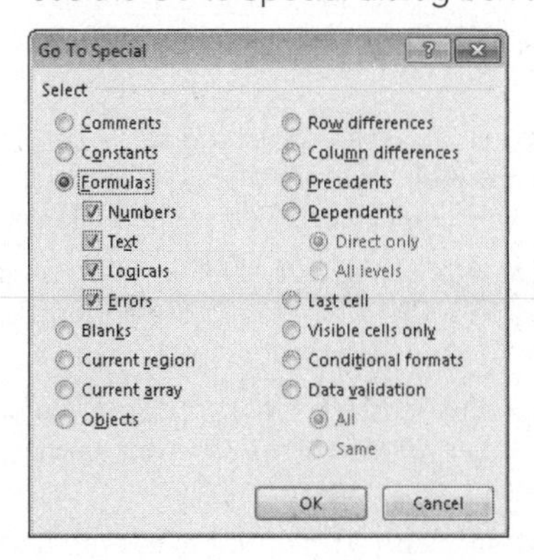

After you make your choice in the dialog box, Excel selects the qualifying subset of cells in the current selection. Often, this subset of cells is a multiple selection. If no cells qualify, Excel lets you know with the message `No cells were found`.

TIP

If you bring up the Go to Special dialog box with only one cell selected, Excel bases its selection on the entire used area of the worksheet. Otherwise, the selection is based on the selected range.

Table 4.1 offers a description of the options available in the Go to Special dialog box. Some of the options are very useful.

TABLE 4.1 Go to Special Options

Option	What it does
Comments	Selects the cells that contain a cell comment.
Constants	Selects all nonempty cells that don't contain formulas. Use the check boxes under the Formulas option to choose which types of nonformula cells to include.
Formulas	Selects cells that contain formulas. Qualify this by selecting the type of result: numbers, text, logical values (`TRUE` or `FALSE`), or errors.
Blanks	Selects all empty cells. If a single cell is selected when the dialog box displays, this option selects the empty cells in the used area of the worksheet.
Current Region	Selects a rectangular range of cells around the active cell. This range is determined by surrounding blank rows and columns. You can also press Ctrl+Shift+*.
Current Array	Selects the entire array. (See Chapter 17 for more on arrays.)
Objects	Selects all embedded objects on the worksheet, including charts and graphics.
Row Differences	Analyzes the selection and selects cells that are different from other cells in each row.
Column Differences	Analyzes the selection and selects the cells that are different from other cells in each column.
Precedents	Selects cells that are referred to in the formulas in the active cell or selection (limited to the active sheet). You can select either direct precedents or precedents at any level. (See Chapter 31 for more information.)
Dependents	Selects cells with formulas that refer to the active cell or selection (limited to the active sheet). You can select either direct dependents or dependents at any level. (See Chapter 31 for more information.)
Last Cell	Selects the bottom-right cell in the worksheet that contains data or formatting. For this option, the entire worksheet is examined, even if a range is selected when the dialog box displays.
Visible Cells Only	Selects only visible cells in the selection. This option is useful when dealing with a filtered list or table.

Option	What it does
Conditional Formats	Selects cells that have a conditional format applied (by choosing Home ➪ Styles ➪ Conditional Formatting). The All option selects all such cells. The Same option selects only the cells that have the same conditional formatting as the active cell.
Data Validation	Selects cells that are set up for data entry validation (by choosing Data ➪ Date Tools ➪ Data Validation). The All option selects all such cells. The Same option selects only the cells that have the same validation rules as the active cell.

TIP

When you select an option in the Go to Special dialog box, be sure to note which suboptions become available. The placement of these suboptions can be misleading. For example, when you select Constants, the suboptions under Formulas become available to help you further refine the results. Likewise, the suboptions under Dependents also apply to Precedents, and those under Data Validation also apply to Conditional Formats.

Selecting cells by searching

Another way to select cells is to choose Home ➪ Editing ➪ Find & Select ➪ Find (or press Ctrl + F), which allows you to select cells by their contents. The Find and Replace dialog box is shown in Figure 4.6. This figure shows additional options that are available when you click the Options button.

FIGURE 4.6

The Find and Replace dialog box, with its options displayed.

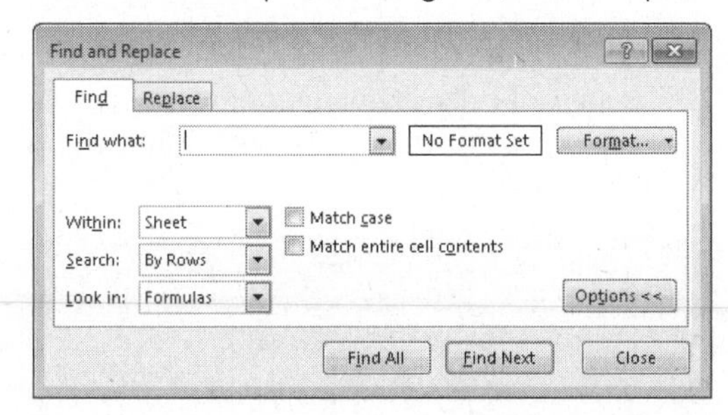

Enter the text that you're looking for; then click Find All. The dialog box expands to display all the cells that match your search criteria. For example, Figure 4.7 shows the dialog box after Excel has located all cells that contain the text *March*. You can click an item in the list, and the screen will scroll so that you can view the cell in context. To select all the cells in the list, first select any single item in the list. Then press Ctrl + A to select them all.

FIGURE 4.7

The Find and Replace dialog box, with its results listed.

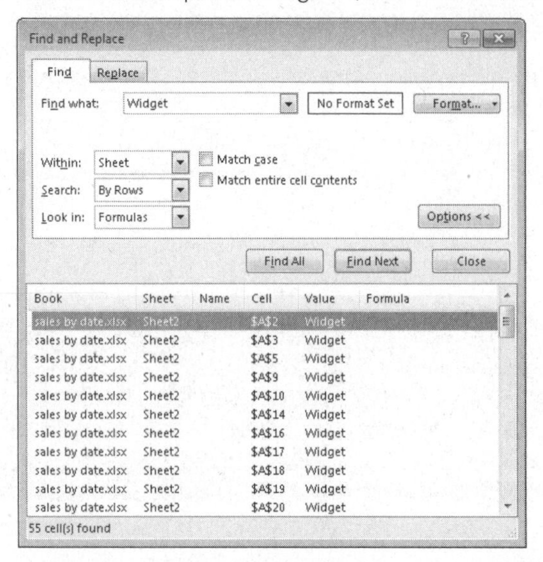

NOTE

The Find and Replace dialog box allows you to return to the worksheet without dismissing the dialog box.

The Find and Replace dialog box supports two wildcard characters:

?	Matches any single character
*	Matches any number of characters

Wildcard characters also work with values when the Match Entire Cell Contents option is selected. For example, searching for `3*` locates all cells that contain a value that begins with 3. Searching for `1?9` locates all three-digit entries that begin with 1 and end with 9. Searching for *00 locates values that end with two zeros.

TIP

To search for a question mark or an asterisk, precede the character with a tilde (~). For example, the following search string finds the text `*NONE*`:

```
~*NONE~*
```

If you need to search for the tilde character, use two tildes.

If your searches don't seem to be working correctly, double-check these three options (which sometimes have a way of changing on their own):

- **Match Case:** If this check box is selected, the case of the text must match exactly. For example, searching for `smith` does not locate `Smith`.
- **Match Entire Cell Contents:** If this check box is selected, a match occurs if the cell contains only the search string (and nothing else). For example, searching for `Excel` doesn't locate a cell that contains `Microsoft Excel`. When using wildcard characters, an exact match is not required.
- **Look In:** This drop-down list has three options: Values, Formulas, and Comments. If, for example, Values is selected, searching for `900` doesn't find a cell that contains `900` if that value is generated by a formula (unless the formula itself contains `900`).

Copying or Moving Ranges

As you create a worksheet, you may find it necessary to copy or move information from one location to another. Excel makes copying or moving ranges of cells easy. Here are some common things you might do:

- Copy a cell to another location.
- Copy a cell to a range of cells. The source cell is copied to every cell in the destination range.
- Copy a range to another range. Both ranges must be the same size.
- Move a range of cells to another location.

The primary difference between copying and moving a range is the effect of the operation on the source range. When you copy a range, the source range is unaffected. When you move a range, the contents are removed from the source range.

Note

Copying a cell normally copies the cell's contents, any formatting that is applied to the original cell (including conditional formatting and data validation), and the cell comment (if it has one). When you copy a cell that contains a formula, the cell references in the copied formulas are changed automatically to be relative to their new destination.

Copying or moving consists of two steps (although shortcut methods are available):

1. **Select the cell or range to copy (the source range), and copy it to the Clipboard.** To move the range instead of copying it, cut the range instead of copying it.
2. **Move the cell pointer to the range that will hold the copy (the destination range), and paste the Clipboard contents.**

CAUTION

When you paste information, Excel overwrites any cells that get in the way without warning you. If you find that pasting overwrote some essential cells, choose Undo from the Quick Access toolbar (or press Ctrl+Z).

NOTE

When you copy a cell or range, Excel surrounds the copied area with an animated border. As long as that border remains animated, the copied information is available for pasting. If you press Esc to cancel the animated border, Excel removes the information from the Clipboard.

Because copying (or moving) is used so often, Excel provides many different methods. I discuss each method in the following sections. Copying and moving are similar operations, so I point out only important differences between the two.

Copying by using Ribbon commands

Choosing Home ➪ Clipboard ➪ Copy transfers a copy of the selected cell or range to the Windows Clipboard and the Office Clipboard. After performing the copy part of this operation, select the cell that will hold the copy and choose Home ➪ Clipboard ➪ Paste.

Instead of choosing Home ➪ Clipboard ➪ Paste, you can just activate the destination cell and press Enter. If you use this technique, Excel removes the copied information from the Clipboard so that it can't be pasted again.

NOTE

If you click the Copy button more than once before you click the Paste button, Excel may automatically display the Office Clipboard taskbar. To prevent this taskbar from appearing, click the Options button at the bottom and then remove the check mark from Show Office Clipboard Automatically.

If you're copying a range, you don't need to select an entire same-sized range before you click the Paste button. You only need to activate the upper-left cell in the destination range.

TIP

The Home ➪ Clipboard ➪ Paste control contains a drop-down arrow that, when clicked, gives you additional paste option icons. The paste preview icons are explained later in this chapter (see "Pasting in special ways").

About the Office Clipboard

Whenever you cut or copy information from a Windows program, Windows stores the information on the Windows Clipboard, which is an area of your computer's memory. Each time that you cut or copy information, Windows replaces the information previously stored on the Clipboard with the new information that you cut or copied. The Windows Clipboard can store data in a variety of formats. Because Windows manages information on the Clipboard, it can be pasted to other Windows applications, regardless of where it originated.

Microsoft Office has its own Clipboard (the Office Clipboard), which is available only in Office programs. To view or hide the Office Clipboard, click the dialog launcher icon in the bottom-right corner of the Home ⇨ Clipboard group.

Whenever you cut or copy information in an Office program, such as Excel or Word, the program places the information on both the Windows Clipboard and the Office Clipboard. However, the program treats information on the Office Clipboard differently from how it treats information on the Windows Clipboard. Instead of replacing information on the Office Clipboard, the program appends the information to the Office Clipboard. With multiple items stored on the Clipboard, you can then paste the items either individually or as a group.

You can find out more about this feature in "Using the Office Clipboard to paste," later in this chapter.

Copying by using shortcut menu commands

If you prefer, you can use the following shortcut menu commands for copying and pasting:

- Right-click the range and choose Copy (or Cut) from the shortcut menu to copy the selected cells to the Clipboard.
- Right-click and choose Paste from the shortcut menu that appears to paste the Clipboard contents to the selected cell or range.

For more control over how the pasted information appears, use one of the paste icons in the shortcut menu (see Figure 4.8).

Instead of using Paste, you can just activate the destination cell and press Enter. If you use this technique, Excel removes the copied information from the Clipboard so that it can't be pasted again.

FIGURE 4.8

The paste icons on the shortcut menu provide more control over how the pasted information appears.

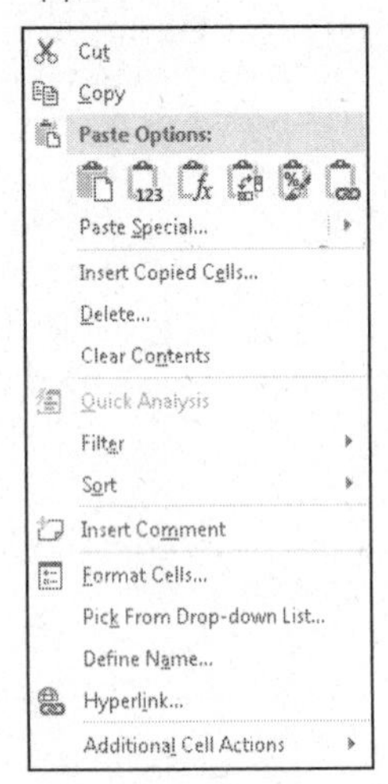

Copying by using shortcut keys

The copy and paste operations also have shortcut keys associated with them:

- Ctrl + C copies the selected cells to both the Windows Clipboard and the Office Clipboard.
- Ctrl + X cuts the selected cells to both the Windows Clipboard and the Office Clipboard.
- Ctrl + V pastes the Windows Clipboard contents to the selected cell or range.

TIP

These are standard key combinations, used by many other Windows applications.

Using Paste Options Buttons When Inserting and Pasting

Some cell and range operations — specifically inserting, pasting, and filling cells by dragging — result in the display of paste option buttons. For example, if you copy a range and then paste it to a different location using Home ➪ Clipboard ➪ Paste, a drop-down options list appears at the lower right of the pasted range. Click the list (or press Ctrl), and you see the options shown in the figure here. These options enable you to specify how the data should be pasted, such as values only or formatting only. In this case, using the paste option buttons is an alternative to using options in the Paste Special dialog box. (Read more about Paste Special in the upcoming section, "Using the Paste Special dialog box.")

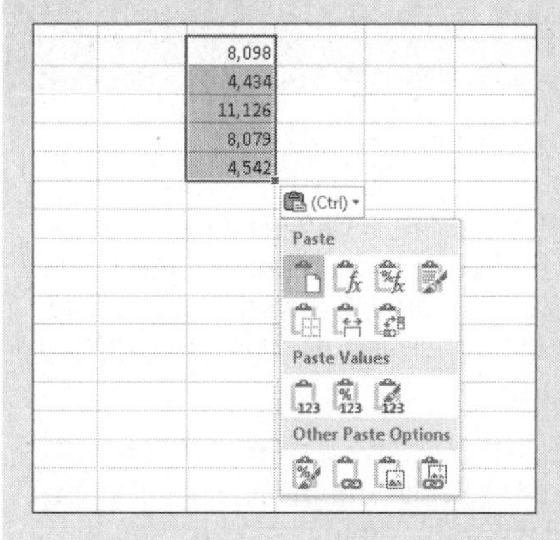

Some users find these paste options buttons helpful, and others think that they're annoying. (Count me in the latter group.) To disable this feature, choose File ➪ Options and click the Advanced tab. Remove the check mark from the two options labeled Show Paste Options Buttons When Content Is Pasted and Show Insert Options Buttons.

Copying or moving by using drag-and-drop

Excel also enables you to copy or move a cell or range by dragging. Unlike other methods of copying and moving, dragging and dropping does not place any information on either the Windows Clipboard or the Office Clipboard.

Caution

The drag-and-drop method of moving does offer one advantage over the cut-and-paste method: Excel warns you if a drag-and-drop move operation will overwrite existing cell contents. Oddly, you do *not* get a warning if a drag-and-drop copy operation will overwrite existing cell contents.

To copy using drag-and-drop, select the cell or range that you want to copy and then press Ctrl and move the mouse to one of the selection's borders (the mouse pointer is augmented with a small plus sign). Then, drag the selection to its new location while you continue to press the Ctrl key. The original selection remains behind, and Excel makes a new copy when you release the mouse button.

To move a range using drag-and-drop, don't press Ctrl while dragging the border.

TIP

If the mouse pointer doesn't turn into an arrow when you point to the border of a cell or range, you need to make a change to your settings. Choose File ⇨ Options to display the Excel Options dialog box, select the Advanced tab, and place a check mark on the option labeled Enable Fill Handle and Cell Drag-and-Drop.

Copying to adjacent cells

Often, you need to copy a cell to an adjacent cell or range. This type of copying is quite common when working with formulas. For example, if you're working on a budget, you might create a formula to add the values in column B. You can use the same formula to add the values in the other columns. Rather than re-enter the formula, you can copy it to the adjacent cells.

Excel provides additional options for copying to adjacent cells. To use these commands, activate the cell that you're copying *and* extend the cell selection to include the cells that you're copying to. Then issue the appropriate command from the following list for one-step copying:

- Home ⇨ Editing ⇨ Fill ⇨ Down (or Ctrl + D) copies the cell to the selected range below.
- Home ⇨ Editing ⇨ Fill ⇨ Right (or Ctrl + R) copies the cell to the selected range to the right.
- Home ⇨ Editing ⇨ Fill ⇨ Up copies the cell to the selected range above.
- Home ⇨ Editing ⇨ Fill ⇨ Left copies the cell to the selected range to the left.

None of these commands places information on either the Windows Clipboard or the Office Clipboard.

TIP

You also can use AutoFill to copy to adjacent cells by dragging the selection's *fill handle* (the small square in the bottom-right corner of the selected cell or range). Excel copies the original selection to the cells that you highlight while dragging. For more control over the AutoFill operation, drag the fill handle with the right mouse button, and you'll get a shortcut menu with additional options.

Copying a range to other sheets

You can use the copy procedures described previously to copy a cell or range to another worksheet, even if the worksheet is in a different workbook. You must, of course, activate the other worksheet before you select the location to which you want to copy.

Excel offers a quicker way to copy a cell or range and paste it to other worksheets in the same workbook.

1. **Select the range to copy.**
2. **Press Ctrl and click the sheet tabs for the worksheets to which you want to copy the information.** Excel displays `[Group]` in the workbook's title bar.
3. **Choose Home ⇨ Editing ⇨ Fill ⇨ Across Worksheets.** A dialog box appears to ask you what you want to copy (All, Contents, or Formats).
4. **Make your choice and then click OK.** Excel copies the selected range to the selected worksheets; the new copy occupies the same cells in the selected worksheets as the original occupies in the initial worksheet.

CAUTION

Be careful with the Home ⇨ Editing ⇨ Fill ⇨ Across Worksheets command because Excel doesn't warn you when the destination cells contain information. You can quickly overwrite lots of cells with this command and not even realize it. So, make sure you check your work, and use Undo if the result isn't what you expected.

Using the Office Clipboard to paste

Whenever you cut or copy information in an Office program, such as Excel, you can place the data on both the Windows Clipboard and the Office Clipboard. When you copy information to the Office Clipboard, you append the information to the Office Clipboard instead of replacing what is already there. With multiple items stored on the Office Clipboard, you can then paste the items either individually or as a group.

To use the Office Clipboard, you first need to open it. Use the dialog launcher on the bottom right of the Home ⇨ Clipboard group to toggle the Clipboard task pane on and off.

TIP

To make the Clipboard task pane open automatically, click the Options button near the bottom of the task pane and choose the Show Office Clipboard Automatically option.

After you open the Clipboard task pane, select the first cell or range that you want to copy to the Office Clipboard and copy it by using any of the preceding techniques. Repeat this process, selecting the next cell or range that you want to copy. As soon as you copy the information, the Office Clipboard task pane shows you the number of items that you've copied and a brief description (it will hold up to 24 items). Figure 4.9 shows the Office Clipboard with four copied items.

FIGURE 4.9

Use the Clipboard task pane to copy and paste multiple items.

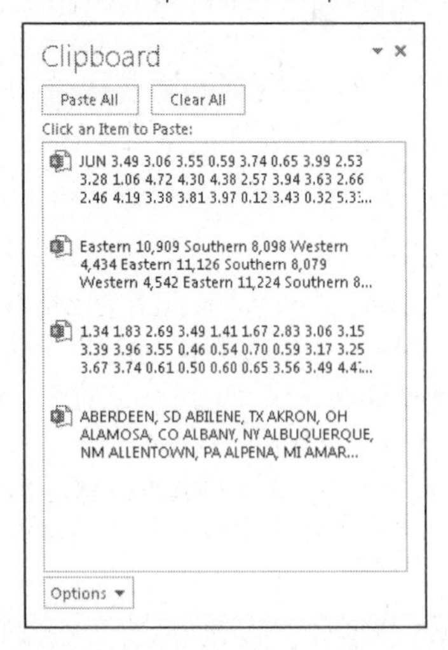

When you're ready to paste information, select the cell into which you want to paste information. To paste an individual item, click it in the Clipboard task pane. To paste all the items that you've copied, click the Paste All button (which is at the top of the Clipboard task pane). The items are pasted, one after the other. The Paste All button is probably more useful in Word, for situations in which you copy text from various sources and then paste it all at once.

You can clear the contents of the Office Clipboard by clicking the Clear All button.

The following items about the Office Clipboard and how it functions are worth noting:

- Excel pastes the contents of the Windows Clipboard (the last item you copied to the Office Clipboard) when you paste by choosing Home ⇨ Clipboard ⇨ Paste, by pressing Ctrl + V, or by right-clicking and choosing Paste from the shortcut menu.
- The last item that you cut or copied appears on both the Office Clipboard and the Windows Clipboard.
- Pasting from the Office Clipboard also places that item on the Windows Clipboard. If you choose Paste All from the Office Clipboard toolbar, you paste all items stored on the Office Clipboard onto the Windows Clipboard as a single item.
- Clearing the Office Clipboard also clears the Windows Clipboard.

CAUTION

The Office Clipboard has a serious problem that makes it virtually worthless for Excel users: If you copy a range that contains formulas, the formulas are not transferred when you paste to a different range. Only the values are pasted. Furthermore, Excel doesn't even warn you about this fact.

Pasting in special ways

You may not always want to copy everything from the source range to the destination range. For example, you may want to copy only the formula results rather than the formulas themselves. Or you may want to copy the number formats from one range to another without overwriting any existing data or formulas.

To control what is copied into the destination range, choose Home ➪ Clipboard ➪ Paste and use the drop-down menu shown in Figure 4.10. When you hover your mouse pointer over an icon, you'll see a preview of the pasted information in the destination range. Click the icon to use the selected paste option.

FIGURE 4.10

Excel offers several pasting options, with preview. Here, the information is copied from D2:E5 and is being pasted beginning at cell D10 using the Transpose option.

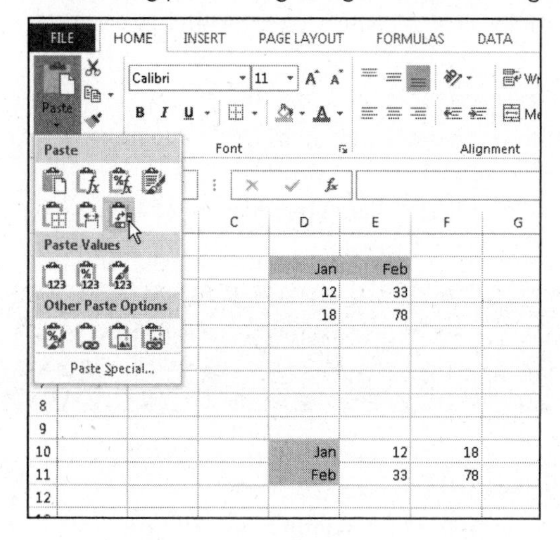

The paste options are

- **Paste (P):** Pastes the cell's contents, formats, and data validation from the Windows Clipboard.
- **Formulas (F):** Pastes formulas but not formatting.
- **Formulas & Number Formatting (O):** Pastes formulas and number formatting only.
- **Keep Source Formatting (K):** Pastes formulas and all formatting.
- **No Borders (B):** Pastes everything except borders that appear in the source range.
- **Keep Source Column Width (W):** Pastes formulas and duplicates the column width of the copied cells.

- **Transpose (T):** Changes the orientation of the copied range. Rows become columns, and columns become rows. Any formulas in the copied range are adjusted so that they work properly when transposed.
- **Merge Conditional Formatting (G):** This icon is displayed only when the copied cells contain conditional formatting. When clicked, it merges the copied conditional formatting with any conditional formatting in the destination range.
- **Values (V):** Pastes the results of formulas. The destination for the copy can be a new range or the original range. In the latter case, Excel replaces the original formulas with their current values.
- **Values & Number Formatting (A):** Pastes the results of formulas plus the number formatting.
- **Values & Source Formatting (E):** Pastes the results of formulas plus all formatting.
- **Formatting (R):** Pastes only the formatting of the source range.
- **Paste Link (N):** Creates formulas in the destination range that refer to the cells in the copied range.
- **Picture (U):** Pastes the copied information as a picture.
- **Linked Picture (I):** Pastes the copied information as a "live" picture that is updated if the source range is changed.
- **Paste Special:** Displays the Paste Special dialog box (described in the next section).

NOTE

After you paste, you're offered another chance to change your mind. A Paste Options drop-down appears at the lower right of the pasted range. Click it (or press Ctrl), and you see the paste option icons again.

Using the Paste Special dialog box

For yet another pasting method, choose Home ➪ Clipboard ➪ Paste ➪ Paste Special to display the Paste Special dialog box (see Figure 4.11). You can also right-click and choose Paste Special from the shortcut menu to display this dialog box. This dialog box has several options, which I explain in the following list.

NOTE

Excel actually has several different Paste Special dialog boxes, each with different options. The one displayed depends on what's copied. This section describes the Paste Special dialog box that appears when a range or cell has been copied.

FIGURE 4.11

The Paste Special dialog box.

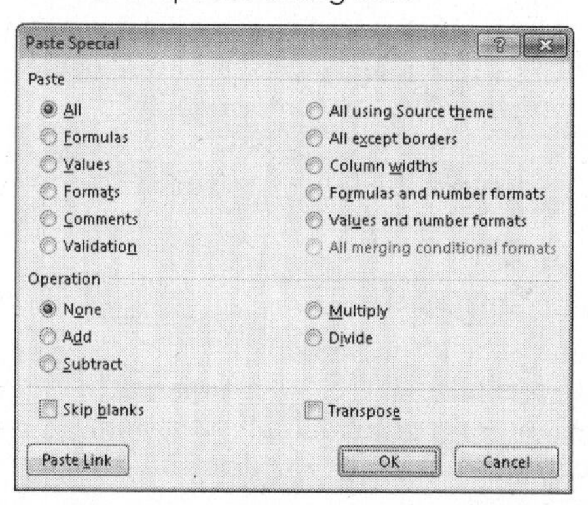

TIP

For the Paste Special command to be available, you need to copy a cell or range. (Choosing Home ⇨ Clipboard ⇨ Cut doesn't work.)

- **All:** Pastes the cell's contents, formats, and data validation from the Windows Clipboard.
- **Formulas:** Pastes values and formulas, with no formatting.
- **Values:** Pastes values and the results of formulas (no formatting). The destination for the copy can be a new range or the original range. In the latter case, Excel replaces the original formulas with their current values.
- **Formats:** Copies only the formatting.
- **Comments:** Copies only the cell comments from a cell or range. This option doesn't copy cell contents or formatting.
- **Validation:** Copies the validation criteria so the same data validation will apply. Data validation is applied by choosing Data ⇨ Data Tools ⇨ Data Validation.
- **All Using Source Theme:** Pastes everything, but uses the formatting from the document theme of the source. This option is relevant only if you're pasting information from a different workbook, and the workbook uses a different document theme than the active workbook.
- **All Except Borders:** Pastes everything except borders that appear in the source range.
- **Column Widths:** Pastes only column width information.
- **Formulas and Number Formats:** Pastes all values, formulas, and number formats (but no other formatting).

- **Values and Number Formats:** Pastes all values and numeric formats but not the formulas themselves.
- **All merging conditional formats:** Merges the copied conditional formatting with any conditional formatting in the destination range. This option is enabled only when you're copying a range that contains conditional formatting.

In addition, the Paste Special dialog box enables you to perform other operations, described in the following sections.

Performing mathematical operations without formulas

The option buttons in the Operation section of the Paste Special dialog box let you perform an arithmetic operation on values and formulas in the destination range. For example, you can copy a range to another range and select the Multiply operation. Excel multiplies the corresponding values in the source range and the destination range and replaces the destination range with the new values.

This feature also works with a single copied cell, pasted to a multi-cell range. Assume that you have a range of values, and you want to increase each value by 5 percent. Enter **105%** into any blank cell and copy that cell to the Clipboard. Then select the range of values and bring up the Paste Special dialog box. Select the Multiply option, and each value in the range is multiplied by 105%.

CAUTION

If the destination range contains formulas, the formulas are also modified. In many cases, this is *not* what you want.

Skipping blanks when pasting

The Skip Blanks option in the Paste Special dialog box prevents Excel from overwriting cell contents in your paste area with blank cells from the copied range. This option is useful if you're copying a range to another area but don't want the blank cells in the copied range to overwrite existing data.

Transposing a range

The Transpose option in the Paste Special dialog box changes the orientation of the copied range. Rows become columns, and columns become rows. Any formulas in the copied range are adjusted so that they work properly when transposed. Note that you can use this check box with the other options in the Paste Special dialog box. Figure 4.12 shows an example of a horizontal range (A1:D5) that was transposed to a different range (A9:E12).

FIGURE 4.12

Transposing a range changes the orientation as the information is pasted into the worksheet.

	A	B	C	D	E	F
1		Jan	Feb	Mar		
2	Region 1	45	53	65		
3	Region 2	41	77	67		
4	Region 3	73	32	51		
5	Region 4	54	43	86		
6						
7						
8						
9		Region 1	Region 2	Region 3	Region 4	
10	Jan	45	41	73	54	
11	Feb	53	77	32	43	
12	Mar	65	67	51	86	
13						
14						

Sheet1

TIP

If you click the Paste Link button in the Paste Special dialog box, you create formulas that link to the source range. As a result, the destination range automatically reflects changes in the source range.

Using Names to Work with Ranges

Dealing with cryptic cell and range addresses can sometimes be confusing, especially when you deal with formulas, which I cover in Chapter 10. Fortunately, Excel allows you to assign descriptive names to cells and ranges. For example, you can give a cell a name such as Interest_Rate, or you can name a range JulySales. Working with these names (rather than cell or range addresses) has several advantages:

- A meaningful range name (such as Total_Income) is much easier to remember than a cell address (such as AC21).
- Entering a name is less error prone than entering a cell or range address, and if you type a name incorrectly in a formula, Excel will display a `#NAME?` error.
- You can quickly move to areas of your worksheet either by using the Name box, located at the left side of the Formula bar (click the arrow to drop down a list of defined names) or by choosing Home ➪ Editing ➪ Find & Select ➪ Go To (or pressing F5) and specifying the range name.
- Creating formulas is easier. You can paste a cell or range name into a formula by using Formula Autocomplete.

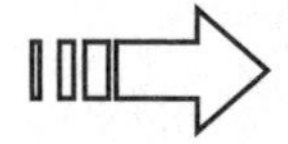

See Chapter 10 for information on Formula Autocomplete.

- Names make your formulas more understandable and easier to use. A formula such as `=Income–Taxes` is more intuitive than `=D20–D40`.

Creating range names in your workbooks

Excel provides several different methods that you can use to create range names. Before you begin, however, you should be aware of a few rules:

- Names can't contain any spaces. You may want to use an underscore character to simulate a space (such as Annual_Total).
- You can use any combination of letters and numbers, but the name must begin with a letter, underscore, or backslash. A name can't begin with a number (such as 3rdQuarter) or look like a cell address (such as QTR3). If these are desirable names, though, you can precede the name with an underscore or a backslash: for example, _3rd Quarter and \QTR3.
- Symbols — except for underscores, backslashes, and periods — aren't allowed.
- Names are limited to 255 characters, but it's a good practice to keep names as short as possible, but still meaningful.

CAUTION

Excel also uses a few names internally for its own use. Although you can create names that override Excel's internal names, you should avoid doing so. To be on the safe side, avoid using the following for names: Print_Area, Print_Titles, Consolidate_Area, and Sheet_Title. To delete a range name or rename a range, see "Managing names," later in this chapter.

Using the Name box

The fastest way to create a name is to use the Name box (to the left of the Formula bar). Select the cell or range to name, click the Name box, and type the name. Press Enter to create the name. (You must press Enter to actually record the name; if you type a name and then click in the worksheet, Excel doesn't create the name.)

If you type an invalid name (such as May21, which is a cell address), Excel activates that address (and doesn't warn you that the name is not valid). If the name you type includes an invalid character, Excel displays an error message. If a name already exists, you can't use the Name box to change the range to which that name refers. Attempting to do so simply selects the range.

The Name box is a drop-down list and shows all names in the workbook. To choose a named cell or range, click the Name box and choose the name. The name appears in the Name box, and Excel selects the named cell or range in the worksheet.

Using the New Name dialog box

For more control over naming cells and ranges, use the New Name dialog box. Start by selecting the cell or range that you want to name. Then choose Formulas ➪ Defined Names ➪ Define Name. Excel displays the New Name dialog box, shown in Figure 4.13. Note that this is a resizable dialog box. Click and drag a border to change the dimensions.

FIGURE 4.13

Create names for cells or ranges by using the New Name dialog box.

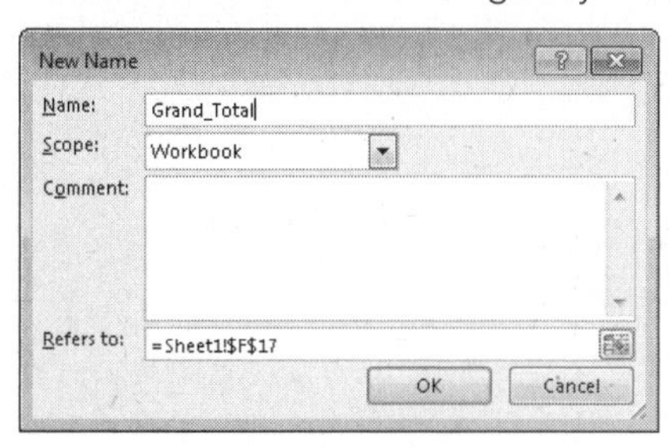

Type a name in the Name text field (or use the name that Excel proposes, if any). The selected cell or range address appears in the Refers To text field. Use the Scope drop-down list to indicate the scope for the name. The *scope* indicates where the name will be valid, and it's either the entire workbook or a particular sheet. If you like, you can add a comment that describes the named range or cell. Click OK to add the name to your workbook and close the dialog box.

Using the Create Names from Selection dialog box

You may have a worksheet that contains text that you want to use for names for adjacent cells or ranges. For example, you may want to use the text in column A to create names for the corresponding values in column B. Excel makes this task easy.

To create names by using adjacent text, start by selecting the name text and the cells that you want to name. (These items can be individual cells or ranges of cells.) The names must be adjacent to the cells that you're naming. (A multiple selection is allowed.) Then choose Formulas ➪ Defined Names ➪ Create from Selection. Excel displays the Create Names from Selection dialog box, shown in Figure 4.14.

The check marks in the Create Names from Selection dialog box are based on Excel's analysis of the selected range. For example, if Excel finds text in the first row of the selection, it proposes that you create names based on the top row. If Excel didn't guess correctly, you can change the check boxes. Click OK, and Excel creates the names. Using the data in Figure 4.14, Excel creates six names: January for cell B1, February for cell B2, and so on.

4

NOTE

If the text contained in a cell would result in an invalid name, Excel modifies the name to make it valid. For example, if a cell contains the text *Net Income* (which is invalid for a name because it contains a space), Excel converts the space to an underscore character. If Excel encounters a value or a numeric formula where text should be, however, it doesn't convert it to a valid name. It simply doesn't create a name — and does not inform you of that fact.

FIGURE 4.14

Use the Create Names from Selection dialog box to name cells using labels that appear in the worksheet.

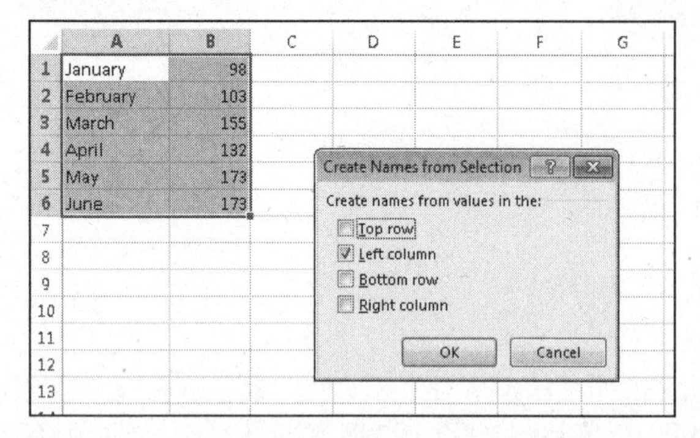

> **CAUTION**
>
> If the upper-left cell of the selection contains text and you choose the Top Row and Left Column options, Excel uses that text for the name of the entire range, excluding the top row and left column. So, after Excel creates the names, take a minute to make sure that they refer to the correct ranges. If Excel creates a name that is incorrect, you can delete or modify it by using the Name Manager (described next).

Managing names

A workbook can have any number of named cells and ranges. If you have many names, you should know about the Name Manager, shown in Figure 4.15.

FIGURE 4.15

Use the Name Manager to work with range names.

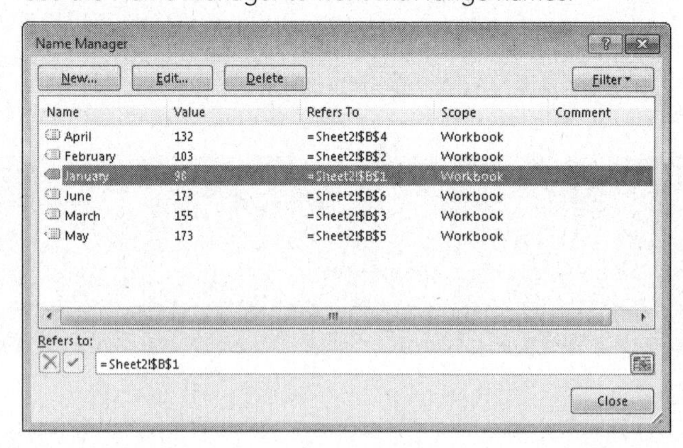

The Name Manager appears when you choose Formulas ➪ Defined Names ➪ Name Manager (or press Ctrl + F3). The Name Manager has the following features:

- **Displays information about each name in the workbook:** You can resize the Name Manager dialog box, widen the columns to show more information, and even rearrange the order of the columns. You can also click a column heading to sort the information by the column.
- **Allows you to filter the displayed names:** Clicking the Filter button lets you show only those names that meet a certain criteria. For example, you can view only the worksheet-level names.
- **Provides quick access to the New Name dialog box:** Click the New button to create a new name without closing the Name Manager.
- **Lets you edit names:** To edit a name, select it in the list and then click the Edit button. You can change the name itself, modify the Refers To range, or edit the comment.
- **Lets you quickly delete unneeded names:** To delete a name, select it in the list and click Delete.

Caution

Be extra careful when deleting names. If the name is used in a formula, deleting the name causes the formula to become invalid. (It displays `#NAME?`.) It seems logical that Excel would replace the name with its actual address – but that doesn't happen. However, deleting a name can be undone, so if you find that formulas return `#NAME?` after you delete a name, choose Undo from the Quick Access toolbar (or press Ctrl+Z) to get the name back.

If you delete the rows or columns that contain named cells or ranges, the names contain an invalid reference. For example, if cell A1 on Sheet1 is named Interest and you delete row 1 or column A, the name Interest then refers to `=Sheet1!#REF!` (that is, to an erroneous reference). If you use Interest in a formula, the formula displays `#REF`.

Tip

The Name Manager is useful, but it has a shortcoming: It doesn't let you display the list of names in a worksheet range so you can view or print them. Such a feat is possible, but you need to look beyond the Name Manager.

To create a list of names in a worksheet, first move the cell pointer to an empty area of your worksheet. The list is created at the active cell position and overwrites any information at that location. Press F3 to display the Paste Name dialog box, which lists all the defined names. Then click the Paste List button. Excel creates a list of all names in the workbook and their corresponding addresses.

Adding Comments to Cells

Documentation that explains certain elements in the worksheet can often be helpful. One way to document your work is to add comments to cells. This feature is useful when you need to describe a particular value or explain how a formula works.

To add a comment to a cell, select the cell and use any of these actions:

- Choose Review ➪ Comments ➪ New Comment.
- Right-click the cell and choose Insert Comment from the shortcut menu.
- Press Shift + F2.

Excel inserts a comment that points to the active cell. Initially, the comment consists of your name, as specified in the General tab of the Excel Options dialog box (choose File ➪ Options to display this dialog box). You can delete your name from the comment, if you like. Enter the text for the cell comment and then click anywhere in the worksheet to hide the comment. You can change the size of the comment by clicking and dragging any of its borders. Figure 4.16 shows a cell with a comment.

FIGURE 4.16

You can add comments to cells to help point out specific items in your worksheets.

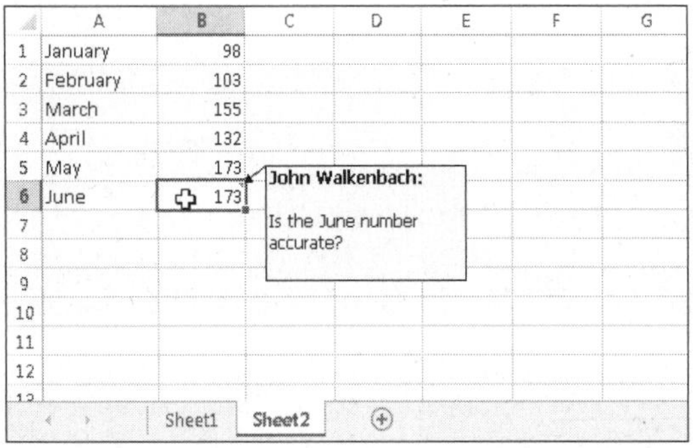

	A	B
1	January	98
2	February	103
3	March	155
4	April	132
5	May	173
6	June	173

John Walkenbach:

Is the June number accurate?

Sheet1 Sheet2

Cells that have a comment display a small red triangle in the upper-right corner. When you move the mouse pointer over a cell that contains a comment (or activate the cell), the comment becomes visible.

You can force a comment to be displayed even when its cell is not activated. Right-click the cell and choose Show/Hide Comments. Although this command refers to "comments" (plural), it affects only the comment in the active cell. To return to normal (make the comment appear only when its cell is activated or the mouse point hovers over it), right-click the cell and choose Hide Comment.

TIP

You can control how comments are displayed. Choose File ➪ Options and then select the Advanced tab of the Excel Options dialog box. In the Display section, select the No Comments or Indicators option from the For Cells with Comments, Show list.

Formatting comments

If you don't like the default look of cell comments, you can make some changes. Right-click the cell and choose Edit Comment. Select the text in the comment and use the commands of the Font and the Alignment groups (on the Home tab) to make changes to the comment's appearance.

For even more formatting options, right-click the comment's border and choose Format Comment from the shortcut menu. Excel responds by displaying the Format Comment dialog box, which allows you to change many aspects of its appearance, including color, border, and margins.

TIP

You can also display an image inside a comment. Right-click the cell and choose Edit Comment. Then right-click the comment's border and choose Format Comment. Select the Colors and Lines tab in the Format Comment dialog box. Click the Color drop-down list and select Fill Effects. In the Fill Effects dialog box, click the Picture tab and then click the Select Picture button to specify a graphics file. Figure 4.17 shows a comment that contains a picture.

FIGURE 4.17

This comment contains a graphics image.

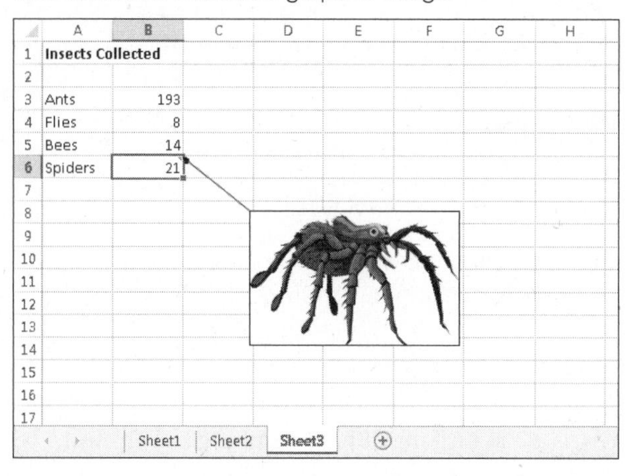

An Alternative to Cell Comments

You can make use of Excel's Data Validation (see Chapter 25) feature to add a different type of comment to a cell. This type of comment appears automatically when the cell is selected. Follow these steps:

1. **Select the cell that will contain the comment.**
2. **Choose Data ➪ Data Tools ➪ Data Validation.** The Data Validation dialog box appears.
3. **Click the Input Message tab.**
4. **Make sure that the Show Input Message When Cell Is Selected check box is selected.**
5. **Type your comment in the Input Message box.**
6. **(Optional) Type a title in the Title box.** This text will appear in bold at the top of the message.
7. **Click OK to close the Data Validation dialog box.**

After performing these steps, the message appears when the cell is activated, and it disappears when any other cell is activated.

Note that this message isn't a "real" comment. For example, a cell that contains this type of message doesn't display a comment indicator, and it's not affected by any of the commands used to work with cell comments. In addition, you can't format these messages in any way, and you can't print them.

Changing a comment's shape

Cell comments are rectangular, but they don't have to be. To change the shape of a cell comment, add a command to your Quick Access toolbar:

1. **Right-click the Quick Access toolbar and choose Customize Quick Access Toolbar.** The Quick Access Toolbar section of the Excel Options dialog box appears.
2. **From the Choose Commands From drop-down list, select Drawing Tools | Format Tab.**
3. **From the list on the left, select Change Shape, and then click Add.**
4. **Click OK to close the Excel Options dialog box.**

After performing these steps, your Quick Access toolbar has a new Change Shape icon.

To change the shape of a comment, make sure that it's visible (right-click the cell and select Show/Hide Comments). Then click the comment's border to select it as a Shape (or Ctrl + click the comment to select it as a Shape). Click the Change Shape button on the Quick Access toolbar and choose a new shape for the comment. Figure 4.18 shows a cell comment with a nonstandard shape.

FIGURE 4.18

Cell comments don't have to be rectangles.

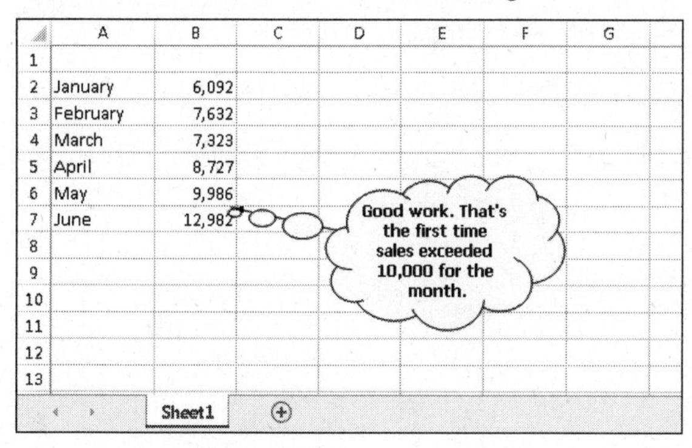

Reading comments

To read all comments in a workbook, choose Review ➪ Comments ➪ Next. Keep clicking Next to cycle through all the comments in a workbook. Choose Review ➪ Comments ➪ Previous to view the comments in reverse order.

Printing comments

Normally, when you print a worksheet that contains cell comments, the comments are not printed. If you would like to print the comments, though, here's how:

1. **Click the dialog box launcher in the Page Layout ➪ Page Setup group.** This is the small icon to the right of the Page Setup group name. Clicking this icon displays the Page Setup dialog box.
2. **In the Page Setup dialog box, click the Sheet tab.**
3. **Make your choice from the Comments drop-down control: At End of Sheet or As Displayed on Sheet (see Figure 4.19).**
4. **Click OK to close the Page Setup dialog box or click the Print button to print the worksheet.**

NOTE

You can also access the Page Setup box from the Print panel of Backstage view.

FIGURE 4.19

Specifying how to print cell comments.

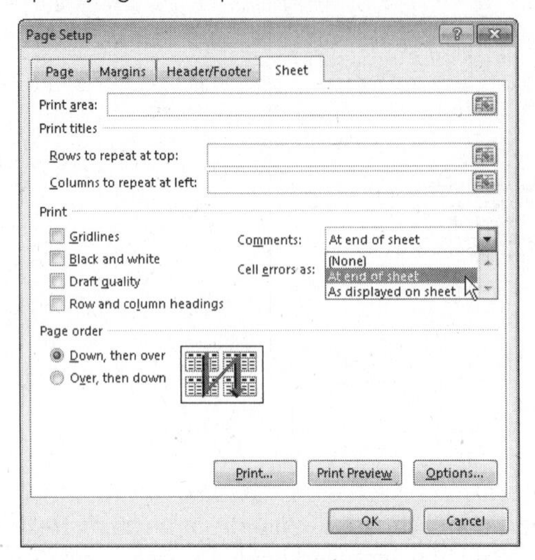

Hiding and showing comments

If you want all cell comments to be visible (regardless of the location of the cell pointer), choose Review ➪ Comments ➪ Show All Comments. This command is a toggle; select it again to hide all cell comments.

To toggle the display of an individual comments, select its cell and then choose Review ➪ Comments ➪ Show/Hide Comment.

Selecting comments

To quickly select all cells in a worksheet that contain a comment, choose Home ➪ Editing ➪ Find & Select ➪ Go to Special. Then choose the Comments option and click OK.

Editing comments

To edit a comment, activate the cell, right-click, and then choose Edit Comment from the shortcut menu. Or select the cell and press Shift + F2. After you make your changes, click any cell.

Deleting comments

To delete a cell comment, activate the cell that contains the comment and then choose Review ➪ Comments ➪ Delete. Or right-click and then choose Delete Comment from the shortcut menu.

CHAPTER 5

Introducing Tables

IN THIS CHAPTER

Understanding how a table differs from a normal range

Working with tables

Using the Total Row

Removing duplicate rows from a table

Sorting and filtering a table

A very common type of spreadsheet contains information in a structured list, also known as a table. A *table* is a rectangular range of data that usually has a row of text headings to describe the contents of each column. Excel's table feature makes common tasks much easier — and a lot better looking. More importantly, the table features may help eliminate some common errors.

This chapter is a basic introduction to Excel tables. As always, I urge you to just dig in and experiment with the various table-related commands. You may be surprised by what you can accomplish with just a few mouse clicks.

What Is a Table?

A *table* is a rectangular range of structured data. Each row in the table corresponds to a single entity. For example, a row can contain information about a customer, a bank transaction, an employee, a product, and so on. Each column contains a specific piece of information. For example, if each row contains information about an employee, the columns can contain data such as name, employee number, hire date, salary, department, and so on. Tables typically have a header row at the top that describes the information contained in each column.

Setting up data like this in a range of cells is very straightforward. The magic happens when you tell Excel to convert a range of data into an "official" table. You do this by selecting any cell within the range and then choosing Insert ➪ Tables ➪ Table.

When you explicitly identify a range as a table, Excel can respond more intelligently to the actions you perform with that range. For example, if you create a chart from a table, the chart will expand automatically as you add new rows to the table. And if you enter a formula into a cell, Excel will propagate the formula to other rows in the table.

Figure 5.1 shows a range of data that has not yet been converted to a table. Notice that this range corresponds to the description I provide earlier: It's a range of structured data with column headers. In this example, each row contains information about a single real estate listing. The range has 10 columns and 125 rows of data.

FIGURE 5.1

This range of data is a good candidate for a table.

	A	B	C	D	E	F	G	H	I	J
1	**Agent**	**Date Listed**	**Area**	**List Price**	**Bedrooms**	**Baths**	**SqFt**	**Type**	**Pool**	**Sold**
2	Jenkins	8/22/2012	N. County	$1,200,500	5	5	4,696	Single Family	TRUE	FALSE
3	Romero	3/28/2012	N. County	$799,000	6	5	4,800	Single Family	FALSE	FALSE
4	Shasta	4/30/2012	Central	$625,000	6	4	3,950	Single Family	TRUE	FALSE
5	Shasta	5/28/2012	S. County	$574,900	5	4	4,700	Single Family	FALSE	FALSE
6	Bennet	5/2/2012	Central	$549,000	4	3	1,940	Single Family	TRUE	FALSE
7	Hamilton	2/18/2012	N. County	$425,900	5	3	2,414	Single Family	TRUE	FALSE
8	Randolph	4/17/2012	N. County	$405,000	3	3	2,444	Single Family	TRUE	TRUE
9	Shasta	3/17/2012	N. County	$398,000	4	2.5	2,620	Single Family	FALSE	FALSE
10	Randolph	8/5/2012	Central	$389,900	4	2.5	2,284	Single Family	FALSE	TRUE
11	Kelly	6/2/2012	Central	$389,500	4	2	1,971	Single Family	FALSE	FALSE
12	Shasta	8/10/2012	N. County	$389,000	4	3	3,109	Single Family	FALSE	FALSE
13	Adams	5/30/2012	N. County	$379,900	3	2.5	2,468	Condo	FALSE	FALSE
14	Adams	8/1/2012	N. County	$379,000	3	3	2,354	Condo	FALSE	TRUE
15	Robinson	3/23/2012	N. County	$379,000	4	3	3,000	Single Family	FALSE	TRUE
16	Chung	4/14/2012	Central	$375,000	4	3	2,467	Single Family	TRUE	FALSE
17	Robinson	11/18/2012	Central	$375,000	4	3	2,368	Single Family	TRUE	TRUE
18	Shasta	7/8/2012	N. County	$374,900	4	3	3,927	Single Family	FALSE	FALSE
19	Lang	4/26/2012	N. County	$369,900	3	2.5	2,030	Condo	TRUE	FALSE
20	Romero	11/21/2012	N. County	$369,900	4	3	1,988	Condo	FALSE	FALSE
21	Shasta	7/16/2012	N. County	$369,900	5	3	2,477	Single Family	FALSE	FALSE

Sheet1

Figure 5.2 shows the range after I converted it to a table by choosing Insert ➪ Tables ➪ Table.

ON THE WEB

If you'd like to practice working with tables, the workbook shown here is available on this book's website. The file is named `real estate table.xlsx`.

FIGURE 5.2

An Excel table.

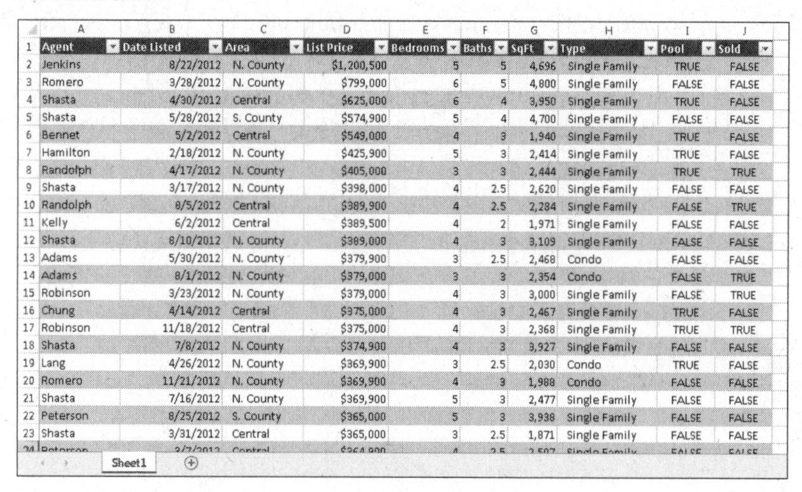

	Agent	Date Listed	Area	List Price	Bedrooms	Baths	SqFt	Type	Pool	Sold
2	Jenkins	8/22/2012	N. County	$1,200,500	5	5	4,696	Single Family	TRUE	FALSE
3	Romero	3/28/2012	N. County	$799,000	6	5	4,800	Single Family	FALSE	FALSE
4	Shasta	4/30/2012	Central	$625,000	6	4	3,950	Single Family	TRUE	FALSE
5	Shasta	5/28/2012	S. County	$574,900	5	4	4,700	Single Family	FALSE	FALSE
6	Bennet	5/2/2012	Central	$549,000	4	3	1,940	Single Family	TRUE	FALSE
7	Hamilton	2/18/2012	N. County	$425,900	5	3	2,414	Single Family	TRUE	FALSE
8	Randolph	4/17/2012	N. County	$405,000	3	3	2,444	Single Family	TRUE	TRUE
9	Shasta	3/17/2012	N. County	$398,000	4	2.5	2,620	Single Family	FALSE	FALSE
10	Randolph	8/5/2012	Central	$389,900	4	2.5	2,284	Single Family	FALSE	TRUE
11	Kelly	6/2/2012	Central	$389,500	4	2	1,971	Single Family	FALSE	FALSE
12	Shasta	8/10/2012	N. County	$389,000	4	3	3,109	Single Family	FALSE	FALSE
13	Adams	5/30/2012	N. County	$379,900	3	2.5	2,468	Condo	FALSE	FALSE
14	Adams	8/1/2012	N. County	$379,000	3	3	2,354	Condo	FALSE	TRUE
15	Robinson	3/23/2012	N. County	$379,000	4	3	3,000	Single Family	FALSE	TRUE
16	Chung	4/14/2012	Central	$375,000	4	3	2,467	Single Family	TRUE	FALSE
17	Robinson	11/18/2012	Central	$375,000	4	3	2,368	Single Family	TRUE	TRUE
18	Shasta	7/8/2012	N. County	$374,900	4	3	3,927	Single Family	FALSE	FALSE
19	Lang	4/26/2012	N. County	$369,900	3	2.5	2,030	Condo	TRUE	FALSE
20	Romero	11/21/2012	N. County	$369,900	4	3	1,988	Condo	FALSE	FALSE
21	Shasta	7/16/2012	N. County	$369,900	5	3	2,477	Single Family	FALSE	FALSE
22	Peterson	8/25/2012	S. County	$365,000	5	3	3,938	Single Family	FALSE	FALSE
23	Shasta	3/31/2012	Central	$365,000	3	2.5	1,871	Single Family	FALSE	FALSE

What's the difference between a standard range and a table? With a table

- Activating any cell in the table gives you access to the Table Tools contextual tab on the Ribbon (see Figure 5.3).

FIGURE 5.3

When you select a cell in a table, you can use the commands located on the Table Tools ⇨ Design tab.

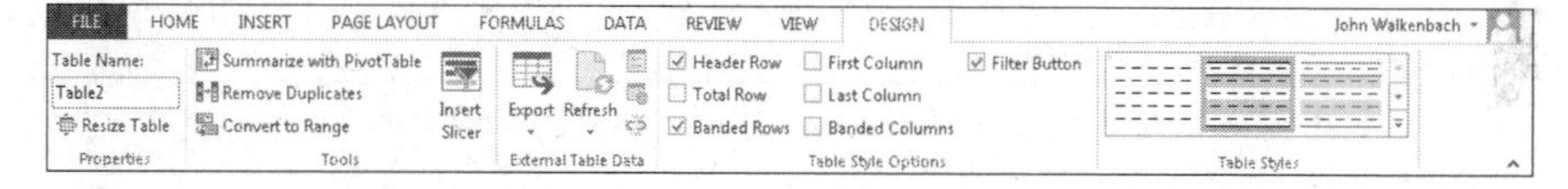

- The cells contain background color and text color formatting. This formatting is optional.
- Each column header contains a Filter Button — a drop-down list that you can use to sort the data or filter the table to display only rows that meet certain criteria. Displaying the Filter Button is optional.
- You can create easy to use Slicers to simplify filtering data.
- If the active cell is within the table, when you scroll down the sheet so that the header row disappears, the table headers replace the column letters in the worksheet header.

5

- Tables support calculated columns. A single formula in a column is automatically propagated to all cells in the column.
- Tables support structured references. Instead of using cell references, formulas can use table names and column headers.
- The lower-right corner of the lower-right cell contains a small control that you can click and drag to extend the table's size, either horizontally (add more columns) or vertically (add more rows).
- Selecting rows and columns within the table is simplified.

All these concepts will become clearer later on.

Creating a Table

Most of the time, you'll create a table from an existing range of data. However, Excel also allows you to create a table from an empty range so that you can fill in the details later. The following instructions assume that you already have a range of data that's suitable for a table.

1. **Make sure that the range doesn't contain any completely blank rows or columns; otherwise, Excel will not guess the table range correctly.**
2. **Select any cell within the range.**
3. **Choose Insert ➪ Tables ➪ Table (or press Ctrl + T).** Excel responds with its Create Table dialog box, shown in Figure 5.4. Excel tries to guess the range, as well as whether the table has a header row. Most of the time, it guesses correctly. If not, make your corrections before you click OK.

FIGURE 5.4

Use the Create Table dialog box to verify that Excel guessed the table dimensions correctly.

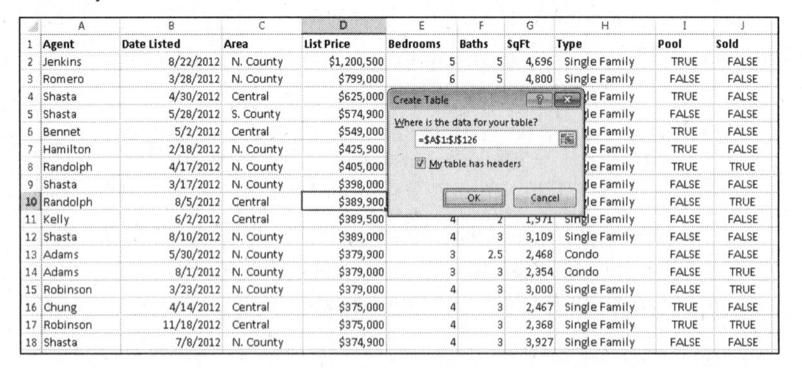

	A	B	C	D	E	F	G	H	I	J
1	Agent	Date Listed	Area	List Price	Bedrooms	Baths	SqFt	Type	Pool	Sold
2	Jenkins	8/22/2012	N. County	$1,200,500	5	5	4,696	Single Family	TRUE	FALSE
3	Romero	3/28/2012	N. County	$799,000	6	5	4,800	Single Family	FALSE	FALSE
4	Shasta	4/30/2012	Central	$625,000				le Family	TRUE	FALSE
5	Shasta	5/28/2012	S. County	$574,900				le Family	FALSE	FALSE
6	Bennet	5/2/2012	Central	$549,000				le Family	TRUE	FALSE
7	Hamilton	2/18/2012	N. County	$425,900				le Family	TRUE	FALSE
8	Randolph	4/17/2012	N. County	$405,000				le Family	TRUE	TRUE
9	Shasta	3/17/2012	N. County	$398,000				le Family	FALSE	FALSE
10	Randolph	8/5/2012	Central	$389,900				le Family	FALSE	TRUE
11	Kelly	6/2/2012	Central	$389,500	4	2	1,971	Single Family	FALSE	FALSE
12	Shasta	8/10/2012	N. County	$389,000	4	3	3,109	Single Family	FALSE	FALSE
13	Adams	5/30/2012	N. County	$379,900	3	2.5	2,468	Condo	FALSE	FALSE
14	Adams	8/1/2012	N. County	$379,000	3	3	2,354	Condo	FALSE	TRUE
15	Robinson	3/23/2012	N. County	$379,000	4	3	3,000	Single Family	FALSE	TRUE
16	Chung	4/14/2012	Central	$375,000	4	3	2,467	Single Family	TRUE	FALSE
17	Robinson	11/18/2012	Central	$375,000	4	3	2,368	Single Family	TRUE	TRUE
18	Shasta	7/8/2012	N. County	$374,900	4	3	3,927	Single Family	FALSE	FALSE

The range is converted to a table (using the default table style), and the Table Tools➪Design tab of the Ribbon appears.

NOTE

Excel may not guess the table's dimensions correctly if the table isn't separated from other information by at least one empty row or column. If Excel guesses incorrectly, just specify the exact range for the table in the Create Table dialog box. Better yet, click Cancel and rearrange your worksheet such that the table is separated from your other data by at least one blank row or column.

To create a table from an empty range, just select the range and choose Insert➪Tables➪Table. Excel creates the table, adds generic column headers (such as Column1 and Column2), and applies table formatting to the range. Almost always, you'll want to replace the generic column headers with more meaningful text.

Changing the Look of a Table

When you create a table, Excel applies the default table style. The actual appearance depends on which document theme is used in the workbook (see Chapter 6). If you prefer a different look, you can easily change the entire look of the table.

Select any cell in the table and choose Table Tools➪Design➪Table Styles. The Ribbon shows one row of styles, but if you click the bottom of the scrollbar to the right, the Table Styles group expands, as shown in Figure 5.5. The styles are grouped into three categories: Light, Medium, and Dark. Notice that you get a "live" preview as you move your mouse among the styles. When you see one you like, just click to make it permanent. And yes, some are really ugly and practically illegible.

For a different set of color choices, choose Page Layout➪Themes➪Themes to select a different document theme.

For more information about themes, see Chapter 6.

5

FIGURE 5.5

Excel offers many different table styles.

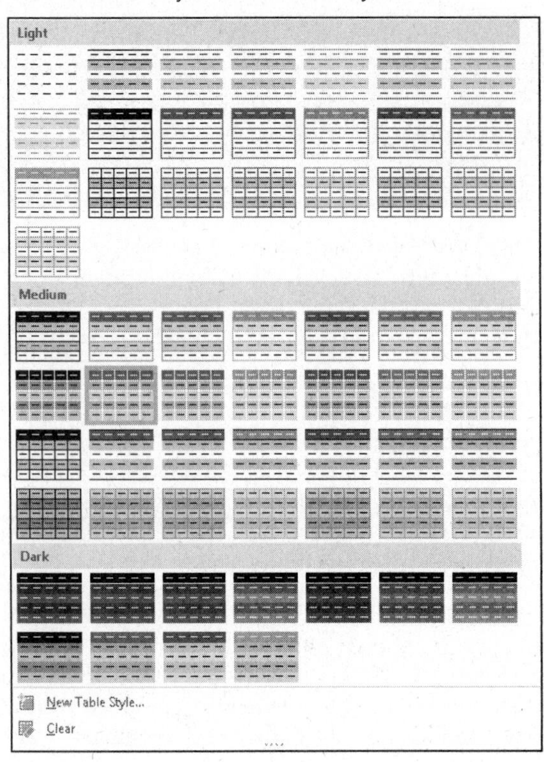

You can change some elements of the style by using the check box controls in the Table Tools ➪ Design ➪ Table Style Options group. These controls determine whether various elements of the table are displayed, and whether some formatting options are in effect:

- **Header Row:** Toggles the display of the Header Row.
- **Total Row:** Toggles the display of the Total Row.
- **First Column:** Toggles special formatting for the first column. Depending on the table style used, this command might have no effect.
- **Last Column:** Toggles special formatting for the last column. Depending on the table style used, this command might have no effect.
- **Banded Rows:** Toggles the display of *banded* (alternating color) rows.
- **Banded Columns:** Toggles the display of banded columns.
- **Filter Button:** Toggles the display of the drop-down buttons in the table's header row.

TIP

If applying table styles isn't working, it's probably because the range was already formatted before you converted it to a table. Table formatting doesn't override normal formatting. To clear existing background fill colors, select the entire table and choose Home ➪ Font ➪ Fill Color ➪ No Fill. To clear existing font colors, choose Home ➪ Font ➪ Font Color ➪ Automatic. To clear existing borders, choose Home ➪ Font ➪ Borders ➪ No Borders. After you issue these commands, the table styles should work as expected.

If you'd like to create a custom table style, choose Table Tools ➪ Design ➪ Table Styles ➪ New Table Style to display the New Table Quick Style dialog box shown in Figure 5.6. You can customize any or all of the 12 table elements. Select an element from the list, click Format, and specify the formatting for that element. When you're finished, give the new style a name and click OK. Your custom table style will appear in the Table Styles gallery in the Custom category. Unfortunately, custom table styles are available only in the workbook in which they were created.

FIGURE 5.6

Use this dialog box to create a new table style.

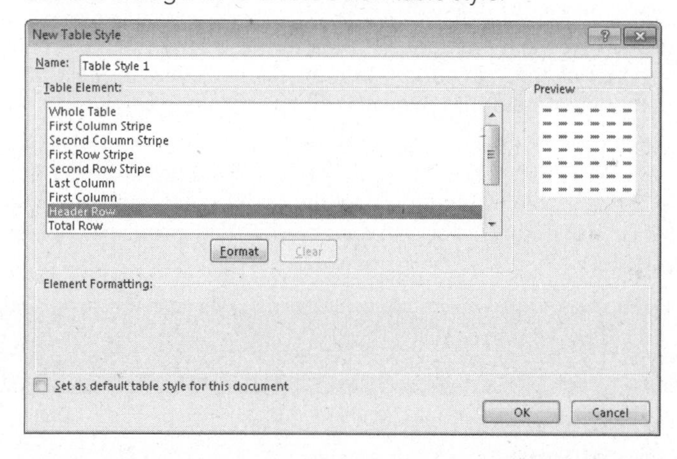

TIP

If you want to make changes to an existing table style, locate it in the Ribbon and right-click. Choose Duplicate from the shortcut menu. Excel displays the Modify Table Quick Style dialog box with all the settings from the specified table style. Make your changes, give the style a new name, and click OK to save it as a custom table style.

Working with Tables

This section describes some common actions you'll take with tables.

Navigating in a table

Selecting cells in a table works just like selecting cells in a normal range. One difference is when you use the Tab key. Pressing Tab moves to the cell to the right, but when you reach the last column, pressing Tab again moves to the first cell in the next row.

Selecting parts of a table

When you move your mouse around in a table, you may notice that the pointer changes shapes. These shapes help you select various parts of the table.

- **To select an entire column:** Move the mouse to the top of a cell in the header row, and the mouse pointer changes to a down-pointing arrow. Click to select the data in the column. Click a second time to select the entire table column (including the Header Row and the Total Row, if it has one). You can also press Ctrl + spacebar (once or twice) to select a column.
- **To select an entire row:** Move the mouse to the left of a cell in the first column, and the mouse pointer changes to a right-pointing arrow. Click to select the entire table row. You can also press Shift + spacebar to select a table row.
- **To select the entire table:** Move the mouse to the upper-left part of the upper-left cell. When the mouse pointer turns into a diagonal arrow, click to select the data area of the table. Click a second time to select the entire table (including the Header Row and the Total Row). You can also press Ctrl + A (once or twice) to select the entire table.

TIP

Right-clicking a cell in a table displays several selection options in the shortcut menu.

Adding new rows or columns

To add a new column to the end of a table, select a cell in the column to the right of the table and start entering the data. Excel automatically extends the table horizontally and adds a generic column name for the new column.

Similarly, if you enter data in the row below a table, Excel extends the table vertically to include the new row.

NOTE

An exception to automatically extending tables is when the table is displaying a Total Row. If you enter data below the Total Row, the table won't be extended and the data won't be part of the table.

To add rows or columns within the table, right-click and choose Insert from the shortcut menu. The Insert shortcut menu command displays additional menu items:

- Table Columns to the Left
- Table Columns to the Right
- Table Rows Above
- Table Rows Below

TIP

When the cell pointer is in the bottom-right cell of a table, pressing Tab inserts a new row at the bottom of the table, above the Total Row (if the table has one).

When you move your mouse to the resize handle at the bottom-right cell of a table, the mouse pointer turns into a diagonal line with two arrowheads. Click and drag down to add more rows to the table. Click and drag to the right to add more columns.

When you insert a new column, the Header Row displays a generic description, such as Column1, Column2, and so on. Typically, you'll want to change these names to more descriptive labels. Just select the cell and overwrite the generic text with your new text.

Deleting rows or columns

To delete a row (or column) in a table, select any cell in the row (or column) to be deleted. To delete multiple rows or columns, select a range of cells. Then right-click and choose Delete⇨Table Rows (or Delete⇨Table Columns).

Moving a table

To move a table to a new location in the same worksheet, move the mouse pointer to any of its borders. When the mouse pointer turns into a cross with four arrows, click and drag the table to its new location.

To move a table to a different worksheet (which could be in a different workbook), you can drag and drop it as well — as long as the destination worksheet is visible onscreen.

Or, you can use these steps to move a table to different worksheet or workbook:

1. **Press Ctrl + A *twice* to select the entire table.**
2. **Press Ctrl + X to cut the selected cells.**
3. **Activate the new worksheet and select the upper-left cell for the table.**
4. **Press Ctrl + V to paste the table.**

Excel Remembers

When you do something with a complete column in a table, Excel remembers that and extends that "something" to all new entries added to that column. For example, if you apply currency formatting to a column and then add a new row, Excel applies currency formatting to the new value in that column.

The same thing applies to other operations, such as conditional formatting, cell protection, data validation, and so on. And if you create a chart using the data in a table, the chart will be extended automatically if you add new data to the table.

Working with the Total Row

The Total Row in a table contains formulas that summarize the information in the columns. When you create a table, the Total Row isn't turned on. To display the Total Row, choose Table Tools ➪ Design ➪ Table Style Options and put a check mark next to Total Row.

By default, a Total Row displays the sum of the values in a column of numbers. In some cases, you'll want a different type of summary formula. When you select a cell in the Total Row, a drop-down arrow appears in the cell. Click the arrow, and you can select from a number of other summary formulas (see Figure 5.7):

FIGURE 5.7

Several types of summary formulas are available for the Total Row.

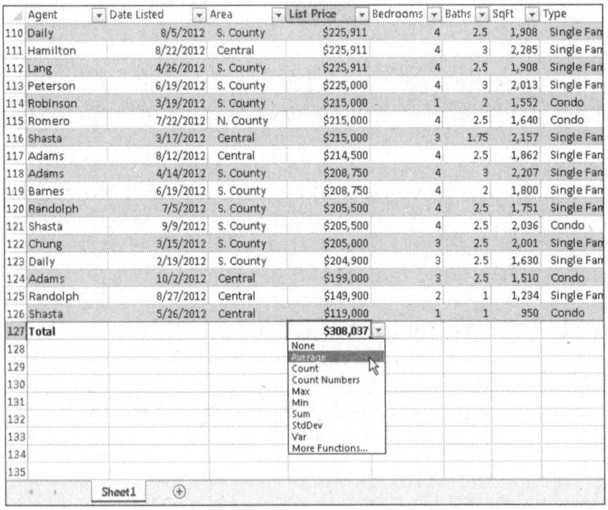

	Agent	Date Listed	Area	List Price	Bedrooms	Baths	SqFt	Type
110	Daily	8/5/2012	S. County	$225,911	4	2.5	1,908	Single Fan
111	Hamilton	8/22/2012	Central	$225,911	4	3	2,285	Single Fan
112	Lang	4/26/2012	S. County	$225,911	4	2.5	1,908	Single Fan
113	Peterson	6/19/2012	S. County	$225,000	4	3	2,013	Single Fan
114	Robinson	3/19/2012	S. County	$215,000	1	2	1,552	Condo
115	Romero	7/22/2012	N. County	$215,000	4	2.5	1,640	Condo
116	Shasta	3/17/2012	Central	$215,000	3	1.75	2,157	Single Fan
117	Adams	8/12/2012	Central	$214,500	4	2.5	1,862	Single Fan
118	Adams	4/14/2012	S. County	$208,750	4	3	2,207	Single Fan
119	Barnes	6/19/2012	S. County	$208,750	4	2	1,800	Single Fan
120	Randolph	7/5/2012	S. County	$205,500	4	2.5	1,751	Single Fan
121	Shasta	9/9/2012	S. County	$205,500	4	2.5	2,036	Condo
122	Chung	3/15/2012	S. County	$205,000	3	2.5	2,001	Single Fan
123	Daily	2/19/2012	S. County	$204,900	3	2.5	1,630	Single Fan
124	Adams	10/2/2012	Central	$199,000	3	2.5	1,510	Condo
125	Randolph	8/27/2012	Central	$149,900	2	1	1,234	Single Fan
126	Shasta	5/26/2012	Central	$119,000	1	1	950	Condo
127	**Total**			**$308,037**				

None
Average
Count
Count Numbers
Max
Min
Sum
StdDev
Var
More Functions...

Sheet1

- **None:** No formula.
- **Average:** Displays the average of the numbers in the column.
- **Count:** Displays the number of entries in the column. (Blank cells are not counted.)
- **Count Numbers:** Displays the number of numeric values in the column. (Blank cells, text cells, and error cells are not counted.)
- **Max:** Displays the maximum value in the column.
- **Min:** Displays the minimum value in the column.
- **Sum:** Displays the sum of the values in the column.
- **StdDev:** Displays the standard deviation of the values in the column. (*Standard deviation* is a statistical measure of how "spread out" the values are.)
- **Var:** Displays the variance of the values in the column. (*Variance* is another statistical measure of how "spread out" the values are.)
- **More Functions:** Displays the Insert Function dialog box so that you can select a function that isn't in the list.

CAUTION

If you have a formula that refers to a value in the Total Row of a table, the formula returns an error if you hide the Total Row. But if you make the Total Row visible again, the formula works as it should.

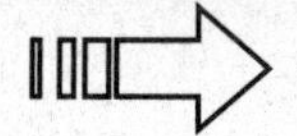

For more information about formulas, including the use of formulas in a table column, see Chapter 10.

Removing duplicate rows from a table

If data in a table was compiled from multiple sources, the table may contain duplicate items. Most of the time, you want to eliminate the duplicates. In the past, removing duplicate data was essentially a manual task, but it's very easy if the data is in a table.

Start by selecting any cell in your table. Then choose Table Tools ➪ Design ➪ Tools ➪ Remove Duplicates. Excel responds with Remove Duplicates dialog box shown in Figure 5.8. The dialog box lists all the columns in your table. Place a check mark next to the columns that you want to be included in the duplicate search. Most of the time, you'll want to select all the columns, which is the default. Click OK, and Excel weeds out the duplicate rows and displays a message that tells you how many duplicates it removed.

When you select all columns in the Remove Duplicates dialog box, Excel will delete a row only if the content of every column is duplicated. In some situations, you may not care about matching some columns, so you would deselect those columns in the Remove Duplicates dialog box. When duplicate rows are found, the first row is kept and subsequent duplicate rows are deleted.

FIGURE 5.8

Removing duplicate rows from a table is easy.

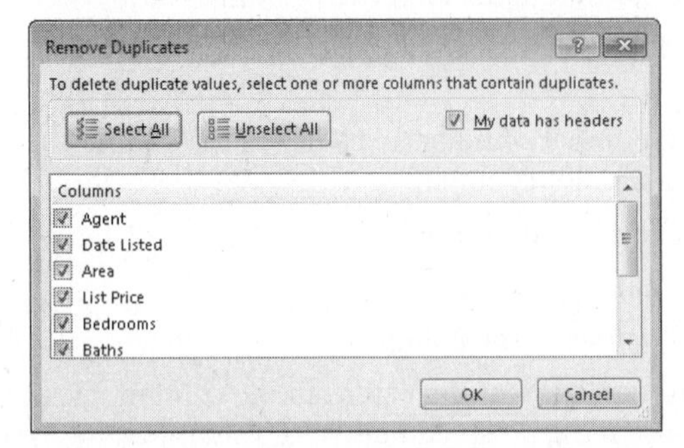

TIP

Data does not have to be in the form of a designated table to remove duplicates. To remove duplicate rows from a normal range, choose Data ➪ Data Tools ➪ Remove Duplicates.

CAUTION

It's important to understand that duplicate values are determined by the value *displayed* in the cell — not necessarily the value *stored* in the cell. For example, assume that two cells contain the same date. One of the dates is formatted to display as 5/15/2012, and the other is formatted to display as May 15, 2012. When removing duplicates, Excel considers these dates to be different.

Sorting and filtering a table

Each item in the Header Row of a table contains a drop-down arrow known as a Filter Button. When clicked, the Filter Button displays sorting and filtering options (see Figure 5.9).

NEW FEATURE

A new feature in Excel 2013 lets you toggle the display of Filter Buttons in a table's Header Row. Choose Table Tools ➪ Design ➪ Table Style Options ➪ Filter Button to display or hide the drop-down arrows.

FIGURE 5.9

Each column in a table has sorting and filtering options.

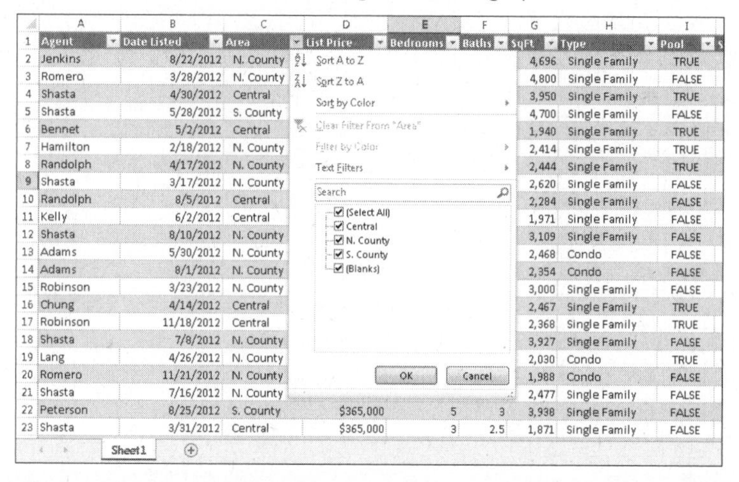

Sorting a table

Sorting a table rearranges the rows based on the contents of a particular column. You may want to sort a table to put names in alphabetical order. Or, maybe you want to sort your sales staff by the totals sales made.

To sort a table by a particular column, click the Filter Button in the column header and choose one of the sort commands. The exact command varies, depending on the type of data in the column.

You can also select Sort by Color to sort the rows based on the background or text color of the data. This option is relevant only if you've overridden the table style colors with custom formatting.

You can sort on any number of columns. The trick is to sort the least significant column first and then proceed until the most significant column is sorted last. For example, in the real estate table, you may want to sort the list by agent. And within each agent's group, sort the rows by area. And within each area, sort the rows by list price. For this type of sort, first sort by the List Price column, then sort by the Area column, and then sort by the Agent column. Figure 5.10 shows the table sorted in this manner.

FIGURE 5.10

A table, after performing a three-column sort.

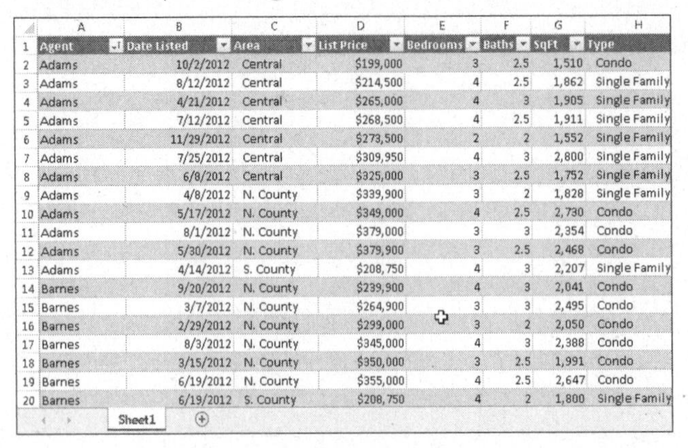

	A	B	C	D	E	F	G	H
1	Agent	Date Listed	Area	List Price	Bedrooms	Baths	SqFt	Type
2	Adams	10/2/2012	Central	$199,000	3	2.5	1,510	Condo
3	Adams	8/12/2012	Central	$214,500	4	2.5	1,862	Single Family
4	Adams	4/21/2012	Central	$265,000	4	3	1,905	Single Family
5	Adams	7/12/2012	Central	$268,500	4	2.5	1,911	Single Family
6	Adams	11/29/2012	Central	$273,500	2	2	1,552	Single Family
7	Adams	7/25/2012	Central	$309,950	4	3	2,800	Single Family
8	Adams	6/8/2012	Central	$325,000	3	2.5	1,752	Single Family
9	Adams	4/8/2012	N. County	$339,900	3	2	1,828	Single Family
10	Adams	5/17/2012	N. County	$349,000	4	2.5	2,730	Condo
11	Adams	8/1/2012	N. County	$379,000	3	3	2,354	Condo
12	Adams	5/30/2012	N. County	$379,900	3	2.5	2,468	Condo
13	Adams	4/14/2012	S. County	$208,750	4	3	2,207	Single Family
14	Barnes	9/20/2012	N. County	$239,900	4	3	2,041	Condo
15	Barnes	3/7/2012	N. County	$264,900	3	3	2,495	Condo
16	Barnes	2/29/2012	N. County	$299,000	3	2	2,050	Condo
17	Barnes	8/3/2012	N. County	$345,000	4	3	2,388	Condo
18	Barnes	3/15/2012	N. County	$350,000	3	2.5	1,991	Condo
19	Barnes	6/19/2012	N. County	$355,000	4	2.5	2,647	Condo
20	Barnes	6/19/2012	S. County	$208,750	4	2	1,800	Single Family

Sheet1

NOTE

When a column is sorted, the Filter Button in the header row displays a different graphic to remind you that the table is sorted by that column.

Another way of performing a multiple-column sort is to use the Sort dialog box (choose Home ➪ Editing ➪ Sort & Filter ➪ Custom Sort). Or right-click any cell in the table and choose Sort ➪ Custom Sort from the shortcut menu.

In the Sort dialog box, use the drop-down lists to specify the sort specifications. In this example, you start with Agent. Then click the Add Level button to insert another set of search controls. In this new set of controls, specify the sort specifications for the Area column. Then add another level and enter the specifications for the List Price column. Figure 5.11 shows the dialog box after entering the specifications for the three-column sort. This technique produces exactly the same sort as described in the previous paragraph.

FIGURE 5.11

Using the Sort dialog box to specify a three-column sort.

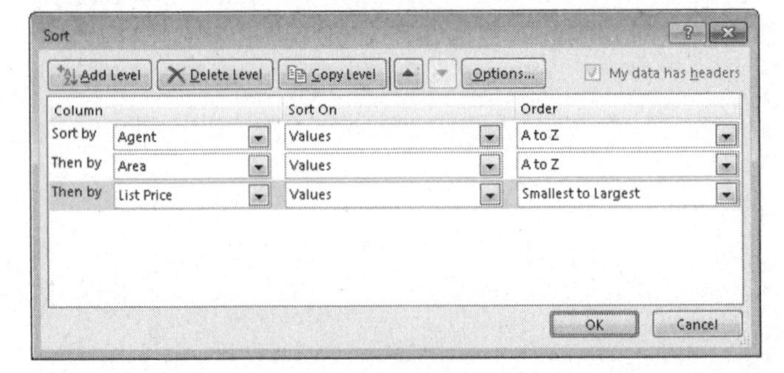

Filtering a table

Filtering a table refers to displaying only the rows that meet certain conditions. (The other rows are hidden.)

Note that entire rows are hidden. Therefore, if you have other data to the left or right of your table, that information will also be hidden. If you plan to filter your list, don't include any other data to the left or right of your table.

Using the real estate table, assume that you're only interested in the data for the N. County area. Click the Filter Button in the Area Row Header and remove the check mark from Select All, which unselects everything. Then, place a check mark next to N. County and click OK. The table, shown in Figure 5.12, is now filtered to display only the listings in the N. County area. Notice that some of the row numbers are missing. These rows are hidden and contain data that does not meet the specified criteria.

FIGURE 5.12

This table is filtered to show only the information for N. County.

	A	B	C	D	E	F	G	H	I	J
1	Agent	Date Listed	Area	List Price	Bedrooms	Baths	SqFt	Type	Pool	Sold
9	Adams	4/8/2012	N. County	$339,900	3	2	1,828	Single Family	TRUE	TRUE
10	Adams	5/17/2012	N. County	$349,000	4	2.5	2,730	Condo	TRUE	TRUE
11	Adams	8/1/2012	N. County	$379,000	3	3	2,354	Condo	FALSE	TRUE
12	Adams	5/30/2012	N. County	$379,900	3	2.5	2,468	Condo	FALSE	FALSE
14	Barnes	9/20/2012	N. County	$239,900	4	3	2,041	Condo	FALSE	FALSE
15	Barnes	3/7/2012	N. County	$264,900	3	3	2,495	Condo	FALSE	FALSE
16	Barnes	2/29/2012	N. County	$299,000	3	2	2,050	Condo	FALSE	FALSE
17	Barnes	8/3/2012	N. County	$345,000	4	3	2,388	Condo	TRUE	TRUE
18	Barnes	3/15/2012	N. County	$350,000	3	2.5	1,991	Condo	FALSE	TRUE
19	Barnes	6/19/2012	N. County	$355,000	4	2.5	2,647	Condo	TRUE	FALSE
23	Bennet	6/24/2012	N. County	$229,500	6	3	2,700	Single Family	TRUE	FALSE
24	Bennet	4/14/2012	N. County	$229,900	3	3	2,266	Condo	FALSE	FALSE
25	Bennet	5/20/2012	N. County	$229,900	4	3	2,041	Condo	FALSE	FALSE
44	Hamilton	2/18/2012	N. County	$425,900	5	3	2,414	Single Family	TRUE	FALSE
47	Jenkins	4/15/2012	N. County	$238,000	4	2.5	1,590	Condo	FALSE	TRUE
48	Jenkins	4/2/2012	N. County	$248,500	4	2.5	2,101	Single Family	TRUE	TRUE
49	Jenkins	4/24/2012	N. County	$349,900	4	3	2,290	Single Family	TRUE	TRUE
50	Jenkins	8/22/2012	N. County	$1,200,500	5	5	4,696	Single Family	TRUE	FALSE
62	Lang	8/16/2012	N. County	$264,900	3	2.5	2,062	Condo	FALSE	FALSE
63	Lang	7/15/2012	N. County	$349,000	4	3	3,930	Single Family	TRUE	FALSE
64	Lang	6/16/2012	N. County	$359,000	3	2.5	2,210	Single Family	FALSE	FALSE
65	Lang	4/26/2012	N. County	$369,900	3	2.5	2,030	Condo	TRUE	FALSE
74	Peterson	6/11/2012	N. County	$235,990	4	2	1,656	Condo	TRUE	FALSE
75	Peterson	4/8/2012	N. County	$259,900	4	3	1,734	Condo	FALSE	TRUE
76	Peterson	3/31/2012	N. County	$309,900	5	3	2,447	Condo	TRUE	FALSE
89	Randolph	4/14/2012	N. County	$259,900	3	2.5	2,122	Condo	FALSE	TRUE

Sheet1

Also notice that the Filter Button in the Area column now shows a different graphic — an icon that indicates the column is filtered.

You can filter by multiple values in a column using multiple check marks. For example, to filter the table to show only N. County and Central, place a check mark next to both values in the drop-down list in the Area Row Header.

You can filter a table using any number of columns. For example, you may want to see only the N. County listings in which the Type is Single Family. Just repeat the operation using the Type column. All tables then display only the rows in which the Area is N. County and the Type is Single Family.

For additional filtering options, select Text Filters (or Number Filters, if the column contains values). The options are fairly self-explanatory, and you have a great deal of flexibility in displaying only the rows that you're interested in. For example, you can display rows in which the List Price is greater than or equal to $200,000, but less than $300,000 (see Figure 5.13).

FIGURE 5.13

Specifying a more complex numeric filter.

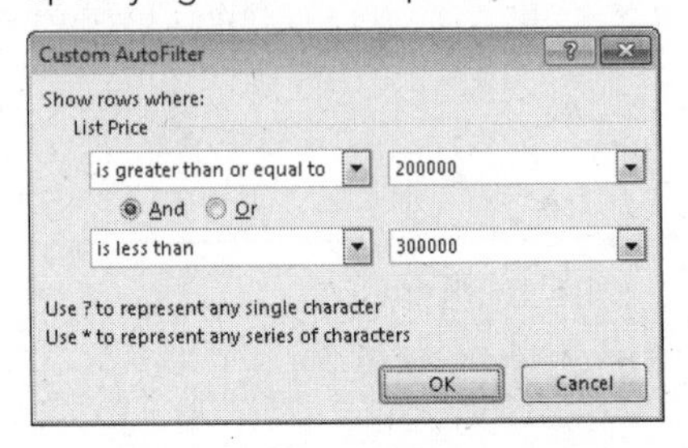

In addition, you can right-click a cell and use the Filter command on the shortcut menu. This menu item leads to several additional filtering options.

NOTE

As you may expect, when you use filtering, the Total Row is updated to show the total only for the visible rows.

When you copy data from a filtered table, only the visible data is copied. In other words, rows that are hidden by filtering don't get copied. This filtering makes it very easy to copy a subset of a larger table and paste it to another area of your worksheet. Keep in mind, though, that the pasted data is not a table — it's just a normal range. You can, however, convert the copied range to a table.

To remove filtering for a column, click the drop-down in the Row Header and select Clear Filter. If you've filtered using multiple columns, it may be faster to remove all filters by choosing Home ⇨ Editing ⇨ Sort & Filter ⇨ Clear.

Filtering a table with Slicers

Another way to filter a table is to use one or more Slicers. This method is less flexible, but more visually appealing. Slicers are particularly useful when the table will be viewed by novices or those who find the normal filtering techniques too complicated. Slicers are very visual, and it's easy to see exactly what type of filtering is in effect. A disadvantage of Slicers is that they take up a lot of room on the screen.

New Feature

Slicers for tables is a new feature in Excel 2013. This feature was introduced in Excel 2010, but it worked only for pivot table filtering.

To add one or more Slicers, activate any cell in the table and choose Table Tools ⇨ Design ⇨ Tools ⇨ Insert Slicer. Excel responds with a dialog box that displays each header in the table (see Figure 5.14).

FIGURE 5.14

Use the Insert Slicers dialog box to specify which Slicers to create.

Place a check mark next to the field(s) that you want to filter. You can create a Slicer for each column, but that's rarely needed. In most cases, you'll want to be able to filter the table by only a few fields. Click OK, and Excel creates a Slicer for each field you specified.

A Slicer contains a button for every unique item in the field. In the real estate listing example, the Slicer for the Agent field contains 14 buttons, because the table has records for 14 different agents.

Note

Slicers may not be appropriate for columns that contain numeric data. For example, the real estate listing table has 78 different values in the List Price column. Therefore, a Slicer for this column would have 78 buttons. There's no way to group the values into numeric ranges. This is an example of how a Slicer is not as flexible as normal filtering using Filter Buttons.

To use a Slicer, just click one of the buttons. The table displays only the rows that correspond to the button. You can also press Ctrl to select multiple buttons and press Shift to select a continuous group of buttons — which would be useful for selecting a range of List Price values.

If your table has more than one Slicer, it's filtered by the selected buttons in each Slicer. To remove filtering for a particular Slicer, click the icon in the upper-right corner of the Slicer.

Use the tools in the Slicer Tools ➪ Options context menu to change the appearance or layout of a Slicer. You have quite a bit of flexibility.

Figure 5.15 shows a table with two slicers. The table is filtered to show only the records for Adams and Jenkins in the N. County area.

FIGURE 5.15

The table is filtered by two Slicers.

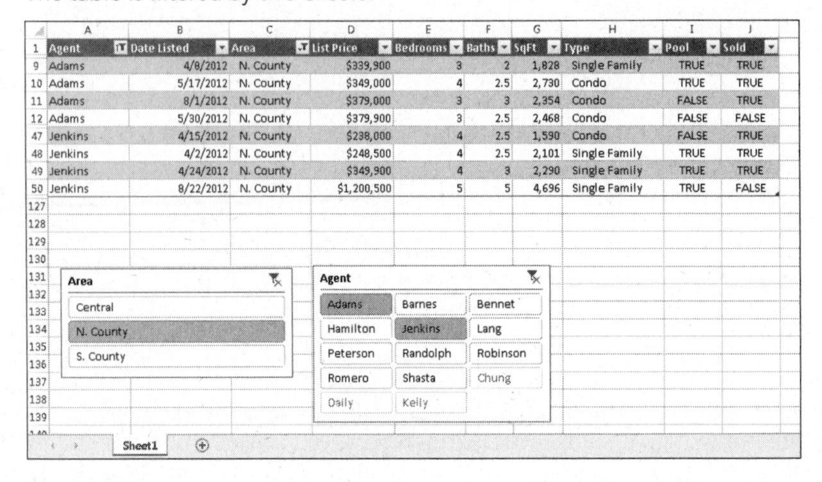

	Agent	Date Listed	Area	List Price	Bedrooms	Baths	SqFt	Type	Pool	Sold
9	Adams	4/8/2012	N. County	$339,900	3	2	1,828	Single Family	TRUE	TRUE
10	Adams	5/17/2012	N. County	$349,000	4	2.5	2,730	Condo	TRUE	TRUE
11	Adams	8/1/2012	N. County	$379,000	3	3	2,354	Condo	FALSE	TRUE
12	Adams	5/30/2012	N. County	$379,900	3	2.5	2,468	Condo	FALSE	FALSE
47	Jenkins	4/15/2012	N. County	$238,000	4	2.5	1,590	Condo	FALSE	TRUE
48	Jenkins	4/2/2012	N. County	$248,500	4	2.5	2,101	Single Family	TRUE	TRUE
49	Jenkins	4/24/2012	N. County	$349,900	4	3	2,290	Single Family	TRUE	TRUE
50	Jenkins	8/22/2012	N. County	$1,200,500	5	5	4,696	Single Family	TRUE	FALSE

Converting a table back to a range

If you need to convert a table back to a normal range, just select a cell in the table and choose Table Tools ➪ Design ➪ Tools ➪ Convert to Range. The table style formatting remains intact, but the range no longer functions as a table.

CHAPTER

6

Worksheet Formatting

IN THIS CHAPTER

- Understanding how formatting can improve your worksheets
- Getting to know the formatting tools
- Using formatting in your worksheets
- Using named styles for easier formatting
- Understanding document themes

Formatting your worksheet is like the icing on a cake — it may not be absolutely necessary, but it can make the end product a lot more attractive. In an Excel worksheet, formatting can also make it easier for others to understand the worksheet's purpose.

Stylistic formatting isn't essential for every workbook that you develop — especially if it's for your own use only. On the other hand, it takes only a few moments to apply some simple formatting, and, after you apply it, the formatting will remain in place without further effort on your part.

In Chapter 5, I show how easy it is to apply formatting to a table. The information in this chapter applies to normal ranges. I show you how to work with the Excel formatting tools: fonts, colors, and styles, such as bold and italic. I also cover custom styles that you can create to make formatting large amounts of material in a similar way easier.

Getting to Know the Formatting Tools

Figure 6.1 shows how even simple formatting can significantly improve a worksheet's readability. The unformatted worksheet (on the left) is perfectly functional but not very readable compared with the formatted worksheet (on the right).

On the Web

This workbook is available on this book's website. The file is named `loan payments.xlsx`.

FIGURE 6.1

In just a few minutes, some simple formatting can greatly improve the appearance of your worksheets.

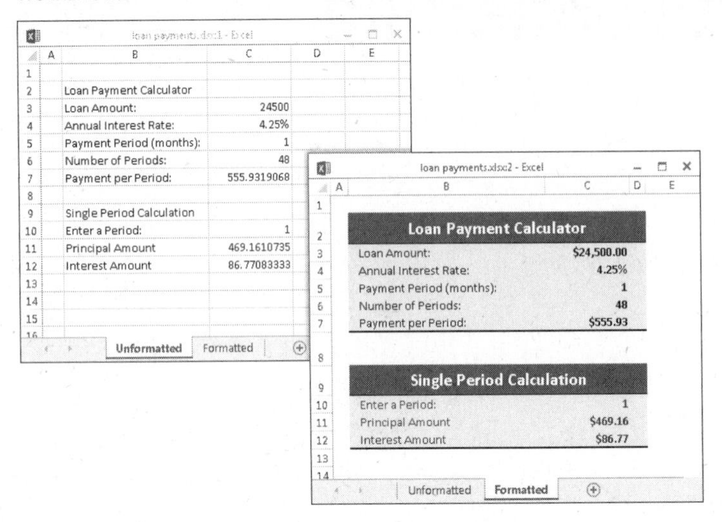

The Excel cell formatting tools are available in three locations:

- On the Home tab of the Ribbon
- On the Mini toolbar that appears when you right-click a range or a cell
- From the Format Cells dialog box

In addition, many common formatting commands have keyboard shortcuts that you can use.

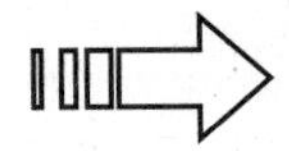

Excel also enables you to format cells based on the cell's contents. Chapter 21 discusses conditional formatting.

Using the formatting tools on the Home tab

The Home tab of the Ribbon provides quick access to the most commonly used formatting options. Start by selecting the cell or range; then use the appropriate tool in the Font, Alignment, or Number groups.

Using these tools is very intuitive, and the best way to familiarize yourself with them is to experiment. Enter some data, select some cells, and then click the controls to change the appearance. Note that some of these controls are actually drop-down lists. Click the small arrow on the button, and the button expands to display your choices.

Using the Mini toolbar

When you right-click a cell or a range selection, you get a shortcut menu. In addition, the Mini toolbar appears above or below the shortcut menu. Figure 6.2 shows how this toolbar looks. The Mini toolbar for cell formatting contains the most commonly used controls from the Home tab of the Ribbon.

FIGURE 6.2

The Mini toolbar appears above or below the right-click shortcut menu.

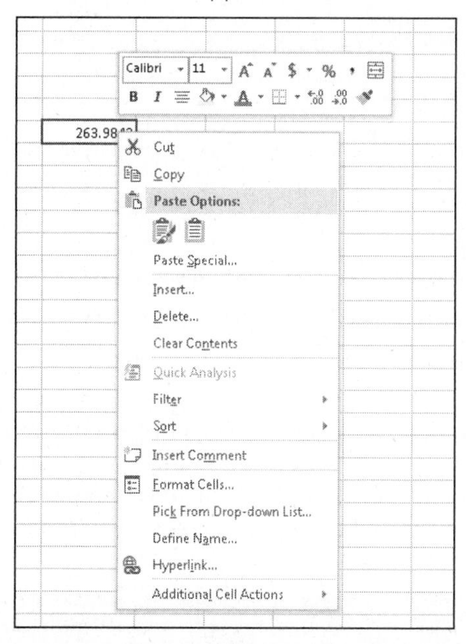

If you use a tool on the Mini toolbar, the shortcut menu disappears, but the toolbar remains visible so you can apply other formatting if you like. To hide the Mini toolbar, just click in any cell or press Escape.

Some people find the Mini toolbar distracting. Unfortunately, Excel doesn't provide a direct way to turn it off. The General tab of the Excel Options dialog box (which appears when you choose File ➪ Options) does offer the Show Mini Toolbar on Selection option, but this option applies only to selecting text while editing a cell. If you really want to get rid of the Mini Toolbar, see the sidebar, "Mini Toolbar Be Gone."

Mini Toolbar Be Gone

If you find the Mini toolbar annoying, you can search all day and not find an option to turn it off. The General tab of the Excel Options dialog box has an option labeled Show Mini Toolbar on Selection, but this option applies to selecting characters while editing a cell. The only way to turn off the Mini toolbar when you right-click is to execute a VBA macro:

```
Sub ZapMiniToolbar()
   Application.ShowMenuFloaties = True
End Sub
```

If you execute this VBA macro, the result is persistent. In other words, the Mini toolbar will not appear, even if you close and restart Excel. The only way to get the Mini toolbar back is to execute another VBA statement that sets the `ShowMenuFloaties` property to `False`.

By the way, the statement might seem wrong, but it works. Contrary to what you would think, setting that property to `True` turns *off* the Mini toolbar. It's a bug that appeared in Excel 2007 and was not fixed in subsequent versions because correcting it would cause many macros to fail. (See Part VI for more information about VBA macros.)

Using the Format Cells dialog box

The formatting controls available on the Home tab of the Ribbon are sufficient most of the time, but some types of formatting require that you use the Format Cells dialog box. This tabbed dialog box lets you apply nearly any type of stylistic formatting, as well as number formatting. The formats that you choose in the Format Cells dialog box apply to the cells that you have selected at the time. Later sections in this chapter cover the tabs of the Format Cells dialog box.

Note

When you use the Format Cells dialog box, you don't see the effects of your formatting choices until you click OK. With every new release of Excel, I expect to see the Format Cells dialog box implemented as a more convenient task pane. But I'm always disappointed. Maybe next time.

After selecting the cell or range to format, you can display the Format Cells dialog box by using any of the following methods:

- Press Ctrl + 1.
- Click the dialog box launcher in Home ➪ Font, Home ➪ Alignment, or Home ➪ Number. (The dialog box launcher is the small downward-pointing arrow icon displayed to the right of the group name in the Ribbon.) When you display the Format Cells dialog box using a dialog box launcher, the dialog box is displayed with the appropriate tab visible.

- Right-click the selected cell or range and choose Format Cells from the shortcut menu.
- Click the More command in some of the drop-down controls in the Ribbon. For example, the Home ➪ Font ➪ Border ➪ More Borders drop-down includes an item named More Borders.

The Format Cells dialog box contains six tabs: Number, Alignment, Font, Border, Fill, and Protection. The following sections contain more information about the formatting options available in this dialog box.

Using Different Fonts to Format Your Worksheet

You can use different fonts, sizes, or text attributes in your worksheets to make various parts — such as the headers for a table — stand out. You also can adjust the font size. For example, using a smaller font allows for more information on a single screen or printed page.

By default, Excel uses 11 point (pt) Calibri font. A *font* is described by its typeface (Calibri, Cambria, Arial, Times New Roman, Courier New, and so on), as well as by its size, measured in points. (Seventy-two points equal one inch.) Excel's row height, by default, is 15 pt. Therefore, 11 pt type entered into 15 pt rows leaves a small amount of blank space between the characters in adjacent rows.

Tip

If you haven't manually changed a row's height, Excel automatically adjusts the row height based on the tallest text that you enter into the row.

Tip

If you plan to distribute a workbook to other users, remember that Excel does not embed fonts. Therefore, you should stick with the standard fonts that are included with Windows or Microsoft Office. If you open a workbook and your system doesn't have the font used in the workbook, Windows attempts to use a similar font. Sometimes this attempt works okay, and sometimes it doesn't.

Use the Font and Font Size tools on the Home tab of the Ribbon (or on the Mini toolbar) to change the font or size for selected cells.

Updating Old Fonts

Office 2007 introduced several new fonts, and the default font has been changed for all the Office applications in subsequent releases. In versions prior to Excel 2007, the default font was 10 pt Arial. In Excel 2007, Excel 2010, and Excel 2013, the default font for the Office theme is 11 pt Calibri. Most people will agree that Calibri is much easier to read, and it gives the worksheet a more modern appearance.

If you open a workbook created in a pre-2007 version of Excel, the default font will not be changed, even if you apply a document style (by choosing Page Layout ➪ Themes ➪ Themes). But here's an easy way to update the fonts in a workbook that was created using an older version of Excel:

1. **Press Ctrl+N to open a new, empty workbook.** The new workbook will use the default document theme.
2. **Open your old workbook file.**
3. **Choose Home ➪ Styles ➪ Cell Styles ➪ Merge Styles.** Excel displays its Merge Styles dialog box.
4. **In the Merge Styles dialog box, select the new workbook that you created in Step 1.**
5. **Click OK.**
6. **Click Yes in response to Excel's question regarding merging styles that have the same name.**

This technique changes the font and size for all unformatted cells. If you've applied font formatting to some cells (for example, made them bold), the font for those cells will not be changed (but you can change the font manually for those cells). If you don't like the new look of your workbook, just close the workbook without saving the changes.

You also can use the Font tab in the Format Cells dialog box to choose fonts, as shown in Figure 6.3. This tab enables you to control several other font attributes that aren't available elsewhere. Besides choosing the font, you can change the font style (bold, italic), underlining, color, and effects (strikethrough, superscript, or subscript). If you select the Normal Font check box, Excel displays the selections for the font defined for the Normal style. I discuss styles later in this chapter (see "Using Named Styles for Easier Formatting").

Figure 6.4 shows several different examples of font formatting. In this figure, gridlines were turned off to make the underlining more visible. Notice, in the figure, that Excel provides four different underlining styles. In the two non-accounting underline styles, only the cell contents are underlined. In the two accounting underline styles, the entire width of the cells is always underlined.

FIGURE 6.3

The Font tab of the Format Cells dialog box gives you many additional font attribute options.

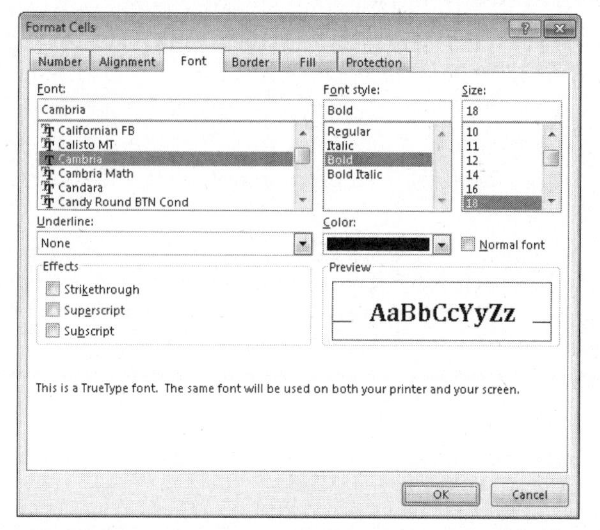

FIGURE 6.4

You can choose many different font formatting options for your worksheets.

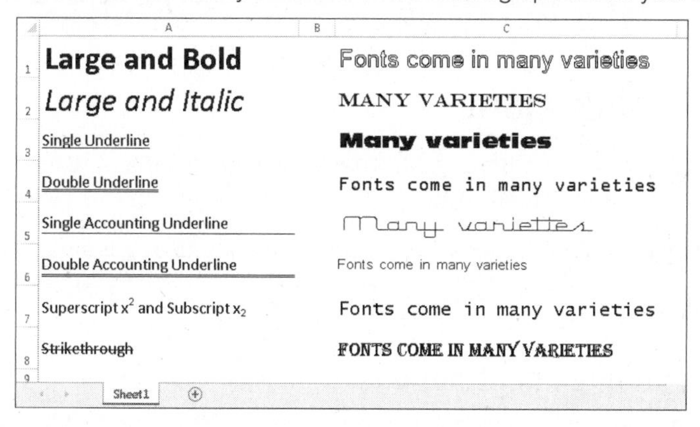

If you prefer to keep your hands on the keyboard, you can use the following shortcut keys to format a selected range quickly:

- **Ctrl + B:** Bold
- **Ctrl + I:** Italic
- **Ctrl + U:** Underline
- **Ctrl + 5:** Strikethrough

Using Multiple Formatting Styles in a Single Cell

If a cell contains text (as opposed to a value or a formula), you can apply formatting to individual characters in the cell. To do so, switch to Edit mode (press F2, or double-click the cell) and then select the characters that you want to format. You can select characters either by dragging the mouse over them or by pressing the Shift key as you press the left or right arrow key.

This technique is useful if you need to apply superscript or subscript formatting to a few characters in the cell (refer to Figure 6.4 for examples).

After you select the characters to format, use any of the standard formatting techniques, including options in the Format Cells dialog box. To display the Format Cells dialog box when editing a cell, press Ctrl+1. The changes apply only to the selected characters in the cell. This technique doesn't work with cells that contain values or formulas.

These shortcut keys act as a toggle. For example, you can turn bold on and off by repeatedly pressing Ctrl + B.

NOTE

Beginning with Excel 2007, the Document Themes feature attempts to assist nondesigners in creating attractive worksheets. I discuss document themes later in this chapter (see "Understanding Document Themes").

Changing Text Alignment

The contents of a cell can be aligned horizontally and vertically. By default, Excel aligns numbers to the right and text to the left. All cells use bottom alignment, by default.

Overriding these defaults is a simple matter. The most commonly used alignment commands are in the Alignment group on the Home tab of the Ribbon. Use the Alignment tab of the Format Cells dialog box for even more options (see Figure 6.5).

Choosing horizontal alignment options

Horizontal alignment options, which control how cell contents are distributed across the width of the cell (or cells), are available from the Format Cells dialog box:

- **General:** Aligns numbers to the right, aligns text to the left, and centers logical and error values. This option is the default alignment.
- **Left:** Aligns the cell contents to the left side of the cell. If the text is wider than the cell, the text spills over to the cell on the right. If the cell on the right isn't empty, the text is truncated and not completely visible. Also available on the Ribbon.

- **Center:** Centers the cell contents in the cell. If the text is wider than the cell, the text spills over to cells on either side if they're empty. If the adjacent cells aren't empty, the text is truncated and not completely visible. Also available on the Ribbon.
- **Right:** Aligns the cell contents to the right side of the cell. If the text is wider than the cell, the text spills over to the cell on the left. If the cell on the left isn't empty, the text is truncated and not completely visible. Also available on the Ribbon.
- **Fill:** Repeats the contents of the cell until the cell's width is filled. If cells to the right also are formatted with Fill alignment, they also are filled.
- **Justify:** Justifies the text to the left and right of the cell. This option is applicable only if the cell is formatted as wrapped text and uses more than one line.
- **Center across Selection:** Centers the text over the selected columns. This option is useful for precisely centering a heading over a number of columns.
- **Distributed:** Distributes the text evenly across the selected column.

FIGURE 6.5

The full range of alignment options are available on the Alignment tab of the Format Cells dialog box.

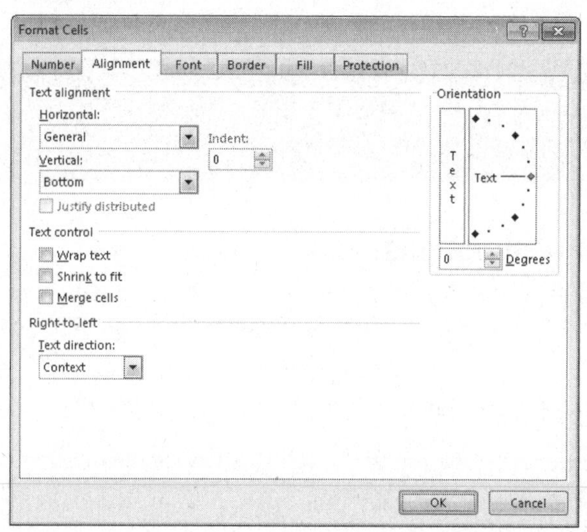

NOTE

If you choose Left, Right, or Distributed, you can also adjust the Indent setting, which adds space between the cell border and the text.

Figure 6.6 shows examples of text that uses three types of horizontal alignment: Left, Justify, and Distributed (with an indent).

FIGURE 6.6

The same text, displayed with three types of horizontal alignment.

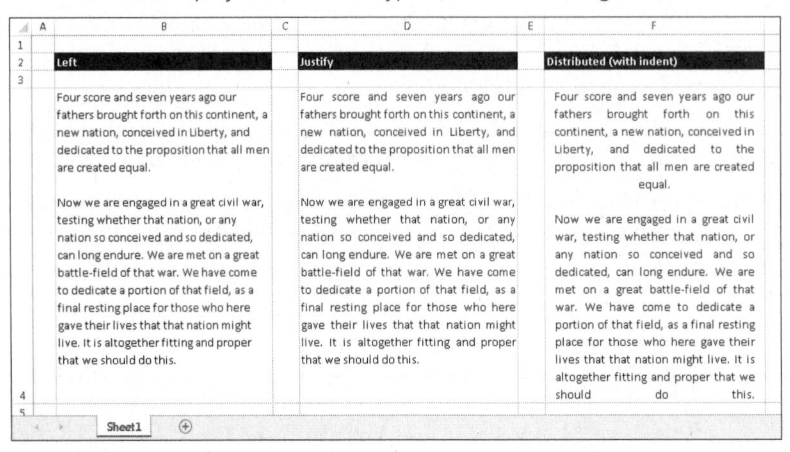

On the Web

If you want to experiment with text alignment settings, this workbook is available at this book's website. The file is named `text alignment.xlsx`.

Choosing vertical alignment options

Vertical alignment options typically aren't used as often as horizontal alignment options. In fact, these settings are useful only if you've adjusted row heights so that they're considerably taller than normal.

Here are the vertical alignment options available in the Format Cells dialog box:

- **Top:** Aligns the cell contents to the top of the cell. Also available on the Ribbon.
- **Center:** Centers the cell contents vertically in the cell. Also available on the Ribbon.
- **Bottom:** Aligns the cell contents to the bottom of the cell. Also available on the Ribbon.
- **Justify:** Justifies the text vertically in the cell; this option is applicable only if the cell is formatted as wrapped text and uses more than one line. This setting can be used to increase the line spacing.
- **Distributed:** Distributes the text evenly vertically in the cell. This setting seems to have the same effect as Justify.

Wrapping or shrinking text to fit the cell

If you have text too wide to fit the column width but you don't want that text to spill over into adjacent cells, you can use either the Wrap Text option or the Shrink to Fit option to accommodate that text. The Wrap Text option is also available on the Ribbon.

The Wrap Text option displays the text on multiple lines in the cell, if necessary. Use this option to display lengthy headings without having to make the columns too wide, and without reducing the size of the text.

The Shrink to Fit option reduces the size of the text so that it fits into the cell without spilling over to the next cell. I've never had much luck with this command. Unless the text is just slightly too long, the result is almost always illegible.

NOTE

If you apply Wrap Text formatting to a cell, you can't use the Shrink to Fit formatting.

Merging worksheet cells to create additional text space

A handy formatting option is the ability to merge two or more cells. When you merge cells, you don't combine the contents of cells. Rather, you combine a group of cells into a single cell that occupies the same space. The worksheet shown in Figure 6.7 contains four sets of merged cells. Range C2:I2 has been merged into a single cell, and so have ranges J2:P2, B4:B8, and B9:B13. In the latter two cases, the text direction has also been changed (see "Displaying text at an angle," later in this chapter).

FIGURE 6.7

Merge worksheet cells to make them act as if they were a single cell.

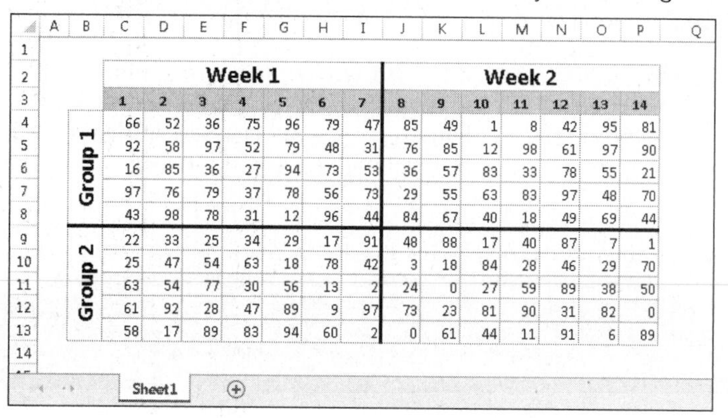

	A	B	C	D	E	F	G	H	I	J	K	L	M	N	O	P	Q
1																	
2			Week 1							Week 2							
3			1	2	3	4	5	6	7	8	9	10	11	12	13	14	
4		Group 1	66	52	36	75	96	79	47	85	49	1	8	42	95	81	
5			92	58	97	52	79	48	31	76	85	12	98	61	97	90	
6			16	85	36	27	94	73	53	36	57	83	33	78	55	21	
7			97	76	79	37	78	56	73	29	55	63	83	97	48	70	
8			43	98	78	31	12	96	44	84	67	40	18	49	69	44	
9		Group 2	22	33	25	34	29	17	91	48	88	17	40	87	7	1	
10			25	47	54	63	18	78	42	3	18	84	28	46	29	70	
11			63	54	77	30	56	13	2	24	0	27	59	89	38	50	
12			61	92	28	47	89	9	97	73	23	81	90	31	82	0	
13			58	17	89	83	94	60	2	0	61	44	11	91	6	89	
14																	

Sheet1

You can merge any number of cells occupying any number of rows and columns. In fact, you can merge all 17,179,869,184 cells in a worksheet into a single cell — although I can't think of any good reason to do so, except maybe to play a trick on a co-worker.

The range that you intend to merge should be empty, except for the upper-left cell. If any of the other cells that you intend to merge are not empty, Excel displays a warning. If you continue, all the data (except in the upper-left cell) will be deleted.

You can use the Alignment tab of the Format Cells dialog box to merge cells, but using the Merge & Center control on the Ribbon (or on the Mini toolbar) is simpler. To merge cells, select the cells that you want to merge and then click the Merge & Center button. The cells will be merged, and the content in the upper-left cells will be centered horizontally. The Merge & Center button acts as a toggle. To unmerge cells, select the merged cells and click the Merge & Center button again.

After you merge cells, you can change the alignment to something other than Center by using the controls in the Home➪Alignment group.

The Home➪Alignment➪Merge & Center control contains a drop-down list with these additional options:

- **Merge Across:** When a multirow range is selected, this command creates multiple merged cells — one for each row.
- **Merge Cells:** Merges the selected cells without applying the Center attribute.
- **Unmerge Cells:** Unmerges the selected cells.

Displaying text at an angle

In some cases, you may want to create more visual impact by displaying text at an angle within a cell. You can display text horizontally, vertically, or at any angle between 90 degrees up and 90 degrees down.

From the Home➪Alignment➪Orientation drop-down list, you can apply the most common text angles. For more control, use the Alignment tab of the Format Cells dialog box. In the Format Cells dialog box (refer to Figure 6.5), use the Degrees spinner control — or just drag the pointer in the gauge. You can specify a text angle between –90 and +90 degrees.

Figure 6.8 shows an example of text displayed at a 45-degree angle.

Note

Rotated text may look a bit distorted onscreen, but the printed output is usually of much better quality.

FIGURE 6.8

Rotate text for additional visual impact.

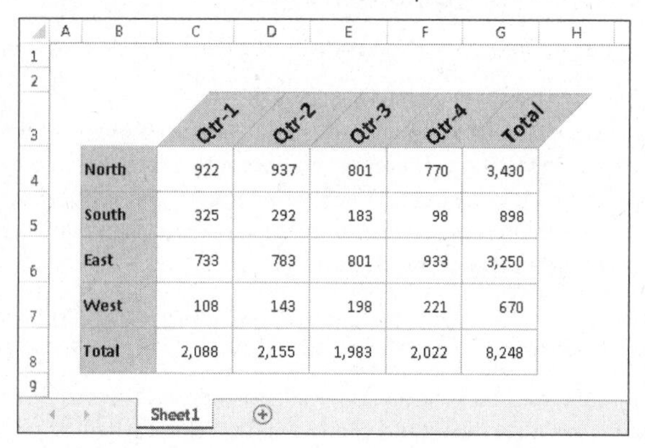

	Qtr-1	Qtr-2	Qtr-3	Qtr-4	Total
North	922	937	801	770	3,430
South	325	292	183	98	898
East	733	783	801	933	3,250
West	108	143	198	221	670
Total	2,088	2,155	1,983	2,022	8,248

Controlling the text direction

Not all languages use the same character direction. Although most Western languages are read left to right, other languages are read right to left. You can use the Text Direction option to select the appropriate setting for the language you use. This command is available only in the Alignment tab of the Format Cells dialog box.

Don't confuse the Text Direction setting with the Orientation setting (discussed in the previous section). Changing the text orientation is common. Changing the text direction is used only in very specific situations.

NOTE

Changing the Text Direction setting won't have any effect unless you have the proper language drivers installed on your system. For example, you must install Japanese language support to use right-to-left text direction Japanese characters. Use the Language tab of the Excel Options dialog box to determine which languages are installed.

Using Colors and Shading

Excel provides the tools to create some very colorful worksheets. You can change the color of the text or add colors to the backgrounds of the worksheet cells.

NOTE

Prior to Excel 2007, workbooks were limited to a palette of 56 colors. Subsequent versions allow a virtually unlimited number of colors.

Using Colors with Table Styles

In Chapter 5, I discuss the handy Table feature. One advantage to using tables is that it's very easy to apply table styles. You can change the look of your table with a single mouse click.

It's important to understand how table styles work with existing formatting. A simple rule is that applying a style to a table doesn't override existing formatting. For example, assume that you have a range of data that uses yellow as the background color for the cells. When you convert that range to a table (by choosing Insert ➪ Tables ➪ Table), the default table style (alternating row colors) isn't visible. Instead, the table will display the previously applied yellow background.

To make table styles visible with this table, you need to remove the manually applied background cell colors. Select the entire table and then choose Home ➪ Font ➪ Fill Color ➪ No Fill.

You can apply any type of formatting to a table, and that formatting will override the table style formatting. For example, you may want to make a particular cell stand out by using a different fill color.

You control the color of the cell's text by choosing Home ➪ Font ➪ Font Color. Control the cell's background color by choosing Home ➪ Font ➪ Fill Color. Both of these color controls are also available on the Mini toolbar, which appears when you right-click a cell or range.

TIP

To hide the contents of a cell, make the background color the same as the font text color. The cell contents are still visible in the Formula bar when you select the cell. Keep in mind, however, that some printers may override this setting, and the text may be visible when printed.

Even though you have access to an unlimited number of colors, you might want to stick with the ten theme colors (and their light/dark variations) displayed in the various color selection controls. In other words, avoid using the More Color option, which lets you select a color. Why? First of all, those ten colors were chosen because they "go together" (well, at least *somebody* thought they did). Another reason involves document themes. If you switch to a different document theme for your workbook, nontheme colors aren't changed. In some cases, the result may be less than pleasing, aesthetically. (See "Understanding Document Themes," later in this chapter, for more information about themes.)

Adding Borders and Lines

Borders (and lines within the borders) are another visual enhancement that you can add around groups of cells. Borders are often used to group a range of similar cells or to delineate rows or columns. Excel offers 13 preset styles of borders, as you can see in the Home ➪ Font ➪ Borders drop-down list shown in Figure 6.9. This control works with the selected cell or range and enables you to specify which, if any, border style to use for each border of the selection.

FIGURE 6.9

Use the Borders drop-down list to add lines around worksheet cells.

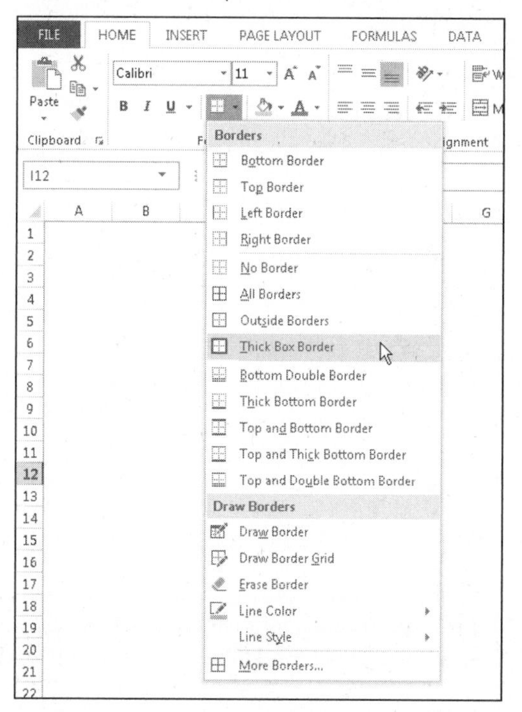

You may prefer to draw borders rather than select a preset border style. To do so, use the Draw Border or Draw Border Grid command from the Home⇨Font⇨Borders drop-down list. Selecting either command lets you create borders by dragging your mouse. Use the Line Color or Line Style commands to change the color or style. When you're finished drawing borders, press Esc to cancel the border-drawing mode.

Another way to apply borders is to use the Border tab of the Format Cells dialog box, which is shown in Figure 6.10. One way to display this dialog box is to select More Borders from the Borders drop-down list.

Before you display the Format Cells dialog box, select the cell or range to which you want to add borders. First, choose a line style and then choose the border position for the line style by clicking one of the Border icons (these icons are toggles).

Notice that the Border tab has three preset icons, which can save you some clicking. If you want to remove all borders from the selection, click None. To put an outline around the selection, click Outline. To put borders inside the selection, click Inside.

FIGURE 6.10

Use the Border tab of the Format Cells dialog box for more control over cell borders.

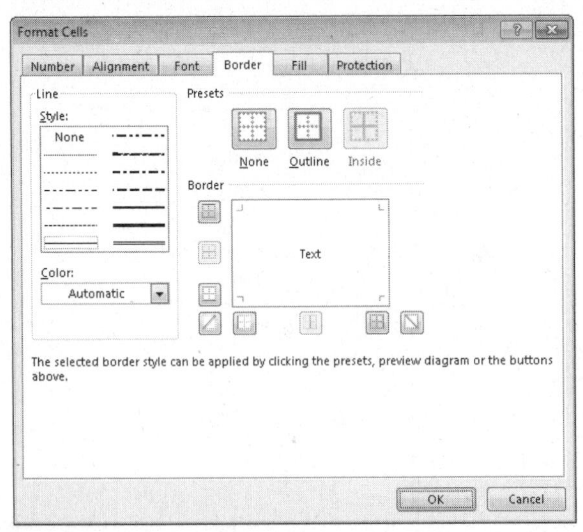

Excel displays the selected border style in the dialog box; there is no live preview. You can choose different styles for different border positions; you can also choose a color for the border. Using this dialog box may require some experimentation, but you'll get the hang of it.

When you apply two diagonal lines, the cells look like they've been crossed out.

TIP

If you use border formatting in your worksheet, you may want to turn off the grid display to make the borders more pronounced. Choose View ➪ Show ➪ Gridlines to toggle the gridline display.

Adding a Background Image to a Worksheet

In some situations, you might want to use a graphics file to serve as a background for a worksheet. This effect is similar to the wallpaper that you may display on your Windows desktop or as a background for a web page.

To add a background to a worksheet, choose Page Layout ➪ Page Setup ➪ Background. Excel displays a dialog box that enables you to select a graphics file. All common graphic file formats are supported, but animated GIFs display as static images. When you locate a file, click Insert. Excel tiles the graphic across your worksheet. Some images are specifically designed to be tiled, such as the one shown in Figure 6.11. This type of image is often used for web pages, and it creates a seamless background.

FIGURE 6.11

You can add almost any image file as a worksheet background image.

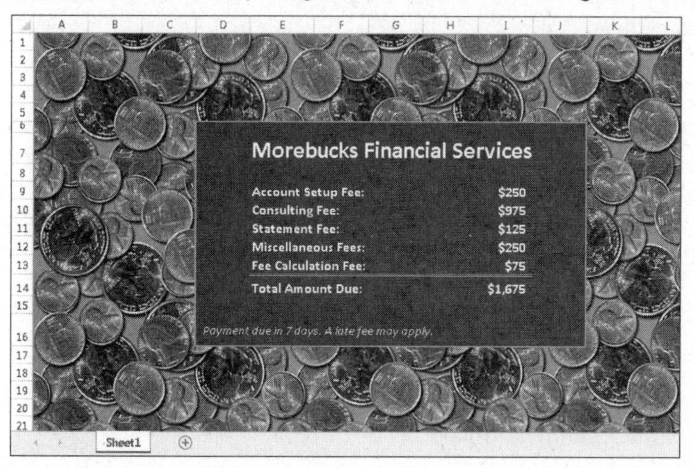

Morebucks Financial Services
Account Setup Fee: $250
Consulting Fee: $975
Statement Fee: $125
Miscellaneous Fees: $250
Fee Calculation Fee: $75
Total Amount Due: $1,675
Payment due in 7 days. A late fee may apply.
Sheet1

ON THE WEB

This workbook, named `background image.xlsx`, is available on this book's website.

When you use a background image, you'll probably want to turn off the gridline display because the gridlines show through the graphic. Some backgrounds make viewing text difficult, so you may want to use a solid background color for cells that contain text.

Keep in mind that using a background image will increase the size of your workbook, because the image is stored in the workbook file.

Copying Formats by Painting

Perhaps the quickest way to copy the formats from one cell to another cell or range is to use the Format Painter button (the button with the paintbrush image) of the Home ⇨ Clipboard group.

1. **Select the cell or range that has the formatting attributes you want to copy.**
2. **Click the Format Painter button.** The mouse pointer changes to include a paintbrush.
3. **Select the cells to which you want to apply the formats.**
4. **Release the mouse button, and Excel applies the same set of formatting options that were in the original range.**

If you double-click the Format Painter button, you can paint multiple areas of the worksheet with the same formats. Excel applies the formats that you copy to each cell or range that you select. To get out of Paint mode, click the Format Painter button again (or press Esc).

NOTE
The graphic background on a worksheet is for onscreen display only — it isn't printed when you print the worksheet.

Using Named Styles for Easier Formatting

One of the most underutilized features in Excel is named styles. Named styles make it very easy to apply a set of predefined formatting options to a cell or range. In addition to saving time, using named styles also helps to ensure a consistent look.

A style can consist of settings for up to six different attributes:

- Number format
- Font (type, size, and color)
- Alignment (vertical and horizontal)
- Borders
- Pattern
- Cell protection (locked and hidden)

The real power of styles is apparent when you change a component of a style. All cells that use that named style automatically incorporate the change. Suppose that you apply a particular style to a dozen cells scattered throughout your worksheet. Later, you realize that these cells should have a font size of 14 pt rather than 12 pt. Rather than change each cell, simply edit the style. All cells with that particular style change automatically.

Applying styles

Excel includes a good selection of predefined named styles that work in conjunction with document themes. Figure 6.12 shows the effect of choosing Home ➪ Styles ➪ Cell Styles. Note that this display is a *live preview* — as you move your mouse over the style choices, the selected cell or range temporarily displays the style. When you see a style you like, click it to apply the style to the selection.

NOTE
If Excel's window is wide enough, you won't see the Cell Styles command in the Ribbon. Instead, you'll see four or more formatted style boxes. Click the drop-down arrow to the right of these boxes to display all the defined styles.

NOTE
By default, all cells use the Normal style. If you modify the Normal style, all cells that haven't been assigned a different style will reflect the new formatting.

FIGURE 6.12

Excel displays samples of predefined cell styles.

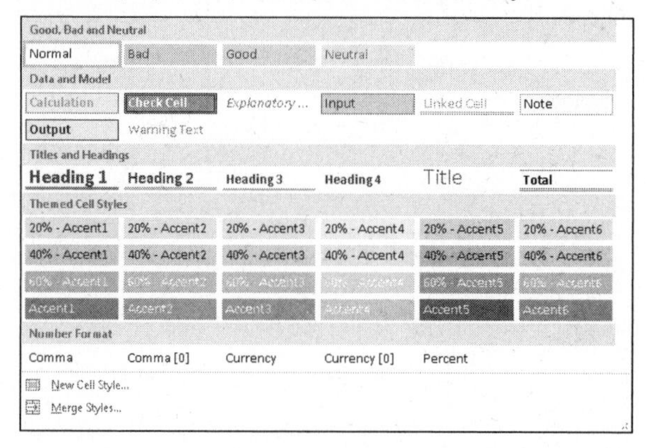

After you apply a style to a cell, you can apply additional formatting to it by using any formatting method discussed in this chapter. Formatting modifications that you make to the cell don't affect other cells that use the same style.

You have quite a bit of control over styles. In fact, you can do any of the following:

- Modify an existing style.
- Create a new style.
- Merge styles from another workbook into the active workbook.

The following sections describe these procedures.

Modifying an existing style

To change an existing style, choose Home ➪ Styles ➪ Cell Styles. Right-click the style you want to modify and choose Modify from the shortcut menu. Excel displays the Style dialog box, shown in Figure 6.13. In this example, the Style dialog box shows the settings for the Office theme Normal style — which is the default style for all cells. The style definitions vary, depending on which document theme is active.

Here's a quick example of how you can use styles to change the default font used throughout your workbook.

1. **Choose Home ➪ Styles ➪ Cell Styles.** Excels displays the list of styles for the active workbook.
2. **Right-click Normal and choose Modify.** Excel displays the Style dialog box (refer to Figure 6.13), with the current settings for the Normal style.
3. **Click the Format button.** Excel displays the Format Cells dialog box.

4. **Click the Font tab and choose the font and size that you want as the default.**
5. **Click OK to return to the Style dialog box.** Notice that the Font item displays the font choice you made.
6. **Click OK again to close the Style dialog box.**

FIGURE 6.13

Use the Style dialog box to modify named styles.

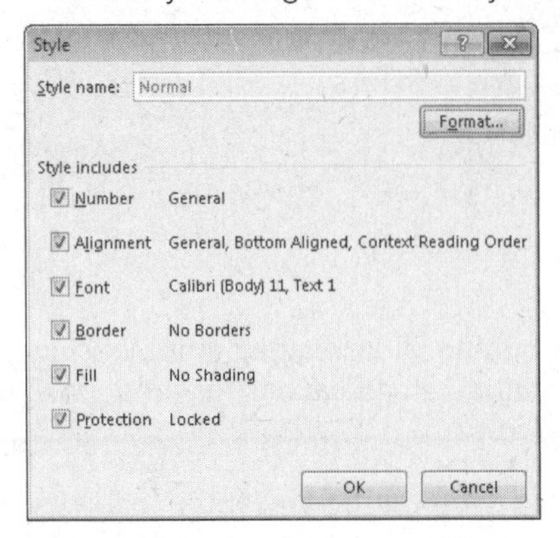

The font for all cells that use the Normal style changes to the font that you specified. You can change any formatting attributes for any style.

Creating new styles

In addition to using Excel's built-in styles, you can create your own styles. This feature can be quite handy because it enables you to apply your favorite formatting options very quickly and consistently.

To create a new style, follow these steps:

1. **Select a cell and apply all the formatting that you want to include in the new style.** You can use any of the formatting that is available in the Format Cells dialog box (refer to Figures 6.3 and 6.5).
2. **After you format the cell to your liking, choose Home ➪ Styles ➪ Cell Styles, and choose New Cell Style.** Excel displays its Style dialog box (refer to Figure 6.13), along with a proposed generic name for the style. Note that Excel displays the words `By Example` to indicate that it's basing the style on the current cell.
3. **Enter a new style name in the Style Name field.** The check boxes display the current formats for the cell. By default, all check boxes are selected.

4. **(Optional) If you don't want the style to include one or more format categories, remove the check(s) from the appropriate check box(es).**
5. **Click OK to create the style and to close the dialog box.**

After you perform these steps, the new custom style is available when you choose Home➪Styles➪Cell Styles. Custom styles are available only in the workbook in which they were created. To copy your custom styles to another workbook, see the section that follows.

Note

The Protection option in the Style dialog box controls whether users will be able to modify cells for the selected style. This option is effective only if you've also turned on worksheet protection, by choosing Review➪Changes➪Protect Sheet.

Merging styles from other workbooks

Custom styles are stored with the workbook in which they were created. If you've created some custom styles, you probably don't want to go through all the work to create copies of those styles in each new Excel workbook. A better approach is to merge the styles from a workbook in which you previously created them.

To merge styles from another workbook, open both the workbook that contains the styles that you want to merge and the workbook that will contain the merged styles. Activate the second workbook and choose Home➪Styles➪Cell Styles, and then choose Merge Styles. Excel displays the Merge Styles dialog box that shows a list of all open workbooks. Select the workbook that contains the styles you want to merge and click OK. Excel copies styles from the workbook that you selected into the active workbook.

Controlling styles with templates

When you start Excel, it loads with several default settings, including the settings for stylistic formatting. If you spend a lot of time changing the default elements for every new workbook, you should know about templates.

Here's an example. You may prefer that gridlines aren't displayed in worksheets. And maybe you prefer Wrap Text to be the default setting for alignment. Templates provide an easy way to change defaults.

The trick is to create a workbook with the Normal style modified in the way that you want it. Then save the workbook as a template (with an `.xltx` extension). After doing so, you can choose this template as the basis for new workbook.

Refer to Chapter 8 for more information about templates.

Understanding Document Themes

In an attempt to help users create more professional-looking documents, the Office designers incorporated a feature known as *document themes*. Using themes is an easy (and almost foolproof) way to specify the colors, fonts, and a variety of graphic effects in a document. And best of all, changing the entire look of your document is a breeze. A few mouse clicks is all it takes to apply a different theme and change the look of your workbook.

Importantly, the concept of themes is incorporated into other Office applications. Therefore, a company can easily create a standard look and feel for all its documents.

NOTE

Themes don't override specific formatting that you apply. For example, assume that you apply the Accent 1 named style to a range. Then you change the font color for a few cells in that range. If you change to a different theme, the manually applied fonts won't be modified to use the new theme fonts. Bottom line: If you plan to take advantage of themes, stick with default formatting choices.

Figure 6.14 shows a worksheet that contains a SmartArt diagram, a table, a chart, a range formatted with the Heading 1 named style, and a range formatted with Explanatory Text name style. These items all use the default theme, which is the Office Theme.

FIGURE 6.14

The elements in this worksheet use the default theme.

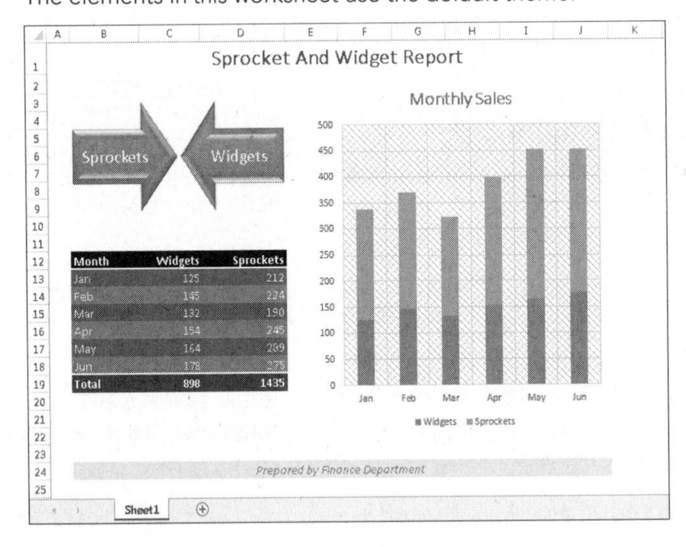

Figure 6.15 shows the same worksheet after applying a different document theme. The different theme changed the fonts, colors (which may not be apparent in the figure), and the graphic effects for the SmartArt diagram.

FIGURE 6.15

The worksheet, after applying a different theme.

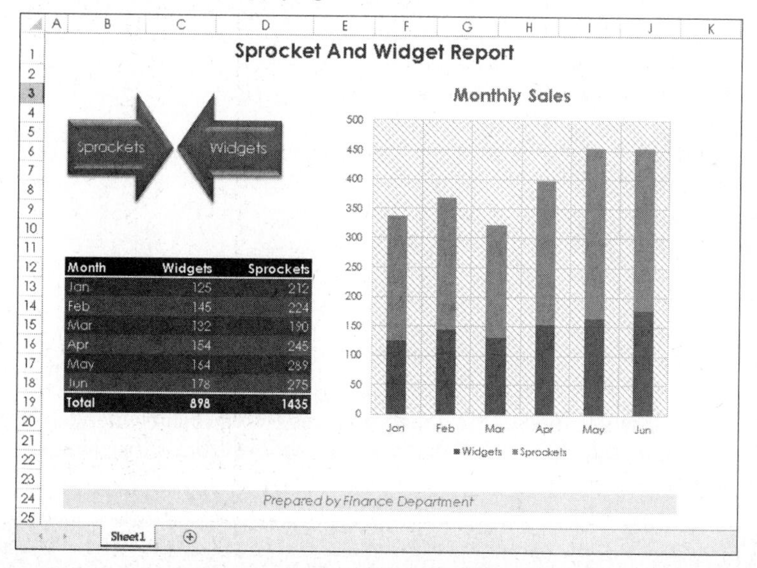

> **ON THE WEB**
>
> If you'd like to experiment with using various themes, the workbook shown in Figure 6.14 and Figure 6.15 is available on this book's website. The file is named `theme examples.xlsx`.

Applying a theme

Figure 6.16 shows the theme choices that appear when you choose Page ➪ Layout ➪ Themes ➪ Themes. This display is a live preview. As you move your mouse over the theme choices, the active worksheet displays the theme. When you see a theme you like, click it to apply the theme to all worksheets in the workbook.

> **NOTE**
>
> A theme applies to the *entire workbook*. You can't use different themes on different worksheets within a workbook.

FIGURE 6.16

Built-in Excel theme choices.

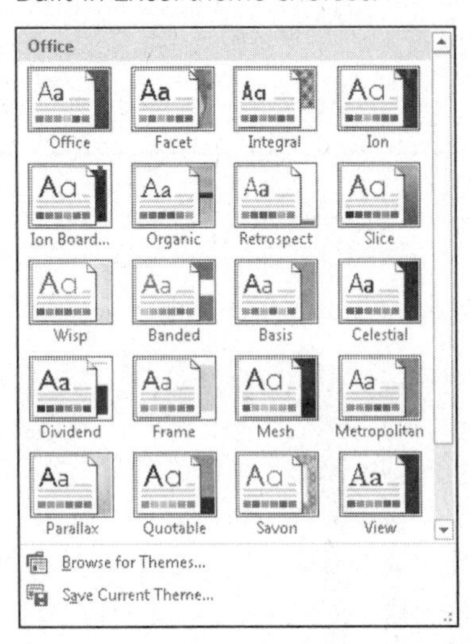

When you specify a particular theme, the gallery choices for various elements reflect the new theme. For example, the chart styles that you can choose from vary, depending on which theme is active.

NOTE

Because themes use different fonts and font sizes, changing to a different theme may affect the layout of your worksheet. For example, after applying a new theme, a worksheet that printed on a single page may spill over to a second page. Therefore, you may need to make some adjustments after you apply a new theme.

Customizing a theme

Notice that the Themes group on the Page Layout tab contains three other controls: Colors, Fonts, and Effects. You can use these controls to change just one of the three components of a theme. For example, you might like the colors and effects in the Office theme but would prefer different fonts. To change the font set, apply the Office theme and then specify your preferred font set by choosing Page Layout ➪ Themes ➪ Font.

Each theme uses two fonts (one for headers, and one for the body), and in some cases, these two fonts are the same. If none of the theme choices is suitable, choose Page Layout ➪ Themes ➪ Font ➪ Customize Fonts to specify the two fonts you prefer (see Figure 6.17).

FIGURE 6.17

Use this dialog box to specify two fonts for a theme.

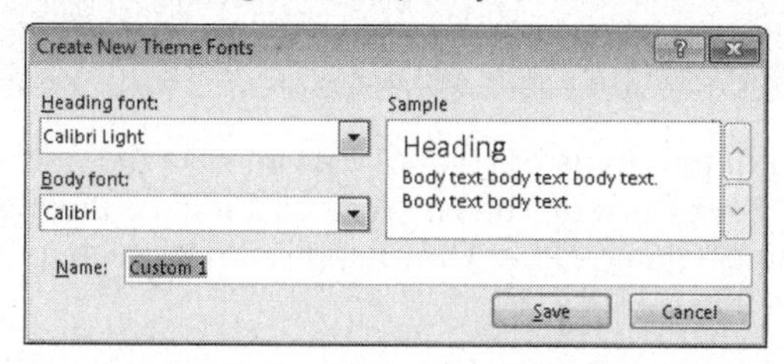

> **TIP**
>
> When you choose Home ➪ Font ➪ Font, the two fonts for the current theme are listed first in the drop-down list.

Choose Page Layout ➪ Themes ➪ Colors to select a different set of colors. And, if you're so inclined, you can even create a custom set of colors by choosing Page Layout ➪ Themes ➪ Colors ➪ Customize Colors. This command displays the Create New Theme Colors dialog box, shown in Figure 6.18. Note that each theme consists of 12 colors. Four of the colors are for text and backgrounds, six are for accents, and two are for hyperlinks. As you specify different colors, the preview panel in the dialog box updates.

FIGURE 6.18

If you're feeling creative, you can specify a set of custom colors for a theme.

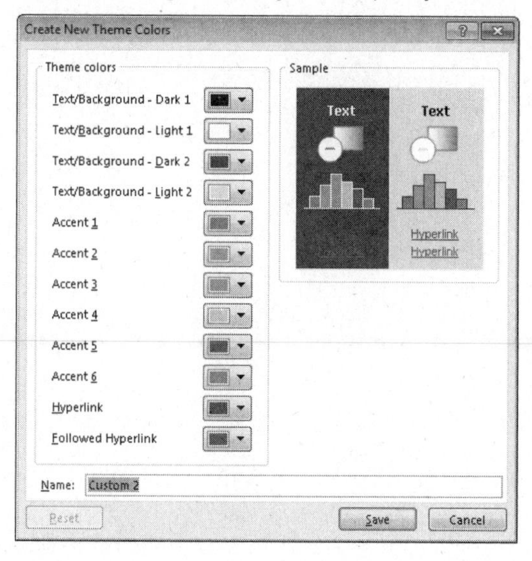

NOTE

Theme effects operate on graphic elements, such as SmartArt, Shapes, and charts. You can choose a different set of theme effects, buy you can't customize theme effects.

If you've customized a theme using different fonts or colors, you can save the new theme by choosing Page Layout⇨Themes⇨Save Current Theme. Your customized themes appear in the theme list in the Custom category. Other Office applications, such as Word and PowerPoint, can use these theme files.

Understanding Excel Files

IN THIS CHAPTER

Creating a new workbook

Opening an existing workbook

Saving and closing workbooks

Sharing workbooks with people who use an older version of Excel

This chapter describes the operations that you perform with workbook files: opening, saving, closing, and so on. It discusses how Excel uses files and provides an overview of the various types of files. Most of the file operations discussed here occur in the *Backstage view,* the screen that you see when you click the File button above the Excel Ribbon.

Creating a New Workbook

When you start Excel 2013, it displays a Start Screen that lists recently used files and shows templates that you can use as the basis for a new workbook. One of the template options is "Blank workbook," which gives you an empty workbook.

New Feature

The Start Screen is new to Excel 2013. If you prefer to skip the Start Screen and always start with an empty workbook, choose File ➪ Options. In the Excel Options dialog box, click the General tab and remove the check mark from the option labeled Show the Start Screen When This Application Starts.

After you start Excel, the empty workbook is called Book1. This workbook exists only in memory and hasn't been saved to disk. By default, this workbook contains one worksheet named Sheet1. If you're starting a project from scratch, you can use this blank workbook.

While you're working in Excel, you can create a new (empty) workbook at any time. Excel provides two ways to create a new workbook:

- Choose File ➪ New, which displays a screen that lets you create a blank workbook or a workbook based on a template. To create a new blank workbook, click Blank Workbook.
- Press Ctrl + N. This shortcut is the fastest way to start a new workbook if you're not using a template.

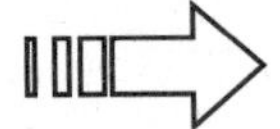

See Chapter 8 for more information on using and creating templates.

Opening an Existing Workbook

Here are some of the ways to open a workbook that's already been saved:

- Choose File ➪ Open ➪ Recent Workbooks and then select the file you want from the Recent Workbooks list. Only the most recently used files are listed. You can specify the number of files to display (maximum of 50) in the Advanced section of the Excel Options dialog box.
- Choose File ➪ Open ➪ Computer. You'll see a list of folders on the right. Click a folder, or click Browse. In either case, Excel displays the Open dialog box so you can locate the file you want to open.
- Locate the Excel workbook file via a Windows Explorer file list. Just double-click the filename (or icon), and the workbook opens in Excel. If Excel isn't running, Windows automatically starts Excel and loads the workbook file.
- Choose File ➪ Open and browse other online locations in the list of places. The list will vary, and may include online SkyDrive locations, SharePoint locations, and others.

TIP

When you choose File ➪ Open ➪ Recent Workbooks, each file in the recent workbooks list displays a pushpin icon on the right when you hover the mouse pointer over the filename. Click the pushpin icon, and that file becomes "pinned" to the list and will always appear at the top of the list. This handy feature ensures that important files always appear on the recent workbooks list – even if you haven't opened the file recently.

Also, notice that you can right-click a workbook in the list and choose Remove from List. Choose Clear Unpinned Workbooks to clear the list and start fresh.

To open a workbook from the Open dialog box, use the folder tree display on the left to locate the folder that contains the file, and then select the workbook file from the list on the right. After you locate and select the file, click Open, and the file opens. Or just double-click the filename to open it.

Notice that the Open button is actually a drop-down list. Click the arrow, and you see the additional options:

- **Open:** Opens the file normally.
- **Open Read-Only:** Opens the selected file in read-only mode. When a file is opened in this mode, you can't save changes with the original filename.
- **Open as Copy:** Opens a copy of the selected file. If the file is named `budget.xlsx`, the workbook that opens is named `Copy(1)budget.xlsx`.
- **Open in Browser:** Opens the file in your default web browser. If the file can't be opened in a browser, this option is disabled.
- **Open in Protected View:** Opens the file in a special mode that doesn't allow editing. In this view, most of the Excel Ribbon commands are disabled. Read more about this new feature in the nearby sidebar, "About Protected View."
- **Open and Repair:** Attempts to open a file that may be damaged and recover information contained in it.
- **Show Previous Versions:** Shows a list of previous versions of the workbook, if any.

TIP

In the Open dialog box, you can hold down the Ctrl key and select multiple workbooks. When you click Open, all the selected workbook files open.

Right-clicking a filename in the Open dialog box displays a shortcut menu with many extra Windows commands. For example, you can copy, delete, or rename the file, modify its properties, and so on.

Filtering filenames

At the bottom of the Open dialog box is a button with a drop-down list. When the Open dialog box is displayed, this button shows All Excel Files (and a long list of file extensions). The Open dialog box displays only those files that match the extensions. In other words, you see only standard Excel files.

If you want to open a file of a different type, click the arrow in the drop-down list and select the file type that you want to open. This changes the filtering and displays only files of the type that you specify.

You can also type a filter directly in the File Name box. For example, typing the following will display only files that have an `.xlsx` extension (press Enter after typing the filter): ***.xlsx**.

About Protected View

Excel 2010 introduced a security feature known as *Protected View*. Although it might seem like Excel is trying to keep you from opening your own files, Protected View is all about protecting you from malware. *Malware* refers to something that can harm your system. Hackers have figured out several ways to manipulate Excel files in a way that harmful code can be executed. Protected View essentially prevents these types of attacks by opening a file in a protected environment (a "sandbox").

If you open an Excel workbook that you downloaded from the web, you'll see a colorful message above the Formula bar. In addition, the Excel title bar displays `[Protected View]`. Choose File➪Info to find out why Excel opened the file in Protected View.

If you're certain that the file is safe, click Enable Editing. If you don't enable editing, you'll be able to view the contents of the workbook, but you won't be able to make any changes to it.

If the workbook contains macros, you'll see another message after you enable editing: `Security Warning. Macros have been disabled.` If you're sure that the macros are harmless, click Enable Content.

Protected View, by default, kicks in for the following:

- Files downloaded from the Internet
- Attachments opened from Outlook
- Files open from potentially unsafe locations, such as your Temporary Internet Files folder
- File that are blocked by File Block Policy (a Windows feature that allows administrators to define potentially dangerous files)
- Files that were digitally signed, but the signature has expired

In some situations, you don't care about working with the document. You just want to print it. In that case, choose File➪Print, and then click the Enable Printing button.

Also, note that you can copy a range of cells from a workbook in Protected View, and paste it into a different workbook.

You have some control over the types of files that trigger Protected View. To change the settings, choose File➪Options, and click Trust Center. Then click the Trust Center Settings button and click the Protected View tab in the Trust Center dialog box.

Choosing your file display preferences

The Open dialog box can display your workbook filenames in several different styles: as a list, with complete details, as icons, and so on. You control the style by clicking the Change Your View icon and then selecting a display style from the drop-down list.

Opening Workbooks Automatically

Many people work on the same workbooks each day. If this describes you, you'll be happy to know that Excel can open specific workbook files automatically whenever you start Excel. Any workbooks placed in the `XLStart` folder open automatically.

The location of the `XLStart` folder varies, depending on your Windows version. To determine the location of the `XLStart` folder on your system, follow these steps:

1. **Choose File➪Options, and select the Trust Center tab.**
2. **Click the Trust Center Settings button.** The Trust Center dialog box appears.
3. **In the Trust Center dialog box, select the Trusted Locations tab.** You'll see a list of trusted locations.
4. **Look for the path for the location described as User Startup.** The path might look something like this:

```
C:\Users\<username>\AppData\Roaming\Microsoft\Excel\XLSTART\
```

Another XLStart folder may be located here:

```
C:\Program Files\Microsoft Office15\Root\Office15\XLStart\
```

Any workbook files (excluding template files) stored in either of these `XLStart` folders open automatically when Excel starts. If one or more files open automatically from an `XLStart` folder, Excel won't start with a blank workbook.

You can specify an alternate startup folder in addition to the `XLStart` folder. Choose File➪Options and select the Advanced tab. Scroll down to the General section and enter a new folder name in the At Startup, Open All Files In field. Then, when you start Excel, it automatically opens all workbook files in both the `XLStart` folders and the alternate folder that you specified.

Saving a Workbook

When you're working in Excel, your workbook is vulnerable to day-ruining events such as power failures and system crashes. Therefore, you should save your work often. Saving a file takes only a few seconds, but re-creating hours of lost work takes many hours.

Excel provides four ways to save your workbook:

- Click the Save icon on the Quick Access toolbar (it looks like an old-fashioned floppy disc).
- Press Ctrl+S.
- Press Shift+F12.
- Choose File➪Save.

CAUTION

Saving a file overwrites the previous version of the file on your hard drive. If you open a workbook and then completely mess it up, don't save the file! Instead, close the workbook without saving it and then reopen the good copy on your hard drive.

If your workbook has already been saved, it's saved again using the same filename in the same location. If you want to save the workbook to a new file or to a different location, choose File⇨Save As (or press F12).

If your workbook has never been saved, you'll be taken to the Save As pane in the Backstage view. Here, you can specify a location, and you'll be prompted for a filename, which you specify in the Save As dialog box. A new (unsaved) workbook has a default name, such as Book1 or Book2. Although Excel allows you to use these generic workbook names for filenames, you'll almost always want to specify a more descriptive filename in the Save As dialog box.

The Save As dialog box is similar to the Open dialog box. Select the desired folder in the folder list on the left. After you select the folder, enter the filename in the File Name field. You don't need to specify a file extension — Excel adds it automatically, based on the file type specified in the Save as Type field. By default, files are saved in the standard Excel file format, which uses an `.xlsx` file extension.

TIP

To change the default file format for saving files, choose File⇨Options to access the Excel Options dialog box. Click the Save tab and change the setting for the Save Files in This Format option. For example, if your workbooks must be compatible with older versions of Excel (versions before Excel 2007), you can change the default format to Excel 97-2003 Workbook (*.xls). Doing so eliminates the need to select the older file type every time you save a new workbook.

CAUTION

If your workbook contains VBA macros, saving it with an `.xlsx` file extension will erase all the macros. It must be saved with an `.xlsm` extension (or saved in the XLS or XLSB format). If your workbook has macros, Excel will *still* propose to save it as an XLSX file. It other words, Excel suggests a file format that will destroy your macros! It will, however, warn you that the macros will be lost.

If a file with the same name already exists in the folder that you specify, Excel asks whether you want to overwrite that file with the new file. Be careful! You can't recover the previous file after you overwrite it.

Using AutoRecover

If you've used computers for any length of time, you've probably lost some work. You forgot to save a file, or maybe the power went out and your unsaved work was lost. Or maybe you were working on something and didn't think it was important, so you closed it without saving — and later realized that it *was* important. A feature introduced in Excel 2010 called AutoRecover might make these types of "d'oh!" moments less frequent.

As you work in Excel, your work is periodically saved, automatically. It happens in the background so you don't even know that it's happening. If necessary, you can access these autosaved versions of your work. And this even applies to workbooks that you never explicitly saved.

The AutoRecover feature consists of two components:

- Versions of a workbook are saved automatically, and you can view them.
- Workbooks that you closed without saving are saved as draft versions.

Recovering versions of the current workbook

To see whether any previous versions of the active workbook are available, choose File⇨Info. The Versions section lists the available old versions (if any) of the current workbook. In some cases, more than one autosaved version will be listed. In other cases, no autosaved versions will be available.

You can open an autosaved version by clicking its name. Remember that opening an autosaved version *won't* automatically replace the current version of your workbook. Therefore, you can decide whether the autosaved version is preferable to the current version. Or, you can just copy some information that may have been accidentally deleted and paste it to your current workbook.

When you close the workbook, the autosaved versions are deleted.

Recovering unsaved work

When you close a workbook without saving your changes, Excel asks whether you're sure. If that unsaved workbook has an autosaved version, the "Are you sure?" dialog box informs you of that fact.

To recover a workbook that you closed without saving, choose File⇨Info⇨Manage Versions⇨Recover Unsaved Workbooks. You'll see a list of all draft versions of your workbooks. You can open them and (if you're lucky) recover something that you needed. Note that the unsaved workbooks are stored in the XLSB file format and are read-only files. If you want to save one of these files, you need to provide a new name.

Draft versions are deleted after four days or when you edit the file.

Configuring AutoRecover

Normally, AutoRecover files are saved every ten minutes. You can adjust the AutoRecover save time in the Save tab of the Excel Options dialog box. You can specify a save interval between 1 and 120 minutes.

File-Naming Rules

Excel workbook files are subject to the same rules that apply to other Windows files. A filename can be up to 255 characters, including spaces. This length enables you to give meaningful names to your files. You can't, however, use any of the following characters in your filenames:

\ (slash)
? (question mark)
: (colon)
* (asterisk)
" (quote)
< (less than)
> (greater than)
| (vertical bar)

You can use uppercase and lowercase letters in your names to improve readability, but the filenames aren't case sensitive. For example, `My 2013 Budget.xlsx` and `MY 2013 BUDGET.xlsx` are equivalent names.

If you work with sensitive documents, you might prefer that previous versions don't get saved automatically on your computer. The Save tab of the Excel Options dialog box lets you disable this feature completely or disable it just for a specific workbook.

Password-Protecting a Workbook

In some cases, you may want to specify a password for your workbook. When a user attempts to open a password-protected workbook, a password must be entered before the file is opened.

To set a password for a workbook, follow these steps:

1. **Choose File⇨Info, and click the Protect Workbook button.** This button displays some additional options in a drop-down list.
2. **Choose Encrypt with Password from the list.** Excel displays the Encrypt Document dialog box, shown in Figure 7.1.

FIGURE 7.1

The Encrypt Document dialog box is where you specify a password for your workbook.

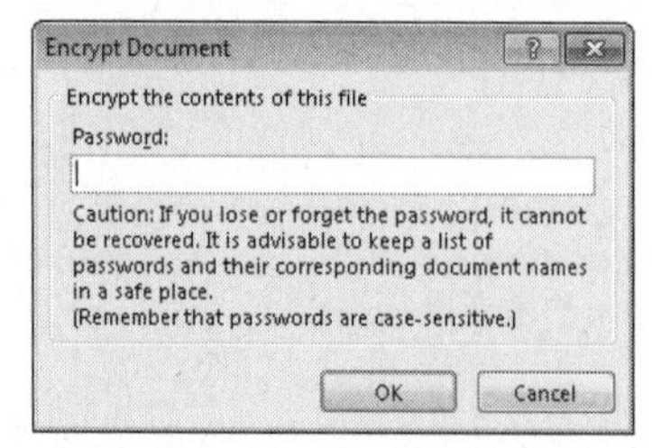

3. **Enter the password, and then enter it again.**
4. **Click OK, and save the workbook.**

When you reopen the workbook, you'll be prompted for a password.

Caution

Passwords are case sensitive. Be careful when using password protection because it's impossible to open the workbook (using normal methods) if you forget the password. Also, remember that Excel passwords can be cracked, so it's not a perfect security measure.

Organizing Your Files

If you have hundreds of Excel files, you might have a problem locating the workbook that you need. Using descriptive filenames can help. Using folders and subfolders (with descriptive names) also makes it easier to find the particular file you need. In some cases, though, that's not enough.

Fortunately, Excel lets you assign a variety of descriptive information (sometimes known as *metadata*) to a workbook. These are known as document properties. This information includes such items as the author, tags, and categories.

When you choose File➪Info, you can view (or modify) the document properties for the active workbook. This information is shown on the right side of the screen.

Tip

To access even more properties for your workbook, click the down arrow on Properties and choose Advanced Properties. Another option on the Properties drop-down list is Show Document Panel. Choosing this command displays the properties in a panel below the Ribbon.

When you use the Open dialog box, you can specify additional columns to display. Start by clicking the More Options drop-down arrow (at the top of the Open dialog box), and then choose Details. Right-click any column header (for example, Name or Date Modified) to see a list of other properties to include. Click the More option to display the Choose Details dialog box, which contains a longer list of properties (see Figure 7.2).

You can sort the file list in the Open dialog box by a particular column by clicking a column heading. Also, notice that each heading is actually a drop-down list. Click the drop-down arrow, and you can filter the list to show only files that match the selected properties.

FIGURE 7.2

The Choose Details dialog box, where you choose additional properties to display in the file list.

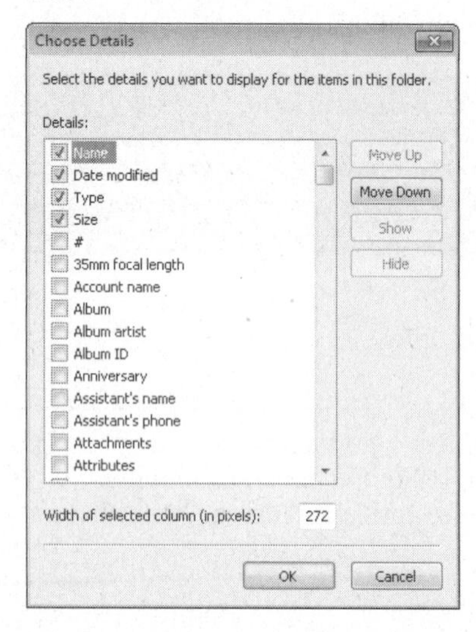

Using document properties lets you work with files as if they were in a database. The key, of course, is taking the time to ensure that the document properties are actually assigned and are accurate.

TIP

If you would like to be prompted to ensure that the document properties are correct, choose Developer ➪ Modify ➪ Document Panel. In the Document Information Panel dialog box, select the Always Show Document Information Panel on Document Open and Initial Save check box. If the Developer tab isn't visible, use the Customize Ribbon panel in the Excel Options dialog box to display it.

NOTE

This discussion of document properties just barely scratches the surface. For example, you can display additional properties and even specify a custom document information panel template that contains information specific to your needs. A complete discussion is beyond the scope of this book.

Using Workspace Files

If you have a project that uses multiple workbooks, you probably get tired of opening the same files every time you work on the project. The solution? Create a workspace file:

1. **Open all the workbooks used for your project.**
2. **Arrange the workbook windows the way you like them.**
3. **Choose View➪Window➪Save Workspace to display the Save Workspace dialog box.**
4. **Excel proposes the name** resume.xlw, **but you can specify any name you like. Just make sure that you use the** .xlw **extension.**
5. **Click Save.** The workspace file is created.

After creating a workspace file, you can open it by choosing File➪Open. In the Open dialog box, specify Workspaces (*.xlw) from the Files of Type drop-down list. Better yet, pin it to the top of the recent files list so it will always be easily accessible.

NOTE

A workspace file contains only the filenames and window position information – not the workbooks. If you want to share these project files with someone, sending the `.xlw` workspace file won't accomplish that goal. You need to include all the files that comprise the workspace.

Other Workbook Info Options

The Info pane of Backstage view displays more file-related options. To display this pane, choose File➪Info. These options, described in the following sections, may be useful if you plan to distribute your workbook to others. Note that not all workbooks display all the options described in the following sections. Only the relevant options are shown.

Protect Workbook options

The File➪Info➪Protect Workbook drop-down list contains the following options:

- **Mark as Final:** Use this option to designate the workbook as "final." The document is saved as a read-only file to prevent changes. This isn't a security feature. Rather, the Mark as Final command is useful to let others know that you're sharing a completed version of a workbook.
- **Encrypt with Password:** Use this command to specify a password that is required to open the workbook. (See "Password-Protecting a Workbook," earlier in this chapter.)

- **Protect Current Sheet:** This command lets you protect various elements of a worksheet. It displays the same dialog box as the Review ⇨ Changes ⇨ Protect Sheet command.

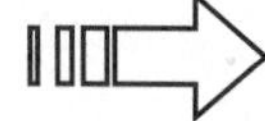

See Chapter 30 for more information about protecting worksheets.

- **Protect Workbook Structure:** This command lets you protect the structure of a workbook. It displays the same dialog box as Review ⇨ Changes ⇨ Protect Workbook.

See Chapter 30 for more information on protecting the structure of a workbook.

- **Restrict Access:** Use this option to specify those who may open the document. This feature requires a fee-based service called *Information Rights Management*.
- **Add a Digital Signature:** This command allows you to "sign" a workbook digitally.

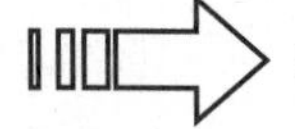

See Chapter 30 for more information about digital signatures.

Check for Issues options

The File ⇨ Info ⇨ Check for Issues drop-down list contains the following options:

- **Inspect Document:** This command displays the Document Inspector dialog box. The Document Inspector can alert you to some potentially private information that may be contained in your workbook — perhaps information that's contained in hidden rows or columns or hidden worksheets. If you plan on making a workbook available to a large audience, it's an excellent idea to use the Document Inspector for a final check.
- **Check Accessibility:** This command checks the workbook for potential problems that might occur for people with disabilities. The results of the check are displayed in a task pane in the workbook.
- **Check Compatibility:** This command is useful if you need to save your workbook in an older file format. It displays a very helpful Compatibility Checker dialog box that lists potential compatibility problems. This dialog box also appears when you save a workbook using an older file format. (For more information, see "Excel File Compatibility," later in this chapter.)

Compatibility Mode section

If the active workbook is an old workbook opened in compatibility mode, you'll see the Compatibility Mode section in the Info pane. To convert the workbook to the current Excel file format, click the Convert button.

CAUTION
Be aware that this command deletes the original version of the file — which seems like a rather drastic measure. It's probably wise to make a copy of your workbook before you use this command.

Closing Workbooks

After you're finished with a workbook, you can close it to free the memory that it uses. Other workbooks will remain open. When you close the last open workbook, you also close Excel.

You can close a workbook by using any of the following methods:

- Choose File⇨Close.
- Click the Close button (the X) in the window's title bar.
- Double-click the Excel icon on the left side of the workbook's title bar. This icon is visible only if the workbook window is not maximized.
- Press Ctrl + F4.
- Press Ctrl + W.

If you've made any changes to your workbook since it was last saved, Excel asks whether you want to save the changes to the workbook before closing it.

Safeguarding Your Work

Nothing is more frustrating than spending hours creating a complicated Excel workbook only to have it destroyed by a power failure, a hard drive crash, or even human error. Fortunately, protecting yourself from these disasters is not a difficult task.

Earlier in the chapter, I discuss the AutoRecover feature that makes Excel save a backup copy of your workbook at regular intervals (see "Using AutoRecover,"). AutoRecover is a good idea, but it certainly isn't the only backup protection you should use. If a workbook is important, you need to take extra steps to ensure its safety. The following backup options help ensure the safety of individual files:

- **Keep a backup copy of the file on the same drive.** Although this option offers some protection if you make a mess of the workbook, it won't do you any good if the entire hard drive crashes.
- **Keep a backup copy on a different hard drive.** This method assumes, of course, that your system has more than one hard drive. This option offers more protection than the preceding method, because the likelihood that both hard drives will fail is remote. If the entire system is destroyed or stolen, however, you're out of luck.

- **Keep a backup copy on a network server.** This method assumes that your system is connected to a server on which you can write files. This method is fairly safe. If the network server is located in the same building, however, you're at risk if the entire building burns down or is otherwise destroyed.
- **Keep a backup copy on an Internet backup site.** Several websites specialize in storing backup files.
- **Keep a backup copy on a removable medium.** This is probably the safest method. Using a removable medium, such as a USB drive enables you to physically take the backup to another location. So, if your system (or the entire building) is damaged, your backup copy remains intact.

Excel File Compatibility

It's important to understand the limitations regarding version compatibility. Even though your colleague is able to open your file, there is no guarantee that everything will function correctly or look the same.

Checking compatibility

If you save your workbook to an older file format (such as `.xls`, for versions prior to Excel 2007), Excel automatically runs the Compatibility Checker. The Compatibility Checker identifies the elements of your workbook that will result in loss of functionality or fidelity (cosmetics).

Figure 7.3 shows the Compatibility Checker dialog box. Click the Select Versions to Show button to limit the compatibility checking to a specific version of Excel.

The bottom part of the Compatibility Checker lists the potential compatibility problems. To display the results in a more readable format, click the Copy to New Sheet button.

Keep in mind that compatibility problems also can occur with Excel 2007 and Excel 2010 even though these versions use the same file format as Excel 2013. You can't expect features that are new to Excel 2013 to work in earlier versions. For example, if you add Slicers to table (a new feature in Excel 2013) and send it to a colleague who uses Excel 2010, the Slicers won't be displayed. In addition, formulas that use any of the new worksheet functions will return an error. The Compatibility Checker identifies these types of problems.

FIGURE 7.3

The Compatibility Checker is a useful tool for those who share workbooks with other people.

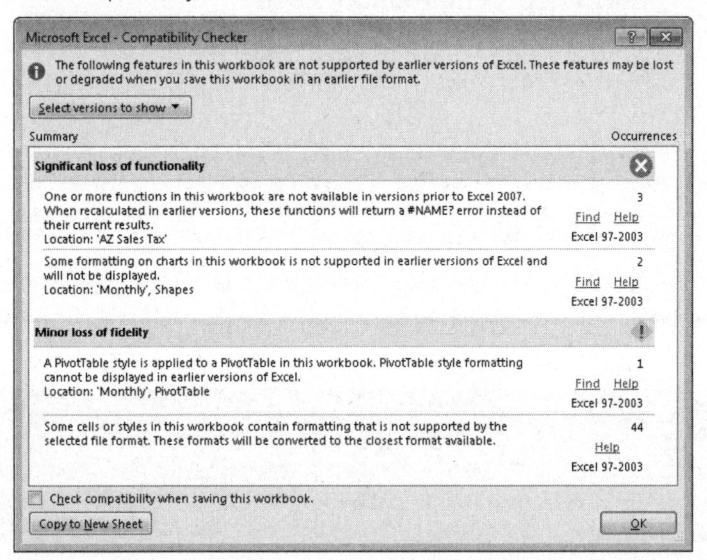

NOTE

Excel 2013 can open all files created with earlier versions of Excel.

Recognizing the Excel 2013 file formats

The Excel file formats (all of which were introduced in Excel 2007) are

- XLSX: A workbook file that does not contain macros
- XLSM: A workbook file that contains macros
- XLTX: A workbook template file that does not contain macros
- XLTM: A workbook template file that contains macros
- XLSA: An add-in file
- XLSB: A binary file similar to the old XLS format but able to accommodate the new features
- XLSK: A backup file

With the exception of XLSB, these are all "open" XML files, which means that the file format is not proprietary and other applications can read and write these types of files.

The Office Compatibility Pack

Normally, those who use an earlier version of Excel can't open workbooks saved in the new Excel file formats. But, fortunately, Microsoft has released a free Compatibility Pack for Office 2003 and Office XP.

If an Office 2003 or Office XP user installs the Compatibility Pack, he can open files created in Office 2007 or Office 2010 and save files in the new format. The Office programs that are affected are Excel, Word, and PowerPoint. This software doesn't endow the older versions with any new features — it just gives them the capability to open and save files in the new format.

To download the Compatibility Pack from Microsoft, search the web for *Office Compatibility Pack.*

Tip

XML files are actually zip-compressed text files. If you rename one of these files to have a `.zip` extension, you'll be able to examine the contents using any of several zip file utilities – including the zip file support built into Windows. Taking a look at the innards of an Excel workbook is an interesting exercise for curious-minded users.

Saving a file for use with an older version of Excel

To save a file for use with an older version of Excel, choose File⇨Save As. In the Save As dialog box, select one of the following from the Save as Type drop-down list:

- **Excel 97–2003 Workbook (*.xls):** If the file will be used by someone who has Excel 97, Excel 2000, Excel 2002, or Excel 2003
- **Microsoft Excel 5.0/95 Workbook (*.xls):** If the file will be used by someone who has Excel 5 or Excel 95

CHAPTER 8

Using and Creating Templates

IN THIS CHAPTER

Understanding Excel templates

Working with the default templates

Creating custom templates

A *template* is essentially a model that serves as the basis for something else. An Excel template is a special type of workbook that's used as the basis to create other workbooks. This chapter discusses some of the templates available from Microsoft and describes how to create your own template files. Creating a template takes some time, but in the long run, doing so may save you a lot of work.

Exploring Excel Templates

The best way to become familiar with Excel template files is to jump in and try a few. Excel 2013 gives you quick access to hundreds of template files.

Viewing templates

To explore the Excel templates, choose File ➪ New. The template thumbnails displayed on the screen that appears are just a small sampling of those that are available. Enter a descriptive word, and search for more.

NOTE

The searching is done at Microsoft Office Online, so you must be connected to the Internet in order to search for templates.

For example, enter *invoice*, and click the Search button. Excel displays many more thumbnails, and you can narrow the search by using the category filters on the right.

Figure 8.1 shows the results of a template search.

FIGURE 8.1

The New page in Backstage view allows you to search for templates.

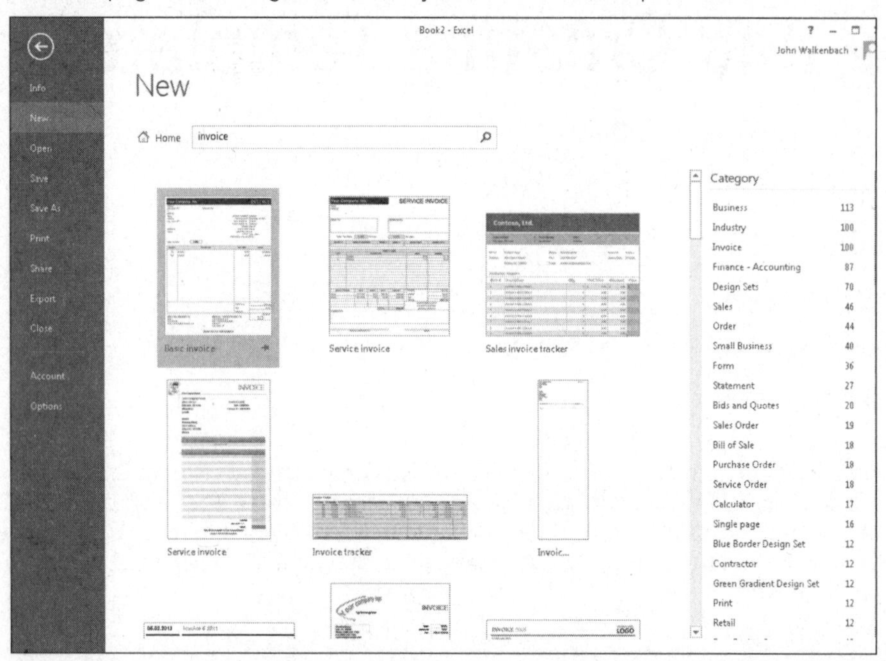

NOTE

Microsoft Office Online has a wide variety of templates, and some are better than others. If you download a few duds, don't give up. Even though a template may not be perfect, you may be able to modify a template to meet your needs. Modifying an existing template is often easier than creating a workbook from scratch.

Creating a workbook from a template

To create a workbook based on a template, just locate a template that looks like it might do the job, and click the thumbnail. Excel displays a box with a larger image, the source for the template, and some additional information. If it still looks good, click the Create button. Otherwise, click one of the arrows to view details for the next (or previous) template in the list.

When you click the Create button, Excel downloads the template and then creates a new workbook based on that template.

What you do next depends on the template. Every template is different, but most are self-explanatory. Some workbooks require customization. Just replace the generic information with your own information.

> **NOTE**
> It's important to understand that you're not working with the template file. Instead, you're working with a workbook that was *created* from the template file. If you make any changes, you're not changing the template – you're changing the workbook that's based on the template. After you download a template from Microsoft Office Online, that template is saved for future use (you won't have to download it again). Downloaded templates appear as thumbnails when you choose File ➪ New.

Figure 8.2 shows a workbook created from a template. This workbook needs to be customized in several areas. But if this template will be used again, it's more efficient to customize the *template* rather than every workbook created from the template.

If you want to save the newly created workbook, click the Save button. Excel proposes a filename based on the template's name, but you can use any filename you like.

FIGURE 8.2

A workbook created from a template.

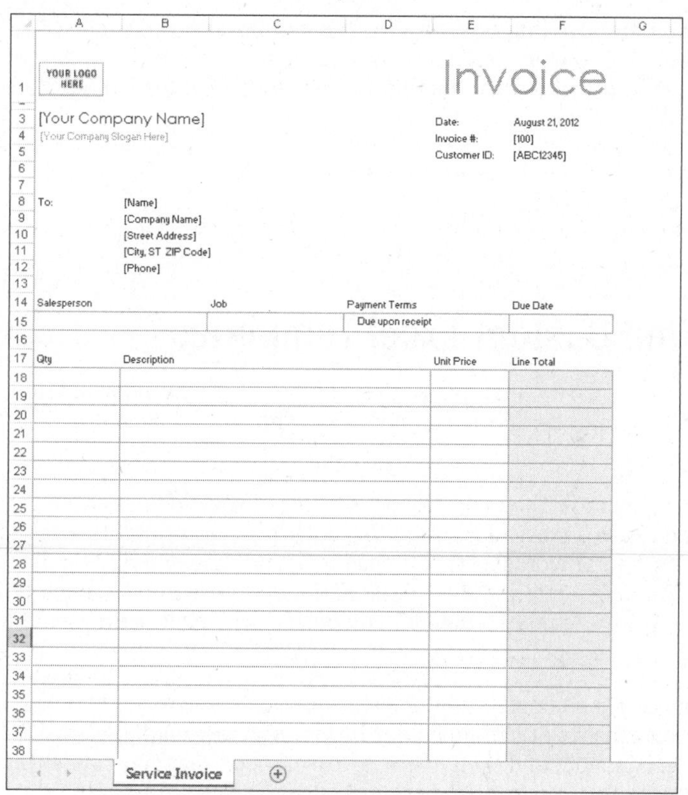

Modifying a template

A template file that you download is just like a workbook file. You can open a template file, make changes to it, and then resave it. For example, with the invoice template shown in Figure 8.2, you may want to modify the template so that it shows your company information and logo and uses your actual sales tax rate. Then, when you use that template in the future, the workbook created from it will already be customized.

To open a template for editing, choose File➪Open (not File➪New) and locate the template file (it will have an `.xltx`, `.xltm`, or `.xlt` extension). When you open a template file by choosing File➪Open, you're opening the actual template file — you are *not* creating a workbook from the template file.

One way to find the location of your downloaded template files is to look at your trusted locations list:

1. **Choose Tools➪Options.** The Excel Options dialog box appears.
2. **Choose Trust Center, and click the Trust Center Settings button.** The Trust Center dialog box appears.
3. **In the Trust Center dialog box, choose Trusted Locations.** You'll see a list of trusted locations. Downloaded templates are stored in the location described as User Templates. If you want to modify (or delete) a downloaded template, this is where you'll find it.

On my system, downloaded templates are stored here:

```
C:\Users\<username>\AppData\Roaming\Microsoft\Templates
```

Understanding Custom Excel Templates

So far, this chapter has focused on templates that were created by others and downloaded to your computer. The remainder of the chapter deals with *custom templates* — templates that you create.

Why create custom templates? The main reason is to make your job easier. For example, you may always like to use a particular header or footer on your printouts. Consequently, the first time that you print a worksheet, you need to spend time entering the header and footer information. Although entering the header and footer doesn't take much time, wouldn't it be easier if Excel simply remembered your favorite page settings and used them automatically?

The solution is to modify the template that Excel uses to create new workbooks. In this case, the modification consists of inserting your header into the template. Save the template file using a special name, and then every new workbook that you create (including the workbook created when Excel starts) has your customized page settings.

Excel supports three types of templates, which I discuss in the following sections:

- **The default workbook template:** Used as the basis for new workbooks.
- **The default worksheet template:** Used as the basis for new worksheets inserted into a workbook.
- **Custom workbook templates:** Usually, these ready-to-run workbooks include formulas, but they can be as simple or as complex as you like. Typically, these templates are set up so that a user can simply plug in values and get immediate results. The Microsoft Office Online templates (discussed earlier in this chapter) are examples of this type of template.

Working with the default templates

The term *default template* may be a little misleading. If you haven't created your own template files to control the default settings, Excel uses its own internal settings — not an actual template file. In other words, Excel uses your template files to set the defaults for new workbooks or worksheets, if these files exist. But if you haven't created these files, Excel is perfectly happy to use its own settings.

Using the workbook template to change workbook defaults

Every new workbook that you create starts out with some default settings. For example, the workbook has one worksheet, the worksheet has gridlines, the page header and footer are blank, text appears in the font defined in the default Normal style, columns are 8.43 units wide, and so on. If you're not happy with any of the default workbook settings, you can change them by creating a workbook template.

8

Making changes to Excel's default workbook is fairly easy to do, and it can save you lots of time in the long run. Here's how to change Excel's workbook defaults:

1. **Open a new workbook.**
2. **Add or delete sheets to give the workbook the number of worksheets that you want.**
3. **Make any other changes that you want to make, which can include column widths, named styles, page setup options, and many of the settings that are available in the Excel Options dialog box.** To change the default formatting for cells, choose Home ➪ Styles ➪ Cell Styles and then modify the settings for the Normal style. For example, you can change the default font, size, or number format.
4. **When your workbook is set up to your liking, choose File ➪ Save As.** The Save As dialog box appears.
5. **Select Excel Template (*.xltx) from the Save As Type list.** If your template contains any VBA macros, select Excel Macro-Enabled Template (*.xltm).
6. **Enter** book **for the filename.**

CAUTION

Excel will offer a name, such as `Book1.xltx`. You must change this name to `book.xltx` (or `book.xltm`) if you want Excel to use your template to set the workbook defaults.

7. **Save the file in your XLStart folder (not in the templates folder that Excel proposes).**

TIP

One way to find the location of your `XLStart` folder is to look at your trusted locations list. Choose Tools ➪ Options to display the Excel Options dialog box. Then choose Trust Center, and click the Trust Center Settings button. In the Trust Center dialog box choose Trusted Locations, and you'll see a list of trusted locations. The location for your `book.xltx` file is the location described as User StartUp. On my system, the folder is

```
C:\Users\<username>\AppData\Roaming\Microsoft\Excel\XLSTART
```

8. **Close the file.**

After you perform the preceding steps, the new default workbook is based on the `book.xltx` (or `book.xltm`) workbook template. You can create a workbook based on your template by using any of these methods:

- Press Ctrl+N.
- Open Excel without first selecting a workbook to open. This option works only if you disable the option to show the Start Screen when Excel starts. This option is specified in the General tab of the Excel Options dialog box (choose File ➪ Open to display the Excel Options dialog box).

NOTE

The `book.xltx` template is not used if you choose File ➪ New and choose Blank Workbook from the list of templates. That command results in a default workbook. I'm not sure if this is a bug or if it's by design. In any case, it provides a way to override the custom `book.xltx` template if you need to.

Creating a worksheet template

You can also create a single sheet template named `sheet.xltx`. Use the same procedure described for `book.xltx`. The `sheet.xltx` template is used when you insert a new worksheet.

Editing your template

After you create your `book.xltx` template, you may discover that you need to change it. You can open the template file and edit it just like any other workbook. After you make your changes, save the file to its original location and close it.

Resetting the default workbook

If you create a book.xltx file and then decide that you'd rather use the standard default settings, simply delete (or rename) the book.xltx template file. Excel then uses its built-in default settings for new workbooks.

Creating custom templates

The book.xltx template discussed in the preceding section is a special type of template that determines default settings for new workbooks. This section discusses other types of templates, referred to as *custom workbook templates,* which are simply workbooks that you set up as the basis for new specific types of workbooks.

Creating a custom workbook template can eliminate repeating work. Assume that you create a monthly sales report that consists of your company's sales by region, plus several summary calculations and charts. You can create a template file that consists of everything except the input values. Then, when it's time to create your report, you can open a workbook based on the template, fill in the blanks, and be finished.

Note

You could, of course, just use the previous month's workbook and save it with a different name. This is prone to errors, however, because you easily can forget to use the Save As command and accidentally overwrite the previous month's file. Another option is to choose File ⇨ Open, and choose Open as Copy in the Open dialog box (this command appears when you click the arrow on the Open button). Opening a file as a copy creates a new workbook from an existing one, but it uses a different name to ensure that the old file is not overwritten.

When you create a workbook that's based on a template, the default workbook name is the template name with a number appended. For example, if you create a new workbook based on a template named Sales Report.xltx, the workbook's default name is Sales Report1.xlsx. The first time that you save a workbook that's created from a template, Excel displays the Save As dialog box so that you can give the workbook a different name if you want to.

A custom template is essentially a normal workbook. It can use any Excel feature, such as charts, formulas, and macros. Usually, a template is set up so that the user can enter values and get immediate results. In other words, most templates include everything but the data, which is entered by the user.

Note

If your template contains macros, it must be saved as an Excel Macro-Enabled Template, with an .xltm extension.

Locking Formula Cells in a Template File

If novices will use the template, you might consider locking all the formula cells to make sure that the formulas aren't deleted or modified. By default, all cells are locked and can't be changed when the worksheet is protected. The following steps describe how to unlock the nonformula cells:

1. **Choose Home⇨Editing⇨Find & Select⇨Go to Special.** The Go to Special dialog box appears.
2. **Select Constants and click OK.** This step selects all nonformula cells.
3. **Press Ctrl+1.** The Format Cells dialog box appears.
4. **Select the Protection tab.**
5. **Remove the check mark from the Locked check box.**
6. **Click OK to close the Format Cells dialog box.**
7. **Choose Review⇨Changes⇨Protect Sheet.** The Protect Sheet dialog box appears.
8. **Specify a password (optional), and click OK.**

After you perform these steps, you can't modify the formula cells — unless the sheet is unprotected.

Saving your custom templates

To save a workbook as a template, choose File⇨Save As and select Template (*.xltx) from the Save as Type drop-down list. If the workbook contains any VBA macros, select Excel Macro-Enabled Template (*.xltm). Save the template in your `Templates` folder — which Excel automatically suggests — or a folder within that `Templates` folder.

If you later discover that you want to modify the template, choose File⇨Open to open and edit the template.

Using custom templates

To create a workbook based on a custom template, choose File⇨New, and then click Personal (below the search box). You'll see thumbnails of all your custom worksheet templates. Double-click a template, and Excel creates a workbook based on the template.

Getting ideas for creating templates

This section provides a few ideas that may spark your imagination for creating templates. The following is a partial list of the settings that you can adjust and use in your custom templates:

- **Multiple formatted worksheets:** You can, for example, create a workbook template that has two worksheets — one formatted to print in landscape mode and one formatted to print in portrait mode.
- **Style:** The best approach is to choose Home➪Styles➪Cell Styles and modify the attributes of the Normal style. For example, you can change the font, font size, alignment, and so on.
- **Custom number formats:** If you create number formats that you use frequently, you can store them in a template.
- **Column widths and row heights:** You may prefer that columns be wider or narrower, or you may want the rows to be taller.
- **Print settings:** Change these settings in the Page Layout tab. You can adjust the page orientation, paper size, margins, and several other attributes.
- **Header and footer:** You enter custom headers or footers in Page Layout view (choose View➪Workbook Views➪Page Layout).
- **Sheet settings:** These options are in the Show group on the View tab and on the Advanced tab of the Excel Options dialog box (in the Display Options for This Worksheet section). Options include row and column header, page break display, gridlines, and more.

Of course, you can also create complete workbooks and save them as templates. For example, if you frequently need to produce a specific report, you may want to create a template that has everything for the report except for the data you need to enter. By saving your master copy as a template, you're less likely to overwrite the original file when you save the file after entering your data.

CHAPTER

9

Printing Your Work

IN THIS CHAPTER

Changing your worksheet view

Adjusting your print settings for better results

Preventing some cells from being printed

Using the Custom Views feature

Creating PDF files

Despite predictions of the "paperless office," reports printed on paper remain commonplace, and office printers will be around for a long time. Many worksheets that you develop with Excel will eventually end up as hard-copy reports. You'll find that printing from Excel is quite easy and that you can generate attractive, well-formatted reports with minimal effort. In addition, Excel has many options that provide you with a great deal of control over the printed page. These options are explained in this chapter.

Basic Printing

If you want to print a copy of a worksheet with no fuss and bother, use the Quick Print option. One way to access this command is to choose File⇨Print (which displays the Print pane of Backstage view), and then click the Print button.

If you like the idea of one-click printing, take a few seconds to add a new button to your Quick Access toolbar: Click the downward-pointing arrow on the right of the Quick Access toolbar and then choose Quick Print from the drop-down list. Excel adds the Quick Print icon to your Quick Access toolbar.

Clicking the Quick Print button prints the current worksheet on the currently selected printer, using the default print settings. If you've changed any of the default print settings (by using the Page Layout tab), Excel uses the new settings; otherwise, it uses the following default settings:

- Prints the active worksheet (or all selected worksheets), including any embedded charts or objects
- Prints one copy

- Prints the entire active worksheet
- Prints in portrait mode
- Doesn't scale the printed output
- Uses letter-size paper with 0.75-inch margins for the top and bottom and 0.70-inch margins for the left and right margins (for the U.S. version)
- Prints with no headers or footers
- Doesn't print cell comments
- Prints with no cell gridlines
- For wide worksheets that span multiple pages, prints down and then over

When you print a worksheet, Excel prints only the active area of the worksheet. In other words, it won't print all 17 billion cells — just those that have data in them. If the worksheet contains any embedded charts or other graphic objects (such as SmartArt or Shapes), they're also printed.

TIP

To quickly determine the active area of the worksheet, press Ctrl+End to move to the last active cell in the worksheet. The active area is between cell A1 and the last active cell. You may notice that Ctrl+End isn't always accurate. For example, if you've deleted some rows, Ctrl+End will take you to the last row that you deleted. However, when the sheet is printed, the active area is reset, so the empty rows are not printed.

Using Print Preview

When you choose File ⇨ Print (or press Ctrl+P), Backstage view displays a preview of your printed output, exactly as it will be printed. Initially, Excel displays the first page of your printed output. To view subsequent pages, use the page controls along the bottom of the preview pane (or, use the vertical scrollbar along the right side of the screen).

The Print Preview window has a few other commands (at the bottom) that you can use while previewing your output. For multipage printout, use the page number controls to quickly jump to a particular page. The Show Margins button toggles the display of margins, and Zoom to Page ensures that a complete page is displayed.

When the Show Margins option is in effect, Excel adds markers to the preview that indicate column borders and margins. You can drag the column or margin markers to make changes that appear onscreen. Changes that you make to column widths in preview mode are also made in the actual worksheet.

Print Preview is certainly useful, but you may prefer to use Page Layout view to preview your output (see "Changing Your Page View").

Changing Your Page View

Page Layout view shows your worksheet divided into pages. In other words, you can visualize your printed output while you work.

Page Layout view is one of three worksheet views, which are controlled by the three icons on the right side of the status bar. You could also use the commands in the View ➪ Workbook Views group on the Ribbon to switch views. The three view options are

- **Normal:** The default view of the worksheet. This view may or may not show page breaks.
- **Page Layout:** Shows individual pages.
- **Page Break Preview:** Allows you to manually adjust page breaks.

Just click one of the icons to change the view. You can also use the Zoom slider to change the magnification from 10% (a very tiny, bird's-eye view) to 400% (very large, for showing fine detail).

The following sections describe how these views can help with printing.

Normal view

Most of the time when you work in Excel, you use Normal view. Normal view can display page breaks in the worksheet. The page breaks are indicated by horizontal and vertical dotted lines. These page break lines adjust automatically if you change the page orientation, add or delete rows or columns, change row heights, change column widths, and so on. For example, if you find that your printed output is too wide to fit on a single page, you can adjust the column widths (keeping an eye on the page break display) until the columns are narrow enough to print on one page.

9

Note

Page breaks aren't displayed until you print (or preview) the worksheet at least one time. Page breaks are also displayed if you set a print area by choosing Page Layout ➪ Page Setup ➪ Print Area.

Tip

If you'd prefer not to see the page break display in Normal view, choose FIle ➪ Options and select the Advanced tab. Scroll down to the Display Options for This Worksheet section and remove the check mark from Show Page Breaks. This setting applies only to the active worksheet. Unfortunately, the option to turn off page break display is not on the Ribbon, and it's not even available for inclusion on the Quick Access toolbar. This is another one of those little annoyances that I expect Microsoft to fix one of these times.

Figure 9.1 shows a worksheet in Normal view, zoomed out to show multiple pages. Notice the dotted lines that indicate page breaks.

FIGURE 9.1

In Normal view, dotted lines indicate page breaks.

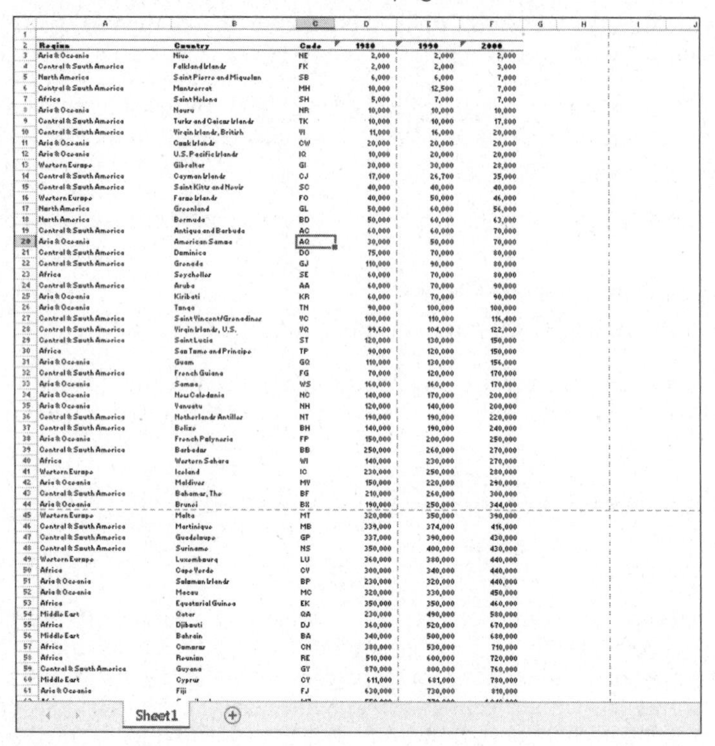

Page Layout view

Page Layout view is the ultimate print preview. Unlike the preview in Backstage view (choose File⇨Print), this mode is not a view-only mode. You have complete access to all Excel commands. In fact, you can use Page Layout view all the time if you like.

Figure 9.2 shows a worksheet in Page Layout view, zoomed out to show multiple pages. Notice that the page header and footer (if any) appear on each page, and repeated rows and columns (if any) also display — giving you a true preview of the printed output.

FIGURE 9.2

In Page Layout view, the worksheet resembles printed pages.

> **TIP**
>
> If you move the mouse to the corner of a page while in Page Layout view, you can click to hide the white space in the margins. Doing so gives you all the advantages of Page Layout view, but you can see more information onscreen because the unused margin space is hidden.

Page Break Preview

Page Break Preview displays the worksheet and shows where the page breaks occur. Figure 9.3 shows an example. This view mode is different from Normal view mode with page breaks turned on: The key difference is that you can drag the page breaks. Unlike Page Layout view, Page Break Preview does not display headers and footers.

FIGURE 9.3

Page Break Preview mode gives you a bird's-eye view of your worksheet and shows exactly where the page breaks occur.

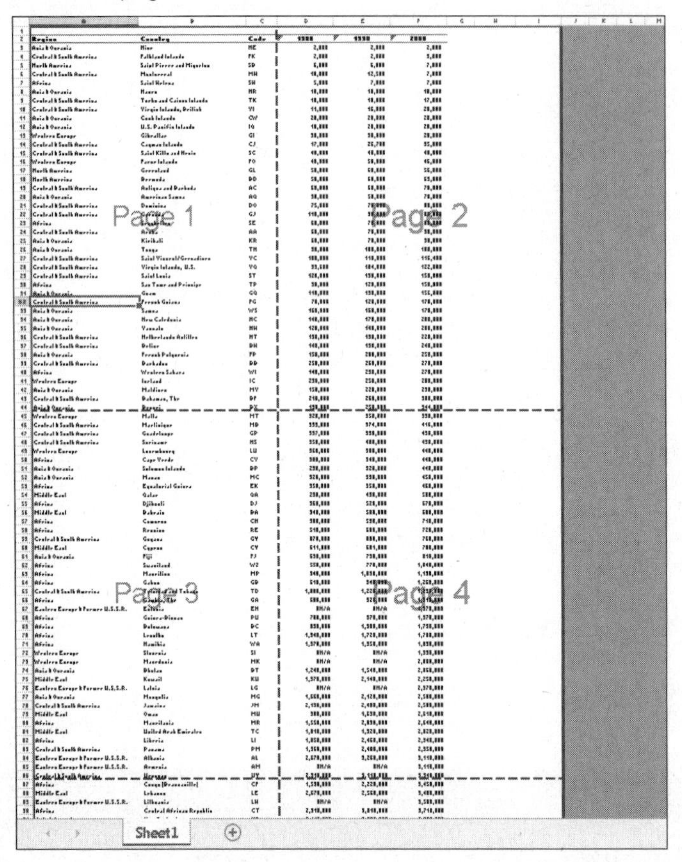

When you enter Page Break Preview, Excel performs the following:

- Changes the zoom factor so that you can see more of the worksheet.
- Displays the page numbers overlaid on the pages.
- Displays the current print range with a white background; nonprinting data appears with a gray background.
- Displays all page breaks as draggable dashed lines.

When you change the page breaks by dragging, Excel automatically adjusts the scaling so that the information fits on the pages, per your specifications.

TIP
In Page Break Preview, you still have access to all Excel commands. You can change the zoom factor if you find the text to be too small.

To exit Page Break Preview, just click one of the other View icons on the status bar.

Adjusting Common Page Setup Settings

Clicking the Quick Print button (or choosing File➪Print➪Print) may produce acceptable results in many cases, but a little tweaking of the print settings can often improve your printed reports. You can adjust print settings in three places:

- The Print settings screen in Backstage view, displayed when you choose File➪Print.
- The Page Layout tab of the Ribbon.
- The Page Setup dialog box, displayed when you click the dialog launcher in the lower-right corner of the Page Layout➪Page Setup group on the Ribbon. You can also access the Page Setup dialog box from the Print settings screen in Backstage view.

Table 9.1 summarizes the locations where you can make various types of print-related adjustments in Excel 2013.

TABLE 9.1 Where to Change Printer Settings

Setting	Print Settings Screen	Page Layout Tab of Ribbon	Page Setup Dialog Box
Number of copies	X		
Printer to use	X		
What to print	X		
Specify worksheet print area		X	X
1-sided or 2-sided	X		
Collated	X		
Orientation	X	X	X
Paper size	X	X	X
Adjust margins	X	X	X
Specify manual page breaks		X	
Specify repeating rows and/or columns			X

continued

TABLE 9.1 *(continued)*

Setting	Print Settings Screen	Page Layout Tab of Ribbon	Page Setup Dialog Box
Set print scaling		X	X
Print or hide gridlines		X	X
Print or hide row and column headings		X	X
Specify the first page number			X
Center output on page			X
Specify header/footers and options			X
Specify how to print cell comments			X
Specify page order			X
Specify black-and-white output			X
Specify how to print error cells			X
Launch dialog box for printer-specific settings	X		X

Table 9.1 might make printing seem more complicated than it really is. The key point to remember is this: If you can't find a way to make a particular adjustment, it's probably available from the Page Setup dialog box.

Choosing your printer

To switch to a different printer or output device, choose File⇨Print, and use the drop-down control in the Printer section to select a different installed printer.

NOTE

To adjust printer settings, click the Printer Properties link to display a property box for the selected printer. The exact dialog box that you see depends on the printer. The Properties dialog box lets you adjust printer-specific settings, such as the print quality and the paper source. In most cases, you won't have to change any of these settings, but if you're having print-related problems, you may want to check the settings.

Specifying what you want to print

Sometimes you may want to print only a part of the worksheet rather than the entire active area. Or you may want to reprint selected pages of a report without printing all the pages. Choose File⇨Print, and use the controls in the Settings section to specify what to print.

You have several options:

- **Print Active Sheets:** Prints the active sheet or sheets that you selected. (This option is the default.) You can select multiple sheets to print by pressing Ctrl and clicking the sheet tabs. If you select multiple sheets, Excel begins printing each sheet on a new page.
- **Print Entire Workbook:** Prints the entire workbook, including chart sheets.
- **Print Selection:** Prints only the range that you selected before choosing File➪Print.
- **Print Selected Chart:** Appears only if a chart is selected. If this option is chosen, only the chart will be printed.
- **Print Selected Table:** Appears only if the cell pointer is within a table (created by choosing Insert➪Tables➪Table) when the Print Setting screen is displayed. If this option is chosen, only the table will be printed.

TIP

You can also choose Page Layout➪Page Setup➪Print Area➪Set Print Area to specify the range(s) to print. Before you choose this command, select the range(s) that you want to print. To clear the print area, choose Page Layout➪Page Setup➪Print Area➪Clear Print Area. To override the print area, select the Ignore Print Area check box in the list of Print What options.

NOTE

The print area does not have to be a single range. You make a multiple selection before you set the print area. Each area will print on a separate page.

If your printed output uses multiple pages, you can select which pages to print by indicating the number of the first and last pages to print by using Pages controls in the Settings section. You can either use the spinner controls or type the page numbers in the edit boxes.

Changing page orientation

Page orientation refers to how output is printed on the page. Choose Page Layout➪Page Setup➪Orientation➪Portrait to print tall pages (the default) or Page Layout➪Page Setup➪Orientation➪Landscape to print wide pages. Landscape orientation is useful when you have a wide range that doesn't fit on a vertically oriented page.

If you change the orientation, the onscreen page breaks adjust automatically to accommodate the new paper orientation.

Page orientation settings are also available when you choose File➪Print.

Specifying paper size

Choose Page Layout ➪ Page Setup ➪ Size to specify the paper size you're using. The paper size settings are also available when you choose File ➪ Print.

NOTE

Even though Excel displays a variety of paper sizes, your printer may not be capable of using all of them.

Printing multiple copies of a report

Use the Copies control at the top of the Print tab in Backstage View to specify the number of copies to print. Just enter the number of copies you want and then click Print.

TIP

If you're printing multiple copies of a report, make sure that the Collated option is selected so that Excel prints the pages in order for each set of output. If you're printing only one page, Excel ignores the Collated setting.

Adjusting the page margins

Margins are the unprinted areas along the sides, top, and bottom of a printed page. Excel provides four "quick margin" settings, and you can also specify the exact margin size you require. All printed pages have the same margins. You can't specify different margins for different pages.

In Page Layout view, a ruler is displayed above the column header and to the left of the row header. Use your mouse to drag the margins in the ruler. Excel adjusts the page display immediately. Use the horizontal ruler to adjust the left and right margins, and use the vertical ruler to adjust the top and bottom margins.

From the Page Layout ➪ Page Setup ➪ Margins drop-down list, you can select Normal, Wide, Narrow, or the Last Custom Setting. These options are also available when you choose File ➪ Print. If none of these settings does the job, choose Custom Margins to display the Margins tab of the Page Setup dialog box, shown in Figure 9.4.

To change a margin, click the appropriate spinner (or you can enter a value directly). The margin settings that you specify in the Page Setup dialog box will then be available in the Page Layout ➪ Page Setup ➪ Margins drop-down list, referred to as Last Custom Setting.

NOTE

The Preview box in the center of the Page Setup dialog box is a bit deceiving because it doesn't really show you how your changes look in relation to the page; instead, it displays a darker line to let you know which margin you're adjusting.

FIGURE 9.4

The Margins tab of the Page Setup dialog box.

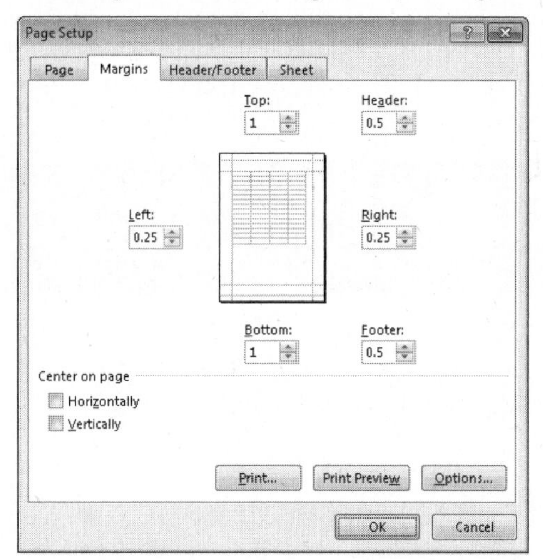

You can also adjust margins in the preview window in Backstage view (choose File ➪ Print). Click the Show Margins button in the bottom-right corner to display the margins in the preview pane. Then drag the margin indicators to adjust the margins.

In addition to the page margins, you can adjust the distance of the header from the top of the page and the distance of the footer from the bottom of the page. These settings should be less than the corresponding margin; otherwise, the header or footer may overlap with the printed output.

By default, Excel aligns the printed page at the top and left margins. If you want the output to be centered vertically or horizontally, select the appropriate check box in the Center on Page section of the Margins tab.

Understanding page breaks

When printing lengthy reports, controlling where pages break is often important. For example, you probably don't want a row to print on a page by itself, nor do you want a table header row to be the last line on a page. Fortunately, Excel gives you precise control over page breaks.

Excel handles page breaks automatically, but sometimes you may want to force a page break — either a vertical or a horizontal one — so that the report prints the way you want. For example, if your worksheet consists of several distinct sections, you may want to print each section on a separate sheet of paper.

Inserting a page break

To insert a horizontal page break line, move the cell pointer to the cell that will begin the new page. Make sure that you place the pointer in column A, though; otherwise, you'll insert a vertical page break *and* a horizontal page break. For example, if you want row 14 to be the first row of a new page, select cell A14. Then choose Page Layout ➪ Page Setup ➪ Breaks ➪ Insert Page Break.

NOTE

Page breaks are visualized differently, depending on which view mode you're using (see "Changing Your Page View," earlier in this chapter).

To insert a vertical page break line, move the cell pointer to the cell that will begin the new page. In this case, though, make sure to place the pointer in row 1. Choose Page Layout ➪ Page Setup ➪ Breaks ➪ Insert Page Break to create the page break.

Removing manual page breaks

To remove a page break you've added, move the cell pointer to the first row beneath (or the first column to the right) of the manual page break and then choose Page Layout ➪ Page Setup ➪ Breaks ➪ Remove Page Break.

To remove all manual page breaks in the worksheet, choose Page Layout ➪ Page Setup ➪ Breaks ➪ Reset All Page Breaks.

Printing row and column titles

If your worksheet is set up with titles in the first row and descriptive names in the first column, it can be difficult to identify data that appears on printed pages where those titles don't appear. To resolve this problem, you can choose to print selected rows or columns as titles on each page of the printout.

Row and column titles serve pretty much the same purpose on a printout as frozen panes do in navigating within a worksheet. Keep in mind, however, that these features are independent of each other. In other words, freezing panes doesn't affect the printed output.

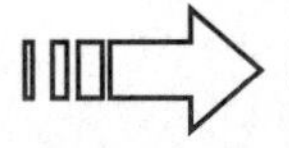

See Chapter 3 for more information on freezing panes.

CAUTION

Don't confuse print titles with headers; these are two different concepts. *Headers* appear at the top of each page and contain information, such as the worksheet name, date, or page number. *Row and column titles* describe the data being printed, such as field names in a database table or list.

You can specify particular rows to repeat at the top of every printed page or particular columns to repeat at the left of every printed page. To do so, choose Page Layout ➪ Page Setup ➪ Print Titles. Excel displays the Sheet tab of the Page Setup dialog box, shown in Figure 9.5.

FIGURE 9.5

Use the Sheet tab of the Page Setup dialog box to specify rows or columns that will appear on each printed page.

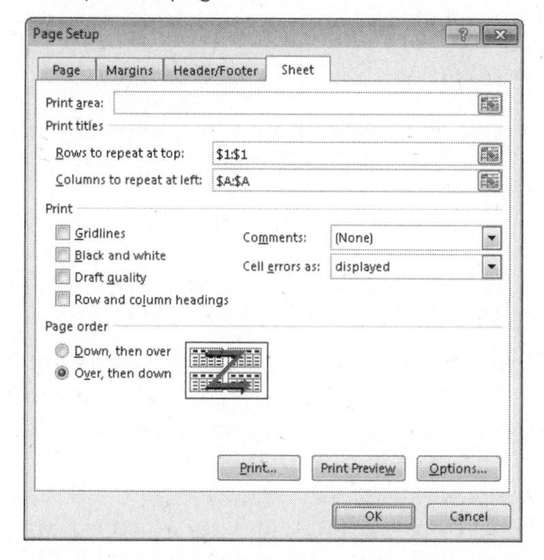

Activate the appropriate box (either Rows to Repeat at Top or Columns to Repeat at Left) and then select the rows or columns in the worksheet. Or you can enter these references manually. For example, to specify rows 1 and 2 as repeating rows, enter **1:2**.

NOTE

When you specify row and column titles and use Page Layout view, these titles will repeat on every page (just as when the document is printed). However, the cells used in the title can be *selected* only on the page in which they first appear.

Scaling printed output

In some cases, you may need to force your printed output to fit on a specific number of pages. You can do so by enlarging or reducing the size. To enter a scaling factor, choose Page Layout ➪ Scale to Fit ➪ Scale. You can scale the output from 10% up to 400%. To return to normal scaling, enter **100%**.

To force Excel to print using a specific number of pages, choose Page Layout ➪ Scale to Fit ➪ Width and Page Layout ➪ Scale to Fit ➪ Height. When you change either one of these settings, the corresponding scale factor is displayed in the Scale control.

Caution

Excel doesn't ensure legibility. It will gladly scale your output to be so small that no one can read it.

Printing cell gridlines

Typically, cell gridlines aren't printed. If you want your printout to include the gridlines, choose Page Layout ➪ Sheet Options ➪ Gridlines ➪ Print.

Alternatively, you can insert borders around some cells to simulate gridlines.

See Chapter 6 for information about borders.

Printing row and column headers

By default, row and column headers for a worksheet are not printed. If you want your printout to include these items, choose Page Layout ➪ Sheet Options ➪ Headings ➪ Print.

Using a background image

Would you like to have a background image on your printouts? Unfortunately, you can't. You may have noticed the Page Layout ➪ Page Setup ➪ Background command. This button displays a dialog box that lets you select an image to display as a background. Placing this control among the other print-related commands is very misleading. Background images placed on a worksheet are never printed.

Tip

In lieu of a true background image, you can insert a Shape, WordArt, or a picture on your worksheet and then adjust its transparency. Then copy the image to all printed pages. Alternatively, you can insert an object in a page header or footer (see the nearby sidebar, "Inserting a Watermark").

Inserting a Watermark

A *watermark* is an image (or text) that appears on each printed page. A watermark can be a faint company logo, or a word such as *DRAFT*. Excel doesn't have an official command to print a watermark, but you can add a watermark by inserting a picture in the page header or footer. Here's how:

1. **Locate an image on your hard drive that you want to use for the watermark.**
2. **Choose View➪Workbook Views➪Page Layout View.**
3. **Click the center section of the header.**
4. **Choose Header & Footer Tools➪Design➪Header & Footer Elements Picture.** The Insert Pictures dialog box appears.
5. **Click Browse and locate the image from Step 1 (or locate a suitable image from other sources listed).**
6. **Click outside the header to see your image.**
7. **To center the image in the middle of the page, click the center section of the header and add some carriage returns before the** &[Picture] **code.** You'll need to experiment to determine the number of carriage returns required to push the image into the body of the document.
8. **If you need to adjust the image (for example, make it lighter), click the center section of the header and then choose Header & Footer Tools➪Design➪Header & Footer Elements➪Format Picture. Use the Image controls in the Picture tab of the Format Picture dialog box to adjust the image.** You may need to experiment with the settings to make sure that the worksheet text is legible.

The accompanying figure shows an example of a header image (a copyright symbol) used as a watermark. You can do a similar thing with text, of course.

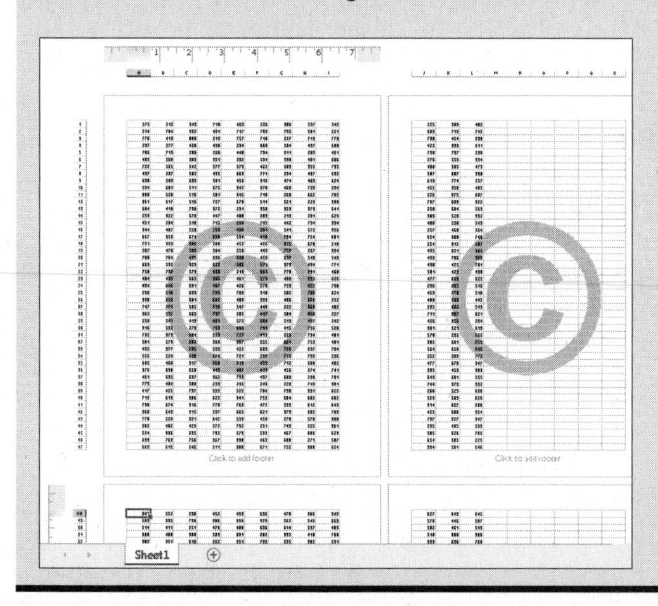

9

Adding a Header or Footer to Your Reports

A *header* is information that appears at the top of each printed page. A *footer* is information that appears at the bottom of each printed page. By default, new workbooks do not have headers or footers.

You can specify headers and footers by using the Header/Footer tab of the Page Setup dialog box. Or simplify the task by switching to Page Layout view, where you can click the section labeled Click to Add Header or Click to Add Footer.

Note

If you're working in Normal view, you can choose Insert ➪ Text ➪ Header & Footer. Excel switches to Page Layout view and activates the center section of the page header.

You can then type the information and apply any type of formatting you like. Note that headers and footers consist of three sections: left, center, and right. For example, you can create a header that prints your name at the left margin, the worksheet name centered in the header, and the page number at the right margin.

Tip

If you want a consistent header or footer for all your documents, create a `book.xltx` template with your headers or footers specified. A `book.xltx` template is used as the basis for new workbooks.

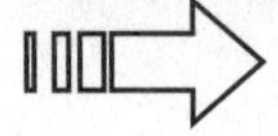

See Chapter 8 for details on creating a template.

When you activate the header or footer section in Page Layout view, the Ribbon displays a new contextual tab: Header & Footer Tools ➪ Design. Use the controls on this tab to work with headers and footers.

Selecting a predefined header or footer

You can choose from a number of predefined headers or footers by using either of the two drop-down lists in the Header & Footer Tools ➪ Design ➪ Header & Footer group. Notice that some items in these lists consist of multiple parts, separated by a comma. Each part goes into one of the three header or footer sections (left, center, or right). Figure 9.6 shows an example of a header that uses all three sections.

FIGURE 9.6

This three-part header is one of Excel's predefined headers.

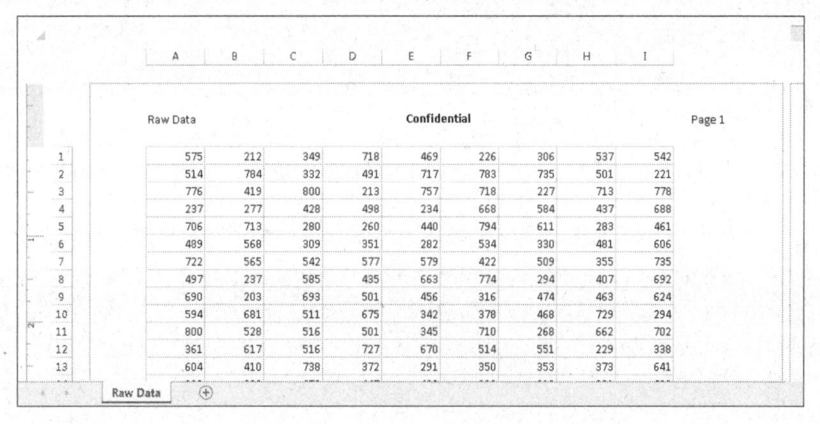

Understanding header and footer element codes

When a header or footer section is activated, you can type whatever text you like into the section. Or to insert variable information, you can insert any of several element codes by clicking a button in the Header & Footer Tools ➪ Design ➪ Header & Footer Elements group. Each button inserts a code into the selected section. For example, to insert the current date, click the Current Date button. Table 9.2 lists the buttons and their functions.

TABLE 9.2 Header and Footer Buttons and Their Functions

Button	Code	Function
Page Number	`&[Page]`	Displays the page number
Number of Pages	`&[Pages]`	Displays the total number of pages to be printed
Current Date	`&[Date]`	Displays the current date
Current Time	`&[Time]`	Displays the current time
File Path	`&[Path]&[File]`	Displays the workbook's complete path and filename
File Name	`&[File]`	Displays the workbook name
Sheet Name	`&[Tab]`	Displays the sheet's name
Picture	Not applicable	Enables you to add a picture
Format Picture	Not applicable	Enables you to change an added picture's settings

You can combine text and codes and insert as many codes as you like into each section.

NOTE
If the text that you enter uses an ampersand (&), you must enter the ampersand twice (because Excel uses an ampersand to signal a code). For example, to enter the text *Research & Development* into a section of a header or footer, type Research && Development.

You can also use different fonts and sizes in your headers and footers. Just select the text that you want to change and then use the formatting tools in the Home ➪ Font group. Or use the controls on the Mini toolbar, which appears automatically when you select the text. If you don't change the font, Excel uses the font defined for the Normal style.

TIP
You can use as many lines as you like. Press Enter to force a line break for multiline headers or footers. If you use multiline headers or footers, you may need to adjust the top or bottom margin so the text won't overlap with the worksheet data (see "Adjusting the page margins," earlier in this chapter).

Unfortunately, you can't print the contents of a specific cell in a header or footer. For example, you may want Excel to use the contents of cell A1 as part of a header. To do so, you need to enter the cell's contents manually — or write a VBA macro to perform this operation before the sheet is printed.

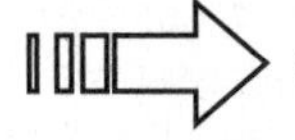

See Chapter 42 for an example of a macro that inserts the contents of a cell into a page header.

Other header and footer options

When a header or footer is selected in Page Layout view, the Header & Footer ➪ Design ➪ Options group contains controls that let you specify other options:

- **Different First Page:** If checked, you can specify a different header/footer for the first printed page.
- **Different Odd & Even Pages:** If checked, you can specify a different header/footer for odd and even pages.
- **Scale with Document:** If checked, the font size in the header and footer will be sized accordingly if the document is scaled when printed. This option is enabled, by default.
- **Align with Page Margins:** If checked, the left header and footer will be aligned with the left margin, and the right header and footer will be aligned with the right margin. This option is enabled, by default.

Copying Page Setup Settings across Sheets

Each Excel worksheet has its own print setup options (orientation, margins, headers and footers, and so on). These options are specified in the Page Setup group of the Page Layout tab.

When you add a new sheet to a workbook, it contains the default page setup settings. Here's an easy way to transfer the settings from one worksheet to additional worksheets:

1. **Activate the sheet that contains the desired setup information.** This is the source sheet.
2. **Select the target sheets.** Ctrl + click the sheet tabs of the sheets you want to update with the settings from the source sheet.
3. **Click the dialog box launcher in the lower-right corner of the Page Layout ➪ Page Setup group.**
4. **When the Page Setup dialog box appears, click OK to close it.**
5. **Ungroup the sheets by right-clicking any selected sheet and choosing Ungroup Sheets from the shortcut menu.** Because multiple sheets are selected when you close the Page Setup dialog box, the settings of the source sheet will be transferred to all target sheets.

NOTE

Two settings located on the Sheet tab of the Page Setup dialog box are not transferred: Print Area and Print Titles. In addition, pictures in the header or footer are not transferred.

Preventing Certain Cells from Being Printed

If your worksheet contains confidential information, you may want to print the worksheet but not the confidential parts. You can use several techniques to prevent certain parts of a worksheet from printing:

- **Hide rows or columns.** When you hide rows or columns, the hidden rows or columns aren't printed. Choose Home ➪ Cells ➪ Format drop-down list to hide the selected rows or columns.
- **Hide cells or ranges.**
  - You can hide cells or ranges by making the text color the same color as the background color. Be aware, however, that this method may not work for all printers.
  - You can hide cells by using a custom number format that consists of three semicolons (;;;). See Chapter 25 for more information about using custom number formats.

- **Mask an area.** You can mask a confidential area of a worksheet by covering it with a rectangle Shape. Choose Insert ➪ Illustrations ➪ Shapes and click the Rectangle Shape. You'll probably want to adjust the fill color to match the cell background and remove the border.

If you find that you must regularly hide data before you print certain reports, consider using the Custom Views feature, discussed later in this chapter (see "Creating Custom Views of Your Worksheet"). This feature allows you to create a named view that doesn't show the confidential information.

Preventing Objects from Being Printed

To prevent objects on the worksheet (such as charts, Shapes, and SmartArt) from being printed, you need to access the Properties tab of the object's Format dialog box (see Figure 9.7):

FIGURE 9.7

Use the Properties tab of the object's Format dialog box to prevent objects from printing.

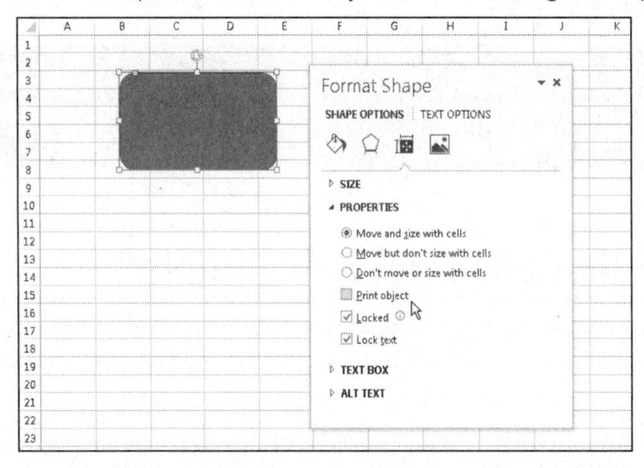

1. **Right-click the object and choose Format *xxxx* from the shortcut menu.** (*xxxx* varies, depending on the object.)
2. **In the Format dialog box that opens for the object, click the Size & Properties icon.**
3. **Expand the Properties section of the dialog box.**
4. **Remove the check mark for Print Object.**

NOTE

For a chart, you must right-click the chart's Chart Area (the background of the chart). Or double-click the chart's border to display the Format Chart Area dialog box. Then expand the Properties section and remove the check mark from Print Object.

Creating Custom Views of Your Worksheet

If you need to create several different printed reports from the same Excel workbook, setting up the specific settings for each report can be a tedious job. For example, you may need to print a full report in landscape mode for your boss. Another department may require a simplified report using the same data, but with some hidden columns in portrait mode. You can simplify the process by creating custom named views of your worksheets that include the proper settings for each report.

The Custom Views feature enables you to give names to various views of your worksheet. You can quickly switch among these named views. A *view* includes settings for the following:

- Print settings, as specified in the Page Layout ⇨ Page Setup, Page Layout ⇨ Scale to Fit, and Page ⇨ Page Setup ⇨ Sheet Options groups
- Hidden rows and columns
- The worksheet view (Normal, Page Layout, Page Break preview)
- Selected cells and ranges
- The active cell
- The zoom factor
- Window sizes and positions
- Frozen panes

If you find that you're constantly fiddling with these settings before printing and then changing them back, using named views can save you some work.

CAUTION

Unfortunately, the Custom Views feature doesn't work if the workbook (not just the worksheet) contains at least one table. When a workbook that contains a table is active, the Custom View command is disabled. This limitation severely limits the usefulness of the Custom Views feature.

To create a named view, follow these steps:

1. **Set up the view settings the way you want them.** For example, hide some columns.
2. **Choose View ⇨ Workbook Views ⇨ Custom Views.** The Custom Views dialog box appears.

3. **Click the Add button.** The Add View dialog box (shown in Figure 9.8) appears.

FIGURE 9.8

Use the Add View dialog box to create a named view.

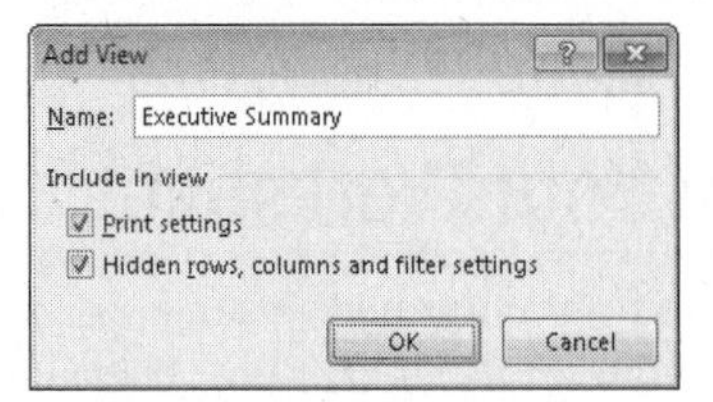

4. **Provide a descriptive name.** You can also specify what to include in the view by using the two check boxes. For example, if you don't want the view to include print settings, remove the check mark from Print Settings.
5. **Click OK to save the named view.**

Then, when you're ready to print, open the Custom Views dialog box to see all named views. To select a particular view, just select it from the list and click the Show button. To delete a named view from the list, click the Delete button.

Creating PDF files

The PDF file format is widely used as a way to present information in a read-only manner, with precise control over the layout. If you need to share your work with someone who doesn't have Excel, creating a PDF is often a good solution. Free software to display PDFs is available from a number of sources.

NOTE

Excel can create PDFs, but it can't open them. Word 2013 can create and open PDFs.

XPS is another "electronic paper" format, developed by Microsoft as an alternative to the PDF format. At this time, there is very little third-party support for the XPS format.

To save a worksheet in PDF or XPS format, choose File ➪ Export ➪ Create PDF/XPS Document ➪ Create a PDF/XPS. Excel displays its Publish as PDF or XPS dialog box, in which you can specify a filename and location and set some other options.

Part II

Working with Formulas and Functions

Formulas and worksheet functions are essential to manipulating data and obtaining useful information from your Excel workbooks. The chapters in this part present a wide variety of formula examples that use many Excel functions. Two of the chapters are devoted to array formulas. These chapters are intended primarily for advanced users who need to perform calculations that may otherwise be impossible.

IN THIS PART

CHAPTER

10

Introducing Formulas and Functions

IN THIS CHAPTER

- Understanding formula basics
- Entering formulas and functions into your worksheets
- Understanding how to use references in formulas
- Correcting common formula errors
- Using advanced naming techniques
- Getting tips for working with formulas

Formulas are what make a spreadsheet program so useful. If it weren't for formulas, a spreadsheet would simply be a fancy word-processing document that has great support for tabular information.

You use formulas in your Excel worksheets to calculate results from the data stored in the worksheet. When data changes, the formulas calculate updated results with no extra effort on your part. This chapter introduces formulas and functions and helps you get up to speed with this important element.

Understanding Formula Basics

A *formula* consists of special code entered into a cell. It performs a calculation of some type and returns a result, which is displayed in the cell. Formulas use a variety of operators and worksheet functions to work with values and text. The values and text used in formulas can be located in other cells, which makes changing data easy and gives worksheets their dynamic nature. For example, you can see multiple scenarios quickly by changing the data in a worksheet and letting your formulas do the work.

A formula can consist of any of these elements:

- Mathematical operators, such as + (for addition) and * (for multiplication)
- Cell references (including named cells and ranges)
- Values or text
- Worksheet functions (such as SUM or AVERAGE)

After you enter a formula, the cell displays the calculated result of the formula. The formula itself appears in the Formula bar when you select the cell, however.

Here are a few examples of formulas:

`=150*.05`	Multiplies 150 times 0.05. This formula uses only values, and it always returns the same result. You could just enter the value 7.5 into the cell.
`=A3`	Returns the value in cell A3. No calculation is performed.
`=A1+A2`	Adds the values in cells A1 and A2.
`=Income-Expenses`	Subtracts the value in the cell named `Expenses` from the value in the cell named `Income`.
`=SUM(A1:A12)`	Adds the values in the range A1:A12, using the `SUM` function.
`=A1=C12`	Compares cell A1 with cell C12. If the cells are identical, the formula returns `TRUE`; otherwise, it returns `FALSE`.

Note that every formula begins with an equal sign (=). The initial equal sign allows Excel to distinguish a formula from plain text.

Using operators in formulas

Excel formulas support a variety of operators. *Operators* are symbols that indicate what mathematical operation you want the formula to perform. Table 10.1 lists the operators that Excel recognizes. In addition to these, Excel has many built-in functions that enable you to perform additional calculations.

TABLE 10.1 Operators Used in Formulas

Operator	Name
+	Addition
–	Subtraction
*	Multiplication
/	Division
^	Exponentiation

Operator	Name
&	Concatenation
=	Logical comparison (equal to)
>	Logical comparison (greater than)
<	Logical comparison (less than)
>=	Logical comparison (greater than or equal to)
<=	Logical comparison (less than or equal to)
<>	Logical comparison (not equal to)

You can, of course, use as many operators as you need to perform the desired calculation.

Here are some examples of formulas that use various operators.

Formula	What It Does
="Part-"&"23A"	Joins (concatenates) the two text strings to produce Part-23A.
=A1&A2	Concatenates the contents of cell A1 with cell A2. Concatenation works with values as well as text. If cell A1 contains 123 and cell A2 contains 456, this formula would return the text 123456.
=6^3	Raises 6 to the third power (216).
=216^(1/3)	Raises 216 to the $\frac{1}{3}$ power. This is mathematically equivalent to calculating the cube root of 216, which is 6.
=A1<A2	Returns TRUE if the value in cell A1 is less than the value in cell A2. Otherwise, it returns FALSE. Logical comparison operators also work with text. If A1 contains Bill and A2 contains Julia, the formula would return TRUE because Bill comes before Julia in alphabetical order.
=A1<=A2	Returns TRUE if the value in cell A1 is less than or equal to the value in cell A2. Otherwise, it returns FALSE.
=A1<>A2	Returns TRUE if the value in cell A1 isn't equal to the value in cell A2. Otherwise, it returns FALSE.

Understanding operator precedence in formulas

When Excel calculates the value of a formula, it uses certain rules to determine the order in which the various parts of the formula are calculated. You need to understand these rules so your formulas produce accurate results.

Table 10.2 lists the Excel operator precedence. This table shows that exponentiation has the highest precedence (performed first) and logical comparisons have the lowest precedence (performed last).

TABLE 10.2 Operator Precedence in Excel Formulas

Symbol	Operator	Precedence
^	Exponentiation	1
*	Multiplication	2
/	Division	2
+	Addition	3
–	Subtraction	3
&	Concatenation	4
=	Equal to	5
<	Less than	5
>	Greater than	5

You can use parentheses to override Excel's built-in order of precedence. Expressions within parentheses are always evaluated first. For example, the following formula uses parentheses to control the order in which the calculations occur. In this case, cell B3 is subtracted from cell B2, and the result is multiplied by cell B4:

```
=(B2-B3)*B4
```

If you enter the formula without the parentheses, Excel computes a different answer. Because multiplication has a higher precedence, cell B3 is multiplied by cell B4. Then this result is subtracted from cell B2, which isn't what was intended.

The formula without parentheses looks like this:

```
=B2-B3*B4
```

It's a good idea to use parentheses even when they aren't strictly necessary. Doing so helps to clarify what the formula is intended to do. For example, the following formula makes it perfectly clear that B3 should be multiplied by B4, and the result subtracted from cell B2. Without the parentheses, you would need to remember Excel's order of precedence.

```
=B2-(B3*B4)
```

You can also *nest* parentheses within formulas — that is, put them inside other parentheses. If you do so, Excel evaluates the most deeply nested expressions first — and then works its way out. Here's an example of a formula that uses nested parentheses:

```
=((B2*C2)+(B3*C3)+(B4*C4))*B6
```

This formula has four sets of parentheses — three sets are nested inside the fourth set. Excel evaluates each nested set of parentheses and then sums the three results. This result is then multiplied by the value in cell B6.

Although the preceding formula uses four sets of parentheses, only the outer set is really necessary. If you understand operator precedence, it should be clear that you can rewrite this formula as:

```
=(B2*C2+B3*C3+B4*C4)*B6
```

But most would agree that using the extra parentheses makes the calculation much clearer.

Every left parenthesis, of course, must have a matching right parenthesis. If you have many levels of nested parentheses, keeping them straight can sometimes be difficult. If the parentheses don't match, Excel displays a message explaining the problem — and won't let you enter the formula.

Caution

In some cases, if your formula contains mismatched parentheses, Excel may propose a correction to your formula. Figure 10.1 shows an example of a proposed correction. You may be tempted simply to accept Excel's suggestion, but be careful – in many cases, the proposed formula, although syntactically correct, isn't the formula you intended, and it will produce an incorrect result.

FIGURE 10.1

Excel sometimes suggests a syntactically correct formula, but not the formula you had in mind.

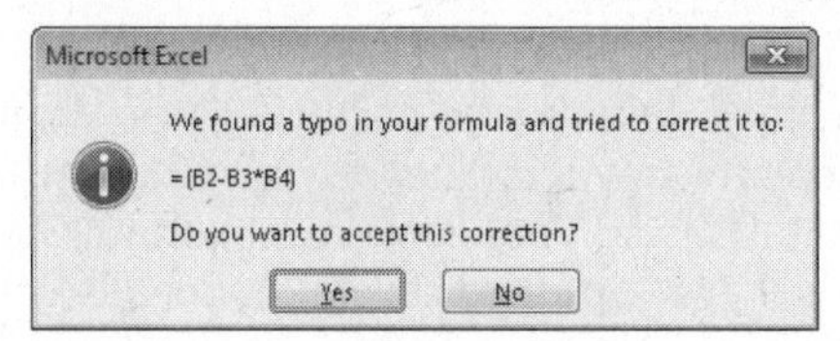

Tip

When you're editing a formula, Excel lends a hand in helping you match parentheses by displaying matching parentheses in the same color.

Using functions in your formulas

Many formulas you create use worksheet functions. These functions enable you to greatly enhance the power of your formulas and perform calculations that are difficult (or even impossible) if you use only the operators discussed previously. For example, you can use the `TAN` function to calculate the tangent of an angle. You can't do this complicated calculation by using the mathematical operators alone.

Examples of formulas that use functions

A worksheet function can simplify a formula significantly.

Here's an example. To calculate the average of the values in ten cells (A1:A10) without using a function, you'd have to construct a formula like this:

```
=(A1+A2+A3+A4+A5+A6+A7+A8+A9+A10)/10
```

Not very pretty, is it? Even worse, you would need to edit this formula if you added another cell to the range. Fortunately, you can replace this formula with a much simpler one that uses one of Excel's built-in worksheet functions, AVERAGE:

```
=AVERAGE(A1:A10)
```

The following formula demonstrates how using a function can enable you to perform calculations that are not otherwise possible. Say you need to determine the largest value in a range. A formula can't tell you the answer without using a function. Here's a formula that uses the MAX function to return the largest value in the range A1:D100:

```
=MAX(A1:D100)
```

Functions also can sometimes eliminate manual editing. Assume that you have a worksheet that contains 1,000 names in cells A1:A1000, and the names appear in all-capital letters. Your boss sees the listing and informs you that the names will be mail-merged with a form letter. All-uppercase letters is not acceptable; for example, JOHN F. SMITH must now appear as John F. Smith. You *could* spend the next several hours re-entering the list (ugh), or you could use a formula, such as the following, which uses the PROPER function to convert the text in cell A1 to the proper case:

```
=PROPER(A1)
```

Enter this formula once in cell B1 and then copy it down to the next 999 rows. Then select B1:B1000 and choose Home➪Clipboard➪Copy to copy the range. Next, with B1:B1000 still selected, choose Home➪Clipboard➪Paste Values (V) to convert the formulas to values. Delete the original column, and you've just accomplished several hours of work in less than a minute.

One last example should convince you of the power of functions. Suppose you have a worksheet that calculates sales commissions. If the salesperson sold more than $100,000 of product, the commission rate is 7.5 percent; otherwise, the commission rate is 5.0 percent. Without using a function, you would have to create two different formulas and make sure that you use the correct formula for each sales amount. A better solution is to write a formula that uses the IF function to ensure that you calculate the correct commission, regardless of sales amount:

```
=IF(A1<100000,A1*5%,A1*7.5%)
```

New Functions in Excel 2013

New Feature

Excel 2013 includes more than 50 new worksheet functions.

Nearly all the new functions are highly specialized functions that will appeal to those in engineering or math-related fields.

But there are some new functions that might appeal to a more general audience:

- `ISFORMULA`: Returns `TRUE` if the referenced cell contains a formula
- `FORMULATEXT`: Returns the formula in the referenced cell, as text
- `SHEET`: Returns the sheet number of the referenced sheet. For example, =SHEET("Sheet3") returns the sheet number for Sheet3.
- `SHEETS`: Returns the number of sheets in a workbook. For example, `=SHEETS()` returns the number of sheets in the workbook.
- `IFNA`: If a reference contains an `#NA` error, returns other text you specify

Keep in mind that these functions are not backward compatible. If you use any of these new functions, they won't work if the file is opened with an earlier version of Excel.

This formula performs some simple decision making. The formula checks the value of cell A1. If this value is less than 100,000, the formula returns cell A1 multiplied by 5 percent. Otherwise, it returns what's in cell A1 multiplied by 7.5 percent. This example uses three arguments, separated by commas. I discuss this in the upcoming section, "Function arguments."

Function arguments

In the preceding examples, you may have noticed that all the functions used parentheses. The information inside the parentheses is the *list of arguments.*

Functions vary in how they use arguments. Depending on what it has to do, a function may use

- No arguments
- One argument
- A fixed number of arguments
- An indeterminate number of arguments
- Optional arguments

An example of a function that doesn't use an argument is the NOW function, which returns the current date and time. Even if a function doesn't use an argument, you must still provide a set of empty parentheses, like this:

```
=NOW()
```

If a function uses more than one argument, you must separate each argument with a comma. The examples at the beginning of the chapter used cell references for arguments. Excel is quite flexible when it comes to function arguments, however. An argument can consist of a cell reference, literal values, literal text strings, expressions, and even other functions. Here are some examples of functions that use various types of arguments:

- **Cell reference:** `=SUM(A1:A24)`
- **Literal value:** `=SQRT(121)`
- **Literal text string:** `=PROPER("john smith")`
- **Expression:** `=SQRT(183+12)`
- **Other functions:** `=SQRT(SUM(A1:A24))`

NOTE

A comma is the list separator character for the U.S. version of Excel. Some other versions may use a semicolon. The list separator is a Windows setting, which can be adjusted in the Windows Control Panel (the Regional and Language Options dialog box).

More about functions

All told, Excel includes more than 450 functions. And if that's not enough, you can download or purchase additional specialized functions from third-party suppliers — and even create your own custom functions (by using VBA) if you're so inclined.

Some users feel a bit overwhelmed by the sheer number of functions, but you'll probably find that you use only a dozen or so on a regular basis. And as you'll see, the Excel Insert Function dialog box (described later in this chapter) makes it easy to locate and insert a function, even if it's not one that you use frequently.

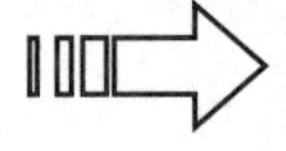

You'll find many examples of Excel's built-in functions in Chapters 11 through 18. Appendix A contains a complete listing of Excel's worksheet functions, with a brief description of each. Chapter 39 covers the basics of creating custom functions with VBA.

Entering Formulas into Your Worksheets

Every formula must begin with an equal sign to inform Excel that the cell contains a formula rather than text. Excel provides two ways to enter a formula into a cell: manually, or by pointing to cell references. The following sections discuss each way in detail.

Using Formula AutoComplete

The Formula AutoComplete feature makes entering formulas easier than ever. Here's a quick walk-through that demonstrates how it works. The goal is to create a formula that uses the `AGGREGATE` function to calculate the average value in a range that I named `TestScores`. The `AVERAGE` function will not work in this situation because the range contains an error value.

1. **Select the cell that will hold the formula, and type an equal sign (=) to signal the start of a formula.**
2. **Type the letter *A*.** You get a list of functions and names that begin with *A* (see the figure). This feature is not case sensitive, so you can use either uppercase or lowercase characters.

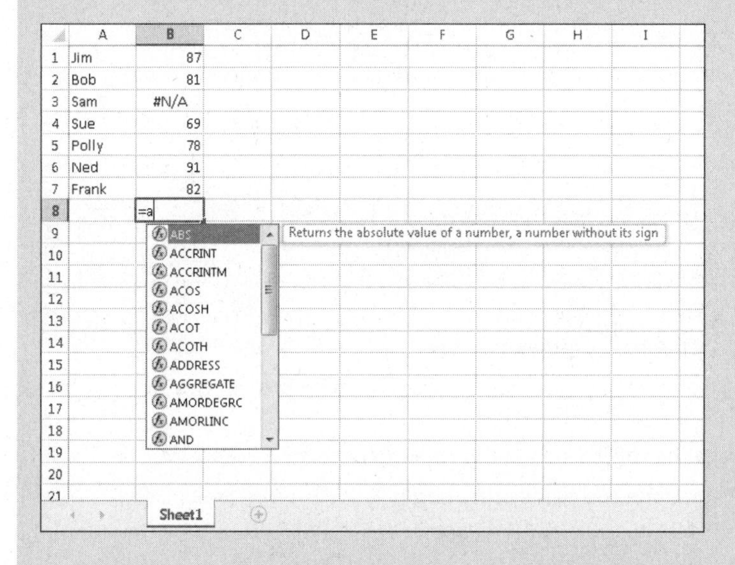

3. **Scroll through the list, or type another letter to narrow down the choices.**
4. **When AGGREGATE is highlighted, press Tab to select it.** Excel adds the opening parenthesis and displays another list that contains options for the first argument for `AGGREGATE`, as shown in the figure.

continued

continued

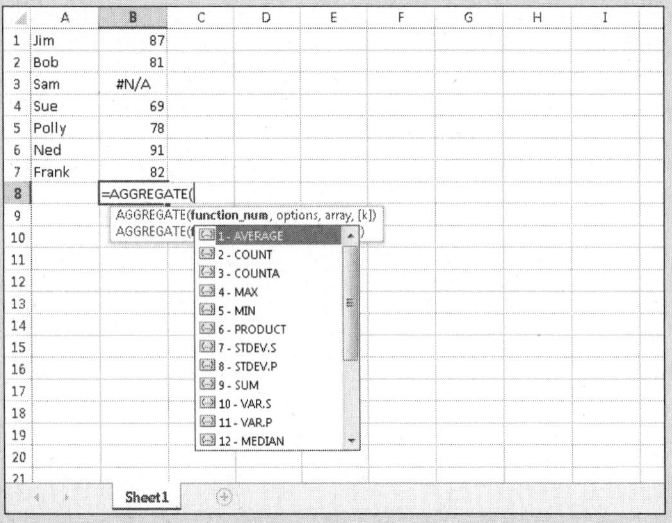

	A	B	C	D	E	F	G	H	I
1	Jim	87							
2	Bob	81							
3	Sam	#N/A							
4	Sue	69							
5	Polly	78							
6	Ned	91							
7	Frank	82							
8		=AGGREGATE(							

AGGREGATE(**function_num**, options, array, [k])
AGGREGATE(

1 - AVERAGE
2 - COUNT
3 - COUNTA
4 - MAX
5 - MIN
6 - PRODUCT
7 - STDEV.S
8 - STDEV.P
9 - SUM
10 - VAR.S
11 - VAR.P
12 - MEDIAN

Sheet1

5. **Select** 1 - AVERAGE **and then press Tab.** Excel inserts `1`, which is the code for calculating the average.
6. **Type a comma to separate the next argument.**
7. **When Excel displays a list of items for the** AGGREGATE **function's second argument, select** 2 - Ignore Error Values **and then press Tab.**
8. **Type a comma to separate the third argument (the range of test scores).**
9. **Type a *T* to get a list of functions and names that begin with *T*; you're looking for** TestScores, **so narrow it down a bit by typing the second character, *E*.**
10. **Highlight** TestScores, **and then press Tab.**
11. **Type a closing parenthesis and then press Enter.**

The completed formula is

```
=AGGREGATE(1,2,TestScores)
```

Formula AutoComplete includes the following items (and each type is identified by a separate icon):

- Excel built-in functions
- User-defined functions (functions defined by the user through VBA or other methods)
- Defined names (cells or range named using the Formulas⇨Defined Names⇨Define Name command)
- Enumerated arguments that use a value to represent an option (only a few functions use such arguments, and `AGGREGATE` is one of them)
- Table structure references (used to identify portions of a table)

Excel provides additional assistance when you create formulas by displaying a drop-down list that contains function names and range names. The items displayed in the list are determined by what you've already typed. For example, if you're entering a formula and then type the letters *SU,* you'll see the drop-down list shown in Figure 10.2. If you type an additional letter, the list is shortened to show only the matching functions. To have Excel autocomplete an entry in that list, use the navigation keys to highlight the entry, and then press Tab. Notice that highlighting a function in the list also displays a brief description of the function. See the sidebar "Using Formula AutoComplete" for an example of how this feature works.

FIGURE 10.2

Excel displays a drop-down list when you enter a formula.

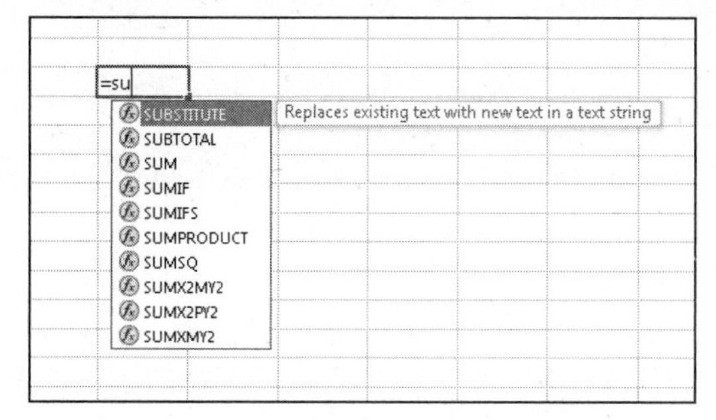

Entering formulas manually

Entering a formula manually involves, well, entering a formula manually. In a selected cell, you simply type an equal sign (=) followed by the formula. As you type, the characters appear in the cell and in the Formula bar. You can, of course, use all the normal editing keys when entering a formula.

Entering formulas by pointing

Even though you can enter formulas by typing in the entire formula, Excel provides another method of entering formulas that is generally easier, faster, and less error prone. This method still involves some manual typing, but you can simply *point* to the cell references instead of typing their values manually. For example, to enter the formula `=A1+A2` into cell A3, follow these steps:

1. **Move the cell pointer to cell A3.**
2. **Type an equal sign (=) to begin the formula.** Notice that Excel displays `Enter` in the status bar (lower left of your screen).

10

3. **Press the up arrow twice.** As you press this key, Excel displays a moving border around cell A1, and the cell reference appears in cell A3 and in the Formula bar. In addition, Excel displays `Point` in the status bar.
4. **Type a plus sign (+).** A solid color border replaces the faint border, and Enter reappears in the status bar.
5. **Press the up arrow again.** The moving border encompasses cell A2 and adds that cell address to the formula.
6. **Press Enter to end the formula.**

New Feature

Excel 2013 color-codes the range addresses and ranges when you're entering or editing a formula. This helps you quickly spot the cells that are used in a formula.

Tip

When creating a formula by pointing, you can also point to the data cells by using your mouse.

Pasting range names into formulas

If your formula uses named cells or ranges, you can either type the name in place of the address, or choose the name from a list and have Excel insert the name for you automatically. Two ways to insert a name into a formula are available:

- **Select the name from the drop-down list.** To use this method, you must know at least the first character of the name. When you're entering the formula, type the first character and then select the name from the drop-down list.
- **Press F3.** The Paste Name dialog box appears. Select the name from the list and then click OK (or just double-click the name). Excel enters the name into your formula. If no names are defined, pressing F3 has no effect.

Figure 10.3 shows an example. The worksheet contains two defined names: `Expenses` and `Sales`. The Paste Name dialog box is being used to insert a name (`Sales`) into the formula being entered in cell B9.

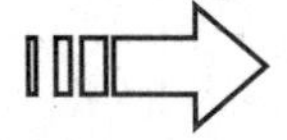

See Chapter 4 for information about creating names for cells and ranges.

FIGURE 10.3

Use the Paste Name dialog box to quickly enter a defined name into a formula.

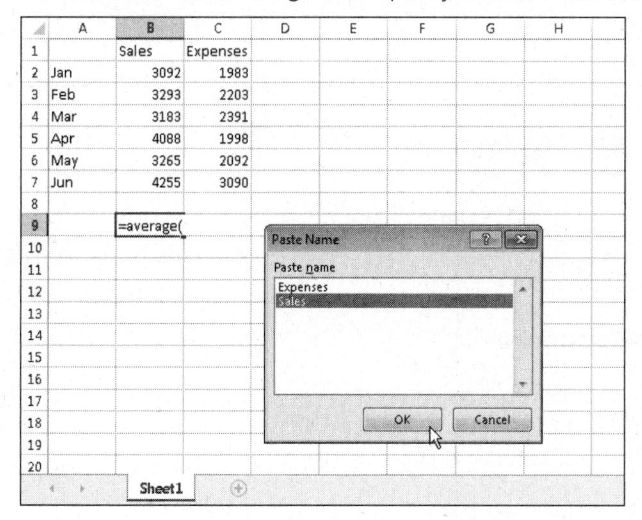

Inserting functions into formulas

The easiest way to enter a function into a formula is to use Formula AutoComplete (the drop-down list that Excel displays while you type a formula). To use this method, however, you must know at least the first character of the function's name.

Another way to insert a function is to use tools in the Function Library group on the Formulas tab on the Ribbon (see Figure 10.4). This method is especially useful if you can't remember which function you need. When entering a formula, click the function category (Financial, Logical, Text, and so on) to get a list of the functions in that category. Click the function you want, and Excel displays its Function Arguments dialog box. This is where you enter the function's arguments. In addition, you can click the Help on This Function link to learn more about the selected function.

FIGURE 10.4

You can insert a function by selecting it from one of the function categories.

Yet another way to insert a function into a formula is to use the Insert Function dialog box (see Figure 10.5). You can access this dialog box in several ways:

FIGURE 10.5

The Insert Function dialog box.

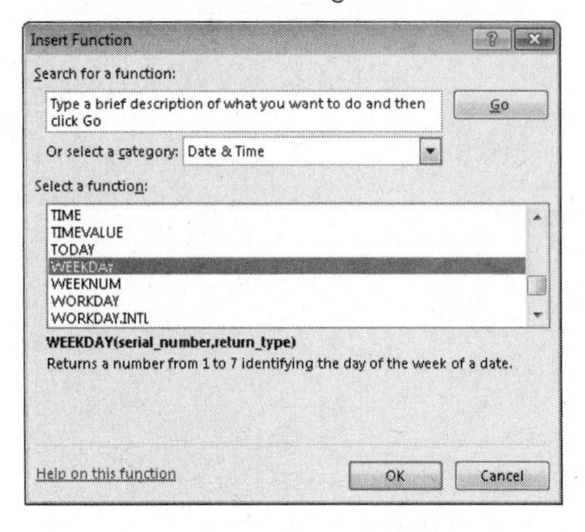

- Choose Formulas ➪ Function Library ➪ Insert Function.
- Use the Insert Function command, which appears at the bottom of each drop-down list in the Formulas ➪ Function Library group.
- Click the Insert Function icon, which is directly to the left of the Formula bar. This button displays *fx*.
- Press Shift + F3.

The Insert Function dialog box shows a drop-down list of function categories. Select a category, and the functions in that category are displayed in the list box. To access a function that you recently used, select Most Recently Used from the drop-down list.

If you're not sure which function you need, you can search for the appropriate function by using the Search for a Function field at the top of the dialog box.

1. **Enter your search terms and click Go.** You get a list of relevant functions. When you select a function from the Select a Function list, Excel displays the function (and its argument names) in the dialog box along with a brief description of what the function does.
2. **When you locate the function you want to use, highlight it and click OK.** Excel then displays its Function Arguments dialog box, as shown in Figure 10.6.

FIGURE 10.6

The Function Arguments dialog box.

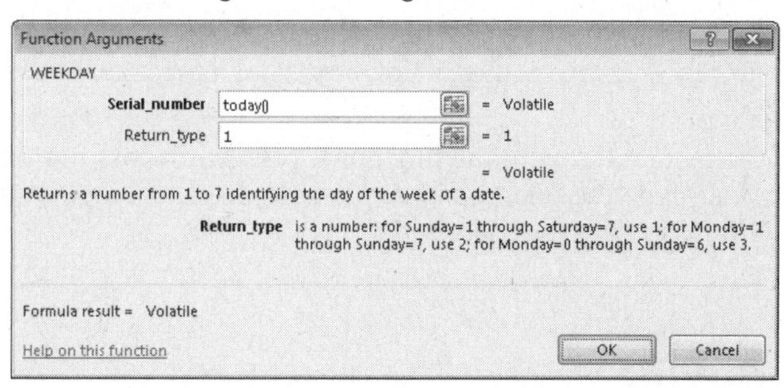

3. **Specify the arguments for the function.** The Function Arguments dialog box will vary, depending on the function you're inserting, and it will show one text box for each of the function's arguments. To use a cell or range reference as an argument, you can enter the address manually or click inside the argument box and then select (that is, point to) the cell or range in the sheet.
4. **After you specify all the function arguments, click OK.**

TIP

Yet another way to insert a function while you're entering a formula is to use the Function List to the left of the Formula bar. When you're entering or editing a formula, the space typically occupied by the Name box displays a list of the functions you've used most recently. After you select a function from this list, Excel displays the Function Arguments dialog box.

Function entry tips

Here are some additional tips to keep in mind when you use the Insert Function dialog box to enter functions:

- You can use the Insert Function dialog box to insert a function into an existing formula. Just edit the formula and move the insertion point to the location at which you want to insert the function. Then open the Insert Function dialog box (using any of the methods described earlier) and select the function.
- You can also use the Function Arguments dialog box to modify the arguments for a function in an existing formula. Click the function in the Formula bar and then click the Insert Function button (the *fx* button, to the left of the Formula bar).
- If you change your mind about entering a function, click the Cancel button.
- The number of boxes you see in the Function Arguments dialog box depends on the number of arguments used in the function you selected. If a function uses no arguments, you won't see any boxes. If the function uses a variable number of arguments (such as the AVERAGE function), Excel adds a new box every time you enter an optional argument.

- As you provide arguments in the Function Argument dialog box, the value of each argument is displayed to the right of each box.
- A few functions, such as `INDEX`, have more than one form. If you choose such a function, Excel displays another dialog box that lets you choose which form you want to use.
- As you become familiar with the functions, you can bypass the Insert Function dialog box and type the function name directly. Excel prompts you with argument names as you enter the function.

Editing Formulas

After you enter a formula, you can (of course) edit that formula. You may need to edit a formula if you make some changes to your worksheet and then have to adjust the formula to accommodate the changes. Or the formula may return an error value, in which case you need to edit the formula to correct the error.

Here are some of the ways to get into cell edit mode:

- Double-click the cell, which enables you to edit the cell contents directly in the cell.
- Press F2, which enables you to edit the cell contents directly in the cell.
- Select the cell that you want to edit, and then click in the Formula bar. This enables you to edit the cell contents in the Formula bar.
- If the cell contains a formula that returns an error, Excel will display a small triangle in the upper-left corner of the cell. Activate the cell, and you'll see a Smart Tag. Click the Smart Tag, and you can choose one of the options for correcting the error. (The options will vary according to the type of error in the cell.)

Tip

You can control whether Excel displays these formula-error-checking Smart Tags in the Formulas section of the Excel Options dialog box. To display this dialog box, choose File ➪ Options. If you remove the check mark from Enable Background Error Checking, Excel no longer displays these Smart Tags.

While you're editing a formula, you can select multiple characters either by dragging the mouse cursor over them or by pressing Shift while you use the navigation keys.

Tip

If you have a formula that you can't seem to edit correctly, you can convert the formula to text and tackle it again later. To convert a formula to text, just remove the initial equal sign (=). When you're ready to try again, type the initial equal sign to convert the cell contents back to a formula.

Using Cell References in Formulas

Most formulas you create include references to cells or ranges. These references enable your formulas to work dynamically with the data contained in those cells or ranges. For example, if your formula refers to cell A1 and you change the value contained in A1, the formula result changes to reflect the new value. If you didn't use references in your formulas, you would need to edit the formulas themselves in order to change the values used in the formulas.

Using relative, absolute, and mixed references

When you use a cell (or range) reference in a formula, you can use three types of references:

- **Relative:** The row and column references can change when you copy the formula to another cell because the references are actually offsets from the current row and column. By default, Excel creates relative cell references in formulas.
- **Absolute:** The row and column references don't change when you copy the formula because the reference is to an actual cell address. An absolute reference uses two dollar signs in its address: one for the column letter and one for the row number (for example, $A$5).
- **Mixed:** Either the row or column reference is relative, and the other is absolute. Only one of the address parts is absolute (for example, $A4 or A$4).

The type of cell reference is important only if you plan to copy the formula to other cells. The following examples illustrate this point.

Figure 10.7 shows a simple worksheet. The formula in cell D2, which multiplies the quantity by the price, is

```
=B2*C2
```

FIGURE 10.7

Copying a formula that contains relative references.

	A	B	C	D	E
1	Item	Quantity	Price	Total	
2	Chair	4	$125.00	$500.00	
3	Desk	4	$695.00	$2,780.00	
4	Lamp	3	$39.95	$119.85	
5					
6					
7					

Sheet1 S ...

10

This formula uses relative cell references. Therefore, when the formula is copied to the cells below it, the references adjust in a relative manner. For example, the formula in cell D3 is

```
=B3*C3
```

But what if the cell references in D2 contained absolute references, like this?

```
=$B$2*$C$2
```

In this case, copying the formula to the cells below would produce incorrect results. The formula in cell D3 would be exactly the same as the formula in cell D2.

Now I'll extend the example to calculate sales tax, which is stored in cell B7 (see Figure 10.8). In this situation, the formula in cell D2 is

```
=(B2*C2)*$B$7
```

FIGURE 10.8

Formula references to the sales tax cell should be absolute.

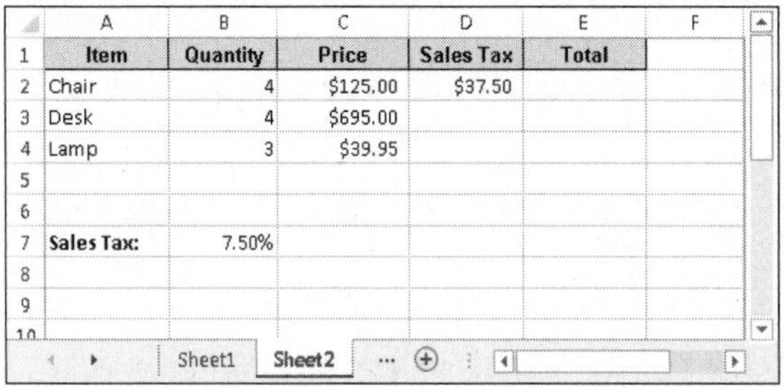

	A	B	C	D	E	F
1	Item	Quantity	Price	Sales Tax	Total	
2	Chair	4	$125.00	$37.50		
3	Desk	4	$695.00			
4	Lamp	3	$39.95			
5						
6						
7	Sales Tax:	7.50%				
8						
9						
10						

Sheet1 Sheet2

The quantity is multiplied by the price, and the result is multiplied by the sales tax rate stored in cell B7. Notice that the reference to B7 is an absolute reference. When the formula in D2 is copied to the cells below it, cell D3 will contain this formula:

```
=(B3*C3)*$B$7
```

Here, the references to cells B2 and C2 were adjusted, but the reference to cell B7 was not — which is exactly what I want because the address of the cell that contains the sales tax never changes.

Figure 10.9 demonstrates the use of mixed references. The formulas in the C3:F7 range calculate the area for various lengths and widths. The formula in cell C3 is

```
=$B3*C$2
```

FIGURE 10.9

Using mixed cell references.

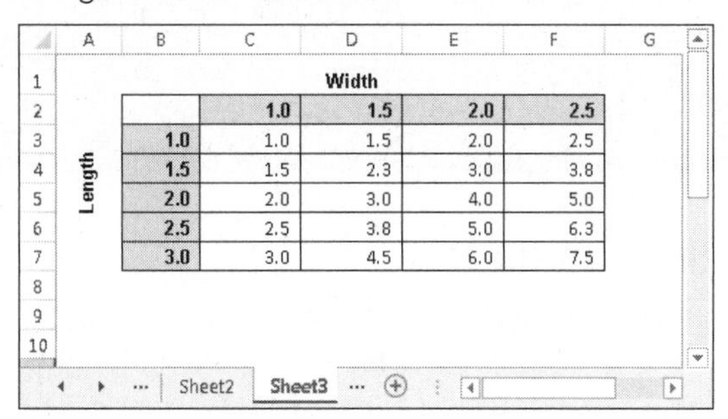

		Width		
Length	1.0	1.5	2.0	2.5
1.0	1.0	1.5	2.0	2.5
1.5	1.5	2.3	3.0	3.8
2.0	2.0	3.0	4.0	5.0
2.5	2.5	3.8	5.0	6.3
3.0	3.0	4.5	6.0	7.5

Notice that both cell references are mixed. The reference to cell B3 uses an absolute reference for the column ($B), and the reference to cell C2 uses an absolute reference for the row ($2). As a result, this formula can be copied down and across, and the calculations will be correct. For example, the formula in cell F7 is

```
=$B7*F$2
```

If C3 used either absolute or relative references, copying the formula would produce incorrect results.

On the Web

A workbook that demonstrates the various types of references is available on this book's website. The file is named `cell references.xlsx`.

Note

When you cut and paste a formula (move it to another location), the cell references in the formula aren't adjusted. Again, this is usually what you want to happen. When you move a formula, you generally want it to continue to refer to the original cells.

Changing the types of your references

You can enter *nonrelative* references (that is, absolute or mixed) manually by inserting dollar signs in the appropriate positions of the cell address. Or you can use a handy shortcut: the F4 key. When you've entered a cell reference (by typing it or by pointing), you can press F4 repeatedly to have Excel cycle through all four reference types.

For example, if you enter **=A1** to start a formula, pressing F4 converts the cell reference to `=$A$1`. Pressing F4 again converts it to `=A$1`. Pressing it again displays `=$A1`. Pressing it one more time returns to the original `=A1`. Keep pressing F4 until Excel displays the type of reference that you want.

NOTE

When you name a cell or range, Excel (by default) uses an absolute reference for the name. For example, if you give the name `SalesForecast` to B1:B12, the Refers To box in the New Name dialog box lists the reference as `$B$1:$B$12`. This is almost always what you want. If you copy a cell that has a named reference in its formula, the copied formula contains a reference to the original name.

Referencing cells outside the worksheet

Formulas can also refer to cells in other worksheets — and the worksheets don't even have to be in the same workbook. Excel uses a special type of notation to handle these types of references.

Referencing cells in other worksheets

To use a reference to a cell in another worksheet in the same workbook, use this format:

```
SheetName!CellAddress
```

In other words, precede the cell address with the worksheet name, followed by an exclamation point. Here's an example of a formula that uses a cell on the `Sheet2` worksheet:

```
=A1*Sheet2!A1
```

This formula multiplies the value in cell A1 on the current worksheet by the value in cell A1 on `Sheet2`.

TIP

If the worksheet name in the reference includes one or more spaces, you must enclose it in single quotation marks. (Excel does that automatically if you use the point-and-click method when creating the formula.) For example, here's a formula that refers to a cell on a sheet named `All Depts`:

```
=A1*'All Depts'! A1
```

Referencing cells in other workbooks

To refer to a cell in a different workbook, use this format:

```
=[WorkbookName]SheetName!CellAddress
```

In this case, the workbook name (in square brackets), the worksheet name, and an exclamation point precede the cell address. The following is an example of a formula that uses a cell reference in the `Sheet1` worksheet in a workbook named `Budget`:

```
=[Budget.xlsx]Sheet1!A1
```

If the workbook name in the reference includes one or more spaces, you must enclose it (and the sheet name) in single quotation marks. For example, here's a formula that refers to a cell on `Sheet1` in a workbook named `Budget For 2013`:

```
=A1*'[Budget For 2013.xlsx]Sheet1'!A1
```

When a formula refers to cells in a different workbook, the other workbook doesn't have to be open. If the workbook is closed, however, you must add the complete path to the reference so that Excel can find it. Here's an example:

```
=A1*'C:\My Documents\[Budget For 2013.xlsx]Sheet1'!A1
```

A linked file can also reside on another system that's accessible on your corporate network. The following formula refers to a cell in a workbook in the `files` directory of a computer named `DataServer`.

```
='\\DataServer\files\[budget.xlsx]Sheet1'!$D$7
```

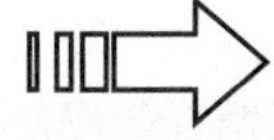

See Chapter 28 for more information about linking workbooks.

> **TIP**
> To create formulas that refer to cells in a different worksheet, point to the cells rather than enter their references manually. Excel takes care of the details regarding the workbook and worksheet references. The workbook you're referencing in your formula must be open if you're going to use the pointing method.

> **NOTE**
> If you point to a different worksheet or workbook when creating a formula, you'll notice that Excel always inserts absolute cell references. Therefore, if you plan to copy the formula to other cells, make sure that you change the cell references to relative before you copy.

Using Formulas in Tables

A table is a specially designated range of cells, set up with column headers. In this section, I describe how formulas work with tables.

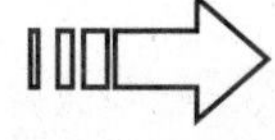

See Chapter 5 for an introduction to the Excel table features.

10

Summarizing data in a table

Figure 10.10 shows a simple table with three columns. I entered the data and then converted the range to a table by choosing Insert⇨Tables⇨Table. Note that I didn't define any names, but the table is named `Table1` by default.

FIGURE 10.10

A simple table with three columns of information.

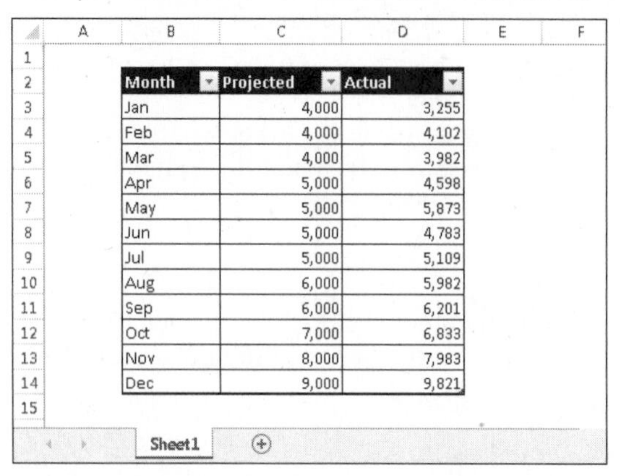

Month	Projected	Actual
Jan	4,000	3,255
Feb	4,000	4,102
Mar	4,000	3,982
Apr	5,000	4,598
May	5,000	5,873
Jun	5,000	4,783
Jul	5,000	5,109
Aug	6,000	5,982
Sep	6,000	6,201
Oct	7,000	6,833
Nov	8,000	7,983
Dec	9,000	9,821

On the Web

This workbook is available on this book's website. It is named `table formulas.xlsx`.

If you'd like to calculate the total projected and total actual sales, you don't even need to write a formula. Simply click a button to add a row of summary formulas to the table:

1. **Activate any cell in the table.**
2. **Place a check mark next to Table Tools ➪ Design ➪ Table Style Options ➪ Total Row.**
3. **Activate a cell in the Total Row and use the drop-down list to select the type of summary formula to use (see Figure 10.11).** For example, to calculate the sum of the Actual column, select `SUM` from the drop-down list in cell D15. Excel creates this formula:

   ```
   =SUBTOTAL(109,[Actual])
   ```

For the `SUBTOTAL` function, `109` is an enumerated argument that represents `SUM`. The second argument for the `SUBTOTAL` function is the column name, in square brackets. Using the column name within brackets creates "structured" references within a table. (I discuss this further in the upcoming section, "Referencing data in a table.")

Note

You can toggle the Total Row display via Table Tools ➪ Design ➪ Table Style Options ➪ Total Row. If you turn it off, the summary options you selected will be displayed again when you turn it back on.

FIGURE 10.11

A drop-down list enables you to select a summary formula for a table column.

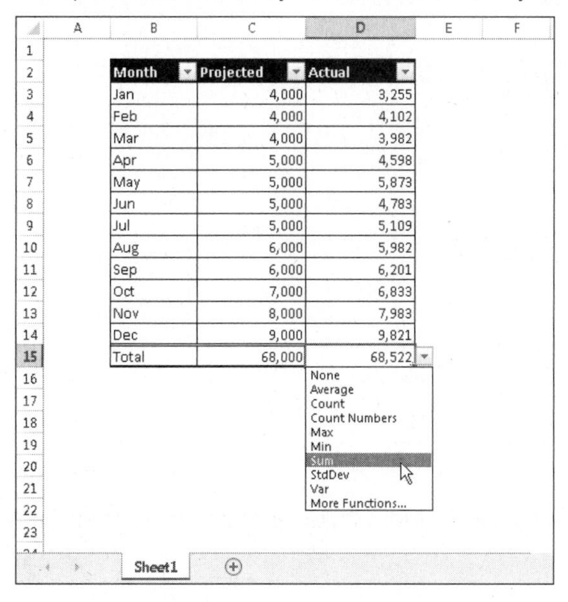

Month	Projected	Actual
Jan	4,000	3,255
Feb	4,000	4,102
Mar	4,000	3,982
Apr	5,000	4,598
May	5,000	5,873
Jun	5,000	4,783
Jul	5,000	5,109
Aug	6,000	5,982
Sep	6,000	6,201
Oct	7,000	6,833
Nov	8,000	7,983
Dec	9,000	9,821
Total	68,000	68,522

Using formulas within a table

In many cases, you'll want to use formulas within a table to perform calculations that use other columns in the table. For example, in the table shown in Figure 10.11, you may want a column that shows the difference between the Actual and Projected amounts. To add this formula:

1. **Activate cell E2 and type** Difference **for the column header.** Excel automatically expands the table for you to include the new column.
2. **Move to cell E3 and type an equal sign to signify the beginning of a formula.**
3. **Press the left arrow key.** Excel displays `[@Actual]`, which is the column heading, in the Formula bar.
4. **Type a minus sign and then press the left arrow key twice.** Excel displays `[@Projected]` in your formula.
5. **Press Enter to end the formula.** Excel copies the formula to all rows in the table.

Figure 10.12 shows the table with the new column.

10

FIGURE 10.12

The Difference column contains a formula.

Month	Projected	Actual	Difference
Jan	4,000	3,255	-745
Feb	4,000	4,102	102
Mar	4,000	3,982	-18
Apr	5,000	4,598	-402
May	5,000	5,873	873
Jun	5,000	4,783	-217
Jul	5,000	5,109	109
Aug	6,000	5,982	-18
Sep	6,000	6,201	201
Oct	7,000	6,833	-167
Nov	8,000	7,983	-17
Dec	9,000	9,821	821
Total	68,000	68,522	

Examine the table, and you find this formula for all cells in the `Difference` column:

```
=[@Actual]-[@Projected]
```

Although the formula was entered into the first row of the table, that's not necessary. Any time a formula is entered into an empty table column, it will automatically fill all the cells in that column. And if you need to edit the formula, Excel will automatically copy the edited formula to the other cells in the column.

NOTE

The at symbol (`@`) that precedes the column header represents "this row." So, `[@Actual]` means "the value in the Actual column in this row."

These steps use the pointing technique to create the formula. Alternatively, you could have entered the formula manually using standard cell references rather than column headers. For example, you could have entered the following formula in cell E3:

```
=D3-C3
```

If you type the cell references, Excel will still copy the formula to the other cells automatically.

One thing should be clear, however, about formulas that use the column headers instead of cell references: They're much easier to understand.

TIP

When you add a formula to a column in a table, Excel displays a Smart Tag. To override the automatic column formulas, click the Smart Tag and choose Stop Automatically Creating Calculated Columns. Use this option if you need different formulas for different rows within the table.

Referencing data in a table

Excel offers some other ways to refer to data that's contained in a table by using the table name and column headers.

> **NOTE**
>
> Remember that you don't need to create names for tables and columns. The data in the table itself has a range name, which is created automatically when you create the table (for example, `Table1`), and you can refer to data within the table by using the column headers — which are *not* range names.

You can, of course, use standard cell references to refer to data in a table, but using the table name and column headers has a distinct advantage: The names adjust automatically if the table size changes by adding or deleting rows. In addition, formulas that use table names and column headers will adjust automatically if you change the name of the table or give a new name to a column.

Refer to the table shown in Figure 10.11. This table is named `Table1`. To calculate the sum of all the data in the table, enter this formula into a cell outside the table:

```
=SUM(Table1)
```

This formula will always return the sum of all the data (excluding calculated Total Row values, if any), even if rows or columns are added or deleted. And if you change the name of `Table1`, Excel will adjust formulas that refer to that table automatically. For example, if you renamed `Table1` to `AnnualData` (by using the Name Manager, or by choosing Table Tools ➪ Design ➪ Properties ➪ Table Name), the preceding formula would change to

```
=SUM(AnnualData)
```

Most of the time, a formula will refer to a specific column in the table. The following formula returns the sum of the data in the `Actual` column:

```
=SUM(Table1[Actual])
```

Notice that the column name is enclosed in square brackets. Again, the formula adjusts automatically if you change the text in the column heading.

Even better, Excel provides some helpful assistance when you create a formula that refers to data within a table. Figure 10.13 shows the formula AutoComplete helping to create a formula by showing a list of the elements in the table. Notice that, in addition to the column headers in the table, Excel lists other table elements that you can reference: `#All`, `#Data`, `#Headers`, `#Totals`, and `@ - This Row`.

FIGURE 10.13

The formula AutoComplete feature is useful when creating a formula that refers to data in a table.

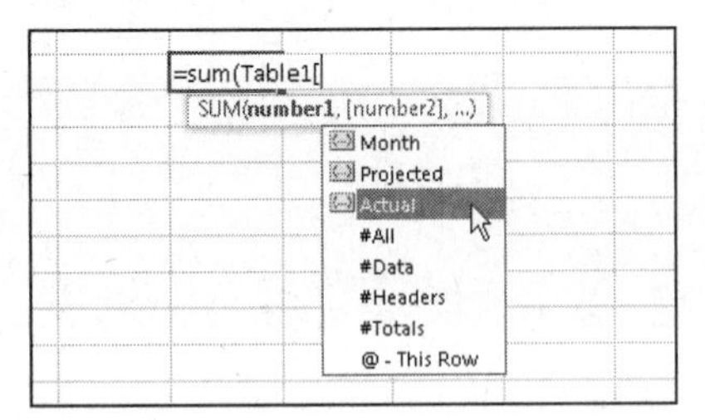

Correcting Common Formula Errors

Sometimes, when you enter a formula, Excel displays a value that begins with a hash mark (#). This is a signal that the formula is returning an error value. You have to correct the formula (or correct a cell that the formula references) to get rid of the error display.

TIP

If the entire cell is filled with hash-mark characters, the column isn't wide enough to display the value. You can either widen the column or change the number format of the cell.

In some cases, Excel won't even let you enter an erroneous formula. For example, the following formula is missing the closing parenthesis:

```
=A1*(B1+C2
```

If you attempt to enter this formula, Excel informs you that you have unmatched parentheses, and it proposes a correction. Often, the proposed correction is accurate, but you can't count on it.

Table 10.3 lists the types of error values that may appear in a cell that has a formula. Formulas may return an error value if a cell to which they refer has an error value. This is known as the *ripple effect* — a single error value can make its way into lots of other cells that contain formulas that depend on that one cell.

TABLE 10.3 Excel Error Values

Error Value	Explanation
#DIV/0!	The formula is trying to divide by zero. This also occurs when the formula attempts to divide by what's in a cell that is empty (that is, by nothing).
#NAME?	The formula uses a name that Excel doesn't recognize. This can happen if you delete a name that's used in the formula or if you have unmatched quotes when using text.

Error Value	Explanation
#N/A	The formula is referring (directly or indirectly) to a cell that uses the NA function to signal that data is not available. Some functions (for example, VLOOKUP) can also return #N/A.
#NULL!	The formula uses an intersection of two ranges that don't intersect. (This concept is described later in the chapter.)
#NUM!	A problem with a value exists; for example, you specified a negative number where a positive number is expected.
#REF!	The formula refers to a cell that isn't valid. This can happen if the cell has been deleted from the worksheet.
#VALUE!	The formula includes an argument or operand of the wrong type. (An *operand* is a value or cell reference that a formula uses to calculate a result.)

Handling circular references

When you're entering formulas, you may occasionally see a warning message like the one shown in Figure 10.14, indicating that the formula you just entered will result in a *circular reference*. A circular reference occurs when a formula refers to its own value — either directly or indirectly. For example, you create a circular reference if you enter **=A1+A2+A3** into cell A3 because the formula in cell A3 refers to cell A3. Every time the formula in A3 is calculated, it must be calculated again because A3 has changed. The calculation could go on forever.

FIGURE 10.14

If you see this warning, you know that the formula you entered will result in a circular reference.

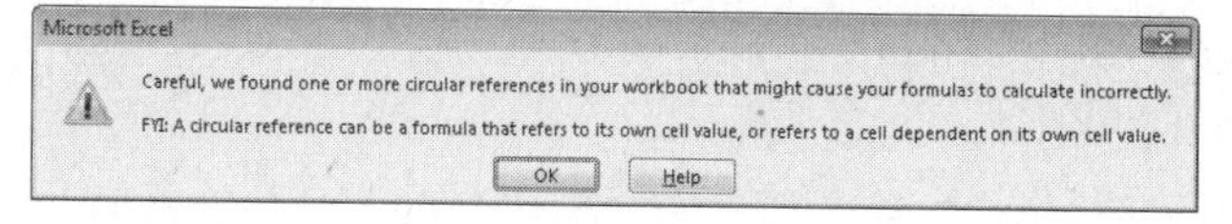

When you get the circular reference message after entering a formula, Excel gives you two options:

- Click OK, and Excel displays a Help screen that tells you more about circular references.
- Click Cancel to enter the formula as is.

Regardless of which option you choose, Excel displays a message in the left side of the status bar to remind you that a circular reference exists.

10

CAUTION

Excel won't tell you about a circular reference if the Enable Iterative Calculation setting is in effect. You can check this setting in the Formulas section of the Excel Options dialog box. If Enable Iterative Calculation is turned on, Excel performs the circular calculation exactly the number of times specified in the Maximum Iterations field (or until the value changes by less than 0.001 or whatever value is in the Maximum Change field). In a few situations, you may use a circular reference intentionally. In these cases, the Enable Iterative Calculation setting must be on. However, it's best to keep this setting turned off so that you're warned of circular references. Usually, a circular reference indicates an error that you must correct.

Often, a circular reference is quite obvious and easy to identify and correct. But when a circular reference is indirect (as when a formula refers to another formula that refers to yet another formula that refers back to the original formula), it may require a bit of detective work to get to the problem.

Specifying when formulas are calculated

You've probably noticed that Excel calculates the formulas in your worksheet immediately. If you change any cells that the formula uses, Excel displays the formula's new result with no effort on your part. All this happens when Excel's Calculation mode is set to Automatic. In Automatic Calculation mode (which is the default mode), Excel follows these rules when it calculates your worksheet:

- When you make a change — enter or edit data or formulas, for example — Excel calculates immediately those formulas that depend on new or edited data.
- If Excel is in the middle of a lengthy calculation, it temporarily suspends the calculation when you need to perform other worksheet tasks; it resumes calculating when you're finished with your other worksheet tasks.
- Formulas are evaluated in a natural sequence. In other words, if a formula in cell D12 depends on the result of a formula in cell D11, Excel calculates cell D11 before calculating cell D12.

Sometimes, however, you may want to control when Excel calculates formulas. For example, if you create a worksheet with thousands of complex formulas, you'll find that processing can slow to a snail's pace while Excel does its thing. In such a case, set Excel's calculation mode to Manual — which you can do by choosing Formulas ⇨ Calculation ⇨ Calculation Options ⇨ Manual (see Figure 10.15).

TIP

If your worksheet uses any data tables, you may want to select the Automatically Except for Data Tables option. Large data tables calculate notoriously slowly. ***Note:*** A data table is not the same as a table created by choosing Insert ⇨ Tables ⇨ Table.

FIGURE 10.15

You can control when Excel calculates formulas.

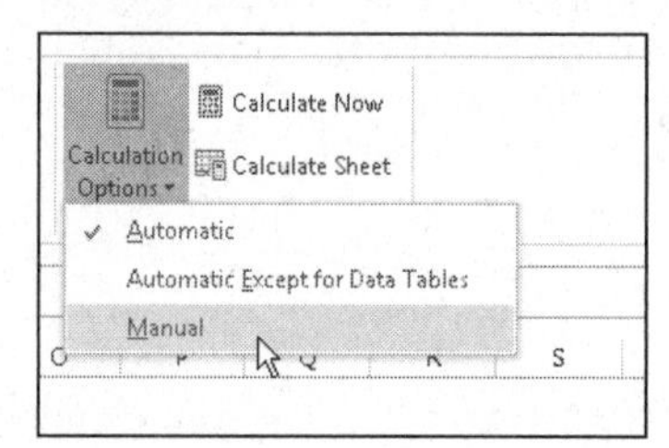

See Chapter 35 for more on data tables.

When you're working in Manual Calculation mode, Excel displays `Calculate` in the status bar when you have any uncalculated formulas. You can use the following shortcut keys to recalculate the formulas:

- **F9:** Calculates the formulas in all open workbooks.
- **Shift + F9:** Calculates only the formulas in the active worksheet. Other worksheets in the same workbook aren't calculated.
- **Ctrl + Alt + F9:** Forces a complete recalculation of all formulas.

NOTE

Excel's Calculation mode isn't specific to a particular worksheet. When you change the Calculation mode, it affects all open workbooks, not just the active workbook.

Using Advanced Naming Techniques

Using range names can make your formulas easier to understand and modify and even help prevent errors. Dealing with a meaningful name such as `AnnualSales` is much easier than dealing with a range reference, such as AB12:AB68.

See Chapter 4 for basic information regarding working with names.

Excel offers a number of advanced techniques that make using names even more useful. I discuss these techniques in the sections that follow. This information is for those who are interested in exploring some of the aspects of Excel that most users don't even know about.

Using names for constants

Many Excel users don't realize that you can give a name to an item that doesn't appear in a cell. For example, if formulas in your worksheet use a sales tax rate, you would probably insert the tax rate value into a cell and use this cell reference in your formulas. To make things easier, you would probably also name this cell something similar to `SalesTax`.

Here's how to provide a name for a value that doesn't appear in a cell:

1. **Choose Formulas⇨Defined Names⇨Define Name.** The New Name dialog box appears.
2. **Enter the name (in this case,** SalesTax**) into the Name field.**
3. **Select a scope in which the name will be valid (either the entire workbook or a specific worksheet).**
4. **Click the Refers To text box, delete its contents, and replace the old contents with a value (such as** .075**).**
5. **(Optional) Use the Comment box to provide a comment about the name.**
6. **Click OK to close the New Name dialog box and create the name.**

You just created a name that refers to a constant rather than a cell or range. Now if you type **=SalesTax** into a cell that's within the scope of the name, this simple formula returns `0.075` — the constant that you defined. You can also use this constant in a formula, such as `=A1*SalesTax`.

Tip

A constant also can be text. For example, you can define a constant for your company's name.

Note

Named constants don't appear in the Name box or in the Go To dialog box. This makes sense because these constants don't reside anywhere tangible. They do appear in the drop-down list that's displayed when you enter a formula — which is handy because you use these names in formulas.

Using names for formulas

In addition to creating named constants, you can also create named formulas. Like named constants, named formulas don't appear in the worksheet.

You create named formulas the same way you create named constants — by using the New Name dialog box. For example, you might create a named formula that calculates the monthly interest rate from an annual rate; Figure 10.16 shows an example. In this case, the name `MonthlyRate` refers to the following formula:

```
=Sheet3!$B$1/12
```

FIGURE 10.16

Excel allows you to name a formula that doesn't exist in a worksheet cell.

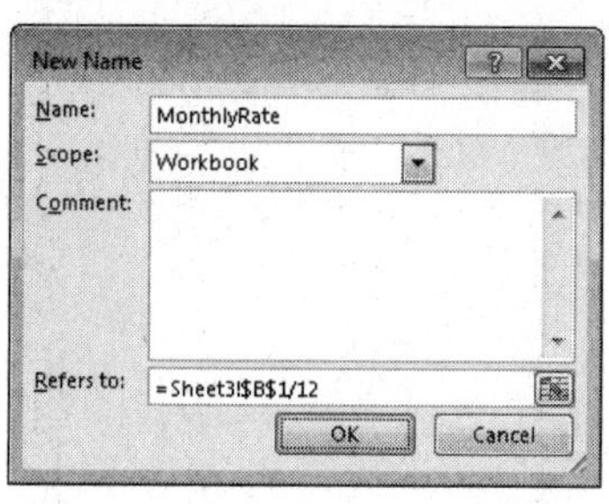

When you use the name `MonthlyRate` in a formula, it uses the value in B1 divided by 12. Notice that the cell reference is an absolute reference.

Naming formulas gets more interesting when you use relative references rather than absolute references. When you use the pointing technique to create a formula in the Refers To field of the New Name dialog box, Excel always uses absolute cell references — which is unlike its behavior when you create a formula in a cell.

For example, activate cell B1 on `Sheet1` and create the name Cubed for the following formula:

```
=Sheet1!A1^3
```

In this example, the relative reference points to the cell to the left of the cell in which the name is used. Therefore, make certain that cell B1 is the active cell *before* you open the New Name dialog box; this is very important. The formula contains a relative reference; when you use this named formula in a worksheet, the cell reference is always relative to the cell that contains the formula. For example, if you enter **=Cubed** into cell D12, cell D12 displays the contents of cell C12 raised to the third power (C12 is the cell directly to the left of cell D12).

Using range intersections

This section describes a concept known as *range intersections* (individual cells that two ranges have in common). Excel uses an *intersection operator* — a space character — to determine the overlapping references in two ranges. Figure 10.17 shows a simple example.

The formula in cell B9 is

```
=C1:C6 A3:E3
```

10

FIGURE 10.17

You can use a range intersection formula to determine values.

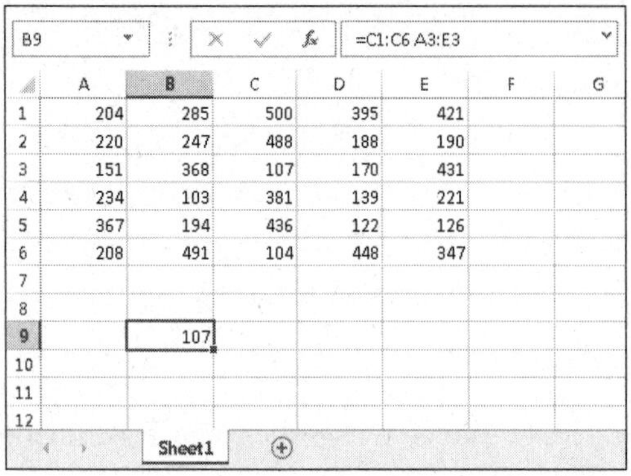

B9 =C1:C6 A3:E3

	A	B	C	D	E	F	G
1	204	285	500	395	421		
2	220	247	488	188	190		
3	151	368	107	170	431		
4	234	103	381	139	221		
5	367	194	436	122	126		
6	208	491	104	448	347		
7							
8							
9		107					
10							
11							
12							

Sheet1

This formula returns `107`, the value in cell C3 — that is, the value at the intersection of the two ranges.

The intersection operator is one of three reference operators used with ranges. Table 10.4 lists these operators.

TABLE 10.4 **Reference Operators for Ranges**

Operator	What It Does
: (colon)	Specifies a range.
, (comma)	Specifies the union of two ranges. This operator combines multiple range references into a single reference.
Space	Specifies the intersection of two ranges. This operator produces cells that are common to two ranges.

The real value of knowing about range intersections is apparent when you use names. Examine Figure 10.18, which shows a table of values. I selected the entire table and then chose Formulas ➪ Defined Names ➪ Create from Selection to create names automatically by using the top row and left column.

FIGURE 10.18

When you use names, using a range intersection formula to determine values is even more useful.

	A	B	C	D	E	F
1		Quarter1	Quarter2	Quarter3	Quarter4	
2	North	93	102	122	131	
3	South	134	130	140	132	
4	East	229	209	248	287	
5	West	67	87	76	77	
6						
7						

Sheet1 Sheet2

Excel created the following names:

```
North    =Sheet1!$B$2:$E$2    Quarter1    =Sheet1!$B$2:$B$5
South    =Sheet1!$B$3:$E$3    Quarter2    =Sheet1!$C$2:$C$5
West     =Sheet1!$B$4:$E$4    Quarter3    =Sheet1!$D$2:$D$5
East     =Sheet1!$B$5:$E$5    Quarter4    =Sheet1!$E$2:$E$5
```

With these names defined, you can create formulas that are easy to read and use. For example, to calculate the total for Quarter 4, just use this formula:

```
=SUM(Quarter4)
```

To refer to a single cell, use the intersection operator. Move to any blank cell and enter the following formula:

```
=Quarter1 West
```

This formula returns the value for the first quarter for the `West` region. In other words, it returns the value that exists where the `Quarter1` range intersects with the `West` range. Naming ranges in this manner can help you create very readable formulas.

Applying names to existing references

When you create a name for a cell or a range, Excel doesn't automatically use the name in place of existing references in your formulas. For example, suppose you have the following formula in cell F10:

```
=A1-A2
```

If you define a name `Income` for A1 and `Expenses` for A2, Excel won't automatically change your formula to `=Income-Expenses`. Replacing cell or range references with their corresponding names is fairly easy, however.

To apply names to cell references in formulas after the fact, start by selecting the range that you want to modify. Then choose Formulas ➪ Defined Names ➪ Define Name ➪ Apply Names. The Apply Names dialog box (shown in Figure 10.19) appears. Select the names that you want to apply by clicking them, and then click OK. Excel replaces the range references with the names in the selected cells.

FIGURE 10.19

Use the Apply Names dialog box to replace cell or range references with defined names.

	A	B	C	D	E
1		Quarter1	Quarter2	Quarter3	Quarter4
2	North	93	102	122	131
3	South	134	130	140	132
4	East	229	209	248	287
5	West	67	87	76	77
6		523	528	586	627

Working with Formulas

In this section, I offer a few additional tips and pointers relevant to formulas.

Not hard-coding values

When you create a formula, think twice before you use any specific value in the formula. For example, if your formula calculates sales tax (which is 6.5%), you may be tempted to enter a formula, such as the following:

```
=A1*.065
```

A better approach is to insert the sales tax rate in a cell — and use the cell reference. Or you can define the tax rate as a named constant, using the technique presented earlier in this chapter. Doing so makes modifying and maintaining your worksheet easier. For example, if the sales tax rate changed to 6.75%, you would have to modify every formula that used the old value. If you store the tax rate in a cell, however, you simply change that one cell, and Excel updates all the formulas.

Using the Formula bar as a calculator

If you need to perform a quick calculation, you can use the Formula bar as a calculator. For example, enter the following formula — but don't press Enter:

```
=(145*1.05)/12
```

If you press Enter, Excel enters the formula into the cell. But because this formula always returns the same result, you may prefer to store the formula's *result* rather than the formula itself. To do so, press F9 and watch the result appear in the Formula bar. Press Enter to store the result in the active cell. (This technique also works if the formula uses cell references or worksheet functions.)

Making an exact copy of a formula

When you copy a formula, Excel adjusts its cell references when you paste the formula to a different location. Sometimes, you may want to make an exact copy of the formula. One way to do this is to convert the cell references to absolute values, but this isn't always desirable. A better approach is to select the formula in Edit mode and then copy it to the Clipboard as text. You can do this in several ways. Here's a step-by-step example of how to make an exact copy of the formula in A1 and copy it to A2:

1. **Double-click A1 (or press F2) to get into Edit mode.**
2. **Drag the mouse to select the entire formula.** You can drag from left to right or from right to left. To select the entire formula with the keyboard, press End, followed by Shift+Home.
3. **Choose Home ➪ Clipboard ➪ Copy (or press Ctrl+C).** This copies the selected text (which will become the copied formula) to the Clipboard.
4. **Press Esc to leave Edit mode.**
5. **Select cell A2.**
6. **Choose Home ➪ Clipboard ➪ Paste (or press Ctrl+V) to paste the text into cell A2.**

You can also use this technique to copy just *part* of a formula, if you want to use that part in another formula. Just select the part of the formula that you want to copy by dragging the mouse, and then use any of the available techniques to copy the selection to the Clipboard. You can then paste the text to another cell.

Formulas (or parts of formulas) copied in this manner won't have their cell references adjusted when they're pasted into a new cell. That's because the formulas are being copied as text, not as actual formulas.

10

TIP

You can also convert a formula to text by adding an apostrophe (') in front of the equal sign. Then copy the formula as usual, and paste it to its new location. Remove the apostrophe from the pasted formula, and it will be identical to the original formula. And don't forget to remove the apostrophe from the original formula as well.

Converting formulas to values

If you have a range of formulas that will always produce the same result (that is, *dead formulas*), you may want to convert them to values. If, say, range A1:A20 contains formulas that have calculated results that will never change — or that you don't want to change. For example, if you use the RANDBETWEEN function to create a set of random numbers and you don't want Excel to recalculate those random numbers each time you press Enter, you can convert the formulas to values. Just follow these steps:

1. **Select A1:A20.**
2. **Choose Home ⇨ Clipboard ⇨ Copy (or press Ctrl + C).**
3. **Choose Home ⇨ Clipboard ⇨ Paste Values (V).**
4. **Press Esc to cancel Copy mode.**

CHAPTER

11

Creating Formulas That Manipulate Text

IN THIS CHAPTER

Seeing how Excel handles text entered into cells

Looking at Excel worksheet functions that handle text

Getting examples of advanced text formulas

Excel is, of course, best known for its ability to crunch numbers. It's also quite versatile, however, with handling text. As you know, you can enter text for such things as row and column headings, customer names and addresses, part numbers, and just about anything else. In addition (as you may expect), you can use formulas to manipulate the text contained in cells.

This chapter contains many examples of formulas that use a variety of functions to manipulate text. Some of these formulas perform feats that you may not have thought possible.

A Few Words about Text

When you enter data into a cell, Excel immediately goes to work and determines whether you're entering a formula, a number (including a date or time), or anything else. That "anything else" is considered text.

NOTE

You may hear the term *string* used instead of *text*. You can use these terms interchangeably. Sometimes they even appear together, as in *text string*.

A single cell can hold up to 32,000 characters — roughly equivalent to the number of characters in this chapter. But Excel is not a word processor, and I can't think of a reason why anyone would need to even come close to that number.

When a Number Isn't Treated as a Number

If you import data into Excel, you may be aware of a common problem: Sometimes the imported values are treated as text.

Depending on your error-checking settings, Excel may display error indicators to identify numbers stored as text. An error indicator appears as a small rectangle in the upper-left corner of the cells. Activate the cell, and click the icon, which expands to show a list of options. To force the number to be treated as an actual number, select Convert to Number from the list of options.

To control which error-checking rules are in effect, choose File ➪ Options, and then select the Formulas tab. You can enable any or all of the nine error types.

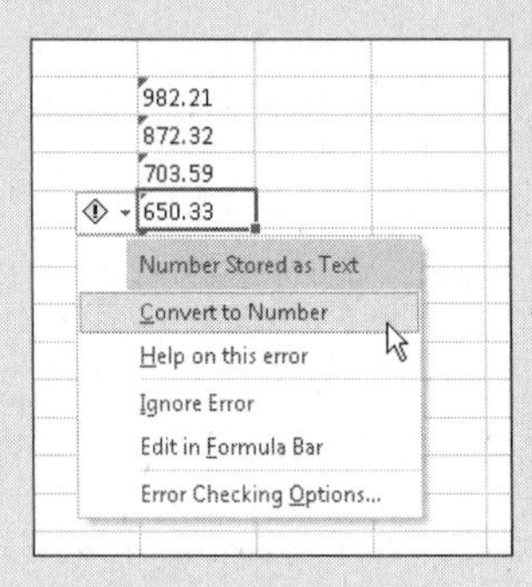

Here's another way to convert these nonnumbers to actual values. Activate any empty cell and choose Home ➪ Clipboard ➪ Copy (or press Ctrl+C). Then select the range that contains the values you need to fix. Choose Home ➪ Clipboard ➪ Paste Special. In the Paste Special dialog box, select the Add operation and then click OK. This procedure essentially adds zero to each cell — and, in the process, forces Excel to treat the nonnumbers as actual values.

If you need to display lots of text in a worksheet, consider using a text box. Choose Insert ➪ Text ➪ Text Box, click the worksheet to create the text box, and then start typing. Working with large amounts of text in a text box is easier than editing cells. In addition, you can easily move, resize, or change the dimensions of a text box. However, if you need to work with the text using formulas and functions, the text must reside in cells.

Text Functions

Excel has an excellent assortment of worksheet functions that can handle text. You can access these functions just where you'd expect: from the Text control in the Function Library group of the Formulas tab.

A few other functions that are relevant to text manipulation appear in other function categories.

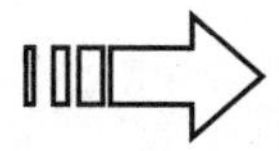

See Appendix A for a listing of the functions in the Text category. Or you can peruse these functions in the Insert Function dialog box. Activate an empty cell, and choose Formulas ➪ Function Library ➪ Insert Function. In the Insert Function dialog box, select the Text category and scroll through the list. To find out more about a particular function, click the Help on This Function link.

Many of the text functions are not limited to text: They can also operate with cells that contain numeric values. You'll find that Excel is very accommodating when it comes to treating numbers as text.

The examples discussed in this section demonstrate some common (and useful) things you can do with text. You may need to adapt some of these examples for your own use.

Working with character codes

Every character you see on your screen has an associated code number. For Windows systems, Excel uses the standard ANSI character set. The ANSI character set consists of 255 characters, numbered (not surprisingly) from 1 through 255. An ANSI character requires one byte of storage. Excel also supports an extended character set known as Unicode, in which each character requires two bytes of storage.

Figure 11.1 shows an Excel worksheet that displays all the 255 ANSI characters. This example uses the Wingdings 3 font. (Other fonts may have different characters.)

FIGURE 11.1

The ANSI character set (for the Wingdings 3 font).

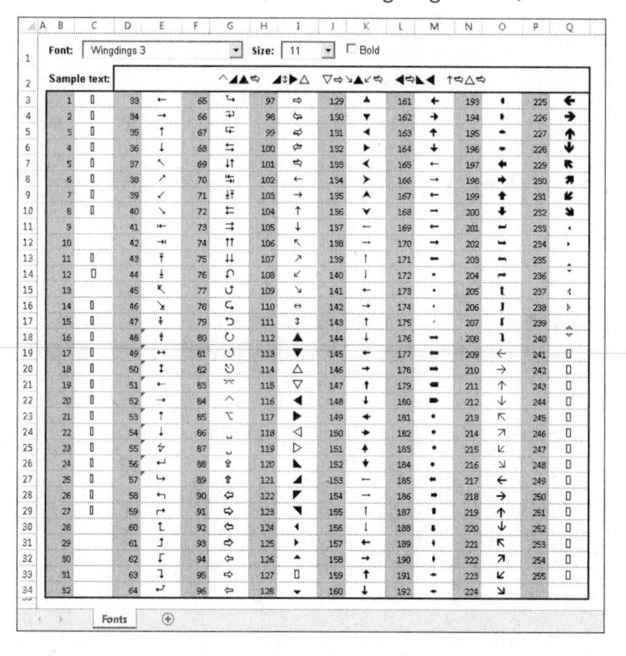

On the Web

This book's website includes a copy of this workbook, which also includes some simple VBA macros that enable you to display the character set for any font installed on your system. The file is named `character set.xlsm`.

Two functions come into play when dealing with character codes: `CODE` and `CHAR`. These functions may not be very useful by themselves, but they can prove quite useful in conjunction with other functions. I discuss these functions in the following sections.

New Feature

Excel 2013 introduces two new functions that are similar to `CODE` and `CHAR`, but work with Unicode characters. The new functions are `UNICODE` and `UNICHAR`.

The CODE function

The Excel `CODE` function returns the character code for its argument. The formula that follows returns `65`, the character code for uppercase *A:*

```
=CODE("A")
```

If the argument for `CODE` consists of more than one character, the function uses only the first character. Therefore, this formula also returns `65`:

```
=CODE("Abbey Road")
```

The CHAR function

The `CHAR` function is essentially the opposite of the `CODE` function. Its argument should be a value between 1 and 255, and the function returns the corresponding character. The following formula, for example, returns the letter *A:*

```
=CHAR(65)
```

To demonstrate the opposing nature of the `CODE` and `CHAR` functions, try entering this formula:

```
=CHAR(CODE("A"))
```

This formula, which is illustrative rather than useful, returns the letter *A*. First, it converts the character to its code value (`65`), and then it converts this code back to the corresponding character.

Assume that cell A1 contains the letter *A* (uppercase). The following formula returns the letter *a* (lowercase):

```
=CHAR(CODE(A1)+32)
```

Inserting Special Characters

If you need to insert special characters not found on your keyboard, you can use the Symbol dialog box (choose Insert ⇨ Symbols ⇨ Symbol). This dialog box simplifies inserting special characters (including Unicode characters) into cells. For example, you may want to display the Greek letter *pi* (π) in your worksheet. From the Symbol dialog box, select the Symbol font (see the accompanying figure). Examine the characters, locate the pi character, and click Insert. You'll see (in the Character Code area of the Symbol dialog box) that this character has a numerical code of 112.

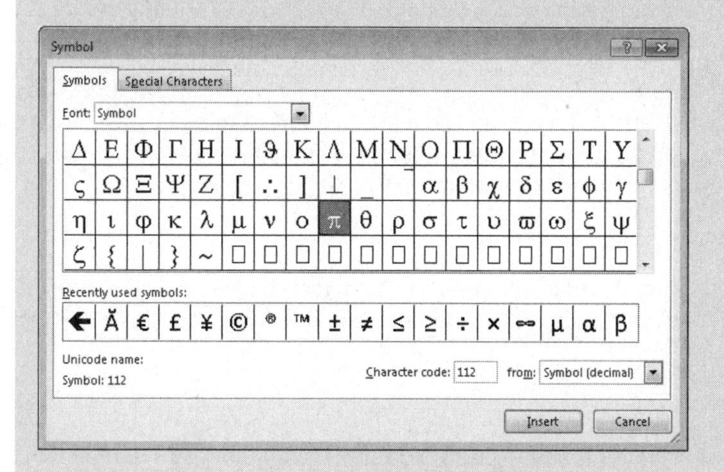

In addition, Excel has several built-in AutoCorrect symbols. For example, if you type **(c)** followed by a space or the Enter key, Excel converts it to a copyright symbol (©).

To see the other symbols that you can enter this way, display the AutoCorrect dialog box. To display this dialog box, choose File ⇨ Options and select the Proofing tab in the Excel Options dialog box. Then click the AutoCorrect Options button. You can then scroll through the list to see which autocorrections are enabled (and delete those that you don't want).

If you find that Excel makes an autocorrection that you don't want, press Ctrl+Z immediately to undo the autocorrection.

This formula takes advantage of the fact that the alphabetic characters all appear in alphabetical order within the character set; lowercase letters follow uppercase letters (with a few other characters tossed in between). Each lowercase letter is exactly 32 character positions higher than its corresponding uppercase letter.

Determining whether two strings are identical

You can create a simple logical formula to determine whether two cells contain the same entry. For example, use this formula to determine whether cell A1 has the same contents as cell A2:

```
=A1=A2
```

This formula will return either `TRUE` or `FALSE`, depending on the contents of cells A1 and A2. However, Excel is a bit lax in its comparisons when text is involved. Consider the case in which A1 contains the word `January` (initial capitalization), and A2 contains `JANUARY` (all uppercase). You'll find that the previous formula returns `TRUE` even though the contents of the two cells are not really the same — the comparison is not case sensitive.

Often, you don't need to worry about the case of the text. If you need to make an exact, case-sensitive comparison, though, use the `EXACT` function. The following formula returns `TRUE` *only* if cells A1 and A2 contain *exactly* the same entry:

```
=EXACT(A1,A2)
```

When you compare text, be careful with trailing space characters, which are often difficult to identify. The following formula returns `FALSE` because the first string contains a trailing space:

```
=EXACT("Canada ","Canada")
```

When an extra space is at the end of text in a cell, it's impossible to tell that it's there. So, if your text comparison formulas don't seem to be working, a trailing space could be the problem.

Joining two or more cells

Excel uses an ampersand (`&`) as its concatenation operator. *Concatenation* is simply a fancy term that describes what happens when you join the contents of two or more cells. For example, if cell A1 contains the text `Tucson` and cell A2 contains the text `Arizona`, the following formula will return `TucsonArizona`:

```
=A1&A2
```

Notice that the two strings are joined together without an intervening space. To add a space between the two entries (to get `Tucson Arizona`), use a formula like this one:

```
=A1&" "&A2
```

Or, even better, use a comma and a space to produce `Tucson, Arizona`:

```
=A1&", "&A2
```

If you'd like to force the second string to be on a new line, concatenate the strings using `CHAR(10)`, which inserts a line break character. Also, make sure that you apply the Wrap Text format to the cell. The following example joins the text in cell A1 and the text in cell B1, with a line break in between:

```
=A1&CHAR(10)&B1
```

TIP

To apply Wrap Text formatting, select the cells and then choose Home ➪ Alignment ➪ Wrap Text.

You can also concatenate characters returned by the `CHAR` function. The following formula returns the string `Stop` by concatenating four characters returned by the `CHAR` function:

```
=CHAR(83)&CHAR(116)&CHAR(111)&CHAR(112)
```

Here's a final example of using the `&` operator. In this case, the formula combines text with the result of an expression that returns the maximum value in column C:

```
="The largest value in Column C is " & MAX(C:C)
```

NOTE

Excel also has a `CONCATENATE` function, which takes up to 255 arguments. For example:

```
=CONCATENATE(A1,B1,C1,D1)
```

This function simply combines the arguments into a single string. You can use this function if you like, but using the `&` operator results in shorter formulas.

Displaying formatted values as text

The `TEXT` function enables you to display a value in a specific number format. Figure 11.2 shows a simple worksheet. The formula in cell D3 is

```
="The net profit is " & B3
```

FIGURE 11.2

The formula in D3 doesn't display the formatted number.

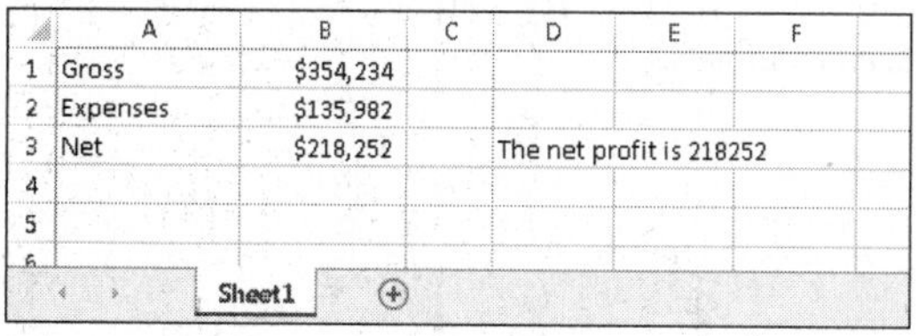

	A	B	C	D	E	F
1	Gross	$354,234				
2	Expenses	$135,982				
3	Net	$218,252		The net profit is 218252		
4						
5						

Sheet1

This formula essentially combines a text string with the contents of cell B3 and displays the result. Note, however, that the formula displays the contents of B3 as a raw value (no formatting). To improve readability, you might want to display the contents of B3 by using a `Currency` number format.

NOTE

Contrary to what you might expect, applying a number format to the cell that contains the formula has no effect. This is because the formula returns a string, not a value. You can, however, use the `TEXT` function to apply formatting. The `TEXT` function supports most (but not all) of Excel's standard custom number formatting strings.

Here's a revised formula that uses the `TEXT` function to apply formatting to the value in B3:

```
="The net profit is " & TEXT(B3," $#,##0")
```

This formula displays the text along with a nicely formatted value:

```
The net profit is $281,252
```

The second argument for the `TEXT` function consists of a standard Excel number format string. You can enter any valid number format code for this argument.

The preceding example uses a simple cell reference (B3). Of course, you can use an expression instead. Here's an example that combines text with a number resulting from a computation:

```
="Average Expenditure: "& TEXT(AVERAGE(A:A),"$#,##0.00")
```

This formula might return a string such as:

```
Average Expenditure: $7,794.57
```

Here's another example that uses the `NOW` function (which returns the current date and time). The `TEXT` function displays the date and time, nicely formatted.

```
="Report printed on "&TEXT(NOW(),"mmmm d, yyyy at h:mm AM/PM")
```

The formula might display the following:

```
Report printed on March 22, 2013 at 3:23 PM
```

See Chapter 25 for details on Excel number formats.

Displaying formatted currency values as text

The Excel DOLLAR function converts a number to text using the currency format. It takes two arguments: the number to convert and the number of decimal places to display. The DOLLAR function uses the regional currency symbol (for example, a dollar sign [$]).

You can sometimes use the DOLLAR function in place of the TEXT function. The TEXT function, however, is much more flexible because it doesn't limit you to a specific number format.

The following formula returns Total: $1,287.37 (the second argument for the DOLLAR function specifies the number of decimal places):

```
="Total: "&DOLLAR(1287.367, 2)
```

NOTE

If you're looking for a function that converts a number into spelled-out text (such as "One hundred twelve and 32/100"), you won't find such a function. Well, Excel does have a BAHTTEXT function, but it converts the number into the Thai language. Why Excel doesn't include an English language version of this function remains a mystery.

Repeating a character or string

The REPT function repeats a text string (first argument) any number of times you specify (second argument). For example, this seasonal formula returns HoHoHo:

```
=REPT("Ho",3)
```

You can also use this function to create crude horizontal dividers between cells. This example displays a squiggly line, 20 characters in length:

```
=REPT("~",20)
```

Creating a text histogram

A clever use for the REPT function is to create a simple *histogram* (or frequency distribution chart) directly in a worksheet. Figure 11.3 shows an example of such a histogram. You'll find this type of graphical display especially useful when you need a visual summary of many values and a standard chart is unwieldy.

The Data Bars conditional formatting feature is a much better way to display a simple histogram directly in cells. (See Chapter 21 for details.)

The formulas in column D graphically depict the sales numbers in column B by displaying a series of characters in the Wingdings 2 font. This example uses character code 162 (a solid rectangle). A formula using the `REPT` function determines the number of characters displayed. The formula in cell D2 is

```
=REPT(CHAR(162),B2/100)
```

FIGURE 11.3

Using the `REPT` function to create a histogram in a worksheet range.

	A	B	C	D	E
1	Month	Units Sold		Chart	
2	January	834			
3	February	1,132			
4	March	1,243			
5	April	1,094			
6	May	902			
7	June	1,543			
8	July	1,654			
9	August	2,123			
10	September	1,566			
11	October	1,434			
12	November	1,321			
13	December	1,654			
14					

Sheet1 Sheet2

Assign the Wingdings font to cell D2, and then copy the formulas down the column to accommodate all the data. Depending on the numerical range of your data, you may need to change the scaling. Experiment by replacing the `100` value in the formulas. You can substitute any character you like for the solid rectangle in the formula to produce a different character in the chart.

ON THE WEB

The workbook shown in Figure 11.3 is available at this book's website. The file is named `text histogram.xlsx`; it also contains another example of this technique.

Padding a number

You're probably familiar with a common security measure (frequently used on printed checks) in which numbers are padded with asterisks on the right. The following formula displays the value in cell A1, along with enough asterisks to make a total of 24 characters:

```
=(A1 & REPT("*",24-LEN(A1)))
```

If you'd prefer to pad the number with asterisks on the left instead, use this formula:

```
=REPT("*",24-LEN(A1))&A1
```

The following formula displays 12 asterisks on both sides of the number:

```
=REPT("*",12)&A1&REPT("*",12)
```

The preceding formulas are a bit deficient because they don't show any number formatting. This revised version displays the value in A1 (formatted), along with the asterisk padding on the right:

```
=(TEXT(A1,"$#,##0.00")&REPT("*",24-LEN(TEXT(A1,"$#,##0.00"))))
```

Figure 11.4 shows this formula in action.

FIGURE 11.4

Using a formula to pad a number with asterisks.

	A	B	C	D
1	$198.34	$198.34*****************		
2	$9.00	$9.00*******************		
3	$0.98	$0.98*******************		
4	$1,098.45	$1,098.45***************		
5	$0.00	$0.00*******************		
6	($129.67)	-$129.67****************		
7				

Sheet1 | Sheet2

You can also pad a number by using a custom number format. To repeat the next character in that format until it fills the column width, include an asterisk (*) in the custom number format code. For example, use this number format to pad the number with dashes:

```
$#,##0.00*-
```

To pad the number with asterisks, use two asterisks in the number format code, like this:

```
$#,##0.00**
```

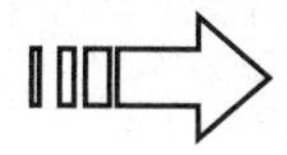

See Chapter 25 for more information about custom number formats, including additional examples using the asterisk format code.

Removing excess spaces and nonprinting characters

Often, data imported into an Excel worksheet contains excess spaces or strange (often unprintable) characters. Excel provides you with two functions to help whip your data into shape: TRIM and CLEAN:

- TRIM removes all leading and trailing spaces and replaces internal strings of multiple spaces with a single space.
- CLEAN removes all nonprinting characters from a string. These "garbage" characters often appear when you import certain types of data.

This example uses the `TRIM` function. The formula returns `Fourth Quarter Earnings` (with no excess spaces):

```
=TRIM("    Fourth     Quarter      Earnings      ")
```

Counting characters in a string

The `LEN` function takes one argument and returns the number of characters in the argument. For example, assume that the string `September Sales` is contained in cell A1. The following formula returns `15`:

```
=LEN(A1)
```

Notice that space characters are included in the character count.

The following formula returns the total number of characters in the range A1:A3:

```
=LEN(A1)+LEN(A2)+LEN(A3)
```

You see example formulas that demonstrate how to count the number of specific characters within a string later in this chapter. Chapter 13 covers counting techniques in greater detail.

Changing the case of text

Excel provides three handy functions to change the case of text:

- `UPPER` converts the text to ALL UPPERCASE.
- `LOWER` converts the text to all lowercase.
- `PROPER` converts the text to Proper Case (the first letter in each word is capitalized, as in a proper name).

These functions are quite straightforward. The formula that follows, for example, converts the text in cell A1 to proper case.

```
=PROPER(A1)
```

If cell A1 contained the text `MR. JOHN Q. PUBLIC`, the formula would return `Mr. John Q. Public`.

These functions operate only on alphabetic characters; they simply ignore all other characters and return them unchanged.

These functions aren't perfect, and they sometimes produce undesired results. For example, this formula returns `Don'T`:

```
=PROPER("don't")
```

Apparently, the `PROPER` function is programmed to always capitalize the letter following an apostrophe. If the argument is `"o'reilly"`, the function works perfectly.

Transforming Data with Formulas

Many of the examples in this chapter describe how to use functions to transform data in some way. For example, you can use the `UPPER` function to transform text into uppercase. Often, you'll want to replace the original data with the transformed data. Specifically, follow these steps:

1. **Insert a new temporary column for formulas to transform the original data.**
2. **Create your formulas in the temporary column.**
3. **Select the formula cells.**
4. **Choose Home⇨Clipboard⇨Copy (or press Ctrl+C).**
5. **Select the original data cells.**
6. **Choose Home⇨Clipboard⇨Paste⇨Values (V).**

This procedure replaces the original data with the transformed data; then you can delete the temporary column that holds the formulas.

Extracting characters from a string

Excel users often need to extract characters from a string. For example, you may have a list of employee names (first and last names) and need to extract the last name from each cell. Excel provides several useful functions for extracting characters:

- `LEFT` returns a specified number of characters from the beginning of a string.
- `RIGHT` returns a specified number of characters from the end of a string.
- `MID` returns a specified number of characters beginning at a specified position within a string.

The following formula returns the last ten characters from cell A1; if A1 contains fewer than ten characters, the formula returns all text in the cell:

```
=RIGHT(A1,10)
```

This next formula uses the `MID` function to return five characters from cell A1, beginning at character position 2. In other words, it returns characters 2 through 6.

```
=MID(A1,2,5)
```

The following example returns the text in cell A1 with only the first letter in uppercase. It uses the `LEFT` function to extract the first character and convert it to uppercase. This character then concatenates to another string that uses the `RIGHT` function to extract all but the first character (converted to lowercase). Here's what it looks like:

```
=UPPER(LEFT(A1))&RIGHT(LOWER(A1),LEN(A1)-1)
```

If cell A1 contained the text `FIRST QUARTER`, the formula would return `First quarter`.

NOTE

This is different from the result obtained using the `PROPER` function. The `PROPER` function makes the first character in each word uppercase.

Replacing text with other text

In some situations, you may need a formula to replace a part of a text string with some other text. For example, you may import data that contains asterisks, and you need to convert the asterisks to some other character. You could use choose Home ⇨ Editing ⇨ Find & Select ⇨ Replace to make the replacement. If you prefer a formula-based solution, you can take advantage of either of two functions:

- `SUBSTITUTE` replaces specific text in a string. Use this function when you know the character(s) to be replaced but not the position.
- `REPLACE` replaces text that occurs in a specific location within a string. Use this function when you know the position of the text to be replaced but not the actual text.

The following formula uses the `SUBSTITUTE` function to replace 2012 with 2013 in the string `2012 Budget`. The formula returns `2013 Budget`.

```
=SUBSTITUTE("2012 Budget","2012","2013")
```

The following formula uses the `SUBSTITUTE` function to remove all spaces from a string. In other words, it replaces all space characters with an empty string. The formula returns `2013OperatingBudget`.

```
=SUBSTITUTE("2013 Operating Budget"," ","")
```

The following formula uses the `REPLACE` function to replace one character beginning at position 5 with nothing. In other words, it removes the fifth character (a hyphen) and returns `Part544`.

```
=REPLACE("Part-544",5,1,"")
```

Finding and searching within a string

The `FIND` and `SEARCH` functions enable you to locate the starting position of a particular substring within a string:

- `FIND` finds a substring within another text string and returns the starting position of the substring. You can specify the character position at which to begin searching. Use this function for case-sensitive text comparisons. Wildcard comparisons are not supported.

- SEARCH finds a substring within another text string and returns the starting position of the substring. You can specify the character position at which to begin searching. Use this function for non-case-sensitive text or when you need to use wildcard characters.

The following formula uses the FIND function and returns 7, the position of the first *m* in the string. Notice that this formula is case sensitive.

```
=FIND("m","Big Mama Thornton",1)
```

The formula that follows, which uses the SEARCH function, returns 5, the position of the first *m* (either uppercase or lowercase):

```
=SEARCH("m","Big Mama Thornton",1)
```

You can use the following wildcard characters within the first argument for the SEARCH function:

- Question mark (?) matches any single character.
- Asterisk (*) matches any sequence of characters.

TIP

If you want to find an actual question mark or asterisk character, type a tilde (~) before the question mark or asterisk.

The next formula examines the text in cell A1 and returns the position of the first three-character sequence that has a hyphen in the middle of it. In other words, it looks for any character followed by a hyphen and any other character. If cell A1 contains the text Part-A90, the formula returns 4.

```
=SEARCH("?-?",A1,1)
```

Searching and replacing within a string

You can use the REPLACE function in conjunction with the SEARCH function to replace part of a text string with another string. In effect, you use the SEARCH function to find the starting location used by the REPLACE function.

For example, assume that cell A1 contains the text Annual Profit Figures. The following formula searches for the six-letter word Profit and replaces it with the word Loss:

```
=REPLACE(A1,SEARCH("Profit",A1),6,"Loss")
```

This next formula uses the SUBSTITUTE function to accomplish the same effect in a more efficient manner:

```
=SUBSTITUTE(A1,"Profit","Loss")
```

Advanced Text Formulas

The examples in this section appear more complex than the examples in the preceding section. As you can see, though, these examples can perform some very useful text manipulations. Space limitations prevent a detailed explanation of how these formulas work, but this section gives you a basic introduction.

On the Web

You can access all the examples in this section by downloading the file from this book's website. The file is named `text formula examples.xlsx`.

Counting specific characters in a cell

This formula counts the number of *B*s (uppercase only) in the string in cell A1:

```
=LEN(A1)-LEN(SUBSTITUTE(A1,"B",""))
```

This formula works by using the `SUBSTITUTE` function to create a new string (in memory) that has all the *B*s removed. Then the length of this string is subtracted from the length of the original string. The result reveals the number of *B*s in the original string.

The following formula is a bit more versatile: It counts the number of *B*s (both uppercase and lowercase) in the string in cell A1. Using the `UPPER` function to convert the string makes this formula work with both uppercase and lowercase characters:

```
=LEN(A1)-LEN(SUBSTITUTE(UPPER(A1),"B",""))
```

Counting the occurrences of a substring in a cell

The formulas in the preceding section count the number of occurrences of a particular character in a string. The following formula works with more than one character. It returns the number of occurrences of a particular substring (contained in cell B1) within a string (contained in cell A1). The substring can consist of any number of characters.

```
=(LEN(A1)-LEN(SUBSTITUTE(A1,B1,"")))/LEN(B1)
```

For example, if cell A1 contains the text `Blonde On Blonde` and B1 contains the text `Blonde`, the formula returns `2`.

The comparison is case sensitive, so if B1 contains the text `blonde`, the formula returns `0`. The following formula is a modified version that performs a case-insensitive comparison by converting the characters to uppercase:

```
=(LEN(A1)-LEN(SUBSTITUTE(UPPER(A1),UPPER(B1),"")))/LEN(B1)
```

Extracting the first word of a string

To extract the first word of a string, a formula must locate the position of the first space character and then use this information as an argument for the `LEFT` function. The following formula does just that:

```
=LEFT(A1,FIND(" ",A1)-1)
```

This formula returns all the text prior to the first space in cell A1. However, the formula has a slight problem: It returns an error if cell A1 consists of a single word. A slightly more complex formula that checks for the error using the `IFERROR` function solves that problem:

```
=IFERROR(LEFT(A1,FIND(" ",A1)-1),A1)
```

CAUTION

The preceding formula uses the `IFERROR` function, which was introduced in Excel 2007. If your workbook will be used with previous versions of Excel, use this formula:

```
=IF(ISERR(FIND(" ",A1)),A1,LEFT(A1,FIND(" ",A1)-1))
```

Extracting the last word of a string

Extracting the last word of a string is more complicated because the `FIND` function only works from left to right. Therefore, the problem is locating the *last* space character. The formula that follows, however, solves this problem by returning the last word of a string (all text following the last space character):

```
=RIGHT(A1,LEN(A1)-FIND("*",SUBSTITUTE(A1," ","*",LEN(A1)-LEN(SUBSTITUTE(A1,
   " ","")))))
```

This formula, however, has the same problem as the first formula in the preceding section: It fails if the string does not contain at least *one* space character. The following modified formula uses the `IFERROR` function to test for an error (that is, no spaces). If the first argument returns an error, the formula returns the complete contents of cell A1:

```
=IFERROR(RIGHT(A1,LEN(A1)-FIND("*",SUBSTITUTE(A1," ","*",LEN(A1)-
   LEN(SUBSTITUTE(A1," ",""))))),A1)
```

Following is a modification that doesn't use the `IFERROR` function. This formula works for all versions of Excel:

```
=IF(ISERR(FIND(" ",A1)),A1,RIGHT(A1,LEN(A1)-FIND("*",SUBSTITUTE(A1,
   " ","*",LEN(A1)-LEN(SUBSTITUTE(A1," ",""))))))
```

Extracting all but the first word of a string

The following formula returns the contents of cell A1, except for the first word:

```
=RIGHT(A1,LEN(A1)-FIND(" ",A1,1))
```

If cell A1 contains `2013 Operating Budget`, the formula returns `Operating Budget`.

The following formula, which uses the `IFERROR` function, returns the entire contents of cell A1 if the cell doesn't have a space character:

```
=IFERROR(RIGHT(A1,LEN(A1)-FIND(" ",A1,1)),A1)
```

Here's a modification that works in all versions of Excel:

```
=IF(ISERR(FIND(" ",A1)),A1,RIGHT(A1,LEN(A1)-FIND(" ",A1,1)))
```

Extracting first names, middle names, and last names

Suppose you have a list consisting of people's names in a single column. You have to separate these names into three columns: one for the first name, one for the middle name or initial, and one for the last name. This task is more complicated than you may think because it must handle the situation for a missing middle initial. However, you can still do it.

> **Note**
>
> The task becomes a *lot* more complicated if the list contains names with titles (such as *Mr.* or *Dr.*) or names followed by additional details (such as *Jr.* or *III*). In fact, the following formulas will *not* handle these complex cases. However, they still give you a significant head start if you're willing to do a bit of manual editing to handle special cases. For a way to remove these titles, see the next section, "Removing titles from names."

The following formulas all assume that the name appears in cell A1.

You can easily construct a formula to return the first name:

```
=LEFT(A1,FIND(" ",A1)-1)
```

This formula returns the last name:

```
=RIGHT(A1,LEN(A1)-FIND("*",SUBSTITUTE(A1," ","*",LEN(A1)-LEN(SUBSTITUTE(A1,
   " ","")))))
```

The next formula extracts the middle name and requires that you use the other formulas to extract the first name and the last name. It assumes that the first name is in B1 and the last name is in D1. Here's what it looks like:

```
=IF(LEN(B1&D1)+2>=LEN(A1),"",MID(A1,LEN(B1)+2,LEN(A1)-LEN(B1&D1)-2))
```

As you can see in Figure 11.5, the formulas work fairly well. There are a few problems, however, notably names that contain one word or four words. But, as I mentioned earlier, you can clean up these cases manually.

FIGURE 11.5

This worksheet uses formulas to extract the first name, last name, and middle name (or initial) from a list of names in column A.

	A	B	C	D
1	**Full Name**	**First**	**Middle**	**Last**
2	John Q. Public	John	Q.	Public
3	Lisa Smith	Lisa		Smith
4	J. R. Robins	J.	R.	Robins
5	Dr. Lester B. Jones	Dr.	Lester B.	Jones
6	J. R. R. Tolkien	J.	R. R.	Tolkien
7	Franklin H. Lee	Franklin	H.	Lee
8	Melvina Mary Jane Pryce	Melvina	Mary Jane	Pryce
9	Suzette I. Thorson	Suzette	I.	Thorson
10	J. Frank	J.		Frank
11	Amanda M. Rowe	Amanda	M.	Rowe
12	Madonna	#VALUE!	#VALUE!	#VALUE!
13	Aaron E. Pacheco	Aaron	E.	Pacheco
14	Dennis Michael Batie	Dennis	Michael	Batie
15	Lloyd Benedict Arnold	Lloyd	Benedict	Arnold
16	Agnes K. Saterfiel	Agnes	K.	Saterfiel
17	Robert M. Simmons	Robert	M.	Simmons
18	Joseph Q. Glenn	Joseph	Q.	Glenn
19	Jeffrey George Bishop	Jeffrey	George	Bishop
20	Henrietta D. Markowski	Henrietta	D.	Markowski
21	William R. Gordon	William	R.	Gordon
22	Khalilah Gorski	Khalilah		Gorski
23	Tammy Faye. Lindsey	Tammy	Faye.	Lindsey
24	Wilfred A. Moy	Wilfred	A.	Moy
25	Carla V. Richards-Walker	Carla	V.	Richards-Walker
26	Joseph Q. Ramsey	Joseph	Q.	Ramsey
27	Lina B. Poston	Lina	B.	Poston
28	James Trott	James		Trott
29	Annita J. Alvarado	Annita	J.	Alvarado

Sheet1

On the Web

This workbook, named `extract names.xlsx`, is available on this book's website.

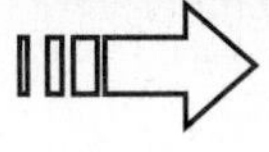

Excel provides two methods to extract text from strings without using formulas: the Text to Columns feature, and the Flash Fill feature (new to Excel 2013). Refer to Chapter 32 for more information about these features.

Removing titles from names

You can use the following formula to remove three common titles *(Mr., Ms.,* and *Mrs.)* from a name. For example, if cell A1 contains `Mr. Fred Munster`, the formula would return `Fred Munster`.

```
=IF(OR(LEFT(A1,2)="Mr",LEFT(A1,3)="Mrs",LEFT(A1,2)="Ms"),RIGHT(A1,LEN(A1)
   -FIND(" ",A1)),A1)
```

Creating an ordinal number

An *ordinal number* is an adjective form of a number. Examples include 1st, 2nd, 5th, 23rd, and so on.

The formula that follows displays the value in cell A1 as an ordinal number:

```
=A13&IF(OR(VALUE(RIGHT(A1,2))={11,12,13}),"th",
IF(OR(VALUE(RIGHT(A1))={1,2,3}),CHOOSE(RIGHT(A1),
"st","nd","rd"),"th"))
```

The formula is rather complex because it must determine whether the number will end in `th`, `st`, `nd`, or `rd`. This formula also uses literal arrays (enclosed in brackets).

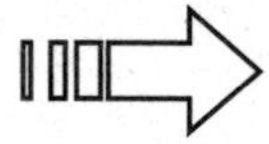

See Chapter 18 for more on literal arrays.

Counting the number of words in a cell

The following formula returns the number of words in cell A1:

```
=LEN(TRIM(A1))-LEN(SUBSTITUTE( (A1)," ",""))+1
```

The formula uses the `TRIM` function to remove excess spaces. It then uses the `SUBSTITUTE` function to create a new string (in memory) that has all the space characters removed. The length of this string is subtracted from the length of the original (trimmed) string to get the number of spaces. This value is then incremented by 1 to get the number of words.

Note that this formula will return `1` if the cell is empty. The following modification solves that problem:

```
=IF(LEN(A1)=0,0,LEN(TRIM(A1))-LEN(SUBSTITUTE(TRIM(A1)," ",""))+1)
```

CHAPTER

12

Working with Dates and Times

IN THIS CHAPTER

Getting an overview of dates and times in Excel

Using Excel date-related functions

Working with Excel time-related functions

Many worksheets contain dates and times in cells. For example, you might track information by date or create a schedule based on time. Beginners often find that working with dates and times in Excel can be frustrating. To work with dates and times, you need a good understanding of how Excel handles time-based information. This chapter provides the information you need to create powerful formulas that manipulate dates and times.

NOTE

The dates in this chapter correspond to the U.S. English language date format: month/day/year. For example, the date 3/1/1952 refers to March 1, 1952, not January 3, 1952. I realize that this setup is illogical, but that's the way Americans have been trained. I trust that the non-American readers of this book can make the adjustment.

How Excel Handles Dates and Times

This section presents a quick overview of how Excel deals with dates and times. It covers Excel's date and time serial number system. I also provide some tips for entering and formatting dates and times.

Understanding date serial numbers

To Excel, a date is simply a number. More precisely, a date is a *serial number* that represents the number of days since the fictitious date of January 0, 1900. A serial number of 1 corresponds to January 1, 1900; a serial number of 2 corresponds to January 2, 1900; and so on. This system makes it possible to create formulas that perform calculations with dates. For example, you can create a formula to calculate the number of days between two dates (just subtract one from the other).

Excel support dates from January 1, 1900, through December 31, 9999 (serial number = 2,958,465).

You may wonder about January 0, 1900. This *nondate* (which corresponds to date serial number 0) is actually used to represent times that aren't associated with a particular day. This concept becomes clear later in this chapter (see "Entering times").

To view a date serial number as a date, you must format the cell as a date. Choose Home⇨Number⇨Number Format. This drop-down control provides you with two date formats. To select from additional date formats, see "Formatting dates and times," later in this chapter.

Entering dates

You can enter a date directly as a serial number (if you know the serial number) and then format it as a date. More often, you enter a date by using any of several recognized date formats. Excel automatically converts your entry into the corresponding date serial number (which it uses for calculations), and it also applies the default date format to the cell so that it displays as an actual date rather than as a cryptic serial number.

Choose Your Date System: 1900 or 1904

Excel supports two date systems: the 1900 date system and the 1904 date system. Which system you use in a workbook determines what date serves as the basis for dates. The 1900 date system uses January 1, 1900, as the day assigned to date serial number 1. The 1904 date system uses January 1, 1904, as the base date. By default, Excel for Windows uses the 1900 date system, and pre-2011 versions of Excel for Mac use the 1904 date system.

NOTE

Microsoft made a change. Excel 2011 for Mac uses the 1900 date system by default. Presumably subsequent Mac versions will as well.

Excel for Windows supports the 1904 date system for compatibility with Mac files. You can choose the date system for the active workbook in the Advanced section of the Excel Options dialog box. (It's in the When Calculating This Workbook subsection.) Generally, you should use the default 1900 date system. And you should exercise caution if you use two different date systems in workbooks that are linked. For example, assume that Book1 uses the 1904 date system and contains the date 1/15/1999 in cell A1. Assume that Book2 uses the 1900 date system and contains a link to cell A1 in Book1. Book2 displays the date as 1/14/1995. Both workbooks use the same date serial number (34713), but they're interpreted differently.

One advantage to using the 1904 date system is that it enables you to display negative time values. With the 1900 date system, a calculation that results in a negative time (for example, 4:00 PM–5:30 PM) cannot be displayed. When using the 1904 date system, the negative time displays as –1:30 (that is, a difference of 1 hour and 30 minutes).

For example, if you need to enter June 18, 2013 into a cell, you can enter the date by typing **June 18, 2013** (or any of several different date formats). Excel interprets your entry and stores the value 41443, the date serial number for that date. It also applies the default date format, so the cell contents may not appear exactly as you typed them.

NOTE

Depending on your regional settings, entering a date in a format such as June 18, 2013, may be interpreted as a text string. In such a case, you need to enter the date in a format that corresponds to your regional settings, such as 18 June 2013.

When you activate a cell that contains a date, the Formula bar shows the cell contents formatted by using the default date format — which corresponds to your system's *short date format*. The Formula bar doesn't display the date's serial number. If you need to find out the serial number for a particular date, format the cell with a nondate number format.

TIP

To change the default date format, you need to change a systemwide setting. From the Windows Control Panel, select Regional and Language Options. The exact procedure varies, depending on the version of Windows you use. Look for the drop-down list that enables you to change the Short Date Format. The setting you choose determines the default date format that Excel uses to display dates in the Formula bar.

Table 12.1 shows a sampling of the date formats that Excel recognizes (using the U.S. settings). Results will vary if you use a different regional setting.

TABLE 12.1 Date Entry Formats Recognized by Excel

Entry	Excel Interpretation (U.S. Settings)
6-18-13	June 18, 2013
6-18-2013	June 18, 2013
6/18/13	June 18, 2013
6/18/2013	June 18, 2013
6-18/13	June 18, 2013
June 18, 2013	June 18, 2013
Jun 18	June 18 of the current year
June 18	June 18 of the current year
6/18	June 18 of the current year
6-18	June 18 of the current year
18-Jun-2013	June 18, 2013
2013/6/18	June 18, 2013

Searching for Dates

If your worksheet uses many dates, you may need to search for a particular date by using the Find and Replace dialog box (Home ➪ Editing ➪ Find & Select ➪ Find, or Ctrl+F). Excel is rather picky when it comes to finding dates. You must enter the date as it appears in the Formula bar. For example, if a cell contains a date formatted to display as June 19, 2013, the date appears in the Formula bar using your system's short date format (for example, 6/19/2013). Therefore, if you search for the date as it appears in the cell, Excel won't find it. But it will find the cell if you search for date in the format that appears in the Formula bar.

As you can see in Table 12.1, Excel is rather flexible when it comes to recognizing dates entered into a cell. It's not perfect, however. For example, Excel does *not* recognize any of the following entries as dates:

- June 18 2013
- Jun-18 2013
- Jun-18/2013

Rather, it interprets these entries as text. If you plan to use dates in formulas, make sure that Excel can recognize the date you enter as a date; otherwise, the formulas that refer to these dates will produce incorrect results.

If you attempt to enter a date that lies outside of the supported date range, Excel interprets it as text. If you attempt to format a serial number that lies outside the supported range as a date, the value displays as a series of hash marks (#########).

Understanding time serial numbers

When you need to work with time values, you extend the Excel date serial number system to include decimals. In other words, Excel works with times by using fractional days. For example, the date serial number for June 1, 2013, is 41426. Noon (halfway through the day) is represented internally as 41426.5.

The serial number equivalent of one minute is approximately 0.00069444. The following formula calculates this number by multiplying 24 hours by 60 minutes, and dividing the result into 1. The denominator consists of the number of minutes in a day (1,440).

```
=1/(24*60)
```

Similarly, the serial number equivalent of one second is approximately 0.00001157, obtained by the following formula:

```
=1/(24*60*60)
```

In this case, the denominator represents the number of seconds in a day (86,400).

In Excel, the smallest unit of time is one 1,000th of a second. The time serial number shown here represents 23:59:59.999 (one 1,000th of a second before midnight):

```
0.99999999
```

Table 12.2 shows various times of day along with each associated time serial number.

TABLE 12.2 Times of Day and Their Corresponding Serial Numbers

Time of Day	Time Serial Number
12:00:00 AM (midnight)	0.00000000
1:30:00 AM	0.06250000
7:30:00 AM	0.31250000
10:30:00 AM	0.43750000
12:00:00 PM (noon)	0.50000000
1:30:00 PM	0.56250000
4:30:00 PM	0.68750000
6:00:00 PM	0.75000000
9:00:00 PM	0.87500000
10:30:00 PM	0.93750000

Entering times

As with entering dates, you normally don't have to worry about the actual time serial numbers. Just enter the time into a cell using a recognized format. Table 12.3 shows some examples of time formats that Excel recognizes.

TABLE 12.3 Time Entry Formats Recognized by Excel

Entry	Excel Interpretation
11:30:00 am	11:30 AM
11:30:00 AM	11:30 AM
11:30 pm	11:30 PM
11:30	11:30 AM
13:30	1:30 PM

Because the preceding samples don't have a specific day associated with them, Excel uses a date serial number of 0, which corresponds to the nonday January 0, 1900. Often, you'll want to combine a date and time. Do so by using a recognized date entry format, followed by a space, and then a recognized time entry format. For example, if you enter **6/18/2013 11:30** in a cell, Excel interprets it as 11:30 a.m. on June 18, 2013. Its date/time serial number is 41443.4791666667.

When you enter a time that exceeds 24 hours, the associated date for the time increments accordingly. For example, if you enter **25:00:00** in a cell, it's interpreted as 1:00 a.m. on January 1, 1900. The day part of the entry increments because the time exceeds 24 hours. Keep in mind that a time value without a date uses January 0, 1900, as the date.

Similarly, if you enter a date *and* a time (and the time exceeds 24 hours), the date that you entered is adjusted. If you enter **9/18/2013 25:00:00**, for example, it's interpreted as 9/19/2013 1:00:00 a.m.

If you enter a time only (without an associated date) into an unformatted cell, the maximum time that you can enter into a cell is 9999:59:59 (just less than 10,000 hours). Excel adds the appropriate number of days. In this case, 9999:59:59 is interpreted as 3:59:59 p.m. on 02/19/1901. If you enter a time that exceeds 10,000 hours, the entry is interpreted as a text string rather than a time.

Formatting dates and times

You have a great deal of flexibility in formatting cells that contain dates and times. For example, you can format the cell to display the date part only, the time part only, or both the date and time parts.

You format dates and times by selecting the cells and then using the Number tab of the Format Cells dialog box, shown in Figure 12.1. To display this dialog box, click the dialog box launcher icon in the Number group of the Home tab, or click the Number Format control and choose More Number Formats from the list that appears.

The Date category shows built-in date formats, and the Time category shows built-in time formats. Some formats include both date and time displays. Just select the desired format from the Type list, and then click OK.

TIP

When you create a formula that refers to a cell containing a date or a time, Excel sometimes automatically formats the formula cell as a date or a time. Often, this automation is very helpful; other times, it's completely inappropriate and downright annoying. To return the number formatting to the default General format, choose Home ⇨ Number ⇨ Number Format and choose General from the drop-down list. Or just press Ctrl+Shift+~ (tilde).

If none of the built-in formats meets your needs, you can create a custom number format. Select the Custom category and then type the custom format codes into the Type box.

See Chapter 25 for information on creating custom number formats.

FIGURE 12.1

Use the Number tab of the Format Cells dialog box to change the appearance of dates and times.

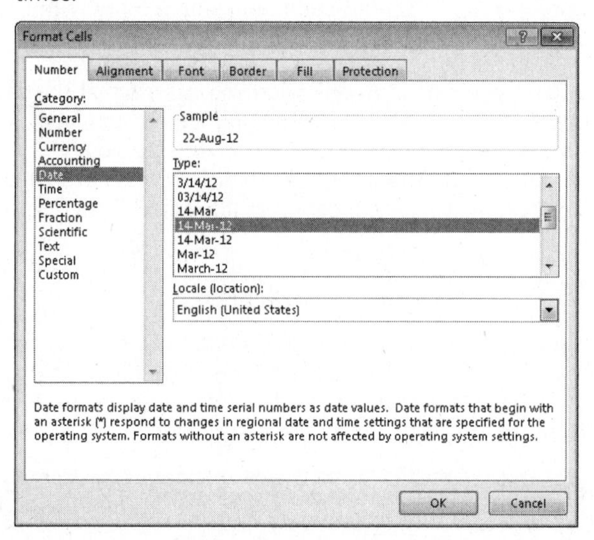

Problems with dates

Excel has some problems when it comes to dates. Many of these problems stem from the fact that Excel was designed many years ago. Excel designers basically emulated the Lotus 1-2-3 program's limited date and time features, which contain a nasty bug that was duplicated intentionally in Excel (described next). If Excel were being designed from scratch today, I'm sure it would be much more versatile in dealing with dates. Unfortunately, users are currently stuck with a product that leaves much to be desired in the area of dates.

Excel's leap year bug

A *leap year,* which occurs every four years, contains an additional day (February 29). Specifically, years that are evenly divisible by 100 are not leap years, unless they are also evenly divisible by 400. Although the year 1900 was not a leap year, Excel treats it as such. In other words, when you type **2/29/1900** into a cell, Excel interprets it as a valid date and assigns a serial number of 60.

If you type **2/29/1901**, however, Excel correctly interprets it as a mistake and doesn't convert it to a date. Instead, it simply makes the cell entry a text string.

How can a product used daily by millions of people contain such an obvious bug? The answer is historical. The original version of Lotus 1-2-3 contained a bug that caused it to treat 1900 as a leap year. When Excel was released some time later, the designers knew about this bug and chose to reproduce it in Excel to maintain compatibility with Lotus worksheet files.

Why does this bug still exist in later versions of Excel? Microsoft asserts that the disadvantages of correcting this bug outweigh the advantages. If the bug were eliminated, it would mess up millions of existing workbooks. In addition, correcting this problem would possibly affect compatibility between Excel and other programs that use dates. As it stands, this bug really causes very few problems because most users don't use dates prior to March 1, 1900.

Pre-1900 dates

The world, of course, didn't begin on January 1, 1900. People who use Excel to work with historical information often need to work with dates before January 1, 1900. Unfortunately, the only way to work with pre-1900 dates is to enter the date into a cell as text. For example, you can enter **July 4, 1776** into a cell, and Excel won't complain.

Tip

If you plan to sort information by old dates, you should enter your text dates with a four-digit year, followed by a two-digit month, and then a two-digit day — for example, 1776-07-04. You won't be able to work with these text strings as dates, but this format *will* enable accurate sorting.

Using text as dates works in some situations, but the main problem is that you can't perform any manipulation on a date that's entered as text. For example, you can't change its numeric formatting, you can't determine which day of the week this date occurred on, and you can't calculate the date that occurs seven days later.

On the Web

The website for this book contains a workbook named `XDATE demo.xlsm`. This workbook contains eight custom worksheet functions that I wrote in VBA. You will need to enable macros when you open this workbook. These functions enable you to work with any date in the years 0100 through 9999. Figure 12.2 shows a worksheet that uses these extended date functions in columns E though G to perform calculations that involve pre-1900 dates.

Inconsistent date entries

You need to be careful when entering dates by using two digits for the year. When you do so, Excel has some rules that kick in to determine which century to use. And those rules vary, depending on the version of Excel that you use.

FIGURE 12.2

My Extended Date Functions add-in enables you to work with pre-1900 dates.

President Birthdays

Num	President	Year	Month	Day	XDATE	XDATEDOW	XDATEYEARDIF
1	George Washington	1732	2	22	Feb 22, 1732	Friday	280
2	John Adams	1735	10	30	Oct 30, 1735	Sunday	276
3	Thomas Jefferson	1743	4	13	Apr 13, 1743	Saturday	269
4	James Madison	1751	3	16	Mar 16, 1751	Tuesday	261
5	James Monroe	1758	4	28	Apr 28, 1758	Friday	254
6	John Quincy Adams	1767	7	11	Jul 11, 1767	Saturday	245
7	Andrew Jackson	1767	3	15	Mar 15, 1767	Sunday	245
8	Martin Van Buren	1782	12	5	Dec 05, 1782	Thursday	229
9	William Henry Harrison	1773	2	9	Feb 09, 1773	Tuesday	239
10	John Tyler	1790	3	29	Mar 29, 1790	Monday	222
11	James Knox Polk	1795	11	2	Nov 02, 1795	Monday	216
12	Zachary Taylor	1784	11	24	Nov 24, 1784	Wednesday	227
13	Millard Fillmore	1800	1	7	Jan 07, 1800	Tuesday	212
14	Franklin Pierce	1804	11	23	Nov 23, 1804	Friday	207
15	James Buchanan	1791	4	23	Apr 23, 1791	Saturday	221
16	Abraham Lincoln	1809	2	12	Feb 12, 1809	Sunday	203
17	Andrew Johnson	1808	12	29	Dec 29, 1808	Thursday	203
18	Ulysses Simpson Grant	1822	4	27	Apr 27, 1822	Saturday	190
19	Rutherford Birchard Hayes	1822	10	4	Oct 04, 1822	Friday	189
20	James Abram Garfield	1831	11	19	Nov 19, 1831	Saturday	180
21	Chester Alan Arthur	1829	10	5	Oct 05, 1829	Monday	182
22	Grover Cleveland	1837	3	18	Mar 18, 1837	Saturday	175
23	Benjamin Harrison	1833	8	20	Aug 20, 1833	Tuesday	179

Sheet1

Two-digit years between 00 and 29 are interpreted as 21st-century dates, and two-digit years between 30 and 99 are interpreted as 20th-century dates. For example, if you enter **12/15/28**, Excel interprets your entry as December 15, 2028. But if you enter **12/15/30**, Excel sees it as December 15, 1930, because Windows uses a default boundary year of 2029. You can keep the default as is or change it via the Windows Control Panel. From the Regional and Language Options dialog box, click the Customize button to display the Customize Regional Options dialog box. Select the Date tab and then specify a different year.

TIP

The best way to avoid any surprises is to simply enter *all* years using all four digits for the year.

Date-Related Worksheet Functions

Excel has quite a few functions that work with dates. These functions are accessible by choosing Formulas ➪ Function Library ➪ Date & Time.

Table 12.4 summarizes the date-related functions available in Excel.

TABLE 12.4 Date-Related Functions

Function	Description
DATE	Returns the serial number of a particular date
DATEVALUE	Converts a date in the form of text to a serial number
DAY	Converts a serial number to a day of the month
DAYS***	Returns the number of days between two dates
DAYS360	Calculates the number of days between two dates based on a 360-day year
EDATE*	Returns the serial number of the date that represents the indicated number of months before or after the start date
EOMONTH*	Returns the serial number of the last day of the month before or after a specified number of months
ISOWEEKNUM***	Returns the ISO week number for a date
MONTH	Converts a serial number to a month
NETWORKDAYS*	Returns the number of whole work days between two dates
NETWORKDAYS.INTL**	An international version of the NETWORKDAYS function, which allows nonstandard weekend days
NOW	Returns the serial number of the current date and time
TODAY	Returns the serial number of today's date
WEEKDAY	Converts a serial number to a day of the week
WEEKNUM*	Returns the week number in the year
WORKDAY*	Returns the serial number of the date before or after a specified number of workdays
WORKDAY.INTL**	An international version of the WORKDAY function, which allows non-standard weekend days.
YEAR	Converts a serial number to a year
YEARFRAC*	Returns the year fraction representing the number of whole days between start_date and end_date

* In versions prior to Excel 2007, these functions are available only when the Analysis ToolPak add-in is installed.

** Indicates a function introduced in Excel 2010.

*** Indicates a function introduced in Excel 2013.

Displaying the current date

The following formula uses the TODAY function to display the current date in a cell:

```
=TODAY()
```

You can also display the date combined with text. The formula that follows, for example, displays text, such as `Today is Tuesday, April 9, 2013`:

```
="Today is "&TEXT(TODAY(),"dddd, mmmm d, yyyy")
```

It's important to understand that the `TODAY` function is not a date stamp. The function is updated whenever the worksheet is calculated. For example, if you enter either of the preceding formulas into a worksheet, the formulas display the current date. And when you open the workbook tomorrow, they will display the current date (*not* the date when you entered the formula).

TIP

To enter a date stamp into a cell, press Ctrl+; (semicolon). This action enters the date directly into the cell and doesn't use a formula. Therefore, the date won't change.

Displaying any date

You can easily enter a date into a cell by simply typing it while using any of the date formats that Excel recognizes. You can also create a date by using the `DATE` function, which takes three arguments: the year, the month, and the day. The following formula, for example, returns a date comprising the year in cell A1, the month in cell B1, and the day in cell C1:

```
=DATE(A1,B1,C1)
```

NOTE

The `DATE` function accepts invalid arguments and adjusts the result accordingly. For example, the following formula uses `13` as the month argument and returns January 1, 2013. The month argument is automatically translated as month 1 of the following year.

```
=DATE(2012,13,1)
```

Often, you'll use the `DATE` function with other functions as arguments. For example, the following formula uses the `YEAR` and `TODAY` functions to return the date for July 4 of the current year:

```
=DATE(YEAR(TODAY()),7,4)
```

The `DATEVALUE` function converts a text string that looks like a date into a date serial number. The following formula returns 40508, which is the date serial number for August 22, 2013:

```
=DATEVALUE("8/22/2013")
```

To view the result of this formula as a date, you need to apply a date number format to the cell.

CAUTION

Be careful when using the DATEVALUE function. A text string that looks like a date in your country may not look like a date in another country. The preceding example works fine if your system is set for U.S. date formats, but it returns an error for other regional date formats because Excel is looking for the 8th day of the 22nd month!

Generating a series of dates

Often, you want to insert a series of dates into a worksheet. For example, in tracking weekly sales, you may want to enter a series of dates, each separated by seven days. These dates will serve to identify the sales figures.

In some cases, you can use the Excel AutoFill feature to insert a series of dates. Enter the first date and drag the cell's fill handle while holding down the right mouse button. Release the mouse button and select an option from the shortcut menu (see Figure 12.3) — Fill Days, Fill Weekdays, Fill Months, or Fill Years. Notice that Excel does not provide a Fill Weeks option.

FIGURE 12.3

Using AutoFill to create a series of dates.

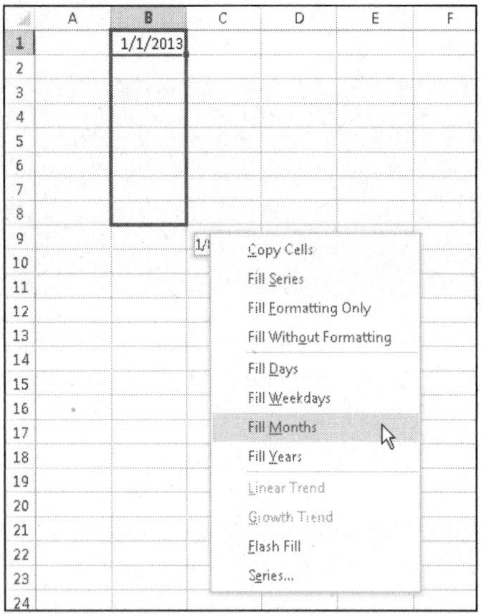

For more flexibility enter the first *two* dates in the series — for example, the starting day for week 1 and the starting day for week 2. Then select both cells and drag the fill handle down the column. Excel will complete the date series, with each date separated by the interval represented by the first two dates.

The advantage of using formulas (instead of AutoFill) to create a series of dates is that when you change the first date, the others update automatically. You need to enter the starting date in a cell and then use formulas (copied down the column) to generate the additional dates.

The following examples assume that you enter the first date of the series into cell A1 and the formula into cell A2. You can then copy this formula down the column as many times as needed.

To generate a series of dates separated by seven days, use this formula:

```
=A1+7
```

To generate a series of dates separated by one month, you need to use a more complicated formula because months don't all have the same number of days. This formula creates a series of dates, separated by one month:


```
=DATE(YEAR(A1),MONTH(A1)+1,DAY(A1))
```

To generate a series of dates separated by one year, use this formula:

```
=DATE(YEAR(A1)+1,MONTH(A1),DAY(A1))
```

To generate a series of weekdays only (no Saturdays or Sundays), use the following formula. This formula assumes that the date in cell A1 is not a weekend day.

```
=IF(WEEKDAY(A1)=6,A1+3,A1+1)
```

Converting a nondate string to a date

You may import data that contains dates coded as text strings. For example, the following text represents August 21, 2013 (a four-digit year followed by a two-digit month, followed by a two-digit day):

```
20130821
```

To convert this string to an actual date, you can use a formula, such as the following. (This formula assumes that the coded data is in cell A1.)

```
=DATE(LEFT(A1,4),MID(A1,5,2),RIGHT(A1,2))
```

This formula uses text functions (`LEFT`, `MID`, and `RIGHT`) to extract the digits, and then it uses these extracted digits as arguments for the `DATE` function.

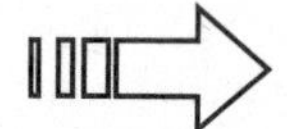

See Chapter 11 for more information about using formulas to manipulate text.

Calculating the number of days between two dates

A common type of date calculation determines the number of days between two dates. For example, say you have a financial worksheet that calculates interest earned on a deposit account. The interest earned depends on the number of days the account is open. If your sheet contains the open date and the close date for the account, you can calculate the number of days the account was open.

Because dates are stored as consecutive serial numbers, you can use simple subtraction to calculate the number of days between two dates. For example, if cells A1 and B1 both contain a date, the following formula returns the number of days between these dates:

```
=A1-B1
```

If cell B1 contains a more recent date than the date in cell A1, the result will be negative. If you don't care about which date is earlier and want to avoid displaying a negative value, use this formula:

```
=ABS(A1-B1)
```

New Feature

You can also use the `DAYS` worksheet function, introduced in Excel 2013. It offers no advantage that I can see, but here's an example of how to use it to calculate the number of days between two dates:

```
=DAYS(A1,B1)
```

Sometimes, calculating the difference between two days is more difficult. To demonstrate, consider the common fence-post analogy. If somebody asks you how many units make up a fence, you can respond with either of two answers: the number of fence posts or the number of gaps between the fence posts. The number of fence posts is always one more than the number of gaps between the posts.

To bring this analogy into the realm of dates, suppose that you start a sales promotion on February 1 and end the promotion on February 9. How many days was the promotion in effect? Subtracting February 1 from February 9 produces an answer of eight days. Actually, though, the promotion lasted nine days. In this case, the correct answer involves counting the fence posts, not the gaps. The formula to calculate the length of the promotion (assuming that you have appropriately named cells) appears like this:

```
=EndDay-StartDay+1
```

Calculating the number of workdays between two dates

When calculating the difference between two dates, you may want to exclude weekends and holidays. For example, you may need to know how many business days fall in the month of November. This calculation should exclude Saturdays, Sundays, and holidays. The `NETWORKDAYS` function can help out.

> **NOTE**
> In versions prior to Excel 2007, the `NETWORKDAYS` function was available only when the Analysis ToolPak add-in was installed. This function is now part of Excel and doesn't require an add-in. This is relevant if you plan to share your workbook with someone who uses an older version of Excel.

The `NETWORKDAYS` function calculates the difference between two dates, excluding weekend days (Saturdays and Sundays). As an option, you can specify a range of cells that contain the dates of holidays, which are also excluded. Excel has no way of determining which days are holidays, so you must provide this information in a range.

Figure 12.4 shows a worksheet that calculates the workdays between two dates. The range A2:A11 contains a list of holiday dates. The two formulas in column C calculate the workdays between the dates in column A and column B. For example, the formula in cell C15 is

```
=NETWORKDAYS(A15,B15,A2:A11)
```

FIGURE 12.4

Using the `NETWORKDAYS` function to calculate the number of workdays between two dates.

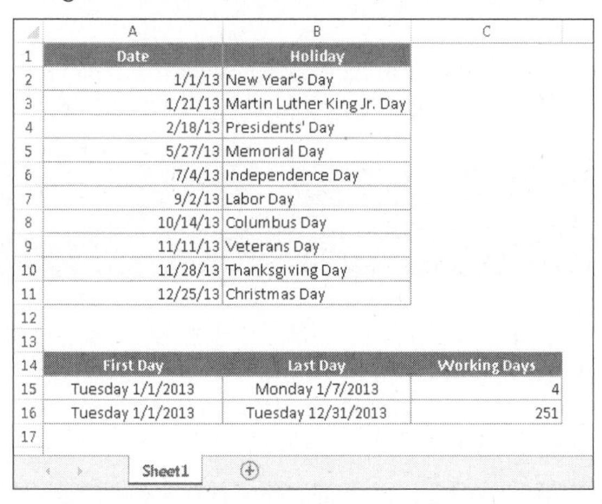

	A	B	C
1	Date	Holiday	
2	1/1/13	New Year's Day	
3	1/21/13	Martin Luther King Jr. Day	
4	2/18/13	Presidents' Day	
5	5/27/13	Memorial Day	
6	7/4/13	Independence Day	
7	9/2/13	Labor Day	
8	10/14/13	Columbus Day	
9	11/11/13	Veterans Day	
10	11/28/13	Thanksgiving Day	
11	12/25/13	Christmas Day	
12			
13			
14	First Day	Last Day	Working Days
15	Tuesday 1/1/2013	Monday 1/7/2013	4
16	Tuesday 1/1/2013	Tuesday 12/31/2013	251
17			

Sheet1

This formula returns `4`, which means that the seven-day period beginning with January 1 contains four workdays. In other words, the calculation excludes one holiday, one Saturday, and one Sunday. The formula in cell C16 calculates the total number of workdays in the year.

> **ON THE WEB**
> This workbook is available on the book's website. The file is named `work days.xlsx`.

NOTE

Excel 2010 introduced an updated version of the NETWORKDAYS function, named NETWORKDAYS.INTL. This newer version of the function is useful if you consider weekend days to be days other than Saturday and Sunday.

Offsetting a date using only workdays

The WORKDAY function is the opposite of the NETWORKDAYS function. For example, if you start a project on January 4 and the project requires ten working days to complete, the WORKDAY function can calculate the date you will finish the project.

NOTE

In versions prior to Excel 2007, the WORKDAY function was available only when the Analysis ToolPak add-in was installed. The function is now part of Excel and doesn't require an add-in.

The following formula uses the WORKDAY function to determine the date that is ten working days from January 4, 2013. A workday consists of a weekday (Monday through Friday).

```
=WORKDAY("1/4/2013",10)
```

The formula returns a date serial number, which must be formatted as a date. The result is January 18, 2013 (four weekend dates fall between January 4 and January 18).

CAUTION

The preceding formula may return a different result, depending on your regional date setting. (The hard-coded date may be interpreted as April 1, 2013.) A better formula is

The second argument for the WORKDAY function can be negative. And, as with the NETWORKDAYS function, the WORKDAY function accepts an optional third argument (a reference to a range that contains a list of holiday dates).

NOTE

Excel 2010 introduced an updated version of the WORKDAY function, named WORKDAY.INTL. This newer version of the function is useful if you consider weekend days to be days other than Saturday and Sunday.

Calculating the number of years between two dates

The following formula calculates the number of years between two dates. This formula assumes that cells A1 and B1 both contain dates:

```
=YEAR(A1)-YEAR(B1)
```

This formula uses the YEAR function to extract the year from each date and then subtracts one year from the other. If cell B1 contains a more recent date than the date in cell A1, the result is negative.

Note that this function doesn't calculate *full* years. For example, if cell A1 contains 12/31/2012 and cell B1 contains 01/01/2013, the formula returns a difference of one year even though the dates differ by only one day. (See the next section for another way to calculate the number of full years.)

Calculating a person's age

A person's age indicates the number of full years that the person has been alive. The formula in the previous section (for calculating the number of years between two dates) won't calculate this value correctly. You can use two other formulas, however, to calculate a person's age.

The following formula returns the age of the person whose date of birth you enter into cell A1. This formula uses the YEARFRAC function.

```
=INT(YEARFRAC(TODAY(),A1,1))
```

NOTE

In versions prior to Excel 2007, the YEARFRAC function was available only when the Analysis ToolPak add-in was installed. The function is now part of Excel and does not require an add-in.

The following formula uses the DATEDIF function to calculate an age. (See the sidebar, "Where's the DATEDIF Function?")

```
=DATEDIF(A1,TODAY(),"Y")
```

Where's the DATEDIF Function?

One of Excel's mysteries is the DATEDIF function. You may notice that this function doesn't appear in the drop-down function list for the Date & Time category, nor does it appear in the Insert Function dialog box. Therefore, when you use this function, you must always enter it manually.

The DATEDIF function has its origins in Lotus 1-2-3, and apparently Excel provides it for compatibility purposes. For some reason, Microsoft wants to keep this function a secret. The function has been available since Excel 5, but Excel 2000 is the only version that ever documented it in its Help system.

DATEDIF is a handy function that calculates the number of days, months, or years between two dates. The function takes three arguments: start_date, end_date, and a code that represents the time unit of interest. Here's an example of a formula that uses the DATEDIF function (it assumes cells A1 and A2 contain a date). The formula returns the number of complete years between those two dates.

```
=DATEDIF(A1,A2,"y")
```

continued

continued

The following table displays valid codes for the third argument. (You must enclose the codes in quotation marks.)

Unit Code	Returns
"y"	The number of complete years in the period.
"m"	The number of complete months in the period.
"d"	The number of days in the period.
"md"	The difference between the days in start_date and end_date. The months and years of the dates are ignored.
"ym"	The difference between the months in start_date and end_date. The days and years of the dates are ignored.
"yd"	The difference between the days of start_date and end_date. The years of the dates are ignored.

The start_date argument must be earlier than the end_date argument or else the function returns an error.

Determining the day of the year

January 1 is the first day of the year, and December 31 is the last day. But what about all those days in between? The following formula returns the day of the year for a date stored in cell A1:

```
=A1-DATE(YEAR(A1),1,0)
```

Here's a similar formula that returns the day of the year for the current date:

```
=TODAY()-DATE(YEAR(TODAY()),1,0)
```

The following formula returns the number of days remaining in the year after a particular date (assumed to be in cell A1):

```
=DATE(YEAR(A1),12,31)-A1
```

Here's the formula modified to use the current date:

```
=DATE(YEAR(TODAY()),12,31)-TODAY()
```

When you enter either formula, Excel applies date formatting to the cell. You need to apply a nondate number format to view the result as a number.

To convert a particular day of the year (for example, the 90th day of the year) to an actual date in a specified year, use the following formula, which assumes that the year is stored in cell A1 and that the day of the year is stored in cell B1:

```
=DATE(A1,1,B1)
```

This formula takes advantage of the fact that the DATE function accepts invalid dates (such as the 90th day of January) and adjusts automatically. The 90th day of January is actually the 90th day of the year.

Determining the day of the week

The WEEKDAY function accepts a date argument and returns an integer between 1 and 7 that corresponds to the day of the week. The following formula, for example, returns 3 because the first day of the year 2013 falls on a Tuesday:

```
=WEEKDAY(DATE(2013,1,1))
```

The WEEKDAY function uses an optional second argument that specifies the day numbering system for the result. If you specify 2 as the second argument, the function returns 1 for Monday, 2 for Tuesday, and so on. If you specify 3 as the second argument, the function returns 0 for Monday, 1 for Tuesday, and so on.

TIP

You can also determine the day of the week for a cell that contains a date by applying a custom number format. A cell that uses the following custom number format displays the day of the week, spelled out:

```
dddd
```

Determining the week of the year

To determine the week of the year for a date, use the WEEKNUM function. The following function returns the week number for the data in cell A1:

```
=WEEKNUM(A1)
```

When you use the WEEKNUM function, you can specify a second optional argument to indicate the type of week numbering system you prefer. The second argument can be one of ten values, which are described in the Help system.

NEW FEATURE

Excel includes a new function, ISOWEEKNUM. This function returns the same result as WEEKNUM with a second argument of 21.

Determining the date of the most recent Sunday

You can use the following formula to return the date for the previous Sunday. If the current day is a Sunday, the formula returns the current date:

```
=TODAY()-MOD(TODAY()-1,7)
```

To modify this formula to find the date of a day other than Sunday, change the `1` to a different number between `2` (for Monday) and `7` (for Saturday).

Determining the first day of the week after a date

This formula returns the specified day of the week that occurs after a particular date. For example, use this formula to determine the date of the first Monday after a particular date. The formula assumes that cell A1 contains a date and cell A2 contains a number between 1 and 7 (`1` for Sunday, `2` for Monday, and so on).

```
=A1+A2-WEEKDAY(A1)+(A2<WEEKDAY(A1))*7
```

If cell A1 contains `June 1, 2013` (a Saturday), and cell A2 contains `2` (for Monday), the formula returns `June 3, 2013`. This is the first Monday following June 1, 2013.

Determining the *n*th occurrence of a day of the week in a month

You may need a formula to determine the date for a particular occurrence of a weekday. For example, suppose that your company payday falls on the second Friday of each month and you need to determine the paydays for each month of the year. The following formula makes this type of calculation:

```
=DATE(A1,A2,1)+A3-WEEKDAY(DATE(A1,A2,1))+(A4-(A3>=WEEKDAY(DATE(A1,A2,1))))*7
```

The formula in this section assumes that

- Cell A1 contains a year.
- Cell A2 contains a month.
- Cell A3 contains a day number (`1` for Sunday, `2` for Monday, and so on).
- Cell A4 contains the occurrence number (for example, `2` to select the second occurrence of the weekday specified in cell A3).

If you use this formula to determine the date of the second Friday in November 2013, it returns `November 8, 2013`.

NOTE

If the value in cell A4 exceeds the number of the specified day in the month, the formula returns a date from a subsequent month. For example, if you attempt to determine the date of the fifth Friday in October 2013 (there is no such date), the formula returns the first Friday in November.

Calculating dates of holidays

Determining the date for a particular holiday can be tricky. Some, such as New Year's Day and Independence Day in the United States are no-brainers because they always occur on the same date. For these kinds of holidays, you can simply use the `DATE` function. To enter New Year's Day (which always falls on January 1) for a specific year in cell A1, you can enter this function:

```
=DATE(A1,1,1)
```

Other holidays are defined in terms of a particular occurrence of a particular weekday in a particular month. For example, Labor Day falls on the first Monday in September.

Figure 12.5 shows a workbook with formulas that calculate the date for 11 U.S. holidays. The formulas, which reference the year in cell A1, are listed in the sections that follow.

FIGURE 12.5

Using formulas to determine the date for various holidays.

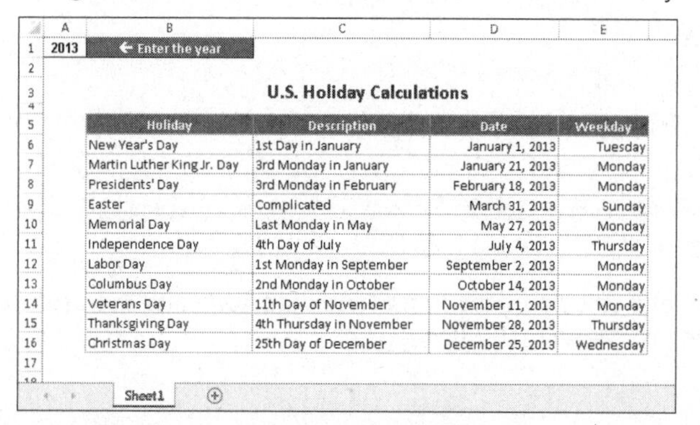

2013 ← Enter the year

U.S. Holiday Calculations

Holiday	Description	Date	Weekday
New Year's Day	1st Day in January	January 1, 2013	Tuesday
Martin Luther King Jr. Day	3rd Monday in January	January 21, 2013	Monday
Presidents' Day	3rd Monday in February	February 18, 2013	Monday
Easter	Complicated	March 31, 2013	Sunday
Memorial Day	Last Monday in May	May 27, 2013	Monday
Independence Day	4th Day of July	July 4, 2013	Thursday
Labor Day	1st Monday in September	September 2, 2013	Monday
Columbus Day	2nd Monday in October	October 14, 2013	Monday
Veterans Day	11th Day of November	November 11, 2013	Monday
Thanksgiving Day	4th Thursday in November	November 28, 2013	Thursday
Christmas Day	25th Day of December	December 25, 2013	Wednesday

Sheet1

On the Web

The workbook shown in Figure 12.5 also appears on the companion website. The file is named `holidays.xlsx`.

New Year's Day

This holiday always falls on January 1:

```
=DATE(A1,1,1)
```

Martin Luther King, Jr., Day

This holiday occurs on the third Monday in January. This formula calculates Martin Luther King, Jr., Day for the year in cell A1:

```
=DATE(A1,1,1)+IF(2<WEEKDAY(DATE(A1,1,1)),7-WEEKDAY(DATE(A1,1,1))+2,2-WEEKDAY
   (DATE(A1,1,1)))+((3-1)*7)
```

Presidents' Day

Presidents' Day occurs on the third Monday in February. This formula calculates Presidents' Day for the year in cell A1:

```
=DATE(A1,2,1)+IF(2<WEEKDAY(DATE(A1,2,1)),7-WEEKDAY(DATE(A1,2,1))+2,2-WEEKDAY
   (DATE(A1,2,1)))+((3-1)*7)
```

Easter

Calculating the date for Easter is difficult because of the complicated manner in which Easter is determined. Easter Day is the first Sunday after the next full moon occurs after the vernal equinox. I found these formulas to calculate Easter on the web. I have no idea how they work. And they don't work if your workbook uses the 1904 date system. (Read about the difference between the 1900 and the 1904 date system earlier in this chapter.)

```
=DOLLAR(("4/"&A1)/7+MOD(19*MOD(A1,19)-7,30)*14%,)*7-6
```

This one is slightly shorter, but equally obtuse:

```
=FLOOR("5/"&DAY(MINUTE(A1/38)/2+56)&"/"&A1,7)-34
```

Memorial Day

The last Monday in May is Memorial Day. This formula calculates Memorial Day for the year in cell A1:

```
=DATE(A1,6,1)+IF(2<WEEKDAY(DATE(A1,6,1)),7-WEEKDAY(DATE(A1,6,1))+2,2-WEEKDAY
   (DATE(A1,6,1)))+((1-1)*7)-7
```

Notice that this formula actually calculates the first Monday in June and then subtracts 7 from the result to return the last Monday in May.

Independence Day

This holiday always falls on July 4:

```
=DATE(A1,7,4)
```

Labor Day

Labor Day occurs on the first Monday in September. This formula calculates Labor Day for the year in cell A1:

```
=DATE(A1,9,1)+IF(2<WEEKDAY(DATE(A1,9,1)),7-WEEKDAY(DATE(A1,9,1))+2,2-WEEKDAY
   (DATE(A1,9,1)))+((1-1)*7)
```

Columbus Day

This holiday occurs on the second Monday in October. This formula calculates Columbus Day for the year in cell A1:

```
=DATE(A1,10,1)+IF(2<WEEKDAY(DATE(A1,10,1)),7-WEEKDAY(DATE(A1,10,1))+2,2-WEEKDAY
   (DATE(A1,10,1)))+((2-1)*7)
```

Veterans Day

This holiday always falls on November 11:

```
=DATE(A1,11,11)
```

Thanksgiving Day

Thanksgiving Day is celebrated on the fourth Thursday in November. This formula calculates Thanksgiving Day for the year in cell A1:

```
=DATE(A1,11,1)+IF(5<WEEKDAY(DATE(A1,11,1)),7-WEEKDAY(DATE(A1,11,1))+5,5-WEEKDAY(
   DATE(A1,11,1)))+((4-1)*7)
```

Christmas Day

This holiday always falls on December 25:

```
=DATE(A1,12,25)
```


Determining the last day of a month

To determine the date that corresponds to the last day of a month, you can use the DATE function. However, you need to increment the month by 1 and use a day value of 0. In other words, the "0th" day of the next month is the last day of the current month.

The following formula assumes that a date is stored in cell A1. The formula returns the date that corresponds to the last day of the month.

```
=DATE(YEAR(A1),MONTH(A1)+1,0)
```

You can use a variation of this formula to determine how many days are in a specified month. The following formula returns an integer that corresponds to the number of days in the month for the date in cell A1:

```
=DAY(DATE(YEAR(A1),MONTH(A1)+1,0))
```

Determining whether a year is a leap year

To determine whether a particular year is a leap year, you can write a formula that determines whether the 29th day of February occurs in February or March. You can take advantage of the fact that the Excel DATE function adjusts the result when you supply an invalid argument — for example, a day of 29 when February contains only 28 days.

The following formula returns TRUE if the year in cell A1 is a leap year. Otherwise, it returns FALSE.

```
=IF(MONTH(DATE(A1,2,29))=2,TRUE,FALSE)
```

CAUTION
This function returns the wrong result (`TRUE`) if the year is 1900 (see "Excel's leap year bug," earlier in this chapter).

The following formula is a bit more complicated, but it correctly identifies 1900 as a non-leap year. This formula assumes that cell A1 contains a year.

```
=IF(OR(MOD(A1,400)=0,AND(MOD(A1,4)=0,MOD(A1,100)<>0)),TRUE, FALSE)
```

Determining a date's quarter

For financial reports, you may find it useful to present information in terms of quarters. The following formula returns an integer between `1` and `4` that corresponds to the calendar quarter for the date in cell A1:

```
=ROUNDUP(MONTH(A1)/3,0)
```

This formula divides the month number by 3 and then rounds up the result.

Time-Related Functions

Excel also includes a number of functions that enable you to work with time values in your formulas. This section contains examples that demonstrate the use of these functions.

Table 12.5 summarizes the time-related functions available in Excel. These functions work with date serial numbers. When you use the Insert Function dialog box, these functions appear in the Date & Time function category.

TABLE 12.5 Time-Related Functions

Function	Description
HOUR	Returns the hour part of a serial number
MINUTE	Returns the minute part of a serial number
NOW	Returns the serial number of the current date and time
SECOND	Returns the second part of a serial number
TIME	Returns the serial number of a specified time
TIMEVALUE	Converts a time in the form of text to a serial number

Displaying the current time

This formula displays the current time as a time serial number (or as a serial number without an associated date):

```
=NOW()-TODAY()
```

You need to format the cell with a time format to view the result as a recognizable time. The quickest way is to choose Home ➪ Number ➪ Format Number and select Time from the drop-down list.

Or just use the following formula, which returns the current date and time. You can apply a number format that shows the time only.

```
=NOW()
```


NOTE

Formulas that use the NOW function are updated only when the worksheet is calculated. The time comes from your computer's clock, so if the clock is wrong, the formula will return an incorrect time.

TIP

To enter a time stamp (that doesn't change) into a cell, press Ctrl+Shift+: (colon).

Displaying any time

One way to enter a time value into a cell is to just type it, making sure that you include at least one colon (:). You can also create a time by using the TIME function. For example, the following formula returns a time comprising the hour in cell A1, the minute in cell B1, and the second in cell C1:

```
=TIME(A1,B1,C1)
```

Like the DATE function, the TIME function accepts invalid arguments and adjusts the result accordingly. For example, the following formula uses 80 as the minute argument and returns 10:20:15 AM. The 80 minutes are simply added to the hour, with 20 minutes remaining.

```
=TIME(9,80,15)
```

CAUTION

If you enter a value greater than `24` as the first argument for the `TIME` function, the result may not be what you expect. Logically, a formula such as the one that follows should produce a date/time serial number of 1.041667 (that is, one day and one hour).

```
=TIME(25,0,0)
```

In fact, this formula is equivalent to the following:

```
=TIME(1,0,0)
```

You can also use the `DATE` function along with the `TIME` function in a single cell. The formula that follows generates a date and time with a serial number of 41612.7708333333 — which represents 6:30 p.m. on December 4, 2013:

```
=DATE(2013,12,4)+TIME(18,30,0)
```

The `TIMEVALUE` function converts a text string that looks like a time into a time serial number. This formula returns `0.2395833333`, the time serial number for 5:45 a.m.:

```
=TIMEVALUE("5:45 am")
```

To view the result of this formula as a time, you need to apply number formatting to the cell. The `TIMEVALUE` function doesn't recognize all common time formats. For example, the following formula returns an error because Excel doesn't like the periods in "a.m."

```
=TIMEVALUE("5:45 a.m.")
```

Calculating the difference between two times

Because times are represented as serial numbers, you can subtract the earlier time from the later time to get the difference. For example, if cell A2 contains 5:30:00 and cell B2 contains 14:00:00, the following formula returns `08:30:00` (a difference of 8 hours and 30 minutes):

```
=B2-A2
```

If the subtraction results in a negative value, however, it becomes an invalid time; Excel displays a series of hash marks (#######) because a time without a date has a date serial number of 0. A negative time results in a negative serial number, which cannot be displayed — although you can still use the calculated value in other formulas.

If the direction of the time difference doesn't matter, you can use the `ABS` function to return the absolute value of the difference:

```
=ABS(B2-A2)
```

This "negative time" problem often occurs when calculating an elapsed time — for example, calculating the number of hours worked given a start time and an end time. This presents no problem if the two times fall in the same day. But if the work shift spans midnight, the result is an invalid negative time. For example, you may start work at 10:00 p.m. and end work at 6:00 a.m. the next day. Figure 12.6 shows a worksheet that calculates the hours worked. As you can see, the shift that spans midnight presents a problem (cell C3).

FIGURE 12.6

Calculating the number of hours worked returns an error if the shift spans midnight.

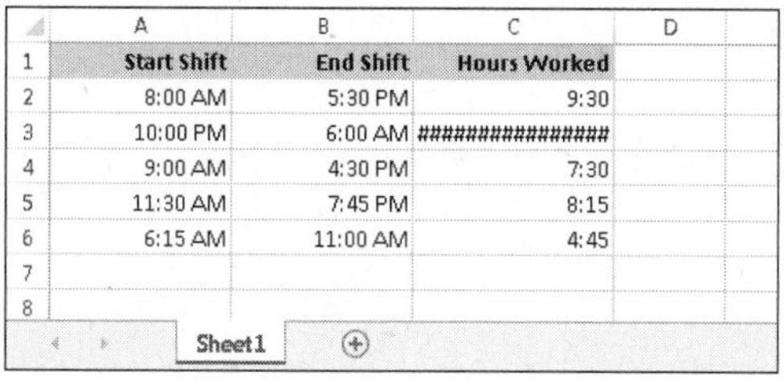

	A	B	C	D
1	Start Shift	End Shift	Hours Worked	
2	8:00 AM	5:30 PM	9:30	
3	10:00 PM	6:00 AM	################	
4	9:00 AM	4:30 PM	7:30	
5	11:30 AM	7:45 PM	8:15	
6	6:15 AM	11:00 AM	4:45	
7				
8				

Sheet1

Using the `ABS` function (to calculate the absolute value) isn't an option in this case because it returns the wrong result (`16`). The following formula, however, *does* work:

```
=IF(B2<A2,B2+1,B2)-A2
```

TIP

Negative times *are* permitted if the workbook uses the 1904 date system. To switch to the 1904 date system, use the Advanced section of the Excel Options dialog box. Select the Use 1904 Date System option. But beware! When changing the workbook's date system, if the workbook uses dates, the dates will be off by four years. (For more information about the 1904 date system, see the sidebar "Choose Your Date System: 1900 or 1904," earlier in this chapter.)

Summing times that exceed 24 hours

Many people are surprised to discover that when you sum a series of times that exceed 24 hours, Excel doesn't display the correct total. Figure 12.7 shows an example. The range B2:B8 contains times that represent the hours and minutes worked each day. The formula in cell B9 is

```
=SUM(B2:B8)
```

FIGURE 12.7

Incorrect cell formatting makes the total appear incorrectly.

	A	B	C	D
1	**Day**	**Hours Worked**		
2	Sunday	0:00		
3	Monday	8:30		
4	Tuesday	8:00		
5	Wednesday	9:00		
6	Thursday	9:30		
7	Friday	4:15		
8	Saturday	2:30		
9	**Total H ours**	**17:45**		
10				
11				

Sheet1 | Sheet2

As you can see, the formula returns a seemingly incorrect total (17 hours, 45 minutes). The total should read 41 hours, 45 minutes. The problem is that the formula is displaying the total as a date/time serial number of 1.7395833, but the cell formatting is not displaying the *date* part of the date/time. In other words, the answer is correct, but it appears incorrect because cell B9 has the wrong number format.

To view a time that exceeds 24 hours, you need to apply a custom number format for the cell so that square brackets surround the *hour* part of the format string. Applying the number format here to cell B9 displays the sum correctly:

```
[h]:mm
```

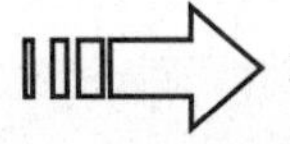

For more information about custom number formats, see Chapter 25.

Figure 12.8 shows another example of a worksheet that manipulates times. This worksheet keeps track of hours worked during a week (regular hours and overtime hours).

ON THE WEB

This workbook is available on this book's website. The filename is `timesheet.xlsm`. The workbook contains a few macros to make it easier to use, so you'll need to enable macros when you open the workbook.

The week's starting date appears in cell D5, and the formulas in column B fill in the dates for the days of the week. Times appear in the range D8:G14, and formulas in column H calculate the number of hours worked each day. For example, the formula in cell H8 is

```
=IF(E8<D8,E8+1-D8,E8-D8)+IF(G8<F8,G8+1-G8,G8-F8)
```

FIGURE 12.8

An employee timesheet workbook.

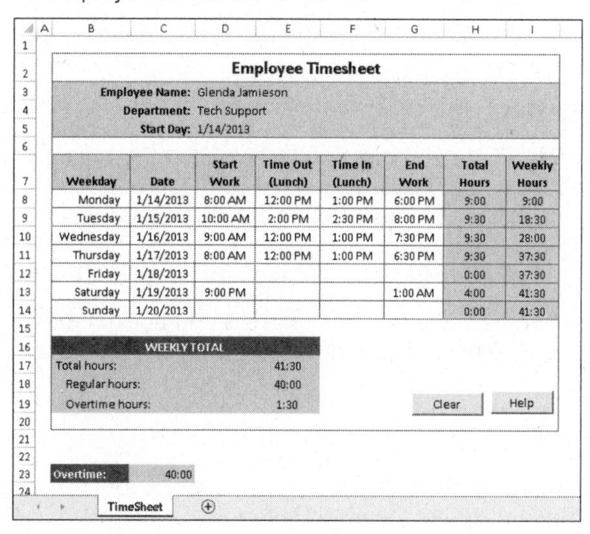

The first part of this formula subtracts the time in column D from the time in column E to get the total hours worked before lunch. The second part subtracts the time in column F from the time in column G to get the total hours worked after lunch. I use `IF` functions to accommodate graveyard shift cases that span midnight — for example, an employee may start work at 10:00 p.m. and begin lunch at 2:00 a.m. Without the `IF` function, the formula returns a negative result.

The following formula in cell H17 calculates the weekly total by summing the daily totals in column H:

```
=SUM(H8:H14)
```

This worksheet assumes that hours in excess of 40 hours in a week are considered overtime hours. The worksheet contains a cell named Overtime, in cell C23. This cell contains a formula that returns `40:00`. If your standard workweek consists of something other than 40 hours, you can change this cell.

The following formula (in cell H18) calculates regular (nonovertime) hours. This formula returns the smaller of two values: the total hours or the overtime hours.

```
=MIN(E17,Overtime)
```

The final formula, in cell H19, simply subtracts the regular hours from the total hours to yield the overtime hours.

```
=E17-E18
```

The times in the range H17:H19 and cell C23 may display time values that exceed 24 hours, so these cells use a custom number format:

```
[h]:mm
```

Converting from military time

Military time is expressed as a four-digit number from 0000 to 2359. For example, 1:00 a.m. is expressed as 0100 hours, and 3:30 p.m. is expressed as 1530 hours. The following formula converts such a number (assumed to be in cell A1) to a standard time:

```
=TIMEVALUE(LEFT(A1,2)&":"&RIGHT(A1,2))
```

The formula returns an incorrect result if the contents of cell A1 do not contain four digits. The following formula corrects the problem, and it returns a valid time for any military time value from `0` to `2359`:

```
=TIMEVALUE(LEFT(TEXT(A1,"0000"),2)&":"&RIGHT(A1,2))
```

Following is a simpler formula that uses the `TEXT` function to return a formatted string and then the `TIMEVALUE` function to express the result in terms of a time:

```
=TIMEVALUE(TEXT(A1,"00\:00"))
```

Converting decimal hours, minutes, or seconds to a time

To convert decimal hours to a time, divide the decimal hours by 24. For example, if cell A1 contains 9.25 (representing hours), this formula returns `09:15:00` (9 hours, 15 minutes):

```
=A1/24
```

To convert decimal minutes to a time, divide the decimal hours by 1,440 (the number of minutes in a day). For example, if cell A1 contains 500 (representing minutes), the following formula returns `08:20:00` (8 hours, 20 minutes):

```
=A1/1440
```

To convert decimal seconds to a time, divide the decimal hours by 86,400 (the number of seconds in a day). For example, if cell A1 contains 65,000 (representing seconds), the following formula returns `18:03:20` (18 hours, 3 minutes, and 20 seconds):

```
=A1/86400
```

Adding hours, minutes, or seconds to a time

You can use the `TIME` function to add any number of hours, minutes, or seconds to a time. For example, assume that cell A1 contains a time. The following formula adds 2 hours and 30 minutes to that time and displays the result:

```
=A1+TIME(2,30,0)
```

You can use the TIME function to fill a range of cells with incremental times. Figure 12.9 shows a worksheet with a series of times in ten-minute increments. Cell A1 contains a time that was entered directly. Cell A2 contains the following formula, which was copied down the column:

```
=A1+TIME(0,10,0)
```

FIGURE 12.9

Using a formula to create a series of incremental times.

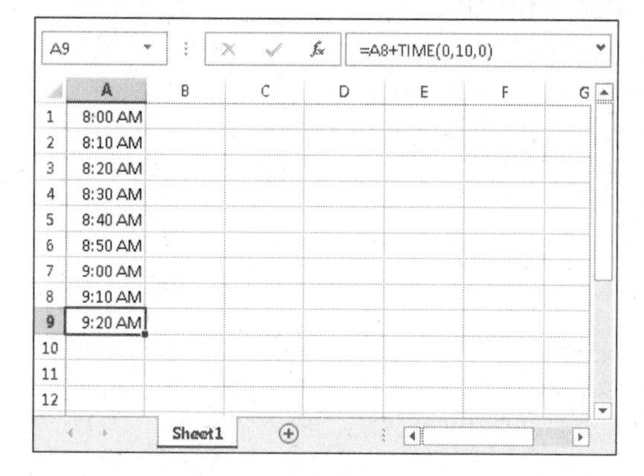

Rounding time values

You may need to create a formula that rounds a time to a particular value. For example, you may need to enter your company's time records rounded to the nearest 15 minutes. This section presents examples of various ways to round a time value.

The following formula rounds the time in cell A1 to the nearest minute:

```
=ROUND(A1*1440,0)/1440
```

The formula works by multiplying the time by 1,440 (to get total minutes). This value is passed to the ROUND function, and the result is divided by 1,440. For example, if cell A1 contains 11:52:34, the formula returns 11:53:00.

The following formula resembles this example, except that it rounds the time in cell A1 to the nearest hour:

```
=ROUND(A1*24,0)/24
```

If cell A1 contains 5:21:31, the formula returns 5:00:00.

The following formula rounds the time in cell A1 to the nearest 15 minutes (a quarter of an hour):

```
=ROUND(A1*24/0.25,0)*(0.25/24)
```

In this formula, 0.25 represents the fractional hour. To round a time to the nearest 30 minutes, change `0.25` to `0.5`, as in the following formula:

```
=ROUND(A1*24/0.5,0)*(0.5/24)
```

Working with non-time-of-day values

Sometimes, you may want to work with time values that don't represent an actual time of day. For example, you may want to create a list of the finish times for a race or record the amount of time you spend in meetings each day. Such times don't represent a time of day. Instead, a value represents the time for an event (in hours, minutes, and seconds). The time to complete a test, for example, may be 35 minutes and 45 seconds. You can enter that value into a cell as:

```
00:35:45
```

Excel interprets such an entry as 12:35:45 a.m., which works fine. (Just make sure that you format the cell so that it appears as you like.) When you enter such times, which don't have an hour component, you must include at least one zero for the hour. If you omit a leading zero for a missing hour, Excel interprets your entry as 35 hours and 45 minutes.

Figure 12.10 shows an example of a worksheet set up to keep track of a person's jogging activity. Column A contains simple dates. Column B contains the distance in miles. Column C contains the time it took to run the distance. Column D contains formulas to calculate the speed in miles per hour. For example, the formula in cell D2 is

```
=B2/(C2*24)
```

Column E contains formulas to calculate the pace, in minutes per mile. For example, the formula in cell E2 is

```
=(C2*60*24)/B2
```

Columns F and G contain formulas that calculate the year-to-date distance (using column B) and the cumulative time (using column C). The cells in column G are formatted using the following number format (which permits time displays that exceed 24 hours):

```
[hh]:mm:ss
```

FIGURE 12.10

This worksheet uses times not associated with a time of day.

	A	B	C	D	E	F	G
1	Date	Distance	Time	Speed (mph)	Pace (min/mile)	YTD Distance	Cumulative Time
2	1/1/2013	1.50	00:18:45	4.80	12.50	1.50	00:18:45
3	1/2/2013	1.50	00:17:40	5.09	11.78	3.00	00:36:25
4	1/3/2013	2.00	00:21:30	5.58	10.75	5.00	00:57:55
5	1/4/2013	1.50	00:15:20	5.87	10.22	6.50	01:13:15
6	1/5/2013	2.40	00:25:05	5.74	10.45	8.90	01:38:20
7	1/6/2013	3.00	00:31:06	5.79	10.37	11.90	02:09:26
8	1/7/2013	3.80	00:41:06	5.55	10.82	15.70	02:50:32
9	1/8/2013	5.00	01:09:00	4.35	13.80	20.70	03:59:32
10	1/9/2013	4.00	00:45:10	5.31	11.29	24.70	04:44:42
11	1/10/2013	3.00	00:29:06	6.19	9.70	27.70	05:13:48
12	1/11/2013	5.50	01:08:30	4.82	12.45	33.20	06:22:18
13							
14							

Sheet1

12

ON THE WEB

You can also access the workbook shown in Figure 12.10 on this book's website. The file is named `jogging log.xlsx`.

CHAPTER

13

Creating Formulas That Count and Sum

IN THIS CHAPTER

Introducing various ways to count and sum cells

Creating basic counting and summing formulas

Working with advanced counting and summing formulas

Developing conditional summing formulas

Many of the most common spreadsheet questions involve counting and summing values and other worksheet elements. It seems that people are always looking for formulas to count or to sum various items in a worksheet. If I've done my job, this chapter answers the vast majority of such questions. It contains many examples that you can easily adapt to your own situation.

Counting and Summing Worksheet Cells

Generally, a *counting formula* returns the number of cells in a specified range that meet certain criteria. A *summing formula* returns the sum of the values of the cells in a range that meet certain criteria.

Table 13.1 lists the Excel worksheet functions that come into play when creating counting and summing formulas. Not all these functions are covered in this chapter. If none of the functions in Table 13.1 can solve your problem, it's likely that an array formula can come to the rescue.

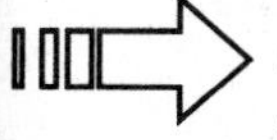

See Chapters 17 and 18 for detailed information and examples of array formulas used for counting and summing.

NOTE

If your data is in the form of a table, you can use autofiltering to accomplish many counting and summing operations. Just set the autofilter criteria, and the table displays only the rows that match your criteria (the nonqualifying rows in the table are hidden). Then you can select formulas to display counts or sums in the table's total row.

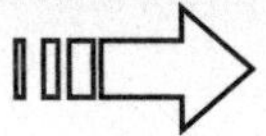

See Chapter 5 for more information on using tables.

TABLE 13.1 Excel Counting and Summing Functions

Function	Description
COUNT	Returns the number of cells that contain a numeric value.
COUNTA	Returns the number of nonblank cells.
COUNTBLANK	Returns the number of blank cells.
COUNTIF	Returns the number of cells that meet a specified criterion.
COUNTIFS*	Returns the number of cells that meet multiple criteria.
DCOUNT	Counts the number of records that meet specified criteria; used with a worksheet database.
DCOUNTA	Counts the number of nonblank records that meet specified criteria; used with a worksheet database.
DSUM	Returns the sum of a column of values that meet specified criteria; used with a worksheet database.
FREQUENCY	Calculates how often values occur within a range of values and returns a vertical array of numbers. Used only in a multicell array formula.
SUBTOTAL	When used with a first argument of 2, 3, 102, or 103, returns a *count* of cells that comprise a subtotal; when used with a first argument of 9 or 109, returns the *sum* of cells that comprise a subtotal.
SUM	Returns the sum of its arguments.
SUMIF	Returns the sum of cells that meet a specified criterion.
SUMIFS*	Returns the sum of cells that meet multiple criteria.
SUMPRODUCT	Multiplies corresponding cells in two or more ranges and returns the sum of those products.

* These functions were introduced in Excel 2007.

Getting a Quick Count or Sum

The Excel status bar can display useful information about the currently selected cells — no formulas required. Normally, the status bar displays the sum and count of the values in the selected range. You can, however, right-click the status bar to bring up a menu with other options. You can choose any or all of the following: Average, Count, Numerical Count, Minimum, Maximum, and Sum.

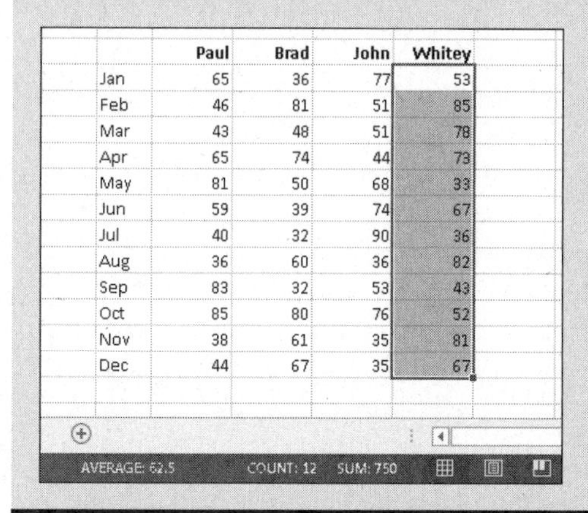

	Paul	Brad	John	Whitey
Jan	65	36	77	53
Feb	46	81	51	85
Mar	43	48	51	78
Apr	65	74	44	73
May	81	50	68	33
Jun	59	39	74	67
Jul	40	32	90	36
Aug	36	60	36	82
Sep	83	32	53	43
Oct	85	80	76	52
Nov	38	61	35	81
Dec	44	67	35	67

Basic Counting Formulas

The basic counting formulas presented in this section are all straightforward and relatively simple. They demonstrate the capability of the Excel counting functions to count the number of cells in a range that meet specific criteria.

Figure 13.1 shows a worksheet that uses formulas (in column E) to summarize the contents of range A1:B10 — a 20-cell range named Data. This range contains a variety of information, including values, text, logical values, errors, and empty cells.

On the Web

This workbook is available on this book's website. The file is named `basic counting.xlsx`.

FIGURE 13.1

Formulas in column E display various counts of the data in A1:B10.

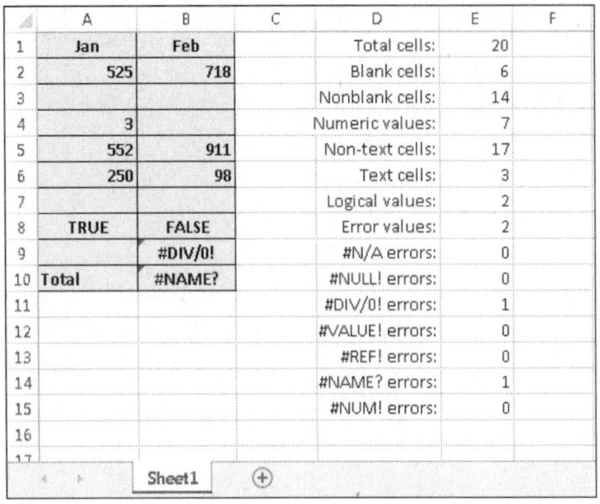

	A	B	C	D	E	F
1	Jan	Feb		Total cells:	20	
2	525	718		Blank cells:	6	
3				Nonblank cells:	14	
4	3			Numeric values:	7	
5	552	911		Non-text cells:	17	
6	250	98		Text cells:	3	
7				Logical values:	2	
8	TRUE	FALSE		Error values:	2	
9		#DIV/0!		#N/A errors:	0	
10	Total	#NAME?		#NULL! errors:	0	
11				#DIV/0! errors:	1	
12				#VALUE! errors:	0	
13				#REF! errors:	0	
14				#NAME? errors:	1	
15				#NUM! errors:	0	
16						

Sheet1

Counting the total number of cells

Oddly, Excel doesn't have a function that simply counts the number of cells in a range reference. To get a count of the total number of cells in a range (empty and nonempty cells), use the following formula. This formula returns the number of cells in a range named Data. It simply multiplies the number of rows (returned by the `ROWS` function) by the number of columns (returned by the `COLUMNS` function).

```
=ROWS(Data)*COLUMNS(Data)
```

About This Chapter's Examples

Most of the examples in this chapter use named ranges for function arguments. When you adapt these formulas for your own use, you'll need to substitute either the actual range address or a range name defined in your workbook. (See Chapter 4 for information about using named ranges.)

Also, some examples consist of array formulas. An *array formula* is a special type of formula that enables you to perform calculations that would not otherwise be possible. You can spot an array formula because it's enclosed in curly brackets when it's displayed in the Formula bar. In addition, I use this syntax for the array formula examples presented in this book. For example:

```
{=Data*2}
```

When you enter an array formula, press Ctrl+Shift+Enter (not just Enter), but *don't* type the curly brackets (Excel inserts the brackets for you). If you need to edit an array formula, don't forget to press Ctrl+Shift+Enter when you finish editing; otherwise, the array formula will revert to a normal formula, and it will return an incorrect result. (See Chapter 17 for an introduction to array formulas.)

This formula will not work if the Data range consists of noncontiguous cells. In other words, Data must be a rectangular range of cells.

Counting blank cells

The following formula returns the number of blank (empty) cells in a range named Data:

```
=COUNTBLANK(Data)
```

This function works only with a contiguous range of cells. If Data is defined as a noncontiguous range, the function returns a #VALUE! error.

The COUNTBLANK function also counts cells containing a formula that returns an empty string. For example, the formula that follows returns an empty string if the value in cell A1 is greater than 5. If the cell meets this condition, the COUNTBLANK function counts that cell.

```
=IF(A1>5,"",A1)
```

You can use the COUNTBLANK function with an argument that consists of entire rows or columns. For example, the following formula returns the number of blank cells in column A:

```
=COUNTBLANK(A:A)
```

The following formula returns the number of empty cells on the entire worksheet named Sheet1. You must enter this formula on a sheet other than Sheet1, or it will create a circular reference.

```
=COUNTBLANK(Sheet1!1:1048576)
```


Counting nonblank cells

To count nonblank cells, use the COUNTA function. The following formula uses the COUNTA function to return the number of nonblank cells in a range named Data:

```
=COUNTA(Data)
```

The COUNTA function counts cells that contain values, text, or logical values (TRUE or FALSE).

NOTE

If a cell contains a formula that returns an empty string, that cell is included in the count returned by COUNTA, even though the cell appears to be blank.

Counting numeric cells

To count only the numeric cells in a range, use the following formula (which assumes the range is named Data):

```
=COUNT(Data)
```

Cells that contain a date or a time are considered to be numeric cells. Cells that contain a logical value (`TRUE` or `FALSE`) aren't considered to be numeric cells.

Counting text cells

To count the number of text cells in a range, you need to use an array formula. The array formula that follows returns the number of text cells in a range named Data:

```
{=SUM(IF(ISTEXT(Data),1))}
```

Counting nontext cells

The following array formula uses the Excel `ISNONTEXT` function, which returns `TRUE` if its argument refers to any nontext cell (including a blank cell). This formula returns the count of the number of cells not containing text (including blank cells):

```
{=SUM(IF(ISNONTEXT(Data),1))}
```

Counting logical values

The following array formula returns the number of logical values (`TRUE` or `FALSE`) in a range named Data:

```
{=SUM(IF(ISLOGICAL(Data),1))}
```

Counting error values in a range

Excel has three functions that help you determine whether a cell contains an error value:

- `ISERROR`: Returns `TRUE` if the cell contains any error value (`#N/A`, `#VALUE!`, `#REF!`, `#DIV/0!`, `#NUM!`, `#NAME?`, or `#NULL!`)
- `ISERR`: Returns `TRUE` if the cell contains any error value except `#N/A`
- `ISNA`: Returns `TRUE` if the cell contains the `#N/A` error value

You can use these functions in an array formula to count the number of error values in a range. The following array formula, for example, returns the total number of error values in a range named Data:

```
{=SUM(IF(ISERROR(data),1))}
```

Depending on your needs, you can use the ISERR or ISNA function in place of ISERROR.

If you want to count specific types of errors, you can use the COUNTIF function. The following formula, for example, returns the number of #DIV/0! error values in the range named Data:

```
=COUNTIF(Data,"#DIV/0!")
```

Note that the COUNTIF functions works only with a contiguous range argument. If Data is a noncontiguous range, the formula returns a #VALUE! error.

Advanced Counting Formulas

Most of the basic examples I present earlier in this chapter use functions or formulas that perform conditional counting. The advanced counting formulas that I present in this section represent more complex examples for counting worksheet cells, based on various types of criteria.

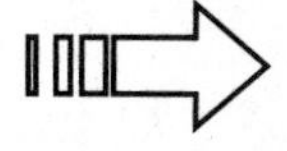

Some of these examples are array formulas. See Chapters 17 and 18 for more information about array formulas.

Counting cells by using the COUNTIF function

The COUNTIF function, which is useful for single-criterion counting formulas, takes two arguments:

- range: The range that contains the values that determine whether to include a particular cell in the count
- criteria: The logical criteria that determine whether to include a particular cell in the count

Table 13.2 lists several examples of formulas that use the COUNTIF function. These formulas all work with a range named Data. As you can see, the criteria argument proves quite flexible. You can use constants, expressions, functions, cell references, and even wildcard characters (* and ?).

Note that the COUNTIF functions works only with a contiguous range argument. If *Data* is defined a noncontiguous range, the formula returns a #VALUE! error.

TABLE 13.2 Examples of Formulas Using the COUNTIF Function

=COUNTIF(Data,12)	Returns the number of cells containing the value 12
=COUNTIF(Data,"<0")	Returns the number of cells containing a negative value
=COUNTIF(Data,"<>0")	Returns the number of cells not equal to 0
=COUNTIF(Data,">5")	Returns the number of cells greater than 5
=COUNTIF(Data,A1)	Returns the number of cells equal to the contents of cell A1
=COUNTIF(Data,">"&A1)	Returns the number of cells greater than the value in cell A1
=COUNTIF(Data,"*")	Returns the number of cells containing text
=COUNTIF(Data,"???")	Returns the number of text cells containing exactly three characters
=COUNTIF(Data,"budget")	Returns the number of cells containing the single word *budget* (not case sensitive)
=COUNTIF(Data,"*budget*")	Returns the number of cells containing the text *budget* anywhere within the text
=COUNTIF(Data,"A*")	Returns the number of cells containing text that begins with the letter *A* (not case sensitive)
=COUNTIF(Data,TODAY())	Returns the number of cells containing the current date
=COUNTIF(Data,">"&AVERAGE(Data))	Returns the number of cells with a value greater than the average of the values
=COUNTIF(Data,">"&AVERAGE(Data)+STDEV(Data)*3)	Returns the number of values exceeding three standard deviations above the mean
=COUNTIF(Data,3)+COUNTIF(Data,-3)	Returns the number of cells containing the value 3 or –3
=COUNTIF(Data,TRUE)	Returns the number of cells containing the logical value TRUE
=COUNTIF(Data,TRUE)+COUNTIF(Data,FALSE)	Returns the number of cells containing a logical value (TRUE or FALSE)
=COUNTIF(Data,"#N/A")	Returns the number of cells containing the #N/A error value

Counting cells based on multiple criteria

In many cases, your counting formula will need to count cells only if two or more criteria are met. These criteria can be based on the cells that are being counted or on a range of corresponding cells.

Figure 13.2 shows a simple worksheet that I use for the examples in this section. This sheet shows sales data categorized by Month, Sales Rep, and Type. The worksheet contains four named ranges that correspond to the labels in row 1.

FIGURE 13.2

This worksheet demonstrates various counting techniques that use multiple criteria.

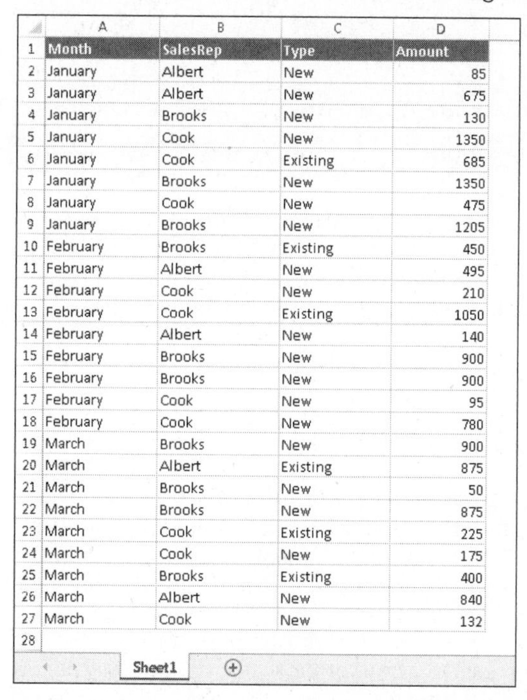

	A	B	C	D
1	Month	SalesRep	Type	Amount
2	January	Albert	New	85
3	January	Albert	New	675
4	January	Brooks	New	130
5	January	Cook	New	1350
6	January	Cook	Existing	685
7	January	Brooks	New	1350
8	January	Cook	New	475
9	January	Brooks	New	1205
10	February	Brooks	Existing	450
11	February	Albert	New	495
12	February	Cook	New	210
13	February	Cook	Existing	1050
14	February	Albert	New	140
15	February	Brooks	New	900
16	February	Brooks	New	900
17	February	Cook	New	95
18	February	Cook	New	780
19	March	Brooks	New	900
20	March	Albert	Existing	875
21	March	Brooks	New	50
22	March	Brooks	New	875
23	March	Cook	Existing	225
24	March	Cook	New	175
25	March	Brooks	Existing	400
26	March	Albert	New	840
27	March	Cook	New	132
28				

On the Web

This workbook is available on this book's website. The file is named `multiple criteria counting.xlsx`.

Note

Several of the examples in this section use the `COUNTIFS` function, which was introduced in Excel 2007. I also present alternative versions of the formulas, which you should use if you plan to share your workbook with others who use an earlier version of Excel.

Using And criteria

An And criterion counts cells if all specified conditions are met. A common example is a formula that counts the number of values that fall within a numerical range. For example, you may want to count cells that contain a value that's greater than 100 *and* less than or equal to 200. For this example, the `COUNTIFS` function will do the job:

```
=COUNTIFS(Amount,">100",Amount,"<=200")
```

NOTE

If the data is contained in a table, you can use table referencing in your formulas. For example, if the table is named Table1, you can rewrite the preceding formula as:

```
=COUNTIFS(Table1[Amount],">100",Table1[Amount],"<=200")
```

This method of writing formulas does not require named ranges. Excel automatically creates names for the table and each column in the table.

The `COUNTIFS` function accepts any number of paired arguments. The first member of the pair is the range to be counted (in this case, the range named Amount); the second member of the pair is the criterion. The preceding example contains two sets of paired arguments and returns the number of cells in which Amount is greater than 100 and less than or equal to 200.

Prior to Excel 2007, you would need to use a formula like this:

```
=COUNTIF(Amount,">100")-COUNTIF(Amount,">200")
```

This formula counts the number of values that are greater than 100 and then subtracts the number of values that are greater than or equal to 200. The result is the number of cells that contain a value greater than 100 and less than or equal to 200. This formula can be confusing because the formula refers to a condition `">200"` even though the goal is to count values that are less than or equal to 200.

Yet another alternate technique is to use an array formula, like the one that follows. You may find it easier to create this type of formula:

```
{=SUM((Amount>100)*(Amount<=200))}
```

NOTE

When you enter an array formula, remember to press Ctrl+Shift+Enter, but don't type the curly brackets. Excel includes the brackets for you.

Sometimes, the counting criteria will be based on cells other than the cells being counted. You may, for example, want to count the number of sales that meet all the following criteria:

- Month is January *and*
- SalesRep is Brooks *and*
- Amount is greater than 1,000.

The following formula (for Excel 2007 and later) returns the number of items that meet all three criteria. Note that the `COUNTIFS` function uses three sets of paired arguments.

```
=COUNTIFS(Month,"January",SalesRep,"Brooks",Amount,">1000")
```

An alternative formula, which works with all versions of Excel, uses the `SUMPRODUCT` function. The following formula returns the same result as the previous formula.

```
=SUMPRODUCT((Month="January")*(SalesRep="Brooks")*(Amount>1000))
```

Yet another way to perform this count is to use an array formula:

```
{=SUM((Month="January")*(SalesRep="Brooks")*(Amount>1000))}
```

Using Or criteria

An Or criterion counts cells if any of the multiple conditions is met. To count cells by using an Or criterion, you can sometimes use multiple `COUNTIF` functions. The following formula, for example, counts the number of sales made in January *or* February:

```
=COUNTIF(Month,"January")+COUNTIF(Month,"February")
```

You can also use the `COUNTIF` function in an array formula. The following array formula, for example, returns the same result as the previous formula:

```
{=SUM(COUNTIF(Month,{"January","February"}))}
```

But if you base your Or criteria on cells other than the cells being counted, the `COUNTIF` function won't work (refer to Figure 13.2). Suppose that you want to count the number of sales that meet at least one of the following criteria:

- Month is January *or*
- SalesRep is Brooks *or*
- Amount is greater than 1,000

If you attempt to create a formula that uses `COUNTIF`, some double counting will occur. The solution is to use an array formula like this:

```
{=SUM(IF((Month="January")+(SalesRep="Brooks")+(Amount>1000),1))}
```

Combining And and Or criteria

In some cases, you may need to combine And criteria and Or criteria when counting. For example, perhaps you want to count sales that meet both of the following criteria:

- Month is January.
- SalesRep is Brooks *or* SalesRep is Cook.

This array formula returns the number of sales that meet the criteria:

```
{=SUM((Month="January")*IF((SalesRep="Brooks")+(SalesRep="Cook"),1))}
```

Counting the most frequently occurring entry

The MODE function returns the most frequently occurring value in a range. Figure 13.3 shows a worksheet with values in range A1:A10 (named Data). The formula that follows returns 10 because that value appears most frequently in the Data range:

```
=MODE(Data)
```

FIGURE 13.3

The MODE function returns the most frequently occurring value in a range.

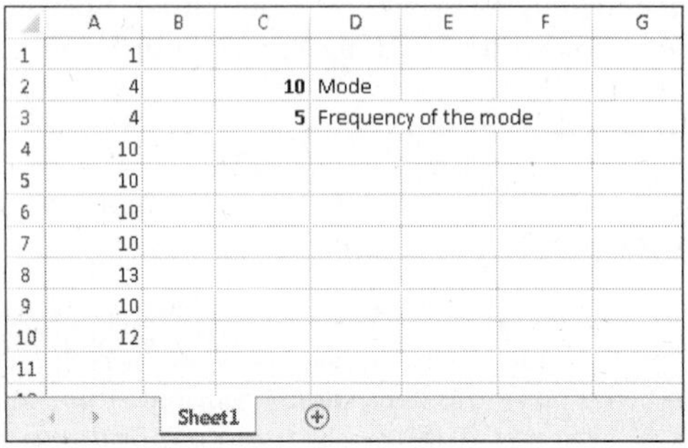

	A	B	C	D	E	F	G
1	1						
2	4		10	Mode			
3	4		5	Frequency of the mode			
4	10						
5	10						
6	10						
7	10						
8	13						
9	10						
10	12						
11							

Sheet1

To count the number of times the most frequently occurring value appears in the range (in other words, the frequency of the mode), use the following formula:

```
=COUNTIF(Data,MODE(Data))
```

This formula returns 5 because the modal value (10) appears five times in the Data range.

The MODE function works only for numeric values. It simply ignores cells that contain text. To find the most frequently occurring text entry in a range, you need to use an array formula.

To count the number of times the most frequently occurring item (text or values) appears in a range named Data, use the following array formula:

```
{=MAX(COUNTIF(Data,Data))}
```

This next array formula operates like the MODE function except that it works with both text and values:

```
{=INDEX(Data,MATCH(MAX(COUNTIF(Data,Data)),COUNTIF(Data,Data),0))}
```

Counting the occurrences of specific text

The examples in this section demonstrate various ways to count the occurrences of a character or text string in a range of cells. Figure 13.4 shows a worksheet used for these examples. Various text strings appear in the range A1:A10 (named Data); cell B1 is named Text.

FIGURE 13.4

This worksheet demonstrates various ways to count character strings in a range.

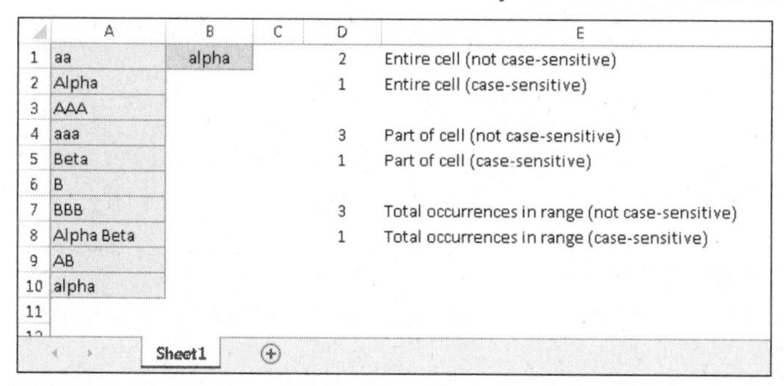

On the Web

This book's website contains a workbook that demonstrates the formulas in this section. The file is named `counting text in a range.xlsx`.

Entire cell contents

To count the number of cells containing the contents of the Text cell (and nothing else), you can use the `COUNTIF` function as the following formula demonstrates.

```
=COUNTIF(Data,Text)
```

For example, if the Text cell contains the string `Alpha`, the formula returns `2` because two cells in the Data range contain this text. This formula is not case sensitive, so it counts both `Alpha` (cell A2) and `alpha` (cell A10). Note, however, that it does not count the cell that contains `Alpha Beta` (cell A8).

The following array formula is similar to the preceding formula, but this one is case sensitive:

```
{=SUM(IF(EXACT(Data,Text),1))}
```

Partial cell contents

To count the number of cells that contain a string that includes the contents of the Text cell, use this formula:

```
=COUNTIF(Data,"*"&Text&"*")
```

For example, if the *Text* cell contains the text `Alpha`, the formula returns `3` because three cells in the Data range contain the text `alpha` (cells A2, A8, and A10). Note that the comparison is not case sensitive.

If you need a case-sensitive count, you can use the following array formula:

```
{=SUM(IF(LEN(Data)-LEN(SUBSTITUTE(Data,Text,""))>0,1))}
```

If the Text cells contain the text `Alpha`, the preceding formula returns `2` because the string appears in two cells (A2 and A8).

Total occurrences in a range

To count the total number of occurrences of a string within a range of cells, use the following array formula:

```
{=(SUM(LEN(Data))-SUM(LEN(SUBSTITUTE(Data,Text,""))))/LEN(Text)}
```

If the Text cell contains the character `B`, the formula returns `7` because the range contains seven instances of the string. This formula is case sensitive.

The following array formula is a modified version that is not case sensitive:

```
{=(SUM(LEN(Data))-SUM(LEN(SUBSTITUTE(UPPER(Data),UPPER(Text),""))))/LEN(Text)}
```

Counting the number of unique values

The following array formula returns the number of unique values in a range named Data:

```
{=SUM(1/COUNTIF(Data,Data))}
```

NOTE

The preceding formula is one of those "classic" Excel formulas that gets passed around on the Internet. I don't know who originated it.

Useful as it is, this formula does have a serious limitation: If the range contains any blank cells, it returns an error. The following array formula solves this problem:

```
{=SUM(IF(COUNTIF(Data,Data)=0,"",1/COUNTIF(Data,Data)))}
```

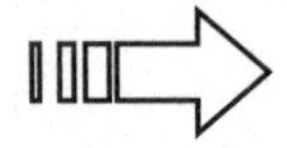

To find out how to create a multicell array formula that returns a list of unique items in a range, see Chapter 18.

ON THE WEB

This book's website contains a workbook that demonstrates this t

Creating a frequency distributi

A *frequency distribution* is a summary table th
range. For example, an instructor may create a fre
would show the count of *A*s, *B*s, *C*s, and so on. Excel p
frequency distributions. You can

- Use the FREQUENCY function.
- Create your own formulas.
- Use the Analysis ToolPak add-in.
- Use a pivot table.

ON THE WEB

A workbook that demonstrates these four techniques is available on this book's website. The file is named `frequency distribution.xlsx`.

The FREQUENCY function

Using the FREQUENCY function to create a frequency distribution can be a bit tricky, and this is probably the most difficult way to create a frequency distribution. The FREQUENCY function always returns an array, so you must use it in an array formula that's entered into a multicell range.

Figure 13.5 shows some data in range A1:E25 (named Data). These values range from 1 to 500. The range G2:G11 contains the bins used for the frequency distribution. Each cell in this bin range contains the upper limit for the bin. In this case, the bins consist of < =50, 51–100, 101–150, and so on. The goal is to count the number of values that fall into each bin.

To create the frequency distribution, select a range of cells that corresponds to the number of cells in the bin range (in this example, select H2:H11 because the bins are in G2:G11). Then enter the following array formula into the selected range (press Ctrl + Shift + Enter it):

```
{=FREQUENCY(Data,G2:G11)}
```

The array formula returns the count of values in the Data range that fall into each bin. To create a frequency distribution that consists of percentages, use the following array formula:

```
{=FREQUENCY(Data,G2:G11)/COUNT(Data)}
```

Figure 13.6 shows two frequency distributions — one in terms of counts and one in terms of percentages. The figure also shows a chart (histogram) created from the frequency distribution.

3.5

…ng a frequency distribution for the data in A1:E25.

	A	B	C	D	E	F	G	H
	55	316	223	185	124		Bins	
	124	93	163	213	314		50	
3	211	41	231	241	212		100	
4	118	113	400	205	254		150	
5	262	1	201	12	101		200	
6	167	479	205	337	118		250	
7	489	15	89	362	148		300	
8	179	248	125	197	177		350	
9	456	153	269	49	127		400	
10	289	500	198	317	300		450	
11	126	114	303	314	270		500	
12	151	279	347	314	170			
13	250	175	93	209	61			
14	166	113	356	124	242			
15	152	384	157	233	99			
16	277	195	436	6	240			
17	147	80	173	211	244			
18	386	93	330	400	141			
19	332	173	129	323	188			
20	338	263	444	84	220			
21	221	402	498	98	2			
22	201	400	3	190	105			
23	35	225	12	265	329			
24	43	302	125	301	444			
25	56	9	135	500	398			
26								

FREQUENCY Func | Formulas | ATP | Pivo ...

FIGURE 13.6

Frequency distributions created by using the `FREQUENCY` function.

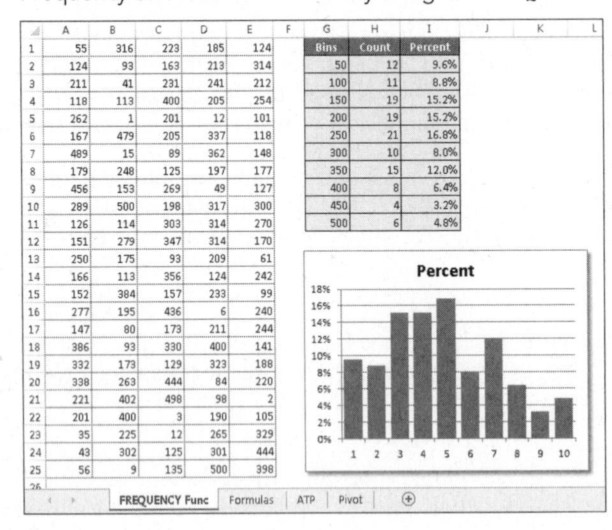

	A	B	C	D	E	F	G	H	I
1	55	316	223	185	124		Bins	Count	Percent
2	124	93	163	213	314		50	12	9.6%
3	211	41	231	241	212		100	11	8.8%
4	118	113	400	205	254		150	19	15.2%
5	262	1	201	12	101		200	19	15.2%
6	167	479	205	337	118		250	21	16.8%
7	489	15	89	362	148		300	10	8.0%
8	179	248	125	197	177		350	15	12.0%
9	456	153	269	49	127		400	8	6.4%
10	289	500	198	317	300		450	4	3.2%
11	126	114	303	314	270		500	6	4.8%
12	151	279	347	314	170				
13	250	175	93	209	61				
14	166	113	356	124	242				
15	152	384	157	233	99				
16	277	195	436	6	240				
17	147	80	173	211	244				
18	386	93	330	400	141				
19	332	173	129	323	188				
20	338	263	444	84	220				
21	221	402	498	98	2				
22	201	400	3	190	105				
23	35	225	12	265	329				
24	43	302	125	301	444				
25	56	9	135	500	398				

Using formulas to create a frequency distribution

Figure 13.7 shows a worksheet that contains test scores for 50 students in column B (the range is named Grades). Formulas in columns G and H calculate a frequency distribution for letter grades. The minimum and maximum values for each letter grade appear in columns D and E. For example, a test score between 80 and 89 (inclusive) earns a B. In addition, a chart displays the distribution of the test scores.

FIGURE 13.7

Creating a frequency distribution of test scores.

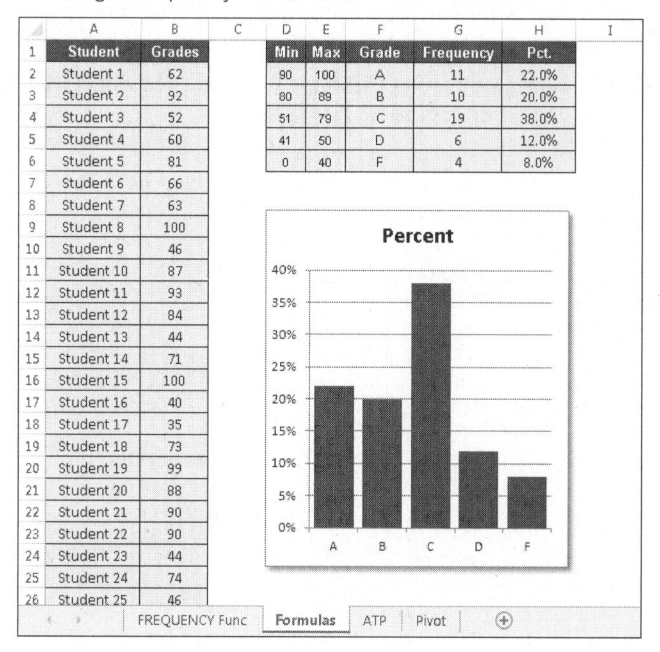

Student	Grades
Student 1	62
Student 2	92
Student 3	52
Student 4	60
Student 5	81
Student 6	66
Student 7	63
Student 8	100
Student 9	46
Student 10	87
Student 11	93
Student 12	84
Student 13	44
Student 14	71
Student 15	100
Student 16	40
Student 17	35
Student 18	73
Student 19	99
Student 20	88
Student 21	90
Student 22	90
Student 23	44
Student 24	74
Student 25	46

Min	Max	Grade	Frequency	Pct.
90	100	A	11	22.0%
80	89	B	10	20.0%
51	79	C	19	38.0%
41	50	D	6	12.0%
0	40	F	4	8.0%

The formula in cell G2 that follows counts the number of scores that qualify for an A:

```
=COUNTIFS(Grades,">="&D2,Grades,"<="&E2)
```

You may recognize this formula from a previous section in this chapter (see "Counting cells based on multiple criteria"). This formula was copied to the four cells below G2.

Note

The preceding formula uses the `COUNTIFS` function, which first appeared in Excel 2007. For compatibility with previous Excel versions, use this array formula:

```
{=SUM((Grades>=D2)*(Grades<=E2))}
```

The formulas in column H calculate the percentage of scores for each letter grade. The formula in H2, which was copied to the four cells below H2, is

```
=G2/SUM($G$2:$G$6)
```

Using the Analysis ToolPak to create a frequency distribution

The Analysis ToolPak add-in, distributed with Excel, provides another way to calculate a frequency distribution:

1. **Enter your bin values in a range.**
2. **Choose Data ➪ Analysis ➪ Analysis.** The Data Analysis dialog box appears. If this command is not available, see the sidebar, "Is the Analysis ToolPak Installed?".
3. **In the Data Analysis dialog box, select Histogram, and then click OK.** The Histogram dialog box, shown in Figure 13.8, appears.

FIGURE 13.8

The Analysis ToolPak's Histogram dialog box.

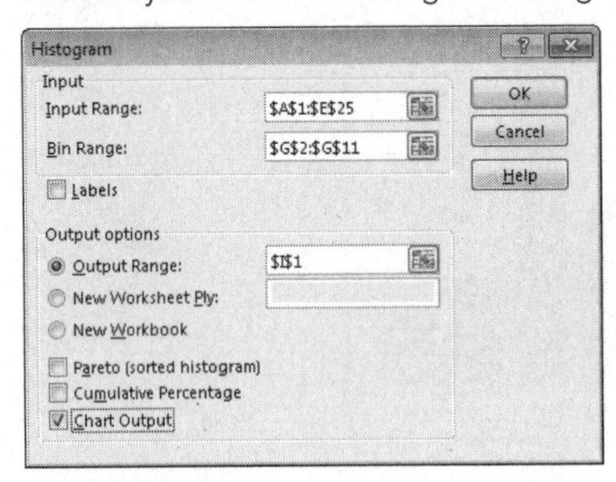

4. **Specify the ranges for your data (Input Range), bins (Bin Range), and results (Output Range), and then select any options and click OK.** Figure 13.9 shows a frequency distribution (and chart) created with the Histogram option.

CAUTION

Note that the frequency distribution consists of values, not formulas. Therefore, if you make any changes to your input data, you need to rerun the Histogram procedure to update the results.

FIGURE 13.9

A frequency distribution and chart generated by the Analysis ToolPak's Histogram option.

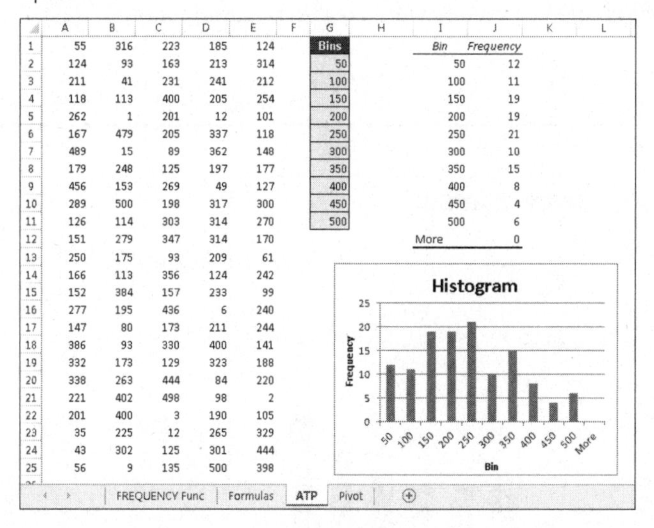

	A	B	C	D	E	F	G	H	I	J
1	55	316	223	185	124		Bins		*Bin*	*Frequency*
2	124	93	163	213	314		50		50	12
3	211	41	231	241	212		100		100	11
4	118	113	400	205	254		150		150	19
5	262	1	201	12	101		200		200	19
6	167	479	205	337	118		250		250	21
7	489	15	89	362	148		300		300	10
8	179	248	125	197	177		350		350	15
9	456	153	269	49	127		400		400	8
10	289	500	198	317	300		450		450	4
11	126	114	303	314	270		500		500	6
12	151	279	347	314	170				More	0
13	250	175	93	209	61					
14	166	113	356	124	242					
15	152	384	157	233	99					
16	277	195	436	6	240					
17	147	80	173	211	244					
18	386	93	330	400	141					
19	332	173	129	323	188					
20	338	263	444	84	220					
21	221	402	498	98	2					
22	201	400	3	190	105					
23	35	225	12	265	329					
24	43	302	125	301	444					
25	56	9	135	500	398					

Is the Analysis ToolPak Installed?

To make sure that the Analysis ToolPak add-in is installed, click the Data tab. If the Ribbon displays the Data Analysis command in the Analysis group, you're all set. If not, you'll need to install the add-in:

1. **Choose File⇨Options.** The Excel Options dialog box appears.
2. **Click the Add-ins tab on the left.**
3. **Select Excel Add-Ins from the Manage drop-down list.**
4. **Click Go to display the Add-Ins dialog box.**
5. **Place a check mark next to Analysis ToolPak.**
6. **Click OK.**

If you've enabled the Developer tab, you can display the Add-Ins dialog box by choosing Developer⇨Add-Ins⇨Add-Ins.

Note: In the Add-Ins dialog box, you see an additional add-in, Analysis ToolPak – VBA. This add-in is for programmers, and you don't need to install it.

Using a pivot table to create a frequency distribution

If your data is in the form of a table, you may prefer to use a pivot table and a pivot chart to create a histogram. Figure 13.10 shows the student grade data summarized in a pivot table and a pivot chart. The counts were created by grouping.

FIGURE 13.10

Using a pivot chart to display a histogram.

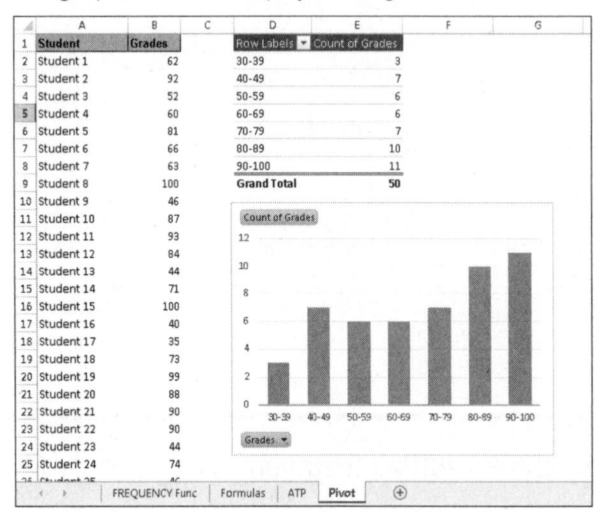

I cover pivot tables in detail in Chapters 33 and 34.

Summing Formulas

The examples in this section demonstrate how to perform common summing tasks by using formulas. The formulas range from very simple to relatively complex array formulas that compute sums by using multiple criteria.

Summing all cells in a range

It doesn't get much simpler than this. The following formula returns the sum of all values in a range named Data:

```
=SUM(Data)
```

The SUM function can take up to 255 arguments. The following formula, for example, returns the sum of the values in five noncontiguous ranges:

```
=SUM(A1:A9,C1:C9,E1:E9,G1:G9,I1:I9)
```

You can use complete rows or columns as an argument for the SUM function. The formula that follows, for example, returns the sum of all values in column A. If this formula appears in a cell in column A, it generates a circular reference error.

```
=SUM(A:A)
```

The following formula returns the sum of all values on Sheet1 by using a range reference that consists of all rows. To avoid a circular reference error, this formula must appear on a sheet other than Sheet1.

```
=SUM(Sheet1!1:1048576)
```

The SUM function is very versatile. The arguments can be numerical values, cells, ranges, text representations of numbers (which are interpreted as values), logical values, and even embedded functions. For example, consider the following formula:

```
=SUM(B1,5,"6",,SQRT(4),A1:A5,TRUE)
```

This odd formula, which is perfectly valid, contains all the following types of arguments, listed here in the order of their presentation:

- A single cell reference: B1
- A literal value: 5
- A string that looks like a value: "6"
- A missing argument: , ,
- An expression that uses another function: SQRT(4)
- A range reference: A1:A5
- A logical value: TRUE

CAUTION

The SUM function is versatile, but it's also inconsistent when you use logical values (TRUE or FALSE). Logical values stored in cells are always treated as 0. However, logical TRUE, when used as an argument in the SUM function, is treated as 1.

Computing a cumulative sum

You may want to display a cumulative sum of values in a range — sometimes known as a "running total." Figure 13.11 illustrates a cumulative sum. Column B shows the monthly amounts, and column C displays the cumulative (year-to-date) totals.

FIGURE 13.11

Simple formulas in column C display a cumulative sum of the values in column B.

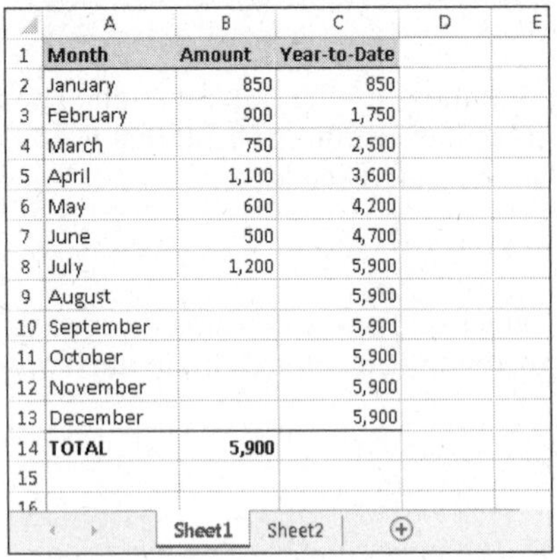

	A	B	C	D	E
1	**Month**	**Amount**	**Year-to-Date**		
2	January	850	850		
3	February	900	1,750		
4	March	750	2,500		
5	April	1,100	3,600		
6	May	600	4,200		
7	June	500	4,700		
8	July	1,200	5,900		
9	August		5,900		
10	September		5,900		
11	October		5,900		
12	November		5,900		
13	December		5,900		
14	**TOTAL**	**5,900**			
15					
16					

Sheet1 | Sheet2

The formula in cell C2 is

```
=SUM(B$2:B2)
```

Notice that this formula uses a *mixed reference* — that is, the first cell in the range reference always refers to the same row (in this case, row 2). When this formula is copied down the column, the range argument adjusts such that the sum always starts with row 2 and ends with the current row. For example, after copying this formula down column C, the formula in cell C8 is

```
=SUM(B$2:B8)
```

You can use an `IF` function to hide the cumulative sums for rows in which data hasn't been entered. The following formula, entered in cell C2 and copied down the column, is

```
=IF(B2<>"",SUM(B$2:B2),"")
```

Figure 13.12 shows this formula at work.

ON THE WEB

This workbook is available on this book's website. The file is named `cumulative sum.xlsx`.

FIGURE 13.12

Using an `IF` function to hide cumulative sums for missing data.

	A	B	C	D	E
1	**Month**	**Amount**	**Year-to-Date**		
2	January	850	850		
3	February	900	1,750		
4	March	750	2,500		
5	April	1,100	3,600		
6	May	600	4,200		
7	June	500	4,700		
8	July	1,200	5,900		
9	August				
10	September				
11	October				
12	November				
13	December				
14	**TOTAL**	**5,900**			
15					

Sheet1 | Sheet2

Ignoring errors when summing

The `SUM` function does not work if the range to be summed includes any errors. For example, if one of the cells to be summed displays `#N/A`, the `SUM` function will also return `#N/A`.

To add the values in a range and ignore the error cells, use the `AGGREGATE` function. For example, to sum a range named Data (which may have error values), use this formula:

```
=AGGREGATE(9,6,Data)
```

The `AGGREGATE` function is very versatile, and can do a lot more than just add values. In this example, the first argument (`9`) specifies `SUM`. The second argument (`6`), means ignore error values.

The arguments are described in the Excel Help. Excel also provides good autocomplete assistance when you enter a formula that uses this function.

CAUTION

The `AGGREGATE` function was introduced in Excel 2010. For compatibility with earlier versions use this array formula:

```
{=SUM(IF(ISERROR(Data),"",Data))}
```

Summing the "top *n*" values

In some situations, you may need to sum the *n* largest values in a range — for example, the top ten values. If your data resides in a table, you can use autofiltering to hide all but the top *n* rows and then display the sum of the visible data in the table's total row.

Another approach is to sort the range in descending order and then use the `SUM` function with an argument consisting of the first *n* values in the sorted range.

A better solution — which doesn't require a table or sorting — uses an array formula like this one:

```
{=SUM(LARGE(Data,{1,2,3,4,5,6,7,8,9,10}))}
```

This formula sums the ten largest values in a range named Data. To sum the ten smallest values, use the `SMALL` function instead of the `LARGE` function:

```
{=SUM(SMALL(Data,{1,2,3,4,5,6,7,8,9,10}))}
```

These formulas use an array constant comprised of the arguments for the `LARGE` or `SMALL` function. If the value of *n* for your top-*n* calculation is large, you may prefer to use the following variation. This formula returns the sum of the top 30 values in the Data range. You can, of course, substitute a different value for 30. Figure 13.13 shows this array formula in use.

```
{=SUM(LARGE(Data,ROW(INDIRECT("1:30"))))}
```

FIGURE 13.13

Using an array formula to calculate the sum of the 30 largest values in a range.

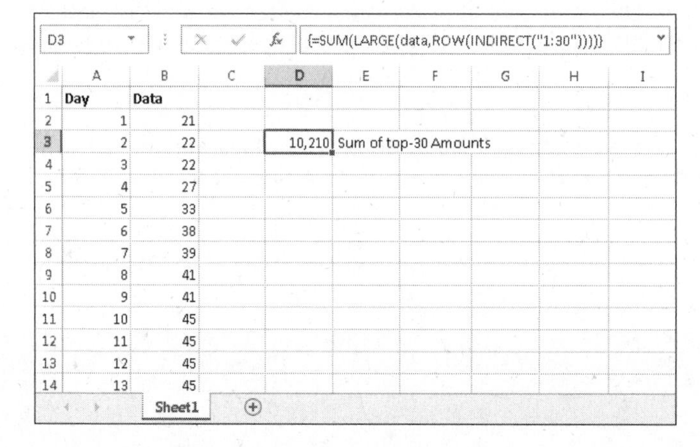

D3 {=SUM(LARGE(data,ROW(INDIRECT("1:30"))))}

	A	B	C	D	E
1	Day	Data			
2	1	21			
3	2	22		10,210	Sum of top-30 Amounts
4	3	22			
5	4	27			
6	5	33			
7	6	38			
8	7	39			
9	8	41			
10	9	41			
11	10	45			
12	11	45			
13	12	45			
14	13	45			

Sheet1

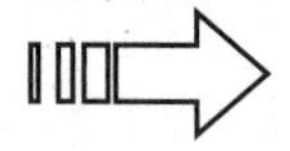

See Chapter 17 for more information about using array constants.

Conditional Sums Using a Single Criterion

Often, you need to calculate a *conditional sum*. With a conditional sum, values in a range that meet one or more conditions are included in the sum. This section presents examples of conditional summing by using a single criterion.

The `SUMIF` function is very useful for single-criterion sum formulas. The `SUMIF` function takes three arguments:

- `range`: The range containing the values that determine whether to include a particular cell in the sum.
- `criteria`: An expression that determines whether to include a particular cell in the sum.
- `sum_range`: Optional. The range that contains the cells you want to sum. If you omit this argument, the function uses the range specified in the first argument.

The examples that follow demonstrate the use of the `SUMIF` function. These formulas are based on the worksheet shown in Figure 13.14, set up to track invoices. Column F contains a formula that subtracts the date in column E from the date in column D. A negative number in column F indicates a past-due payment. The worksheet uses named ranges that correspond to the labels in row 1.

13

FIGURE 13.14

A negative value in column F indicates a past-due payment.

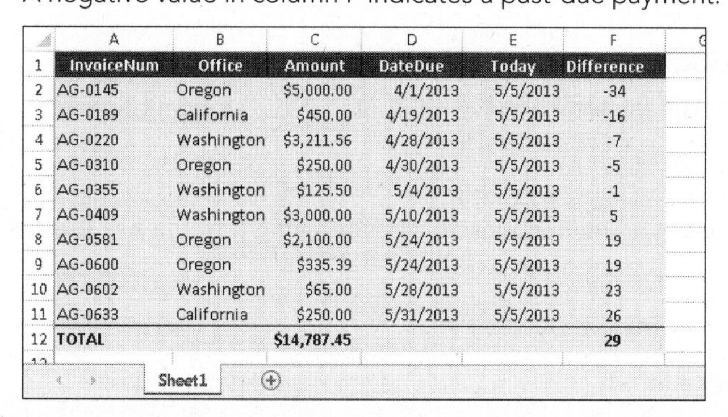

	A	B	C	D	E	F
1	InvoiceNum	Office	Amount	DateDue	Today	Difference
2	AG-0145	Oregon	$5,000.00	4/1/2013	5/5/2013	-34
3	AG-0189	California	$450.00	4/19/2013	5/5/2013	-16
4	AG-0220	Washington	$3,211.56	4/28/2013	5/5/2013	-7
5	AG-0310	Oregon	$250.00	4/30/2013	5/5/2013	-5
6	AG-0355	Washington	$125.50	5/4/2013	5/5/2013	-1
7	AG-0409	Washington	$3,000.00	5/10/2013	5/5/2013	5
8	AG-0581	Oregon	$2,100.00	5/24/2013	5/5/2013	19
9	AG-0600	Oregon	$335.39	5/24/2013	5/5/2013	19
10	AG-0602	Washington	$65.00	5/28/2013	5/5/2013	23
11	AG-0633	California	$250.00	5/31/2013	5/5/2013	26
12	TOTAL		$14,787.45			29

Sheet1

ON THE WEB

All the examples in this section are available at this book's website. The file is named `conditional sum.xlsx`.

Summing only negative values

The following formula returns the sum of the negative values in column F. In other words, it returns the total number of past-due days for all invoices. For this worksheet, the formula returns -63.

```
=SUMIF(Difference,"<0")
```

Because you omit the third argument, the second argument ("<0") applies to the values in the Difference range.

You don't need to hard-code the arguments for the SUMIF function into your formula. For example, you can create a formula, such as the following, which gets the criteria argument from the contents of cell G2:

```
=SUMIF(Difference,G2)
```

This formula returns a new result if you change the criteria in cell G2.

Summing values based on a different range

The following formula returns the sum of the past-due invoice amounts (in column C):

```
=SUMIF(Difference,"<0",Amount)
```

This formula uses the values in the Difference range to determine whether the corresponding values in the Amount range contribute to the sum.

Summing values based on a text comparison

The following formula returns the total invoice amounts for the Oregon office:

```
=SUMIF(Office,"=Oregon",Amount)
```

Using the equal sign in the argument is optional. The following formula has the same result:

```
=SUMIF(Office,"Oregon",Amount)
```

To sum the invoice amounts for all offices *except* Oregon, use this formula:

```
=SUMIF(Office,"<>Oregon",Amount)
```

Summing values based on a date comparison

The following formula returns the total invoice amounts that have a due date after May 1, 2013:

```
=SUMIF(DateDue,">="&DATE(2013,5,1),Amount)
```

Notice that the second argument for the `SUMIF` function is an expression. The expression uses the `DATE` function, which returns a date. Also, the comparison operator, enclosed in quotes, is concatenated (using the `&` operator) with the result of the `DATE` function.

The formula that follows returns the total invoice amounts that have a future due date (including today):

```
=SUMIF(DateDue,">="&TODAY(),Amount)
```

Conditional Sums Using Multiple Criteria

The examples in the preceding section all used a single comparison criterion. The examples in this section involve summing cells based on multiple criteria.

Figure 13.15 shows the sample worksheet again, for your reference. The worksheet also shows the result of several formulas that demonstrate summing by using multiple criteria.

FIGURE 13.15

This worksheet demonstrates summing based on multiple criteria.

	A	B	C	D	E	F
1	InvoiceNum	Office	Amount	DateDue	Today	Difference
2	AG-0145	Oregon	$5,000.00	4/1/2013	5/5/2013	-34
3	AG-0189	California	$450.00	4/19/2013	5/5/2013	-16
4	AG-0220	Washington	$3,211.56	4/28/2013	5/5/2013	-7
5	AG-0310	Oregon	$250.00	4/30/2013	5/5/2013	-5
6	AG-0355	Washington	$125.50	5/4/2013	5/5/2013	-1
7	AG-0409	Washington	$3,000.00	5/10/2013	5/5/2013	5
8	AG-0581	Oregon	$2,100.00	5/24/2013	5/5/2013	19
9	AG-0600	Oregon	$335.39	5/24/2013	5/5/2013	19
10	AG-0602	Washington	$65.00	5/28/2013	5/5/2013	23
11	AG-0633	California	$250.00	5/31/2013	5/5/2013	26
12	**TOTAL**		**$14,787.45**			**29**
13						
14						
15	-63	Total past due days				
16	-63	Total past due days (array formula)				
17						
18	$9,037.06	Total amount past due				
19	$9,037.06	Total amount past due (array formula)				
20						
21	$7,685.39	Total for Oregon only				
22						
23	$7,102.06	Total for all except Oregon				
24						
25	$14,787.45	Total amount with due date beyond May 1				
26						
27	$5,250.00	Total past due amount for Oregon (Excel 2007 or later only)				
28	$5,250.00	Total past due amount for Oregon (array formula)				
29						
30	$5,000.00	Total past due amounts OR amounts for Oregon (array formula)				
31						
32	$5,700.00	Total past due amounts for Oregon and California (array formula)				
33						

Sheet1

Using And criteria

Suppose that you want to get a sum of the invoice amounts that are past due *and* associated with the Oregon office. In other words, the value in the Amount range will be summed only if both of the following criteria are met:

- The corresponding value in the Difference range is negative, *and*
- The corresponding text in the Office range is `Oregon`.

If the worksheet won't be used by anyone running a version prior to Excel 2007, the following formula does the job:

```
=SUMIFS(Amount,Difference,"<0",Office,"Oregon")
```

The following array formula returns the same result and will work in all versions of Excel:

```
{=SUM((Difference<0)*(Office="Oregon")*Amount)}
```

Using Or criteria

Suppose that you want to get a sum of past-due invoice amounts *or* ones associated with the Oregon office. In other words, the value in the Amount range will be summed if either of the following criteria is met:

- The corresponding value in the Difference range is negative, *or*
- The corresponding text in the Office range is `Oregon`.

This example requires an array formula:

```
{=SUM(IF((Office="Oregon")+(Difference<0),1,0)*Amount)}
```

A plus sign (+) joins the conditions; you can include more than two conditions.

Using And and Or criteria

As you may expect, things get a bit tricky when your criteria consists of both And and Or operations. For example, you may want to sum the values in the Amount range when both of the following conditions are met:

- The corresponding value in the Difference range is negative.
- The corresponding text in the Office range is `Oregon` or `California`.

Notice that the second condition actually consists of two conditions joined with Or. The following array formula does the trick:

```
{=SUM((Difference<0)*IF((Office="Oregon")+(Office="California"),1)*Amount)}
```

CHAPTER 14

Creating Formulas That Look Up Values

IN THIS CHAPTER

Introducing formulas that look up values in a table

Identifying the worksheet functions used to perform lookups

Getting acquainted with basic lookup formulas

Delving into more sophisticated lookup formulas

This chapter discusses various techniques that you can use to look up a value in a range of data. Excel has three worksheet functions (`LOOKUP`, `VLOOKUP`, and `HLOOKUP`) designed for this task, but you may find that these functions don't quite cut it.

This chapter provides many lookup examples, including alternative techniques that go well beyond the Excel program's normal lookup capabilities.

Introducing Lookup Formulas

A *lookup formula* returns a value from a table by looking up another related value. A common telephone directory (remember those?) provides a good analogy. If you want to find a person's telephone number, you first locate the name (look it up) and then retrieve the corresponding number.

NOTE

I use the term *table* to describe any rectangular range of data. The range does not necessarily need to be an "official" table, as created by choosing Insert ➪ Tables ➪ Table.

Figure 14.1 shows a worksheet that uses four lookup formulas. This worksheet contains a table of employee data, beginning in row 7. This range is named EmpData. When you enter a last name into cell C2, lookup formulas in D2:G2 retrieve the matching information from the table. If the last name does not appear in Column C, the formulas return #N/A.

FIGURE 14.1

Lookup formulas in row 2 look up the information for the employee name in cell C2.

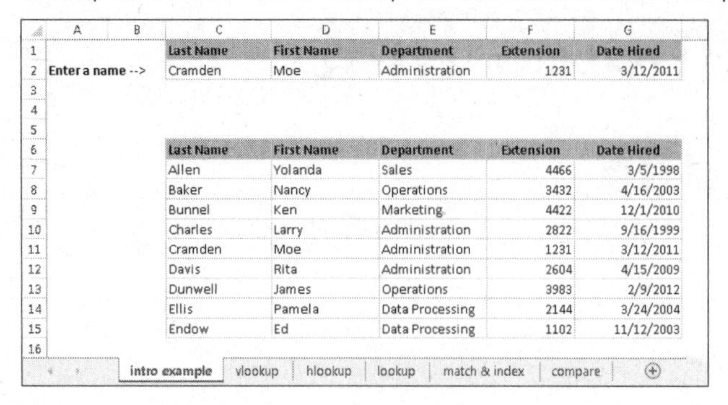

	A	B	C	D	E	F	G
1			Last Name	First Name	Department	Extension	Date Hired
2	Enter a name -->		Cramden	Moe	Administration	1231	3/12/2011
3							
4							
5							
6			Last Name	First Name	Department	Extension	Date Hired
7			Allen	Yolanda	Sales	4466	3/5/1998
8			Baker	Nancy	Operations	3432	4/16/2003
9			Bunnel	Ken	Marketing	4422	12/1/2010
10			Charles	Larry	Administration	2822	9/16/1999
11			Cramden	Moe	Administration	1231	3/12/2011
12			Davis	Rita	Administration	2604	4/15/2009
13			Dunwell	James	Operations	3983	2/9/2012
14			Ellis	Pamela	Data Processing	2144	3/24/2004
15			Endow	Ed	Data Processing	1102	11/12/2003
16							

The following lookup formulas use the `VLOOKUP` function:

```
D2=VLOOKUP(C2,EmpData,2,FALSE)
E2 =VLOOKUP(C2,EmpData,3,FALSE)
F2 =VLOOKUP(C2,EmpData,4,FALSE)
G2=VLOOKUP(C2,EmpData,5,FALSE)
```

This particular example uses four formulas to return information from the EmpData range. In many cases, you want only a single value from the table, so use only one formula.

NOTE

Most of the examples in this chapter use named ranges for function arguments. When you adapt these formulas for your own use, you need to substitute the actual range address or a range name defined in your workbook.

Functions Relevant to Lookups

Several Excel functions are useful when writing formulas to look up information in a table. Table 14.1 lists and describes these functions.

TABLE 14.1 Functions Used in Lookup Formulas

Function	Description
CHOOSE	Returns a specific value from a list of values supplied as arguments.
HLOOKUP	Horizontal lookup. Searches for a value in the top row of a table and returns a value in the same column from a row you specify in the table.

Function	Description
`IF`	Returns one value if a condition you specify is `TRUE`, and returns another value if the condition is `FALSE`.
`IFERROR`*	If the first argument returns an error, the second argument is evaluated and returned. If the first argument does not return an error, then it is evaluated and returned.
`INDEX`	Returns a value (or the reference to a value) from within a table or range.
`LOOKUP`	Returns a value either from a one-row or one-column range. Another form of the `LOOKUP` function works like `VLOOKUP` but is restricted to returning a value from the last column of a range.
`MATCH`	Returns the relative position of an item in a range that matches a specified value.
`OFFSET`	Returns a reference to a range that is a specified number of rows and columns from a cell or range of cells.
`VLOOKUP`	Vertical lookup. Searches for a value in the first column of a table and returns a value in the same row from a column you specify in the table.

* Introduced in Excel 2007.

The examples in this chapter use the functions listed in Table 14.1.

Using the IF Function for Simple Lookups

The `IF` function is very versatile and is often suitable for simple decision-making problems. The accompanying figure shows a worksheet with student grades in column B. Formulas in column C use the `IF` function to return text: either Pass (a score of 65 or higher) or Fail (a score below 65). For example, the formula in cell C2 is

```
=IF(B2>=65,"Pass","Fail")
```

	A	B	C
1	**Student**	**Score**	**Grade**
2	Andy	82	Pass
3	Barbara	57	Fail
4	Chris	73	Pass
5	Dennis	54	Fail
6	Elsie	82	Pass
7	Francine	72	Pass
8			

You can "nest" `IF` functions to provide even more decision-making ability. This formula, for example, returns one of four strings: `Excellent`, `Very Good`, `Fair`, or `Poor`.

```
=IF(B2>=90,"Excellent",IF(B2>=70,"Very Good",IF(B2>=50,"Fair","Poor")))
```

This technique is fine for situations that involve only a few choices. However, using nested `IF` functions can quickly become complicated and unwieldy. The lookup techniques described in this chapter usually provide a much better solution.

14

Basic Lookup Formulas

You can use the Excel basic lookup functions to search a column or row for a lookup value to return another value as a result. Excel provides three basic lookup functions: HLOOKUP, VLOOKUP, and LOOKUP. In addition, the MATCH and INDEX functions are often used together to return a cell or relative cell reference for a lookup value.

The VLOOKUP function

The VLOOKUP function looks up the value in the first column of the lookup table and returns the corresponding value in a specified table column. The lookup table is arranged vertically (which explains the *V* in the function's name). The syntax for the VLOOKUP function is

```
VLOOKUP(lookup_value,table_array,col_index_num,range_lookup)
```

The VLOOKUP function's arguments are as follows:

- lookup_value: The value to be looked up in the first column of the lookup table.
- table_array: The range that contains the lookup table.
- col_index_num: The column number within the table from which the matching value is returned.
- range_lookup: Optional. If TRUE or omitted, an approximate match is returned. (If an exact match is not found, the next largest value that is less than lookup_value is returned.) If FALSE, VLOOKUP will search for an exact match. If VLOOKUP can't find an exact match, the function returns #N/A.

Caution

If the range_lookup argument is TRUE or omitted, the first column of the lookup table must be in ascending order. If lookup_value is smaller than the smallest value in the first column of table_array, VLOOKUP returns #N/A. If the range_lookup argument is FALSE, the first column of the lookup table need not be in ascending order. If an exact match is not found, the function returns #N/A.

Tip

If the lookup_value argument is text and the range_lookup argument is FALSE, the lookup_value can include wildcard characters * and ?.

A very common use for a lookup formula involves an income tax rate schedule (see Figure 14.2). The tax rate schedule shows the income tax rates for various income levels. The following formula (in cell B3) returns the tax rate for the income in cell B2:

```
=VLOOKUP(B2,D2:F7,3)
```

FIGURE 14.2

Using VLOOKUP to look up a tax rate.

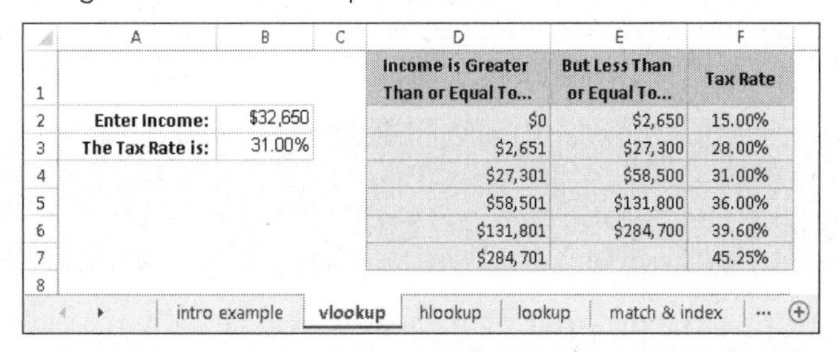

	A	B	C	D	E	F
1				Income is Greater Than or Equal To...	But Less Than or Equal To...	Tax Rate
2	Enter Income:	$32,650		$0	$2,650	15.00%
3	The Tax Rate is:	31.00%		$2,651	$27,300	28.00%
4				$27,301	$58,500	31.00%
5				$58,501	$131,800	36.00%
6				$131,801	$284,700	39.60%
7				$284,701		45.25%
8						

intro example | vlookup | hlookup | lookup | match & index | ...

On the Web

The examples in this section are available at this book's website. They're contained in a file named `basic lookup examples.xlsx`.

The lookup table resides in a range that consists of three columns (D2:F7). Because the last argument for the `VLOOKUP` function is `3`, the formula returns the corresponding value in the third column of the lookup table.

Note that an exact match is not required. If an exact match is not found in the first column of the lookup table, the `VLOOKUP` function uses the next largest value that is less than the lookup value. In other words, the function uses the row in which the value you want to look up is greater than or equal to the row value but less than the value in the next row. In the case of a tax table, this is exactly what you want to happen.

The HLOOKUP function

The `HLOOKUP` function works just like the `VLOOKUP` function except that the lookup table is arranged horizontally instead of vertically. The `HLOOKUP` function looks up the value in the first row of the lookup table and returns the corresponding value in a specified table row.

The syntax for the `HLOOKUP` function is

```
HLOOKUP(lookup_value,table_array,row_index_num,range_lookup)
```

The `HLOOKUP` function's arguments are as follows

- `lookup_value`: The value to be looked up in the first row of the lookup table.
- `table_array`: The range that contains the lookup table.
- `row_index_num`: The row number within the table from which the matching value is returned.

- `range_lookup`: Optional. If `TRUE` or omitted, an approximate match is returned. (If an exact match is not found, the next largest value less than `lookup_value` is returned.) If `FALSE`, `HLOOKUP` will search for an exact match. If `HLOOKUP` can't find an exact match, the function returns `#N/A`.

TIP

If the `lookup_value` argument is text and the `range_lookup` argument is `FALSE`, the `lookup_value` can include wildcard characters `*` and `?`.

Figure 14.3 shows the tax rate example with a horizontal lookup table (in the range E1:J3). The formula in cell B3 is

```
=HLOOKUP(B2,E1:J3,3)
```

FIGURE 14.3

Using `HLOOKUP` to look up a tax rate.

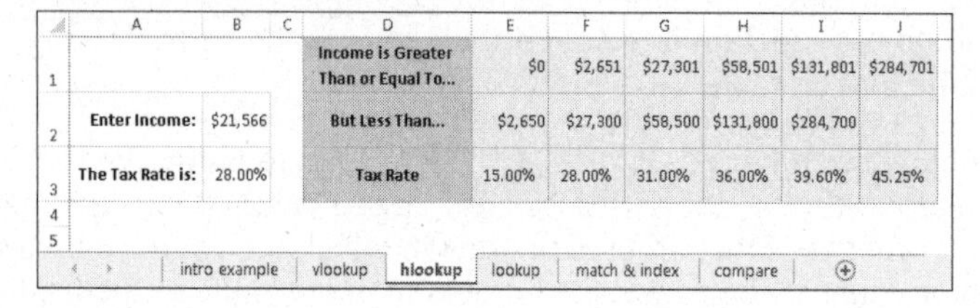

	A	B	C	D	E	F	G	H	I	J
1				Income is Greater Than or Equal To...	$0	$2,651	$27,301	$58,501	$131,801	$284,701
2	Enter Income:	$21,566		But Less Than...	$2,650	$27,300	$58,500	$131,800	$284,700	
3	The Tax Rate is:	28.00%		Tax Rate	15.00%	28.00%	31.00%	36.00%	39.60%	45.25%
4										
5										

The LOOKUP function

The `LOOKUP` function looks in a one-row or one-column range (`lookup_vector`) for a value (`lookup_value`) and returns a value from the same position in a second one-row or one-column range (`result_vector`).

The `LOOKUP` function has the following syntax:

```
LOOKUP(lookup_value,lookup_vector,result_vector)
```

The function's arguments are as follows:

- `lookup_value`: The value to be looked up in the `lookup_vector`.
- `lookup_vector`: A single-column or single-row range that contains the values to be looked up. These values must be in ascending order.
- `result_vector`: The single-column or single-row range that contains the values to be returned. It must be the same size as the `lookup_vector`.

CAUTION

Values in the `lookup_vector` must be in ascending order. If the values in the first column are not arranged in ascending order, the `LOOKUP` function may return an incorrect value. If `lookup_value` is smaller than the smallest value in `lookup_vector`, `LOOKUP` returns `#N/A`.

Figure 14.4 shows the tax table again. This time, the formula in cell B3 uses the `LOOKUP` function to return the corresponding tax rate. The formula in cell B3 is

```
=LOOKUP(B2,D2:D7,F2:F7)
```

FIGURE 14.4

Using `LOOKUP` to look up a tax rate.

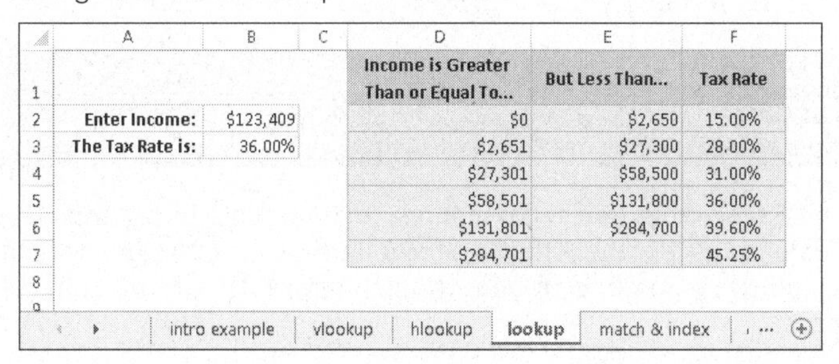

	A	B	C	D	E	F
1				Income is Greater Than or Equal To...	But Less Than...	Tax Rate
2	Enter Income:	$123,409		$0	$2,650	15.00%
3	The Tax Rate is:	36.00%		$2,651	$27,300	28.00%
4				$27,301	$58,500	31.00%
5				$58,501	$131,800	36.00%
6				$131,801	$284,700	39.60%
7				$284,701		45.25%
8						

Note that `LOOKUP` (as opposed to `VLOOKUP`) requires two range references: a range to be looked in, and a range that contains result values. `VLOOKUP`, on the other hand, uses a single range for the lookup table, and the third argument determines which column to use for the result. This argument, of course, can consist of a cell reference.

Combining the MATCH and INDEX functions

The `MATCH` and `INDEX` functions are often used together to perform lookups. The `MATCH` function returns the relative position of a cell in a range that matches a specified value. The syntax for `MATCH` is

```
MATCH(lookup_value,lookup_array,match_type)
```

The `MATCH` function's arguments are as follows:

- `lookup_value`: The value you want to match in `lookup_array`. If `match_type` is `0` and the `lookup_value` is `text`, this argument can include wildcard characters `*` and `?`.
- `lookup_array`: The range being searched.
- `match_type`: An integer (`-1`, `0`, or `1`) that specifies how the match is determined.

If `match_type` is `1`, `MATCH` finds the largest value less than or equal to `lookup_value`. (`lookup_array` must be in ascending order.) If `match_type` is `0`, `MATCH` finds the first value exactly equal to `lookup_value`. If `match_type` is `-1`, `MATCH` finds the smallest value greater than or equal to `lookup_value`. (`lookup_array` must be in descending order.) If you omit the `match_type` argument, this argument is assumed to be `1`.

The `INDEX` function returns a cell from a range. The syntax for the `INDEX` function is

```
INDEX(array,row_num,column_num)
```

The `INDEX` function's arguments are as follows:

- `array`: A range
- `row_num`: A row number within `array`
- `col_num`: A column number within `array`

NOTE

If `array` contains only one row or column, the corresponding `row_num` or `column_num` argument is optional.

Figure 14.5 shows a worksheet with dates, day names, and amounts in columns D, E, and F. When you enter a date in cell B1, the following formula (in cell B2) searches the dates in column D and returns the corresponding amount from column F. The formula in cell B2 is

```
=INDEX(F2:F21,MATCH(B1,D2:D21,0))
```

FIGURE 14.5

Using the `INDEX` and `MATCH` functions to perform a lookup.

	A	B	C	D	E	F	G
1	Date:	1/12/2013		Date	Weekday	Amount	
2	Amount:	189		1/1/2013	Tuesday	23	
3				1/2/2013	Wednesday	179	
4				1/3/2013	Thursday	149	
5				1/4/2013	Friday	196	
6				1/5/2013	Saturday	131	
7				1/6/2013	Sunday	179	
8				1/7/2013	Monday	134	
9				1/8/2013	Tuesday	179	
10				1/9/2013	Wednesday	193	
11				1/10/2013	Thursday	191	
12				1/11/2013	Friday	176	
13				1/12/2013	Saturday	189	
14				1/13/2013	Sunday	163	
15				1/14/2013	Monday	121	
16				1/15/2013	Tuesday	100	
17				1/16/2013	Wednesday	109	
18				1/17/2013	Thursday	151	
19				1/18/2013	Friday	138	
20				1/19/2013	Saturday	114	
21				1/20/2013	Sunday	156	
22							

vlookup | hlookup | lookup | match & index | compare

When a Blank Is Not a Zero

The Excel lookup functions treat empty cells in the result range as zeros. The worksheet in the accompanying figure contains a two-column lookup table, and this formula looks up the name in cell B1 and returns the corresponding amount:

```
=VLOOKUP(B1,D2:E8,2)
```

Note that the Amount cell for Charlie is blank, but the formula returns a 0.

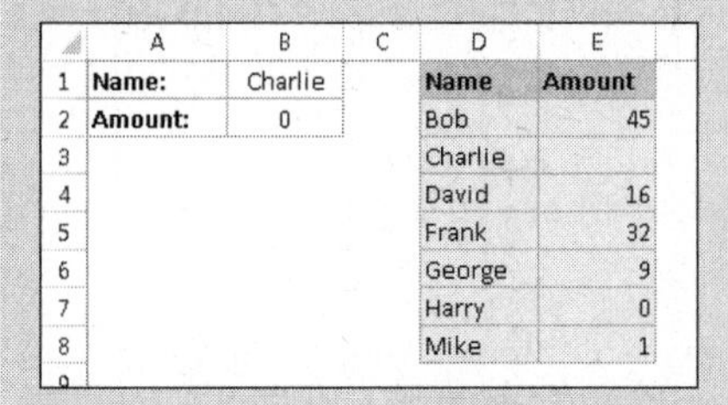

	A	B	C	D	E
1	**Name:**	Charlie		**Name**	**Amount**
2	**Amount:**	0		Bob	45
3				Charlie	
4				David	16
5				Frank	32
6				George	9
7				Harry	0
8				Mike	1

If you need to distinguish zeros from blank cells, you must modify the lookup formula by adding an `IF` function to check whether the length of the returned value is `0`. When the looked-up value is blank, the length of the return value is `0`. In all other cases, the length of the returned value is nonzero. The following formula displays an empty string (a blank) whenever the length of the looked-up value is zero and the actual value whenever the length is anything but zero:

```
=IF(LEN(VLOOKUP(B1,D2:E8,2))=0,"",(VLOOKUP(B1,D2:E8,2)))
```

Alternatively, you can specifically check for an empty string, as in the following formula:

```
=IF(VLOOKUP(B1,D2:E8,2)="","",(VLOOKUP(B1,D2:E8,2)))
```


To understand how this formula works, start with the `MATCH` function. This function searches the range D2:D21 for the date in cell B1. It returns the relative row number where the date is found. This value is then used as the second argument for the `INDEX` function. The result is the corresponding value in F2:F21.

Specialized Lookup Formulas

You can use additional types of lookup formulas to perform more specialized lookups. For example, you can look up an exact value, search in another column besides the first in a lookup table, perform a case-sensitive lookup, return a value from among multiple lookup tables, and perform other specialized and complex lookups.

ON THE WEB

The examples in this section are available on this book's website. The file is named `specialized lookup examples.xlsx`.

Looking up an exact value

As demonstrated in the previous examples, VLOOKUP and HLOOKUP don't necessarily require an exact match between the value to be looked up and the values in the lookup table. An example is looking up a tax rate in a tax table. In some cases, you may require a perfect match. For example, when looking up an employee number, you would require a perfect match for the number.

To look up an exact value only, use the VLOOKUP (or HLOOKUP) function with the optional fourth argument set to FALSE.

Figure 14.6 shows a worksheet with a lookup table that contains employee numbers (column C) and employee names (column D). The lookup table is named EmpList. The formula in cell B2, which follows, looks up the employee number entered in cell B1 and returns the corresponding employee name:

```
=VLOOKUP(B1,EmpList,2,FALSE)
```

FIGURE 14.6

This lookup table requires an exact match.

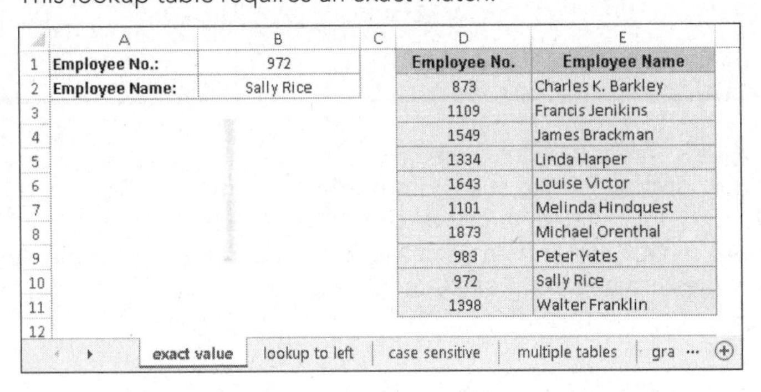

	A	B	C	D	E
1	**Employee No.:**	972		**Employee No.**	**Employee Name**
2	**Employee Name:**	Sally Rice		873	Charles K. Barkley
3				1109	Francis Jenikins
4				1549	James Brackman
5				1334	Linda Harper
6				1643	Louise Victor
7				1101	Melinda Hindquest
8				1873	Michael Orenthal
9				983	Peter Yates
10				972	Sally Rice
11				1398	Walter Franklin
12					

Because the last argument for the VLOOKUP function is FALSE, the function returns a value only if an exact match is found. If the value is not found, the formula returns #N/A. This result, of course, is exactly what you want to happen because returning an approximate match for an employee number makes no sense. Also, notice that the employee numbers in column C are not in ascending order. If the last argument for VLOOKUP is FALSE, the values need not be in ascending order.

Tip

If you prefer to see something other than #N/A when the employee number is not found, you can use the IFERROR function to test for the error result and substitute a different string. The following formula displays the text Not Found rather than #N/A:

```
=IFERROR(VLOOKUP(B1,EmpList,2,FALSE),"Not Found")
```

IFERROR works only with Excel 2007 and later versions. For compatibility with previous versions, use the following formula:

```
=IF(ISNA(VLOOKUP(B1,EmpList,2,FALSE)),"Not Found",VLOOKUP(B1,EmpList,2,FALSE))
```

Looking up a value to the left

The VLOOKUP function always looks up a value in the first column of the lookup range. But what if you want to look up a value in a column other than the first column? It would be helpful if you could supply a negative value for the third argument for VLOOKUP — but Excel doesn't allow it.

Figure 14.7 illustrates the problem. Suppose that you want to look up the batting average (column B, in a range named Averages) of a player in column C (in a range named Players). The player you want data for appears in a cell named LookupValue. The VLOOKUP function won't work because the data isn't arranged correctly. One option is to rearrange your data, but sometimes that's not possible.

FIGURE 14.7

The VLOOKUP function can't look up a value in column B based on a value in column C.

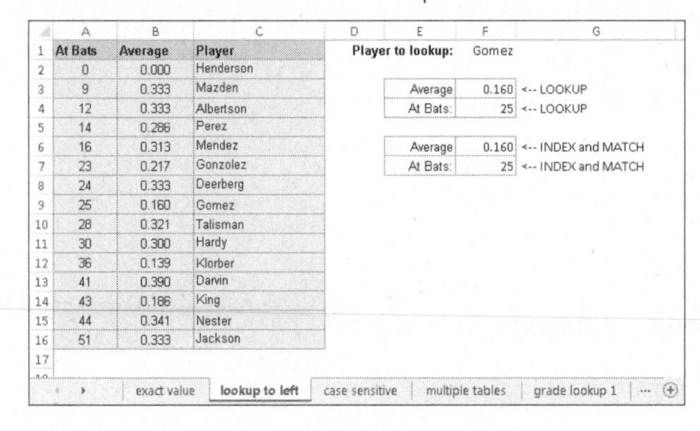

	A	B	C	D	E	F	G
1	At Bats	Average	Player	Player to lookup:		Gomez	
2	0	0.000	Henderson				
3	9	0.333	Mazden		Average	0.160	<-- LOOKUP
4	12	0.333	Albertson		At Bats:	25	<-- LOOKUP
5	14	0.286	Perez				
6	16	0.313	Mendez		Average	0.160	<-- INDEX and MATCH
7	23	0.217	Gonzolez		At Bats:	25	<-- INDEX and MATCH
8	24	0.333	Deerberg				
9	25	0.160	Gomez				
10	28	0.321	Talisman				
11	30	0.300	Hardy				
12	36	0.139	Klorber				
13	41	0.390	Darvin				
14	43	0.186	King				
15	44	0.341	Nester				
16	51	0.333	Jackson				
17							

One solution is to use the LOOKUP function, which requires two range arguments. The following formula (in cell F3) returns the batting average from column B of the player name contained in the cell named LookupValue:

```
=LOOKUP(LookupValue,Players,Averages)
```

Using the LOOKUP function requires that the lookup range (in this case, the Players range) is in ascending order. In addition to this limitation, the formula suffers from a serious problem: If you enter a nonexistent player (in other words, the LookupValue cell contains a value not found in the Players range), the formula returns an incorrect result — and you won't even know it.

A better solution uses the INDEX and MATCH functions. The formula that follows works just like the previous one except that it returns #N/A if the player is not found. Another advantage is that the player names don't have to be sorted.

```
=INDEX(Averages,MATCH(LookupValue,Players,0))
```

Performing a case-sensitive lookup

The Excel lookup functions (LOOKUP, VLOOKUP, and HLOOKUP) are not case sensitive. For example, if you write a lookup formula to look up the text *budget,* the formula considers any of the following a match: *BUDGET, Budget,* or *BuDgEt.*

Figure 14.8 shows a simple example. Range D2:D7 is named Range1, and range E2:E7 is named Range2. The word to be looked up appears in cell B1 (named Value).

FIGURE 14.8

Using an array formula to perform a case-sensitive lookup.

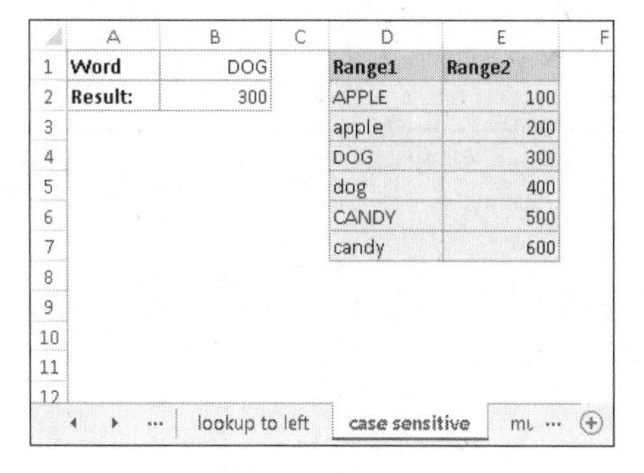

	A	B	C	D	E	F
1	**Word**	DOG		**Range1**	**Range2**	
2	**Result:**	300		APPLE	100	
3				apple	200	
4				DOG	300	
5				dog	400	
6				CANDY	500	
7				candy	600	
8						
9						
10						
11						

The array formula that follows is in cell B2. This formula does a case-sensitive lookup in Range1 and returns the corresponding value in Range2.

```
{=INDEX(Range2,MATCH(TRUE,EXACT(Value,Range1),0))}
```

The formula looks up the word *DOG* (uppercase) and returns 300. The following standard LOOKUP formula (which is not case sensitive) returns 400:

```
=LOOKUP(Value,Range1,Range2)
```

NOTE

When entering an array formula, remember to press Ctrl+Shift+Enter, and do not type the curly brackets.

Looking up a value from multiple lookup tables

You can, of course, have any number of lookup tables in a worksheet. In some situations, your formula may need to decide which lookup table to use. Figure 14.9 shows an example.

FIGURE 14.9

This worksheet demonstrates the use of multiple lookup tables.

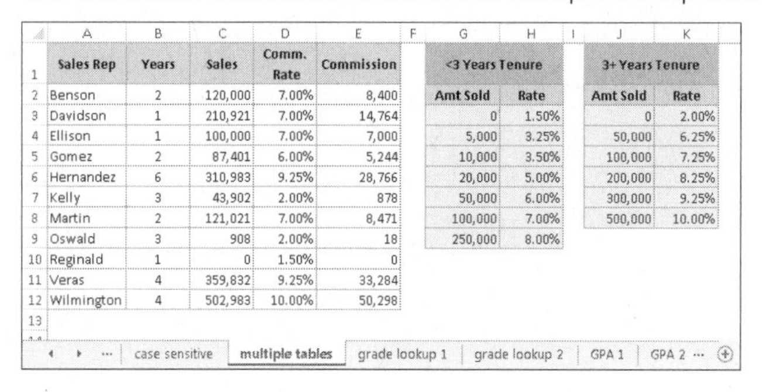

	A	B	C	D	E	F	G	H	I	J	K
1	Sales Rep	Years	Sales	Comm. Rate	Commission		<3 Years Tenure			3+ Years Tenure	
2	Benson	2	120,000	7.00%	8,400		Amt Sold	Rate		Amt Sold	Rate
3	Davidson	1	210,921	7.00%	14,764		0	1.50%		0	2.00%
4	Ellison	1	100,000	7.00%	7,000		5,000	3.25%		50,000	6.25%
5	Gomez	2	87,401	6.00%	5,244		10,000	3.50%		100,000	7.25%
6	Hernandez	6	310,983	9.25%	28,766		20,000	5.00%		200,000	8.25%
7	Kelly	3	43,902	2.00%	878		50,000	6.00%		300,000	9.25%
8	Martin	2	121,021	7.00%	8,471		100,000	7.00%		500,000	10.00%
9	Oswald	3	908	2.00%	18		250,000	8.00%			
10	Reginald	1	0	1.50%	0						
11	Veras	4	359,832	9.25%	33,284						
12	Wilmington	4	502,983	10.00%	50,298						
13											

case sensitive | multiple tables | grade lookup 1 | grade lookup 2 | GPA 1 | GPA 2

This workbook calculates sales commission and contains two lookup tables: G3:H9 (named CommTable1) and J3:K8 (named CommTable2). The commission rate for a particular sales representative depends on two factors: the sales rep's years of service (column B) and the amount sold (column C). Column D contains formulas that look up the commission rate from the appropriate table. For example, the formula in cell D2 is

```
=VLOOKUP(C2,IF(B2<3,CommTable1,CommTable2),2)
```

The second argument for the `VLOOKUP` function consists of an `IF` formula that uses the value in column B to determine which lookup table to use.

The formula in column E simply multiplies the sales amount in column C by the commission rate in column D. The formula in cell E2, for example, is

```
=C2*D2
```

Determining letter grades for test scores

A common use of a lookup table is to assign letter grades for test scores. Figure 14.10 shows a worksheet with student test scores. The range E2:F6 (named GradeList) displays a lookup table used to assign a letter grade to a test score.

Column C contains formulas that use the VLOOKUP function and the lookup table to assign a grade based on the score in column B. The formula in cell C2, for example, is

```
=VLOOKUP(B2,GradeList,2)
```

When the lookup table is small (as in the example shown earlier in Figure 14.10), you can use a literal array in place of the lookup table. The formula that follows, for example, returns a letter grade without using a lookup table. Instead, the information in the lookup table is hard-coded into an array.

```
=VLOOKUP(B2,{0,"F";40,"D";70,"C";80,"B";90,"A"},2)
```

FIGURE 14.10

Looking up letter grades for test scores.

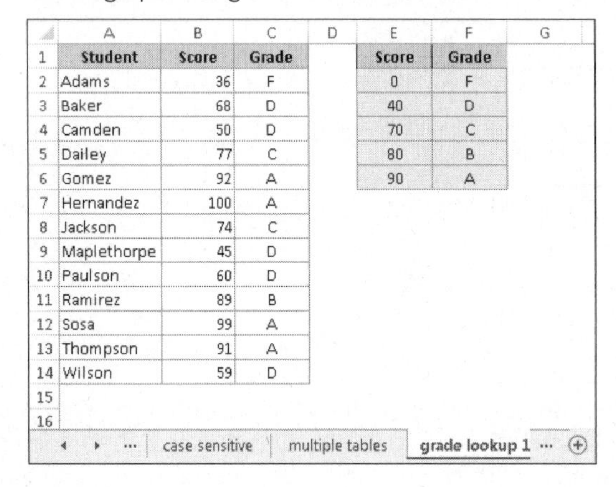

	A	B	C	D	E	F	G
1	Student	Score	Grade		Score	Grade	
2	Adams	36	F		0	F	
3	Baker	68	D		40	D	
4	Camden	50	D		70	C	
5	Dailey	77	C		80	B	
6	Gomez	92	A		90	A	
7	Hernandez	100	A				
8	Jackson	74	C				
9	Maplethorpe	45	D				
10	Paulson	60	D				
11	Ramirez	89	B				
12	Sosa	99	A				
13	Thompson	91	A				
14	Wilson	59	D				
15							
16							

... case sensitive | multiple tables | grade lookup 1 ...

See Chapter 17 for more information about arrays.

Another approach, which uses a more legible formula, is to use the LOOKUP function with two array arguments:

```
=LOOKUP(B2,{0,40,70,80,90},{"F","D","C","B","A"})
```

Calculating a grade-point average

A student's *grade-point average* (GPA) is a numerical measure of the average grade received for classes taken. This discussion assumes a letter grade system, in which each letter grade is assigned a numeric value (A = 4, B = 3, C = 2, D = 1, and F = 0). The GPA comprises an average of the numeric grade values weighted by the credit hours of the course. A one-hour course, for example, receives less weight than a three-hour course. The GPA ranges from 0 (all Fs) to 4.00 (all As).

Figure 14.11 shows a worksheet with information for a student. This student took five courses, for a total of 13 credit hours. Range B2:B6 is named CreditHours. The grades for each course appear in column C. (Range C2:C6 is named Grades.) Column D uses a lookup formula to calculate the grade value for each course. The lookup formula in cell D2, for example, follows. This formula uses the lookup table in G2:H6 (named GradeTable).

```
=VLOOKUP(C2,GradeTable,2,FALSE)
```

FIGURE 14.11

Using multiple formulas to calculate a GPA.

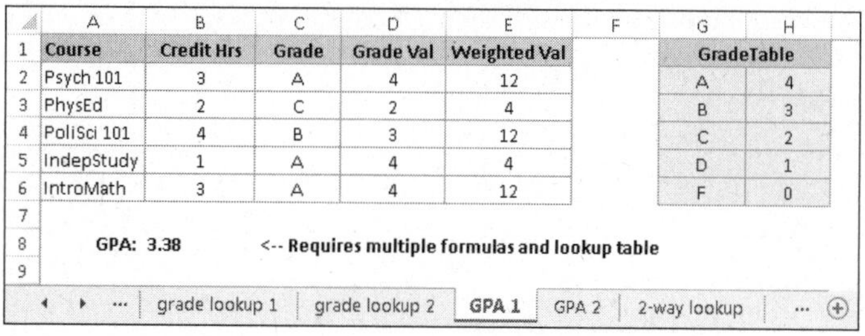

	A	B	C	D	E	F	G	H
1	Course	Credit Hrs	Grade	Grade Val	Weighted Val		GradeTable	
2	Psych 101	3	A	4	12		A	4
3	PhysEd	2	C	2	4		B	3
4	PoliSci 101	4	B	3	12		C	2
5	IndepStudy	1	A	4	4		D	1
6	IntroMath	3	A	4	12		F	0
7								
8	GPA:	3.38		<-- Requires multiple formulas and lookup table				
9								

grade lookup 1 | grade lookup 2 | GPA 1 | GPA 2 | 2-way lookup

Formulas in column E calculate the weighted values. The formula in cell E2 is

```
=D2*B2
```

Cell B8 computes the GPA by using the following formula:

```
=SUM(E2:E6)/SUM(B2:B6)
```

The preceding formulas work fine, but you can streamline the GPA calculation quite a bit. In fact, you can use a single array formula to make this calculation and avoid using the lookup table and the formulas in columns D and E. This array formula does the job:

```
{=SUM((MATCH(Grades,{"F","D","C","B","A"},0)-1)*CreditHours)/SUM(CreditHours)}
```

Performing a two-way lookup

Figure 14.12 shows a worksheet with a table that displays product sales by month. To retrieve sales for a particular month and product, the user enters a month in cell B1 and a product name in cell B2.

FIGURE 14.12

This table demonstrates a two-way lookup.

	A	B	C	D	E	F	G	H	I
1	Month:	July			Widgets	Sprockets	Snapholytes	Combined	
2	Product:	Sprockets		January	2,892	1,771	4,718	9,381	
3				February	3,380	4,711	2,615	10,706	
4	Month Offset:	8		March	3,744	3,223	5,312	12,279	
5	Product Offset:	3		April	3,221	2,438	1,108	6,767	
6	Sales:	3,337		May	4,839	1,999	1,994	8,832	
7				June	3,767	5,140	3,830	12,737	
8				July	5,467	3,337	3,232	12,036	
9	Single-formula -->	3,337		August	3,154	4,895	1,607	9,656	
10				September	1,718	2,040	1,563	5,321	
11				October	1,548	1,061	2,590	5,199	
12				November	5,083	3,558	3,960	12,601	
13				December	5,753	2,839	3,013	11,605	
14				Total	44,566	37,012	35,542	117,120	
15									

... | grade lookup 2 | GPA 1 | GPA 2 | 2-way lookup | 2-column lookup | cell address | ...

To simplify things, the worksheet uses the following named ranges:

- **Month:** B1
- **Product:** B2
- **Table:** D1:H14
- **MonthList:** D1:D14
- **ProductList:** D1:H1

The following formula (in cell B4) uses the `MATCH` function to return the position of the month within the MonthList range. For example, if the month is January, the formula returns `2` because January is the second item in the MonthList range (the first item is a blank cell, D1).

```
=MATCH(Month,MonthList,0)
```

The formula in cell B5 works similarly but uses the ProductList range:

```
=MATCH(Product,ProductList,0)
```

The final formula, in cell B6, returns the corresponding sales amount. It uses the `INDEX` function with the results from cells B4 and B5.

```
=INDEX(Table,B4,B5)
```

You can combine these formulas into a single formula, as shown here:

```
=INDEX(Table,MATCH(Month,MonthList,0),MATCH(Product,ProductList,0))
```

TIP

Another way to accomplish a two-way lookup is to provide a name for each row and column of the table. A quick way to do so is to select the table and choose Formulas ➪ Defined Names ➪ Create from Selection. In the Create Names from Selection dialog box, select the Top Row and Left Column check boxes. After creating the names, you can use a simple formula, such as:

```
= Sprockets July
```

This formula, which uses the range intersection operator (a space), returns July sales for Sprockets.

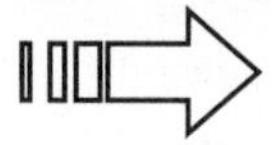

See Chapter 10 for details about the range intersection operator.

Performing a two-column lookup

Some situations may require a lookup based on the values in two columns. Figure 14.13 shows an example.

FIGURE 14.13

This workbook performs a lookup by using information in two columns (D and E).

	A	B	C	D	E	F	G
1	**Make:**	Toyota		**Make**	**Model**	**Code**	
2	**Model:**	Sequoia		Chevy	Suburban	C-094	
3	**Code:**	T-871		Chevy	Tahoe	C-823	
4				Ford	Explorer	F-772	
5				Ford	Escape	F-229	
6				Honda	Pilot	I-897	
7				Honda	CR-V	I-900	
8				Jeep	Compass	J-983	
9				Jeep	Grand Cherokee	J-701	
10				Nissan	Suburban	N-231	
11				Toyota	Sequoia	T-871	
12				Toyota	Land Cruiser	T-981	
13							
14							

The lookup table contains automobile makes and models and a corresponding code for each. The worksheet uses named ranges, as shown here:

- **Code:** F2:F12
- **Make:** B1
- **Model:** B2
- **Makes:** D2:D12
- **Models:** E2:E12

The following array formula displays the corresponding code for an automobile make and model:

```
{=INDEX(Code,MATCH(Make&Model,Makes&Models,0))}
```

This formula works by concatenating the contents of Make and Model and then searching for this text in an array consisting of the concatenated corresponding text in Makes and Models.

Determining the cell address of a value within a range

Most of the time, you want your lookup formula to return a value. You may, however, need to determine the cell address of a particular value within a range. For example, Figure 14.14 shows a worksheet with a range of numbers that occupies a single column (named Data). Cell B1, which contains the value to look up, is named Target.

FIGURE 14.14

The formula in cell B2 returns the address in the Data range for the value in cell B1.

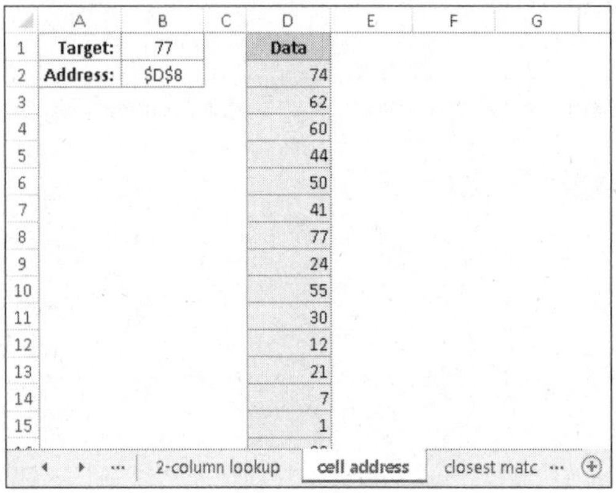

	A	B	C	D	E	F	G
1	Target:	77		Data			
2	Address:	$D$8		74			
3				62			
4				60			
5				44			
6				50			
7				41			
8				77			
9				24			
10				55			
11				30			
12				12			
13				21			
14				7			
15				1			

2-column lookup | cell address | closest matc ...

The formula in cell B2, which follows, returns the address of the cell in the Data range that contains the Target value:

```
=ADDRESS(ROW(Data)+MATCH(Target,Data,0)-1,COLUMN(Data))
```

If the Data range occupies a single row, use this formula to return the address of the Target value:

```
=ADDRESS(ROW(Data),COLUMN(Data)+MATCH(Target,Data,0)-1)
```

If the Data range contains more than one instance of the Target value, the address of the first occurrence is returned. If the Target value isn't found in the Data range, the formula returns #N/A.

Looking up a value by using the closest match

The VLOOKUP and HLOOKUP functions are useful in the following situations:

- You need to identify an exact match for a target value. Use FALSE as the function's fourth argument.
- You need to locate an approximate match. If the function's fourth argument is TRUE or omitted and an exact match is not found, the next largest value less than the lookup value is returned.

But what if you need to look up a value based on the *closest* match? Neither VLOOKUP nor HLOOKUP can do the job.

Figure 14.15 shows a worksheet with student names in column A and values in column B. Range B2:B20 is named Data. Cell E2, named Target, contains a value to search for in the Data range. Cell E3, named ColOffset, contains a value that represents the column offset from the Data range.

FIGURE 14.15

This workbook demonstrates how to perform a lookup by using the closest match.

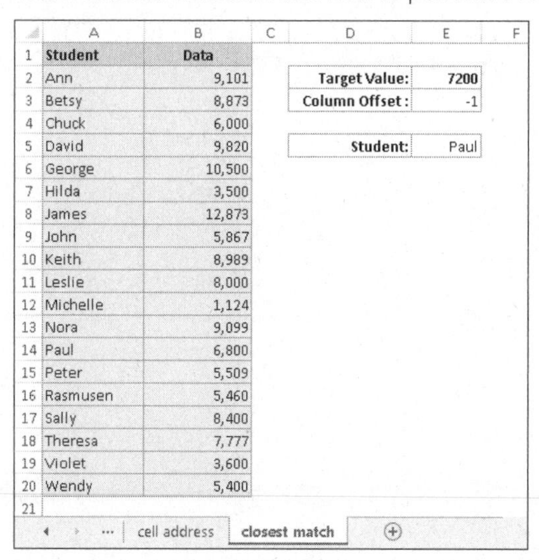

	A	B
1	Student	Data
2	Ann	9,101
3	Betsy	8,873
4	Chuck	6,000
5	David	9,820
6	George	10,500
7	Hilda	3,500
8	James	12,873
9	John	5,867
10	Keith	8,989
11	Leslie	8,000
12	Michelle	1,124
13	Nora	9,099
14	Paul	6,800
15	Peter	5,509
16	Rasmusen	5,460
17	Sally	8,400
18	Theresa	7,777
19	Violet	3,600
20	Wendy	5,400

	D	E
2	Target Value:	7200
3	Column Offset:	-1
5	Student:	Paul

The array formula that follows identifies the closest match to the Target value in the Data range and returns the names of the corresponding student in column A (that is, the column with an offset of –1). The formula returns Paul (with a corresponding value of 6,800, which is the one closest to the Target value of 7,200).

```
{=INDIRECT(ADDRESS(ROW(Data)+MATCH(MIN(ABS(Target-Data)),ABS(Target-Data),0)-
  1,COLUMN(Data)+ColOffset))}
```

If two values in the Data range are equidistant from the Target value, the formula uses the first one in the list.

The value in ColOffset can be negative (for a column to the left of Data), positive (for a column to the right of Data), or 0 (for the actual closest match value in the Data range).

To understand how this formula works, you need to understand the INDIRECT function. This function's first argument is a text string in the form of a cell reference (or a reference to a cell that contains a text string). In this example, the text string is created by the ADDRESS function, which accepts a row and column reference and returns a cell address.

CHAPTER

15

Creating Formulas for Financial Applications

IN THIS CHAPTER

Getting a brief overview of the Excel functions that deal with the time value of money

Looking at formulas that perform various types of loan calculations

Considering formulas that perform various types of investment calculations

Reviewing Excel depreciation functions

It's a safe bet that the most common use of Excel is to perform calculations involving money. Every day, people make hundreds of thousands of financial decisions based on the numbers that are calculated in a spreadsheet. These decisions range from simple (Can I afford to buy a new car?) to complex (Will purchasing XYZ Corporation result in a positive cash flow in the next 18 months?). This chapter discusses basic financial calculations that you can perform with the assistance of Excel.

The Time Value of Money

The face value of money may not always be what it seems. A key consideration is the *time value* of money. This concept involves calculating the value of money in the past, present, or future. It's based on the premise that money increases in value over time because of interest earned by the money. In other words, a dollar invested today will be worth more tomorrow.

For example, imagine that your rich uncle decided to give away some money and asked you to choose one of the following options:

- Receive $8,000 today.
- Receive $9,500 in one year.
- Receive $12,000 in five years.
- Receive $150 per month for five years.

If your goal is to maximize the amount received, you need to take into account not only the face value of the money but also the *time value* of the money when it arrives in your hands.

The time value of money depends on your perspective. In other words, you're either a lender or a borrower. When you take out a loan to purchase an automobile, you're a borrower, and the institution that provides the funds to you is the lender. When you invest money in a bank savings account, you're a lender; you're lending your money to the bank, and the bank is borrowing it from you.

Several concepts contribute to the time value of money:

- **Present value (PV):** This is the principal amount. If you deposit $5,000 in a bank savings account, this amount represents the *principal,* or present value, of the money you invested. If you borrow $15,000 to purchase a car, this amount represents the principal, or present value, of the loan. Present value may be positive or negative.
- **Future value (FV):** This is the principal plus interest. If you invest $5,000 for five years and earn 3% annual interest, your investment is worth $5,796.37 at the end of the five-year term. This amount is the future value of your $5,000 investment. If you take out a three-year car loan for $15,000 and make monthly payments based on a 5.25% annual interest rate, you pay a total of $16,244.97. This amount represents the principal plus the interest you paid. Future value may be positive or negative, depending on the perspective (lender or borrower).
- **Payment (PMT):** This is either principal or principal plus interest. If you deposit $100 per month into a savings account, $100 is the payment. If you have a monthly mortgage payment of $1,025, this amount is made up of principal and interest.
- **Interest rate:** Interest is a percentage of the principal, usually expressed on an annual basis. For example, you may earn 2.5% annual interest on a bank CD (certificate of deposit). Or your mortgage loan may have a 6.75% interest rate.
- **Period:** This represents the point in time when interest is paid or earned (for example, a bank CD that pays interest quarterly, or an auto loan that requires monthly payments).
- **Term:** This is the amount of time of interest. A 12-month bank CD has a term of one year. A 30-year mortgage loan has a term of 360 months.

Loan Calculations

This section describes how to calculate various components of a loan. Think of a loan as consisting of the following components:

- The loan amount
- The interest rate
- The number of payment periods
- The periodic payment amount

If you know any three of these components, you can create a formula to calculate the unknown component.

NOTE
The loan calculations in this section all assume a fixed-rate loan with a fixed term.

Worksheet functions for calculating loan information

This section describes six commonly used financial functions: PMT, PPMT, IPMT, RATE, NPER, and PV. For information about the arguments used in these functions, see Table 15.1.

TABLE 15.1 Financial Function Arguments

Function Argument	Description
Rate	The interest rate per period. If the rate is expressed as an annual interest rate, you must divide it by the number of periods.
Nper	The total number of payment periods.
Per	A particular period. The period must be less than or equal to nper.
Pmt	The payment made each period (a constant value that does not change).
Fv	The future value after the last payment is made. If you omit fv, it is assumed to be 0. (The future value of a loan, for example, is 0.)
Type	Indicates when payments are due — either 0 (due at the end of the period) or 1 (due at the beginning of the period). If you omit type, it is assumed to be 0.
Guess	Used by the RATE function. An initial estimate of what the result will be. The RATE function is calculated by iteration. If the function doesn't converge on a result, changing the guess argument will help.

PMT

The PMT function returns the loan payment (principal plus interest) per period, assuming constant payment amounts and a fixed interest rate. The syntax for the PMT function is

```
PMT(rate,nper,pv,fv,type)
```

The following formula returns the monthly payment amount for a $5,000 loan with a 6% annual percentage rate. The loan has a term of four years (48 months).

```
=PMT(6%/12,48,-5000)
```

This formula returns $117.43, the monthly payment for the loan. The first argument, rate, is the annual rate divided by the number of months in a year. Also, notice that the third argument (pv, for present value) is negative and represents money owed.

PPMT

The `PPMT` function returns the principal part of a loan payment for a given period, assuming constant payment amounts and a fixed interest rate. The syntax for the `PPMT` function is

```
PPMT(rate,per,nper,pv,fv,type)
```

The following formula returns the amount paid to principal for the first month of a $5,000 loan with a 6% annual percentage rate. The loan has a term of four years (48 months).

```
=PPMT(6%/12,1,48,-5000)
```

The formula returns $92.43 for the principal, which is about 78.7% of the total loan payment. If I change the second argument to 48 (to calculate the principal amount for the last payment), the formula returns $116.84, or about 99.5% of the total loan payment.

> **NOTE**
> To calculate the cumulative principal paid between any two payment periods, use the `CUMPRINC` function. This function uses two additional arguments: `start_period` and `end_period`. In Excel versions prior to Excel 2007, `CUMPRINC` is available only when you install the Analysis ToolPak add-in.

IPMT

The `IPMT` function returns the interest part of a loan payment for a given period, assuming constant payment amounts and a fixed interest rate. The syntax for the `IPMT` function is

```
IPMT(rate,per,nper,pv,fv,type)
```

The following formula returns the amount paid to interest for the first month of a $5,000 loan with a 6% annual percentage rate. The loan has a term of four years (48 months).

```
=IPMT(6%/12,1,48,-5000)
```

This formula returns an interest amount of $25.00. By the last payment period for the loan, the interest payment is only $0.58.

> **NOTE**
> To calculate the cumulative interest paid between any two payment periods, use the `CUMIPMT` function. This function uses two additional arguments: `start_period` and `end_period`. In Excel versions prior to Excel 2007, `CUMIPMT` is available only when you install the Analysis ToolPak add-in.

RATE

The `RATE` function returns the periodic interest rate of a loan, given the number of payment periods, the periodic payment amount, and the loan amount. The syntax for the `RATE` function is

```
RATE(nper,pmt,pv,fv,type,guess)
```

The following formula calculates the annual interest rate for a 48-month loan for $5,000 that has a monthly payment amount of $117.43.

```
=RATE(48,117.43,-5000)*12
```

This formula returns 6.00%. Notice that the result of the function is multiplied by 12 to get the annual percentage rate.

NPER

The `NPER` function returns the number of payment periods for a loan, given the loan's amount, interest rate, and periodic payment amount. The syntax for the `NPER` function is

```
NPER(rate,pmt,pv,fv,type)
```

The following formula calculates the number of payment periods for a $5,000 loan that has a monthly payment amount of $117.43. The loan has a 6% annual interest rate.

```
=NPER(6%/12,117.43,-5000)
```

This formula returns 47.997 (that is, 48 months). The monthly payment was rounded to the nearest penny, causing the minor discrepancy.

PV

The `PV` function returns the present value (that is, the original loan amount) for a loan, given the interest rate, the number of periods, and the periodic payment amount. The syntax for the `PV` function is

```
PV(rate,nper,pmt,fv,type)
```

The following formula calculates the original loan amount for a 48-month loan that has a monthly payment amount of $117.43. The annual interest rate is 6%.

```
=PV(6%/12,48,-117.43)
```

This formula returns $5,000.21. The monthly payment was rounded to the nearest penny, causing the $0.21 discrepancy.

A loan calculation example

Figure 15.1 shows a worksheet set up to calculate the periodic payment amount for a loan.

FIGURE 15.1

Using the PMT function to calculate a periodic loan payment amount.

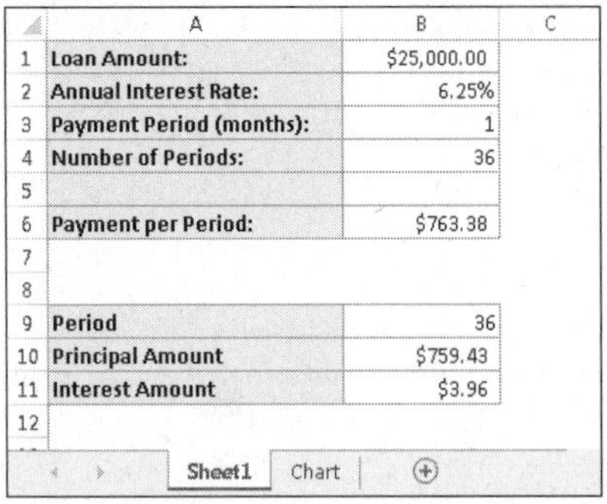

	A	B	C
1	Loan Amount:	$25,000.00	
2	Annual Interest Rate:	6.25%	
3	Payment Period (months):	1	
4	Number of Periods:	36	
5			
6	Payment per Period:	$763.38	
7			
8			
9	Period	36	
10	Principal Amount	$759.43	
11	Interest Amount	$3.96	
12			

Sheet1 | Chart

On the Web

The workbook described in this section is available at this book's website. The file is named `loan payment.xlsx`.

The loan amount is in cell B1, and the annual interest rate is in cell B2. Cell B3 contains the payment period expressed in months. For example, if cell B3 is 1, the payment is due monthly. If cell B3 is 3, the payment is due every three months, or quarterly. Cell B4 contains the number of periods of the loan. The example shown in this figure calculates the payment for a $25,000 loan at 6.25% annual interest with monthly payments for 36 months. The formula in cell B6 is

```
=PMT(B2*(B3/12),B4,-B1)
```

Notice that the first argument is an expression that calculates the *periodic interest rate* by using the annual interest rate and the payment period. Therefore, if payments are made quarterly on a three-year loan, the payment period is 3, the number of periods is 12, and the periodic interest rate would be calculated as the annual interest rate multiplied by $3/12$.

In the worksheet in Figure 15.1, range A9:B11 is set up to calculate the principal and interest amount for a particular payment period. Cell B9 contains the payment period used by the formulas in B10:B11. (The payment period must be less than or equal to the value in cell B4.)

The formula in cell B10, shown here, calculates the amount of the payment that goes toward principal for the payment period in cell B9:

```
=PPMT(B2*(B3/12),B9,B4,-B1)
```

The following formula, in cell B11, calculates the amount of the payment that goes toward interest for the payment period in cell B9:

```
=IPMT(B2*(B3/12),B9,B4,-B1)
```

The sum of B10 and B11 is equal to the total loan payment calculated in cell B6. However, the relative proportion of principal and interest amounts varies with the payment period. (An increasingly larger proportion of the payment is applied toward principal as the loan progresses.) Figure 15.2 shows the principal and interest portions graphically.

FIGURE 15.2

This chart shows how the interest and principal amounts vary during the payment periods of a loan.

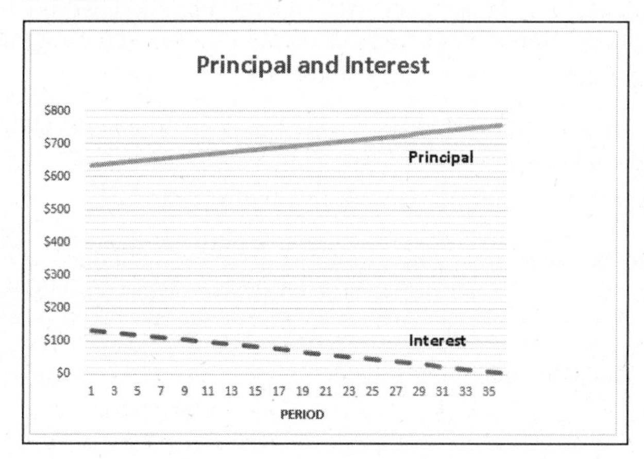

Credit card payments

Do you ever wonder how long it would take to pay off a credit card balance if you make the minimum payment amount each month? Figure 15.3 shows a worksheet set up to make this type of calculation.

FIGURE 15.3

This worksheet calculates the number of payments required to pay off a credit card balance by paying the minimum payment amount each month.

	A	B
1	Credit Card Balance	$1,000.00
2	Annual Interest Rate:	21.25%
3	Minimum Payment Pct:	2.00%
4	Minimum Monthly Payment Amount:	$20.00
5	Your Actual Monthly Payment:	$20.00
6		
7	No. of Payments Required:	123.4
8	Total Amount Paid:	$2,468.42
9	Total Interest Paid:	$1,468.42
10		

Sheet1

ON THE WEB

The workbook shown in Figure 15.3 is available at this book's website. The file is named `credit card payments.xlsx`.

Range B1:B5 stores input values. In this example, the credit card has a balance of $1,000, and the lender charges a 21.25% annual percentage rate (APR). The minimum payment is 2.00% (typical of many credit card lenders). Therefore, the minimum payment amount for this example is $20. You can enter a different payment amount in cell B5, but it must be large enough to pay off the loan. For example, you may choose to pay $50 per month to pay off the balance more quickly. However, paying $10 per month isn't sufficient, and the formulas return an error.

Range B7:B9 holds formulas that perform various calculations. The formula in cell B7, which follows, calculates the number of months required to pay off the balance:

```
=NPER(B2/12,B5,-B1,0)
```

The formula in B8 calculates the total amount you will pay. This formula is

```
=B7*B5
```

The formula in cell B9 calculates the total interest paid:

```
=B8-B1
```

In this example, it would take about 123 months (more than ten years) to pay off the credit card balance if the borrower made only the minimum monthly payment. The total interest paid on the $1,000 loan would be $1,468.42. This calculation assumes, of course, that no additional charges are made on the account. This example may help explain why you receive so many credit card solicitations in the mail.

Figure 15.4 shows some additional calculations for the credit card example. For example, if you want to pay off the credit card in 12 months, you need to make monthly payments of $93.23. (This amount results in total payments of $1,118.81 with total interest of $118.81.) The formula in B13 is

```
=PMT($B$2/12,A13,-$B$1)
```

Creating a loan amortization schedule

A *loan amortization schedule* is a table of values that shows various types of information for each payment period of a loan. Figure 15.5 shows a worksheet that uses formulas to calculate an amortization schedule.

FIGURE 15.4

Column B shows the payment required to pay off the credit card balance for various payoff periods.

Other Payoff Periods (months)	Pmt Required	Total Pmts	Total Interest
2	$513.32	$1,026.64	$26.64
6	$177.15	$1,062.89	$62.89
12	$93.23	$1,118.81	$118.81
24	$51.51	$1,236.20	$236.20
36	$37.80	$1,360.93	$360.93
48	$31.10	$1,492.82	$492.82
60	$27.19	$1,631.65	$631.65
72	$24.68	$1,777.17	$777.17
84	$22.96	$1,929.06	$929.06
96	$21.74	$2,086.97	$1,086.97
108	$20.84	$2,250.54	$1,250.54
120	$20.16	$2,419.38	$1,419.38
132	$19.64	$2,593.09	$1,593.09

FIGURE 15.5

A loan amortization schedule.

Loan Amount:	$18,500.00
Annual Interest Rate:	7.25%
Pmt. Period (months):	1
Number of Periods:	36

Loan Amortization Schedule

Payment Period	Payment Amount	Cumulative Payments	Interest	Cumulative Interest	Principal	Cumulative Principal	Principal Balance
							$18,500.00
1	$573.34	$573.34	$111.77	$111.77	$461.57	$461.57	$18,038.43
2	$573.34	$1,146.69	$108.98	$220.75	$464.36	$925.93	17,574.07
3	$573.34	$1,720.03	$106.18	$326.93	$467.17	$1,393.10	17,106.90
4	$573.34	$2,293.37	$103.35	$430.28	$469.99	$1,863.09	16,636.91
5	$573.34	$2,866.72	$100.51	$530.80	$472.83	$2,335.92	16,164.08
6	$573.34	$3,440.06	$97.66	$628.46	$475.69	$2,811.60	15,688.40
7	$573.34	$4,013.40	$94.78	$723.24	$478.56	$3,290.16	15,209.84
8	$573.34	$4,586.75	$91.89	$815.13	$481.45	$3,771.61	14,728.39
9	$573.34	$5,160.09	$88.98	$904.12	$484.36	$4,255.97	14,244.03
10	$573.34	$5,733.43	$86.06	$990.18	$487.29	$4,743.26	13,756.74
11	$573.34	$6,306.78	$83.11	$1,073.29	$490.23	$5,233.49	13,266.51
12	$573.34	$6,880.12	$80.15	$1,153.44	$493.19	$5,726.68	12,773.32
13	$573.34	$7,453.46	$77.17	$1,230.61	$496.17	$6,222.85	12,277.15

ON THE WEB

This workbook available on this book's website. The file is named `loan amortization schedule.xlsx`.

The loan parameters are entered into C1:C4, and the formulas beginning in row 9 use these values for the calculations. Table 15.2 shows the formulas in row 9 of the schedule. These formulas were copied down to row 488. Therefore, the worksheet can calculate amortization schedules for a loan with as many as 480 payment periods (40 years of monthly payments).

NOTE
Formulas in the rows that extend beyond the number of payments return an error value. The worksheet uses conditional formatting to hide the data in these rows.

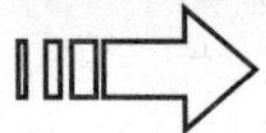

See Chapter 21 for more information about conditional formatting.

TABLE 15.2 Formulas Used to Calculate an Amortization Schedule

Cell	Formula	Description
A9	`=A8+1`	Returns the payment number
B9	`=PMT($B$2*($B$3/12), $B$4,-$B$1)`	Calculates the periodic payment amount
C9	`=C8+B9`	Calculates the cumulative payment amounts
D9	`=IPMT($B$2*($B$3/12), A9,$B$4,-$B$1)`	Calculates the interest portion of the periodic payment
E9	`=E8+D9`	Calculates the cumulative interest paid
F9	`=PPMT($B$2*($B$3/12), A9,$B$4,-$B$1)`	Calculates the principal portion of the periodic payment
G9	`=G8+F9`	Calculates the cumulative amount applied toward principal
H9	`=H8-F9`	Returns the principal balance at the end of the period

Summarizing loan options by using a data table

The Excel Data Table feature is probably one of the most underutilized tools in Excel. Keep in mind that a data table is not the same as a table (created by choosing Insert ➪ Tables ➪ Table). A data table is a handy way to summarize calculations that depend on one or two "changing" cells. In this example, I use a data table to summarize various loan options. This section describes how to create one-way and two-way data tables.

See Chapter 35 for more information about setting up data tables.

ON THE WEB
A workbook that demonstrates one- and two-way data tables is available at this book's website. The file is named `loan data tables.xlsx`.

Creating a one-way data table

A *one-way data table* shows the results of any number of calculations for different values of a single input cell.

Figure 15.6 shows a one-way data table (in B10:I13) that displays three calculations (payment amount, total payments, and total interest) for a loan, using seven interest rates ranging from 7.00% to 8.50%. In this example, the input cell is cell B2.

FIGURE 15.6

Using a one-way data table to display three loan calculations for various interest rates.

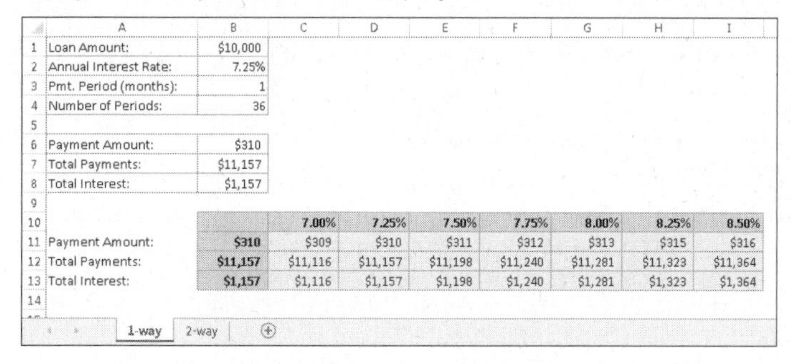

	A	B	C	D	E	F	G	H	I
1	Loan Amount:	$10,000							
2	Annual Interest Rate:	7.25%							
3	Pmt. Period (months):	1							
4	Number of Periods:	36							
5									
6	Payment Amount:	$310							
7	Total Payments:	$11,157							
8	Total Interest:	$1,157							
9									
10			7.00%	7.25%	7.50%	7.75%	8.00%	8.25%	8.50%
11	Payment Amount:	$310	$309	$310	$311	$312	$313	$315	$316
12	Total Payments:	$11,157	$11,116	$11,157	$11,198	$11,240	$11,281	$11,323	$11,364
13	Total Interest:	$1,157	$1,116	$1,157	$1,198	$1,240	$1,281	$1,323	$1,364
14									

To create this one-way data table, follow these steps:

1. **Enter the formulas that return the results for use in the data table.** In this example, the formulas are in B6:B8.
2. **Enter various values for a single input cell in successive columns.** In this example, the input value is interest rate, and the values for various interest rates appear in C10:I10.
3. **Create a reference to the formula cells in the column to the left of the input values.** In this example, the range B11:B13 contains simple formulas that reference other cells. For example, cell B11 contains the following formula:

   ```
   =B6
   ```

4. **Select the rectangular range that contains the entries from the previous steps.** In this example, select B10:I13.
5. **Choose Data ➪ Data Tools ➪ What-If Analysis ➪ Data Table.** The Data Table dialog box, shown in Figure 15.7, appears.

FIGURE 15.7

The Data Table dialog box.

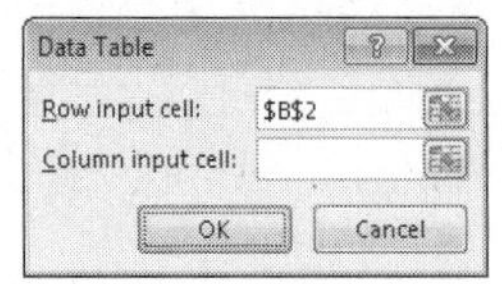

6. **For the Row input cell field, specify the cell reference that corresponds to the variable in your Data Table column header row.** In this example, the Row input cell is B2.
7. **Leave the Column input cell field empty.** The Column input field is used for two-way data tables, described in the next section.
8. **Click OK.** Excel inserts a multi-cell array formula that uses the `TABLE` function with a single argument.
9. **(Optional) Format the data table.** For example, you may want to apply shading to the row and column headers.

Note that Excel enters the multi-cell array formula only in the results portion of the table. The first column and first row of the range you selected in Step 4 are not changed.

> **TIP**
>
> When you create a data table, the leftmost column of the data table (the column that contains the references entered in Step 3) contains the calculated values for the input cell. In this example, those values are repeated in column D. To avoid confusion, you may want to hide the values B11:B13 by making the font color the same color as the background.

Creating a two-way data table

A *two-way data table* shows the results of a single calculation for different values of two input cells. Figure 15.8 shows a two-way data table (in B10:I16) that displays a calculation (payment amount) for a loan, using seven interest rates and six loan amounts — a total of 42 different combinations.

To create this two-way data table, follow these steps:

1. **Enter a formula that returns the results that will be used in the data table.** In this example, the formula is in cell B6. The formulas in B7:B8 are not used.
2. **Enter various values for the first input in successive columns.** In this example, the first input value is interest rate, and the values for various interest rates appear in C10:I10.
3. **Enter various values for the second input cell in successive rows, to the left and below the input values for the first input.** In this example, the second input value is the loan amount, and the values for various loan amounts are in B11:B16.

FIGURE 15.8

Using a two-way data table to display payment amounts for various loan amounts and interest rates.

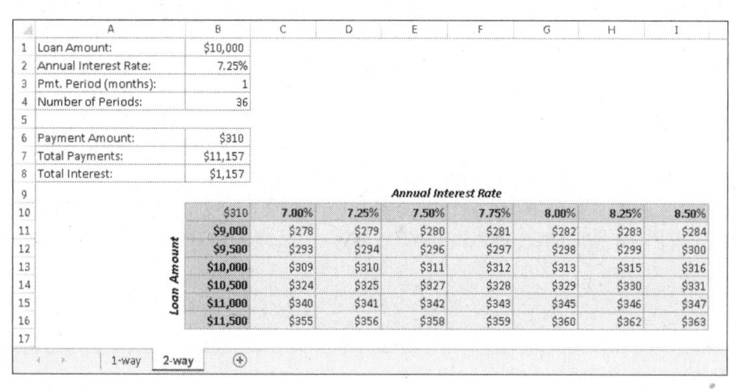

	A	B	C	D	E	F	G	H	I
1	Loan Amount:	$10,000							
2	Annual Interest Rate:	7.25%							
3	Pmt. Period (months):	1							
4	Number of Periods:	36							
5									
6	Payment Amount:	$310							
7	Total Payments:	$11,157							
8	Total Interest:	$1,157							
9					*Annual Interest Rate*				
10		$310	7.00%	7.25%	7.50%	7.75%	8.00%	8.25%	8.50%
11	*Loan Amount*	$9,000	$278	$279	$280	$281	$282	$283	$284
12		$9,500	$293	$294	$296	$297	$298	$299	$300
13		$10,000	$309	$310	$311	$312	$313	$315	$316
14		$10,500	$324	$325	$327	$328	$329	$330	$331
15		$11,000	$340	$341	$342	$343	$345	$346	$347
16		$11,500	$355	$356	$358	$359	$360	$362	$363
17									

4. **Create a reference to the formula that will be calculated in the table.** This reference goes in the upper-left corner of the data table range. In this example, cell B10 contains the following formula:

   ```
   =B6
   ```

5. **Select the rectangular range that contains the entries from the previous steps.** In this example, select B10:I16.
6. **Choose Data ➪ Data Tools ➪ What-If Analysis ➪ Data Table.** Excel displays the Data Table dialog box (refer to Figure 15.7).
7. **For the Row Input Cell field, specify the cell reference that corresponds to the first input cell.** In this example, the Row Input cell is B2.
8. **For the Column Input Cell field, specify the cell reference that corresponds to the second input cell.** In this example, the Column Input cell is B1.
9. **Click OK.** Excel inserts an array formula that uses the `TABLE` function with two arguments.

After you create the two-way data table, you can change the calculated cell by changing the cell reference in the upper-left cell of the data table. In this example, you can change the formula in cell B10 to `=B8` (to display total interest) or `=B7` (to display total payments).

TIP

If you create very large data tables, the calculation speed of your workbook may be slowed down. Excel has a special calculation mode for calculation-intensive data tables. To change the calculation mode, choose Formulas ➪ Calculation ➪ Calculation Options ➪ Automatic Except for Data Tables.

Calculating a loan with irregular payments

So far, the loan calculation examples in this chapter have involved loans with regular periodic payments. In some cases, loan payback is irregular. For example, you may loan some money to a friend without a formal agreement as to how he'll pay the money back. You still collect interest on the loan, so you need a way to perform the calculations based on the actual payment dates.

Figure 15.9 shows a worksheet set up to keep track of such a loan. The annual interest rate for the loan is stored in cell B1 (named APR). The original loan amount and loan date are stored in row 5. Notice that the loan amount is entered as a negative value in cell B5. Formulas, beginning in row 6, track the irregular loan payments and perform calculations.

FIGURE 15.9

This worksheet tracks loan payments that are made on an irregular basis.

	A	B	C	D	E	F	G	H
1	Interest Rate (APR):	5.00%					Loan Payment History	
2								
3								
4	Payment Number	Payment Amount	Payment Date	Amount to Interest	Amount to Principal	Cumulative Payments	Cumulative Interest	Loan Balance
5	Original Loan	($7,500.00)	6/8/2011					$7,500.00
6	1	$200.00	7/25/2011	$48.29	$151.71	$200.00	$48.29	$7,348.29
7	2	$200.00	8/9/2011	$15.10	$184.90	$400.00	$63.39	$7,163.39
8	3	$200.00	9/24/2011	$45.14	$154.86	$600.00	$108.53	$7,008.53
9	4	$100.00	12/9/2011	$72.97	$27.03	$700.00	$181.49	$6,981.49
10	5	$250.00	1/19/2012	$39.21	$210.79	$950.00	$220.70	$6,770.70
11	Addition to Principal	($500.00)	2/1/2012	$12.06	($512.06)	$450.00	$232.76	$7,282.76
12	6	$100.00	2/21/2012	$19.95	$80.05	$550.00	$252.71	$7,202.71
13	7	$100.00	2/27/2012	$5.92	$94.08	$650.00	$258.63	$7,108.63
14	8	$1,000.00	3/7/2012	$8.76	$991.24	$1,650.00	$267.40	$6,117.40
15	9	$250.00	3/22/2012	$12.57	$237.43	$1,900.00	$279.97	$5,879.97
16	10	$200.00	4/8/2012	$13.69	$186.31	$2,100.00	$293.66	$5,693.66
17	11	$200.00	4/25/2012	$13.26	$186.74	$2,300.00	$306.92	$5,506.92
18	12	$1,000.00	5/10/2012	$11.32	$988.68	$3,300.00	$318.23	$4,518.23
19	13	$100.00	5/22/2012	$7.43	$92.57	$3,400.00	$325.66	$4,425.66
20	14	$200.00	6/8/2012	$10.31	$189.69	$3,600.00	$335.97	$4,235.97
21	15	$200.00	6/25/2012	$9.86	$190.14	$3,800.00	$345.83	$4,045.83
22	16	$100.00	7/11/2012	$8.87	$91.13	$3,900.00	$354.70	$3,954.70
23	17	$100.00	7/21/2012	$5.42	$94.58	$4,000.00	$360.12	$3,860.12
24	Addition to Principal	($500.00)	9/7/2012	$25.38	($525.38)	$3,500.00	$385.50	$4,385.50
25	18	$100.00	11/8/2012	$37.25	$62.75	$3,600.00	$422.75	$4,322.75
26	19	$100.00	11/21/2012	$7.70	$92.30	$3,700.00	$430.44	$4,230.44
27	20	$200.00	12/21/2012	$17.39	$182.61	$3,900.00	$447.83	$4,047.83
28	21	$750.00	1/11/2013	$11.64	$738.36	$4,650.00	$459.47	$3,309.47
29	22	$750.00	2/11/2013	$14.05	$735.95	$5,400.00	$473.53	$2,573.53
30	23	$750.00	3/11/2013	$9.87	$740.13	$6,150.00	$483.40	$1,833.40
31	24							

Sheet1

Column B stores the payment amount made on the date in column C. Notice that the payments are not made on a regular basis. Also, notice that in two cases (row 11 and row 24), the payment amount is negative. These entries represent additional borrowed money added to the loan balance. Formulas in columns D and E calculate the amount of the payment credited toward interest and principal. Columns F and G keep a running tally of the cumulative payments and interest amounts. Formulas in column H compute the new loan balance after each payment.

Table 15.3 lists and describes the formulas in row 6. Note that each formula uses an `IF` function to determine whether the payment date in column C is missing. If so, the formula returns an empty string, so no data appears in the cell.

TABLE 15.3 Formulas to Calculate a Loan with Irregular Payments

Cell	Formula	Description
D6	`=IF(C6<>"",(C6-C5)/365*H5*APR,"")`	Calculates the interest, based on the payment date
E6	`=IF(C6<>"",B6-D6,"")`	Subtracts the interest amount from the payment to calculate the amount credited to principal
F6	`=IF(C6<>"",F5+B6,"")`	Adds the payment amount to the running total
G6	`=IF(C6<>"",G5+D6,"")`	Adds the interest to the running total
H6	`=IF(C6<>"",H5-E6,"")`	Calculates the new loan balance by subtracting the principal amount from the previous loan balance

ON THE WEB

This workbook is available at this book's website. The file name is `irregular payments.xlsx`.

Investment Calculations

Investment calculations involve calculating interest on fixed-rate investments, such as bank savings accounts, CDs, and annuities. You can make these interest calculations for investments that consist of a single deposit or multiple deposits.

ON THE WEB

This book's website contains a workbook with all the interest calculation examples in this section. The file is named `investment calculations.xlsx`.

Future value of a single deposit

Many investments consist of a single deposit that earns interest over the term of the investment. This section describes calculations for simple interest and compound interest.

Calculating simple interest

Simple interest refers to the fact that interest payments are not compounded. The basic formula for computing interest is

```
Interest=Principal*Rate*Term
```

For example, suppose that you deposit $1,000 into a bank CD that pays a 3% simple annual interest rate. After one year, the CD matures, and you withdraw your money. The bank adds $30, and you walk away with $1,030. In this case, the interest earned is calculated by multiplying the principal ($1,000) by the interest rate (0.03) by the term (one year).

If the investment term is less than one year, the simple interest rate is adjusted accordingly, based on the term. For example, $1,000 invested in a six-month CD that pays 3% simple annual interest earns $15.00 when the CD matures. In this case, the annual interest rate multiplies by 6/12.

Figure 15.10 shows a worksheet set up to make simple interest calculations. The formula in cell B7, shown here, calculates the interest due at the end of the term:

```
=B3*B4*B5
```

FIGURE 15.10

This worksheet calculates simple interest payments.

	A	B	C
1	**Simple Interest Calculation**		
2			
3	Investment amount:	$1,000.00	
4	Annual interest rate:	3.00%	
5	Investment term (years):	1.00	
6			
7	Interest:	$30.00	
8	Investment at the end of the term:	$1,030.00	
9			
10			
11			

Simple | Compound1 | Compound2 | C ...

The formula in B8 simply adds the interest to the original investment amount.

Calculating compound interest

Most fixed-term investments pay interest by using some type of compound interest calculation. *Compound interest* refers to interest credited to the investment balance, and the investment then earns interest on the interest.

For example, suppose that you deposit $1,000 into a bank CD that pays 3% annual interest rate, compounded monthly. Each month, the interest is calculated on the balance, and that amount is credited to your account. The next month's interest calculation will be based on a higher amount because it also includes the previous month's interest payment. One way to calculate the final investment amount involves a series of formulas (see Figure 15.11).

FIGURE 15.11

Using a series of formulas to calculate compound interest.

	A	B	C
1	**Compound Interest Calculation**		
2	***Monthly compounding***		
3			
4	Investment amount:	$1,000.00	
5	Annual interest rate:	3.00%	
6	Investment term (months):	12	
7			
8	**Month**	**Interest Earned**	**Balance**
9	Beginning Balance		$1,000.00
10	1	$2.50	$1,002.50
11	2	$2.51	$1,005.01
12	3	$2.51	$1,007.52
13	4	$2.52	$1,010.04
14	5	$2.53	$1,012.56
15	6	$2.53	$1,015.09
16	7	$2.54	$1,017.63
17	8	$2.54	$1,020.18
18	9	$2.55	$1,022.73
19	10	$2.56	$1,025.28
20	11	$2.56	$1,027.85
21	12	$2.57	$1,030.42
22			

Simple | Compound1 | Compound2 | com ...

Column B contains formulas to calculate the interest for one month. For example, the formula in B10 is

```
=C9*($B$5*(1/12))
```

The formulas in column C simply add the monthly interest amount to the balance. For example, the formula in C10 is

```
=C9+B10
```

At the end of the 12-month term, the CD balance is $1,030.42. In other words, monthly compounding results in an additional $0.42 (compared with simple interest).

You can use the `FV` (future value) function to calculate the final investment amount without using a series of formulas. Figure 15.12 shows a worksheet set up to calculate compound interest. Cell B6 is an input cell that holds the number of compounding periods per year. For monthly compounding, the value in B6 would be `12`. For quarterly compounding, the value would be `4`. For daily compounding, the value would be `365`. Cell B7 holds the term of the investment expressed in years.

FIGURE 15.12

Using a single formula to calculate compound interest.

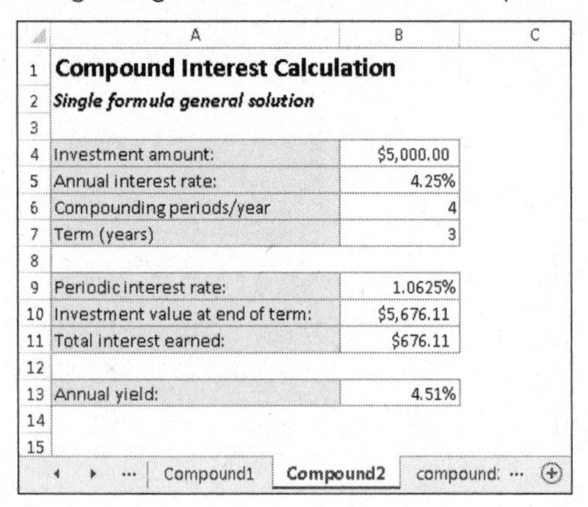

	A	B	C
1	**Compound Interest Calculation**		
2	***Single formula general solution***		
3			
4	Investment amount:	$5,000.00	
5	Annual interest rate:	4.25%	
6	Compounding periods/year	4	
7	Term (years)	3	
8			
9	Periodic interest rate:	1.0625%	
10	Investment value at end of term:	$5,676.11	
11	Total interest earned:	$676.11	
12			
13	Annual yield:	4.51%	
14			
15			

Compound1 | Compound2 | compound: ...

Cell B9 contains the following formula that calculates the periodic interest rate. This value is the interest rate used for each compounding period.

```
=B5*(1/B6)
```

The formula in cell B10 uses the `FV` function to calculate the value of the investment at the end of the term. The formula is

```
=FV(B9,B6*B7,,-B4)
```

The first argument for the `FV` function is the periodic interest rate, which is calculated in cell B9. The second argument represents the total number of compounding periods. The third argument (`pmt`) is omitted, and the fourth argument is the original investment amount (expressed as a negative value).

The total interest is calculated with a simple formula in cell B11:

```
=B10-B4
```

Another formula, in cell B13, calculates the annual yield on the investment:

```
=(B11/B4)/B7
```

For example, suppose that you deposit $5,000 into a three-year CD with a 4.25% annual interest rate compounded quarterly. In this case, the investment has four compounding periods per year, so you enter **4** into cell B6. The term is three years, so you enter **3** into cell B7. The formula in B10 returns $5,676.11.

Perhaps you want to see how this rate stacks up against a competitor's account that offers daily compounding. Figure 15.13 shows a calculation with daily compounding, using a $5,000 investment (compare this with Figure 15.12). As you can see, the difference is very small ($679.88 versus $676.11). Over a period of three years, the account with daily compounding earns a total of $3.77 more interest. In terms of annual yield, quarterly compounding earns 4.51%, and daily compounding earns 4.53%.

FIGURE 15.13

Calculating interest by using daily compounding.

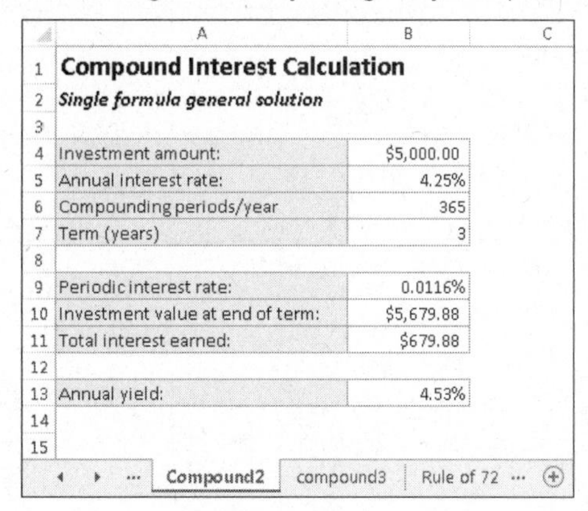

Calculating interest with continuous compounding

The term *continuous compounding* refers to interest that is accumulated continuously. In other words, the investment has an infinite number of compounding periods per year. The following formula calculates the future value of a $5,000 investment at 4.25% compounded continuously for three years:

```
=5000*EXP(4.25%*3)
```

The formula returns $5,679.92, which is an additional $0.04 compared with daily compounding.

NOTE

You can calculate compound interest without using the `FV` function. The general formula to calculate compound interest is

```
Principal*(1+Periodic Rate)^Number of Periods
```

For example, consider a five-year, $5,000 investment that earns an annual interest rate of 4%, compounded monthly. The formula to calculate the future value of this investment is

```
=5000*(1+4%/12)^(12*5)
```

15

The Rule of 72

Need to make an investment decision, but don't have a computer handy? You can use the Rule of 72 to determine the number of years required to double your money at a particular interest rate, using annual compounding. Just divide 72 by the interest rate. For example, consider a $10,000 investment at 4% interest. How many years will it take to turn that 10 grand into 20 grand? Take 72, divide it by 4, and you get 18 years. What if you can get a 5% interest rate? If so, you can double your money in a little over 14 years.

How accurate is the Rule of 72? The table that follows shows Rule of 72 estimated years versus the actual years for various interest rates. As you can see, this simple rule is remarkably accurate. However, for interest rates that exceed 30 percent, the accuracy drops off considerably.

Interest Rate	Rule of 72	Actual
1%	72.00	69.66
2%	36.00	35.00
3%	24.00	23.45
4%	18.00	17.67
5%	14.40	14.21
6%	12.00	11.90
7%	10.29	10.24
8%	9.00	9.01
9%	8.00	8.04
10%	7.20	7.27
15%	4.80	4.96
20%	3.60	3.80
25%	2.88	3.11
30%	2.40	2.64

The Rule of 72 also works in reverse. For example, if you want to double your money in six years, divide 6 into 72; you'll discover that you need to find an investment that pays an annual interest rate of about 12%. Good luck.

Future value of a series of deposits

Now, consider another type of investment, one in which you make a regular series of deposits into an account. This type of investment is known as an *annuity*.

The worksheet functions discussed in the "Loan Calculations" section earlier in this chapter also apply to annuities, but you need to use the perspective of a lender, not a borrower. A simple example of this type of investment is a holiday club savings program offered by some banking institutions. A fixed amount is deducted from each of your paychecks and deposited into an interest-earning account. At the end of the year, you withdraw the money (with accumulated interest) to use for holiday expenses.

Suppose that you deposit $200 at the beginning of each month (for 12 months) into an account that pays 2.5% annual interest compounded monthly. The following formula calculates the future value of your series of deposits:

```
=FV(2.5%/12,12,-200,,1)
```

This formula returns $2,432.75, which represents the total of your deposits ($2,400.00) plus the interest ($32.75). The last argument for the `FV` function is `1`, which means that you make payments at the beginning of the month. Figure 15.14 shows a worksheet set up to calculate annuities. Table 15.4 describes the contents of this sheet.

FIGURE 15.14

This worksheet contains formulas to calculate annuities.

	A	B	C
1	**Annuity Calculator**		
2			
3	**Deposits...**		
4	Initial investment:	$0.00	
5	Periodic deposit amount:	$200.00	
6	No. periodic deposits per year:	12	
7	Deposits made at beginning of period?	TRUE	
8			
9	**Investment Period...**		
10	Length of investment (years):	1	
11			
12	**Interest Rate...**		
13	Annual interest rate:	2.50%	
14			
15	**Calculations**		
16	Initial investment	$0.00	
17	Additional deposits:	$2,400.00	
18	Total amount invested:	$2,400.00	
19	Periodic interest rate:	0.21%	
20	Value of investment at end of term:	$2,432.75	
21	Interest earned on investment:	$32.75	
22			
23			

Sheet1

15

On the Web

The workbook shown in Figure 15.14 is available at this book's website. The file is named `annuity calculator.xlsx`.

TABLE 15.4 The Annuity Calculator Worksheet

Cell	Formula	Description
B4	None (input cell)	Initial investment (can be 0)
B5	None (input cell)	The amount deposited on a regular basis
B6	None (input cell)	The number of deposits made in 12 months
B7	None (input cell)	`TRUE` if you make deposits at the beginning of period; otherwise, `FALSE`
B10	None (input cell)	The length of the investment, in years (can be fractional)
B13	None (input cell)	The annual interest rate
B16	`=B4`	Displays the initial investment amount
B17	`=B5*B6*B10`	Calculates the total of all regular deposits
B18	`=B16+B17`	Adds the initial investment to the sum of the deposits
B19	`=B13*(1/B6)`	Calculates the periodic interest rate
B20	`=FV(B19,B6*B10,-B5,-B4,IF(B7,1,0))`	Calculates the future value of the investment
B21	`=B20-B18`	Calculates the interest earned from the investment

Depreciation Calculations

Excel offers five functions to calculate depreciation of an asset over time. Depreciating an asset places a value on the asset at a point in time, based on the original value and its useful life. The function that you choose depends on the type of *depreciation method* that you use.

Table 15.5 summarizes the Excel depreciation functions and the arguments used by each. For complete details, consult the Excel online Help system.

TABLE 15.5 Excel Depreciation Functions

Function	Depreciation Method	Arguments
SLN	Straight line. The asset depreciates by the same amount each year of its life.	Cost, Salvage, Life
DB	Declining balance. Computes depreciation at a fixed rate.	Cost, Salvage, Life, Period, Month*
DDB	Double declining balance. Computes depreciation at an accelerated rate. Depreciation is highest in the first period and decreases in successive periods.	Cost, Salvage, Life, Period, Factor*
SYD	Sum of the year's digits. Allocates a large depreciation in the earlier years of an asset's life.	Cost, Salvage, Life, Period
VDB	Variable declining balance. Computes the depreciation of an asset for any period (including partial periods) using the double declining balance method or some other method you specify.	Cost, Salvage, Life, Start _Period, End_ Period, Factor*, No Switch*

* Optional

Here are the arguments for the depreciation functions:

- `Cost`: Original cost of the asset.
- `Salvage`: Salvage cost of the asset after it has fully depreciated.
- `Life`: Number of periods over which the asset will depreciate.
- `Period`: Period in the life for which the calculation is being made.
- `Month`: Number of months in the first year; if omitted, Excel uses 12.
- `Start_Period`: Starting period for the depreciation calculation.
- `End_Period`: Ending period for the depreciation calculation.
- `Factor`: Rate at which the balance declines; if omitted, it is assumed to be 2 (that is, double-declining).
- `No Switch`: `TRUE` or `FALSE`. Specifies whether to switch to straight-line depreciation when depreciation is greater than the declining balance calculation.

Figure 15.15 shows depreciation calculations using the `SLN`, `DB`, `DDB`, and `SYD` functions. The asset's original cost, $10,000, is assumed to have a useful life of ten years, with a salvage value of $1,000. The range labeled *Depreciation Amount* shows the annual depreciation of the asset. The range labeled *Value of Asset* shows the asset's depreciated value over its life.

ON THE WEB

This workbook is available at this book's website. The file is named `depreciation calculations.xlsx`.

Figure 15.16 shows a chart that graphs the asset's value. As you can see, the `SLN` function produces a straight line; the other functions produce a curved line because the depreciation is greater in the earlier years of the asset's life.

FIGURE 15.15

A comparison of four depreciation functions.

	A	B	C	D	E
1	Asset:	Office Furniture			
2	Original Cost:	$10,000			
3	Life (years):	10			
4	Salvage Value:	$1,000			
5					
6	*Depreciation Amount*				
7	Year	SLN	DB	DDB	SYD
8	1	$900.00	$2,060.00	$2,000.00	$1,636.36
9	2	$900.00	$1,635.64	$1,600.00	$1,472.73
10	3	$900.00	$1,298.70	$1,280.00	$1,309.09
11	4	$900.00	$1,031.17	$1,024.00	$1,145.45
12	5	$900.00	$818.75	$819.20	$981.82
13	6	$900.00	$650.08	$655.36	$818.18
14	7	$900.00	$516.17	$524.29	$654.55
15	8	$900.00	$409.84	$419.43	$490.91
16	9	$900.00	$325.41	$335.54	$327.27
17	10	$900.00	$258.38	$268.44	$163.64
18					
19					
20	*Value of Asset*				
21	Year	SLN	DB	DDB	SYD
22	0	$10,000.00	$10,000.00	$10,000.00	$10,000.00
23	1	$9,100.00	$7,940.00	$8,000.00	$8,363.64
24	2	$8,200.00	$6,304.36	$6,400.00	$6,890.91
25	3	$7,300.00	$5,005.66	$5,120.00	$5,581.82
26	4	$6,400.00	$3,974.50	$4,096.00	$4,436.36
27	5	$5,500.00	$3,155.75	$3,276.80	$3,454.55
28	6	$4,600.00	$2,505.67	$2,621.44	$2,636.36
29	7	$3,700.00	$1,989.50	$2,097.15	$1,981.82
30	8	$2,800.00	$1,579.66	$1,677.72	$1,490.91
31	9	$1,900.00	$1,254.25	$1,342.18	$1,163.64
32	10	$1,000.00	$995.88	$1,073.74	$1,000.00
33					

Depreciation | VBD

FIGURE 15.16

This chart shows an asset's value over time, using four depreciation functions.

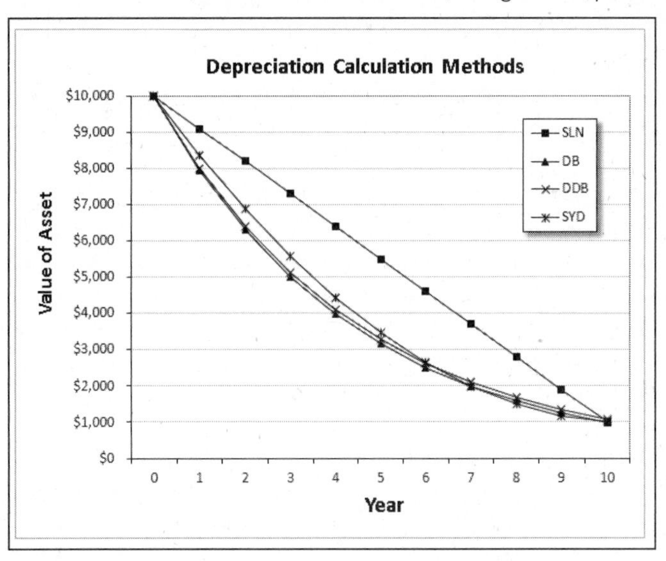

The VBD function is useful if you need to calculate depreciation for multiple periods (for example, years 2 and 3). Figure 15.17 shows a worksheet set up to calculate depreciation using the VBD function. The formula in cell B11 is

```
=VDB(B2,B4,B3,B6,B7,B8,B9)
```

The formula displays the depreciation for the first three years of an asset (starting period of 0 and ending period of 3).

FIGURE 15.17

Using the VBD function to calculate depreciation for multiple periods.

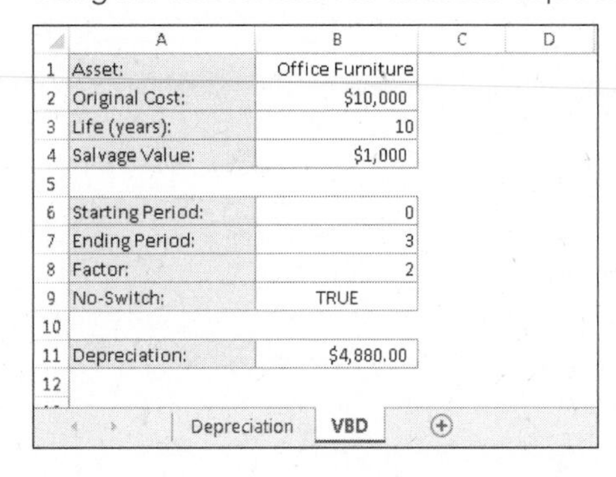

	A	B	C	D
1	Asset:	Office Furniture		
2	Original Cost:	$10,000		
3	Life (years):	10		
4	Salvage Value:	$1,000		
5				
6	Starting Period:	0		
7	Ending Period:	3		
8	Factor:	2		
9	No-Switch:	TRUE		
10				
11	Depreciation:	$4,880.00		
12				

CHAPTER

16

Miscellaneous Calculations

IN THIS CHAPTER

Converting between measurement units

Solving right triangles

Calculating area, surface, circumference, and volume

Demonstrating various ways to round numbers

This chapter contains reference information that may be useful to you at some point. Consider it a cheat sheet to help you remember the stuff you may have learned but have long since forgotten.

Unit Conversions

You know the distance from New York to London in miles, but your European office needs the number in kilometers. What's the conversion factor?

Excel's CONVERT function can convert between a variety of measurements in the following categories:

- Area
- Distance
- Energy
- Force
- Information
- Magnetism
- Power
- Pressure
- Speed
- Temperature
- Time
- Volume (or liquid measure)
- Weight and mass

NOTE

Prior to Excel 2007, the CONVERT function required the Analysis ToolPak add-in. Beginning with Excel 2007, this useful function is built in.

The CONVERT function requires three arguments: the value that you want to convert, the from-unit, and the to-unit. For example, if cell A1 contains a distance expressed in miles, use this formula to convert miles to kilometers:

```
=CONVERT(A1,"mi","km")
```

The second and third arguments are unit abbreviations, which are listed in the Excel Help system. Some of the abbreviations are commonly used, but others aren't. And, of course, you must use the *exact* abbreviation. Furthermore, the unit abbreviations are case sensitive, so the following formula returns an error:

```
=CONVERT(A1,"Mi","km")
```

The CONVERT function is even more versatile than it seems. When using metric units, you can apply a multiplier. In fact, the first example I presented uses a multiplier. The actual unit abbreviation for the third argument is *m* for meters. I added the kilo-multiplier — *k* — to express the result in kilometers.

Sometimes, you need to use a bit of creativity. For example, if you need to convert 100 km/hour into miles/sec, the following formula uses the CONVERT function:

```
=CONVERT(100,"km","mi")/CONVERT(1,"hr","sec")
```

NEW FEATURE

The CONVERT function has been significantly enhanced in Excel 2013 and includes dozens of new units.

Figure 16.1 shows part of a table that lists all the conversion units supported by the CONVERT function. The table can be sorted and filtered, and it also indicates which of the units support the metric prefixes and which are new to Excel 2013.

ON THE WEB

This workbook is available on this book's website. The filename is conversion units table.xlsx.

If you can't find a particular unit that works with the CONVERT function, it's possible that Excel has another function that will do the job. Table 16.1 lists some other functions that convert between measurement units.

FIGURE 16.1

A table that lists all the units supported by the CONVERT function.

	A	B	C	D	E
1	Category	Unit	Abbreviation	Metric Prefixes?	New Excel 2013?
2	Area	International acre	"uk_acre"	FALSE	TRUE
3	Area	U.S. survey/statute acre	"us_acre"	FALSE	TRUE
4	Area	Square angstrom	"ang2" or “ang^2"	FALSE	TRUE
5	Area	Are	"ar"	FALSE	TRUE
6	Area	Square feet	"ft2" or "ft^2"	FALSE	TRUE
7	Area	Hectare	"ha"	FALSE	TRUE
8	Area	Square inches	"in2" or "in^2"	FALSE	TRUE
9	Area	Square light-year	"ly2" or "ly^2"	FALSE	TRUE
10	Area	Square meters	"m2" or "m^2"	TRUE	TRUE
11	Area	Morgen	"Morgen"	FALSE	TRUE
12	Area	Square miles	"mi2" or "mi^2"	FALSE	TRUE
13	Area	Square nautical miles	"Nmi2" or "Nmi^2"	FALSE	TRUE
14	Area	Square Pica	"Picapt2", "Pica2", "Pica^2" or "Picapt^2"	FALSE	TRUE
15	Area	Square yards	"yd2" or "yd^2"	FALSE	TRUE
16	Distance	Meter	"m"	TRUE	FALSE
17	Distance	Statute mile	"mi"	FALSE	FALSE
18	Distance	Nautical mile	"Nmi"	FALSE	FALSE
19	Distance	Inch	"in"	FALSE	FALSE
20	Distance	Foot	"ft"	FALSE	FALSE
21	Distance	Yard	"yd"	FALSE	FALSE
22	Distance	Angstrom	"ang"	FALSE	FALSE
23	Distance	Ell	"ell"	FALSE	TRUE
24	Distance	Light-year	"ly"	FALSE	TRUE
25	Distance	Parsec	"parsec" or "pc"	FALSE	TRUE
26	Distance	Pica (1/72 inch)	"Picapt" or "Pica"	FALSE	TRUE
27	Distance	Pica (1/6 inch)	"pica"	FALSE	FALSE
28	Distance	U.S survey mile (statute mile)	"survey_mi"	FALSE	TRUE
29	Energy	Joule	"J"	TRUE	FALSE
30	Energy	Erg	"e"	TRUE	FALSE
31	Energy	Thermodynamic calorie	"c"	FALSE	FALSE
32	Energy	IT calorie	"cal"	FALSE	FALSE

CONVERT arguments | Prefixes

TABLE 16.1 Other Conversion Functions

Function	Description
ARABIC*	Converts an Arabic number to decimal
BASE*	Converts a decimal number to a specified base
BIN2DEC	Converts a binary number to decimal
BIN2OCT	Converts a binary number to octal
DEC2BIN	Converts a decimal number to binary
DEC2HEX	Converts a decimal number to hexadecimal
DEC2OCT	Converts a decimal number to octal
DEGREES	Converts an angle (in radians) to degrees
HEX2BIN	Converts a hexadecimal number to binary
HEX2DEC	Converts a hexadecimal number to decimal
HEX2OCT	Converts a hexadecimal number to octal
OCT2BIN	Converts an octal number to binary
OCT2DEC	Converts an octal number to decimal
OCT2HEX	Converts an octal number to hexadecimal
RADIANS	Converts an angle (in degrees) to radians

* Function is new to Excel 2013

Need to Convert Other Units?

The `CONVERT` function, of course, doesn't handle every possible unit conversion. To calculate other unit conversions, you need to find the appropriate conversion factor. The Internet is a good source for such information. Use any search engine and enter search terms that correspond to the units you use. Likely, you'll find the information that you need.

Also, you can download a copy of Josh Madison's popular (and free) Convert software (www.joshmadison.com/convert-for-windows). This excellent program can handle just about any conceivable unit conversion that you throw at it.

Solving Right Triangles

A *right triangle* has six components: three sides and three angles. Figure 16.2 shows a right triangle with its various parts labeled. Angles are labeled *A, B,* and *C;* sides are labeled *Hypotenuse, Adjacent,* and *Opposite.* Angle *C* is always 90 degrees (or π/2 radians). If you know any two of these components (excluding angle C, which is always known), you can use formulas to solve for the others.

FIGURE 16.2

A right triangle's components.

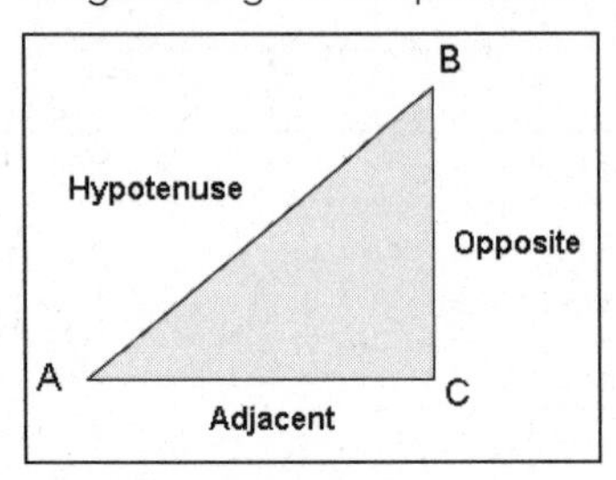

The Pythagorean theorem states that $\text{Opposite}^2 + \text{Adjacent}^2 = \text{Hypotenuse}^2$. Therefore, if you know two sides of a right triangle, you can calculate the remaining side. The formula to calculate a right triangle's opposite side (given the length of the hypotenuse and adjacent side) is as follows:

```
=SQRT((hypotenuse^2)-(adjacent^2))
```

The formula to calculate a right triangle's adjacent side (given the length of the hypotenuse and opposite side) is as follows:

```
=SQRT((hypotenuse^2)-(opposite^2))
```

The formula to calculate a right triangle's hypotenuse (given the length of the adjacent and opposite sides) is as follows:

```
=SQRT((opposite^2)+(adjacent^2))
```

Other useful trigonometric identities are

```
SIN(A) = opposite/hypotenuse
SIN(B) = adjacent/hypotenuse
COS(A) = adjacent/hypotenuse
COS(B) = opposite/hypotenuse
TAN(A) = opposite/adjacent
TAN(B) = adjacent/opposite
```

NOTE

Excel's trigonometric functions all assume that the angle arguments are in radians. To convert degrees to radians, use the `RADIANS` function. To convert radians to degrees, use the `DEGREES` function.

If you know the opposite and adjacent sides, you can use the following formula to calculate the angle formed by the hypotenuse and adjacent side (angle A):

```
=ATAN(opposite/adjacent)
```

The preceding formula returns radians. To convert to degrees, use this formula:

```
=DEGREES(ATAN(opposite/adjacent))
```

If you know the opposite and adjacent sides, you can use the following formula to calculate the angle formed by the hypotenuse and the opposite side (angle B):

```
=PI()/2-ATAN(opposite/adjacent)
```

The preceding formula returns radians. To convert to degrees, use this formula:

```
=90-DEGREES(ATAN(opposite/adjacent))
```

Area, Surface, Circumference, and Volume Calculations

This section contains formulas for calculating the area, surface, circumference, and volume for common two- and three-dimensional shapes.

Calculating the area and perimeter of a square

To calculate the area of a square, square the length of one side. The following formula calculates the area of a square for a cell named *side:*

```
=side^2
```

To calculate the perimeter of a square, multiply one side by 4. The following formula uses a cell named *side* to calculate the perimeter of a square:

```
=side*4
```

Calculating the area and perimeter of a rectangle

To calculate the area of a rectangle, multiply its height by its base. The following formula returns the area of a rectangle, using cells named *height* and *base:*

```
=height*base
```

To calculate the perimeter of a rectangle, multiply the height by 2 and then add it to the width multiplied by 2. The following formula returns the perimeter of a rectangle, using cells named *height* and *width:*

```
=(height*2)+(width*2)
```

Calculating the area and perimeter of a circle

To calculate the area of a circle, multiply the square of the radius by π. The following formula returns the area of a circle. It assumes that a cell named *radius* contains the circle's radius:

```
=PI()*(radius^2)
```

The radius of a circle is equal to one-half of the diameter.

To calculate the circumference of a circle, multiply the diameter of the circle by π. The following formula calculates the circumference of a circle using a cell named *diameter:*

```
=diameter*PI()
```

The diameter of a circle is the radius times 2.

Calculating the area of a trapezoid

To calculate the area of a trapezoid, add the two parallel sides, multiply by the height, and then divide by 2. The following formula calculates the area of a trapezoid, using cells named *parallel_side_1, parallel_side_2,* and *height:*

```
=((parallel_side_1+parallel_side_2)*height)/2
```

Calculating the area of a triangle

To calculate the area of a triangle, multiply the base by the height and then divide by 2. The following formula calculates the area of a triangle, using cells named *base* and *height:*

```
=(base*height)/2
```

Calculating the surface and volume of a sphere

To calculate the surface of a sphere, multiply the square of the radius by π and then multiply by 4. The following formula returns the surface of a sphere, the radius of which is in a cell named *radius:*

```
=PI()*(radius^2)*4
```

To calculate the volume of a sphere, multiply the cube of the radius by 4 times π and then divide by 3. The following formula calculates the volume of a sphere. The cell named *radius* contains the sphere's radius.

```
=((radius^3)*(4*PI()))/3
```

Calculating the surface and volume of a cube

To calculate the surface area of a cube, square one side and multiply by 6. The following formula calculates the surface of a cube using a cell named *side,* which contains the length of a side of the cube:

```
=(side^2)*6
```

To calculate the volume of a cube, raise the length of one side to the third power. The following formula returns the volume of a cube, using a cell named *side:*

```
=side^3
```

Calculating the surface and volume of a rectangular solid

The following formula calculates the surface of a rectangular solid using cells named *height, width*, and *length:*

```
=(length*height*2)+(length*width*2)+(width*height*2)
```

To calculate the volume of a rectangular solid, multiply the height by the width by the length:

```
=height*width*length
```

Calculating the surface and volume of a cone

The following formula calculates the surface of a cone (including the surface of the base). This formula uses cells named *radius* and *height:*

```
=PI()*radius*(SQRT(height^2+radius^2)+radius))
```

To calculate the volume of a cone, multiply the square of the radius of the base by π, multiply by the height, and then divide by 3. The following formula returns the volume of a cone, using cells named *radius* and *height:*

```
=(PI()*(radius^2)*height)/3
```

Calculating the volume of a cylinder

To calculate the volume of a cylinder, multiply the square of the radius of the base by π and then multiply by the height. The following formula calculates the volume of a cylinder, using cells named *radius* and *height:*

```
=(PI()*(radius^2)*height)
```

Calculating the volume of a pyramid

Calculate the area of the base, multiply by the height, and then divide by 3. This formula calculates the volume of a pyramid. It assumes cells named *width* (the width of the base), *length* (the length of the base), and *height* (the height of the pyramid).

```
=(width*length*height)/3
```

Rounding Numbers

Excel provides quite a few functions that round values in various ways. Table 16.2 summarizes these functions.

Caution

It's important to understand the difference between rounding a value and formatting a value. When you format a number to display a specific number of decimal places, formulas that refer to that number use the actual value, which may differ from the displayed value. When you round a number, formulas that refer to that value use the rounded number.

TABLE 16.2 Excel Rounding Functions

Function	Description
CEILING	Rounds a number up (away from zero) to the nearest specified multiple.
DOLLARDE	Converts a dollar price expressed as a fraction into a decimal number.
DOLLARFR	Converts a dollar price expressed as a decimal into a fractional number.
EVEN	Rounds a number up (away from zero) to the nearest even integer.
FLOOR	Rounds a number down (toward zero) to the nearest specified multiple.
INT	Rounds a number down to make it an integer.
ISO.CEILING*	Rounds a number up to the nearest integer or to the nearest multiple of significance. Similar to CEILING but works correctly with negative arguments.
MROUND	Rounds a number to a specified multiple.
ODD	Rounds a number up (away from zero) to the nearest odd integer.
ROUND	Rounds a number to a specified number of digits.
ROUNDDOWN	Rounds a number down (toward zero) to a specified number of digits.
ROUNDUP	Rounds a number up (away from zero) to a specified number of digits.
TRUNC	Truncates a number to a specified number of significant digits.

* Introduced in Excel 2010

The following sections provide examples of formulas that use various types of rounding.

Basic rounding formulas

The ROUND function is useful for basic rounding to a specified number of digits. You specify the number of digits in the second argument for the ROUND function. For example, the formula that follows returns 123.40 (the value is rounded to one decimal place):

```
=ROUND(123.37,1)
```

If the second argument for the ROUND function is zero, the value is rounded to the nearest integer. The formula that follows, for example, returns 123.00:

```
=ROUND(123.37,0)
```

The second argument for the ROUND function can also be negative. In such a case, the number is rounded to the left of the decimal point. The following formula, for example, returns 120.00:

```
=ROUND(123.37,-1)
```

The ROUND function rounds either up or down. But how does it handle a number such as 12.5, rounded to no decimal places? You'll find that the ROUND function rounds such numbers away from zero. The formula that follows, for instance, returns 13.0:

```
=ROUND(12.5,0)
```

The next formula returns –13.00 (the rounding occurs away from zero):

```
=ROUND(-12.5,0)
```

To force rounding to occur in a particular direction, use the ROUNDUP or ROUNDDOWN functions. The following formula, for example, returns 12.0. The value rounds down.

```
=ROUNDDOWN(12.5,0)
```

The formula that follows returns 13.0. The value rounds up to the nearest whole value.

```
=ROUNDUP(12.43,0)
```

Rounding to the nearest multiple

The MROUND function is useful for rounding values to the nearest multiple. For example, you can use this function to round a number to the nearest 5. The following formula returns 135:

```
=MROUND(133,5)
```

Rounding currency values

Often, you need to round currency values. For example, you may need to round a dollar amount to the nearest penny. A calculated price may be something like $45.78923. In such a case, you'll want to round the calculated price to the nearest penny. This may sound simple, but there are actually three ways to round such a value:

- Round it up to the nearest penny.
- Round it down to the nearest penny.
- Round it to the nearest penny (the rounding may be up or down).

The following formula assumes that a dollar-and-cents value is in cell A1. The formula rounds the value to the nearest penny. For example, if cell A1 contains $12.421, the formula returns $12.42.

```
=ROUND(A1,2)
```

If you need to round the value up to the nearest penny, use the CEILING function. The following formula rounds the value in cell A1 up to the nearest penny. For example, if cell A1 contains $12.421, the formula returns $12.43.

```
=CEILING(A1,0.01)
```

To round a dollar value down, use the FLOOR function. The following formula, for example, rounds the dollar value in cell A1 down to the nearest penny. If cell A1 contains $12.421, the formula returns $12.42.

```
=FLOOR(A1,0.01)
```

To round a dollar value up to the nearest nickel, use this formula:

```
=CEILING(A1,0.05)
```

You've probably noticed that many retail prices end in $0.99. If you have an even dollar price and you want it to end in $0.99, just subtract $0.01 from the price. Some higher-ticket items are always priced to end with $9.99. To round a price to the nearest $9.99, first round it to the nearest $10.00 and then subtract a penny. If cell A1 contains a price, use a formula like this to convert it to a price that ends in $9.99:

```
=ROUND(A1/10,0)*10-0.01
```

For example, if cell A1 contains $345.78, the formula returns $349.99.

A simpler approach uses the MROUND function:

```
=MROUND(A1,10)-0.01
```

Working with fractional dollars

The DOLLARFR and DOLLARDE functions are useful when working with fractional dollar value, as in stock market quotes.

Consider the value $9.25. You can express the decimal part as a fractional value ($9 1/4, $9 2/8, $9 4/16, and so on). The DOLLARFR function takes two arguments: the dollar amount and the denominator for the fractional part. The following formula, for example, returns 9.1 (the .1 decimal represents 1/4):

```
=DOLLARFR(9.25,4)
```

Caution

In most situations, you won't use the value returned by the DOLLARFR function in other calculations. In the preceding example, the result of the function will be interpreted as 9.1, not 9.25. To perform calculations on such a value, you need to convert it back to a decimal value by using the DOLLARDE function.

The DOLLARDE function converts a dollar value expressed as a fraction to a decimal amount. It also uses a second argument to specify the denominator of the fractional part. The following formula, for example, returns 9.25:

```
=DOLLARDE(9.1,4)
```

TIP

The DOLLARDE and DOLLARFR functions aren't limited to dollar values. For example, you can use these functions to work with feet and inches. You might have a value that represents 8½ feet. Use the following formula to express this value in terms of feet and inches. The formula returns 8.06 (which represents 8 feet, 6 inches).

```
=DOLLARFR(8.5,12)
```

Another example is baseball statistics. A pitcher may work 6⅔ innings, and this is usually represented as 6.2. The following formula displays 6.2:

```
=DOLLARFR(6+2/3,3)
```

Using the INT and TRUNC functions

On the surface, the INT and TRUNC functions seem similar. Both convert a value to an integer. The TRUNC function simply removes the fractional part of a number. The INT function rounds a number down to the nearest integer, based on the value of the fractional part of the number.

In practice, INT and TRUNC return different results only when using negative numbers. For example, the following formula returns –14.0:

```
=TRUNC(-14.2)
```

The next formula returns –15.0 because –14.3 is rounded down to the next lower integer:

```
=INT(-14.2)
```

The TRUNC function takes an additional (optional) argument that's useful for truncating decimal values. For example, the formula that follows returns 54.33 (the value truncated to two decimal places):

```
=TRUNC(54.3333333,2)
```

Rounding to an even or odd integer

The ODD and EVEN functions are provided for situations in which you need to round a number up to the nearest odd or even integer. These functions take a single argument and return an integer value. The EVEN function rounds its argument up to the nearest even integer. The ODD function rounds its argument up to the nearest odd integer. Table 16.3 shows some examples of these functions.

TABLE 16.3 Results Using the EVEN and ODD Functions

Number	EVEN Function	ODD Function
–3.6	–4	–5
–3.0	–4	–3
–2.4	–4	–3
–1.8	–2	–3
–1.2	–2	–3
–0.6	–2	–1
0.0	0	1
0.6	2	1
1.2	2	3
1.8	2	3
2.4	4	3
3.0	4	3
3.6	4	5

Rounding to n significant digits

In some cases, you may need to round a value to a particular number of significant digits. For example, you might want to express the value 1,432,187 in terms of two significant digits (that is, as 1,400,000). The value 9,187,877 expressed in terms of three significant digits is 9,180,000.

If the value is a positive number with no decimal places, the following formula does the job. This formula rounds the number in cell A1 to two significant digits. To round to a different number of significant digits, replace the 2 in this formula with a different number.

```
=ROUNDDOWN(A1,2-LEN(A1))
```

For nonintegers and negative numbers, the solution gets a bit trickier. The formula that follows provides a more general solution that rounds the value in cell A1 to the number of significant digits specified in cell A2. This formula works for positive and negative integers and nonintegers.

```
=ROUND(A1,A2-1-INT(LOG10(ABS(A1))))
```

For example, if cell A1 contains 1.27845 and cell A2 contains 3, the formula returns 1.28000 (the value, rounded to three significant digits).

CHAPTER

17

Introducing Array Formulas

IN THIS CHAPTER

Defining arrays and array formulas

Comparing one-dimensional and two-dimensional arrays

Working with array constants

Working with array formulas

Looking at examples of multicell array formulas

Looking at examples of single-cell array formulas

One of Excel's most interesting (and most powerful) features is its ability to work with arrays in formulas. When you understand this concept, you'll be able to create elegant formulas that appear to perform spreadsheet magic.

This chapter introduces the concept of arrays and is required reading for anyone who wants to become a master of Excel formulas. Chapter 18 continues with lots of useful examples.

On the Web

Most of the examples in this chapter are available at this book's website. The filename is `array examples.xlsx`.

Understanding Array Formulas

If you do any computer programming, you've probably been exposed to the concept of an array. An *array* is a collection of items operated on collectively or individually. In Excel, an array can be one dimensional or two dimensional. These dimensions correspond to rows and columns. For example, a one-dimensional array can be stored in a range that consists of one row (a horizontal array) or one column (a vertical array). A two-dimensional array can be stored in a rectangular range of cells. Excel doesn't support three-dimensional arrays (but its VBA programming language does).

As you'll see, arrays don't have to be stored in cells. You can also work with arrays that exist only in Excel's memory. Then you can use an *array formula* to manipulate this information and return a result. Excel supports two types of array formulas:

- **Single-cell array formulas:** Works with arrays stored in ranges or in memory and produces a result displayed in a single cell.
- **Multicell array formulas:** Works with arrays stored in ranges or in memory and produces an array as a result. Because a cell can hold only one value, a multicell array formula is entered into a range of cells.

This section presents two array formula examples: one that occupies multiple cells and another that occupies only one cell.

A multicell array formula

Figure 17.1 shows a simple worksheet set up to calculate product sales. Normally, you'd calculate the value in column D (total sales per product) with a formula such as the one that follows, and then you'd copy this formula down the column.

```
=B2*C2
```

FIGURE 17.1

Column D contains formulas to calculate the total for each product.

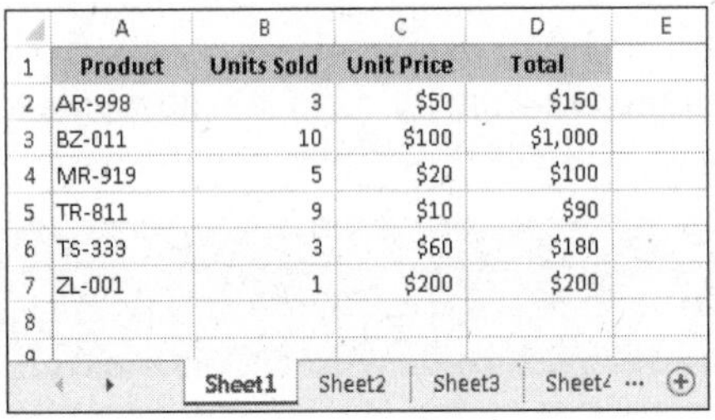

	A	B	C	D	E
1	Product	Units Sold	Unit Price	Total	
2	AR-998	3	$50	$150	
3	BZ-011	10	$100	$1,000	
4	MR-919	5	$20	$100	
5	TR-811	9	$10	$90	
6	TS-333	3	$60	$180	
7	ZL-001	1	$200	$200	
8					

Sheet1 | Sheet2 | Sheet3 | Sheet4 ...

After copying the formula, the worksheet contains six formulas in column D.

An alternative method uses a *single* formula (a multicell array formula) to calculate all six values in D2:D7. This single formula occupies six cells and returns an array of six values.

To create a multicell array formula to perform the calculations, follow these steps:

1. **Select a range to hold the results.** In this case, the range is D2:D7. Because you can't display more than one value in a single cell, six cells are required to display the resulting array — so you select six cells to make this array work.
2. **Type the following formula:**

   ```
   =B2:B7*C2:C7
   ```

3. **Press Ctrl + Shift + Enter to enter the formula.** Normally, you press Enter to enter a formula. Because this is an array formula, however, press Ctrl + Shift + Enter.

CAUTION

You can't insert a multicell array formula into a range that has been designated a table (by choosing Insert ⇨ Tables ⇨ Table). In addition, you can't convert a range that contains a multicell array formula to a table.

The formula is entered into all six selected cells. If you examine the Formula bar, you see the following:

```
{=B2:B7*C2:C7}
```


Excel places curly brackets around the formula to indicate that it's an array formula.

This formula performs its calculations and returns a six-item array. The array formula actually works with two other arrays, both of which happen to be stored in ranges. The values for the first array are stored in B2:B7, and the values for the second array are stored in C2:C7.

This multicell array formula returns exactly the same values as these six normal formulas entered into individual cells in D2:D7:

```
=B2*C2
=B3*C3
=B4*C4
=B5*C5
=B6*C6
=B7*C7
```

Using a multicell array formula rather than individual formulas does offer a few advantages:

- It's a good way to ensure that all formulas in a range are identical.
- Using a multicell array formula makes it less likely that you'll overwrite a formula accidentally. You can't change or delete just one cell in a multicell array formula. Excel displays an error message if you attempt to do so.
- Using a multicell array formula will almost certainly prevent novices from tampering with your formulas.

Using a multicell array formula as described in the preceding list also has some potential disadvantages:

- Inserting a new row into the range is impossible. But in some cases, the inability to insert a row is a positive feature. For example, you might not want users to add rows because it would affect other parts of the worksheet.
- If you add new data to the bottom of the range, you need to modify the array formula to accommodate the new data.

A single-cell array formula

Now it's time to take a look at a single-cell array formula. Check out Figure 17.2, which is similar to Figure 17.1. Notice, however, that the formulas in column D have been deleted. The goal is to calculate the sum of the total product sales without using the individual calculations that were in column D.

FIGURE 17.2

The array formula in cell C9 calculates the total sales without using intermediate formulas.

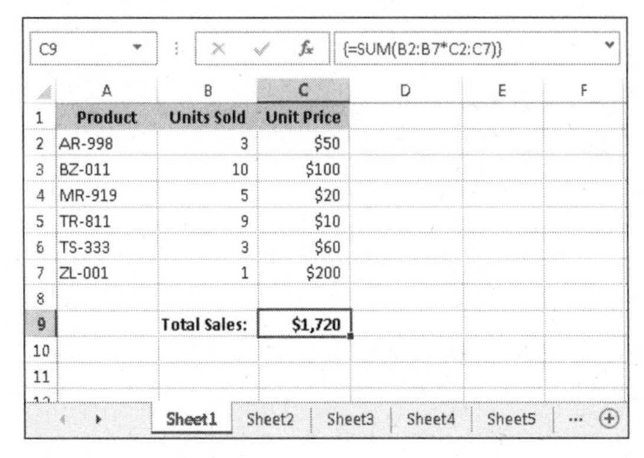

	A	B	C	D	E	F
1	Product	Units Sold	Unit Price			
2	AR-998	3	$50			
3	BZ-011	10	$100			
4	MR-919	5	$20			
5	TR-811	9	$10			
6	TS-333	3	$60			
7	ZL-001	1	$200			
8						
9		Total Sales:	$1,720			
10						
11						

The following array formula is in cell C9:

```
{=SUM(B2:B7*C2:C7)}
```

When you enter this formula, make sure that you press Ctrl + Shift + Enter (and don't type the curly brackets because Excel automatically adds them for you).

This formula works with two arrays, both of which are stored in cells. The first array is stored in B2:B7, and the second array is stored in C2:C7. The formula multiplies the corresponding values in these two arrays and creates a new array (which exists only in memory). The new array consists of six values, which can be represented like this (the reason for using semicolons is explained a bit later):

```
{150;1000;100;90;180;200}
```

The `SUM` function then operates on this new array and returns the sum of its values.

NOTE

In this case, you can use the `SUMPRODUCT` function to obtain the same result without using an array formula:

```
=SUMPRODUCT(B2:B7,C2:C7)
```

As you see, however, array formulas allow many other types of calculations that are otherwise not possible.

Creating an Array Constant

The examples in the preceding section used arrays stored in worksheet ranges. The examples in this section demonstrate an important concept: An array doesn't have to be stored in a range of cells. This type of array, which is stored in memory, is referred to as an *array constant.*

To create an array constant, list its items and surround them with curly brackets. Here's an example of a five-item horizontal array constant:

```
{1,0,1,0,1}
```

The following formula uses the SUM function, with the preceding array constant as its argument. The formula returns the sum of the values in the array (which is 3):

```
=SUM({1,0,1,0,1})
```


Notice that this formula uses an array, but the formula itself isn't an array formula. Therefore, you don't press Ctrl + Shift + Enter to enter the formula — although entering it as an array formula will still produce the same result.

NOTE

When you specify an array directly (as shown previously), you must provide the curly brackets around the array elements. When you enter an array formula, on the other hand, you do not supply the curly brackets.

At this point, you probably don't see any advantage to using an array constant. The following formula, for example, returns the same result as the previous formula. The advantages, however, will become apparent.

```
=SUM(1,0,1,0,1)
```

Here's a formula that uses two array constants:

```
=SUM({1,2,3,4}*{5,6,7,8})
```

The formula creates a new array (in memory) that consists of the product of the corresponding elements in the two arrays. The new array is

```
{5,12,21,32}
```

This new array is then used as an argument for the SUM function, which returns the result (70). The formula is equivalent to the following formula, which doesn't use arrays:

```
=SUM(1*5,2*6,3*7,4*8)
```

Alternatively, you can use the SUMPRODUCT function. The formula that follows is not an array formula, but it uses two array constants as its arguments.

```
=SUMPRODUCT({1,2,3,4},{5,6,7,8})
```

A formula can work with both an array constant and an array stored in a range. The following formula, for example, returns the sum of the values in A1:D1, each multiplied by the corresponding element in the array constant:

```
=SUM((A1:D1*{1,2,3,4}))
```

This formula is equivalent to

```
=SUM(A1*1,B1*2,C1*3,D1*4)
```

An array constant can contain numbers, text, logical values (`TRUE` or `FALSE`), and even error values, such as `#N/A`. Numbers can be in integer, decimal, or scientific format. You must enclose text in double quotation marks. You can use different types of values in the same array constant, as in this example:

```
{1,2,3,TRUE,FALSE,TRUE,"Moe","Larry","Curly"}
```

An array constant can't contain formulas, functions, or other arrays. Numeric values can't contain dollar signs, commas, parentheses, or percent signs. For example, the following is an invalid array constant:

```
{SQRT(32),$56.32,12.5%}
```

Understanding the Dimensions of an Array

As stated previously, an array can be one dimensional or two dimensional. A one-dimensional array's orientation can be horizontal (corresponding to a single row) or vertical (corresponding to a single column).

One-dimensional horizontal arrays

The elements in a one-dimensional horizontal array are separated by commas, and the array can be displayed in a row of cells. The following example is a one-dimensional horizontal array constant:

```
{1,2,3,4,5}
```

Displaying this array in a range requires five consecutive cells in a row. To enter this array into a range, select a range of cells that consists of one row and five columns. Then enter **={1,2,3,4,5}** and press Ctrl+Shift+Enter.

NOTE

If you enter this array into a horizontal range that consists of more than five cells, the extra cells will contain `#N/A` (which denotes unavailable values). If you enter this array into a *vertical* range of cells, only the first item (`1`) will appear in each cell.

The following example is another horizontal array; it has seven elements and is made up of text strings:

```
{"Sun","Mon","Tue","Wed","Thu","Fri","Sat"}
```

To enter this array, select seven cells in a row and type the following (and then press Ctrl + Shift + Enter):

```
={"Sun","Mon","Tue","Wed","Thu","Fri","Sat"}
```


One-dimensional vertical arrays

The elements in a one-dimensional vertical array are separated by semicolons, and the array can be displayed in a column of cells. The following is a six-element vertical array constant:

```
{10;20;30;40;50;60}
```

Displaying this array in a range requires six cells in a column. To enter this array into a range, select a range of cells that consists of six rows and one column. Then enter the following formula, followed by Ctrl + Shift + Enter:

```
={10;20;30;40;50;60}
```

The following is another example of a vertical array; this one has four elements:

```
{"Widgets";"Sprockets";"Doodads";"Thingamajigs"}
```

Two-dimensional arrays

A two-dimensional array uses commas to separate its horizontal elements and semicolons to separate its vertical elements. The following example shows a 3 x 4 array constant:

```
{1,2,3,4;5,6,7,8;9,10,11,12}
```

Displaying this array in a range requires 12 cells. To enter this array into a range, select a range of cells that consists of three rows and four columns. Then type the following formula, and press Ctrl + Shift + Enter:

```
={1,2,3,4;5,6,7,8;9,10,11,12}
```

Figure 17.3 shows how this array appears when entered into a range (in this case, B3:E5).

FIGURE 17.3

A 3 x 4 array entered into a range of cells.

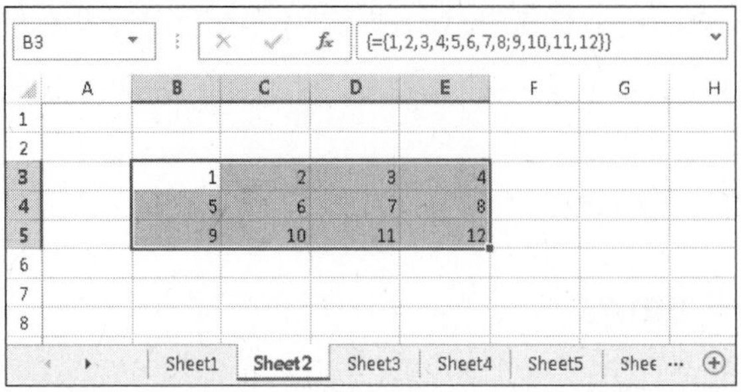

If you enter an array into a range that has more cells than array elements, Excel displays `#N/A` in the extra cells. Figure 17.4 shows a 3 x 4 array entered into a 10 x 5 cell range.

FIGURE 17.4

A 3 x 4 array entered into a 10 x 5 cell range.

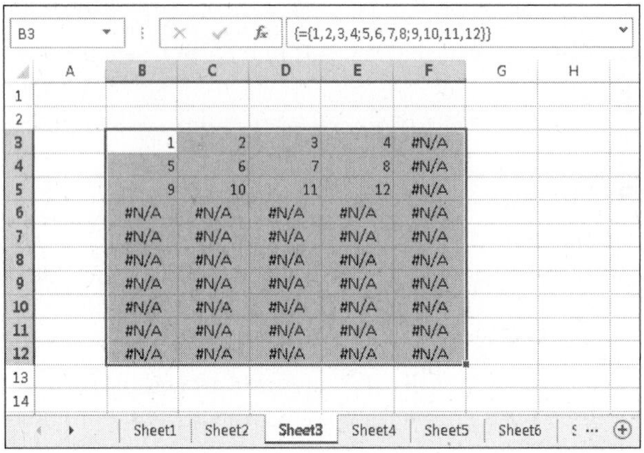

Each row of a two-dimensional array must contain the same number of items. The array that follows, for example, isn't valid, because the third row contains only three items:

```
{1,2,3,4;5,6,7,8;9,10,11}
```

Excel doesn't allow you to enter a formula that contains an invalid array.

Naming Array Constants

You can create an array constant, give it a name, and then use this named array in a formula. Technically, a named array is a named formula.

Chapters 4 and 10 cover the topic of names and named formulas.

Figure 17.5 shows a named array being created from the New Name dialog box. (Access this dialog box by choosing Formulas➪Defined Names➪Define Name.) The name of the array is DayNames, and it refers to the following array constant:

```
{"Sun","Mon","Tue","Wed","Thu","Fri","Sat"}
```


FIGURE 17.5

Creating a named array constant.

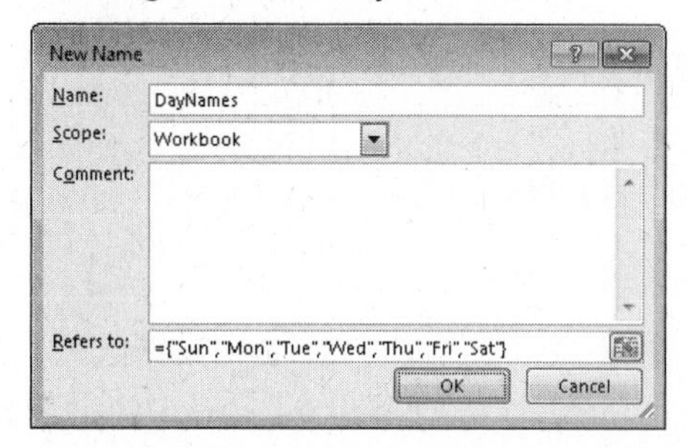

Notice that, in the New Name dialog box, the array is defined (in the Refers To field) using a leading equal sign (=). Without this equal sign, the array is interpreted as a text string rather than an array. Also, you must type the curly brackets when defining a named array constant; Excel doesn't enter them for you.

After creating this named array, you can use it in a formula. Figure 17.6 shows a worksheet that contains a multicell array formula entered into the range B2:H2. The formula is

```
{=DayNames}
```

To enter this formula, select seven cells in a row, type **=DayNames**, and press Ctrl+Shift+Enter.

Because commas separate the array elements, the array has a horizontal orientation. Use semicolons to create a vertical array. Or you can use the Excel `TRANSPOSE` function to insert a horizontal array into a vertical range of cells (see "Transposing an array," later in this chapter). The following array formula, which is entered into a seven-cell vertical range, uses the `TRANSPOSE` function:

```
{=TRANSPOSE(DayNames)}
```

FIGURE 17.6

Using a named array in an array formula.

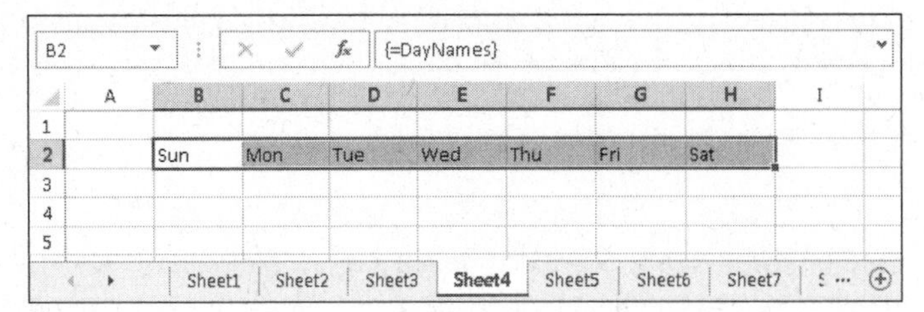

You also can access individual elements from the array by using the Excel `INDEX` function. The following formula, for example, returns `Wed`, the fourth item in the `DayNames` array:

```
=INDEX(DayNames,4)
```

Working with Array Formulas

This section deals with the mechanics of selecting cells that contain arrays and entering and editing array formulas. These procedures differ a bit from working with ordinary ranges and formulas.

Entering an array formula

When you enter an array formula into a cell or range, you must follow a special procedure so Excel knows that you want an array formula rather than a normal formula. You enter a normal formula into a cell by pressing Enter. You enter an array formula into one or more cells by pressing Ctrl + Shift + Enter.

Don't enter the curly brackets when you create an array formula; Excel inserts them for you. If the result of an array formula consists of more than one value, you must select all the cells in the results range *before* you enter the formula. If you fail to do so, only the first element of the result is returned.

Selecting an array formula range

You can manually select the cells that contain a multicell array formula by using the normal cell selection procedures. Or you can use either of the following methods:

- Activate any cell in the array formula range. Choose Home ⇨ Editing ⇨ Find & Select ⇨ Go To, or just press F5. The Go To dialog box appears. In the Go To dialog box, click the Special button and then choose the Current Array option. Click OK to close the dialog box.
- Activate any cell in the array formula range and press Ctrl + / (forward slash) to select the cells that make up the array.

Editing an array formula

If an array formula occupies multiple cells, you must edit the entire range as though it were a single cell. The key point to remember is that you can't change just one element of a multicell array formula. If you attempt to do so, Excel displays the message shown in Figure 17.7.

FIGURE 17.7

Excel's warning message reminds you that you can't edit just one cell of a multicell array formula.

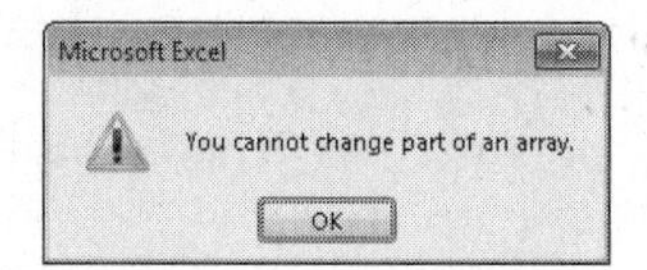

To edit an array formula, select all the cells in the array range and activate the Formula bar as usual (click it or press F2). Excel removes the curly brackets from the formula while you edit it. Edit the formula and then press Ctrl + Shift + Enter to enter the changes. All the cells in the array now reflect your editing changes (and the curly brackets reappear).

The following rules apply to multicell array formulas. If you try to do any of these things, Excel lets you know about it:

- You can't change the contents of any individual cell that makes up an array formula.
- You can't move cells that make up part of an array formula (but you can move an entire array formula).
- You can't delete cells that form part of an array formula (but you can delete an entire array).
- You can't insert new cells into an array range. This rule includes inserting rows or columns that would add new cells to an array range.
- You can't use multicell array formulas inside of a table that was created by choosing Insert ➪ Tables ➪ Table. Similarly, you can't convert a range to a table if the range contains a multicell array formula.

CAUTION

If you accidentally press Ctrl+Enter (instead of Ctrl+Shift+Enter) after editing an array formula, the formula will be entered into each selected cell, but it will no longer be an array formula. And it will probably return an incorrect result. Just reselect the cells, press F2, and then press Ctrl+Shift+Enter.

Although you can't change any individual cell that makes up a multicell array formula, you can apply formatting to the entire array or to only parts of it.

Array Formulas: The Downside

If you've followed along in this chapter, you probably understand some of the advantages of using array formulas. The main advantage, of course, is that an array formula enables you to perform otherwise impossible calculations. As you gain more experience with arrays, however, you undoubtedly will also discover some disadvantages.

Array formulas are one of the least understood features of Excel. Consequently, if you plan to share a workbook with someone who may need to make modifications, you should probably avoid using array formulas. Encountering an array formula when you don't know what it is can be very confusing.

You might also discover that you can easily forget to enter an array formula by pressing Ctrl+Shift+Enter. (And don't forget: If you edit an existing array, you must remember to use this key combination to complete the edits.) Except for logical errors, this is probably the most common problem that users have with array formulas. If you press Enter by mistake after editing an array formula, just press F2 to get back into Edit mode and then press Ctrl+Shift+Enter.

Another potential problem with array formulas is that they can sometimes slow your worksheet's recalculations, especially if you use very large arrays. On a faster system, this delay in speed may not be a problem. But, conversely, using an array formula is almost always faster than using a custom VBA function. See Chapter 39 for more information about creating custom VBA functions.

Expanding or contracting a multicell array formula

Often, you may need to expand a multicell array formula (to include more cells) or contract it (to include fewer cells). Doing so requires these steps:

1. **Select the entire range that contains the array formula.**
2. **Press F2 to enter Edit mode.**
3. **Press Ctrl + Enter.** This step enters an identical (non-array) formula into each selected cell.
4. **Change your range selection to include additional or fewer cells, but make sure the active cell is in a cell that's part of the original array.**
5. **Press F2 to re-enter Edit mode.**
6. **Press Ctrl + Shift + Enter.**

Using Multicell Array Formulas

This section contains examples that demonstrate additional features of *multicell array formulas* (array formulas that are entered into a range of cells). These features include creating arrays from values, performing operations, using functions, transposing arrays, and generating consecutive integers.

Creating an array from values in a range

The following array formula creates an array from a range of cells. Figure 17.8 shows a workbook with some data entered into A1:C4. The range D8:F11 contains a single array formula:

```
{=A1:C4}
```

FIGURE 17.8

Creating an array from a range.

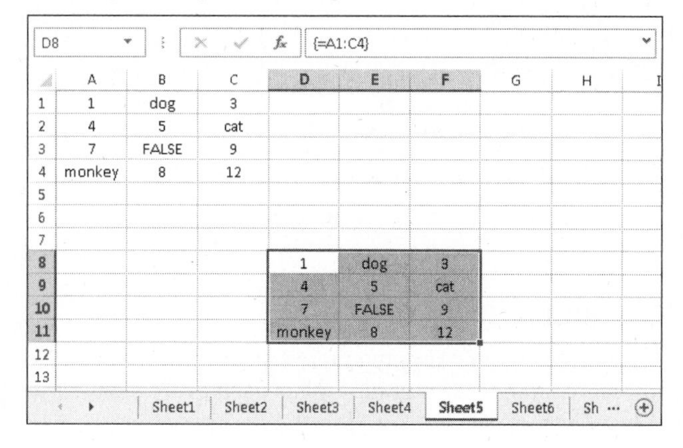

The array in D8:F11 is linked to the range A1:C4. Change any value in A1:C4, and the corresponding cell in D8:F11 reflects that change. It's a one-way link, of course. You can't change a value in D8:F11.

Creating an array constant from values in a range

In the preceding example, the array formula in D8:F11 essentially created a link to the cells in A1:C4. It's possible to sever this link and create an array constant made up of the values in A1:C4:

1. **Select the cells that contain the array formula (the range D8:F11, in this example).**
2. **Press F2 to edit the array formula.**
3. **Press F9 to convert the cell references to values.**
4. **Press Ctrl + Shift + Enter to re-enter the array formula (which now uses an array constant).**

The array constant is

```
{1,"dog",3;4,5,"cat";7,False,9;"monkey",8,12}
```

Figure 17.9 shows how this looks in the Formula bar.

FIGURE 17.9

After you press F9, the Formula bar displays the array constant.

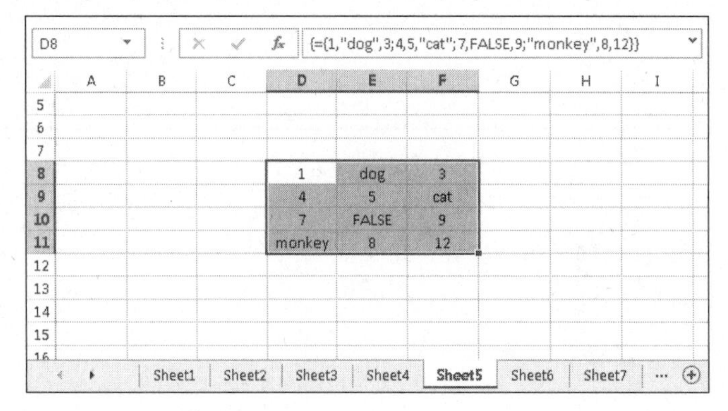

Performing operations on an array

So far, most of the examples in this chapter simply entered arrays into ranges. The following array formula creates a rectangular array and multiplies each array element by 2:

```
{={1,2,3,4;5,6,7,8;9,10,11,12}*2}
```

Figure 17.10 shows the result when you enter this formula into a range:

FIGURE 17.10

Performing a mathematical operation on an array.

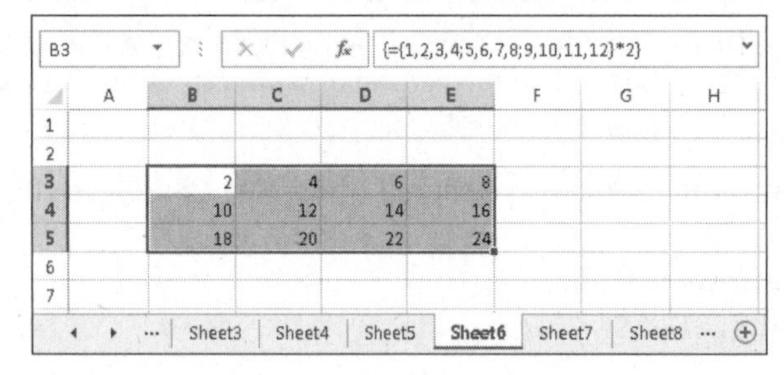

The following array formula multiplies each array element by itself:

```
{={1,2,3,4;5,6,7,8;9,10,11,12}*{1,2,3,4;5,6,7,8;9,10,11,12}}
```

The following array formula is a simpler way of obtaining the same result. Figure 17.11 shows the result when you enter this formula into a range:

```
{={1,2,3,4;5,6,7,8;9,10,11,12}^2}
```

FIGURE 17.11

Multiplying each array element by itself.

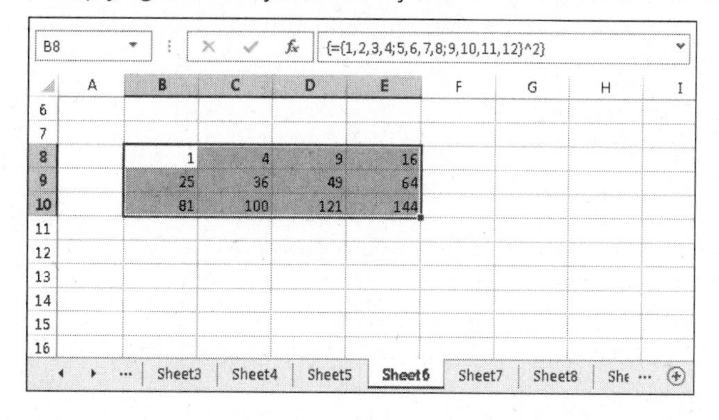

If the array is stored in a range (such as B8:E10), the array formula returns the square of each value in the range, as follows:

```
{=B8:E10^2}
```

Using functions with an array

As you may expect, you can also use worksheet functions with an array. The following array formula, which you can enter into a ten-cell vertical range, calculates the square root of each array element in the array constant:

```
{=SQRT({1;2;3;4;5;6;7;8;9;10})}
```

If the array is stored in a range, a multicell array formula such as the one that follows returns the square root of each value in the range:

```
{=SQRT(A1:A10)}
```

Transposing an array

When you transpose an array, you essentially convert rows to columns and columns to rows. In other words, you can convert a horizontal array to a vertical array (and vice versa). Use the `TRANSPOSE` function to transpose an array.

Consider the following one-dimensional horizontal array constant:

```
{1,2,3,4,5}
```

You can enter this array into a vertical range of cells by using the TRANSPOSE function. To do so, select a range of five cells that occupy five rows and one column. Then enter the following formula and press Ctrl + Shift + Enter:

```
=TRANSPOSE({1,2,3,4,5})
```

The horizontal array is transposed, and the array elements appear in the vertical range.

Transposing a two-dimensional array works in a similar manner. Figure 17.12 shows a two-dimensional array entered into a range normally and entered into a range by using the TRANSPOSE function. The formula in A1:D3 is

```
{={1,2,3,4;5,6,7,8;9,10,11,12}}
```

FIGURE 17.12

Using the TRANSPOSE function to transpose a rectangular array.

A6 | {=TRANSPOSE(A1:D3)}

	A	B	C	D	E	F	G	H
1	1	2	3	4				
2	5	6	7	8				
3	9	10	11	12				
4								
5								
6	1	5	9					
7	2	6	10					
8	3	7	11					
9	4	8	12					
10								
11								
12								
13								

Sheet5 | Sheet6 | Sheet7 | Sheet8 | Sheet9 | Sheet1C

The formula in A6:C9 is

```
{=TRANSPOSE({1,2,3,4;5,6,7,8;9,10,11,12})}
```

You can, of course, use the TRANSPOSE function to transpose an array stored in a range. The following formula, for example, uses an array stored in A1:C4 (four rows, three columns). You can enter this array formula into a range that consists of three rows and four columns.

```
{=TRANSPOSE(A1:C4)}
```

Generating an array of consecutive integers

As you see in Chapter 18, generating an array of consecutive integers for use in a complex array formula is often useful. The ROW function, which returns a row number, is ideal for this. Consider the array formula shown here, entered into a vertical range of 12 cells:

```
{=ROW(1:12)}
```

This formula generates a 12-element array that contains integers from 1 to 12. To demonstrate, select a range that consists of 12 rows and one column and enter the array formula into the range. You'll find that the range is filled with 12 consecutive integers (as shown in Figure 17.13).

FIGURE 17.13

Using an array formula to generate consecutive integers.

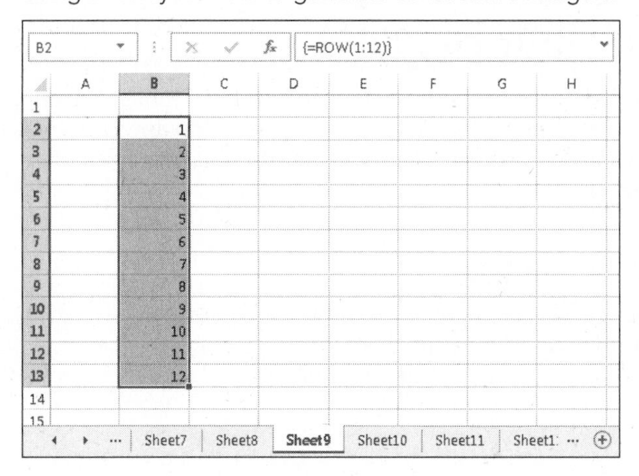

If you want to generate an array of consecutive integers, a formula like the one shown previously is good — but not perfect. To see the problem, insert a new row above the range that contains the array formula. Excel adjusts the row references so that the array formula now reads

```
{=ROW(2:13)}
```

The formula that originally generated integers from 1 to 12 now generates integers from 2 to 13.

For a better solution, use this formula:

```
{=ROW(INDIRECT("1:12"))}
```

This formula uses the `INDIRECT` function, which takes a text string as its argument. Excel does not adjust the references contained in the argument for the `INDIRECT` function. Therefore, this array formula *always* returns integers from 1 to 12.

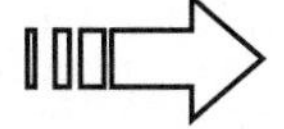

Chapter 18 contains several examples that use the technique for generating consecutive integers.

Worksheet Functions That Return an Array

Several of the Excel worksheet functions use arrays; you must enter a formula that uses one of these functions into multiple cells as an array formula. These functions are `FORECAST`, `FREQUENCY`, `GROWTH`, `LINEST`, `LOGEST`, `MINVERSE`, `MMULT`, and `TREND`. Consult the Excel Help system for more information.

Using Single-Cell Array Formulas

The examples in the preceding section all used a multicell array formula — a single array formula that's entered into a range of cells. The real power of using arrays becomes apparent when you use single-cell array formulas. This section contains examples of array formulas that occupy a single cell.

Counting characters in a range

Suppose that you have a range of cells that contains text entries (see Figure 17.14). If you need to get a count of the total number of characters in that range, the "traditional" method involves creating a formula like the one that follows and copying it down the column:

```
=LEN(A1)
```

FIGURE 17.14

The goal is to count the number of characters in a range of text.

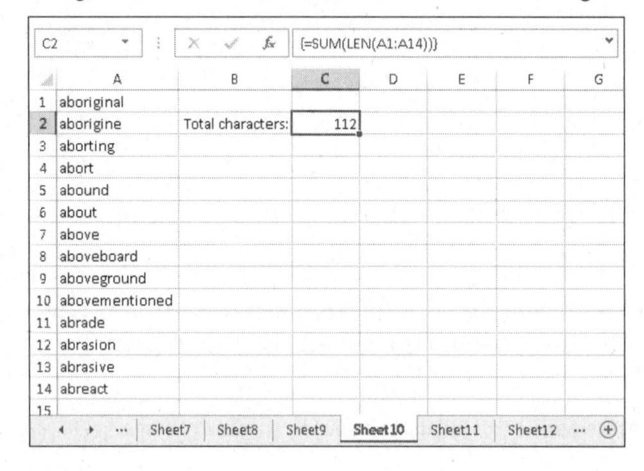

Then you use a `SUM` formula to calculate the sum of the values returned by these intermediate formulas.

The following array formula does the job without using any intermediate formulas:

```
{=SUM(LEN(A1:A14))}
```

The array formula uses the LEN function to create a new array (in memory) that consists of the number of characters in each cell of the range. In this case, the new array is

```
{10,9,8,5,6,5,5,10,11,14,6,8,8,7}
```

The array formula is then reduced to

```
=SUM({10,9,8,5,6,5,5,10,11,14,6,8,8,7})
```

The formula returns the sum of the array elements, 112.

Summing the three smallest values in a range

If you have values in a range named Data, you can determine the smallest value by using the SMALL function:

```
=SMALL(Data,1)
```

You can determine the second smallest and third smallest values by using these formulas:

```
=SMALL(Data,2)
=SMALL(Data,3)
```

To add the three smallest values, you could use a formula like this:

```
=SUM(SMALL(Data,1), SMALL(Data,2), SMALL(Data,3)
```

This formula works fine, but using an array formula is more efficient. The following array formula returns the sum of the three smallest values in a range named Data:

```
{=SUM(SMALL(Data,{1,2,3}))}
```

The formula uses an array constant as the second argument for the SMALL function. This generates a new array, which consists of the three smallest values in the range. This array is then passed to the SUM function, which returns the sum of the values in the new array.

Figure 17.15 shows an example in which the range A1:A10 is named Data. The SMALL function is evaluated three times, each time with a different second argument. The first time, the SMALL function has a second argument of 1, and it returns -5. The second time, the second argument for the SMALL function is 2, and it returns 0 (the second smallest value in the range). The third time, the SMALL function has a second argument of 3 and returns the third smallest value of 2.

FIGURE 17.15

An array formula returns the sum of the three smallest values in A1:A10.

D2 | {=SUM(SMALL(A1:A10,{1,2,3}))}

	A	B	C	D	E	F	G
1	12						
2	-5		Sum of three smallest:	-3			
3	3						
4	2						
5	0						
6	6						
7	13						
8	7						
9	4						
10	8						
11							
12							

Sheet7 | Sheet8 | Sheet9 | Sheet10 | Sheet11 | Sheet12

Therefore, the array that's passed to the `SUM` function is

```
{-5,0,2)
```

The formula returns the sum of the array (`-3`).

Counting text cells in a range

Suppose that you need to count the number of text cells in a range. The `COUNTIF` function seems like it might be useful for this task — but it's not. `COUNTIF` is useful only if you need to count values in a range that meet some criterion (for example, values greater than 12).

To count the number of text cells in a range, you need an array formula. The following array formula uses the `IF` function to examine each cell in a range. It then creates a new array (of the same size and dimensions as the original range) that consists of 1s and 0s, depending on whether the cell contains text. This new array is then passed to the `SUM` function, which returns the sum of the items in the array. The result is a count of the number of text cells in the range:

```
{=SUM(IF(ISTEXT(A1:D5),1,0))}
```

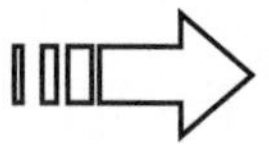

This general array formula type (that is, an `IF` function nested in a `SUM` function) is very useful for counting. See Chapter 13 for additional examples of `IF` and `SUM` functions.

Figure 17.16 shows an example of the preceding formula in cell C7. The array created by this formula is:

```
{0,1,1,1;1,0,0,0;1,0,0,0;1,0,0,0;1,0,0,0}
```

FIGURE 17.16

An array formula returns the number of text cells in the range.

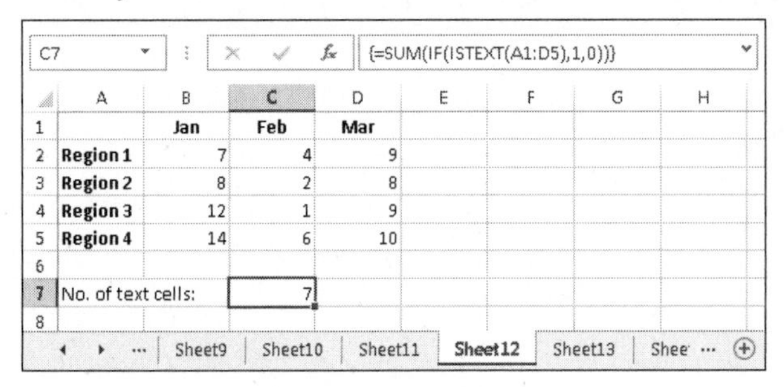

	A	B	C	D
1		Jan	Feb	Mar
2	Region 1	7	4	9
3	Region 2	8	2	8
4	Region 3	12	1	9
5	Region 4	14	6	10
6				
7	No. of text cells:		7	

Notice that this array contains four rows of three elements (the same dimensions as the range).

Here is a slightly more efficient variation on this formula:

```
{=SUM(ISTEXT(A1:D5)*1)}
```

This formula eliminates the need for the `IF` function and takes advantage of the fact that

```
TRUE * 1 = 1
```

and

```
FALSE * 1 = 0
```

Eliminating intermediate formulas

One key benefit of using an array formula is that you can often eliminate intermediate formulas in your worksheet, which makes your worksheet more compact and eliminates the need to display irrelevant calculations. Figure 17.17 shows a worksheet that contains pre-test and post-test scores for students. Column D contains formulas that calculate the changes between the pre-test and the post-test scores. Cell D17 contains a formula, shown here, that calculates the average of the values in column D:

```
=AVERAGE(D2:D15)
```

With an array formula, you can eliminate column D. The following array formula calculates the average of the changes but does not require the formulas in column D:

```
{=AVERAGE(C2:C15-B2:B15)}
```

FIGURE 17.17

Without an array formula, calculating the average change requires intermediate formulas in column D.

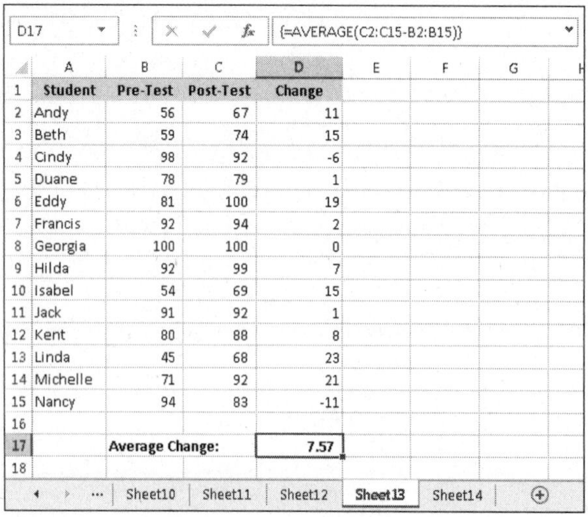

D17 | {=AVERAGE(C2:C15-B2:B15)}

	A	B	C	D	E	F	G
1	Student	Pre-Test	Post-Test	Change			
2	Andy	56	67	11			
3	Beth	59	74	15			
4	Cindy	98	92	-6			
5	Duane	78	79	1			
6	Eddy	81	100	19			
7	Francis	92	94	2			
8	Georgia	100	100	0			
9	Hilda	92	99	7			
10	Isabel	54	69	15			
11	Jack	91	92	1			
12	Kent	80	88	8			
13	Linda	45	68	23			
14	Michelle	71	92	21			
15	Nancy	94	83	-11			
16							
17		Average Change:		7.57			
18							

Sheet10 | Sheet11 | Sheet12 | Sheet13 | Sheet14

How does it work? The formula uses two arrays, the values of which are stored in two ranges (B2:B15 and C2:C15). The formula creates a *new* array that consists of the differences between each corresponding element in the other arrays. This new array is stored in Excel's memory, not in a range. The `AVERAGE` function then uses this new array as its argument and returns the result.

The new array, calculated from the two ranges, consists of the following elements:

```
{11,15,-6,1,19,2,0,7,15,1,8,23,21,-11}
```

The formula, therefore, is equivalent to

```
=AVERAGE({11,15,-6,1,19,2,0,7,15,1,8,23,21,-11})
```

Excel evaluates the function and displays the results, 7.57.

You can use additional array formulas to calculate other measures for the data in this example. For example, the following array formula returns the largest change (that is, the greatest improvement). This formula returns `23`, which represents Linda's test scores.

```
{=MAX(C2:C15-B2:B15)}
```

The following array formula returns the smallest value in the Change column. This formula returns –11, which represents Nancy's test scores.

```
{=MIN(C2:C15-B2:B15)}
```

Using an array in lieu of a range reference

If your formula uses a function that requires a range reference, you may be able to replace that range reference with an array constant. This is useful in situations in which the values in the referenced range do not change.

> **NOTE**
> A notable exception to using an array constant in place of a range reference in a function is with the database functions that use a reference to a criteria range (for example, DSUM). Unfortunately, using an array constant instead of a reference to a criteria range does not work.

Figure 17.18 shows a worksheet that uses a lookup table to display a word that corresponds to an integer. For example, looking up a value of 9 returns Nine from the lookup table in D1:E10. The formula in cell C1 is

```
=VLOOKUP(B1,D1:E10,2,FALSE)
```

FIGURE 17.18

You can replace the lookup table in D1:E10 with an array constant.

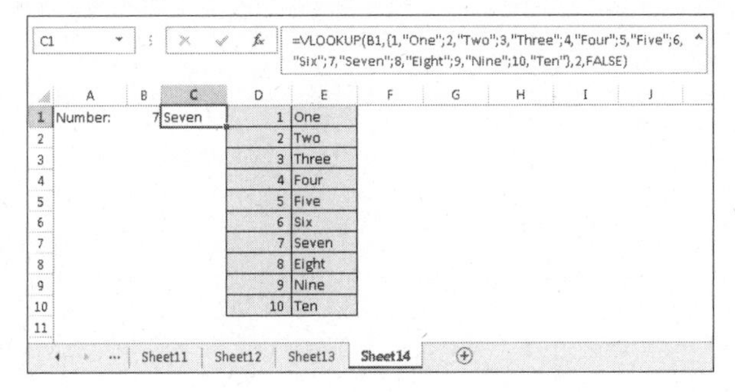

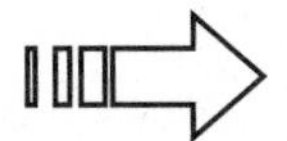

For information about lookup formulas, see Chapter 14.

You can use a two-dimensional array in place of the lookup range. The following formula returns the same result as the previous formula, but it does not require the lookup range in D1:E1:

```
=VLOOKUP(B1,{1,"One";2,"Two";3,"Three";4,"Four";5,"Five";6,"Six";7,"Seven";8,
   "Eight";9,"Nine";10,"Ten"},2,FALSE)
```

This chapter introduced arrays. Chapter 18 explores the topic further and provides some additional examples.

CHAPTER

18

Performing Magic with Array Formulas

IN THIS CHAPTER

Looking at more examples of single-cell array formulas

Seeing more examples of multicell array formulas

Returning an array from a custom VBA function

The preceding chapter provides an introduction to arrays and array formulas and presented some basic examples to whet your appetite. This chapter continues the saga and provides many useful examples that further demonstrate the power of this feature.

I selected the examples in this chapter to provide a good assortment of the various uses for array formulas. You can use most of them as is. You will, of course, need to adjust the range names or references used. Also, you can modify many of the examples easily to work in a slightly different manner.

Working with Single-Cell Array Formulas

As I describe in the preceding chapter, you enter single-cell array formulas into a single cell (not into a range of cells). These array formulas work with arrays contained in a range or that exist in memory. This section provides some additional examples of such array formulas.

ON THE WEB

The examples in this section are available on this book's website. The file is named `single-cell array formulas.xlsx`.

Summing a range that contains errors

You may have discovered that the `SUM` function doesn't work if you attempt to sum a range that contains one or more error values (such as `#DIV/0!` or `#N/A`). Figure 18.1 shows an example. The formula in cell D11 returns an error value because the range that it sums (D4:D10) contains errors.

The following array formula, in cell D13, overcomes this problem and returns the sum of the values, even if the range contains error values:

```
{=SUM(IFERROR(D4:D10,""))}
```

This formula works by creating a new array that contains the original values but without the errors. The `IFERROR` function effectively filters out error values by replacing them with an empty string. The `SUM` function then works on this "filtered" array. This technique also works with other functions, such as `AVERAGE`, `MIN`, and `MAX`.

NOTE

The `IFERROR` function was introduced in Excel 2007. Following is a modified version of the formula that's compatible with older versions of Excel:

```
{=SUM(IF(ISERROR(D4:D10),"",D4:D10))}
```

The `AGGREGATE` function, which was introduce in Excel 2010, provides another way to sum a range that contains one or more error values, without using an array formula. Here's an example:

```
=AGGREGATE(9,2,C4:C10)
```

The first argument, `9`, is the code for `SUM`. The second argument, `2`, is the code for "ignore error values." The `AGGREGATE` function can also be used to calculate an average, minimum, maximum, and so on.

FIGURE 18.1

An array formula can sum a range of values, even if the range contains errors.

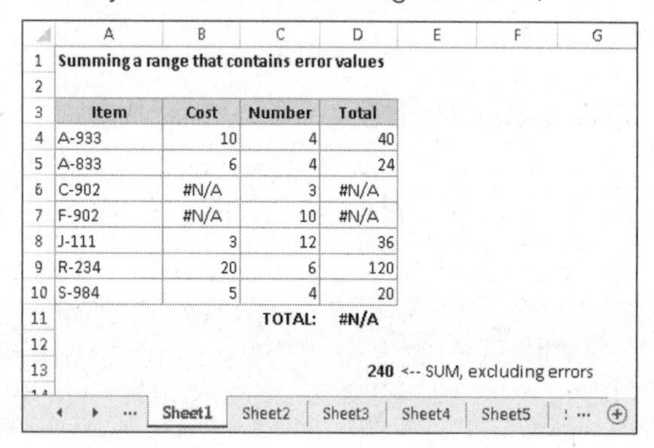

	A	B	C	D	E	F	G
1	**Summing a range that contains error values**						
2							
3	**Item**	**Cost**	**Number**	**Total**			
4	A-933	10	4	40			
5	A-833	6	4	24			
6	C-902	#N/A	3	#N/A			
7	F-902	#N/A	10	#N/A			
8	J-111	3	12	36			
9	R-234	20	6	120			
10	S-984	5	4	20			
11			**TOTAL:**	**#N/A**			
12							
13				**240**	<-- SUM, excluding errors		

Sheet1 | Sheet2 | Sheet3 | Sheet4 | Sheet5

Counting the number of error values in a range

The following array formula is similar to the previous example, but it returns a count of the number of error values in a range named Data:

```
{=SUM(IF(ISERROR(Data),1,0))}
```

This formula creates an array that consists of 1s (if the corresponding cell contains an error) and 0s (if the corresponding cell does not contain an error value).

You can simplify the formula a bit by removing the third argument for the `IF` function. If this argument isn't specified, the `IF` function returns `FALSE` if the condition is not satisfied (that is, the cell does not contain an error value). In this context, Excel treats `FALSE` as a `0` value. The array formula shown here performs exactly like the previous formula, but it doesn't use the third argument for the `IF` function:

```
{=SUM(IF(ISERROR(Data),1))}
```

Actually, you can simplify the formula even more:

```
{=SUM(ISERROR(Data)*1)}
```

This version of the formula relies on the fact that

```
TRUE * 1 = 1
```

and

```
FALSE * 1 = 0
```

Summing the *n* largest values in a range

The following array formula returns the sum of the ten largest values in a range named Data:

```
{=SUM(LARGE(Data,ROW(INDIRECT("1:10"))))}
```

The `LARGE` function is evaluated ten times, each time with a different second argument (`1`, `2`, `3`, and so on up to `10`). The results of these calculations are stored in a new array, and that array is used as the argument for the `SUM` function.

To sum a different number of values, replace the `10` in the argument for the `INDIRECT` function with another value.

If the number of cells to sum is contained in cell C17, use the following array formula, which uses the concatenation operator (`&`) to create the range address for the `INDIRECT` function:

```
{=SUM(LARGE(Data,ROW(INDIRECT("1:"&C17))))}
```

To sum the *n* smallest values in a range, use the `SMALL` function instead of the `LARGE` function.

Using the `INDIRECT` function to generate a series of consecutive integers is discussed in Chapter 17.

Computing an average that excludes zeros

Figure 18.2 shows a simple worksheet that calculates average sales. The formula in cell B13 is

```
=AVERAGE(B4:B11)
```

FIGURE 18.2

The calculated average includes cells that contain a 0.

	A	B	C	D	E
1	**Exclude zero from average**				
2					
3	**Sales Person**	**Sales**			
4	Abner	23,991			
5	Baker	15,092			
6	Charleston	0			
7	Davis	11,893			
8	Ellerman	32,116			
9	Flugelhart	29,089			
10	Gallaway	0			
11	Harrison	33,211			
12					
13	Average with zeros:		18,174		
14	Average without zeros (array formula):		24,232		
15					

... | Sheet3 | Sheet4 | Sheet5 | Sheet6 | Sheet7 | ...

Two of the sales staff had the week off, however, so including their 0 sales in the calculated average doesn't accurately describe the average sales per representative.

NOTE

The AVERAGE function ignores blank cells, but it does not ignore cells that contain 0.

The following array formula returns the average of the range but excludes the cells containing 0:

```
{=AVERAGE(IF(B5:B12<>0,B5:B12))}
```

This formula creates a new array that consists only of the nonzero values in the range. The AVERAGE function then uses this new array as its argument.

You can also get the same result with a regular (nonarray) formula:

```
=SUM(B5:B12)/COUNTIF(B5:B12,"<>0")
```

This formula uses the COUNTIF function to count the number of nonzero values in the range. This value is divided into the sum of the values.

> **NOTE**
>
> The only reason to use an array formula to calculate an average that excludes zero values is for compatibility with versions prior to Excel 2007. A simpler approach is to use the `AVERAGEIF` function in a nonarray formula:
>
> ```
> =AVERAGEIF(B5:B12,"<>0",B5:B12)
> ```

Determining whether a particular value appears in a range

To determine whether a particular value appears in a single column of cells, you can use the `LOOKUP` function. But if the range consists of multiple columns, you'll need to use a different approach.

Figure 18.3 shows a worksheet with a list of names in A5:E24 (named NameList). An array formula in cell D3 checks the name entered into cell C3 (named TheName). If the name exists in the list of names, the formula displays the text `Found`; otherwise, it displays `Not Found`.

FIGURE 18.3

Using an array formula to determine whether a range contains a particular value.

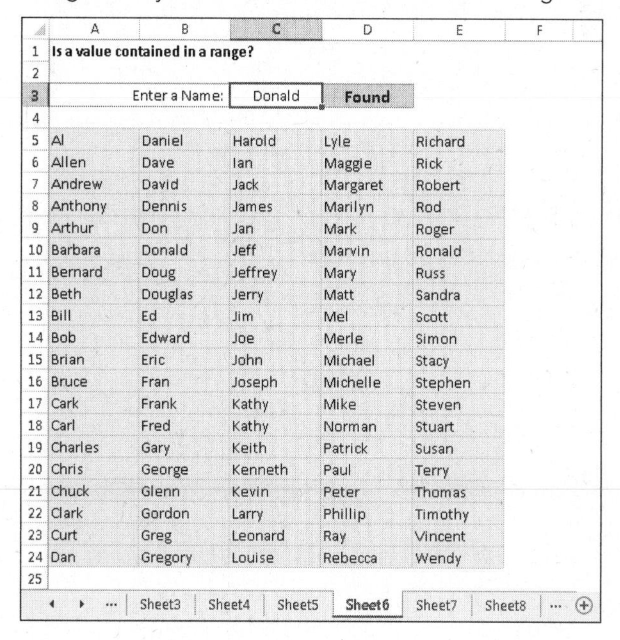

	A	B	C	D	E	F
1	**Is a value contained in a range?**					
2						
3		Enter a Name:	Donald	**Found**		
4						
5	Al	Daniel	Harold	Lyle	Richard	
6	Allen	Dave	Ian	Maggie	Rick	
7	Andrew	David	Jack	Margaret	Robert	
8	Anthony	Dennis	James	Marilyn	Rod	
9	Arthur	Don	Jan	Mark	Roger	
10	Barbara	Donald	Jeff	Marvin	Ronald	
11	Bernard	Doug	Jeffrey	Mary	Russ	
12	Beth	Douglas	Jerry	Matt	Sandra	
13	Bill	Ed	Jim	Mel	Scott	
14	Bob	Edward	Joe	Merle	Simon	
15	Brian	Eric	John	Michael	Stacy	
16	Bruce	Fran	Joseph	Michelle	Stephen	
17	Cark	Frank	Kathy	Mike	Steven	
18	Carl	Fred	Kathy	Norman	Stuart	
19	Charles	Gary	Keith	Patrick	Susan	
20	Chris	George	Kenneth	Paul	Terry	
21	Chuck	Glenn	Kevin	Peter	Thomas	
22	Clark	Gordon	Larry	Phillip	Timothy	
23	Curt	Greg	Leonard	Ray	Vincent	
24	Dan	Gregory	Louise	Rebecca	Wendy	
25						

The array formula in cell D3 is

```
{=IF(OR(TheName=NameList),"Found","Not Found")}
```

This formula compares TheName to each cell in the NameList range. It builds a new array that consists of logical `TRUE` or `FALSE` values. The `OR` function returns `TRUE` if any one of the values in the new array is `TRUE`. The `IF` function uses this result to determine which message to display.

A simpler form of this formula follows. This formula displays `TRUE` if the name is found; otherwise, it returns `FALSE`.

```
{=OR(TheName=NameList)}
```

Yet another approach uses the `COUNTIF` function in a nonarray formula:

```
=IF(COUNTIF(NameList,TheName)>0,"Found","Not Found")
```

Counting the number of differences in two ranges

The following array formula compares the corresponding values in two ranges (named MyData and YourData) and returns the number of differences in the two ranges. If the contents of the two ranges are identical, the formula returns `0`.

```
{=SUM(IF(MyData=YourData,0,1))}
```

Figure 18.4 shows an example.

FIGURE 18.4

Using an array formula to count the number of differences in two ranges.

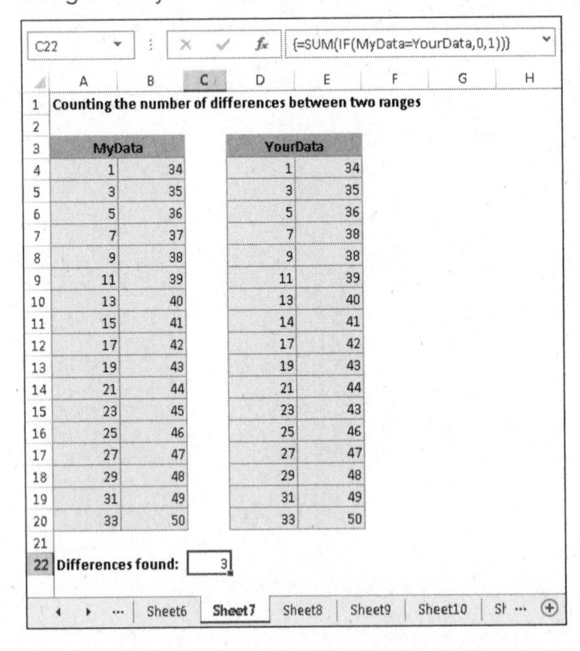

MyData		YourData	
1	34	1	34
3	35	3	35
5	36	5	36
7	37	7	38
9	38	9	38
11	39	11	39
13	40	13	40
15	41	14	41
17	42	17	42
19	43	19	43
21	44	21	44
23	45	23	43
25	46	25	46
27	47	27	47
29	48	29	48
31	49	31	49
33	50	33	50

NOTE

Each of the two ranges can consist of more than one column, but they must be the same size and of the same dimensions.

This formula works by creating a new array of the same size as the ranges being compared. The IF function fills this new array with 0s and 1s: 1 if a difference is found, and 0 if the corresponding cells are the same. The SUM function then returns the sum of the values in the array.

The following array formula, which is simpler, is another way of calculating the same result:

```
{=SUM(1*(MyData<>YourData))}
```

This version of the formula relies on the fact that

```
TRUE * 1 = 1
```

and

```
FALSE * 1 = 0
```


Returning the location of the maximum value in a range

The following array formula returns the row number of the maximum value in a single-column range named Data:

```
{=MIN(IF(Data=MAX(Data),ROW(Data), "")))}
```

The IF function creates a new array that corresponds to the Data range. If the corresponding cell contains the maximum value in Data, the array contains the row number; otherwise, it contains an empty string. The MIN function uses this new array as its second argument, and it returns the smallest value, which corresponds to the row number of the maximum value in Data.

I use the MIN function to handle ties. If the Data range contains more than one cell that has the maximum value, the row of the *first* occurrence of the maximum cell is returned. If you change MIN to MAX, then the formula returns the last occurrence of the maximum cell.

The following array formula is similar to the previous one, but it returns the actual cell address of the maximum value in the Data range. It uses the ADDRESS function, which takes two arguments: a row number and a column number.

```
{=ADDRESS(MIN(IF(Data=MAX(Data),ROW(Data), "")),COLUMN(Data))}
```

The previous formulas work only with a single-column range. The following variation works with any sized range and returns the address of the largest value in the range named Data:

```
{=ADDRESS(MIN(IF(Data=MAX(Data),ROW(Data), "")),MIN(IF(Data=MAX(Data),
   COLUMN(Data), ""))))}
```

If the range contains two or more cells that are tied for the maximum value, this formula returns the address of the first occurrence.

Finding the row of a value's *n*th occurrence in a range

The following array formula returns the row number within a single-column range named Data that contains the *n*th occurrence of the value in a cell named Value:

```
{=SMALL(IF(Data=Value,ROW(Data), ""),n)}
```

The `IF` function creates a new array that consists of the row number of values from the Data range that are equal to Value. Values from the Data range that aren't equal to Value are replaced with an empty string. The `SMALL` function works on this new array and returns the *n*th smallest row number.

The formula returns `#NUM!` if the Value is not found or if *n* exceeds the number of occurrences of Value in the range.

Returning the longest text in a range

The following array formula displays the text string in a range (named Data) that has the most characters. If multiple cells contain the longest text string, the first cell is returned.

```
{=INDEX(Data,MATCH(MAX(LEN(Data)),LEN(Data),FALSE),1)}
```

This formula works with two arrays, both of which contain the length of each item in the Data range. The `MAX` function determines the largest value, which corresponds to the longest text item. The `MATCH` function calculates the offset of the cell that contains the maximum length. The `INDEX` function returns the contents of the cell containing the most characters.

Figure 18.5 shows an example. This function works only if the Data range consists of a single column.

Determining whether a range contains valid values

You may have a list of items that you need to check against another list. For example, you may import a list of part numbers into a range named MyList, and you want to ensure that all the part numbers are valid. You can do so by comparing the items in the imported list to the items in a master list of part numbers (named Master). Figure 18.6 shows an example.

FIGURE 18.5

Using an array formula to return the longest text in a range.

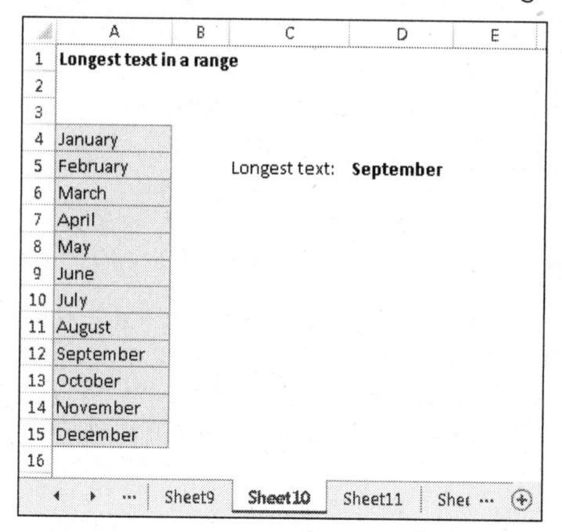

FIGURE 18.6

Using array formula to count and identify items that aren't in a list.

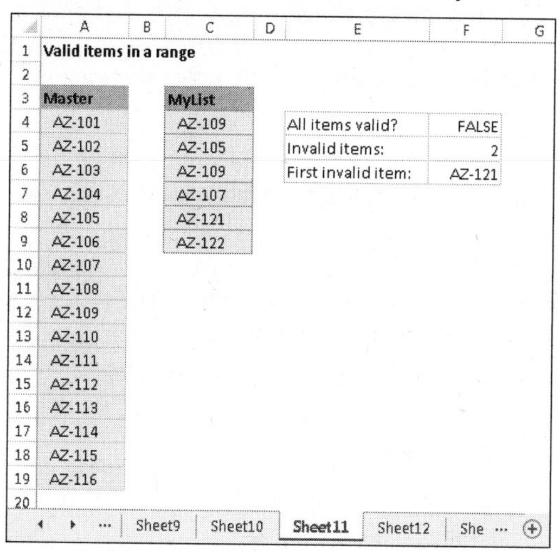

The following array formula returns TRUE if every item in the range named MyList is found in the range named Master. Both ranges must consist of a single column, but they don't need to contain the same number of rows.

```
{=ISNA(MATCH(TRUE,ISNA(MATCH(MyList,Master,0)),0))}
```

The array formula that follows returns the number of invalid items. In other words, it returns the number of items in MyList that do not appear in Master.

```
{=SUM(1*ISNA(MATCH(MyList,Master,0)))}
```

To return the first invalid item in MyList, use the following array formula:

```
{=INDEX(MyList,MATCH(TRUE,ISNA(MATCH(MyList,Master,0)),0))}
```

Summing the digits of an integer

I can't think of any practical application for the example in this section, but it's a good demonstration of the potential power of an array formula. The following array formula calculates the sum of the digits in a positive integer, which is stored in cell A1. For example, if cell A1 contains the value `409`, the formula returns `13` (the sum of 4, 0, and 9).

```
{=SUM(MID(A1,ROW(INDIRECT("1:"&LEN(A1))),1)*1)}
```

To understand how this formula works, start with the `ROW` function, as shown here:

```
{=ROW(INDIRECT("1:"&LEN(A1)))}
```

This function returns an array of consecutive integers beginning with 1 and ending with the number of digits in the value in cell A1. For example, if cell A1 contains the value `409`, the `LEN` function returns `3`, and the array generated by the `ROW` functions is

```
{1,2,3}
```

For more information about using the `INDIRECT` function to return this array, see Chapter 17.

This array is then used as the second argument for the `MID` function. The `MID` part of the formula, simplified a bit and expressed as values, is the following:

```
{=MID(409,{1,2,3},1)*1}
```

This function generates an array with three elements:

```
{4,0,9}
```

By simplifying again and adding the `SUM` function, the formula looks like this:

```
{=SUM({4,0,9})}
```

This formula produces the result of 13.

NOTE

The values in the array created by the `MID` function are multiplied by 1 because the `MID` function returns a string. Multiplying by 1 forces a numeric value result. Alternatively, you can use the `VALUE` function to force a numeric string to become a numeric value.

Notice that the formula doesn't work with a negative value because the negative sign is not a numeric value. Also, the formula fails if the cell contains nonnumeric values (such as 123A6). The following formula solves this problem by checking for errors in the array and replacing them with zero:

```
{=SUM(IFERROR(MID(A1,ROW(INDIRECT("1:"&LEN(A1))),1)*1,0))}
```

NOTE

This formula uses the `IFERROR` function, which was introduced in Excel 2007.

Figure 18.7 shows a worksheet that uses both versions of this formula.

FIGURE 18.7

Two versions of an array formula calculate the sum of the digits in an integer.

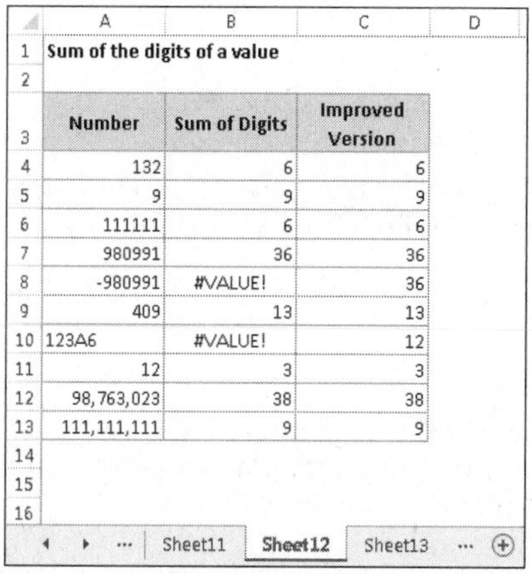

	A	B	C	D
1	Sum of the digits of a value			
2				
3	Number	Sum of Digits	Improved Version	
4	132	6	6	
5	9	9	9	
6	111111	6	6	
7	980991	36	36	
8	-980991	#VALUE!	36	
9	409	13	13	
10	123A6	#VALUE!	12	
11	12	3	3	
12	98,763,023	38	38	
13	111,111,111	9	9	
14				
15				
16				

Sheet11 | Sheet12 | Sheet13

Summing rounded values

Figure 18.8 shows a simple worksheet that demonstrates a common spreadsheet problem: rounding errors. As you can see, the grand total in cell E7 appears to display an incorrect amount (it's off by a penny). The values in column E use a number format that displays two decimal places. The actual values, however, consist of additional decimal places that do not display due to rounding (as a result of the number format). The net effect of these rounding errors is a seemingly incorrect total. The total, which is actually $168.320997, displays as $168.32.

FIGURE 18.8

Using an array formula to correct rounding errors.

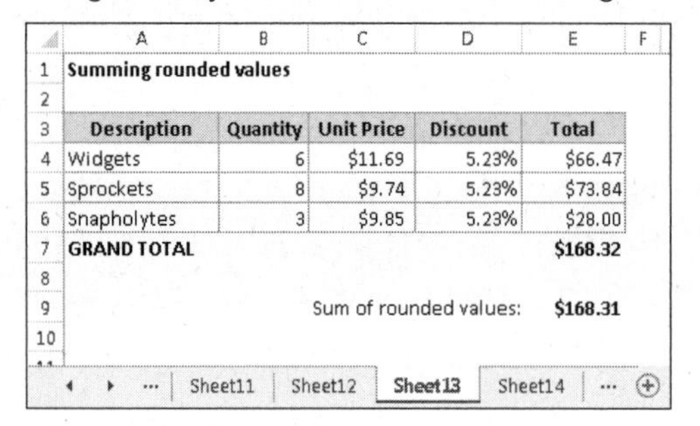

	A	B	C	D	E	F
1	**Summing rounded values**					
2						
3	**Description**	**Quantity**	**Unit Price**	**Discount**	**Total**	
4	Widgets	6	$11.69	5.23%	$66.47	
5	Sprockets	8	$9.74	5.23%	$73.84	
6	Snapholytes	3	$9.85	5.23%	$28.00	
7	**GRAND TOTAL**				**$168.32**	
8						
9			Sum of rounded values:		**$168.31**	
10						

Sheet11 | Sheet12 | Sheet13 | Sheet14

The following array formula creates a new array that consists of values in column E, rounded to two decimal places:

```
{=SUM(ROUND(E4:E6,2))}
```

This formula returns $168.31.

You can also eliminate these types of rounding errors by using the `ROUND` function in the formula that calculates each row total in column E (which does not require an array formula).

Summing every *n*th value in a range

Suppose that you have a range of values and you want to compute the sum of every third value in the list — the first, the fourth, the seventh, and so on. One solution is to hard-code the cell addresses in a formula. A better solution, though, is to use an array formula.

In Figure 18.9, the values are stored in a range named Data, and the value of *n* is in cell D2 (named *n*).

The following array formula returns the sum of every *n*th value in the range:

```
{=SUM(IF(MOD(ROW(INDIRECT("1:"&COUNT(Data)))-1,n)=0,Data,""))}
```

This formula returns `70`, which is the sum of every third value in the range.

This formula generates an array of consecutive integers, and the `MOD` function uses this array as its first argument. The second argument for the `MOD` function is the value of *n*. The `MOD` function creates another array that consists of the remainders when each row number is divided by *n*. When the array item is `0` (that is, the row is evenly divisible by *n*), the corresponding item in the *Data* range will be included in the sum.

FIGURE 18.9

An array formula returns the sum of every *n*th value in the range.

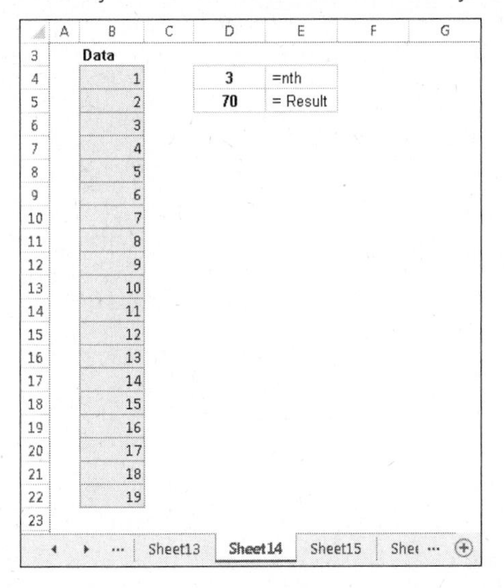

You find that this formula fails when *n* is `0` (that is, when it sums no items). The modified array formula that follows uses an `IF` function to handle this case:

```
{=IF(n=0,0,SUM(IF(MOD(ROW(INDIRECT("1:"&COUNT(Data)))-1,n)=0,Data,"")))}
```

This formula works only when the Data range consists of a single column of values. It does not work for a multicolumn range or for a single row of values.

To make the formula work with a horizontal range, you need to transpose the array of integers generated by the `ROW` function. The `TRANSPOSE` function is just the ticket. The modified array formula that follows works only with a horizontal Data range:

```
{=IF(n=0,0,SUM(IF(MOD(TRANSPOSE(ROW(INDIRECT("1:"&COUNT(Data))))-
   1,n)=0,Data,""))))}
```

Removing nonnumeric characters from a string

The following array formula extracts a number from a string that contains text. For example, consider the string *ABC145Z*. The formula returns the numeric part, `145`.

```
{=MID(A1,MATCH(0,(ISERROR(MID(A1,ROW(INDIRECT("1:"&LEN(A1))),1)*1)*1),0),
   LEN(A1)-SUM((ISERROR(MID(A1,ROW(INDIRECT("1:"&LEN(A1))),1)*1)*1)))}
```

This formula works only with a single embedded number. For example, it fails with a string like *X45Z99* because the string contains two embedded numbers.

Using the Excel Formula Evaluator

If you want to better understand how some of these complex array formulas work, consider using a handy tool: the Formula Evaluator. Select the cell that contains the formula and then choose Formulas ➪ Formula Auditing ➪ Evaluate Formula. The Evaluate Formula dialog box, shown in the figure here, appears.

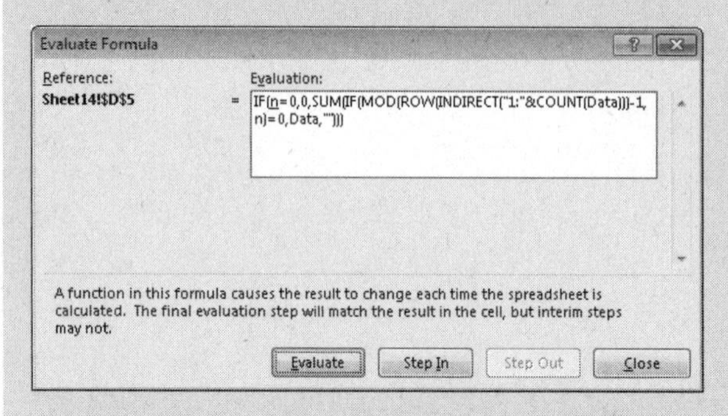

Click the Evaluate button repeatedly to see the intermediate results as the formula is being calculated. It's like watching a formula calculate in slow motion.

Determining the closest value in a range

The formula in this section performs an operation that none of Excel's lookup functions can do. The array formula that follows returns the value in a range named Data that is closest to another value (named Target):

```
{=INDEX(Data,MATCH(SMALL(ABS(Target-Data),1),ABS(Target-Data),0))}
```

If two values in the Data range are equidistant from the Target value, the formula returns the first one in the list. Figure 18.10 shows an example of this formula. In this case, the Target value is `45`. The array formula in cell D4 returns `48` — the value closest to 45.

Returning the last value in a column

Suppose that you have a worksheet that you update frequently by adding new data to columns. You may need a way to reference the last value in column A (the value most recently entered). If column A contains no empty cells, the solution is relatively simple and doesn't require an array formula:

```
=OFFSET(A1,COUNTA(A:A)-1,0)
```

FIGURE 18.10

An array formula returns the closest match.

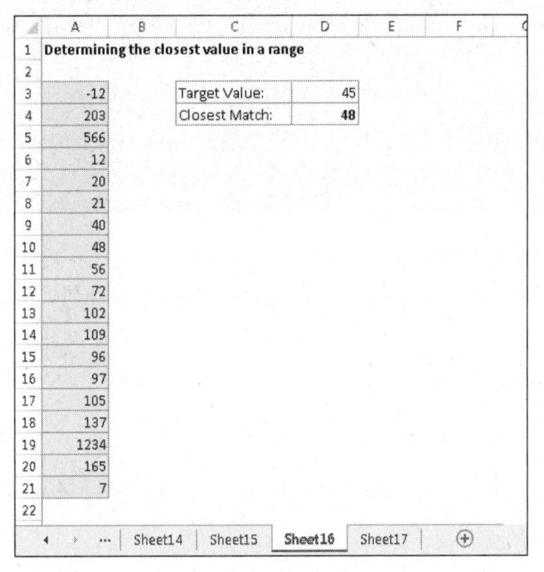

	A	B	C	D
1	**Determining the closest value in a range**			
2				
3	-12		Target Value:	45
4	203		Closest Match:	**48**
5	566			
6	12			
7	20			
8	21			
9	40			
10	48			
11	56			
12	72			
13	102			
14	109			
15	96			
16	97			
17	105			
18	137			
19	1234			
20	165			
21	7			
22				

Sheet14 | Sheet15 | **Sheet16** | Sheet17

This formula uses the COUNTA function to count the number of nonempty cells in column A. This value (–1) is used as the second argument for the OFFSET function. For example, if the last value is in row 100, COUNTA returns 100. The OFFSET function returns the value in the cell 99 rows down from cell A1 in the same column.

If column A has one or more empty cells interspersed, which is frequently the case, the preceding formula won't work because the COUNTA function doesn't count the empty cells.

The following array formula returns the contents of the last nonempty cell in the first 500 rows of column A:

```
{=INDEX(A1:A500,MAX(ROW(A1:A500)*(A1:A500<>"")))}
```

You can, of course, modify the formula to work with a column other than column A. To use a different column, change the column references from A to whatever column you need. If the last nonempty cell occurs in a row beyond row 500, you need to change the two instances of 500 to a larger number. The fewer rows referenced in the formula, the faster the calculation speed. Note that the formula does not work if the column contains any error values.

CAUTION

You can't use this formula, as written, in the same column with which it's working. Attempting to do so generates a circular reference. You can, however, modify it. For example, to use the function in cell A1, change the references so that they begin with row 2 instead of row 1.

> **Tip**
>
> As I was finishing up this chapter, I found an alternate (nonarray) formula that returns the last value in a column. This formula returns the last nonempty cell in column A:
>
> ```
> =LOOKUP(2,1/(A:A<>""),A:A )
> ```
>
> The only problem is that I don't understand how it works. But it seems to be perfectly reliable and is probably more efficient than the array formula. It differs from the array formula in one way: It ignores error values. So it actually returns the last nonempty, non-error cell in a column.

Returning the last value in a row

The following array formula is similar to the previous formula, but it returns the last nonempty cell in a row (in this case, row 1):

```
{=INDEX(1:1,MAX(COLUMN(1:1)*(1:1<>"")))}
```

To use this formula for a different row, change the 1:1 reference to correspond to the row.

Figure 18.11 shows an example for the last value in a column, and the last value in a row.

FIGURE 18.11

Using array formulas to return the last nonempty cell in a column or row.

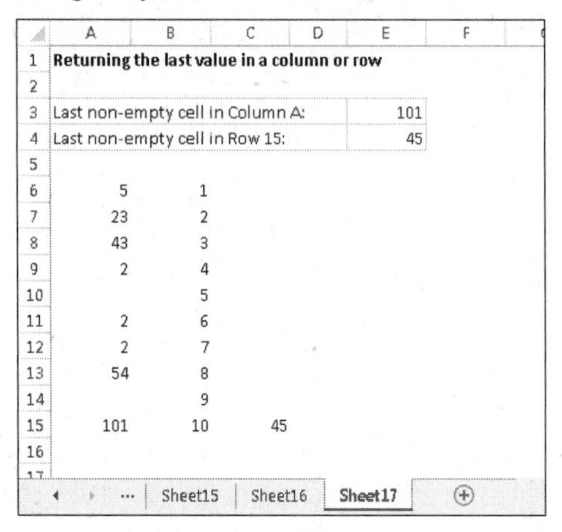

	A	B	C	D	E	F
1	**Returning the last value in a column or row**					
2						
3	Last non-empty cell in Column A:				101	
4	Last non-empty cell in Row 15:				45	
5						
6	5	1				
7	23	2				
8	43	3				
9	2	4				
10		5				
11	2	6				
12	2	7				
13	54	8				
14		9				
15	101	10	45			
16						

An alternative, nonarray formula that returns the last nonempty non-error cell in a row is:

```
=LOOKUP(2,1/(1:1<>""),1:1 )
```

Working with Multicell Array Formulas

The preceding chapter introduced array formulas entered into multicell ranges. In this section, I present a few more multicell array formulas. Most of these formulas return some or all the values in a range, but rearranged in some way.

When you enter a multicell array formula, you must select the entire range first. Then type the formula and press Ctrl + Shift + Enter.

ON THE WEB

The examples in this section are available on this book's website. The file is named `multicell array formulas.xlsx`.

Returning only positive values from a range

The following array formula works with a single-column vertical range (named Data). The array formula is entered into a range that's the same size as Data and returns only the positive values in the Data range. (Zeroes and negative numbers are ignored.)

```
{=INDEX(Data,SMALL(IF(Data>0,ROW(INDIRECT("1:"&ROWS(Data)))),ROW(INDIRECT
   ("1:"&ROWS(Data)))))}
```


As you can see in Figure 18.12, this formula works, but not perfectly. The Data range is A4:A23, and the array formula is entered into C4:C23. However, the array formula displays `#NUM!` error values for cells that don't contain a value.

This modified array formula, entered into range E4:E23, uses the `IFERROR` function to avoid the error value display:

```
{=IFERROR(INDEX(Data,SMALL(IF(Data>0,ROW(INDIRECT("1:"&ROWS(Data)))),ROW
   (INDIRECT("1:"&ROWS(Data))))),"")}
```

The `IFERROR` function was introduced in Excel 2007. For compatibility with older versions, use this formula:

```
{=IF(ISERR(SMALL(IF(Data>0,ROW(INDIRECT("1:"&ROWS(Data)))),ROW(INDIRECT
   ("1:"&ROWS(Data))))),"",INDEX(Data,SMALL(IF(Data>0,ROW(INDIRECT("1:"&ROWS
   (Data)))),ROW(INDIRECT("1:"&ROWS(Data))))))}
```

FIGURE 18.12

Using an array formula to return only the positive values in a range.

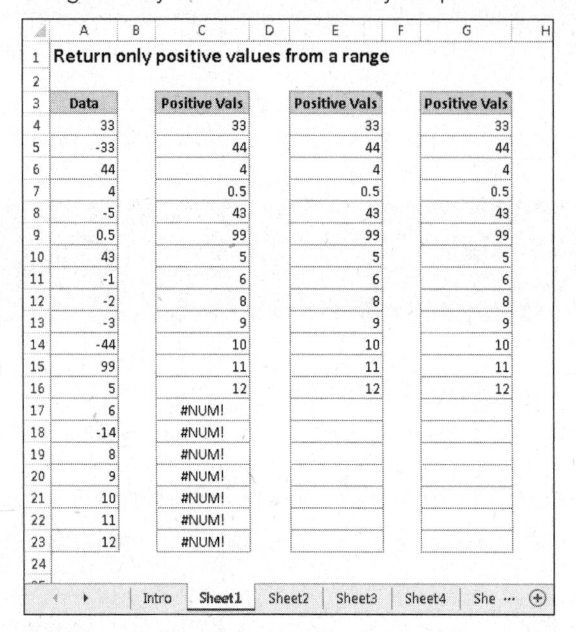

Return only positive values from a range

Data	Positive Vals	Positive Vals	Positive Vals
33	33	33	33
-33	44	44	44
44	4	4	4
4	0.5	0.5	0.5
-5	43	43	43
0.5	99	99	99
43	5	5	5
-1	6	6	6
-2	8	8	8
-3	9	9	9
-44	10	10	10
99	11	11	11
5	12	12	12
6	#NUM!		
-14	#NUM!		
8	#NUM!		
9	#NUM!		
10	#NUM!		
11	#NUM!		
12	#NUM!		

Returning nonblank cells from a range

The following formula is a variation on the formula in the preceding section. This array formula works with a single-column vertical range named Data. The array formula is entered into a range of the same size as Data and returns only the nonblank cells in the Data range.

```
{=IFERROR(INDEX(Data,SMALL(IF(Data<>"",ROW(INDIRECT("1:"&ROWS(Data)))),ROW
   (INDIRECT("1:"&ROWS(Data))))),"")}
```

For compatibility with versions prior to Excel 2007, use this formula:

```
{=IF(ISERR(SMALL(IF(Data<>"",ROW(INDIRECT("1:"&ROWS(Data)))),ROW(INDIRECT
   ("1:"&ROWS(Data))))),"",INDEX(Data,SMALL(IF(Data<>"",ROW(INDIRECT("1:"&ROWS
   (Data)))),ROW(INDIRECT("1:"&ROWS(Data))))))}
```

Reversing the order of cells in a range

In Figure 18.13, cells C4:C13 contain a multicell array formula that reverses the order of the values in the range A4:A13 (which is named Data).

The array formula is

```
{=IF(INDEX(Data,ROWS(Data)-ROW(INDIRECT("1:"&ROWS(Data)))+1)="","",INDEX(Data,
   ROWS(Data)-ROW(INDIRECT("1:"&ROWS(Data)))+1))}
```

FIGURE 18.13

A multicell array formula displays the entries in A4:A13 in reverse order.

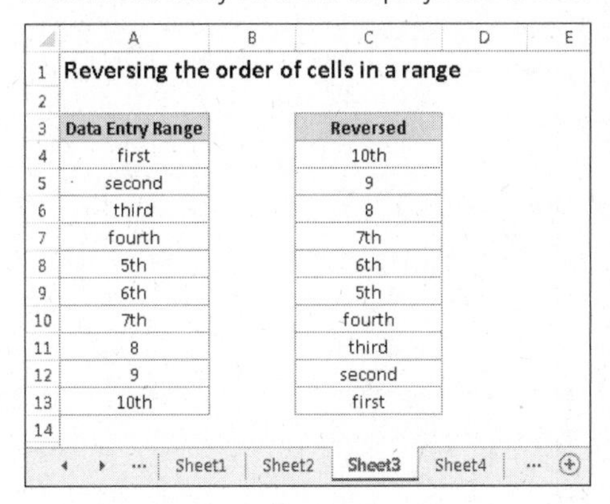

	A	B	C	D	E
1	**Reversing the order of cells in a range**				
2					
3	**Data Entry Range**		**Reversed**		
4	first		10th		
5	second		9		
6	third		8		
7	fourth		7th		
8	5th		6th		
9	6th		5th		
10	7th		fourth		
11	8		third		
12	9		second		
13	10th		first		
14					

Sorting a range of values dynamically

Figure 18.14 shows a data entry range in column A (named Data). As the user enters values into that range, the values are displayed sorted from largest to smallest in column C. The array formula in column C is rather simple:

```
{=LARGE(Data,ROW(INDIRECT("1:"&ROWS(Data))))}
```

If you prefer to avoid the `#NUM!` error display, use this formula:

```
=IFERROR(LARGE(Data,ROW(INDIRECT("1:"&ROWS(Data)))),"")
```

If you require compatibility with versions prior to Excel 2007, the formula gets a bit more complex:

```
{=IF(ISERR(LARGE(Data,ROW(INDIRECT("1:"&ROWS(Data))))),"",LARGE(Data,ROW
   (INDIRECT("1:"&ROWS(Data)))))}
```

Note that this formula works only with values. The file at this book's website has a similar array formula example that works only with text.

FIGURE 18.14

A multicell array formula displays the values in column A, sorted.

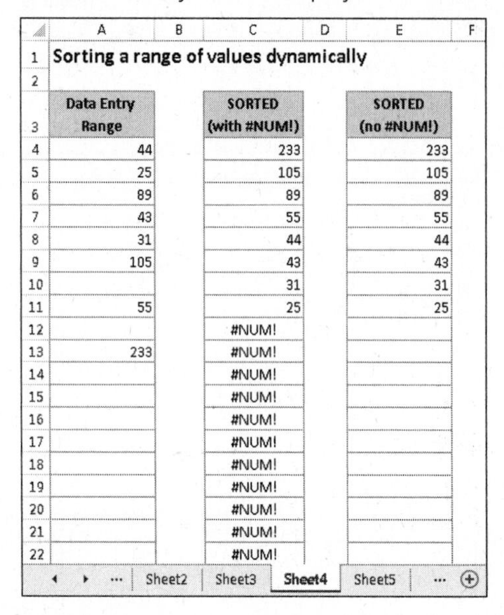

	A	B	C	D	E	F
1	Sorting a range of values dynamically					
2						
3	Data Entry Range		SORTED (with #NUM!)		SORTED (no #NUM!)	
4	44		233		233	
5	25		105		105	
6	89		89		89	
7	43		55		55	
8	31		44		44	
9	105		43		43	
10			31		31	
11	55		25		25	
12			#NUM!			
13	233		#NUM!			
14			#NUM!			
15			#NUM!			
16			#NUM!			
17			#NUM!			
18			#NUM!			
19			#NUM!			
20			#NUM!			
21			#NUM!			
22			#NUM!			

Sheet2 | Sheet3 | Sheet4 | Sheet5

Returning a list of unique items in a range

If you have a single-column range named Data, the following array formula returns a list of the unique items in the range (the list with no duplicated items):

```
{=INDEX(Data,SMALL(IF(MATCH(Data,Data,0)=ROW(INDIRECT("1:"&ROWS(Data))),MATCH
  (Data,Data,0),""),ROW(INDIRECT("1:"&ROWS(Data)))))}
```

This formula doesn't work if the Data range contains any blank cells. The unfilled cells of the array formula display `#NUM!`.

The following modified version eliminates the `#NUM!` display by using the `IFERROR` function.

```
{=IFERROR(INDEX(Data,SMALL(IF(MATCH(Data,Data,0)=ROW(INDIRECT
("1:"&ROWS(data))),MATCH(Data,Data,0),""),ROW(INDIRECT
("1:"&ROWS(Data))))),"")}
```

Figure 18.15 shows an example. Range A4:A22 is named Data, and the array formula is entered into range C4:C22. Range E4:E22 contains the array formula that uses the `IFERROR` function.

FIGURE 18.15

Using an array formula to return unique items from a list.

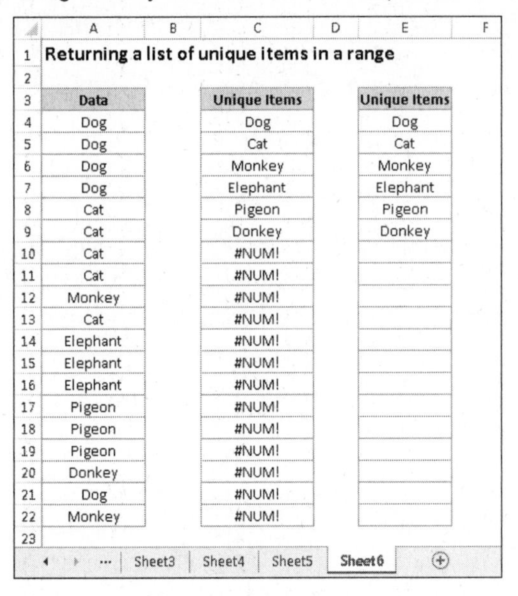

Data	Unique Items	Unique Items
Dog	Dog	Dog
Dog	Cat	Cat
Dog	Monkey	Monkey
Dog	Elephant	Elephant
Cat	Pigeon	Pigeon
Cat	Donkey	Donkey
Cat	#NUM!	
Cat	#NUM!	
Monkey	#NUM!	
Cat	#NUM!	
Elephant	#NUM!	
Elephant	#NUM!	
Elephant	#NUM!	
Pigeon	#NUM!	
Pigeon	#NUM!	
Pigeon	#NUM!	
Donkey	#NUM!	
Dog	#NUM!	
Monkey	#NUM!	

Displaying a calendar in a range

Figure 18.16 shows the results of one of my favorite multicell array formulas, a "live" calendar displayed in a range of cells. If you change the date at the top, the calendar recalculates to display the dates for the month and year.

FIGURE 18.16

Displaying a calendar by using a single array formula.

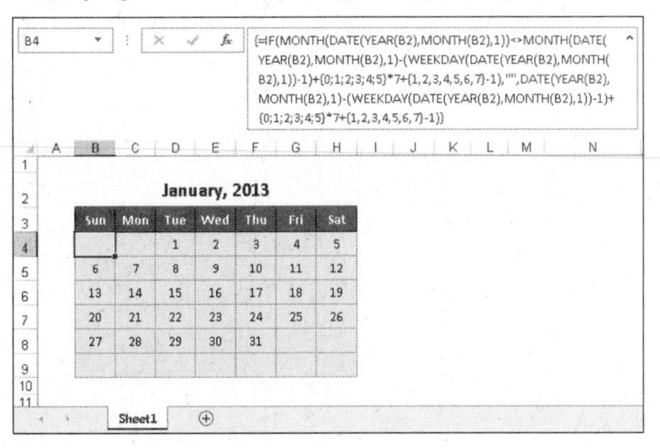

Sun	Mon	Tue	Wed	Thu	Fri	Sat
		1	2	3	4	5
6	7	8	9	10	11	12
13	14	15	16	17	18	19
20	21	22	23	24	25	26
27	28	29	30	31		

On the Web

This workbook is available at this book's website. The file is named `array formula calendar.xlsx`. In addition, you'll find a workbook (`yearly calendar.xlsx`) that uses this technique to display a calendar for a complete year.

After you create this calendar, you can easily copy it to other worksheets or workbooks.

To create this calendar in the range B2:H9, follow these steps:

1. **Select B2:H2 and merge the cells by choosing Home➪Alignment➪Merge & Center.**
2. **Enter a date into the merged range.** The day of the month isn't important.
3. **Enter the abbreviated day names in the range B3:H3.**
4. **Select B4:H9 and enter this array formula.** ***Remember:*** To enter an array formula, press Ctrl + Shift + Enter (not just Enter).

   ```
   {=IF(MONTH(DATE(YEAR(B2),MONTH(B2),1))<>MONTH(DATE(YEAR(B2),MONTH
   (B2),1)-(WEEKDAY(DATE(YEAR(B2),MONTH(B2),1))-1)+{0;1;2;3;4;5}*7+
   {1,2,3,4,5,6,7}-1),"",DATE(YEAR(B2),MONTH(B2),1)-(WEEKDAY(DATE
   (YEAR(B2),MONTH(B2),1))-1)+{0;1;2;3;4;5}*7+{1,2,3,4,5,6,7}-1)}
   ```

5. **Format the range B4:H9 to use this custom number format: d.** This step formats the dates to show only the day. Use the Custom category in the Number tab of the Format Cells dialog box to specify this custom number format.
6. **Adjust the column widths and format the cells as you like.**
7. **Change the month and year in cell B2.** The calendar updates automatically.

After creating this calendar, you can copy the range to any other worksheet or workbook.

The array formula actually returns date values, but the cells are formatted to display only the day portion of the date. Also, notice that the array formula uses array constants.

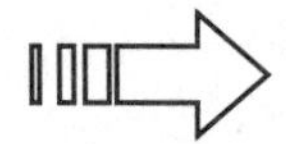

See Chapter 17 for more information about array constants.

Part III

Creating Charts and Graphics

The five chapters in this part deal with charts and graphics — including Sparkline graphics. You'll discover how to use Excel's graphics capabilities to display your data in a chart. In addition, you'll learn to use Excel's other drawing tools to enhance your worksheets.

IN THIS PART

CHAPTER

19

Getting Started Making Charts

IN THIS CHAPTER

Charting overview

Seeing how Excel handles charts

Comparing embedded charts and chart sheets

Identifying the parts of a chart

Looking at examples of each chart type

When most people think of Excel, they think of crunching rows and columns of numbers. But as you probably know already, Excel is no slouch when it comes to presenting data visually in the form of charts. In fact, Excel is probably the most commonly used software in the world for creating charts.

This chapter presents an introductory overview of Excel's charting ability. Chapter 20 continues with some more advanced techniques.

What Is a Chart?

A *chart* is a visual representation of numeric values. Charts (also known as *graphs*) have been an integral part of spreadsheets since the early days of Lotus 1-2-3. Charts generated by early spreadsheet products were quite crude, but they've improved significantly over the years. Excel provides you with the tools to create a wide variety of highly customizable professional-quality charts.

Displaying data in a well-conceived chart can make your numbers more understandable. Because a chart presents a picture, charts are particularly useful for summarizing a series of numbers and their interrelationships. Making a chart can often help you spot trends and patterns that may otherwise go unnoticed. If you're unfamiliar with the elements of a chart, see the sidebar later in this chapter, "The Parts of a Chart."

Figure 19.1 shows a worksheet that contains a simple column chart that depicts a company's sales volume by month. Viewing the chart makes it very apparent that sales were down in the summer months (June through August), but they increased steadily during the final four months of the year. You could, of course, arrive at this same conclusion simply by studying the numbers. But viewing the chart makes the point much more quickly.

FIGURE 19.1

A simple column chart depicts the monthly sales volume.

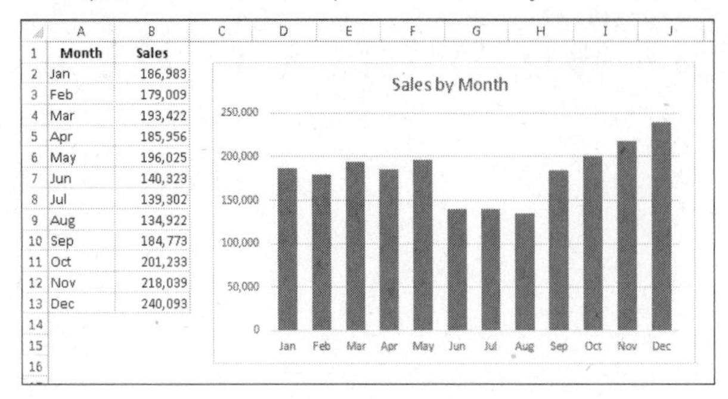

Month	Sales
Jan	186,983
Feb	179,009
Mar	193,422
Apr	185,956
May	196,025
Jun	140,323
Jul	139,302
Aug	134,922
Sep	184,773
Oct	201,233
Nov	218,039
Dec	240,093

A column chart is just one of many different types of charts that you can create with Excel. Later in this chapter, I discuss all chart types so you can make the right choice for your data.

Understanding How Excel Handles Charts

Before you can create a chart, you must have some numbers — sometimes known as *data*. The data, of course, is stored in the cells in a worksheet. Normally, the data that a chart uses resides in a single worksheet, but that's not a strict requirement. A chart can use data that's stored in a different worksheet or even in a different workbook.

A chart is essentially an object that Excel creates upon request. This object consists of one or more data series, displayed graphically. The appearance of the data series depends on the selected chart type. For example, if you create a line chart that uses two data series, the chart contains two lines, each representing one data series. The data for each series is stored in a separate row or column. Each point on the line is determined by the value in a single cell and is represented by a marker. You can distinguish each of the lines by its thickness, line style, color, or data markers (squares, circles, and so on).

Figure 19.2 shows a line chart that plots two data series across a 12-month period. I used different data markers (squares versus circles) to identify the two series, as shown in the legend at the bottom of the chart. The chart clearly shows the sales in the Western Region are declining steadily, while Eastern Region sales are increasing a bit after remaining level for several months.

A key point to keep in mind is that charts are *dynamic*. In other words, a chart series is linked to the data in your worksheet. If the data changes, the chart is updated automatically to reflect those changes.

FIGURE 19.2

This line chart displays two data series.

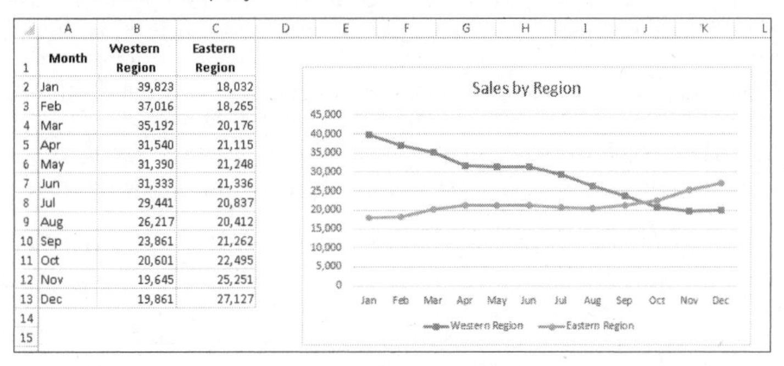

Month	Western Region	Eastern Region
Jan	39,823	18,032
Feb	37,016	18,265
Mar	35,192	20,176
Apr	31,540	21,115
May	31,390	21,248
Jun	31,333	21,336
Jul	29,441	20,837
Aug	26,217	20,412
Sep	23,861	21,262
Oct	20,601	22,495
Nov	19,645	25,251
Dec	19,861	27,127

After you create a chart, you can always change its type, change the formatting, add or remove specific elements (such as the title or legend), add new data series to it, or change an existing data series so that it uses data in a different range.

A chart is either embedded in a worksheet or displayed on a separate chart sheet. It's very easy to move an embedded chart to a chart sheet (and vice versa).

Embedded charts

An *embedded chart* basically floats on top of a worksheet, on the worksheet's drawing layer. The charts shown previously in this chapter are both embedded charts.

As with other drawing objects (such as Shapes or SmartArt), you can move an embedded chart, resize it, change its proportions, adjust its borders, and perform other operations. Using embedded charts enables you to print the chart next to the data that it uses.

To make any changes to the actual chart in an embedded chart object, you must click it to *activate* the chart. When a chart is activated, Excel displays the Chart Tools context tab. The Ribbon provides many tools for working with charts, and even more tools are available in the Format task pane.

New Feature

Excel 2013 incorporates some additional features that make it even easier to make your chart look exactly how you want it. When you select a chart, you see three icons to the right of the chart that adjust various aspects of the chart. I describe these new tools later in this chapter.

With one exception, every chart starts out as an embedded chart. The exception is when you create a default chart by selecting the data and pressing F11. In that case, the chart is created on a chart sheet.

Chart sheets

When a chart is on a chart sheet, you view it by clicking its sheet tab. A chart sheets contains a single chart. Chart sheets and worksheets can be interspersed in a workbook.

To move an embedded chart to a chart sheet, click the chart to select it and then choose Chart Tools ➪ Design ➪ Location ➪ Move Chart. The Move Chart dialog box, shown in Figure 19.3, appears. Select the New Sheet option and provide a name for the chart sheet (or accept Excel's default name). Click OK, the chart is moved, and the new chart sheet is activated.

FIGURE 19.3

The Move Chart dialog box lets you move a chart to a chart sheet.

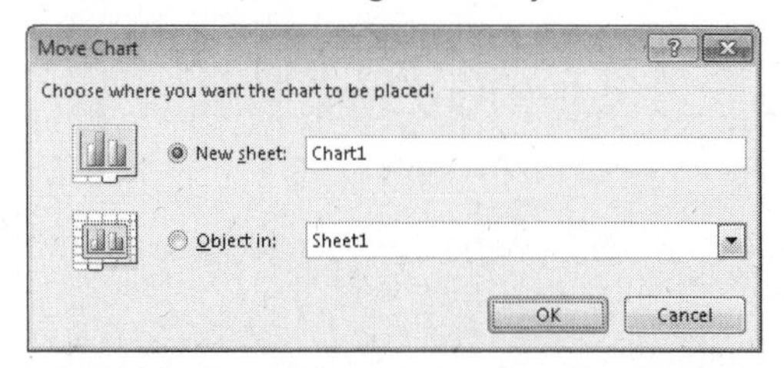

TIP

This operation also works in the opposite direction: You can select a chart on a chart sheet and relocate it to a worksheet as an embedded chart. In the Move Chart dialog box, choose Object In, and then select the worksheet from the drop-down list.

When you place a chart on a chart sheet, the chart occupies the entire sheet. If you plan to print a chart on a page by itself, using a chart sheet is often your better choice. If you have many charts, you may want to put each one on a separate chart sheet to avoid cluttering your worksheet. This technique also makes locating a particular chart easier because you can change the names of the chart sheets' tabs to provide a description of the chart that it contains.

The Excel Ribbon changes when a chart sheet is active, similar to the way it changes when you select an embedded chart. You have access to the same editing tools for embedded charts and charts on chart sheets.

If the chart isn't fully visible in the window, you can use the scroll bars to scroll it, or adjust the zoom factor to make it smaller. You can also change its orientation (tall or wide) by choosing Page Layout ➪ Page Setup ➪ Orientation.

Parts of a Chart

Refer to the accompanying chart as you read the following description of the chart's elements.

The particular chart is a *combination chart* that displays two *data series:* Sales Calls and Units Sold. Sales Calls are plotted as vertical columns, and the Units Sold are plotted as a line with square markers. Each column (or marker on the line) represents a single *data point* (the value in a cell). The chart data is stored in the range A1:C7.

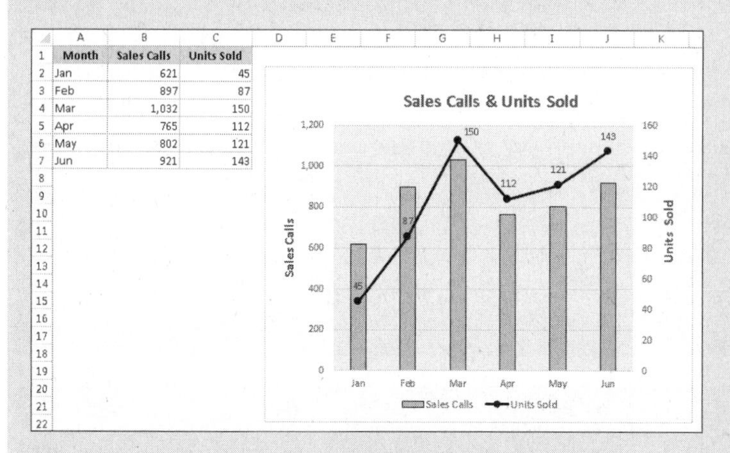

Month	Sales Calls	Units Sold
Jan	621	45
Feb	897	87
Mar	1,032	150
Apr	765	112
May	802	121
Jun	921	143

It has a horizontal axis, known as the *category axis.* This axis represents the category for each data point (January, February, and so on).

It has two vertical axes, known as *value axes,* and each one has a different scale. The axis on the left is for the columns (Sales Calls), and the axis on the right is for the line (Units Sold).

The value axes also display scale values. The axis on the left displays scale values from 0 to 1,200, in major unit increments of 200. The value axis on the right uses a different scale: 0 to 160, in increments of 20.

Why two value axes? A chart with two value axes is appropriate because the two data series vary dramatically in scale. If the Sales data were plotted using the left axis, the line would barely be visible.

Most charts provide some method of identifying the data series or data points. A legend, for example, is often used to identify the various series in a chart. In this example, the legend appears on the bottom of the chart. Some charts also display data labels to identify specific data points. This chart displays data labels for the Units Sold series, but not for the Sales Calls series. In addition, most charts (including the example chart) contain a chart title and additional labels to identify the axes or categories.

It also contains horizontal gridlines (which correspond to the left value axis). Gridlines are basically extensions of the value axis scale, which makes it easier for the viewer to determine the magnitude of the data points.

All charts have a chart area (the entire background area of the chart) and a plot area. The plot area shows the actual chart, and in this example, the plot area has a different background color.

Charts can have additional parts or fewer parts, depending on the chart type. For example, a pie chart has slices and no axes. A 3-D chart may have walls and a floor. You can also add many other types of items to a chart. For example, you can add a trend line or display error bars. In other words, after you create a chart, you have a great deal of flexibility in customizing it.

Creating a Chart

Creating a chart is fairly simple:

1. **Make sure that your data is appropriate for a chart.**
2. **Select the range that contains your data.**
3. **Select the Insert tab and select a chart type from the Charts group.** These icons display drop-down lists that display subtypes. Excel creates the chart and places it in the center of the window.
4. **(Optional) Use the various tools and commands to change the look or layout of the chart or add or delete chart elements.**

New Feature

Excel 2013 includes a new option in the Insert ➪ Charts groups: Recommended Charts. If you choose this option, the Insert Chart dialog box appears with two tabs. The Recommended Charts tab contains a list of suggested chart types appropriate for your data; sometimes this feature can be useful, but you can't always assume that all the recommended charts are suitable. The second tab, All Charts, gives you access to all of Excel's chart types. The charts displayed in the Insert Chart dialog box are not generic thumbnails; the charts depict your actual data.

Tip

You can create a chart with a single keystroke. Select the range to be used in the chart and then press Alt+F1 (for an embedded chart) or F11 (for a chart on a chart sheet). Excel displays the chart of the selected data, using the default chart type. The default chart type is a column chart, but you can change it. To change the default chart type, select any chart and choose Chart Tools ➪ Design ➪ Change Chart Type. The Change Chat Type dialog box appears. Choose a chart type from the list on the left, and then right-click a chart in the row of thumbnails and choose Set As Default Chart.

Hands On: Creating and Customizing a Chart

This section contains a step-by-step example of creating a chart and applying some customizations. If you've never created a chart, this is a good opportunity to get a feel for how the process works.

Figure 19.4 shows a worksheet with a range of data. This data shows customer survey results by month, broken down by customers in three age groups. In this case, the data resides in a table (created by choosing Insert ➪ Tables ➪ Table), but that's not a requirement to create a chart.

On the Web

This workbook, named `hands-on example.xlsx`, is available on this book's website.

FIGURE 19.4

The source data for the hands-on chart example.

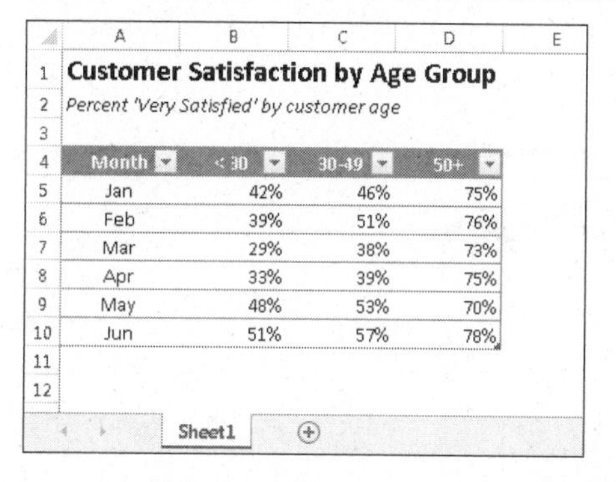

Customer Satisfaction by Age Group

Percent 'Very Satisfied' by customer age

Month	< 30	30-49	50+
Jan	42%	46%	75%
Feb	39%	51%	76%
Mar	29%	38%	73%
Apr	33%	39%	75%
May	48%	53%	70%
Jun	51%	57%	78%

Sheet1

Selecting the data

The first step is to select the data for the chart. Your selection should include such items as labels and series identifiers (row and column headings). For this example, select the entire table (range A4:D10). This range includes the category labels but not the title (which is in A1).

TIP

If you want to chart all data in a table (or a rectangular range separated from other data), you can select just a single cell. Excel will almost always guess the range for the chart accurately. If you don't want to plot all data in the table, just select the specific columns or rows.

NOTE

The data that you use in a chart need not be in contiguous cells. You can press Ctrl and make a multiple selection. The initial data, however, must be on a single worksheet. If you need to plot data that exists on more than one worksheet, you can add more series after the chart is created. In all cases, however, data for a single chart series must reside on one sheet.

Choosing a chart type

After you select the data, select a chart type from the Insert ➪ Charts group. Each control in this group is a drop-down list, which lets you further refine your choice by selecting a subtype.

For this example, let Excel recommend a chart type. Choose Insert ➪ Charts ➪ Recommended Charts. Excel displays the dialog box shown in Figure 19.5. This dialog box shows several recommended charts, using your actual data. Select the first choice, Clustered Column, and click OK. Excel inserts the chart in the middle of the workbook window. You can move the chart by dragging any of its borders. You can also resize it by clicking and dragging in one of its corners. Figure 19.6 shows the chart after I moved it next to the data range.

FIGURE 19.5

Letting Excel recommend a chart type.

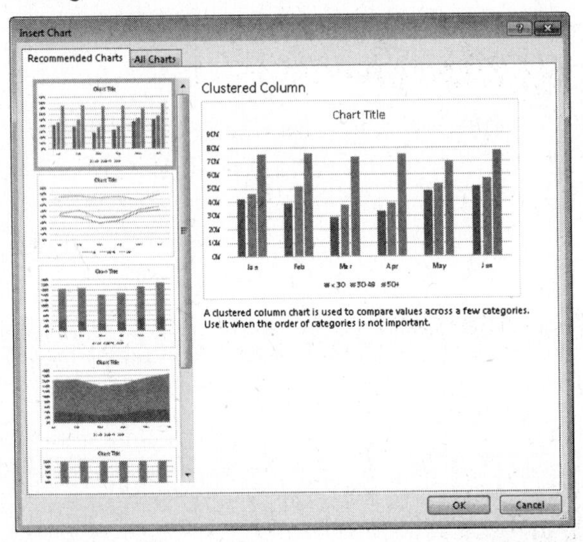

FIGURE 19.6

A clustered column chart created from the data in the table.

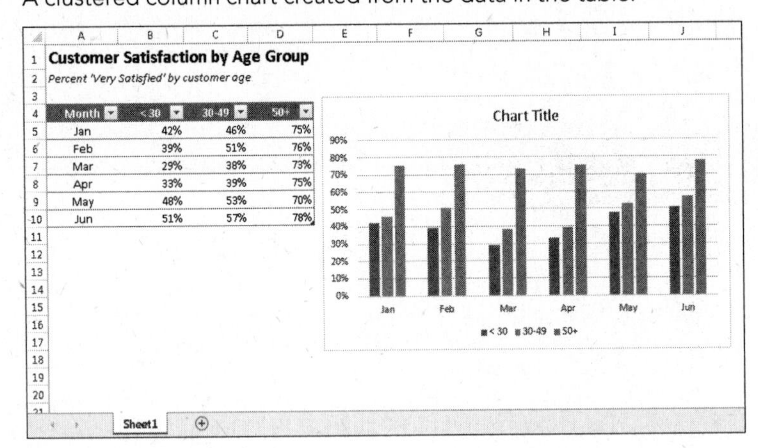

Customer Satisfaction by Age Group

Percent 'Very Satisfied' by customer age

Month	< 30	30-49	50+
Jan	42%	46%	75%
Feb	39%	51%	76%
Mar	29%	38%	73%
Apr	33%	39%	75%
May	48%	53%	70%
Jun	51%	57%	78%

Experimenting with different styles

The chart looks pretty good, but it's just one of several predefined styles for a clustered column chart.

To see some other looks for the chart, select the chart (click it) and check out a few other predefined styles in the Chart Tools ➪ Design ➪ Chart Styles group. Just hover your mouse over a thumbnail image, and your chart temporarily takes on the new style. If you find a style you like, click the thumbnail to make it permanent. Notice that this Ribbon group also includes a Change Colors tool, which lets you quickly modify the colors used in the chart.

New Feature

You can also access the chart styles and colors by using the Chart Styles icon, which appears to the right of the chart when you select it (the icon displays a paintbrush). The choices are presented in a scrollable list. The choices are exactly the same as those displayed in the Chart Tools ➪ Design ➪ Chart Styles group.

Experimenting with different layouts

Every chart type has a set of layouts that you can choose from. A layout contains additional chart elements, such as a title, data labels, axes, and so on. You can add your own elements to your chart, but often, using a predefined layout saves time. Even if the layout isn't exactly what you want, it may be close enough that you need to make only a few adjustments.

To try a different predefined layout, select the chart and choose Chart Tools ➪ Design ➪ Chart Layouts ➪ Quick Layout.

To manually add or remove elements from the chart, click the Chart Elements icon, which appears to the right of the chart and has an image of a plus sign. Note that each item expands to provide more options, such as the location of the element within the chart. The Chart Elements icon contains the same option as the Chart Tools ➪ Design ➪ Chart Layouts ➪ Add Chart Element control.

Figure 19.7 shows the chart after selecting a different style and changing the colors. I chose a layout that displays the legend on the right and includes axis titles. I customized the generic title and vertical axis title and deleted the horizontal axis title because it's obvious that it displays months.

Tip

You can link the chart title to a cell so the title always displays the contents of a particular cell. To create a link to a cell, click the chart title, type an equal sign (=), click the cell, and press Enter. Excel displays the link in the Formula bar. In the example, the text in cell A1 is perfect for the chart title.

FIGURE 19.7

The chart, after selecting a different style and layout.

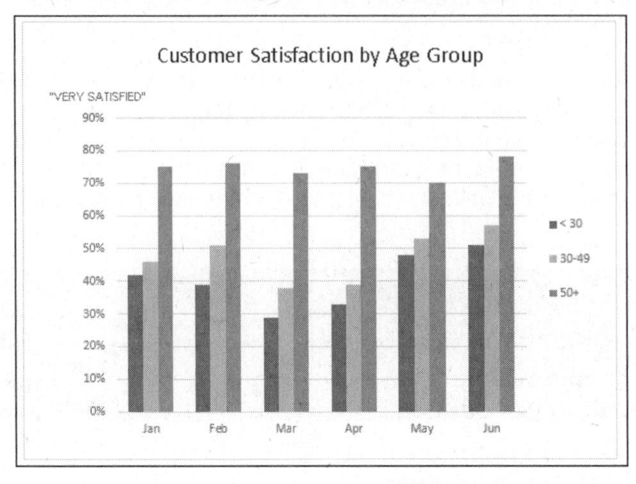

Experiment with the Chart Tools ➪ Design Ribbon to make other changes to the chart. Also try the tools that appear to the right of the chart when you click it. For example, you can remove the gridlines add axis titles, relocate the legend, and so on. Making these changes is easy and fairly intuitive.

Up until now, the changes made to the chart have been strictly cosmetic. The following sections describe how to make more substantial changes to a chart.

Trying another view of the data

The chart, at this point, shows six clusters (months) of three data points in each (age groups). Would the data be easier to understand if you plotted the information in the opposite way?

Try it. Select the chart and then choose Chart Tools ➪ Design ➪ Data ➪ Switch Row/Column. Figure 19.8 shows the result of this change.

NOTE

The orientation of the data has a drastic effect on the look of your chart. Excel has its own rules that it uses to determine the initial data orientation when you create a chart. If Excel's orientation doesn't match your expectation, it's easy enough to change.

The chart, with this new orientation, reveals information that wasn't so apparent in the original version. The < 30 and 30–49 age groups both show a decline in satisfaction for March and April. The 50 + age group didn't have this problem, however.

FIGURE 19.8

The chart, after changing the row and column orientation.

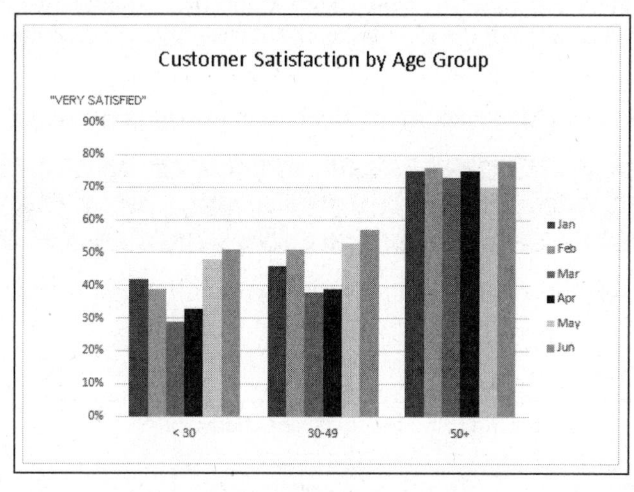

Trying other chart types

Although a clustered column chart seems to work well for this data, there's no harm in checking out some other chart types. Choose Design ➪ Type ➪ Change Chart Type to experiment with other chart types. This command displays the Change Chart Type dialog box, shown in Figure 19.9. The figure shows how the data would look as a line chart.

FIGURE 19.9

Use this dialog box to change the chart type.

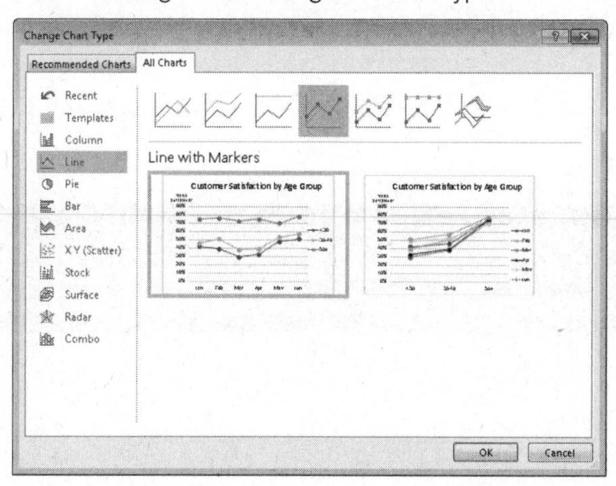

The main chart categories are listed on the left, and the subtypes are shown as a horizontal row of icons. Select an icon and the display shows how the chart will look in both data orientations. When you find a suitable chart type, click OK and Excel changes the chart. Notice that this dialog box has a tab at the top that lets you access Excel's recommended chart types for the data.

If you don't like the result after clicking OK, select Undo from the Quick Access toolbar.

> **TIP**
>
> You can also change the chart type by selecting the chart and using the controls in the Insert ⇨ Charts group.

Figure 19.10 shows a few different chart type options using the customer satisfaction data.

FIGURE 19.10

The customer satisfaction data, displayed using four different chart types.

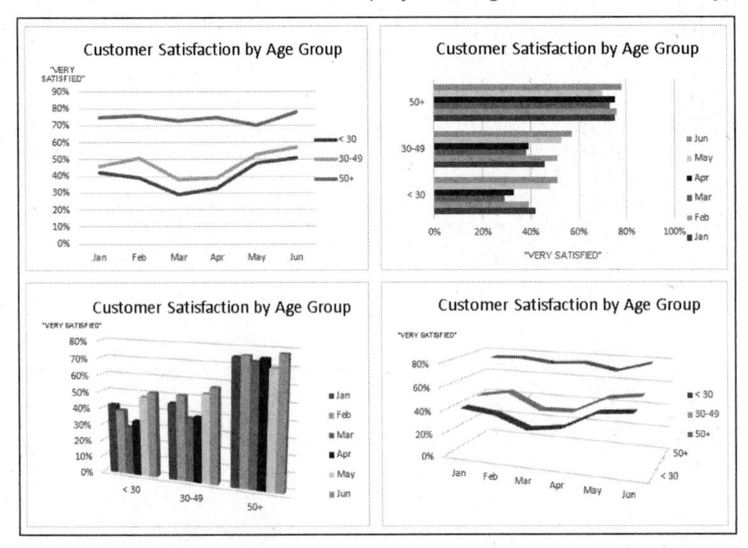

> **TIP**
>
> The styles displayed in the gallery depend on the workbook's theme. When you choose Page Layout ⇨ Themes ⇨ Themes to apply a different theme, you'll have a new selection of chart styles and colors designed for the selected theme.

Working with Charts

This section covers some common chart modifications:

- Resizing and moving charts
- Copying a chart
- Deleting a chart
- Adding chart elements
- Moving and deleting chart elements
- Formatting chart elements
- Printing charts

NOTE
Before you can modify a chart, the chart must be activated. To activate an embedded chart, click it. Doing so activates the chart and selects the element that you click. To activate a chart on a chart sheet, just click its sheet tab.

Resizing a chart

If your chart is an embedded chart, you can freely resize it with your mouse. Click the chart's border. Square handles appear on the chart's corners and edges. When the mouse pointer turns into a double arrow, click and drag to resize the chart.

When a chart is selected, choose Chart Tools ➪ Format ➪ Size and use the two controls to adjust the height and width of the chart. Use the spinners or type the dimensions directly into the Height and Width controls.

Moving a chart

To move an embedded chart to a different location on a worksheet, click the chart and drag one of its borders. You can use standard cut-and-paste techniques to move an embedded chart. In fact, this is the only way to move a chart from one worksheet to another. Select the chart and choose Home ➪ Clipboard ➪ Cut (or press Ctrl + X). Then activate a cell near the desired location and choose Home ➪ Clipboard ➪ Paste (or press Ctrl + V). The new location can be in a different worksheet or even in a different workbook. If you paste the chart to a different workbook, the chart will be linked to the data in the original workbook.

To move an embedded chart to a chart sheet (or vice versa), select the chart and choose Chart Tools ➪ Design ➪ Location ➪ Move Chart; the Move Chart dialog box appears. Choose New Sheet and provide a name for the chart sheet (or use the Excel proposed name).

Copying a chart

To make an exact copy of an embedded chart on the same worksheet, click the chart's border, press and hold the Ctrl key, and drag. Release the mouse button, and a new copy of the chart is created.

To make a copy of a chart sheet, use the same procedure, but drag the chart sheet's tab.

You also can use standard copy-and-paste techniques to copy a chart. Select the chart (an embedded chart or a chart sheet) and choose Home ➪ Clipboard ➪ Copy (or press Ctrl + C). Then activate a cell near the desired location and choose Home ➪ Clipboard ➪ Paste (or press Ctrl + V). The new location can be in a different worksheet or even in a different workbook. If you paste the chart to a different workbook, it will be linked to the data in the original workbook.

Deleting a chart

To delete an embedded chart, press Ctrl and click the chart (to select the chart as an object). Then press Delete. When the Ctrl key is pressed, you can select multiple charts, and then delete them all with a single press of the Delete key.

To delete a chart sheet, right-click its sheet tab and choose Delete from the shortcut menu. To delete multiple chart sheets, select them by pressing Ctrl while you click the sheet tabs.

Adding chart elements

To add new elements to a chart (such as a title, legend, data labels, or gridlines), activate the chart and use the controls in the Chart Elements icon, which appears to the right of the chart. Note that each item expands to display additional options.

You can also use the Add Chart Element control on the Chart Tools ➪ Design ➪ Chart Layouts tab.

Moving and deleting chart elements

Some elements within a chart can be moved: titles, legend, and data labels. To move a chart element, simply click it to select it and then drag its border.

The easiest way to delete a chart element is to select it and then press Delete. You can also use the controls on the Chart Elements icon, which appears to the right of the chart.

Note

A few chart elements consist of multiple objects. For example, the data labels element consists of one label for each data point. To move or delete one data label, click once to select the entire element and then click a second time to select the specific data label. You can then move or delete the single data label.

Exploring the Format Task Pane

The Format task pane can be a bit deceiving. It contains many options that aren't visible, and you sometimes have to do quite a bit of clicking to find the formatting option you're looking for. The accompanying figure shows the task pane for the chart title. The name of the task pane depends on which chart element is selected. The task pane varies quite a bit, depending on which chart element is selected.

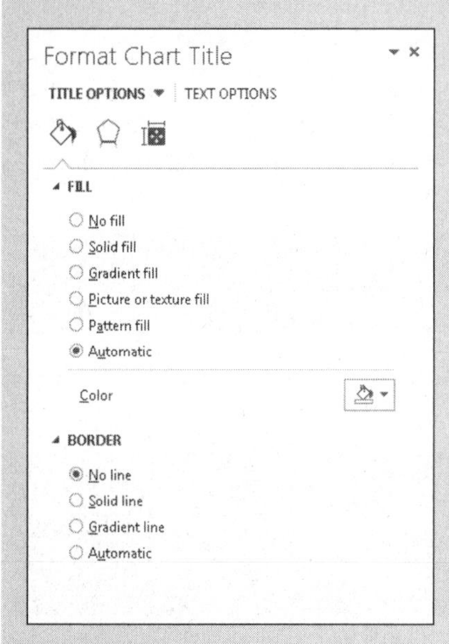

Notice that the task pane displays two tabs along the top: Title Options and Text Options. Click the Title Options tab, and you see three icons: Fill & Line, Effects, and Size & Properties. Each of these icons has its own set of controls, which can be expanded or contracted.

Similarly, the Text Options tab has three icons: Text Fill & Outline, Text Effects, and Textbox. Again, each of these icons has its own set of options.

So, if you want to change the color of the text in a chart's title by using the Format Chart Title task pane, you would follow these steps:

1. **If the Format task pane is displayed, click the chart's title; if the task pane is not displayed, double-click the chart's title.**
2. **In the Format Chart Title task pane, select the Text Options tab.**
3. **Click the Text Fill & Outline icon.**
4. **Expand the Text Fill section.**
5. **Choose a color from the Color control.**

At first, the Format task pane will seem complicated and confusing. But as you get acquainted with it, it gets much easier to use.

Also, keep in mind that many formatting choices are available on the Ribbon. For example, a quicker way to change the text color in a chart title is to select the title, click the Home tab on the Ribbon, and use the Font Color control.

Formatting chart elements

Many users are content to stick with the predefined chart styles and layouts. For more precise customizations, Excel allows you to work with individual chart elements and apply additional formatting. You can use the Ribbon commands for some modifications, but the easiest way to format chart elements is to right-click the element and choose Format <*Element*> from the shortcut menu. The exact command depends on the element you select. For example, if you right-click the chart's title, the shortcut menu command is Format Chart Title.

The Format command displays a task pane with options for the selected element. Changes that you make are displayed immediately. When you select a new chart element, the dialog box changes to display the properties for the newly selected element. You can keep this task pane displayed while you work on the chart. It can be docked along the left or right part of the window or made free floating and sizable.

TIP

If the Format task pane isn't displayed, you can double-click a chart element to display it.

Refer to the "Exploring the Format Task Pane" sidebar for an explanation of how the Format task panes work.

TIP

If you apply formatting to a chart element and decide that it wasn't such a good idea, you can revert to the original formatting for the particular chart style. Right-click the chart element and choose Reset to Match Style from the shortcut menu. To reset the entire chart, select the chart area when you issue the command.

See Chapter 20 for more information about customizing and formatting charts.

Printing charts

Printing embedded charts is nothing special; you print them the same way that you print a worksheet. As long as you include the embedded chart in the range that you want to print, Excel prints the chart as it appears onscreen. When printing a sheet that contains embedded charts, it's a good idea to preview first (or use Page Layout view) to ensure that your charts don't span multiple pages. If you created the chart on a chart sheet, Excel always prints the chart on a page by itself.

TIP

If you select an embedded chart and choose File ➪ Print, Excel prints the chart on a page by itself and does *not* print the worksheet.

If you don't want a particular embedded chart to appear on your printout, access the Format Chart Area task pane and select the Size & Properties icon. Then Expand the Properties section and clear the Print Object check box.

Understanding Chart Types

People who create charts usually do so to make a point or to communicate a specific message. Often, the message is explicitly stated in the chart's title or in a text box within the chart. The chart itself provides visual support.

Choosing the correct chart type is often a key factor in the effectiveness of the message. Therefore, it's often well worth your time to experiment with various chart types to determine which one conveys your message best.

In almost every case, the underlying message in a chart is some type of comparison. Examples of some general types of comparisons include

- **Comparing an item to other items:** A chart may compare sales in each of a company's sales regions.
- **Comparing data over time:** A chart may display sales by month and indicate trends over time.
- **Making relative comparisons:** A common pie chart can depict relative proportions in terms of pie "slices."
- **Comparing data relationships:** An XY chart is ideal for this comparison. For example, you might show the relationship between monthly marketing expenditures and sales.
- **Comparing frequency:** You can use a common histogram, for example, to display the number (or percentage) of students who scored within a particular grade range.
- **Identifying outliers or unusual situations:** If you have thousands of data points, creating a chart may help identify data that isn't representative.

Choosing a chart type

A common question among Excel users is "How do I know which chart type to use for my data?" Unfortunately, this question has no cut-and-dried answer. Perhaps the best answer is a vague one: Use the chart type that gets your message across in the simplest way. A good starting point is Excel's recommended charts. Select your data and choose Insert ➪ Charts ➪ Recommended Charts to see the chart types that Excel suggests. Remember that these suggestions are not always the best choices.

NOTE

In the Ribbon, the Charts group of the Insert tab shows the Recommended Charts button, plus eight other drop-down buttons. Some of these drop-down buttons display multiple chart types. For example, stock, surface, and radar charts are all available from a single drop-down button. Similarly, scatter charts and bubble charts share a single button. Probably the easiest way to choose a particular chart type is to select Insert ➪ Charts ➪ Recommended Charts, which displays the Insert Chart dialog box. Select the All Charts tab and you'll have a concise list of all chart types and sub-chart types.

Figure 19.11 shows the same set of data plotted by using six different chart types. Although all six charts represent the same information (monthly website visitors), they look quite different from one another.

FIGURE 19.11

The same data, plotted by using six chart types.

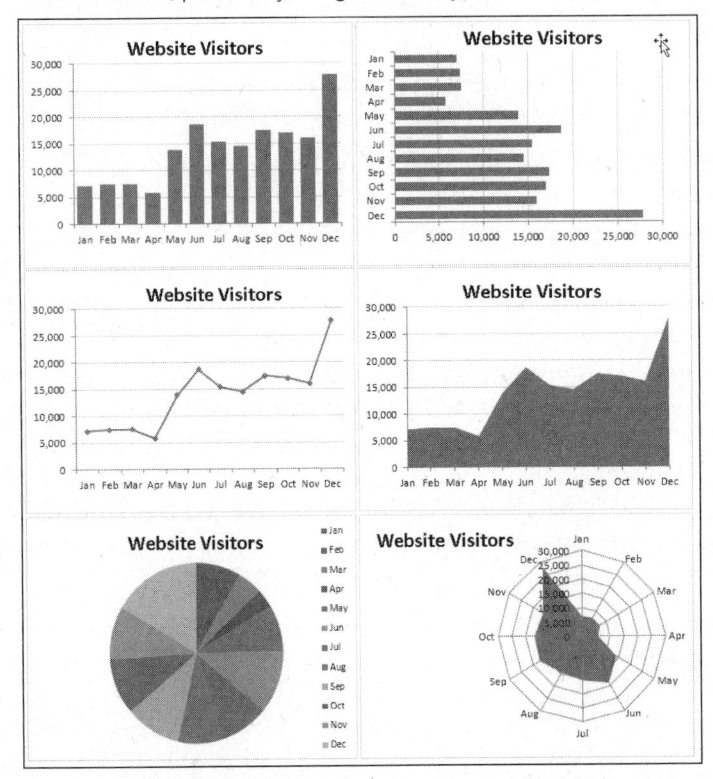

On the Web

This workbook is available this book's website. The file is named `six chart types.xlsx`.

The column chart (upper left) is probably the best choice for this particular set of data because it clearly shows the information for each month in discrete units. The bar chart (upper right) is similar to a column chart, but the axes are swapped. Most people are more accustomed to seeing time-based information extend from left to right rather than from top to bottom, so this isn't the optimal choice.

The line chart (middle left) may not be the best choice because it can imply that the data is continuous — that points exist in between the 12 actual data points. This same argument may be made against using an area chart (middle right).

The pie chart (lower left) is simply too confusing and does nothing to convey the time-based nature of the data. Pie charts are most appropriate for a data series in which you want to emphasize proportions among a relatively small number of data points. If you have too many data points, a pie chart can be impossible to interpret.

The radar chart (lower right) is clearly inappropriate for this data. People aren't accustomed to viewing time-based information in a circular direction!

NOTE

Excel's first recommendation for this data is a line chart, followed by column chart and area chart. This is a case where I disagree with Excel.

Fortunately, changing a chart's type is easy, so you can experiment with various chart types until you find the one that represents your data accurately, clearly, and as simply as possible.

The remainder of this chapter contains more information about the various Excel chart types. The examples and discussion may give you a better handle on determining the most appropriate chart type for your data.

Column charts

Probably the most common chart type is the *column chart*, which displays each data point as a vertical column, the height of which corresponds to the value. The value scale is displayed on the vertical axis, which is usually on the left side of the chart. You can specify any number of data series, and the corresponding data points from each series can be stacked on top of each other. Typically, each data series is depicted in a different color or pattern.

Column charts are often used to compare discrete items, and they can depict the differences between items in a series or items across multiple series. Excel offers seven column-chart subtypes.

ON THE WEB

A workbook that contains the charts in this section is available on this book's website. The file is named `column charts.xlsx`.

Figure 19.12 shows an example of a clustered column chart that depicts monthly sales for two products. From this chart, it's clear that Sprocket sales have always exceeded Widget sales. In addition, Widget sales have been declining over the five-month period, whereas Sprocket sales are increasing.

FIGURE 19.12

This clustered column chart compares monthly sales for two products.

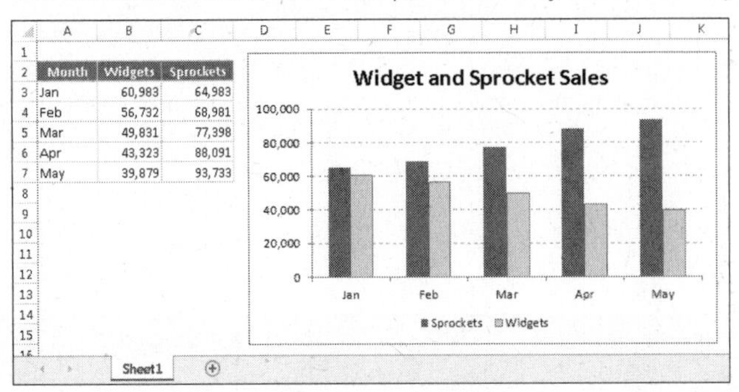

The same data, in the form of a stacked column chart, is shown in Figure 19.13. This chart has the added advantage of depicting the combined sales over time. It shows that total sales have remained fairly steady each month, but the relative proportions of the two products have changed.

FIGURE 19.13

This stacked column chart displays sales by product and depicts the total sales.

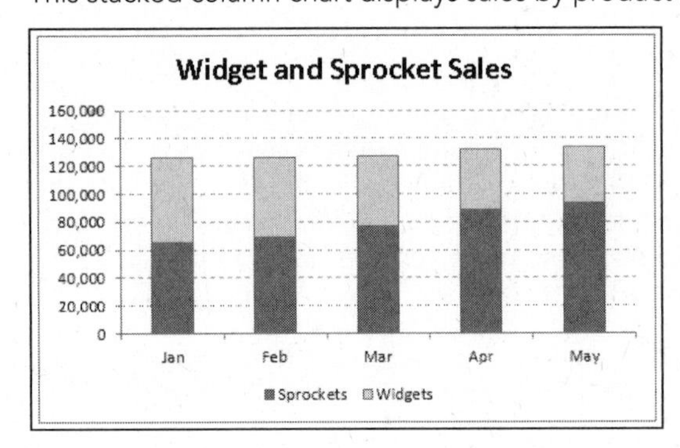

Figure 19.14 shows the same sales data plotted as a 100% stacked column chart. This chart type shows the relative contribution of each product by month. Notice that the vertical axis displays percentage values, not sales amounts. This chart provides no information about the actual sales volumes, but such information could be provided using data labels. This type of chart is often a good alternative to using several pie charts. Instead of using a pie to show the relative sales volume in each year, the chart uses a column for each year.

FIGURE 19.14

This 100% stacked column chart displays monthly sales as a percentage.

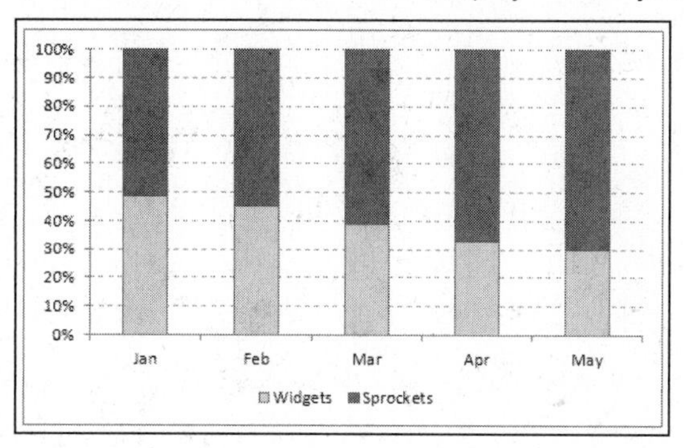

The data is plotted with a 3-D clustered column chart in Figure 19.15. The name is a bit deceptive, because the chart uses only two dimensions, not three. Many people use this type of chart because it has more visual pizzazz. Compare this chart with a "true" 3-D column chart (which has a second category axis), shown in Figure 19.16. This type of chart may be appealing visually, but precise comparisons are difficult because of the distorted perspective view.

FIGURE 19.15

A 3-D column chart.

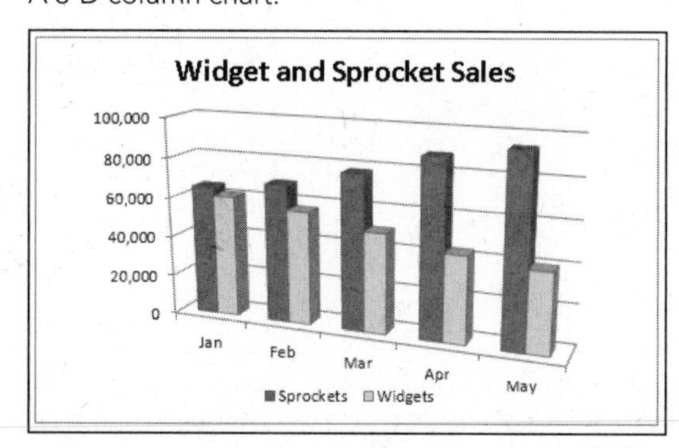

For the 3-D columns, you can choose a different column shape in the Format Data Series dialog box. Excel offers variations such as cylinder, cone, and pyramids.

FIGURE 19.16

A true 3-D column chart.

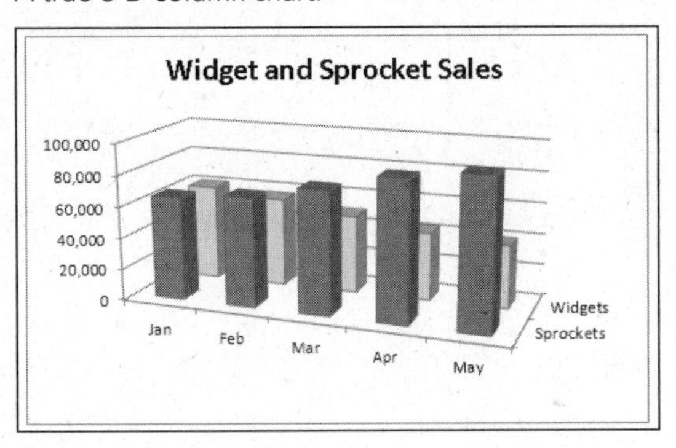

Bar charts

A *bar chart* is essentially a column chart that has been rotated 90 degrees clockwise. One distinct advantage to using a bar chart is that the category labels may be easier to read. Figure 19.17 shows a bar chart that displays a value for each of ten survey items. The category labels are lengthy, and displaying them legibly with a column chart would be difficult. Excel offers six bar chart subtypes.

FIGURE 19.17

If you have lengthy category labels, a bar chart may be a good choice.

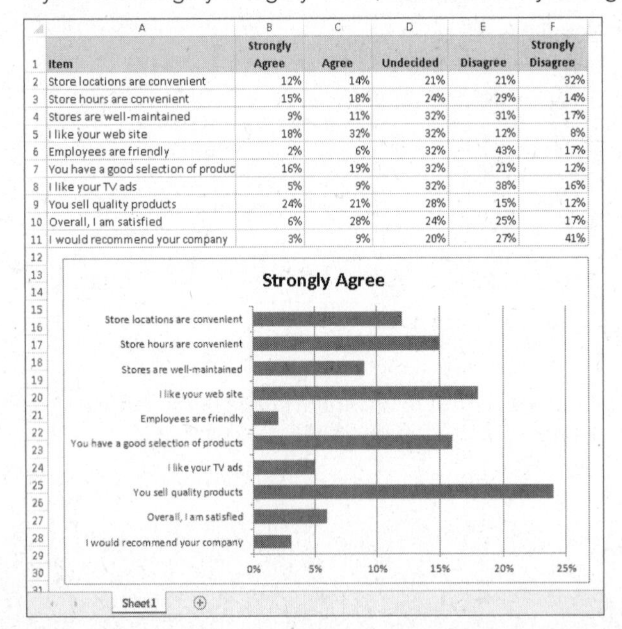

Item	Strongly Agree	Agree	Undecided	Disagree	Strongly Disagree
Store locations are convenient	12%	14%	21%	21%	32%
Store hours are convenient	15%	18%	24%	29%	14%
Stores are well-maintained	9%	11%	32%	31%	17%
I like your web site	18%	32%	32%	12%	8%
Employees are friendly	2%	6%	32%	43%	17%
You have a good selection of produc	16%	19%	32%	21%	12%
I like your TV ads	5%	9%	32%	38%	16%
You sell quality products	24%	21%	28%	15%	12%
Overall, I am satisfied	6%	28%	24%	25%	17%
I would recommend your company	3%	9%	20%	27%	41%

On the Web

A workbook that contains the chart in this section is available on this book's website. The file is named `bar charts.xlsx`.

Note

Unlike a column chart, no subtype displays multiple series along a third axis. (That is, Excel does not provide a 3-D Bar Chart subtype.) You can add a 3-D look to a bar chart, but it will be limited to two axes.

You can include any number of data series in a bar chart. In addition, the bars can be "stacked" from left to right.

Line charts

Line charts are often used to plot continuous data and are useful for identifying trends. For example, plotting daily sales as a line chart may enable you to identify sales fluctuations over time. Normally, the category axis for a line chart displays equal intervals. Excel supports seven line chart subtypes.

See Figure 19.18 for an example of a line chart that depicts 53 years of monthly data (636 data points). Although the data varies quite a bit on a monthly basis, the chart clearly depicts the cycles.

FIGURE 19.18

A line chart often can help you spot trends in your data.

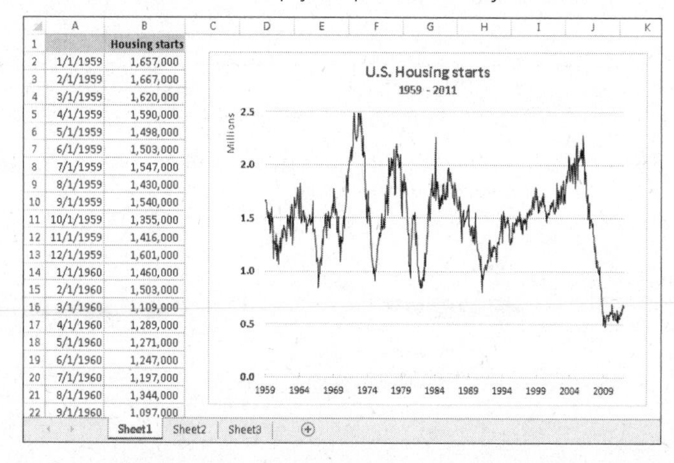

On the Web

A workbook that contains the charts in this section is available on this book's website. The file is named `line charts.xlsx`.

A line chart can use any number of data series, and you distinguish the lines by using different colors, line styles, or markers. Figure 19.19 shows a line chart that has three series. The series are distinguished by markers (circles, squares, and triangles) and different line colors. When the chart is printed on a non-color printer, the markers are the only way to identify the lines.

FIGURE 19.19

This line chart displays three series.

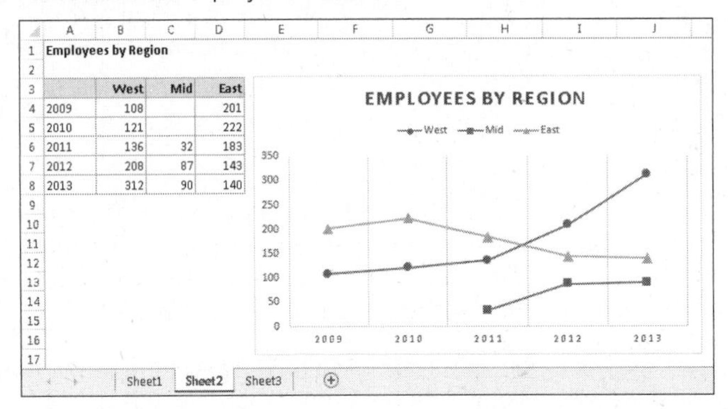

The final line chart example, shown in Figure 19.20, is a 3-D line chart. Although it has a nice visual appeal, it's certainly not the clearest way to present the data. In fact, it's fairly worthless.

FIGURE 19.20

This 3-D line chart does not present the data very well.

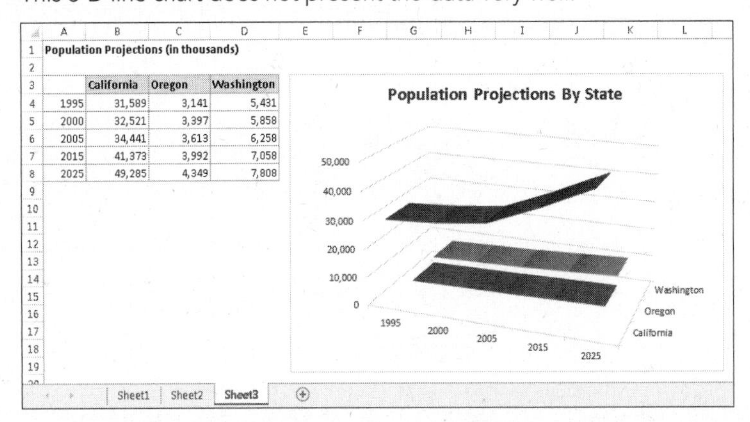

Pie charts

A *pie chart* is useful when you want to show relative proportions or contributions to a whole. A pie chart uses only one data series. Pie charts are most effective with a small number of data points. Generally, a pie chart should use no more than five or six data points (or slices). A pie chart with too many data points can be very difficult to interpret.

CAUTION

The values used in a pie chart must all be positive numbers. If you create a pie chart that uses one or more negative values, the negative values will be converted to positive values — which is probably not what you intended!

You can "explode" one or more slices of a pie chart for emphasis (see Figure 19.21). Activate the chart and click any pie slice to select the entire pie. Then click the slice that you want to explode and drag it away from the center.

FIGURE 19.21

A pie chart with one slice exploded.

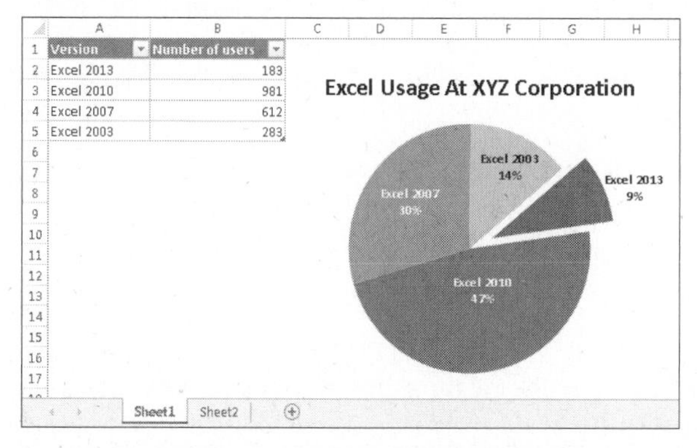

ON THE WEB

A workbook that contains the charts in this section is available on this book's website. The file is named `pie charts.xlsx`.

The pie of pie and bar of pie chart types enable you to display a secondary chart that provides more detail for one of the pie slices. Figure 19.22 shows an example of a bar of pie chart. The pie chart shows the breakdown of four expense categories: Rent, Supplies, Miscellaneous, and Salary. The secondary bar chart provides an additional regional breakdown of the Salary category.

FIGURE 19.22

A bar of pie chart that shows detail for one of the pie slices.

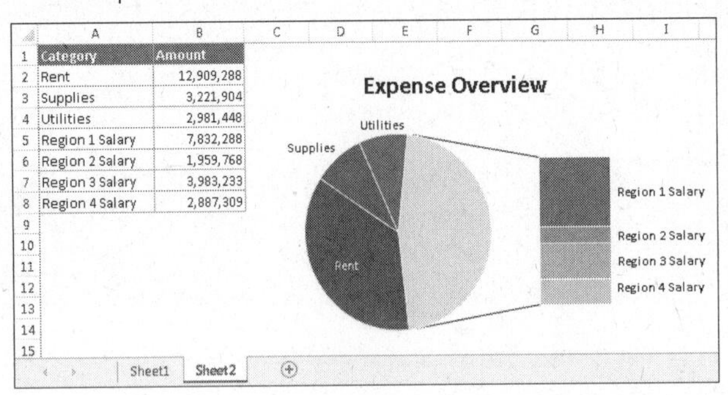

The data used in the chart resides in A2:B8. When the chart was created, Excel made a guess as to which categories belong to the secondary chart. In this case, the guess was to use the last three data points for the secondary chart — and the guess was incorrect.

To correct the chart, right-click any of the pie slices and choose Format Data Series. In the Format Data Series task pane, select the Series Options icon and make the changes. In this example, I chose Split Series by Position and specified that the second plot contains four values in the series.

XY (scatter) charts

Another common chart type is an *XY chart* (also known as scattergrams or scatter plots). An XY chart differs from most other chart types in that both axes display values. (An XY chart has no category axis.)

This type of chart often is used to show the relationship between two variables. Figure 19.23 shows an example of an XY chart that plots the relationship between sales calls made (horizontal axis) and sales (vertical axis). Each point in the chart represents one month. The chart shows that these two variables are positively related: Months in which more calls were made typically had higher sales volumes.

ON THE WEB

A workbook that contains the charts in this section is available on this book's website. The file is named `xy charts.xlsx`.

NOTE

Although these data points correspond to time, the chart doesn't convey any time-related information. In other words, the data points are plotted based only on their two values.

FIGURE 19.23

An XY chart shows the relationship between two variables.

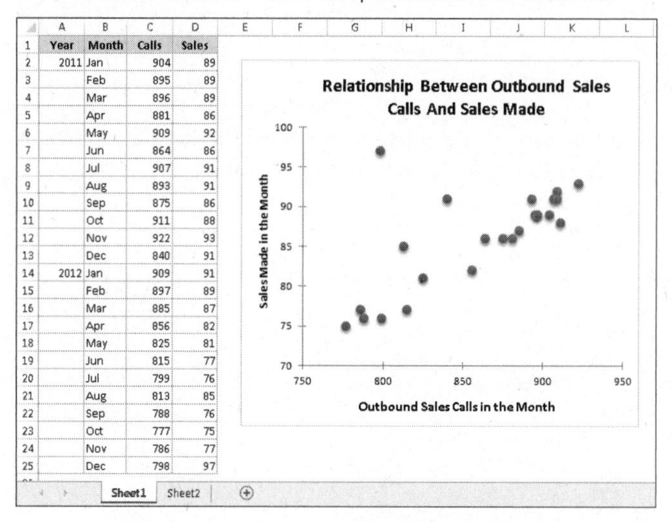

Year	Month	Calls	Sales
2011	Jan	904	89
	Feb	895	89
	Mar	896	89
	Apr	881	86
	May	909	92
	Jun	864	86
	Jul	907	91
	Aug	893	91
	Sep	875	86
	Oct	911	88
	Nov	922	93
	Dec	840	91
2012	Jan	909	91
	Feb	897	89
	Mar	885	87
	Apr	856	82
	May	825	81
	Jun	815	77
	Jul	799	76
	Aug	813	85
	Sep	788	76
	Oct	777	75
	Nov	786	77
	Dec	798	97

Figure 19.24 shows another XY chart, this one with lines that connect the XY points. This chart plots a hypocycloid curve with 200 data points. It's set up with three parameters. Change any of the parameters, and you'll get a completely different curve. This is a very minimalist chart. I deleted all the chart elements except the data series itself.

FIGURE 19.24

A hypocycloid curve, plotted as an XY chart.

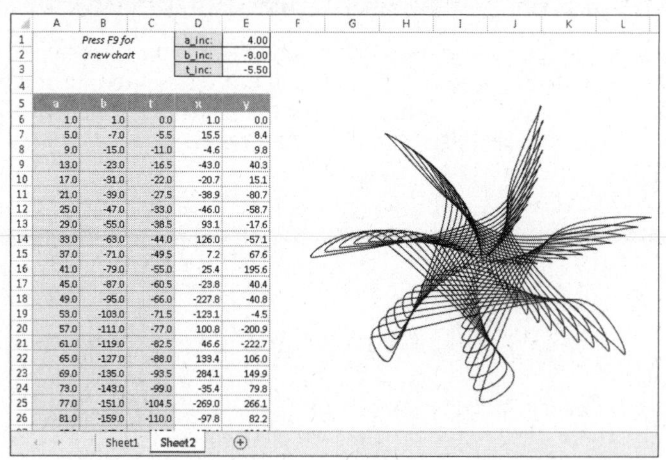

Press F9 for a new chart

a_inc:	4.00
b_inc:	-8.00
t_inc:	-5.50

a	b	t	x	y
1.0	1.0	0.0	1.0	0.0
5.0	-7.0	-5.5	15.5	8.4
9.0	-15.0	-11.0	-4.6	9.8
13.0	-23.0	-16.5	-43.0	40.3
17.0	-31.0	-22.0	-20.7	15.1
21.0	-39.0	-27.5	-38.9	-80.7
25.0	-47.0	-33.0	-46.0	-58.7
29.0	-55.0	-38.5	93.1	-17.6
33.0	-63.0	-44.0	126.0	-57.1
37.0	-71.0	-49.5	7.2	67.6
41.0	-79.0	-55.0	25.4	195.6
45.0	-87.0	-60.5	-23.8	40.4
49.0	-95.0	-66.0	-227.8	-40.8
53.0	-103.0	-71.5	-123.1	-4.5
57.0	-111.0	-77.0	100.8	-200.9
61.0	-119.0	-82.5	46.6	-222.7
65.0	-127.0	-88.0	133.4	106.0
69.0	-135.0	-93.5	284.1	149.9
73.0	-143.0	-99.0	-35.4	79.8
77.0	-151.0	-104.5	-269.0	266.1
81.0	-159.0	-110.0	-97.8	82.2

If this type of design looks familiar, it's because a hypocycloid curve is the basis for a popular children's drawing toy.

Area charts

Think of an *area chart* as a line chart in which the area below the line has been colored in. Figure 19.25 shows an example of a stacked area chart. Stacking the data series enables you to clearly see the total, plus the contribution by each series.

FIGURE 19.25

A stacked area chart.

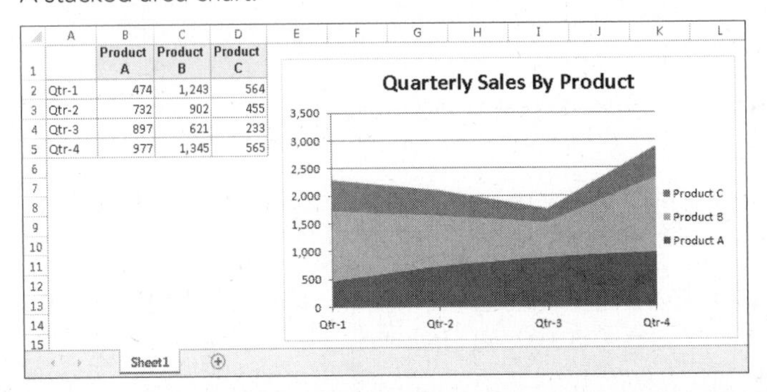

	Product A	Product B	Product C
Qtr-1	474	1,243	564
Qtr-2	732	902	455
Qtr-3	897	621	233
Qtr-4	977	1,345	565

> **ON THE WEB**
> A workbook that contains the charts in this section is available on this book's website. The file is named `area charts.xlsx`.

Figure 19.26 shows the same data, plotted as a 3-D area chart. As you can see, it's not an example of an effective chart. The data for products B and C are obscured. In some cases, the problem can be resolved by rotating the chart or using transparency. But usually the best way to salvage a chart like this is to select a new chart type.

FIGURE 19.26

This 3-D area chart is not a good choice.

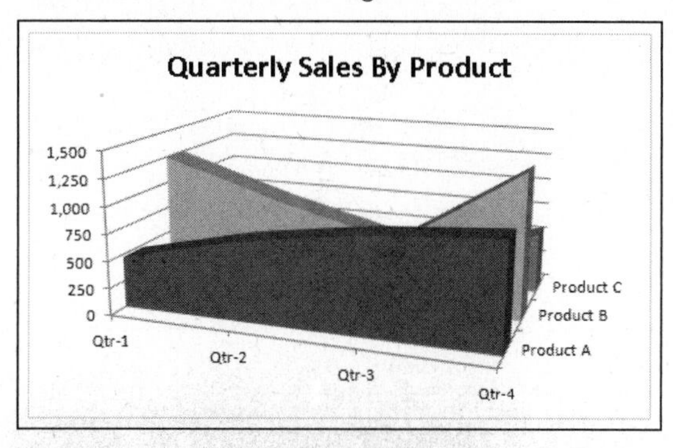

Radar charts

You may not be familiar with this type of chart. A *radar chart* is a specialized chart that has a separate axis for each category, and the axes extend outward from the center of the chart. The value of each data point is plotted on the corresponding axis.

Figure 19.27 shows an example of a radar chart. This chart plots two data series across 12 categories (months) and shows the seasonal demand for snow skis versus water skis. Note that the water-ski series partially obscures the snow-ski series.

FIGURE 19.27

Plotting ski sales using a radar chart with 12 categories and two series.

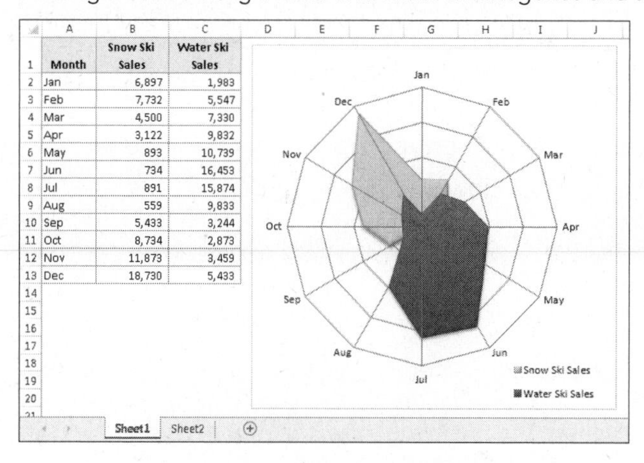

Month	Snow Ski Sales	Water Ski Sales
Jan	6,897	1,983
Feb	7,732	5,547
Mar	4,500	7,330
Apr	3,122	9,832
May	893	10,739
Jun	734	16,453
Jul	891	15,874
Aug	559	9,833
Sep	5,433	3,244
Oct	8,734	2,873
Nov	11,873	3,459
Dec	18,730	5,433

On the Web

A workbook that contains the charts in this section is available at this book's website. The file is named `radar charts.xlsx`.

Using a radar chart to show seasonal sales may be an interesting approach, but it's certainly not the best chart type. As you can see in Figure 19.28, a stacked bar chart shows the information much more clearly.

FIGURE 19.28

A stacked bar chart is a better choice for the ski sales data.

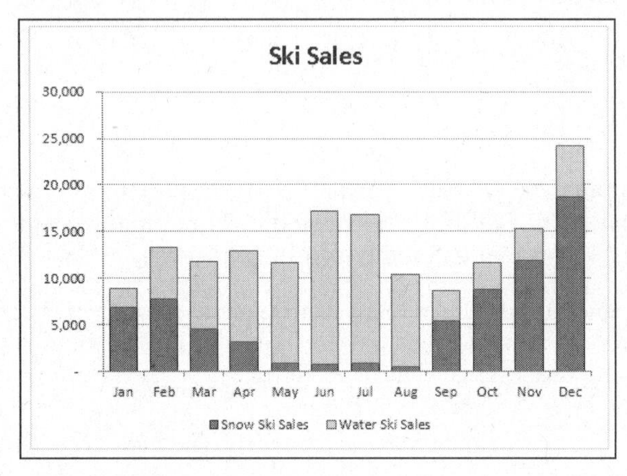

A more appropriate use for radar charts is shown in Figure 19.29. These four charts each plot a color. More precisely, each chart shows the RGB components (the contributions of red, green, and blue) that make up a color. Each chart has one series and three categories. The categories extend from 0 to 255.

Note

If you view the charts in color, you'll see that they actually depict the color that they describe. The data series colors were applied manually.

Surface charts

Surface charts display two or more data series on a surface. As Figure 19.30 shows, these charts can be quite interesting. Unlike other charts, Excel uses color to distinguish values, not to distinguish the data series. The number of colors used is determined by the major unit scale setting for the value axis. Each color corresponds to one major unit.

FIGURE 19.29

These radar charts depict the red, green, and blue contributions for each of four colors.

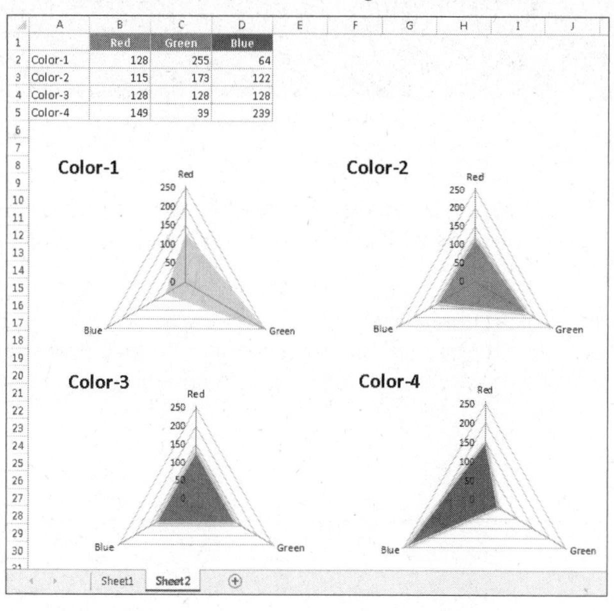

	Red	Green	Blue
Color-1	128	255	64
Color-2	115	173	122
Color-3	128	128	128
Color-4	149	39	239

FIGURE 19.30

A surface chart.

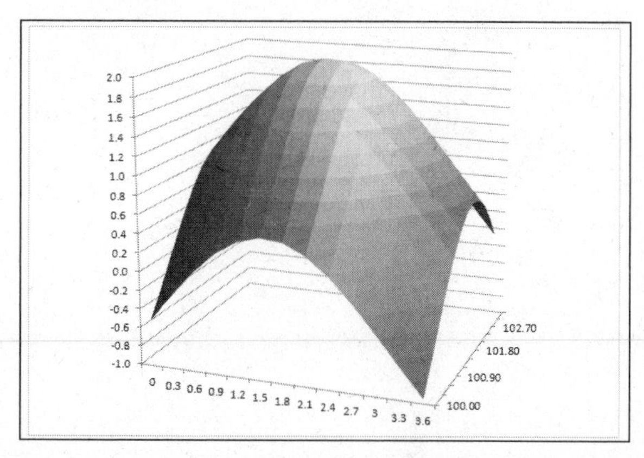

ON THE WEB

A workbook that contains the charts in this section is available on this book's website. The file is named `surface charts.xlsx`.

> **NOTE**
>
> A surface chart does not plot 3-D data points. The series axis for a surface chart, as with all other 3-D charts, is a category axis – not a value axis. In other words, if you have data that is represented by *x*, *y*, and *z* coordinates, it can't be plotted accurately on a surface chart unless the *x* and *y* values are equally spaced.

Bubble charts

Think of a *bubble chart* as an XY chart that can display an additional data series, which is represented by the size of the bubbles. As with an XY chart, both axes are value axes (there is no category axis).

Figure 19.31 shows an example of a bubble chart that depicts the results of a weight-loss program. The horizontal value axis represents the original weight, the vertical value axis shows the number of weeks in the program, and the size of the bubbles represents the amount of weight lost.

FIGURE 19.31

A bubble chart.

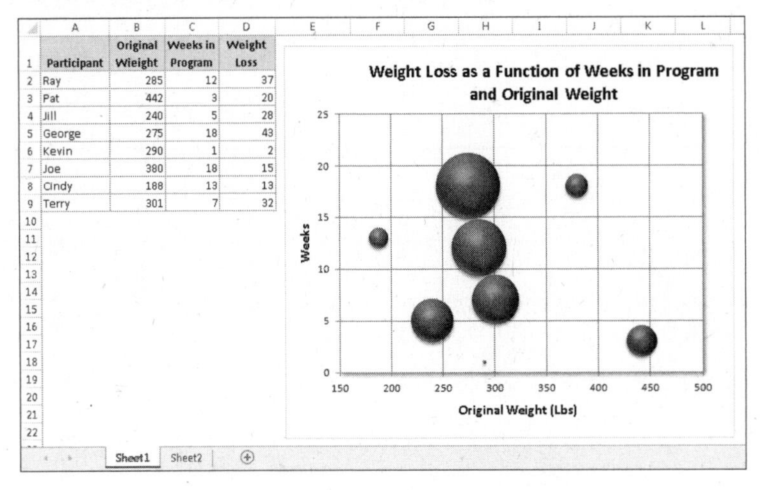

Participant	Original Wieight	Weeks in Program	Weight Loss
Ray	285	12	37
Pat	442	3	20
Jill	240	5	28
George	275	18	43
Kevin	290	1	2
Joe	380	18	15
Cindy	188	13	13
Terry	301	7	32

On the Web

A workbook that contains the charts in this section is available on this book's website. The file is named `bubble charts.xlsx`.

Figure 19.32 shows another bubble chart, made up of nine series that represent mouse face parts. The size and position of each bubble required some experimentation.

FIGURE 19.32

This bubble chart depicts a mouse.

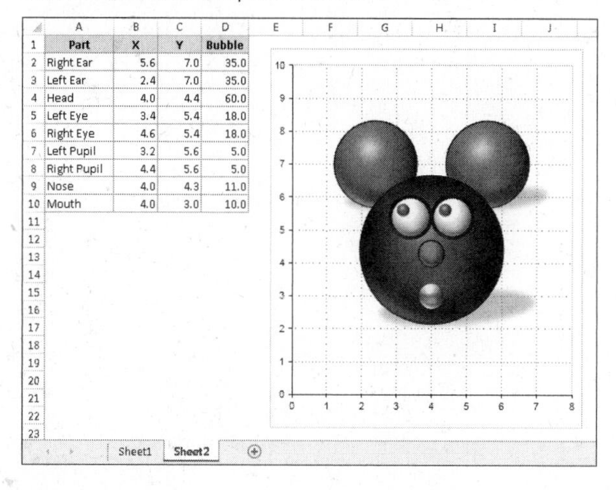

Part	X	Y	Bubble
Right Ear	5.6	7.0	35.0
Left Ear	2.4	7.0	35.0
Head	4.0	4.4	60.0
Left Eye	3.4	5.4	18.0
Right Eye	4.6	5.4	18.0
Left Pupil	3.2	5.6	5.0
Right Pupil	4.4	5.6	5.0
Nose	4.0	4.3	11.0
Mouth	4.0	3.0	10.0

Stock charts

Stock charts are most useful for displaying stock-market information. These charts require three to five data series, depending on the subtype.

Figure 19.33 shows an example of each of the four stock chart types. The two charts on the bottom display the trade volume and use two value axes. The daily volume, represented by columns, uses the axis on the left. The *up-bars,* sometimes referred to as *candlesticks,* are the vertical lines that depict the difference between the opening and closing price. A black up-bar indicates that the closing price was lower than the opening price.

FIGURE 19.33

The four stock chart subtypes.

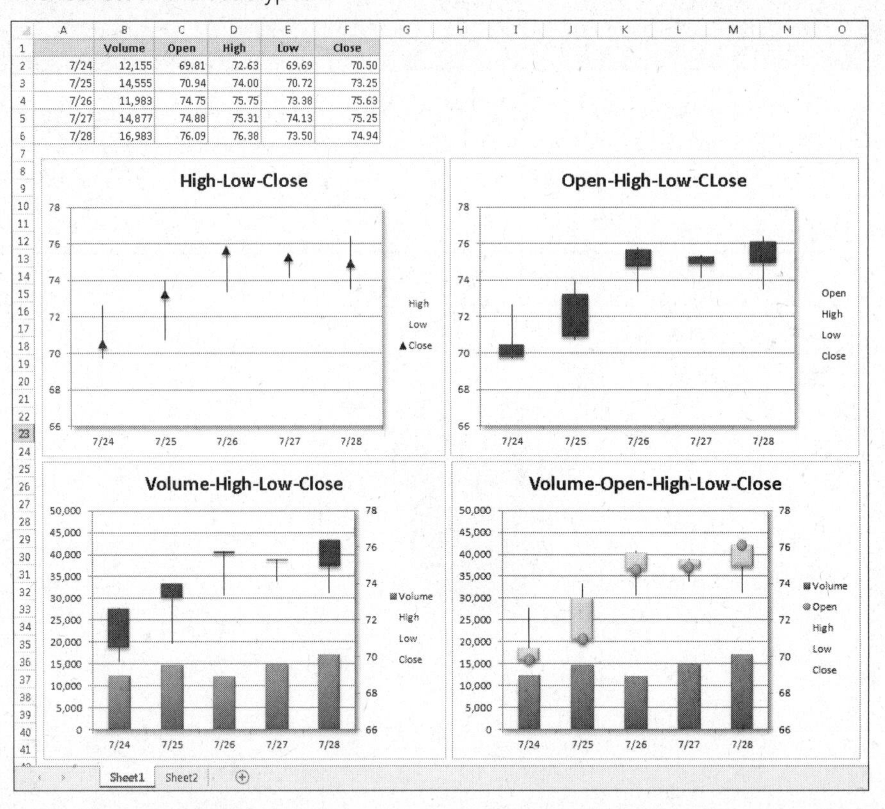

On the Web

A workbook that contains the charts in this section is available on this book's website. The file is named `stock charts.xlsx`.

Stock charts aren't just for stock price data. Figure 19.34 shows a stock chart that depicts the high, low, and average temperatures for each day in May. This is a high-low-close chart.

FIGURE 19.34

Plotting temperature data with a stock chart.

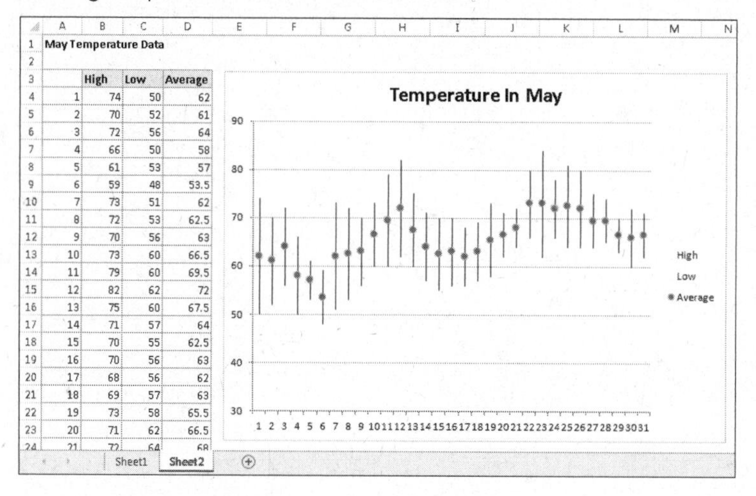

Learning More

This chapter introduced Excel charts, including examples of the types of charts that you can create. For many people, the information in this chapter is sufficient to create a wide variety of charts.

Those who require control over every aspect of their charts can find the information they need in the next chapter. It picks up where this one leaves off and covers the details involved in creating the perfect chart.

CHAPTER 20

Learning Advanced Charting

IN THIS CHAPTER

- Understanding chart customization
- Changing basic chart elements
- Working with data series
- Discovering some chart-making tricks

Excel makes creating a basic chart very easy. Select your data, choose a chart type, and you're finished. You may take a few extra seconds and select one of the prebuilt chart styles and maybe even select one of the chart layouts. But if your goal is to create the most effective chart possible, you probably want to take advantage of the additional customization techniques available in Excel.

Customizing a chart involves changing its appearance, as well as possibly adding new elements to it. These changes can be purely cosmetic (such as changing colors, modifying line widths, or adding a shadow) or quite substantial (say, changing the axis scales or adding a second value axis). Chart elements that you might add include such features as a data table, a trend line, or error bars.

The preceding chapter introduced charting in Excel and described how to create basic charts. This chapter takes the topic to the next level. You learn how to customize your charts to the maximum so that they look exactly as you want. You also pick up some slick charting tricks that will make your charts even more impressive.

Selecting Chart Elements

Modifying a chart is similar to everything else you do in Excel: First, you make a selection (in this case, select a chart element), and then you issue a command to do something with the selection.

You can select only one chart element (or one group of chart elements) at a time. For example, if you want to change the font for two axis labels, you must work on each set of axis labels separately.

Excel provides three ways, described in the following sections, to select a particular chart element:

- Mouse
- Keyboard
- Chart Elements control

Selecting with the mouse

To select a chart element with your mouse, just click the element. The chart element appears with small circles at the corners.

TIP

Some chart elements are a bit tricky to select. To ensure that you select the chart element that you intended to select, view the Chart Element control, located in the Chart Tools ➪ Format ➪ Current Selection group of the Ribbon (see Figure 20.1). Or, if the Format task pane is displayed, you can identify the selected chart element by the title of the task pane. Press Ctrl+1 to display the Format task pane.

FIGURE 20.1

The Chart Element control (in the upper-left corner) displays the name of the selected chart element. In this example, the Legend is selected.

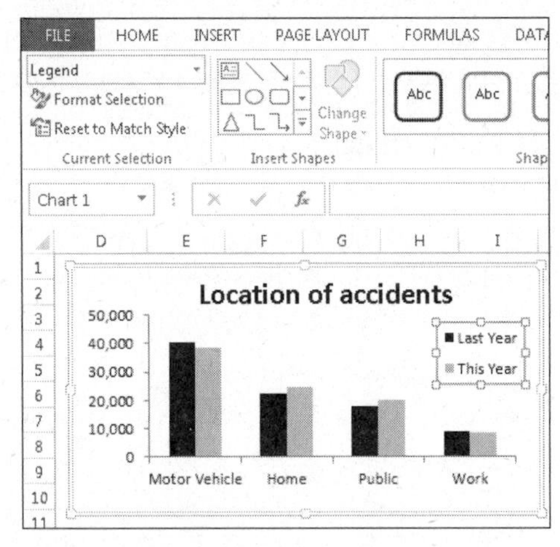

When you move the mouse over a chart, a small *chart tip* displays the name of the chart element under the mouse pointer. When the mouse pointer is over a data point, the chart tip also displays the value of the data point.

TIP

If you find these chart tips annoying, you can turn them off. Choose File ➪ Options and select the Advanced tab in the Excel Options dialog box. Locate the Chart section and clear either or both the Show Chart Element Names on Hover or the Show Data Point Values on Hover check boxes.

Some chart elements (such as a series, a legend, and data labels) consist of multiple items. For example, a chart series element is made up of individual data points. To select a particular data point, click twice: First, click the series to select it, and then click the specific element within the series (for example, a column or a line chart marker). Selecting the element enables you to apply formatting to only a particular data point in a series.

You may find that some chart elements are difficult to select with the mouse. If you rely on the mouse for selecting a chart element, you may have to click it several times before the desired element is actually selected. Fortunately, Excel provides other ways to select a chart element, and it's worth your while to be familiar with them. Keep reading to see how.

Selecting with the keyboard

When a chart is active, you can use the up-arrow and down-arrow navigation keys on your keyboard to cycle among the chart's elements. Again, keep your eye on the Chart Elements control to ensure that the selected chart element is what you think it is.

- **When a chart series is selected:** Use the left-arrow and right-arrow keys to select an individual item within the series.
- **When a set of data labels is selected:** You can select a specific data label by using the left-arrow or right-arrow key.
- **When a legend is selected:** Select individual elements within the legend by using the left-arrow or right-arrow keys.

Selecting with the Chart Element control

The Chart Element control is located in the Chart Tools ➪ Format ➪ Current Selection group. This control displays the name of the currently selected chart element. It's a drop-down control, and you can also use it to select a particular element in the active chart (see Figure 20.2).

The Chart Element control also appears in the Mini toolbar, which is displayed when you right-click a chart element.

The Chart Element control enables you to select only the top-level elements in the chart. To select an individual data point within a series, for example, you need to select the series and then use the navigation keys (or your mouse) to select the desired data point.

FIGURE 20.2

Using the Chart Element drop-down control to select a chart element — in this case, the Vertical Axis Major Gridlines.

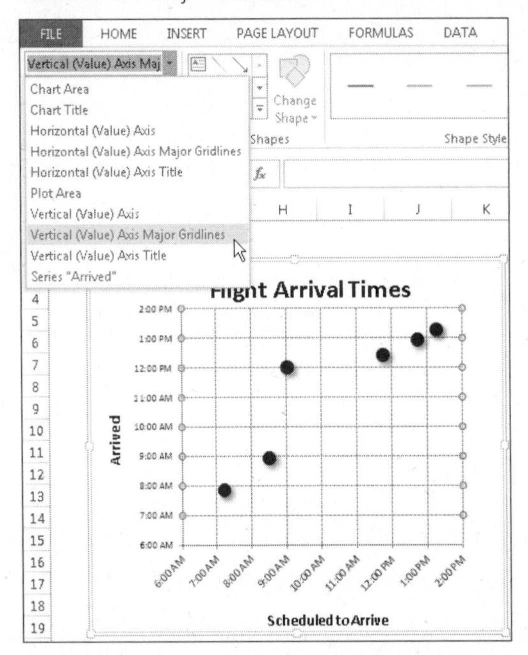

NOTE

When a single data point is selected, the Chart Element control *will* display the name of the selected element even though it's not actually available for selection from the drop-down list.

TIP

If you do a lot of work with charts, you may want to add the Chart Element control to your Quick Access toolbar. That way, it will always be visible regardless of which Ribbon tab is showing. To add the control to your Quick Access toolbar, right-click the down arrow in the control and choose Add to Quick Access Toolbar.

User Interface Choices for Modifying Chart Elements

You have four main ways of working with chart elements: the Format task pane, the icons that display to the right of the chart, the Ribbon, and the Mini toolbar.

Using the Format task pane

When a chart element is selected, use the element's Format task pane to format or set options for the element. Each chart element has a unique Format task pane that contains controls specific to the element (although many Format task panes have controls in common). To access the Format task pane, use any of these methods:

- Double-click the chart element.
- Right-click the chart element and then choose Format *xxxx* from the shortcut menu (where *xxxx* is the name of the element).
- Select a chart element and then choose Chart Tools ➪ Format ➪ Current Selection ➪ Format Selection.
- Select a chart element and press Ctrl + 1.

Any of these actions displays the Format task pane from which you can make many changes to the selected chart element. For example, Figure 20.3 shows the task pane that appears when a chart's value axis is selected. The task pane is free floating, not docked. Note that a scrollbar is displayed, which means that all the options can't fit in the vertical space for the task pane.

FIGURE 20.3

Use the Format task pane to set the properties of a selected chart element — in this case, the chart's value axis.

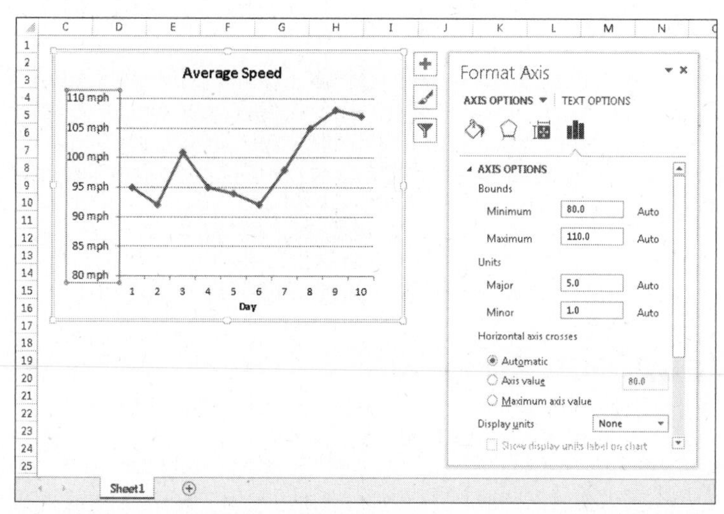

New Feature

The Format task pane is a new feature in Excel 2013. Previously, this type of chart formatting was done in a tabbed dialog box.

TIP

Normally, the Format task pane is docked on the right side of the window. But you can click the title and drag it anywhere you like and also resize it. To re-dock the task pane, drag it to the right side of the window. If you select a different chart element, the Format task pane changes to display the options appropriate for the new element.

Using the chart customization buttons

When a chart is selected, three buttons appear to the right of the chart. These buttons, when clicked, expand to show various options. The icons are

- **Chart Elements:** Use these tools to hide or display specific elements in the chart. Note that each item can be expanded to show additional options. To expand an item in the Chart Elements list, hover your mouse over the item and click the arrow that appears.
- **Chart Styles:** Use this icon to select from prebuilt chart styles or change the color scheme of the chart.
- **Chart Filters:** Use this icon to hide or display data series and specific points in a data series, or hide and display categories.

NEW FEATURE

The chart customization buttons are a new feature in Excel 2013.

Using the Ribbon

When a chart element is selected, you can also use the commands on the Ribbon to change some aspects of its formatting. For example, to change the color of the bars in a column chart, use the commands from the Chart Tools ⇨ Format ⇨ Shape Styles group. For some types of chart element formatting, you need to leave the Chart Tools tab. For example, to adjust font-related properties, use the commands from the Home ⇨ Font group.

The Ribbon controls do *not* comprise a comprehensive set of tools for chart elements. The Format task pane usually presents options that aren't available on the Ribbon.

Using the Mini toolbar

When you right-click an element in a chart, Excel displays a shortcut menu and the Mini toolbar. The Mini toolbar contains icons (Style, Fill, Outline) that, when clicked, display formatting options. For some chart elements, the Style icon isn't relevant, so the Mini toolbar displays the Chart Elements control (which you can use to select another chart element).

Figure 20.4 shows the Mini toolbar that appears after right-clicking a chart's title.

FIGURE 20.4

When you right-click a chart element, the Mini toolbar appears above the shortcut menu.

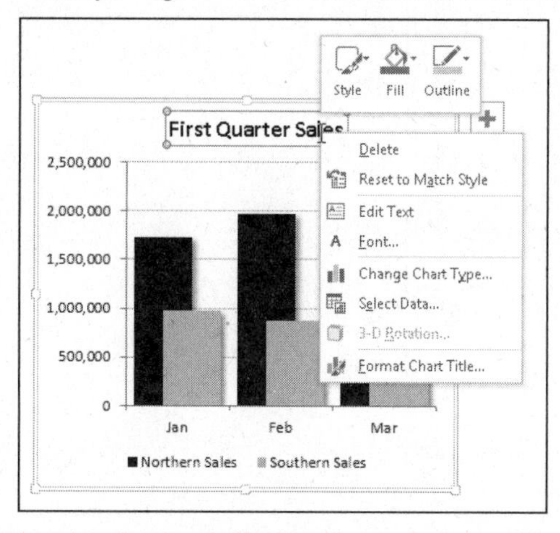

Modifying the Chart Area

The *Chart Area* is an object that contains all other elements in the chart. You can think of it as a chart's master background or container.

The only modifications that you can make to the Chart Area are cosmetic. You can change its fill color, outline, or effects such as shadows and soft edges.

NOTE

If you set the Chart Area of an embedded chart to use No Fill, the underlying cells are visible. Figure 20.5 shows a chart that uses No Fill and No Outline in its Chart Area. The Plot Area, Legend, and Chart Title *do* use a fill color. Adding a shadow to these other elements makes them appear to be floating above the worksheet.

The Chart Area element also controls all the fonts used in the chart. For example, if you want to change every font in the chart, you don't need to format each text element separately. Just select the Chart Area and then make the change from options of the Home⇨Font group or the Format Chart Area task pane.

FIGURE 20.5

The Chart Area element uses No Fill, so the underlying cells are visible.

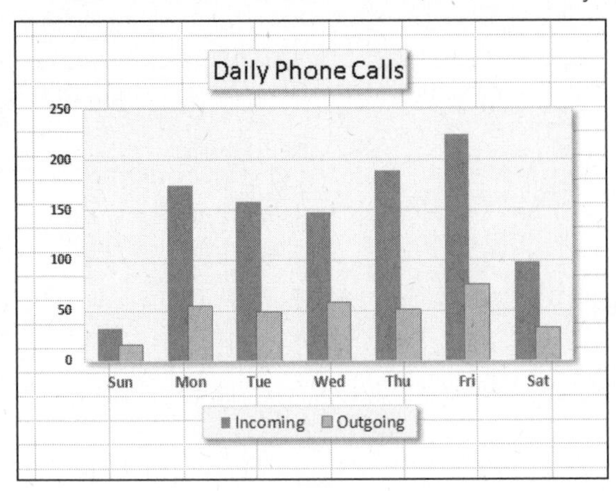

Modifying the Plot Area

The *Plot Area* is the part of the chart that contains the actual chart. More specifically, the Plot Area is a container for the chart series.

TIP

If you set the Shape Fill property to No Fill, the Plot Area will be transparent. Therefore, the fill color applied to the Chart Area will show through.

You can move and resize the Plot Area. Select the Plot Area and then drag a border to move it. To change the size of the Plot Area, drag one of the corner handles.

Different chart types vary in how they respond to changes in the Plot Area dimensions. For example, you can't change the relative dimensions of the Plot Area of a pie chart or a radar chart. The Plot Area of these charts is always square. With other chart types, though, you can change the aspect ratio of the Plot Area by changing either the height or the width.

Figure 20.6 shows a chart in which the Plot Area was resized to make room for an inserted Shape that contains text.

Resetting Chart Element Formatting

If you go overboard formatting a chart element, you can always reset it to its original state. Just select the element and choose Chart Tools ➪ Format ➪ Current Selection ➪ Reset to Match Style. Or right-click the chart element and choose Reset to Match Style from the shortcut menu.

To reset all formatting changes in the entire chart, select the Chart Area before you issue the Reset to Match Style command.

FIGURE 20.6

Reducing the size of the Plot Area makes room for the Shape.

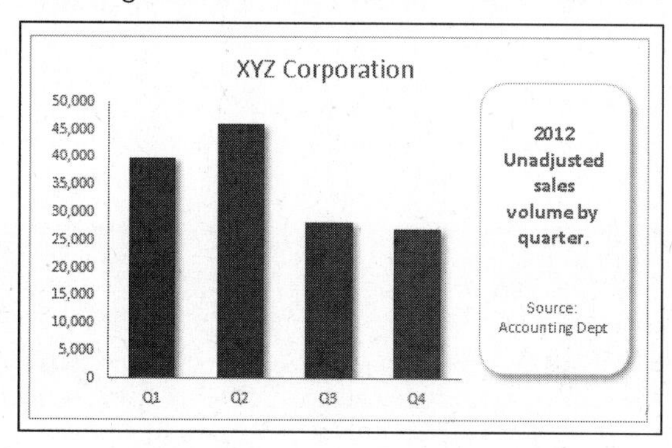

In some cases, the size of the Plot Area changes automatically when you adjust other elements of your chart. For example, if you add a legend to a chart, the size of the Plot Area may be reduced to accommodate the legend.

TIP

Changing the size and position of the Plot Area can have a dramatic effect on the overall look of your chart. When you're fine-tuning a chart, you'll probably want to experiment with various sizes and positions for the Plot Area.

Working with Titles in a Chart

A chart can have several different types of titles:

- Chart title
- Category axis title
- Value axis title

- Secondary category axis title
- Secondary value axis title
- Depth axis title (for true 3-D charts)

The number of titles that you can use depends on the chart type. For example, a pie chart supports only a chart title because it has no axes.

The easiest way to add a chart title is to use the Chart Elements button (the plus sign), which appears to the right of the chart. Activate the chart, click the Chart Elements button and enable the Chart Title item. To specify a location, move the mouse over the Chart Title item and click the arrow. You can then specify the location for the Chart Title. Click More Options to display the Format Chart Title task pane.

The same basic procedure applies to Axis Titles. You have additional options to specify which axis title(s) you want.

After you add a title, you can replace the default text and drag the title to a different position. However, you can't change the size of a title by dragging its borders. The only way to change the size of a title is to change the font size.

TIP

The chart title or any of the axis titles can also use a cell reference. For example, you can create a link so the chart always displays the text contained in cell A1 as its title. To create a link, select the title, type an equal sign (=), point to the cell, and press Enter. After you create the link, the Formula bar displays the cell reference when you select the title.

Working with a Legend

A chart's *legend* consists of text and keys that identify the data series in the chart. A *key* is a small graphic that corresponds to the chart's series (one key for each series).

To add a legend to your chart, activate the chart and click the Chart Elements icon to the right of the chart. Place a check mark next to Legend. To specify a location for the legend, click the arrow next to the Legend item and choose a location (Right, Top, Left, or Bottom). After you add a legend, you can drag it to move it anywhere you like.

TIP

If you move a legend manually, you may need to adjust the size of the chart's Plot Area.

The quickest way to remove a legend is to select the legend and then press Delete.

You can select individual items within a legend and format them separately. For example, you may want to make the text bold to draw attention to a particular data series. To select an element in the legend, first select the legend and then click the desired element.

Adding Free-Floating Text to a Chart

Text in a chart is not limited to titles. In fact, you can add free-floating text anywhere you want. To do so, activate the chart and choose Insert ⇨ Text ⇨ Text Box. Click in the chart to create the text box and enter the text. You can resize the text box, move it, change its formatting, and so on. You can also add a Shape to the chart and then add text to the Shape (if the Shape is one that accepts text). Refer to Figure 20.6 for an example of an inserted Shape with text.

If you didn't include legend text when you originally selected the cells to create the chart, Excel displays Series 1, Series 2, and so on in the legend. To add series names, choose Chart Tools ⇨ Design ⇨ Data ⇨ Select Data to display the Select Data Source dialog box (see Figure 20.7). Select the series name and click the Edit button. In the Edit Series dialog box, type the series name or enter a cell reference that contains the series name. Repeat for each series that needs naming.

FIGURE 20.7

Use the Select Data Source dialog box to change the name of a data series.

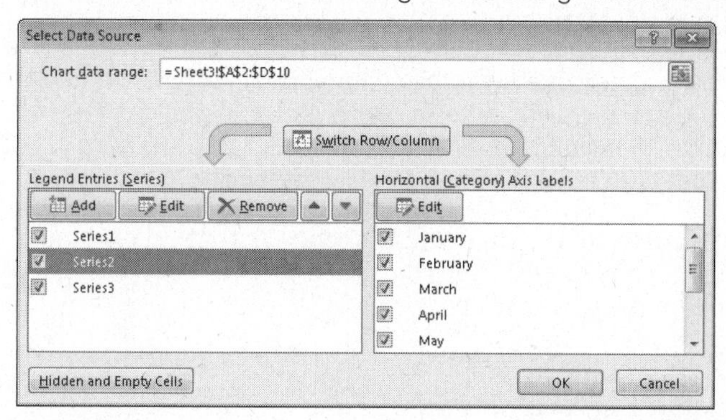

In some cases, you may prefer to omit the legend and use callouts to identify the data series. Figure 20.8 shows a chart with no legend. Instead, it uses Shapes to identify each series. These Shapes are from the Callouts section of the Chart Tools ⇨ Format ⇨ Insert Shapes gallery.

FIGURE 20.8

Using Shapes as callouts in lieu of a legend.

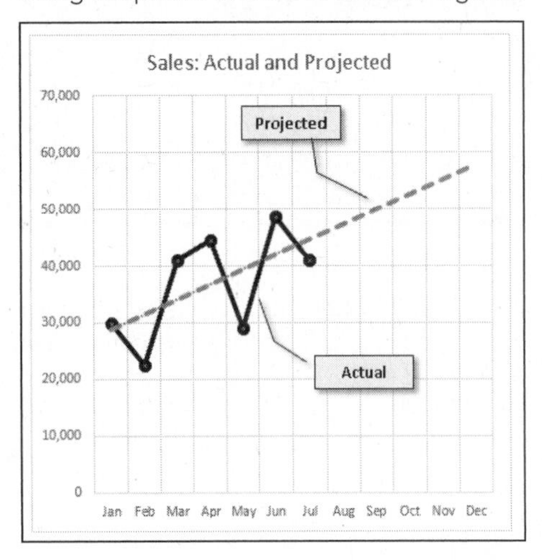

Working with Gridlines

Gridlines can help the viewer determine what the chart series represents numerically. Gridlines simply extend the tick marks on an axis. Some charts look better with gridlines; others appear more cluttered. Sometimes, horizontal gridlines alone are enough, although XY charts often benefit from both horizontal and vertical gridlines.

To add or remove gridlines, activate the chart and click the Chart Elements button to the right of the chart. Place a checkmark next to Gridlines. To specify the type of gridlines, click the arrow to the right of the Gridlines item.

NOTE

Each axis has two sets of gridlines: major and minor. Major units display a label. Minor units are located between the labels.

To modify the color or thickness of a set of gridlines, click one of the gridlines and use the commands from the Chart Tools ➪ Format ➪ Shape Styles group. Or use the controls in the Format Major (or Format Minor) Gridlines task pane.

If gridlines seem too overpowering, consider changing them to a lighter color or use one of the dashed line options.

Copying Chart Formatting

You created a killer chart and spent hours customizing it. Now you need to create another one just like it, but with a different set of data. What are your options? You have several choices:

- **Copy the formatting.** Create your new chart with the default formatting. Then select your original chart and choose Home ➪ Clipboard ➪ Copy (or press Ctrl+C). Click your new chart and choose Home ➪ Clipboard ➪ Paste ➪ Paste Special. In the Paste Special dialog box, select the Formats option.
- **Copy the chart and change the data sources.** Press Ctrl while you click the original chart and drag. This creates an exact copy of your chart. Then choose Chart Tools ➪ Design ➪ Data ➪ Select Data. In the Select Data Source dialog box, specify the data for the new chart in the Chart Data Range field.
- **Create a chart template.** Select your chart, right-click the Chart Area, and choose Save as Template from the shortcut menu. Excel prompts you for a name. When you create your next chart, use this template as the chart type. For more information about using chart templates, see "Creating Chart Templates," later in this chapter.

Modifying the Axes

Charts vary in the number of axes that they use. Pie and doughnut charts have no axes. All 2-D charts have two axes, but can have three (if you use a secondary value axis) or four (if you use a secondary category axis in an XY chart). True 3-D charts have three axes.

Excel gives you a great deal of control over these axes, via the Format Axis task pane. The content of this task pane varies depending on the type of axis selected.

Value axis

To change a value axis, right-click it and choose Format Axis. Figure 20.9 shows one panel (Axis Options) of the Format Axis task pane, for a value axis. In this case, the Tick Marks section is expanded and the other three sections are contracted. The other icons along the top of this task pane deal with cosmetic and number formatting for the axis.

By default, Excel determines the minimum and maximum axis values automatically, based on the numerical range of the data. To override this automatic axis scaling, enter your own minimum and maximum values in the Bounds section. If you change theses values, the word *Auto* changes to a Reset button. Click Reset to revert to automatic axis scaling.

FIGURE 20.9

The Format Axis task pane for a value axis.

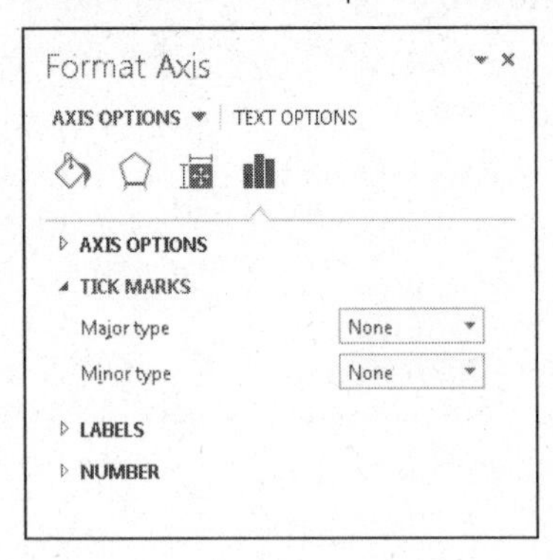

Excel also adjusts the major and minor axis units automatically. Again, you can override Excel's choice and specify different units.

Adjusting the bounds of a value axis can dramatically affect the chart's appearance. Manipulating the scale, in some cases, can present a false picture of the data. Figure 20.10 shows two line charts that depict the same data. The chart on the left uses Excel's default (Auto) axis bounds values, which extend from 1,600 to 1,950. In the chart on the right, the Minimum bound value was set to 0, and the Maximum bound value was set to 3,000. The first chart makes the differences in the data seem more prominent. The second chart gives the impression that there isn't much change over time.

FIGURE 20.10

These two charts show the same data but use a different value axis bounds.

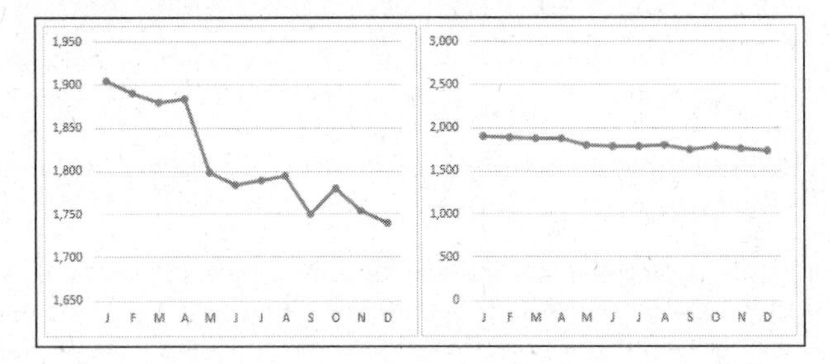

The actual scale that you use depends on the situation. There are no hard-and-fast rules regarding setting scale values except that you shouldn't misrepresent data by manipulating the chart to prove a point that doesn't exist.

TIP

If you're preparing several charts that use similarly scaled data, keeping the bounds the same is a good idea so that the charts can be compared more easily.

Another option in the Format Axis task pane is Values in Reverse Order. The left chart in Figure 20.11 uses default axis settings. The right chart uses the Values in Reverse Order option, which reverses the scale's direction. Notice that the Category Axis is at the top. If you would prefer that it remain at the bottom of the chart, select the Maximum Axis Value option for the Horizontal Axis Crosses setting.

FIGURE 20.11

The right chart uses the Values in Reverse Order option.

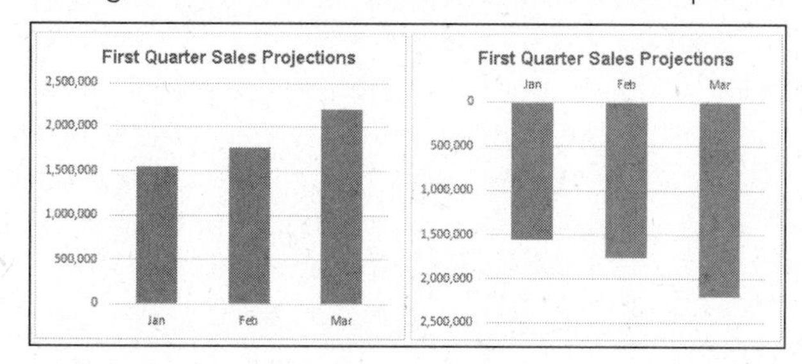

If the values to be plotted cover a very large numerical range, you may want to use a logarithmic scale for the value axis. A log scale is most often used for scientific applications. Figure 20.12 shows two charts. The top chart uses a standard scale, and the bottom chart uses a logarithmic scale.

NOTE

The Base setting is 10, so each scale value in the chart is ten times greater than the one below it. Increasing the major unit to 100 results in a scale in which each tick mark value is 100 times greater than the one below it. You can specify a base value between 2 and 1,000.

ON THE WEB

This workbook, `log scale.xlsx`, is available on this book's website.

20

FIGURE 20.12

These charts display the same data, but the bottom chart uses a logarithmic scale.

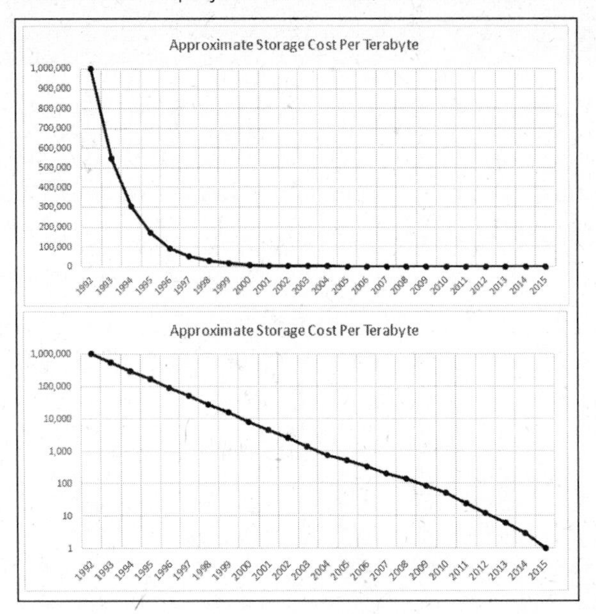

If your chart uses very large numbers, you may want to change the Display Units settings. Figure 20.13 shows a chart (top) that uses very large numbers. The chart below it uses the Display Units as Millions settings, with the option to Show Display Units Labels on Chart. I added "of Miles" to the label.

To adjust the tick marks displayed on an axis, click the Tick Marks section of the Format Axis dialog box to expand that section. The Major and Minor Tick Mark options control how the tick marks are displayed. *Major tick marks* are the axis tick marks that normally have labels next to them. *Minor tick marks* fall between the major tick marks.

If you expand the Labels section, you can position the axis labels at three different locations: Next to Axis, High, and Low. Each axis extends from –10 to +10. When you combine these settings with the Axis Crosses At option, you have a great deal of flexibility, as shown in Figure 20.14.

FIGURE 20.13

The chart on the bottom uses display units of millions.

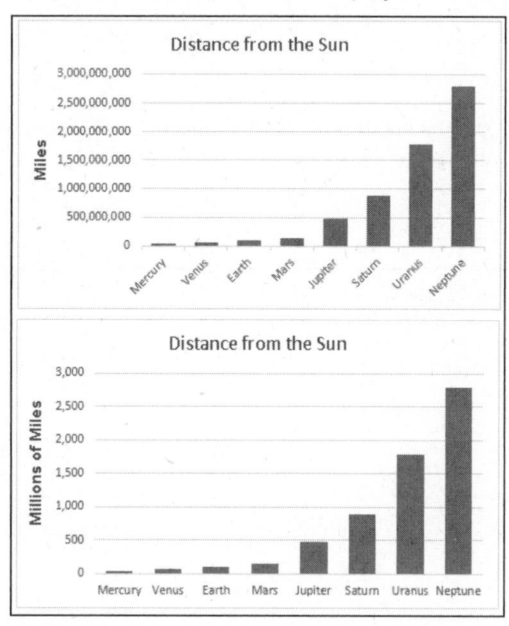

FIGURE 20.14

Various ways to display axis labels and crossing points.

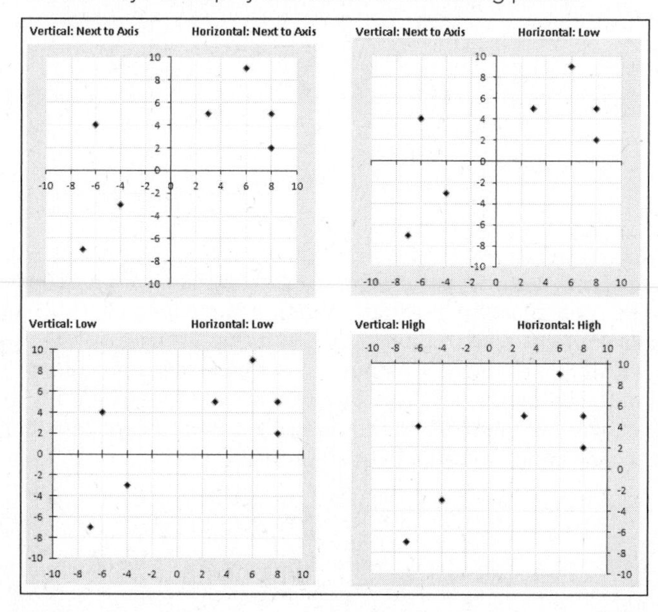

The final section of the task pane, Number, lets you specify the number formatting for the value axis. Normally, the number formatting is linked to the source data, but you can override that.

Category axis

Figure 20.15 shows part of the Axis Options section of the Format Axis task pane when a category axis is selected. Some options are the same as those for a value axis.

FIGURE 20.15

Some of the options available for a category axis.

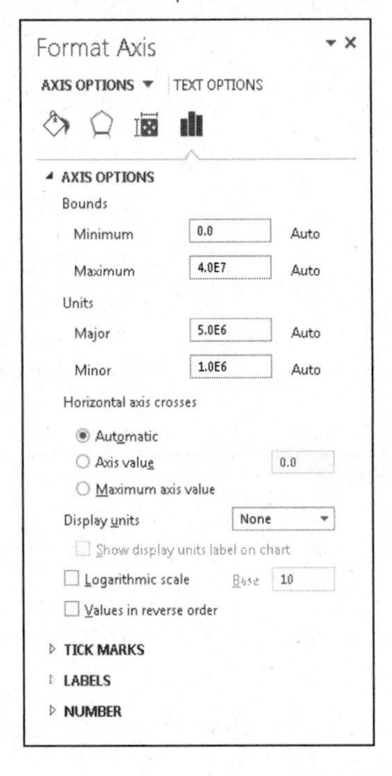

An important setting is the Axis Type: Text or Date. When you create a chart, Excel recognizes if your category axis contains date or time values. If it does, it uses a Date category axis. Figure 20.16 shows a simple example. Column A contains dates, and column B contains the values plotted in the column chart. The data consists of values for only 10 dates, yet Excel created the chart with 30 intervals on the category axis. It recognized that the category axis values were dates and created an equal-interval scale.

FIGURE 20.16

Excel recognizes dates and creates a time-based category axis.

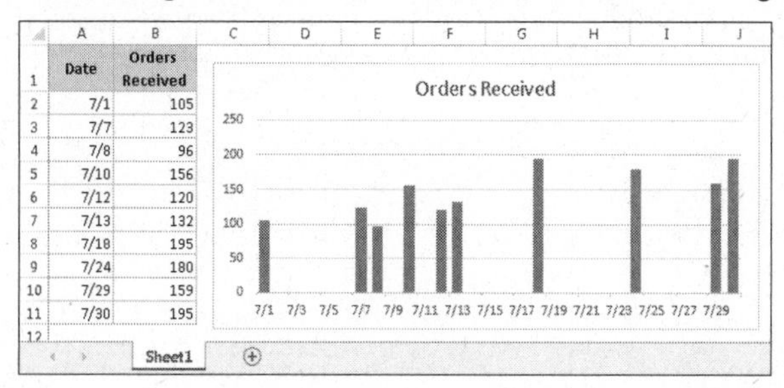

You can override Excel's decision to use a Date category axis by choosing the Text Axis option for Axis Type. Figure 20.17 shows the chart after making this change. In this case, using a time-based category axis (as shown in Figure 20.16) presents a much truer picture of the data.

FIGURE 20.17

Overriding the Excel time-based category axis.

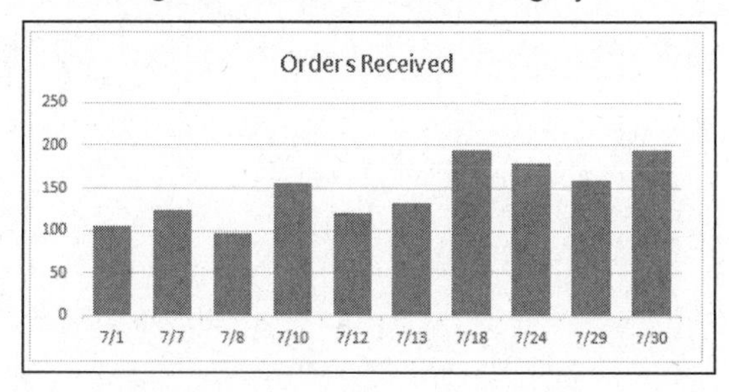

Excel chooses how to orient the category labels, but you can override its choice. Figure 20.18 shows a column chart with month labels. Because of the lengthy category labels, Excel displays the text at an angle. If you make the chart wider, the labels will then appear horizontally. You can also adjust the labels using the Alignment controls in the Size & Properties section of the Format Axis task pane.

FIGURE 20.18

Excel determines how to display category axis labels.

In some cases, you really don't need every category label. You can adjust the Interval between Labels settings to skip some labels (and cause the text to display horizontally). Figure 20.19 shows such a chart; the Interval between Labels setting is 3.

FIGURE 20.19

Changing the Interval between Labels setting makes labels display horizontally.

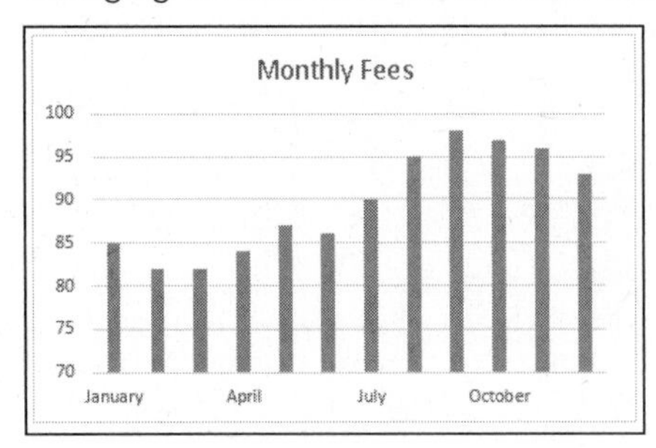

Keep in mind that a category axis labels can consist of more than one column. Figure 20.20 shows a chart that displays three columns of text for the category axis. I selected the range A1:E10, created a column chart, and Excel figured out the category axis.

Don't Be Afraid to Experiment (But on a Copy)

I'll let you in on a secret: The key to mastering charts in Excel is experimentation, otherwise known as trial and error. Excel's charting options can be overwhelming, even to experienced users. This book doesn't even pretend to cover all the charting features and options. Your job, as a potential charting master, is to dig deep and try out the various options in your charts. With a bit of creativity, you can create original-looking charts.

After you create a basic chart, make a copy of the chart for your experimentation. That way, if you mess it up, you can always revert to the original and start again. To make a copy of an embedded chart, click the chart and press Ctrl+C. Then activate a cell and press Ctrl+V. To make a copy of a chart sheet, press Ctrl while you click the sheet tab and then drag it to a new location among the other tabs.

FIGURE 20.20

This chart uses three columns of text for the category axis labels.

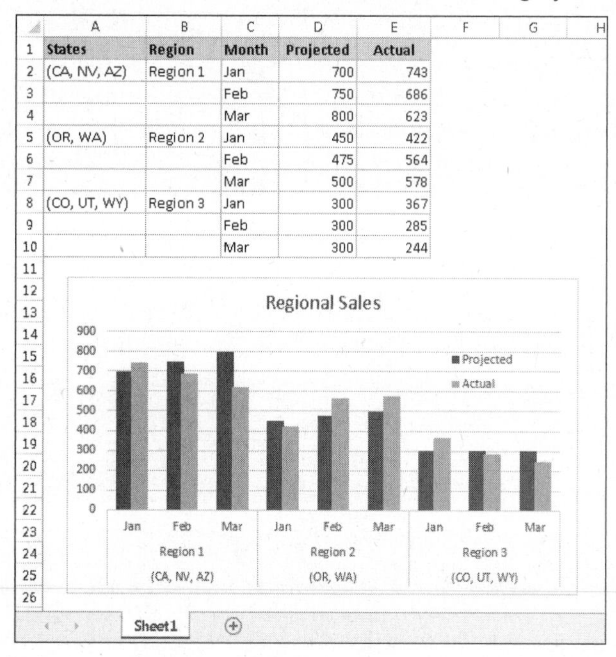

States	Region	Month	Projected	Actual
(CA, NV, AZ)	Region 1	Jan	700	743
		Feb	750	686
		Mar	800	623
(OR, WA)	Region 2	Jan	450	422
		Feb	475	564
		Mar	500	578
(CO, UT, WY)	Region 3	Jan	300	367
		Feb	300	285
		Mar	300	244

Working with Data Series

Every chart consists of one or more data series. This data translates into chart columns, bars, lines, pie slices, and so on. This section discusses some common operations that involve a chart's data series.

When you select a data series in a chart, Excel does the following:

- Displays the series name in the Chart Elements control (located in the Chart Tools ➪ Format ➪ Current Selection group
- Displays the `Series` formula in the Formula bar
- Highlights the cells used for the selected series by outlining them in color

You can make changes to a data series by using options on the Ribbon or from the Format Data Series task pane. This task pane varies, depending on the type of data series you're working on (column, line, pie, and so on).

Caution

If the Format task pane isn't already displayed, the easiest way to display the Format Data Series task pane is to double-click the chart series. Be careful, however: If a data series is already selected, double-clicking brings up the Format Data Point dialog box. Changes that you make affect only one point in the data series. To edit the *entire series,* make sure that a chart element other than the data series is selected before you double-click the data series. Or just press Ctrl+1 to display the task pane.

Deleting or hiding a data series

To delete a data series in a chart, select the data series and press Delete. The data series disappears from the chart. The data in the worksheet, of course, remains intact.

Note

You can delete all data series from a chart. If you do so, the chart appears empty. It retains its settings, however. Therefore, you can add a data series to an empty chart, and it again looks like a chart.

New Feature

Excel 2013 offers a new option: hiding a data series. Activate a chart and click the Chart Filters button on the right. Remove the check mark from the data series that you want to hide, click Apply, and that data series is hidden — but it's still associated with the chart, so you can unhide it later. You can't hide all the series, though. At least one must be visible. The Chart Filters button also lets you hide individual points in a series.

Adding a new data series to a chart

If you want to add another data series to an existing chart, one approach is to re-create the chart and include the new data series. However, adding the data to the existing chart is usually easier, and your chart retains any customization that you've made.

Figure 20.21 shows a column chart that has one data series (Pre-Test). The Post-Test scores just became available and were entered into the worksheet in column C. Now the chart needs to be updated to include the new data series.

FIGURE 20.21

This chart needs a new data series.

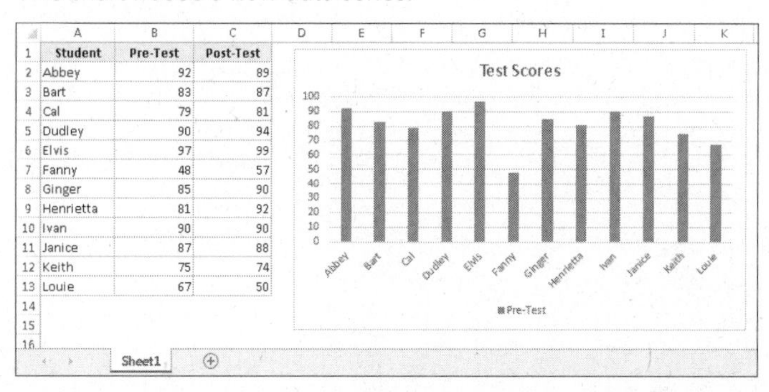

Excel provides three ways to add a new data series to a chart:

- **Use the Select Data Source dialog box.** Activate the chart and choose Chart Tools ➪ Design ➪ Data ➪ Select Data. In the Select Data Source dialog box, click the Add button, and Excel displays the Edit Series dialog box. Specify the Series Name (as a cell reference or text) and the range that contains the Series Values. The Select Data Source dialog box is also accessible from the shortcut menu displayed by right-clicking many elements in a chart.
- **Drag the range outline.** If the data series to be added is contiguous with other data in the chart, you can click the Chart Area in the chart. Excel highlights and outlines the data in the worksheet. Click one of the corners of the outline and drag to highlight the new data. This method works only for embedded charts.
- **Copy and paste.** Select the range to add and press Ctrl + C to copy it to the Clipboard. Then activate the chart and press Ctrl + V to paste the data into the chart.

TIP

If the chart was originally made from data in a table (created via Insert ➪ Tables ➪ Table), the chart is updated automatically when you add new rows or columns to the table (or remove rows or columns). If you have a chart that is updated frequently with new data, you can save time and effort by creating the chart from data in a table.

20

Changing data used by a series

You may find that you need to modify the range that defines a data series. For example, say you need to add new data points or remove old ones from the data set. The following sections describe several ways to change the range used by a data series.

Changing the data range by dragging the range outline

If you have an embedded chart, the easiest way to change the data range for a data series is to drag the range outline. When you select a series in a chart, Excel outlines the data range used by that series. You can drag the small dot in the lower-right corner of the range outline to extend or contract the data series. In Figure 20.22, the range outline will be dragged to include two additional data points.

FIGURE 20.22

Changing a chart's data series by dragging the range outline.

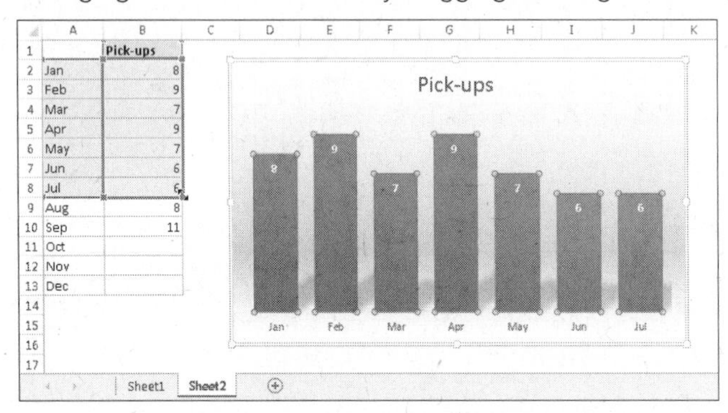

You can also click and drag one of the sides of the outline to move the outline to a different range of cells.

In some cases, you'll also need to adjust the range that contains the category labels as well. The labels are also outlined, and you can drag the outline to expand or contract the range of labels used in the chart.

If your chart is on a chart sheet, you need to use one of the two methods described next.

Using the Edit Series dialog box

Another way to update the chart to reflect a different data range is to use the Edit Series dialog box. A quick way to display this dialog box is to right-click the series in the chart and then choose Select Data from the shortcut menu. The Select Source Data dialog box appears. Select the data series in the list, and click Edit to display the Edit Series dialog box, shown in Figure 20.23.

You can change the entire data range used by the chart by adjusting the range references in the Chart Data Range field. Or select a series from the list and click Edit to modify the selected series.

FIGURE 20.23

The Edit Series dialog box.

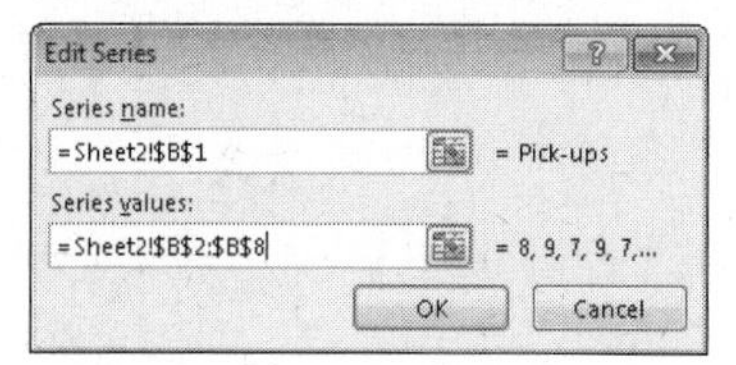

Editing the Series formula

Every data series in a chart has an associated SERIES formula, which appears in the Formula bar when you select a data series in a chart. If you understand how a SERIES formula is constructed, you can edit the range references in the SERIES formula directly to change the data used by the chart.

NOTE

The SERIES formula is not a real formula: In other words, you can't use it in a cell, and you can't use worksheet functions within the SERIES formula. You can, however, edit the arguments in the SERIES formula.

A SERIES formula has the following syntax:

```
=SERIES(series_name, category_labels, values, order, sizes)
```

The arguments that you can use in the SERIES formula include

- series_name: (Optional) A reference to the cell that contains the series name used in the legend. If the chart has only one series, the name argument is used as the title. This argument can also consist of text in quotation marks. If omitted, Excel creates a default series name (for example, Series 1).
- category_labels: (Optional) A reference to the range that contains the labels for the category axis. If omitted, Excel uses consecutive integers beginning with 1. For XY charts, this argument specifies the X values. A noncontiguous range reference is also valid. The ranges' addresses are separated by commas and enclosed in parentheses. The argument could also consist of an array of comma-separated values (or text in quotation marks) enclosed in curly brackets.
- values: (Required) A reference to the range that contains the values for the series. For XY charts, this argument specifies the Y values. A noncontiguous range reference is also valid. The range addresses are separated by a comma and enclosed in parentheses. The argument could also consist of an array of comma-separated values enclosed in curly brackets.
- order: (Required) An integer that specifies the plotting order of the series. This argument is relevant only if the chart has more than one series. Using a reference to a cell is not allowed.

- `sizes`: (Only for bubble charts) A reference to the range that contains the values for the size of the bubbles in a bubble chart. A noncontiguous range reference is also valid. The range addresses are separated by commas and enclosed in parentheses. The argument can also consist of an array of values enclosed in curly brackets.

Range references in a `SERIES` formula are always absolute (contain two dollar signs), and they always include the sheet name. For example

```
=SERIES(Sheet1!$B$1,,Sheet1!$B$2:$B$7,1)
```

TIP

You can substitute range names for the range references. If you do so, Excel changes the reference in the `SERIES` formula to include the workbook name (if it's a workbook-level name) or to include the worksheet name (if it's a sheet-level name). For example if you use a workbook-level range named `MyData` (in a workbook named `budget.xlsx`), the `SERIES` formula looks like this

```
=SERIES(Sheet1!$B$1,,budget.xlsx!MyData,1)
```

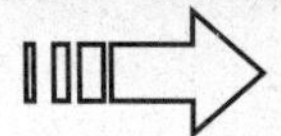

For more information about named ranges, see Chapter 4.

Displaying data labels in a chart

Sometimes, you may want your chart to display the actual numerical value for each data point. To add labels to data series in a chart, select the series and click the Add Elements button on the right side of the chart. Place a check mark next to Data Labels. Click the arrow next to the Data Labels item to specify the position for the labels.

To add data labels for all series, use the same procedure, but start by selecting something other than a data series.

Figure 20.24 shows three minimalist charts with data labels.

To change the type of information that appears in data labels, select the data labels for a series and use the Format Data Labels task pane (if the task pane isn't visible, press Ctrl + 1). Then use the Label Options section to customize the data labels. For example, you can include the series name and the category name along with the value.

The data labels are linked to the worksheet, so if your data changes, the labels also change. If you want to override the data label with other text, select the label and enter the new text.

NEW FEATURE

Excel 2013 finally introduces a feature that's been on the wish lists of many users for at least 15 years: the ability to specify an arbitrary range to be used as data labels for a series. In the Format Data Labels task pane, select Value from Cells (in the Label Options section) and click Select Range to specify the range that contains the data point labels.

FIGURE 20.24

These charts use data labels and don't display axes.

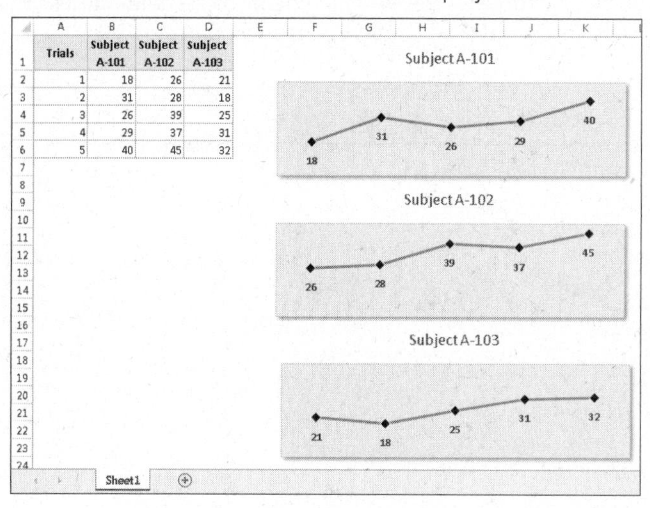

Figure 20.25 shows an XY chart that uses data labels stored in a range. In previous versions of Excel, adding these data labels had to be done manually or with the assistance of a macro.

FIGURE 20.25

Data labels linked to text in an arbitrary range.

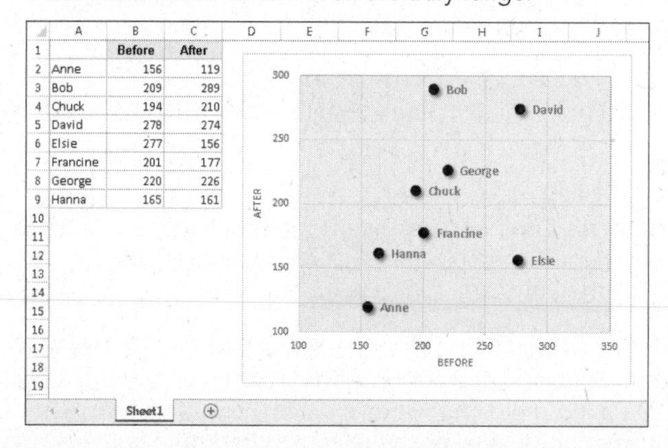

TIP

Often, the data labels aren't positioned properly. For example, a label may be obscured by another data point or another label. If you select an individual data label, you can drag the label to a better location. To select an individual data label, click once to select them all and then click the single data label.

Handling missing data

Sometimes, data that you're charting may be missing one or more data points. As shown in Figure 20.26, Excel offers three ways to handle the missing data:

FIGURE 20.26

Three options for dealing with missing data.

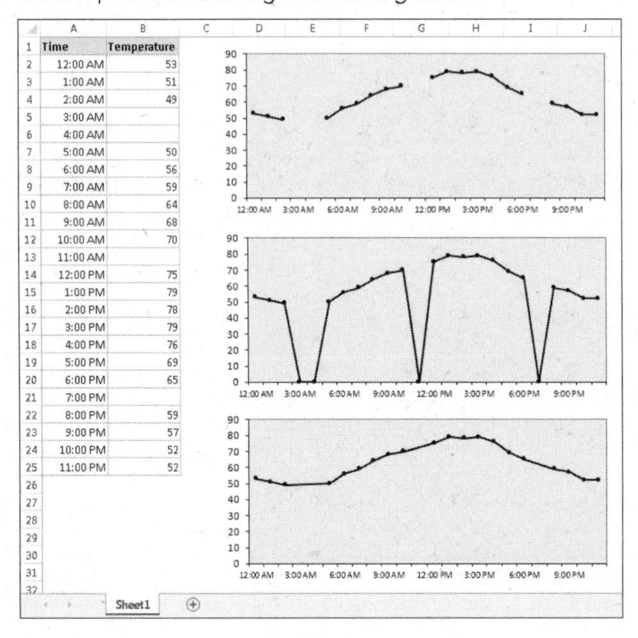

- **Gaps:** Missing data is simply ignored, and the data series will have a gap. This is the default.
- **Zero:** Missing data is treated as zero.
- **Connect Data Points with Line:** Missing data is interpolated, calculated by using data on either side of the missing point(s). This option is available for line charts, area charts, and XY charts only.

To specify how to deal with missing data for a chart, choose Chart Tools ➪ Design ➪ Data ➪ Select Data. In the Select Data Source dialog box, click the Hidden and Empty Cells button. Excel displays its Hidden and Empty Cell Settings dialog box. Make your choice in the dialog box. The option that you choose applies to the entire chart, and you can't set a different option for different series in the same chart.

TIP

Normally, a chart doesn't display data that's in a hidden row or column. You can use the Hidden and Empty Cell Settings dialog box to force a chart to use hidden data, though.

Adding error bars

Some chart types support error bars. *Error bars* often are used to indicate "plus or minus" information that reflects uncertainty in the data. Error bars are appropriate for area, bar, column, line, and XY charts only.

To add error bars, select a data series and then click the Add Elements icon to the right of the chart. Add a check mark next to Error Bars. Click the arrow next to the Error Bars item to specify the type of error bars. If necessary, you can fine-tune the error bar settings from the Format Error Bars task pane. The types of error bars are

- **Fixed value:** The error bars are fixed by an amount that you specify.
- **Percentage:** The error bars are a percentage of each value.
- **Standard Deviation(s):** The error bars are in the number of standard deviation units that you specify. (Excel calculates the standard deviation of the data series.)
- **Standard Error:** The error bars are one standard error unit. (Excel calculates the standard error of the data series.)
- **Custom:** You set the error bar units for the upper or lower error bars. You can enter either a value or a range reference that holds the error values that you want to plot as error bars.

The chart shown in Figure 20.27 displays error bars based on percentage.

FIGURE 20.27

This line chart series displays error bars based on percentage.

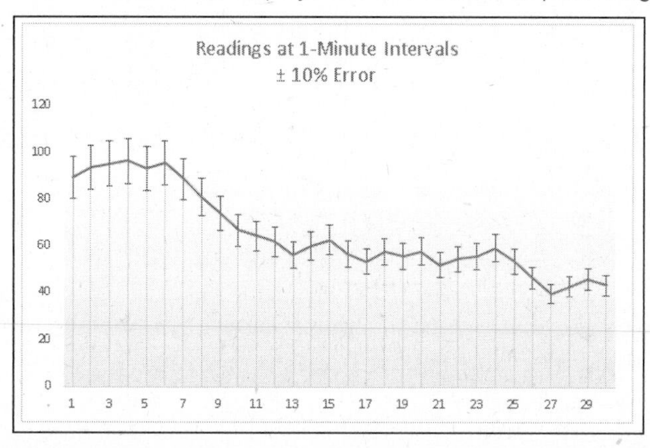

TIP

A data series in an XY chart can have error bars for both the X values and the Y values.

20

Adding a trendline

When you're plotting data over time, you may want to display a trendline that describes the data. A *trendline* points out general trends in your data. In some cases, you can forecast future data with trendlines.

To add a trendline, select the data series and click the Add Elements button, to the right of the chart. Place a check mark next to Trendline. To specify the type of trendline, click the arrow to the right of the Trendline item. The type of trendline that you choose depends on your data. Linear trends are most common, but some data can be described more effectively with another type.

Figure 20.28 shows a line chart with two linear trendlines. Although the raw data is quite variable, the trendlines show that income is increasing and expenses are decreasing (but at a slower rate).

FIGURE 20.28

A line chart with two linear trendlines.

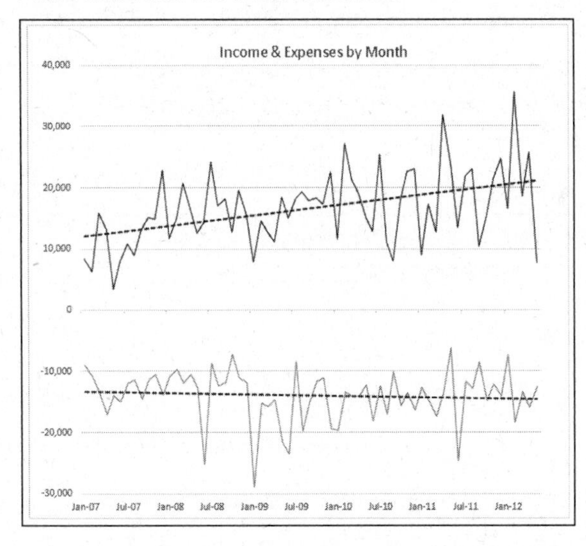

For more control over a trendline, use the Format Trendline task pane.

Figure 20.29 shows another trendline example, in an XY chart. The trendline depicts the relationship between height and weight for 15 people.

FIGURE 20.29

The trendline depicts the relationship between height and weight.

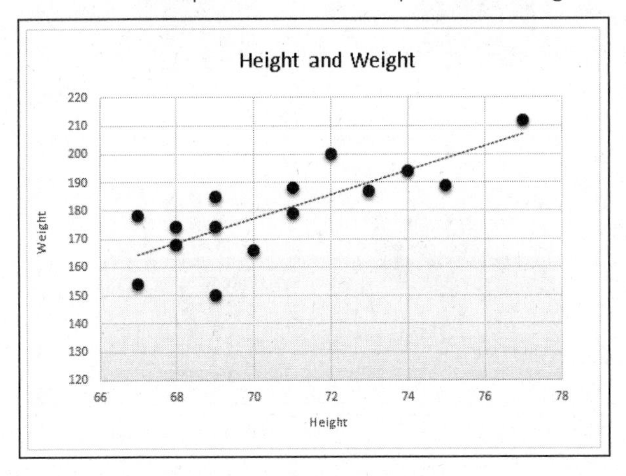

Modifying 3-D charts

3-D charts have a few additional elements that you can customize. For example, most 3-D charts have a floor and walls, and true 3-D charts also have an additional category axis. You can select these chart elements and format them to your liking using the Format task pane.

One area in which Excel 3-D charts differ from 2-D charts is in the perspective — or *viewpoint* — from which you see the chart. In some cases, the data may be viewed better if you change the order of the series.

Figure 20.30 shows six views of 3-D column chart with two data series. The top-left chart is the original, and the others are variations. In some of the charts, I changed the series order to make the columns more visible. As you can see, you can accidentally distort the chart to make it virtually worthless in terms of visualizing information. If accuracy of presentation is important, a 3-D chart is hardly ever the best choice.

Changing the viewing angle of a 3-D chart may reveal portions of the chart that are otherwise hidden. To rotate a 3-D chart, use the Format Chart Area task pane. Then choose Chart Options ⇨ Effects and expand the 3-D Rotation section. You can make your rotations and perspective changes by clicking the appropriate controls.

FIGURE 20.30

Variations on a simple 3-D column chart.

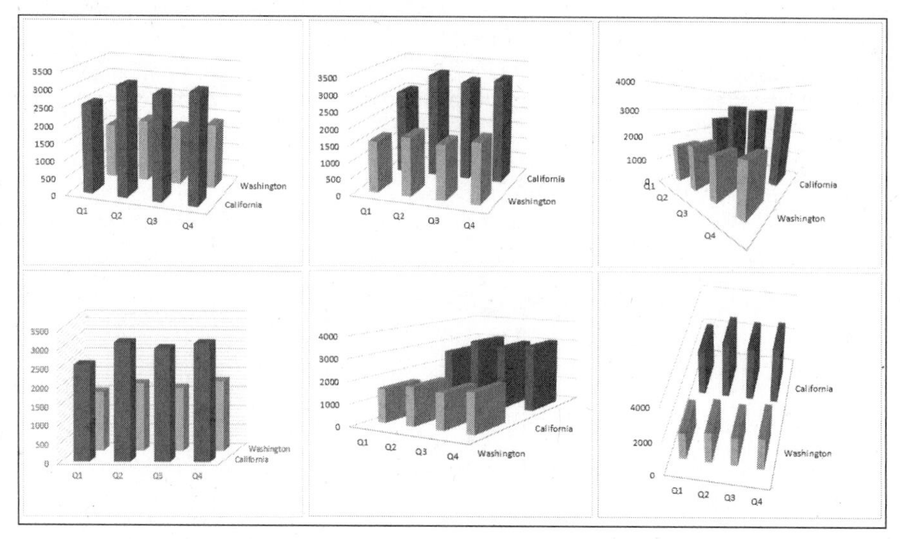

Creating combination charts

A *combination chart* is a single chart that consists of series that use different chart types. A combination chart may also include a second value axis. For example, you may have a chart that shows both columns and lines, with two value axes. The value axis for the columns is on the left, and the value axis for the line is on the right. A combination chart requires at least two data series.

NEW FEATURE

In previous version, creating a combo chart required several manual and often nonintuitive steps. Excel 2013 has made it much easier to create combination charts.

Figure 20.31 shows a column chart with two data series. The values for the Precipitation series are very low — so low that they're barely visible on the Value Axis scale. This is a good candidate for a combination chart.

The following steps describe how to use the data to create a combination (column and line) that uses a second Value Axis.

1. **Move the cell pointer to any cell in the data area, and choose Insert➪Charts➪Recommended Charts.** The Insert Chart dialog box appears.
2. **Select the All Charts tab.**
3. **In the list of chart types, click Combo.**
4. **For the Avg Temp series, specify Clustered Column as the chart type.**

5. **For the Precipitation series, specify Line as the chart type, and click the Secondary Axis check box.**
6. **Click OK to insert the chart.**

Figure 20.32 shows the Insert Chart dialog box after specifying the parameters for each series.

FIGURE 20.31

The Precipitation series is barely visible.

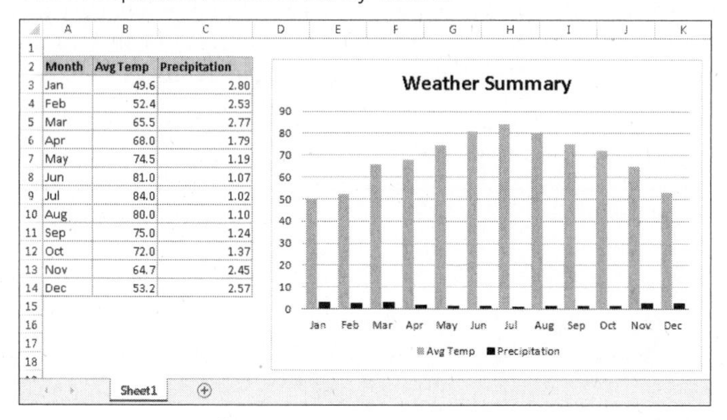

Month	Avg Temp	Precipitation
Jan	49.6	2.80
Feb	52.4	2.53
Mar	65.5	2.77
Apr	68.0	1.79
May	74.5	1.19
Jun	81.0	1.07
Jul	84.0	1.02
Aug	80.0	1.10
Sep	75.0	1.24
Oct	72.0	1.37
Nov	64.7	2.45
Dec	53.2	2.57

FIGURE 20.32

Using the Insert Chart dialog box to create a combination chart.

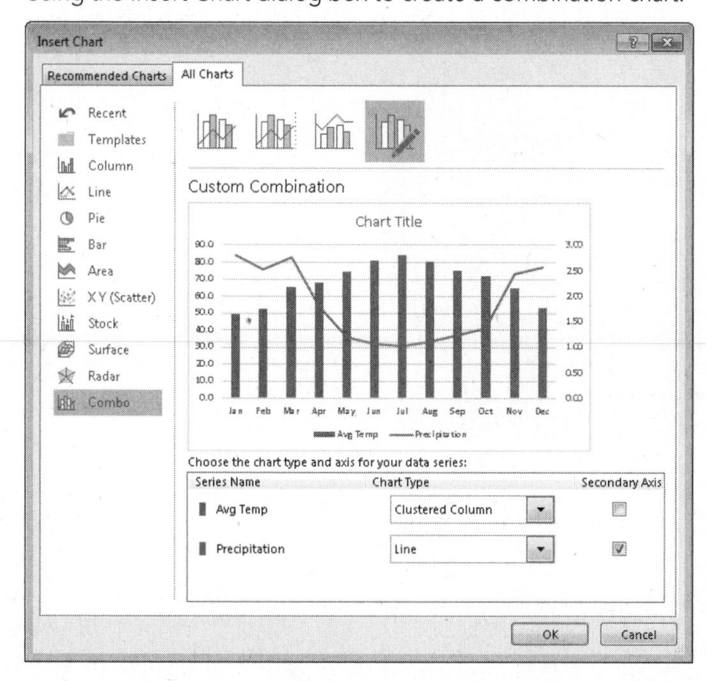

> **On the Web**
>
> This workbook is available on this book's website. The filename is `weather combination chart.xlsx`.

> **Note**
>
> In some cases, you can't combine chart types. For example, you can't create a combination chart that involves a bubble chart or a 3-D chart. In the Insert Chart dialog box, Excel displays only the chart types that can be used.

Figure 20.33 demonstrates just how far you can go with a combination chart. This chart combines five different chart types: Pie, Area, Column, Line, and XY. I can't think of any situation that would warrant such a chart, but it's an interesting demo.

FIGURE 20.33

A five-way combination chart.

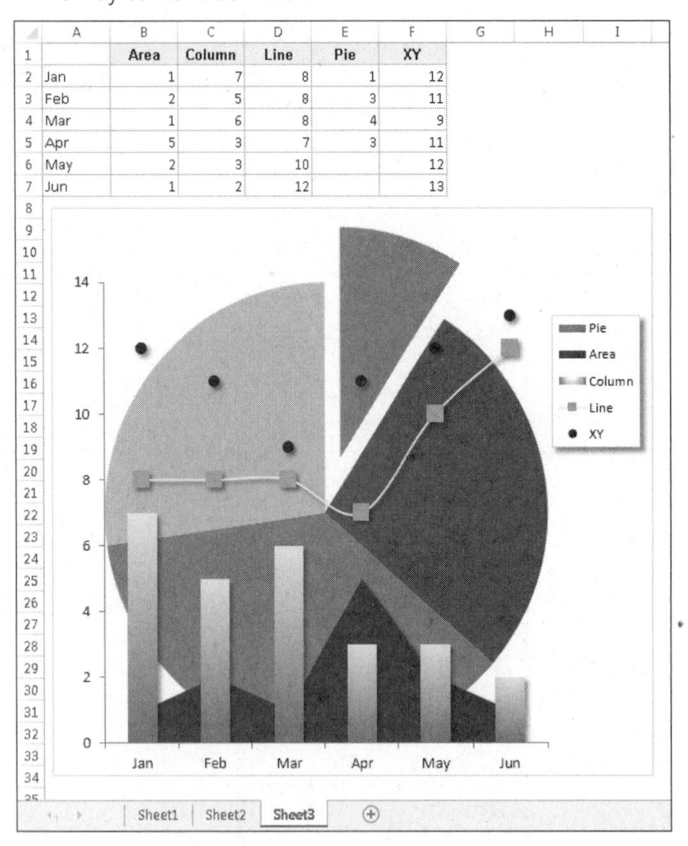

Displaying a data table

In some cases, you may want to display a *data table,* which displays the chart's data in tabular form, directly in the chart.

To add a data table to a chart, activate the chart and click the Add Element button to the right of the chart. Place a check mark next to Data Table. Click the arrow to the right of the Data Table item for a few options. Figure 20.34 shows a combination chart that includes a data table.

FIGURE 20.34

This combination chart includes a data table that displays the values of the data points.

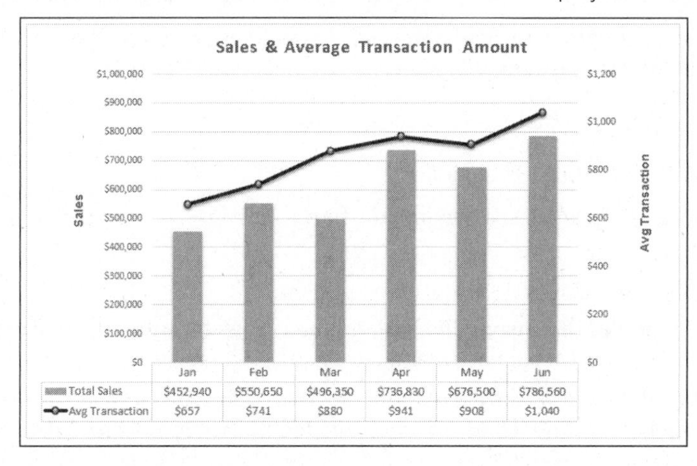

Not all chart types support data tables. If the Data Table option isn't available, that means the chart doesn't support this feature.

TIP

Using a data table is probably best suited for charts on chart sheets. If you need to show the data used in an embedded chart, you can do so using data in cells, which provides you with a lot more flexibility in terms of formatting.

Creating Chart Templates

This section describes how to create custom chart templates. A template includes customized chart formatting and settings. When you create a new chart, you can choose to use your template rather than a built-in chart type.

If you find that you're continually customizing your charts in the same way, you can probably save some time by creating a template. Or, if you create lots of combination charts, you can create a combination chart template and avoid making the manual adjustments required for a combination chart.

To create a chart template, follow these steps:

1. **Create a chart to serve as the basis for your template.** The data you use for this chart isn't critical, but for best results, it should be typical of the data that you'll eventually be plotting with your custom chart type.
2. **Apply any formatting and customizations that you like.** This step determines the appearance of the charts created from the template.
3. **Activate the chart and right-click the Chart Area or the Plot Area, and choose Save as Template from the shortcut menu.** The Save Chart Template dialog box appears.
4. **Provide a name for the template and click Save.** Make sure you don't change the proposed directory for the file.

To create a chart based on a template, follow these steps:

1. **Select the data to be used in the chart.**
2. **Choose Insert ➪ Charts ➪ Recommended Charts.** The Insert Chart dialog box appears.
3. **Select the All Charts tab.**
4. **From the left side of the Insert Chart dialog box, select Templates.** Excel displays a thumbnail for each custom template that has been created.
5. **Click the thumbnail that represents the template you want to use, and then click OK.** Excel creates the chart based on the template you selected.

Note

You can also apply a template to an existing chart. Select the chart and choose Chart Tools ➪ Design ➪ Type ➪ Change Chart Type to display the Change Chart Type dialog box — which is identical to the Insert Chart dialog box.

Learning Some Chart-Making Tricks

This section describes some interesting (and perhaps useful) chart-making tricks. Some of these tricks use little-known features, and several tricks enable you to make charts that you may have considered impossible to create.

Creating picture charts

Excel makes it easy to incorporate a pattern, texture, or graphics file for elements in your chart.

Figure 20.35 shows a chart that uses a photo as the background for a chart's Chart Area element.

FIGURE 20.35

The Chart Area contains a photo.

To display an image in a chart element, use the Fill section in the element's Format task pane. Select the Picture or Texture Fill option and then click the button that corresponds to the image source (File, Clipboard, or Online). If you use the Clipboard button, make sure that you copied your image first. The other two options prompt you for the image.

Figure 20.36 shows two more examples: a pie chart that uses a clip art image as its fill; and a column chart that uses a Shape, which was inserted on a worksheet and then copied to the Clipboard.

FIGURE 20.36

The left chart uses clip art, and the right chart uses a Shape that was copied to the Clipboard and pasted to the chart's data series.

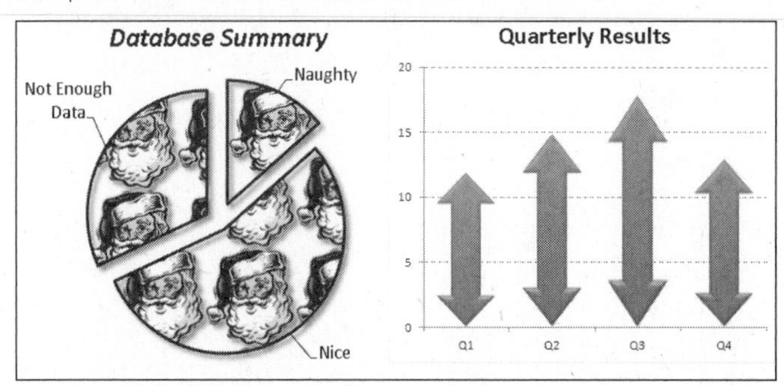

New Feature

A new feature in Excel 2013 also lets you use a graphic images and textures for text in a chart. For example, select a chart's title, and then use the Text Options ⇨ Text Fill options in the Format Chart Title task pane.

On the Web

The examples in this section are available on this book's website. The filename is `picture charts.xlsx`.

Using images in a chart offers unlimited potential for creativity. The key, of course, is to resist the temptation to go overboard. Usually, a chart's primary goal is to convey information, not to impress the viewer with your artistic skills.

Caution

Using images, especially photos, in charts can dramatically increase the size of your workbooks.

Creating a thermometer chart

You're probably familiar with a "thermometer" type display that shows the percentage of a task that has been completed. Creating such a display in Excel is very easy. The trick involves creating a chart that uses a single cell (which holds a percentage value) as a data series.

Figure 20.37 shows a worksheet set up to track daily progress toward a goal: 1,000 new customers in a 15-day period. Cell B18 contains the goal value, and cell B19 contains a simple formula that calculates the sum. Cell B21 contains a formula that calculates the percent of goal:

```
=B19/B18
```

As you enter new data in column B, the formulas display the current results.

On the Web

A workbook with this example is available on this book's website. The filename is `thermometer chart.xlsx`.

To make the thermometer chart, select cell B21 and create a column chart from that single cell. Notice the blank cell above cell B21. Without this blank cell, Excel uses the entire data block for the chart, not just the single cell. Because B21 is isolated from the other data, only the single cell is used.

FIGURE 20.37

This single-point chart displays progress toward a goal.

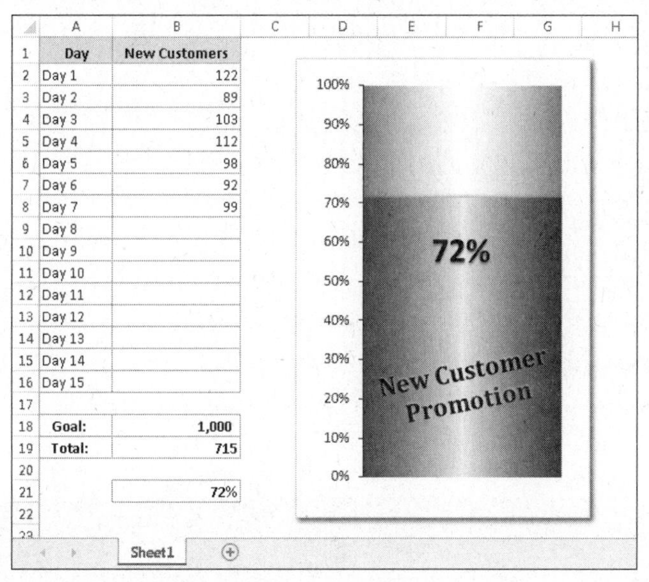

	A	B
1	Day	New Customers
2	Day 1	122
3	Day 2	89
4	Day 3	103
5	Day 4	112
6	Day 5	98
7	Day 6	92
8	Day 7	99
9	Day 8	
10	Day 9	
11	Day 10	
12	Day 11	
13	Day 12	
14	Day 13	
15	Day 14	
16	Day 15	
17		
18	Goal:	1,000
19	Total:	715
20		
21		72%

Other changes required are to

- Select the horizontal category axis and press Delete to remove the category axis from the chart.
- Remove the legend.
- Add a text box, linked to cell B21 to display the percent accomplished.
- In the Format Data Series task pane (Series Options section), set the Gap width to 0, which makes the column occupy the entire width of the plot area.
- Select the Value Axis and display the Format Value Axis task pane. In the Axis Options section, set the Minimum to 0 and the Maximum to 1.

Make any other cosmetic adjustments to get the look you desire.

Creating a gauge chart

Figure 20.38 shows another chart based on a single cell. It's a pie chart set up to resemble a gauge. Although this chart displays only one value (entered in cell B1), it actually uses three data points (in A4:A6).

FIGURE 20.38

This chart resembles a speedometer gauge and displays a value between 0 and 100 percent.

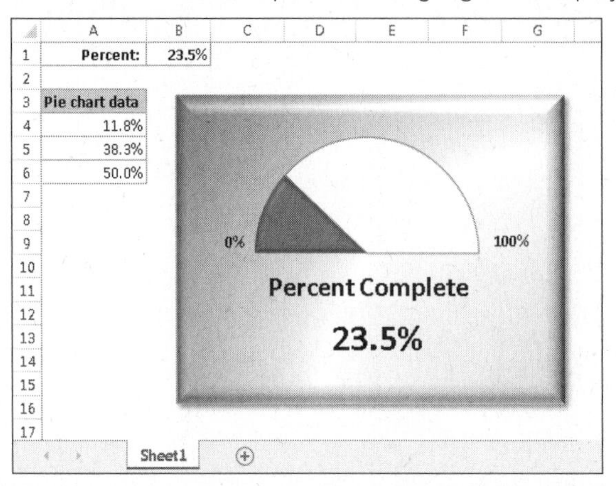

ON THE WEB

A workbook with this example is available on this book's website. The filename is `gauge chart.xlsx`.

One slice of the pie — the slice at the bottom — always consists of 50 percent. I rotated the pie so that the 50 percent slice was at the bottom. Then I hid that slice by specifying No Fill and No Border for the data point.

The other two slices are apportioned based on the value in cell B1. The formula in cell A4 is

```
=MIN(B1,100%)/2
```

This formula uses the `MIN` function to display the smaller of two values: either the value in cell B1 or 100 percent. It then divides this value by 2 because only the top half of the pie is relevant. Using the `MIN` function prevents the chart from displaying more than 100 percent.

The formula in cell A5 simply calculates the remaining part of the pie — the part to the right of the gauge's "needle":

```
=50%-A4
```

The chart's title was moved below the half-pie. The chart also contains a text box, linked to cell B1, that displays the percent completed.

Displaying conditional colors in a column chart

This section describes how to create a column chart in which the color of each column depends on the value that it's displaying. Figure 20.39 shows such a chart (more impressive when you see it in color). The data used to create the chart is in range A1:F14.

FIGURE 20.39

The color of the column varies with the value.

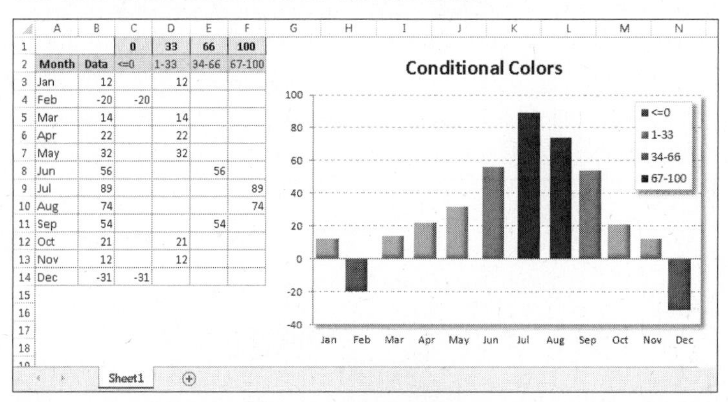

	A	B	C	D	E	F
1			0	33	66	100
2	Month	Data	<=0	1-33	34-66	67-100
3	Jan	12		12		
4	Feb	-20	-20			
5	Mar	14		14		
6	Apr	22		22		
7	May	32		32		
8	Jun	56			56	
9	Jul	89				89
10	Aug	74				74
11	Sep	54			54	
12	Oct	21		21		
13	Nov	12		12		
14	Dec	-31	-31			

ON THE WEB

A workbook with this example is on this book's website. The filename is `conditional colors.xlsx`.

This chart actually displays four data series, but some data is missing for each series. The data for the chart is entered in column B. Formulas in columns C:F determine which series the number belongs to by referencing the cut-off values in Row 1. For example, the formula in cell C3 is

```
=IF(B3<=$C$1,B3,"")
```

If the value in column B is less than the value in cell C1, the value goes in this column. The formulas are set up such that a value in column B goes into only one column in the row.

The formula in cell D3 is a bit more complex because it must determine whether cell C3 is greater than the value in cell C1 and less than or equal to the value in cell D1:

```
=IF(AND($B3>C$1,$B3<=D$1),$B3,"")
```

The four data series are overlaid on top of each other in the chart. The trick involves setting the Series Overlap value to a large number. This setting determines the spacing between the series. Use the Series Options section of the Format Data Series task pane to adjust this setting. That section has another setting, Gap Width. In this case, the Gap Width essentially controls the width of the columns.

20

NOTE

Series Overlap and Gap Width apply to the entire chart. If you change the setting for one series, the other series change to the same value.

Creating a comparative histogram

With a bit of creativity, you can create charts that you may have considered impossible. For example, Figure 20.40 shows a chart sometimes referred to as a *comparative histogram chart.* Such charts often display population data.

FIGURE 20.40

A comparative histogram.

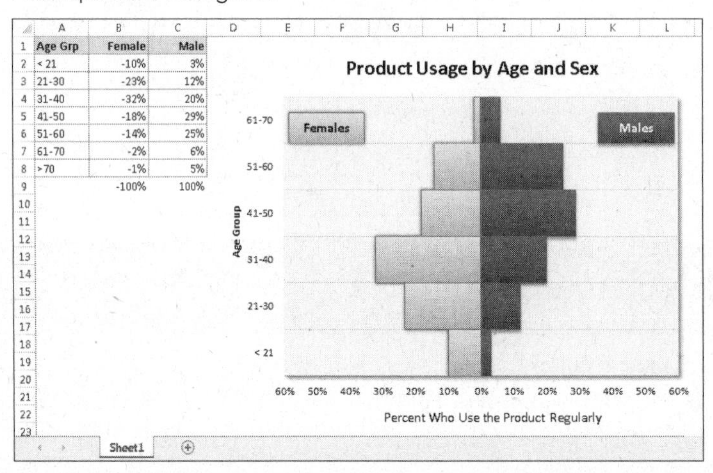

ON THE WEB

A workbook with this example is available on this book's website. The filename is `comparative histogram.xlsx`.

Here's how to create the chart:

1. **Enter the data in A1:C8, as shown in Figure 20.40.** Notice that the values for females are entered as negative values, which is very important.
2. **Select A1:C8 and create a bar chart.** Use the subtype labeled Clustered Bar.
3. **Select the horizontal axis and display the Format Axis task pane.**
4. **Expand the Number section and specify the 0%;0%;0% custom number format in the Format Code box.** This custom number format eliminates the negative signs in the percentages.
5. **Select the vertical axis and display the Format Axis task pane.**
6. **In the Axis Options section, set all tick marks to None and set the Axis Labels option to Low.** This setting keeps the vertical axis in the center of the chart but displays the axis labels at the left side.

7. **Select either data series and display the Format Data Series task pane.**
8. **In the Series Options section, set the Series Overlap to 100% and the Gap Width to 0%.**
9. **Delete the legend and add two text boxes to the chart (Females and Males) to substitute for the legend.**
10. **Apply other formatting and labels as desired.**

Creating a Gantt chart

A *Gantt chart* is a horizontal bar chart often used in project management applications. Although Excel doesn't support Gantt charts per se, creating a simple Gantt chart is possible. The key is getting your data set up properly.

Figure 20.41 shows a Gantt chart that depicts the schedule for a project, which is in the range A2:C13. The horizontal axis represents the total time span of the project, and each bar represents a project task. The viewer can quickly see the duration for each task and identify overlapping tasks.

FIGURE 20.41

You can create a simple Gantt chart from a bar chart.

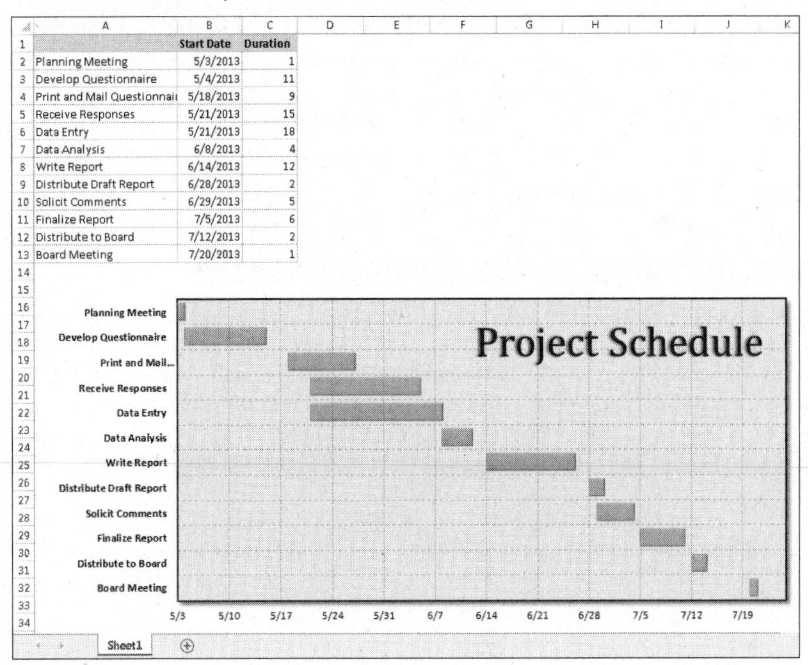

	A	B	C
1		Start Date	Duration
2	Planning Meeting	5/3/2013	1
3	Develop Questionnaire	5/4/2013	11
4	Print and Mail Questionnai	5/18/2013	9
5	Receive Responses	5/21/2013	15
6	Data Entry	5/21/2013	18
7	Data Analysis	6/8/2013	4
8	Write Report	6/14/2013	12
9	Distribute Draft Report	6/28/2013	2
10	Solicit Comments	6/29/2013	5
11	Finalize Report	7/5/2013	6
12	Distribute to Board	7/12/2013	2
13	Board Meeting	7/20/2013	1

On the Web

A workbook with this example is available on this book's website. The filename is `gantt chart.xlsx`.

Column A contains the task name, column B contains the corresponding start date, and column C contains the duration of the task, in days. Note that column A does not have a column header. That's very important. If cell A1 contains text, Excel will use columns A and B for the category axis labels.

Follow these steps to create this chart:

1. **Select the range A1:C13, and create a stacked bar chart.**
2. **Delete the legend.**
3. **Select the category (vertical) axis and display the Format Axis task pane.**
4. **In the Axis Options section, specify Categories in Reverse Order to display the tasks in order, starting at the top; choose Horizontal Axis Crosses at Maximum Category to display the dates at the bottom.**
5. **Select the Start Date data series and display the Format Data Series task pane.**
6. **In the Series Options section, set the Series Overlap to 100%; in the Fill section, specify No Fill; in the Border section, specify No Line.** These steps effectively hide the data series.
7. **Select the value (horizontal) axis and display the Format Axis task pane.**
8. **In the Axis Options section, adjust the Minimum and Maximum settings to accommodate the dates that you want to display on the axis.** You can enter a date value, and Excel converts it to a date serial number. In the example, the Minimum is 5/3/2013 and the Maximum is 7/24/2013.
9. **Apply other formatting as desired.**

Plotting mathematical functions with one variable

An XY chart is useful for plotting various mathematical and trigonometric functions. For example, Figure 20.42 shows a plot of the `SIN` function. The chart plots *y* for values of *x* (expressed in radians) from –5 to +5 in increments of 0.5. Each pair of *x* and *y* values appears as a data point in the chart, and the points connect with a line.

The function is expressed as

```
y = SIN(x)
```

The corresponding formula in cell B2 (which is copied to the cells below) is

```
=SIN(A2)
```

> **ON THE WEB**
>
> This book's website contains a general-purpose, single-variable plotting application. The file is named `function plot 2D.xlsx`.

FIGURE 20.42

This chart plots the `SIN(x)`.

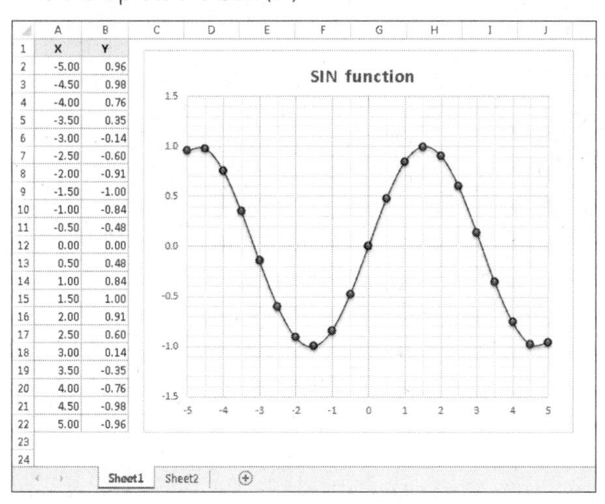

X	Y
-5.00	0.96
-4.50	0.98
-4.00	0.76
-3.50	0.35
-3.00	-0.14
-2.50	-0.60
-2.00	-0.91
-1.50	-1.00
-1.00	-0.84
-0.50	-0.48
0.00	0.00
0.50	0.48
1.00	0.84
1.50	1.00
2.00	0.91
2.50	0.60
3.00	0.14
3.50	-0.35
4.00	-0.76
4.50	-0.98
5.00	-0.96

Plotting mathematical functions with two variables

The preceding section describes how to plot functions that use a single variable (`x`). You also can plot functions that use two variables. For example, the following function calculates a value of `z` for various values of two variables (`x` and `y`):

```
z = SIN(x)*COS(y)
```

Figure 20.43 shows a surface chart that plots the value of `z` for 21 `x` values and 21 `y` values, ranging from –2.0 to +2.0. Both `x` and `y` use an increment of 0.2.

The formula in cell B2, copied across and down, is

```
=SIN($A2)*COS(B$1)
```

> **ON THE WEB**
>
> This book's website contains a general-purpose, two-variable plotting application. The file is named `function plot 3D.xlsm`. This workbook contains a few simple VBA macros to allow you to change the chart's rotation and elevation.

FIGURE 20.43

Using a surface chart to plot a function with two variables.

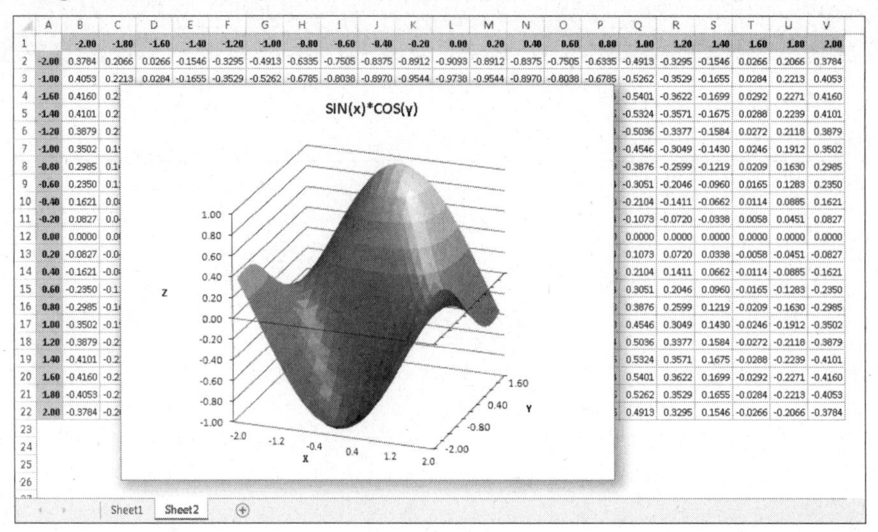

CHAPTER

21

Visualizing Data Using Conditional Formatting

IN THIS CHAPTER

Getting an overview of Excel's conditional formatting feature

Using the graphical conditional formats

Using conditional formatting formulas

Finding tips for using conditional formatting

This chapter explores the topic of conditional formatting, one of Excel's most versatile features. You can apply conditional formatting to a cell so that the cell looks different, depending on its contents.

Conditional formatting is a useful tool for visualizing numeric data. In some cases, conditional formatting may be a viable alternative to creating a chart.

About Conditional Formatting

Conditional formatting enables you to apply cell formatting selectively and automatically, based on the contents of the cells. For example, you can apply conditional formatting in such a way that all negative values in a range have a light-yellow background color. When you enter or change a value in the range, Excel examines the value and checks the conditional formatting rules for the cell. If the value is negative, the background is shaded; otherwise, no formatting is applied.

Conditional formatting is an easy way to quickly identify erroneous cell entries or cells of a particular type. You can use a format (such as bright-red cell shading) to make particular cells easy to identify.

Figure 21.1 shows a worksheet with nine ranges, each with a different type of conditional formatting rule applied. Here's a brief explanation of each:

FIGURE 21.1

This worksheet demonstrates a few conditional formatting rules.

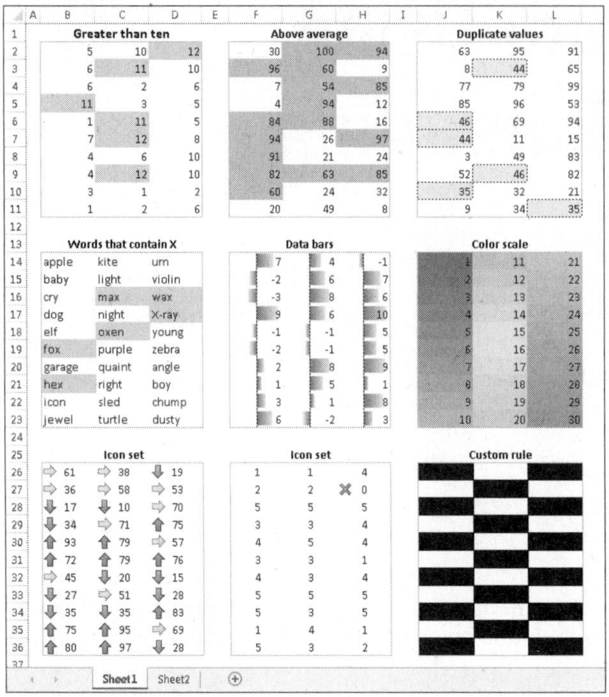

	A	B	C	D	E	F	G	H	I	J	K	L
1			Greater than ten				Above average				Duplicate values	
2		5	10	12		30	100	94		63	95	91
3		6	11	10		96	60	9		8	44	65
4		6	2	6		7	54	85		77	79	99
5		11	3	5		4	94	12		85	96	53
6		1	11	5		84	88	16		46	69	94
7		7	12	8		94	26	97		44	11	15
8		4	6	10		91	21	24		3	49	83
9		4	12	10		82	63	85		52	46	82
10		3	1	2		60	24	32		35	32	21
11		1	2	6		20	49	8		9	34	35
12												
13			Words that contain X				Data bars				Color scale	
14		apple	kite	urn		7	4	-1		1	11	21
15		baby	light	violin		-2	6	7		2	12	22
16		cry	max	wax		-3	8	6		3	13	23
17		dog	night	X-ray		9	6	10		4	14	24
18		elf	oxen	young		-1	-1	5		5	15	25
19		fox	purple	zebra		-2	-1	5		6	16	26
20		garage	quaint	angle		2	8	9		7	17	27
21		hex	right	boy		1	5	1		8	18	28
22		icon	sled	chump		3	1	8		9	19	29
23		jewel	turtle	dusty		6	-2	3		10	20	30
24												
25			Icon set				Icon set				Custom rule	
26		61	38	19		1	1	4				
27		36	58	53		2	2	0				
28		17	10	70		5	5	5				
29		34	71	75		3	3	4				
30		93	79	57		4	5	4				
31		72	79	76		3	3	1				
32		45	20	15		4	3	4				
33		27	51	28		5	5	5				
34		35	35	83		5	3	5				
35		75	95	69		1	4	1				
36		80	97	28		5	3	2				

Sheet1 | Sheet2

- **Greater than ten:** Values greater than ten are highlighted with a different background color. This rule is just one of many numeric-value-related rules that you can apply.
- **Above average:** Values that are higher than the average value are highlighted.
- **Duplicate values:** Values that appear in the range more than once are highlighted.
- **Words that contain X:** If the cell contains X (upper- or lowercase), the cell is highlighted.
- **Data bars:** Each cell displays a horizontal bar, the length of which is proportional to its value.
- **Color scale:** The background color varies, depending on the value of the cells. You can choose from several different color scales or create your own.
- **Icon set:** One of several icon sets. It displays a small graphic in the cell. The graphic varies, depending on the cell value.
- **Icon set:** Another icon set, with all but one icon in the set hidden.
- **Custom rule:** The rule for this checkerboard pattern is based on a formula:

```
=MOD(ROW(),2)=MOD(COLUMN(),2)
```

ON THE WEB

This workbook, named `conditional formatting examples.xlsx`, is available at this book's website.

Specifying Conditional Formatting

To apply a conditional formatting rule to a cell or range, select the cells and then use one of the commands from the Home ➪ Styles ➪ Conditional Formatting drop-down list to specify a rule. The choices are

- **Highlight Cell Rules:** Examples include highlighting cells that are greater than a particular value, between two values, contain specific text string, contain a date, or are duplicated.
- **Top Bottom Rules:** Examples include highlighting the top ten items, the items in the bottom 20%, and items that are above average.
- **Data Bars:** Applies graphic bars directly in the cells, proportional to the cell's value.
- **Color Scales:** Applies background color, proportional to the cell's value.
- **Icon Sets:** Displays icons directly in the cells. The icons depend on the cell's value.
- **New Rule:** Enables you to specify other conditional formatting rules, including rules based on a logical formula.
- **Clear Rules:** Deletes all the conditional formatting rules from the selected cells.
- **Manage Rules:** Displays the Conditional Formatting Rules Manager dialog box, in which you create new conditional formatting rules, edit rules, or delete rules.

Formatting types you can apply

When you select a conditional formatting rule, Excel displays a dialog box specific to that rule. These dialog boxes have one thing in a common: a drop-down list with common formatting suggestions.

Figure 21.2 shows the dialog box that appears when you choose Home ➪ Styles ➪ Conditional Formatting ➪ Highlight Cells Rules ➪ Between. This particular rule applies the formatting if the value in the cell falls between two specified values. In this case, you enter the two values (or specify cell references), and then use choices from the drop-down list to set the type of formatting to display if the condition is met.

FIGURE 21.2

One of several different conditional formatting dialog boxes.

The formatting suggestions in the drop-down list are just a few of thousands of different formatting combinations. If none of Excel's suggestions are what you want, choose the Custom Format option to display the Format Cells dialog box. You can specify the format in any or all of the four tabs: Number, Font, Border, and Fill.

NOTE

The Format Cells dialog box used for conditional formatting is a modified version of the standard Format Cells dialog box. It doesn't have the Alignment and Protection tabs, and some of the Font formatting options are disabled. The dialog box also includes a Clear button that clears any formatting already selected.

Making your own rules

For maximum control, Excel provides the New Formatting Rule dialog box, shown in Figure 21.3. Access this dialog box by choosing Home⇨Styles⇨Conditional Formatting⇨New Rules.

FIGURE 21.3

Use the New Formatting Rule dialog box to create your own conditional formatting rules.

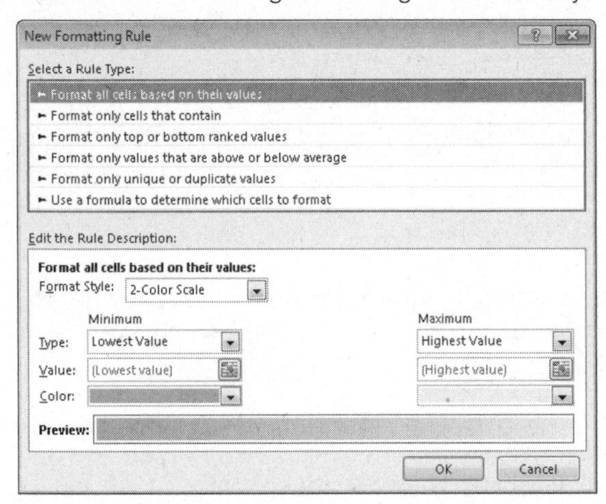

Use the New Formatting Rule dialog box to re-create all the conditional format rules available via the Ribbon, as well as new rules. First, select a general rule type from the list at the top of the dialog box. The bottom part of the dialog box varies, depending on your selection at the top. After you specify the rule, click the Format button to specify the type of formatting to apply if the condition is met. An exception is the first rule type (Format All Cells Based on Their Values), which doesn't have a Format button (it uses graphics rather than cell formatting).

Here is a summary of the rule types:

- **Format all cells based on their values:** Use this rule type to create rules that display data bars, color scales, or icon sets.
- **Format only cells that contain:** Use this rule type to create rules that format cells based on mathematical comparisons (greater than, less than, greater than or equal to, less than or equal to, equal to, not equal to, between, not between). You can also create rules based on text, dates, blanks, nonblanks, and errors.
- **Format only top- or bottom-ranked values:** Use this rule type to create rules that involve identifying cells in the top *n*, top *n*%, bottom *n*, and bottom *n*%.
- **Format only values that are above or below average:** Use this rule type to create rules that identify cells that are above average, below average, or within a specified standard deviation from the average.
- **Format only unique or duplicate values:** Use this rule type to create rules that format unique or duplicate values in a range.
- **Use a formula to determine which cells to format:** Use this rule type to create rules based on a logical formula (see "Creating Formula-Based Rules," later in this chapter).

Conditional Formats That Use Graphics

This section describes the three conditional formatting options that display graphics: data bars, color scales, and icon sets. These types of conditional formatting can be useful for visualizing the values in a range.

Using data bars

The *data bars conditional format* displays horizontal bars directly in the cell. The length of the bar is based on the value of the cell, relative to the other values in the range.

A simple data bar

Figure 21.4 shows an example of data bars. It's a list of tracks on 37 Bob Dylan albums, with the length of each track in column D. I applied data bar conditional formatting to the values in column D. You can tell at a glance which tracks are longer.

On the Web

The examples in the section are available on this book's website. The workbook is named `data bars examples.xlsx`.

FIGURE 21.4

The length of the data bars is proportional to the track length in the cell in column D.

	A	B	C	D
1	Artist	Album	Title	Length
2	Bob Dylan	Planet Waves	Never Say Goodbye	0:02:53
3	Bob Dylan	Bob Dylan	Fixin' To Die Blues	0:02:21
4	Bob Dylan	Tell Tale Signs (Disc 1)	Huck's Tune (from "Lucky You" Soundtrack)	0:04:04
5	Bob Dylan	World Gone Wrong	Blood in My Eyes	0:05:04
6	Bob Dylan	Good As I Been to You	Blackjack Davey	0:05:50
7	Bob Dylan	Good As I Been to You	Froggie Went a Courtin'	0:06:23
8	Bob Dylan	Self Portrait	The Mighty Quinn (Quinn the Eskimo)	0:02:48
9	Bob Dylan	Good As I Been to You	Canadee-I-O	0:04:23
10	Bob Dylan	Bringing it All Back Home	Outlaw Blues	0:03:06
11	Bob Dylan	World Gone Wrong	Love Henry	0:04:24
12	Bob Dylan	Down in the Groove	Had A Dream About You, Baby	0:02:50
13	Bob Dylan	Tell Tale Signs (Disc 1)	Dignity (Piano Demo, Oh Mercy)	0:02:12
14	Bob Dylan	Tell Tale Signs (Disc 1)	Someday Baby (Alternate Version, Modern Times)	0:05:57
15	Bob Dylan	Bob Dylan	Freight Train Blues	0:02:19
16	Bob Dylan	Tell Tale Signs (Disc 1)	High Water (for Charley Patton) (Live, 2003)	0:06:46
17	Bob Dylan	The Freewheelin' Bob Dylan	Don't Think Twice, It's All Right	0:03:40
18	Bob Dylan	Tempest	Tempest	0:13:54
19	Bob Dylan	Another Side of Bob Dylan	I Shall Be Free No. 10	0:04:47
20	Bob Dylan	Highway 61 Revisited	Just Like Tom Thumb's Blues	0:05:32
21	Bob Dylan	30th Anniversary Concert	When I Paint My Masterpiece	0:04:23
22	Bob Dylan	Bob Dylan	Highway 51 blues	0:02:53
23	Bob Dylan	The Freewheelin' Bob Dylan	Down The Highway	0:03:27
24	Bob Dylan	MTV Unplugged	Shooting Star	0:04:06
25	Bob Dylan	Dylan	Lily of the West	0:03:47
26	Bob Dylan	Together Through Life	If You Ever Go To Houston	0:05:48
27	Bob Dylan	Down in the Groove	Rank Strangers To Me	0:02:57

Sheet1 Pivot Sheet2

TIP

When you adjust the column width, the bar lengths adjust accordingly. The differences among the bar lengths are more prominent when the column is wider.

Excel provides quick access to 12 data bar styles via Home ⇨ Styles ⇨ Conditional Formatting ⇨ Data Bars. For additional choices, click the More Rules option, which displays the New Formatting Rule dialog box. Use this dialog box to

- Show the bar only (hide the numbers).
- Specify Minimum and Maximum values for the scaling.
- Change the appearance of the bars.
- Specify how negative values and the axis are handled.
- Specify the direction of the bars.

NOTE

Oddly, if you add data bars using one of the 12 data bar styles, the colors used for data bars are *not* theme colors. If you apply a new document theme, the data bar colors do not change. However, if you add the data bars by using the New Formatting Rule dialog box, the colors you choose *are* theme colors.

Using data bars in lieu of a chart

Using the data bars conditional formatting can sometimes serve as a quick alternative to creating a chart. Figure 21.5 shows a three-column range (in B3:D14) with data bars conditional formatting in column D (column D contains references to the values in column C). The conditional formatting in column D uses the Show Bars Only option, so the values are not displayed.

FIGURE 21.5

Comparing data bars conditional formatting (top) with a bar chart.

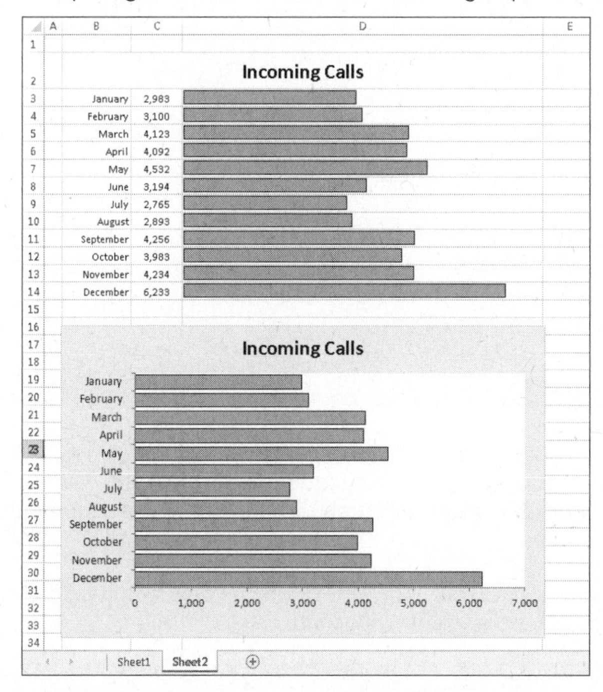

Figure 21.5 also shows an actual bar chart created from the same data. The bar chart takes about the same amount of time to create and is a lot more flexible. But for a quick-and-dirty chart, data bars may be a good option — especially when you need to create several such charts.

Using color scales

The *color scale conditional formatting option* varies the background color of a cell based on the cell's value, relative to other cells in the range.

A color scale example

Figure 21.6 shows examples of color scale conditional formatting. The example on the left depicts monthly sales for three regions. Conditional formatting was applied to the range B4:D15. The conditional formatting uses a three-color scale, with red for the lowest value, yellow for the midpoint, and green for the highest value. Values in between are displayed using a color within the gradient. It's clear that the Central region consistently has lower sales volumes, but the conditional formatting doesn't help identify monthly difference for a particular region.

FIGURE 21.6

Two examples of color scale conditional formatting.

	A	B	C	D	E	F	G	H	I
1	**A single conditional formatting rule**					**A separate rule for each region**			
2									
3	**Month**	**Western**	**Central**	**Eastern**		**Month**	**Western**	**Central**	**Eastern**
4	January	214,030	103,832	225,732		January	214,030	103,832	225,732
5	February	204,414	105,061	239,422		February	204,414	105,061	239,422
6	March	200,001	104,422	227,916		March	200,001	104,422	227,916
7	April	201,579	97,888	228,718		April	201,579	97,888	228,718
8	May	203,468	94,898	221,195		May	203,468	94,898	221,195
9	June	200,109	99,822	216,163		June	200,109	99,822	216,163
10	July	190,427	99,974	226,600		July	190,427	99,974	226,600
11	August	199,367	96,711	217,985		August	199,367	96,711	217,985
12	September	190,330	94,881	204,144		September	190,330	94,881	204,144
13	October	186,350	97,790	216,165		October	186,350	97,790	216,165
14	November	193,635	91,465	215,013		November	193,635	91,465	215,013
15	December	197,792	90,786	224,877		December	197,792	90,786	224,877
16									

Sheet1 Sheet2

The example on the right shows the same data, but conditional formatting was applied to each region separately. This approach facilitates comparisons within a region and can also help identify high or low sales months.

Neither one of these approaches is necessarily better. The way you set up conditional formatting depends entirely on what you're trying to visualize.

ON THE WEB

This workbook, named `color scale example.xlsx`, is available at this book's website.

Excel provides four two-color scale presets and four three-color scales presets, which you can apply to the selected range by choosing Home ➪ Styles ➪ Conditional Formatting ➪ Color Scales.

To customize the colors and other options, choose Home ➪ Styles ➪ Conditional Formatting ➪ Color Scales ➪ More Rules. The New Formatting Rule dialog box, shown in Figure 21.7, appears. Adjust the settings, and watch the Preview box to see the effects of your changes.

FIGURE 21.7

Use the New Formatting Rule dialog box to customize a color scale.

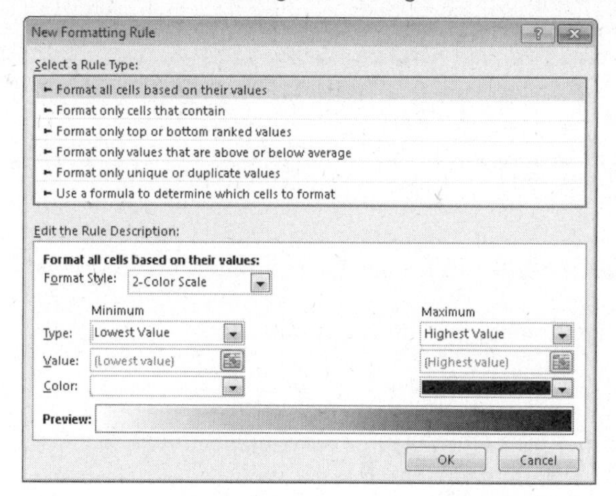

An extreme color scale example

It's important to understand that color scale conditional formatting uses a gradient. For example, if you format a range using a two-color scale, you'll get a lot more than two colors. You'll also get colors within the gradient between the two specified colors.

Figure 21.8 shows an extreme example that uses color scale conditional formatting on a range of more than 6,000 cells. The worksheet contains average daily temperatures for an 18-year period. Each row contains 365 (or 366) temperatures for the year. The columns are very narrow so the entire year can be visualized.

FIGURE 21.8

This worksheet uses color scale conditional formatting to display daily temperatures.

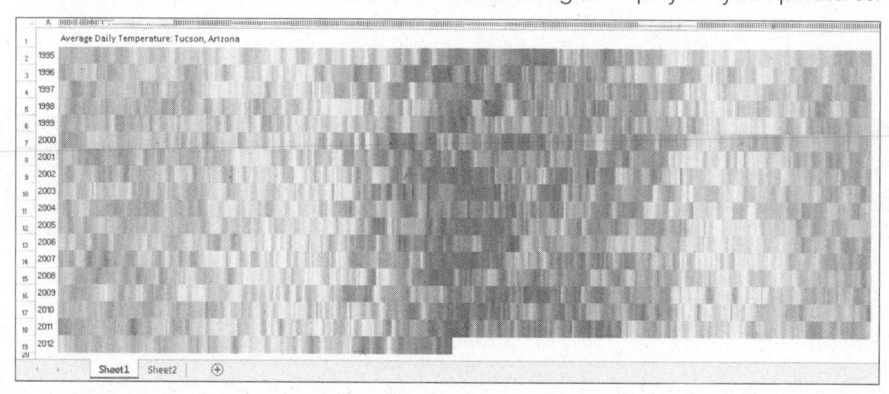

On the Web

This workbook, named `extreme color scale.xlsx`, is available at this book's website. The workbook contains a second example of extreme color scale.

Using icon sets

Yet another conditional formatting option is to display an icon in the cell. The icon displayed depends on the value of the cell.

To assign an icon set to a range, select the cells and choose Home➪Styles➪Conditional Formatting➪Icon Sets. Excel provides 20 icon sets to choose from. The number of icons in the sets ranges from three to five. You can't create a custom icon set.

An icon set example

Figure 21.9 shows an example that uses an icon set. The symbols graphically depict the status of each project, based on the value in column C.

FIGURE 21.9

Using an icon set to indicate the status of projects.

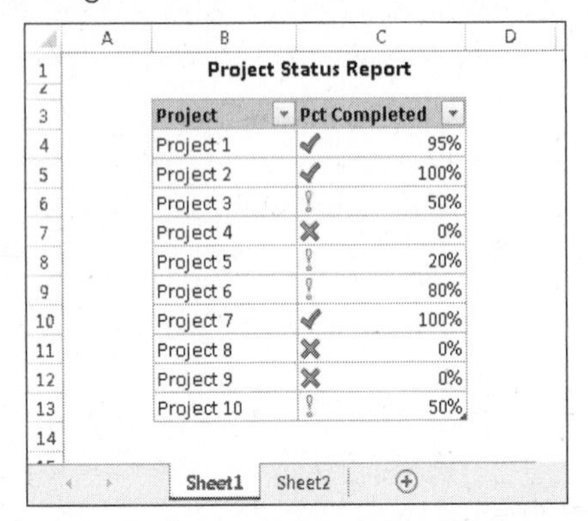

Project Status Report

Project	Pct Completed
Project 1	95%
Project 2	100%
Project 3	50%
Project 4	0%
Project 5	20%
Project 6	80%
Project 7	100%
Project 8	0%
Project 9	0%
Project 10	50%

On the Web

The icon set examples in this section are available on this book's website. The workbook is named `icon set examples.xlsx`.

By default, the symbols are assigned using percentiles. For a three-symbol set, the items are grouped into three percentiles. For a four-symbol set, they're grouped into four percentiles. And for a five-symbol set, the items are grouped into five percentiles.

If you would like more control over how the icons are assigned, choose Home➪Styles➪Conditional Formatting➪Icon Sets➪More Rules to display the New Formatting Rule dialog box. To modify an existing rule, choose Home ➪ Styles ➪ Conditional Formatting ➪ Manage Rules. Then select the rule to modify and click the Edit Rule button.

Figure 21.10 shows how to modify the icon set rules such that only projects that are 100% completed get the check mark icons. Projects that are 0% completed get the X icon. All other projects get no icon.

FIGURE 21.10

Changing the icon assignment rule.

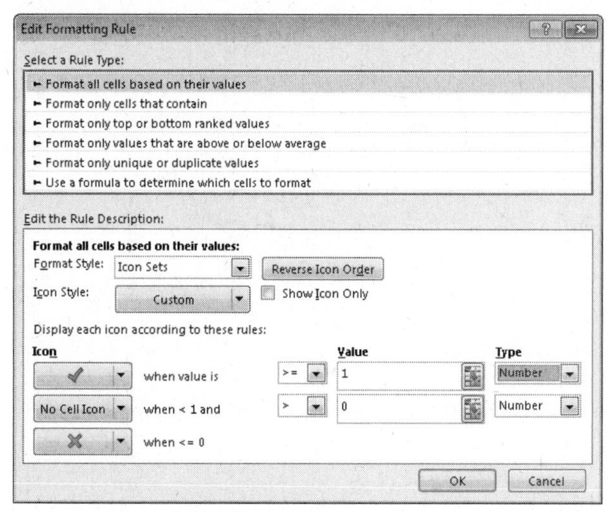

Figure 21.11 shows project status list after making this change.

FIGURE 21.11

Using a modified rule and eliminating an icon makes the table more readable.

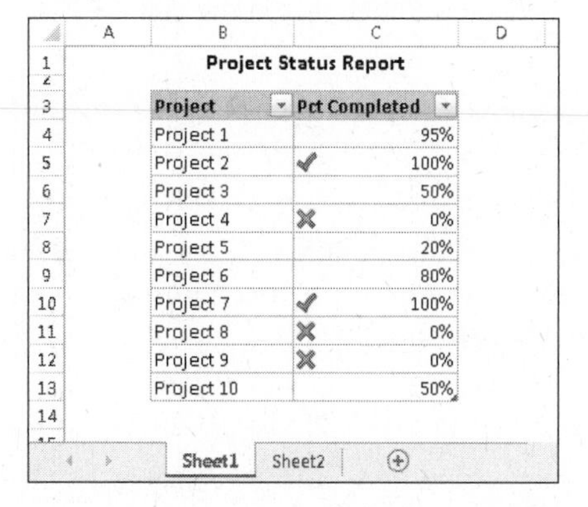

Project Status Report

Project	Pct Completed
Project 1	95%
Project 2	✔ 100%
Project 3	50%
Project 4	✖ 0%
Project 5	20%
Project 6	80%
Project 7	✔ 100%
Project 8	✖ 0%
Project 9	✖ 0%
Project 10	50%

Another icon set example

Figure 21.12 shows a table that contains two test scores for each student. The Change column contains a formula that calculates the difference between the two tests. The Trend column uses an icon set to display the trend graphically.

FIGURE 21.12

The arrows depict the trend from Test 1 to Test 2.

Student	Test1	Test2	Change	Trend
Amy	59	65	6	↑
Bob	82	78	-4	→
Calvind	98	92	-6	↓
Doug	56	69	13	↑
Ephraim	98	89	-9	↓
Frank	67	75	8	↑
Gretta	78	87	9	↑
Harold	87	92	5	↑
Inez	56	85	29	↑
June	87	72	-15	↓
Kenny	87	88	1	→
Lance	92	92	0	→
Marvin	82	73	-9	↓
Noel	98	100	2	→
Opie	84	73	-11	↓
Paul	94	93	-1	→
Quinton	68	92	24	↑
Rasmus	91	90	-1	→
Sam	85	86	1	→
Ted	72	92	20	↑
Ursie	80	75	-5	↓
Valerie	77	65	-12	↓
Wally	64	45	-19	↓
Xerxes	59	63	4	→
Yolanda	89	99	10	↑
Zippy	85	82	-3	→

Sheet1 Sheet2

This example uses the icon set named 3 Arrows, and I customized the rule:

- **Up Arrow:** When value is >= 5
- **Level Arrow:** When value < 5 and > -5
- **Down Arrow:** When value is <= -5

In other words, a difference of no more than five points in either direction is considered an even trend. An improvement of at least five points is considered a positive trend, and a decline of five points or more is considered a negative trend.

NOTE

The Trend column contains a formula that references the Change column. I used the Show Icon Only option in the Trend column, which also centers the icon in the column.

In some cases, using icon sets can cause your worksheet to look a bit cluttered. Displaying an icon for every cell in a range might result in visual overload.

Figure 21.13 shows a portion of the test results table after hiding the level arrow by choosing No Cell Icon in the Edit Formatting Rule dialog box.

FIGURE 21.13

Hiding one of the icons makes the table less cluttered.

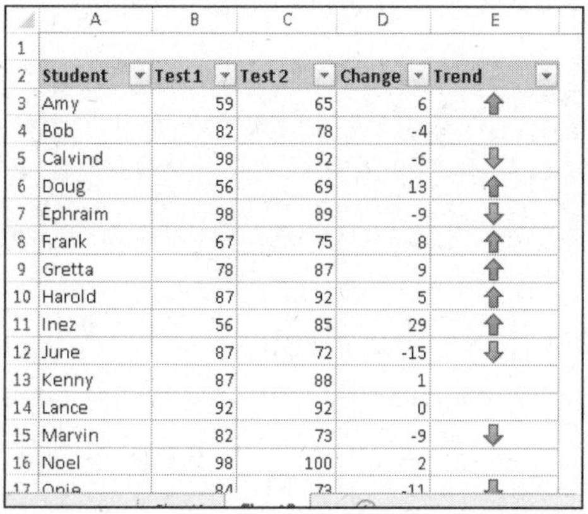

	A	B	C	D	E
1					
2	Student	Test1	Test2	Change	Trend
3	Amy	59	65	6	↑
4	Bob	82	78	-4	
5	Calvind	98	92	-6	↓
6	Doug	56	69	13	↑
7	Ephraim	98	89	-9	↓
8	Frank	67	75	8	↑
9	Gretta	78	87	9	↑
10	Harold	87	92	5	↑
11	Inez	56	85	29	↑
12	June	87	72	-15	↓
13	Kenny	87	88	1	
14	Lance	92	92	0	
15	Marvin	82	73	-9	↓
16	Noel	98	100	2	
17	Opie	84	73	-11	↓

Creating Formula-Based Rules

Excel's conditional formatting feature is versatile, but sometimes it's just not quite versatile enough. Fortunately, you can extend its versatility by writing conditional formatting formulas.

The examples later in this section describe how to create conditional formatting formulas to

- Identify text entries
- Identify dates that fall on a weekend
- Format cells that are in odd-numbered rows or columns (for dynamic alternate row or columns shading)
- Format groups of rows (for example, shade every two groups of rows)
- Display a sum only when all precedent cells contain values

Some of these formulas may be useful to you. If not, they may inspire you to create other conditional formatting formulas.

On the Web

This book's website contains all the examples in this section. The file is named `conditional formatting formulas.xlsx`.

To specify conditional formatting based on a formula, select the cells and then choose Home ➪ Styles ➪ Conditional Formatting ➪ New Rule. The New Formatting Rule dialog box appears. Click the rule type Use a Formula to Determine Which Cells to Format, and then specify the formula.

You can type the formula directly into the box or enter a reference to a cell that contains a logical formula. As with normal Excel formulas, the formula you enter here must begin with an equal sign (=).

Note

The formula must be a logical formula that returns either `TRUE` or `FALSE`. If the formula evaluates to `TRUE`, the condition is satisfied and the conditional formatting is applied. If the formula evaluates to `FALSE`, the conditional formatting is not applied.

Understanding relative and absolute references

If the formula that you enter into the Conditional Formatting dialog box contains a cell reference, that reference is considered a *relative reference,* based on the upper-left cell in the selected range.

For example, suppose that you want to set up a conditional formatting condition that applies shading to cells in range A1:B10 only if the cell contains text. None of Excel's conditional formatting options can do this task, so you need to create a formula that will return `TRUE` if the cell contains text and `FALSE` otherwise. Follow these steps:

1. **Select the range A1:B10 and ensure that cell A1 is the active cell.**
2. **Choose Home ➪ Styles ➪ Conditional Formatting ➪ New Rule.** The New Formatting Rule dialog box appears.
3. **Click the Use a Formula to Determine Which Cells to Format rule type.**
4. **Enter the following formula in the Formula box:**

   ```
   =ISTEXT(A1)
   ```
5. **Click the Format button.** The Format Cells dialog box appears.
6. **From the Fill tab, specify the cell shading that will be applied if the formula returns TRUE.**
7. **Click OK to return to the New Formatting Rule dialog box (see Figure 21.14).**

FIGURE 21.14

Creating a conditional formatting rule based on a formula.

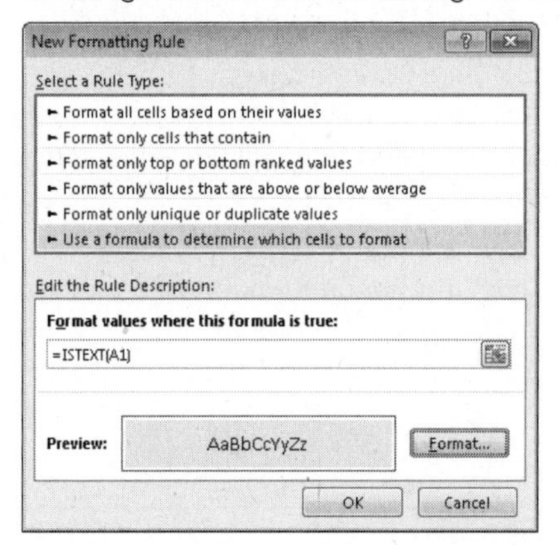

8. **Click OK to close the New Formatting Rule dialog box.**

Notice that the formula entered in Step 4 contains a relative reference to the upper-left cell in the selected range.

Generally, when entering a conditional formatting formula for a range of cells, you'll use a reference to the active cell, which is typically the upper-left cell in the selected range. One exception is when you need to refer to a specific cell. For example, suppose that you select range A1:B10, and you want to apply formatting to all cells in the range that exceed the value in cell C1. Enter this conditional formatting formula:

```
=A1>$C$1
```

In this case, the reference to cell C1 is an *absolute reference;* it will not be adjusted for the cells in the selected range. In other words, the conditional formatting formula for cell A2 looks like this:

```
=A2>$C$1
```

The relative cell reference is adjusted, but the absolute cell reference is not.

Conditional formatting formula examples

Each of these examples uses a formula entered directly into the New Formatting Rule dialog box, after selecting the Use a Formula to Determine Which Cells to Format rule type. You decide the type of formatting that you apply conditionally.

Identifying weekend days

Excel provides a number of conditional formatting rules that deal with dates, but it doesn't let you identify dates that fall on a weekend. Use this formula to identify weekend dates:

```
=OR(WEEKDAY(A1)=7,WEEKDAY(A1)=1)
```

This formula assumes that a range is selected and that cell A1 is the active cell.

Highlighting a row based on a value

Figure 21.15 shows a worksheet that contains a conditional formula in the range A3:G28. If a name entered in cell B1 is found in the first column, the entire row for that name is highlighted.

FIGURE 21.15

Highlighting a row, based on a matching name.

	A	B	C	D	E	F	G	H
1	**Name:**	Oliver						
2								
3	Alice	7	118	61	55	85	26	
4	Bob	198	134	180	3	132	63	
5	Carl	2	46	59	63	59	26	
6	Denise	190	121	12	26	68	97	
7	Elvin	174	42	176	68	124	14	
8	Francis	129	114	83	103	129	129	
9	George	9	128	24	44	139	108	
10	Harald	168	183	200	167	134	83	
11	Ivan	165	141	95	91	100	144	
12	June	116	171	109	84	148	15	
13	Kathy	131	43	197	82	103	163	
14	Larry	139	30	171	122	34	196	
15	Mary	31	171	185	162	171	17	
16	Noel	78	126	190	78	123	2	
17	Oliver	157	98	100	75	137	10	
18	Patrick	120	144	106	39	39	119	
19	Quincey	156	200	58	74	37	76	
20	Raul	58	147	160	182	11	79	
21	Shiela	79	183	5	161	104	23	
22	Todd	91	54	100	174	198	78	
23	Ursula	53	140	188	58	54	36	
24	Vince	121	13	2	139	148	101	
25	Walter	132	65	123	129	174	90	
26	Xenu	162	127	86	51	164	35	
27	Yolanda	60	116	107	117	189	200	
28	Zed	103	142	103	165	89	37	

... | Weekends | **Row Highlight** | AltRow | Checkerboard | Grc ...

The conditional formatting formula is:

```
=$A3=$B$1
```

Notice that a mixed reference is used for cell A3. Because the column part of the reference is absolute, the comparison is always done using the contents of column A.

Displaying alternate-row shading

The conditional formatting formula that follows was applied to the range A1:D18, as shown in Figure 21.16, to apply shading to alternate rows.

```
=MOD(ROW(),2)=0
```

FIGURE 21.16

Using conditional formatting to apply formatting to alternate rows.

	A	B	C	D	E
1	945	32	76	956	
2	176	795	573	874	
3	790	689	904	439	
4	653	873	379	656	
5	762	795	783	347	
6	670	514	706	321	
7	594	304	64	608	
8	321	722	510	275	
9	743	628	174	158	
10	494	462	979	616	
11	933	25	871	737	
12	821	49	209	156	
13	474	755	451	96	
14	146	175	813	297	
15	939	981	669	512	
16	824	769	16	668	
17	767	650	302	111	
18	375	998	438	59	
19					
20					

AltRow | Checkerboard | Grc ...

Alternate row shading can make your spreadsheets easier to read. If you add or delete rows within the conditional formatting area, the shading is updated automatically.

This formula uses the ROW function (which returns the row number) and the MOD function (which returns the remainder of its first argument divided by its second argument). For cells in even-numbered rows, the MOD function returns 0, and cells in that row are formatted.

For alternate shading of columns, use the COLUMN function instead of the ROW function.

Creating checkerboard shading

The following formula is a variation on the example in the preceding section. It applies formatting to alternate rows and columns, creating a checkerboard effect.

```
=MOD(ROW(),2)=MOD(COLUMN(),2)
```

Shading groups of rows

Here's another row shading variation. The following formula shades alternate groups of rows. It produces four shaded rows, followed by four unshaded rows, followed by four more shaded rows, and so on.

```
=MOD(INT((ROW()-1)/4)+1,2)=1
```

Figure 21.17 shows an example.

FIGURE 21.17

Conditional formatting produces these groups of alternating shaded rows.

	A	B	C	D	E
1	537	630	667	44	
2	318	569	338	475	
3	732	412	999	200	
4	504	349	705	32	
5	538	149	531	575	
6	372	635	378	729	
7	273	663	994	334	
8	573	234	5	116	
9	188	831	906	56	
10	721	441	142	571	
11	93	389	338	118	
12	70	840	497	238	
13	654	558	399	812	
14	724	774	464	240	
15	861	310	618	385	
16	58	924	146	202	
17	826	59	568	47	
18	535	257	398	678	
19	934	582	649	68	
20	567	411	371	34	
21	410	650	15	9	
22	951	858	68	573	
23					

Groups4 | AllData

For different sized groups, change the 4 to some other value. For example, use this formula to shade alternate groups of two rows:

```
=MOD(INT((ROW()-1)/2)+1,2)=1
```

Displaying a total only when all values are entered

Figure 21.18 shows a range with a formula that uses the SUM function in cell C6. Conditional formatting is used to display the sum only when all of the four cells above aren't blank. The conditional formatting formula for cell C6 (and cell C5, which contains a label) is

```
=COUNT($C$2:$C$5)=4
```

FIGURE 21.18

The sum is displayed only when all four values have been entered.

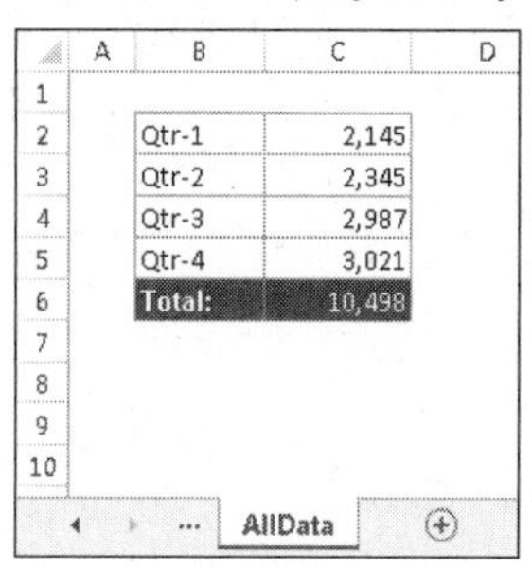

This formula returns `TRUE` only if C2:C5 contains no empty cells. The conditional formatting applied is a dark background color. The text color is white, so it's legible only when the conditional formatting rule is satisfied.

Figure 21.19 shows the worksheet when one of the values is missing.

FIGURE 21.19

A missing value causes the sum to be hidden.

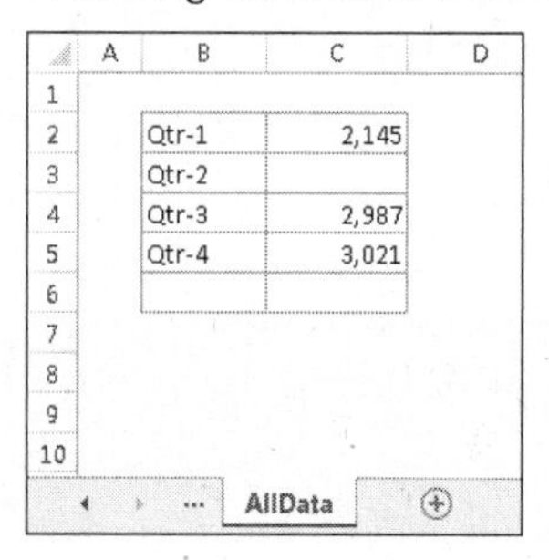

Working with Conditional Formats

This section describes some additional information about conditional formatting that you may find useful.

Managing rules

The Conditional Formatting Rules Manager dialog box is useful for checking, editing, deleting, and adding conditional formats. First select any cell in the range that contains conditional formatting. Then choose Home ➪ Styles ➪ Conditional Formatting ➪ Manage Rules.

You can specify as many rules as you like by clicking the New Rule button. As you can see in Figure 21.20, cells can even use data bars, color scales, and icon sets all at the same time — although I can't think of a good reason to do so.

FIGURE 21.20

This range uses data bars, color scales, and icon sets.

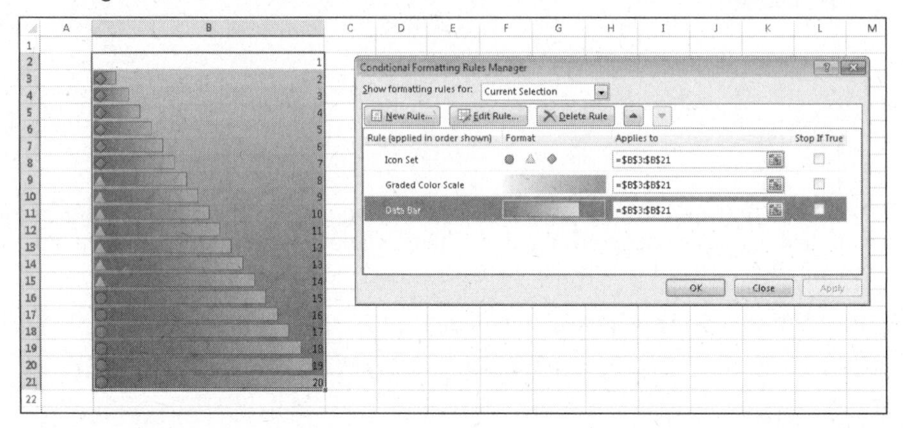

Copying cells that contain conditional formatting

Conditional formatting information is stored with a cell much like standard formatting information is stored with a cell. As a result, when you copy a cell that contains conditional formatting, you also copy the conditional formatting.

TIP

To copy only the formatting (including conditional formatting), copy the cells and then use the Paste Special dialog box and select the Formats option. Or choose Home ⇨ Clipboard ⇨ Paste ⇨ Formatting (R).

If you insert rows or columns within a range that contains conditional formatting, the new cells have the same conditional formatting.

Deleting conditional formatting

When you press Delete to delete the contents of a cell, you don't delete the conditional formatting for the cell (if any). To remove all conditional formats (as well as all other cell formatting), select the cell and then choose Home ⇨ Editing ⇨ Clear ⇨ Clear Formats. Or choose Home ⇨ Editing ⇨ Clear ⇨ Clear All to delete the cell contents and the conditional formatting.

To remove only conditional formatting (and leave the other formatting intact), choose Home⇨Styles⇨Conditional Formatting⇨Clear Rules.

Locating cells that contain conditional formatting

You can't always tell, just by looking at a cell, whether it contains conditional formatting. You can, however, use the Go to Special dialog box to select such cells.

1. **Choose Home⇨Editing⇨Find & Select⇨Go to Special.** The Go to Special dialog box appears.
2. **In the Go to Special dialog box, select the Conditional Formats option.**
3. **To select all cells on the worksheet containing conditional formatting, select the All option; to select only the cells that contain the same conditional formatting as the active cell, select the Same option.**
4. **Click OK.** Excel selects the cells for you.

NOTE

The Excel Find and Replace dialog box includes a feature that allows you to search your worksheet to locate cells that contain specific formatting. This feature does *not* locate cells that contain formatting resulting from conditional formatting.

CHAPTER

22

Creating Sparkline Graphics

IN THIS CHAPTER

Introducing the Sparkline graphics feature

Adding Sparklines to a worksheet

Customizing Sparklines

Making a Sparkline display only the most recent data

A *Sparkline* is a small chart that's displayed in a single cell. A Sparkline allows you to quickly spot time-based trends or variations in data. Because they're so compact, Sparklines are almost always used in a group.

Although Sparklines look like miniature charts (and can sometimes take the place of a chart), this feature is completely separate from the charting feature. For example, charts are placed on a worksheet's draw layer, and a single chart can display several series of data. A Sparkline is displayed inside a cell and displays only one series of data.

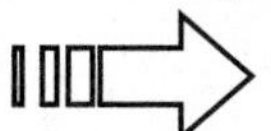

See Chapters 19 and 20 for information about *real* charts.

This chapter introduces Sparklines and presents examples that demonstrate how they can be used in your worksheets.

NOTE

Sparklines were introduced in Excel 2010. If you create a workbook that uses Sparklines, and that workbook is opened using a previous version of Excel, the Sparkline cells will be empty.

ON THE WEB

All examples in this chapter are available at this book's website. The filename is `sparkline examples.xlsx`.

Sparkline Types

Excel supports three types of Sparklines. Figure 22.1 shows examples of each, displayed in column H. Each Sparkline depicts the six data points to the left.

FIGURE 22.1

Three groups of Sparklines.

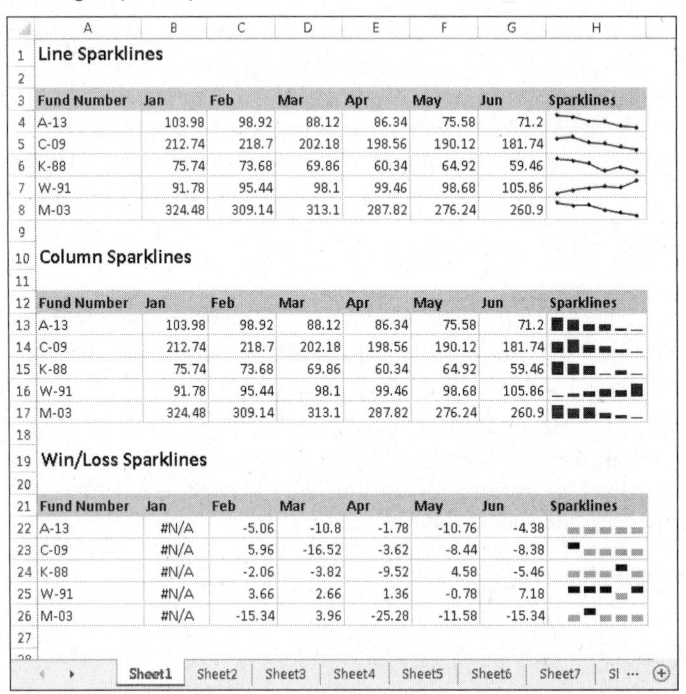

Line Sparklines

Fund Number	Jan	Feb	Mar	Apr	May	Jun	Sparklines
A-13	103.98	98.92	88.12	86.34	75.58	71.2	
C-09	212.74	218.7	202.18	198.56	190.12	181.74	
K-88	75.74	73.68	69.86	60.34	64.92	59.46	
W-91	91.78	95.44	98.1	99.46	98.68	105.86	
M-03	324.48	309.14	313.1	287.82	276.24	260.9	

Column Sparklines

Fund Number	Jan	Feb	Mar	Apr	May	Jun	Sparklines
A-13	103.98	98.92	88.12	86.34	75.58	71.2	
C-09	212.74	218.7	202.18	198.56	190.12	181.74	
K-88	75.74	73.68	69.86	60.34	64.92	59.46	
W-91	91.78	95.44	98.1	99.46	98.68	105.86	
M-03	324.48	309.14	313.1	287.82	276.24	260.9	

Win/Loss Sparklines

Fund Number	Jan	Feb	Mar	Apr	May	Jun	Sparklines
A-13	#N/A	-5.06	-10.8	-1.78	-10.76	-4.38	
C-09	#N/A	5.96	-16.52	-3.62	-8.44	-8.38	
K-88	#N/A	-2.06	-3.82	-9.52	4.58	-5.46	
W-91	#N/A	3.66	2.66	1.36	-0.78	7.18	
M-03	#N/A	-15.34	3.96	-25.28	-11.58	-15.34	

- **Line:** Similar to a line chart. As an option, the line can display with a marker for each data point. The first group in Figure 22.1 shows line Sparklines, with markers. A quick glance reveals that, with the exception of Fund Number W-91, the funds have been losing value over the six-month period.
- **Column:** Similar to a column chart. The second group in Figure 22.1 shows the same data displayed with column Sparklines.
- **Win/Loss:** A "binary"-type chart that displays each data point as a high block or a low block. The third group shows win/loss Sparklines. Notice that the data is different. Each cell displays the *change* from the previous month. In the Sparkline, each data point is depicted as a high block (win) or a low block (loss). In this example, a positive change from the previous month is a win, and a negative change from the previous month is a loss.

Why Sparklines?

If the term *Sparkline* seems odd, don't blame Microsoft. Edward Tufte coined the term *sparkline*, and in his book, *Beautiful Evidence* (Graphics Press), he describes it as follows:

> Sparklines: Intense, simple, word-sized graphics

In the case of Excel, Sparklines are cell-sized graphics. As you see in this chapter, Sparklines aren't limited to lines.

Creating Sparklines

Figure 22.2 shows some data to be summarized with Sparklines. To create Sparkline graphics, follow these steps:

FIGURE 22.2

Data to be summarized with Sparklines.

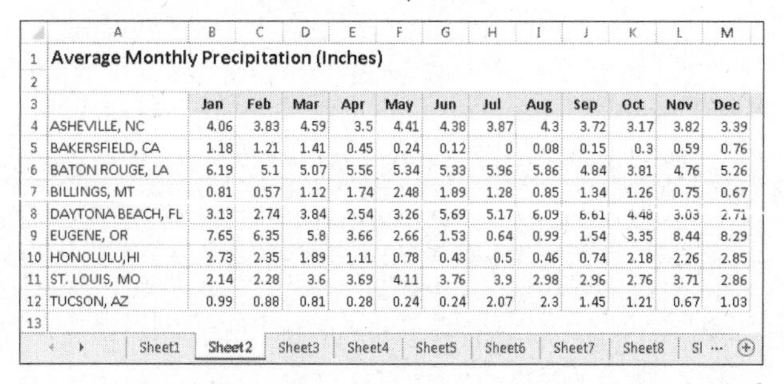

Average Monthly Precipitation (Inches)

	Jan	Feb	Mar	Apr	May	Jun	Jul	Aug	Sep	Oct	Nov	Dec
ASHEVILLE, NC	4.06	3.83	4.59	3.5	4.41	4.38	3.87	4.3	3.72	3.17	3.82	3.39
BAKERSFIELD, CA	1.18	1.21	1.41	0.45	0.24	0.12	0	0.08	0.15	0.3	0.59	0.76
BATON ROUGE, LA	6.19	5.1	5.07	5.56	5.34	5.33	5.96	5.86	4.84	3.81	4.76	5.26
BILLINGS, MT	0.81	0.57	1.12	1.74	2.48	1.89	1.28	0.85	1.34	1.26	0.75	0.67
DAYTONA BEACH, FL	3.13	2.74	3.84	2.54	3.26	5.69	5.17	6.09	6.61	4.48	3.03	2.71
EUGENE, OR	7.65	6.35	5.8	3.66	2.66	1.53	0.64	0.99	1.54	3.35	8.44	8.29
HONOLULU,HI	2.73	2.35	1.89	1.11	0.78	0.43	0.5	0.46	0.74	2.18	2.26	2.85
ST. LOUIS, MO	2.14	2.28	3.6	3.69	4.11	3.76	3.9	2.98	2.96	2.76	3.71	2.86
TUCSON, AZ	0.99	0.88	0.81	0.28	0.24	0.24	2.07	2.3	1.45	1.21	0.67	1.03

1. **Select the data that will be depicted (data only, not column headings); if you're creating multiple Sparklines, select all the data.** In this example, start by selecting B4:M12.
2. **With the data selected, choose Insert ➪ Sparklines, and click one of the three Sparkline types: Line, Column, or Win/Loss.** The Create Sparklines dialog box, shown in Figure 22.3, appears.

FIGURE 22.3

Use the Create Sparklines dialog box to specify the data range and the location for the Sparkline graphics.

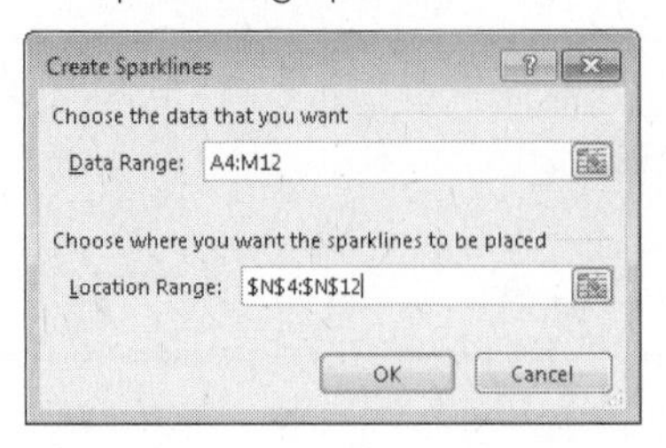

3. **Specify the location for the Sparklines.** Typically, you'll put the Sparklines next to the data, but that's not a requirement. Most of the time, you'll use an empty range to hold the Sparklines. However, Excel doesn't prevent your from inserting Sparklines into cells that already contain data. The Sparkline location that you specify must match the source data in terms of number of rows or number of columns. For this example, specify N4:N12 as the Location Range.
4. **Click OK.** Excel creates the Sparklines graphics of the type you specified.

The Sparklines are linked to the data, so if you change any of the values in the data range, the Sparkline graphic will update. Often, you'll want to increase the column width or row height to improve the readability of the Sparklines.

TIP

Most of the time, you'll create Sparklines on the same sheet that contains the data. If you want to create Sparklines on a different sheet, start by activating the sheet where the Sparklines will be displayed. Then, in the Create Sparklines dialog box, specify the source data either by pointing or by typing the complete sheet reference (for example, Sheet1A1:C12). The Create Sparklines dialog box lets you specify a different sheet for the Data Range, but not for the Location Range. Or, you can just create the Sparklines on the same sheet as the data, and then cut and paste the cells to a different worksheet.

Figure 22.4 shows column Sparklines for the precipitation data.

FIGURE 22.4

Column Sparklines summarize the precipitation data for nine cities.

	A	B	C	D	E	F	G	H	I	J	K	L	M	N
1	**Average Monthly Precipitation (Inches)**													
2														
3		**Jan**	**Feb**	**Mar**	**Apr**	**May**	**Jun**	**Jul**	**Aug**	**Sep**	**Oct**	**Nov**	**Dec**	
4	ASHEVILLE, NC	4.06	3.83	4.59	3.5	4.41	4.38	3.87	4.3	3.72	3.17	3.82	3.39	
5	BAKERSFIELD, CA	1.18	1.21	1.41	0.45	0.24	0.12	0	0.08	0.15	0.3	0.59	0.76	
6	BATON ROUGE, LA	6.19	5.1	5.07	5.56	5.34	5.33	5.96	5.86	4.84	3.81	4.76	5.26	
7	BILLINGS, MT	0.81	0.57	1.12	1.74	2.48	1.89	1.28	0.85	1.34	1.26	0.75	0.67	
8	DAYTONA BEACH, FL	3.13	2.74	3.84	2.54	3.26	5.69	5.17	6.09	6.61	4.48	3.03	2.71	
9	EUGENE, OR	7.65	6.35	5.8	3.66	2.66	1.53	0.64	0.99	1.54	3.35	8.44	8.29	
10	HONOLULU,HI	2.73	2.35	1.89	1.11	0.78	0.43	0.5	0.46	0.74	2.18	2.26	2.85	
11	ST. LOUIS, MO	2.14	2.28	3.6	3.69	4.11	3.76	3.9	2.98	2.96	2.76	3.71	2.86	
12	TUCSON, AZ	0.99	0.88	0.81	0.28	0.24	0.24	2.07	2.3	1.45	1.21	0.67	1.03	
13														

Sheet1 | Sheet2 | Sheet3 | Sheet4 | Sheet5 | Sheet6 | Sheet7 | Sheet8 | Sheet9

Understanding Sparkline Groups

In most situations, you'll probably create a *group* of Sparklines — one for each row or column of data. A worksheet can hold any number of Sparkline groups. Excel remembers each group, and you can work with the group as a single unit. For example, you can select one Sparkline in a group, and then modify the formatting of all Sparklines in the group. When you select one Sparkline cell, Excel displays an outline of all the other Sparklines in the group.

You can, however, perform some operations on an individual Sparkline in a group:

- **Change the Sparkline's data source.** Select the Sparkline cell and choose Sparkline Tools ➪ Design ➪ Sparkline ➪ Edit Data ➪ Edit Single Sparkline's Data. Excel displays a dialog box that lets you change the data source for the selected Sparkline.
- **Delete the Sparkline.** Select the Sparkline cell and choose Sparkline Tools ➪ Design ➪ Group ➪ Clear ➪ Clear Selected Sparklines.

Both operations are available from the shortcut menu that appears when you right-click a Sparkline cell.

You can also ungroup a set of Sparklines by selecting any Sparkline in the group and choosing Sparkline Tools ➪ Design ➪ Group ➪ Ungroup. After you ungroup a set of Sparklines, you can work with each Sparkline individually.

Customizing Sparklines

When you activate a cell that contains a Sparkline, Excel displays an outline around all the Sparklines in its group. You can then use the commands on the Sparkline Tools ➪ Design tab to customize the group of Sparklines.

Sizing Sparkline cells

When you change the width or height of a cell that contains a Sparkline, the Sparkline adjusts accordingly. In addition, you can insert a Sparkline into merged cells.

Figure 22.5 shows the same Sparkline, displayed at four sizes resulting from column width, row height, and merged cells. As you can see, the size and proportions of the cell (or merged cells) make a big difference in the appearance.

Handling hidden or missing data

By default, if you hide rows or columns that are used in a Sparkline graphic, the hidden data does not appear in the Sparkline. Also, missing data (an empty cell) is displayed as a gap in the graphic.

FIGURE 22.5

A Sparkline at various sizes.

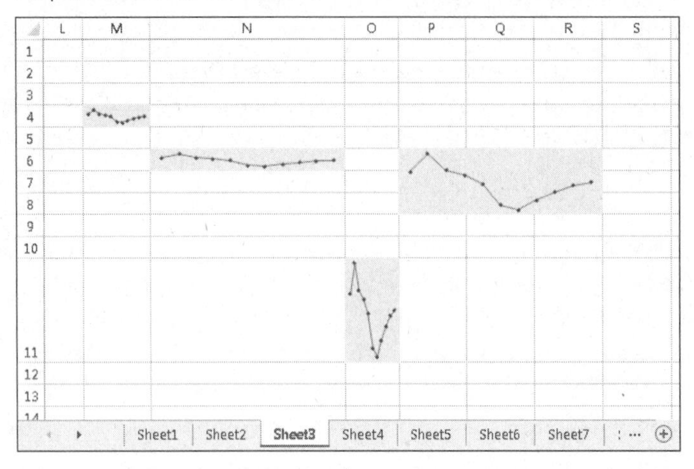

To change these settings, choose Sparkline Tools ⇨ Design ⇨ Sparkline ⇨ Edit Data ⇨ Hidden and Empty Cells. In the Hidden and Empty Cell Settings dialog box that appears (see Figure 22.6), specify how to handle hidden data and empty cells.

FIGURE 22.6

The Hidden and Empty Cell Settings dialog box.

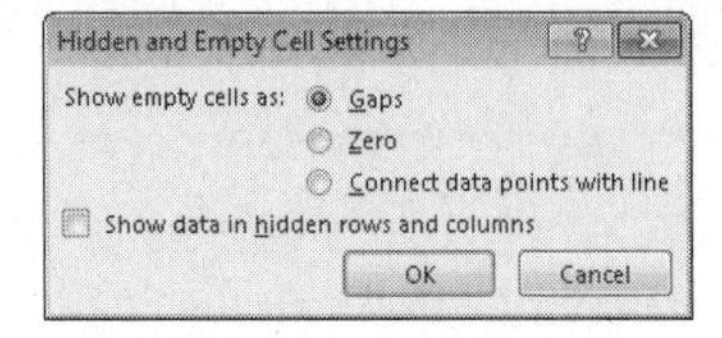

Changing the Sparkline type

As I mentioned earlier, Excel supports three Sparkline types: Line, Column, and Win/Loss. After you create a Sparkline or group of Sparklines, you can easily change the type by selecting the Sparkline and clicking one of the three icons in the Sparkline Tools ⇨ Design ⇨ Type group. If the selected Sparkline is part of a group, all Sparklines in the group are changed to the new type.

TIP

If you've customized the appearance, Excel remembers your customization settings for each type if you switch among Sparkline types.

Changing Sparkline colors and line width

After you've created a Sparkline, changing the color is easy. Use the controls in the Sparkline Tools ➪ Design ➪ Style group.

NOTE

Colors used in Sparkline graphics are tied to the document theme. Therefore, if you change the theme (by choosing Page Layout ➪ Themes ➪ Themes), the Sparkline colors will change to the new theme colors.

See Chapter 6 for more information about document themes.

For Line Sparklines, you can also specify the line width. Choose Sparkline Tools ➪ Design ➪ Style ➪ Sparkline Color ➪ Weight.

Highlighting certain data points

Use the commands in the Sparkline Tools ➪ Design ➪ Show group to customize the Sparklines to highlight certain aspects of the data. The options are

- **High Point:** Apply a different color to the highest data point in the Sparkline.
- **Low Point:** Apply a different color to the lowest data point in the Sparkline.
- **Negative Points:** Apply a different color to negative values in the Sparkline.
- **First Point:** Apply a different color to the first data point in the Sparkline.
- **Last Point:** Apply a different color to the last data point in the Sparkline.
- **Markers:** Show data markers in the Sparkline. This option is available only for Line Sparklines.

You control the color of the highlighting by using the Marker Color control in the Sparkline Tools ➪ Design ➪ Style group. Unfortunately, you can't change the size of the markers in Line Sparklines.

Figure 22.7 shows some Line Sparklines with various types of highlighting applied.

FIGURE 22.7

Highlighting options for Line Sparklines.

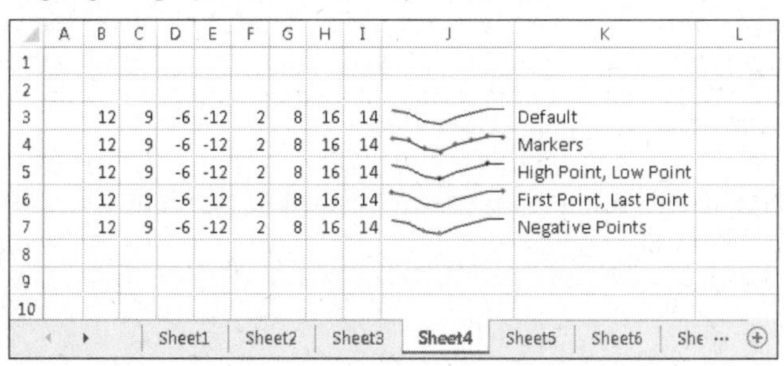

	A	B	C	D	E	F	G	H	I	J	K	L
1												
2												
3		12	9	-6	-12	2	8	16	14		Default	
4		12	9	-6	-12	2	8	16	14		Markers	
5		12	9	-6	-12	2	8	16	14		High Point, Low Point	
6		12	9	-6	-12	2	8	16	14		First Point, Last Point	
7		12	9	-6	-12	2	8	16	14		Negative Points	
8												
9												
10												

Adjusting Sparkline axis scaling

When you create one or more Sparklines, they all use (by default) automatic axis scaling. In other words, the minimum and maximum vertical axis values are determined automatically for each Sparkline in the group, based on the numeric range of the data used by the Sparkline.

The Sparkline Tools ⇨ Design ⇨ Group ⇨ Axis command lets you override this automatic behavior and control the minimum and maximum value for each Sparkline or for a group of Sparklines. For even more control, you can use the Custom Value option and specify the minimum and maximum for the Sparkline group.

NOTE

Sparklines don't actually display a vertical axis, so you're essentially adjusting an invisible axis.

Figure 22.8 shows two groups of Sparklines. The group at the top uses the default axis settings (Automatic for Each Sparkline). Each Sparkline shows the six-month trend for the product, but there is no indication of the magnitude of the values.

FIGURE 22.8

The bottom group of Sparklines shows the effect of using the same axis minimum and maximum values for all Sparklines in a group.

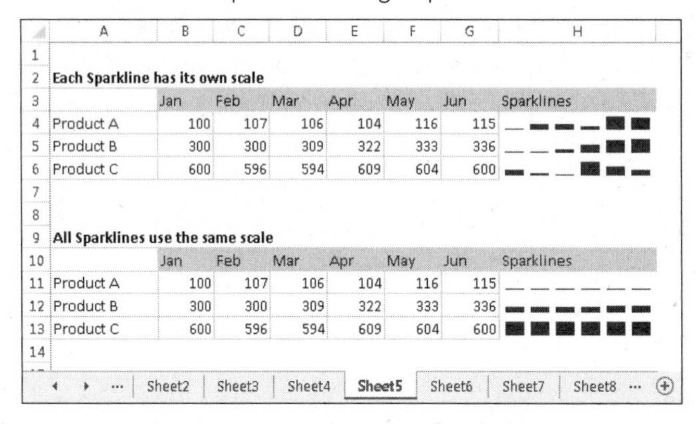

Each Sparkline has its own scale

	Jan	Feb	Mar	Apr	May	Jun	Sparklines
Product A	100	107	106	104	116	115	
Product B	300	300	309	322	333	336	
Product C	600	596	594	609	604	600	

All Sparklines use the same scale

	Jan	Feb	Mar	Apr	May	Jun	Sparklines
Product A	100	107	106	104	116	115	
Product B	300	300	309	322	333	336	
Product C	600	596	594	609	604	600	

For the Sparkline group at the bottom (which uses the same data), I changed the vertical axis minimum and maximum to use the Same for All Sparklines setting. With these settings in effect, the magnitude of the values *across* the products is apparent — but the trend across the months within a product is not apparent.

The axis scaling option you choose depends upon what aspect of the data you want to emphasize.

Faking a reference line

One useful feature that's missing in the Excel implementation of Sparklines is a reference line. For example, it might be useful to show performance relative to a goal. If the goal is displayed as a reference line in a Sparkline, the viewer can quickly see whether the performance for a period exceeded the goal.

You can, however, transform the data and then use a Sparkline axis as a fake reference line. Figure 22.9 shows an example. Students have a monthly reading goal of 500 pages. The range of data shows the actual pages read, with Sparklines in column H. The Sparklines show the six-month page data, but it's impossible to tell who exceeded the goal and when they did it.

FIGURE 22.9

Sparklines display the number of pages read per month.

	A	B	C	D	E	F	G	H
1	**Pages Read**							
2	Monthly Goal:		500					
3								
4				**Pages Read**				
5		**Jan**	**Feb**	**Mar**	**Apr**	**May**	**Jun**	
6	Ann	450	412	632	663	702	512	
7	Bob	309	215	194	189	678	256	
8	Chuck	608	783	765	832	483	763	
9	Dave	409	415	522	598	421	433	
10	Ellen	790	893	577	802	874	763	
11	Frank	211	59	0	0	185	230	
12	Giselle	785	764	701	784	214	185	
13	Henry	350	367	560	583	784	663	
14								

Sheet3 | Sheet4 | Sheet5 | Sheet6 | Sheet7 | Sheet8

Figure 22.10 shows another approach: Transforming the data such that meeting the goal is expressed as a `1`, and failing to meet the goal is expressed as a `-1`. I used the following formula (in cell B18) to transform the original data:

```
=IF(B6>$C$2,1,-1)
```

I copied this formula to the other cells in B18:G25 range.

Using the transformed data, I created Win/Loss Sparklines to visualize the results. This approach is better than the original, but it doesn't convey any magnitude differences. For example, you can't tell whether the student missed the goal by 1 page or by 500 pages.

FIGURE 22.10

Using Win/Loss Sparklines to display goal achievement.

Pages Read (Did or Did Not Meet Goal)

	Jan	Feb	Mar	Apr	May	Jun
Ann	-1	-1	1	1	1	1
Bob	-1	-1	-1	-1	1	-1
Chuck	1	1	1	1	-1	1
Dave	-1	-1	1	1	-1	-1
Ellen	1	1	1	1	1	1
Frank	-1	-1	-1	-1	-1	-1
Giselle	1	1	1	1	-1	-1
Henry	-1	-1	1	1	1	1

Figure 22.11 shows a better approach. Here, I transformed the original data by subtracting the goal from the pages read. The formula in cell B31 is

```
=B6-$C$2
```

FIGURE 22.11

The axis in the Sparklines represents the goal.

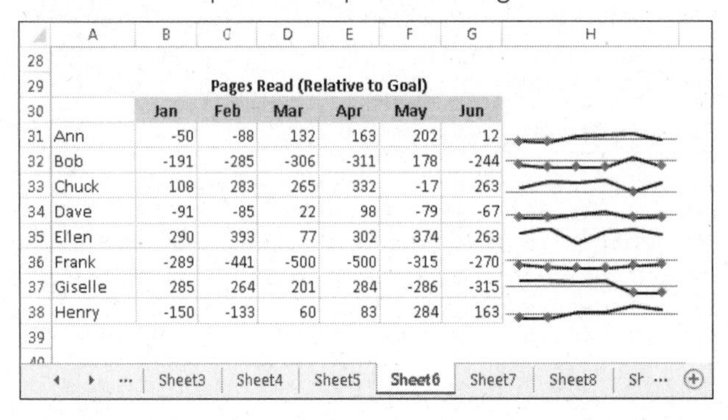

Pages Read (Relative to Goal)

	Jan	Feb	Mar	Apr	May	Jun
Ann	-50	-88	132	163	202	12
Bob	-191	-285	-306	-311	178	-244
Chuck	108	283	265	332	-17	263
Dave	-91	-85	22	98	-79	-67
Ellen	290	393	77	302	374	263
Frank	-289	-441	-500	-500	-315	-270
Giselle	285	264	201	284	-286	-315
Henry	-150	-133	60	83	284	163

I copied this formula to the other cells in the B31:G38 range, and created a group of Line Sparklines, with the axis turned on. I also enabled the Negative Points option so that negative values (failure to meet the goal) clearly stand out.

Specifying a Date Axis

Normally, data displayed in a Sparkline is assumed to be at equal intervals. For example, a Sparkline might display a daily account balance, sales by month, or profits by year. But what if the data isn't at equal intervals?

Figure 22.12 shows data, by date, along with a Sparklines graphic created from column B. Notice that some dates are missing, but the Sparkline shows the columns as if the values were spaced at equal intervals.

FIGURE 22.12

The Sparkline displays the values as if they are at equal time intervals.

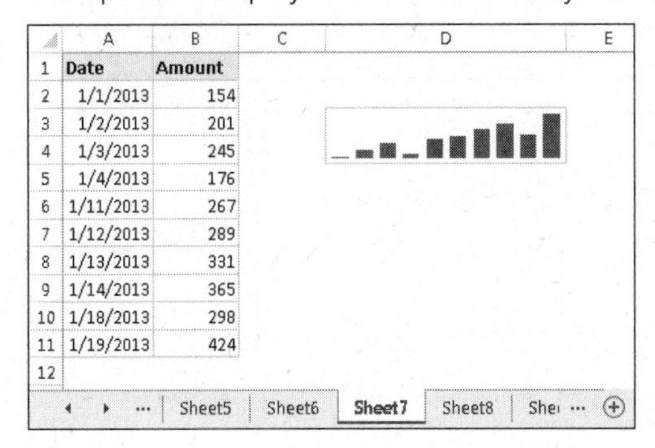

Date	Amount
1/1/2013	154
1/2/2013	201
1/3/2013	245
1/4/2013	176
1/11/2013	267
1/12/2013	289
1/13/2013	331
1/14/2013	365
1/18/2013	298
1/19/2013	424

To better depict the data, the solution is to specify a date axis. Select the Sparkline and choose Sparkline Tools ➪ Design ➪ Group ➪ Axis ➪ Date Axis Type. Excel displays a dialog box, asking for the range that contains the dates. In this example, specify range A2:A11. Click OK, and the Sparkline displays gaps for the missing dates (see Figure 22.13).

FIGURE 22.13

After specifying a date axis, the Sparkline shows the values accurately.

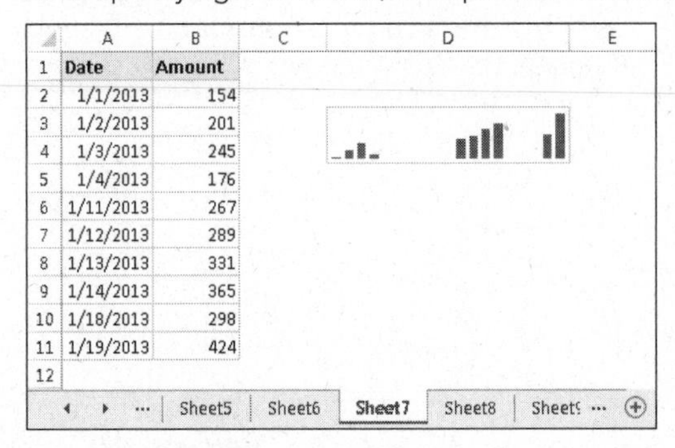

Date	Amount
1/1/2013	154
1/2/2013	201
1/3/2013	245
1/4/2013	176
1/11/2013	267
1/12/2013	289
1/13/2013	331
1/14/2013	365
1/18/2013	298
1/19/2013	424

Auto-Updating Sparklines

If a Sparkline uses data in a normal range of cells, adding new data to the beginning or end of the range does *not* force the Sparkline to use the new data. You need to use the Edit Sparklines dialog box to update the data range (choose Sparkline Tools ➪ Design ➪ Sparkline ➪ Edit Data). But, if the Sparkline data is in a column within a table (created by choosing Insert ➪ Tables ➪ Table), then the Sparkline will use new data that's added to the end of the table.

Figure 22.14 shows an example. The Sparkline was created using the data in the Rate column of the table. When you add the new rate for September, the Sparkline will automatically update its Data Range.

FIGURE 22.14

Creating a Sparkline from data in a table.

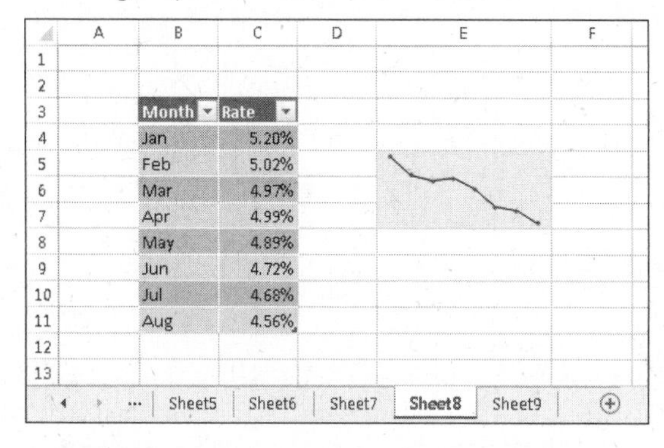

Month	Rate
Jan	5.20%
Feb	5.02%
Mar	4.97%
Apr	4.99%
May	4.89%
Jun	4.72%
Jul	4.68%
Aug	4.56%

Displaying a Sparkline for a Dynamic Range

The example in this section describes how to create a Sparkline that display only the most recent data points in a range. Figure 22.15 shows a worksheet that tracks daily sales. The Sparkline, in merged cells E4:E5, displays only the seven most recent data points in column B. When new data is added to column B, the Sparkline will adjust to show only the most recent seven days of sales.

FIGURE 22.15

Using a dynamic range name to display only the last seven data points in a Sparkline.

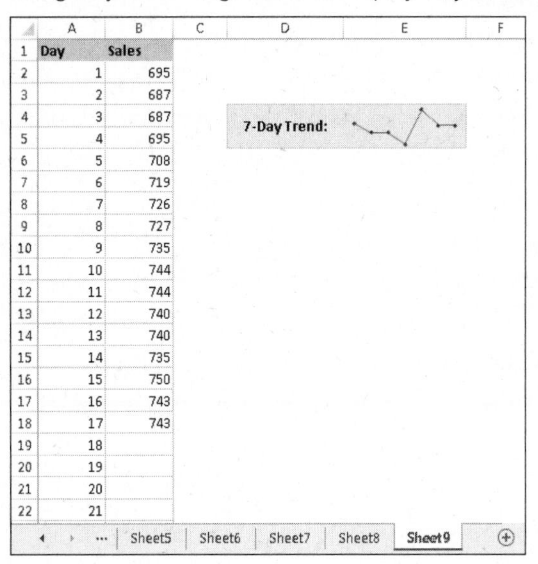

	A	B
1	Day	Sales
2	1	695
3	2	687
4	3	687
5	4	695
6	5	708
7	6	719
8	7	726
9	8	727
10	9	735
11	10	744
12	11	744
13	12	740
14	13	740
15	14	735
16	15	750
17	16	743
18	17	743
19	18	
20	19	
21	20	
22	21	

I started by creating a dynamic range name. Here's how:

1. **Choose Formulas ➪ Defined Names ➪ Define Name, specify Last7 as the Name, and enter the following formula in the Refers To field:**

   ```
   =OFFSET($B$2,COUNTA($B:$B)-7-1,0,7,1)
   ```

   This formula calculates a range by using the `OFFSET` function. The first argument is the first cell in the range (B2). The second argument is the number of cells in the column (minus the number to be returned and minus 1 to accommodate the label in B1).

   This name always refers to the last seven nonempty cells in column B. To display a different number of data points, change both instances of `7` to a different value.

2. **Chose Insert ➪ Sparklines ➪ Line.**
3. **In the Data Range field, type** Last7 **(the dynamic range name); specify cell E4 as the Location Range.** The Sparkline shows the data in range B11:B17.
4. **Add new data to column B.** The Sparkline adjusts to display only the last seven data points.

Need More about Sparklines?

This chapter describes pretty much everything there is to know about Excel Sparklines. You may be left asking, "Is that all there is?" Unfortunately, yes.

The Sparklines feature in Excel certainly leaves much to be desired. For example, you're limited to three types (Line, Column, and Win/Loss). It would be useful to have access to other Sparkline types, such as a column chart with no gaps, an area chart, and a stacked bar chart. Although Excel provides some basic formatting options, many users would prefer to have more control over the appearance of their Sparklines.

If you like the idea of Sparklines — and you're disappointed by the implementation in Excel 2013 — check out some add-ins that provide Sparklines in Excel. These products provide many additional Sparkline types, and most provide many additional customization options. Search the web for *Sparklines Excel*, and you'll find several add-ins to choose from.

CHAPTER

23

Enhancing Your Work with Pictures and Drawings

IN THIS CHAPTER

Inserting and customizing Shapes

Getting an overview of SmartArt and WordArt

Working with other types of graphics

When it comes to visual presentation, Excel has a lot more up its sleeve than charts. As you may know, you can insert a wide variety of graphics into your worksheet to add pizzazz to an otherwise boring report.

This chapter describes the non-chart-related graphic tools available in Excel. These tools consist of Shapes, SmartArt, WordArt, and imported or pasted images. In addition to enhancing your worksheets, you'll find that working with these objects can be a nice diversion. When you need a break from crunching numbers, you might enjoy creating an artistic masterpiece using Excel's graphic tools.

On the Web

Most of the examples in this chapter are available at this book's website.

Using Shapes

Microsoft Office, including Excel, provides access to a variety of customizable graphic images known as *Shapes*. You might want to insert Shapes to create simple diagrams, display text, or just add some visual appeal to a worksheet.

Keep in mind that Shapes can add unnecessary clutter to a worksheet. Perhaps the best advice is to use Shapes sparingly. Ideally, Shapes can help draw attention to some aspect of your worksheet. They shouldn't be the main attraction.

Inserting a Shape

You can add a Shape to a worksheet's draw layer by choosing Insert ➪ Illustrations ➪ Shapes, which opens the Shapes gallery, shown in Figure 23.1. Shapes are organized into categories, and the category at the top displays the Shapes that you've used recently. To insert a Shape on a worksheet, you can do one of the following:

FIGURE 23.1

The Shapes gallery.

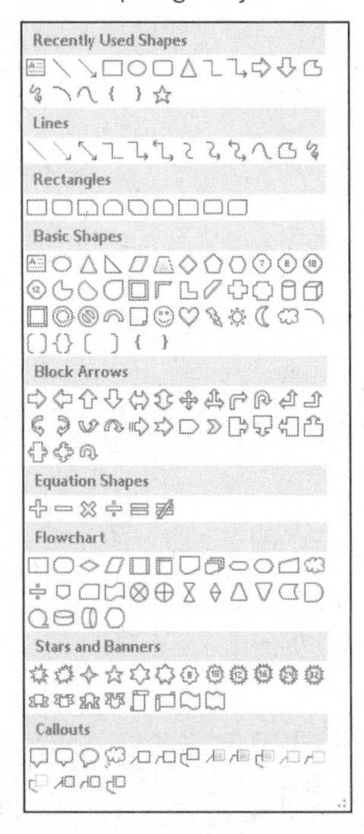

- **Click the Shape in the Shapes gallery and then click in the worksheet.** A default-sized shape is added to your worksheet.
- **Click the Shape and then drag in the worksheet.** This allows you to create a larger or smaller Shape, or a Shape with different proportions than the default.

When you release the mouse button, the object is selected, and its name appears in the Name field (as shown in Figure 23.2).

TIP

You can also insert a Shape into a chart. Just select the chart before you choose the Shape from the gallery and then click inside the chart to insert the Shape. The Shape is embedded in the chart. If you move the chart, the Shape comes along. The Shape also adjusts when you change the size of the chart.

FIGURE 23.2

This Shape was drawn on the worksheet. Its name (Sun 1) appears in the Name field.

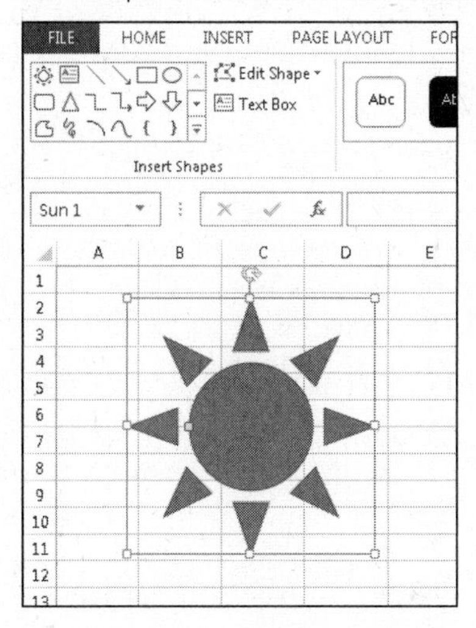

A few Shapes require a slightly different approach. For example, when adding a FreeForm Shape (from the Lines category), you can click repeatedly to create lines. Or click and drag to create a nonlinear shape. Double-click to finish drawing and create the Shape. The Curve Shape (in the Lines category) also requires several clicks while drawing. If you choose the Scribble Shape, you just drag the mouse pointer across the worksheet to create your masterpiece. If you connect the ends, it will be a filled Shape.

Here are a few tips to keep in mind when creating Shapes:

- Every Shape has a name. Some have generic names like Shape 1 and Shape 2, but others are given more descriptive names (for example, Rectangle 1). To change the name of a Shape, select it, type a new name in the Name field, and press Enter.
- To select a specific Shape on a worksheet, just click it.
- When you create a Shape by dragging, hold down the Shift key to maintain the object's default proportions.
- You can control how objects appear onscreen in the Advanced tab of the Excel Options dialog box (choose File ⇨ Options). This setting appears in the Display Options for This Workbook section. Normally, the All option is selected under For Objects Show. You can hide all objects by choosing Nothing (Hide Objects). Hiding objects may speed things up if your worksheet contains complex objects that take a long time to redraw.

About the Drawing Layer

Every worksheet and chart sheet has a *drawing layer*. This invisible surface can hold Shapes, SmartArt, WordArt, graphic images, embedded charts, inserted objects, and so on.

You can move, resize, copy, and delete objects placed on the drawing layer, with no effect on any other elements in the worksheet. Objects on the drawing layer have properties that relate to how they're moved and sized when underlying cells are moved and sized. When you right-click a graphic object and choose Size and Position from the shortcut menu, Excel displays the Format task pane for the object. Expand the Properties section to adjust how the object moves or resizes with its underlying cells (see the accompanying figure).

Your choices are as follows:

- **Move and Size with Cells:** If this option is selected, the object appears to be attached to the cells beneath it. For example, if you insert rows above the object, the object moves down. If you increase the column width, the object gets wider.
- **Move But Don't Size with Cells:** If this option is selected, the object moves whenever rows or columns are inserted, but it never changes its size when you change row heights or column widths.
- **Don't Move or Size with Cells:** This option makes the object completely independent of the underlying cells.

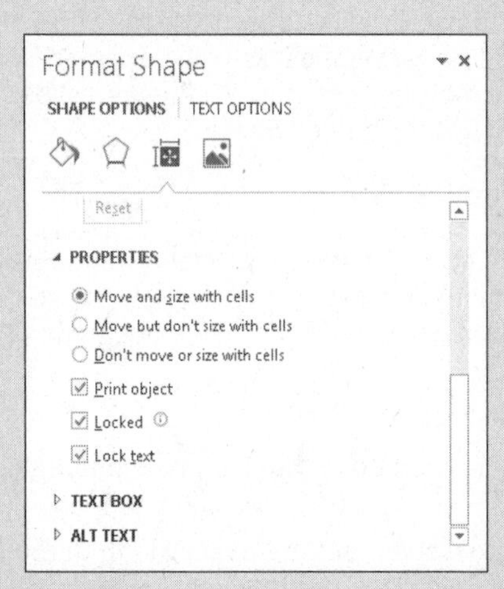

The preceding options control how an object is moved or sized with respect to the underlying cells.

Excel also lets you *attach* an object to a cell. To do so, choose File ➪ Options to open the Excel Options dialog box, click the Advanced tab, and select the Cut, Copy, and Sort Inserted Objects with Their Parent Cells check box. After you do so, graphic objects on the drawing layer are attached to the underlying cells. If you copy a range of cells that includes an object, the object is also copied. Note that this is a general option that affects all objects and, by default, this option is enabled.

Adding text to a Shape

Many Shape objects can display text. To add text to such a Shape, select the Shape and start typing the text.

To change the formatting for all text in a Shape, click the Shape object to select it. You can then use the formatting commands on the Font and Alignment groups of the Home tab of the Ribbon. To change the formatting of specific characters within the text, select only those characters, and use the Ribbon controls. Or, right-click and use the Mini toolbar to format the selected text. In addition, you can dramatically change the look of the text by using the tools in the Drawing Tools ➪ Format ➪ WordArt Styles group. You can read more about WordArt later in this chapter.

Formatting Shapes

When you select a Shape, the Drawing Tools ➪ Format contextual tab is available, with the following groups of commands:

- **Insert Shapes:** Insert new Shapes; change a Shape to a different Shape.
- **Shape Styles:** Change the overall style of a Shape; modify the Shape's fill, outline, or effects.
- **WordArt Styles:** Modify the appearance of the text within a Shape.
- **Arrange:** Adjust the "stack order" of Shapes, align Shapes, group multiple Shapes, and rotate Shapes.
- **Size:** Change the size of a Shape by typing dimensions.

Additional commands are available from the Shape's shortcut menu (which you access by right-clicking the Shape). In addition, you can use your mouse to perform some operations directly: for example, resize or rotate a Shape.

Figure 23.3 shows a worksheet with some Shapes that use various types of formatting.

FIGURE 23.3

A variety of Shapes.

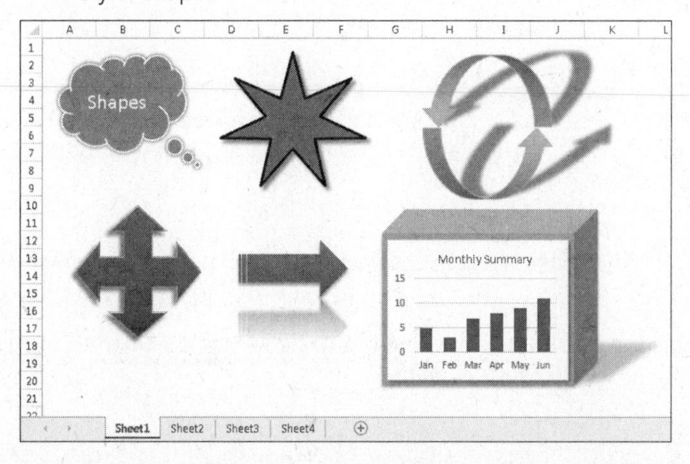

Selecting and Hiding Objects

An easy way to select an object is to use the Selection task pane. Just select any Shape and then choose Drawing Tools⇨Format⇨Arrange⇨Selection Pane. Or if a Shape isn't selected you can choose Home⇨Editing⇨Find & Select⇨Selection Pane.

Like with all task panes, you can undock this pane from the side of the window and make it free-floating. The accompanying figure shows the Selection task pane as a floating window.

Each object on the active worksheet is listed in the Selection task pane. Just click the object's name to select it. To select multiple objects, press Ctrl while you click the names.

To hide an object, click the "eye" icon to the right of its name. Use the buttons at the top of the task pane to quickly hide (or show) all items.

As an alternative to the Ribbon, you can use the Format Shape task pane. Right-click the Shape and choose Format Shape from the shortcut menu. The task pane contains some additional formatting options that aren't on the Ribbon. Changes appear immediately, and you can keep the Format Shape task pane open while you work.

I could probably write 20 pages about formatting Shapes, but it would be a waste of paper and certainly not a very efficient way of learning about Shape formatting. The best way, by far, to learn about formatting Shapes is to experiment. Create some shapes, click some commands, and see what happens. The commands are fairly intuitive, and you can always use Undo if a command doesn't do what you expected it to do.

Stacking Shapes

Shapes (as well as other objects on the drawing layer) are arranged in a stack. Each object that is added is placed at the top of the stack. Therefore, a large Shape can be stacked on top of a smaller Shape, completely obscuring it.

The Selection task pane lists the objects in order (the first object listed is at the top of the stack). You can drag and drop item names in the Selection task pane to change the stack order.

Another way to change the stack order of a Shape is to right-click the Shape and choose one of these commands from the shortcut menu:

- **Bring to Front⇨Bring to Front:** Sends the Shape to the top of the stack
- **Bring to Front⇨Bring Forward:** Sends the Shape one level higher
- **Send to Back⇨Send to Back:** Sends the Shape to the bottom of the stack
- **Send to Back⇨Send Backward:** Sends the Shape one level lower

These commands are also available in the Drawing Tools⇨Format⇨Arrange group of the Ribbon.

Grouping objects

Excel lets you *group* (combine) two or more Shape objects into a single object. For example, if you create a design that uses four separate Shapes, you can combine them into a group. Then, you can manipulate this group as a single object (move it, resize it, apply formatting, and so on).

To group objects, press Ctrl while you click the objects to be included in the group. Then right-click any of the selected Shapes and choose Group⇨Group from the shortcut menu.

Tip

You can also group a chart with a Shape. Just drag a chart on to a Shape, select both objects, right-click and choose Group⇨Group. You need to change the stack order if the chart is behind the Shape. This is a good way to make your charts stand out from the crowd. Figure 23.3 shows an example of a Shape grouped with a chart.

When objects are grouped, you can still work with an individual object in the group. Click once to select the group; then click again to select the object.

To ungroup a group, right-click the group object and choose Group⇨Ungroup from the shortcut menu. This command breaks the object into its original components.

Aligning and spacing objects

When you have several objects on a worksheet, you may want to align and evenly space these objects. You can, of course, drag the objects with your mouse (which isn't very precise). Or you can use the navigation arrow keys to move a selected object one pixel at a time. The fastest way to align and space objects is to let Excel do it for you.

To align multiple objects, start by selecting them (press Ctrl and click the objects). Then use the tools in the Drawing Tools⇨Format⇨Arrange⇨Align drop-down list.

Note

Unfortunately, you can't specify which object is used as the basis for the alignment. When you're aligning objects to the left (or right), they're always aligned with the leftmost (or rightmost) object that's selected. When you're aligning objects to the top (or bottom), they're always aligned with the topmost (or bottommost) object. Aligning the centers (or middles) of objects will align them along an axis halfway between the left and right (or top and bottom) extremes of the selected shapes. After you align the Shapes, they remain selected so it's easy to drag them all to the desired location.

You can instruct Excel to distribute three or more objects so that they're equally spaced horizontally or vertically. Choose Drawing Tools ➪ Format ➪ Arrange ➪ Align, and then select either Distribute Horizontally or Distribute Vertically.

Reshaping Shapes

Excel has many Shapes to choose from, but sometimes the Shape you need isn't in the gallery. In such a case, you may be able to modify one of the existing shapes using one of these techniques:

- **Rotate the Shape.** When you select a Shape, it displays a small circular arrow. Click and drag this arrow to rotate the Shape.
- **Group multiple Shapes.** You may be able to create the Shape you need by combining two or more Shapes and then grouping them (see "Grouping objects," earlier in this chapter).
- **Reconfigure the Shape.** Many Shapes display one or more small yellow squares when the Shape is selected. You can click and drag this square to change the Shape's outline. The exact behavior varies with the Shape, so you should experiment and see what happens. Figure 23.4 shows six variations of an up-down arrow. This particular shape, when selected, has two yellow squares, which allows lots of variations.
- **Create a Freeform Shape.** Select the Freeform Shape (in the Lines category of the Shapes gallery) to create a custom Shape. Figure 23.5 shows a Freeform Shape, with eyes and a mouth added. The shadow effect completes the masterpiece.

FIGURE 23.4

Six variations on a Shape.

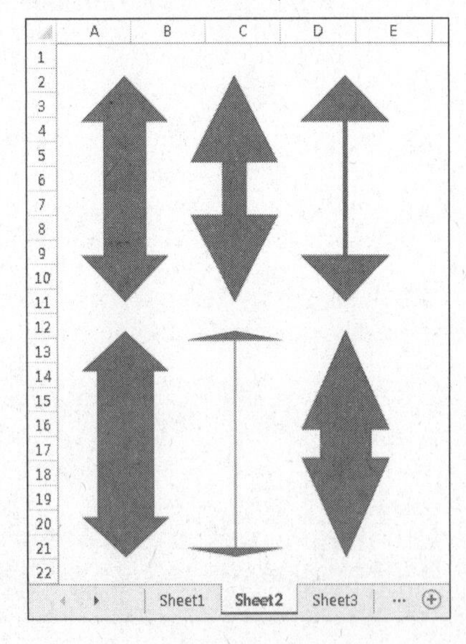

FIGURE 23.5

When none of the existing Shapes will do, create your own Freeform Shape.

- **Editing a Shape's Points.** Another way to create a unique Shape is to edit its points. Select the Shape and choose Drawing Tools ➪ Format ➪ Insert Shapes ➪ Edit Shape ➪ Edit Points. You can then drag the points to reconfigure the Shape. Figure 23.6 shows an example of a Shape (named Frame) that has been edited beyond all recognition.

FIGURE 23.6

A Shape, before and after editing its points.

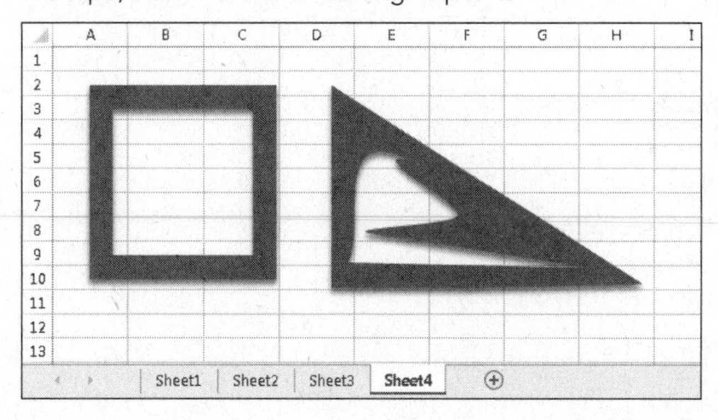

Exporting Graphic Objects

If you create a graphic in Excel using Shapes, SmartArt, or WordArt, you may want to save the graphic as a separate file for use in another program. Unfortunately, Excel doesn't provide a direct way to export a graphic, but here's a useful trick. First, a bit of setup work is required:

1. **Right-click the Quick Access toolbar and choose Customize the Quick Access Toolbar.** The Quick Access Toolbar tab of the Excel Options dialog box appears.
2. **In the upper-left drop-down control, choose Commands Not in the Ribbon.**
3. **In the list box, scroll down and select Web Options, and then click the Add button.**
4. **In the list box, select Web Page Preview, and then click the Add button.**
5. **Click OK to close the Excel Options dialog box.** Your Quick Access toolbar will have two new buttons.

Here's how to use these tools to export graphic objects (including charts) from a worksheet.

1. **Make sure that your graphics appear the way you want.**
2. **Click the Web Page Preview button in the Quick Access toolbar.** A copy of your workbook is converted to an HTML file and is displayed in your default browser.
3. **In the browser, right-click a graphic object, choose Save Image As, and specify a location for the file.** Your browser may have a different but equivalent command. Or you can just drag the graphic image to your desktop.

If the quality of the images in your browser is lacking, click the Web Options button in your Quick Access toolbar.

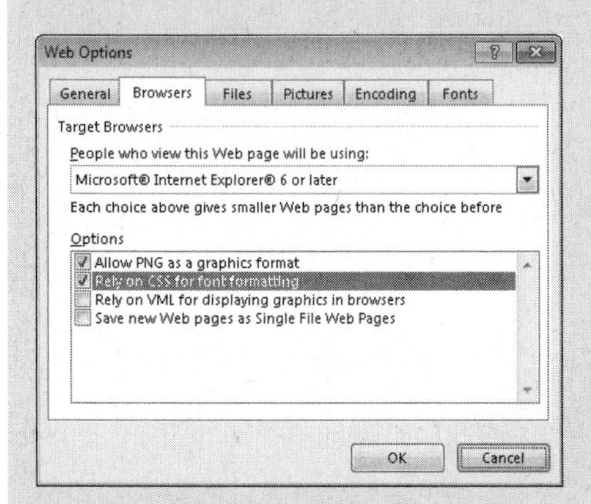

In the Web Options dialog box, click the Browser tab and make sure Allow PNG as a Graphics Format is enabled. If graphics don't appear in your browser at all, remove the check mark from Rely on VML for Displaying Graphics in Browser. Next, click the Pictures tab and choose the 120 Pixels Per Inch option. Click OK and do the web preview again. You should see better-quality graphics (transparent PNG files).

Printing objects

By default, objects are printed along with the worksheet. To avoid printing a Shape, right-click the Shape and choose Size and Position. In the Format Shape task pane, expand the Properties section and then clear the Print Object check box.

Using SmartArt

Excel's Shapes are certainly impressive, but the SmartArt feature is downright amazing. Using SmartArt, you can insert a wide variety of highly customizable diagrams into a worksheet, and you can change the overall look of the diagram with a few mouse clicks. This feature was introduced in Office 2007 and is probably more useful for PowerPoint users. But many Excel users will be able to make good use of SmartArt.

Inserting SmartArt

To insert SmartArt into a worksheet, choose Insert ⇨ SmartArt. Excel displays the dialog box shown in Figure 23.7. The diagrams are arranged in categories along the left. When you find one that looks appropriate, click it for a larger view in the panel on the right, which also provides some usage tips. Then click OK to insert the graphic.

FIGURE 23.7

Inserting a SmartArt graphic.

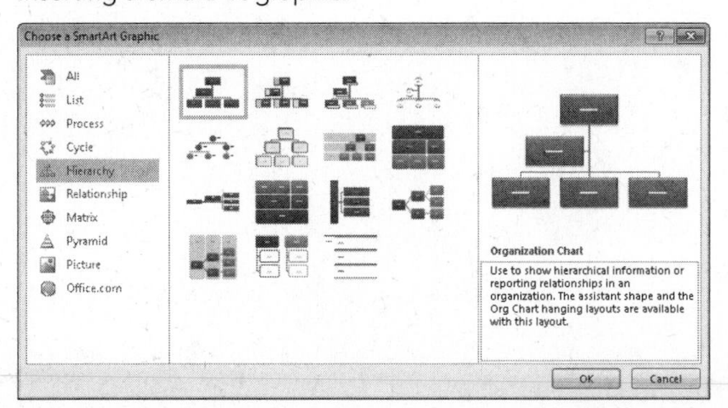

NOTE

Don't be concerned about the number of elements contained in the SmartArt graphics. You can customize the SmartArt to display the number of elements you need.

Figure 23.8 shows a SmartArt diagram after I customized it and added text. When you insert or select a SmartArt diagram, Excel displays its SmartArt Tools contextual tab, which provides many customization options.

FIGURE 23.8

This SmartArt shows a simple organizational chart.

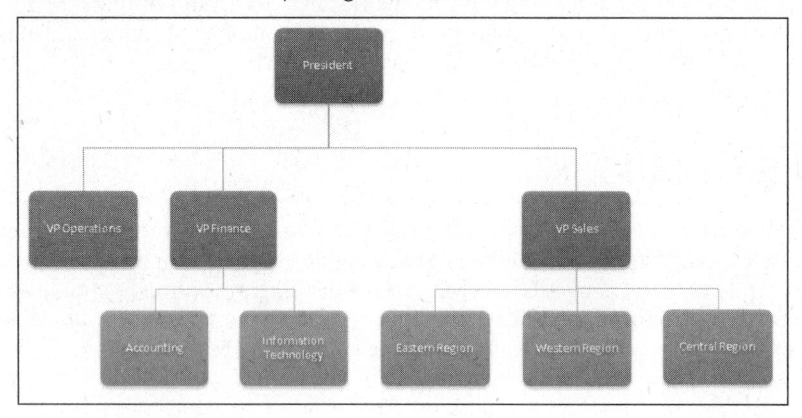

Customizing SmartArt

Figure 23.9 shows a SmartArt graphic (named Vertical Equation, from the Process category) immediately after I inserted it into a worksheet. The Type Your Text Here window makes it very easy to enter text into the elements of the image. If you prefer, you can click one of the [Text] areas in the image and type the text directly.

FIGURE 23.9

This SmartArt needs to be customized.

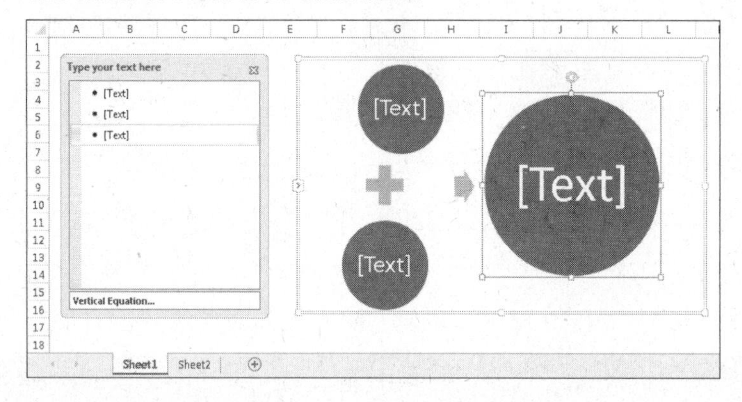

Figure 23.10 shows the SmartArt after I added some text.

FIGURE 23.10

The SmartArt now has text.

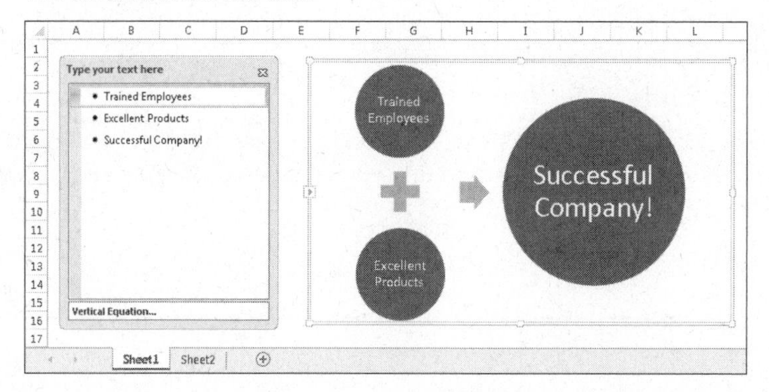

This particular diagram depicts two items combining into a third item. Suppose that your boss sees this graphic and tells you that you need a third item: Advanced Technology. To add an element to the SmartArt graphic, just select an item and choose SmartArt Tools ➪ Design ➪ Create Graphic ➪ Add Shape. Or you can just select an item and press Enter. Figure 23.11 shows the modified SmartArt.

FIGURE 23.11

The SmartArt, after adding a new element.

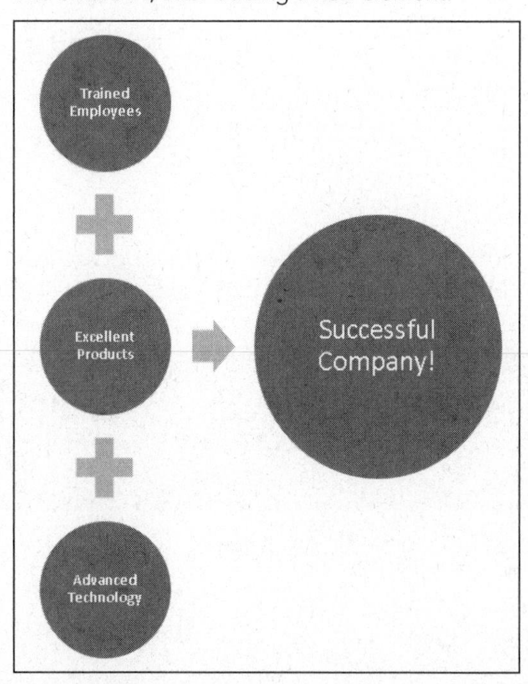

When working with SmartArt, keep in mind that you can move, resize, or format individually any element within the graphic. Select the element and then use the tools on the SmartArt Tools ➪ Format tab.

Changing the layout

You can easily change the layout of a SmartArt diagram. Select the object and then choose SmartArt Tools ➪ Design ➪ Layouts. Any text that you've entered remains intact. Figure 23.12 shows a few alternate layouts for the previous example.

FIGURE 23.12

A few different layouts for the SmartArt.

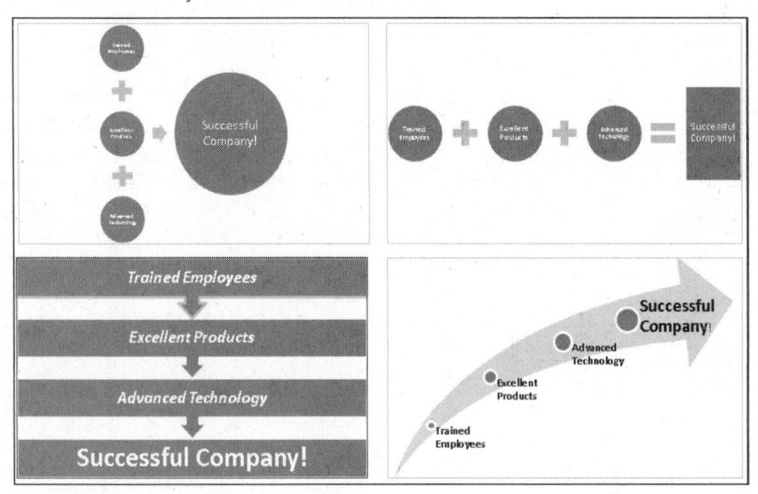

Changing the style

After you decide on a layout, you may want to consider other styles or colors available in the SmartArt Tools ➪ Design ➪ SmartArt Styles group. Figure 23.13 shows the diagram after I chose a different style and changed the colors.

> **TIP**
>
> SmartArt styles available vary depending upon the document theme assigned to the workbook. To change a workbook's theme, choose Page Layout ➪ Themes ➪ Themes. Switching to a different theme can have a dramatic impact on the appearance of SmartArt diagrams.

FIGURE 23.13

A few mouse clicks changed the style of this diagram.

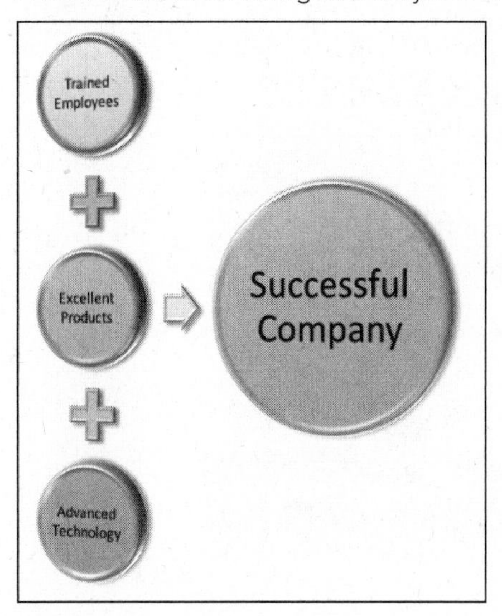

Learning more about SmartArt

This section provided a basic introduction to SmartArt. The topic is probably complex enough to warrant an entire book, but I recommend simply experimenting with the commands.

Using WordArt

You can use WordArt to create graphical effects in text. Figure 23.14 shows a few examples of WordArt.

To insert a WordArt graphic on a worksheet, choose Insert ➪ Text ➪ WordArt and then select a style from the gallery. Excel inserts an object with the placeholder text `Your text here`. Replace that text with your own, resize it, and apply other formatting if you like.

When you select a WordArt image, Excel displays its Drawing Tools contextual menu. Use the controls to vary the look of your WordArt. Or right-click and choose Format Shape to use the task pane.

FIGURE 23.14

WordArt examples.

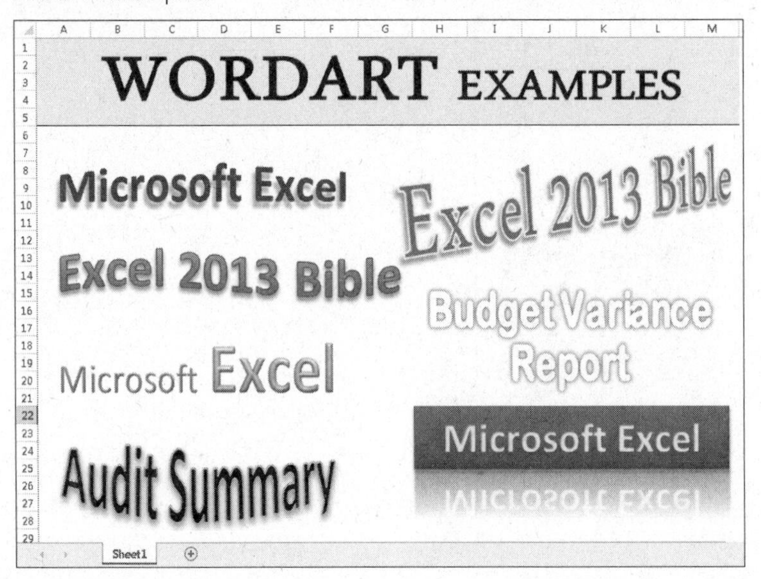

Word Art consists of two components: The text, and the Shape that contains the text. The Format Shape task pane has two headings (Shape Options and Text Options). The Ribbon controls in the Drawing Tools ➪ Format ➪ Shape Styles group operate on the Shape that contains the text — *not the text*. To apply text formatting, use the controls in the Drawing Tools ➪ Format ➪ WordArt Styles group. You can also use some of the standard formatting controls on the Home tab or the Mini toolbar.

Working with Other Graphic Types

Excel can import a wide variety of graphics into a worksheet. You have several choices:

- **Inserting an image from your computer:** If the graphic image that you want to insert is available in a file, you can easily import the file into your worksheet. Choose Insert ➪ Illustrations ➪ Picture. The Insert Picture dialog box appears, allowing you to browse for the file. Oddly, you can't drag and drop an image into a worksheet.
- **Inserting an image from an online source:** Choose Insert ➪ Illustrations ➪ Online Pictures. The Insert Picture window appears, allowing you to search for an image. Figure 23.15 shows the results of an image search.
- **Copying and pasting:** If an image is on the Windows Clipboard, you can paste it into a worksheet by choosing Home ➪ Clipboard ➪ Paste (or by pressing Ctrl + V).

FIGURE 23.15

Use the Insert Picture window to search for images online.

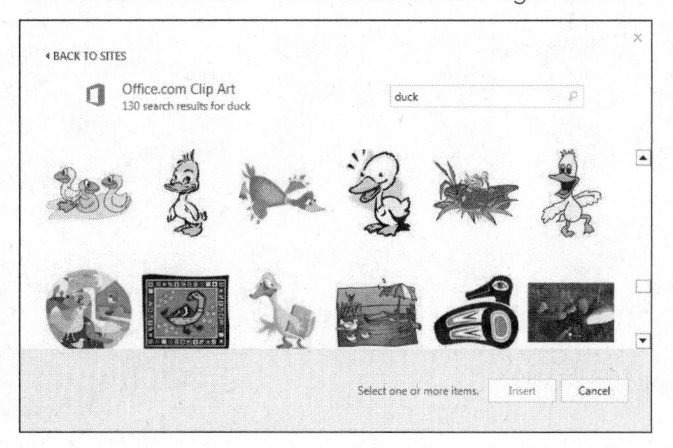

About graphics files

Graphics files come in two main categories:

- **Bitmap:** Bitmap images are made up of discrete dots. They usually look pretty good at their original size but often lose clarity if you increase the size. Examples of common bitmap file formats include BMP, PNG, JPEG, TIFF, and GIF.
- **Vector:** Vector-based images, on the other hand, are comprised of points and paths that are represented by mathematical equations, so they retain their crispness regardless of their size. Examples of common vector file formats include CGM, WMF, and EPS.

You can find millions of graphics files free for the taking on the Internet. Be aware, however, that some graphic files have copyright restrictions.

CAUTION

Using bitmap graphics in a worksheet can dramatically increase the size of your workbook.

When you insert a picture on a worksheet, you can modify the picture in a number of ways from the Picture Tools ➪ Format contextual tab, which becomes available when you select a picture object. For example, you can adjust the color, contrast, and brightness. In addition, you can add borders, shadows, reflections, and so on — similar to the operations available for Shapes.

And don't overlook the Picture Tools ➪ Format ➪ Picture Styles group. These commands can transform your image in some very interesting ways. Figure 23.16 shows various styles for a picture.

In addition, you can right-click and choose Format Picture to use the controls in the Format Picture task pane.

FIGURE 23.16

Displaying a picture in a number of different styles.

A feature introduced in Office 2010 is Artistic Effects. This command can apply a number of Photoshop-like effects to an image. To access this feature, select an image and choose Picture Tools➪Format➪Adjust➪Artistic Effects. Each effect is somewhat customizable, so if you're not happy with the default effect, try adjusting some options.

You might be surprised by some of the image enhancements that are available — including the ability to remove the background from photos. The best way to learn theses features is to dig in and experiment. Even if you have no need for image enhancement, you might find that it's a fun diversion when you need a break from working with numbers.

Figure 23.17 shows a photo before and after applying some artistic effects and removing the background.

FIGURE 23.17

A photo, before and after manipulating it with Excel.

Taking Linked Pictures of Ranges

One of Excel's best-kept secrets is its ability to copy and paste "live" pictures of cells and charts. You can copy a cell or range and then paste a picture (as an object) of the cell or range on any worksheet or chart. If you change the contents of a cell that's in a picture, the picture changes. The accompanying image shows a picture of a range after applying some picture effects. For best results, apply a fill color of white to all cells that don't have a specific fill color.

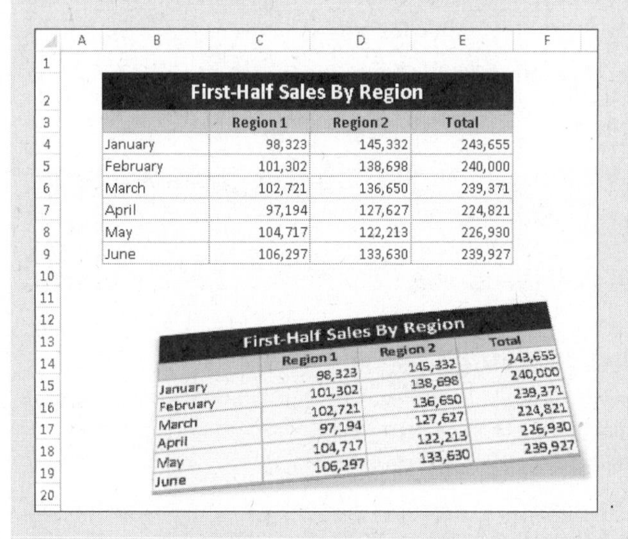

First-Half Sales By Region

	Region 1	Region 2	Total
January	98,323	145,332	243,655
February	101,302	138,698	240,000
March	102,721	136,650	239,371
April	97,194	127,627	224,821
May	104,717	122,213	226,930
June	106,297	133,630	239,927

To "take a picture" of a range

1. **Select the range.**
2. **Press Ctrl+C to copy the range.**
3. **Activate another cell.**
4. **Choose Home⇨Clipboard⇨Paste⇨Linked Picture (I).**

The result is a live picture of the range you selected in Step 1.

If you use this feature frequently, you can save some time by adding the Excel Camera tool to your Quick Access toolbar:

1. **Right-click the Quick Access toolbar, and choose Customize Quick Access Toolbar from the shortcut menu that appears.** The Excel Options dialog box appears, with the Quick Access Toolbar tab selected.
2. **Select Command Not in the Ribbon from the drop-down list on the left.**
3. **Select Camera from the list and click Add.**
4. **Click OK to close the Excel Options dialog box.**

After you add the Camera tool to your Quick Access toolbar, you can select a range of cells and click the Camera tool to take a "picture" of the range. Then click in the worksheet, and Excel places a live picture of the selected range on the worksheet's draw layer. If you make changes to the original ranges, the changes are shown in the picture of the range.

Inserting screenshots

Excel can also capture and insert a screenshot of any program currently running on your computer (including another Excel window). To use the screenshot feature, follow these steps:

1. **Make sure that the window you want to use displays the content that you want.**
2. **Choose Insert ⇨ Illustrations ⇨ Screenshot.** You'll see a gallery that contains thumbnails of all windows open on your computer (except the current Excel window).
3. **Click the image you want.** Excel inserts it into your worksheet.

You can use any of the normal picture tools to work with screenshots.

New Feature

If you don't want to capture a complete window, choose Screen Clipping in Step 2. Then click and drag your mouse to select the area of the screen to capture. This feature is new in Excel 2013.

Displaying a worksheet background image

If you want to use a graphics image for a worksheet's background (similar to wallpaper on the Windows Desktop), choose Page Layout ⇨ Page Setup ⇨ Background and select a graphics file. The selected graphics file is tiled on the worksheet.

Unfortunately, worksheet background images are for onscreen display only. These images do not appear when the worksheet is printed.

Using the Equation Editor

The final section in this chapter deals with the Equation Editor, which was introduced in Excel 2010. Use this feature to insert a nicely formatted mathematical equation as a graphic object.

Figure 23.18 shows an example of an equation in a worksheet. Keep in mind that these equations do not perform calculations — they're for display purposes only.

The best way to become familiar with the Equation Editor is to insert one of the premade equations. Choose Insert ⇨ Symbols ⇨ Equation, and choose one of equations from the gallery. The equation is inserted in your worksheet.

When you select an Equation object, you have access to two contextual tabs:

- **Drawing Tools:** Used to format the container object
- **Equation Tools:** Used to edit the equation

FIGURE 23.18

An equation created by the Equation Editor.

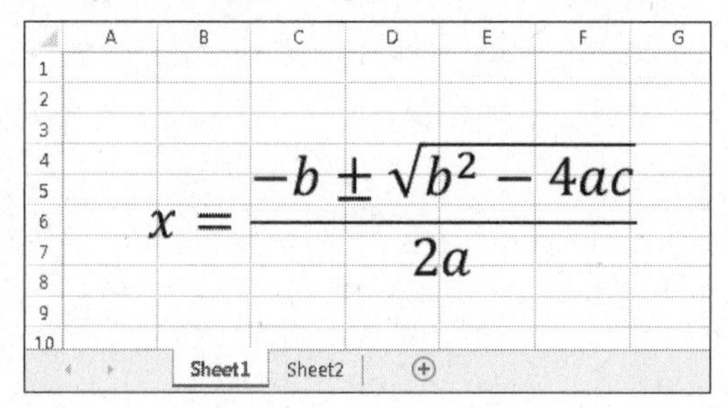

The Equation Tools ➪ Design tab contains three groups of controls:

- **Tools:** Used to insert a new equation, or control how the equation is displayed. Click the dialog box launcher in the bottom-right corner of the Tools group to display the Equation Options dialog box, where you can specify how the equation is copied and also define keyboard shortcuts (click Math AutoCorrect).
- **Symbols:** Contains common mathematical symbols and operators that you can use in your equations.
- **Structures:** Contains templates for various structures that are used in equations.

Describing how to use the Equation tools is more difficult than actually using them. Generally, you add a structure and then edit the various parts by adding text or symbols. You can put structures inside of structures, and there is no limit to the complexity of the equations. It might be a bit tricky at first, but it doesn't take long before you understand how it works.

Figure 23.19 shows two equations that illustrate an old calculus joke.

FIGURE 23.19

Two Equation objects on a worksheet.

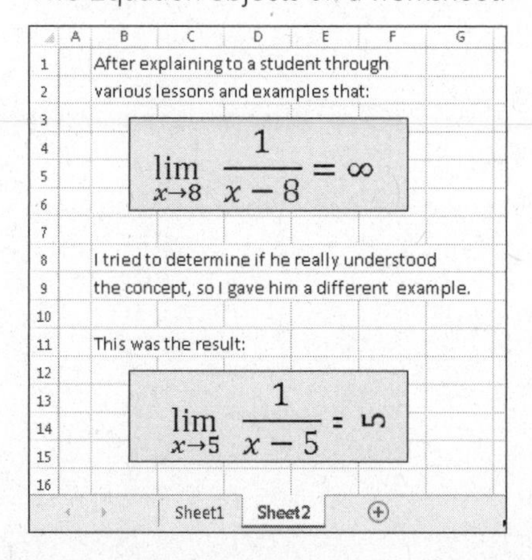

Part IV

Using Advanced Excel Features

A number of Excel features can be fairly called "advanced" features if for no better reason than the ways in which they expand the definitions of what a spreadsheet program can do. The chapters in this part cover some useful features that you may not have used in the past but may find very valuable.

IN THIS PART

CHAPTER

24

Customizing the Excel User Interface

IN THIS CHAPTER

Customizing the Quick Access toolbar

Customizing the Ribbon

A software program's *user interface* consists of all the ways that the user interacts with the software. In Excel, the user interface consists of

- The Ribbon
- The Quick Access toolbar
- Right-click shortcut menus
- Dialog boxes
- Task panes
- Keyboard shortcuts

This chapter describes how to make changes to two Excel user interface components: the Quick Access toolbar and the Ribbon. You might want to customize these elements to make Excel more suited to the way you use it.

Customizing the Quick Access Toolbar

The Quick Access toolbar is always visible, regardless of which Ribbon tab is selected. After you customize the Quick Access toolbar, your frequently used commands will always be one click away.

Note

The only situation in which the Quick Access toolbar is not visible is in full-screen mode, which is enabled by clicking the Ribbon Display Options button in the Excel title bar, and choosing Auto-hide Ribbon. Full-screen mode works differently in Excel 2013 than it did in previous versions. To temporarily display the Quick Access toolbar (and Ribbon) in full-screen mode, click the title bar. To cancel full-screen mode, click the Ribbon Display Options button in the Excel title bar, and choose Show Tabs or Show Tabs and Commands.

About the Quick Access toolbar

By default, the Quick Access toolbar is located on the left side of Excel title bar, above the Ribbon (see Figure 24.1). Unless you customize it, this toolbar includes three tools:

- **Save:** Saves the active workbook
- **Undo:** Reverses the effect of the last action
- **Redo:** Reverses the effect of the last undo

If you prefer, you can move the Quick Access toolbar below the Ribbon. To do so, right-click the Quick Access toolbar and choose Show Quick Access Toolbar below the Ribbon. Moving the Quick Access toolbar below the Ribbon uses additional vertical space on your screen. In other words, you'll be able to see one less row of your worksheet if you move the Quick Access toolbar from its default location. Unlike traditional toolbars, the Quick Access toolbar cannot be made free-floating, so you can't move it to a convenient location. It always appears either above or below the Ribbon.

FIGURE 24.1

The default location for the Quick Access toolbar is on the left side of the Excel title bar.

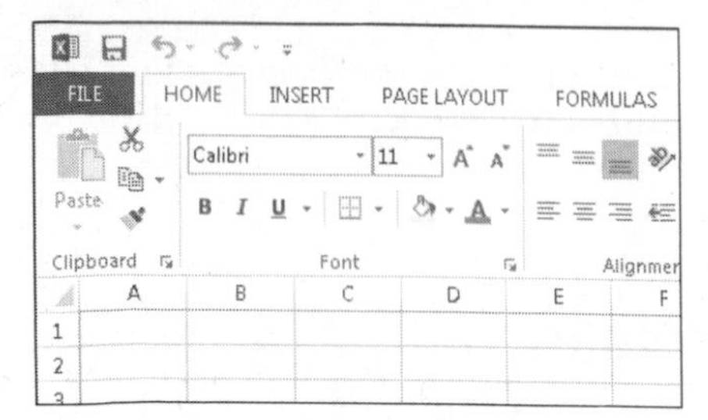

Commands on the Quick Access toolbar always appear as small icons, with no text. An exception to this rule is drop-down controls that display text. For example, if you add the Font control from the Home ⇨ Font group, it appears as a drop-down control in the Quick Access toolbar. When you hover your mouse pointer over an icon, you see the name of the command and a brief description.

Customizing the Quick Access toolbar consists of adding new commands to it. If you find that you use some Excel commands frequently, you can make these commands easily accessible by adding them to your Quick Access toolbar. You can also rearrange the order of the icons.

As far as I can tell, there is no limit to the number of commands that you can add. The Quick Access toolbar always displays only a single line of icons. If the number of icons exceeds the Excel window width, it displays an additional icon at the end: More Controls. Click the More Controls icon, and the hidden Quick Access toolbar icons appear in a pop-up window.

Adding new commands to the Quick Access toolbar

You can add a new command to the Quick Access toolbar in three ways:

- Click the Quick Access toolbar drop-down control, which is located on the right side of the Quick Access toolbar (see Figure 24.2). The list contains a few commonly used commands. Select a command from the list, and Excel adds it to your Quick Access toolbar.
- Right-click any control on the Ribbon and choose Add to Quick Access Toolbar. The control is added to your Quick Access toolbar, positioned to the right of the last control.
- Use the Quick Access Toolbar tab in the Excel Options dialog box. A quick way to access this dialog box is to right-click any Ribbon control and choose Customize Quick Access Toolbar.

FIGURE 24.2

This drop-down list is one way to add a new command to the Quick Access toolbar.

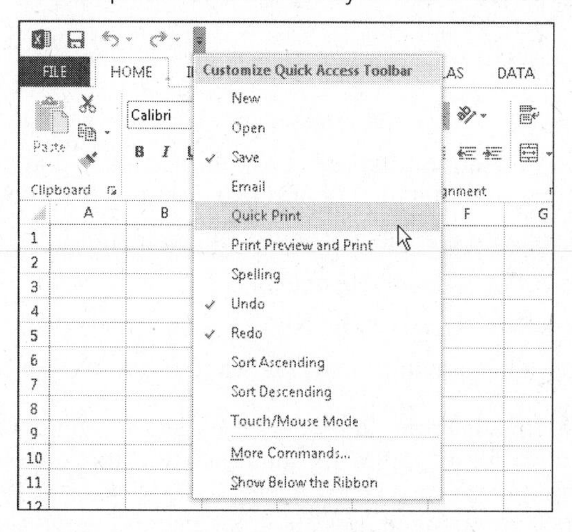

The remainder of this section discusses the Quick Access Toolbar tab of the Excel Options dialog box, shown in Figure 24.3.

The left side of the dialog box displays a list of Excel commands, and the right side shows the commands currently on your Quick Access toolbar. Above the command list on the left is the Choose Commands From drop-down list, from which you can filter the list. Select an item from the drop-down list, and the list displays only the commands for that item. In Figure 24.3, the list shows commands in the Popular Commands category.

FIGURE 24.3

Use the Quick Access Toolbar tab in the Excel Options dialog box to customize the Quick Access toolbar.

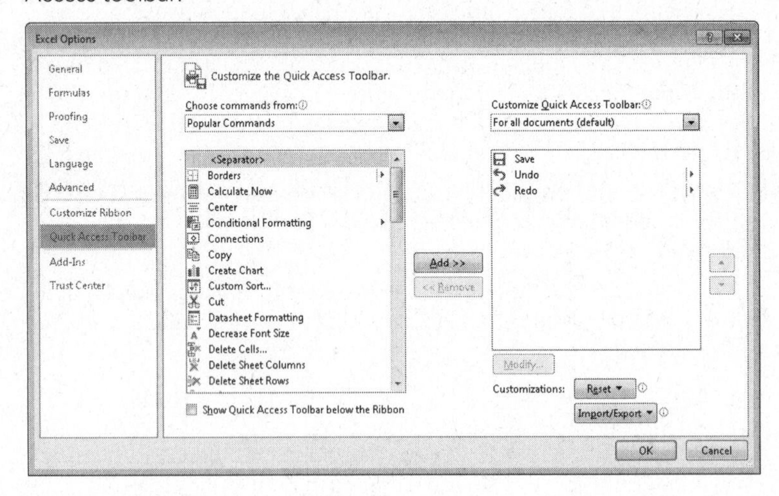

Some of the items in the drop-down list are

- **Popular Commands:** Displays commands that Excel users commonly use.
- **Commands Not in the Ribbon:** Displays a list of commands that you can't access from the Ribbon. Many, but not all, are obsolete or not very useful.
- **All Commands:** Displays a complete list of Excel commands.
- **Macros:** Displays a list of all available macros.
- **File Tab:** Displays the commands available in the Backstage view.
- **Home Tab:** Displays all commands available when the Home tab is active.

In addition, the Choose Commands From drop-down list contains an item for every other tab, including the context tabs (for example, the additional tabs that are displayed when a chart is selected). To add an item to your Quick Access toolbar, select it from the list on the left and then click Add. The command appears in the list on the right. At the top of each list is an item called <Separator>. Adding this item to your Quick Access toolbar results in a vertical bar to help you group commands.

The commands are listed in alphabetical order. Sometimes, you need to do some guessing to find a particular command.

TIP

By default, Quick Access toolbar customizations are visible for all documents. You can create a Quick Access toolbar configuration that's specific to a particular workbook. In other words, the commands on the Quick Access toolbar appear only when a particular workbook is active. Start by activating the workbook, and then display the Customize Quick Access Toolbar tab of the Excel Options dialog box. When you add a command to the Quick Access toolbar, use the drop-down list in the upper right to specify the workbook (only the active workbook is available as a choice).

NOTE

Some commands simply aren't available. For example, I would like the Quick Access toolbar to display the command to toggle page break display on a worksheet. As far as I can tell, the only way to issue that command is to display the Advanced tab of the Excel Options dialog box, and then scroll down until you find the Show Page Breaks check box. Also, you won't find commands from a task pane, unless those commands are also available on the Ribbon.

When you select Macros from the Choose Commands From drop-down, Excel lists all available macros. You can attach a macro to a Quick Access toolbar icon so that when you click the icon, the macro is executed. If you add a macro to your Quick Access toolbar, you can click the Modify button to change the text and choose a different icon for the macro.

When you finish making your Quick Access toolbar customizations, click OK to close the Excel Options dialog box. The new icon will appear on the Quick Access toolbar.

TIP

The only times you ever *need* to use the Quick Access Toolbar tab of the Excel Options dialog box is when you want to add a command that's not on the Ribbon, add a command that executes a macro, or rearrange the order of the icons. In all other situations, it's much easier to locate the command in the Ribbon, right-click the command, and choose Add to Quick Access Toolbar.

Other Quick Access toolbar actions

Other Quick Access toolbar actions include the following:

- **Rearranging the Quick Access toolbar icons:** If you want to change the order of your Quick Access toolbar icons, you can do so from the Quick Access Toolbar tab of the Excel Options dialog box. Select the command and then use the Up and Down arrow buttons on the right to move the icon.

Sharing User Interface Customizations

In the Excel Options dialog box, the Quick Access Toolbar tab and the Customize Ribbon tab both have an Import/Export button. You can use this button to save and open files that contain user interface customizations. For example, you might create a new Ribbon tab and want to share it with your officemates.

Click the Import/Export button, and you get two options:

- **Import Customization File:** You're prompted to locate the file. Before you load a file, you're asked whether you want to replace all existing Ribbon and Quick Access toolbar customizations.
- **Export All Customizations:** You're prompted to provide a filename and location for the file.

The information is stored in a file that has a `*.exportedUI` extension.

Unfortunately, importing and exporting is not implemented very well. Excel doesn't allow you to save or load only the Quick Access toolbar customizations or only the Ribbon customizations. Both types of customizations are exported and imported. Therefore, you can't share your Quick Access toolbar customizations without also sharing your Ribbon customizations.

- **Removing Quick Access toolbar icons:** The easiest way to remove an icon from your Quick Access toolbar is to right-click the icon and choose Remove from Quick Access Toolbar. You can also use the Quick Access Toolbar tab of the Excel Options dialog box. Just select the command in the list on the right and click Remove.
- **Resetting the Quick Access toolbar:** If you want to return the Quick Access toolbar to its default state, display the Quick Access Toolbar tab of the Excel Options dialog box and click the Reset button. Then choose Reset Only Quick Access Toolbar. The Quick Access toolbar then displays its three default commands.

Caution
You can't undo resetting the Quick Access toolbar.

Customizing the Ribbon

The Ribbon is Excel's primary user interface component. It consists of tabs along the top. When you click a tab, it displays a set of relevant commands, and the commands are arranged in groups.

Why you may want to customize the Ribbon

Most users have no need to customize the Ribbon. If you find that you tend to use the same command over and over, though — and you're constantly clicking tabs to access these commands — then you might benefit from customizing the Ribbon in such a way that the commands you need are on the same tab.

What can be customized

You can customize tabs on the Ribbon by

- Adding new custom tabs
- Deleting custom tabs
- Changing the order of the tabs
- Changing the name of tabs
- Hiding built-in tabs

You can customize groups on the Ribbon by

- Adding new custom groups
- Adding commands to custom groups
- Removing commands from custom groups
- Removing groups from tabs
- Moving a group to a different tab
- Changing the order of the groups within a tab
- Changing the name of a group

Those are fairly comprehensive lists of customization options, but there are some actions that you *can't* do:

- Remove built-in tabs (but you *can* hide them).
- Remove specific commands from built-in groups (but you can remove entire groups).
- Change the order of commands in a built-in group.

Note

Unfortunately, you can't customize the Ribbon (or Quick Access toolbar) by using VBA macros. However, developers can write RibbonX code and store it in workbook files. When the file is open, the Ribbon is modified to display new commands. Writing RibbonX code is relatively complicated and beyond the scope of this book.

How to customize the Ribbon

Customizing the Ribbon is done via the Customize Ribbon panel of the Excel Options dialog box (see Figure 24.4). The quickest way to display this dialog box is to right-click anywhere on the Ribbon and choose Customize the Ribbon.

FIGURE 24.4

The Customize Ribbon tab of the Excel Options dialog box.

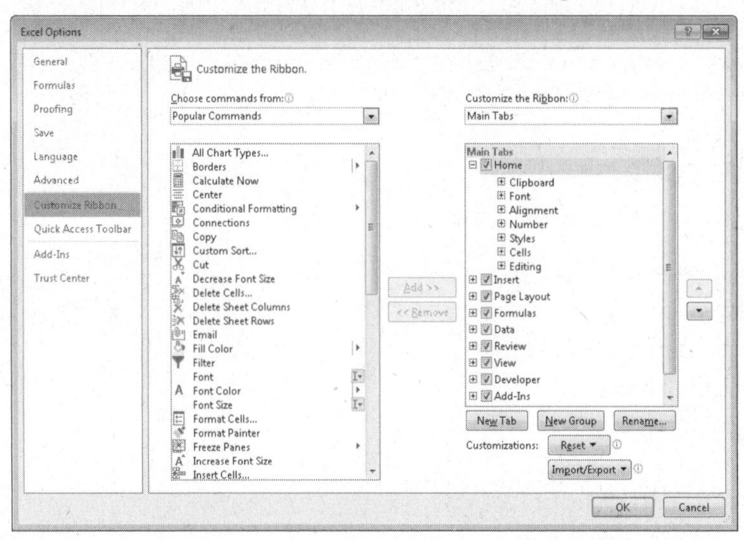

Creating a new tab

If you'd like to create a new tab, click the New Tab button. Excel creates a tab named New Tab (Custom) and a new group in the tab named New Group (Custom).

You'll almost always want to give the tab (and the group) better names. Select the item and click Rename. Use the Move Up and Move Down arrow buttons on the right to reposition the new tab, if necessary.

REMEMBER

You don't need to add a new tab just because you want to add new commands to the Ribbon. You can create a new group for an existing tab.

Creating a new group

To create a new group, select the tab that will hold the new group and click the New Group button. Excel creates a new group named New Group (Custom). Use the Rename button to provide a more descriptive name, and use the Move Up and Move Down arrow buttons on the right to reposition the group within the tab.

Adding commands to a new group

Adding commands to the Ribbon is very similar to adding commands to the Quick Access toolbar, which I describe earlier in this chapter. Commands that you add must be placed in a new group. Here's the general procedure:

1. **Use the Choose Command From drop-down list on the left to display various groups of commands.**
2. **Select the command in the list box on the left.**
3. **Use the Customize the Ribbon drop-down list on the right to choose a group of tabs.** *Main Tabs* refer to the tabs that are always visible; *Tool Tabs* refer to the contextual tabs that appear when a particular object is selected.
4. **In the list box on the right, select the tab and the group where you want to put the command.** You'll need to click the plus-sign control to expand the tab name so that it displays its group names.

REMEMBER

You can add commands only to groups that you've created.

5. **Click the Add button to add the selected command from the left to the selected group on the right.**

To rearrange the order of tabs, groups, or commands, select the item and use the Move Up and Move Down buttons on the right. Note that you can move a group into a different tab.

NOTE

Although you can't remove a built-in tab, you can hide the tab by clearing the check box next to its name.

Figure 24.5 shows a part of a customized Ribbon. In this case, I added two groups to the View tab (to the right of the Zoom group): Extra Commands (with three new commands) and Text to Speech (with five new commands).

FIGURE 24.5

The View tab, with two new groups added.

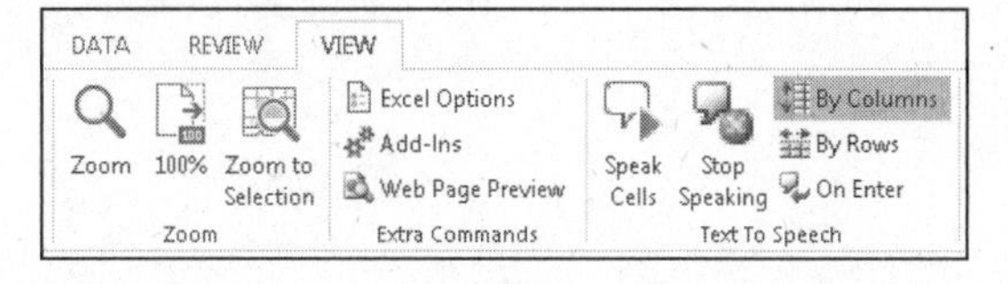

Resetting the Ribbon

To restore all or part of the Ribbon to its default state, right-click any part of the Ribbon and choose Customize the Ribbon from the shortcut menu. Excel displays the Customize Ribbon tab of the Excel Options dialog box. Click the Reset button to display two options: Reset Only Selected Ribbon Tab and Reset All Customizations. If you choose the latter, the Ribbon will be returned to its default state and you'll also lose any Quick Access toolbar customizations that you made.

CHAPTER

25

Using Custom Number Formats

IN THIS CHAPTER

Getting an overview of custom number formatting

Creating a custom number format

Listing all custom number format codes

Looking at examples of custom number formats

When you enter a number into a cell, you can display that number in a variety of different formats. Excel has quite a few built-in number formats, but sometimes you may find that none of them is exactly what you need.

This chapter describes how to create custom number formats and provides many examples that you can use as is or adapt to your needs.

About Number Formatting

By default, all cells use the General number format. This format is basically "what you type is what you get." But if the cell isn't wide enough to show the entire number, the General format rounds numbers with decimals and uses scientific notation for large numbers. In many cases, the General number format works just fine, but most people prefer to specify a different number format for consistency.

The key thing to remember about number formatting is that it affects only how a value is *displayed.* The actual number remains intact, and any formulas that use a formatted number use the actual number.

NOTE

An exception to this rule occurs if you specify the Set Precision as Displayed option on the Advanced tab in the Excel Options dialog box. If that option is in effect, formulas use the values that are actually displayed in the cells as the result of a number format applied to the cells. In general, using this option is not a good idea because it changes the underlying values in your worksheet.

One more thing to keep in mind: If you use the Find and Replace dialog box (Home ➪ Editing ➪ Find & Select ➪ Find), characters that are displayed as a result of number formatting (for example, a currency symbol) are not searchable by default. To be able to locate information based on formatting, use the Look In Values option in the Find and Replace dialog box.

Automatic number formatting

Excel is smart enough to perform some formatting for you automatically. For example, if you enter **12.3%** into a cell, Excel assumes that you want to use a percentage format and applies it automatically. If you use commas to separate thousands (such as 123,456), Excel applies comma formatting for you. And if you precede your value with a currency symbol, Excel formats the cell for currency.

NOTE

You have an option when it comes to entering values into cells formatted as percentages. Access the Excel Options dialog box and click the Advanced tab. If the Enable Automatic Percent Entry check box is selected (the default setting), you can simply enter a normal value into a cell that has been formatted to display as a percent (for example, enter 12.5 for 12.5%). If this check box isn't selected, you must enter the value as a decimal (for example, .125 for 12.5%).

Excel automatically applies a built-in number format to a cell based on the following criteria:

- If a number contains a slash (/), it may be converted to a date format or a fraction format.
- If a number contains a hyphen (-), it may be converted to a date format.
- If a number contains a colon (:) or is followed by a space and the letter *A* or *P* (uppercase or lowercase), it may be converted to a time format.
- If a number contains the letter *E* (uppercase or lowercase), it may be converted to scientific notation (also known as exponential format). If the number doesn't fit into the column width, it may also be converted to this format.

TIP

Automatic number formatting can be very frustrating. For example, if you enter a part number 10-12 into a cell, Excel will convert it to a date. Even worse, there is no way to convert it back to your original entry! To avoid automatic number formatting when you enter a value, preformat the data input range with the desired number format or format the cell as Text. Another option is to precede your entry with an apostrophe. The apostrophe makes the entry text, so number formatting is not applied to the cell.

Formatting numbers by using the Ribbon

The Number group on the Home tab of the Ribbon contains several controls for applying common number formats quickly. The Number Format drop-down control gives you quick access to 11 common number formats. In addition, the Number group contains some buttons. When you click one of these buttons, the selected cells take on the specified number format. Table 25.1 summarizes the formats that these buttons perform in the U.S. English version of Excel.

NOTE

Some of these buttons actually apply predefined styles to the selected cells. Access Excel's styles by using the Style gallery, in the Styles group on the Home tab. You can modify the styles by right-clicking the style name and choosing Modify from the shortcut menu. See Chapter 6 for details.

TABLE 25.1 Number-Formatting Buttons on the Ribbon

Button Name	Formatting Applied
Accounting Number Format	Adds a dollar sign to the left, separates thousands with a comma, and displays the value with two digits to the right of the decimal point. This is a drop-down control, so you can select other common currency symbols.
Percent Style	Displays the value as a percentage, with no decimal places. This button applies a style to the cell.
Comma Style	Separates thousands with a comma and displays the value with two digits to the right of the decimal place. It's like the Accounting number format, but without the currency symbol. This button applies a style to the cell.
Increase Decimal	Increases the number of digits to the right of the decimal point by one.
Decrease Decimal	Decreases the number of digits to the right of the decimal point by one.

Using shortcut keys to format numbers

Another way to apply number formatting is to use shortcut keys. Table 25.2 summarizes the shortcut key combinations that you can use to apply common number formatting to the selected cells or range. Notice that these are the shifted versions of the number keys along the top of a typical keyboard.

TABLE 25.2 Number-Formatting Keyboard Shortcuts

Key Combination	Formatting Applied
Ctrl+Shift+~	General number format (that is, unformatted values).
Ctrl+Shift+!	Two decimal places, thousands separator, and a hyphen for negative values.
Ctrl+Shift+@	Time format with the hour, minute, and AM or PM.
Ctrl+Shift+#	Date format with the day, month, and year.
Ctrl+Shift+$	Currency format with two decimal places. (Negative numbers appear in parentheses.)
Ctrl+Shift+%	Percentage format with no decimal places.
Ctrl+Shift+^	Scientific notation number format with two decimal places.

Using the Format Cells dialog box to format numbers

For maximum control of number formatting, use the Number tab in the Format Cells dialog box. You can access this dialog box in any of several ways:

- Click the dialog box launcher at the bottom right of the Home➪Number group.
- Choose Home➪Number➪Number Format➪More Number Formats.
- Press Ctrl+1.

The Number tab in the Format Cells dialog box contains 12 categories of number formats from which to choose. When you select a category from the list box, the right side of the dialog box changes to display appropriate options.

Here are the number format categories, along with some general comments:

- **General:** The default format; it displays numbers as integers, decimals, or in scientific notation if the value is too wide to fit into the cell.
- **Number:** Specify the number of decimal places, whether to use your system thousands separator (for example, a comma) to separate thousands, and how to display negative numbers.
- **Currency:** Specify the number of decimal places, choose a currency symbol, and display negative numbers. This format always uses the system thousands separator symbol (for example, a comma) to separate thousands.
- **Accounting:** Differs from the Currency format in that the currency symbols always line up vertically, regardless of the number of digits displayed in the value.
- **Date:** Choose from a variety of date formats and select the locale for your date formats.
- **Time:** Choose from a number of time formats and select the locale for your time formats.
- **Percentage:** Choose the number of decimal places; always displays a percent sign.
- **Fraction:** Choose from among nine fraction formats.
- **Scientific:** Displays numbers in exponential notation (with an *E*): `2.00E+05 = 200,000`. You can choose the number of decimal places to display to the left of *E*.
- **Text:** When applied to a value, causes Excel to treat the value as text (even if it looks like a value). This feature is useful for such items as numerical part numbers and credit card numbers.
- **Special:** Contains additional number formats. The list varies, depending on the locale you choose. For the English (United States) locale, the formatting options are Zip Code, Zip Code +4, Phone Number, and Social Security Number.
- **Custom:** Define custom number formats not included in any of the other categories.

NOTE

If the cell displays a series of hash marks after you apply a number format (such as #########), it usually means that the column isn't wide enough to display the value by using the number format that you selected. Either make the column wider (by dragging the right border of the column header) or change the number format. A series of hash marks also can mean that the cell contains an invalid date or time.

Creating a Custom Number Format

When you create a custom number format, it can be used to format any cells in the workbook. You can create about 200 custom number formats in each workbook.

Figure 25.1 shows the Custom category in the Number tab of the Format Cells dialog box. Here, you can create number formats not included in any of the other categories. Excel gives you a great deal of flexibility in creating custom number formats.

FIGURE 25.1

The Custom category of the Number tab in the Format Cells dialog box.

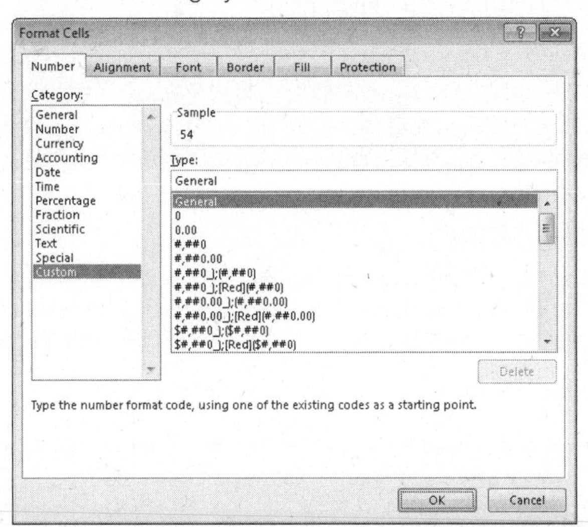

TIP

Custom number formats are stored with the workbook in which they are defined. To make the custom format available in a different workbook, you can just copy a cell that uses the custom format to the other workbook.

You construct a number format by specifying a series of codes as a *number format string*. You enter this code sequence in the Type field after you select the Custom category on the Number tab of the Format Cells dialog box. Here's an example of a simple number format code:

```
0.000
```

This code consists of placeholders and a decimal point; it tells Excel to display the value with three digits to the right of the decimal place. Here's another example:

```
00000
```

This custom number format has five placeholders and displays the value with five digits (no decimal point). This format is good to use when the cell holds a five-digit zip code. (In fact, this is the code actually used by the Zip Code format in the Special category.) When you format the cell with this number format and then enter a Zip Code, such as 06604, the value is displayed with the leading zero. If you enter this number into a cell with the General number format, it displays 6604 (no leading zero).

Scroll through the list of number formats in the Custom category in the Format Cells dialog box to see many more examples. In many cases, you can use one of these codes as a starting point, and you'll need to customize it only slightly.

On the Web

The website for this book contains a workbook with many custom number format examples (see Figure 25.2). The file is named `number formats.xlsx`.

Parts of a number format string

A custom format string can have up to four sections, which enables you to specify different format codes for positive numbers, negative numbers, zero values, and text. You do so by separating the codes with a semicolon. The codes are arranged in the following order:

```
Positive format; Negative format; Zero format; Text format
```

If you don't use all four sections of a format string, Excel interprets the format string as follows:

- **If you use only one section:** The format string applies to all numeric types of entries.
- **If you use two sections:** The first section applies to positive values and zeros, and the second section applies to negative values.
- **If you use three sections:** The first section applies to positive values, the second section applies to negative values, and the third section applies to zeros.
- **If you use all four sections:** The last section applies to text stored in the cell.

FIGURE 25.2

Examples of custom number formatting.

Custom Format	Cell Entry	How it Appears
Using text		
#,##0 "US Dollars"	1500	1,500 US Dollars
"Answer: "General	1500	Answer: 1500
"The amount is "#,##0" dollars"	1500	The amount is 1,500 dollars
Scaling large numbers		
#,##0,	123456789	123,457
#,##0,	12345678912	12,345,679
#,##0,	1234	1
Data Validation		
0.00;"No negative values!"	123	123.00
0.00;"No negative values!"	-123	No negative values!
0.00;"No negative values!"	0	0.00
Zero with Dashes		
#,##0_);(#,##0);-0-_)	0	-0-
#,##0_);(#,##0);-0-_)	12.2	12
#,##0_);(#,##0);-0-_)	-12	(12)
Telephone Numbers		
(###) ###-###	8005551212	(800) 555-1212
###"/"###-####	8005551212	800/555-1212
Social Security Numbers		
###-##-####	421897322	421-89-7322
"SSN" ###-##-####	421897322	SSN 421-89-7322
Date Formats		
mmmm-yyyy	9/29/2012	September-2012
mmmm d, yyyy	9/29/2012	September 29, 2012
dddd	9/29/2012	Saturday
mmmm d, yyyy (dddd)	9/29/2012	September 29, 2012 (Saturday)
"It's" dddd	9/29/2012	It's Saturday
Different colors and formatting		
[Red][<1]0.0%;[Blue][>=1]#,##0;General	1	1
[Red][<1]0.0%;[Blue][>=1]#,##0;General	-1	-100.0%

Sheet1

The following is an example of a custom number format that specifies a different format for each of these types:

```
[Green]General;[Red]General;[Black]General;[Blue]General
```

This custom number format example takes advantage of the fact that colors have special codes. A cell formatted with this custom number format displays its contents in a different color, depending on the value. When a cell is formatted with this custom number format, a positive number is green, a negative number is red, a zero is black, and text is blue.

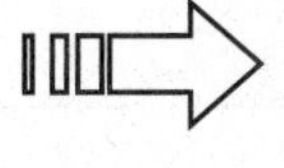

If you want to apply cell formatting automatically (such as text or background color) based on the cell's contents, a much better solution is to use the Excel Conditional Formatting feature. Chapter 21 covers conditional formatting.

Custom number format codes

Table 25.3 lists the formatting codes available for custom formats, along with brief descriptions. I use most of these codes in examples later in this chapter.

TABLE 25.3 Codes Used to Create Custom Number Formats

Code	Comments
General	Displays the number in General format.
#	Digit placeholder. Displays only significant digits, and does not display insignificant zeros.
0 (zero)	Digit placeholder. Displays insignificant zeros if a number has fewer digits than there are zeros in the format.
?	Digit placeholder. Adds spaces for insignificant zeros on either side of the decimal point so that decimal points align when formatted with a fixed-width font. You can also use ? for fractions that have varying numbers of digits.
.	Decimal point.
%	Percentage.
,	Thousands separator.
E-, E+, e-, e+	Scientific notation.
$, -, +, /, (,), :, space	Displays this character.
\	Displays the next character in the format.
*	Repeats the next character, to fill the column width.
_ (underscore)	Leaves a space equal to the width of the next character.
"text"	Displays the text inside the double quotation marks.
@	Text placeholder.
[color]	Displays the characters in the color specified. Can be any of the following text strings (not case sensitive): Black, Blue, Cyan, Green, Magenta, Red, White, or Yellow.
[Color n]	Displays the corresponding color in the color palette, where n is a number from 0 to 56.
[condition value]	Set your own criterion for each section of a number format.

Table 25.4 lists the codes used to create custom formats for dates and times.

Changing the Default Number Format for a Workbook

As I mention earlier, the default number format is General. If you prefer a different default number format, you have two choices: Preformat the cells with the number format of your choice, or change the number format for the Normal style.

You can preformat specific cells, entire rows or columns, or even the entire worksheet. Just select the range and use any of the techniques described in this chapter to apply a number format to the selected cells.

Instead of preformatting an entire worksheet, however, a better solution is to change the number format for the Normal style. Unless you specify otherwise, all cells use the Normal style. Therefore, by changing the number format for the Normal style, you're essentially creating a new default number format for the workbook. The modified style applies to all new worksheets that you insert into the workbook.

Change the Normal style by displaying the Style gallery. Right-click the Normal style icon (in the Home ➪ Styles group) and choose Modify to display the Style dialog box. In the Style dialog box, click the Format button and then choose the new number format that you want to use for the Normal style.

TABLE 25.4 Codes Used in Creating Custom Formats for Dates and Times

Code	Comments
m	Displays the month as a number without leading zeros (1–12).
mm	Displays the month as a number with leading zeros (01–12).
mmm	Displays the month as an abbreviation (Jan–Dec).
mmmm	Displays the month as a full name (January–December).
mmmmm	Displays the first letter of the month (J–D).
d	Displays the day as a number without leading zeros (1–31).
dd	Displays the day as a number with leading zeros (01–31).
ddd	Displays the day as an abbreviation (Sun–Sat).
dddd	Displays the day as a full name (Sunday–Saturday).
yy or yyyy	Displays the year as a two-digit number (00–99) or as a four-digit number (1900–9999).
h or hh	Displays the hour as a number without leading zeros (0–23) or as a number with leading zeros (00–23).
m or mm	When used with a colon in a time format, displays the minute as a number without leading zeros (0–59) or as a number with leading zeros (00–59).
s or ss	Displays the second as a number without leading zeros (0–59) or as a number with leading zeros (00–59).
[ ]	Displays hours greater than 24 or minutes or seconds greater than 60.
AM/PM	Displays the hour using a 12-hour clock; if no AM/PM indicator is used, the hour uses a 24-hour clock.

Where Did Those Number Formats Come From?

Excel may create custom number formats without your realizing it. When you use the Increase Decimal or Decrease Decimal button on the Home ⇨ Number group of the Ribbon (or on the Mini toolbar), Excel creates new custom number formats, which appear on the Number tab in the Format Cells dialog box. For example, if you click the Increase Decimal button five times, the following custom number formats are created:

```
0.0
0.000
0.0000
0.000000
```

A format string for two decimal places is not created because that format string is built in.

Custom Number Format Examples

The remainder of this chapter consists of useful examples of custom number formats. You can use most of these format codes as is. Others may require slight modification to meet your needs.

Scaling values

You can use a custom number format to scale a number. For example, if you work with very large numbers, you may want to display the numbers in thousands (that is, display 1,200,000 as 1,200). The actual number, of course, will be used in calculations that involve that cell. The formatting affects only how it is displayed.

Displaying values in thousands

The following format string displays values without the last three digits to the left of the decimal place and no decimal places. In other words, the value appears as if it's divided by 1,000 and rounded to no decimal places.

```
#,###,
```

A variation of this format string follows. A value with this number format appears as if it's divided by 1,000 and rounded to two decimal places.

```
#,###.00,
```

Table 25.5 shows examples of these number formats:

TABLE 25.5 Examples of Displaying Values in Thousands

Value	Number Format	Display
123456	#,###,	123
1234565	#,###,	1,235
–323434	#,###,	-323
123123.123	#,###,	123
499	#,###,	(blank)
500	#,###,	1
123456	#,###.00,	123.46
1234565	#,###.00,	1,234.57
–323434	#,###.00,	-323.43
123123.123	#,###.00,	123.12
499	#,###.00,	.50
500	#,###.00,	.50

Displaying values in hundreds

The following format string displays values in hundreds, with two decimal places. A value with this number format appears as if it's divided by 100 and rounded to two decimal places.

```
0"."00
```

Table 25.6 shows examples of these number formats:

TABLE 25.6 Examples of Displaying Values in Hundreds

Value	Number Format	Display
546	0"."00	5.46
100	0"."00	1.00
9890	0"."00	98.90
500	0"."00	5.00
–500	0"."00	-5.00
0	0"."00	0.00

25

Displaying values in millions

The following format string displays values in millions with no decimal places. A value with this number appears as if it's divided by 1,000,000 and rounded to no decimal places.

```
#,###,,
```

A variation of this format string follows. A value with this number appears as if it's divided by 1,000,000 and rounded to two decimal places.

```
#,###.00,,
```

Here's another variation. This format string adds the letter *M* to the end of the value.

```
#,###,,M
```

The following format string is a bit more complex. It adds the letter *M* to the end of the value and also displays negative values in parentheses, as well as displaying zeros.

```
#,###.0,,"M"_);(#,###.0,,"M)";0.0"M"_)
```

Table 25.7 shows examples of these format strings.

TABLE 25.7 Examples of Displaying Values in Millions

Value	Number Format	Display
123456789	#,###,,	123
1.23457E+11	#,###,,	123,457
1000000	#,###,,	1
5000000	#,###,,	5
–5000000	#,###,,	-5
0	#,###,,	(blank)
123456789	#,###.00,,	123.46
1.23457E+11	#,###.00,,	123,457.00
1000000	#,###.00,,	1.00
5000000	#,###.00,,	5.00
–5000000	#,###.00,,	-5.00
0	#,###.00,,	.00
123456789	#,###,,"M"	123M
1.23457E+11	#,###,,"M"	123,457M
1000000	#,###,,"M"	1M
5000000	#,###,,"M"	5M
–5000000	#,###,,"M"	-5M
0	#,###,,"M"	M
123456789	#,###.0,,"M"_);(#,###.0,,"M)";0.0"M"_)	123.5M
1.23457E+11	#,###.0,,"M"_);(#,###.0,,"M)";0.0"M"_)	123,456.8M
1000000	#,###.0,,"M"_);(#,###.0,,"M)";0.0"M"_)	1.0M
5000000	#,###.0,,"M"_);(#,###.0,,"M)";0.0"M"_)	5.0M
–5000000	#,###.0,,"M"_);(#,###.0,,"M)";0.0"M"_)	(5.0M)
0	#,###.0,,"M"_);(#,###.0,,"M)";0.0"M"_)	0.0M

Appending zeros to a value

The following format string displays a value with three additional zeros and no decimal places. A value with this number format appears as if it's rounded to no decimal places and then multiplied by 1,000.

```
#",000"
```

Examples of this format string, plus a variation that adds six zeros, are shown in Table 25.8.

TABLE 25.8 Examples of Displaying a Value with Extra Zeros

Value	Number Format	Display
1	#",000"	1,000
1.5	#",000"	2,000
43	#",000"	43,000
–54	#",000"	-54,000
5.5	#",000"	6,000
0.5	#",000,000"	1,000,000
0	#",000,000"	,000,000
1	#",000,000"	1,000,000
1.5	#",000,000"	2,000,000
43	#",000,000"	43,000,000
–54	#",000,000"	-54,000,000
5.5	#",000,000"	6,000,000
0.5	#",000,000"	1,000,000

Displaying leading zeros

To display leading zeros, create a custom number format that uses the 0 character. For example, if you want all numbers to display with ten digits, use the number format string that follows. Values with fewer than ten digits will display with leading zeros.

```
0000000000
```

You also can force all numbers to display with a fixed number of leading zeros. The format string that follows, for example, appends three zeros to the beginning of each number:

```
"000"#
```

Specifying conditions

The following custom number format displays text, based on the value of the cell.

```
[<10]"Too low";[>10]"Too high";"Just right"
```

If the value is less than 10, it displays `Too low`. If the value is greater than 10, it displays `Too high`. If the value is exactly 10, it displays `Just right`. Note that you can specify only one or two conditions, plus an "other."

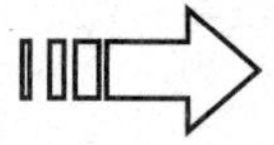

Generally, using Excel's conditional formatting feature is a better solution for formatting that's based on a value. See Chapter 21 for details.

Displaying fractions

Excel supports quite a few built-in fraction number formats (select the Fraction category on the Number tab in the Format Cells dialog box). For example, to display the value .125 as a fraction with 8 as the denominator, select As Eighths (4/8) from the Type list (see Figure 25.3).

FIGURE 25.3

Selecting a number format to display a value as a fraction.

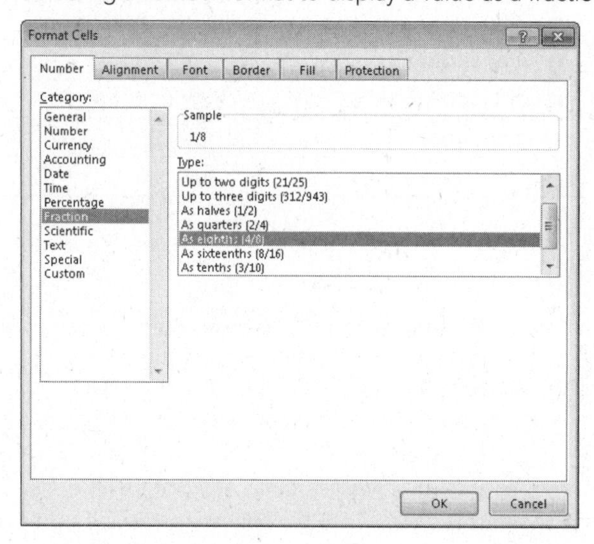

You can use a custom format string to create other fractional formats. For example, the following format string displays a value in 50ths:

```
# ??/50
```

To display the fraction reduced to its lowest terms, use a question mark after the slash symbol. For example, the value 0.125 can be expressed as 2/16, and 2/16 can be reduced to 1/8. Here's an example of a number format that displays the value as a fraction reduced to its simplest terms:

```
# ?/?
```

If you omit the leading hash mark, the value is displayed without a leading value. For example, the value 2.5 would display as 5/2 using this number format code:

```
?/?
```

The following format string displays a value in terms of fractional dollars. For example, the value 154.87 is displayed as `154 and 87/100 Dollars`.

```
0 "and "??/100 "Dollars"
```

The following example displays the value in sixteenths, with a quotation mark appended to the right. This format string is useful when you deal with fractions of inches (for example, 2/16").

```
# ??/16\"
```

Displaying a negative sign on the right

The following format string displays negative values with the negative sign to the right of the number. Positive values have an additional space on the right, so both positive and negative numbers align properly on the right.

```
#,##0.00_-;#,##0.00-
```

To make the negative numbers more prominent, you can add a color code to the negative part of the number format string:

```
#,##0.00_-;[Red]#,##0.00-
```

Formatting dates and times

When you enter a date into a cell, Excel formats the date using the system short date format. You can change this format by using the Windows Control Panel (Regional and Language Options).

Excel provides many useful, built-in date and time formats. Table 25.9 shows some other date and time formats that you may find useful. The first column of the table shows the date/time serial number.

TABLE 25.9 Useful Built-In Date and Time Formats

Value	Number Format	Display
41456	mmmm d, yyyy (dddd)	July 1, 2013 (Monday)
41456	"It's" dddd!	It's Monday!
41456	dddd, mm/dd/yyyy	Monday, 07/01/2013
41456	"Month: "mmm	Month: July
41456	General (m/d/yyyy)	41456 (7/1/2013)
0.345	h "Hours"	8 Hours
0.345	h:mm "o'clock"	8:16 o'clock
0.345	h:mm a/p"m"	8:16 am
0.78	h:mm a/p".m."	6:43 p.m.

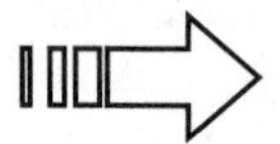

See Chapter 12 for more information about the Excel date and time serial number system.

Displaying text with numbers

The ability to display text with a value is sometimes useful. To add text, just create the number format string as usual (or use a built-in number format as a starting point) and put the text within quotation marks. The following number format string, for example, displays a value with the text `(US Dollars)` added to the end:

```
#,##0.00 "(US Dollars)"
```

Here's another example that displays text before the number:

```
"Average: "0.00
```

If you use the preceding number format, you'll find that the negative sign appears before the text for negative values. To display number signs properly, use this variation:

```
"Average: "0.00;"Average: "-0.00
```

The following format string displays a value with the words `Dollars and Cents`. For example, the number 123.45 displays as `123 Dollars and .45 Cents`. Technically, the decimal point should not appear in the amount before `Cents`, but there's no way to eliminate it.

```
0 "Dollars and" .00 "Cents"
```

Testing Custom Number Formats

The TEXT function displays a number using a number format string specified as the second argument. The TEXT function uses exactly the same number formatting codes as standard number formatting. Use this to your advantage when creating a custom number format.

The figure shows a worksheet with four entries in column A: a positive value, zero, a negative value, and text. Cell B1 contains a custom formatting string. Cell C1 contains this formula, which was copied to the three cells below.

```
=TEXT(A1,$B$1)
```

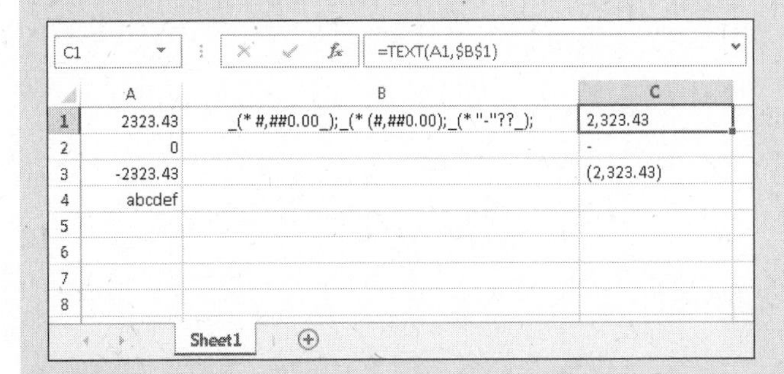

When you modify the number formatting string in cell B1, the cells in column C update.

This technique works well, and editing a number format string in a cell is much easier than doing it directly in the Format Cells dialog box. However, the technique has two limitations:

- The TEXT function does not handle color codes.
- The TEXT function does not handle the asterisk code (used to repeat text).

When you're satisfied, just copy the text in B1 and paste it into the Format Cells dialog box. Then you can apply this custom format for any cells.

Suppressing certain types of entries

You can use number formatting to hide certain types of entries. For example, the following format string displays text but not values:

```
;;
```

This format string displays values but not text or zeros:

```
0.0;-0.0;;
```

This format string displays everything except zeros:

```
0.0;-0.0;;@
```

You can use the following format string to completely hide the contents of a cell:

```
;;;
```

Note that when the cell is activated, however, the cell's contents are visible on the Formula bar.

Filling a cell with a repeating character

The asterisk (*) symbol specifies a repeating character in a number format string. The repeating character completely fills the cell and adjusts if the column width changes. The following format string, for example, displays the contents of a cell padded on the right with dashes:

```
General*-;-General*-;General*-;General*-
```

CHAPTER

26

Using Data Validation

IN THIS CHAPTER

Getting an overview of Excel's data validation feature

Looking at practical examples of using data validation formulas

This chapter explores a very useful Excel feature: data validation. Data validation enables you to add rules for what's acceptable in specific cells and allows you to add dynamic elements to your worksheet without using any macro programming.

About Data Validation

The Excel *data validation* feature allows you to set up rules that dictate what can be entered into a cell. For example, you may want to limit data entry in a particular cell to whole numbers between 1 and 12. If the user makes an invalid entry, you can display a custom message, such as the one shown in Figure 26.1.

FIGURE 26.1

Displaying a message when the user makes an invalid entry.

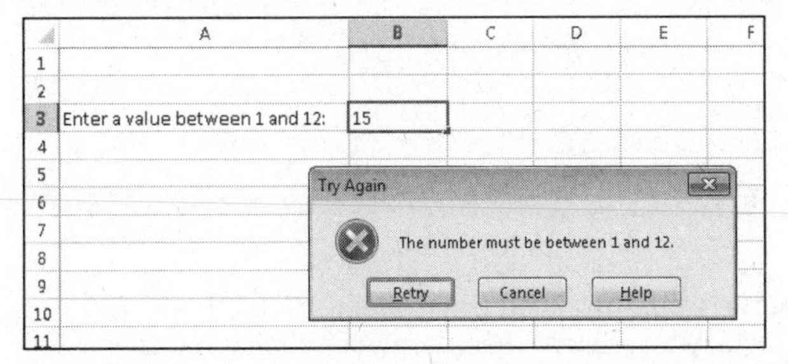

Excel makes it easy to specify the validation criteria. You can also use a formula for more complex criteria.

CAUTION

The Excel data validation feature suffers from a potentially serious problem: If the user copies a cell that does *not* use data validation and pastes it to a cell that *does* use data validation, the data validation rules are deleted. In other words, the cell then accepts any type of data. This has always been a problem, and Microsoft still hasn't fixed it in Excel 2013.

Specifying Validation Criteria

To specify the type of data allowable in a cell or range, follow these steps:

1. **Select the cell or range.**
2. **Choose Data ➪ Data Tools ➪ Data Validation.** The Data Validation dialog box appears (see Figure 26.2).

FIGURE 26.2

The three tabs of the Data Validation dialog box.

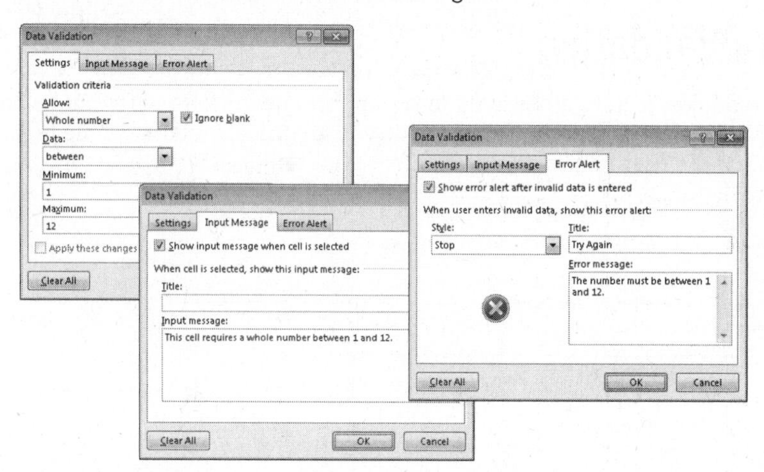

3. **Select the Settings tab.**
4. **Choose an option from the Allow drop-down list.** The contents of the Data Validation dialog box change, displaying controls based on your choice. To specify a formula, select Custom.
5. **Specify the conditions by using the displayed controls.** Your selection in Step 4 determines what other controls you can access.

6. **(Optional) Select the Input Message tab and specify which message to display when a user selects the cell.** You can use this optional step to tell the user what type of data is expected. If this step is omitted, no message will appear when the user selects the cell.
7. **(Optional) Select the Error Alert tab and specify which error message to display when a user makes an invalid entry.** The selection for Style determines what choices users have when they make invalid entries. To prevent an invalid entry, choose Stop. If this step is omitted, a standard message will appear if the user makes an invalid entry.

CAUTION

Even with data validation in effect, a user can enter invalid data. If the Style setting on the Error Alert tab of the Data Validation dialog box is set to anything other than Stop, invalid data *can* be entered. You can identify invalid entries by having Excel circle them (explained in the next section).

8. **Click OK.** The cell or range contains the validation criteria you specified.

Types of Validation Criteria You Can Apply

From the Settings tab of the Data Validation dialog box, you can specify a wide variety of data validation criteria. The following options are available from the Allow drop-down list. Keep in mind that the other controls on the Settings tab vary, depending on your choice from the Allow drop-down list.

- **Any Value:** Selecting this option removes any existing data validation. Note, however, that the input message, if any, still displays if the box is checked on the Input Message tab.
- **Whole Number:** The user must enter a whole number. You specify a valid range of whole numbers by using the Data drop-down list. For example, you can specify that the entry must be a whole number greater than or equal to 100.
- **Decimal:** The user must enter a number. You specify a valid range of numbers by refining the criteria from choices in the Data drop-down list. For example, you can specify that the entry must be greater than or equal to 0 and less than or equal to 1.
- **List:** The user must choose from a drop-down list of entries you provide. This option is very useful, and I discuss it in detail later in this chapter (see "Creating a drop-down list").
- **Date:** The user must enter a date. You specify a valid date range from choices in the Data drop-down list. For example, you can specify that the entered data must be greater than or equal to January 1, 2013, and less than or equal to December 31, 2013.
- **Time:** The user must enter a time. You specify a valid time range from choices in the Data drop-down list. For example, you can specify that the entered data must be later than 12:00 p.m.

- **Text Length:** The length of the data (number of characters) is limited. You specify a valid length by using the Data drop-down list. For example, you can specify that the length of the entered data be 1 (a single alphanumeric character).
- **Custom:** To use this option, you must supply a logical formula that determines the validity of the user's entry (a logical formula returns either `TRUE` or `FALSE`). You can enter the formula directly into the Formula control (which appears when you select the Custom option), or you can specify a cell reference that contains a formula. This chapter contains examples of useful formulas.

The Settings tab of the Data Validation dialog box contains two other check boxes:

- **Ignore Blank:** If selected, blank entries are allowed.
- **Apply These Changes to All Other Cells with the Same Setting:** If selected, the changes you make apply to all other cells that contain the original data validation criteria.

TIP

The Data ⇨ Data Tools ⇨ Data Validation drop-down list contains an item named Circle Invalid Data. When you select this item, circles appear around cells that contain incorrect entries. If you correct an invalid entry, the circle disappears. To get rid of the circles, choose Data ⇨ Data Tools ⇨ Data Validation ⇨ Clear Validation Circles. In Figure 26.3, valid entries are defined as values between 1 and 100. Values that not within this numerical range are circled.

FIGURE 26.3

Excel can draw circles around invalid entries (in this case, cells that contain values less than 1 or greater than 100).

	A	B	C	D	E	F	G	H	I	J
1	73	57	11	11	1	35	78	99	76	
2	104	24	1	60	76	59	15	97	33	
3	51	93	97	100	19	-10	31	100	92	
4	40	40	78	49	19	61	31	77	4	
5	62	11	2	26	89	55	12	13	69	
6	9	97	32	105	21	20	15	16	0	
7	58	28	80	50	43	21	6	95	93	
8	24	102	13	25	23	13	57	41	24	
9	67	16	87	62	51	22	45	87	104	
10	57	86	4	35	33	96	59	8	49	
11	26	38	43	74	100	75	66	27	32	
12	9	17	-6	80	22	80	3	88	71	
13	12	64	36	22	72	71	74	24	8	
14	86	69	91	67	83	48	42	53	64	
15	36	33	90	70	48	96	13	96	21	
16	57	103	87	63	102	79	65	21	108	
17	11	49	44	-7	7	4	25	19	97	
18										

Sheet1 Sheet2

Creating a Drop-Down List

One of the most common uses of data validation is to create a drop-down list in a cell. Figure 26.4 shows an example that uses the month names in A1:A12 as the list source.

FIGURE 26.4

This drop-down list (with an Input Message) was created using data validation.

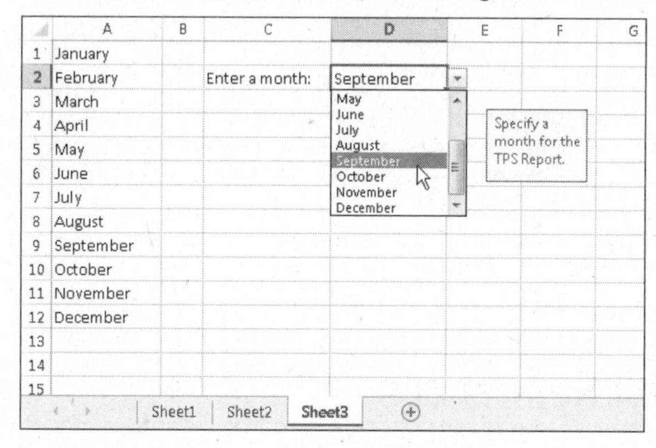

To create a drop-down list in a cell

1. **Enter the list items into a single-row or single-column range.** These items will appear in the drop-down list.
2. **Select the cell that will contain the drop-down list and then choose Data ➪ Data Tools ➪ Data Validation.** The Data Validation dialog box appears.
3. **From the Settings tab, select the List option (from the Allow drop-down list) and specify the range that contains the list, using the Source control.** The range can be in a different worksheet, but it must be in the same workbook.
4. **Make sure that the In-Cell Dropdown check box is selected.**
5. **Set any other Data Validation options as desired.**
6. **Click OK.** The cell displays an input message (if specified) and a drop-down arrow when it's activated. Click the arrow and choose an item from the list that appears.

TIP

If you have a short list, you can enter the items directly into the Source control of the Settings tab of the Data Validation dialog box. (This control appears when you choose the List option in the Allow drop-down list.) Just separate each item with list separators specified in your regional settings (a comma if you use the U.S. regional settings).

Using Formulas for Data Validation Rules

For simple data validation, the data validation feature is quite straightforward and easy to use. The real power of this feature, though, becomes apparent when you use data validation formulas.

The formula that you specify must be a logical formula that returns either `TRUE` or `FALSE`. If the formula evaluates to `TRUE`, the data is considered valid and remains in the cell. If the formula evaluates to `FALSE`, a message box appears that displays the message that you specify on the Error Alert tab of the Data Validation dialog box.

Specify a formula in the Data Validation dialog box by selecting the Custom option from the Allow drop-down list of the Settings tab. Enter the formula directly into the Formula control, or enter a reference to a cell that contains a formula. The Formula control appears on the Settings tab of the Data Validation dialog box when the Custom option is selected.

I present several examples of formulas used for data validation in the section "Data Validation Formula Examples," later in this chapter.

Understanding Cell References

If the formula that you enter into the Data Validation dialog box contains a cell reference, that reference is considered a *relative reference,* based on the upper-left cell in the selected range.

The following example clarifies this concept. Suppose that you want to allow only an odd number to be entered into the range B2:B10. None of the Excel data validation rules can limit entry to odd numbers, so a formula is required.

Follow these steps:

1. **Select the range (B2:B10 for this example) and ensure that cell B2 is the active cell.**
2. **Choose Data ➪ Data Tools ➪ Data Validation.** The Data Validation dialog box appears.
3. **Select the Settings tab and select the Custom option (from the Allow drop-down list).**
4. **Enter the following formula in the Formula field, as shown in Figure 26.5:**

   ```
   =ISODD(B2)
   ```

   This formula uses the `ISODD` function, which returns `TRUE` if its numeric argument is an odd number. Notice that the formula refers to the active cell, which is cell B2.

FIGURE 26.5

Entering a data validation formula.

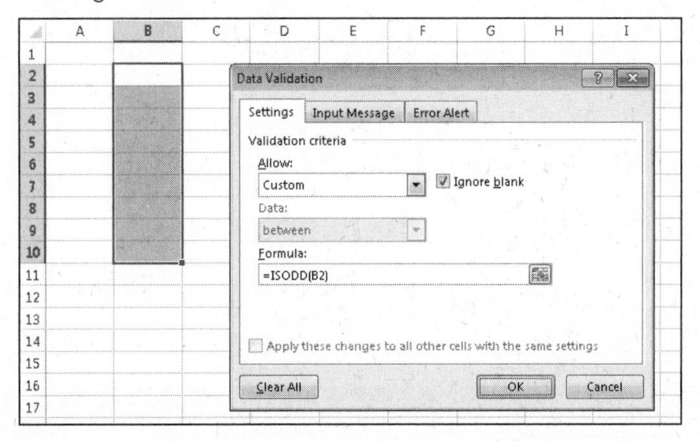

5. **On the Error Alert tab, choose Stop for the Style and then type** An odd number is required here **as the Error Message.**
6. **Click OK to close the Data Validation dialog box.**

Notice that the formula entered contains a reference to the upper-left cell in the selected range. This data validation formula was applied to a range of cells, so you might expect that each cell would contain the same data validation formula. Because you entered a relative cell reference as the argument for the `ISODD` function, Excel adjusts the formula for the other cells in the B2:B10 range. To demonstrate that the reference is relative, select cell B5 and examine its formula displayed in the Data Validation dialog box. You'll see that the formula for this cell is

```
=ISODD(B5)
```

NOTE

An alternative method is to enter the logical formula in a cell and then enter a cell reference in the Formula field in the Data Validation dialog box. For this example, cell C2 would contain `=ISODD(B2)`, and that formula would be copied down the column to cell C10. Then the Formula field in the Data Validation dialog box would have this formula: `=C2`. Most of the time, entering the formula into the Formula field is easier and more efficient.

Generally, when entering a data validation formula for a range of cells, you use a reference to the active cell, which is normally the upper-left cell in the selected range. An exception is when you need to refer to a specific cell. For example, suppose that you select range A1:B10, and you want your data validation to allow only values that are greater than the value in cell C1. You would use this formula:

```
=A1>$C$1
```

In this case, the reference to cell C1 is an *absolute reference;* it will not be adjusted for the cells in the selected range — which is just what you want. The data validation formula for cell A2 looks like this:

```
=A2>$C$1
```

The relative cell reference is adjusted, but the absolute cell reference is not.

Data Validation Formula Examples

The following sections contain a few data validation examples that use a formula entered directly into the Formula control on the Settings tab of the Data Validation dialog box. These examples help you understand how to create your own Data Validation formulas.

On the Web

All the examples in this section are available at this book's website. The file is named `data validation examples.xlsx`.

Accepting text only

Excel has a data validation option to limit the length of text entered into a cell, but it doesn't have an option to force text (rather than a number) into a cell. To force a cell or range to accept only text (no values), use the following data validation formula:

```
=ISTEXT(A1)
```

This formula assumes that the active cell in the selected range is cell A1.

Accepting a larger value than the previous cell

The following data validation formula enables the user to enter a value only if it's greater than the value in the cell directly above it:

```
=A2>A1
```

This formula assumes that A2 is the active cell in the selected range. Note that you can't use this formula for a cell in row 1.

Accepting nonduplicate entries only

The following data validation formula does not permit the user to make a duplicate entry in the range A1:C20:

```
=COUNTIF($A$1:$C$20,A1)=1
```

This is a logical formula that returns TRUE if the value in the cell occurs only one time in the A1:C20 range. Otherwise, it returns FALSE, and the Duplicate Entry dialog box is displayed.

This formula assumes that A1 is the active cell in the selected range. Note that the first argument for COUNTIF is an absolute reference. The second argument is a relative reference, and it adjusts for each cell in the validation range. Figure 26.6 shows this validation criterion in effect, using a custom error alert message. The user is attempting to enter 19 into cell B5.

FIGURE 26.6

Using data validation to prevent duplicate entries in a range.

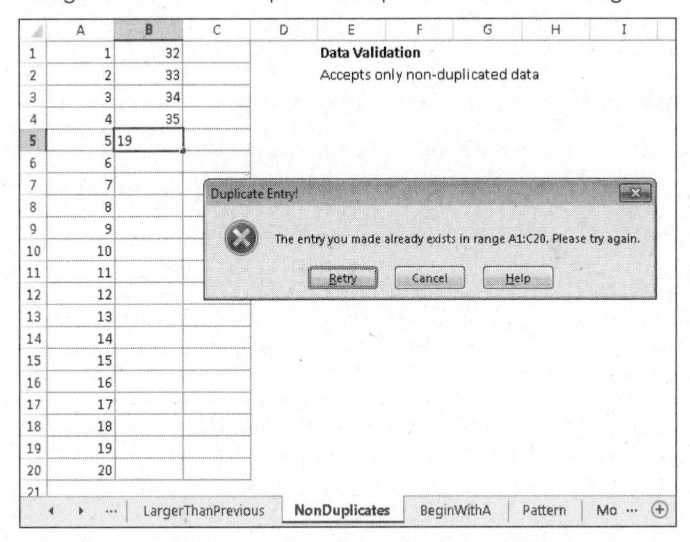

Accepting text that begins with a specific character

The following data validation formula demonstrates how to check for a specific character. In this case, the formula ensures that the user's entry is a text string that begins with the letter *A* (uppercase or lowercase).

```
=LEFT(A1)="a"
```

This is a logical formula that returns TRUE if the first character in the cell is the letter *A*. Otherwise, it returns FALSE. This formula assumes that the active cell in the selected range is cell A1.

The following formula is a variation of this validation formula. It uses wildcard characters in the second argument of the COUNTIF function. In this case, the formula ensures that the entry begins with the letter *A* and contains exactly five characters:

```
=COUNTIF(A1,"A????")=1
```

Accepting dates by the day of the week

The following data validation formula ensures that the cell entry is a date, and that the date is a Monday:

```
=WEEKDAY(A1)=2
```

This formula assumes that the active cell in the selected range is cell A1. It uses the WEEKDAY function, which returns 1 for Sunday, 2 for Monday, and so on.

Accepting only values that don't exceed a total

Figure 26.7 shows a simple budget worksheet, with the budget item amounts in the range B1:B6. The planned budget is in cell E5, and the user is attempting to enter a value in cell B4 that would cause the total (cell E6) to exceed the budget. The following data validation formula ensures that the sum of the budget items does not exceed the budget:

```
=SUM($B$1:$B$6)<=$E$5
```

FIGURE 26.7

Using data validation to ensure that the sum of a range does not exceed a certain value.

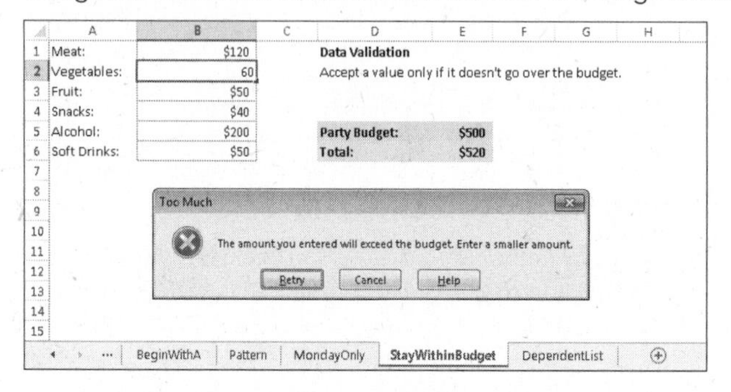

Creating a dependent list

As I describe previously, you can use data validation to create a drop-down list in a cell (see "Creating a Drop-Down List," earlier in this chapter). This section explains how to use a drop-down list to control the entries that appear in a second drop-down list. In other words, the second drop-down list is dependent upon the value selected in the first drop-down list.

Figure 26.8 shows a simple example of a dependent list created by using data validation. Cell E2 contains data validation that displays a three-item list from the range A1:C1 (Vegetables, Fruits, and Meats). When the user chooses an item from the list, the second list (in cell F2) displays the appropriate items.

FIGURE 26.8

The items displayed in the list in cell F2 depend on the list item selected in cell E2.

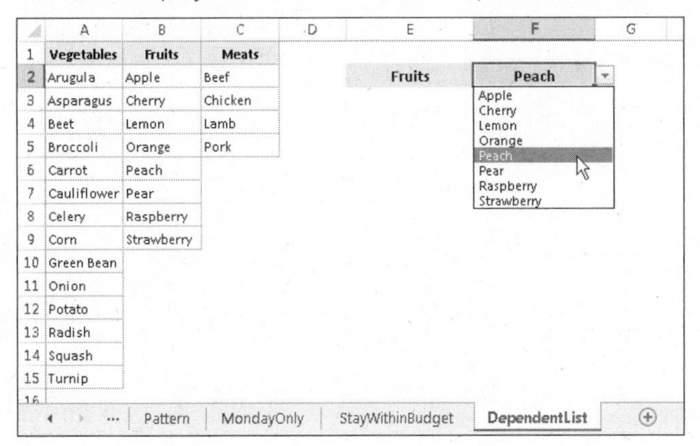

This worksheet uses three named ranges:

- **Vegetables:** A2:A15
- **Fruits:** B2:B9
- **Meats:** C2:C5

Cell F2 contains data validation that uses this formula:

```
=INDIRECT($E$2)
```

Therefore, the drop-down list displayed in F2 depends on the value displayed in cell E2.

CHAPTER

27

Creating and Using Worksheet Outlines

IN THIS CHAPTER

Introducing worksheet outlines

Creating an outline

Using outlines

If you use a word processor, you may be familiar with the concept of an outline. Most word processors (including Microsoft Word) have an outline mode that lets you view only the headings and subheadings in your document. You can easily expand a heading to show the text below it. Using an outline makes visualizing the structure of your document easy.

Excel also is capable of using outlines, and understanding this feature can make working with certain types of worksheets much easier for you.

Introducing Worksheet Outlines

You'll find that some worksheets are more suitable for outlines than others. You can use outlines to create summary reports in which you don't want to show all the details. If your worksheet uses hierarchical data with subtotals, it's probably a good candidate for an outline.

The best way to understand how worksheet outlining works is to look at an example. Figure 27.1 shows a simple sales summary sheet without an outline. Formulas are used to calculate subtotals by region and by quarter.

FIGURE 27.1

A simple sales summary with subtotals.

	A	B	C	D	E	F	G	H	I	J
1	**State**	**Jan**	**Feb**	**Mar**	***Qtr-1***	**Apr**	**May**	**Jun**	***Qtr-2***	***Total***
2	California	1,118	1,960	1,252	***4,330***	1,271	1,557	1,679	***4,507***	**8,837**
3	Washington	1,247	1,238	1,028	***3,513***	1,345	1,784	1,574	***4,703***	**8,216**
4	Oregon	1,460	1,954	1,726	***5,140***	1,461	1,764	1,144	***4,369***	**9,509**
5	Arizona	1,345	1,375	1,075	***3,795***	1,736	1,555	1,372	***4,663***	**8,458**
6	**West Total**	**5,170**	**6,527**	**5,081**	**16,778**	**5,813**	**6,660**	**5,769**	**18,242**	**35,020**
7	New York	1,429	1,316	1,993	***4,738***	1,832	1,740	1,191	***4,763***	**9,501**
8	New Jersey	1,735	1,406	1,224	***4,365***	1,706	1,320	1,290	***4,316***	**8,681**
9	Massachusetts	1,099	1,233	1,110	***3,442***	1,637	1,512	1,006	***4,155***	**7,597**
10	Florida	1,705	1,792	1,225	***4,722***	1,946	1,327	1,357	***4,630***	**9,352**
11	**East Total**	**5,968**	**5,747**	**5,552**	**17,267**	**7,121**	**5,899**	**4,844**	**17,864**	**35,131**
12	Kentucky	1,109	1,078	1,155	***3,342***	1,993	1,082	1,551	***4,626***	**7,968**
13	Oklahoma	1,309	1,045	1,641	***3,995***	1,924	1,499	1,941	***5,364***	**9,359**
14	Missouri	1,511	1,744	1,414	***4,669***	1,243	1,493	1,820	***4,556***	**9,225**
15	Illinois	1,539	1,493	1,211	***4,243***	1,165	1,013	1,445	***3,623***	**7,866**
16	Kansas	1,973	1,560	1,243	***4,776***	1,495	1,125	1,387	***4,007***	**8,783**
17	**Central Total**	**7,441**	**6,920**	**6,664**	**21,025**	**7,820**	**6,212**	**8,144**	**22,176**	**43,201**
18	**Grand Total**	**18,579**	**19,194**	**17,297**	**55,070**	**20,754**	**18,771**	**18,757**	**58,282**	**113,352**
19										
20										

Sheet1 | Normalized

Figure 27.2 shows the same worksheet after I created the outline. Notice that Excel adds a new section to the left of the screen. This section contains outline controls that enable you to determine which level to view. This particular outline has three levels: States, Regions (each region consists of states grouped into categories such as West, East, and Central), and Grand Total (the sum of each region's subtotal).

FIGURE 27.2

The worksheet after creating an outline.

1 2 3

	A	B	C	D	E	F	G	H	I	J
1	**State**	**Jan**	**Feb**	**Mar**	***Qtr-1***	**Apr**	**May**	**Jun**	***Qtr-2***	***Total***
2	California	1,118	1,960	1,252	4,330	1,271	1,557	1,679	4,507	8,837
3	Washington	1,247	1,238	1,028	3,513	1,345	1,784	1,574	4,703	8,216
4	Oregon	1,460	1,954	1,726	5,140	1,461	1,764	1,144	4,369	9,509
5	Arizona	1,345	1,375	1,075	3,795	1,736	1,555	1,372	4,663	8,458
6	**West Total**	**5,170**	**6,527**	**5,081**	**16,778**	**5,813**	**6,660**	**5,769**	**18,242**	**35,020**
7	New York	1,429	1,316	1,993	4,738	1,832	1,740	1,191	4,763	9,501
8	New Jersey	1,735	1,406	1,224	4,365	1,706	1,320	1,290	4,316	8,681
9	Massachusetts	1,099	1,233	1,110	3,442	1,637	1,512	1,006	4,155	7,597
10	Florida	1,705	1,792	1,225	4,722	1,946	1,327	1,357	4,630	9,352
11	**East Total**	**5,968**	**5,747**	**5,552**	**17,267**	**7,121**	**5,899**	**4,844**	**17,864**	**35,131**
12	Kentucky	1,109	1,078	1,155	3,342	1,993	1,082	1,551	4,626	7,968
13	Oklahoma	1,309	1,045	1,641	3,995	1,924	1,499	1,941	5,364	9,359
14	Missouri	1,511	1,744	1,414	4,669	1,243	1,493	1,820	4,556	9,225
15	Illinois	1,539	1,493	1,211	4,243	1,165	1,013	1,445	3,623	7,866
16	Kansas	1,973	1,560	1,243	4,776	1,495	1,125	1,387	4,007	8,783
17	**Central Total**	**7,441**	**6,920**	**6,664**	**21,025**	**7,820**	**6,212**	**8,144**	**22,176**	**43,201**
18	**Grand Total**	**18,579**	**19,194**	**17,297**	**55,070**	**20,754**	**18,771**	**18,757**	**58,282**	**113,352**
19										

Sheet1 | Normalized

Figure 27.3 depicts the outline after clicking the 2 button, which displays the second level of details. Now, the outline shows only the totals for the regions (the detail rows are hidden). You can partially expand the outline to show the detail for a particular region by clicking one of the plus-sign buttons. Collapsing the outline to level 1 shows only the headers and the Grand Total row.

Excel can create outlines in both directions. In the preceding examples, the outline is a row (vertical) outline. Figure 27.4 shows the same model after a column (horizontal) outline was added. When both outlines are in effect, Excel also displays outline controls at the top.

FIGURE 27.3

The worksheet after collapsing the outline to the second level.

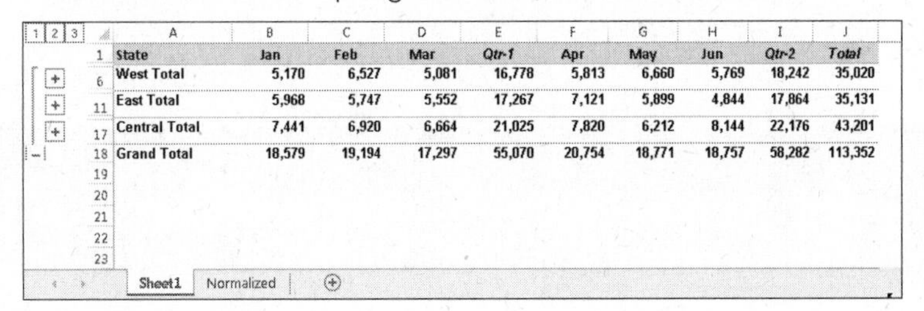

	A	B	C	D	E	F	G	H	I	J
1	State	Jan	Feb	Mar	Qtr-1	Apr	May	Jun	Qtr-2	Total
6	West Total	5,170	6,527	5,081	16,778	5,813	6,660	5,769	18,242	35,020
11	East Total	5,968	5,747	5,552	17,267	7,121	5,899	4,844	17,864	35,131
17	Central Total	7,441	6,920	6,664	21,025	7,820	6,212	8,144	22,176	43,201
18	Grand Total	18,579	19,194	17,297	55,070	20,754	18,771	18,757	58,282	113,352
19										
20										
21										
22										
23										

Sheet1 | Normalized

FIGURE 27.4

The worksheet after adding a column outline.

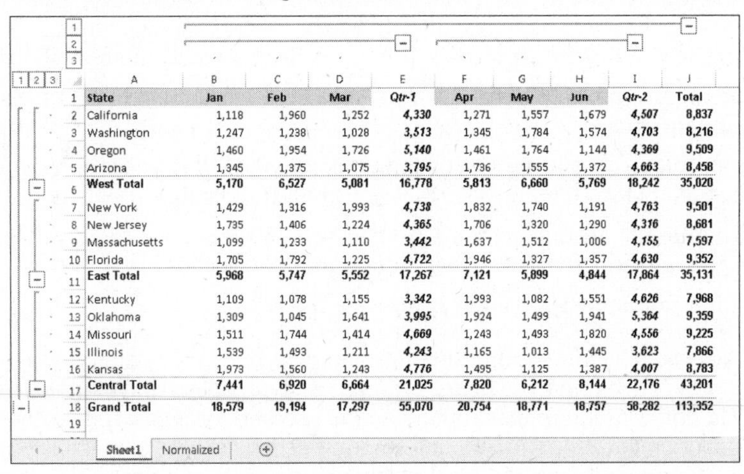

	A	B	C	D	E	F	G	H	I	J
1	State	Jan	Feb	Mar	Qtr-1	Apr	May	Jun	Qtr-2	Total
2	California	1,118	1,960	1,252	4,330	1,271	1,557	1,679	4,507	8,837
3	Washington	1,247	1,238	1,028	3,513	1,345	1,784	1,574	4,703	8,216
4	Oregon	1,460	1,954	1,726	5,140	1,461	1,764	1,144	4,369	9,509
5	Arizona	1,345	1,375	1,075	3,795	1,736	1,555	1,372	4,663	8,458
6	West Total	5,170	6,527	5,081	16,778	5,813	6,660	5,769	18,242	35,020
7	New York	1,429	1,316	1,993	4,738	1,832	1,740	1,191	4,763	9,501
8	New Jersey	1,735	1,406	1,224	4,365	1,706	1,320	1,290	4,316	8,681
9	Massachusetts	1,099	1,233	1,110	3,442	1,637	1,512	1,006	4,155	7,597
10	Florida	1,705	1,792	1,225	4,722	1,946	1,327	1,357	4,630	9,352
11	East Total	5,968	5,747	5,552	17,267	7,121	5,899	4,844	17,864	35,131
12	Kentucky	1,109	1,078	1,155	3,342	1,993	1,082	1,551	4,626	7,968
13	Oklahoma	1,309	1,045	1,641	3,995	1,924	1,499	1,941	5,364	9,359
14	Missouri	1,511	1,744	1,414	4,669	1,243	1,493	1,820	4,556	9,225
15	Illinois	1,539	1,493	1,211	4,243	1,165	1,013	1,445	3,623	7,866
16	Kansas	1,973	1,560	1,243	4,776	1,495	1,125	1,387	4,007	8,783
17	Central Total	7,441	6,920	6,664	21,025	7,820	6,212	8,144	22,176	43,201
18	Grand Total	18,579	19,194	17,297	55,070	20,754	18,771	18,757	58,282	113,352
19										

Sheet1 | Normalized

If you create both a row outline and a column outline in a worksheet, you can work with each outline independently of the other. For example, you can show the row outline at the second level and the column outline at the first level. Figure 27.5 shows the model with both outlines collapsed at the second level. The result is a nice high-level summary table that gives regional totals by quarter.

FIGURE 27.5

The worksheet with both outlines collapsed at the second level.

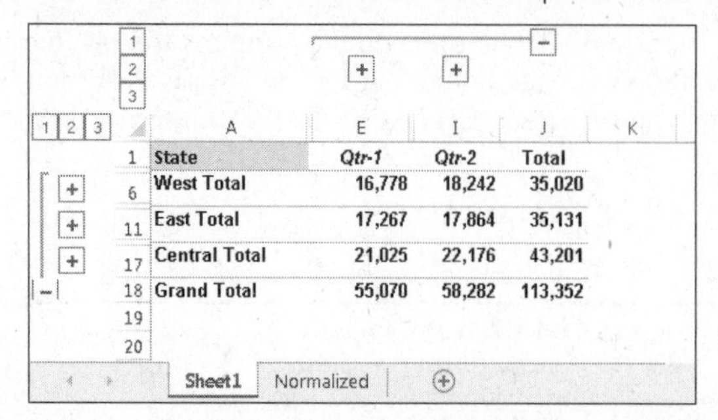

ON THE WEB

You can find the workbook used in the preceding examples on this book's website. The file is named `outline example.xlsx`.

Keep in mind the following points about worksheet outlines:

- **A worksheet can have only one outline.** If you need to create more than one outline, move the data to a new worksheet.
- **You can either create an outline manually or have Excel do it for you automatically.** If you choose the latter option, you may need to do some preparation to get the worksheet in the proper format. (The next section covers both methods.)
- **You can create an outline either for all data on a worksheet or just for a selected data range.**
- **You can remove an outline with a single command.** (Read how in the upcoming section, "Removing an outline.") However, the data remains.
- **You can hide the outline symbols (to free screen space) but retain the outline.** I show you how in the "Hiding the outline symbols" section, later in this chapter.
- **An outline can have up to eight nested levels.**

Worksheet outlines can be quite useful. If your main objective is to summarize a large amount of data, though, you may be better off using a pivot table. A pivot table is much more flexible and doesn't require that you create the subtotal formulas; it does the summarizing for you automatically. The ultimate solution depends upon your data source. If you're entering data from scratch, the most flexible approach is to enter it in a normalized table format, and create a pivot table.

I discuss pivot tables (and normalized data) in Chapters 33 and 34.

Creating an Outline

This section describes the two ways to create an outline: automatically and manually. Before you create an outline, you need to ensure that data is appropriate for an outline and that the formulas are set up properly.

Preparing the data

What type of data is appropriate for an outline? Generally, the data should be arranged in a hierarchy, such as a budget that consists of an arrangement similar to the following:

Company
  Division
    Department
      Budget Category
        Budget Item

In this case, each budget item (for example, airfare and hotel expenses) is part of a budget category (for example, travel expenses). Each department has its own budget, and the departments are rolled up into divisions. The divisions make up the company. This type of arrangement is well suited for a row outline.

The data arrangement suitable for an outline is essentially a summary table of your data. In some situations, your data will be "normalized" data — one data point per row. You can easily create a pivot table to summarize such data, and a pivot table is much more flexible than dealing with an outline.

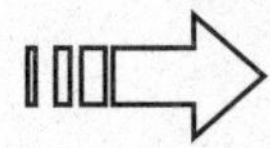

See Chapters 34 and 35 for more information on pivot tables.

After you create such an outline, you can view the information at any level of detail that you want by clicking the outline controls. When you need to create reports for different levels of management, consider using an outline. For example, upper management may want to see only the division totals, division managers may want to see totals by department, and each department manager needs to see the full details for his or her department.

Keep in mind that using an outline isn't a security feature. The data that's hidden when an outline is collapsed can easily be revealed when the outline is expanded.

You can include time-based information that is rolled up into larger units (such as months and quarters) in a column outline. Column outlines work just like row outlines, however, and the levels don't have to be time based.

Before you create an outline, you need to make sure that all the summary formulas are entered correctly and consistently. In this context, *consistently* means that the formulas are in the same relative location. Generally, formulas that compute summary formulas (such as subtotals) are entered below the data to which they refer. In some cases, however, the summary formulas are entered above the referenced cells. Excel can handle either method, but you must be consistent throughout the range that you outline. If the summary formulas aren't consistent, automatic outlining won't produce the results that you want.

NOTE

If your summary formulas aren't consistent (that is, some are above and some are below the data), you still can create an outline, but you must do it manually.

Creating an outline automatically

Excel can create an outline for you automatically in a few seconds, whereas it may take you ten minutes or more to do the same thing manually.

NOTE

If you've created a table for your data (by choosing Insert ➪ Tables ➪ Table), Excel can't create an outline automatically. You can create an outline from a table, but you must do so manually.

To have Excel create an outline, move the cell pointer anywhere within the range of data that you're outlining. Then, choose Data ➪ Outline ➪ Group ➪ Auto Outline. Excel analyzes the formulas in the range and creates the outline. Depending on the formulas that you have, Excel creates a row outline, a column outline, or both.

If the worksheet already has an outline, Excel asks whether you want to modify the existing outline. Click Yes to force Excel to remove the old outline and create a new one.

NOTE

Excel automatically creates an outline when you choose Data ➪ Outline ➪ Subtotal, which inserts subtotal formulas automatically.

Creating an outline manually

Usually, letting Excel create the outline is the best approach. It's much faster and less error prone. If the outline that Excel creates isn't what you have in mind, however, you can create an outline manually.

When Excel creates a row outline, the summary rows must all be below the data or all above the data: They can't be mixed. Similarly, for a column outline, the summary columns must all be to the right of the data or to the left of the data. If your worksheet doesn't meet these requirements, you have two choices:

- Rearrange the worksheet so that it does meet the requirements.
- Create the outline manually.

You also need to create an outline manually if the range doesn't contain any formulas. You may have imported a file and want to use an outline to display it better. Because Excel uses the positioning of the formulas to determine how to create the outline, it can't make an outline without formulas.

Creating an outline manually consists of creating groups of rows (for row outlines) or groups of columns (for column outlines). To create a group of rows, follow these steps:

1. **Select the rows that you want to include in the group.** One way to do this is to click a row number and then drag to select other adjacent rows.

CAUTION
Don't select the row that has the summary formulas. You don't want these rows to be included in the group.

2. **Choose Data➪Outline➪Group➪Group.** Excel displays outline symbols for the group.
3. **Repeat this process for each group that you want to create.** When you collapse the outline, Excel hides rows in the group, but the summary row, which isn't in the group, remains in view.

NOTE
If you select a range of cells (rather than entire rows or columns) before you create a group, Excel displays a dialog box asking what you want to group. It then groups entire rows or columns based on the range that you select.

You can also select groups of groups to create multilevel outlines. When you create multi-level outlines, always start with the innermost groupings and then work your way out. If you realize that you grouped the wrong rows, you can ungroup the group by selecting the rows and choosing Data➪Outline➪Ungroup➪Ungroup.

Here are keyboard shortcuts you can use that speed up grouping and ungrouping:

- **Alt + Shift + right arrow:** Groups selected rows or columns
- **Alt + Shift + left arrow:** Ungroups selected rows or columns

Creating outlines manually can be confusing at first, but if you stick with it, you'll become a pro in no time.

Figure 27.6 shows a worksheet with a three-level outline of this book. I had to create it manually because it has no formulas, just text.

FIGURE 27.6

An outline of this book, created manually.

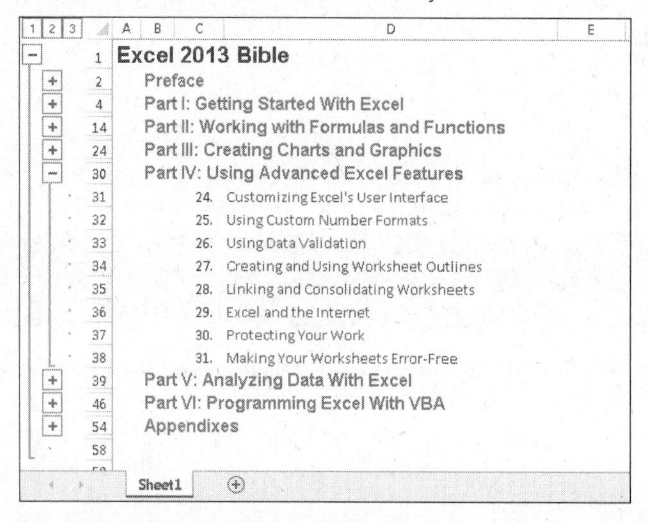

ON THE WEB

This workbook is available on this book's website. The file is named `book outline.xlsx`.

Working with Outlines

This section discusses the basic operations that you can perform with a worksheet outline.

Displaying levels

To display various outline levels, click the appropriate outline symbol. These symbols consist of buttons with numbers on them (1, 2, and so on) or a plus sign (+) or a minus sign (-). Refer to Figure 27.5, which shows these symbols for a row and column outline.

Clicking the 1 button collapses the outline so that it displays no detail (just the highest summary level of information), clicking the 2 button expands the outline to show one level, and so on. The number of numbered buttons depends on the number of outline levels. Choosing a level number displays the detail for that level, plus any levels with lower numbers. To display all levels (the most detail), click the highest-level number.

You can expand a particular section by clicking its plus-sign button, or you can collapse a particular section by clicking its minus-sign button. In short, you have complete control over the details that Excel exposes or hides in an outline.

If you prefer, you can use the Hide Detail and Show Detail commands on the Data⇨Outline group to hide and show details, respectively.

TIP

If you constantly adjust the outline to show different reports, consider using the Custom Views feature to save a particular view and give it a name. Then you can quickly switch among the named views. Choose View⇨Workbook Views⇨Custom Views.

Adding data to an outline

You may need to add additional rows or columns to an outline. In some cases, you may be able to insert new rows or columns without disturbing the outline, and the new rows or columns become part of the outline. In other cases, you'll find that the new row or column is not part of the outline. If you create the outline automatically, choose Data⇨Outline⇨Group⇨Auto Outline. Excel makes you verify that you want to modify the existing outline. If you create the outline manually, you need to make the adjustments manually, as well.

Removing an outline

After you no longer need an outline, you can remove it by choosing Data⇨Outline⇨Ungroup⇨Clear Outline. Excel fully expands the outline by displaying all hidden rows and columns, and the outline symbols disappear. Be careful before you remove an outline, however. You can't make it reappear by clicking the Undo button; you must re-create the outline from scratch.

Adjusting the outline symbols

When you create a manual outline, Excel puts the outline symbols below the summary rows. This can be very unintuitive because you need to click the symbol in the row *below* the section that you want to expand.

If you prefer that the outline symbols appear in the same row as the summary row, click the dialog box launcher in the lower right of the Data⇨Outline group. Excel displays the dialog box shown in Figure 27.7. Remove the check mark from the Summary Rows Below Detail option, and click OK. The outline will now display the outline symbols in a more logical position.

FIGURE 27.7

Use the Settings dialog box to adjust the position of the outline symbols.

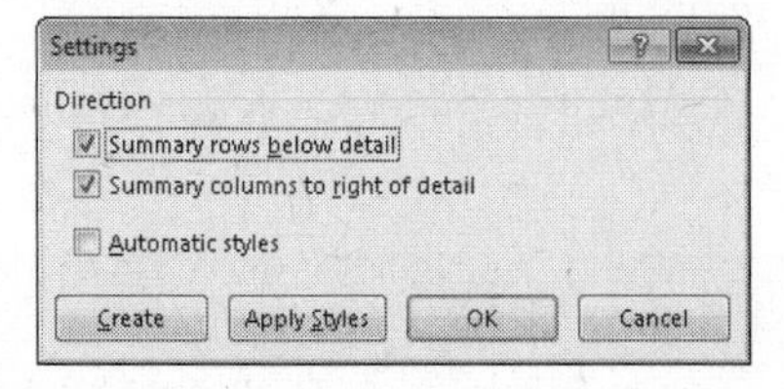

Hiding the outline symbols

The outline symbols Excel displays when an outline is present take up quite a bit of space. (The exact amount depends on the number of levels.) If you want to see as much as possible onscreen, you can temporarily hide these symbols without removing the outline. Press Ctrl + 8 to toggle the outline symbols on and off. When the outline symbols are hidden, you can't expand or collapse the outline.

NOTE

When you hide the outline symbols, the outline still is in effect, and the worksheet displays the data at the current outline level (that is, some rows or columns may be hidden).

The Custom Views feature, which saves named views of your outline, also saves the status of the outline symbols as part of the view, enabling you to name some views with the outline symbols and other views without them.

CHAPTER

28

Linking and Consolidating Worksheets

IN THIS CHAPTER

Using various methods to link workbooks

Consolidating multiple worksheets

In this chapter, I discuss two procedures that you might find helpful: linking and consolidation. *Linking* is the process of using references to cells in external workbooks to get data into your worksheet. *Consolidation* combines or summarizes information from two or more worksheets (which can be in multiple workbooks).

Linking Workbooks

As you may know, Excel allows you to create formulas that contain references to other workbook files. In such a case, the workbooks are linked in such a way that one depends upon the other. The workbook that contains the external reference formulas is the *dependent* workbook (because it contains formulas that depend upon another workbook). The workbook that contains the information used in the external reference formula is the *source* workbook (because it's the source of the information).

When you consider linking workbooks, you may ask yourself the following question: If Workbook A needs to access data in another workbook (Workbook B), why not just enter the data into Workbook A in the first place? In some cases, you can. But the real value of linking becomes apparent when the source workbook is being continually updated by another person or group. Creating a link in Workbook A to Workbook B means that in Workbook A, you always have access to the most recent information in Workbook B because Workbook A is updated whenever Workbook B changes.

Linking workbooks also can be helpful if you need to consolidate different files. For example, each regional sales manager may store data in a separate workbook. You can create a summary workbook that first uses link formulas to retrieve specific data from each manager's workbook and then calculates totals across all regions.

Linking also is useful as a way to break up a large workbook into smaller files. You can create smaller workbooks that are linked with a few key external references.

Linking has its downside, however. External reference formulas are somewhat fragile, and accidentally severing the links that you create is relatively easy. You can prevent this mistake if you understand how linking works. Later in the chapter, I discuss some problems that may arise, as well as how to avoid them (see "Avoiding Potential Problems with External Reference Formulas").

On the Web

The website for this book contains two linked files that you can use to get a feel for how linking works. The files are named `source.xlsx` and `dependent.xlsx`. As long as these files remain in the same folder, the links will be maintained.

Creating External Reference Formulas

You can create an external reference formula by using several different techniques:

- **Type the cell references manually.** These references may be lengthy because they include workbook and sheet names and possibly even drive and path information. These references can also point to workbooks stored on the Internet. The advantage of manually typing the cell references is that the source workbook doesn't have to be open. The disadvantage is that it's very error prone. Mistyping a single character makes the formula return an error (or possibly return a wrong value from the file).
- **Point to the cell references.** If the source workbook is open, you can use the standard pointing techniques to create formulas that use external references.
- **Paste the links.** Copy your data to the Clipboard. Then, with the source workbook open, choose Home➪Clipboard➪Paste➪Paste Link (N). Excel pastes the copied data as external reference formulas.
- **Choose Data➪Data Tools➪Consolidate.** For more on this method, see the section "Consolidating worksheets by using the Consolidate command," later in this chapter.

Understanding link formula syntax

The general syntax for an external reference formula is as follows:

```
=[WorkbookName]SheetName!CellAddress
```

Precede the cell address with the workbook name (in brackets), followed by the worksheet name and an exclamation point. Here's an example of a formula that uses cell A1 in the Sheet1 worksheet of a workbook named Budget:

```
=[Budget.xlsx]Sheet1!A1
```

If the workbook name or the sheet name in the reference includes one or more spaces, you must enclose the text in single quotation marks. For example, here's a formula that refers to cell A1 on Sheet1 in a workbook named `Annual Budget.xlsx`:

```
='[Annual Budget.xlsx]Sheet1'!A1
```

When a formula links to a different workbook, you don't need to open the other workbook. However, if the workbook is closed and not in the current folder, you must add the complete path to the reference. For example:

```
='C:\Data\Excel\Budget\[Annual Budget.xlsx]Sheet1'!A1
```

If the workbook is stored on the Internet, the formula will also include the URL. For example:

```
='https://d.docs.live.net/86a6d7c1f41bd208/Documents/[Annual Budget.xlsx]
  Sheet1'!A1
```

NOTE

Single quotes are always required when the link includes a path or a URL, even if the path or URL includes no spaces.

Creating a link formula by pointing

Entering external reference formulas manually usually isn't the best approach because you can easily make an error. Instead, have Excel build the formula for you, as follows:

1. **Open the source workbook.**
2. **Select the cell in the dependent workbook that will hold the formula.**
3. **Type an equal sign (=)**
4. **Activate the source workbook and select the cell or range and press Enter.** The dependent workbook is reactivated.

When you point to the cell or range, Excel automatically takes care of the details and creates a syntactically correct external reference. When using this method, the cell reference is always an absolute reference (such as `$A$1`). If you plan to copy the formula to create additional link formulas, you need to change the absolute reference to a relative reference by removing the dollar signs for the cell address.

As long as the source workbook remains open, the external reference doesn't include the path (or URL) to the workbook. If you close the source workbook, however, the external reference formulas change to include the full path (or URL).

Pasting links

Pasting links provides another way to create external reference formulas. This method is applicable when you want to create formulas that simply reference other cells. Follow these steps:

1. **Open the source workbook.**
2. **Select the cell or range that you want to link, and then copy it to the Clipboard.** Ctrl + C is the quickest way.
3. **Activate the dependent workbook and select the cell in which you want the link formula to appear.** If you're pasting a copied range, just select the upper-left cell.
4. **Choose Home ➪ Clipboard ➪ Paste ➪ Paste Link (N).**

Working with External Reference Formulas

This section discusses some key points that you need to know about when working with links. Understanding these details can help prevent some common errors.

Creating links to unsaved workbooks

Excel enables you to create link formulas to unsaved workbooks (and even to nonexistent workbooks). Assume that you have two workbooks open (Book1 and Book2), and you haven't saved either of them. If you create a link formula to Book1 in Book2 and then save Book2, Excel displays a confirmation dialog box like the one shown in Figure 28.1.

FIGURE 28.1

This confirmation message indicates that the workbook you're saving contains references to a workbook that you haven't yet saved.

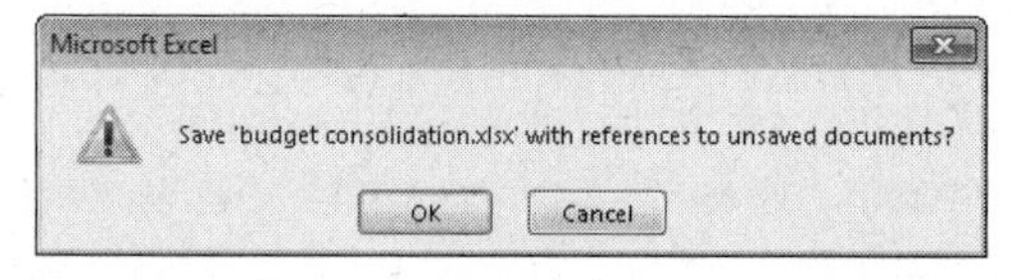

Typically, you don't want to save a workbook that has links to an unsaved document. To avoid this prompt, save the source workbook first.

You can also create links to documents that don't exist. You may want to do so if you'll be using a source workbook from a colleague, but the file hasn't yet arrived. When you enter an external reference formula that refers to a nonexistent workbook, Excel displays its Update Values dialog box, which resembles the Open dialog box. If you click Cancel, the formula retains the workbook name that you entered, but it returns a `#REF!` error.

Security Warning for Links

Excel 2010 introduced a new security feature related to links. The first time you open a workbook that contains links to other files, you see a security warning below the Ribbon. The links won't be updated unless you click the Enable Content button.

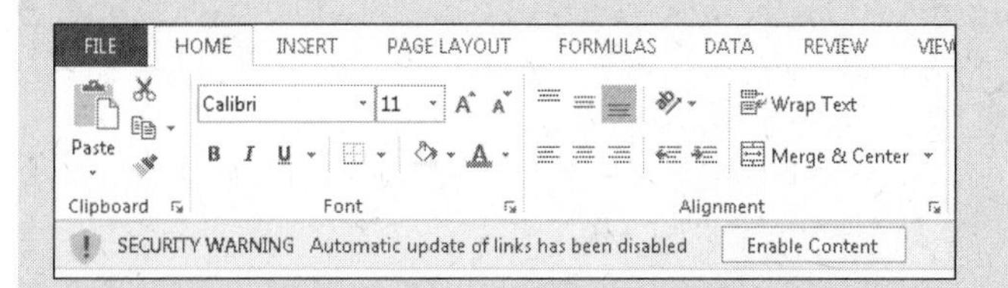

However, Excel remembers that you've deemed the workbook safe, so you won't see that Security Warning again. If you want to disable these Security Warnings, follow these steps:

1. **Choose File⇨Options.** The Excel Options dialog box appears.
2. **Select the Trust Center tab, and click the Trust Center Settings button.** The Trust Center dialog box appears.
3. **Select the External Content tab, and change the option for Security Settings for Workbook Links.**

When the source workbook becomes available, you can choose Data⇨Connections⇨Edit Links to update the link (see "Updating links," later in this chapter). After doing so, the error goes away, and the formula displays its proper value.

Opening a workbook with external reference formulas

When you open a workbook that contains links, Excel displays a dialog box (shown in Figure 28.2) that asks you what to do. Your options are

FIGURE 28.2

Excel displays this dialog box when you open a workbook that contains links to other files.

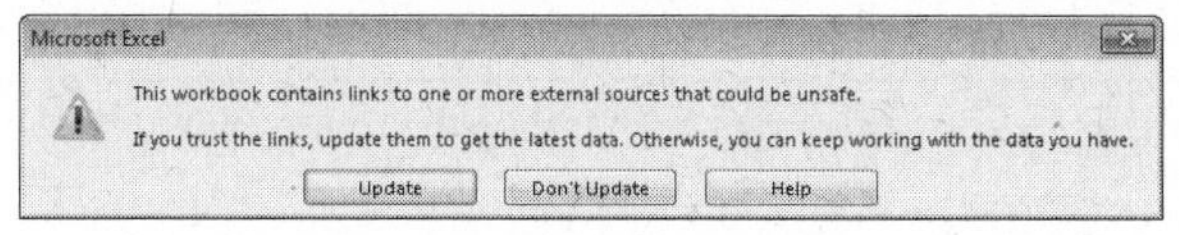

- **Update:** The links are updated with the current information in the source file(s).
- **Don't Update:** The links are not updated, and the workbook displays the previous values returned by the link formulas.
- **Help:** The Excel Help screen displays so you can read about links.

What if you choose to update the links, but the source workbook is no longer available? If Excel can't locate a source workbook that's referred to in a link formula, it displays its Edit Links dialog box, shown in Figure 28.3. Click the Change Source button to specify a different workbook, or click the Break Link to destroy the link.

FIGURE 28.3

The Edit Links dialog box.

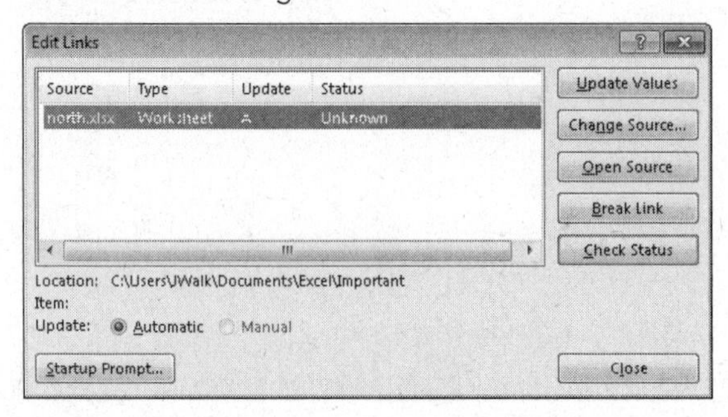

You can also access the Edit Links dialog box by choosing Data ➪ Connections ➪ Edit Links. The Edit Links dialog box lists all source workbooks, plus other types of links to other documents.

TIP

To prevent Excel from displaying the dialog box in Figure 28.2, open the Excel Options dialog box, select the Advanced tab, and remove the check mark from Ask to Update Automated Links. That disables the dialog box for all workbooks.

Changing the startup prompt

When you open a workbook that contains one or more external reference formulas, Excel, by default, displays the dialog box that asks how you want to handle the links (refer to Figure 28.2). You can eliminate this prompt by changing a setting in the Startup Prompt dialog box (see Figure 28.4).

FIGURE 28.4

Use the Startup Prompt dialog box to specify how Excel handles links when the workbook is opened.

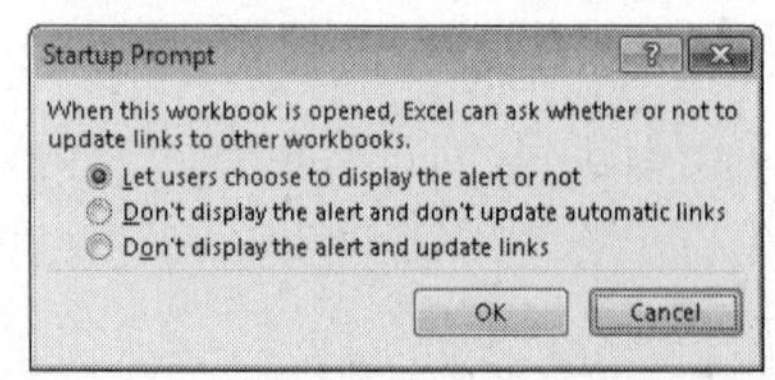

To display the Startup Prompt dialog box, choose Data ➪ Connections ➪ Edit Links. The Edit Links dialog box (refer to Figure 28.3) appears. In the Edit Links dialog box, click the Startup Prompt button and then select the option that describes how you want to handle the links.

Updating links

If you want to ensure that your link formulas have the latest values from their source workbooks, you can force an update. For example, say that you just discovered that someone made changes to the source workbook and saved the latest version to your network server. In such a case, you may want to update the links to display the current data.

To update linked formulas with their current value, open the Edit Links dialog box (Data ➪ Connections ➪ Edit Links), choose the appropriate source workbook in the list, and then click the Update Values button. Excel updates the link formulas with the latest version of the source workbook.

NOTE

Excel always sets worksheet links to the Automatic Update option in the Edit Links dialog box, and you can't change them to Manual, which means that Excel updates the links only when you open the workbook. Excel doesn't automatically update links when the source file changes (unless the source workbook is open).

Changing the link source

In some cases, you may need to change the source workbook for your external references. For example, say you have a worksheet that has links to a file named Preliminary Budget, but you later receive a finalized version named Final Budget.

You can change the link source using the Edit Links dialog box (choose Data ➪ Connections ➪ Edit Links). Select the source workbook that you want to change, and click the Change Source button. Excel displays its Change Source dialog box, from which you can select a new source file. After you select the file, all external reference formulas that referred to the old file are updated.

Severing links

If you have external references in a workbook and then decide that you no longer need the links, you can convert the external reference formulas to values, thereby severing the links. To do so, access the Edit Links dialog box (choose Data ➪ Connections ➪ Edit Links), select the linked file in the list, and then click Break Link.

CAUTION

Excel prompts you to verify your intentions because you can't undo this operation.

Avoiding Potential Problems with External Reference Formulas

Using external reference formulas can be quite useful, but the links may be unintentionally severed. As long as the source file hasn't been deleted, you can almost always re-establish lost links. If you open the workbook and Excel can't locate the file, you see a dialog box that enables you to specify the workbook and re-create the links. You also can change the source file by clicking the Change Source button in the Edit Links dialog box (choose Data ➪ Connections ➪ Edit Links). The following sections discuss some pointers that you must remember when you use external reference formulas.

Renaming or moving a source workbook

If you (or someone else) renames the source document or moves it to a different folder, Excel won't be able to update the links. You need to use the Edit Links dialog box and specify the new source document (see "Changing the link source," earlier in this chapter).

NOTE

If the source and dependent folder reside in the same folder, you can move both of the files to a different folder. In such a case, the links remain intact.

Using the Save As command

If both the source workbook and the dependent workbook are open, Excel doesn't display the full path to the source file in the external reference formulas. If you use the File ➪ Save As command to give the source workbook a new name, Excel modifies the external references to use the new workbook name. In some cases, this change may be what you want. But in other cases, it may not.

Here's an example of how using File ➪ Save As can cause a problem: You finished working on a source workbook and save the file. Then you decide to be safe and make a backup copy on a different drive, using File ➪ Save As. The formulas in the dependent workbook now refer to the backup copy, not the original source file. This is *not* what you want.

Bottom line? Be careful when you choose File ➪ Save As with a workbook that is the source of a link in another open workbook.

Modifying a source workbook

If you open a workbook that is a source workbook for another workbook, be extremely careful if the dependent workbook isn't open. For example, if you add a new row to the source workbook, the cells all move down one row. When you open the dependent workbook, it continues to use the old cell references — which is probably not what you want.

NOTE

It's easy to determine the source workbooks for a particular dependent workbook: Just examine the files listed in the Edit Links dialog box (choose Data ⇨ Connections ⇨ Edit Links). However, it's not possible to determine whether a particular workbook is used as the source for another workbook.

You can avoid this problem by

- **Always opening the dependent workbook(s) when you modify the source workbook:** If you do so, Excel adjusts the external references in the dependent workbook when you make changes to the source workbook.
- **Using names rather than cell references in your link formula:** This approach is the safest.

The following link formula refers to cell C21 on Sheet1 in the `budget.xlsx` workbook:

```
=[budget.xlsx]Sheet1!$C$21
```

If cell C21 is named Total, you can write the formula using that name:

```
=budget.xlsx!Total
```

Using a name ensures that the link retrieves the correct value, even if you add or delete rows or columns from the source workbook.

By the way, notice that filename isn't enclosed in brackets. That's because Total is assumed to be a workbook-level name and doesn't need to be qualified with a sheet name. If Total were a sheet-level name (defined on Sheet1), the formula would be:

```
=[budget.xlsx]Sheet1!Total
```

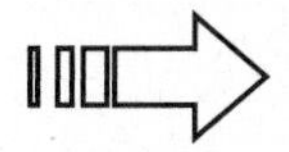

See Chapter 4 for more information about creating names for cells and ranges.

Intermediary links

Excel doesn't place many limitations on the complexity of your network of external references. For example, Workbook A can contain external references that refer to Workbook B, which can contain an external reference that refers to Workbook C. In this case, a value in Workbook A can ultimately depend on a value in Workbook C. Workbook B is an *intermediary link.*

I don't recommend using intermediary links, but if you must use them, be aware that Excel doesn't update external reference formulas if the dependent workbook isn't open. In the preceding example, assume that Workbooks A and C are open. If you change a value in Workbook C, Workbook A won't reflect the change because you didn't open Workbook B (the intermediary link).

Time to Rethink Your Consolidation Strategy?

If you're reading this chapter, there's a good chance you're looking for a way to combine data from multiple sources. The consolidation methods I describe can work — but they may not be the most efficient way to approach the problem.

A typical budget is actually a summary. It's usually much easier to work with "normalized" data, which consists of one row per data item. Then you can use Excel's most sophisticated tool (a pivot table) to consolidate and summarize the information.

For example, a budget for Region 1 might show a value for training expenses for the IT department for January. Instead of just entering this number into a grid, you gain a lot of flexibility by putting it into a table with multiple columns that describe the number. For example, this single item can be represented as a row in a normalized table with these six headings: Region, Department, Expense Description, Month, Year, and Budget Amount.

If each regional manager submitted his budget information in this format, it would be a simple matter to combine the data in a single worksheet and then create a pivot table that displays a summary in just about any layout you want.

Consolidating Worksheets

The term *consolidation*, in the context of worksheets, refers to several operations that involve multiple worksheets or multiple workbook files. In some cases, consolidation involves creating link formulas. Here are two common examples of consolidation:

- The budget for each department in your company is stored in a single workbook, with a separate worksheet for each department. You need to consolidate the data and create a company-wide budget on a single sheet.
- Each department head submits a budget to you in a separate workbook file. Your job is to consolidate these files into a company-wide budget.

These types of tasks can be very difficult or quite easy. The task is easy if the information is laid out *exactly* the same in each worksheet. If the worksheets aren't laid out identically, they may be similar enough. In the second example, some budget files submitted to you may be missing categories that aren't used by a particular department. In this case, you can use a handy feature in Excel that matches data by using row and column titles. I discuss this feature in "Consolidating worksheets by using the Consolidate command," later in this chapter.

If the worksheets bear little or no resemblance to each other, your best bet may be to edit the sheets so that they correspond to one another. Or return the files to the department heads and ask that they submit them using a standardized format. Better yet, redesign your workflow to use normalized tables that can be used as the source for pivot tables.

You can use any of the following techniques to consolidate information from multiple workbooks:

- Use external reference formulas.
- Copy the data, and choose Home ➪ Clipboard ➪ Paste ➪ Paste Link (N).
- Use the Consolidate dialog box, which you get to by choosing Data ➪ Data Tools ➪ Consolidate.

Consolidating worksheets by using formulas

Consolidating with formulas simply involves creating formulas that use references to other worksheets or other workbooks. Here are the primary advantages to using this method of consolidation:

- If the values in the source worksheets change, the formulas are updated automatically.
- The source workbooks don't need to be open when you create the consolidation formulas.

If you're consolidating the worksheets in the same workbook and all the worksheets are laid out identically, the consolidation task is simple. You can just use standard formulas to create the consolidations. For example, to compute the total for cell A1 in worksheets named Sheet2 through Sheet10, enter the following formula:

```
=SUM(Sheet2:Sheet10!A1)
```

You can enter this formula manually or use the multisheet selection technique. You can then copy this formula to create summary formulas for other cells.

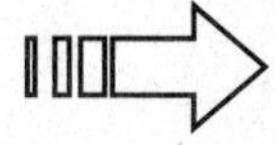

See Chapter 4 for more on multisheet selection.

If the consolidation involves other workbooks, you can use external reference formulas to perform your consolidation. For example, if you want to add the values in cell A1 from Sheet1 in two workbooks (named Region1 and Region2), you can use the following formula:

```
=[Region1.xlsx]Sheet1!B2+[Region2.xlsx]Sheet1!B2
```

You can include any number of external references in this formula, up to the 8,000-character limit for a formula. However, if you use many external references, such a formula can be quite lengthy and confusing if you need to edit it.

If the worksheets that you're consolidating aren't laid out the same, you can still use formulas, but you need to ensure that each formula refers to the correct cell — a task that is both tedious and error prone.

Consolidating worksheets by using Paste Special

Another method of consolidating information is to use the Paste Special dialog box. This technique takes advantage of the fact that the Paste Special dialog box can perform a mathematical operation when it pastes data from the Clipboard. For example, you can use the Add option to add the copied data to the selected range. Figure 28.5 shows the Paste Special dialog box.

FIGURE 28.5

Choosing the Add operation in the Paste Special dialog box.

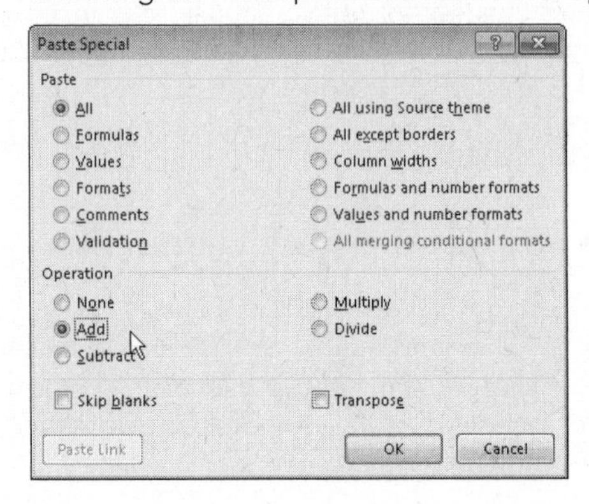

This method is applicable only when all the worksheets that you're consolidating are open. The disadvantage is that the consolidation isn't dynamic. In other words, it doesn't generate formulas that refer to the original source data. So, if any data that was consolidated changes, the consolidation is no longer accurate.

Here's how to use this method:

1. **Copy the data from the first source range.**
2. **Activate the dependent workbook and select a location for the consolidated data.** A single cell is sufficient.
3. **Choose Home ➪ Clipboard ➪ Paste ➪ Paste Special.** The Paste Special dialog box appears.
4. **Choose the Values option and the Add operation, and then click OK.**

Repeat these steps for each source range that you want to consolidate. Make sure that the consolidation location in Step 2 is the same for each paste operation.

CAUTION

This method is probably the worst way of consolidating data. It can be rather error prone, and the lack of formulas means that here is no "trail." If an error is discovered, it may be difficult or impossible to determine the source of the error.

Consolidating worksheets by using the Consolidate dialog box

For the ultimate in data consolidation, use the Consolidate dialog box. This method is very flexible, and in some cases, it even works if the source worksheets aren't laid out identically. This technique can create consolidations that are *static* (no link formulas) or *dynamic* (with link formulas). The Data Consolidate feature supports the following methods of consolidation:

- **By position:** This method is accurate only if the worksheets are laid out identically.
- **By category:** Excel uses row and column labels to match data in the source worksheets. Use this option if the data is laid out differently in the source worksheets or if some source worksheets are missing rows or columns.

Figure 28.6 shows the Consolidate dialog box, which appears when you choose Data ➪ Data Tools ➪ Consolidate. Following is a description of the controls in this dialog box:

FIGURE 28.6

The Consolidate dialog box enables you to specify ranges to consolidate.

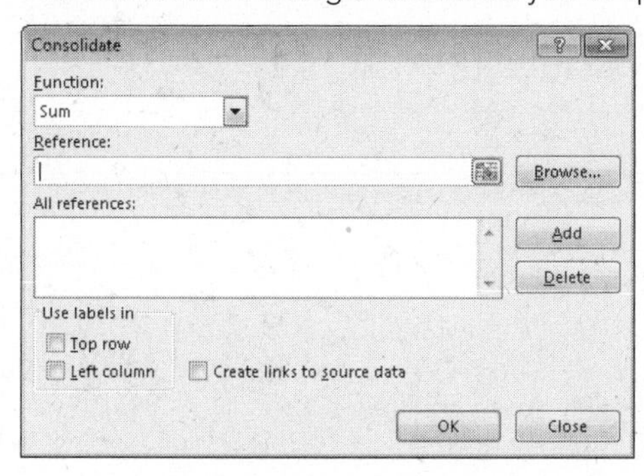

- **Function drop-down list:** Specify the type of consolidation. `Sum` is the most commonly used consolidation function, but you can also select from ten other options.
- **Reference box:** Specify a range from a source file that you want to consolidate. You can enter the range reference manually or use any standard pointing technique (if the workbook is open). Named ranges are also acceptable. After you enter the range in this box, click Add to add it to the All References list. If you consolidate by position, don't include labels in the range; if you consolidate by category, *do* include labels in the range.
- **All References list box:** Contains the list of references that you've added with the Add button.
- **Use Labels In check boxes:** Use to instruct Excel to perform the consolidation by examining the labels in the top row, the left column, or both positions. Use these options when you consolidate by category.

- **Create Links to Source Data check box:** When you select this option, Excel adds summary formulas for each label and creates an outline. If you don't select this option, the consolidation doesn't use formulas, and an outline isn't created.
- **Browse button:** Click to display a dialog box that enables you to select a workbook to open. It inserts the filename in the Reference box, but you have to supply the range reference. You'll find that your job is much easier if all the workbooks to be consolidated are open.
- **Add button:** Click to add the reference in the Reference box to the All References list. Make sure that you click this button after you specify each range.
- **Delete button:** Click to delete the selected reference from the All References list.

A workbook consolidation example

The simple example in this section demonstrates the power of the Data Consolidate feature. Figure 28.7 shows three single-sheet workbooks that will be consolidated. These worksheets report three months of product sales. Notice, however, that they don't all report on the same products. In addition, the products aren't even listed in the same order. In other words, these worksheets aren't laid out identically. Creating consolidation formulas manually would be a very tedious task.

FIGURE 28.7

Three worksheets to be consolidated.

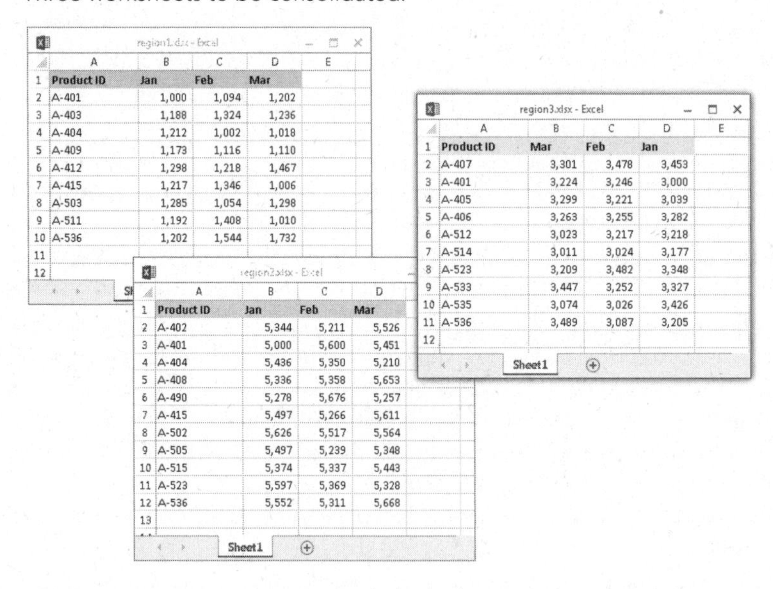

Product ID	Jan	Feb	Mar
A-401	1,000	1,094	1,202
A-403	1,188	1,324	1,236
A-404	1,212	1,002	1,018
A-409	1,173	1,116	1,110
A-412	1,298	1,218	1,467
A-415	1,217	1,346	1,006
A-503	1,285	1,054	1,298
A-511	1,192	1,408	1,010
A-536	1,202	1,544	1,732

Product ID	Jan	Feb	Mar
A-402	5,344	5,211	5,526
A-401	5,000	5,600	5,451
A-404	5,436	5,350	5,210
A-408	5,336	5,358	5,653
A-490	5,278	5,676	5,257
A-415	5,497	5,266	5,611
A-502	5,626	5,517	5,564
A-505	5,497	5,239	5,348
A-515	5,374	5,337	5,443
A-523	5,597	5,369	5,328
A-536	5,552	5,311	5,668

region3.xlsx - Excel

Product ID	Mar	Feb	Jan
A-407	3,301	3,478	3,453
A-401	3,224	3,246	3,000
A-405	3,299	3,221	3,039
A-406	3,263	3,255	3,282
A-512	3,023	3,217	3,218
A-514	3,011	3,024	3,177
A-523	3,209	3,482	3,348
A-533	3,447	3,252	3,327
A-535	3,074	3,026	3,426
A-536	3,489	3,087	3,205

On the Web

These workbooks are available on this book's website. The files are named `region1.xlsx`, `region2.xlsx`, and `region3.xlsx`.

To consolidate this information, start with a new workbook. You don't need to open the source workbooks, but consolidation is easier if they're open. Follow these steps to consolidate the workbooks:

1. **Choose Data ➪ Data Tools ➪ Consolidate.** The Consolidate dialog box appears.
2. **Select the type of consolidation summary that you want to use from the Function drop-down list.** Use `Sum` for this example.
3. **Enter the reference for the first worksheet to consolidate.** If the workbook is open, you can point to the reference; if it isn't open, click the Browse button to locate the file on disk. The reference must include a range. You can use a range that includes complete columns, such as A:K. This range is larger than the actual range to consolidate, but using this range ensures that the consolidation will still work if new rows and columns are added to the source file. When the reference in the Reference box is correct, click Add to add it to the All References list.
4. **Enter the reference for the second worksheet.** You can point to the range in the Region2 workbook, or you can simply edit the existing reference by changing Region1 to Region2 and then clicking Add. This reference is added to the All References list.
5. **Enter the reference for the third worksheet.** Again, you can edit the existing reference by changing Region2 to Region3 and then clicking Add. This final reference is added to the All References list.
6. **Because the worksheets aren't laid out the same, select the Left Column and the Top Row check boxes to force Excel to match the data by using the labels.**
7. **Select the Create Links to Source Data check box to make Excel create an outline with external references.**
8. **Click OK to begin the consolidation.**

Excel creates the consolidation, beginning at the active cell. Notice that Excel created an outline, which is collapsed to show only the subtotals for each product. If you expand the outline (by clicking the number 2 or the plus-sign symbols in the outline), you can see the details. Examine it further, and you discover that each detail cell is an external reference formula that uses the appropriate cell in the source file. Therefore, the consolidated results are updated automatically when values are changed in any of the source workbooks.

Figure 28.8 shows the result of the consolidation, and Figure 28.9 shows the summary information (with the outline collapsed to hide the details).

FIGURE 28.8

The result of consolidating the information in three workbooks.

	A	B	C	D	E	F	G
1			Jan	Feb	Mar		
2		Region2	5,344	5,211	5,526		
3	A-402		5,344	5,211	5,526		
4		Region3	3,453	3,478	3,301		
5	A-407		3,453	3,478	3,301		
6		Region1	1,000	1,094	1,202		
7		Region2	5,000	5,600	5,451		
8		Region3	3,000	3,246	3,224		
9	A-401		9,000	9,940	9,877		
10		Region1	1,188	1,324	1,236		
11	A-403		1,188	1,324	1,236		
12		Region1	1,212	1,002	1,018		
13		Region2	5,436	5,350	5,210		
14	A-404		6,648	6,352	6,228		
15		Region1	1,173	1,116	1,110		
16	A-409		1,173	1,116	1,110		
17		Region1	1,298	1,218	1,467		
18	A-412		1,298	1,218	1,467		
19		Region2	5,336	5,358	5,653		
20	A-408		5,336	5,358	5,653		
21		Region2	5,278	5,676	5,257		
22	A-490		5,278	5,676	5,257		
23		Region1	1,217	1,346	1,006		
24		Region2	5,497	5,266	5,611		
25	A-415		6,714	6,612	6,617		
26		Region1	1,285	1,054	1,298		
27	A-503		1,285	1,054	1,298		
28		Region1	1,192	1,408	1,010		
29	A-511		1,192	1,408	1,010		
30		Region2	5,626	5,517	5,564		
31	[illegible]		[illegible]	[illegible]	[illegible]		

Sheet1

For more information on Excel outlines, see Chapter 27.

Refreshing a consolidation

When you choose the option to create formulas, the external references in the consolidation workbook are created only for data that exists at the time of the consolidation. Therefore, if new rows are added to any of the original workbooks, the consolidation must be redone. Fortunately, the consolidation parameters are stored with the workbook, so it's a simple matter to rerun the consolidation if necessary. That's why specifying complete columns and including extra columns (in Step 3 in the preceding section) is a good idea.

Excel remembers the references that you entered in the Consolidate dialog box and saves them with the workbook. That way, if you want to refresh a consolidation, you won't have to re-enter the references. Just display the Consolidate dialog box, verify that the ranges are correct, and then click OK.

FIGURE 28.9

Collapsing the outline to show only the totals.

	A	B	C	D	E	F
1			Jan	Feb	Mar	
3	A-402		5,344	5,211	5,526	
5	A-407		3,453	3,478	3,301	
9	A-401		9,000	9,940	9,877	
11	A-403		1,188	1,324	1,236	
14	A-404		6,648	6,352	6,228	
16	A-409		1,173	1,116	1,110	
18	A-412		1,298	1,218	1,467	
20	A-408		5,336	5,358	5,653	
22	A-490		5,278	5,676	5,257	
25	A-415		6,714	6,612	6,617	
27	A-503		1,285	1,054	1,298	
29	A-511		1,192	1,408	1,010	
31	A-502		5,626	5,517	5,564	
33	A-505		5,497	5,239	5,348	
35	A-515		5,374	5,337	5,443	
37	A-405		3,039	3,221	3,299	
39	A-406		3,282	3,255	3,263	
41	A-512		3,218	3,217	3,023	
43	A-514		3,177	3,024	3,011	
46	A-523		8,945	8,851	8,537	
48	A-533		3,327	3,252	3,447	
50	A-535		3,426	3,026	3,074	
54	A-536		9,959	9,942	10,889	
55						

Sheet1

More about consolidation

Excel is very flexible regarding the sources that you can consolidate. You can consolidate data from the following:

- **Open workbooks.**
- **Closed workbooks:** You need to enter the reference manually, but you can use the Browse button to get the filename part of the reference.
- **The same workbook in which you're creating the consolidation.**

And, of course, you can mix and match any of the preceding choices in a single consolidation.

If you perform the consolidation by matching labels, be aware that the matches must be exact. For example, *Jan* doesn't match *January*. The matching is not case sensitive, however, so *April* does match *APRIL*. In addition, the labels can be in any order, and they don't need to be in the same order in all the source ranges.

If you don't select the Create Links to Source Data check box, Excel generates a static consolidation. (It doesn't create formulas.) Therefore, if the data on any of the source worksheets changes, the consolidation won't update automatically. To update the summary information, you need to choose Data ⇨ Data Tools ⇨ Consolidate again.

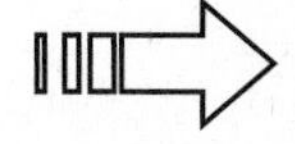

If you do select the Create Links to Source Data check box, Excel creates a standard worksheet outline that you can manipulate by using the techniques described in Chapter 27.

CHAPTER

29

Excel and the Internet

IN THIS CHAPTER

Saving a workbook to an internet location

Saving Excel files in HTML format

Creating hyperlinks

Importing data from a web page

Most people who use a computer are connected to the Internet. The web has become an important way to share, collaborate, and gather information from myriad sources. To help you with these tasks, Excel has the capability to create files that you can use on the Internet and also to gather and process data from the web. This chapter covers topics related to Excel and the Internet.

Saving a Workbook on the Internet

Excel 2013 makes it very easy to save your work to your SkyDrive or to a SharePoint site. Doing so lets you access the workbook from any computer that has Internet access, no matter where you are. And the computer doesn't have to have Excel installed. Sign in to your SkyDrive or SharePoint account, and you can download the file and work on it locally or view it (and perhaps do minor editing) directly in your web browser using the Excel Web App.

To save a file to the Internet, choose File ⇨ Save As, and then select SkyDrive or SharePoint in the Places section of the Save As screen. Click Browse, and choose a directory for the file. If you want, you can share the workbook with others — but only one person at a time can edit the file. You must be signed in to your SkyDrive or SharePoint account in order to save a file to one of these locations.

Figure 29.1 shows an Excel workbook that was saved to a SkyDrive account. It's displayed in a browser using the Excel Web App. The file is a two-sheet workbook, with sheet tabs at the bottom. As you can see, the Excel Web App includes a modified Ribbon, and it works much like the standard desktop version of Excel.

FIGURE 29.1

A workbook displayed in a browser using the Excel Web App.

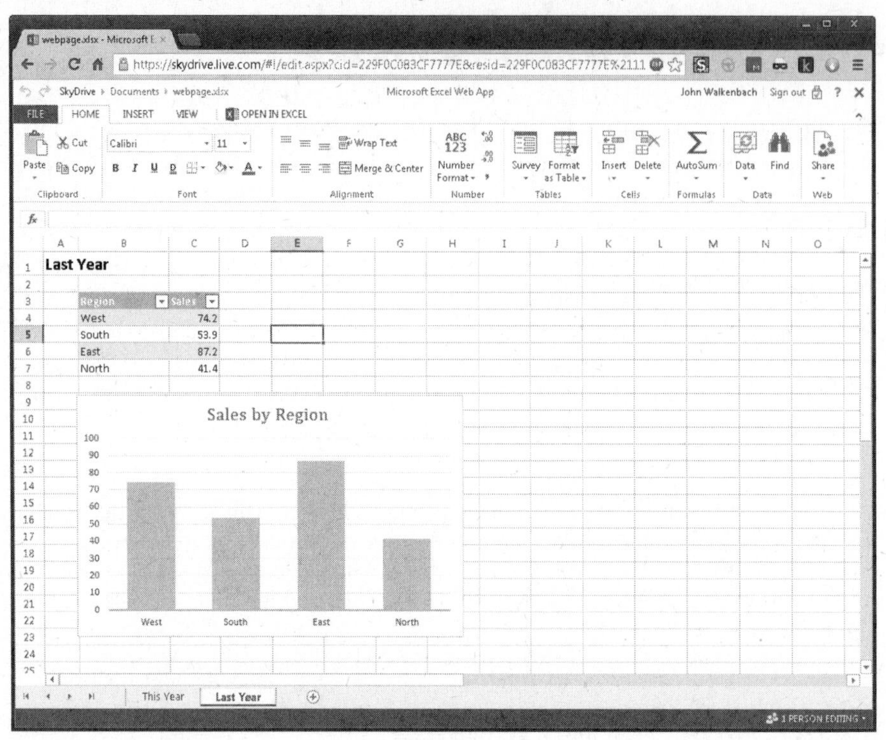

Compared to the desktop version, the Excel Web App has quite a few limitations. For example, formatting options are limited, it can't run VBA macros, it can't create pivot tables — but you can view and manipulate them. There's also a size limitation. If your file is too large, you can't open it with the Excel Web App. But overall, it's very impressive software.

Saving Workbooks in HTML Format

Hypertext Markup Language (HTML) is the language of the World Wide Web. When you browse the web, most documents that your browser retrieves and displays are in HTML format. An HTML file consists of text information plus special tags that describe how the text is to be formatted. The browser interprets the tags, applies the formatting, and displays the information.

You can save an Excel workbook so that it's viewable in a web browser. When you save an Excel workbook for viewing on the web, you have two options:

- **An HTML file:** Produces a static web page, plus a folder that contains support files. You can create the HTML file from the entire workbook or from a specific sheet.
- **A single file web page:** Produces a MIME HTML file (`*.mht`; `*.mhtml`). Not all browsers can open these files.

These options are described in the following sections. Both examples use a simple two-sheet workbook file. Each sheet has a table and a chart. Figure 29.2 shows one of these worksheets.

FIGURE 29.2

This workbook will be saved in Excel web formats.

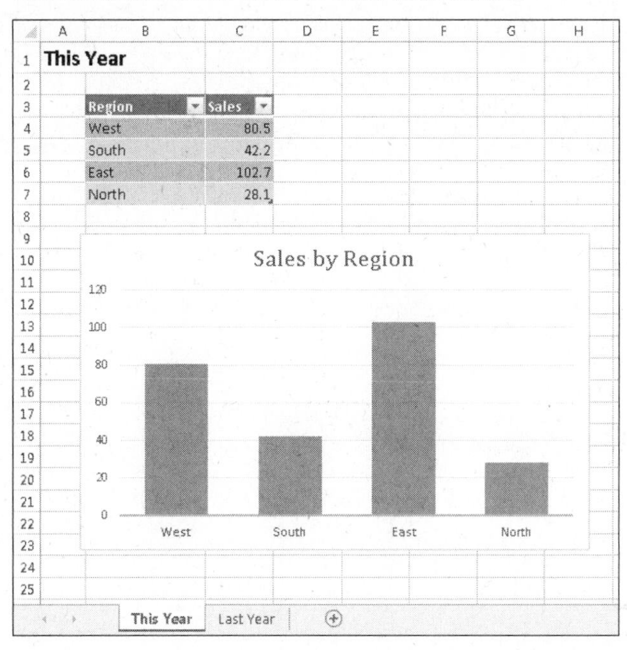

Keep in mind that these files are intended to be only displayed by a web browser. They are *not* interactive files. In other words, the user can't make any changes while viewing the file.

TIP

To create an interactive version, save your workbook to your SkyDrive site. Then you can share the workbook and it can be opened using the Excel Web App.

ON THE WEB

This workbook, named `webpage.xlsx`, is available at this book's website.

Creating an HTML file

To save a workbook as an HTML file:

1. **(Optional but recommended) Save the workbook as a normal Excel file.**
2. **Choose File⇨Save As.** The Save As dialog box appears.
3. **Select Web Page (*.htm; *.html) from the Save as Type drop-down list.**
4. **Specify what to save (either entire workbook or the active sheet).**
5. **Specify a filename and then choose a location for the file.**
6. **Click Save to create the HTML file.** Excel may display a message warning you that some features in the workbook are not compatible with the web page format. You can ignore this message.

Caution

Although Excel can open the HTML files that it creates, essential information is lost. For example, formulas are lost, and charts appear as static graphic images. Therefore, if you might need to make changes later on, make sure you keep a copy of your work in a standard Excel file format.

Figure 29.3 shows how Sheet1 of the example file looks in a browser — Google Chrome, in this case. Notice that the workbook's sheet tabs appear along the bottom, and you can switch sheets just as you do in Excel.

FIGURE 29.3

Viewing the HTML file in a browser.

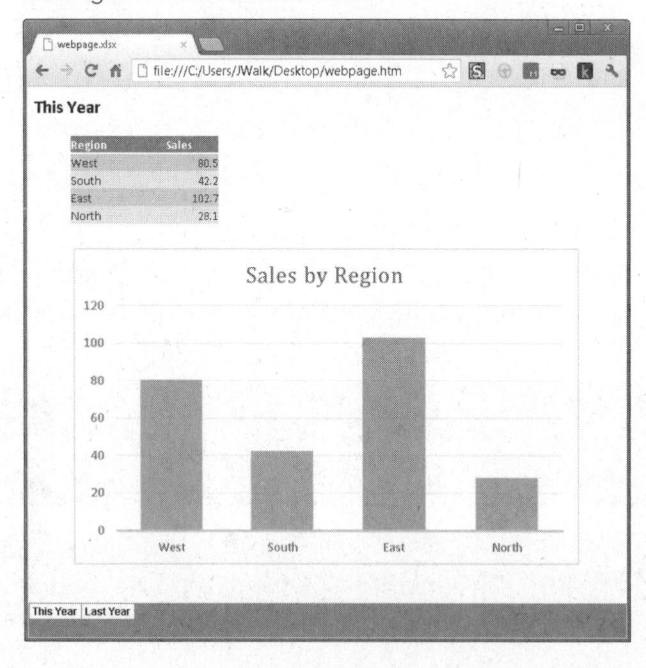

In addition to the webpage.htm file, Excel also created a folder named webpage_files. This folder contains additional files that must be kept with the main HTML file. Therefore, if you post such a file on a web server, don't forget to also post the accompanying directory.

TIP

If you create a lot of HTML files from Excel workbooks, you should add the Web Page Preview tool to your Quick Access toolbar. Right-click the Quick Access toolbar and choose Customize Quick Access Toolbar. Choose the Commands Not in the Ribbon category, and then add Web Page Preview. Clicking that command provides an instant preview (in your default web browser) of the active workbook.

Creating a single-file web page

In the previous section, I discuss how creating an HTML file with Excel also creates a folder of additional files. The procedure for creating a web page that uses a single file is exactly the same, except for Step 3. In Step 3, select Single File Web Page (*.mht; *.mhtml) from the Save as Type drop-down list.

Figure 29.4 shows the example file displayed in Internet Explorer.

FIGURE 29.4

Viewing the single-file web page in Internet Explorer.

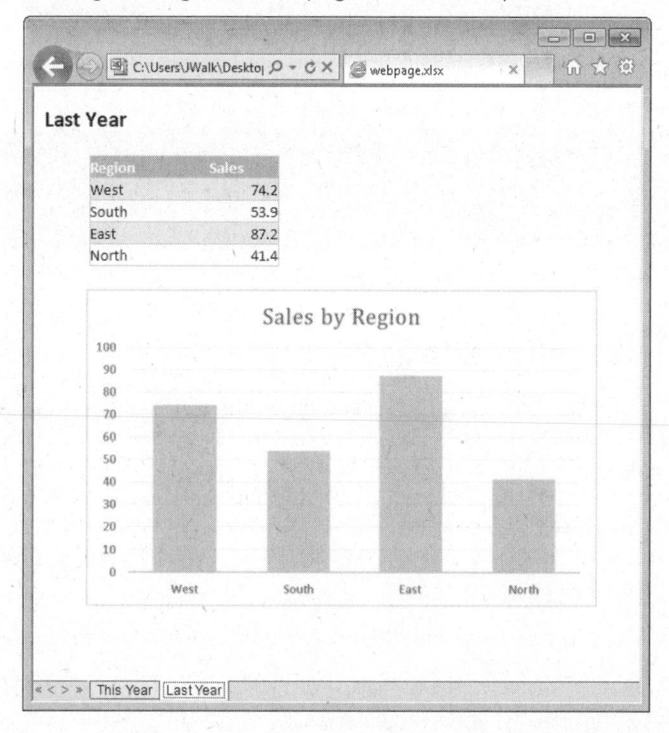

Setting Web Options

If you save your work in HTML format, you should be aware of some additional options. In the Save As dialog box, click Tools and then choose Web Options to display the Web Options dialog box. You can also access this dialog box from the Advanced tab of the Excel Options dialog box (the button is in the General section). From this dialog box, you can control some aspects of the HTML file, such as target browser version (Internet Explorer only), target monitor resolution, and fonts.

For the best-quality images, make sure you choose Allow PNG as a Graphics Format (it's on the Browsers tab).

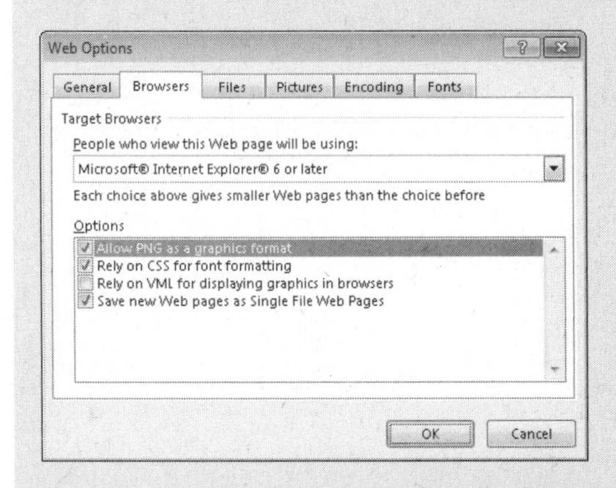

CAUTION
As I mentioned earlier, not all browsers can open single-file MHTM files. Two that can are Microsoft Internet Explorer and Google Chrome. Other browsers (such as Mozilla Firefox) may require an add-on to display these files.

Opening an HTML File

Excel can open most HTML files, which can be stored on your local drive or on a web server. Choose File➪Open and locate the HTML file. If the file is on a web server, you'll need to copy the URL and paste it into the File Name field in the Open dialog box. Files opened directly from a web server are opened in read-only mode. How the HTML code renders in Excel varies considerably. Sometimes, the HTML file may look exactly as it does in a browser. Other times, it may bear little resemblance, especially if the HTML file uses Cascading Style Sheets (CSS) for layout.

After opening an HTML file, you can work with the information using the normal Excel tools.

Another way to open an HTML file from a web server is to use a web query, which is discussed later in this chapter (see "Using Web Queries").

Working with Hyperlinks

A *hyperlink* is clickable text that provides a quick way to jump to other workbooks and files. You can set up hyperlinks to display files stored on your own computer, your network, and the web. For example, you can create a series of hyperlinks to serve as a table of contents for a workbook. Or you can insert a hyperlink that displays a web page in your default web browser.

Inserting a hyperlink

You can create hyperlinks from cell text or graphic objects, such as shapes and pictures. To create a text hyperlink in a cell, select the cell and choose Insert ➪ Links ➪ Hyperlink (or press Ctrl + K). The Insert Hyperlink dialog box, shown in Figure 29.5, appears.

FIGURE 29.5

Use the Insert Hyperlink dialog box to add hyperlinks to your Excel worksheets.

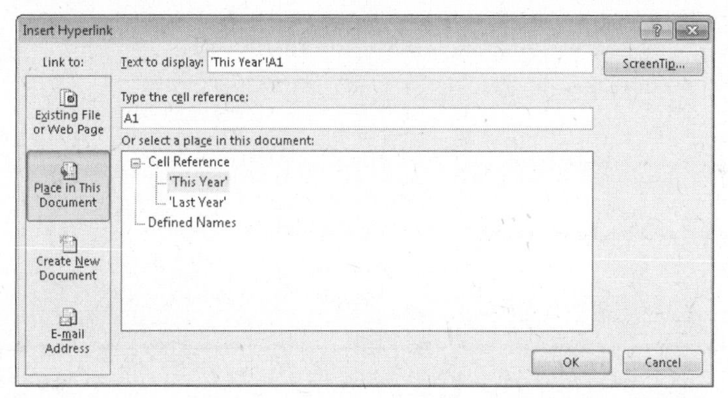

Select an icon in the Link To column that represents the type of hyperlink you want to create. You can create hyperlinks to a file on your hard drive, a web page on the Internet, a new document, or a location in your current workbook. In addition, you can create a hyperlink that consists of an e-mail address. Then specify the location of the file that you want to link to. The dialog box changes, depending upon the icon selected. If you like, click the ScreenTip button to provide some additional text that appears as a mouse-hover-activated ToolTip. Click OK, and Excel creates the hyperlink in the active cell.

Figure 29.6 shows a worksheet with hyperlinks that function as a table of contents for a workbook. Clicking a link activates a worksheet in the workbook. The example also shows an e-mail address that, when clicked, activates the default e-mail program.

Using the Research Task Pane

Somewhat related to the topic of this chapter is the Research task pane, which is displayed by choosing Review ➪ Proofing ➪ Research. When this task pane is displayed, you can perform a variety of web searches directly from Excel. These include dictionary and thesaurus services, plus a complete web search using Bing or another search engine. Clicking a hyperlink in the search results displays the website in your browser.

FIGURE 29.6

Hyperlinks in a workbook.

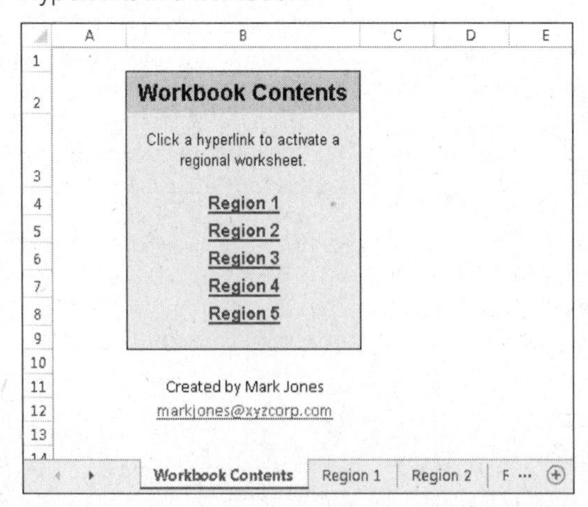

ON THE WEB

This workbook is available on this book's website. The file is named `hyperlinks.xlsx`.

The appearance of hyperlinks in cells is controlled by two styles in the Style Gallery. The Hyperlink style controls the appearance of hyperlinks that haven't been clicked, and the Followed Hyperlink style controls the appearance of "visited" hyperlinks. To change the appearance of your hyperlinks, modify either or both of those styles.

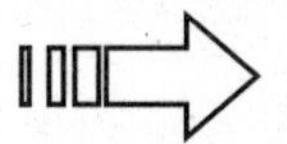

See Chapter 6 for information about using and modifying document styles.

To add a hyperlink to a Shape, select the Shape and then choose Insert ➪ Links ➪ Hyperlink (or press Ctrl + K). Specify the required information in the Insert Hyperlink dialog box, as outlined earlier in this section.

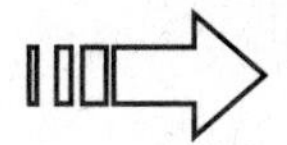

You can read more about Shapes in Chapter 23.

Using hyperlinks

When you hover your mouse pointer over a cell that contains a hyperlink, the mouse pointer turns into a hand. Click the hyperlink, and you're taken to the hyperlinked document.

TIP

To select a cell that has a hyperlink with your mouse (without following the hyperlink), position your mouse over the cell, click, and hold for a second or two before you release the mouse button. Or just activate a nearby cell and use the navigation keys to select the cell that contains the hyperlink.

When you hover your pointer over a Shape that contains a hyperlink, the mouse pointer turns into a hand. To follow a hyperlink from a Shape, just point to the Shape and click.

If the hyperlink contains an e-mail address, your default e-mail program launches so that you can send an e-mail to the address specified when you created the hyperlink.

Using Web Queries

Excel enables you to pull in data contained in an HTML file by performing a web query. The data is transferred to a worksheet, where you can manipulate it any way you like. Web queries are especially useful for data that is frequently updated, such as stock market quotes.

The term *web query* is a bit misleading because this operation is not limited to the web. You can perform a web query on a local HTML file, a file stored on a network server, or a file stored on a web server on the Internet. To retrieve information from a web server, you must be connected to the Internet. After the information is retrieved, an Internet connection is not required to work with the information (unless you need to refresh the query).

NOTE
Performing a web query doesn't actually open the HTML file in Excel. Instead, it copies the information from the HTML file.

The best part about a web query is that Excel remembers where the data came from. Therefore, after you create a web query, you can *refresh* the query to pull in the most recent data.

To create a web query, follow these steps:

1. **Choose Data ➪ Get External Data ➪ From Web.** The New Web Query dialog box appears. This dialog box is resizable and functions as a web browser.
2. **Type the URL of the HTML file in the Address field.** The HTML file can be on the Internet, on a corporate intranet, or on a local or network drive. The file is displayed in the New Web Query dialog box, and each table in the document is indicated by an arrow in a yellow box (see Figure 29.7).

FIGURE 29.7

Use the New Web Query dialog box to specify the source of the data.

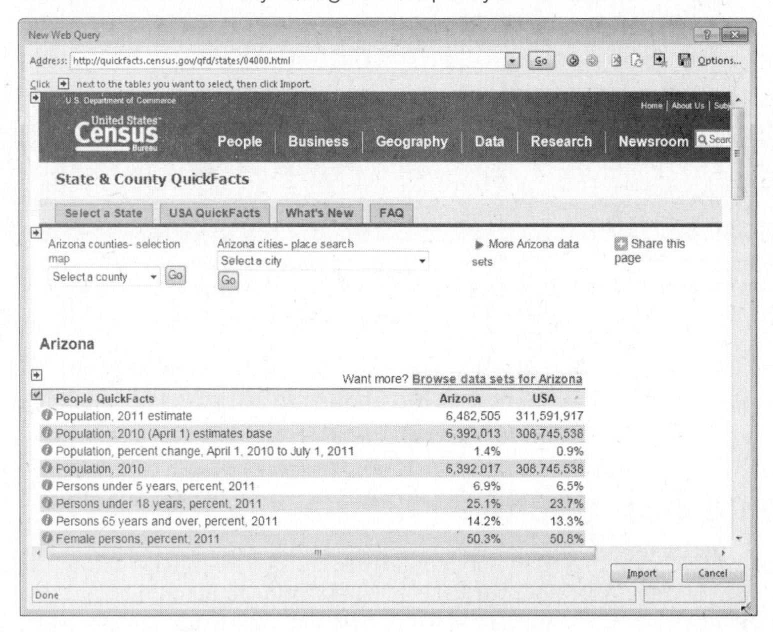

3. **Click one or more arrows to select the table(s) you want to import.**
4. **You can also control how the imported data is formatted. In the New Web Query dialog box, click Options (upper right).** The Web Query Options dialog

box appears. Select the desired formatting, and then click OK to return to the New Web Query dialog box.

5. **When you're ready to retrieve the information, click Import.** The Import Data dialog box appears.
6. **Choose where you want to place the data.** The information on the web page is retrieved and placed on your worksheet.

NOTE

Excel's web query feature works by identifying tables (specified using the <TABLE> tag) in the document. Increasingly, website designers use CSS to display tabular information. Excel doesn't recognize these as tables and, therefore, does not display a yellow arrow so you can retrieve only the table. Therefore, you may have to retrieve the entire document and then delete everything except the table that you want.

After you create your web query, you have some additional options. Right-click any cell in the data range and choose Data Range Properties from the shortcut menu. The External Data Range Properties dialog box, shown in Figure 29.8, appears. These settings control when the data is refreshed, how it's formatted, and what happens if the amount of data changes when the query is refreshed.

FIGURE 29.8

Use the External Data Range Properties dialog box to specify how Excel handles the imported data.

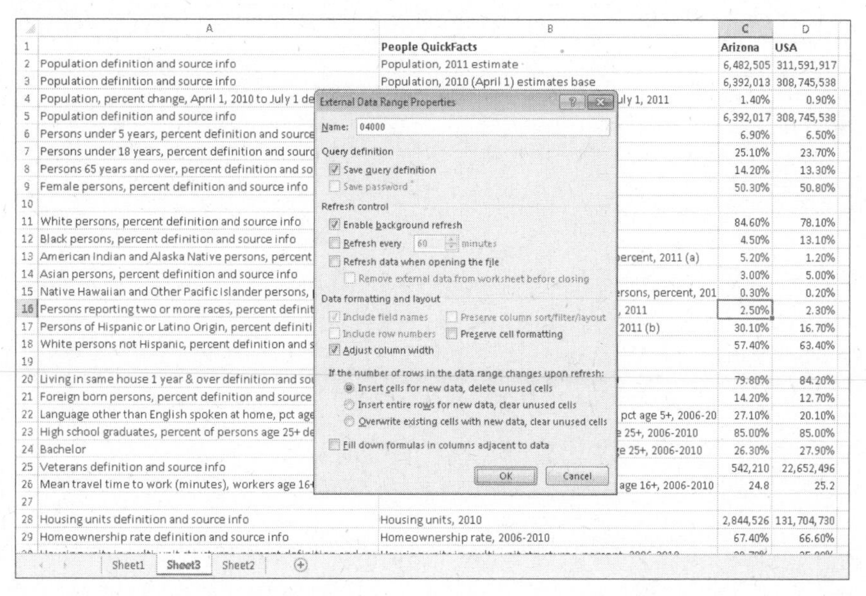

To force a refresh at any time, right-click any cell in the data range and choose Refresh. The data in your worksheet is replaced by the latest of content of the web page.

E-Mail Features

Excel makes it easy to e-mail your work to others. You can access the e-mail features from the Share tab of Backstage view (choose File➪Share).

You can send the active workbook to one or more recipients via e-mail. The file can be the actual workbook, a PDF file, or an XPS file. If the workbook is saved to a shared location, you can send a link to the file (rather than the actual file). An additional option lets you fax the workbook (assuming that your system has a fax service provider).

CHAPTER

30

Protecting Your Work

IN THIS CHAPTER

Protecting worksheets

Protecting workbooks

Protecting Visual Basic Projects

Creating PDFs and checking documents

The concept of "protection" gets a lot of attention in the Excel forums. It seems that many users want to learn how to protect various workbook elements from being overwritten or copied. Excel has several protection-related features, and those features are covered in this chapter.

Types of Protection

Excel's protection-related features fall into three categories:

- **Worksheet protection:** Protecting a worksheet from being modified or restricting the modifications to certain users
- **Workbook protection:** Protecting a workbook from having sheets inserted or deleted, and requiring the use of a password to open the workbook
- **Visual Basic (VB) protection:** Using a password to prevent others from viewing or modifying your VBA code

Caution

Before I discuss these features, you should understand the notion of security. Using a password to protect some aspect of your work doesn't guarantee that it's secure. Password-cracking utilities (and some simple tricks) have been around for a long time. Using passwords work in the vast majority of cases, but if someone is truly intent on getting to your data, he can usually find a way. If absolute security is critical, perhaps Excel isn't the proper tool.

About Information Rights Management

Excel supports an Information Rights Management (IRM) feature, which allows you to specify access permissions for workbooks. Using IRM may help prevent sensitive information from being printed, e-mailed, or copied by unauthorized people. When IRM is applied to a workbook, the permission information is stored in the document file itself.

To use IRM, you must install the Microsoft Windows Rights Management Services (RMS) — an extra-cost product that isn't included with Microsoft Office. You can access the IRM settings by choosing File⇨Info⇨Protect Workbooks⇨Restrict Access.

IRM is not covered in this book. If your company uses RMS, consult your system administrator for more information about how this feature is used within your organization.

Protecting a Worksheet

You may want to protect a worksheet for a variety of reasons. One very common reason is to prevent yourself or others from accidentally deleting formulas or other critical data. A typical scenario is to protect a worksheet so that the data can be changed, but the formulas can't be changed.

To protect a worksheet, activate the worksheet and choose Review⇨Changes⇨Protect Sheet. Excel displays the Protect Sheet dialog box, shown in Figure 30.1. Providing a password is optional. If you enter a password, that password will be required to unprotect the worksheet. If you accept the default options in the Protect Sheet dialog box (and if you haven't unlocked any cells), none of the cells on the worksheet can be modified.

FIGURE 30.1

Use the Protect Sheet dialog box to protect a worksheet.

To unprotect a protected sheet, choose Review⇨Changes⇨Unprotect Sheet. If the sheet was protected with a password, you're prompted to enter that password.

Unlocking cells

In many cases, you'll want to allow *some* cells to be changed when the worksheet is protected. For example, your worksheet may have some input cells that are used by formula cells. In such a case, you would want the user to be able to change the input cells, but not the formula cells. Every cell has a Locked attribute, and that attribute determines whether the cell can be changed when the sheet is protected.

By default, all cells are locked. To change the Locked attribute, select the cell or range, right-click, and choose Format Cells from the shortcut menu (or press Ctrl + 1). Select the Protection tab of the Format Cells dialog box, clear the Locked check box, and then click OK (see Figure 30.2).

FIGURE 30.2

Use the Protection tab in the Format Cells dialog box to change the Locked attribute of a cell or range.

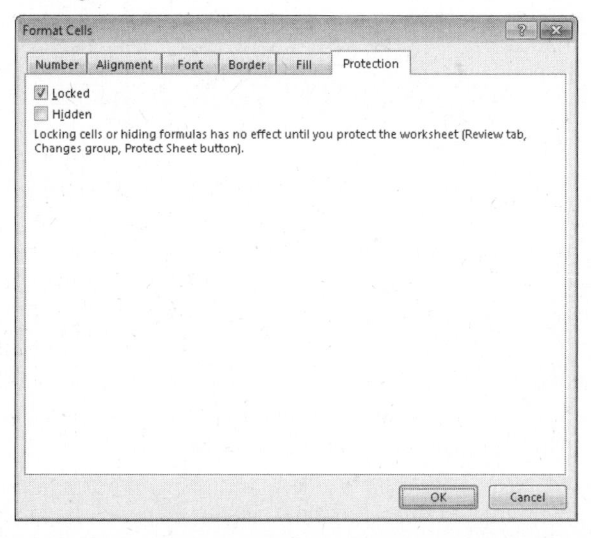

NOTE

The Protection tab of the Format Cells dialog box has another attribute: Hidden. If this check box is selected, the contents of the cell don't appear in the Formula bar when the sheet is protected. The cell isn't hidden in the worksheet. You may want to set the Hidden attribute for formula cells to prevent users from seeing the formula when the cell is selected.

After you unlock the desired cells, choose Review ⇨ Changes ⇨ Protect Sheet to protect the sheet. After doing so, you can change the unlocked cells, but if you attempt to change a locked cell, Excel displays the warning alert shown in Figure 30.3.

FIGURE 30.3

Excel warns you if you attempt to change a locked cell.

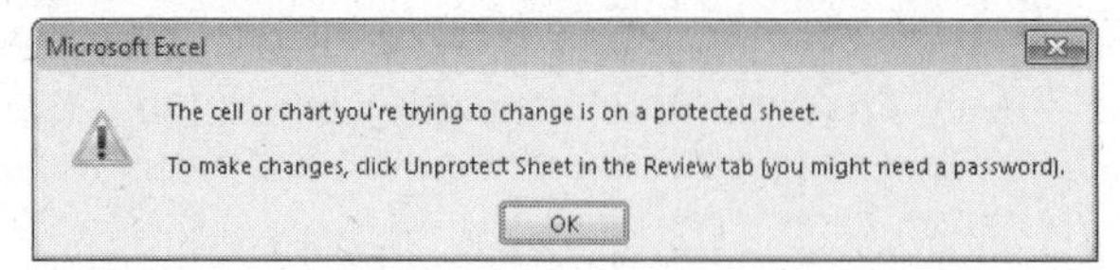

Sheet protection options

The Protect Sheet dialog box has several options, which determine what the user can do when the worksheet is protected.

- **Select Locked Cells:** If checked, the user can select locked cells using the mouse or the keyboard. This setting is enabled by default.
- **Select Unlocked Cells:** If checked, the user can select unlocked cells using the mouse or the keyboard. This setting is enabled by default.
- **Format Cells:** If checked, the user can apply formatting to locked cells.
- **Format Columns:** If checked, the user can hide or change the width of columns.
- **Format Rows:** If checked, the user can hide or change the height of rows.
- **Insert Columns:** If checked, the user can insert new columns.
- **Insert Rows:** If checked, the user can insert new rows.
- **Insert Hyperlinks:** If checked, the user can insert hyperlinks (even in locked cells).
- **Delete Columns:** If checked, the user can delete columns.
- **Delete Rows:** If checked, the user can delete rows.
- **Sort:** If checked, the user can sort data in a range as long as the range doesn't contain any locked cells.
- **Use AutoFilter:** If checked, the user can use existing autofiltering.
- **Use PivotTable & PivotChart:** If checked, the user can change the layout of pivot tables or create new pivot tables. This setting also applies to pivot charts.
- **Edit Objects:** If checked, the user can make changes to objects (such as Shapes) and charts, as well as insert or delete comments.
- **Edit Scenarios:** If checked, the user can use scenarios.

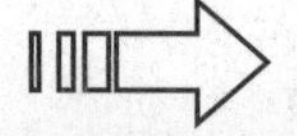

See Chapter 35 for more on creating and using scenarios.

TIP

When the worksheet is protected and the Select Unlocked Cells option is set, pressing Tab moves to the next unlocked cell, making data entry much easier.

Assigning user permissions

Excel also offers the ability to assign user-level permissions to different areas on a protected worksheet. You can specify which users can edit a particular range while the worksheet is protected. As an option, you can require a password to make changes.

This feature is rarely used, and the setup procedure is rather complicated. But if you need this level of protection, setting it up might be worth the effort.

1. **Unprotect the worksheet if it's protected.**
2. **Choose Review ➪ Changes ➪ Allow Users to Edit Ranges.** The Allow Users to Edit Ranges dialog box, shown in Figure 30.4, appears.

FIGURE 30.4

The Allow Users to Edit Ranges dialog box.

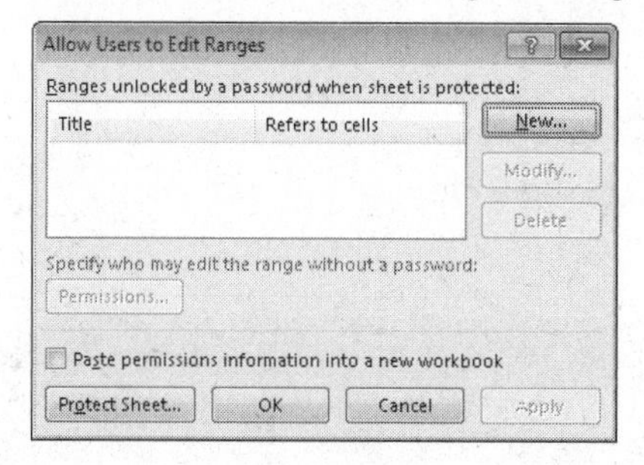

3. **Click the New button and follow the prompts in the series of dialog boxes that follow.**
4. **Protect the sheet.**

Protecting a Workbook

Excel provides two ways to protect a workbook:

- Require a password to open the workbook.
- Prevent users from adding sheets, deleting sheets, hiding sheets, and unhiding sheets.

I discuss each of these methods in the sections that follow.

Requiring a password to open a workbook

Excel lets you save a workbook with a password. After doing so, whoever tries to open the workbook must enter the password.

To add a password to a workbook, follow these steps:

1. **Choose File ➪ Info ➪ Protect Workbook ➪ Encrypt with Password.** The Encrypt Document dialog box, shown in Figure 30.5, appears.

FIGURE 30.5

Specify a workbook password in the Encrypt Document dialog box.

2. **Type a password and click OK.**
3. **Type the password again and click OK.**
4. **Save the workbook.**

NOTE
You need to perform these steps only once. You don't need to specify the password every time you resave the workbook.

To remove a password from a workbook, repeat the same procedure. In Step 2, however, delete the existing password symbols from the Encrypt Document dialog box, click OK, and save your workbook.

Figure 30.6 shows the Password dialog box that appears when you try to open a file saved with a password.

FIGURE 30.6

Opening this workbook requires a password.

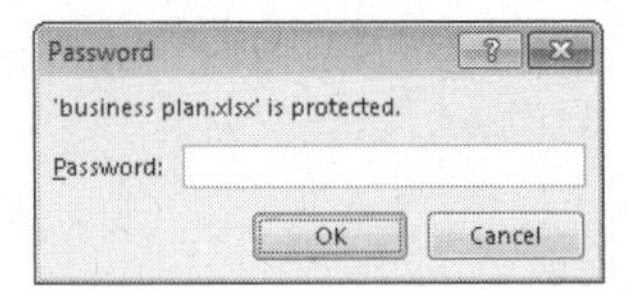

Excel provides another way to add a password to a document:

1. **Choose File⇨Save As.** The Save As dialog box appears.
2. **Click the Tools button and choose General Options.** The General Options dialog appears.
3. **Enter a password in the Password to Open field.**
4. **Click OK.** You're asked to re-enter the password before you return to the Save As dialog box.
5. **In the Save As dialog box, make sure that the filename, location, and type are correct; then click Save.**

NOTE

The General Options dialog box has another password field: Password to Modify. If you specify a password for this field, the file opens in *read-only mode* (it can't be saved under the same name) unless the user knows the password. If you use the Read-Only Recommended check box without a password, Excel *suggests* that the file be opened in read-only mode, but the user can override this suggestion.

Protecting a workbook's structure

To prevent others (or yourself) from performing certain actions in a workbook, you can protect the workbook's structure. When a workbook's structure is protected, the user may not

- Add a sheet.
- Delete a sheet.
- Hide a sheet.
- Unhide a sheet.
- Rename a sheet.
- Move a sheet.

To protect a worksheet's structure

1. **Choose Review⇨Changes⇨Protect Workbook.** The Protect Structure and Windows dialog box, shown in Figure 30.7, appears.

FIGURE 30.7

The Protect Structure and Windows dialog box.

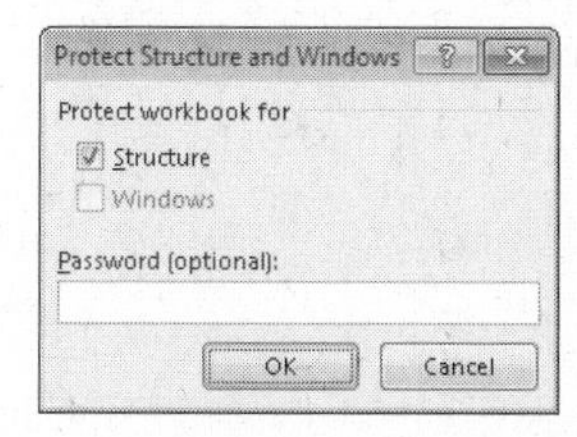

2. **Select the Structure check box.**
3. **(Optional) Enter a password.**
4. **Click OK.**

To unprotect the workbook's structure, choose Review➪Changes➪Unprotect Workbook. If the workbook's structure was protected with a password, you're prompted to enter the password.

> **Note**
> In previous versions of Excel, you could also protect a workbook's windows. This type of protection prevented others (or yourself) from changing the size and position of a workbook's windows. Because of the new single document interface in Excel 2013, the ability to protect windows is no longer available.

VB Project Protection

If your workbook contains any VBA macros, you may want to protect the VB Project to prevent others from viewing or modifying your macros. To protect a VB Project

1. **Press Alt + F11 to activate the VB Editor.**
2. **Select your project in the Projects window.**
3. **Choose Tools - <*Project Name*> Properties (where <*Project Name*> corresponds to your Project name).** The Project Properties dialog box appears.
4. **Select the Protection tab (see Figure 30.8).**

FIGURE 30.8

Protecting a VB Project with a password.

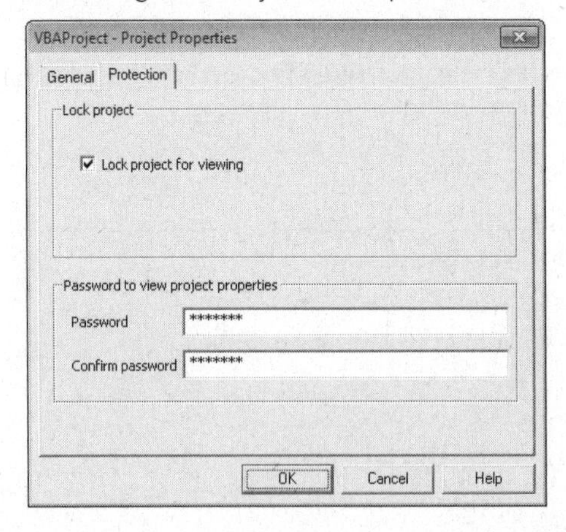

5. **Select the Lock Project for Viewing check box.**
6. **Enter a password (twice).**
7. **Click OK and then save your file.** When the file is closed and then re-opened, a password will be required to view or modify the VBA code.

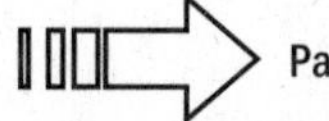
Part VI discusses VBA macros.

Related Topics

This section covers additional topics related to protecting and distributing your work.

Saving a worksheet as a PDF file

The Portable Document Format (PDF) file format is widely used as a way to present information in a read-only manner, with precise control over the layout. Software to display PDF files is available from a number of sources. Excel can create PDF files, but it can't open them.

XPS is another "electronic paper" format, developed by Microsoft as an alternative to the PDF format. At this time, there is very little third-party support for the XPS format.

Save a worksheet in PDF or XPS format by choosing File ➪ Export ➪ Create PDF/XPS Document ➪ Create a PDF/XPS. The Publish as PDF or XPS dialog box appears; here, you can specify a filename and location and set some other options.

Marking a workbook final

Excel lets you mark a workbook as final. This action makes two changes to the workbook:

- It makes the workbook read-only so that the file can't be saved using the same name.
- It makes the workbook view-only so that nothing may be changed.

When you open a finalized document, you see a message below the Ribbon. You can override its final status by clicking the Edit Anyway button.

To finalize a workbook, choose File ➪ Info ➪ Protect Workbook ➪ Mark as Final. A dialog box appears, where you can confirm your choice.

CAUTION
Marking a document as final is *not* a security measure. Anyone who opens the workbook can cancel the mark-as-final designation. Therefore, this method doesn't guarantee that others will not change the workbook.

Inspecting a workbook

If you plan to distribute a workbook to others, you may want to have Excel check the file for hidden data and personal information. This tool can locate hidden information about you, your organization, or the workbook. In some situations, you may not want to share this information with others.

To inspect a workbook, choose File➪Info➪Check for Issues➪Inspect Document. The Document Inspector dialog box, shown in Figure 30.9, appears. Click Inspect, and Excel displays the results of the inspection and gives you the opportunity to remove the items it finds.

FIGURE 30.9

The Document Inspector dialog box identifies hidden and personal information in a workbook.

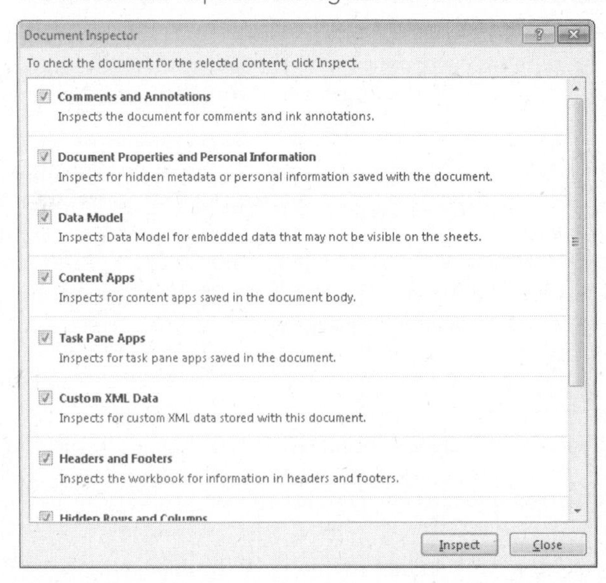

CAUTION

If Excel identifies items in the Document Inspector, it doesn't necessarily mean that they *should* be removed. In other words, you shouldn't blindly use the Remove All buttons to remove the items that Excel locates. For example, you may have a hidden sheet that serves a critical purpose. Excel will identify that hidden sheet and make it very easy for you to delete it. To be on the safe side, always make a backup copy of your workbook before running the Document Inspector.

Two other commands are available in the File➪Info➪Check for Issues menu:

- **Check Accessibility:** Checks the workbook for content that people with disabilities might find difficult to read. The results are displayed in a task pane. See Figure 30.10 for an example.

FIGURE 30.10

Output from the Accessibility Checker is displayed in a task pane.

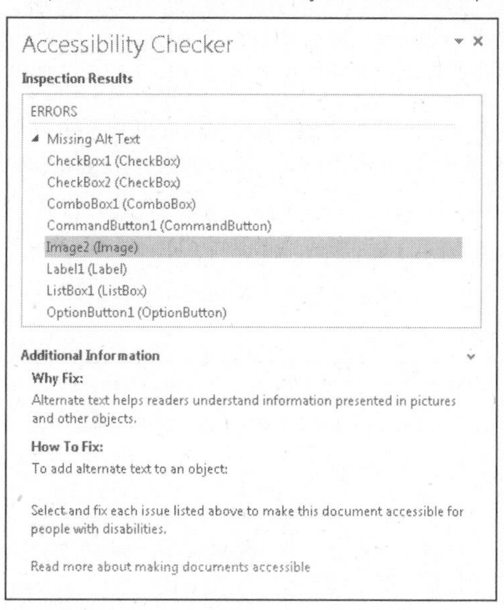

- **Check Compatibility:** Checks the workbook for the presence of features that may not work in previous versions of Excel.

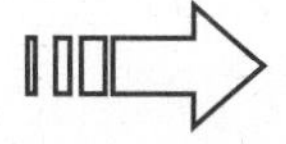

See Chapter 7 for more about checking file compatibility.

Using a digital signature

Excel lets you add a *digital signature* to a workbook. Using a digital signature is somewhat analogous to signing a paper document. A digital signature helps to assure the authenticity of the workbook and ensures that the content hasn't been modified since it was signed.

After you sign a workbook, the signature is valid until you make changes and resave the file.

Getting a digital ID

To digitally sign a workbook, you must obtain a certificate from a certified authority that is able to verify the authenticity of your signature. Prices vary, depending on the certificate-granting company.

Another option is to create your own digital ID, but others will not be able to verify the authenticity. Creating your own digital ID is useful if you want to ensure that no one tampers with one of your signed workbooks.

Signing a workbook

Excel supports two types of digital signatures: a visible signature and an invisible signature.

To add a visible digital signature, choose Insert ➪ Text ➪ Signature Line ➪ Microsoft Office Signature Line. The Signature Setup dialog box appears, and you're prompted for the information for the signature. After you add the signature box, double-click it, and the Sign dialog box appears; here, you actually sign the document either by typing your name or uploading a scanned image of your signature. After signing the document, it will be marked as final. Any change to the file will invalidate the signature.

Figure 30.11 shows a document with a visible digital signature.

FIGURE 30.11

This document has a digital signature.

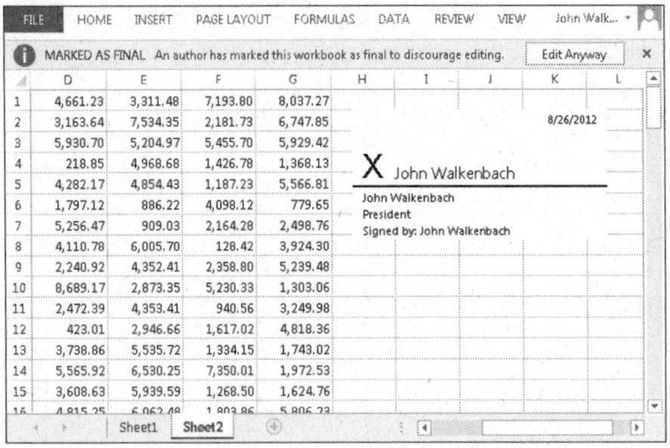

To add an invisible digital signature, choose File ➪ Info ➪ Protect Workbook ➪ Add a Digital Signature. If the signed workbook is changed in any way, the digital signature is invalidated.

CHAPTER

31

Making Your Worksheets Error Free

IN THIS CHAPTER

Identify and correcting common formula errors

Using Excel auditing tools

Using formula AutoCorrect

Tracing cell relationships

Checking spelling and related features

It goes without saying that you want your Excel worksheets to produce accurate results. Unfortunately, it's not always easy to be certain that the results are correct — especially if you deal with large, complex worksheets. This chapter introduces the tools and techniques available to help identify, correct, and prevent errors.

Finding and Correcting Formula Errors

Making a change in a worksheet — even a relatively minor change — may produce a ripple effect that introduces errors in other cells. For example, accidentally entering a value into a cell that previously held a formula is all too easy to do. This simple error can have a major impact on other formulas, and you may not discover the problem until long after you make the change — or you may never discover the problem.

Formula errors tend to fall into one of the following general categories:

- **Syntax errors:** You have a problem with the syntax of a formula. For example, a formula may have mismatched parentheses, or a function may not have the correct number of arguments.
- **Logical errors:** A formula doesn't return an error, but it contains a logical flaw that causes it to return an incorrect result.
- **Incorrect reference errors:** The logic of the formula is correct, but the formula uses an incorrect cell reference. As a simple example, the range reference in a `Sum` formula may not include all the data that you want to sum.

- **Semantic errors:** An example is a function name that is spelled incorrectly. Excel will attempt to interpret it as a name and will display the `#NAME?` error.
- **Circular references:** A circular reference occurs when a formula refers to its own cell, either directly or indirectly. Circular references are useful in a few cases, but most of the time, a circular reference indicates a problem.
- **Array formula entry error:** When entering (or editing) an array formula, you must press Ctrl + Shift + Enter to enter the formula. If you fail to do so, Excel doesn't recognize the formula as an array formula, and you may get an error or incorrect results.

Refer to Chapter 17 for an introduction to array formulas.

- **Incomplete calculation errors:** The formulas simply aren't calculated fully. To ensure that your formulas are fully calculated, press Ctrl + Alt + Shift + F9.

Syntax errors are usually the easiest to identify and correct. In most cases, you'll know when your formula contains a syntax error. For example, Excel won't permit you to enter a formula with mismatched parentheses. Other syntax errors also usually result in an error display in the cell.

The following sections describe common formula problems and offers advice on identifying and correcting them.

Mismatched parentheses

In a formula, every left parenthesis must have a corresponding right parenthesis. If your formula has mismatched parentheses, Excel usually won't permit you to enter it. An exception to this rule involves a simple formula that uses a function. For example, if you enter the following formula (which is missing a closing parenthesis), Excel accepts the formula and provides the missing parenthesis.

```
=SUM(A1:A500
```

A formula may have an equal number of left and right parentheses, but the parentheses may not match properly. For example, consider the following formula, which converts a text string such that the first character is uppercase and the remaining characters are lowercase. This formula has five pairs of parentheses, and they match properly.

```
=UPPER(LEFT(A1))&RIGHT(LOWER(A1),LEN(A1)-1)
```

The following formula also has five pairs of parentheses, but they're mismatched. The result displays a syntactically correct formula that simply returns the wrong result.

```
=UPPER(LEFT(A1)&RIGHT(LOWER(A1),LEN(A1)-1))
```

Often, parentheses that are in the wrong location will result in a *syntax error,* which is usually a message that tells you that you entered too many or too few arguments for a function.

Using Formula AutoCorrect

When you enter a formula that has a syntax error, Excel attempts to determine the problem and offers a suggested correction. The accompanying figure shows an example of a proposed correction.

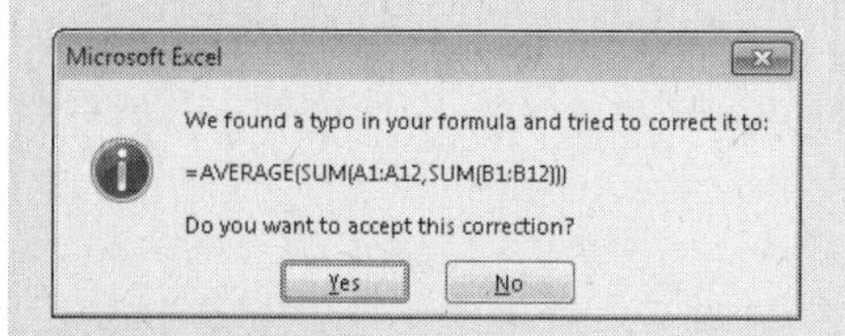

Be careful when accepting corrections for your formulas from Excel because it doesn't always guess correctly. For example, I entered the following formula (which has mismatched parentheses):

```
=AVERAGE(SUM(A1:A12,SUM(B1:B12))
```

Excel then proposed the following correction to the formula:

```
=AVERAGE(SUM(A1:A12,SUM(B1:B12)))
```

You may be tempted to accept the suggestion without even thinking. In this case, the proposed formula is syntactically correct — but not what I intended. The correct formula is

```
=AVERAGE(SUM(A1:A12),SUM(B1:B12))
```

TIP

Excel can help you out with mismatched parentheses. When you're editing a formula and you move the cursor over a parenthesis, Excel displays it (and its matching parenthesis) in bold for about one-half second. In addition, Excel color-codes pairs of nested parentheses while you're editing a formula.

Cells are filled with hash marks

A cell is filled with a series of hash marks (#) for one of two reasons:

- **The column is not wide enough to accommodate the formatted numeric value.** To correct it, you can make the column wider or use a different number format (see Chapter 25).
- **The cell contains a formula that returns an invalid date or time.** For example, Excel doesn't support dates prior to 1900 or the use of negative time values. A formula that returns either of these values results in a cell filled with hash marks. Widening the column won't fix it.

Blank cells are not blank

Some Excel users have discovered that by pressing the spacebar, the contents of a cell seem to erase. Actually, pressing the spacebar inserts an invisible space character, which isn't the same as erasing the cell.

For example, the following formula returns the number of nonempty cells in range A1:A10. If you "erase" any of these cells by using the spacebar, these cells are included in the count, and the formula returns an incorrect result.

```
=COUNTA(A1:A10)
```

If your formula doesn't ignore blank cells the way that it should, check to make sure that the blank cells are really blank cells. Here's how to search for cells that contain only blank characters:

1. **Press Ctrl + F.** The Find and Replace dialog box appears.
2. **Click the Options button to expand the dialog box so it displays additional options.**
3. **In the Find What box, enter `* *`.** That's an asterisk, followed by a space, followed by another asterisk.
4. **Make sure the Match Entire Cell Contents check box is selected.**
5. **Click Find All.** If any cells that contain only space characters are found, Excel lists the cell address at the bottom of the Find and Replace dialog box.

Extra space characters

If you have formulas or use procedures that rely on comparing text, be careful that your text doesn't contain additional space characters. Adding an extra space character is particularly common when data has been imported from another source.

Excel automatically removes trailing spaces from values that you enter, but trailing spaces in text entries are not deleted. It's impossible to tell just by looking at a cell whether it contains one or more trailing space characters.

The `TRIM` function removes leading spaces, trailing spaces, and multiple spaces within a text string. Figure 31.1 shows some text in column A. The formula in B1, which was copied down the column is

```
=TRIM(A1)=A1
```

This formula returns `FALSE` if the text in column A contains leading spaces, trailing spaces, or multiple spaces. In this case, the word *Dog* in cell A2 contains a trailing space.

Tracing Error Values

Often, an error in one cell is the result of an error in a precedent cell. For help in identifying the cell causing an error value to appear, activate the cell that contains the error and then choose Formulas ➪ Formula Auditing ➪ Error Checking ➪ Trace Error. Excel draws arrows to indicate which cell is the source of the error.

	A	B	C	D	E
1		Total	Units	Per Unit	
2	Jan	1,555	19	81.84	
3	Feb	2,454	29	84.62	
4	Mar	1,930	27	71.48	
5	Apr	1,266	21	60.29	
6	May	3,027	31	97.65	
7	Jun	1,170	0	#DIV/0!	
8	Jul	3,747	43	87.14	
9	Aug	4,941	63	78.43	
10	Sep	2,505	39	64.23	
11	Oct	2,862	42	68.14	
12	Nov	1,867	28	66.68	
13	Dec	3,043	39	78.03	
14					
15					
16	Average	2,531	31.75	#DIV/0!	
17					
18					
19					
20					

Sheet1 | Sheet2 | Sheet3 | Sheet- ...

After you identify the error, choose Formulas ➪ Formula Auditing ➪ Remove Arrows to get rid of the arrow display.

FIGURE 31.1

Using a formula to identify cells that contain extra space characters.

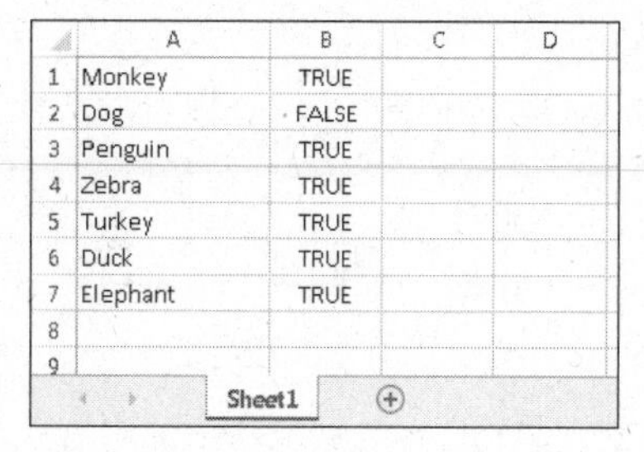

	A	B	C	D
1	Monkey	TRUE		
2	Dog	FALSE		
3	Penguin	TRUE		
4	Zebra	TRUE		
5	Turkey	TRUE		
6	Duck	TRUE		
7	Elephant	TRUE		
8				

Sheet1

Formulas returning an error

A formula may return any of the following error values:

- #DIV/0!
- #N/A
- #NAME?
- #NULL!
- #NUM!
- #REF!
- #VALUE!

The following sections summarize possible problems that may cause these errors.

TIP

Excel allows you to choose how error values are printed. To access this feature, display the Page Setup dialog box and select the Sheet tab. You can choose to print error values as displayed (the default), or as blank cells, dashes, or #N/A. To display the Page Setup dialog box, click the dialog box launcher of the Page Layout ➪ Page Setup group.

#DIV/0! errors

Division by zero is not a valid operation. If you create a formula that attempts to divide by zero, Excel displays its familiar `#DIV/0!` error value.

Because Excel considers a blank cell to be zero, you also get this error if your formula divides by a missing value. This problem is common when you create formulas for data that you haven't entered yet, as shown in Figure 31.2. The formula in cell D4, which was copied to the cells below it, is

```
=C4/B4
```

This formula calculates the ratio of the values in columns C and B. Data isn't available for all days, so the formula returns a `#DIV/0!` error.

To avoid the error display, you can use an `IF` function to check for a blank cell in column B:

```
=IF(B4=0,"",C4/B4)
```

This formula displays an empty string if cell B4 is blank or contains `0`; otherwise, it displays the calculated value.

FIGURE 31.2

#DIV/0! errors occur when the data in column B is missing.

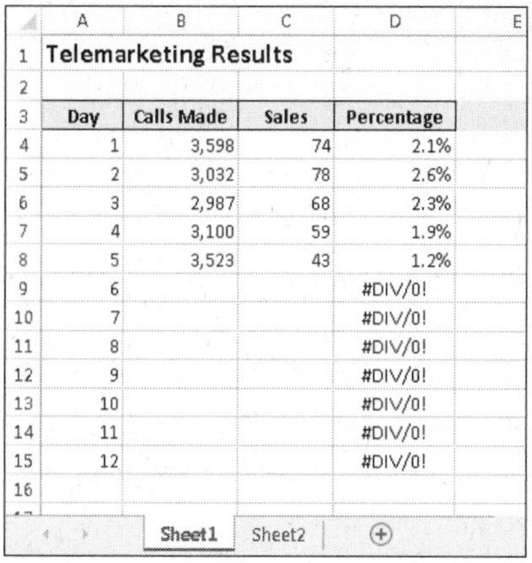

	A	B	C	D	E
1	Telemarketing Results				
2					
3	Day	Calls Made	Sales	Percentage	
4	1	3,598	74	2.1%	
5	2	3,032	78	2.6%	
6	3	2,987	68	2.3%	
7	4	3,100	59	1.9%	
8	5	3,523	43	1.2%	
9	6			#DIV/0!	
10	7			#DIV/0!	
11	8			#DIV/0!	
12	9			#DIV/0!	
13	10			#DIV/0!	
14	11			#DIV/0!	
15	12			#DIV/0!	
16					

Sheet1 | Sheet2

Another approach is to use an IFERROR function to check for *any* error condition. The following formula, for example, displays an empty string if the formula results in any type of error:

```
=IFERROR(C4/B4,"")
```

NOTE

The IFERROR function was introduced in Excel 2007. For compatibility with previous versions of Excel, use this formula:

```
=IF(ISERROR(C4/B4),"",C4/B4)
```

#N/A errors

The #N/A error occurs if any cell referenced by a formula displays #N/A.

NOTE

Some users like to use =NA() or #N/A explicitly for missing data. This method makes it perfectly clear that the data is not available and hasn't been deleted accidentally.

The #N/A error also occurs when a LOOKUP function (HLOOKUP, LOOKUP, MATCH, or VLOOKUP) can't find a match.

If you would like to display an empty string instead of #N/A use the IFNA function in a formula like this:

```
=IFNA(VLOOKUP(A1,C1:F50,4,FALSE),"")
```

Note

The `IFNA` function is new to Excel 2013. For compatibility with previous versions use a formula like this:

```
=IF(ISNA(VLOOKUP(A1,C1:F50,4,FALSE)),"",VLOOKUP(A1,C1:F50,4,FALSE))
```

#NAME? errors

The `#NAME?` error occurs under these conditions:

- The formula contains an undefined range or cell name.
- The formula contains text that Excel *interprets* as an undefined name. A misspelled function name, for example, generates a `#NAME?` error.
- The formula contains text that isn't enclosed in quotation marks.
- The formula contains a range reference that omits the colon between the cell addresses.
- The formula uses a worksheet function that's defined in an add-in, and the add-in is not installed.

Caution

Excel has a bit of a problem with range names. If you delete a name for a cell or range and the name is used in a formula, the formula continues to use the name, even though it's no longer defined. As a result, the formula displays `#NAME?`. You might expect Excel to automatically convert the names to their corresponding cell references, but this doesn't happen.

#NULL! errors

A `#NULL!` error occurs when a formula attempts to use an intersection of two ranges that don't actually intersect. Excel's intersection operator is a space. The following formula, for example, returns `#NULL!` because the two ranges don't intersect:

```
=SUM(B5:B14 A16:F16)
```

The following formula doesn't return `#NULL!` but displays the contents of cell B9, which represents the intersection of the two ranges:

```
=SUM(B5:B14 A9:F9)
```

You also see a `#NULL!` error if you accidentally omit an operator in a formula. For example, this formula is missing the second operator:

```
= A1+A2 A3
```

#NUM! errors

A formula returns a `#NUM!` error if any of the following occurs:

- You pass a nonnumeric argument to a function when a numeric argument is expected (for example, $1,000 instead of 1000).
- You pass an invalid argument to a function. For example, this formula returns `#NUM!`:

  `=SQRT(-12)`
- A function that uses iteration can't calculate a result. Examples of functions that use iteration are `IRR` and `RATE`.
- A formula returns a value that is too large or too small. Excel supports values between -1E-307 and 1E+307.

#REF! errors

A `#REF!` error occurs when a formula uses an invalid cell reference. This error can occur in the following situations:

- You delete the row column of a cell that is referenced by the formula. For example, the following formula displays a `#REF!` error if row 1, column A, or column B is deleted:

  `=A1/B1`
- You delete the worksheet of a cell that is referenced by the formula. For example, the following formula displays a `#REF!` error if Sheet2 is deleted:

  `=Sheet2!A1`
- You copy a formula to a location that invalidates the relative cell references. For example, if you copy the following formula from cell A2 to cell A1, the formula returns `#REF!` because it attempts to refer to a nonexistent cell.

  `=A1-1`
- You cut a cell (choose Home⇨Clipboard⇨Cut) and then paste it to a cell that's referenced by a formula. The formula will display `#REF!`.

#VALUE! errors

A `#VALUE!` error is very common and can occur under the following conditions:

- An argument for a function is of an incorrect data type, or the formula attempts to perform an operation using incorrect data. For example, a formula that adds a value to a text string returns the `#VALUE!` error.
- A function's argument is a range when it should be a single value.
- A custom worksheet function is not calculated. You can press Ctrl+Alt+F9 to force a recalculation.
- A custom worksheet function attempts to perform an operation that is not valid. For example, custom functions can't modify the Excel environment or make changes to other cells.
- You forget to press Ctrl+Shift+Enter when entering an `Array` formula.

Pay Attention to the Colors

When you edit a cell that contains a formula, Excel color-codes the cell and range references in the formula. Excel also outlines the cells and ranges used in the formula by using corresponding colors. Therefore, you can see at a glance the cells that are used in the formula.

You also can manipulate the colored outline to change the cell or range reference. To change the references used in a formula, drag the outline's border or fill handle (at the lower right of the outline). This technique is often easier than editing the formula.

Absolute/relative reference problems

As I describe in Chapter 10, a cell reference can be relative (for example, `A1`), absolute (for example, `$A$1`), or mixed (for example, `$A1` or `A$1`). The type of cell reference that you use in a formula is relevant only if the formula will be copied to other cells.

A common problem is using a relative reference when you should use an absolute reference. As shown in Figure 31.3, cell C1 contains a tax rate, which is used in the formulas in column C. The formula in cell C4 is

```
=B4+(B4*$C$1)
```

FIGURE 31.3

Formulas in the range C4:C7 use an absolute reference to cell C1.

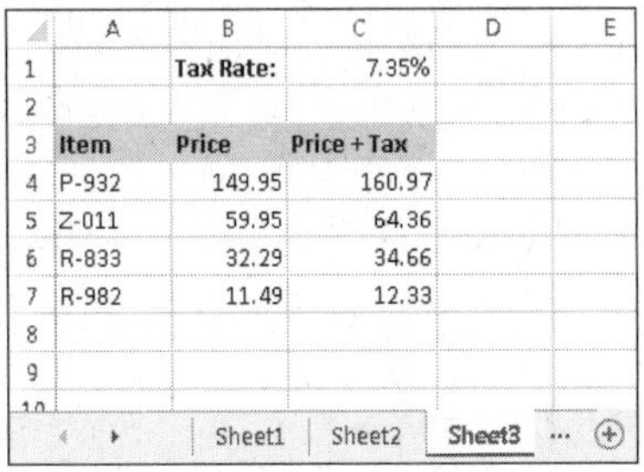

	A	B	C	D	E
1		Tax Rate:	7.35%		
2					
3	Item	Price	Price + Tax		
4	P-932	149.95	160.97		
5	Z-011	59.95	64.36		
6	R-833	32.29	34.66		
7	R-982	11.49	12.33		
8					
9					

Sheet1 | Sheet2 | Sheet3

Notice that the reference to cell C1 is an absolute reference. When the formula is copied to other cells in column C, the formula continues to refer to cell C1. If the reference to cell C1 were a relative reference, the copied formulas would return an incorrect result.

Operator precedence problems

As I describe in Chapter 10, Excel has some straightforward rules about the order in which mathematical operations are performed. When in doubt (or when you simply need to clarify your intentions), you should use parentheses to ensure that operations are performed in the correct order. For example, the following formula multiplies A1 by A2 and then adds 1 to the result. The multiplication is performed first because it has a higher order of precedence.

```
=1+A1*A2
```

The following is a clearer version of this formula. The parentheses aren't necessary, but in this case, the order of operations is perfectly obvious.

```
=1+(A1*A2)
```

Notice that the negation operator symbol is exactly the same as the subtraction operator symbol. This, as you may expect, can cause some confusion. Consider these two formulas:

```
=-3^2
=0-3^2
```

The first formula, as expected, returns `9`. The second formula, however, returns `-9`. Squaring a number always produces a positive result, so how is it that Excel can return the `-9` result?

In the first formula, the minus sign is a *negation* operator and has the highest precedence. However, in the second formula, the minus sign is a *subtraction* operator, which has a lower precedence than the exponentiation operator. Therefore, the value `3` is squared, and then the result is subtracted from `0` (zero), which produces a negative result.

Using parentheses, as shown in the following formula, causes Excel to interpret the operator as a minus sign rather than a negation operator. This formula returns `-9`.

```
=-(3^2)
```

Formulas are not calculated

If you use custom worksheet functions written in VBA, you may find that formulas that use these functions fail to get recalculated and may display incorrect results. For example, assume that you wrote a VBA function that returns the number format of a referenced cell. If you change the number format, the function will continue to display the previous number format. That's because changing a number format doesn't trigger a recalculation.

To force a single formula to be recalculated, select the cell, press F2, and then press Enter. To force a recalculation of all formulas, press Ctrl + Alt + F9.

Actual versus displayed values

You may encounter a situation in which values in a range don't appear to add up properly. For example, Figure 31.4 shows a worksheet with the following formula entered into each cell in the range B2:B4:

```
=1/3
```

FIGURE 31.4

A simple demonstration of numbers that appear to add up incorrectly.

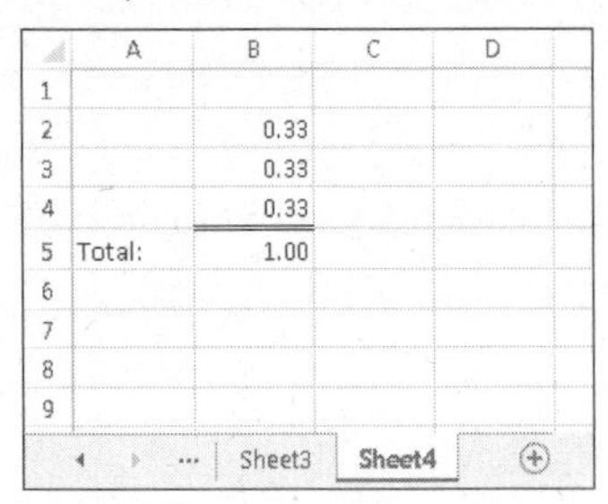

Cell B5 contains the following formula:

```
=SUM(B2:B4)
```

All the cells are formatted to display with three decimal places. As you can see, the formula in cell B5 appears to display an incorrect result. (You may expect it to display `0.99`.) The formula, of course, *does* return the correct result. The formula uses the *actual* values in the range B2:B4 not the *displayed* values.

You can instruct Excel to use the displayed values by selecting the Set Precision as Displayed check box of the Advanced section of the Excel Options dialog box. (Choose File⇨Options to display this dialog box.)

CAUTION

Be very careful with the Set Precision as Displayed option. This option also affects normal values (nonformulas) that have been entered into cells. For example, if a cell contains the value `4.68` and is displayed with no decimal places (that is, `5`), selecting the Precision as Displayed check box converts 4.68 to 5.00. This change is permanent, and you can't restore the original value if you later clear the Set Precision as Displayed check box. A better approach is to use the `ROUND` function to round off the values to the desired number of decimal places.

Floating point number errors

Computers, by their very nature, don't have infinite precision. Excel stores numbers in binary format by using 8 bytes, which can handle numbers with 15-digit accuracy. Some numbers can't be expressed precisely by using 8 bytes, so the number is stored as an approximation.

To demonstrate how this lack of precision may cause problems, enter the following formula into cell A1:

```
=(5.1-5.2)+1
```

The result should be `0.9`. However, if you format the cell to display 15 decimal places, you discover that Excel calculates the formula with a result of `0.899999999999999`.

This result occurs because the operation in parentheses is performed first, and this intermediate result stores in binary format by using an approximation. The formula then adds 1 to this value, and the approximation error is propagated to the final result.

In many cases, this type of error doesn't present a problem. However, if you need to test the result of that formula by using a logical operator, it *may* present a problem. For example, the following formula (which assumes that the previous formula is in cell A1) returns `FALSE`:

```
=A1=.9
```

One solution to this type of error is to use the `ROUND` function. The following formula, for example, returns `TRUE` because the comparison is made by using the value in A1 rounded to one decimal place.

```
=ROUND(A1,1)=0.9
```

Here's another example of a "precision" problem. Try entering the following formula:

```
=(1.333-1.233)-(1.334-1.234)
```

This formula should return `0`, but it actually returns `-2.220446E-16` (a number very close to zero).

If that formula is in cell A1, the following formula returns `Not Zero`.

```
=IF(A1=0,"Zero","Not Zero")
```

One way to handle these "very close to zero" rounding errors is to use a formula like this:

```
=IF(ABS(A1)<1E-6,"Zero","Not Zero")
```

This formula uses the less-than operator (<) to compare the absolute value of the number with a very small number. This formula returns `Zero`.

"Phantom link" errors

You may open a workbook and see a message like the one shown in Figure 31.5. This message sometimes appears even when a workbook contains no linked formulas. Often, these phantom links are created when you copy a worksheet that contains names.

FIGURE 31.5

Excel's way of asking whether you want to update links in a workbook.

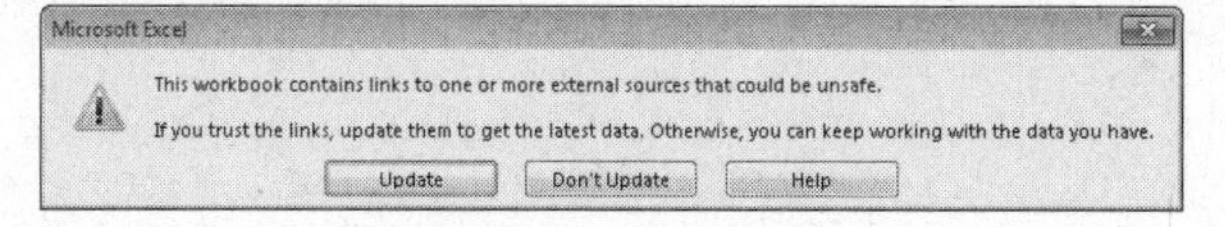

First, try choosing File ➪ Info ➪ Edit Links to Files to display the Edit Links dialog box. Then select each link and click Break Link. If that doesn't solve the problem, this phantom link may be caused by an erroneous name. Choose Formulas ➪ Defined Names ➪ Name Manager and scroll through the list of names in the Name Manager dialog box. If you see a name that refers to #REF!, delete the name. The Name Manager dialog box has a Filter button that lets you filter the names. For example, you can filter the lists to display only the names with errors.

Using Excel Auditing Tools

Excel includes a number of tools that can help you track down formula errors. This section describes the auditing tools built in to Excel.

Identifying cells of a particular type

The Go to Special dialog box (shown in Figure 31.6) is a handy tool that enables you to locate cells of a particular type. To display this dialog box, choose Home ➪ Editing ➪ Find & Select ➪ Go to Special.

FIGURE 31.6

The Go to Special dialog box.

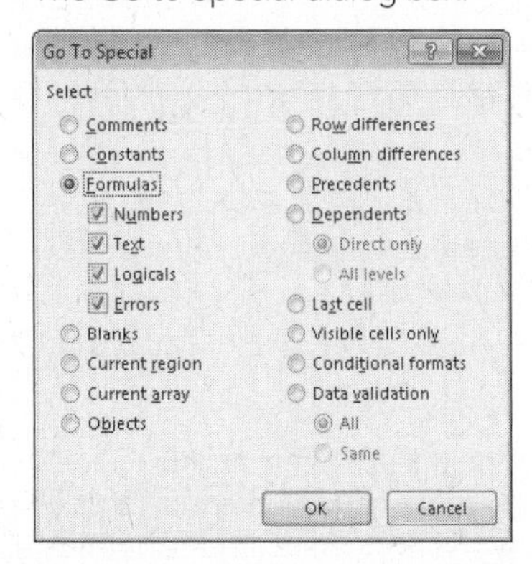

NOTE

If you select a multicell range before displaying the Go to Special dialog box, the command operates only within the selected cells. If a single cell is selected, the command operates on the entire worksheet.

You can use the Go to Special dialog box to select cells of a certain type, which can often help you identify errors. For example, if you choose the Formulas option, Excel selects all the cells that contain a formula. If you zoom the worksheet out to a small size, you can get a good idea of the worksheet's organization (see Figure 31.7). To zoom a worksheet, use the zoom controls on the right side of the status bar or press Ctrl while you move the scroll wheel on your mouse.

FIGURE 31.7

Zooming out and selecting all formula cells can give you a good overview of how the worksheet is designed.

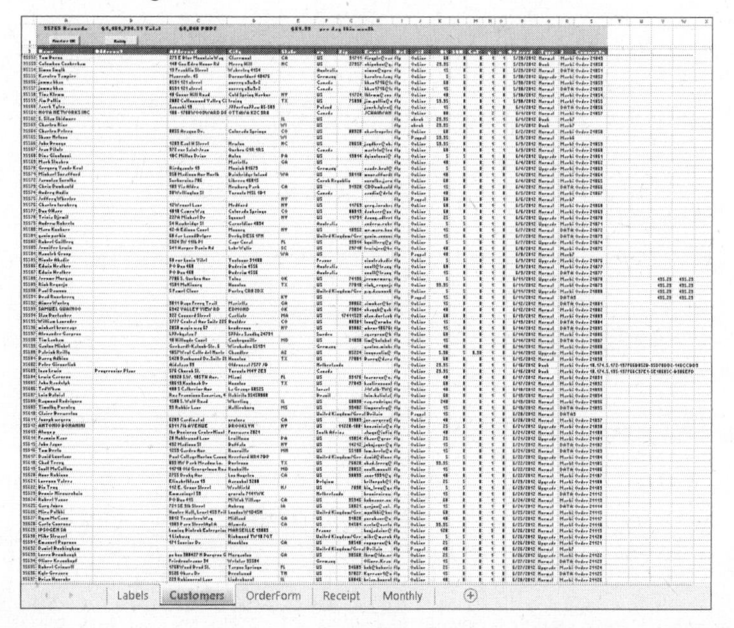

> **TIP**
>
> Selecting the formula cells may also help you spot a common error: namely, a formula that has been replaced accidentally with a value. If you find a cell that's not selected amid a group of selected formula cells, chances are good that the cell previously contained a formula that has been replaced by a value.

Viewing formulas

You can become familiar with an unfamiliar workbook by displaying the formulas rather than the results of the formulas. To toggle the display of formulas, choose Formulas ➪ Formula Auditing ➪ Show Formulas. You may want to create a second window for the workbook before issuing this command. This way, you can see the formulas in one window and the results of the formula in the other window. Choose View ➪ Window ➪ New Window to open a new window.

Using the Inquire Add-in

Some versions of Excel 2013 include a useful auditing add-in called Inquire. To install Inquire, follow these steps:

1. **Choose File⇨Options.** The Excel Options dialog box appears.
2. **Select the Add-ins tab.**
3. **At the bottom of the dialog box, choose COM Add-ins from the Manage drop-down list, and click Go.** The COM Add-Ins dialog box appears.
4. **Place a check mark next to Inquire Add-in and click OK.** The add-in will be loaded automatically when Excel starts.

Note: If Inquire is not listed, that means your version of Excel does not include the add-in.

Inquire is accessible from the Inquire tab on the Ribbon. You can use this add-in to

- Compare versions of a workbook
- Analyze a workbook for potential problem and inconsistencies
- Display interactive diagnostics (shown here)
- Visualize links between workbook and worksheets
- Clear excess cell formatting
- Manage passwords

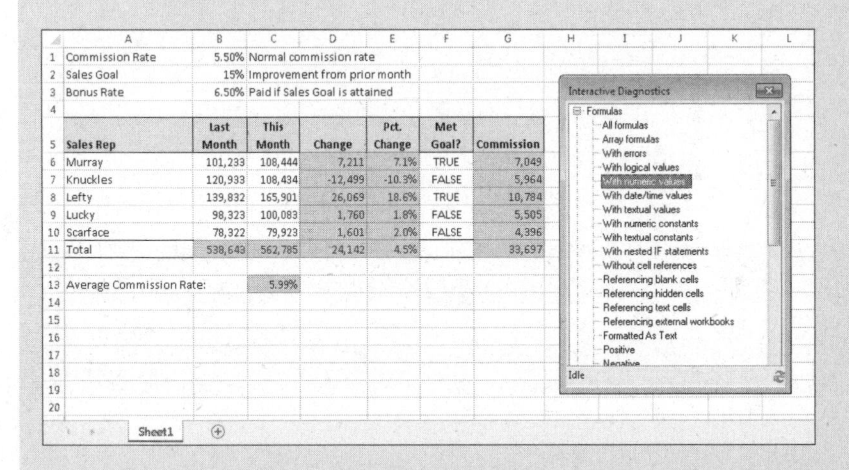

TIP

You can also press Ctrl+` (the accent grave key, typically located above the Tab key) to toggle between Formula view and Normal view.

Figure 31.8 shows an example of a worksheet displayed in two windows. The window on the top shows Normal view (formula results), and the window on the bottom displays the formulas. Choosing View ➪ Window ➪ View Side by Side, which allows synchronized scrolling, is also useful for viewing two windows.

FIGURE 31.8

Displaying formulas (bottom window) and their results (top window).

	A	B	C	D	E	F	G
1	Commission Rate	5.50%	Normal commission rate				
2	Sales Goal	15%	Improvement from prior month				
3	Bonus Rate	6.50%	Paid if Sales Goal is attained				
4							
5	Sales Rep	Last Month	This Month	Change	Pct. Change	Met Goal?	Commission
6	Murray	101,233	108,444	7,211	7.1%	TRUE	7,049
7	Knuckles	120,933	108,434	-12,499	-10.3%	FALSE	5,964
8	Lefty	139,832	165,901	26,069	18.6%	TRUE	10,784
9	Lucky	98,323	100,083	1,760	1.8%	FALSE	5,505
10	Scarface	78,322	79,923	1,601	2.0%	FALSE	4,396
11	Total	538,643	562,785	24,142	4.5%		33,697
12							
13	Average Commission Rate:		5.99%				
14							

Sheet1

commission calc.xlsx:2 - Excel

	A	B	C	D	E	F	G
1	Commission Rate	0.055	Normal commission				
2	Sales Goal	0.15	Improvement from p				
3	Bonus Rate	0.065	Paid if Sales Goal is a				
4							
5	Sales Rep	Last Month	This Month	Change	Pct. Change	Met Goal?	Commission
6	Murray	101233	108444	=C6-B6	=D6/B6	=E6>=$B$3	=IF(F6,$B$3,$B$1)*C6
7	Knuckles	120933	108434	=C7-B7	=D7/B7	=E7>=$B$3	=IF(F7,$B$3,$B$1)*C7
8	Lefty	139832	165901	=C8-B8	=D8/B8	=E8>=$B$3	=IF(F8,$B$3,$B$1)*C8
9	Lucky	98323	100083	=C9-B9	=D9/B9	=E9>=$B$3	=IF(F9,$B$3,$B$1)*C9
10	Scarface	78322	79923	=C10-B10	=D10/B10	=E10>=$B$3	=IF(F10,$B$3,$B$1)*C10
11	Total	=SUM(B6:B10)	=SUM(C6:C10)	=SUM(D6:D10)	=D11/B11		=SUM(G6:G10)
12							
13	Average Commission Rate:		=G11/C11				
14							

Sheet1

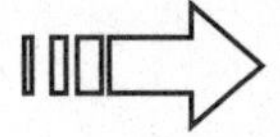

See Chapter 4 for more information about this command.

Tracing cell relationships

To understand how to trace cell relationships, you need to familiarize yourself with the following two concepts:

- **Cell precedents:** Applicable only to cells that contain a formula, a formula cell's precedents are all the cells that contribute to the formula's result. A *direct precedent* is a cell that you use directly in the formula. An *indirect precedent* is a cell that isn't used directly in the formula but is used by a cell that you refer to in the formula.
- **Cell dependents:** These formula cells depend upon a particular cell. A cell's dependents consist of all formula cells that use the cell. Again, the formula cell can be a *direct dependent* or an *indirect dependent*.

For example, consider this simple formula entered into cell A4:

```
=SUM(A1:A3)
```

Cell A4 has three precedent cells (A1, A2, and A3), which are all direct precedents. Cells A1, A2, and A3 all have at least one dependent cell (cell A4), and they're all direct dependents.

Identifying cell precedents for a formula cell often sheds light on why the formula isn't working correctly. Conversely, knowing which formula cells depend on a particular cell is also helpful. For example, if you're about to delete a formula, you may want to check whether it has any dependents.

Identifying precedents

You can identify cells used by a formula in the active cell in a number of ways:

- **Press F2.** The cells that are used directly by the formula are outlined in color, and the color corresponds to the cell reference in the formula. This technique is limited to identifying cells on the same sheet as the formula.
- **Choose Home ➪ Editing ➪ Find & Select ➪ Go to Special to display the Go to Special dialog box.** Select the Precedents option and then select either Direct Only (for direct precedents only) or All Levels (for direct and indirect precedents). Click OK, and Excel selects the precedent cells for the formula. This technique is limited to identifying cells on the same sheet as the formula.
- **Press Ctrl + [.** This selects all direct precedent cells on the active sheet.
- **Press Ctrl + Shift + {.** This selects all precedent cells (direct and indirect) on the active sheet.
- **Choose Formulas ➪ Formula Auditing ➪ Trace Precedents.** Excel will draw arrows to indicate the cell's precedents. Click this button multiple times to see additional levels of precedents. Choose Formulas ➪ Formula Auditing ➪ Remove Arrows to hide the arrows. Figure 31.9 shows a worksheet with precedent arrows drawn to indicate the precedents for the formula in cell C13.

Identifying dependents

You can identify formula cells that use a particular cell in a number of ways:

- **Choose Home ➪ Editing ➪ Find & Select ➪ Go to Special to display the Go to Special dialog box.** Select the Dependents option and then select either Direct Only (for direct dependents only) or All Levels (for direct and indirect dependents). Click OK. Excel selects the cells that depend upon the active cell. This technique is limited to identifying cells on the active sheet only.
- **Press Ctrl +].** This selects all direct dependent cells on the active sheet.
- **Press Ctrl + Shift + }.** This selects all dependent cells (direct and indirect) on the active sheet.
- **Choose Formulas ➪ Formula Auditing ➪ Trace Dependents.** Excel will draw arrows to indicate the cell's dependents. Click this button multiple times to see additional levels of dependents. Choose Formulas ➪ Formula Auditing ➪ Remove Arrows to hide the arrows.

FIGURE 31.9

This worksheet displays arrows that indicate cell precedents for the formula in cell C13.

	A	B	C	D	E	F	G	H
1	Commission Rate	5.50%	Normal commission rate					
2	Sales Goal	15%	Improvement from prior month					
3	Bonus Rate	6.50%	Paid if Sales Goal is attained					
4								
5	Sales Rep	Last Month	This Month	Change	Pct. Change	Met Goal?	Commission	
6	Murray	101,233	108,444	7,211	7.1%	TRUE	7,049	
7	Knuckles	120,933	108,434	-12,499	-10.3%	FALSE	5,964	
8	Lefty	139,832	165,901	26,069	18.6%	TRUE	10,784	
9	Lucky	98,323	100,083	1,760	1.8%	FALSE	5,505	
10	Scarface	78,322	79,923	1,601	2.0%	FALSE	4,396	
11	Total	538,643	562,785	24,142	4.5%		33,697	
12								
13	Average Commission Rate:		5.99%					
14								

Sheet1

Tracing error values

If a formula displays an error value, Excel can help you identify the cell that is causing that error value. An error in one cell is often the result of an error in a precedent cell. Activate a cell that contains an error value and then choose Formulas ➪ Formula Auditing ➪ Error Checking ➪ Trace Error. Excel draws arrows to indicate the error source.

Fixing circular reference errors

If you accidentally create a circular reference formula, Excel displays a warning message — `Circular Reference` — with the cell address, in the status bar, and also draws arrows on the worksheet to help you identify the problem. If you can't figure out the source of the problem, choose Formulas ➪ Formula Auditing ➪ Error Checking ➪ Circular References. This command displays a list of all cells that are involved in the circular references. Start by selecting the first cell listed and then work your way down the list until you figure out the problem.

Using the background error-checking feature

Some people may find it helpful to take advantage of the Excel automatic error-checking feature. This feature is enabled or disabled via the Enable Background Error Checking check box, found on the Formulas tab of the Excel Options dialog box, shown in Figure 31.10. In addition, you can use the check boxes in the Error Checking Rules section to specify which types of errors to check.

FIGURE 31.10

Excel can check your formulas for potential errors.

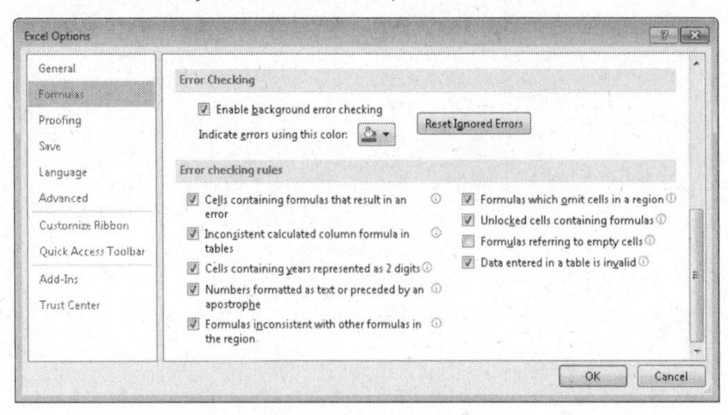

When error checking is turned on, Excel continually evaluates the formulas in your worksheet. If a potential error is identified, Excel places a small triangle in the upper-left corner of the cell. When the cell is activated, a drop-down control appears. Clicking this drop-down control provides you with options. Figure 31.11 shows the options that appear when you click the drop-down control in a cell that contains a `#DIV/0!` error. The options vary, depending on the type of error.

FIGURE 31.11

After you click an error, drop-down control gives you a list of options.

	A	B	C	D	E
1	Telemarketing Results				
2					
3	Day	Calls Made	Sales	Percentage	
4	1	3,598	74	2.1%	
5	2	3,032	78	2.6%	
6	3	2,987	68	2.3%	
7	4	3,100	59	1.9%	
8	5	3,523	43	1.2%	
9	6			#DIV/0!	
10	7			#DIV/0!	
11	8			#DIV/0!	
12	9				
13	10				
14	11				
15	12				

Divide by Zero Error
Help on this error
Show Calculation Steps...
Ignore Error
Edit in Formula Bar
Error Checking Options...

Sheet1 | Sheet2 | Sheet3 | Sheet4

In many cases, you'll choose to ignore an error by selecting the Ignore Error option. Selecting this option eliminates the cell from subsequent error checks. However, all previously ignored errors can be reset so that they appear again. (Use the Reset Ignored Errors button on the Formulas tab of the Excel Options dialog box.)

You can choose Formulas ➪ Formula Auditing ➪ Error Checking to display a dialog box that describes each potential error cell in sequence, much like using a spell-checking command. This command is available even if you disable background error checking. Figure 31.12 shows the Error Checking dialog box. This dialog box is *modeless:* that is, you can still access your worksheet when the Error Checking dialog box is displayed.

FIGURE 31.12

Use the Error Checking dialog box to cycle through potential errors identified by Excel.

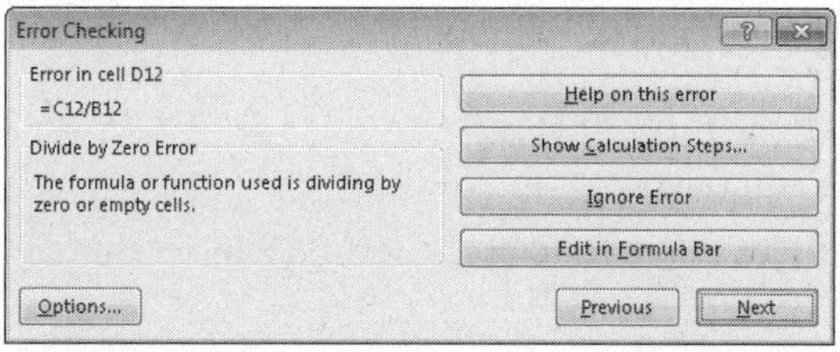

CAUTION

The error-checking feature isn't perfect. In fact, it's not even close to perfect. In other words, you can't assume that you have an error-free worksheet simply because Excel doesn't identify any potential errors! Also, be aware that this error-checking feature won't catch a very common type of error: namely, overwriting a formula cell with a value.

Using Formula Evaluator

Formula Evaluator lets you see the various parts of a nested formula evaluated in the order in which the formula is calculated. To use Formula Evaluator, select the cell that contains the formula and then choose Formula ➪ Formula Auditing ➪ Evaluate Formula to display the Evaluate Formula dialog box (see Figure 31.13).

Click the Evaluate button to show the result of calculating the expressions within the formula. Each click of the button performs another calculation. This feature may seem a bit complicated at first, but if you spend some time working with it, you'll understand how it works and see the value.

FIGURE 31.13

The Evaluate Formula dialog box shows a formula being calculated one step at a time.

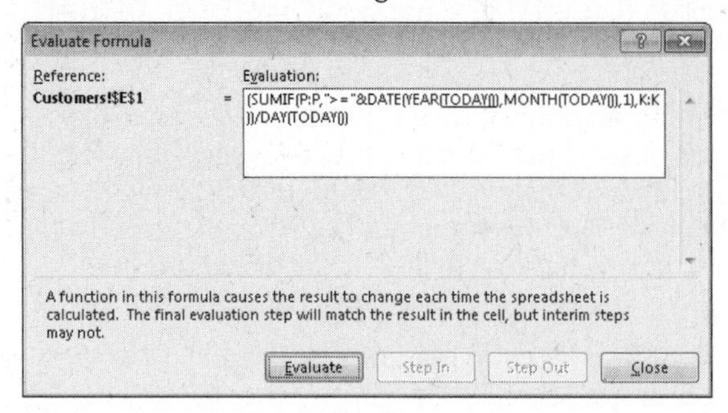

Excel provides another way to evaluate a part of a formula:

1. **Select the cell that contains the formula.**
2. **Press F2 to get into Cell Edit mode.**
3. **Use your mouse to highlight the portion of the formula you want to evaluate.** Or press Shift and use the navigation keys.
4. **Press F9.**

The highlighted portion of the formula displays the calculated result. You can evaluate other parts of the formula or press Esc to cancel and return your formula to its previous state.

CAUTION

Be careful when using this technique because if you press Enter (rather than Esc), the formula will be modified to use the calculated values.

Searching and Replacing

Excel has a powerful search-and-replace feature that makes it easy to locate information in a worksheet or across multiple worksheets in a workbook. As an option, you can also search for text and replace it with other text.

To access the Find and Replace dialog box, start by selecting the range that you want to search. If you select any single cell, Excel searches the entire sheet. Choose Home ➪ Editing ➪ Find & Select ➪ Find (or press Ctrl + F). You'll see the Find and Replace dialog box, shown in Figure 31.14. If you're simply looking for information in the worksheet, select the Find tab. If you want to replace existing text with new text, use the Replace tab. Also note that you can use the Options button to display (or hide) additional options. The dialog box shown in the figure displays these additional options.

FIGURE 31.14

Use the Find and Replace dialog box to locate information in a worksheet or workbook.

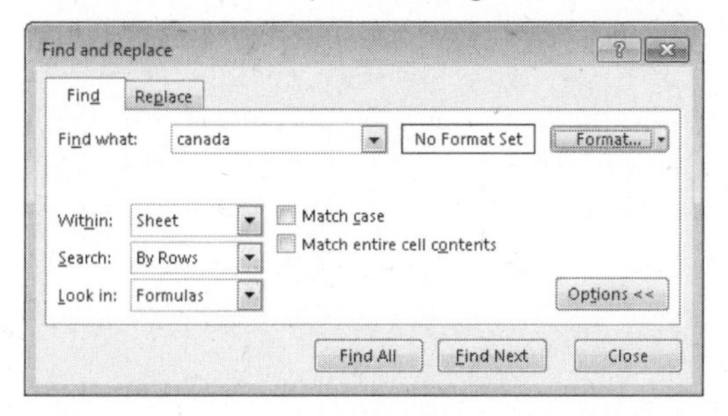

Searching for information

Enter the information to search for in the Find What text box and then specify any of the following options.

- **Within drop-down list:** Specify where to search (the current sheet or the entire workbook).
- **Search drop-down list:** Specify the direction (by rows or by columns).
- **Look In drop-down list:** Specify what cell parts to search (formulas, values, or comments).
- **Match Case check box:** Specify whether the search should be case sensitive.
- **Match Entire Cell Contents check box:** Specify whether the entire cell contents must be matched.
- **Format button:** Click to search for cells that have a particular formatting (see the upcoming "Searching for formatting" section).

Click Find Next to locate the matching cells one at a time or click Find All to locate all matches. If you use the Find All button, the Find and Replace dialog box expands to display the addresses of all matching cells in a list (see Figure 31.15). When you select an entry in this list, Excel scrolls the worksheet so that you can view it in context.

TIP

After using Find All, press Ctrl+A to select all the found cells.

NOTE

Because the Find and Replace dialog box is modeless, you can access the worksheet and make changes without the need to dismiss the dialog box.

FIGURE 31.15

Displaying the result of a search in the Find and Replace dialog box.

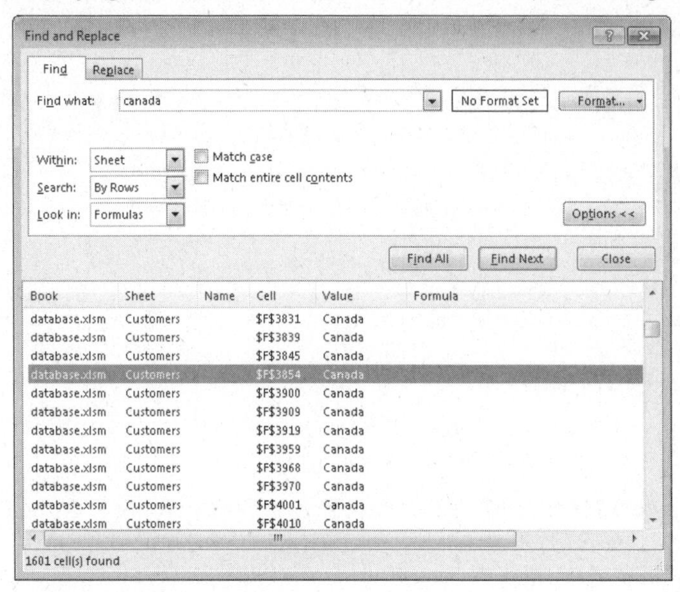

Replacing information

To replace text with other text, use the Replace tab in the Find and Replace dialog box. Enter the text to be replaced in the Find What field, and then enter the new text in the Replace With field. Specify other options as described in the previous section.

Click Find Next to locate the first matching item and then click Replace to do the replacement. When you click the Replace button, Excel locates the next matching item. To override the replacement, click Find Next. To replace all items without verification, click Replace All. If the replacement didn't occur as you planned, you can use the Undo button on the Quick Access toolbar (or press Ctrl + Z).

TIP

To delete information, enter the text to be deleted in the Find What field but leave the Replace With field empty.

Searching for formatting

From the Find and Replace dialog box, you can also locate cells that contain a particular type of formatting. As an option, you can replace that formatting with another type of formatting. For example, assume that you want to locate all cells that are formatted as bold and then change that formatting to bold and italic. Follow these steps:

1. **Choose Home ➪ Editing ➪ Find & Select ➪ Replace or press Ctrl + H.** The Find and Replace dialog box appears.
2. **Make sure that the Replace tab is displayed.** If necessary, click the Options button to expand the dialog box.
3. **If the Find What and Replace With fields are not empty, delete their contents.**
4. **Click the top Format button.** The Find Format dialog box appears. This dialog box resembles the standard Format Cells dialog box.
5. **Select the Font tab.**
6. **Select Bold in the Font Style list, and then click OK.**
7. **Click the bottom Format button.** The Replace Format dialog box appears.
8. **Select the Font tab.**
9. **Select Bold Italic from the Font Style list, and then click OK.** At this point, the Find and Replace dialog box resembles Figure 31.16. Notice that it displays previews of the formatting that will be found and replaced.

FIGURE 31.16

Use the Find and Replace dialog box to change formatting.

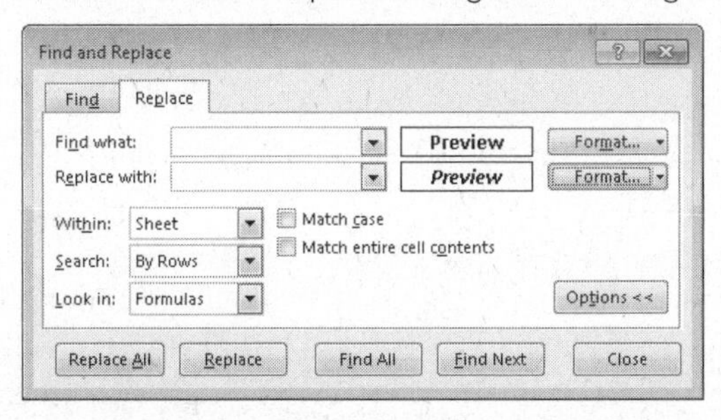

10. **In the Find and Replace dialog box, click Replace All.** Excel locates all cells that have bold formatting and changes the formatting to bold italic.

You can also find formatting based on a particular cell. In the Find Format dialog box, click the Choose Format from Cell button and then click the cell that contains the formatting you're looking for.

> **CAUTION**
>
> The Find and Replace dialog box can't find background color formatting in tables that was applied using table styles or formatting that is applied based on conditional formatting.

Spell-Checking Your Worksheets

If you use a word-processing program, you probably take advantage of its spell-checker feature. Spelling mistakes can be just as embarrassing when they appear in a spreadsheet. Fortunately, Microsoft includes a spell checker with Excel.

To access the spell checker, choose Review ➪ Proofing ➪ Spelling, or press F7. To check the spelling in just a particular range, select the range before you activate the spell checker.

If the spell checker finds any words it doesn't recognize as correct, the Spelling dialog box, shown in Figure 31.17, appears.

FIGURE 31.17

Use the Spelling dialog box to locate and correct spelling errors in your worksheets.

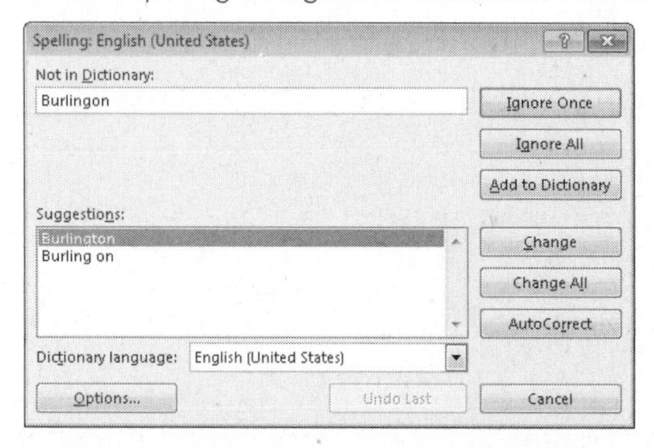

> **NOTE**
> The spell checker checks cell contents, text in graphic objects and charts, and page headers and footers. Even the contents of hidden rows and columns are checked.

The Spelling dialog box works similarly to other spell checkers with which you may be familiar. If Excel encounters a word that isn't in the current dictionary or that is misspelled, it offers a list of suggestions. You can respond by clicking one of these buttons:

- **Ignore Once:** Ignore the word and continues the spell check.
- **Ignore All:** Ignore the word and all subsequent occurrences of it.
- **Add to Dictionary:** Add the word to the dictionary.
- **Change:** Change the word to the selected word in the Suggestions list.
- **Change All:** Change the word to the selected word in the Suggestions list and change all subsequent occurrences of it without asking.
- **AutoCorrect:** Add the misspelled word and its correct spelling (which you select from the list) to the AutoCorrect list.

Using AutoCorrect

AutoCorrect is a handy feature that automatically corrects common typing mistakes. You can also add words to the list that Excel corrects automatically. The AutoCorrect dialog box appears in Figure 31.18. To access this feature, choose File ⇨ Options. In the Excel Options dialog box, select the Proofing tab and then click the AutoCorrect Options button.

FIGURE 31.18

Use the AutoCorrect dialog box to control the spelling corrections Excel makes automatically.

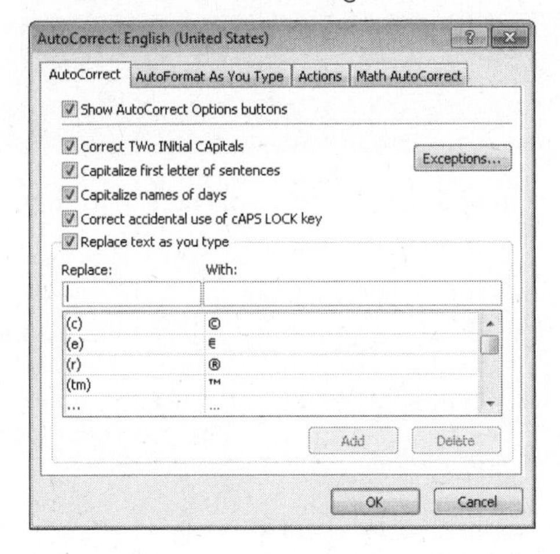

This dialog box has several options:

- **Correct TWo INitial CApitals:** Automatically corrects words with two initial uppercase letters. For example, BUdget is converted to Budget. This mistake is common among fast typists. You can click the Exceptions button to specify a list of exceptions to this rule.
- **Capitalize First Letter of Sentences:** Capitalizes the first letter in a sentence. All other letters are unchanged.
- **Capitalize Names of Days:** Capitalizes the days of the week. If you enter **monday**, Excel converts it to **Monday.**
- **Correct Accidental Use of cAPS LOCK key:** Corrects errors caused if you accidentally pressed the CapsLock key while typing.
- **Replace Text as You Type:** AutoCorrect automatically changes incorrect words as you type them.

Excel includes a long list of AutoCorrect entries for commonly misspelled words. In addition, it has AutoCorrect entries for some symbols. For example, (c) is replaced with ©, and (r) is replaced with ®. You can also add your own AutoCorrect entries. For example, if you find that you frequently misspell the word *January* as *Janruary*, you can create an

AutoCorrect entry so that it's changed automatically. To create a new AutoCorrect entry, enter the misspelled word in the Replace box and the correctly spelled word in the With field. You can also delete entries that you no longer need.

TIP

You also can use the AutoCorrect feature to create shortcuts for commonly used words or phrases. For example, if you work for a company named Consolidated Data Processing Corporation, you can create an AutoCorrect entry for an abbreviation, such as cdp. Then, whenever you type cdp, Excel automatically changes it to Consolidated Data Processing Corporation. Just make sure that you don't use a combination of characters that might normally appear in your text.

NOTE

In some cases, you may want to override the AutoCorrect feature. For example, you may need to literally enter (c) rather than a copyright symbol. Just click the Undo button on the Quick Access toolbar or press Ctrl+Z.

You can use the AutoFormat as You Type tab of the AutoCorrect dialog box to control a few other automatic settings in Excel.

The Actions tab enables what were formerly known as *Smart Tags* for certain types of data in your worksheets. The types of actions Excel recognizes vary depending on the types of software that are installed on your system. For example, if you enable the Financial Symbol action, you can right-click a cell that contains a financial symbol (such as MSFT, for Microsoft), choose Additional Cell Actions, and you'll be presented with a list of options. For example, you can insert a refreshable stock price in your worksheet.

The Math AutoCorrect tab contains shortcuts used to enter symbols when working in the Equation Editor (see Chapter 23).

Part V

Analyzing Data with Excel

Excel is a superb data-analysis tool — if you know how to extract the information you really need. In this part, you'll learn how to obtain, clean up, and analyze data in Excel. As you'll see, many of the data-analysis capabilities in Excel are both surprisingly powerful and easy to use.

IN THIS PART

CHAPTER

32

Importing and Cleaning Data

IN THIS CHAPTER

Importing data into Excel

Manipulating and cleaning data

Using the new Flash Fill feature to extract and concatenate data

Reviewing a checklist for data cleaning

Exporting data to other formats

Data is everywhere. For example, if you run a website, you're collecting data continually and you may not even know it. Every visit to your site generates information that is stored in a file on your server. This file contains lots of useful information, if you take the time to examine it.

That's just one example of data collection. Virtually every automated system collects data and stores it. Most of the time, the system that collects the data is also equipped to verify and analyze the data — but not always. And, of course, data is also collected manually. A telephone survey is a good example.

Excel is good tool for analyzing data, and it's often used to summarize the information and display it in the form of tables and charts. But often, the data that's collected isn't perfect. For one reason or another, it needs to be cleaned up before it can be analyzed.

One very common use for Excel is as a tool to clean up data. Cleaning up data involves getting raw data into a worksheet, and then manipulating it so it conforms to various requirements. In the process, the data will be made consistent so it can be properly analyzed.

This chapter describes various ways to get data into a worksheet and provides some tips to help you clean it up.

Importing Data

Before you can do anything with data, you must get it into a worksheet. Excel is able to import most common text file formats and can also retrieve data from websites.

Importing from a file

This section describes file types that Excel can open directly, using the File➪Open command. Figure 32.1 shows the list of file filter options you can specify in the Open dialog box.

FIGURE 32.1

Filtering by file extension in the Open dialog box.

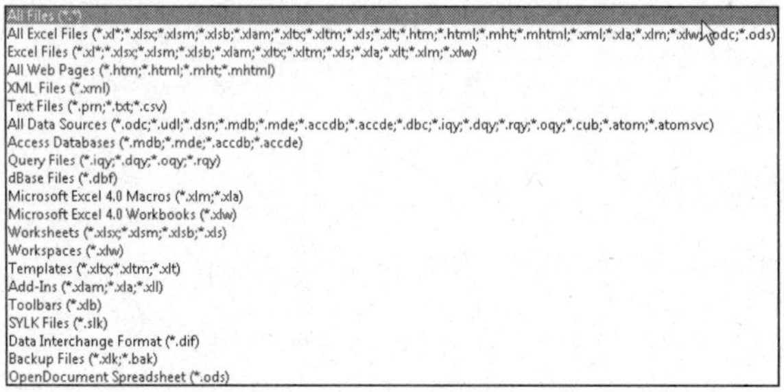

Spreadsheet file formats

In addition to the current file formats (XLSX, XLSM, XLSB, XLTX, XLTM, and XLAM), Excel 2013 can open workbook files from all previous versions of Excel:

- **XLS:** Binary files created by Excel 4, Excel 95, Excel 97, Excel 2000, Excel 2002, and Excel 2003
- **XLM:** Binary files that contain Excel 4 macros (no data)
- **XLT:** Binary files for an Excel template
- **XLA:** Binary files for an Excel add-in

Excel can also open one file format created by other spreadsheet products: ODS, the OpenDocument spreadsheet format. ODS files are produced by a variety of "open" software, including Google Drive, OpenOffice, LibreOffice, StarOffice, and several others.

NOTE

Excel does not support Lotus 1-2-3 files, Quattro Pro files, or Microsoft Works files.

Database file formats

Excel 2013 can open the following database file formats:

- **Access files:** These files have various extensions, including MDB and ACCDB.
- **dBase files:** Produced by dBase III and dBase IV. Excel does not support dBase II files.

In addition, Excel supports various types of database connections that enable you to access data selectively. For example, you can perform a query on a large database to retrieve only the records you need (rather than the entire database).

Text file formats

A text file contains raw characters, with no formatting. Excel can open most types of text files:

- **CSV:** Comma separated values. Columns are delimited with a comma, and rows are delimited with a carriage return.
- **TXT:** Columns are delimited with a tab, and rows are delimited with a carriage return.
- **PRN:** Columns are delimited with multiple space characters, and rows are delimited with a carriage return. Excel imports this type of file into a single column.
- **DIF:** The file format originally used by the VisiCalc spreadsheet. Rarely used.
- **SYLK:** The file format originally used by Multiplan. Rarely used.

Most of these text file types have variants. For example, text files produced on a Mac have different end-of-row characters. Excel can usually handle the variants without a problem.

When you attempt to open a text file in Excel, the Text Import Wizard might kick in to help you specify how you want the data to be retrieved.

Tip

To bypass the Text Import Wizard, press Shift while you click the Open button in the Open dialog box.

When Excel Can't Open a File

If Excel doesn't support a particular file format, don't be too quick to give up. It's likely that others have had the same problem as you. Try searching the web for the file extension, plus the word *Excel*. It's possible that a file converter is available, or maybe someone has figured out how to use an intermediary program to open the file and export it into a format that Excel recognizes.

Importing HTML files

Excel can open most HTML files, which can be stored on your local drive or on a web server. Choose File ➪ Open and locate the HTML file. If the file is on a web server, you'll need to copy the URL and paste it into the File Name field in the Open dialog box.

How the HTML code renders in Excel varies considerably. Sometimes, the HTML file may look exactly as it does in a browser. Other times, it may bear little resemblance, especially if the HTML file uses Cascading Style Sheets (CSS) for layout.

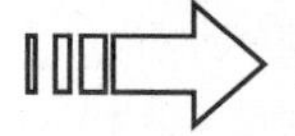

In some cases, you can access data on the web by using a Web Query. I discuss this topic in Chapter 29.

Importing XML files

XML (Extensible Markup Language) is a text file format suitable for structured data. Data is enclosed in tags, which also serve to describe the data.

Excel can open XML files, and simple files will display with little or no effort. Complex XML files will require some work, however. A discussion of this topic is beyond the scope of this book. You'll find information about getting data from XML files in Excel's Help system and online.

Importing a text file into a specified range

If you need to insert a text file into a specific range in a worksheet, you might think that your only choice is to import the text into a new workbook and then to copy the data and paste it into the range where you want it to appear. However, you can do it in a more direct way.

Figure 32.2 shows a small CSV file. The following instructions describe how to import this file, named `monthly.csv`, beginning at cell C3.

FIGURE 32.2

This CSV file will be imported into a range.

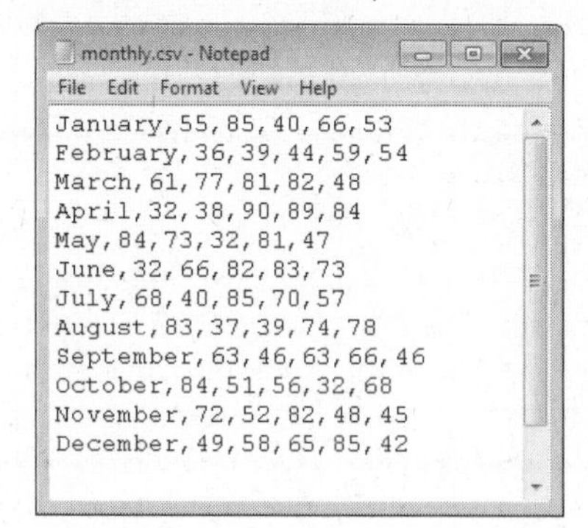

1. **Choose Data ⇨ Get External Data ⇨ From Text.** The Import Text File dialog box appears.
2. **Navigate to the folder that contains the text file.**
3. **Select the file from the list, and then click the Import button.** The Text Import Wizard appears.
4. **Use the Text Import Wizard to specify how the data will be imported. For a CSV file, specify Delimited, with a Comma Delimiter.**
5. **Click the Finish button.** The Import Data dialog box, shown in Figure 32.3, appears.

FIGURE 32.3

Using the Import Data dialog box to import a CSV file.

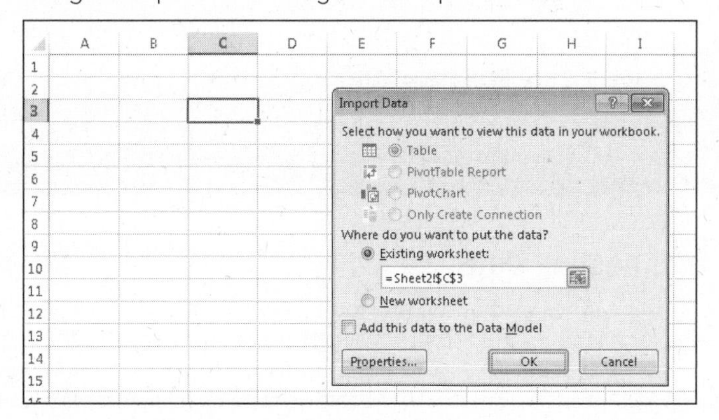

6. **Click the Properties button.** The External Data Range Properties dialog box appears.
7. **Deselect the Save Query Definition check box, and click OK to return to the Import Data dialog box.**
8. **In the Import Data dialog box, specify the location for the imported data.** It can be a cell in an existing worksheet or a new worksheet.
9. **Click OK, and Excel imports the data (see Figure 32.4).**

FIGURE 32.4

This range contains data imported directly from a CSV file.

	A	B	C	D	E	F	G	H
1								
2								
3			January	55	85	40	66	53
4			February	36	39	44	59	54
5			March	61	77	81	82	48
6			April	32	38	90	89	84
7			May	84	73	32	81	47
8			June	32	66	82	83	73
9			July	68	40	85	70	57
10			August	83	37	39	74	78
11			September	63	46	63	66	46
12			October	84	51	56	32	68
13			November	72	52	82	48	45
14			December	49	58	65	85	42
15								

NOTE

You can ignore Step 7 if the data you're importing will be changing. By saving the query definition, you can quickly update the imported data by right-clicking any cell in the range and choosing Refresh Data.

Copying and pasting data

If all else fails, you can try standard copy-and-paste techniques. If you can copy data from an application (for example, a word-processing program or a document displayed in PDF viewer), there's a good chance you can paste it into an Excel workbook. For best results, try pasting using the Home ➪ Clipboard ➪ Paste ➪ Paste Special command, and try various paste options listed. Usually, pasted data will require some cleanup.

Data Clean-up Techniques

This section discusses a variety of techniques that you can use to clean up data in a worksheet.

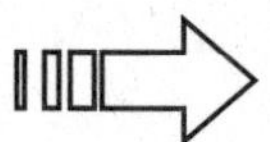

Chapter 11 contains additional examples of text-related formulas that may be helpful when cleaning data.

Removing duplicate rows

If data is compiled from multiple sources, it may contain duplicate rows. Most of the time, you want to eliminate the duplicates. In the past, removing duplicate data was essentially a manual task — although it could be automated by using a confusing advanced filter technique. But now removing duplicate rows is very easy, thanks to Excel's Remove Duplicates command (introduced in Excel 2007).

Start by moving the cell cursor to any cell within your data range. Choose Data ➪ Data Tools ➪ Remove Duplicates, and the Remove Duplicates dialog box, shown in Figure 32.5, appears.

FIGURE 32.5

Use the Remove Duplicates dialog box to delete duplicate rows.

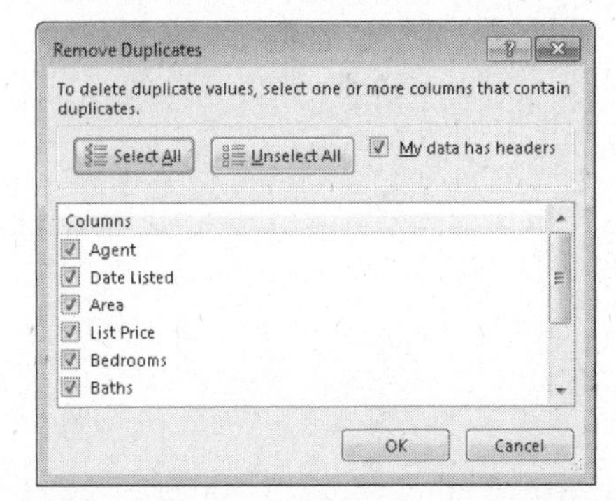

NOTE

If your data is in a table, you can also use Table Tools ➪ Design ➪ Tools ➪ Remove Duplicates. These two commands work exactly the same.

The Remove Duplicates dialog box lists all the columns in your data range or table. Place a check mark next to the columns that you want to be included in the duplicate search. Most of the time, you'll want to select all the columns, which is the default. Click OK, and Excel weeds out the duplicate rows and displays a message that tells you how many duplicates it removed. It would be nice if Excel gave you the option to change your mind, but it doesn't. If Excel deleted too many rows, you can undo the procedure by clicking Undo (or by pressing Ctrl + Z).

When you select all columns in the Remove Duplicates dialog box, Excel will delete a row only if the content of every column is duplicated. In some situations, you may not care about matching some columns, so you would deselect those columns in the Remove Duplicates dialog box. For example, if each row has a unique ID code, Excel would never find any duplicate rows. So, you'd want to uncheck that column in the Remove Duplicates dialog box.

When duplicate rows are found, the first row is kept and subsequent duplicate rows are deleted.

CAUTION

Duplicate values are determined by the value *displayed* in the cell — not necessarily the value *stored* in the cell. For example, assume that two cells contain the same date. One of the dates is formatted to display as 5/15/2012, and the other is formatted to display as May 15, 2012. When removing duplicates, Excel considers these dates to be different. Similarly, values that are formatted differently are considered to be different. So $1,209.32 is not the same as 1209.32. Therefore, you might want to apply formatting to entire columns to ensure that duplicate rows are not overlooked just because of a formatting difference.

Identifying duplicate rows

If you would like to *identify* duplicate rows so you can examine them without automatically deleting them, here's another method. Unlike the technique described in the previous section, this method looks at actual values, not formatted values.

Create a formula to the right of your data that concatenates each of the cells to the left. The formulas below assume that the data is in columns A:F.

Enter this formula in cell G2:

```
=A2&B2&C2&D2&E2&F2
```

Add another formula in cell H2. This formula displays the number of times a value in column G occurs.

```
=COUNTIF(G:G,G2)
```

Copy these formulas down the column for each row of your data.

Column H displays the number of occurrences of that row. Unduplicated rows will display 1. Duplicated rows will display a number that corresponds to the number of times that row appears.

Figure 32.6 shows a simple example. If you don't care about a particular column, just omit it from the formula in column G. For example, if you want to find duplicates regardless of the Status column, just omit D2 from the concatenating formula.

Splitting text

When importing data, you might find that multiple values are imported into a single column. Figure 32.7 shows an example of this type of import problem.

FIGURE 32.6

Using formulas to identify duplicate rows.

	A	B	C	D	E	F	G	H
1	First	Last	State	Status	Member No.	Joined		
2	Elvira	Taylor	CA	Active	10-9730	10/13/2010	ElviraTaylorCAActive10-973040464	1
3	Marva	Allen	CA	Active	11-1438	6/7/2012	MarvaAllenCAActive11-143841067	1
4	Chrystal	Massey	CA	Active	22-8257	2/24/2011	ChrystalMasseyCAActive22-825740598	2
5	Jamie	Dickerson	OR	Active	11-6587	12/20/2012	JamieDickersonORActive11-658741263	1
6	Margarita	Clark	WA	Inactive	14-1270	8/7/2009	MargaritaClarkWAInactive14-127040032	1
7	Deanne	Elliott	WA	Active	14-3518	10/7/2010	DeanneElliottWAActive14-351840458	1
8	Marilyn	Smith	UT	Active	15-1815	12/31/2010	MarilynSmithUTActive15-181540543	1
9	Lucille	Fisher	OR	Active	15-5323	11/18/2008	LucilleFisherORActive15-532339770	1
10	Sharon	Mitchell	OR	Active	16-4523	9/8/2009	SharonMitchellORActive16-452340064	1
11	Linda	Johnson	AZ	Active	16-6377	5/29/2010	LindaJohnsonAZActive16-637740327	1
12	Rosemary	Ross	CO	Active	16-8075	3/16/2012	RosemaryRossCOActive16-807540984	1
13	Deborah	Alexander	WA	Inactive	25-3921	11/15/2008	DeborahAlexanderWAInactive25-39213976	2
14	Lucia	Tucker	OR	Active	17-8198	10/9/2008	LuciaTuckerORActive17-819839730	1
15	Vicky	Scott	CA	Active	18-4433	11/15/2011	VickyScottCAActive18-443340862	1
16	Helen	Long	UT	Active	18-7754	4/22/2009	HelenLongUTActive18-775439925	1
17	Eliza	Gonzalez	AZ	Active	18-8608	9/29/2011	ElizaGonzalezAZActive18-860840815	1
18	Shannon	Young	OR	Active	19-8296	8/27/2008	ShannonYoungORActive19-829639687	1
19	Charlotte	Baker	CA	Active	21-5865	4/6/2011	CharlotteBakerCAActive21-586540639	1
20	Chrystal	Massey	CA	Active	22-8257	2/24/2011	ChrystalMasseyCAActive22-825740598	2
21	Barbara	Hill	AZ	Active	22-9506	8/17/2009	BarbaraHillAZActive22-950640042	1

Sheet1

FIGURE 32.7

The imported data was put in one column, rather than multiple columns.

	A	B	C
1	January 194 118 75 117 76 77 97 70 25 225		
2	February 112 211 74 71 139 62 145 144 200 28		
3	March 181 67 213 172 76 122 180 220 158 53		
4	April 139 63 185 206 205 126 134 119 164 52		
5	May 213 54 120 177 75 162 186 150 210 125		
6	June 70 24 167 207 170 174 204 185 190 195		
7	July 123 115 212 212 63 222 211 40 104 187		
8	August 110 186 58 199 119 67 166 198 110 135		
9	September 148 201 211 204 161 119 208 86 215 162		
10	October 29 59 31 190 30 67 86 97 77 49		
11	November 31 46 143 218 93 202 191 78 101 200		
12	December 84 98 107 189 133 29 77 215 109 69		
13			
14			

monthlydata

TIP

I used a fixed-width font (Courier New) to display the data in Figure 32.7. With the default font, it was not apparent that the data lined up nicely in fixed-width columns.

If the text is all the same length (as in the example), you might be able to write a series of formulas that extract the information to separate columns. The `LEFT`, `RIGHT`, and `MID` functions are useful for this task.

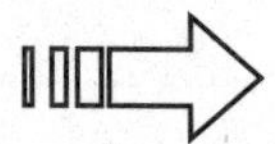

See Chapter 11 for examples of formulas that extract characters from text.

You should also be aware that Excel offers two non-formula methods to assist in splitting data so it occupies multiple columns: Text to Columns and Flash Fill.

Using Text to Columns

The Text to Columns command can parse strings into their component parts.

First, make sure that the column that contains the data to be split up has enough empty columns to the right to accommodate the extracted data. Then select the data to be parsed and choose Data ➪ Data Tools ➪ Text to Columns. Excel displays the Convert Text to Columns Wizard, which consists of a series of dialog boxes that walk you through the steps to convert a single column of data into multiple columns. Figure 32.8 shows the initial step, in which you choose the type of data:

FIGURE 32.8

The first dialog box in the Convert Text to Columns Wizard.

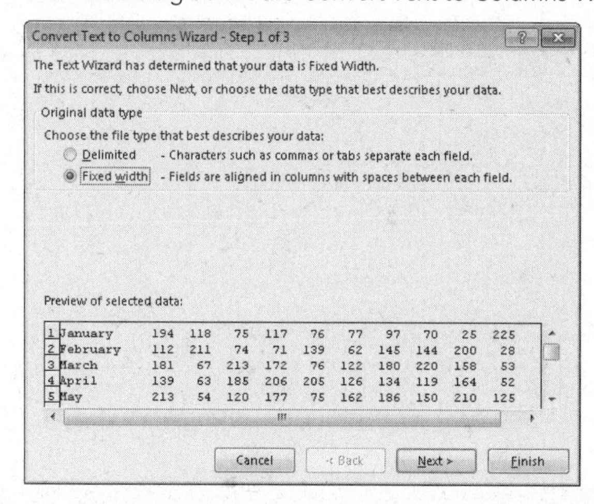

- **Delimited:** The data to be split is separated by delimiters such as commas, spaces, slashes, or other characters.
- **Fixed Width:** Each component occupies exactly the same number of characters.

Make your choice and click Next to move on to Step 2, which depends on the choice you made in Step 1.

If you're working with delimited data, specify the delimiting character or characters. You'll see a preview of the result. If you're working with fixed-width data, specify the column breaks directly in the preview window.

When you're satisfied with the column breaks, click Next to move to Step 3. In this step you can click a column in the preview window and specify general formatting for the column. Click Finish, and Excel splits the data as specified.

Using Flash Fill

The Text to Columns Wizard works well for many types of data. But sometimes you'll encounter data that can't be parsed by that wizard. For example, the Text to Columns Wizard is useless if you have variable-width data that doesn't have delimiters. In such a case, the Flash Fill feature might save the day. But keep in mind that Flash Fill works successfully only when the data is *very* consistent.

New Feature

Flash Fill is a new feature in Excel 2013.

Flash Fill uses pattern recognition to extract data (and also concatenate data). Just enter a few examples in a column that's adjacent to the data, and choose Data ➪ Data Tools ➪ Flash Fill (or press Ctrl + E). Excel analyzes the examples and attempts to fill in the remaining cells. If Excel didn't recognize the pattern you had in mind, press Ctrl + Z, add another example or two, and try again.

Figure 32.9 shows a worksheet with some text in a single column. The goal is to extract the number from each cell and put it into a separate cell. The Text to Columns Wizard can't do it because the space delimiters aren't consistent. It might be possible to write an array formula, but it would be very complicated.

FIGURE 32.9

The goal is to extract the numbers in column A.

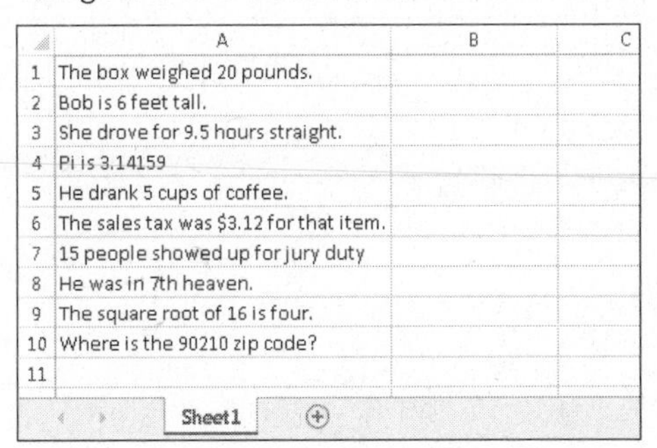

	A	B	C
1	The box weighed 20 pounds.		
2	Bob is 6 feet tall.		
3	She drove for 9.5 hours straight.		
4	Pi is 3.14159		
5	He drank 5 cups of coffee.		
6	The sales tax was $3.12 for that item.		
7	15 people showed up for jury duty		
8	He was in 7th heaven.		
9	The square root of 16 is four.		
10	Where is the 90210 zip code?		
11			

Sheet1

ON THE WEB

This workbook, which also includes other Flash Fill examples, is available on this book's website. The filename is `flash fill demo.xlsx`.

To try using Flash Fill, activate cell B1 and type the first number (20). Move to B2, and type the second number (6). Can Flash Fill identify the remaining numbers and fill them in? Choose Data ➪ Data Tools ➪ Flash Fill (or press Ctrl+E) and Excel fills in the remaining cells in a flash. Figure 32.10 shows the result.

FIGURE 32.10

Using manually entered examples in B1 and B2, Excel makes some incorrect guesses.

	A	B	C
1	The box weighed 20 pounds.	20	
2	Bob is 6 feet tall.	6	
3	She drove for 9.5 hours straight.	5	
4	Pi is 3.14159	14159	
5	He drank 5 cups of coffee.	5	
6	The sales tax was $3.12 for that item.	12	
7	15 people showed up for jury duty	15	
8	He was in 7th heaven.	7	
9	The square root of 16 is four.	16	
10	Where is the 90210 zip code?	90210	
11			

Sheet1

As you see, Excel identified most of the values. Accuracy increases if you provide more examples. For example, provide an example of a decimal number. Delete the suggested values, enter **3.12** in cell B6, and press Ctrl+E. This time, Excel gets them all correct (see Figure 32.11).

FIGURE 32.11

After you enter an example of a decimal number, Excel gets them all correct.

	A	B	C
1	The box weighed 20 pounds.	20	
2	Bob is 6 feet tall.	6	
3	She drove for 9.5 hours straight.	9.5	
4	Pi is 3.14159	3.14159	
5	He drank 5 cups of coffee.	5	
6	The sales tax was $3.12 for that item.	3.12	
7	15 people showed up for jury duty	15	
8	He was in 7th heaven.	7	
9	The square root of 16 is four.	16	
10	Where is the 90210 zip code?	90210	
11			

Sheet1

This simple example demonstrates two important points:

- You must examine your data very carefully after using Flash Fill. Just because the first few rows are correct, you can't assume that Flash Fill worked correctly for all rows.
- Flash Fill increases accuracy when you provide more examples.

Figure 32.12 shows another example, names in column A. The goal is to extract the first, last, and middle name (if it has one). In column B Excel successfully gets all the first names using only two examples (Mark and Tim). Plus, it successfully extracted all the last names (column C), using Russell and Colman. Extracting the middle names or initials (column D) eluded me until I provided examples that included a space on either side of the middle name).

FIGURE 32.12

Using Flash Fill to split names.

	A	B	C	D	E
1	Mark Russell	Mark	Russell		
2	Tim Colman	Tim	Colman		
3	Sam Daniel Bains	Sam	Bains	Daniel	
4	Fred James Foster	Fred	Foster	James	
5	James J. Wehr	James	Wehr	J.	
6	Mitch Nicholls	Mitch	Nicholls		
7	Neal McCaslin	Neal	McCaslin		
8	Ned Poulakis	Ned	Poulakis		
9	Paul T. Wingfield	Paul	Wingfield	T.	
10	Peter Gans	Peter	Gans		
11	Ron E. Hoffman	Ron	Hoffman	E.	
12	Julia Hayes	Julia	Hayes		
13	Richard P Light	Richard	Light	P	
14	Ray Walker	Ray	Walker		
15	Robert F. Mahaney	Robert	Mahaney	F.	
16	Robert Fist	Robert	Fist		
17					

Sheet1 Sheet2

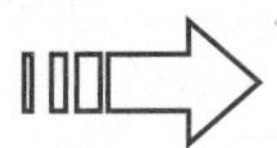

See Chapter 11 for a reliable formula-based solution for splitting names.

To summarize, Excel's new Flash Fill is an interesting idea, but it seems to work reliably only if the data is very consistent. Even when you think it worked correctly, make sure you examine the results carefully. And think twice before trusting it with important data. There's no way to document how the data was extracted. But the main limitation is that (unlike formulas) Flash Fill is not a dynamic technique. If your data changes, the flash-filled column does not update.

NOTE

You can also use the Flash Fill feature to create new data from multiple columns. Just provide a few examples of how you want the data combined, and Excel will figure out the pattern and fill in the column. Using Flash Fill to *create* data seems to work much better than using it to *extract* data. But then again, it's also easier to create formulas to create data from existing columns.

Changing the case of text

Often, you'll want to make text in a column consistent, in terms of case. Excel provides no direct way to change the case of text, but it's easy to do with formulas (see the sidebar "Transforming Data with Formulas").

The three relevant functions are

- `UPPER`: Converts the text to ALL UPPERCASE.
- `LOWER`: Converts the text to all lowercase.
- `PROPER`: Converts the text to Proper Case (the first letter in each word is capitalized, as in a proper name).

These functions are quite straightforward. They operate only on alphabetic characters and just ignore all other characters and return them unchanged.

If you use the `PROPER` function, you'll probably need to do some additional cleanup to handle exceptions. Following are examples of transformations that you probably would consider incorrect:

- The letter following an apostrophe is always capitalized (for example, Don'T). This is done, apparently, to handle names like O'Reilly.
- The `PROPER` function doesn't handle names with an embedded capital letter, such as McDonald.
- "Minor" words such as *and* and *the* are always capitalized. For example, some people would prefer that the fourth word in *United States Of America* not be capitalized.

Often, you can correct some of these problems by using Find and Replace.

Removing extra spaces

It's usually a good idea to ensure that data doesn't have extra spaces. It's impossible to spot a space character at the end of a text string. Extra spaces can cause lots of problems, especially when you need to compare text strings. The text *July* is not the same as the text *July* with a space appended to the end. The first is four characters long, and the second is five characters long.

Transforming Data with Formulas

Many of the data cleanup examples in this chapter describe how to use formulas and functions to transform data in some way. For example, you can use the `UPPER` function to transform text into uppercase. When the data is transformed, you'll have two columns: the original data and the transformed data. Almost always you'll want to replace the original data with the transformed data. Here's how to do it:

1. **Insert a new temporary column for formulas to transform the original data.**
2. **Create your formulas in the temporary column, and make sure that the formulas do what they were intended to do.**
3. **Select the formula cells.**
4. **Choose Home ⇨ Clipboard ⇨ Copy (or press Ctrl+C).**
5. **Select the original data cells.**
6. **Choose Home ⇨ Clipboard ⇨ Paste ⇨ Values (V).**

This procedure replaces the original data with the transformed data. Then you can delete the temporary column that holds the formulas.

Create a formula that uses the `TRIM` function to remove all leading and trailing spaces, and also replace multiple spaces with a single space. This example uses the `TRIM` function. The formula returns `Fourth Quarter Earnings` (with no excess spaces):

```
=TRIM("    Fourth     Quarter      Earnings      ")
```

Data that is imported from a web page often contains a different type of space: a non-breaking space, indicated by ` ` in HTML code. In Excel, this character can be generated by this formula:

```
=CHAR(160)
```

You can use a formula like this to replace those spaces with normal spaces:

```
=SUBSTITUTE(A2,CHAR(160)," ")
```

Or use this formula to replace the non-breaking space character with normal spaces and also remove excess spaces:

```
=TRIM(SUBSTITUTE(A2,CHAR(160)," "))
```

Removing strange characters

Often, data imported into an Excel worksheet contains strange (sometimes unprintable) characters. You can use the `CLEAN` function to remove all nonprinting characters from a string. If the data is in cell A2, this formula will do the job:

```
=CLEAN(A2)
```

NOTE

The CLEAN function can miss some non-printing Unicode characters. It's programmed to remove the first 32 nonprinting characters in the 7-bit ASCII code. Consult the Excel Help system for information on how to remove the non-printing Unicode characters (search Help for the CLEAN function).

Converting values

In some cases you may need to convert values from one system to another. For example, you may import a file that has values in fluid ounces, and they need to be expressed in milliliters. Excel's handy CONVERT function can perform that and many other conversions.

If cell A2 contains a value in ounces, the following formula converts it to milliliters:

```
=CONVERT(A2,"oz","ml")
```

This function is extremely versatile and can handle most common measurement units in the following categories: weight and mass, distance, time, pressure, force, energy, power, magnetism, temperature, volume, liquid, area, bits and bytes, and speed.

See Chapter 16 for more examples that use the CONVERT function.

Excel can also convert between number bases. You may import a file that contains hexadecimal values, and you need to convert them to decimal. Use the HEX2DEC function to perform this conversion. For example, the following formula returns 1,279, the decimal equivalent of its hex argument.

```
=HEX2DEC("4FF")
```

Excel can also convert from binary to decimal (BIN2DEC) and from octal to decimal (OCT2DEC).

Functions that convert from decimal to another number base are: DEC2HEX, DEC2BIN, and DEC2OCT.

NEW FEATURE

Excel 2013 includes a new function, BASE, that converts a decimal number to any number base. Note that there is not a function that works in the opposite direction. Excel does not provide a function that converts any number base to decimal. You're limited to binary, octal, and hexadecimal.

Classifying values

Often, you may have values that need to be classified into a group. For example, if you have ages of people, you might want to classify them into groups such as 17 or younger, 18–24, 25–34, and so on.

The easiest way to perform this classification is with a lookup table. Figure 32.13 shows ages in column A, and classifications in column B. Column B uses the lookup table in D2:E9. The formula in cell B2 is

```
=VLOOKUP(A2,$D$2:$E$9,2)
```


FIGURE 32.13

Using a lookup table to classify ages into age ranges.

	A	B	C	D	E
1	Age	Classification			
2	24	18-24		0	<18
3	42	35-44		18	18-24
4	44	35-44		25	25-34
5	17	<18		35	35-44
6	72	65-74		45	45-54
7	51	45-54		55	55-64
8	40	35-44		65	65-74
9	51	45-54		75	75+
10	34	25-34			
11	51	45-54			
12	81	75+			
13	18	18-24			
14	46	45-54			
15	60	55-64			
16	32	25-34			
17					
18					

Sheet1 Sheet2

This formula was copied to the cells below.

You can also use a lookup table for non-numeric data. Figure 32.14 shows a lookup table that is used to assign a region to a state.

FIGURE 32.14

Using a lookup table to assign a region for a state.

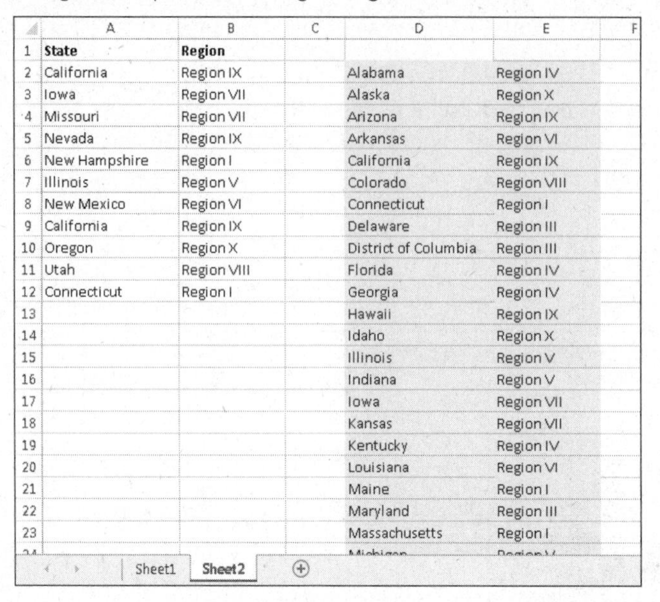

	A	B	C	D	E
1	**State**	**Region**			
2	California	Region IX		Alabama	Region IV
3	Iowa	Region VII		Alaska	Region X
4	Missouri	Region VII		Arizona	Region IX
5	Nevada	Region IX		Arkansas	Region VI
6	New Hampshire	Region I		California	Region IX
7	Illinois	Region V		Colorado	Region VIII
8	New Mexico	Region VI		Connecticut	Region I
9	California	Region IX		Delaware	Region III
10	Oregon	Region X		District of Columbia	Region III
11	Utah	Region VIII		Florida	Region IV
12	Connecticut	Region I		Georgia	Region IV
13				Hawaii	Region IX
14				Idaho	Region X
15				Illinois	Region V
16				Indiana	Region V
17				Iowa	Region VII
18				Kansas	Region VII
19				Kentucky	Region IV
20				Louisiana	Region VI
21				Maine	Region I
22				Maryland	Region III
23				Massachusetts	Region I

Sheet1 | Sheet2

The two-column lookup table is in the range D2:E52. The formula in cell B2, which was copied to the cells below is

```
=VLOOKUP(A2,$D$2:$E$52,2,FALSE)
```

TIP

A side-benefit is that the `VLOOKUP` function will return false if an exact match is not found – a good way to spot misspelled states. Using `FALSE` as the last argument in the function indicates than exact match is required.

Joining columns

To combine data in two more columns, you can usually use the concatenation operator (&) in a formula. For example, the following formula combines the contents of cells A1, B1, and C1:

```
=A1&B1&C1
```

Often, you'll need to insert spaces between the cells — for example, if the columns contain a title, first name, and last name. Concatenating using the formulas above would produce something like *Mr.ThomasJones*. To add spaces (to produce *Mr. Thomas Jones*), modify the formula:

```
=A1&" "&B1&" "&C1
```

You can also use the new Flash Fill feature to join columns without using formulas. Just provide an example or two in an adjacent column, and press Ctrl+E.

Rearranging columns

If you need to rearrange the columns in a worksheet, you could insert a blank column and then drag another column into the new blank column. But then the moved column leaves a gap, which you need to delete.

Here's an easier way:

1. **Click the column header of the column you want to move.**
2. **Choose Home ➪ Clipboard ➪ Cut.**
3. **Click the column header to the right of where you want the column to go.**
4. **Right-click and choose Insert Cut Cells from the shortcut menu.**

Repeat these steps until the columns are in the order you want.

Randomizing the rows

If you need to arrange the rows in random order, here's a quick way to do it. In the column to the right of the data, insert this formula into the first cell and copy it down:

```
=RAND()
```

Then sort the data using this column. The rows will be in random order, and you can delete the column.

Extracting a filename from a URL

In some cases, you may have a list of URLs and need to extract only the filename. The following formula returns the filename from a URL. Assume cell A2 contains this URL:

```
http://example.com/assets/images/horse.jpg
```

The following formula returns `horse.jpg`.

```
=RIGHT(A2,LEN(A2)-FIND("*",SUBSTITUTE(A2,"/","*",LEN(A2)-
   LEN(SUBSTITUTE(A2,"/","")))))
```

This formula returns all text that follows the last slash character. If cell A2 doesn't contain a slash character, the formula returns an error.

To extract the URL without the filename, use this formula:

```
=LEFT(A2,FIND("*",SUBSTITUTE(A2,"/","*",LEN(A2)-LEN(SUBSTITUTE(A2,"/","")))))
```

NOTE

This type of extraction is a good use for the new Flash Fill feature (see "Splitting Text," earlier in this chapter).

Matching text in a list

You may have some data that you need to check against another list. For example, you may want to identify the data rows in which data in a particular column appears in a different list. Figure 32.15 shows a simple example. The data is in columns A:C. The goal is to identify the rows in which the Member Num appears in the Resigned Members list, in column F. These rows can then be deleted.

FIGURE 32.15

The goal is to identify member numbers that are in the resigned members list in column F.

	A	B	C	D	E	F	G
1	Name	Member Num	State			Resigned Members	
2	Alice Jones	39-5954	AZ			11-6587	
3	Jennifer Green	46-2010	UT			16-4523	
4	Rhoda Davis	93-1595	AZ			16-8075	
5	Rita Morris	35-5121	WA			21-5865	
6	Debra Hopkins	91-2687	UT			23-5078	
7	Marcela Garcia	93-4652	AZ	Resigned		36-9582	
8	Viola Jenkins	74-4701	CA			39-2953	
9	Charlotte Baker	21-5865	CA	Resigned		40-8172	
10	Angela Gonzalez	79-8010	AZ			42-6818	
11	Michelle Young	93-7380	WA			45-8343	
12	Linda Johnson	16-6377	AZ			58-2363	
13	Annette Williamson	94-2032	CA			58-8192	
14	Ruth Mckinney	58-8192	WA	Resigned		65-3095	
15	Mary Gibson	27-3637	CO			67-5960	
16	Christine Warren	81-8640	AZ			78-4209	
17	Stacey Martin	82-8709	CO			78-8201	
18	Shirley Clarke	99-6607	AZ			81-1158	
19	Rosemary Ross	16-8075	CO	Resigned		86-7291	
20	Waltraud Adams	55-5367	AZ			87-2700	
21	Nancy Martinez	82-4869	CA			93-4652	
22	Dominique Jackson	28-9592	AZ			97-2586	
23	Deanne Elliott	14-3518	WA				
24	Vanessa Hill	31-8125	UT				

Sheet2

ON THE WEB

This workbook, named `match names.xlsx`, is available on this book's website.

Here's a formula entered in cell D2, and copied down that will do the job:

```
=IF(COUNTIF($F$2:$F$22,B2)>0,"Resigned","" )
```

This formula displays the word *Resigned* if the Member Num in column B is found in the Resigned Members list. If the Member number is not found, it returns an empty string. If the list is sorted by column D, the rows for all resigned members will appear together and can be quickly deleted.

This technique can be adapted to other types of list-matching tasks.

Changing vertical data to horizontal data

Figure 32.16 shows a common type of data layout that you might see when importing a file. Each record consists of three consecutive cells in a single column: Name, Department, and Location. The goal is to convert this data so each record appears in three columns.

FIGURE 32.16

Vertical data that needs to be converted to three columns.

	A	B
1	Lori Howard	
2	Accounting	
3	Main Office	
4	Jacqueline Espinoza	
5	Sales	
6	West Branch	
7	Jose Collins	
8	Accounting	
9	Main Office	
10	Bernice Ryan	
11	Sales	
12	East Branch	
13	Diana Brown	
14	Accounting	
15	West Branch	
16	Jay J. Davis	
17	Research	
18	Main Office	
19	Shandi Johnson	
20	Accounting	
21	Main Office	
22		

There are several ways to convert this type of data, but here's a method that's fairly easy. It requires a small amount of setup, but the work is done with a single formula, which is copied to a range.

Start by creating some numeric vertical and horizontal "headers," as shown in Figure 32.17. Column C contains numbers that correspond to the first row of each data item (in this case, the Name). In this example, I put the following values in column C: 1, 4, 7, 10, 13, 16, and 19. You can use a simple formula to generate this series of numbers.

FIGURE 32.17

Headers that are used to convert the vertical data into rows.

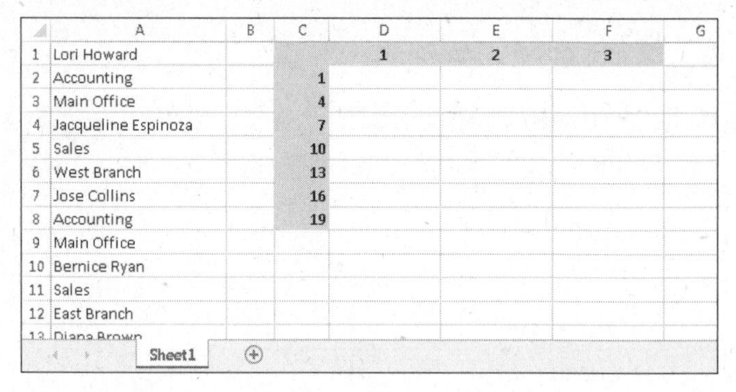

	A	B	C	D	E	F	G
1	Lori Howard			1	2	3	
2	Accounting		1				
3	Main Office		4				
4	Jacqueline Espinoza		7				
5	Sales		10				
6	West Branch		13				
7	Jose Collins		16				
8	Accounting		19				
9	Main Office						
10	Bernice Ryan						
11	Sales						
12	East Branch						
13	Diana Brown						

The horizontal range of headers consists of consecutive integers, starting with 1. In this example, each record contains three cells of data, so the horizontal header contains 1, 2, and 3.

ON THE WEB

This workbook, named `vertical data.xlsx`, is available on this book's website.

And now, the formula, which goes in cell D2:

```
=OFFSET($A$1,$C2+D$1-2,0)
```

Copy this formula across to the next two columns and down to the next six rows. The result is shown in Figure 32.18.

FIGURE 32.18

A single formula transforms the vertical data into rows.

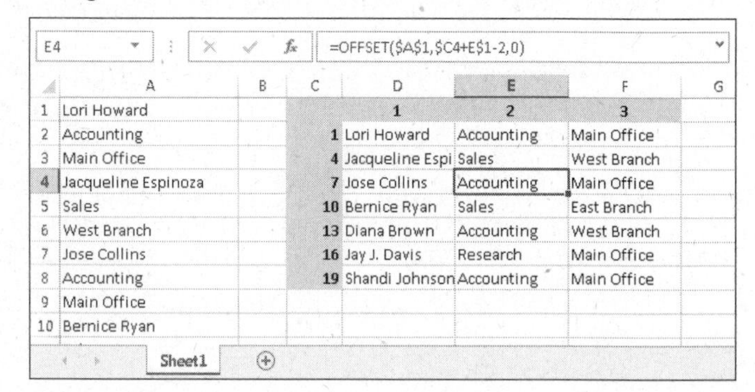

E4 =OFFSET($A$1,$C4+E$1-2,0)

	A	B	C	D	E	F	G
1	Lori Howard			1	2	3	
2	Accounting		1	Lori Howard	Accounting	Main Office	
3	Main Office		4	Jacqueline Espi	Sales	West Branch	
4	Jacqueline Espinoza		7	Jose Collins	Accounting	Main Office	
5	Sales		10	Bernice Ryan	Sales	East Branch	
6	West Branch		13	Diana Brown	Accounting	West Branch	
7	Jose Collins		16	Jay J. Davis	Research	Main Office	
8	Accounting		19	Shandi Johnson	Accounting	Main Office	
9	Main Office						
10	Bernice Ryan						

You can easily adapt this technique to work with vertical data that contains a different number of rows. For example, if each record contained ten rows of data, the column C header values would be 1, 11, 21, 31, and so on. The horizontal headers would consist of values 1 through 10 rather than 1 through 3.

Notice that the formula uses an absolute reference to cell A1. That reference won't change when the formula is copied, so all the formulas use cell A1 as the base. If the data begins in a different cell, change `$A$1` to the address of the first cell.

The formula also uses "mixed" referencing in the second argument of the `OFFSET` function. The C2 reference has a dollar sign in front of C, so column C is the absolute part of the reference. In the D1 reference, the dollar sign is before the 1, so row 1 is the absolute part of the reference.

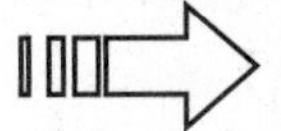

See Chapter 10 for more about using mixed references in formulas.

Filling gaps in an imported report

When you import data, you can sometimes end up with a worksheet that looks something like the one shown in Figure 32.19. This type of report formatting is common. As you can see, an entry in column A applies to several rows of data. If you sort this type of list, the missing data messes things up, and you can no longer tell who sold what when.

FIGURE 32.19

This report contains gaps in the Sales Rep column.

	A	B	C	D	E
1					
2	**Sales Rep**	**Month**	**Units Sold**	**Amount**	
3	Jane	Jan	182	$15,101	
4		Feb	3350	$34,230	
5		Mar	114	$9,033	
6	George	Jan	135	$8,054	
7		Feb	401	$9,322	
8		Mar	357	$32,143	
9	Beth	Jan	509	$29,239	
10		Feb	414	$38,993	
11		Mar	53	$309	
12	Dan	Jan	323	$9,092	
13		Feb	283	$12,332	
14		Mar	401	$32,933	
15					
16					

Sheet1

If the report is small, you can enter the missing cell values manually or by using a series of Home ➪ Editing ➪ Fill ➪ Down commands (or the Ctrl + D shortcut). But if you have a large list that's in this format, here's a better way:

1. **Select the range that has the gaps (A3:A14, in this example).**
2. **Choose Home ➪ Editing ➪ Find & Select ➪ Go to Special.** The Go to Special dialog box appears.
3. **Select the Blanks option and click OK.** This action selects the blank cells in the original selection.
4. **In the formula bar, type an equal sign (=) followed by the address of the first cell with an entry in the column (=A3, in this example), and press Ctrl+Enter.**
5. **Reselect the original range and press Ctrl+C to copy the selection.**
6. **Choose Home ➪ Clipboard ➪ Paste ➪ Paste Values to convert the formulas to values.**

After you complete these steps, the gaps are filled in with the correct information, and your worksheet looks similar to the one shown in Figure 32.20.

FIGURE 32.20

The gaps are gone, and this list can now be sorted.

	A	B	C	D	E
1					
2	Sales Rep	Month	Units Sold	Amount	
3	Jane	Jan	182	$15,101	
4	Jane	Feb	3350	$34,230	
5	Jane	Mar	114	$9,033	
6	George	Jan	135	$8,054	
7	George	Feb	401	$9,322	
8	George	Mar	357	$32,143	
9	Beth	Jan	509	$29,239	
10	Beth	Feb	414	$38,993	
11	Beth	Mar	53	$309	
12	Dan	Jan	323	$9,092	
13	Dan	Feb	283	$12,332	
14	Dan	Mar	401	$32,933	
15					

Sheet1

Checking spelling

If you use a word-processing program, you probably take advantage of its spell checker feature. Spelling mistakes can be embarrassing when they appear in a text document, but they can cause serious problems with they occur within your data. For example, if you tabulate data by month, a misspelled month name will make it appear that a year has 13 months.

To access the Excel spell checker, choose Review ⇨ Proofing ⇨ Spelling, or press F7. To check the spelling in just a particular range, select the range before you activate the spell checker.

If the spell checker finds any words it doesn't recognize as correct, it displays the Spelling dialog box. The options are fairly self-explanatory.

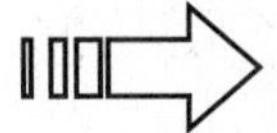

See Chapter 31 for more about the Spelling dialog box.

Replacing or removing text in cells

You may need to systematically replace (or remove) certain characters in a column of data. For example, you may need to replace all backslash characters with forward slash characters. In many cases, you can use Excel's Find and Replace dialog box to accomplish this task. To remove text using the Find and Replace dialog box, just leave the Replace With field empty.

In other situations, you may need a formula-based solution. Consider the data shown in Figure 32.21. The goal is to replace the second hyphen character with a colon. Using Find and Replace wouldn't work because there isn't any way to specify that only the second hyphen should be replaced.

FIGURE 32.21

To replace only the second hyphen in these cells, Find and Replace is not an option.

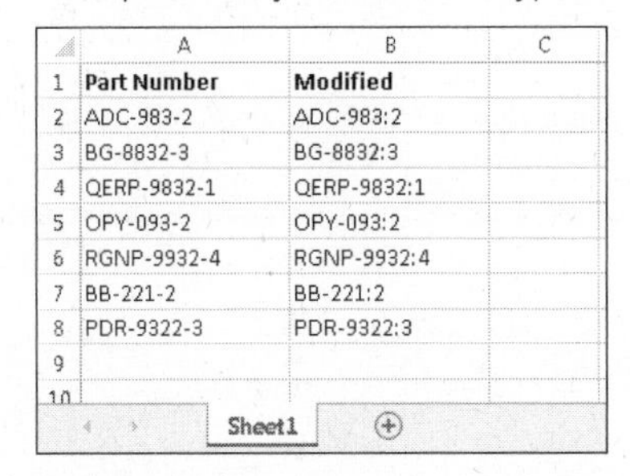

	A	B	C
1	**Part Number**	**Modified**	
2	ADC-983-2	ADC-983:2	
3	BG-8832-3	BG-8832:3	
4	QERP-9832-1	QERP-9832:1	
5	OPY-093-2	OPY-093:2	
6	RGNP-9932-4	RGNP-9932:4	
7	BB-221-2	BB-221:2	
8	PDR-9322-3	PDR-9322:3	
9			
10			

Sheet1

In this case, the solution is a fairly simple formula that replaces the second occurrence of a hyphen with a colon:

```
=SUBSTITUTE(A2,"-",":",2)
```

To remove the second occurrence of a hyphen, just omit the third argument for the SUBSTITUTE function:

```
=SUBSTITUTE(A2,"-",,2)
```

This is another example where Flash Fill can also do the job.

Try PUP for Data Cleaning

My Power Utility Pak add-in consists of more than 50 general-purpose Excel utilities — including several tools that can assist you when cleaning up data. The one I use most often is called Text Tools.

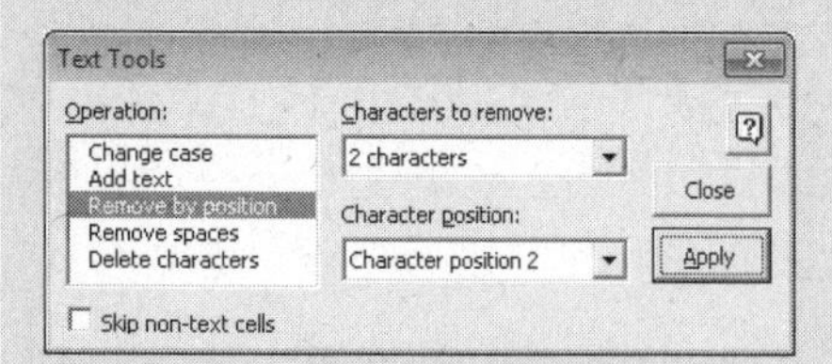

Text Tools has options to

- **Change the case of text:** Uppercase, lowercase, proper case, sentence case, and toggle case.
- **Add text to cells:** Specify text to add before the first character, after the last character, or after a specific character number.
- **Remove by position:** Specify the number of characters to remove and the location within the cell.
- **Remove spaces:** Leading spaces, trailing spaces, excess spaces, or all spaces.
- **Delete characters:** Non-printing, alpha, non-alpha, numeric, or non-numeric.

Text Tools is a stay-on top dialog box, so it's always handy. It operates directly on the text, so no formulas are required. It's fast, and it even has an undo feature.

You can download a free 30-day trial from my website (www.spreadsheetpage.com). Or use the coupon in the back of the book to purchase a discounted license.

Note

If you've worked with programming languages, you may be familiar with the concept of regular expressions. A *regular expression* is a way to match strings of text using very concise (and often confusing) codes. Excel doesn't support regular expressions, but if you search the web you'll find ways to incorporate regular expressions in VBA, plus a few add-ins that provide this feature in the workbook environment.

Adding text to cells

If you need to add text to a cell, one solution is to use a new column of formulas. Here are some examples:

- The following formula adds: "ID:" and a space to the beginning of a cell:

  ```
  ="ID: "&A2
  ```

- The following formula adds ".mp3" to the end of a cell:

  ```
  =A2&".mp3"
  ```

- The following formula inserts a hyphen after the third character in a cell:

  ```
  =LEFT(A2,3)&"-"&RIGHT(A2,LEN(A2)-3)
  ```

You can also use the new Flash Fill feature to add text to cells.

Fixing trailing minus signs

Imported data sometimes displays negative values with a trailing minus sign. For example, a negative value may appear as **3,498–** rather than the more common **–3,498**. Excel does not convert these values. In fact, it considers them to be non-numeric text.

The solution is so simple it may even surprise you:

1. **Select the data that has the trailing minus signs.** The selection can also include positive values.
2. **Choose Data⇨Data Tools⇨Text to Columns.** The Text to Columns dialog box appears.
3. **Click Finish.**

This procedure works because of a default setting in the Advanced Text Import Settings dialog box (which you don't even see, normally). To display this dialog box, shown in Figure 32.22, go to Step 3 in the Text to Columns Wizard dialog box and click Advanced.

FIGURE 32.22

The Trailing Minus for Negative Numbers option makes it very easy to fix trailing minus signs in a range of data.

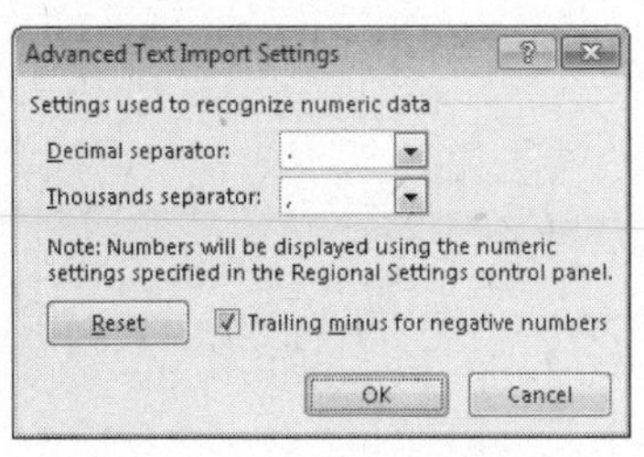

A Data Cleaning Checklist

This section contains a list of items that could cause problems with data. Not all these are relevant to every set of data.

- Does each column have a unique and descriptive header?
- Is each column of data formatted consistently?
- Did you check for duplicate or missing rows?
- For text data, are the words consistent in terms of case?
- Did you check for spelling errors?
- Does the data contain any extra spaces?
- Are the columns arranged in the proper (or logical) order?
- Are any cells blank that shouldn't be blank?
- Did you correct any trailing minus signs?
- Are the columns wide enough to display all data?

Exporting Data

The chapter begins with a section on importing data, so it's only appropriate to end it with a discussion of exporting data to a file that's not a standard Excel file.

Exporting to a text file

When you choose File⇨Save as, the Save As dialog box lets you choose from a variety of text file formats. The three types are:

- **CSV:** Comma separated value files
- **TXT:** Tab delimited files
- **PRN:** Formatted text

I discuss these file types in the sections that follow.

CSV files

When you export a worksheet to a CSV file, the data is saved as displayed. In other words, if a cell contains 12.8312344 but is formatted to display with two decimal places, the value will be saved as 12.83.

Cells are delimited with a comma character, and rows are delimited with a carriage return and line feed.

NOTE

If you export a file using the Mac variant, rows are delimited with a carriage return only (no line feed character).

Note that if a cell contains a comma, the cell value is saved within quotation marks. If a cell contains a quotation mark character, that character appears twice.

TXT files

Exporting a workbook to a TXT file is almost identical to the CSV file format described earlier. The only difference is that cells are separated by a tab character rather than a comma.

If your worksheet contains any Unicode characters, you should export the file using the Unicode variant. Otherwise, Unicode characters will be saved as question mark characters.

PRN files

A PRN file is very much like a printed image of the worksheet. The cells are separated by multiple space characters. Also, a line is limited to 240 characters. If a line exceeds that limit, the remainder appears on the next line. PRN files are rarely used.

Exporting to other file formats

Excel also lets you save your work in several other formats:

- **Data Interchange Format:** These files have a DIF extension. Not used very often.
- **Symbolic Link:** These files have a SYLK extension. Not used very often.
- **Portable Document Format:** These files have a PDF extension. This is a very common "read-only" file format.
- **XML Paper Specification Document:** These files have an XPS extension. Microsoft's alternative to PDF files. Not used very often.
- **Web Page:** These files have an HTM extension. Often, saving a file as a workbook will generate a directory of ancillary files required to render the page accurately.
- **OpenDocument Spreadsheet:** These files have an ODS extension. They're compatible with various open source spreadsheet programs.

CHAPTER 33

Introducing Pivot Tables

IN THIS CHAPTER

Understanding pivot tables

Identifying types of data appropriate for a pivot table

Getting clear on pivot table terminology

Creating pivot tables

Looking at pivot table examples that answer specific questions about data

The PivotTable feature is perhaps the most technologically sophisticated component in Excel. With only a few mouse clicks, you can slice and dice a data table in dozens of different ways and produce just about any type of summary you can think of.

If you haven't yet discovered the power of pivot tables, this chapter provides an introduction, and Chapter 34 continues with many examples that demonstrate how easy it is to create powerful data summaries using pivot tables.

About Pivot Tables

A *pivot table* is essentially a dynamic summary report generated from a database. The database can reside in a worksheet (in the form of a table) or in an external data file. A pivot table can help transform endless rows and columns of numbers into a meaningful presentation of the data — and do it so quickly you'll be amazed.

For example, a pivot table can create frequency distributions and cross-tabulations of several different data dimensions. In addition, you can display subtotals and any level of detail that you want.

Perhaps the most innovative aspect of a pivot table is its interactivity. After you create a pivot table, you can rearrange the information in almost any way imaginable and even insert special formulas that perform new calculations. You even can create post hoc groupings of summary items (for example, combine Northern Region totals with Western Region totals). And the icing on the cake: With a few mouse clicks, you can apply formatting to a pivot table to convert it into an attractive report.

One minor drawback to using a pivot table is that, unlike a formula-based summary report, a pivot table does not update automatically when you change information in the source data. This drawback doesn't pose a serious problem, however, because a single click of the Refresh button forces a pivot table to update itself with the latest data.

Pivot tables were introduced in Excel 97, and this feature improves with every new version of Excel. Unfortunately, many users avoid this feature because they think it's too complicated. My goal in this chapter is to dispel that myth.

A pivot table example

The best way to understand the concept of a pivot table is to see one. Start with Figure 33.1, which shows a portion of the data used in creating the pivot table in this chapter. This range happens to be in a table, but that's not a requirement for creating a pivot table.

FIGURE 33.1

This table is used to create a pivot table.

	A	B	C	D	E	F	G	H
1	Date	Weekday	Amount	AcctType	OpenedBy	Branch	Customer	
2	Nov-01	Friday	5,000	IRA	New Accts	Central	Existing	
3	Nov-01	Friday	14,571	CD	Teller	Central	New	
4	Nov-01	Friday	500	Checking	New Accts	Central	Existing	
5	Nov-01	Friday	15,000	CD	New Accts	Central	Existing	
6	Nov-01	Friday	4,623	Savings	New Accts	North County	Existing	
7	Nov-01	Friday	8,721	Savings	New Accts	Westside	New	
8	Nov-01	Friday	15,276	Savings	New Accts	North County	Existing	
9	Nov-01	Friday	5,000	Savings	New Accts	Westside	Existing	
10	Nov-01	Friday	15,759	CD	Teller	Westside	Existing	
11	Nov-01	Friday	12,000	CD	New Accts	Westside	Existing	
12	Nov-01	Friday	7,177	Savings	Teller	North County	Existing	
13	Nov-01	Friday	6,837	Savings	New Accts	Westside	Existing	
14	Nov-01	Friday	3,171	Checking	New Accts	Westside	Existing	
15	Nov-01	Friday	50,000	Savings	New Accts	Central	Existing	
16	Nov-01	Friday	4,690	Checking	New Accts	North County	New	
17	Nov-01	Friday	12,438	Checking	New Accts	Central	Existing	
18	Nov-01	Friday	5,000	Checking	New Accts	North County	Existing	
19	Nov-01	Friday	7,000	Savings	New Accts	North County	New	
20	Nov-01	Friday	11,957	Checking	New Accts	Central	Existing	
21	Nov-01	Friday	13,636	CD	New Accts	North County	Existing	
22	Nov-01	Friday	16,000	CD	New Accts	Central	New	
23	Nov-01	Friday	5,879	Checking	New Accts	Central	Existing	
24	Nov-01	Friday	4,000	Savings	New Accts	Central	Existing	
25	Nov-01	Friday	10,000	CD	Teller	North County	Existing	
26	Nov-01	Friday	7,427	Checking	New Accts	North County	Existing	
27	Nov-01	Friday	4,500	Checking	New Accts	North County	New	
28	Nov-01	Friday	12,962	Checking	Teller	Central	Existing	
29	Nov-01	Friday	500	Checking	New Accts	Central	New	
30	Nov-01	Friday	5,364	Checking	Teller	Central	New	
31	Nov-01	Friday	45,000	CD	Teller	North County	Existing	
32	Nov-01	Friday	14,867	Checking	Teller	North County	Existing	
33	Nov-01	Friday	13,061	Checking	Teller	Central	New	
34	Nov-01	Friday	11,779	CD	Teller	Central	New	
35	Nov-02	Saturday	4,995	Checking	New Accts	Central	New	

data | pt1 | pt2 | q1 | q2 | q3 | q4 | q5 | q6 | q7

This table consists of a month's worth of new account information for a three-branch bank. The table contains 712 rows, and each row represents a new account opened at the bank. The table has the following columns:

- The date the account was opened
- The day of the week the account was opened
- The opening amount
- The account type (CD, checking, savings, or IRA)
- Who opened the account (a teller or a new-account representative)
- The branch at which it was opened (Central, Westside, or North County)
- The type of customer (an existing customer or a new customer)

On the Web

This workbook, named `bank accounts.xlsx`, is available on this book's website.

The bank accounts database contains quite a bit of information. In its current form, though, the data doesn't reveal much. To make the data more useful, you need to summarize it. Summarizing a database is essentially the process of answering questions about the data. Following are a few questions that may be of interest to the bank's management:

- What is the daily total new deposit amount for each branch?
- Which day of the week accounts for the most deposits?
- How many accounts were opened at each branch, broken down by account type?
- What's the dollar distribution of the different account types?
- What types of accounts do tellers open most often?
- How does the Central branch compare with the other two branches?
- In which branch do tellers open the most checking accounts for new customers?

You can, of course, spend time sorting the data and creating formulas to answer these questions. But almost always, a pivot table is a better choice. Creating a pivot table takes only a few seconds, doesn't require a single formula, and produces a nice-looking report. In addition, pivot tables are much less prone to error than creating formulas. (Later in this chapter, you'll see several pivot tables that answer the preceding questions.)

Figure 33.2 shows a pivot table created from the bank data. This pivot table shows the amount of new deposits, broken down by branch and account type. This particular summary is one of dozens of summaries that you can produce from this data.

FIGURE 33.2

A simple pivot table.

	A	B	C	D	E	F
1						
2						
3	**Sum of Amount**	**AcctType**				
4	**Branch**	**CD**	**Checking**	**IRA**	**Savings**	**Grand Total**
5	Central	1,359,385	802,403	68,380	885,757	3,115,925
6	North County	1,137,911	392,516	134,374	467,414	2,132,215
7	Westside	648,549	292,995	10,000	336,088	1,287,632
8	**Grand Total**	**3,145,845**	**1,487,914**	**212,754**	**1,689,259**	**6,535,772**
9						
10						
11						
12						

data | pt1 | pt2 | q1 | q2 | q3 | q4 | q5 | q6 | q7

Figure 33.3 shows another pivot table generated from the bank data. This pivot table uses a drop-down Report Filter for the Customer item (in row 2). In the figure, the pivot table displays the data only for Existing customers. (The user can also select New or All from the drop-down control.)

FIGURE 33.3

A pivot table that uses a report filter.

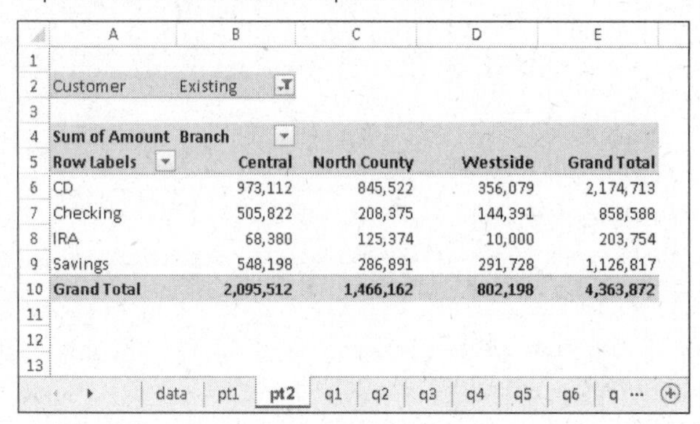

	A	B	C	D	E
1					
2	Customer	Existing			
3					
4	**Sum of Amount**	**Branch**			
5	**Row Labels**	**Central**	**North County**	**Westside**	**Grand Total**
6	CD	973,112	845,522	356,079	2,174,713
7	Checking	505,822	208,375	144,391	858,588
8	IRA	68,380	125,374	10,000	203,754
9	Savings	548,198	286,891	291,728	1,126,817
10	**Grand Total**	**2,095,512**	**1,466,162**	**802,198**	**4,363,872**
11					
12					
13					

data | pt1 | pt2 | q1 | q2 | q3 | q4 | q5 | q6 | q ...

Notice the change in the orientation of the table? For this pivot table, branches appear as column labels, and account types appear as row labels. This change, which took about five seconds to make, is another example of the flexibility of a pivot table.

Why "Pivot?"

Are you curious about the term *pivot*?

Pivot, as a verb, means to rotate or revolve. If you think of your data as a physical object, a pivot table lets you rotate the data summary and look at it from different angles or perspectives. A pivot table allows you to move fields around easily, nest fields within each other, and even create ad hoc groups of items.

If you were handed a strange object and asked to identify it, you'd probably look at it from several different angles in an attempt to figure it out. Working with a pivot table is similar to investigating a strange object. In this case, the object happens to be your data. A pivot table invites experimentation, so feel free to rotate and manipulate the pivot table until you're satisfied. You may be surprised at what you discover.

Data appropriate for a pivot table

A pivot table requires that your data be in the form of a rectangular database table. You can store the database in either a worksheet range (which can be a table or just a normal range) or an external database file. And although Excel can generate a pivot table from any database, not all databases benefit.

Generally speaking, fields in a database table consist of two types of information:

- **Data:** Contains a value or data to be summarized. For the bank account example, the Amount field is a data field.
- **Category:** Describes the data. For the bank account data, the Date, Weekday, AcctType, OpenedBy, Branch, and Customer fields are category fields because they describe the data in the Amount field.

Note

A database table that's appropriate for a pivot table is said to be "normalized." In other words, each record (or row) contains information that describes the data.

A single database table can have any number of data fields and category fields. When you create a pivot table, you usually want to summarize one or more of the data fields. Conversely, the values in the category fields appear in the pivot table as rows, columns, or filters.

Exceptions exist, however, and you may find the Excel PivotTable feature useful even for databases that don't contain actual numerical data fields.

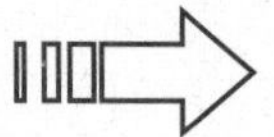

Chapter 34 has an example of a pivot table created from non-numeric data.

Figure 33.4 shows an example of an Excel range that is *not* appropriate for a pivot table. You might recognize this data from the outline example in Chapter 27. Although the range contains descriptive information about each value, it does *not* consist of normalized data. In fact, this range actually resembles a pivot table summary, but it's much less flexible.

FIGURE 33.4

This range is not appropriate for a pivot table.

	A	B	C	D	E	F	G	H	I	J
1	**State**	**Jan**	**Feb**	**Mar**	***Qtr-1***	**Apr**	**May**	**Jun**	***Qtr-2***	**Total**
2	California	1,118	1,960	1,252	***4,330***	1,271	1,557	1,679	***4,507***	**8,837**
3	Washington	1,247	1,238	1,028	***3,513***	1,345	1,784	1,574	***4,703***	**8,216**
4	Oregon	1,460	1,954	1,726	***5,140***	1,461	1,764	1,144	***4,369***	**9,509**
5	Arizona	1,345	1,375	1,075	***3,795***	1,736	1,555	1,372	***4,663***	**8,458**
6	**West Total**	**5,170**	**6,527**	**5,081**	**16,778**	**5,813**	**6,660**	**5,769**	**18,242**	**35,020**
7	New York	1,429	1,316	1,993	***4,738***	1,832	1,740	1,191	***4,763***	**9,501**
8	New Jersey	1,735	1,406	1,224	***4,365***	1,706	1,320	1,290	***4,316***	**8,681**
9	Massachusetts	1,099	1,233	1,110	***3,442***	1,637	1,512	1,006	***4,155***	**7,597**
10	Florida	1,705	1,792	1,225	***4,722***	1,946	1,327	1,357	***4,630***	**9,352**
11	**East Total**	**5,968**	**5,747**	**5,552**	**17,267**	**7,121**	**5,899**	**4,844**	**17,864**	**35,131**
12	Kentucky	1,109	1,078	1,155	***3,342***	1,993	1,082	1,551	***4,626***	**7,968**
13	Oklahoma	1,309	1,045	1,641	***3,995***	1,924	1,499	1,941	***5,364***	**9,359**
14	Missouri	1,511	1,744	1,414	***4,669***	1,243	1,493	1,820	***4,556***	**9,225**
15	Illinois	1,539	1,493	1,211	***4,243***	1,165	1,013	1,445	***3,623***	**7,866**
16	Kansas	1,973	1,560	1,243	***4,776***	1,495	1,125	1,387	***4,007***	**8,783**
17	**Central Total**	**7,441**	**6,920**	**6,664**	**21,025**	**7,820**	**6,212**	**8,144**	**22,176**	**43,201**
18	**Grand Total**	**18,579**	**19,194**	**17,297**	**55,070**	**20,754**	**18,771**	**18,757**	**58,282**	**113,352**

Sheet1 | Normalized

Figure 33.5 shows the same data, but normalized. This range contains 78 rows of data — one for each of the six monthly sales values for the 13 states. Notice that each row contains category information for the sales value. This table is an ideal candidate for a pivot table and contains all information necessary to summarize the information by region or quarter.

Figure 33.6 shows a pivot table created from the normalized data. As you can see, it's virtually identical to the non-normalized data shown in Figure 33.4. Working with normalized data provides ultimate flexibility in designing reports.

On the Web

This workbook, named `normalized data.xlsx`, is available on this book's website.

FIGURE 33.5

This range contains normalized data and is appropriate for a pivot table.

	A	B	C	D	E
1	**State**	**Region**	**Month**	**Qtr**	**Sales**
2	Arizona	West	Jan	Qtr-1	1,345
3	Arizona	West	Feb	Qtr-1	1,375
4	Arizona	West	Mar	Qtr-1	1,075
5	Arizona	West	Apr	Qtr-2	1,736
6	Arizona	West	May	Qtr-2	1,555
7	Arizona	West	Jun	Qtr-2	1,372
8	California	West	Jan	Qtr-1	1,118
9	California	West	Feb	Qtr-1	1,960
10	California	West	Mar	Qtr-1	1,252
11	California	West	Apr	Qtr-2	1,271
12	California	West	May	Qtr-2	1,557
13	California	West	Jun	Qtr-2	1,679
14	Florida	East	Jan	Qtr-1	1,705
15	Florida	East	Feb	Qtr-1	1,792
16	Florida	East	Mar	Qtr-1	1,225
17	Florida	East	Apr	Qtr-2	1,946
18	Florida	East	May	Qtr-2	1,327
19	Florida	East	Jun	Qtr-2	1,357
20	Illinois	Central	Jan	Qtr-1	1,539
21	Illinois	Central	Feb	Qtr-1	1,493
22	Illinois	Central	Mar	Qtr-1	1,211
23	Illinois	Central	Apr	Qtr-2	1,165
24	Illinois	Central	May	Qtr-2	1,013
25	Illinois	Central	Jun	Qtr-2	1,445
26	Kansas	Central	Jan	Qtr-1	1,973
27	Kansas	Central	Feb	Qtr-1	1,560
28	Kansas	Central	Mar	Qtr-1	1,243

Not Normalized | **Normalized**

FIGURE 33.6

A pivot table created from normalized data.

	H	I	J	K	L	M	N	O	P	Q
2	**Sum of Sales**	**Col**								
3		**QTR1**	**QTR1**	**QTR1**	**QTR1 Total**	**QTR2**	**QTR2**	**QTR2**	**QTR2 Total**	**Grand Total**
4	**Row Labels**	**Jan**	**Feb**	**Mar**		**Apr**	**May**	**Jun**		
5	Central	7,441	6,920	6,664	21,025	7,820	6,212	8,144	22,176	43,201
6	Illinois	1,539	1,493	1,211	4,243	1,165	1,013	1,445	3,623	7,866
7	Kansas	1,973	1,560	1,243	4,776	1,495	1,125	1,387	4,007	8,783
8	Kentucky	1,109	1,078	1,155	3,342	1,993	1,082	1,551	4,626	7,968
9	Missouri	1,511	1,744	1,414	4,669	1,243	1,493	1,820	4,556	9,225
10	Oklahoma	1,309	1,045	1,641	3,995	1,924	1,499	1,941	5,364	9,359
11	East	5,968	5,747	5,552	17,267	7,121	5,899	4,844	17,864	35,131
12	Florida	1,705	1,792	1,225	4,722	1,946	1,327	1,357	4,630	9,352
13	Massachusetts	1,099	1,233	1,110	3,442	1,637	1,512	1,006	4,155	7,597
14	New Jersey	1,735	1,406	1,224	4,365	1,706	1,320	1,290	4,316	8,681
15	New York	1,429	1,316	1,993	4,738	1,832	1,740	1,191	4,763	9,501
16	West	5,170	6,527	5,081	16,778	5,813	6,660	5,769	18,242	35,020
17	Arizona	1,345	1,375	1,075	3,795	1,736	1,555	1,372	4,663	8,458
18	California	1,118	1,960	1,252	4,330	1,271	1,557	1,679	4,507	8,837
19	Oregon	1,460	1,954	1,726	5,140	1,461	1,764	1,144	4,369	9,509
20	Washington	1,247	1,238	1,028	3,513	1,345	1,784	1,574	4,703	8,216
21	**Grand Total**	**18,579**	**19,194**	**17,297**	**55,070**	**20,754**	**18,771**	**18,757**	**58,282**	**113,352**

Sheet1

Creating a Pivot Table Automatically

How easy is it to create a pivot table? This task requires practically no effort if you choose a Recommended PivotTable.

New Feature

Recommended PivotTables is a new feature in Excel 2013.

If your data is in a worksheet, select any cell within the data range choose Insert ➪ Tables ➪ Recommended PivotTables, Excel quickly scans your data and the Recommended PivotTables dialog box presents thumbnails that depict some pivot tables that you can choose from. Figure 33.7 shows the Recommended PivotTables dialog box for the bank account data.

FIGURE 33.7

Selecting a Recommended PivotTable.

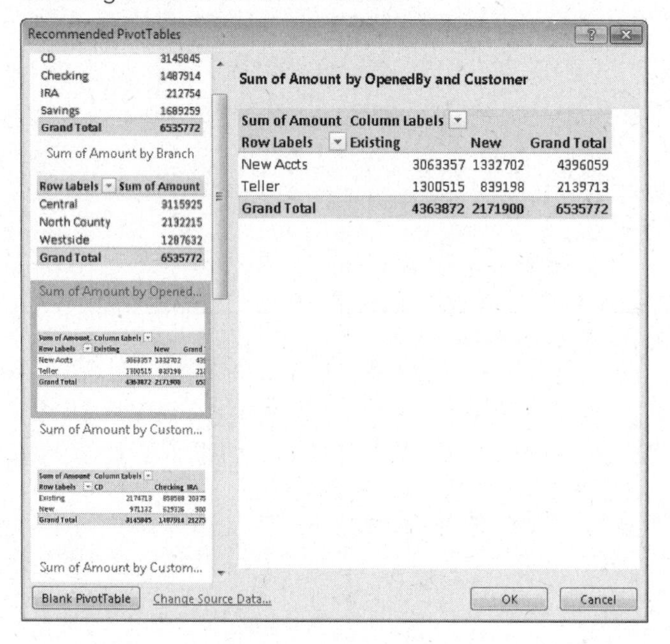

The pivot table thumbnails use your actual data, and there's a good chance that one of them will be exactly what you're looking for — or at least very close to what you're looking for. Select a thumbnail, click OK, and Excel creates the pivot table on a new worksheet.

When any cell in a pivot table is selected, Excel displays the PivotTable Fields task pane. You can use this task pane to make changes to the layout of the pivot table.

NOTE

If your data is in an external database, start by selecting a blank cell. When you choose Insert ⇨ Tables ⇨ Recommended PivotTables, the Choose Data Source dialog box appears. Select Use An External Data Source, and then click Choose Connection to specify the data source. You'll see the thumbnails of the list of recommended pivot tables.

If none of the Recommended PivotTables is suitable, you have two choices:

- Create a pivot table that's close to what you want, and then use the PivotTable Fields task pane to modify it.
- Click the Blank PivotTable button (at the bottom of the Recommended PivotTables dialog box) and create a pivot table manually.

Creating a Pivot Table Manually

Using a recommended pivot table is easy, but you might prefer to create a pivot table manually. If you use a version prior to Excel 2013, manually creating a pivot table is your only option.

In this section, I describe the basic steps required to create a pivot table, using the bank account data described earlier in this chapter. Creating a pivot table is an interactive process. It's not at all uncommon to experiment with various layouts until you find one that you're satisfied with. If you're unfamiliar with the elements of a pivot table, see the sidebar, "Pivot Table Terminology."

Specifying the data

If your data is in a worksheet range, select any cell in that range and then choose Insert ⇨ Tables ⇨ PivotTable. The Create PivotTable dialog box, shown in Figure 33.8, appears.

FIGURE 33.8

In the Create PivotTable dialog box, you tell Excel where the data is and where you want the pivot table.

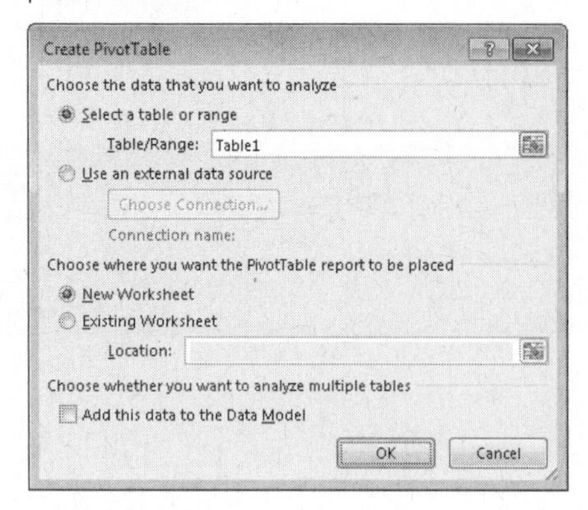

Excel attempts to guess the range, based on the location of the active cell. If you're creating a pivot table from an external data source, you need to select that option and then click Choose Connection to specify the data source.

TIP

If you're creating a pivot table from data in a worksheet, it's a good idea to first create a table for the range (choose Insert ⇨ Tables ⇨ Table). Then, if you expand the table by adding new rows of data, Excel will refresh the pivot table without the need to manually indicate the new data range.

Specifying the location for the pivot table

Use the bottom section of the Create PivotTable dialog box to indicate the location for your pivot table. The default location is on a new worksheet, but you can specify any range on any worksheet, including the worksheet that contains the data.

Click OK, and Excel creates an empty pivot table and displays a PivotTable Fields task pane, as shown in Figure 33.9.

TIP

The PivotTable Fields task pane is typically docked on the right side of the Excel window. Drag its title bar to move it anywhere you like. Also, if you click a cell outside the pivot table, the task pane is temporarily hidden.

FIGURE 33.9

Use the PivotTable Fields task pane to build the pivot table.

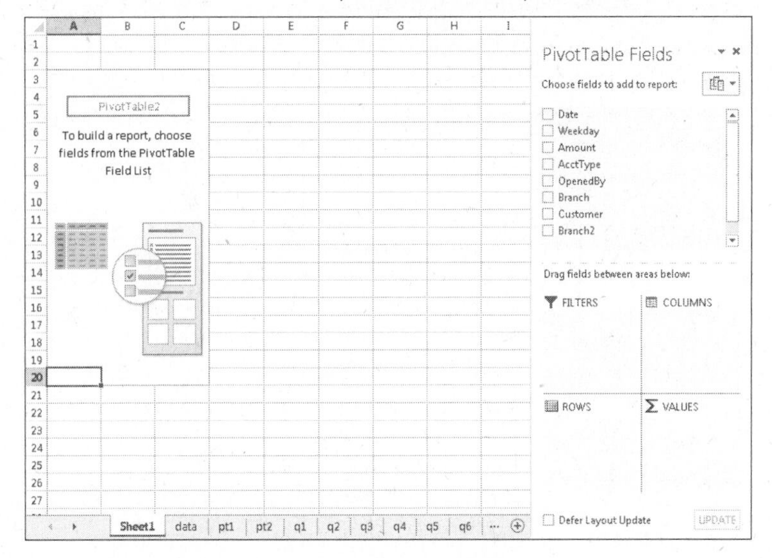

Laying out the pivot table

Next, set up the actual layout of the pivot table. You can do so by using of the following techniques:

- Drag the field names (at the top of the PivotTable Fields task pane) to one of the four boxes at the bottom of the task pane.
- Place a check mark next to the item at the top of the PivotTable Fields task pane. Excel places the field into one of the four boxes at the bottom. You can drag it to a different box, if necessary.
- Right-click a field name at the top of the PivotTable Fields task pane and choose its location from the shortcut menu (for example, Add to Row Labels).

The following steps create the pivot table presented earlier in this chapter (see "A pivot table example"). For this example, I drag the items from the top of the PivotTable Fields task pane to the areas in the bottom of the PivotTable Fields task pane.

1. **Drag the Amount field into the Values area.** At this point, the pivot table displays the total of all the values in the Amount column.
2. **Drag the AcctType field into the Rows area.** Now the pivot table shows the total amount for each of the account types.
3. **Drag the Branch field into the Columns area.** The pivot table shows the amount for each account type, cross-tabulated by branch (see Figure 33.10). The pivot table updates itself automatically with every change you make in the PivotTable Fields task pane.

Pivot Table Terminology

Understanding the terminology associated with pivot tables is the first step in mastering this feature. Refer to the accompanying figure to get your bearings.

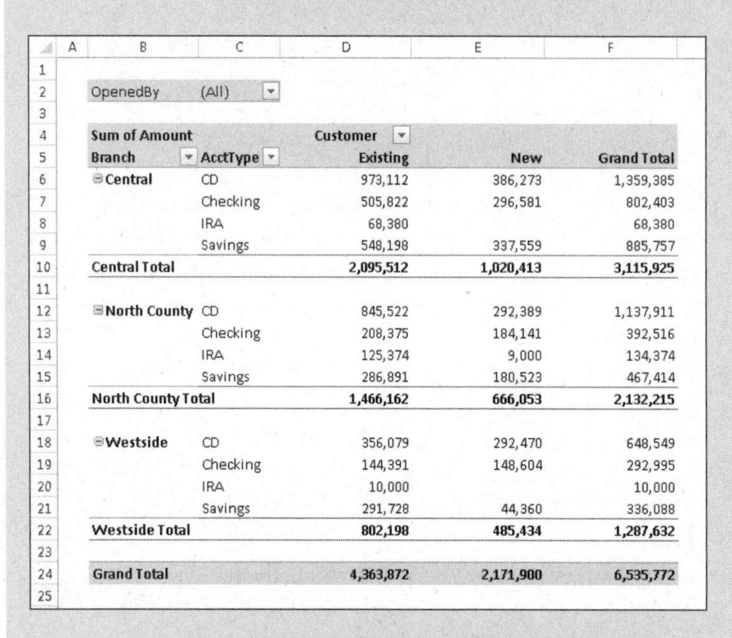

	A	B	C	D	E	F
1						
2		OpenedBy	(All)			
3						
4		**Sum of Amount**		**Customer**		
5		**Branch**	**AcctType**	**Existing**	**New**	**Grand Total**
6		**Central**	CD	973,112	386,273	1,359,385
7			Checking	505,822	296,581	802,403
8			IRA	68,380		68,380
9			Savings	548,198	337,559	885,757
10		**Central Total**		**2,095,512**	**1,020,413**	**3,115,925**
11						
12		**North County**	CD	845,522	292,389	1,137,911
13			Checking	208,375	184,141	392,516
14			IRA	125,374	9,000	134,374
15			Savings	286,891	180,523	467,414
16		**North County Total**		**1,466,162**	**666,053**	**2,132,215**
17						
18		**Westside**	CD	356,079	292,470	648,549
19			Checking	144,391	148,604	292,995
20			IRA	10,000		10,000
21			Savings	291,728	44,360	336,088
22		**Westside Total**		**802,198**	**485,434**	**1,287,632**
23						
24		**Grand Total**		**4,363,872**	**2,171,900**	**6,535,772**
25						

- **Column labels:** A field that has a column orientation in the pivot table. Each item in the field occupies a column. In the figure, Customer represents a column field that contains two items (Existing and New). You can have nested column fields.
- **Grand totals:** A row or column that displays totals for all cells in a row or column in a pivot table. You can specify that grand totals be calculated for rows, columns, or both (or neither). The pivot table in the figure shows grand totals for both rows and columns.
- **Group:** A collection of items treated as a single item. You can group items manually or automatically (group dates into months, for example). The pivot table in the figure does not have any defined groups.
- **Item:** An element in a field that appears as a row or column header in a pivot table. In the figure, Existing and New are items for the Customer field. The Branch field has three items: Central, North County, and Westside. AcctType has four items: CD, Checking, IRA, and Savings.
- **Refresh:** Recalculates the pivot table after making changes to the source data.
- **Row labels:** A field that has a row orientation in the pivot table. Each item in the field occupies a row. You can have nested row fields. In the figure, Branch and AcctType both represent row fields.

- **Source data:** The data used to create a pivot table. It can reside in a worksheet or an external database.
- **Subtotals:** A row or column that displays subtotals for detail cells in a row or column in a pivot table. The pivot table in the figure displays subtotals for each branch, below the data. You can also display subtotals above the data or hide subtotals.
- **Table Filter:** A field that has a page orientation in the pivot table — similar to a slice of a three-dimensional cube. You can display one item, multiple items, or all items in a page field at one time. In the figure, OpenedBy represents a page field that displays All (that is, not filtered).
- **Values area:** The cells in a pivot table that contain the summary data. Excel offers several ways to summarize the data (sum, average, count, and so on).

FIGURE 33.10

After a few simple steps, the pivot table shows a summary of the data.

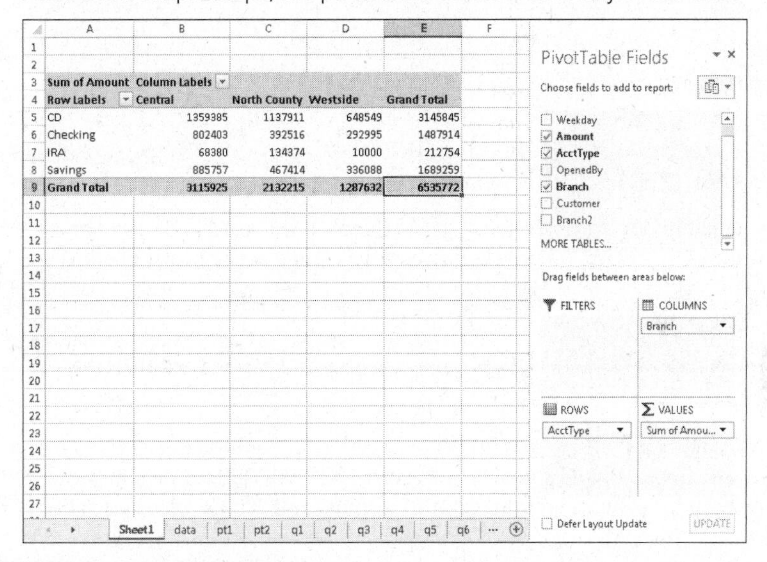

Sum of Amount	Column Labels			
Row Labels	Central	North County	Westside	Grand Total
CD	1359385	1137911	648549	3145845
Checking	802403	392516	292995	1487914
IRA	68380	134374	10000	212754
Savings	885757	467414	336088	1689259
Grand Total	3115925	2132215	1287632	6535772

Formatting the pivot table

Notice that the pivot table uses General number formatting. To change the number format for all data, right-click any value and choose Number Format from the shortcut menu. Then use the Format Cells dialog box to change the number format for the displayed data.

Pivot Table Calculations

Pivot table data is most frequently summarized using a sum. However, you can display your data using a number of different summary techniques, specified in the Value Field Settings dialog box. The quickest way to display this dialog box is to right-click any value in the pivot table, and choose Value Field Settings from the shortcut menu. This dialog box has two tabs: Summarize Values By and Show Values As.

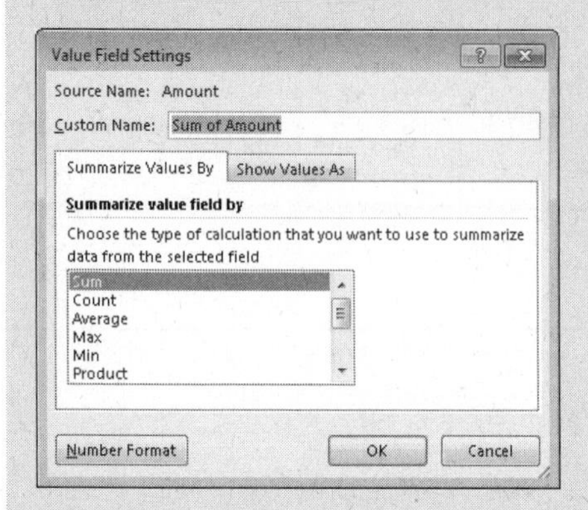

Use the Summarize Values By tab to select a different summary function. Your choices are Sum, Count, Average, Max, Min, Product, Count Numbers, StdDev, StdDevp, Var, and Varp.

To display your values in a different form, use the drop-down control on the Show Values As tab. You have many options to choose from, including as a percentage of the total or subtotal.

This dialog box also provides a way to apply a number format to the values. Just click the button and choose your number format.

You can apply any of several built-in styles to a pivot table. Select any cell in the pivot table and then choose PivotTable Tools ⇨ Design ⇨ PivotTable Styles to select a style. Fine-tune the display by using the controls in the PivotTable Tools ⇨ Design ⇨ PivotTable Style Options group.

You can also use the controls from the PivotTable ⇨ Design ⇨ Layout group to control various elements in the pivot table. You can adjust any of the following elements:

- **Subtotals:** Hide subtotal, or choose where to display them (above or below the data).
- **Grand Totals:** Choose which types, if any, to display.

- **Report Layout:** Choose from three different layout styles (compact, outline, or tabular). You can also choose to hide repeating labels.
- **Blank Row:** Add a blank row between items to improve readability.

The PivotTable Tools ➪ Analyze ➪ Show group contains additional options that affect the appearance of your pivot table. For example, you use the Show Field Headers button to toggle the display of the field headings.

Still more pivot table options are available from the PivotTable Options dialog box. To display this dialog box, choose PivotTable Tools ➪ Analyze ➪ PivotTable ➪ Options. Or right-click any cell in the pivot table and choose PivotTable Options from the shortcut menu.

The best way to become familiar with all these layout and formatting options is to experiment.

Modifying the pivot table

After you create a pivot table, changing it is easy. For example, you can add further summary information by using the PivotTable Fields task pane. Figure 33.11 shows the pivot table after I dragged a second field (OpenedBy) to the Rows section in the PivotTable Fields task pane.

FIGURE 33.11

Two fields are used for row labels.

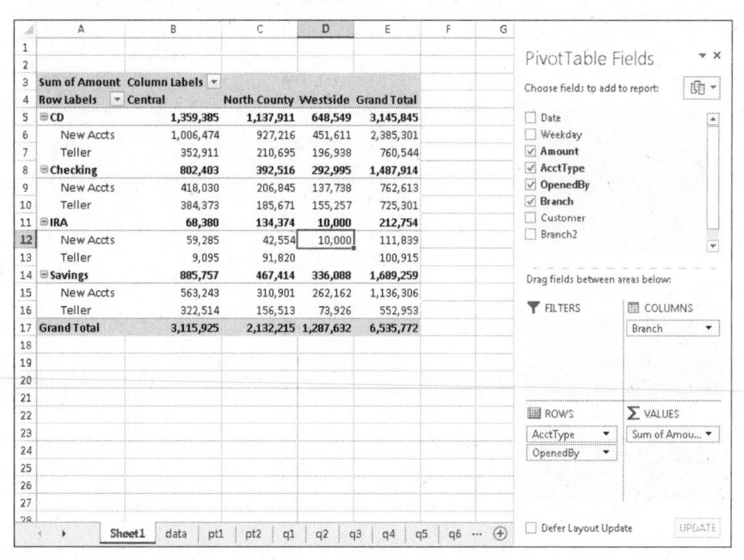

Here are some tips on other pivot table modifications you can make:

- To remove a field from the pivot table, select it in the bottom part of the PivotTable Fields task pane and then drag it away.
- If an area has more than one field, you can change the order in which the fields are listed by dragging the field names. Doing so determines how nesting occurs and affects the appearance of the pivot table.
- To temporarily remove a field from the pivot table, remove the check mark from the field name in the top part of the PivotTable Fields task pane. The pivot table is redisplayed without that field. Place the check mark back on the field name, and it appears in its previous section.
- If you add a field to the Filters section, the field items appear in a drop-down list, which allows you to filter the displayed data by one or more items. Figure 33.12 shows an example. I dragged the Date field to the Filters area. The pivot table is now showing the data only for a single day (which I selected from the drop-down list in cell B1).

FIGURE 33.12

The pivot table is filtered by date.

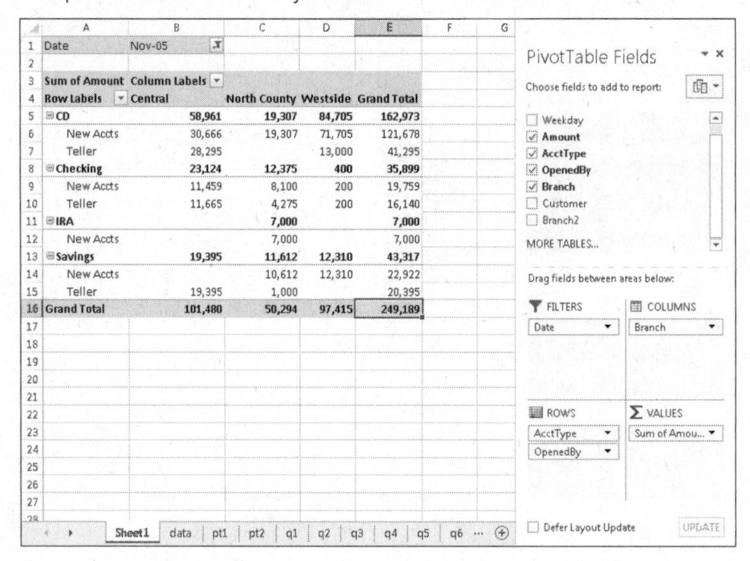

Date	Nov-05			
Sum of Amount	Column Labels			
Row Labels	Central	North County	Westside	Grand Total
CD	58,961	19,307	84,705	162,973
New Accts	30,666	19,307	71,705	121,678
Teller	28,295		13,000	41,295
Checking	23,124	12,375	400	35,899
New Accts	11,459	8,100	200	19,759
Teller	11,665	4,275	200	16,140
IRA		7,000		7,000
New Accts		7,000		7,000
Savings	19,395	11,612	12,310	43,317
New Accts		10,612	12,310	22,922
Teller	19,395	1,000		20,395
Grand Total	101,480	50,294	97,415	249,189

Copying a Pivot Table's Content

A pivot table is very flexible, but it does have some limitations. For example, you can't add new rows or columns, change any of the calculated values, or enter formulas within the pivot table. If you want to manipulate a pivot table in ways not normally permitted, make a copy of it so it's no longer linked to its data source.

To copy a pivot table, select the entire table and choose Home ➪ Clipboard ➪ Copy (or press Ctrl+C). Then select a new worksheet and choose Home Clipboard ➪ Paste ➪ Paste Values. The pivot table formatting is not copied — even if you repeat the operation and use the Formats option in the Paste Special dialog box.

To copy the pivot table and its formatting, use the Office Clipboard to paste. If the Office Clipboard is not displayed, click the dialog box launcher in the bottom right of the Home ➪ Clipboard group.

The contents of the pivot table are copied to the new location so that you can do whatever you like to them.

Note that the copied information is *not* a pivot table, and it is no longer linked to the source data. If the source data changes, your copied pivot table will not reflect these changes.

More Pivot Table Examples

To demonstrate the flexibility of this feature, I created some additional pivot tables. The examples use the bank account data and answer the questions posed earlier in this chapter (see "A pivot table example").

What is the daily total new deposit amount for each branch?

Figure 33.13 shows the pivot table that answers this question.

- The Branch field is in the Columns section.
- The Date field is in the Rows section.
- The Amount field is in the Values section and is summarized by `Sum`.

Note that the pivot table can also be sorted by any column. For example, you can sort the Grand Total column in descending order to find out which day of the month had the largest amount of new funds. To sort, just right-click any cell in the column to sort and choose Sort from the shortcut menu.

FIGURE 33.13

This pivot table shows daily totals for each branch.

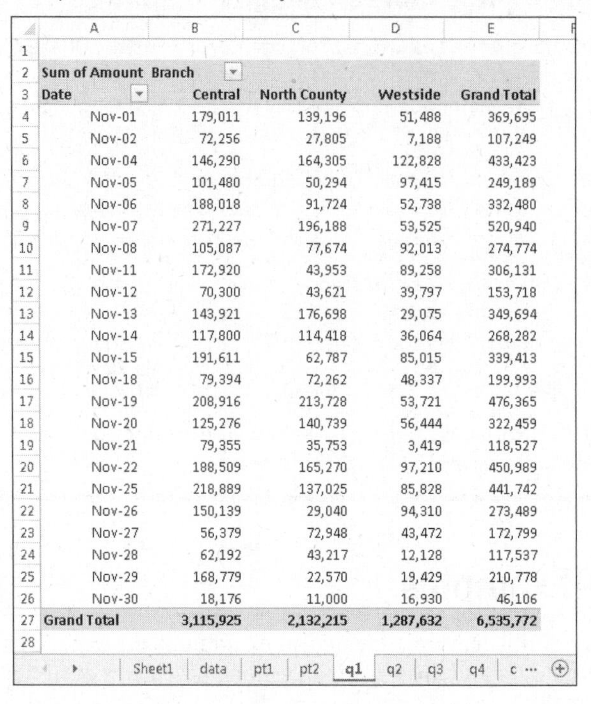

Sum of Amount	Branch			
Date	Central	North County	Westside	Grand Total
Nov-01	179,011	139,196	51,488	369,695
Nov-02	72,256	27,805	7,188	107,249
Nov-04	146,290	164,305	122,828	433,423
Nov-05	101,480	50,294	97,415	249,189
Nov-06	188,018	91,724	52,738	332,480
Nov-07	271,227	196,188	53,525	520,940
Nov-08	105,087	77,674	92,013	274,774
Nov-11	172,920	43,953	89,258	306,131
Nov-12	70,300	43,621	39,797	153,718
Nov-13	143,921	176,698	29,075	349,694
Nov-14	117,800	114,418	36,064	268,282
Nov-15	191,611	62,787	85,015	339,413
Nov-18	79,394	72,262	48,337	199,993
Nov-19	208,916	213,728	53,721	476,365
Nov-20	125,276	140,739	56,444	322,459
Nov-21	79,355	35,753	3,419	118,527
Nov-22	188,509	165,270	97,210	450,989
Nov-25	218,889	137,025	85,828	441,742
Nov-26	150,139	29,040	94,310	273,489
Nov-27	56,379	72,948	43,472	172,799
Nov-28	62,192	43,217	12,128	117,537
Nov-29	168,779	22,570	19,429	210,778
Nov-30	18,176	11,000	16,930	46,106
Grand Total	3,115,925	2,132,215	1,287,632	6,535,772

Sheet1 | data | pt1 | pt2 | q1 | q2 | q3 | q4 | c ...

Which day of the week accounts for the most deposits?

Figure 33.14 shows the pivot table that answers this question.

FIGURE 33.14

This pivot table shows new account totals by day of the week.

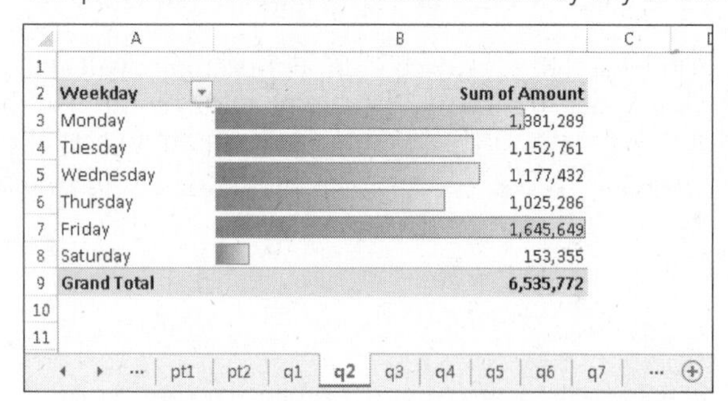

Weekday	Sum of Amount
Monday	1,381,289
Tuesday	1,152,761
Wednesday	1,177,432
Thursday	1,025,286
Friday	1,645,649
Saturday	153,355
Grand Total	6,535,772

... | pt1 | pt2 | q1 | q2 | q3 | q4 | q5 | q6 | q7 | ...

- The Weekday field is in the Rows section.
- The Amount field is in the Values section and is summarized by `Sum`.

I added conditional formatting data bars to make it easier to see how the days compare.

See Chapter 21 for more information about conditional formatting.

How many accounts were opened at each branch, broken down by account type?

Figure 33.15 shows a pivot table that answers this question.

FIGURE 33.15

This pivot table uses the `Count` function to summarize the data.

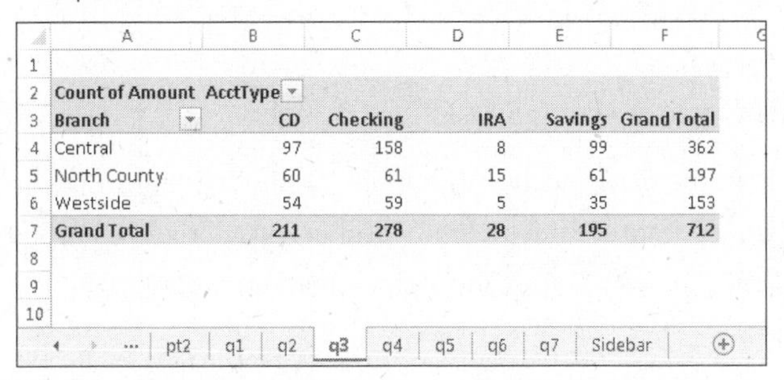

Count of Amount	AcctType				
Branch	CD	Checking	IRA	Savings	Grand Total
Central	97	158	8	99	362
North County	60	61	15	61	197
Westside	54	59	5	35	153
Grand Total	211	278	28	195	712

- The AcctType field is in the Columns section.
- The Branch field is in the Rows section.
- The Amount field is in the Values section and is summarized by `Count`.

So far, the pivot table examples have all used the `Sum` summary function. In this case, I changed the summary function to `Count`. To change the summary function to `Count`, right-click any cell in the Values area and choose Summarize Values By⇨Count from the shortcut menu.

What's the dollar distribution of the different account types?

Figure 33.16 shows a pivot table that answers this question. For example, 253 (or 35.53%) of the new accounts were for an amount of $5,000 or less.

FIGURE 33.16

This pivot table counts the number of accounts that fall into each value range.

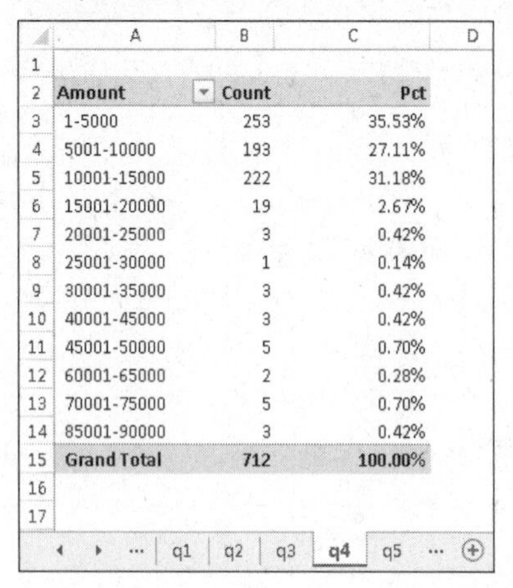

Amount	Count	Pct
1-5000	253	35.53%
5001-10000	193	27.11%
10001-15000	222	31.18%
15001-20000	19	2.67%
20001-25000	3	0.42%
25001-30000	1	0.14%
30001-35000	3	0.42%
40001-45000	3	0.42%
45001-50000	5	0.70%
60001-65000	2	0.28%
70001-75000	5	0.70%
85001-90000	3	0.42%
Grand Total	712	100.00%

This pivot table is unusual because it uses only one field: Amount.

- The Amount field is in the Rows section (grouped, to show dollar ranges).
- The Amount field is also in the Values section and is summarized by `Count`.
- A third instance of the Amount field is the Values section, summarized by `Percent of Column Total`.

When I initially added the Amount field to the Rows section, the pivot table showed a row for each unique dollar amount. To group the values, I right-clicked one of the Row labels and chose Group from the shortcut menu. Then I used the Grouping dialog box to set up bins of $5,000 increments. Note that the Grouping dialog box does not appear if you select more than one Row labels.

The second instance of the Amount field (in the Values section) is summarized by `Count`. I right-clicked a value and chose Summarize Data By ➪ Count from the shortcut menu.

I added another instance of Amount to the Values section, and I set it up to display the percentage. I right-clicked a value in column C and chose Show Values As ➪ % of Column Total. This option is also available in the Show Values As tab of the Value Field Settings dialog box.

What types of accounts do tellers open most often?

The pivot table in Figure 33.17 shows that the most common account opened by tellers is a Checking account.

FIGURE 33.17

This pivot table uses a Filter to show only the Teller data.

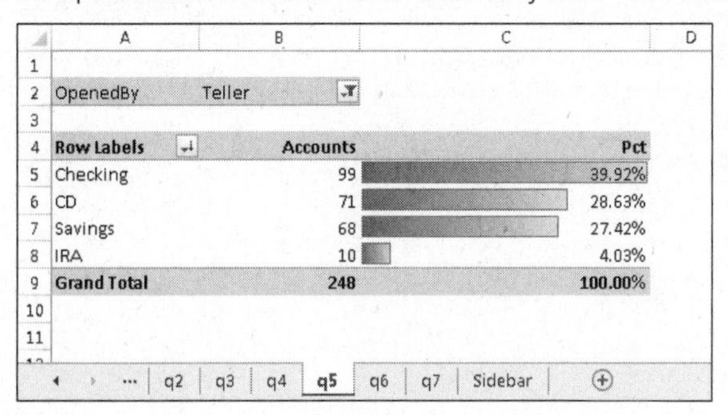

OpenedBy	Teller	
Row Labels	**Accounts**	**Pct**
Checking	99	39.92%
CD	71	28.63%
Savings	68	27.42%
IRA	10	4.03%
Grand Total	**248**	**100.00%**

- The AcctType field is in the Rows section.
- The OpenedBy field is in the Filters section.
- The Amount field is in the Values section (summarized by `Count`).
- A second instance of the Amount field is in the Values section (summarized by `% of Column Total`).

This pivot table uses the OpenedBy field as a Filter and is showing the data only for Tellers. I sorted the data so that the largest value is at the top, and I also used conditional formatting to display data bars for the percentages.

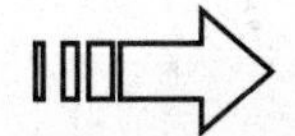

See Chapter 21 for more information about conditional formatting.

How does the Central branch compare with the other two branches?

Figure 33.18 shows a pivot table that sheds some light on this rather vague question. It shows how the Central branch compares with the other two branches *combined*.

- The AcctType field is in the Rows section.
- The Branch field is in the Columns section.
- The Amount field is in the Values section.

I selected North County and Westside labels, right-clicked, and chose Group. This combines those two branches into a new category. Grouping also creates a new field in the PivotTable Fields task pane. In this case the new field is named Branch2. I changed the label in the pivot table to `Other Branches`.

FIGURE 33.18

This pivot table (and pivot chart) compares the Central branch with the other two branches combined.

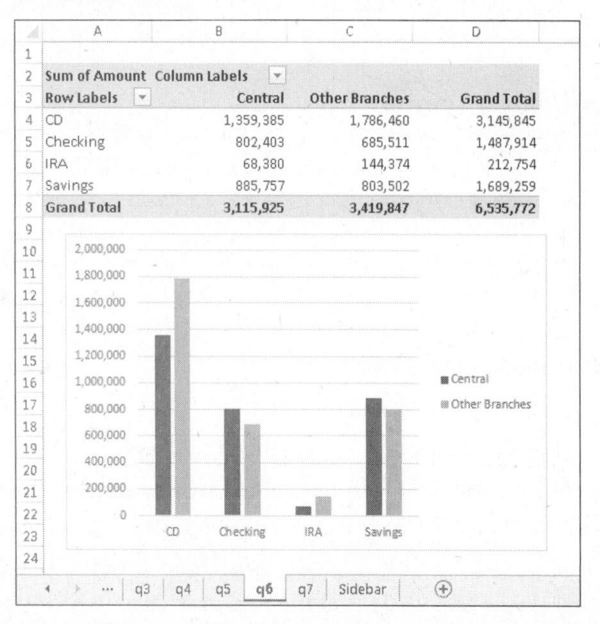

Sum of Amount	Column Labels		
Row Labels	Central	Other Branches	Grand Total
CD	1,359,385	1,786,460	3,145,845
Checking	802,403	685,511	1,487,914
IRA	68,380	144,374	212,754
Savings	885,757	803,502	1,689,259
Grand Total	3,115,925	3,419,847	6,535,772

NOTE

The new field, Branch2, is also available for use in other pivot tables created from the data.

After grouping the North County and Westside branches, the pivot table allows easy comparison between the Central branch and the other branches combined.

I also created a pivot chart for good measure.

See Chapter 34 for more information about pivot charts.

In which branch do tellers open the most checking accounts for new customers?

Figure 33.19 shows a pivot table that answers this question. At the Central branch, tellers opened 23 checking accounts for new customers.

FIGURE 33.19

This pivot table uses three Filters.

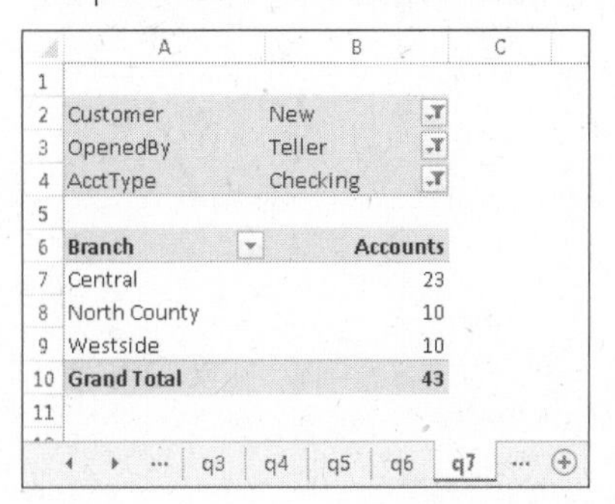

- The Customer field is in the Filters section.
- The OpenedBy field is in the Filters section.
- The AcctType field is in the Filters section.
- The Branch field is in the Rows section.
- The Amount field is in the Values section, summarized by `Count`.

This pivot table uses three Report Filters. The Customer field is filtered to show only New, the OpenedBy field is filtered to show only Teller, and the AcctType field is filtered to show only Checking.

Learning More

The examples in this chapter should give you an appreciation for the power and flexibility of Excel pivot tables. The next chapter digs a bit deeper and covers some advanced features — with lots of examples.

CHAPTER 34

Analyzing Data with Pivot Tables

IN THIS CHAPTER

Creating a pivot table from non-numeric data

Grouping items in a pivot table

Creating a calculated field or a calculated item in a pivot table

Understanding the new Date Model feature

Creating an attractive report using a pivot table

The previous chapter introduces pivot tables. There, I present several examples to demonstrate the types of pivot table summaries that you can generate from a set of data.

This chapter continues the discussion and explores the details of creating effective pivot tables. Creating a basic pivot table is very easy, and the examples in this chapter demonstrate additional pivot table features that you may find helpful. I urge you to try these techniques with your own data. If you don't have suitable data, use the files available on this book's website.

Working with Non-Numeric Data

Most pivot tables are created from numeric data, but pivot tables are also useful with some types of non-numeric data. Because you can't sum non-numbers, this technique involves counting.

Figure 34.1 shows a table and a pivot table generated from the table. The table is a list of 400 employees, along with their location and gender. As you can see, the table has no numeric values, but you can create a useful pivot table that counts the items rather than sums them. The pivot table cross-tabulates the Location field by the Sex field for the 400 employees and shows the count for each combination of location and gender.

FIGURE 34.1

This table doesn't have any numeric fields, but you can use it to generate a pivot table, shown next to the table.

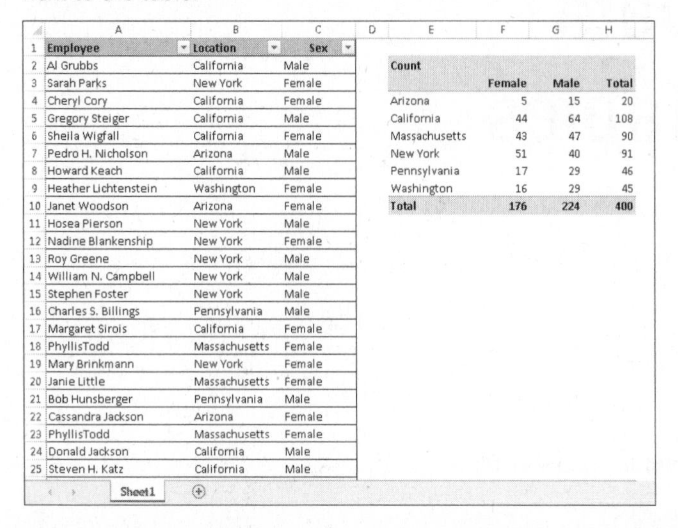

	Employee	Location	Sex
2	Al Grubbs	California	Male
3	Sarah Parks	New York	Female
4	Cheryl Cory	California	Female
5	Gregory Steiger	California	Male
6	Sheila Wigfall	California	Female
7	Pedro H. Nicholson	Arizona	Male
8	Howard Keach	California	Male
9	Heather Lichtenstein	Washington	Female
10	Janet Woodson	Arizona	Female
11	Hosea Pierson	New York	Male
12	Nadine Blankenship	New York	Female
13	Roy Greene	New York	Male
14	William N. Campbell	New York	Male
15	Stephen Foster	New York	Male
16	Charles S. Billings	Pennsylvania	Male
17	Margaret Sirois	California	Female
18	PhyllisTodd	Massachusetts	Female
19	Mary Brinkmann	New York	Female
20	Janie Little	Massachusetts	Female
21	Bob Hunsberger	Pennsylvania	Male
22	Cassandra Jackson	Arizona	Female
23	PhyllisTodd	Massachusetts	Female
24	Donald Jackson	California	Male
25	Steven H. Katz	California	Male

Count	Female	Male	Total
Arizona	5	15	20
California	44	64	108
Massachusetts	43	47	90
New York	51	40	91
Pennsylvania	17	29	46
Washington	16	29	45
Total	**176**	**224**	**400**

Sheet1

ON THE WEB

A workbook that demonstrates the pivot table created from non-numeric data is available on this book's website. The file is named `employee list.xlsx`.

Here are the PivotTable Fields task pane settings I used for this pivot table:

- The Sex field is used for the Columns.
- The Location field is used for the Rows.
- Location is also used for the Values and is summarized by `Count`.
- The pivot table has the field headers turned off, by using the Field Headers toggle control in the PivotTable Tools ➪ Analyze ➪ Show group.

NOTE

The Employee field is not used. This example uses the Location field for the Values section, but you can actually use any of the three fields because the pivot table is displaying a count.

Figure 34.2 shows the pivot table after making some additional changes:

FIGURE 34.2

The pivot table, after making a few changes.

	Female		Male		Total Ct	Total Pct
	Ct	Pct	Ct	Pct		
Arizona	5	2.8%	15	6.7%	20	5.0%
California	44	25.0%	64	28.6%	108	27.0%
Massachusetts	43	24.4%	47	21.0%	90	22.5%
New York	51	29.0%	40	17.9%	91	22.8%
Pennsylvania	17	9.7%	29	12.9%	46	11.5%
Washington	16	9.1%	29	12.9%	45	11.3%
Total	**176**	**100.0%**	**224**	**100.0%**	**400**	**100.0%**

- I added a second instance of the Location field to the Values section. To display percentages, I right-clicked a value in that column and chose Show Values As ➪ Percent of Column Total.
- I changed the field names in the pivot table to Ct and Pct.
- I selected a pivot table style that makes it easier to distinguish the columns.

Grouping Pivot Table Items

One of the most useful features of a pivot table is the ability to combine items into groups. You can group items that appear in the Rows or Columns section in the PivotTable Fields task pane. Excel offers two ways to group items:

- **Manually:** After creating the pivot table, select the items to be grouped and then choose PivotTable Tools ➪ Analyze ➪ Group ➪ Group Selection. Or you can select the items, right-click, and choose Group from the shortcut menu.
- **Automatically:** If the items are numeric (or dates), use the Grouping dialog box to specify how you would like to group the items. Select any single item and then choose PivotTable Tools ➪ Analyze ➪ Group ➪ Group Field. Or right-click a single item and choose Group from the shortcut menu. In either case, the Grouping dialog box appears. Use this dialog box to specify how to group the items.

34

NOTE

If you plan on creating multiple pivot tables that use different groupings, make sure you read the sidebar "Multiple Groups from the Same Data Source."

A manual grouping example

Figure 34.3 shows the pivot table example from the previous sections, with two groups created from the Row Labels. To create the first group, I held down the Ctrl key while I selected Arizona, California, and Washington. Then I right-clicked and chose Group from the shortcut menu. Then I selected the three other states and created a second group. I replaced the default group names (Group 1 and Group 2) with more meaningful names (Western Region and Eastern Region).

FIGURE 34.3

A pivot table with two groups.

Count			
	Female	Male	Total
⊟Western Region			
Arizona	5	15	20
California	44	64	108
Washington	16	29	45
⊟Eastern Region			
Massachusetts	43	47	90
New York	51	40	91
Pennsylvania	17	29	46
Total	176	224	400

You can create any number of groups and even create groups of groups.

Excel provides a number of options for displaying a pivot table, and you may want to experiment with these options when you use groups. These commands are on the PivotTable Tools⇨Design tab of the Ribbon. There are no rules for choosing a particular option. The key is to try a few and see which makes your pivot table look the best. In addition, try various options in the PivotTable Tools⇨Design tab. Often, the style that you choose can greatly enhance readability.

Figure 34.4 shows pivot tables using various options for displaying subtotals, grand totals, and styles.

On the Web

A workbook that contains these grouping examples is available on this book's website. The file is named `grouping examples.xlsx`.

Automatic grouping examples

When a field contains numbers, dates, or times, Excel can create groups automatically. The two examples in this section demonstrate automatic grouping.

Grouping by date

Figure 34.5 shows a portion of a simple table with two fields: Date and Sales. This table has 730 rows and covers the dates between January 1, 2012, and December 31, 2013. The goal is to summarize the sales information by month.

FIGURE 34.4

Pivot tables with options for subtotals and grand totals.

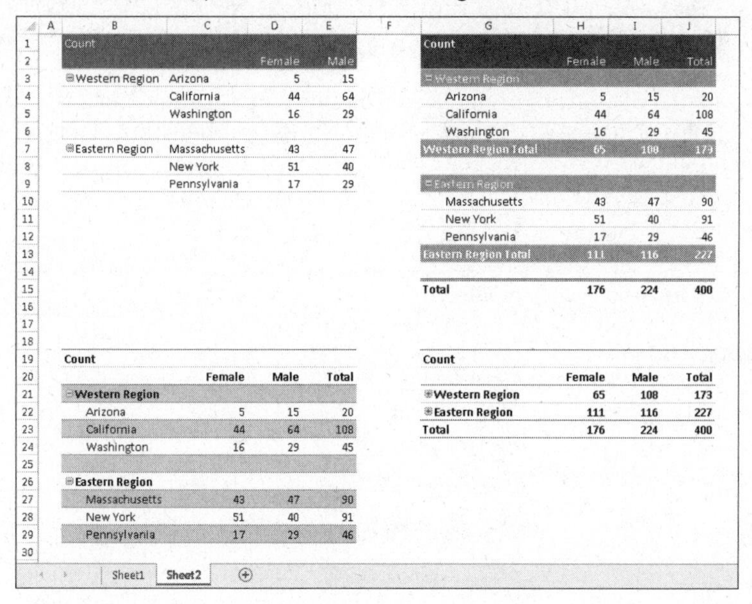

Count		Female	Male
Western Region	Arizona	5	15
	California	44	64
	Washington	16	29
Eastern Region	Massachusetts	43	47
	New York	51	40
	Pennsylvania	17	29

Count	Female	Male	Total
Western Region			
Arizona	5	15	20
California	44	64	108
Washington	16	29	45
Western Region Total	65	108	173
Eastern Region			
Massachusetts	43	47	90
New York	51	40	91
Pennsylvania	17	29	46
Eastern Region Total	111	116	227
Total	176	224	400

Count	Female	Male	Total
Western Region			
Arizona	5	15	20
California	44	64	108
Washington	16	29	45
Eastern Region			
Massachusetts	43	47	90
New York	51	40	91
Pennsylvania	17	29	46

Count	Female	Male	Total
Western Region	65	108	173
Eastern Region	111	116	227
Total	176	224	400

Sheet1 Sheet2

FIGURE 34.5

You can use a pivot table to summarize the sales data by month.

Date	Sales
1/1/2012	3,830
1/2/2012	3,763
1/3/2012	4,362
1/4/2012	3,669
1/5/2012	3,942
1/6/2012	4,488
1/7/2012	4,416
1/8/2012	3,371
1/9/2012	3,628
1/10/2012	4,548
1/11/2012	5,493
1/12/2012	5,706
1/13/2012	6,579
1/14/2012	6,333
1/15/2012	6,101
1/16/2012	5,289
1/17/2012	5,349
1/18/2012	5,814
1/19/2012	6,501
1/20/2012	6,513

Sheet1

ON THE WEB

A workbook demonstrating how to group pivot table items by date is available on this book's website. The file is named `grouping sales by date.xlsx`.

Figure 34.6 shows part of a pivot table created from the data. The Date field is in the Rows section, and the Sales field is in the Values section. Not surprisingly, the pivot table looks exactly like the input data because the dates have not been grouped.

FIGURE 34.6

The pivot table, before grouping by month.

	A	B	C	D	E	F
1	Date	Sales				
2	1/1/2012	3,830		Row Labels	Sum of Sales	
3	1/2/2012	3,763		1/1/2012	3830	
4	1/3/2012	4,362		1/2/2012	3763	
5	1/4/2012	3,669		1/3/2012	4362	
6	1/5/2012	3,942		1/4/2012	3669	
7	1/6/2012	4,488		1/5/2012	3942	
8	1/7/2012	4,416		1/6/2012	4488	
9	1/8/2012	3,371		1/7/2012	4416	
10	1/9/2012	3,628		1/8/2012	3371	
11	1/10/2012	4,548		1/9/2012	3628	
12	1/11/2012	5,493		1/10/2012	4548	
13	1/12/2012	5,706		1/11/2012	5493	
14	1/13/2012	6,579		1/12/2012	5706	
15	1/14/2012	6,333		1/13/2012	6579	
16	1/15/2012	6,101		1/14/2012	6333	
17	1/16/2012	5,289		1/15/2012	6101	
18	1/17/2012	5,349		1/16/2012	5289	
19	1/18/2012	5,814		1/17/2012	5349	
20	1/19/2012	6,501		1/18/2012	5814	
21	1/20/2012	6,513		1/19/2012	6501	
22	1/21/2012	5,970		1/20/2012	6513	
23	1/22/2012	5,791		1/21/2012	5970	
24	1/23/2012	5,478		1/22/2012	5791	
25	1/24/2012	6,564		1/23/2012	5478	
26	1/25/2012	6,642		1/24/2012	6564	

Sheet1

To group the items by month, select any date and choose PivotTable Tools ➪ Analyze ➪ Group ➪ Group Field (or right-click and choose Group from the shortcut menu). The Grouping dialog box, shown in Figure 34.7, appears. Excel supplies values for the Starting At and Ending At fields. The values cover the entire range of data, and you can change them if you like.

FIGURE 34.7

Use the Grouping dialog box to group pivot table items by dates.

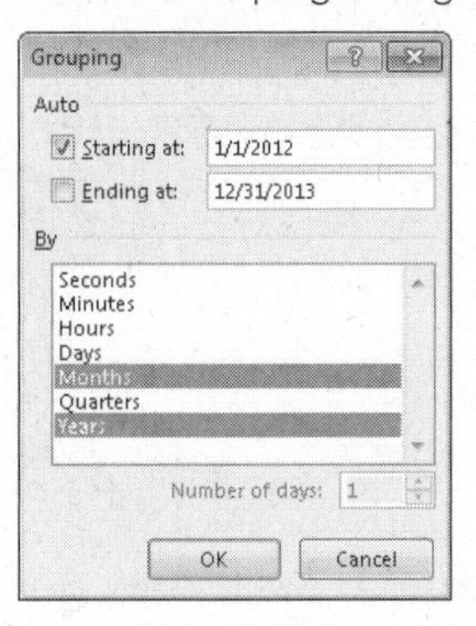

In the By list box, select Months and Years and verify that the starting and ending dates are correct for your data. Click OK. The Date items in the pivot table are grouped by years and by months, as shown in Figure 34.8.

FIGURE 34.8

The pivot table, after grouping by month and year.

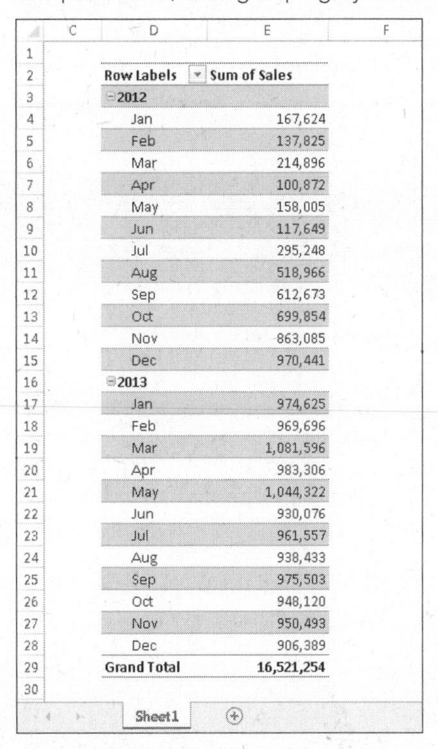

Row Labels	Sum of Sales
⊟2012	
Jan	167,624
Feb	137,825
Mar	214,896
Apr	100,872
May	158,005
Jun	117,649
Jul	295,248
Aug	518,966
Sep	612,673
Oct	699,854
Nov	863,085
Dec	970,441
⊟2013	
Jan	974,625
Feb	969,696
Mar	1,081,596
Apr	983,306
May	1,044,322
Jun	930,076
Jul	961,557
Aug	938,433
Sep	975,503
Oct	948,120
Nov	950,493
Dec	906,389
Grand Total	16,521,254

Multiple Groups from the Same Data Source

If you create multiple pivot tables from the same data source, you may have noticed that grouping a field in one pivot table affects the other pivot tables. Specifically, all the other pivot tables automatically use the same grouping. Sometimes, this is exactly what you want. Other times, it's not at all what you want. For example, you might like to see two pivot table reports: one that summarizes data by month and year, and another that summarizes the data by quarter and year.

The reason grouping affects other pivot tables is because all the pivot tables are using the same pivot table "cache." Unfortunately, there is no direct way to force a pivot table to use a new cache. But there *is* a way to trick Excel into using a new cache. The trick involves giving multiple range names to the source data.

For example, name your source range `Table1`, and then give the same range a second name: `Table2`. The easiest way to name a range is to use the Name box, to the left of the Formula bar. Select the range, type a name in the Name box, and press Enter. Then, with the range still selected, type a different name, and press Enter. Excel will display only the first name, but you can verify that both names exist by choose Formulas ➪ Define Names ➪ Name Manager.

When you create the first pivot table, specify `Table1` as the Table/Range. When you create the second pivot table, specify `Table2` as the Table/Range. Each pivot table will use a separate cache, and you can create groups in one pivot table, independent of the other pivot table.

You can use this trick with existing pivot tables. Make sure that you give the data source a different name. Then select the pivot table and choose PivotTable Tools ➪ Analyze ➪ Data ➪ Change Data Source. In the Change PivotTable Data Source dialog box, type the new name that you gave to the range. This will cause Excel to create a new pivot cache for the pivot table.

NOTE

If you select only Months in the By list box in the Grouping dialog box, months in different years combine together. For example, the January item would display the sum of sales for 2012 and 2013.

Figure 34.9 shows another view of the data, grouped by quarter and by year.

Grouping by time

Figure 34.10 shows a set of data in columns A:B. Each row is a reading from a measurement instrument, taken at one-minute intervals throughout an entire day. The table has 1,440 rows, each representing one minute. The pivot table summarizes the data by hour.

FIGURE 34.9

This pivot table shows sales by quarter and by year.

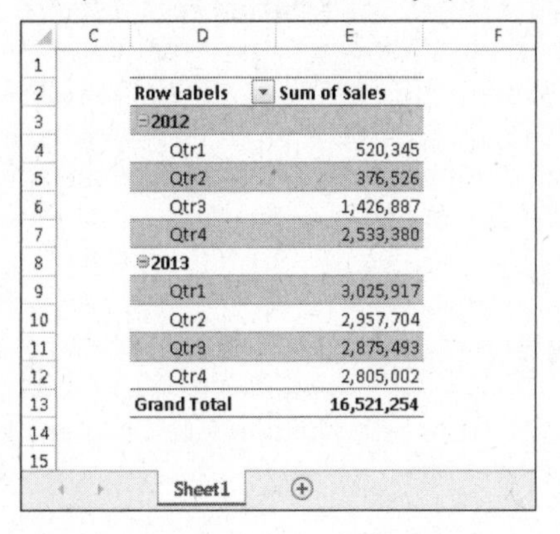

Row Labels	Sum of Sales
2012	
Qtr1	520,345
Qtr2	376,526
Qtr3	1,426,887
Qtr4	2,533,380
2013	
Qtr1	3,025,917
Qtr2	2,957,704
Qtr3	2,875,493
Qtr4	2,805,002
Grand Total	**16,521,254**

FIGURE 34.10

This pivot table is grouped by Hours.

Time	Reading
6/15/2013 0:00	105.32
6/15/2013 0:01	105.35
6/15/2013 0:02	104.37
6/15/2013 0:03	106.40
6/15/2013 0:04	106.42
6/15/2013 0:05	105.45
6/15/2013 0:06	107.46
6/15/2013 0:07	109.49
6/15/2013 0:08	110.54
6/15/2013 0:09	110.54
6/15/2013 0:10	110.55
6/15/2013 0:11	109.56
6/15/2013 0:12	107.60
6/15/2013 0:13	107.68
6/15/2013 0:14	109.69
6/15/2013 0:15	107.76
6/15/2013 0:16	107.81
6/15/2013 0:17	108.83
6/15/2013 0:18	109.85
6/15/2013 0:19	111.94
6/15/2013 0:20	114.04
6/15/2013 0:21	112.12
6/15/2013 0:22	112.21
6/15/2013 0:23	112.25
6/15/2013 0:24	113.34
6/15/2013 0:25	112.41

	Average	Minimum	Maximum
12 AM	110.50	104.37	116.21
1 AM	118.57	112.72	127.14
2 AM	124.39	115.75	130.36
3 AM	122.74	112.85	132.90
4 AM	129.29	123.99	133.52
5 AM	132.91	125.88	141.04
6 AM	139.67	132.69	146.06
7 AM	128.18	117.53	139.65
8 AM	119.24	112.10	129.38
9 AM	134.36	129.11	142.79
10 AM	136.16	130.91	142.89
11 AM	122.79	108.63	138.10
12 PM	111.76	106.43	116.71
1 PM	104.91	98.48	111.86
2 PM	119.71	110.37	130.55
3 PM	131.83	121.92	139.65
4 PM	131.05	123.36	137.94
5 PM	138.90	133.05	145.06
6 PM	134.71	129.29	139.89
7 PM	123.09	113.97	135.23
8 PM	118.13	112.64	125.65
9 PM	112.64	108.09	117.72
10 PM	103.19	96.13	110.49
11 PM	106.01	100.03	111.76
Grand Total	**123.11**	**96.13**	**146.06**

ON THE WEB

This workbook, named `time-based grouping.xlsx`, is available on this book's website.

Here are the settings I used for this pivot table:

- The Values area has three instances of the Reading field and each instance displays a different summary method (Average, Minimum, and Maximum). To change the summary method for a column, right-click any cell in the column and choose the Summarize Values By and then appropriate option.
- The Time field is in the Rows section, and I used the Grouping dialog box to group by Hours.

Creating a Frequency Distribution

Excel provides a number of ways to create a frequency distribution (see Chapter 13), but none of these methods is easier than using a pivot table.

Figure 34.11 shows part of a table of 221 students and the test score for each. The goal is to determine how many students are in each ten-point range (1–10, 11–20, and so on).

FIGURE 34.11

Creating a frequency distribution for these test scores is simple.

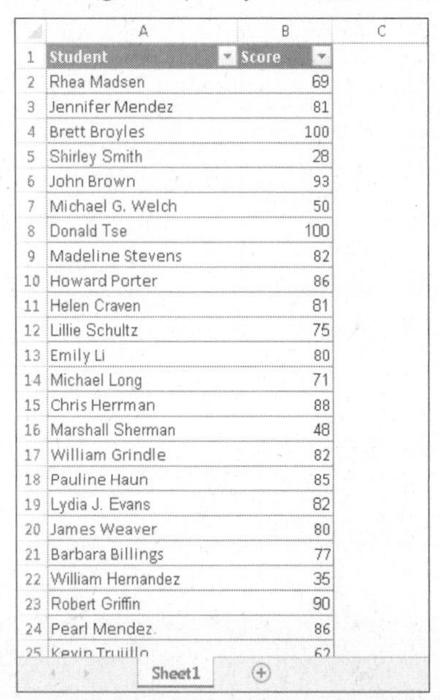

	A	B	C
1	Student	Score	
2	Rhea Madsen	69	
3	Jennifer Mendez	81	
4	Brett Broyles	100	
5	Shirley Smith	28	
6	John Brown	93	
7	Michael G. Welch	50	
8	Donald Tse	100	
9	Madeline Stevens	82	
10	Howard Porter	86	
11	Helen Craven	81	
12	Lillie Schultz	75	
13	Emily Li	80	
14	Michael Long	71	
15	Chris Herrman	88	
16	Marshall Sherman	48	
17	William Grindle	82	
18	Pauline Haun	85	
19	Lydia J. Evans	82	
20	James Weaver	80	
21	Barbara Billings	77	
22	William Hernandez	35	
23	Robert Griffin	90	
24	Pearl Mendez	86	
25	Kevin Trujillo	62	

Sheet1

ON THE WEB

This workbook, named `frequency distribution.xlsx`, is available on this book's website.

The pivot table is simple:

- The Score field is in the Rows section (grouped).
- Another instance of the Score field is in the Values section (summarized by Count).

The Grouping dialog box that generated the bins specified that the groups start at 1, end at 100, and are incremented by 10.

NOTE

By default, Excel does not display items with a count of zero. In this example, no test scores are less than 21, so the 1–10 and 11–20 items were hidden. To force the display of empty bins, right-click any cell and choose Field Settings from the shortcut menu. In the Field Settings dialog box. Click the Layout & Print tab, and select Show Items with No Data.

Figure 34.12 show the frequency distribution of the test scores, along with a pivot chart (see "Creating Pivot Charts," later in this chapter). I filtered the Scores so the pivot table (and chart) do not show the <1 category and the >101 category.

FIGURE 34.12

The pivot table and pivot chart show the frequency distribution for the test scores.

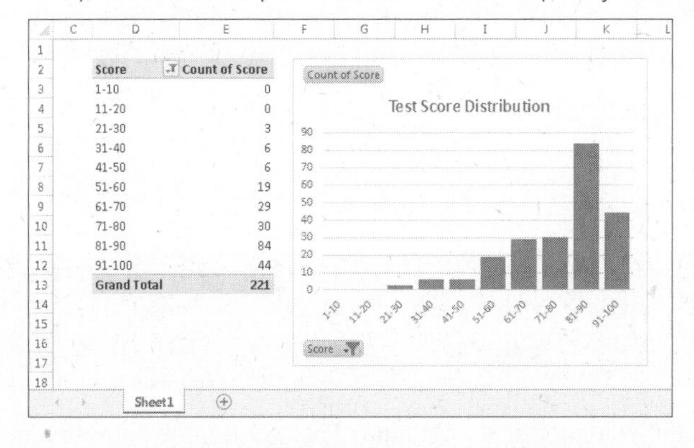

NOTE

This example uses the Excel Grouping dialog box to create the groups automatically. If you don't want to group in equal-sized bins, you can create your own groups. For example, you may want to assign letter grades based on the test score. Select the rows for the first group, right-click, and then choose Group from the shortcut menu. Repeat these steps for each additional group. Then replace the default group names with more meaningful names.

Creating a Calculated Field or Calculated Item

Perhaps the most confusing aspect of pivot tables is calculated fields versus calculated items. Many pivot table users simply avoid dealing with calculated fields and items. However, these features can be useful, and they really aren't that complicated once you understand how they work.

First, some basic definitions:

- **A calculated field:** A new field created from other fields in the pivot table. If your pivot table source is a worksheet table, an alternative to using a calculated field is to add a new column to the table and create a formula to perform the desired calculation. A calculated field must reside in the Values area of the pivot table. You can't use a calculated field in the Columns area, in the Rows area, or in the Filter area.
- **A calculated item:** Uses the contents of other items within a field of the pivot table. If your pivot table source is a worksheet table, an alternative to using a calculated item is to insert one or more rows and write formulas that use values in other rows. A calculated item must reside in the Columns area, Rows area, or Filters area of a pivot table. You can't use a calculated item in the Values area.

The formulas used to create calculated fields and calculated items aren't standard Excel formulas. In other words, you don't enter the formulas into cells. Rather, you enter these formulas in a dialog box, and they're stored along with the pivot table data.

The examples in this section use the worksheet table shown in Figure 34.13. The table consists of five columns and 48 rows. Each row describes monthly sales information for a particular sales representative. For example, Amy is a sales rep for the North region, and she sold 239 units in January for total sales of $23,040.

On the Web

A workbook demonstrating calculated fields and items is available on this book's website. The file is named `calculated fields and items.xlsx`.

Figure 34.14 shows a pivot table created from the data. This pivot table shows Sales (Values area), cross-tabulated by Month (Rows area) and by SalesRep (Columns area).

FIGURE 34.13

This data demonstrates calculated fields and calculated items.

	A	B	C	D	E
1	SalesRep	Region	Month	Sales	Units Sold
2	Amy	North	Jan	$23,040	239
3	Amy	North	Feb	$24,131	79
4	Amy	North	Mar	$24,646	71
5	Amy	North	Apr	$22,047	71
6	Amy	North	May	$24,971	157
7	Amy	North	Jun	$24,218	92
8	Amy	North	Jul	$25,735	175
9	Amy	North	Aug	$23,638	87
10	Amy	North	Sep	$25,749	557
11	Amy	North	Oct	$24,437	95
12	Amy	North	Nov	$25,355	706
13	Amy	North	Dec	$25,899	180
14	Bob	North	Jan	$20,024	103
15	Bob	North	Feb	$23,822	267
16	Bob	North	Mar	$24,854	96
17	Bob	North	Apr	$22,838	74
18	Bob	North	May	$25,320	231
19	Bob	North	Jun	$24,733	164
20	Bob	North	Jul	$21,184	68
21	Bob	North	Aug	$23,174	114
22	Bob	North	Sep	$25,999	84
23	Bob	North	Oct	$22,639	260
24	Bob	North	Nov	$23,949	109
25	Bob	North	Dec	$23,179	465
26	Chuck	South	Jan	$19,886	95
27	Chuck	South	Feb	$23,494	148
28	Chuck	South	Mar	$21,824	83
29	Chuck	South	Apr	$22,058	96
30	Chuck	South	May	$20,280	453
31	Chuck	South	Jun	$23,965	760

Data

FIGURE 34.14

This pivot table was created from the sales data.

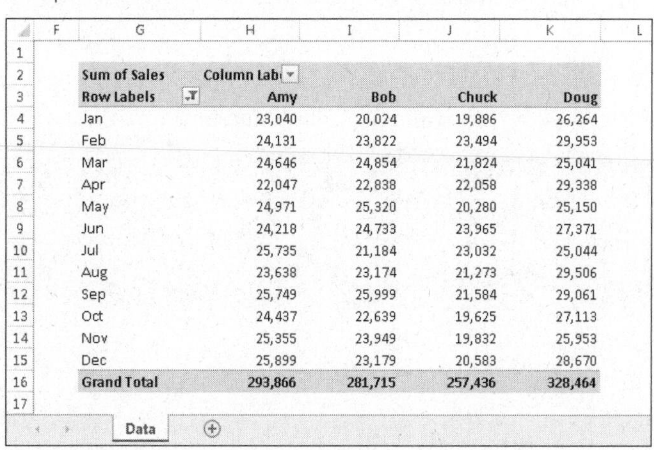

Sum of Sales	Column Labels			
Row Labels	Amy	Bob	Chuck	Doug
Jan	23,040	20,024	19,886	26,264
Feb	24,131	23,822	23,494	29,953
Mar	24,646	24,854	21,824	25,041
Apr	22,047	22,838	22,058	29,338
May	24,971	25,320	20,280	25,150
Jun	24,218	24,733	23,965	27,371
Jul	25,735	21,184	23,032	25,044
Aug	23,638	23,174	21,273	29,506
Sep	25,749	25,999	21,584	29,061
Oct	24,437	22,639	19,625	27,113
Nov	25,355	23,949	19,832	25,953
Dec	25,899	23,179	20,583	28,670
Grand Total	**293,866**	**281,715**	**257,436**	**328,464**

Data

The examples that follow create

- A calculated field, to compute average sales per unit
- Four calculated items, to compute the quarterly sales commission

Creating a calculated field

Because a pivot table is a special type of range, you can't insert new rows or columns within the pivot table, which means that you can't insert formulas to perform calculations with the data in a pivot table. However, you can create calculated fields for a pivot table. A *calculated field* consists of a calculation that can involve other fields.

A calculated field is basically a way to display new information (derived from other fields) in a pivot table. It's an alternative to creating a new column field in your source data. In many cases, you may find it easier to insert a new column in the source range with a formula that performs the desired calculation. A calculated field is most useful when the data comes from a source that you can't easily manipulate — such as an external database.

In the sales example, suppose that you want to calculate the average sales amount per unit. You can compute this value by dividing the Sales field by the Units Sold field. The result shows a new field (a calculated field) for the pivot table.

Use the following procedure to create a calculated field that consists of the Sales field divided by the Units Sold field:

1. **Select any cell within the pivot table.**
2. **Choose PivotTable Tools ➪ Analyze ➪ Calculations ➪ Fields, Items & Sets ➪ Calculated Field.** The Insert Calculated Field dialog box appears.
3. **Enter a descriptive name in the Name box and specify the formula in the Formula box (see Figure 34.15).** The formula can use worksheet functions and other fields from the data source. For this example, the calculated field name is Average Unit Price, and the formula is

   ```
   =Sales/'Units Sold'
   ```
4. **Click Add to add this new field.**
5. **Click OK to close the Insert Calculated Field dialog box.**

NOTE

You can create the formula manually by typing it or by double-clicking items in the Fields list box. Double-clicking an item transfers it to the Formula field. Because the Units Sold field contains a space, Excel adds single quotes around the field name.

FIGURE 34.15

The Insert Calculated Field dialog box.

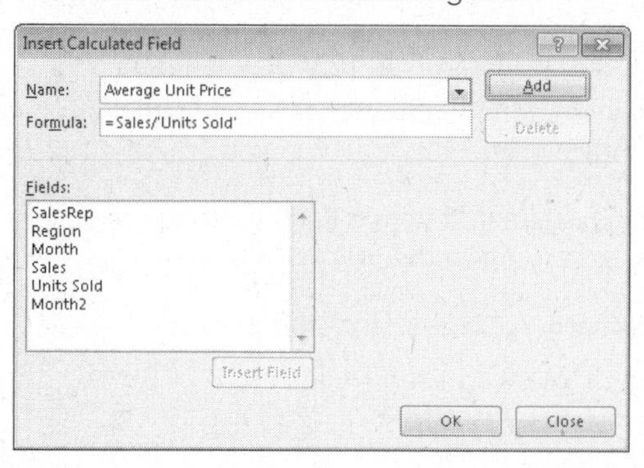

After you create the calculated field, Excel adds it to the Values area of the pivot table (and it also appears in the PivotTable Fields task pane). You can treat it just like any other field, with one exception: You can't move it to the Rows, Columns, or Filters areas. It must remain in the Values area.

Figure 34.16 shows the pivot table after adding the calculated field. The new field displayed Sum of Average Unit Price, but I shortened this label to Avg Price.

FIGURE 34.16

This pivot table uses a calculated field.

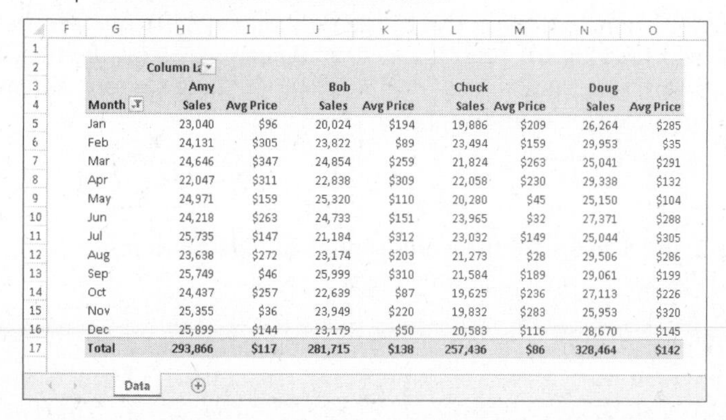

	Column La							
	Amy		Bob		Chuck		Doug	
Month	Sales	Avg Price	Sales	Avg Price	Sales	Avg Price	Sales	Avg Price
Jan	23,040	$96	20,024	$194	19,886	$209	26,264	$285
Feb	24,131	$305	23,822	$89	23,494	$159	29,953	$35
Mar	24,646	$347	24,854	$259	21,824	$263	25,041	$291
Apr	22,047	$311	22,838	$309	22,058	$230	29,338	$132
May	24,971	$159	25,320	$110	20,280	$45	25,150	$104
Jun	24,218	$263	24,733	$151	23,965	$32	27,371	$288
Jul	25,735	$147	21,184	$312	23,032	$149	25,044	$305
Aug	23,638	$272	23,174	$203	21,273	$28	29,506	$286
Sep	25,749	$46	25,999	$310	21,584	$189	29,061	$199
Oct	24,437	$257	22,639	$87	19,625	$236	27,113	$226
Nov	25,355	$36	23,949	$220	19,832	$283	25,953	$320
Dec	25,899	$144	23,179	$50	20,583	$116	28,670	$145
Total	**293,866**	**$117**	**281,715**	**$138**	**257,436**	**$86**	**328,464**	**$142**

TIP

The formulas that you develop can also use worksheet functions, but the functions can't refer to cells or named ranges.

34

Inserting a calculated item

The preceding section describes how to create a calculated field. Excel also enables you to create a *calculated item* for a pivot table field. Keep in mind that a calculated field can be an alternative to adding a new field (column) to your data source. A calculated item, on the other hand, is an alternative to adding a new row to the data source — a row that contains a formula that refers to other rows.

In this example, you create four calculated items. Each item represents the commission earned on the quarter's sales, according to the following schedule:

- **Quarter 1:** 10% of January, February, and March sales
- **Quarter 2:** 11% of April, May, and June sales
- **Quarter 3:** 12% of July, August, and September sales
- **Quarter 4:** 12.5% of October, November, and December sales

NOTE

Modifying the source data to obtain this information would require inserting 16 new rows, each with formulas (four formulas for each sales rep). So, for this example, creating four calculated items may be an easier task.

To create a calculated item to compute the commission for January, February, and March, follow these steps:

1. **Move the cell pointer to the Row Labels or Column Labels area of the pivot table and choose PivotTable Tools ➪ Analyze ➪ Calculations ➪ Fields, Items & Sets ➪ Calculated Item.** The Insert Calculated Item dialog box appears.
2. **Enter a name for the new item in the Name field and specify the formula in the Formula field (see Figure 34.17).** The formula can use items in other fields, but it can't use worksheet functions. For this example, the new item is named Qtr1 Commission, and the formula appears as follows:

   ```
   =10%*(Jan+Feb+Mar)
   ```
3. **Click Add.**
4. **Repeat Steps 2 and 3 to create three additional calculated items:**

   Qtr2 Commission: `= 11%*(Apr+May+Jun)`

   Qtr3 Commission: `= 12%*(Jul+Aug+Sep)`

   Qtr4 Commission: `= 12.5%*(Oct+Nov+Dec)`
5. **Click OK to close the dialog box.**

NOTE

A calculated item, unlike a calculated field, does not appear in the PivotTable Fields task pane. Only fields appear in the field list.

FIGURE 34.17

The Insert Calculated Item dialog box.

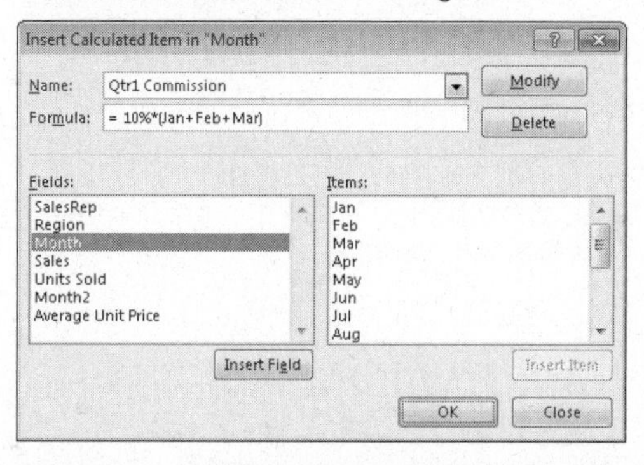

CAUTION

If you use a calculated item in your pivot table, you may need to turn off the Grand Total display for columns to avoid double counting. In this example, the Grand Total includes the calculated items, so the commission amounts are included with the sales amounts. To turn off Grand Totals, choose PivotTable Tools ➪ Design ➪ Layout ➪ Grand Totals.

After you create the calculated items, they appear in the pivot table. Figure 34.18 shows the pivot table after adding the four calculated items. Notice that the calculated items are added to the end of the Month items. You can rearrange the items by selecting the cell and dragging its border. Another option is to create two groups: one for the sales numbers, and one for the commission calculations. Figure 34.19 shows the pivot table after creating the two groups and adding subtotals.

FIGURE 34.18

This pivot table uses calculated items for quarterly totals.

	F	G	H	I	J	K	L
38		Row Labels	Amy	Bob	Chuck	Doug	Grand Total
39		Jan	23,040	20,024	19,886	26,264	89,214
40		Feb	24,131	23,822	23,494	29,953	101,400
41		Mar	24,646	24,854	21,824	25,041	96,365
42		Apr	22,047	22,838	22,058	29,338	96,281
43		May	24,971	25,320	20,280	25,150	95,721
44		Jun	24,218	24,733	23,965	27,371	100,287
45		Jul	25,735	21,184	23,032	25,044	94,995
46		Aug	23,638	23,174	21,273	29,506	97,591
47		Sep	25,749	25,999	21,584	29,061	102,393
48		Oct	24,437	22,639	19,625	27,113	93,814
49		Nov	25,355	23,949	19,832	25,953	95,089
50		Dec	25,899	23,179	20,583	28,670	98,331
51		Qtr1 Commission	7,182	6,870	6,520	8,126	28,698
52		Qtr2 Commission	7,124	7,289	6,630	8,186	29,229
53		Qtr3 Commission	7,512	7,036	6,589	8,361	29,498
54		Qtr4 Commission	7,569	6,977	6,004	8,174	28,723
55							

Data

34

FIGURE 34.19

The pivot table, after creating two groups and adding subtotals.

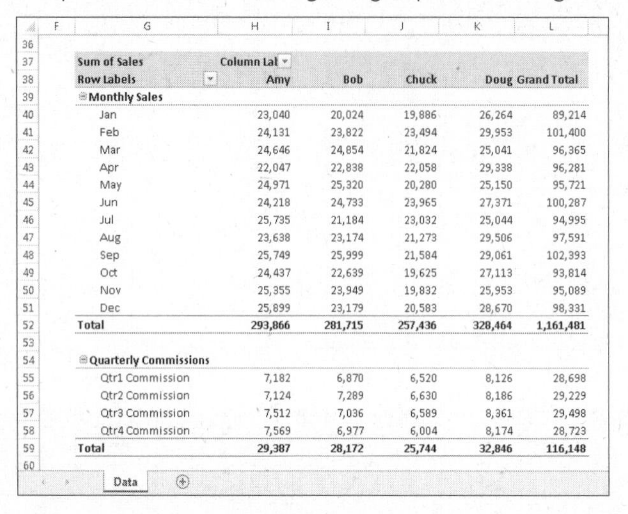

Sum of Sales	Column Lat				
Row Labels	Amy	Bob	Chuck	Doug	Grand Total
Monthly Sales					
Jan	23,040	20,024	19,886	26,264	89,214
Feb	24,131	23,822	23,494	29,953	101,400
Mar	24,646	24,854	21,824	25,041	96,365
Apr	22,047	22,838	22,058	29,338	96,281
May	24,971	25,320	20,280	25,150	95,721
Jun	24,218	24,733	23,965	27,371	100,287
Jul	25,735	21,184	23,032	25,044	94,995
Aug	23,638	23,174	21,273	29,506	97,591
Sep	25,749	25,999	21,584	29,061	102,393
Oct	24,437	22,639	19,625	27,113	93,814
Nov	25,355	23,949	19,832	25,953	95,089
Dec	25,899	23,179	20,583	28,670	98,331
Total	293,866	281,715	257,436	328,464	1,161,481
Quarterly Commissions					
Qtr1 Commission	7,182	6,870	6,520	8,126	28,698
Qtr2 Commission	7,124	7,289	6,630	8,186	29,229
Qtr3 Commission	7,512	7,036	6,589	8,361	29,498
Qtr4 Commission	7,569	6,977	6,004	8,174	28,723
Total	29,387	28,172	25,744	32,846	116,148

Filtering Pivot Tables with Slicers

A *Slicer* is an interactive control that makes it easy to filter data in a pivot table. Figure 34.20 shows a pivot table with three Slicers. Each Slicer represents a particular field. In this case, the pivot table is displaying data for existing customers, opened by tellers at the Central branch.

FIGURE 34.20

Using Slicers to filter the data displayed in a pivot table.

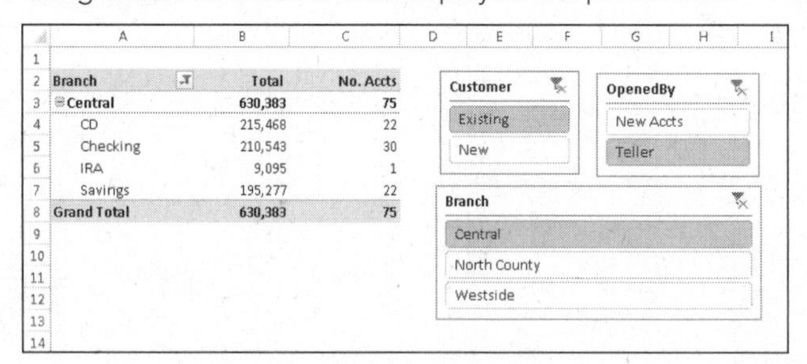

Branch	Total	No. Accts
Central	630,383	75
CD	215,468	22
Checking	210,543	30
IRA	9,095	1
Savings	195,277	22
Grand Total	630,383	75

The same type of filtering can be accomplished by using the field labels in the pivot table, but Slicers are intended for those who might not understand how to filter data in a pivot table. Slicers can also be used to create an attractive and easy-to-use interactive "dashboard."

A Reverse Pivot Table

The Excel Pivot Table feature creates a summary table from a list. But what if you want to perform the opposite operation? Often, you may have a two-way summary table, and it would be convenient if the data were in the form of a normalized list.

In the figure here, range A1:E13 contains a summary table with 48 data points. Notice that this summary table is similar to a pivot table. Column G:I shows part of a 48-row table that was derived from the summary table. In other words, every value in the original summary table gets converted to a row, which also contains the region name and month. This type of table is useful because it can be sorted and manipulated in other ways. And you can create a pivot table from this transformed table.

	North	South	East	West
Jan	132	233	314	441
Feb	143	251	314	447
Mar	172	252	345	450
Apr	184	290	365	452
May	212	299	401	453
Jun	239	317	413	457
Jul	249	350	427	460
Aug	263	354	448	468
Sep	291	373	367	472
Oct	294	401	392	479
Nov	302	437	495	484
Dec	305	466	504	490

Month	Region	Sales
Jan	North	132
Jan	South	233
Jan	East	314
Jan	West	441
Feb	North	143
Feb	South	251
Feb	East	314
Feb	West	447
Mar	North	172
Mar	South	252
Mar	East	345
Mar	West	450
Apr	North	184
Apr	South	290
Apr	East	365
Apr	West	452
May	North	212
May	South	299
May	East	401
May	West	453
Jun	North	239

The companion website contains a workbook, `reverse pivot.xlsm`, which has a VBA macro that will convert any two-way summary table into a three-column normalized table.

To add one or more Slicers to a worksheet, start by selecting any cell in a pivot table. Then choose Insert ➪ Filter ➪ Slicer. The Insert Slicers dialog box appears, with a list of all fields in the pivot table. Place a check mark next to the Slicers you want, and then click OK.

NEW FEATURE

In Excel 2013, Slicers aren't limited to pivot tables. Slicer can also be used with a table (created with Insert ➪ Tables ➪ Table).

Slicers can be moved and resized, and you can change the look. To remove the effects of filtering by a particular Slicer, click the icon in the Slicer's upper-right corner.

To use a Slicer to filter data in a pivot table, just click a button. To display multiple values, press Ctrl while you click the buttons in a Slicer. Press Shift and click to select a series of consecutive buttons.

Figure 34.21 shows a pivot table and a pivot chart. Two Slicers are used to filter the data (by state and by month). In this case, the pivot table and pivot chart show only the data for Kansas, Missouri, and New York, for the months of January through March. Slicers provide a quick and easy way to create an interactive chart.

FIGURE 34.21

Using Slicers to filter a pivot table by state and by month.

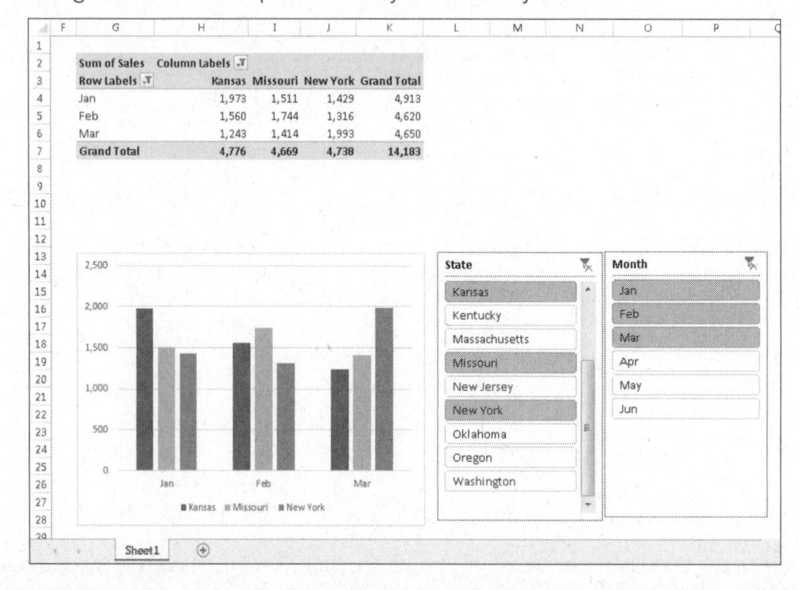

On the Web

This workbook, named `pivot table slicers.xlsx`, is available on this book's website.

Filtering Pivot Tables with a Timeline

A *Timeline* is conceptually similar to a Slicer, but this control is designed to simplify time-based filtering in a pivot table.

New Feature

Timelines are new to Excel 2013.

A Timeline is relevant only if your pivot table has a field that's formatted as a date. This feature does not work with times. To add a Timeline, select a cell in a pivot table and choose Insert ➪ Filter ➪ Timeline. A dialog box appears listing all date-based fields. If your pivot table doesn't have a field formatted as a date, Excel displays an error.

Figure 34.22 shows a pivot table created from the data in columns A:E. This pivot table uses a Timeline, set to allow date filtering by quarters. Click a button that corresponds to the quarter you want to view, and the pivot table is updated immediately. To select a range of quarters, press Shift while you click the buttons. Other filtering options (selectable from the drop-down in the upper-right corner) are Year, Month, and Day. In the figure, the pivot table displays data from the first two quarters of 2012.

FIGURE 34.22

Using a Timeline to filter a pivot table by date.

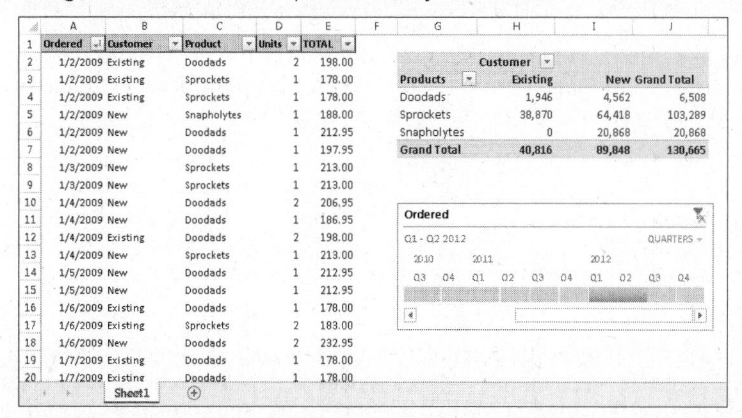

Ordered	Customer	Product	Units	TOTAL
1/2/2009	Existing	Doodads	2	198.00
1/2/2009	Existing	Sprockets	1	178.00
1/2/2009	Existing	Sprockets	1	178.00
1/2/2009	New	Snapholytes	1	188.00
1/2/2009	New	Doodads	1	212.95
1/2/2009	New	Doodads	1	197.95
1/3/2009	New	Sprockets	1	213.00
1/3/2009	New	Sprockets	1	213.00
1/4/2009	New	Doodads	2	206.95
1/4/2009	New	Doodads	1	186.95
1/4/2009	Existing	Doodads	2	198.00
1/4/2009	New	Sprockets	1	213.00
1/5/2009	New	Doodads	1	212.95
1/5/2009	New	Doodads	1	212.95
1/6/2009	Existing	Doodads	1	178.00
1/6/2009	Existing	Sprockets	2	183.00
1/6/2009	New	Doodads	2	232.95
1/7/2009	Existing	Doodads	1	178.00
1/7/2009	Existing	Doodads	1	178.00

	Customer		
Products	Existing	New	Grand Total
Doodads	1,946	4,562	6,508
Sprockets	38,870	64,418	103,289
Snapholytes	0	20,868	20,868
Grand Total	40,816	89,848	130,665

ON THE WEB

A workbook that uses a Timeline is available on this book's website. The filename is `pivot table timeline.xlsx`.

You can, of course, use both Slicers and a Timeline for a pivot table. A Timeline has the same type of formatting options as Slicers, so you can create an attractive interactive dashboard that simplifies pivot table filtering.

Referencing Cells within a Pivot Table

After you create a pivot table, you may want to create formulas that reference one or more cells within a pivot table. Figure 34.23 shows a simple pivot table that displays income and expense information for three years. In this pivot table, the Month field is hidden, so the pivot table shows the year totals.

FIGURE 34.23

The formulas in column F reference cells in the pivot table.

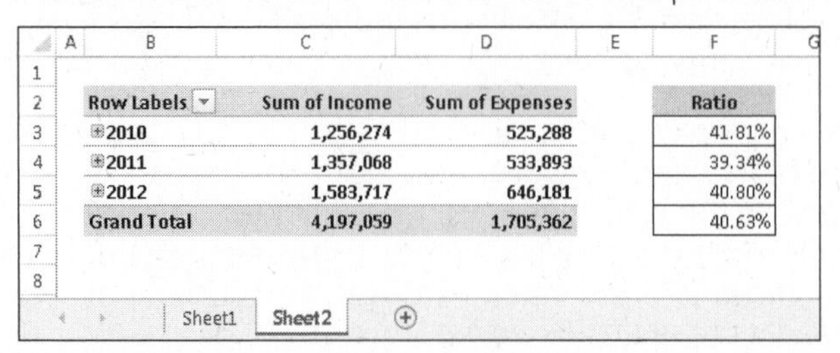

Row Labels	Sum of Income	Sum of Expenses		Ratio
2010	1,256,274	525,288		41.81%
2011	1,357,068	533,893		39.34%
2012	1,583,717	646,181		40.80%
Grand Total	4,197,059	1,705,362		40.63%

ON THE WEB

This workbook, named `pivot table referencing.xlsx`, is available on this book's website.

Column F contains formulas, and this column is not part of the pivot table. These formulas calculate the expense-to-income ratio for each year. I created these formulas by pointing to the cells. You may expect to see this formula in cell F3:

```
=D3/C3
```

In fact, the formula in cell F5 is

```
=GETPIVOTDATA("Sum of Expenses",$B$2,"Year",2010)/GETPIVOTDATA("Sum of
   Income",$B$2,"Year",2010)
```

When you use the pointing technique to create a formula that references a cell in a pivot table, Excel replaces those simple cell references with a much more complicated `GETPIVOTDATA` function. If you type the cell references manually (instead of pointing to them), Excel doesn't use the `GETPIVOTDATA` function. The reason? Using the `GETPIVOTDATA` function helps ensure that the formula will continue to reference the intended cells if the pivot table layout is changed.

Figure 34.24 shows the pivot table after expanding the years to show the month detail. As you can see, the formulas in column F still show the correct result even though the referenced cells are in a different location. Had I used simple cell references, the formula would return incorrect results after expanding the years.

CAUTION

Using the `GETPIVOTDATA` function has one caveat: The data that it retrieves must be visible. If you modify the pivot table so that the value used by `GETPIVOTDATA` is no longer visible, the formula returns an error.

FIGURE 34.24

After expanding the pivot table, formulas that use the `GETPIVOTDATA` function continue to display the correct result.

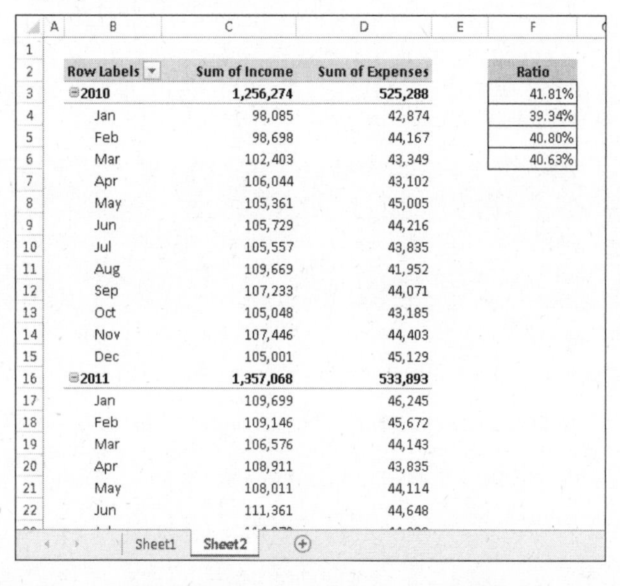

Row Labels	Sum of Income	Sum of Expenses		Ratio
2010	1,256,274	525,288		41.81%
Jan	98,085	42,874		39.34%
Feb	98,698	44,167		40.80%
Mar	102,403	43,349		40.63%
Apr	106,044	43,102		
May	105,361	45,005		
Jun	105,729	44,216		
Jul	105,557	43,835		
Aug	109,669	41,952		
Sep	107,233	44,071		
Oct	105,048	43,185		
Nov	107,446	44,403		
Dec	105,001	45,129		
2011	1,357,068	533,893		
Jan	109,699	46,245		
Feb	109,146	45,672		
Mar	106,576	44,143		
Apr	108,911	43,835		
May	108,011	44,114		
Jun	111,361	44,648		

TIP

If, for some reason, you want to prevent Excel from using the `GETPIVOTDATA` function when you point to pivot table cells when creating a formula, choose PivotTable Tools ➪ Analyze ➪ PivotTable ➪ Options ➪ Generate GetPivot Data. This command is a toggle.

Creating Pivot Charts

A *pivot chart* is a graphical representation of a data summary displayed in a pivot table. If you're familiar with creating charts in Excel, you'll have no problem creating and customizing pivot charts. All Excel charting features are available in a pivot chart.

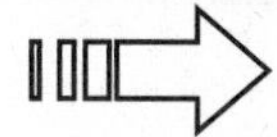

I cover charting in Chapters 19 and 20.

Excel provides several ways to create a pivot chart:

- Select any cell in an existing pivot table and then choose PivotTable Tools ➪ Analyze ➪ Tools ➪ PivotChart.

- Select any cell in an existing pivot table and then choose Insert ➪ Charts ➪ PivotChart.
- Choose Insert ➪ Charts ➪ PivotChart ➪ PivotChart. If the cell pointer is not within a pivot table, Excel prompts you for the data source and creates a pivot chart.
- Choose Insert ➪ Charts ➪ Pivot Chart ➪ PivotChart & PivotTable. Excel prompts you for the data source and creates a pivot table and a pivot chart. This command is available only when the cell pointer is not within a pivot table.

New Feature

In the past, when you created a pivot chart, the pivot chart was always based on a pivot table. With Excel 2013, you can create a stand-alone pivot chart that doesn't require a pivot table. However, you have much more flexibility if you create a pivot chart from a pivot table. For example, if you create a stand-alone pivot chart, you can't group items.

A pivot chart example

Figure 34.25 shows part of a table that tracks daily sales by region. The Date field contains dates for the entire year (excluding weekends), the Region field contains the region name (Eastern, Southern, or Western), and the Sales field contains the sales amount.

FIGURE 34.25

This data will be used to create a pivot chart.

	A	B	C	D
1	Date	Region	Sales	
2	1/2/2013	Eastern	10,909	
3	1/3/2013	Eastern	11,126	
4	1/4/2013	Eastern	11,224	
5	1/5/2013	Eastern	11,299	
6	1/6/2013	Eastern	11,265	
7	1/9/2013	Eastern	11,328	
8	1/10/2013	Eastern	11,494	
9	1/11/2013	Eastern	11,328	
10	1/12/2013	Eastern	11,598	
11	1/13/2013	Eastern	11,868	
12	1/16/2013	Eastern	11,702	
13	1/17/2013	Eastern	11,846	
14	1/18/2013	Eastern	11,898	
15	1/19/2013	Eastern	11,871	
16	1/20/2013	Eastern	12,053	
17	1/23/2013	Eastern	12,073	
18	1/24/2013	Eastern	12,153	
19	1/25/2013	Eastern	12,226	
20	1/26/2013	Eastern	12,413	
21	1/27/2013	Eastern	12,663	
22	1/30/2013	Eastern	12,571	

data | Sheet1

ON THE WEB

This workbook, named `sales by region pivot chart.xlsx`, is available on this book's website.

Although you can create a pivot chart without a pivot table, I find it much easier to create a pivot table first. Figure 34.26 shows the pivot table. The Date field is in the Rows area, and the daily dates have been grouped into months. The Region field is in the Columns area. The Sales field is in the Values area.

FIGURE 34.26

This pivot table summarizes sales by region and by month.

Sum of Sales	Region		
Month	Eastern	Southern	Western
Jan	259,416	171,897	99,833
Feb	255,487	135,497	100,333
Mar	296,958	147,425	107,884
Apr	248,956	131,401	110,628
May	293,192	132,165	144,889
Jun	281,641	122,156	133,153
Jul	263,899	110,844	147,484
Aug	283,917	107,935	176,325
Sep	252,049	101,233	181,518
Oct	273,592	104,542	212,932
Nov	292,585	98,041	232,032
Dec	288,378	95,986	239,514
Grand Total	**3,290,070**	**1,459,122**	**1,886,525**

data | Sheet1

The pivot table is certainly easier to interpret than the raw data, but the trends would be easier to spot in a chart.

To create a pivot chart, select any cell in the pivot table and choose PivotTable Tools ➪ Analyze ➪ Tools ➪ PivotChart. The Insert Chart dialog box appears, from which you can choose a chart type. For this example, select a Line With Markers chart and then click OK. Excel creates the pivot chart shown in Figure 34.27. The chart makes it easy to see an upward sales trend for the Western division, a downward trend for the Southern division, and relatively flat sales for the Eastern division.

A pivot chart includes field buttons that let you filter the chart's data. To remove some or all of the field buttons, select the pivot chart and use the Field Buttons control in the PivotChart Tools ➪ Analyze ➪ Show/Hide group.

FIGURE 34.27

The pivot chart uses the data displayed in the pivot table.

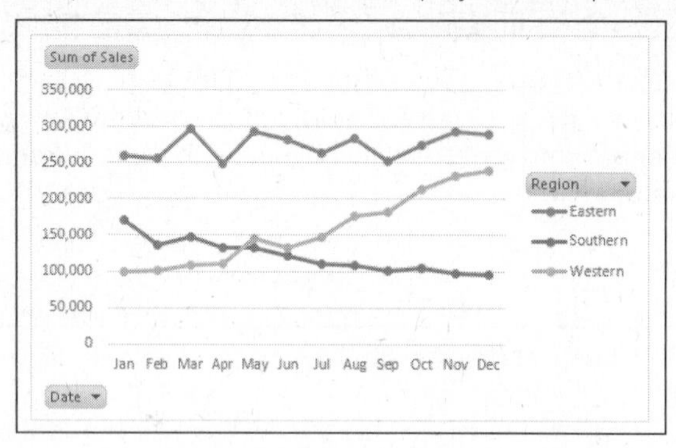

When you select a pivot chart, the Ribbon displays a new contextual tab: PivotChart Tools. The commands in the Design and Format tabs are virtually identical to those for a standard Excel chart, so you can manipulate the pivot chart any way you like.

If you modify the underlying pivot table, the chart adjusts automatically to display the new summary data. Figure 34.28 shows the pivot chart after I changed the Date grouping to quarters.

FIGURE 34.28

If you modify the pivot table, the pivot chart is also changed.

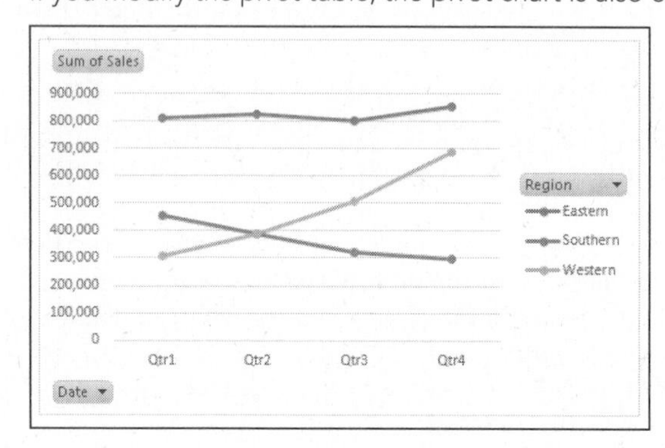

More about pivot charts

Keep in mind these points when using pivot charts:

- **A pivot table and a pivot chart are joined in a two-way link.** If you make structural or filtering changes to one, the other is also changed.
- **When you activate a pivot chart, the PivotTable Fields task pane changes to the PivotChart Fields task pane.** In this task pane, Legend (Series) replaces the Columns area, and Axis (Category) replaces the Rows area.
- **The field buttons in a pivot chart contain the same controls as the pivot chart's field headers.** These controls allow you to filter the data that's displayed in the pivot table and pivot chart. If you make changes to the pivot chart using these buttons, those changes are also reflected in the pivot table.
- **If you have a pivot chart linked to a pivot table and you delete the underlying pivot table, the pivot chart remains.** The pivot chart's Series formulas contain the original data, stored in arrays.
- **By default, pivot charts are embedded in the sheet that contains the pivot table.** To move the pivot chart to a different worksheet (or to a Chart sheet), choose PivotChart Tools ➪ Analyze ➪ Actions ➪ Move Chart.
- **You can create multiple pivot charts from a pivot table, and you can manipulate and format the charts separately.** However, all the charts display the same data.
- **A normal chart, when selected, displays the icons to the right: Chart Elements, Chart Styles, and Chart Filters.** A pivot chart does not display the Chart Filters icon.
- **Slicers and Timelines also work with pivot charts.** See the examples earlier in this chapter.
- **Don't forget about themes.** You can choose Page Layout ➪ Themes ➪ Themes to change the workbook theme, and your pivot table and pivot chart will both reflect the new theme.

Another Pivot Table Example

The pivot table example in this section demonstrates some useful ways to work with pivot tables.

Figure 34.29 shows part of a table with 3,144 data rows, one for each county in the United States. The fields are

FIGURE 34.29

This table contains data for each county in the United States.

	A	B	C	D	E	F	G
1	County	State Name	Region	Census 2000	Census 1990	Land Area	WaterArea
2	Los Angeles	California	Region IX	9,519,338	8,863,164	4,060.87	691.45
3	Cook	Illinois	Region V	5,376,741	5,105,067	945.68	689.36
4	Harris	Texas	Region VI	3,400,578	2,818,199	1,728.83	48.87
5	San Diego	California	Region IX	2,813,833	2,498,016	4,199.89	325.62
6	Orange	California	Region IX	2,846,289	2,410,556	789.40	158.57
7	Kings	New York	Region II	2,465,326	2,300,664	70.61	26.29
8	Maricopa	Arizona	Region IX	3,072,149	2,122,101	9,203.14	21.13
9	Wayne	Michigan	Region V	2,061,162	2,111,687	614.15	58.05
10	Queens	New York	Region II	2,229,379	1,951,598	109.24	69.04
11	Dade	Florida	Region IV	2,253,362	1,937,094	1,946.21	77.85
12	Dallas	Texas	Region VI	2,218,899	1,852,810	879.60	28.96
13	Philadelphia	Pennsylvania	Region III	1,517,550	1,585,577	135.09	7.55
14	King	Washington	Region X	1,737,034	1,507,319	2,126.04	180.48
15	Santa Clara	California	Region IX	1,682,585	1,497,577	1,290.69	13.32
16	New York	New York	Region II	1,537,195	1,487,536	22.96	10.81
17	San Bernardino	California	Region IX	1,709,434	1,418,380	20,052.50	52.82
18	Cuyahoga	Ohio	Region V	1,393,978	1,412,140	458.49	787.07
19	Middlesex	Massachusetts	Region I	1,465,396	1,398,468	823.46	24.08
20	Allegheny	Pennsylvania	Region III	1,281,666	1,336,449	730.17	14.54
21	Suffolk	New York	Region II	1,419,369	1,321,864	912.20	1,460.87
22	Nassau	New York	Region II	1,334,544	1,287,348	286.69	166.39
23	Alameda	California	Region IX	1,443,741	1,279,182	737.57	83.57
24	Broward	Florida	Region IV	1,623,018	1,255,488	1,205.40	114.24
25	Bronx	New York	Region II	1,332,650	1,203,789	42.03	15.40

data | pivot | formulas

- **County:** The name of the county
- **State Name:** The state of the county
- **Region:** The region (Roman numeral ranging from I to X)
- **Census 2000:** The population of the county, according to the 2000 Census
- **Census 1990:** The population of the county, according to the 1990 Census
- **LandArea:** The area, in square miles (excluding water-covered area)
- **WaterArea:** The area, in square miles, covered by water

ON THE WEB

This workbook, named `county data.xlsx`, is available on this book's website.

Figure 34.30 shows a pivot table created from the county data. The pivot table uses the Region and State Name fields for the Rows section and uses Census 2000 and Census 1990 in the Values section.

FIGURE 34.30

This pivot table was created from the county data.

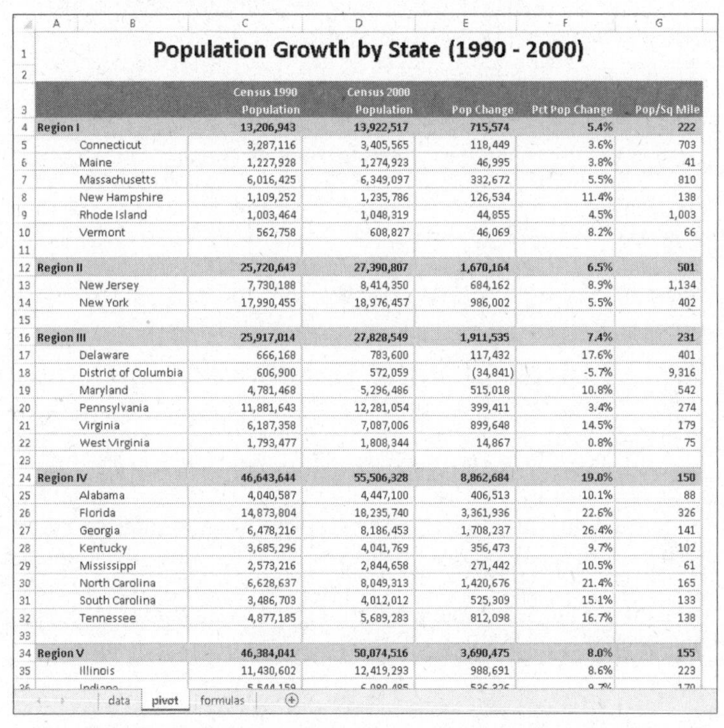

Population Growth by State (1990 - 2000)

	Census 1990 Population	Census 2000 Population	Pop Change	Pct Pop Change	Pop/Sq Mile
Region I	**13,206,943**	**13,922,517**	**715,574**	**5.4%**	**222**
Connecticut	3,287,116	3,405,565	118,449	3.6%	703
Maine	1,227,928	1,274,923	46,995	3.8%	41
Massachusetts	6,016,425	6,349,097	332,672	5.5%	810
New Hampshire	1,109,252	1,235,786	126,534	11.4%	138
Rhode Island	1,003,464	1,048,319	44,855	4.5%	1,003
Vermont	562,758	608,827	46,069	8.2%	66
Region II	**25,720,643**	**27,390,807**	**1,670,164**	**6.5%**	**501**
New Jersey	7,730,188	8,414,350	684,162	8.9%	1,134
New York	17,990,455	18,976,457	986,002	5.5%	402
Region III	**25,917,014**	**27,828,549**	**1,911,535**	**7.4%**	**231**
Delaware	666,168	783,600	117,432	17.6%	401
District of Columbia	606,900	572,059	(34,841)	-5.7%	9,316
Maryland	4,781,468	5,296,486	515,018	10.8%	542
Pennsylvania	11,881,643	12,281,054	399,411	3.4%	274
Virginia	6,187,358	7,087,006	899,648	14.5%	179
West Virginia	1,793,477	1,808,344	14,867	0.8%	75
Region IV	**46,643,644**	**55,506,328**	**8,862,684**	**19.0%**	**150**
Alabama	4,040,587	4,447,100	406,513	10.1%	88
Florida	14,873,804	18,235,740	3,361,936	22.6%	326
Georgia	6,478,216	8,186,453	1,708,237	26.4%	141
Kentucky	3,685,296	4,041,769	356,473	9.7%	102
Mississippi	2,573,216	2,844,658	271,442	10.5%	61
North Carolina	6,628,637	8,049,313	1,420,676	21.4%	165
South Carolina	3,486,703	4,012,012	525,309	15.1%	133
Tennessee	4,877,185	5,689,283	812,098	16.7%	138
Region V	**46,384,041**	**50,074,516**	**3,690,475**	**8.0%**	**155**
Illinois	11,430,602	12,419,293	988,691	8.6%	223

I created three calculated fields to display additional information:

- **Change (displayed as Pop Change):** The difference between Census 2000 and Census 1990
- **Pct Change (displayed as Pct Pop Change):** The population change expressed as a percentage of the 1990 population
- **Density (displayed as Pop/Sq Mile):** The population per square mile of land

34

TIP

To view (or document) calculated fields and calculated items in a pivot table, choose PivotTable Tools ➪ Analyze ➪ Calculations ➪ Fields, Items & Sets ➪ List Formulas. Excel inserts a new worksheet with information about your calculated fields and items. Figure 34.31 shows an example.

FIGURE 34.31

This worksheet lists calculated fields and items for the pivot table.

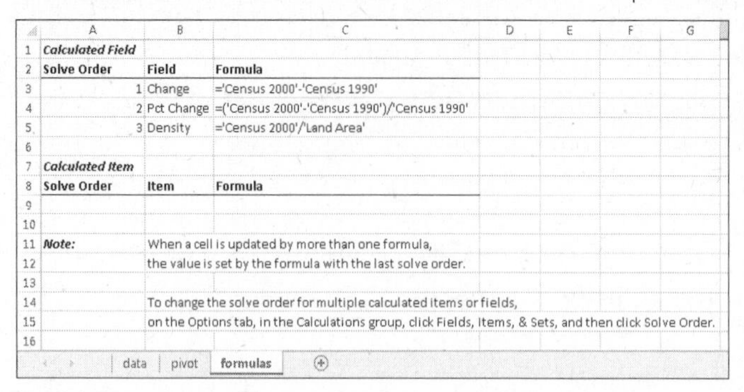

	A	B	C
1	*Calculated Field*		
2	**Solve Order**	**Field**	**Formula**
3	1	Change	='Census 2000'-'Census 1990'
4	2	Pct Change	=('Census 2000'-'Census 1990')/'Census 1990'
5	3	Density	='Census 2000'/'Land Area'
6			
7	*Calculated Item*		
8	**Solve Order**	**Item**	**Formula**
9			
10			
11	*Note:*	When a cell is updated by more than one formula,	
12		the value is set by the formula with the last solve order.	
13			
14		To change the solve order for multiple calculated items or fields,	
15		on the Options tab, in the Calculations group, click Fields, Items, & Sets, and then click Solve Order.	
16			

This pivot table is sorted on two columns. The main sort is by Region, and states within each region are sorted alphabetically. To sort, just select a cell that contains a data point to be included in the sort. Right-click and choose from the shortcut menu.

Sorting by Region requires some additional effort because Roman numerals are not in alphabetical order. Therefore, I had to create a custom list. To create a custom sort list, access the Excel Options dialog box, select the Advanced tab, and click Edit Custom Lists. Click New List, type your list entries, and click Add. Figure 34.32 shows the custom list I created for the region names.

FIGURE 34.32

This custom list ensures that the Region names are sorted correctly.

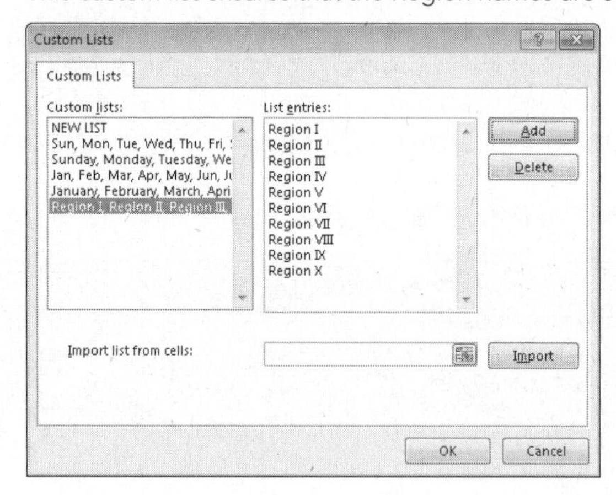

Producing a Report with a Pivot Table

By using a pivot table, you can convert a huge table of data into an attractive printed report. Figure 34.33 shows a small portion of a pivot table that I created from a table that has more than 67,000 rows of data. This data happens to be my digital music collection, and each row contains information about a single music file: the genre, the artist name, the track name, the album name, the duration, and the file size. I chose this example because it's the largest file I have that's actually interesting.

FIGURE 34.33

Part of a 161-page pivot table report.

	Under The Volcano	58 Mb	0:40:45
Steve Martin		**180 Mb**	**1:25:20**
	Rare Bird Alert	77 Mb	0:41:31
	The Crow New Songs for the 5-String Banjo	103 Mb	0:43:49
Tony Furtada		**44 Mb**	**0:37:34**
	Swamped	44 Mb	0:37:34
Tony Rice		**59 Mb**	**0:37:18**
	California Autumn	59 Mb	0:37:18
Various - Bluegrass		**754 Mb**	**8:28:43**

Page 7 of 161

		Adventures In Music #15 Bluegrass	58 Mb	0:59:51
		Dawg Tales_ Acoustic Tribute to David Grisman	79 Mb	0:50:44
		Definitive Blugrass Collection (Disc 1)	58 Mb	0:37:10
		Definitive Blugrass Collection (Disc 2)	61 Mb	0:38:50
		Hand-Picked (CD 1) 25 Years of Bluegrass on Rounder Records	115 Mb	1:13:45
		Hand-Picked (CD 2) 25 Years of Bluegrass on Rounder Records	120 Mb	1:16:23
		Heartland An Appalachian Anthology	105 Mb	1:06:08
		The Great Dobro Sessions	117 Mb	1:13:33
		The Rebel Records Sampler	42 Mb	0:32:19
	Wayne Henderson		**130 Mb**	**1:21:25**
		Les Pick	71 Mb	0:44:37
		Rugby Guitar	60 Mb	0:36:48
	Yo-Yo Ma, Stuart Duncan, Edgar Meyer, Chris Thile		**136 Mb**	**0:57:19**
		The Goat Rodeo Sessions	136 Mb	0:57:19
Blues Acoustic			**11,467 Mb**	**106:42:49**
	Alberta Hunter		**226 Mb**	**1:49:43**
		Amtrak Blues	61 Mb	0:39:26
		Downhearted Blues	165 Mb	1:10:17
	Beth Scalet		**4 Mb**	**0:03:48**
		Blues In Paradise	4 Mb	0:03:48
	Big Joe Duskin		**74 Mb**	**0:50:31**
		Big Joe Jumps Again!	74 Mb	0:50:31
	Black Ace		**84 Mb**	**1:09:41**
		I'm The Boss Card In Your Hand	84 Mb	1:09:41
	Bluff City Backsliders		**71 Mb**	**0:45:48**
		Bluff City Backsliders	71 Mb	0:45:48
	Bo Ramsey		**7 Mb**	**0:10:06**
		Downloads	7 Mb	0:10:06
	Bob Brozman		**103 Mb**	**1:02:40**
		Devil's Slide	103 Mb	1:02:40
	Brother Yusef		**117 Mb**	**0:49:22**
		Blues By Request	117 Mb	0:49:22
	Buddy Guy & Junior Wells		**192 Mb**	**1:41:23**
		Alone & Acoustic	93 Mb	0:59:31
		Going Back To Acoustic	98 Mb	0:41:52
	Cadillac John & Bill Abel		**107 Mb**	**0:45:33**
		Crazy About You	107 Mb	0:45:33
	Cherry Lee Mewis		**106 Mb**	**0:43:48**
		Little Girl Blue	106 Mb	0:43:48
	Chris Thomas King		**102 Mb**	**0:54:01**
		Red Mud	102 Mb	0:54:01
	Chris Whitley		**97 Mb**	**1:06:06**
		Dirt Floor	37 Mb	0:27:06
		Perfect Day	60 Mb	0:39:00

34

The pivot table report created from this data is 161 pages long, and it took about five minutes to set up (and only a little longer to fine-tune it).

ON THE WEB

This workbook, named `music list.xlsx`, is available on this book's website.

Here's a quick summary of how I created this report:

1. **I selected a cell in the table and chose Insert ➪ Tables ➪ PivotTable.** The Create PivotTable dialog box appeared.
2. **I clicked OK to accept the default settings.**
3. **In the new worksheet, I used the PivotTable Fields task pane and dragged the following fields to the Rows area: Genre, Artist, and Album.**
4. **I dragged the following fields to the Values area: Title, Size, and Duration.**
5. **I used the Data Field Settings dialog box to summarize Title as Count, Size as Sum, and Duration as Sum.**
6. **I wanted the information in the Size column to display in megabytes (not kilobytes), so I formatted the column using this custom number format:**

   ```
   ###,###, "Mb";;
   ```

7. **I wanted the information in the Duration column to display as hours, minutes, and seconds, so I formatted the column using this custom number format:**

   ```
   [h]:mm:ss;;
   ```

8. **I edited the column headings.** For example, I replaced *Count of Track* with *Tracks.*
9. **I changed the layout to outline format by choosing PivotTable Tools ➪ Design ➪ Layout ➪ Report Layout ➪ Show in Outline Form.**
10. **I turned off the field headers by choosing PivotTable Tools ➪ Analyze ➪ Show ➪ Field Headers.**
11. **I turned off the buttons by choosing PivotTable Tools ➪ Analzye ➪ Show ➪ +/– Buttons.**
12. **I applied a built-in style by choosing PivotTable Tools ➪ Design ➪ PivotTable Styles.**
13. **I went into Page Layout view and adjusted the column widths so that the report would fit horizontally on the page.**
14. **I added to Slicers (Genre and Artist) to make it easy to display specific music types.**

Note that you can expand and contract fields. For example, to hide the albums under each artist, select any artist and choose PivotTable Tools ➪ Analyze ➪ Active Field ➪ Collapse Field. To hide all the artist names (and just display the genres), select any genre cell and choose PivotTable Tools ➪ Analyze ➪ Active Field ➪ Collapse Field. Use the Expand Field command to unhide hidden fields.

Using the Data Model

So far, this chapter has focused exclusively on pivot tables that are created from a single table of data. A feature called the *Data Model* brings new power to pivot charts. With the Data Model, you can use multiple tables of data in a single pivot table. You'll need to create one or more "table relationships" so the data can be tied together.

NEW FEATURE

The Data Model is a new feature in Excel 2013.

Figure 34.34 shows parts of three tables that are in a single workbook (each sheet is in its own worksheet and is shown in a separate window). The tables are named Orders, Customers, and Regions. The Orders table contains information about product orders. The Customers table contains information about the company's customers. The Regions table contains a region identifier for each state.

FIGURE 34.34

These three tables will be used for a pivot table, using the Data Model.

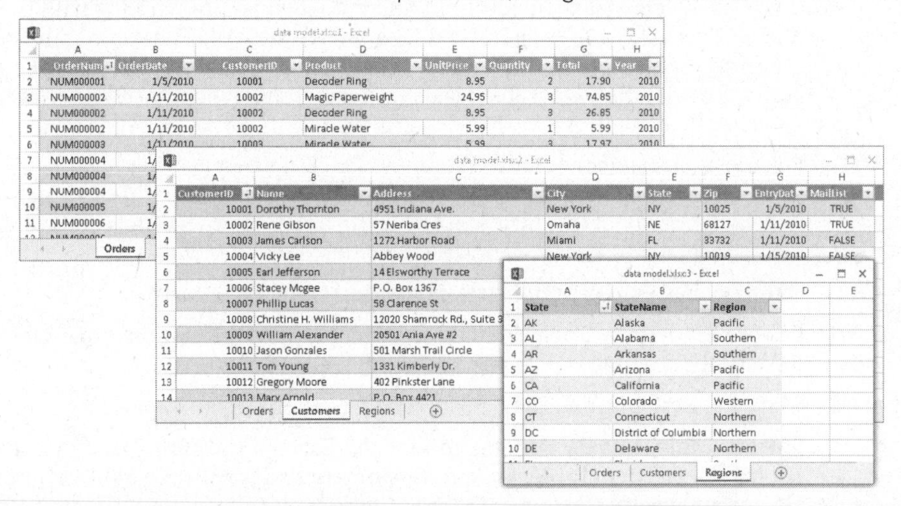

Notice that the Orders and Customers tables have a CustomerID column in common, and the Customers and Regions tables have a State column in common. The common columns will be used to form relationship among the tables.

Notice that these are "one-to-many" relationships. For every row in the Orders table, there is exactly one corresponding row in the Customers table, and that row is determined by the CustomerID column. Similarly, for every row in the Customers table, there is exactly one corresponding row in the Regions table, and that row is determined by the State column.

34

On the Web

The example in this section is available on this book's website. The workbook is named `data model.xlsx`.

Note

A pivot table created using the Data Model has some restrictions, as opposed to a pivot table created from a single table. Most notably, you can't create groups. In addition, you can't create calculated fields or calculated items.

For this example, the goal is to summarize sales by state, by region, and by year. Notice that the sales and date information is in the Order table, the state information is in the Customers table, and the region names are in the Regions table. Therefore, all three tables will be used for this pivot table.

Start by creating a pivot table (in a new worksheet) from the Orders table. Follow these steps:

1. **Select any cell within the table and choose Insert ➪ Tables ➪ Pivot Tables.** The Create PivotTable dialog box appears.
2. **Select the Add This Data to the Data Model check box.** Notice that the PivotTable Fields task pane is a bit different when you're working with the Data Model. The task pane contains two tabs: Active and All. The Active tab lists only the Orders table. The All tab lists all the tables in the workbook. To make things easier, activate the PivotTable Fields task pane, right-click the Customers table, and choose Show in Active Tab. Then do the same for the Regions table.

   Figure 34.35 shows the Active tab of the PivotTable Fields task pane, with all three tables expanded to show their column headers. Notice that I also changed the configuration of this task pane by using the drop-down Tools control. I chose Fields Section and Areas Section Side-by-Side.

   The next step is to set up the relationships among the tables.
3. **Choose PivotTable Tools ➪ Analyze ➪ Calculations ➪ Relationships.** The Manage Relationships dialog box appears.
4. **Click the New button.** The Create Relationship dialog box appears.
5. **For the Table, specify Orders, and for the Foreign Column specify Customer ID; for the Related Table, specify Customers and for the Related Column (Primary) specify CustomerID (see Figure 34.36).**

FIGURE 34.35

The PivotTable Fields task pane, with three active tables.

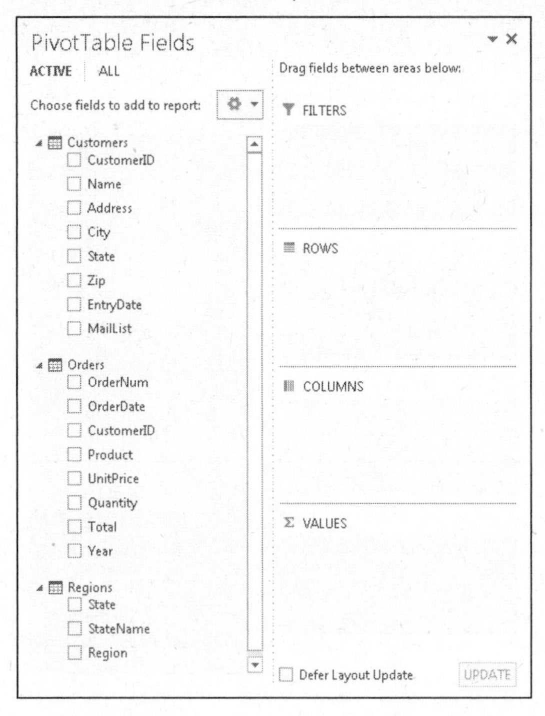

FIGURE 34.36

Creating a relationship between two tables.

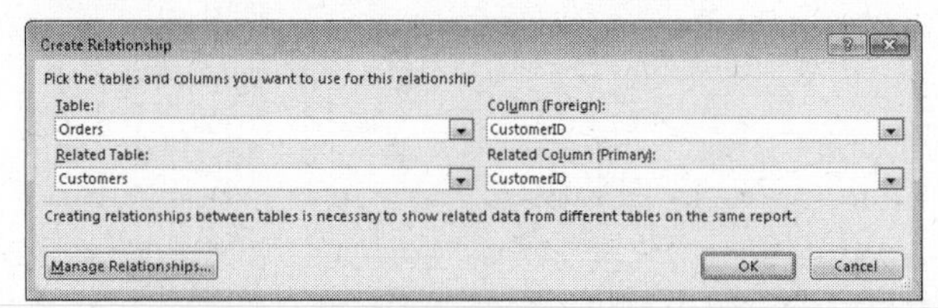

6. **Click OK to return to the Manage Relationships dialog box.**
7. **Click New again and set up a relationship between the Customers table and the Regions table.** Both will use the State column. The Manage Relationships dialog box will now show two relationships.

NOTE

If you don't set up the table relationships in advance, Excel will prompt you to do so when you add a field to the pivot table that's from a different table than you started with.

8. **With the table relationship established, it's simply a matter of dragging the field names to the appropriate section of the PivotTable Fields task pane:**
   - Drag the Total field to the Values area.
   - Drag the Year field to the Columns area.
   - Drag the Region field to the Rows area.
   - Drag the StateName field to the Rows area.

   Figure 34.37 shows part of the pivot table. I added two slicers to enable filtering the table by customers who are on the mailing list, and by product.

FIGURE 34.37

The pivot table, after adding two slicers.

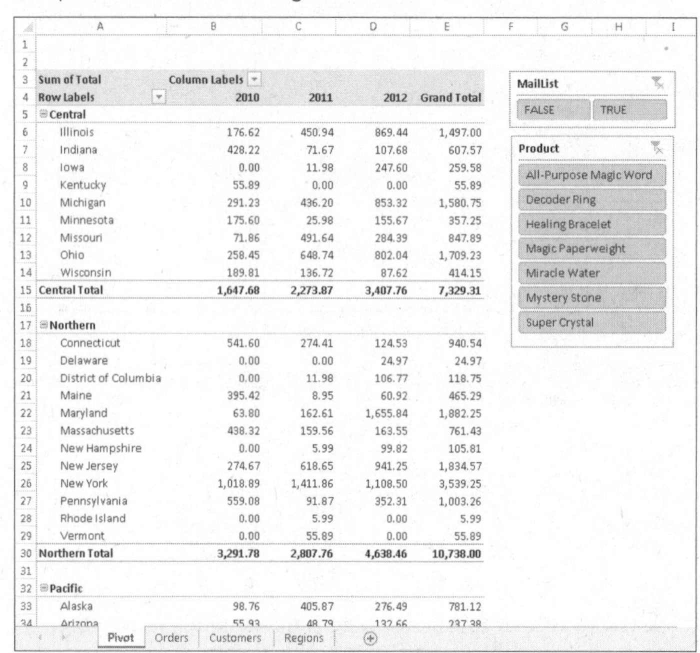

Sum of Total	Column Labels			
Row Labels	2010	2011	2012	Grand Total
Central				
Illinois	176.62	450.94	869.44	1,497.00
Indiana	428.22	71.67	107.68	607.57
Iowa	0.00	11.98	247.60	259.58
Kentucky	55.89	0.00	0.00	55.89
Michigan	291.23	436.20	853.32	1,580.75
Minnesota	175.60	25.98	155.67	357.25
Missouri	71.86	491.64	284.39	847.89
Ohio	258.45	648.74	802.04	1,709.23
Wisconsin	189.81	136.72	87.62	414.15
Central Total	1,647.68	2,273.87	3,407.76	7,329.31
Northern				
Connecticut	541.60	274.41	124.53	940.54
Delaware	0.00	0.00	24.97	24.97
District of Columbia	0.00	11.98	106.77	118.75
Maine	395.42	8.95	60.92	465.29
Maryland	63.80	162.61	1,655.84	1,882.25
Massachusetts	438.32	159.56	163.55	761.43
New Hampshire	0.00	5.99	99.82	105.81
New Jersey	274.67	618.65	941.25	1,834.57
New York	1,018.89	1,411.86	1,108.50	3,539.25
Pennsylvania	559.08	91.87	352.31	1,003.26
Rhode Island	0.00	5.99	0.00	5.99
Vermont	0.00	55.89	0.00	55.89
Northern Total	3,291.78	2,807.76	4,638.46	10,738.00
Pacific				
Alaska	98.76	405.87	276.49	781.12
Arizona	55.93	48.79	132.66	237.38

TIP

When you create a pivot chart using the Data Model, you can convert the pivot table to formulas. Select any cell in the pivot table and choose PivotTable Tools ➪ Analyze ➪ OLAP Tools ➪ Convert to Formulas. The pivot table is replaced by cells that use formulas. These formulas use `CUBEMEMBER` and `CUBEVALUE` functions. Although the range is no longer a pivot table, the formulas update when the data changes.

Learning More about Pivot Tables

The two pivot table chapters in this book provide a good introduction, and most users should have enough knowledge to create and modify pivot tables and pivot charts. But these chapters barely scratch the surface. Excel's pivot table feature could easily be the topic for an entire book.

Two relevant topics I haven't covered are

- **Using external data sources:** All the examples in this book use data stored in an Excel workbook. You can also create pivot tables from external databases.
- **The PowerPivot add-in:** Enables you to integrate large external databases and create "business intelligence" reports and dashboards. PowerPivot works independently of Excel's built-in pivot table features.

CHAPTER 35

Performing Spreadsheet What-If Analysis

IN THIS CHAPTER

Considering a what-if example

Identifying types of what-if analyses

Looking at manual what-if analyses

Creating one-input and two-input data tables

Using Scenario Manager

One of the most appealing aspects of Excel is its ability to create dynamic models. A *dynamic model* uses formulas that instantly recalculate when you change values in cells that are used by the formulas. When you change values in cells in a systematic manner and observe the effects on specific formula cells, you're performing a type of *what-if* analysis.

What-if analysis is the process of asking such questions as "What if the interest rate on the loan changes to 7.5% rather than 7.0%?" or "What if we raise our product prices by 5%?"

If you set up your worksheet properly, answering such questions is simply a matter of plugging in new values and observing the results of the recalculation. Excel provides useful tools to assist you in your what-if endeavors.

A What-If Example

Figure 35.1 shows a simple worksheet model that calculates information pertaining to a mortgage loan. The worksheet is divided into two sections: the input cells and the result cells (which contain formulas).

FIGURE 35.1

This simple worksheet model uses four input cells to produce the results.

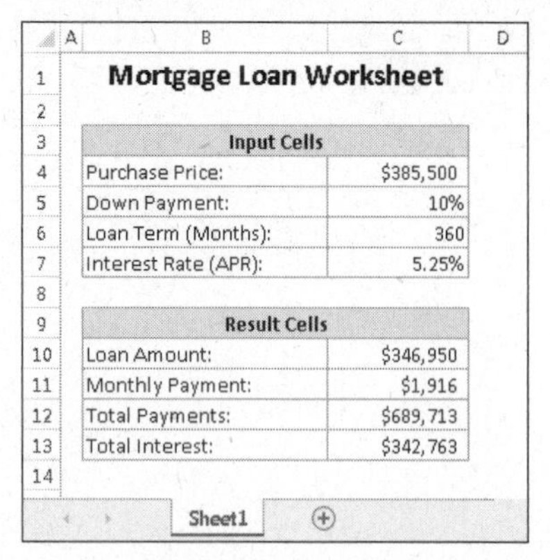

Mortgage Loan Worksheet

Input Cells	
Purchase Price:	$385,500
Down Payment:	10%
Loan Term (Months):	360
Interest Rate (APR):	5.25%

Result Cells	
Loan Amount:	$346,950
Monthly Payment:	$1,916
Total Payments:	$689,713
Total Interest:	$342,763

Sheet1

ON THE WEB

This workbook is available on this book's website. The filename is `mortgage loan.xlsx`.

With this worksheet, you can easily answer the following what-if questions:

- What if I can negotiate a lower purchase price on the property?
- What if the lender requires a 20% down payment?
- What if I can get a 40-year mortgage?
- What if the interest rate increases to 5.50%?

You can answer these questions by simply changing the values in the cells in range C4:C7 and observing the effects in the dependent cells (C10:C13). You can, of course, vary any number of input cells simultaneously.

Types of What-If Analyses

Not surprisingly, Excel can handle much more sophisticated models than the preceding example. To perform a what-if analysis using Excel, you have three basic options:

- **Manual what-if analysis:** Plug in new values and observe the effects on formula cells.
- **Data tables:** Create a special type of table that displays the results of selected formula cells as you systematically change one or two input cells.
- **Scenario Manager:** Create named scenarios and generate reports that use outlines or pivot tables.

I discuss each of these types of what-if analysis in the rest of this chapter.

Avoid Hard-Coding Values in a Formula

The mortgage calculation example, simple as it is, demonstrates an important point about spreadsheet design: You should always set up your worksheet so that you have maximum flexibility to make changes. Perhaps the most fundamental rule of spreadsheet design is the following:

> Do not hard-code values in a formula. Instead, store the values in separate cells and use cell references in the formula.

The term *hard-code* refers to the use of actual values, or *constants,* in a formula. In the mortgage loan example, all the formulas use references to cells, not actual values.

You *could* use the value 360, for example, for the loan term argument of the `pmt` function in cell C11 of Figure 35.1. Using a cell reference has two advantages: First, you have no doubt about the values that the formula uses (they aren't buried in the formula). Second, you can easily change the value — which is easier than editing the formula.

Using values in formulas may not seem like much of an issue when only one formula is involved, but just imagine what would happen if this value were hard-coded into several hundred formulas that were scattered throughout a worksheet.

Performing manual what-if analysis

A manual what-if analysis doesn't require too much explanation. In fact, the example that opens this chapter demonstrates how it's done. Manual what-if analysis is based on the idea that you have one or more input cells that affect one or more key formula cells. You change the value in the input cells and see what happens to the formula cells. You may want to print the results or save each scenario to a new workbook. The term *scenario* refers to a specific set of values in one or more input cells.

Manual what-if analysis is very common. People often use this technique without even realizing that they're doing a type of what-if analysis. This method of performing what-if analysis certainly has nothing wrong with it, but you should be aware of some other techniques.

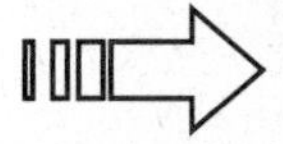

If your input cells are not located near the formula cells, consider using a Watch Window to monitor the formula results in a movable window. I discuss this feature in Chapter 3.

Creating data tables

This section describes one of Excel's most underutilized features: data tables. A *data table* is a dynamic range that summarizes formula cells for varying input cells. You can create a data table fairly easily, but data tables have some limitations. In particular, a data table can deal with only one or two input cells at a time. This limitation becomes clear as you view the examples.

NOTE

Scenario Manager, discussed later in this chapter (see "Using Scenario Manager"), can produce a report that summarizes any number of input cells and result cells.

Don't confuse a data table with a standard table (created by choosing Insert ⇨ Tables ⇨ Table). These two features are completely independent.

Creating a one-input data table

A *one-input data table* displays the results of one or more formulas for various values of a single input cell. Figure 35.2 shows the general layout for a one-input data table. You need to set up the table yourself, manually. This is not something that Excel will do for you.

FIGURE 35.2

How a one-input data table is set up.

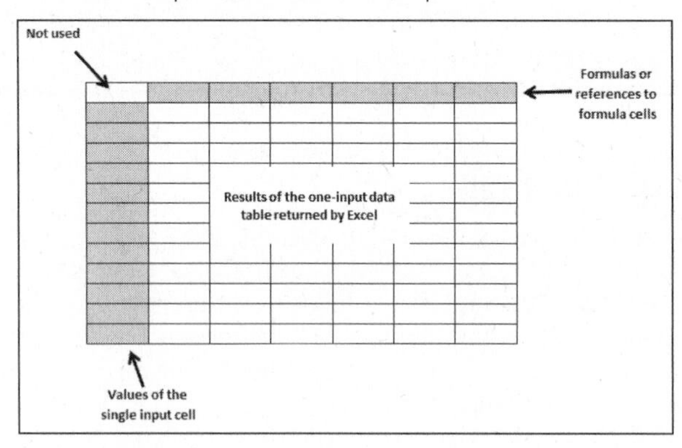

You can place the data table anywhere in a worksheet. The left column contains various values for the single input cell. The top row contains references to formulas located elsewhere in the worksheet. You can use a single formula reference or any number of formula references. The upper-left cell of the table remains empty. Excel calculates the values that result from each value of the input cell and places them under each formula reference.

This example uses the mortgage loan worksheet from earlier in the chapter (see "A What-If Example"). The goal of this exercise is to create a data table that shows the values of the four formula cells (loan amount, monthly payment, total payments, and total interest) for various interest rates ranging from 4.5% to 6.5%, in 0.25% increments.

ON THE WEB

This workbook is available on this book's website. The file is named `mortgage loan data table.xlsx`.

Figure 35.3 shows the setup for the data table area. Row 3 consists of references to the formulas in the worksheet. For example, cell F3 contains the formula `=C10`, and cell G3 contains the formula `=C11`. Row 2 contains optional descriptive labels, and these are not actually part of the data table. Column E contains the values of the single input cell (interest rate) that Excel will use in the table.

FIGURE 35.3

Preparing to create a one-input data table.

	A	B	C	D	E	F	G	H	I
1		**Mortgage Loan Worksheet**							
2						*Loan Amt*	*Mo Pmt*	*Total Pmts*	*Total Int*
3		**Input Cells**				$346,950	$1,916	$689,713	$342,763
4		Purchase Price:	$385,500		4.50%				
5		Down Payment:	10%		4.75%				
6		Loan Term:	360		5.00%				
7		Interest Rate (Months):	5.25%	*Interest rate*	5.25%				
8					5.50%				
9		**Result Cells**			5.75%				
10		Loan Amount:	$346,950		6.00%				
11		Monthly Payment:	$1,916		6.25%				
12		Total Payments:	$689,713		6.50%				
13		Total Interest:	$342,763						

data table

To create the table, select the data table range (in this case, E3:I12) and then choose Data ➪ Data Tools ➪ What-If Analysis ➪ Data Table. The Data Table dialog box, shown in Figure 35.4, appears.

FIGURE 35.4

The Data Table dialog box.

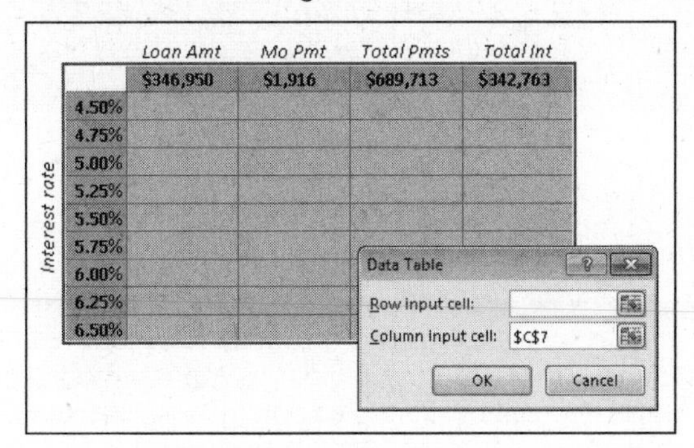

You must specify the worksheet cell that contains the input value. Because variables for the input cell appear in the left column in the data table, you place this cell reference in the Column Input Cell field. Enter **C7** or point to the cell in the worksheet. Leave the Row Input Cell field blank. Click OK, and Excel fills in the table with the calculated results (see Figure 35.5).

FIGURE 35.5

The result of the one-input data table.

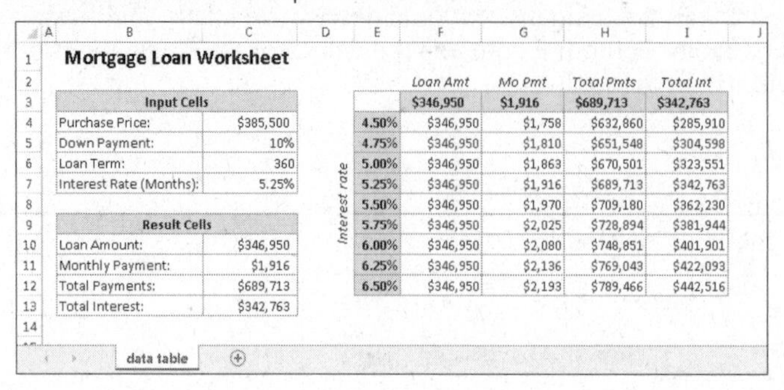

Mortgage Loan Worksheet

Input Cells	
Purchase Price:	$385,500
Down Payment:	10%
Loan Term:	360
Interest Rate (Months):	5.25%

Result Cells	
Loan Amount:	$346,950
Monthly Payment:	$1,916
Total Payments:	$689,713
Total Interest:	$342,763

Interest rate	Loan Amt	Mo Pmt	Total Pmts	Total Int
	$346,950	$1,916	$689,713	$342,763
4.50%	$346,950	$1,758	$632,860	$285,910
4.75%	$346,950	$1,810	$651,548	$304,598
5.00%	$346,950	$1,863	$670,501	$323,551
5.25%	$346,950	$1,916	$689,713	$342,763
5.50%	$346,950	$1,970	$709,180	$362,230
5.75%	$346,950	$2,025	$728,894	$381,944
6.00%	$346,950	$2,080	$748,851	$401,901
6.25%	$346,950	$2,136	$769,043	$422,093
6.50%	$346,950	$2,193	$789,466	$442,516

Using this table, you can now see the calculated loan values for varying interest rates. Notice that the Loan Amt column (column F) doesn't vary. That's because the formula in cell C10 doesn't depend on the interest rate.

If you examine the contents of the cells that Excel entered as a result of this command, you'll see that the data is generated with a multicell array formula:

```
{=TABLE(,C7)}
```

As I discuss in Chapter 17, an *array formula* is a single formula that can produce results in multiple cells. Because the table uses formulas, Excel updates the table that you produce if you change the cell references in the first row or plug in different interest rates in the first column.

NOTE

You can arrange a one-input table vertically (as in this example) or horizontally. If you place the values of the input cell in a row, you enter the input cell reference in the Row Input Cell field of the Data Table dialog box.

Creating a two-input data table

As the name implies, a *two-input data table* lets you vary *two* input cells. You can see the setup for this type of table in Figure 35.6. Although it looks similar to a one-input table, the two-input table has one critical difference: It can show the results of only one formula at a time. With a one-input table, you can place any number of formulas, or references to formulas, across the top row of the table. In a two-input table, this top row holds the values for the second input cell. The upper-left cell of the table contains a reference to the single result formula.

FIGURE 35.6

The setup for a two-input data table.

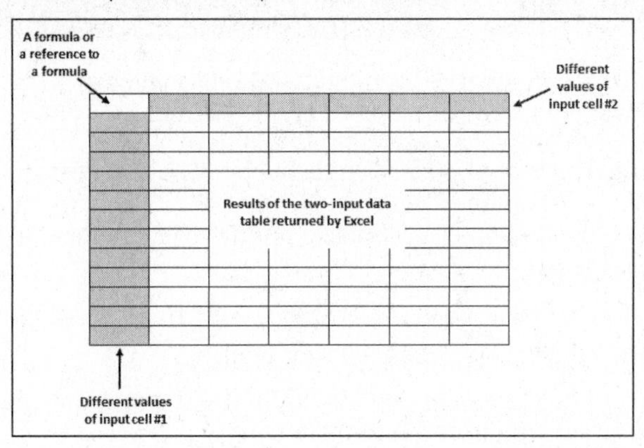

Using the mortgage loan worksheet, you could create a two-input data table that shows the results of a formula (say, monthly payment) for various combinations of two input cells (such as interest rate and down-payment percent). To see the effects on other formulas, you simply create multiple data tables — one for each formula cell that you want to summarize.

The example in this section uses the worksheet shown in Figure 35.7 to demonstrate a two-input data table. In this example, a company wants to conduct a direct-mail promotion to sell its product. The worksheet calculates the net profit from the promotion.

FIGURE 35.7

This worksheet calculates the net profit from a direct-mail promotion.

	A	B
1	Direct Mail Profit Model	
2		
3	Input Cells	
4	Number mailed:	275,000
5	Response rate:	2.50%
6		
7	Parameters	
8	Printing costs per unit:	$0.15
9	Mailing costs per unit:	$0.28
10	Responses:	6,875
11	Profit per response:	$18.50
12	Gross profit:	$127,188
13	Printing + mailing costs:	$118,250
14	Net Profit	$8,937
15		

Sheet1

35

ON THE WEB

This workbook, named `direct mail data table.xlsx`, is on this book's website.

This model uses two input cells: the number of promotional pieces mailed and the anticipated response rate. The following items appear in the Parameters area:

- **Printing costs per unit:** The cost to print a single mailer. The unit cost varies with the quantity: $0.20 each for quantities less than 200,000; $0.15 each for quantities of 200,001 through 300,000; and $0.10 each for quantities of more than 300,000. The following formula is used:

  ```
  =IF(B4<200000,0.2,IF(B4<300000,0.15,0.1))
  ```

- **Mailing costs per unit:** A fixed cost, $0.28 per unit mailed.
- **Responses:** The number of responses, calculated from the response rate and the number mailed. The formula in this cell is the following:

  ```
  =B4*B5
  ```

- **Profit per response:** A fixed value. The company knows that it will realize an average profit of $18.50 per order.
- **Gross profit:** This is a simple formula that multiplies the profit-per-response by the number of responses:

  ```
  =B10*B11
  ```

- **Print + mailing costs:** This formula calculates the total cost of the promotion:

  ```
  =B4*(B8+B9)
  ```

- **Net Profit:** This formula calculates the bottom line — the gross profit minus the printing and mailing costs.

If you enter values for the two input cells, you see that the net profit varies quite a bit, often going negative to produce a net loss.

Figure 35.8 shows the setup of a two-input data table that summarizes the net profit at various combinations of quantity and response rate; the table appears in the range E4:M14. Cell E4 contains a formula that references the Net Profit cell:

```
=B14
```

To create the data table, follow these steps:

1. **Enter the response rate values in F4:M4.**
2. **Enter the number mailed values in E5:E14.**
3. **Select the range E4:M14 and choose Data ➪ Data Tools ➪ What-If Analysis ➪ Data Table.** The Data Table dialog box appears.

FIGURE 35.8

Preparing to create a two-input data table.

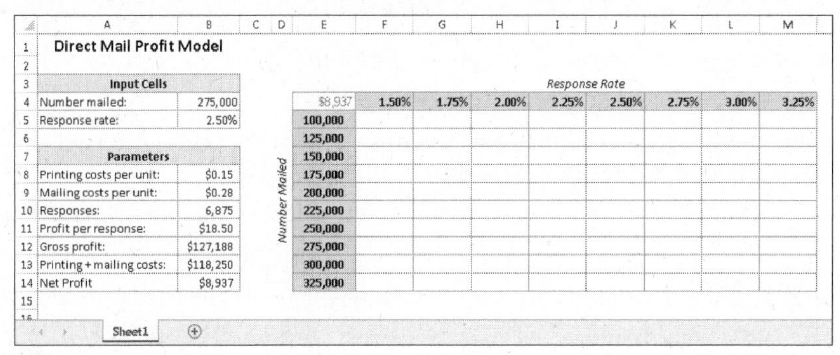

Direct Mail Profit Model

Input Cells	
Number mailed:	275,000
Response rate:	2.50%

Parameters	
Printing costs per unit:	$0.15
Mailing costs per unit:	$0.28
Responses:	6,875
Profit per response:	$18.50
Gross profit:	$127,188
Printing + mailing costs:	$118,250
Net Profit	$8,937

Response Rate / Number Mailed

$8,937	1.50%	1.75%	2.00%	2.25%	2.50%	2.75%	3.00%	3.25%
100,000								
125,000								
150,000								
175,000								
200,000								
225,000								
250,000								
275,000								
300,000								
325,000								

4. **Specify B5 as the Row input cell (the response rate) and cell B4 as the Column input (the number mailed).**
5. **Click OK.** Excel fills in the data table.

Figure 35.9 shows the result. As you can see, quite a few of the combinations of response rate and quantity mailed result in a loss rather than a profit.

FIGURE 35.9

The result of the two-input data table.

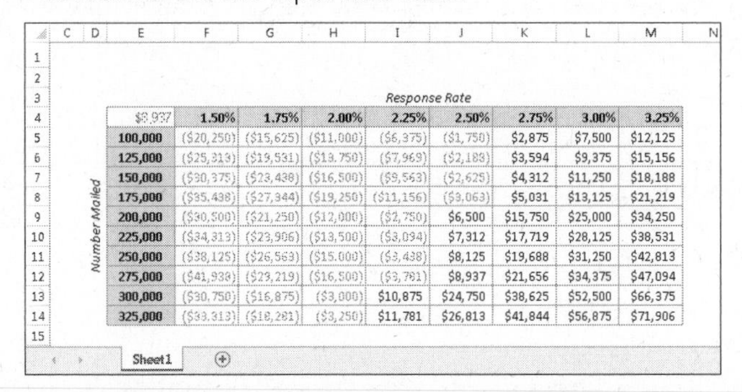

Response Rate / Number Mailed

$8,937	1.50%	1.75%	2.00%	2.25%	2.50%	2.75%	3.00%	3.25%
100,000	($20,250)	($15,625)	($11,000)	($6,375)	($1,750)	$2,875	$7,500	$12,125
125,000	($25,313)	($19,531)	($13.750)	($7,969)	($2,183)	$3,594	$9,375	$15,156
150,000	($30,375)	($23,438)	($16,500)	($9,563)	($2,625)	$4,312	$11,250	$18,188
175,000	($35.438)	($27,344)	($19,250)	($11,156)	($3,063)	$5,031	$13,125	$21,219
200,000	($30,500)	($21,250)	($12,000)	($2,750)	$6,500	$15,750	$25,000	$34,250
225,000	($34,313)	($23,906)	($13,500)	($3,094)	$7,312	$17,719	$28,125	$38,531
250,000	($38,125)	($26,563)	($15.000)	($3,438)	$8,125	$19,688	$31,250	$42,813
275,000	($41,938)	($29,219)	($16,500)	($3,781)	$8,937	$21,656	$34,375	$47,094
300,000	($30.750)	($16,875)	($3,000)	$10,875	$24,750	$38,625	$52,500	$66,375
325,000	($33.313)	($18,281)	($3,250)	$11,781	$26,813	$41,844	$56,875	$71,906

As with the one-input data table, this data table is dynamic. You can change the formula in cell E4 to refer to another cell (such as gross profit). Or you can enter some different values for Response Rate and Number Mailed.

Using Scenario Manager

Data tables are useful, but they have a few limitations:

- You can vary only one or two input cells at a time.
- Setting up a data table is not very intuitive.
- A two-input table shows the results of only one formula cell (although you can create additional tables for more formulas).
- In many situations, you're interested in a few select combinations, not an entire table that shows all possible combinations of two input cells.

The Scenario Manager is a fairly easy way to automate some aspects of your what-if models. You can store different sets of input values (called *changing cells* in the terminology of Scenario Manager) for any number of variables and give a name to each set. You can then select a set of values by name, and Excel displays the worksheet by using those values. You can also generate a summary report that shows the effect of various combinations of values on any number of result cells. These summary reports can be an outline or a pivot table.

For example, your annual sales forecast may depend upon several factors. Consequently, you can define three scenarios: best case, worst case, and most likely case. You then can switch to any of these scenarios by selecting the named scenario from a list. Excel substitutes the appropriate input values in your worksheet and recalculates the formulas.

Defining scenarios

To introduce you to Scenario Manager, this section starts with an example that uses a simplified production model, as shown in Figure 35.10.

FIGURE 35.10

A simple production model to demonstrate Scenario Manager.

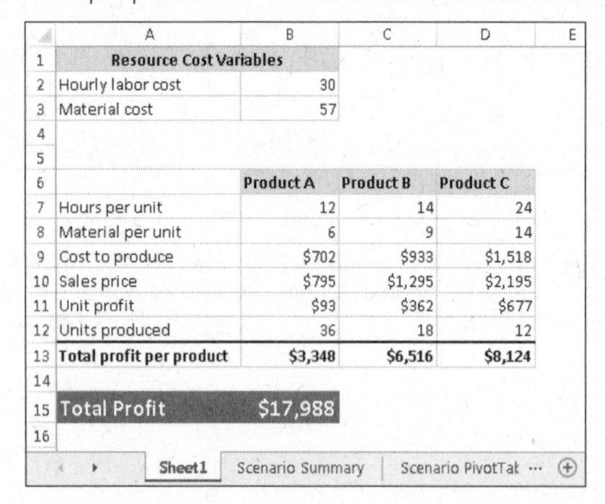

	A	B	C	D	E
1	Resource Cost Variables				
2	Hourly labor cost	30			
3	Material cost	57			
4					
5					
6		Product A	Product B	Product C	
7	Hours per unit	12	14	24	
8	Material per unit	6	9	14	
9	Cost to produce	$702	$933	$1,518	
10	Sales price	$795	$1,295	$2,195	
11	Unit profit	$93	$362	$677	
12	Units produced	36	18	12	
13	Total profit per product	$3,348	$6,516	$8,124	
14					
15	Total Profit	$17,988			
16					

Sheet1 | Scenario Summary | Scenario PivotTat ...

On the Web

This workbook, named `production model scenarios.xlsx`, is available on this book's website.

This worksheet contains two input cells: the hourly labor cost (cell B2) and the unit cost for materials (cell B3). The company produces three products, and each product requires a different number of hours and a different amount of materials to produce.

Formulas calculate the total profit per product (row 13) and the total combined profit (cell B15). Management — trying to predict the total profit, but uncertain what the hourly labor cost and material costs will be — has identified three scenarios, listed in Table 35.1.

TABLE 35.1 Three Scenarios for the Production Model

Scenario	Hourly Cost	Materials Cost
Best Case	30	57
Worst Case	38	62
Most Likely	34	59

The Best Case scenario has the lowest hourly cost and lowest materials cost. The Worst Case scenario has high values for both the hourly cost and the materials cost. The third scenario, Most Likely Case, has intermediate values for both of these input cells. The managers need to be prepared for the worst case, however, and they're interested in what would happen under the Best Case scenario.

Choose Data ➪ Data Tools ➪ What-If Analysis ➪ Scenario Manager to display the Scenario Manager dialog box. When you first open this dialog box, it tells you that no scenarios are defined — which is not too surprising because you're just starting. As you add named scenarios, they appear in the Scenarios list in this dialog box.

Tip

It's a good idea to create names for the changing cells and all the result cells that you want to examine. Excel uses these names in the dialog boxes and in the reports that it generates. If you use names, keeping track of what's going on is much easier; names also make your reports more readable.

To add a scenario, click the Add button in the Scenario Manager dialog box. Excel displays its Add Scenario dialog box, shown in Figure 35.11.

FIGURE 35.11

Use the Add Scenario dialog box to create a named scenario.

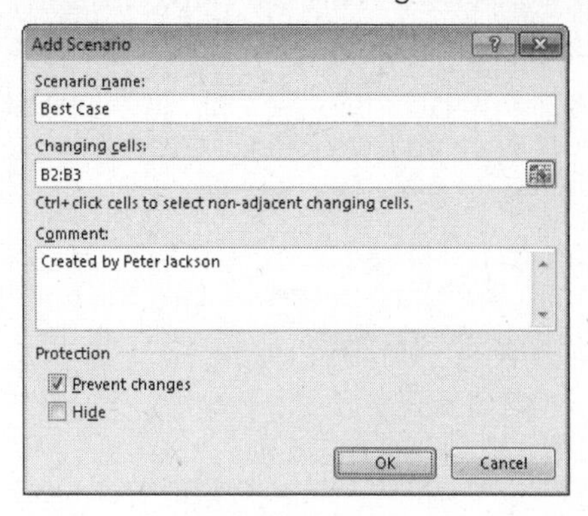

This dialog box consists of four parts:

- **Scenario Name:** You can give the scenario any name that you like — preferably something meaningful.
- **Changing Cells:** The input cells for the scenario. You can enter the cell addresses directly or point to them. If you've created a name for the cells, type the name. Nonadjacent cells are allowed; if pointing to multiple cells, press Ctrl while you click the cells. Each named scenario can use the same set of changing cells or different changing cells. The number of changing cells for a scenario is limited to 32.
- **Comment:** By default, Excel displays the name of the person who created the scenario and the date when it was created. You can change this text, add new text to it, or delete it.
- **Protection:** The two Protection options (preventing changes and hiding a scenario) are in effect only when you protect the worksheet and choose the Scenario option in the Protect Sheet dialog box. Protecting a scenario prevents anyone from modifying it; a hidden scenario doesn't appear in the Scenario Manager dialog box.

In this example, define the three scenarios that are listed in Table 36.1. The changing cells are Hourly_Cost (B2) and Materials_Cost (B3).

After you enter the information in the Add Scenario dialog box, click OK. Excel then displays the Scenario Values dialog box, shown in Figure 35.12. This dialog box displays one field for each changing cell that you specified in the previous dialog box. Enter the values for each cell in the scenario. If you click OK, you return to the Scenario Manager dialog box, which then displays your named scenario in its list. If you have more scenarios to create, click the Add button to return to the Add Scenario dialog box.

Using the Scenarios Drop-Down List

The Scenarios drop-down list shows all the defined scenarios and enables you to quickly display a scenario. Oddly, this useful tool doesn't appear on the Ribbon. But if you use Scenario Manager, you can add the Scenarios control to your Quick Access toolbar. Here's how:

1. **Right-click the Quick Access toolbar and choose Customize Quick Access Toolbar from the shortcut menu.** The Excel Options dialog box appears, with the Quick Access Toolbar tab selected.
2. **From the Choose Commands From drop-down list, select Commands Not in the Ribbon.**
3. **Scroll down the list and select Scenario.**
4. **Click the Add button.**
5. **Click OK to close the Excel Options dialog box.**

Alternatively, you can add the Scenarios control to the Ribbon. See Chapter 24 for additional details on customizing the Quick Access toolbar and the Ribbon.

FIGURE 35.12

You enter the values for the scenario in the Scenario Values dialog box.

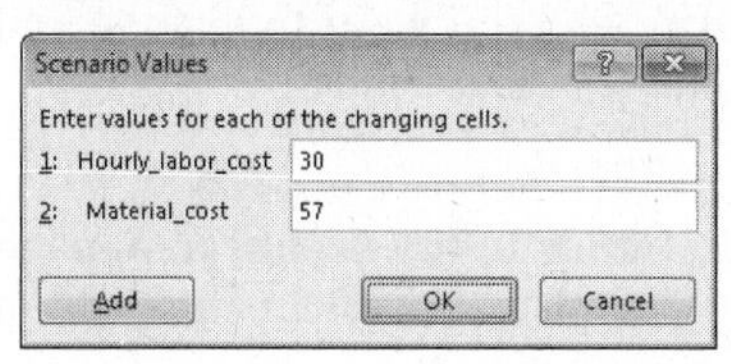

Displaying scenarios

After you define all the scenarios and return to the Scenario Manager dialog box, the dialog box displays the names of your defined scenarios. Select one of the scenarios and then click the Show button (or double-click the Scenario name). Excel inserts the corresponding values into the changing cells and calculates the worksheet to show the results for that scenario. Figure 35.13 shows an example of selecting a scenario.

35

FIGURE 35.13

Selecting a scenario to display.

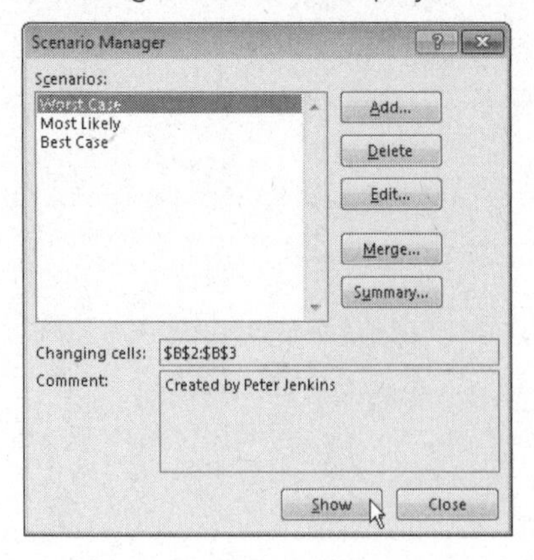

Modifying scenarios

After you've created scenarios, you may need to change them. To do so, follow these steps:

1. **Click the Edit button in the Scenario Manager dialog box to change one or more of the values for the changing cells of a scenario.**
2. **From the Scenarios list, select the scenario that you want to change and then click the Edit button.** The Edit Scenario dialog box appears.
3. **Click OK.** The Scenario Values dialog box appears.
4. **Make your changes and then click OK to return to the Scenario Manager dialog box.** Notice that Excel automatically updates the Comments box with new text that indicates when the scenario was modified.

Merging scenarios

In workgroup situations, you may have several people working on a spreadsheet model, and several people may have defined various scenarios. The marketing department, for example, may have its opinion of what the input cells should be, the finance department may have another opinion, and your CEO may have yet another opinion.

Excel makes it easy to merge these various scenarios into a single workbook. Before you merge scenarios, make sure that the workbook from which you're merging is open:

1. **Click the Merge button in the Scenario Manager dialog box.**
2. **From the Merge Scenarios dialog box that appears, choose the workbook that contains the scenarios you're merging in the Book drop-down list.**
3. **Choose the sheet that contains the scenarios you want to merge from the Sheet list box, and click Add.** Notice that the dialog box displays the number of scenarios in each sheet as you scroll through the Sheet list box.
4. **Click OK.** You return to the previous dialog box, which now displays the scenario names that you merged from the other workbook.

Generating a scenario report

If you've created multiple scenarios, you may want to document your work by creating a scenario summary report. When you click the Summary button in the Scenario Manager dialog box, Excel displays the Scenario Summary dialog box.

You have a choice of report types:

- **Scenario Summary:** The summary report appears in the form of a worksheet outline.
- **Scenario PivotTable:** The summary report appears in the form of a pivot table.

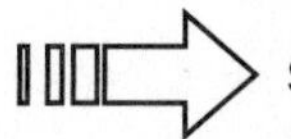

See Chapter 27 for more information about outlines and Chapter 33 for an introduction to pivot tables.

For simple cases of scenario management, a standard Scenario Summary report is usually sufficient. If you have many scenarios defined with multiple result cells, however, you may find that a Scenario PivotTable provides more flexibility.

The Scenario Summary dialog box also asks you to specify the *result cells* (the cells that contain the formulas in which you're interested). For this example, select B13:D13 and B15 (a multiple selection) to make the report show the profit for each product, plus the total profit.

NOTE

As you work with Scenario Manager, you may discover its main limitation: namely, that a scenario can use no more than 32 changing cells. If you attempt to use more cells, you get an error message.

Excel creates a new worksheet to store the summary table. Figure 35.14 shows the Scenario Summary form of the report. If you gave names to the changing cells and result cells, the table uses these names; otherwise, it lists the cell references.

FIGURE 35.14

A Scenario Summary report produced by Scenario Manager.

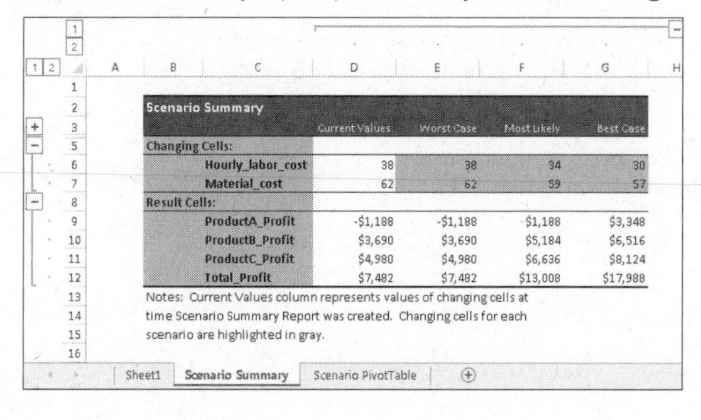

Scenario Summary	Current Values	Worst Case	Most Likely	Best Case
Changing Cells:				
Hourly_labor_cost	38	38	34	30
Material_cost	62	62	59	57
Result Cells:				
ProductA_Profit	-$1,188	-$1,188	$1,188	$3,348
ProductB_Profit	$3,690	$3,690	$5,184	$6,516
ProductC_Profit	$4,980	$4,980	$6,636	$8,124
Total_Profit	$7,482	$7,482	$13,008	$17,988

Notes: Current Values column represents values of changing cells at time Scenario Summary Report was created. Changing cells for each scenario are highlighted in gray.

CHAPTER

36

Analyzing Data Using Goal Seeking and Solver

IN THIS CHAPTER

Performing what-if analysis — in reverse

Single-cell goal seeking

Introducing Solver

Looking at Solver examples

The preceding chapter discusses *what-if analysis* — the process of changing input cells to observe the results on other dependent cells. This chapter looks at that process from the opposite perspective: finding the value of one or more input cells that produces a desired result in a formula cell.

What-If Analysis, in Reverse

Consider the following what-if question: "What is the total profit if sales increase by 20%?" If you set up your worksheet model properly, you can change the value in one or more cells to see what happens to the profit cell. The examples in this chapter take the opposite approach. If you know what a formula result *should* be, Excel can tell you the values that you need to enter in one or more input cells to produce that result. In other words, you can ask a question such as "How much do sales need to increase to produce a profit of $1.2 million?" Excel provides two tools that are relevant:

- **Goal Seek:** Determines the value that you need to enter in a single input cell to produce a result that you want in a dependent (formula) cell.
- **Solver:** Determines the values that you need to enter in multiple input cells to produce a result that you want. Moreover, because you can specify certain constraints to the problem, you gain significant problem-solving ability.

Single-Cell Goal Seeking

Single-cell goal seeking is a rather simple concept. Excel determines what value in an input cell produces a desired result in a formula cell. The following example shows you how single-cell goal seeking works.

A goal-seeking example

Figure 36.1 shows the mortgage loan worksheet used in the preceding chapter. This worksheet has four input cells (C4:C7) and four formula cells (C10:C13). Originally, this worksheet was used for a what-if analysis example. This example demonstrates the opposite approach. Rather than supply different input cell values to look at the calculated formulas, this example lets Excel determine one of the input values that will produce the desired result.

FIGURE 36.1

This worksheet is a good demonstration of goal seeking.

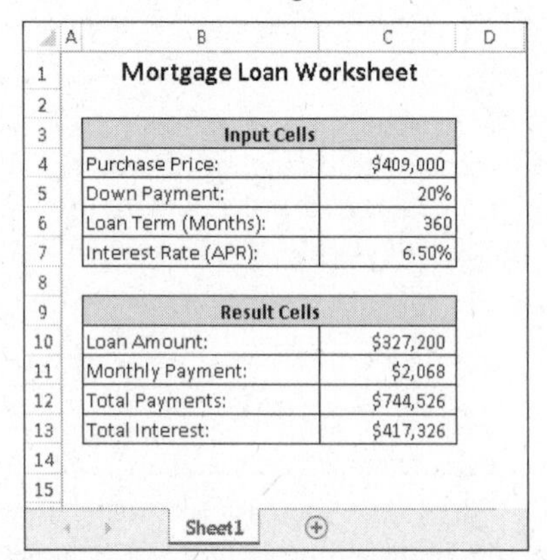

Mortgage Loan Worksheet

Input Cells	
Purchase Price:	$409,000
Down Payment:	20%
Loan Term (Months):	360
Interest Rate (APR):	6.50%

Result Cells	
Loan Amount:	$327,200
Monthly Payment:	$2,068
Total Payments:	$744,526
Total Interest:	$417,326

ON THE WEB

This workbook is available on this book's website. The file is named `mortgage loan.xlsx`.

Assume that you're in the market for a new home and you know that you can afford an $1,800 monthly mortgage payment. You also know that a lender can issue a 30-year fixed-rate mortgage loan for 6.50%, based on an 80% loan-to-value (that is, a 20% down payment). The question is: "What is the maximum purchase price I can handle?" In other words, what value in cell C4 (purchase price) causes the formula in cell C11 (monthly payment) to result in $1,800? In this simple example, you could plug values into cell C4 until C11 displays $1,800. With more complex models, Excel can usually determine the answer much more efficiently.

To answer the question posed in the preceding paragraph, first set up the input cells to match what you already know. Specifically:

- Enter **20%** in cell C5 (the down payment percent).
- Enter **360** in cell C6 (the loan term, in months).
- Enter **6.5%** in cell C7 (the annual interest rate).

Next, choose Data ➪ Data Tools ➪ What-If Analysis ➪ Goal Seek. The Goal Seek dialog box, shown in Figure 36.2, appears. Completing this dialog box is similar to forming a sentence. You want to set cell C11 to 1800 by changing cell C4. Enter this information in the dialog box either by typing the cell references or by pointing with the mouse. Click OK to begin the goal-seeking process.

FIGURE 36.2

The Goal Seek dialog box.

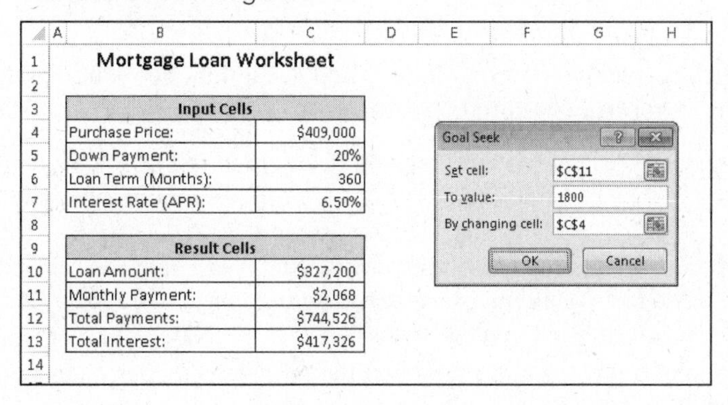

In less than a second, Excel displays the Goal Seek Status box, shown in Figure 36.3, which shows the target value and the value that Excel calculated. In this case, Excel found an exact value. The worksheet now displays the found value in cell C4 ($355,974). As a result of this value, the monthly payment amount is $1,800. At this point, you have two options:

- Click OK to replace the original value with the found value.
- Click Cancel to restore your worksheet to the form that it had before you chose Goal Seek.

FIGURE 36.3

Goal Seek has found a solution.

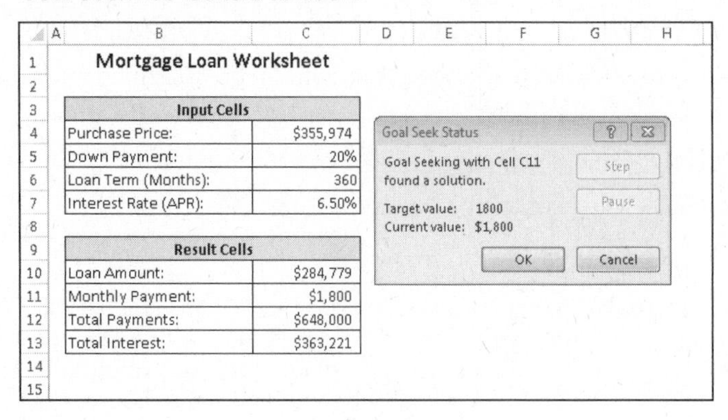

More about goal seeking

Excel can't always find a value that produces the result that you're seeking. Sometimes, a solution simply doesn't exist. In such a case, the Goal Seek Status box informs you of that fact.

Other times, however, Excel may report that it can't find a solution, but you're pretty sure that one exists. If that's the case, you can try the following options:

- Change the current value of the By Changing Cell field in the Goal Seek dialog box (refer to Figure 36.2) to a value that is closer to the solution, and then reissue the command.
- Adjust the Maximum iterations setting on the Formulas tab of the Excel Options dialog box (choose File ⇨ Options). Increasing the number of iterations (or calculations) makes Excel try more possible solutions.
- Double-check your logic and make sure that the formula cell does, indeed, depend upon the specified changing cell.

NOTE

Like all computer programs, Excel has limited precision. To demonstrate this limitation, enter =A1^2 into cell A2. Then use the Goal Seek dialog box to find the value in cell A1 (which is empty) that makes the formula return `16`. Excel comes up with a value of 4.00002269, which is close to the square root of 16, but certainly not exact. You can adjust the precision on the Formulas tab of the Excel Options dialog box (make the Maximum Change value smaller).

NOTE

In some cases, multiple values of the input cell produce the same desired result. For example, the formula `=A1^2` returns `16` if cell A1 contains either –4 or +4. If you use goal seeking when multiple solutions are possible, Excel gives you the solution that is closest to the current value.

Introducing Solver

The Excel Goal Seek feature is a useful tool, but it clearly has limitations. It can solve for only one adjustable cell, and it returns only a single solution. Excel's powerful Solver tool extends this concept by enabling you to do the following:

- Specify multiple adjustable cells.
- Specify constraints on the values that the adjustable cells can have.
- Generate a solution that maximizes or minimizes a particular worksheet cell.
- Generate multiple solutions to a problem.

Although goal seeking is a relatively simple operation, using Solver can be much more complicated. In fact, Solver is probably one of the most difficult (and potentially frustrating) features in Excel. I'm the first to admit that Solver isn't for everyone. In fact, most Excel users have no use for this feature. However, many users find that having this much power is worth spending the extra time to learn about it.

Appropriate problems for Solver

Problems that are appropriate for Solver fall into a relatively narrow range. They typically involve situations that meet the following criteria:

- A target cell depends upon other cells and formulas. Typically, you want to maximize or minimize this target cell or set it equal to some value.
- The target cell depends on a group of cells (called *changing cells*) that Solver can adjust to affect the target cell.
- The solution must adhere to certain limitations, or *constraints*.

After you set up your worksheet appropriately, you can use Solver to adjust the changing cells and produce the result that you want in your target cell — and simultaneously meet all the constraints that you defined.

No Solver Command?

You access Solver by choosing Data ➪ Analysis ➪ Solver. If this command isn't available, you need to install the Solver add-in. It's a simple process:

1. **Choose File ➪ Options.** The Excel Options dialog box appears.
2. **Select the Add-Ins tab.**
3. **At the bottom of the dialog box, select Excel Add-Ins from the Manage drop-down list and then click Go.** The Add-Ins dialog box appears.
4. **Place a check mark next to Solver Add-In, and then click OK.**

After performing these steps, the Solver add-in loads whenever you start Excel.

A simple Solver example

I start with a simple example to introduce Solver and then present some increasingly complex examples to demonstrate what this feature can do.

Figure 36.4 shows a worksheet that is set up to calculate the profit for three products. Column B shows the number of units of each product, Column C shows the profit per unit for each product, and Column D contains formulas that calculate the total profit for each product by multiplying the units by the profit per unit.

FIGURE 36.4

Use Solver to determine the number of units to maximize the total profit.

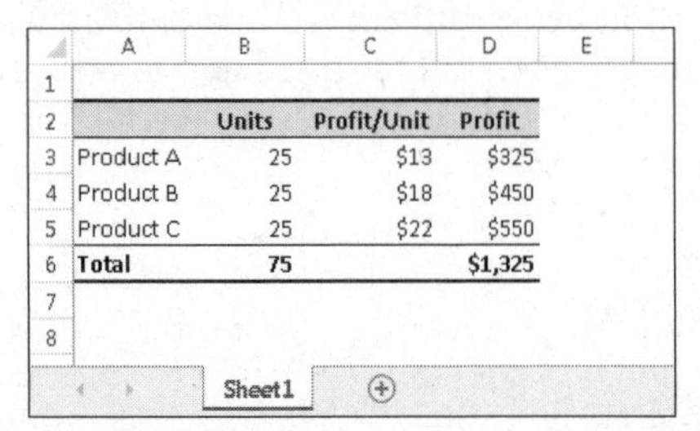

	Units	Profit/Unit	Profit
Product A	25	$13	$325
Product B	25	$18	$450
Product C	25	$22	$550
Total	**75**		**$1,325**

On the Web

This workbook, named `three products.xlsx`, is available on this book's website.

You don't need an MBA to realize that the greatest profit comes from Product C. Therefore, to maximize total profit, the logical solution is to produce only Product C. If things were really this simple, you wouldn't need tools such as Solver. As in most situations, this company has some constraints that must be met:

- The combined production capacity is 300 total units per day.
- The company needs 50 units of Product A to fill an existing order.
- The company needs 40 units of Product B to fill an anticipated order.
- Because the market for Product C is relatively limited, the company doesn't want to produce more than 40 units of this product.

These four constraints make the problem more realistic and a bit more challenging. In fact, it's a perfect problem for Solver.

I go into more detail in a moment, but here's the basic procedure for using Solver:

1. **Set up the worksheet with values and formulas.** Make sure that you format cells logically; for example, if you can't produce partial units of your products, format those cells to contain numbers with no decimal values.

2. **Choose Data ➪ Analysis ➪ Solver.** The Solver Parameters dialog box appears.
3. **Specify the target cell (also known as the objective).**
4. **Specify the range that contains the changing cells.**
5. **Specify the constraints.**
6. **Change the Solver options, if necessary.**
7. **Let Solver solve the problem.**

To start Solver to tackle this example, choose Data ➪ Analysis ➪ Solver. The Solver Parameters dialog box appears. Figure 36.5 shows this dialog box, set up to solve the problem.

FIGURE 36.5

The Solver Parameters dialog box.

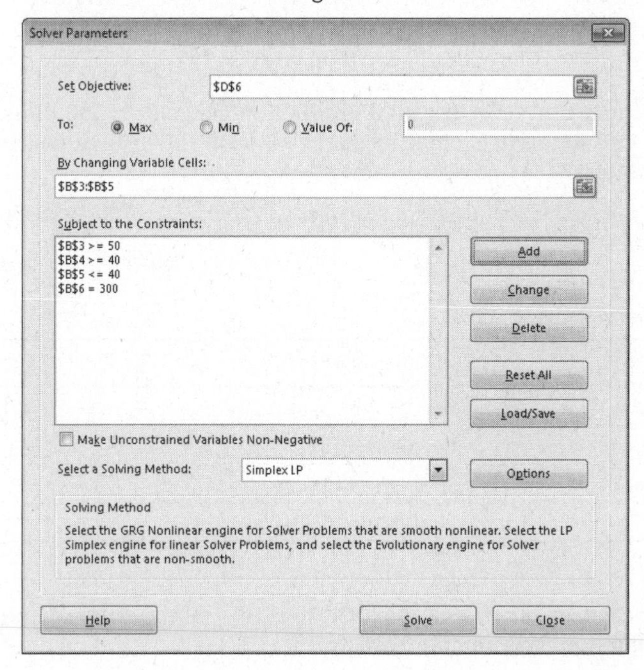

In this example, the target cell is D6 — the cell that calculates the total profit for three products.

1. **Enter** D6 **in the Set Objective field of the Solver Parameters dialog box.**
2. **Because the objective is to maximize this cell, select the Max option button.**

3. **Specify the changing cells (which are in the range B3:B5) in the By Changing Variable Cells field.** The next step is to specify the constraints on the problem. The constraints are added one at a time and appear in the Subject to the Constraints list.
4. **To add a constraint, click the Add button.** The Add Constraint dialog box, shown in Figure 36.6, appears. This dialog box has three parts: a Cell Reference, an operator, and a Constraint value.

FIGURE 36.6

The Add Constraint dialog box.

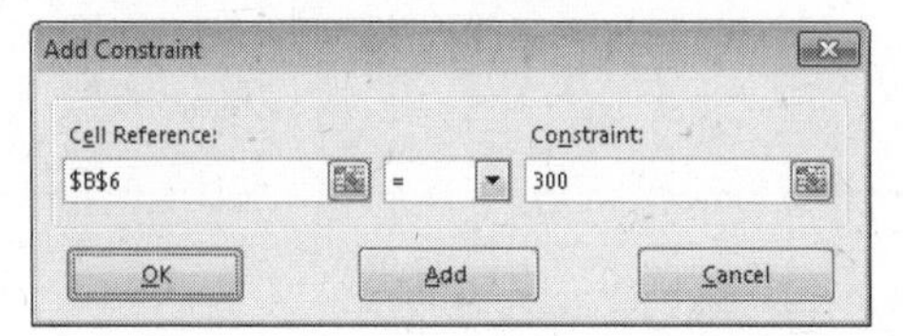

5. **To set the first constraint (that the total production capacity is 300 units), enter** B6 **as the Cell Reference, choose equal (=) from the drop-down list of operators, and enter** 300 **as the Constraint value.**
6. **Click Add, and enter the remaining constraints.** Table 37.1 summarizes the constraints for this problem.

TABLE 37.1 Constraints Summary

Constraint	Expressed As
Capacity is 300 units	B6=300
At least 50 units of Product A	B3>=50
At least 40 units of Product B	B4>=40
No more than 40 units of Product C	B5<=40

7. **After you enter the last constraint, click OK to return to the Solver Parameters dialog box, which now lists the four constraints.**
8. **For the Solving Method, use Simplex LP.**
9. **Click the Solve button to start the solution process.** You can watch the progress onscreen, and Excel soon announces that it has found a solution. The Solver Results dialog box is shown in Figure 36.7.

FIGURE 36.7

Solver displays this dialog box when it finds a solution to the problem.

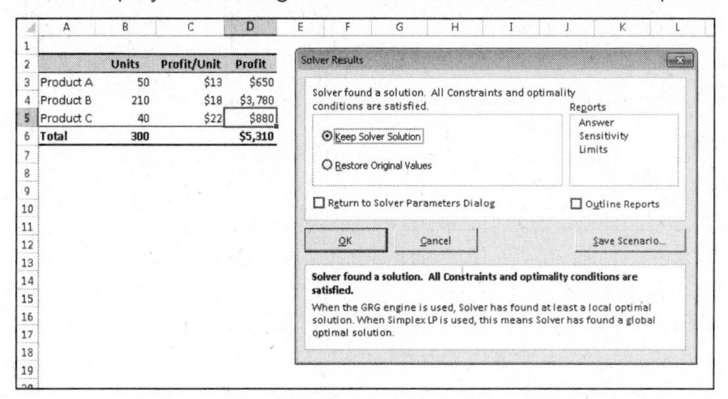

At this point, you have the following options:

- Keep the solution that Solver found.
- Restore the original changing cell values.
- Create any or all of the three reports that describe what Solver did.
- Click the Save Scenario button to save the solution as a scenario so that Scenario Manager can use it.

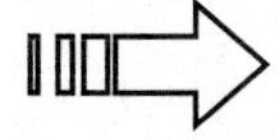

See Chapter 35 for more on Scenario Manager.

The Reports section of the Solver Results dialog box lets you select any or all of three optional reports. If you specify any report options, Excel creates each report on a new worksheet, with an appropriate name. Figure 36.8 shows an Answer Report. In the Constraints section of the report, three of the four constraints are *binding*, which means that these constraints were satisfied at their limit with no more room to change.

This simple example illustrates how Solver works. The fact is, you could probably solve this particular problem manually just as quickly. That, of course, isn't always the case.

CAUTION

When you close the Solver Results dialog box (by clicking either OK or Cancel), the Undo stack is cleared. In other words, you can't undo any changes that Solver makes to your workbook.

FIGURE 36.8

One of three reports that Solver can produce.

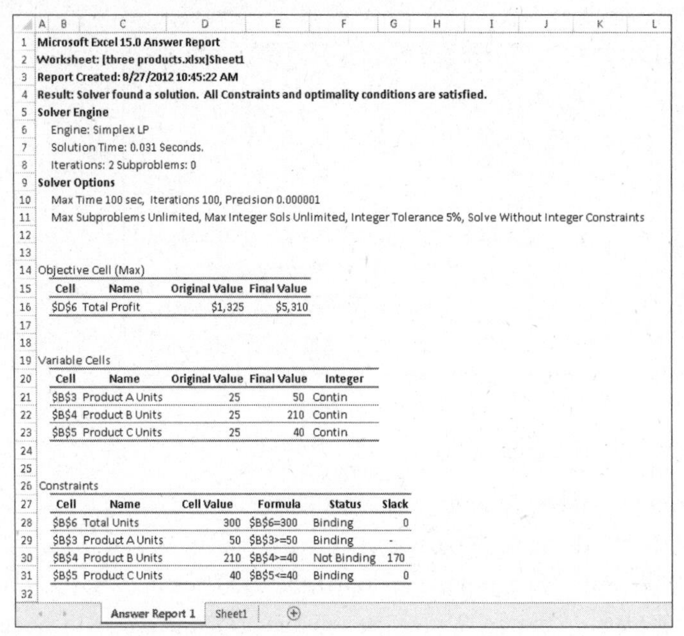

Microsoft Excel 15.0 Answer Report
Worksheet: [three products.xlsx]Sheet1
Report Created: 8/27/2012 10:45:22 AM
Result: Solver found a solution. All Constraints and optimality conditions are satisfied.
Solver Engine
Engine: Simplex LP
Solution Time: 0.031 Seconds.
Iterations: 2 Subproblems: 0
Solver Options
Max Time 100 sec, Iterations 100, Precision 0.000001
Max Subproblems Unlimited, Max Integer Sols Unlimited, Integer Tolerance 5%, Solve Without Integer Constraints

Objective Cell (Max)

Cell	Name	Original Value	Final Value
$D$6	Total Profit	$1,325	$5,310

Variable Cells

Cell	Name	Original Value	Final Value	Integer
$B$3	Product A Units	25	50	Contin
$B$4	Product B Units	25	210	Contin
$B$5	Product C Units	25	40	Contin

Constraints

Cell	Name	Cell Value	Formula	Status	Slack
$B$6	Total Units	300	$B$6=300	Binding	0
$B$3	Product A Units	50	$B$3>=50	Binding	-
$B$4	Product B Units	210	$B$4>=40	Not Binding	170
$B$5	Product C Units	40	$B$5<=40	Binding	0

Answer Report 1 | Sheet1

More about Solver

Before presenting more complex examples, this section discusses the Solver Options dialog box. From this dialog box, you control many aspects of the solution process, as well as load and save model specifications in a worksheet range.

Usually, you want to save a model only when you're using more than one set of Solver parameters with your worksheet. This is because Excel saves the first Solver model automatically with your worksheet (using hidden names). If you save additional models, Excel stores the information in the form of formulas that correspond to the specifications. (The last cell in the saved range is an array formula that holds the options settings.)

It's not unusual for Solver to report that it can't find a solution, even when you know that one should exist. Often, you can change one or more of the Solver options and try again. When you click the Options button in the Solver Parameters dialog box, the Solver Options dialog box, shown in Figure 36.9, appears.

FIGURE 36.9

You can control many aspects of how Solver solves a problem.

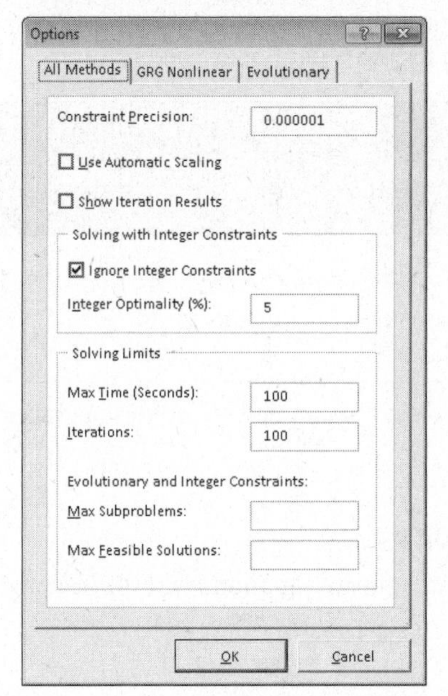

This list describes Solver's options:

- **Constraint Precision:** Specify how close the Cell Reference and Constraint formulas must be to satisfy a constraint. Excel may solve the problem more quickly if you specify less precision.
- **Use Automatic Scaling:** Use when the problem involves large differences in magnitude — when you attempt to maximize a percentage, for example, by varying cells that are very large.
- **Show Iteration Results:** Instruct Solver to pause and display the results after each iteration by selecting this check box.
- **Ignore Integer Constraints:** When this check box is selected, Solver ignores constraints that specify that a particular cell must be an integer. Using this option may allow Solver to find a solution that can't be found otherwise.
- **Max Time:** Specify the maximum amount of time (in seconds) that you want Solver to spend on a problem. If Solver reports that it exceeded the time limit, you can increase the amount of time that it spends searching for a solution.
- **Iterations:** Enter the maximum number of trial solutions that you want Solver to perform.

- **Max Subproblems:** For complex problems. Specify the maximum number of subproblems that may be explored by the Evolutionary algorithm.
- **Max Feasible Solutions:** For complex problems. Specify the maximum number of feasible solutions that may be explored by the Evolutionary algorithm.

Note

The other two tabs in the Options dialog box contain additional options used by the GRG Nonlinear and Evolutionary algorithms.

Solver Examples

The remainder of this chapter consists of examples of using Solver for various types of problems.

Solving simultaneous linear equations

This example describes how to solve a set of three linear equations with three variables. Here's an example of a set of linear equations:

$$4x + y - 2z = 0$$

$$2x - 3y + 3z = 9$$

$$-6x - 2y + z = 0$$

The question that Solver will answer is: *What values of* x, y, *and* z *satisfy all three equations?*

Figure 36.10 shows a workbook set up to solve this problem. This workbook has three named cells, which makes the formulas more readable:

- *x*: C11
- *y*: C12
- *z*: C13

The three named cells are all initialized to 1.0 (which certainly doesn't solve the equations).

On the Web

This workbook, named `linear equations.xlsx`, is available on this book's website.

FIGURE 36.10

Solver will attempt to solve this series of linear equations.

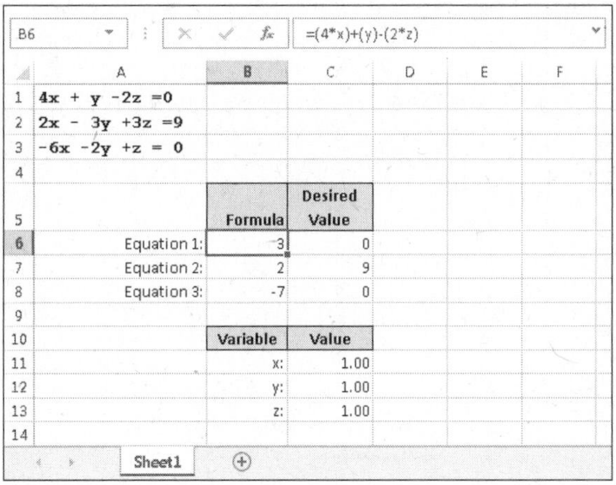

B6 =(4*x)+(y)-(2*z)

	A	B	C	D	E	F
1	4x + y -2z =0					
2	2x - 3y +3z =9					
3	-6x -2y +z = 0					
4						
5		Formula	Desired Value			
6	Equation 1:	3	0			
7	Equation 2:	2	9			
8	Equation 3:	-7	0			
9						
10		Variable	Value			
11		x:	1.00			
12		y:	1.00			
13		z:	1.00			
14						

Sheet1

The three equations are represented by formulas in the range B6:B8:

- B6: `=(4*x)+(y)-(2*z)`
- B7: `=(2*x)-(3*y)+(3*z)`
- B8: `=-(6*x)-(2*y)+(z)`

These formulas use the values in the *x*, *y*, and *z* named cells. The range C6:C8 contains the desired result for these three formulas.

Solver will adjust the values in *x*, *y*, and *z* — that is, the changing cells in C11:C13 — subject to these constraints:

```
B6=C6
B7=C7
B8=C8
```

NOTE

This problem doesn't have a target cell because it's not trying to maximize or minimize anything. However, the Solver Parameters dialog box insists that you specify a formula for the Set Objective field. Therefore, just enter a reference to any cell that has a formula.

Figure 36.11 shows the solution. The *x* (`0.75`), *y* (`-2.0`), and *z* (`0.5`) values satisfy all three equations.

NOTE

A set of linear equations may have one solution, no solution, or an infinite number of solutions.

FIGURE 36.11

Solver solved the simultaneous equations.

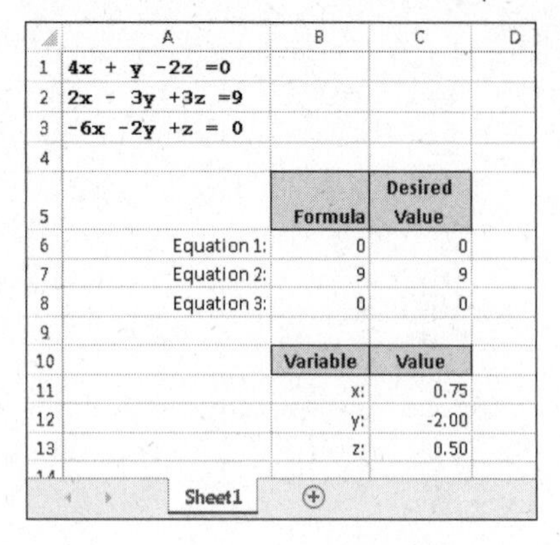

Minimizing shipping costs

This example involves finding alternative options for shipping materials, while keeping total shipping costs at a minimum (see Figure 36.12). A company has warehouses in Los Angeles, St. Louis, and Boston. Retail outlets throughout the United States place orders, which the company then ships from one of the warehouses. The company wants to meet the product needs of all six retail outlets from available inventory and keep total shipping charges as low as possible.

ON THE WEB

This workbook, named `shipping costs.xlsx`, is available on this book's website.

This workbook is rather complicated, so I'll explain each part individually:

- **Shipping Costs Table:** This table, in range B2:E8, is a matrix that contains per-unit shipping costs from each warehouse to each retail outlet. The cost to ship a unit from Los Angeles to Denver, for example, is $58.
- **Product needs of each retail store:** This information appears in C12:C17. For example, Denver needs 150 units, Houston needs 225, and so on. C18 contains a formula that calculates the total needed.
- **Number to ship from:** Range D12:F17 holds the adjustable cells that Solver varies. These cells are all initialized with a value of 25 to give Solver a starting value. Column G contains formulas that sum the number of units the company needs to ship to each retail outlet.
- **Warehouse inventory:** Row 21 contains the amount of inventory at each warehouse, and row 22 contains formulas that subtract the amount shipped (row 18) from the inventory.

- **Calculated shipping costs:** Row 24 contains formulas that calculate the shipping costs. Cell D24 contains the following formula, which is copied to the two cells to the right of Cell D24:

  ```
  =SUMPRODUCT(C3:C8,D12:D17)
  ```

Cell G24 is the bottom line, the total shipping costs for all orders.

FIGURE 36.12

This worksheet determines the least expensive way to ship products from warehouses to retail outlets.

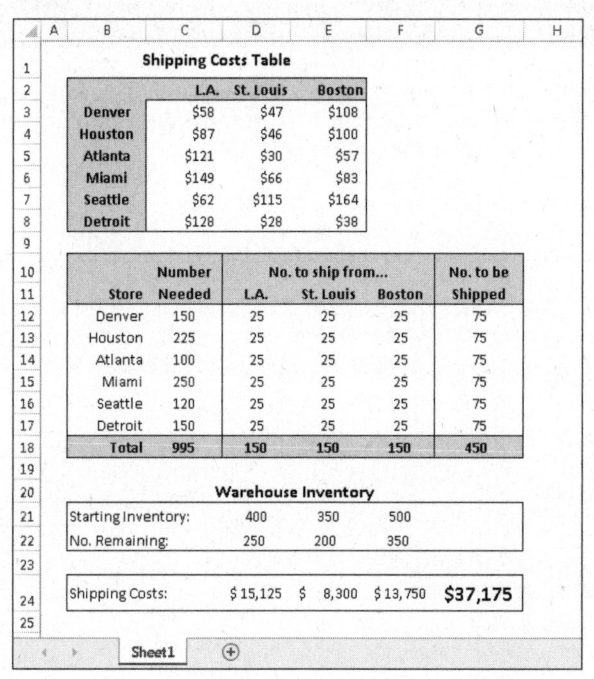

Shipping Costs Table

	L.A.	St. Louis	Boston
Denver	$58	$47	$108
Houston	$87	$46	$100
Atlanta	$121	$30	$57
Miami	$149	$66	$83
Seattle	$62	$115	$164
Detroit	$128	$28	$38

	Number	No. to ship from...			No. to be
Store	Needed	L.A.	St. Louis	Boston	Shipped
Denver	150	25	25	25	75
Houston	225	25	25	25	75
Atlanta	100	25	25	25	75
Miami	250	25	25	25	75
Seattle	120	25	25	25	75
Detroit	150	25	25	25	75
Total	995	150	150	150	450

Warehouse Inventory

Starting Inventory:	400	350	500	
No. Remaining:	250	200	350	
Shipping Costs:	$ 15,125	$ 8,300	$ 13,750	**$37,175**

Sheet1

Solver fills in values in the range D12:F17 in such a way that minimizes shipping costs while still supplying each retail outlet with the desired number of units. In other words, the solution minimizes the value in cell G24 by adjusting the cells in D12:F17, subject to the following constraints:

- **The number of units needed by each retail outlet must equal the number shipped.** (In other words, all the orders are filled.) These constraints are represented by the following specifications:

  ```
  C12=G12    C14=G14    C16=G16
  C13=G13    C15=G15    C17=G17
  ```

- **The number of units remaining in each warehouse's inventory must not be negative.** (In other words, they can't ship more than what's available.) This is represented by the following constraint specifications:

  D22>=0   E22>=0   F22>=0

- **The adjustable cells can't be negative because shipping a negative number of units makes no sense.** The Solve Parameters has a handy option: Make Unconstrained Variables Non-Negative. Make sure this setting is enabled.

NOTE

Before you solve this problem with Solver, you may want to attempt to solve this problem manually, by entering values in D12:F17 that minimize the shipping costs. And, of course, you need to make sure that all the constraints are met. Doing so may help you better appreciate Solver.

Setting up the problem is the difficult part. For example, you must enter nine constraints. When you have specified all the necessary information, click the Solve button to put Solver to work. Solver displays the solution shown in Figure 36.13.

FIGURE 36.13

The solution that was created by Solver.

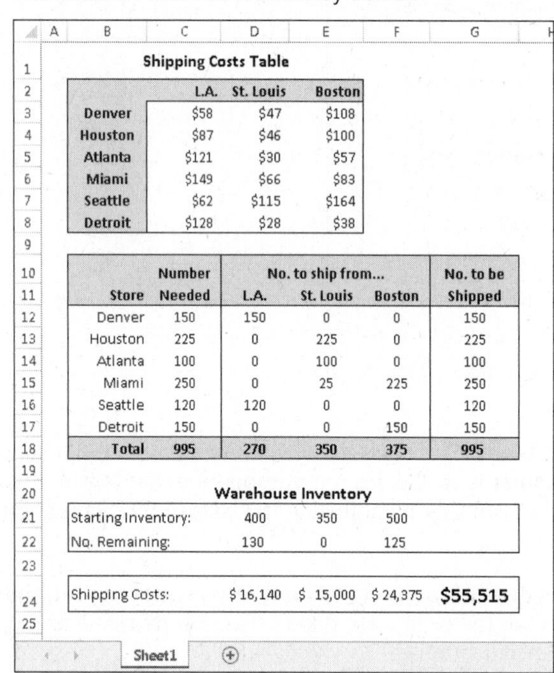

Shipping Costs Table

	L.A.	St. Louis	Boston
Denver	$58	$47	$108
Houston	$87	$46	$100
Atlanta	$121	$30	$57
Miami	$149	$66	$83
Seattle	$62	$115	$164
Detroit	$128	$28	$38

	Number	No. to ship from...			No. to be
Store	Needed	L.A.	St. Louis	Boston	Shipped
Denver	150	150	0	0	150
Houston	225	0	225	0	225
Atlanta	100	0	100	0	100
Miami	250	0	25	225	250
Seattle	120	120	0	0	120
Detroit	150	0	0	150	150
Total	995	270	350	375	995

Warehouse Inventory

Starting Inventory:	400	350	500	
No. Remaining:	130	0	125	
Shipping Costs:	$ 16,140	$ 15,000	$ 24,375	$55,515

Sheet1

Learning More about Solver

Solver is a complex tool, and this chapter barely scratches the surface. If you'd like to learn more about Solver, I highly recommend the website for Frontline Systems (`www.solver.com`). Frontline Systems is the company that developed Solver for Excel. Its website has several tutorials and lots of helpful information, including a detailed manual that you can download. You can also find additional Solver products for Excel that can handle much more complex problems.

The total shipping cost is $55,515, and all the constraints are met. Notice that shipments to Miami come from both St. Louis and Boston.

Allocating resources

The example in this section is a common type of problem that's ideal for Solver. Essentially, problems of this sort involve optimizing the volumes of individual production units that use varying amounts of fixed resources. Figure 36.14 shows a simplified example for a toy company.

FIGURE 36.14

Using Solver to maximize profit when resources are limited.

	A	B	C	D	E	F	G	H	I
1				XYZ Toys Inc.					
2		Materials Needed							
3	**Material**	**Toy A**	**Toy B**	**Toy C**	**Toy D**	**Toy E**	**Amt. Avail.**	**Amt. Used**	**Amt. Left**
4	Red Paint	0	1	0	1	3	625	250	375
5	Blue Paint	3	1	0	1	0	640	250	390
6	White Paint	2	1	2	0	2	1,100	350	750
7	Plastic	1	5	2	2	1	875	550	325
8	Wood	3	0	3	5	5	2,200	800	1,400
9	Glue	1	2	3	2	3	1,500	550	950
10	Unit Profit	$15	$30	$20	$25	$25			
11	No. to Make	**50**	**50**	**50**	**50**	**50**			
12	Profit	$750	$1,500	$1,000	$1,250	$1,250			
13	**Total Profit**	$5,750							
14									

Sheet1

ON THE WEB

This workbook is available on this book's website. The file is named `allocating resources.xlsx`.

This company makes five different toys, which use six different materials in varying amounts. For example, Toy A requires 3 units of blue paint, 2 units of white paint, 1 unit of plastic, 3 units of wood, and 1 unit of glue. Column G shows the current inventory of each type of material. Row 10 shows the unit profit for each toy.

The number of toys to make is shown in the range B11:F11. These are the values that Solver determines (the changing cells). The goal of this example is to determine how to allocate the resources to maximize the total profit (B13). In other words, Solver determines how many units of each toy to make. The constraints in this example are relatively simple:

- **Ensure that production doesn't use more resources than are available.** This can be accomplished by specifying that each cell in column I is greater than or equal to zero.
- **Ensure that the quantities produced aren't negative.** This can be accomplished by specifying the Make Unconstrained Variables Non-Negative option.

Figure 36.15 shows the results that are produced by Solver. It shows the product mix that generates $12,365 in profit and uses all resources in their entirety, except for glue.

FIGURE 36.15

Solver determined how to use the resources to maximize the total profit.

	A	B	C	D	E	F	G	H	I
1				XYZ Toys Inc.					
2				Materials Needed					
3	Material	Toy A	Toy B	Toy C	Toy D	Toy E	Amt. Avail.	Amt. Used	Amt. Left
4	Red Paint	0	1	0	1	3	625	625	0
5	Blue Paint	3	1	0	1	0	640	640	0
6	White Paint	2	1	2	0	2	1,100	1,100	0
7	Plastic	1	5	2	2	1	875	875	0
8	Wood	3	0	3	5	5	2,200	2,200	0
9	Glue	1	2	3	2	3	1,500	1,353	147
10	Unit Profit	$15	$30	$20	$25	$25			
11	No. to Make	**194**	**19**	**158**	**40**	**189**			
12	Profit	$2,903	$573	$3,168	$1,008	$4,713			
13	**Total Profit**	**$12,365**							
14									

Sheet1

Optimizing an investment portfolio

This example demonstrates how to use Solver to help maximize the return on an investment portfolio. A portfolio consists of several investments, each of which has a different yield. In addition, you may have some constraints that involve reducing risk and diversification goals. Without such constraints, a portfolio problem becomes a no-brainer: Put all your money in the investment with the highest yield.

This example involves a *credit union* (a financial institution that takes members' deposits and invests them in loans to other members, bank CDs, and other types of investments). The credit union distributes part of the return on these investments to the members in the form of *dividends,* or interest on their deposits.

This hypothetical credit union must adhere to some regulations regarding its investments, and the board of directors has imposed some other restrictions. These regulations and restrictions comprise the problem's constraints. Figure 36.16 shows a workbook set up for this problem.

FIGURE 36.16

This worksheet is set up to maximize a credit union's investments, given some constraints.

	A	B	C	D	E
1	**Portfolio Amount:**	$5,000,000			
2					
3					
4	**Investment**	**Pct Yield**	**Amount Invested**	**Yield**	**Pct. of Portfolio**
5	New Car Loans	6.90%	1,000,000	69,000	20.00%
6	Used Car Loans	8.25%	1,000,000	82,500	20.00%
7	Real Estate Loans	8.90%	1,000,000	89,000	20.00%
8	Unsecured Loans	13.00%	1,000,000	130,000	20.00%
9	Bank CDs	4.60%	1,000,000	46,000	20.00%
10	**TOTAL**		$5,000,000	$416,500	100.00%
11					
12			Total Yield:	**8.33%**	
13					
14			Auto Loans	40.00%	

Sheet1

On the Web

This workbook is available on this book's website. The file is named `investment portfolio.xlsx.`

Allocating the $5 million portfolio is subject to these constraints:

- **The amount that the credit union invests in new-car loans must be at least three times the amount that the credit union invests in used-car loans.** (Used-car loans are riskier investments.) This constraint is represented as

  `C5>=C6*3`

- **Car loans should make up at least 15% of the portfolio.** This constraint is represented as

  `D14>=.15`

- **Unsecured loans should make up no more than 25% of the portfolio.** This constraint is represented as

  `E8<=.25`

- **At least 10% of the portfolio should be in bank CDs.** This constraint is represented as:

  ```
  E9>=.10
  ```

- **The total amount invested is $5,000,000.**
- **All investments should be positive or zero.**

The changing cells are C5:C9, and the goal is to maximize the total yield in cell D12. Starting values of 1,000,000 have been entered in the changing cells. When you run Solver with these parameters, it produces the solution shown in Figure 36.17, which has a total yield of 9.25%.

FIGURE 36.17

The results of the portfolio optimization.

	A	B	C	D	E
1	**Portfolio Amount:**	$5,000,000			
2					
3					
4	**Investment**	**Pct Yield**	**Amount Invested**	**Yield**	**Pct. of Portfolio**
5	New Car Loans	6.90%	562,500	38,813	11.25%
6	Used Car Loans	8.25%	187,500	15,469	3.75%
7	Real Estate Loans	8.90%	2,500,000	222,500	50.00%
8	Unsecured Loans	13.00%	1,250,000	162,500	25.00%
9	Bank CDs	4.60%	500,000	23,000	10.00%
10	**TOTAL**		$5,000,000	$462,281	100.00%
11					
12			Total Yield:	**9.25%**	
13					
14			Auto Loans	15.00%	

Sheet1

CHAPTER

37

Analyzing Data with the Analysis ToolPak

IN THIS CHAPTER

Getting an overview of the Analysis ToolPak

Using the Analysis ToolPak

Meeting the Analysis ToolPak tools

Although Excel was designed primarily for business users, people in other disciplines, including education, research, statistics, and engineering, also use the software. One way Excel addresses these nonbusiness users is with its Analysis ToolPak add-in. However, many features in the Analysis ToolPak are valuable for business applications as well.

The Analysis ToolPak: An Overview

The Analysis ToolPak is an add-in that provides analytical capability that normally isn't available in Excel.

These analysis tools offer many features that may be useful to those in the scientific, engineering, and educational communities — not to mention business users whose needs extend beyond the normal spreadsheet fare.

This section provides a quick overview of the types of analyses that you can perform with the Analysis ToolPak. This chapter covers each of the following tools:

- Analysis of variance (three types)
- Correlation
- Covariance
- Descriptive statistics
- Exponential smoothing
- F-Test

- Fourier analysis
- Histogram
- Moving average
- Random number generation
- Rank and percentile
- Regression
- Sampling
- T-Test (three types)
- Z-Test

As you can see, the Analysis ToolPak add-in brings a great deal of functionality to Excel. These procedures have limitations, however. In some cases, you may prefer to create your own formulas to do some calculations.

Installing the Analysis ToolPak Add-in

The Analysis ToolPak is implemented as an add-in. Before you can use it, though, you need to make sure that the add-in is installed. Select the Data tab. If you see an Analysis group, showing Data Analysis, the Analysis ToolPak is installed. If you can't access Data⇨Analysis⇨Data Analysis, install the add-in by following these steps:

1. **Choose File⇨Options.** The Excel Options dialog box appears.
2. **Select the Add-Ins tab.**
3. **At the bottom of the dialog box, select Excel Add-Ins from the Manage drop-down list and then click Go.** The Add-Ins dialog box appears.
4. **Place a check mark next to Analysis ToolPak.**
5. **Click OK to close the Add-Ins dialog box.**

Using the Analysis Tools

Using the procedures in the Analysis ToolPak add-in is relatively straightforward as long as you're familiar with the particular analysis type. To use any of these tools, choose Data⇨Analysis⇨Data Analysis, and the Data Analysis dialog box, shown in Figure 37.1, appears. Scroll through the list until you find the analysis tool that you want to use, and then click OK. A dialog box specific to the procedure that you select appears.

FIGURE 37.1

Select your tool from the Data Analysis dialog box.

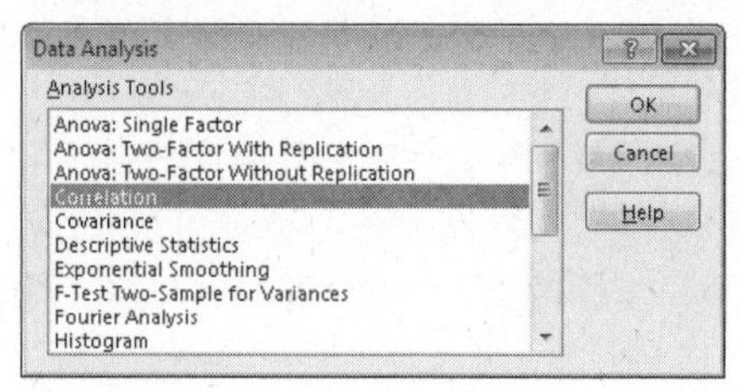

Usually, you need to specify one or more Input ranges, plus an Output range (one cell is sufficient). Alternatively, you can choose to place the results on a new worksheet or in a new workbook. The procedures vary in the amount of additional information required. In many dialog boxes, you may be able to indicate whether your Data range includes labels. If so, you can specify the entire range, including the labels, and indicate to Excel that the first column (or row) contains labels. Excel then uses these labels in the tables that it produces. Most tools also provide different output options that you can select, based on your needs.

CAUTION

The Analysis ToolPak isn't consistent in how it generates its output. In some cases, the procedures use formulas, so you can change your data, and the results update automatically. In other procedures, Excel stores the results as values, so if you change your data, the results don't reflect your changes.

Introducing the Analysis ToolPak Tools

This section describes each tool in the Analysis ToolPak and provides an example. I don't describe every available option in these procedures. If you need to use the advanced analysis tools, you probably already know how to use most of the options not covered here.

Before you use any of these tools, I suggest that you read the appropriate section in Excel's Help system.

ON THE WEB

This book's website contains a workbook that shows output from all the tools discussed in this section. The file is named `atp examples.xlsx`.

Analysis of Variance

Analysis of Variance (sometimes abbreviated as *Anova*) is a statistical test that determines whether two or more samples were drawn from the same population. Using tools in the Analysis ToolPak, you can perform three types of analysis of variance:

- **Single-factor:** A one-way analysis of variance, with only one sample for each group of data
- **Two-factor with replication:** A two-way analysis of variance, with multiple samples (or replications) for each group of data
- **Two-factor without replication:** A two-way analysis of variance, with a single sample (or replication) for each group of data

Figure 37.2 shows the dialog box for a single-factor analysis of variance. Alpha represents the statistical confidence level for the test.

FIGURE 37.2

Specifying parameters for a single-factor analysis of variance.

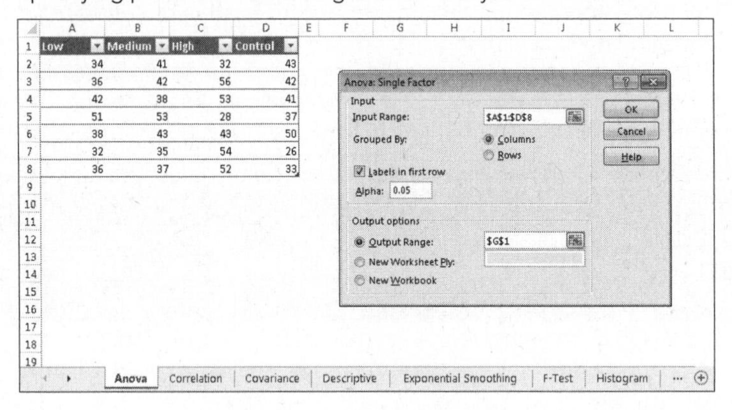

The output for this test consists of the means and variances for each of the samples, the value of *F*, the critical value of *F*, and the significance of *F* (P-value).

Correlation

Correlation is a widely used statistic that measures the degree to which two sets of values vary together. For example, if higher values in one data set are typically associated with higher values in the second data set, the two data sets have a positive correlation. The degree of correlation is expressed as a coefficient that ranges from −1.0 (a perfect negative correlation) to +1.0 (a perfect positive correlation). A correlation coefficient of 0 indicates that the two variables aren't correlated.

Figure 37.3 shows the Correlation dialog box. Specify the input range, which can include any number of variables, arranged in rows or columns.

FIGURE 37.3

The Correlation dialog box.

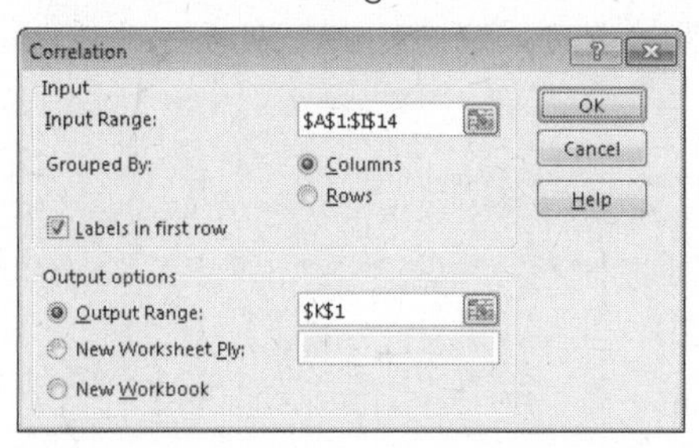

The output consists of a correlation matrix that shows the correlation coefficient for each variable paired with every other variable.

NOTE

The resulting correlation matrix doesn't use formulas to calculate the results. Therefore, if any data changes, the correlation matrix isn't valid. You can use the CORREL function to create a correlation matrix that changes automatically when you change data.

Covariance

The Covariance tool produces a matrix that is similar to the one generated by the Correlation tool. *Covariance*, like correlation, measures the degree to which two variables vary together. Specifically, *covariance* is the average of the product of the deviations of each data point pair from their respective means.

Because the Covariance tool does not generate formulas, you may prefer to calculate a covariance matrix using the COVAR function.

Descriptive Statistics

The Descriptive Statistics tool produces a table that describes your data with some standard statistics. Figure 37.4 shows some sample output.

Because the output for this procedure consists of values (not formulas), you should use this procedure only when you're certain that your data isn't going to change; otherwise, you'll need to re-execute the procedure. You can generate all these statistics by using formulas.

FIGURE 37.4

Descriptive Statistics output.

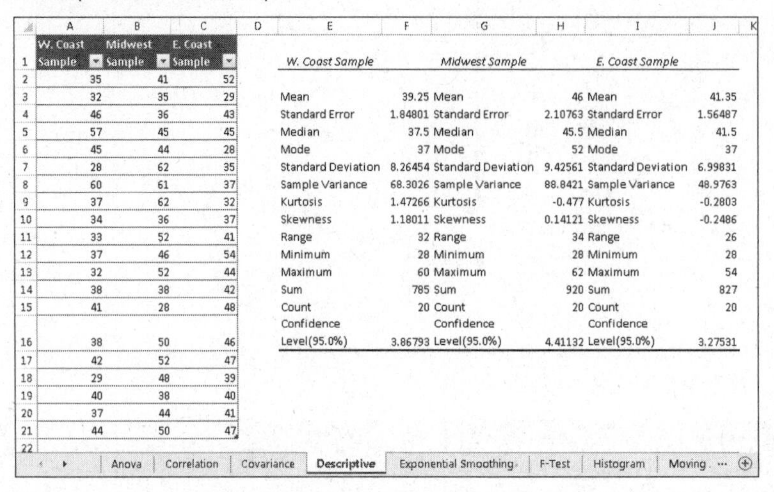

W. Coast Sample	Midwest Sample	E. Coast Sample
35	41	52
32	35	29
46	36	43
57	45	45
45	44	28
28	62	35
60	61	37
37	62	32
34	36	37
33	52	41
37	46	54
32	52	44
38	38	42
41	28	48
38	50	46
42	52	47
29	48	39
40	38	40
37	44	41
44	50	47

W. Coast Sample		*Midwest Sample*		*E. Coast Sample*	
Mean	39.25	Mean	46	Mean	41.35
Standard Error	1.84801	Standard Error	2.10763	Standard Error	1.56487
Median	37.5	Median	45.5	Median	41.5
Mode	37	Mode	52	Mode	37
Standard Deviation	8.26454	Standard Deviation	9.42561	Standard Deviation	6.99831
Sample Variance	68.3026	Sample Variance	88.8421	Sample Variance	48.9763
Kurtosis	1.47266	Kurtosis	-0.477	Kurtosis	-0.2803
Skewness	1.18011	Skewness	0.14121	Skewness	-0.2486
Range	32	Range	34	Range	26
Minimum	28	Minimum	28	Minimum	28
Maximum	60	Maximum	62	Maximum	54
Sum	785	Sum	920	Sum	827
Count	20	Count	20	Count	20
Confidence Level(95.0%)	3.86793	Confidence Level(95.0%)	4.41132	Confidence Level(95.0%)	3.27531

Exponential Smoothing

Exponential Smoothing is a technique for predicting data that is based on the previous data point and the previously predicted data point. You can specify the *damping factor* (also known as a *smoothing constant*), which can range from 0 to 1. This factor determines the relative weighting of the previous data point and the previously predicted data point. You also can request standard errors and a chart.

The exponential smoothing procedure generates formulas that use the damping factor that you specify. Therefore, if the data changes, Excel updates the formulas.

F-test (two-sample test for variance)

An *F-test* is a commonly used statistical test that enables you to compare two population variances. Figure 37.5 shows a small data set and F-test output.

The output for this test consists of the means and variances for each of the two samples, the value of *F*, the critical value of *F*, and the significance of *F*.

FIGURE 37.5

Output from the F-Test tool.

	A	B	C	D	E	F	G	H
1	Group 1	Group 2		F-Test Two-Sample for Variances				
2	96	39						
3	78	53			*Group 1*	*Group 2*		
4	72	51		Mean	75.44444	46.66667		
5	78	48		Variance	109.5278	25		
6	65	51		Observations	9	9		
7	66	42		df	8	8		
8	69	44		F	4.381111			
9	87	42		P(F<=f) one-tail	0.025855			
10	68	50		F Critical one-tai	3.438103			
11								
12								

Descriptive | Exponential Smoothing | F-Test | Histogram | N ...

Fourier Analysis

The Fourier Analysis tool performs a "fast Fourier" transformation of a range of data. Using the Fourier Analysis tool, you can transform a range limited to the following sizes: 1, 2, 4, 8, 16, 32, 64, 128, 256, 512, or 1,024 data points. This procedure accepts and generates complex numbers, which are represented as text string (not numerical values).

Histogram

The Histogram tool is useful for producing data distributions and histogram charts. It accepts an Input range and a Bin range. A *Bin range* is a range of values that specifies the limits for each column of the histogram. If you omit the Bin range, Excel creates ten equal-interval bins for you. The size of each bin is determined by the following formula:

```
=(MAX(input_range)- MIN(input_range))/10
```

Output from the Histogram tool is shown in Figure 37.6. As an option, you can specify that the resulting histogram be sorted by frequency of occurrence in each bin.

If you specify the Pareto (Sorted Histogram) option, the Bin range must contain values and can't contain formulas. If formulas appear in the Bin range, Excel doesn't sort properly, and your worksheet displays error values. The Histogram tool doesn't use formulas, so if you change any of the input data, you need to repeat the histogram procedure to update the results.

For other ways of generating frequency distributions, see Chapters 13 and 34.

FIGURE 37.6

Use the Histogram tool to generate distributions and graphical output.

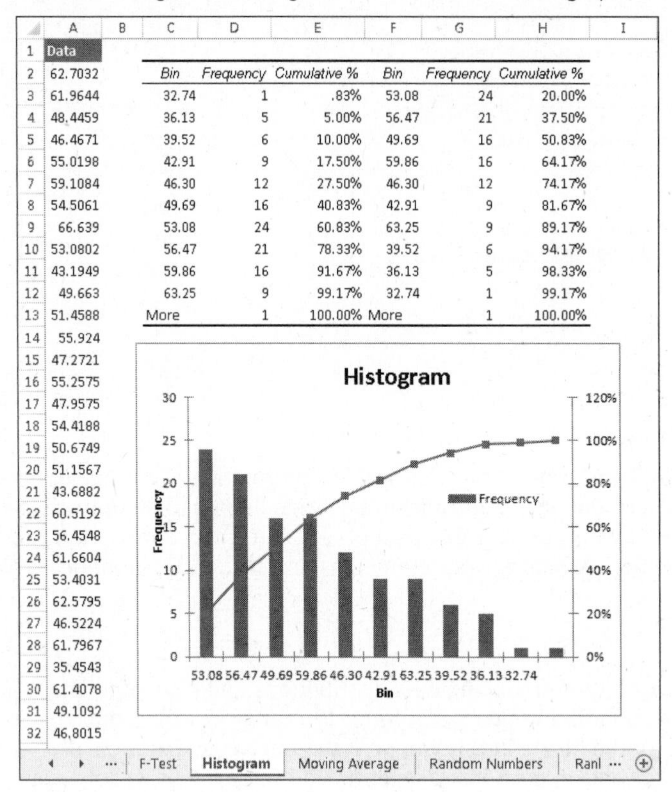

	A	C	D	E	F	G	H
1	Data						
2	62.7032	*Bin*	*Frequency*	*Cumulative %*	*Bin*	*Frequency*	*Cumulative %*
3	61.9644	32.74	1	.83%	53.08	24	20.00%
4	48.4459	36.13	5	5.00%	56.47	21	37.50%
5	46.4671	39.52	6	10.00%	49.69	16	50.83%
6	55.0198	42.91	9	17.50%	59.86	16	64.17%
7	59.1084	46.30	12	27.50%	46.30	12	74.17%
8	54.5061	49.69	16	40.83%	42.91	9	81.67%
9	66.639	53.08	24	60.83%	63.25	9	89.17%
10	53.0802	56.47	21	78.33%	39.52	6	94.17%
11	43.1949	59.86	16	91.67%	36.13	5	98.33%
12	49.663	63.25	9	99.17%	32.74	1	99.17%
13	51.4588	More	1	100.00%	More	1	100.00%
14	55.924						
15	47.2721						
16	55.2575						
17	47.9575						
18	54.4188						
19	50.6749						
20	51.1567						
21	43.6882						
22	60.5192						
23	56.4548						
24	61.6604						
25	53.4031						
26	62.5795						
27	46.5224						
28	61.7967						
29	35.4543						
30	61.4078						
31	49.1092						
32	46.8015						

Moving Average

The Moving Average tool helps you smooth out a data series that has a lot of variability. This procedure is often used in conjunction with a chart. Excel does the smoothing by computing a moving average of a specified number of values. In many cases, a moving average enables you to spot trends that otherwise would be obscured by noise in the data.

Figure 37.7 shows a chart generated by the Moving Average tool. You can, of course, specify the number of values that you want Excel to use for each average. If you select the Standard Errors check box in the Moving Average dialog box, Excel calculates standard errors and places formulas for these calculations next to the moving average formulas. The standard error values indicate the degree of variability between the actual values and the calculated moving averages.

The first few cells in the output are `#N/A` because not enough data points exist to calculate the average for these initial values.

FIGURE 37.7

A chart produced by the Moving Average tool.

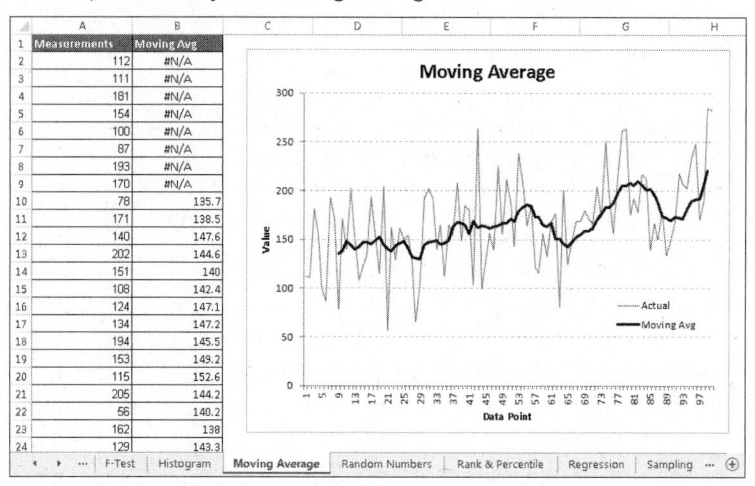

Random Number Generation

Although Excel contains built-in functions to calculate random numbers, the Random Number Generation tool is much more flexible because you can specify what type of distribution you want the random numbers to have. Figure 37.8 shows the Random Number Generation dialog box. The Parameters section varies, depending upon the type of distribution that you select.

FIGURE 37.8

This dialog box enables you to generate a wide variety of random numbers.

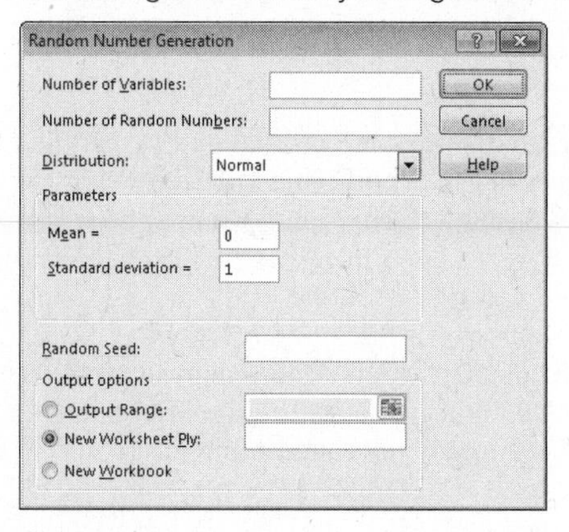

Number of Variables refers to the number of columns that you want, and Number of Random Numbers refers to the number of rows that you want. For example, if you want 200 random numbers arranged in 10 columns of 20 rows, you specify 10 and 20, respectively, in these fields.

In the Random Seed field, you can specify a starting value that Excel uses in its random-number-generating algorithm. Usually, you leave this field blank. If you want to generate the same random number sequence, however, you can specify a seed between 1 and 32,767 (integer values only). You can create the following types of distributions via the Distribution drop-down list in the Random Number Generation dialog box:

- **Uniform:** Every random number has an equal chance of being selected. You specify the upper and lower limits.
- **Normal:** The random numbers correspond to a normal distribution. You specify the mean and standard deviation of the distribution.
- **Bernoulli:** The random numbers are either 0 or 1, determined by the probability of success that you specify.
- **Binomial:** This option returns random numbers based on a Bernoulli distribution over a specific number of trials, given a probability of success that you specify.
- **Poisson:** This option generates values in a Poisson distribution. A *Poisson distribution* is characterized by discrete events that occur in an interval, where the probability of a single occurrence is proportional to the size of the interval. The lambda parameter is the expected number of occurrences in an interval. In a Poisson distribution, lambda is equal to the mean, which also is equal to the variance.
- **Patterned:** This option doesn't generate random numbers. Rather, it repeats a series of numbers in steps that you specify.
- **Discrete:** This option enables you to specify the probability that specific values are chosen. It requires a two-column input range; the first column holds the values, and the second column holds the probability of each value being chosen. The sum of the probabilities in the second column must equal 100 percent.

Rank and Percentile

The Rank and Percentile tool creates a table that shows the ordinal and percentile ranking for each value in a range. You can also generate ranks and percentiles by using Excel functions (those that begin with `RANK` and `PERCENTILE`).

Regression

Use the Regression tool (see Figure 37.9) to calculate a regression analysis from worksheet data. You can use regression to analyze trends, forecast the future, build predictive models, and, often, to make sense out of a series of seemingly unrelated numbers.

FIGURE 37.9

The Regression dialog box.

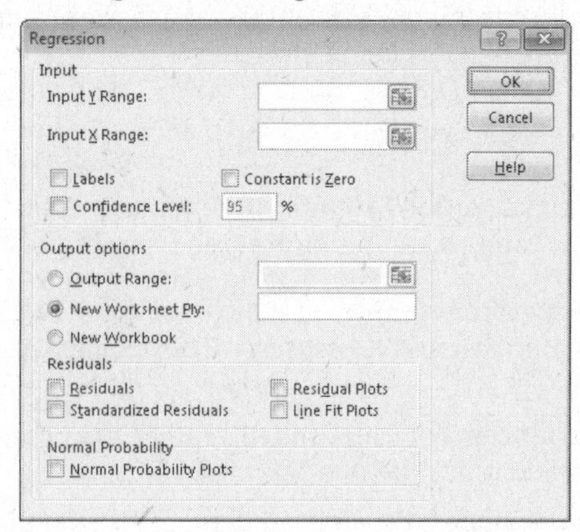

Regression analysis enables you to determine the extent to which one range of data (the dependent variable) varies as a function of the values of one or more other ranges of data (the independent variables). This relationship is expressed mathematically, using values that Excel calculates. You can use these calculations to create a mathematical model of the data and predict the dependent variable by using different values of one or more independent variables. This tool can perform simple and multiple linear regressions and calculate and standardize residuals automatically.

As you can see, the Regression dialog box offers many options:

- **Input Y Range:** The range that contains the dependent variable.
- **Input X Range:** One or more ranges that contain independent variables.
- **Confidence Level:** The confidence level for the regression.
- **Constant Is Zero:** If selected, forces the regression to have a constant of 0 (which means that the regression line passes through the origin; when the X values are 0, the predicted Y value is 0).
- **Residuals:** The four options in this section of the dialog box enable you to specify whether to include residuals in the output. *Residuals* are the differences between observed and predicted values.
- **Normal Probability:** Generates a chart for normal probability plots.

Sampling

The Sampling tool generates a random sample from a range of input values. The Sampling tool can help you to work with a large database by creating a subset of it.

This procedure has two options: periodic and random. If you choose a periodic sample, Excel selects every *n*th value from the Input range, where *n* equals the period that you specify. With a random sample, you simply specify the size of the sample you want Excel to select, and every value has an equal probability of being chosen.

T-Test

Use the T-Test tool to determine whether a statistically significant difference exists between two small samples. The Analysis ToolPak can perform three types of t-tests:

- **Paired two-sample for means:** For paired samples in which you have two observations on each subject (such as a pretest and a post-test). The samples must be the same size.
- **Two-sample assuming equal variances:** For independent, rather than paired, samples. Excel assumes equal variances for the two samples.
- **Two-sample assuming unequal variances:** For independent, rather than paired, samples. Excel assumes unequal variances for the two samples.

Figure 37.10 shows output for the Paired Two Sample for Means t-Test. You specify the significance level (alpha) and the hypothesized difference between the two means (that is, the *null hypothesis*).

FIGURE 37.10

Output from the paired t-Test dialog box.

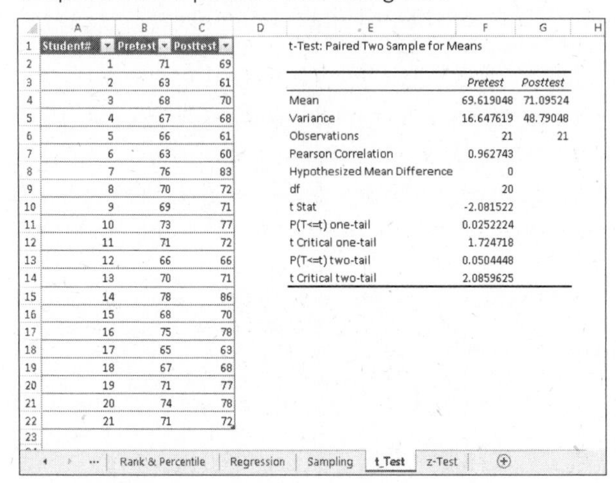

Student#	Pretest	Posttest
1	71	69
2	63	61
3	68	70
4	67	68
5	66	61
6	63	60
7	76	83
8	70	72
9	69	71
10	73	77
11	71	72
12	66	66
13	70	71
14	78	86
15	68	70
16	75	78
17	65	63
18	67	68
19	71	77
20	74	78
21	71	72

t-Test: Paired Two Sample for Means

	Pretest	Posttest
Mean	69.619048	71.09524
Variance	16.647619	48.79048
Observations	21	21
Pearson Correlation	0.962743	
Hypothesized Mean Difference	0	
df	20	
t Stat	-2.081522	
P(T<=t) one-tail	0.0252224	
t Critical one-tail	1.724718	
P(T<=t) two-tail	0.0504448	
t Critical two-tail	2.0859625	

Z-Test (two-sample test for means)

The T-Test tool is used for small samples; the Z-Test tool is used for larger samples or populations. You must know the variances for both input ranges.

Part VI

Programming Excel with VBA

If you've ever wanted to do a bit more or automate routine operations so that you don't always have to perform boring, repetitious tasks manually, this part is for you. This part is also aimed at those Excel users who want to develop Excel-based applications for other users. Visual Basic for Applications (VBA) is the powerful programming language that you can use for these tasks, as well as for more esoteric purposes, such as developing that specialized worksheet function that you simply can't find in Excel.

IN THIS PART

CHAPTER 38

Introducing Visual Basic for Applications

IN THIS CHAPTER

Introducing VBA macros

Creating VBA macros

Recording VBA macros

Writing VBA code

Learning more about VBA

This chapter is an introduction to the Visual Basic for Applications (VBA) macro language — a key component for users who want to customize and automate Excel. This chapter teaches you how to record macros and create simple macro procedures. Subsequent chapters expand upon the topics in this chapter.

Introducing VBA Macros

A *macro* is a sequence of instructions that automates some aspect of Excel so that you can work more efficiently and with fewer errors. You may create a macro, for example, to format and print your month-end sales report. After the macro is developed, you can then execute the macro to perform many time-consuming procedures automatically.

You don't have to be a power user to create and use simple VBA macros. Casual users can simply turn on Excel's macro recorder: Excel records your actions and converts them into a VBA macro. When you execute this macro, Excel performs the actions again. More advanced users, though, can write code that tells Excel to perform tasks that can't be recorded. For example, you can write procedures that display custom dialog boxes, or process data in a series of workbooks, and even create special-purpose add-ins.

What You Can Do with VBA

VBA is an extremely rich programming language with thousands of uses. The following list contains just a few things that you can do with VBA macros. (Not all of these tasks are covered in this book.)

- **Insert boilerplate text.** If you need to enter standard text into a range of cells, you can create a macro to do the typing for you.
- **Automate a procedure that you perform frequently.** For example, you may need to prepare a month-end summary. If the task is straightforward, you can develop a macro to do it for you.
- **Automate repetitive operations.** If you need to perform the same action in 12 different workbooks, you can record a macro while you perform the task once — and then let the macro repeat your action in the other workbooks.
- **Create a custom command.** For example, you can combine several Excel commands so that they're executed from a single keystroke or from a single mouse click.
- **Create a simplified "front end" for users who don't know much about Excel.** For example, you can set up a foolproof data-entry template.
- **Develop a new worksheet function.** Although Excel includes a wide assortment of built-in functions, you can create custom functions that greatly simplify your formulas.
- **Create complete macro-driven applications.** Excel macros can display custom dialog boxes and respond to new commands added to the Ribbon.
- **Create custom add-ins for Excel.** Most add-ins shipped with Excel were created with Excel macros. I used VBA exclusively to create my Power Utility Pak.

Displaying the Developer Tab

If you plan to work with VBA macros, make sure that the Developer tab is present on the Excel Ribbon. The Developer tab, which does not appear by default, contains useful commands for VBA users (see Figure 38.1). To display this tab, follow these steps:

FIGURE 38.1

The Developer tab.

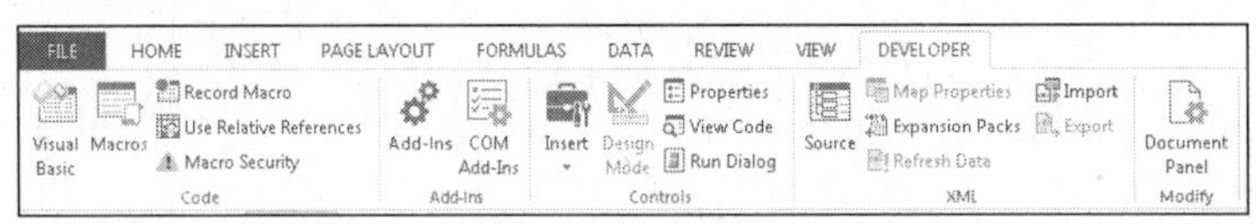

1. **Right-click any Ribbon control and select Customize the Ribbon from the shortcut menu.** The Customize Ribbon tab of the Excel Options dialog box appears.
2. **In the list box on the right, place a check mark next to Developer.**
3. **Click OK to return to Excel.**

About Macro Security

Macros have the potential to cause serious damage to your computer, such as erasing files or installing malware. Consequently, Microsoft has added macro-security features to help prevent macro-related problems.

Figure 38.2 shows the Macro Settings section of the Trust Center dialog box. To display this dialog box, choose Developer ➪ Code ➪ Macro Security.

FIGURE 38.2

The Macro Settings section of the Trust Center dialog box.

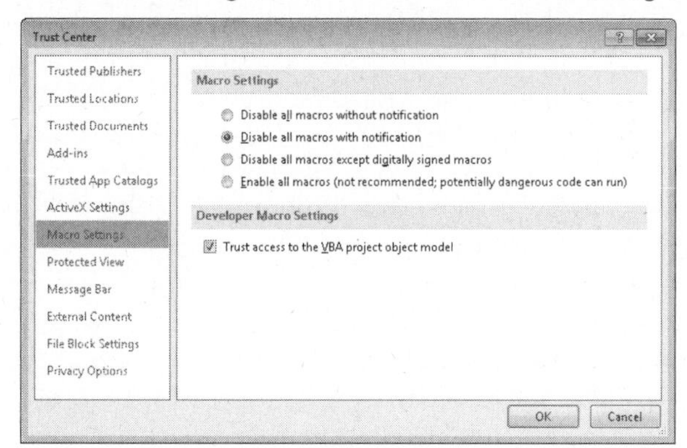

By default, Excel uses the Disable All Macros with Notification option. With this setting in effect, if you open a workbook that contains macros (and the file is not digitally "signed"), the macros will be disabled, and Excel displays a Security Warning above the Formula bar (see Figure 38.3). If you're certain that the workbook comes from a trusted source, click the Enable Content button in the security warning area, and the macros will be enabled. Excel remembers your decision; if you enable the macros, you won't see the Security Warning the next time you open that file.

FIGURE 38.3

Excel displays a Security Warning if a workbook contains macros.

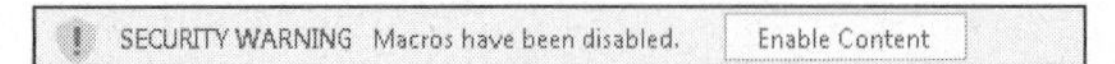
SECURITY WARNING Macros have been disabled.
Enable Content

NOTE

If the Visual Basic (VB) Editor window is open when you open a workbook that contains macros, Excel does not display the Security Warning above the Formula bar. Instead, it displays a dialog box with two buttons: Enable Macros and Disable Macros.

Rather than deal with individual workbooks, you may prefer to designate one or more folders as "trusted locations." All the workbooks in a trusted location are opened without a macro warning. You designate trusted folders in the Trusted Locations section of the Trust Center dialog box.

Saving Workbooks That Contain Macros

If you store one or more VBA macros in a workbook, you must save the file with an XLSM extension.

The first time you save a workbook that contains macros (or even an empty VBA module), the file format defaults to XLSX — and this format can't contain macros. Unless you change the file format to XLSM, Excel displays the warning shown in Figure 38.4. You need to click No, and then choose Excel Macro-Enabled Workbook (*.xlsm) from the Save As Type drop-down list in the Save As dialog box.

FIGURE 38.4

Excel warns you if your workbook contains macros and you attempt to save it in a nonmacro file format.

Microsoft Excel
The following features cannot be saved in macro-free workbooks:
• VB project
To save a file with these features, click No, and then choose a macro-enabled file type in the File Type list.
To continue saving as a macro-free workbook, click Yes.
Yes
No
Help

NOTE

Alternatively, you can save the workbook in the old Excel 97-2003 format (which uses an XLS extension) or the new Excel binary format (which uses an XLSB extension). Both of these file formats can contain macros.

Two Types of VBA Macros

Before getting into the details of creating macros, you need to understand a key distinction. A *VBA macro* (also known as a *procedure*) can be one of two types: a `Sub` or a `Function`. The next two sections discuss the difference.

VBA Sub procedures

You can think of a `Sub` procedure as a new command that either the user or another macro can execute. You can have any number of `Sub` procedures in an Excel workbook. Figure 38.5 shows a simple VBA `Sub` procedure. When this code is executed, VBA inserts the current date into the active cell, applies a number format, makes the cell bold, sets the text color to white, sets the background color to black, and adjusts the column width.

FIGURE 38.5

A simple VBA procedure.

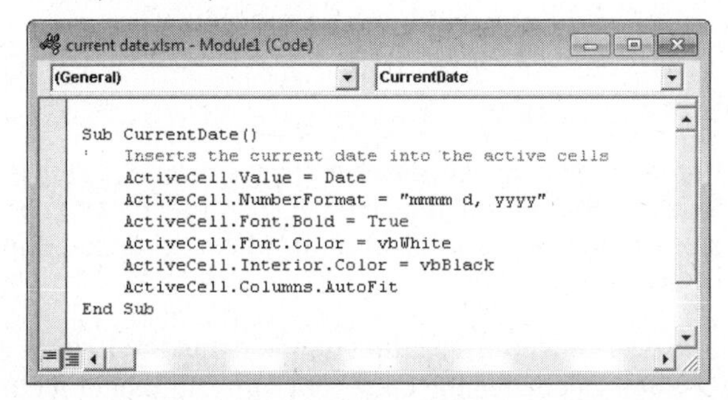

On the Web

A workbook that contains this macro is available on this book's website. It also includes a button that makes it easy to execute the macro. The file is named `current date.xlsm`.

What's New in the Visual Basic Editor?

In a word, nothing. Beginning with Excel 2007, Microsoft made many changes to Excel's user interface. However, the VB Editor has remained untouched. The VBA language has been updated to accommodate the new Excel features, but the VB Editor has no new features, and the toolbars and menus work exactly as they always have. There is one difference in Excel 2013: The Help system is now completely web-based. In order to access VBA Help, you must be connected to the Internet.

Sub procedures always start with the keyword Sub, the macro's name (every macro must have a unique name), and then a pair of parentheses. (The parentheses are required; they're empty unless the procedure uses one or more arguments.) The End Sub statement signals the end of the procedure. The lines in between comprise the procedure's code.

The CurrentDate macro also includes a comment. *Comments* are simply notes to yourself, and they're ignored by VBA. A comment line begins with an apostrophe. You can also put a comment in the same line as a statement. In other words, when VBA encounters an apostrophe, it ignores the rest of the text in the line.

You execute a VBA Sub procedure in any of the following ways:

- Choose Developer ➪ Code ➪ Macros (or press Alt + F8) to display the Macro dialog box. Select the procedure name from the list, and then click Run.
- Press the procedure's shortcut key combination (if it has one).
- Click a button or other shape that has a macro assigned to it.
- If the VB Editor is active, move the cursor anywhere within the code and press F5.
- Execute the procedure by calling it from another VBA procedure.

VBA functions

The second type of VBA procedure is a function. A *function* always returns a single value (just as a worksheet function always returns a single value). A VBA function can be executed by other VBA procedures or used in worksheet formulas, just as you would use Excel's built-in worksheet functions.

Figure 38.6 shows a custom worksheet function. This function is named CubeRoot, and it requires a single argument. CubeRoot calculates the cube root of its argument and returns the result. A Function procedure looks much like a Sub procedure. Notice, however, that function procedures begin with the keyword Function and end with an End Function statement.

FIGURE 38.6

This VBA function returns the cube root of its argument.

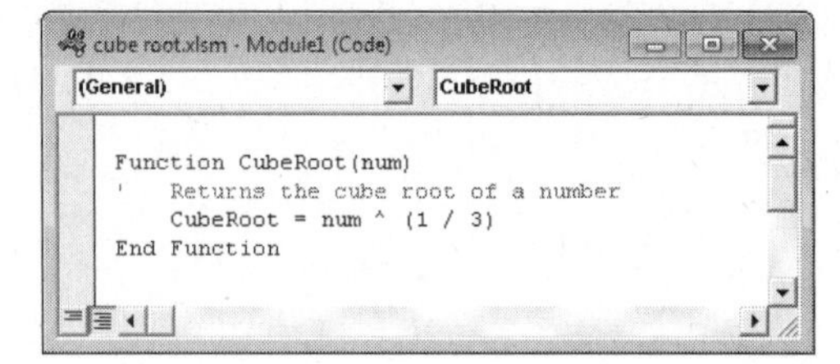

Some Definitions

If you're new to VBA, you may be overwhelmed by the terminology. I've put together some key definitions to help you keep the terms straight. These terms cover VBA and UserForms (custom dialog boxes) — two important elements that are used to customize Excel:

- **Code:** VBA instructions that are produced in a module sheet when you record a macro. You can also enter VBA code manually.
- **Controls:** Objects on a UserForm (or in a worksheet) that you manipulate. Examples include buttons, check boxes, and list boxes.
- **Function:** One of two types of VBA macros that you can create. (The other is a `Sub` procedure.) A function returns a single value. You can use VBA functions in other VBA macros or in your worksheets.
- **Macro:** A set of VBA instructions performed automatically.
- **Method:** An action taken on an object. For example, applying the `Clear` method to a `Range` object erases the contents and formatting of the cells.
- **Module:** A container for VBA code.
- **Object:** An element that you manipulate with VBA. Examples include ranges, charts, drawing objects, and so on.
- **Procedure:** Another name for a macro. A VBA procedure can be a `Sub` procedure or a `Function` procedure.
- **Property:** A particular aspect of an object. For example, a `Range` object has properties, such as `Height`, `Style`, and `Name`.
- Sub **procedure:** One of two types of Visual Basic macros that you can create. The other is a `Function`.
- **UserForm**: A container that holds controls for a custom dialog box and holds VBA code to manipulate the controls.

Chapters 40 and 41 explain UserForms in depth.

- **VBA:** Visual Basic for Applications. The macro language that is available in Excel, as well as in the other Microsoft Office applications.
- **VB Editor:** The window (separate from Excel) that you use to create VBA macros and UserForms. Press Alt+F11 to toggle between Excel and the VB Editor.

Creating VBA functions that you use in worksheet formulas can simplify your formulas and enable you to perform calculations that otherwise may be impossible. Chapter 39 discusses VBA functions in greater detail.

On the Web

A workbook that contains this function is available on this book's website. The file is named `cube root .xlsm`.

Creating VBA Macros

Excel provides two ways to create macros:

- Turn on the macro recorder and record your actions.
- Enter the code directly into a VBA module.

The following sections describe these methods.

Recording VBA macros

In this section, I describe the basic steps that you take to record a VBA macro. In most cases, you can record your actions as a macro and then simply replay the macro; you don't need to look at the code that's automatically generated. If simply recording and playing back macros is as far as you go with VBA, you don't need to be concerned with the language itself (although a basic understanding of how things work doesn't do any harm).

Recording your actions to create VBA code: The basics

The Excel macro recorder translates your actions into VBA code. To start the macro recorder, choose Developer ➪ Code ➪ Record Macro (or click the Record Macro icon on the left side of the status bar). The Record Macro dialog box, shown in Figure 38.7, appears.

FIGURE 38.7

The Record Macro dialog box.

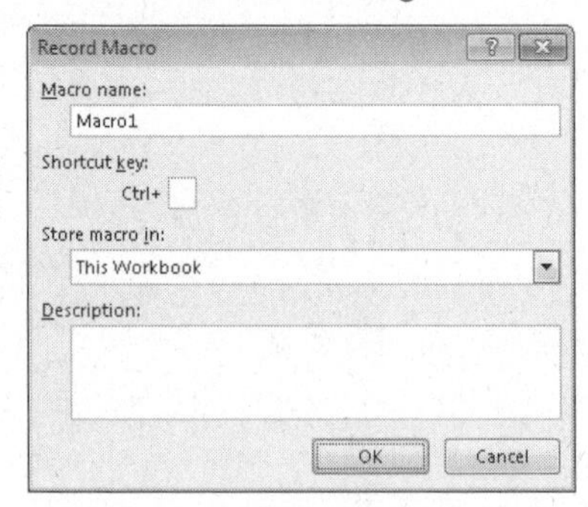

The Record Macro dialog box presents several options:

- **Macro Name:** The name of the macro. Excel proposes generic names, such as Macro1, Macro2, and so on.
- **Shortcut Key:** You can specify a key combination that executes the macro. The key combination always uses the Ctrl key. You can also press Shift when you enter a letter. For example, pressing Shift while you enter the letter *H* makes the shortcut key combination Ctrl + Shift + H.

CAUTION

Shortcut keys assigned to macros take precedence over built-in shortcut keys. For example, if you assign Ctrl+S to a macro, you can't use the key combination to save your workbook when that macro is available.

- **Store Macro In:** The location for the macro. Your choices are the current workbook, your Personal Macro Workbook (see "Storing macros in your Personal Macro Workbook," later in this chapter), or a new workbook.
- **Description:** A description of the macro (optional).

To begin recording your actions, click OK; your actions within Excel are converted to VBA code. When you finish recording the macro, choose Developer ➪ Code ➪ Stop Recording. Or you can click the Stop Recording button on the status bar. This button replaces the Start Recording button while your macro is being recorded.

NOTE

Recording your actions always results in a new `Sub` procedure. You can't create a `Function` procedure by using the macro recorder. Function procedures must be created manually.

Recording a macro: A simple example

This example demonstrates how to record a very simple macro that inserts your name in the active cell.

To create the macro, start with a new workbook and follow these steps:

1. **Activate an empty cell.**

NOTE

Select the cell to be formatted *before* you start recording your macro. This step is important. If you select a cell while the macro recorder is turned on, the actual cell that you select will be recorded into the macro. In such a case, the macro would always format that particular cell, and it would not be a general-purpose macro.

2. **Choose Developer ➪ Code ➪ Record Macro.** The Record Macro dialog box appears. (Refer to Figure 38.7.)

3. **Enter a new single-word name for the macro, to replace the default Macro1 name.** For example, type **MyName** as the name
4. **Assign this macro to the shortcut key Ctrl + Shift + N by entering an uppercase N in the Shortcut Key field.**
5. **Click OK to close the Record Macro dialog box and begin recording your actions.**
6. **Type your name into the selected cell and then press Enter.**
7. **Choose Developer ⇨ Code ⇨ Stop Recording (or click the Stop Recording button on the status bar).**

Examining the macro

The macro was recorded in a new module named `Module1`. To view the code in this module, you must activate the VB Editor. You can activate the VB Editor in either of two ways:

- Press Alt + F11.
- Choose Developer ⇨ Code ⇨ Visual Basic.

In the VB Editor, the Project window displays a list of all open workbooks and add-ins. This list is displayed as a tree diagram, which you can expand or collapse. The code that you recorded previously is stored in Module1 in the current workbook. When you double-click Module1, the code in the module appears in the Code window.

Figure 38.8 shows the recorded macro, as displayed in the Code window.

FIGURE 38.8

The `MyName` procedure was generated by the Excel macro recorder.

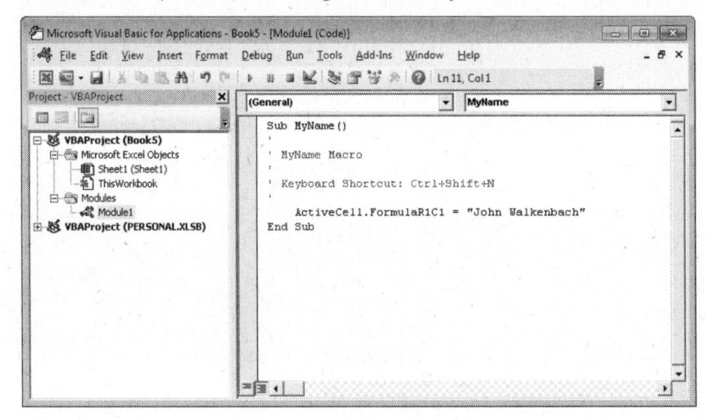

The macro should look something like this (with your name substituted for mine, of course):

```
Sub MyName()
'
' MyName Macro
'
' Keyboard Shortcut: Ctrl+Shift+N
'
    ActiveCell.FormulaR1C1 = "John Walkenbach"
End Sub
```

The macro recorded is a `Sub` procedure that is named `MyName`. The statements tell Excel what to do when the macro is executed.

Notice that Excel inserted some comments at the top of the procedure. These comments are some of the information that appeared in the Record Macro dialog box. These comment lines (which begin with an apostrophe) aren't really necessary, and deleting them has no effect on how the macro runs. If you ignore the comments, you'll see that this procedure has only one VBA statement:

```
ActiveCell.FormulaR1C1 = "John Walkenbach"
```

This single statement causes the name you typed while recording the macro to be inserted into the active cell. The `FormulaR1C1` part is a property of the `Range` object — but I'm getting ahead of myself.

Testing the macro

Before you recorded this macro, you set an option that assigned the macro to the Ctrl+Shift+N shortcut key combination. To test the macro, return to Excel by using either of the following methods:

- Press Alt+F11.
- Click the View Microsoft Excel button on the VB Editor toolbar.

When Excel is active, activate a worksheet. (It can be in the workbook that contains the VBA module or in any other workbook.) Select a cell and press Ctrl+Shift+N. The macro immediately enters your name into the cell.

Editing the macro

After you record a macro, you can make changes to it (although you must know what you're doing). For example, assume that you want your name to be bold. You could rerecord the macro, but this modification is simple, so editing the code is more efficient. Press Alt+F11 to activate the VB Editor window. Then activate Module1 and insert the following statement before the `End Sub` statement:

```
ActiveCell.Font.Bold = True
```

The edited macro appears as follows:

```
Sub MyName()
'
' MyName Macro
'
' Keyboard Shortcut: Ctrl+Shift+N
'
    ActiveCell.FormulaR1C1 = "John Walkenbach"
    ActiveCell.Font.Bold = True
End Sub
```

Test this new macro, and you see that it performs as it should.

Another example

This example demonstrates how to record a time-stamp macro that inserts the current date and time into the active cell.

To create the macro, follow these steps:

1. **Activate an empty cell.**
2. **Choose Developer ➪ Code ➪ Record Macro.** The Record Macro dialog box appears.
3. **Enter a new, single-word name for the macro, to replace the default Macro1 name.** A good name is `TimeStamp`.
4. **Assign this macro to the shortcut key Ctrl + Shift + T by entering an uppercase T in the Shortcut Key field.**
5. **Click OK to close the Record Macro dialog box.**
6. **Enter this formula into the selected cell:**

   `=NOW()`
7. **With the date cell selected, click the Copy button (or press Ctrl + C) to copy the cell to the Clipboard.**
8. **Choose Home ➪ Clipboard ➪ Paste ➪ Values (V).** This step replaces the formula with static text so that the date and time do not update when the worksheet is calculated.
9. **Press Esc to cancel Copy mode.**
10. **Choose Developer ➪ Code ➪ Stop Recording (or click the Stop Recording button on the status bar).**

Running the macro

Activate an empty cell and press Ctrl + Shift + T to execute the macro. There's a pretty good chance that the macro won't work!

The VBA code that is recorded in this macro depends upon a setting on the Advanced tab of the Excel Options dialog box: namely, after Pressing Enter, Move Selection. If this setting is enabled (which is the default), the recorded macro won't work as intended because the active cell was changed when you pressed Enter. Even if you reactivated the date cell while recording (in Step 7), the macro still fails.

Examining the macro

Activate the VB Editor and take a look at the recorded code. Figure 38.9 shows the recorded macro, as displayed in the Code window.

FIGURE 38.9

The TimeStamp procedure was generated by the Excel macro recorder.

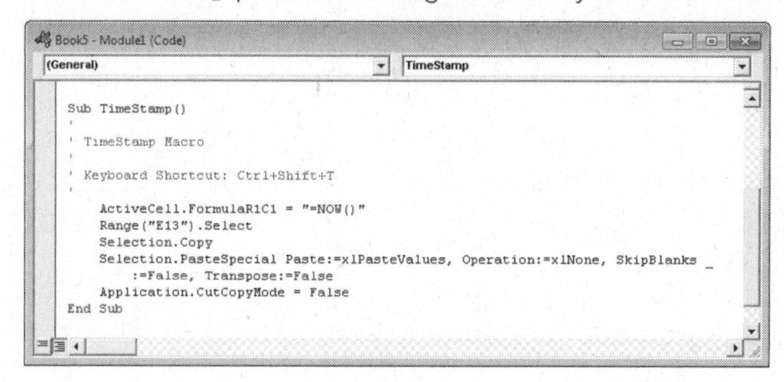
Book5 - Module1 (Code)
(General)
TimeStamp
Sub TimeStamp()
'
' TimeStamp Macro
'
' Keyboard Shortcut: Ctrl+Shift+T
'
ActiveCell.FormulaR1C1 = "=NOW()"
Range("E13").Select
Selection.Copy
Selection.PasteSpecial Paste:=xlPasteValues, Operation:=xlNone, SkipBlanks _
:=False, Transpose:=False
Application.CutCopyMode = False
End Sub

The procedure has five statements. The first inserts the `NOW()` formula into the active cell. The second statement selects cell E13 — an action I performed because the cell pointer moved to the next cell after I entered the formula. The exact cell address depends on where the cell pointer was when the macro was recorded.

The third statement copies the cell. The fourth statement, which is displayed on two lines (the underscore character means that the statement continues on the next line), pastes the Clipboard contents (as a value) to the current selection. The fourth statement cancels the moving border around the selected range.

The problem is that the macro is hard-coded to select cell E13. If you execute the macro when a different cell is active, the code always selects cell E13 before it copies the cell. This is not what you intended, and it causes the macro to fail.

NOTE

You'll also notice that the macro recorded some actions that you didn't make. For example, it specified several options for the `PasteSpecial` operation. Recording actions that you don't specifically make is just a by-product of the method that Excel uses to translate actions into code.

Rerecording the macro

You can fix the macro in several ways. If you understand VBA, you can edit the code so it works properly. Or you can rerecord the macro using relative references.

Delete the existing `TimeStamp` procedure, and rerecord it. Before you start recording, click the Use Relative References command in the Code group of the Developer tab. This control is a toggle, and it's turned off by default.

Figure 38.10 shows the new macro, recorded with relative references in effect.

FIGURE 38.10

This `TimeStamp` macro works correctly.

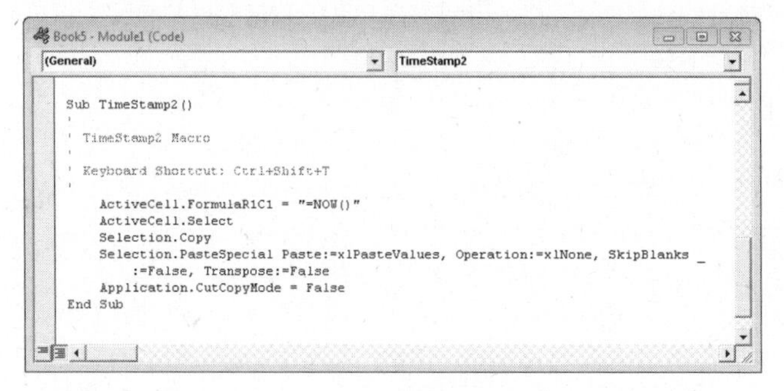
Book5 - Module1 (Code)
(General)
TimeStamp2
Sub TimeStamp2()
' TimeStamp2 Macro
' Keyboard Shortcut: Ctrl+Shift+T
ActiveCell.FormulaR1C1 = "=NOW()"
ActiveCell.Select
Selection.Copy
Selection.PasteSpecial Paste:=xlPasteValues, Operation:=xlNone, SkipBlanks _
:=False, Transpose:=False
Application.CutCopyMode = False
End Sub

Testing the macro

When Excel is active, activate a worksheet. (It can be in the workbook that contains the VBA module or in any other workbook.) Select a cell and press Ctrl+Shift+T. The macro immediately enters the current date and time into the cell. You may need to widen the column to see the date and time.

When the result of macro requires additional manual intervention, that's a sign that the macro could be improved. To widen the column automatically, just add this statement to the end of the macro (before the `End Sub` statement):

```
ActiveCell.EntireColumn.AutoFit
```

More about recording VBA macros

If you followed along with the preceding examples, you should have a better feel for how to record macros — and also a good feel for problems that might occur with even simple macros. If you find the VBA code confusing, don't worry. You don't really have to be concerned with it as long as the macro that you record works correctly. If the macro doesn't work, rerecording the macro rather than editing the code is often easier.

A good way to learn about what gets recorded is to set up your screen so that you can see the code that is being generated in the VB Editor windows. To do so, make sure that the Excel window isn't maximized; then arrange the Excel window and the VB Editor window so both are visible. While you're recording your actions, make sure that the VB Editor window is displaying the module in which the code is being recorded. (You may have to double-click the module name in the Project window.)

TIP

If you do a lot of work with VBA, consider adding a second monitor to your system. Then you can display Excel on one monitor and the VB Editor on the other.

Absolute versus relative recording

If you're going to work with recorded macros, you need to understand the concept of *relative* versus *absolute* recording modes. In a previous example in this chapter, I showed how even a simple macro could fail because of an incorrect recording mode.

Normally, when you record a macro, Excel stores exact references to the cells that you select. (That is, it performs *absolute recording.*) If you select the range B1:B10 while you're recording a macro, for example, Excel records this selection as

```
Range("B1:B10").Select
```


This VBA statement means exactly what it says: "Select the cells in the range B1:B10." When you invoke the macro that contains this statement, the same cells are always selected, regardless of where the active cell is located.

Look in the Developer ➪ Code group of the Ribbon for Use Relative References. When you click this control, Excel changes its recording mode from absolute (the default) to relative. When recording in relative mode, selecting a range of cells is translated differently, depending on where the active cell is located. For example, if you're recording in relative mode and cell A1 is active, selecting the range B1:B10 generates the following statement:

```
ActiveCell.Offset(0, 1).Range("A1:A10").Select
```

This statement can be translated as "From the active cell, move 0 rows down and 1 column right, and then treat this new cell as if it were cell A1. Now select what would be A1:A10." In other words, a macro that is recorded in relative mode starts out by using the active cell as its base and then stores relative references to this cell. As a result, you get different results, depending on the location of the active cell. When you replay this macro, the cells that are selected depend on the active cell. This macro selects a range that is 10 rows by 1 column, offset from the active cell by 0 rows and 1 column.

When Excel is recording in relative mode, the Use Relative Reference control appears with a background color. To return to absolute recording, click the Use Relative Reference control again (and it displays its normal state, with no background color).

Storing macros in your Personal Macro Workbook

Most user-created macros are designed for use in a specific workbook, but you may want to use some macros in all your work. You can store these general-purpose macros in the Personal Macro Workbook so that they're always available to you. The Personal Macro Workbook is loaded whenever you start Excel. This file, named `personal.xlsb`, doesn't exist until you record a macro, using Personal Macro Workbook as the destination.

> **NOTE**
> The Personal Macro Workbook normally is in a hidden window (to keep it out of the way).

To record the macro in your Personal Macro Workbook, select the Personal Macro Workbook option in the Record Macro dialog box before you start recording. This option is in the Store Macro In drop-down box.

If you store macros in the Personal Macro Workbook, you don't have to remember to open the Personal Macro Workbook when you load a workbook that uses macros. When you want to exit, Excel asks whether you want to save changes to the Personal Macro Workbook.

Assigning a macro to a shortcut key

When you begin recording a macro, the Record Macro dialog box gives you an opportunity to provide a shortcut key for the macro. Here's what to do if you'd like to change the shortcut key or provide a shortcut key for a macro that doesn't have one:

1. **Choose Developer ⇨ Code ⇨ Macros (or press Alt + F8).** The Macro dialog box appears.
2. **Select the macro name from the list.**
3. **Click the Options button.** The Macro Options dialog box, shown in Figure 38.11, appears.

FIGURE 38.11

Use the Macro Options dialog box to add or change a shortcut key for a macro.

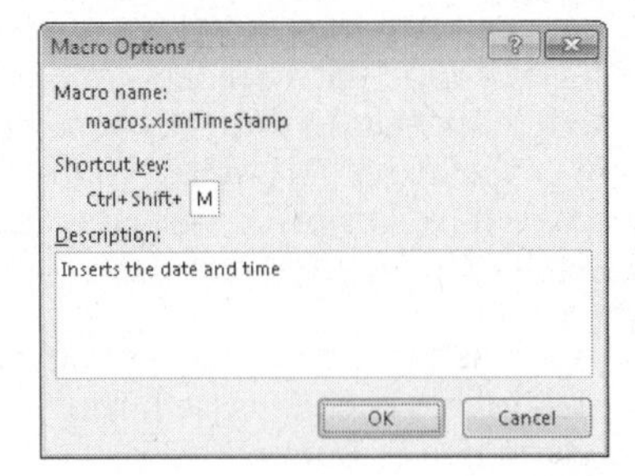

4. **Specify the shortcut key.** Use a single letter (for a Ctrl + letter shortcut), or press Shift and enter an uppercase letter (for a Ctrl + Shift + letter shortcut).
5. **Click OK to return to the Macro dialog box.**
6. **Click Cancel to close the Macro dialog box.**

Assigning a macro to a button

After you record a macro and test it, you may want to assign the macro to a button placed in a worksheet. You can follow these steps to do so:

1. **If the macro is a general-purpose macro that you plan to use in more than one workbook, make sure that the macro is stored in your Personal Macro Workbook.**
2. **Choose Developer ⇨ Controls ⇨ Insert, and then click the icon identified as *Button (Form Control)*.** Move your mouse pointer over the icons, and you see a ToolTip that describes the control (see Figure 38.12).

FIGURE 38.12

Adding a button to a worksheet so that it can be used to execute a macro.

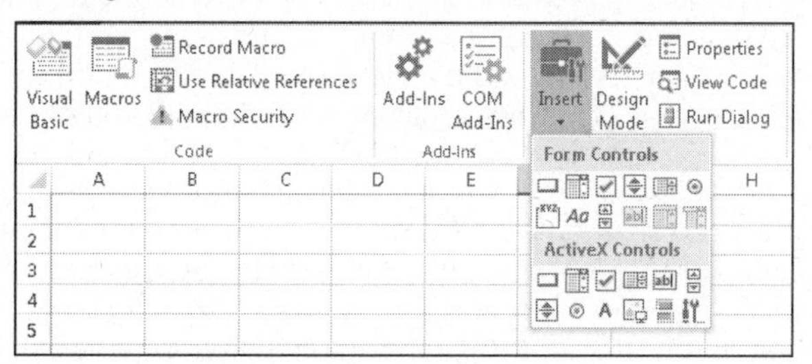

3. **Click the worksheet and drag to draw the button.** When you release the mouse button, the Assign Macro dialog box appears.
4. **Select the macro from the list.**
5. **Click OK to close the Assign Macro dialog box.**
6. **(Optional) Change the text that appears on the button to make it descriptive; right-click the button, choose Edit Text from the shortcut menu, and make your changes.**

After performing these steps, clicking the button executes the assigned macro.

Adding a macro to your Quick Access toolbar

You can also assign a macro to a button on your Quick Access toolbar:

1. **Right-click the Quick Access toolbar, and choose Customize Quick Access Toolbar from the shortcut menu.** The Quick Access Toolbar tab of the Excel Options dialog box appears.
2. **Select Macros from the drop-down list on the left.**
3. **At the top of the list on the right, choose For All Documents, or For xxx (where xxx is the active workbook's name).** This step determines whether the macro will be available for all workbooks, or just the workbook that contains the macro.
4. **Select your macro and click the Add button.**
5. **To change the icon or displayed text, click the Modify button.**

After performing these steps, your Quick Access toolbar will display a button that executes your macro.

Writing VBA code

As demonstrated in the preceding sections, the easiest way to create a simple macro is to record your actions. To develop more complex macros, however, you have to enter the VBA code manually — in other words, write a program. To save time (and assist in the learning process), you can often combine recording with manual code entry.

Before you can begin writing VBA code, you must have a good understanding of such topics as objects, properties, and methods. And it doesn't hurt to be familiar with common programming constructs, such as looping and `If-Then` statements.

This section is an introduction to VBA programming, which is essential if you want to write (rather than record) VBA macros. It isn't intended to be a complete instructional guide. My book *Excel 2013 Power Programming with VBA* (Wiley) covers all aspects of VBA and advanced spreadsheet application development.

The basics: Entering and editing code

Before you can enter code, you must insert a VBA module into the workbook. If the workbook already has a VBA module, you can use the existing module sheet for your new code.

Follow these steps to insert a new VBA module:

1. **Press Alt+F11 to activate the VB Editor window.** The Project window displays a list of all open workbooks and add-ins.
2. **In the Project window, locate and select the workbook you're working in.**
3. **Choose Insert⇨Module.** VBA inserts a new (empty) module into the workbook and displays it in the Code window.

VBA Coding Tips

When you enter code in a module sheet, you're free to use indenting and blank lines to make the code more readable. In fact, this is an excellent habit.

After you enter a line of code (by pressing Enter), it's evaluated for syntax errors. If none is found, the line of code is reformatted, and colors are added to keywords and identifiers. This automatic reformatting adds consistent spaces (before and after an equal sign, for example) and removes extra spaces that aren't needed. If a syntax error is found, you receive a pop-up message, and the line is displayed in a different color (red, by default). You need to correct your error before you can execute the macro.

A single statement can be as long as you need. However, you may want to break the statement into two or more lines. To do so, insert a space followed by an underscore (_). The following code, although written as two lines, is actually a single VBA statement:

```
Sheets("Sheet1").Range("B1").Value = _
  Sheets("Sheet1").Range("A1").Value
```

You can insert comments freely into your VBA code. The comment indicator is an apostrophe single quote character ('). Any text that follows a single quote on that line is ignored. A comment can be a line by itself, or it can be inserted after a statement. The following examples show two comments:

```
' Assign the values to the variables
Rate = .085  'Rate as of November 16
```


A VBA module, which is displayed in a separate window, works like a text editor. You can move through the sheet, select text, insert, copy, cut, paste, and so on.

How VBA works

VBA is by far the most complex feature in Excel, and you can easily get overwhelmed. To set the stage for the details of VBA, here is a concise summary of how VBA works:

- **You perform actions in VBA by writing (or recording) code in a VBA module and then executing the macro in any one of various ways.** VBA modules are stored in an Excel workbook, and a workbook can hold any number of VBA modules. To view or edit a VBA module, you must activate the VB Editor window. (Press Alt+F11 to toggle between Excel and the VB Editor window.)
- **A VBA module consists of procedures.** A *procedure* is computer code that performs some action. The following is an example of a simple `Sub` procedure called `ShowSum`, which adds 1 + 1 and displays the result in a pop-up dialog box:

```
Sub ShowSum()
  Sum = 1 + 1
  MsgBox "The answer is " & Sum
End Sub
```

- **A VBA module also can store function procedures.** A *function procedure* performs calculations and returns a single value. A function can be called from another VBA procedure or can even be used in a worksheet formula. Here's an example of a function named `AddTwo`. This function sums two values, which are supplied as arguments, and returns the result.

```
Function AddTwo(arg1, arg2)
  AddTwo = arg1 + arg2
End Function
```

- **VBA manipulates objects.** Excel provides more than 100 classes of objects that you can manipulate. Examples of objects include a workbook, a worksheet, a range on a worksheet, a chart, and a rectangle shape.
- **Objects are arranged in a hierarchy and can act as containers for other objects.** For example, Excel itself is an object called `Application`, and it contains other objects, such as `Workbook` objects. The `Workbook` object can contain other objects, such as `Worksheet` objects and `Chart` objects. A `Worksheet` object can contain objects such as `Range` objects, `PivotTable` objects, and so on. The arrangement of all these objects is referred to as an *object model.*
- **Objects that are alike form a *collection*.** For example, the `Worksheets` collection consists of all worksheets in a particular workbook. The `ChartObjects` collection consists of all `ChartObjects` on a worksheet. `Collections` are objects in themselves.
- **You refer to an object in your VBA code by specifying its position in the object hierarchy, using a period as a separator.**

  For example, you can refer to a workbook named `Book1.xlsx` as

```
Application.Workbooks("Book1.xlsx")
```

  This expression refers to the `Book1.xlsx` workbook in the `Workbooks` collection. The `Workbooks` collection is contained in the `Application` object (that is, Excel). Extending this to another level, you can refer to Sheet1 in Book1 as follows:

```
Application.Workbooks("Book1.xlsx").Worksheets("Sheet1")
```

  You can take it to still another level and refer to a specific cell as follows:

```
Application.Workbooks("Book1.xlsx").Worksheets("Sheet1").
  Range("A1")
```

- **If you omit specific references, Excel uses the *active* objects.** If `Book1.xlsx` is the active workbook, the preceding reference can be simplified as follows:

```
Worksheets("Sheet1").Range("A1")
```

  If you know that Sheet1 is the active sheet, you can simplify the reference even more:

```
Range("A1")
```

- **Objects have properties.** A *property* can be thought of as a setting for an object. For example, a `Range` object has properties, such as `Value` and `Address`. A

`Chart` object has properties such as `HasTitle` and `Type`. You can use VBA both to determine object properties and to change them.

- **You refer to properties by combining the object with the property, separated by a period.** For example, you can refer to the value in cell A1 on Sheet1 as follows:

```
Worksheets("Sheet1").Range("A1").Value
```

- **You can assign values to variables.** A *variable* is a VBA element that holds a value or text. To assign the value in cell A1 on Sheet1 to a variable called `Interest`, use the following VBA statement:

```
Interest = Worksheets("Sheet1").Range("A1").Value
```

- **Objects have methods.** A *method* is an action that is performed with the object. For example, one of the methods for a `Range` object is `ClearContents`. This method clears the contents of the range.
- **You specify methods by combining the object with the method, separated by a period.** For example, to clear the contents of range A1:C12, use the following statement:

```
Worksheets("Sheet1").Range("A1:C12").ClearContents
```

- **VBA also includes all the constructs of modern programming languages, including typed variables, arrays, looping, debugging aids, and so on.**

The preceding describes VBA in a nutshell. Now you just have to learn the details, some of which are covered in the rest of this chapter.

38

Objects and collections

VBA is an *object-oriented language,* which means that it manipulates objects, such as `Ranges`, `Charts`, `Shapes`, and so on. These objects are arranged in a hierarchy. The `Application` object (which is Excel) contains other objects. For example, the `Application` object contains a number of objects, including the following:

- `AddIns` (a collection of `AddIn` objects)
- `Windows` (a collection of `Window` objects)
- `Workbooks` (a collection of `Workbook` objects)

Most of these objects can contain other objects. For example, a `Workbook` object can contain the following objects:

- `Charts` (a collection of `Chart` sheet objects)
- `Names` (a collection of `Name` objects)
- `Styles` (a collection of `Style` objects)
- `Windows` (a collection of `Window` objects in the workbook)
- `Worksheets` (a collection of `Worksheet` objects)

Each of these objects, in turn, can contain other objects. A `Worksheet` object, for example, can contain the following objects:

- `ChartObjects` (a collection of all `ChartObject` objects)
- `PageSetup` (an object that stores printing information)
- `PivotTables` (a collection of all `PivotTable` objects)

A *collection* consists of all like objects. For example, the collection of all `Workbook` objects is known as the `Workbooks` collection. You can refer to an individual object in a collection by using an index number or a name. For example, if a workbook has three worksheets (named Sheet1, Sheet2, and Sheet3), you can refer to the first object in the `Worksheets` collection in either of these ways:

```
Worksheets(1)
Worksheets("Sheet1")
```

Properties

The objects that you work with have *properties,* which you can think of as attributes of the objects. For example, a `Range` object has properties, such as `Column`, `Row`, `Width`, and `Value`. A `Chart` object has properties, such as `Legend`, `ChartTitle`, and so on. `ChartTitle` is also an object, with properties such as `Font`, `Orientation`, and `Text`. Excel has many objects, and each has its own set of properties. You can write VBA code to do the following:

- Examine an object's current property setting and take some action based on it.
- Change an object's property setting.

You refer to a property in your VBA code by placing a period (a dot) and the property name after the object's name. For example, the following VBA statement sets the `Value` property of a range named *frequency* to `15`. (That is, the statement causes the number `15` to appear in the range's cells.)

```
Range("frequency").Value = 15
```

Some properties are *read-only,* which means that you can examine the property, but you can't change the property. For a single-cell `Range` object, the `Row` and `Column` properties are read-only properties: You can determine where a cell is located (in which row and column), but you can't change the cell's location by changing these properties.

A `Range` object also has a `Formula` property, which is *not* read-only; that is, you can insert a formula into a cell by changing its `Formula` property. The following statement inserts a formula into cell A12 by changing the cell's `Formula` property:

```
Range("A12").Formula = "=SUM(A1:A10)"
```

NOTE

Contrary to what you may think, Excel doesn't have a `Cell` object. When you want to manipulate a single cell, you use the `Range` object (with only one cell in it).

At the top of the object hierarchy is the `Application` object, which is actually Excel, the program. The `Application` object has several useful properties:

- `Application.ActiveWorkbook`: Returns the active workbook (a `Workbook` object) in Excel.
- `Application.ActiveSheet`: Returns the active sheet (a `Sheet` object) of the active workbook.
- `Application.ActiveCell`: Returns the active cell (a `Range` object) object of the active window.
- `Application.Selection`: Returns the object that is currently selected in the active window of the `Application` object. This can be a `Range`, a `Chart`, a `Shape`, or some other selectable object.

You also should understand that properties can return objects. In fact, that's exactly what the preceding examples do. The result of `Application.ActiveCell`, for example, is a `Range` object. Therefore, you can access properties by using a statement such as the following:

```
Application.ActiveCell.Font.Size = 15
```

In this case, the `ActiveCell` property returns a `Range` object. The `Font` property returns a `Font` object, which is contained in the `Range` object. `Size` is a property of the `Font` object. The preceding statement sets the `Size` property to `15` — that is, it causes the font in the currently selected cell to have a size of 15 points (pt).

TIP

Because `Application` properties are so commonly used, you can omit the object qualifier (`Application`). For example, to get the row of the active cell, you can use a statement such as the following:

```
ActiveCell.Row
```

In many cases, you can refer to the same object in a number of different ways. Assume that you have a workbook named `Sales.xlsx` and it's the only workbook open. Furthermore, assume that this workbook has one worksheet, named `Summary`. Your VBA code can refer to the `Summary` sheet in any of the following ways:

```
Workbooks("Sales.xlsx").Worksheets("Summary")
Workbooks(1).Worksheets(1)
Workbooks(1).Sheets(1)
Application.ActiveWorkbook.ActiveSheet
ActiveWorkbook.ActiveSheet
ActiveSheet
```

The method that you use is determined by how much you know about the workspace. For example, if more than one workbook is open, the second or third method isn't reliable. If you want to work with the active sheet (whatever it may be), any of the last three methods would work. To be absolutely sure that you're referring to a specific sheet on a specific workbook, the first method is your best choice.

Methods

Objects also have *methods*. You can think of a method as an action taken with an object. For example, `Range` objects have a `Clear` method. The following VBA statement clears a `Range`, an action that is equivalent to selecting the `Range` and then choosing Home⇨Editing⇨Clear⇨Clear All:

```
Range("A1:C12").Clear
```

In VBA code, methods *look* like properties because they're connected to the object with a "dot." However, methods and properties are different concepts.

Variables

Like all programming languages, VBA enables you to work with variables. In VBA (unlike in some languages), you don't need to declare variables explicitly before you use them in your code (although doing so is definitely a good practice).

NOTE

If your VBA module contains an `Option Explicit` statement at the top of the module, then you *must* declare all variables in the module. Undeclared variables will result in a compile error, and your procedures will not run.

In the following example, the value in cell A1 on Sheet1 is assigned to a variable named `Rate`:

```
Rate = Worksheets("Sheet1").Range("A1").Value
```

After the statement is executed, you can work with the variable `Rate` in other parts of your VBA code.

Controlling execution

VBA uses many constructs that are found in most other programming languages. These constructs are used to control the flow of execution. This section introduces a few of the more common programming constructs.

The If-Then construct

One of the most important control structures in VBA is the `If-Then` construct, which gives your applications decision-making capability. The basic syntax of the `If-Then` structure is

```
If condition Then statements [Else elsestatements]
```

In plain English, if a condition is true, then a group of statements will be executed. If you include the `Else` clause, then another group of statements will be executed if the condition is not true.

The following is an example (which doesn't use the optional `Else` clause). This procedure checks the active cell. If it contains a negative value, the cell's font color is changed to red. Otherwise, nothing happens.

```
Sub CheckCell()
  If ActiveCell.Value < 0 Then ActiveCell.Font.Color = vbGreen
End Sub
```

Here's another multi-line version of that procedure that uses an `Else` clause. Because it uses multiple lines, you must include an `End If` statement. This procedure colors the active cell text red if it's a negative value, and green otherwise.

```
Sub CheckCell()
   If ActiveCell.Value < 0 Then
      ActiveCell.Font.Color = vbRed
   Else
      ActiveCell.Font.Color = vbGreen
   End If
End Sub
```

38

For-Next loops

You can use a `For-Next` loop to execute one or more statements a number of times. Here's an example of a `For-Next` loop:

```
Sub SumSquared()
  Total = 0
  For Num = 1 To 10
    Total = Total + (Num ^ 2)
  Next Num
  MsgBox Total
End Sub
```

This example has one statement between the `For` statement and the `Next` statement. This single statement is executed ten times. The variable `Num` takes on successive values of `1`, `2`, `3`, and so on, up to `10`. The variable `Total` stores the sum of `Num` squared, added to the previous value of `Total`. The result is a value that represents the sum of the first ten integers squared. This result is displayed in a message box.

The With-End With construct

A construct that you sometimes encounter if you record macros is the `With-End With` construct. This is a shortcut way of dealing with several properties or methods of the same object. The following is an example:

```
Sub AlignCells()
  With Selection
    .HorizontalAlignment = xlCenter
    .VerticalAlignment = xlCenter
    .WrapText = False
    .Orientation = xlHorizontal
  End With
End Sub
```

The following macro performs exactly the same operations but doesn't use the `With-End With` construct:

```
Sub AlignCells()
  Selection.HorizontalAlignment = xlCenter
  Selection.VerticalAlignment = xlCenter
  Selection.WrapText = False
  Selection.Orientation = xlHorizontal
End Sub
```

The Select Case construct

The `Select Case` construct is useful for choosing among two or more options. The following example demonstrates the use of a `Select Case` construct. In this example, the active cell is checked. If its value is less than `0`, it's colored red. If it's equal to `0`, it's colored blue. If the value is greater than `0`, it's colored black.

```
Sub CheckCell()
  Select Case ActiveCell.Value
    Case Is < 0
      ActiveCell.Font.Color = vbRed
    Case 0
      ActiveCell.Font.Color = vbBlue
    Case Is > 0
      ActiveCell.Font.Color = vbBlack
  End Select

End Sub
```

Any number of statements can go below each `Case` statement, and they all get executed if the case is true.

A macro that can't be recorded

The following is a VBA macro that can't be recorded because it uses programming concepts that must be entered manually. This macro creates a list of all formulas on the active sheet. The list is stored on a new worksheet.

```
Sub ListFormulas()
' Create a range object
  Set InputRange = ActiveSheet.UsedRange
' Add a new sheet
  Set OutputSheet = Worksheets.Add
' Variable for the output row
  OutputRow = 1
' Loop through the range
  For Each cell In InputRange
    If cell.HasFormula Then
      OutputSheet.Cells(OutputRow, 1) = "'" & cell.Address
      OutputSheet.Cells(OutputRow, 2) = "'" & cell.Formula
      OutputRow = OutputRow + 1
    End If
  Next cell
End Sub
```

On the Web

A workbook that contains this example is available on this book's website. The file is named `list formulas.xlsm`.

Although this macro may look complicated, it's fairly simple when you break it down. Here's how it works:

1. The macro creates an object variable named `InputRange`. This variable corresponds to the used range on the active sheet (avoiding the need to check every cell).
2. It then adds a new worksheet and assigns the worksheet to an object variable named `OutputSheet`. The `OutputRow` variable is set to `1`. This variable is incremented later on.
3. The `For-Next` loop examines each cell in the `InputRange`. If the cell has a formula, the cell's address and formula are written to the `OutputSheet`. The `OutputRow` variable is also incremented.

Figure 38.13 shows the result of running this macro — a handy list of all formulas in the worksheet.

As macros go, this example is okay, but it's certainly not perfect. It's not very flexible, and it doesn't include any error handling. For example, if the workbook structure is protected, trying to add a new sheet will cause an error.

FIGURE 38.13

The `ListFormulas` macro creates a list of all formulas in a worksheet.

	A	B	C	D	E	F	G	H
1	$G$2	=B9/2						
2	$A$8	=SUM(A2:A7)						
3	$B$8	=SUM(B2:B7)						
4	$C$8	=SUM(C2:C7)						
5	$D$8	=SUM(D2:D7)						
6	$A$9	=AVERAGE(A2:A7)						
7	$B$9	=AVERAGE(B2:B7)						
8	$C$9	=AVERAGE(C2:C7)						
9	$D$9	=AVERAGE(D2:D7)						
10	$E$9	=AVERAGE(E2:E7)						
11	$A$15	=RANDBETWEEN(1,1000)						
12	$B$15	=RANDBETWEEN(1,1000)						
13	$C$15	=RANDBETWEEN(1,1000)						
14	$D$15	=RANDBETWEEN(1,1000)						
15	$E$15	=RANDBETWEEN(1,1000)						
16	$A$16	=RANDBETWEEN(1,1000)						
17	$B$16	=RANDBETWEEN(1,1000)						

Sheet1 | Sheet2

Learning More

This chapter is a basic introduction to VBA. If this is your first exposure to VBA, you're probably a bit overwhelmed by objects, properties, and methods. I don't blame you. If you try to access a property that an object doesn't have, you get a run-time error, and your VBA code grinds to a screeching halt until you correct the problem. Fortunately, several good ways are available to learn about objects, properties, and methods.

- **Read the rest of the book.** Subsequent chapters in this section contain additional information and many more examples.
- **Record your actions.** The best way to become familiar with VBA is to turn on the macro recorder and record actions that you make in Excel. You can then examine the code to gain some insights regarding the objects, properties, and methods.
- **Use the Help system.** The main source of detailed information about Excel's objects, methods, and procedures is the VBA Help system. Help is very thorough and easy to access. When you're in a VBA module, just move the cursor to a property or method and press F1. You get help that describes the word that is under the cursor. In Excel 2013, all VBA Help is online, so you must be connected to the Internet to use the Help system.
- **Get another book.** Several books are devoted exclusively to using VBA with Excel. My book, *Excel 2013 Power Programming with VBA* (Wiley), is one.

CHAPTER 39

Creating Custom Worksheet Functions

IN THIS CHAPTER

Getting an overview of VBA functions

Looking at function procedures

Focusing on function procedure arguments

Debugging custom functions

Pasting custom functions

As mentioned in the preceding chapter, you can create two types of VBA procedures: `Sub` procedures and `Function` procedures. This chapter focuses on `Function` procedures.

Overview of VBA Functions

Function procedures that you write in VBA are quite versatile. You can use these functions in two situations:

- You can call the function from a different VBA procedure.
- You can use the function in formulas that you create in a worksheet.

This chapter focuses on creating functions for use in your formulas.

Excel includes more than 400 predefined worksheet functions. With so many from which to choose, you may be curious as to why anyone would need to develop additional functions. The main reason is that creating a custom function can greatly simplify your formulas by making them shorter, and shorter formulas are more readable and easier to work with. For example, you can often replace a complex formula with a single function. Another reason is that you can write functions to perform operations that would otherwise be impossible.

NOTE

This chapter assumes that you're familiar with entering and editing VBA code in the Visual Basic (VB) Editor.

See Chapter 38 for an overview of the VB Editor.

An Introductory Example

Creating custom functions is relatively easy after you understand VBA. Without further ado, here's an example of a VBA function procedure. This function is stored in a VBA module, which is accessible from the VB Editor.

A custom function

This example function, named `NumSign`, uses one argument. The function returns a text string of `Positive` if its argument is greater than zero, `Negative` if the argument is less than zero, and `Zero` if the argument is equal to zero. If the argument is non-numeric, the function returns an empty string. The `NumSign` function is shown in Figure 39.1.

FIGURE 39.1

A simple custom worksheet function.

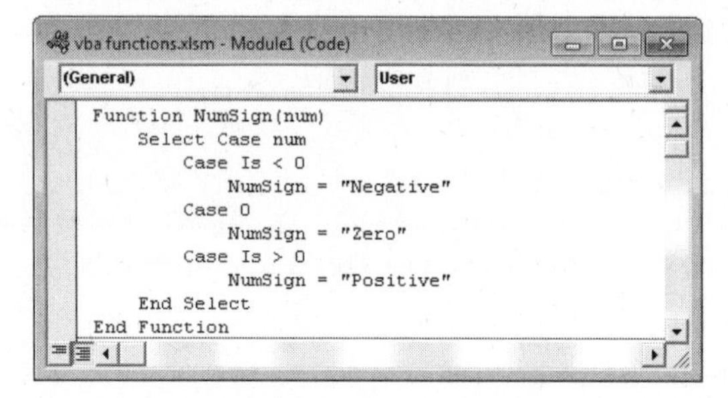

You can, of course, accomplish the same effect with the following worksheet formula, which uses nested `IF` functions:

```
=IF(A1=0,"Zero",IF(A1>0,"Positive","Negative"))
```

Many would agree that the custom function solution is easier to understand and to edit than the worksheet formula.

Using the function in a worksheet

When you enter a formula that uses the NumSign function, Excel executes the function to get the result. This custom function works just like any built-in worksheet function. You can insert it in a formula by choosing Formulas ➪ Function Library ➪ Function Wizard, which displays the Insert Function dialog box. (Custom functions are listed in the User Defined category.) When you select the function from the list, you can then use the Function Arguments dialog box to specify the arguments for the function, as shown in Figure 39.2. You can also nest custom functions and combine them with other elements in your formulas.

FIGURE 39.2

Creating a worksheet formula that uses a custom function.

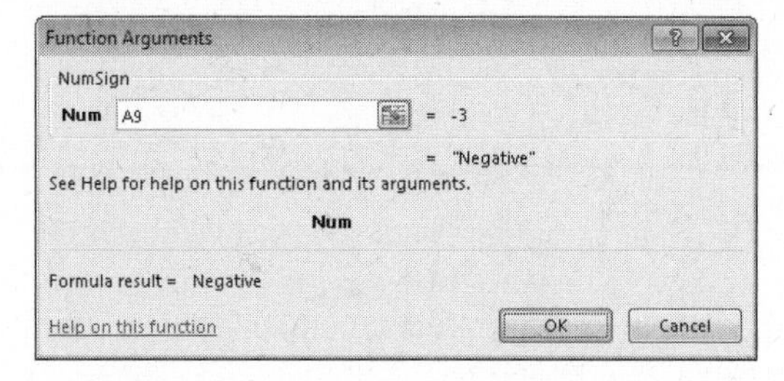

Analyzing the custom function

This section describes the NumSign function. Here again is the code:

```
Function NumSign(num)
    Select Case num
        Case Is < 0
            NumSign = "Negative"
        Case 0
            NumSign = "Zero"
        Case Is > 0
            NumSign = "Positive"
    End Select
End Function
```

Notice that the procedure starts with the keyword Function, followed by the name of the function (NumSign). This custom function uses one argument (num), and the argument's name is enclosed in parentheses. The num argument represents the cell or variable that is to be processed. When the function is used in a worksheet, the argument can be a cell reference (such as A1) or a literal value (such as -123). When the function is used in another procedure, the argument can be a numeric variable, a literal number, or a value that is obtained from a cell.

What a Function Can't Do

Almost everyone who starts creating custom worksheet functions using VBA makes a fatal mistake: They try to get the function to do more than is possible.

A worksheet function returns a value, and the function must be completely "passive." In other words, the function can't change anything on the worksheet. For example, you can't develop a worksheet function that changes the formatting of a cell. (Every VBA programmer has tried, and not one of them has been successful!) If your function attempts to perform an action that isn't allowed, the function simply returns an error.

The preceding paragraph isn't quite true. Over the years I've discovered a few cases in which a VBA function used in a formula can have an effect. For example, it's possible to create a custom worksheet function that adds or deletes cell comments. But, for the most part, functions used in formulas must be passive.

VBA functions that aren't used in worksheet formulas can do anything that a regular `Sub` procedure can do — including changing cell formatting.

The `NumSign` function uses the `Select Case` construct (described in Chapter 38) to take a different action, depending on the value of `num`. If `num` is less than zero, `NumSign` is assigned the text `Negative`. If `num` is equal to zero, `NumSign` is `Zero`. If `num` is greater than zero, `NumSign` is `Positive`. The value returned by a function is always assigned to the function's name.

If you work with this function, you might notice a problem if the argument is non-numeric. In such a case, the function returns `Positive`. In other words, the function has a bug. Following is a revised version that returns an empty string if the argument is non-numeric. This code uses the VBA `IsNumeric` function to check the argument. If it's numeric, the code checks the sign. If the argument is not numeric, the `Else` part of the `If-Then-Else` structure is executed.

```
Function NumSign(num)
    If IsNumeric(num) Then
        Select Case num
          Case Is < 0
            NumSign = "Negative"
          Case 0
            NumSign = "Zero"
          Case Is > 0
            NumSign = "Positive"
        End Select
    Else
       NumSign = ""
    End If
End Function
```

Without using a custom function, you would need the following formula to get the same result:

```
=IF(ISNUMBER(A1),IF(A1<0,"Negative",IF(A1>0,"Positive","Zero")),"")
```

About Function Procedures

A custom `Function` procedure has much in common with a `Sub` procedure. Function procedures have some important differences, however. Perhaps the key difference is that a function returns a *value* (which can be a number or a text string). When writing a `Function` procedure, the value that's returned is the value that has been assigned to the function's name when a function is finished executing.

To create a custom function, follow these steps:

1. **Activate the VB Editor (press Alt + F11).**
2. **Select the workbook in the Project window.**
3. **Choose Insert⇨Module to insert a VBA module.** Or you can use an existing code module. However, it must be a standard VBA module.
4. **Enter the keyword** Function **followed by the function's name and a list of the arguments (if any) in parentheses.** If the function doesn't use an argument, the VB Editor adds a set of empty parentheses.
5. **Insert the VBA code that performs the work — and make sure that the variable corresponding to the function's name has the appropriate value when the function ends.** This is the value that the function returns.
6. **End the function with an End Function statement.**

Note

Step 3 is very important. If you put a function procedure in a code module for ThisWorkbook or a worksheet (for example, Sheet1), the function will not be recognized in a worksheet formula. Excel will display a `#NAME?` error.

Function names that are used in worksheet formulas must adhere to the same rules as variable names.

Executing Function Procedures

You can execute a `Sub` procedure in many ways, but you can execute a `Function` procedure in just two ways:

- Call it from another VBA procedure.
- Use it in a worksheet formula.

Calling custom functions from a procedure

You can call custom functions from a VBA procedure just as you call built-in VBA functions. For example, after you define a function called `CalcTax`, you can enter a statement such as the following:

```
Tax = CalcTax(Amount, Rate)
```

This statement executes the `CalcTax` custom function with `Amount` and `Rate` as its arguments. The function's result is assigned to the `Tax` variable.

Using custom functions in a worksheet formula

You use a custom function in a worksheet formula just as you use built-in functions. However, you must ensure that Excel can locate the function. If the function procedure is in the same workbook, you don't have to do anything special. If the function is defined in a different workbook, you may have to tell Excel where to find the function. The following are the three ways in which you can do this:

- **Precede the function's name with a file reference.** For example, if you want to use a function called `CountNames` that's defined in a workbook named `MyFunctions`, you can use a reference such as the following:

  ```
  =MyFunctions.xlsm!CountNames(A1:A1000)
  ```

  If the workbook name contains a space, you need to add single quotes around the workbook name. For example

  ```
  ='My Functions.xlsm'!CountNames(A1:A1000)
  ```

  If you insert the function with the Insert Function dialog box, the workbook reference is inserted automatically.

- **Set up a reference to the workbook.** If the custom function is defined in a referenced workbook, you don't need to precede the function name with the workbook name. You establish a reference to another workbook by choosing Tools⇨References (in the VB Editor). You're presented with a list of references that includes all open workbooks. Place a check mark in the item that refers to the workbook that contains the custom function. (Click the Browse button if the workbook isn't open.)

- **Create an add-in.** When you create an add-in from a workbook that has function procedures, you don't need to use the file reference when you use one of the functions in a formula; the add-in must be installed, however.

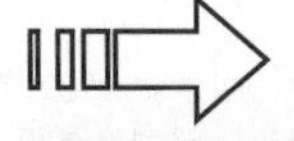

Chapter 44 discusses add-ins.

Note

Function procedures don't appear in the Macro dialog box because you can't execute a function directly. As a result, you need to do extra, upfront work to test your functions while you're developing them. One approach is to set up a simple `Sub` procedure that calls the function. If the function is designed to be used in worksheet formulas, you can enter a simple formula that uses the function to test it while you're developing the function.

Function Procedure Arguments

Keep in mind the following about function procedure arguments:

- Arguments can be variables (including arrays), constants, literals, or expressions.
- Some functions do not have arguments.
- Some functions have a fixed number of required arguments (from 1 to 60).
- Some functions have a combination of required and optional arguments.

The following sections present a series of examples that demonstrate how to use arguments effectively with functions. Coverage of optional arguments is beyond the scope of this book.

On the Web

The examples in this chapter are available on this book's website. The file is named `VBA functions.xlsm`.

A function with no argument

Most functions use arguments, but that's not a requirement. Excel, for example, has a few built-in worksheet functions that don't use arguments, such as `RAND`, `TODAY`, and `NOW`.

The following is a simple example of a function that has no arguments. This function returns the `UserName` property of the `Application` object, which is the name that appears in the Personalize section of the Excel Options dialog box. This function is very simple, but it can be useful because no other way is available to get the user's name to appear in a worksheet formula.

```
Function User()
' Returns the name of the current user
  User = Application.UserName
End Function
```

When you enter the following formula into a worksheet cell, the cell displays the name of the current user:

```
=User()
```

As with Excel's built-in functions, when you use a function with no arguments, you must include a set of empty parentheses.

A function with one argument

The function that follows takes a single argument and uses the Excel text-to-speech generator to "speak" the argument.

```
Function SayIt(txt)
  Application.Speech.Speak (txt)
End Function
```

NOTE
To hear the synthesized voice, your system must be set up to play sound.

For example, if you enter this formula, Excel will "speak" the contents of cell A1 whenever the worksheet is recalculated:

```
=SayIt(A1)
```

You can use this function in a slightly more complex formula, as shown here. In this example, the argument is a text string rather than a cell reference.

```
=IF(SUM(A:A)>1000,SayIt("Goal reached"),)
```

This formula calculates the sum of the values in Column A. If that sum exceeds 1,000, you will hear "Goal reached."

When you use the `SayIt` function in a worksheet formula, the function always returns `0` because a value is not assigned to the function's name.

Another function with one argument

This section contains a more complex function that is designed for a sales manager who needs to calculate the commissions earned by the sales force. The commission rate is based on the amount sold — those who sell more earn a higher commission rate. The function returns the commission amount, based on the sales made (which is the function's only argument — a required argument). The calculations in this example are based on the following table:

Monthly Sales	Commission Rate
0–$9,999	8.0%
$10,000–$19,999	10.5%
$20,000–$39,999	12.0%
$40,000+	14.0%

You can use any of several different methods to calculate commissions for various sales amounts that are entered into a worksheet. You could write a formula such as the following:

```
=IF(AND(A1>=0,A1<=9999.99),A1*0.08,IF(AND(A1>=10000,
A1<=19999.99), A1*0.105,IF(AND(A1>=20000,
A1<=39999.99),A1*0.12,IF(A1>=40000,A1*0.14,0))))
```

This approach isn't the best for a couple of reasons. First, the formula is overly complex and difficult to understand. Second, the values are hard-coded into the formula, making the formula difficult to modify if the commission structure changes.

A better solution is to use a lookup table function to compute the commissions; for example:

```
=VLOOKUP(A1,Table,2)*A1
```

Using the VLOOKUP function requires that you have a table of commission rates set up in your worksheet.

Another option is to create a custom function, such as the following:

```
Function Commission(Sales)
'   Calculates sales commissions
    Tier1 = 0.08
    Tier2 = 0.105
    Tier3 = 0.12
    Tier4 = 0.14
    Select Case Sales
         Case 0 To 9999.99
            Commission = Sales * Tier1
         Case 10000 To 19999.99
            Commission = Sales * Tier2
         Case 20000 To 39999.99
            Commission = Sales * Tier3
         Case Is >= 40000
            Commission = Sales * Tier4
    End Select
End Function
```

After you define the Commission function in a VBA module, you can use it in a worksheet formula. Entering the following formula into a cell produces a result of 3,000. (The amount, 25,000, qualifies for a commission rate of 12%.)


```
=Commission(25000)
```

If the sales amount is in cell D23, the function's argument would be a cell reference, like this:

```
=Commission(D23)
```

A function with two arguments

This example builds on the previous one. Imagine that the sales manager implements a new policy: The total commission paid is increased by 1% for every year that the salesperson has been with the company. For this example, the custom Commission function (defined in the preceding section) has been modified so that it takes two arguments, both of which are required arguments. Call this new function Commission2:

```
Function Commission2(Sales, Years)
'    Calculates sales commissions based on years in service
     Tier1 = 0.08
     Tier2 = 0.105
     Tier3 = 0.12
     Tier4 = 0.14
     Select Case Sales
          Case 0 To 9999.99
            Commission2 = Sales * Tier1
          Case 10000 To 19999.99
            Commission2 = Sales * Tier2
          Case 20000 To 39999.99
            Commission2 = Sales * Tier3
          Case Is >= 40000
            Commission2 = Sales * Tier4
     End Select
     Commission2 = Commission2 + (Commission2 * Years / 100)
End Function
```

The modification was quite simple. The second argument (`Years`) was added to the `Function` statement, and an additional computation was included that adjusts the commission before exiting the function.

The following is an example of how you write a formula by using this function. It assumes that the sales amount is in cell A1, and that the number of years that the salesperson has worked is in cell B1.

```
=Commission2(A1,B1)
```

A function with a range argument

The example in this section demonstrates how to use a worksheet range as an argument. Actually, it's not at all tricky; Excel takes care of the details behind the scenes.

Assume that you want to calculate the average of the five largest values in a range named `Data`. Excel doesn't have a function that can do this calculation, so you can write the following formula:

```
=(LARGE(Data,1)+LARGE(Data,2)+LARGE(Data,3)+
LARGE(Data,4)+LARGE(Data,5))/5
```

This formula uses Excel's `LARGE` function, which returns the *n*th largest value in a range. The preceding formula adds the five largest values in the range named `Data` and then divides the result by 5. The formula works fine, but it's rather unwieldy. Plus, what if you need to compute the average of the top *six* values? You'd need to rewrite the formula and make sure that all copies of the formula also get updated.

Wouldn't it be easier if Excel had a function named `TopAvg`? For example, you could use the following (nonexistent) function to compute the average:

```
=TopAvg (Data,5)
```

This situation is an example of when a custom function can make things much easier for you. The following is a custom VBA function, named `TopAvg`, which returns the average of the top *n* values in a range:

```
Function TopAvg(Data, Num)
' Returns the average of the highest Num values in Data
  Sum = 0
  For i = 1 To Num
    Sum = Sum + WorksheetFunction.Large(Data, i)
  Next i
  TopAvg = Sum / Num
End Function
```

This function takes two arguments: `Data` (which represents a range in a worksheet) and `Num` (the number of values to average). The code starts by initializing the `Sum` variable to `0`. It then uses a `For-Next` loop to calculate the sum of the *n*th largest values in the range. (Note that Excel's `LARGE` function is used within the loop.) You can use an Excel worksheet function in VBA if you precede the function with `WorksheetFunction` and a period. Finally, `TopAvg` is assigned the value of `Sum` divided by `Num`.

You can use all Excel worksheet functions in your VBA procedures *except* those that have equivalents in VBA. For example, VBA has a `Rnd` function that returns a random number. Therefore, you can't use Excel's `RAND` function in a VBA procedure.

A simple but useful function

Useful functions don't have to be complicated. The function in this section is essentially a wrapper for a built-in VBA function called `Split`. The `Split` function makes it very easy to extract an element in a delimited string. The function is named `ExtractElement`:

```
Function ExtractElement(Txt, n, Separator)
' Returns the nth element of a text string, where the
' elements are separated by a specified separator character
    ExtractElement = Split(Application.Trim(Txt), Separator)(n - 1)
End Function
```

The function takes three arguments:

- `Txt`: A delimited text string, or a reference to a cell that contains a delimited text string
- `n`: The element number within the string
- `Separator`: A single character that represents the separator

Here's a formula that uses the `ExtractElement` function:

```
=EXTRACTELEMENT("123-45-678,2,"-")
```

39

The formula returns 45, the second element in the string that's delimited by hyphens.

The delimiter can also be a space character. Here's a formula the extracts the first name from the name in cell A1:

```
=EXTRACTELEMENT(A1,1," ")
```

Debugging Custom Functions

Debugging a Function procedure can be a bit more challenging than debugging a Sub procedure. If you develop a function to use in worksheet formulas, an error in the Function procedure simply results in an error display in the formula cell (usually #VALUE!). In other words, you don't receive the normal run-time error message that helps you to locate the offending statement.

When you're debugging a worksheet formula, using only one instance of the function in your worksheet is the best technique. The following are three methods that you may want to use in your debugging:

- **Place MsgBox functions at strategic locations to monitor the value of specific variables.** Fortunately, message boxes in function procedures pop up when the procedure is executed. But make sure that you have only one formula in the worksheet that uses your function; otherwise, the message boxes appear for each formula that's evaluated.
- **Test the procedure by calling it from a Sub procedure.** Run-time errors display normally, and you can either fix the problem (if you know what it is) or jump right into the debugger.
- **Set a breakpoint in the function and then use the Excel debugger to step through the function.** Press F9, and the statement at the cursor becomes a breakpoint. The code will stop executing, and you can step through the code line by line (by pressing F8). Consult the Help system for more information about using VBA debugging tools.

Inserting Custom Functions

The Excel Insert Function dialog box makes it easy to identify a function and insert it into a formula. This dialog box also displays custom functions written in VBA. After you select a function, the Function Arguments dialog box prompts you for the function's arguments.

NOTE

Function procedures that are defined with the Private keyword do not appear in the Insert Function dialog box. So, if you create a function that will be used only by other VBA procedures, you should declare the function by using the Private keyword.

You also can display a description of your custom function in the Insert Function dialog box. To do so, follow these steps:

1. **Create the function in a module by using the VB Editor.**
2. **Activate Excel.**
3. **Choose Developer ➪ Code ➪ Macros.** The Macro dialog box appears.
4. **Type the name of the function in the Macro Name field.** Notice that functions don't typically appear in this dialog box, so you must enter the function name yourself.
5. **Click the Options button.** The Macro Options dialog box, shown in Figure 39.3, appears.

FIGURE 39.3

Entering a description for a custom function. This description appears in the Insert Function dialog box.

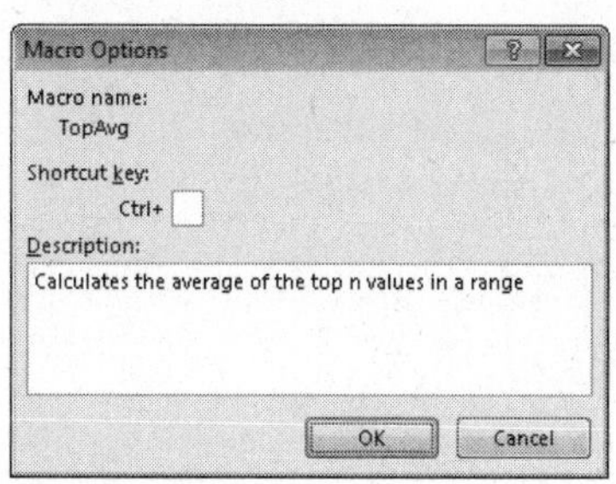

6. **Enter a description of the function and then click OK.** The Shortcut key field is irrelevant for functions.

The description that you enter appears in the Insert Function dialog box.

Another way to provide a description for a custom function is to execute a VBA statement that uses the `MacroOptions` method. The `MacroOptions` method also lets you assign your function to a specific category and even provide a description of the arguments. The argument descriptions display in the Function Arguments dialog box, which appears after you select the function in the Insert Function dialog box. Excel 2010 added the ability to provide descriptions of function arguments.

Figure 39.4 shows the Function Arguments dialog box, which prompts the user to enter arguments for a custom function (`TopAvg`). This function appears in function category 3 (Math and Trig). I added the description, category, and argument descriptions by executing this `Sub` procedure:

```
Sub CreateArgDescriptions()
    Application.MacroOptions Macro:="TopAvg", _
      Description:="Calculates the average of the top n values in a range", _
      Category:=3, _
      ArgumentDescriptions:=Array("The range that contains the data", "The value
  of n")
End Sub
```

The category numbers are listed in the VBA Help system. You execute this procedure only one time. After executing it, the description, category, and argument descriptions are stored in the file.

FIGURE 39.4

Using the Function Arguments dialog box to insert a custom function.

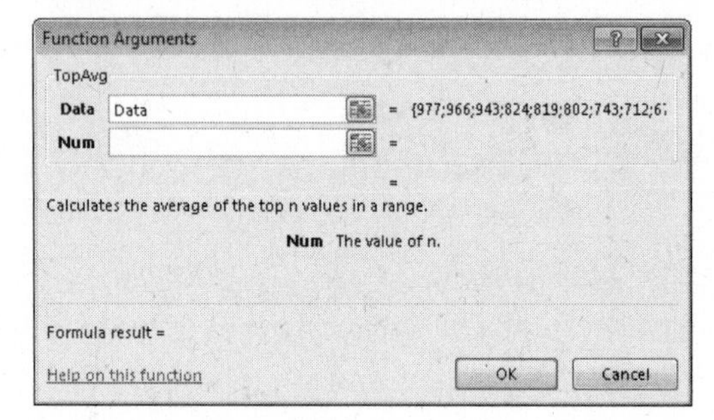

Learning More

The information in this chapter only scratches the surface when it comes to creating custom functions. It should be enough to get you started, however, if you're interested in this topic.

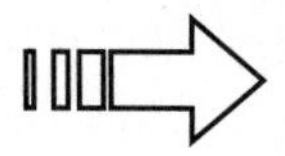

See Chapter 43 for more examples of useful VBA functions. You may be able to use the examples directly or adapt them for your needs.

CHAPTER 40

Creating UserForms

IN THIS CHAPTER

You can't use Excel very long without being exposed to dialog boxes. Excel, like most Windows programs, uses dialog boxes to obtain information, clarify commands, and display messages. If you develop VBA macros, you can create your own dialog boxes that work very much like those that are built in to Excel. These dialog boxes are known as UserForms.

Why Create UserForms?

Some macros that you create behave exactly the same every time that you execute them. For example, you may develop a macro that enters a list of your sales regions into a worksheet range. This macro always produces the same result and requires no additional user input. You may develop other macros, however, that perform differently under different circumstances or that offer options for the user. In such cases, the macro may benefit from a custom dialog box.

The following is an example of a simple macro that makes each cell in the selected range uppercase (but skips cells that have a formula). The procedure uses VBA's built-in `StrConv` function.

```
Sub ChangeCase()
  For Each cell In Selection
    If Not cell.HasFormula Then
      cell.Value = StrConv(cell.Value, vbUpperCase)
    End If
  Next cell
End Sub
```

This macro is useful, but it can be improved. For example, the macro would be more helpful if it could also change the cells to lowercase or *proper case* (only the first letter of each word is uppercase). This modification is not difficult to make, but if you make this change to the macro, you need some method of asking the user what type of change to make to the cells. The solution is to present a dialog box like the one shown in Figure 40.1. This dialog box is a UserForm that was created by using the Visual Basic (VB) Editor, and it's displayed by a VBA macro.

FIGURE 40.1

A UserForm that asks the user to select an option.

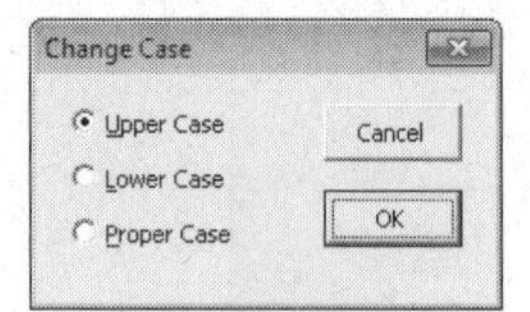

Another solution is to develop three macros, one for each type of text case change. Combining these three operations into a single macro and using a UserForm is a more efficient approach, however. I discuss this example, including how to create the UserForm, in "Another UserForm Example," later in the chapter.

UserForm Alternatives

After you get the hang of it, developing UserForms isn't difficult. But sometimes using the tools that are built into VBA is easier. For example, VBA includes two functions (`InputBox` and `MsgBox`) that enable you to display simple dialog boxes without having to create a UserForm in the VB Editor. You can customize these dialog boxes in some ways, but they certainly don't offer the number of options that are available in a UserForm.

The InputBox function

The `InputBox` function is useful for obtaining a single input from the user. A simplified version of the function's syntax follows:

```
InputBox(prompt[,title][,default])
```

The elements are defined as follows:

- `prompt`: (Required) Text that is displayed in the input box
- `title`: (Optional) Text that appears in the input box's title bar
- `default`: (Optional) The default value

The following is an example of how you can use the `InputBox` function:

```
CName = InputBox("Customer name?","Customer Data")
```

When this VBA statement is executed, Excel displays the dialog box shown in Figure 40.2. Notice that this example uses only the first two arguments for the `InputBox` function and does not supply a default value. When the user enters a value and clicks OK, the value is assigned to the variable `CName`. Your VBA code can then use that variable.

FIGURE 40.2

This dialog box is displayed by the VBA `InputBox` function.

The MsgBox function

The VBA `MsgBox` function is a handy way to display information and to solicit simple input from users. I use the VBA `MsgBox` function in many of this book's examples to display a variable's value. A simplified version of the `MsgBox` syntax is as follows:

```
MsgBox(prompt[,buttons][,title])
```

The elements are defined as follows:

- `prompt`: (Required) Text that is displayed in the message box
- `buttons`: (Optional) The code for the buttons that are to appear in the message box
- `title`: (Optional) Text that appears in the message box's title bar

You can use the `MsgBox` function by itself or assign its result to a variable. If you use it by itself, don't include parentheses around the arguments. The following example displays a message and does not return a result:

```
Sub MsgBoxDemo()
  MsgBox "Click OK to continue"
End Sub
```

Figure 40.3 shows how this message box appears.

FIGURE 40.3

A simple message box, displayed with the VBA `MsgBox` function.

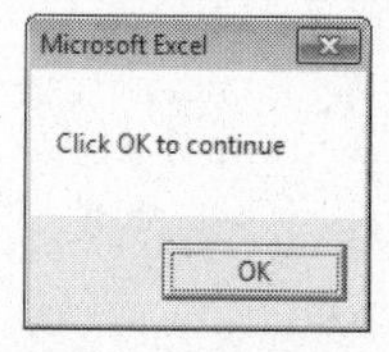

To get a response from a message box, you can assign the result of the `MsgBox` function to a variable. The following code uses some built-in constants (described in Table 40.1) to make it easier to work with the values that are returned by `MsgBox`:

```
Sub GetAnswer()
  Ans = MsgBox("Continue?", vbYesNo)
  Select Case Ans
   Case vbYes
' ...[code if Ans is Yes]...
   Case vbNo
' ...[code if Ans is No]...
  End Select
End Sub
```

When this procedure is executed, the `Ans` variable contains a value that corresponds to `vbYes` or `vbNo`. The `Select Case` statement determines the action to take based on the value of `Ans`.

You can easily customize your message boxes because of the flexibility of the `buttons` argument. Table 40.1 lists the built-in constants that you can use for the `buttons` argument. You can specify which buttons to display, whether an icon appears, and which button is the default.

TABLE 40.1 Constants Used in the MsgBox Function

Constant	Value	Description
vbOKOnly	0	Displays OK button.
vbOKCancel	1	Displays OK and Cancel buttons.
vbAbortRetryIgnore	2	Displays Abort, Retry, and Ignore buttons.
vbYesNoCancel	3	Displays Yes, No, and Cancel buttons.
vbYesNo	4	Displays Yes and No buttons.
vbRetryCancel	5	Displays Retry and Cancel buttons.
vbCritical	16	Displays Critical Message icon.
vbQuestion	32	Displays Query icon (a question mark).
VBExclamation	48	Displays Warning Message icon.
vbInformation	64	Displays Information Message icon.
vbDefaultButton1	0	First button is default.
vbDefaultButton2	256	Second button is default.
vbDefaultButton3	512	Third button is default.

The following example uses a combination of constants to display a message box with a Yes button and a No button (`vbYesNo`), and a question mark icon (`vbQuestion`). The second button (the No button) is designated as the default button (`vbDefaultButton2`), which is the button that is executed if the user presses Enter. For simplicity, these constants are assigned to the `Config` variable, and `Config` is then used as the second argument in the `MsgBox` function.

```
Sub GetAnswer()
  Config = vbYesNo + vbQuestion + vbDefaultButton2
  Ans = MsgBox("Process the monthly report?", Config)
  If Ans = vbYes Then RunReport
  If Ans = vbNo Then Exit Sub
End Sub
```

Figure 40.4 shows how this message box appears when the `GetAnswer Sub` is executed. If the user clicks the Yes button, the routine executes the procedure named `RunReport` (which is not shown). If the user clicks the No button (or presses Enter), the procedure is ended with no action. Because the title argument was omitted in the `MsgBox` function, Excel uses the default title (`Microsoft Excel`).

FIGURE 40.4

The second argument of the `MsgBox` function determines what appears in the message box.

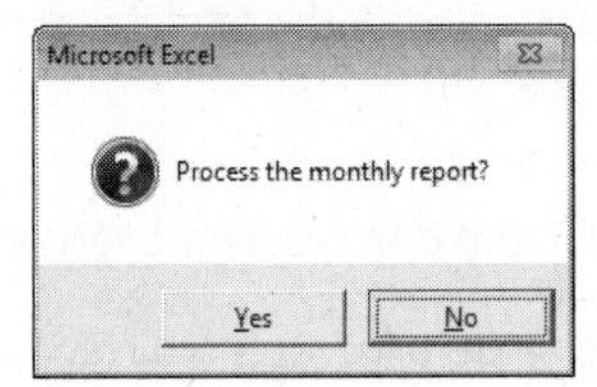

The `Sub` procedure that follows is another example of using the `MsgBox` function:

```
Sub GetAnswer2()
  Msg = "Do you want to process the monthly report?"
  Msg = Msg & vbNewLine & vbNewLine
  Msg = Msg & "Processing the monthly report will take approximately "
  Msg = Msg & "15 minutes. It will generate a 30-page report for all "
  Msg = Msg & "sales offices for the current month."
  Title = "XYZ Marketing Company"
  Config = vbYesNo + vbQuestion
  Ans = MsgBox(Msg, Config, Title)
  If Ans = vbYes Then RunReport
  If Ans = vbNo Then Exit Sub
End Sub
```

This example demonstrates an efficient way to specify a longer message in a message box. A variable (`Msg`) and the concatenation operator (`&`) are used to build the message in a series of statements. `vbNewLine` is a constant that represents a break character. (Using two line breaks inserts a blank line.) The title argument is also used to display a different title in the message box. The `Config` variable stores the constants that generate Yes and No buttons and a question mark icon. Figure 40.5 shows how this message box appears when the procedure is executed.

FIGURE 40.5

A message box with a longer message and a title.

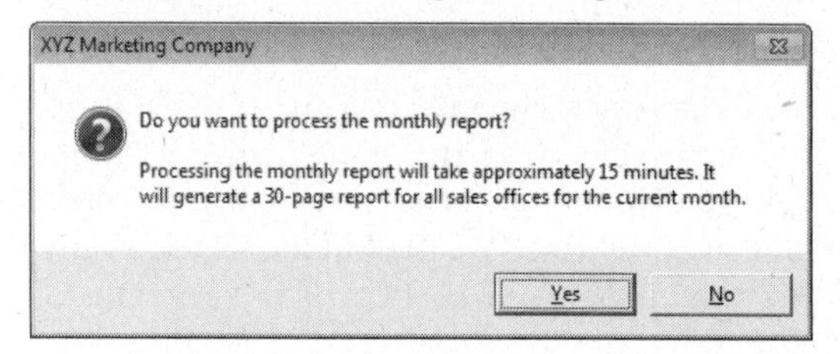

Creating UserForms: An Overview

The `InputBox` and `MsgBox` functions are adequate for many situations, but if you need to obtain more information, you need to create a UserForm.

The following is a list of the general steps that you typically take to create a UserForm:

1. **Determine exactly how the dialog box is going to be used and where it will fit into your VBA macro.**
2. **Activate the VB Editor and insert a new UserForm.**
3. **Add the appropriate controls to the UserForm.**
4. **Create a VBA macro to display the UserForm.** This macro goes in a normal VBA module.
5. **Create event handler VBA procedures that are executed when the user manipulates the controls (for example, clicks the OK button).** These procedures go in the code module for the UserForm.

The following sections provide more details on creating a UserForm.

Working with UserForms

To create a dialog box, you must first insert a new UserForm in the VB Editor window. To activate the VB Editor, choose Developer ➪ Code ➪ Visual Basic (or press Alt+F11). Make sure that the correct workbook is selected in the Project window and then choose Insert ➪ UserForm. The VB Editor displays an empty UserForm, shown in Figure 40.6. When you activate a UserForm, the VB editor displays the Toolbox, which is used to add controls to the UserForm.

FIGURE 40.6

An empty UserForm.

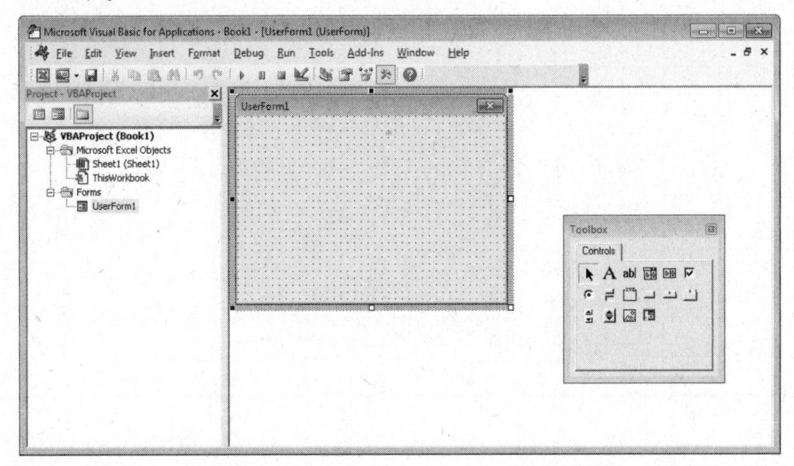

Adding controls

The Toolbox, also shown in Figure 40.6, contains various ActiveX controls that you can add to your UserForm. If the Toolbox is not visible, choose View ➪ Toolbox.

When you move the mouse pointer over a control in the Toolbox, the control's name appears. To add a control, click and drag it into the form. After adding a control, you can move it or change its size.

Table 40.2 lists the Toolbox controls.

TABLE 40.2 Toolbox Controls

Control	Description
`Select Objects`	Lets you select other controls by dragging.
`Label`	Adds a label (a container for text).
`TextBox`	Adds a text box, which allows the user to type text.
`ComboBox`	Adds a combo box (a drop-down list).
`ListBox`	Adds a list box, which allows the user to select an item from a list.
`CheckBox`	Adds a check box to control Boolean options.
`OptionButton`	Adds an option button to allow the user to select from multiple options.
`ToggleButton`	Adds a toggle button to control Boolean options.
`Frame`	Adds a frame (a container for other objects).
`CommandButton`	Adds a command button (a clickable button).
`TabStrip`	Adds a tab strip (a container for other objects).
`MultiPage`	Adds a multipage control (a container for other objects).
`ScrollBar`	Adds a scroll bar, which allows the user to specify a value by dragging a bar.
`SpinButton`	Adds a spin button, which allows the user to specify a value by clicking up or down.
`Image`	Adds a control that can contain an image.
`RefEdit`	Adds a reference edit control, which lets the user select a range.

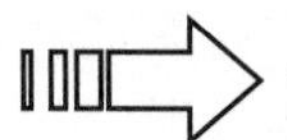

You can also place some of these controls directly on your worksheet. See Chapter 41 for details.

Changing the properties of a control

Every control that you add to a UserForm has several properties that determine how the control looks and behaves. You can change some of these properties (such as `Height` and `Width`) by clicking and dragging the control's border. To change other properties, use the Properties window.

To display the Properties window, choose View➪Properties Window (or press F4). The Properties window displays a list of properties for the selected control. (Each control has a different set of properties.) If you click the UserForm itself, the Properties window displays properties for the form. Figure 40.7 shows the Properties window for a `CommandButton` control.

To change a property, select the property in the Properties window and then enter a new value. Some properties (such as `BackColor`) enable you to select a property from a list. The top of the Properties window contains a drop-down list that enables you to select a control to work with. You can also click a control to select it and display its properties.

FIGURE 40.7

The Properties window for a `CommandButton` control.

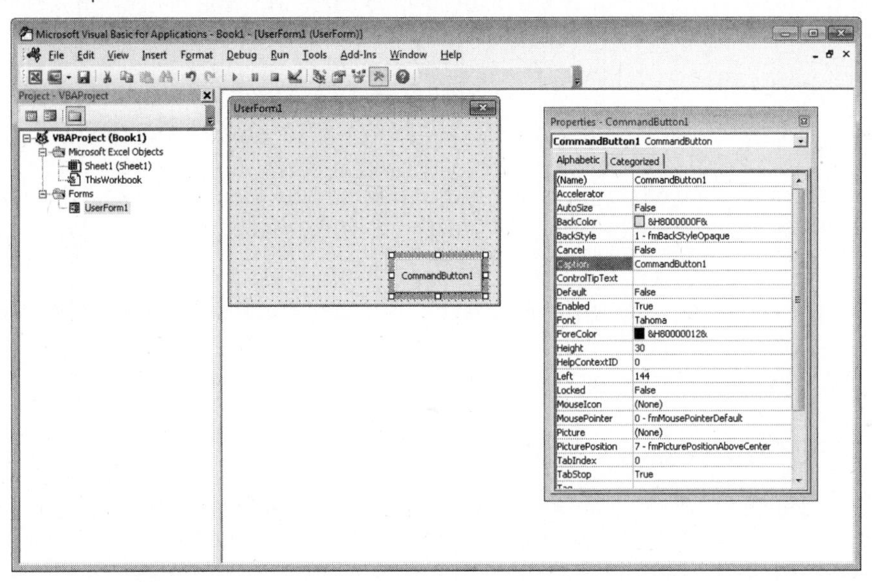

When you set properties via the Properties window, you're setting properties at *design time.* You can also use VBA to change the properties of controls while the UserForm is displayed (that is, at *run time*).

A complete discussion of all the properties is well beyond the scope of this book — and it would indeed be very dull reading. To find out about a particular property, select it in the Properties window and press F1 for help.

Handling events

When you insert a UserForm, that form can also hold VBA `Sub` procedures to handle the events that are generated by the UserForm. An *event* is something that occurs when the user manipulates a control. For example, clicking a button causes an event. Selecting an item in a list box control also triggers an event. To make a UserForm useful, you must write VBA code to do something when an event occurs.

Event handler procedures have names that combine the control with the event. The general form is the control's name, followed by an underscore, and then the event name. For example, the procedure that is executed when the user clicks a button named `MyButton` is `MyButton_Click`.

Displaying a UserForm

You also need to write a procedure to display the UserForm. You use the `Show` method of the `UserForm` object. The following procedure displays the UserForm named `UserForm1`:

```
Sub ShowDialog()
   UserForm1.Show
End Sub
```

This procedure should be stored in a regular VBA module (not the code module for the UserForm). If your VB project doesn't have a regular VBA module, choose Insert ➪ Module to add one.

When the `ShowDialog` procedure is executed, the UserForm is displayed. What happens next depends upon the event handler procedures that you create.

A UserForm Example

The preceding section is, admittedly, rudimentary. This section demonstrates, in detail, how to develop a UserForm. This example is rather simple. The UserForm displays a message to the user — something that can be accomplished more easily by using the `MsgBox` function. However, a UserForm gives you more flexibility in terms of formatting and layout of the message.

On the Web

This workbook is available on this book's website. The file is named `show message.xlsm`.

Creating the UserForm

If you're following along on your computer, start with a new workbook. Then follow these steps:

1. **Choose Developer ➪ Code ➪ Visual Basic (or press Alt + F11).** The VB Editor window appears.
2. **Double-click your workbook's name to activate it.**
3. **Choose Insert ➪ UserForm.** The VB Editor adds an empty form named `UserForm1` and displays the Toolbox.
4. **Press F4 to display the Properties window, and then change the following properties of the UserForm object:**

Property	*Change to*
`Name`	`AboutBox`
`Caption`	`About This Workbook`

5. **Use the Toolbox to add a `Label` object to the UserForm. If the Toolbox is not visible, choose View ➪ Toolbox.**
6. **Select the Label object, and in the Properties window, enter any text that you want for the label's Caption.**
7. **In the Properties window, click the Font property and adjust the font.** You can change the typeface, size, and so on. The changes then appear in the form. Figure 40.8 shows an example of a formatted `Label` control. In this example, the `TextAlign` property was set to the code that center aligns the text.

   ```
   2 - fmTextAlignCenter
   ```

FIGURE 40.8

A `Label` control, after changing its `Font` properties.

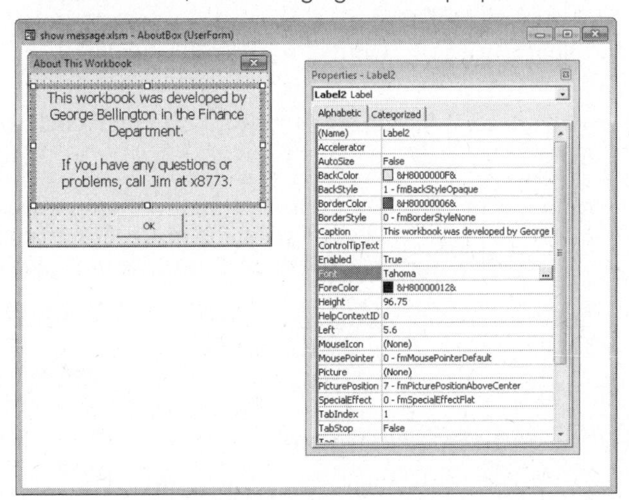

8. **Use the Toolbox and add a CommandButton object to the UserForm; then use the Properties window to change the following properties for the CommandButton:**

Property	*Change to*
`Name`	`OKButton`
`Caption`	`OK`
`Default`	`True`

9. **Make other adjustments so that the form looks good to you.** You can change the size of the form or move or resize the controls.

Testing the UserForm

At this point, the UserForm has all the necessary controls. What's missing is a way to display the UserForm. While you're developing the UserForm, you can press F5 to display it and see how it looks. To close the UserForm, click the Close button (X) in the title bar.

This section explains how to write a VBA `Sub` procedure to display the UserForm when Excel is active.

1. **Insert a VBA module by choosing Insert⇨Module.**
2. **In the empty module, enter the following code:**

```
Sub ShowAboutBox()
   AboutBox.Show
End Sub
```

3. **Press Alt + F11 to activate Excel.**
4. **Choose Developer⇨Code⇨Macros (or press Alt + F8).** The Macros dialog box appears.
5. **Select ShowAboutBox from the list of macros, and then click Run.** The UserForm appears.

If you click the OK button, notice that it doesn't close the UserForm as you may expect. This button needs to have an event handler procedure in order for it to do anything when it's clicked. To dismiss the UserForm, click the Close button (X) in its title bar.

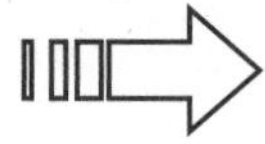

You may prefer to display the UserForm by clicking a `CommandButton` on your worksheet. See Chapter 41 for details on attaching a macro to a worksheet `CommandButton`.

Creating an event handler procedure

An *event handler procedure* is executed when an event occurs. In this case, you need a procedure to handle the `Click` event that's generated when the user clicks the OK button.

1. **Press Alt + F11 to activate the VB Editor.**
2. **Activate the AboutBox UserForm by double-clicking its name in the Project window.**
3. **Double-click the CommandButton control.** The VB Editor activates the code module for the UserForm and inserts some boilerplate code, as shown in Figure 40.9.
4. **Insert the following statement before the End Sub statement:**

```
Unload AboutBox
```

FIGURE 40.9

The code module for the UserForm.

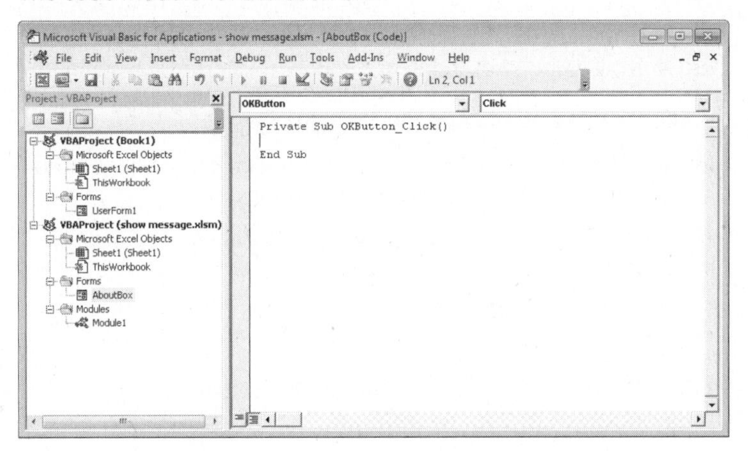

This statement simply dismisses the UserForm by using the `Unload` statement. The complete event handler procedure is

```
Private Sub OKButton_Click()
   Unload AboutBox
End Sub
```

After adding the event procedure, clicking the OK button works as it should.

Another UserForm Example

The example in this section is an enhanced version of the `ChangeCase` procedure presented at the beginning of the chapter. Recall that the original version of this macro changes the text in the selected cells to uppercase characters. This modified version asks the user what type of case change to make: uppercase, lowercase, or proper case (initial capitals).

On the Web

This workbook is available on this book's website. The file is `change case.xlsm`.

Creating the UserForm

This UserForm needs one piece of information from the user: the type of change to make to the text. Because only one option can be selected, `OptionButton` controls are appropriate. Start with an empty workbook and follow these steps to create the UserForm:

1. **Press Alt + F11 to activate the VB Editor window.**
2. **In the VB Editor, choose Insert ➪ UserForm.** The VB Editor adds an empty form named `UserForm1` and displays the Toolbox.
3. **Press F4 to display the Properties window, and then change the following property of the `UserForm` object:**

Property	*Change to*
`Caption`	`Change Case`

4. **Add a CommandButton object to the UserForm and then change the following properties for the CommandButton:**

Property	*Change to*
`Name`	`OKButton`
`Caption`	`OK`
`Default`	`True`

5. **Add another CommandButton object and then change the following properties:**

Property	*Change to*
`Name`	`CancelButton`
`Caption`	`Cancel`
`Cancel`	`True`

6. **Add an OptionButton control and then change the following properties.** (This option is the default, so its `Value` property should be set to `True`.)

Property	*Change to*
`Name`	`OptionUpper`
`Caption`	`Upper Case`
`Value`	`True`

7. **Add a second OptionButton control and then change the following properties:**

Property	*Change to*
`Name`	`OptionLower`
`Caption`	`Lower Case`

8. **Add a third OptionButton control and then change the following properties:**

Property	*Change to*
`Name`	`OptionProper`
`Caption`	`Proper Case`

9. **Adjust the size and position of the controls and the form until your UserForm resembles the UserForm shown in Figure 40.10.** Make sure that the controls do not overlap.

FIGURE 40.10

The UserForm after adding controls and adjusting some properties.

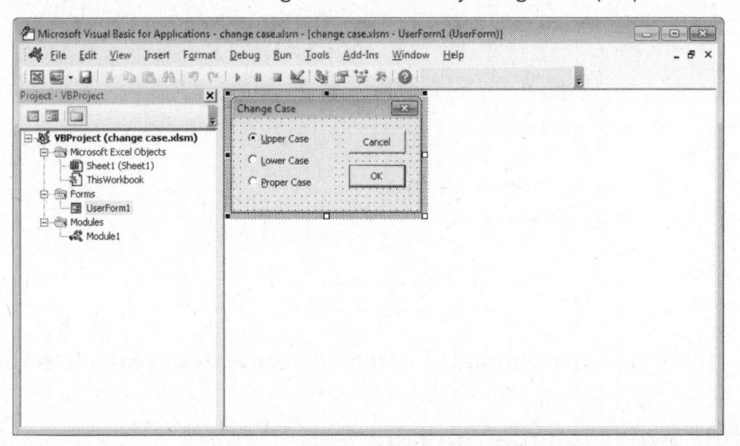

TIP

The VB Editor provides several useful commands to help you size and align the controls. For example, you can make a group of selected controls the same size, or move them so they're all aligned to the left. Select the controls that you want to work with, and then choose a command from the Format menu. These commands are fairly self-explanatory, and the Help system has complete details.

Testing the UserForm

At this point, the UserForm has all the necessary controls. What's missing is a way to display the form. This section explains how to write a VBA procedure to display the UserForm.

1. **Make sure that the VB Editor window is activated.**
2. **Insert a module by choosing Insert ➪ Module.**
3. **In the empty module, enter the following code:**

```
Sub ShowUserForm()
   UserForm1.Show
End Sub
```

4. **Choose Run ➪ Sub/UserForm (or press F5).** The Excel window is activated, and the new UserForm is displayed, as shown in Figure 40.11. The `OptionButton` controls work, but clicking the OK and Cancel buttons has no effect. These two buttons need to have event handler procedures.

FIGURE 40.11

Displaying the UserForm.

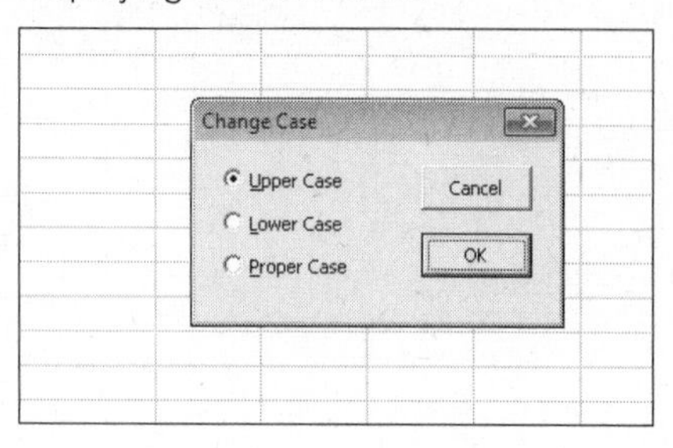

5. **Click the Close button (X) in the title bar to dismiss the UserForm.**

Creating event handler procedures

This section explains how to create two event handler procedures: one to handle the `Click` event for the `CancelButton` `CommandButton` and the other to handle the `Click` event for the `OKButton` `CommandButton`. Event handlers for the `OptionButton` controls are not necessary. The VBA code can determine which of the three `OptionButton` controls is selected.

Event handler procedures are stored in the UserForm code module. To create the procedure to handle the `Click` event for the `CancelButton`, follow these steps:

1. **Activate the UserForm1 form by double-clicking its name in the Project window.**
2. **Double-click the CancelButton control.** The VB Editor activates the code module for the UserForm and inserts an empty procedure.
3. **Insert the following statement before the End Sub statement:**

   ```
   Unload UserForm1
   ```

That's all there is to it. The following is a listing of the entire procedure that's attached to the `Click` event for the `CancelButton`:

```
Private Sub CancelButton_Click()
   Unload UserForm1
End Sub
```

This procedure is executed when the `CancelButton` is clicked. It consists of a single statement that unloads the UserForm1 form.

The next step is to add the code to handle the `Click` event for the `OKButton` control. Follow these steps:

1. **Select OKButton from the drop-down list at the top of the module or reactivate the UserForm and double-click the OKButton control.** The VB Editor begins a new procedure called `OKButton_Click`.
2. **Enter the following code.** The first and last statements have already been entered for you by the VB Editor.

```
Private Sub OKButton_Click()
'   Exit if a range is not selected
    If TypeName(Selection) <> "Range" Then Exit Sub
'       Upper case
    If OptionUpper Then
        For Each cell In Selection
        If Not cell.HasFormula Then
            cell.Value = StrConv(cell.Value, vbUpperCase)
        End If
        Next cell
    End If
'   Lower case
    If OptionLower Then
        For Each cell In Selection
        If Not cell.HasFormula Then
            cell.Value = StrConv(cell.Value, vbLowerCase)
        End If
        Next cell
    End If
'   Proper case
    If OptionProper Then
        For Each cell In Selection
        If Not cell.HasFormula Then
            cell.Value = StrConv(cell.Value, vbProperCase)
        End If
        Next cell
    End If
    Unload UserForm1
End Sub
```

The macro starts by checking the type of selection. If a range is not selected, the procedure ends. The remainder of the procedure consists of three separate blocks. Only one block is executed, determined by which `OptionButton` is selected. The selected `OptionButton` has a value of `True`. Finally, the UserForm is unloaded (dismissed).

Testing the UserForm

To try out the UserForm from Excel, follow these steps:

1. **Activate Excel.**
2. **Enter some text into a range of cells.**
3. **Select the range with the text.**
4. **Choose Developer ➪ Code ➪ Macros (or press Alt + F8).** The Macros dialog box appears.
5. **Select ShowUserForm from the list of macros, and then click Run.** The UserForm appears.
6. **Make your choice, and click OK.**

Try it with a few more selections, including noncontiguous cells. Notice that if you click Cancel, the UserForm is dismissed and no changes are made.

The code does have a problem, though: If you select one or more entire columns, the procedure processes every cell, which can take a very long time. The version of the workbook on the website corrects this problem by working with a subset of the selection that intersects with the workbook's used range.

Making the macro available from a worksheet button

At this point, everything should be working properly. However, you have no quick and easy way to execute the macro. A good way to execute this macro would be from a button on the worksheet. You can use the following steps:

1. **Choose Developer ➪ Controls ➪ Insert and click the Button control in the Form Controls group.**
2. **Click and drag in the worksheet to create the button.** The Assign Macro dialog box appears.
3. **Select the ShowUserForm macro, and then click OK.**
4. **(Optional) At this point, the button is still selected, so you can change the text to make it more descriptive.** You can also right-click the button at any time to change the text.

After performing the preceding steps, clicking the button executes the macro and displays the UserForm.

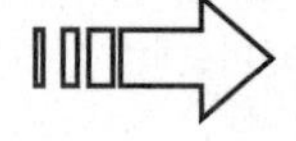

The button in this example is from the Form Controls group. Excel also provides a button in the ActiveX Controls group. See Chapter 41 for more information about the ActiveX Controls group.

Making the macro available on your Quick Access toolbar

If you'd like to use this macro while other workbooks are active, you may want to add a button to your Quick Access toolbar. Follow these steps:

1. **Make sure that the workbook containing the macro is open.**
2. **Right-click anywhere on the Ribbon and choose Customize Quick Access Toolbar from the shortcut menu.** The Excel Options dialog box appears, with the Quick Access Toolbar section selected.
3. **Choose Macros from the Choose Commands From drop-down menu on the left.** You'll see your macro listed.
4. **Select the macro's name, and click Add to add the item to the list on the right.**
5. **(Optional) To change the icon, click Modify and choose a new image.** You can also change the Display Name.
6. **Click OK to close the Excel Options dialog box.** The icon appears on your Quick Access toolbar.

More on Creating UserForms

Creating UserForms can make your macros much more versatile. You can create custom commands that display dialog boxes that look exactly like those that Excel uses. This section contains some additional information to help you develop custom dialog boxes that work like those that are built in to Excel.

Adding accelerator keys

Custom dialog boxes should not discriminate against those who prefer to use the keyboard rather than a mouse. All Excel dialog boxes work equally well with a mouse and a keyboard because each control has an associated accelerator key. The user can press Alt plus the accelerator key to work with a specific dialog box control.

Adding accelerator keys to your UserForms is a good idea. You do this in the Properties window by entering a character for the `Accelerator` property.

The letter that you enter as the accelerator key must be a letter that is contained in the caption of the object. However, it can be *any* letter in the text — not necessarily the first letter. You should make sure that an accelerator key is not duplicated in a UserForm. If you have duplicate accelerator keys, the accelerator key acts on the first control in the tab order of the UserForm. Then, pressing the accelerator key again takes you to the next control.

Some controls (such as edit boxes) don't have a caption property. You can assign an accelerator key to a label that describes the control. Pressing the accelerator key then activates the next control in the tab order (which you should ensure is the edit box).

Controlling tab order

The previous section refers to a UserForm's *tab order*. When you're working with a UserForm, pressing Tab and Shift + Tab cycles through the dialog box's controls. When you create a UserForm, you should make sure that the tab order is correct. Usually, it means that tabbing should move through the controls in a logical sequence.

To view or change the tab order in a UserForm, choose View ➪ Tab Order to display the Tab Order dialog box. You can then select a control from the list; use the Move Up and Move Down buttons to change the tab order for the selected control.

Learning More

Mastering UserForms takes practice. You should closely examine the dialog boxes that Excel uses to get a feeling for how dialog boxes are designed. You can duplicate many of the dialog boxes that Excel uses.

The best way to learn more about creating dialog boxes is by using the VBA Help system. Pressing F1 is the quickest way to display the Help window.

CHAPTER

41

Using UserForm Controls in a Worksheet

IN THIS CHAPTER

Understanding why you may want to use controls on a worksheet

Using controls

Looking at the Controls Toolbox controls

Chapter 40 presents an introduction to UserForms. If you like the idea of using dialog box controls, but you don't like the idea of creating a custom dialog box, this chapter is for you. It explains how to enhance your worksheet with a variety of interactive controls, such as buttons, list boxes, and option buttons.

Why Use Controls on a Worksheet?

The main reason to use controls on a worksheet is to make it easier for the user to provide input. For example, if you create a model that uses one or more input cells, you can create controls to allow the user to select values for the input cells.

Adding controls to a worksheet requires much less effort than creating a dialog box. In addition, you may not have to create any macros because you can link a control to a worksheet cell. For example, if you insert a `CheckBox` control on a worksheet, you can link it to a particular cell. When the `CheckBox` is checked, the linked cell displays `TRUE`. When the `CheckBox` is not checked, the linked cell displays `FALSE`.

Figure 41.1 shows an example that uses three types of controls: a `Checkbox`, two sets of `OptionButtons`, and a `ScrollBar`. The user's selections are used to display a loan amortization schedule on another worksheet. The workbook is very interactive, but it uses no macros.

FIGURE 41.1

This worksheet uses UserForm controls.

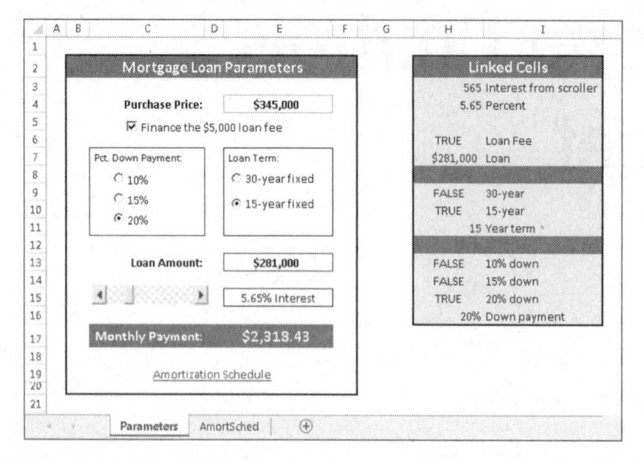

On the Web

This workbook is available on this book's website. The file is named `mortgage loan.xlsx`.

Adding controls to a worksheet can be a bit confusing because Excel offers two different sets of controls, both of which you access by choosing Developer ➪ Controls ➪ Insert:

- **Form controls:** These controls are unique to Excel.
- **ActiveX controls:** These controls are a subset of those that are available for use on UserForms.

Figure 41.2 shows the controls that appear when you choose Developer ➪ Controls ➪ Insert. When you move your mouse pointer over a control, Excel displays a ToolTip that identifies the control.

To add to the confusion, many controls are available from both sources. For example, a control named `ListBox` is listed in both Forms controls and ActiveX controls. However, they're two entirely different controls. In general, Forms controls are easier to use, but ActiveX controls provide more flexibility.

Note

This chapter focuses exclusively on ActiveX controls.

FIGURE 41.2

Excel's two sets of worksheet controls.

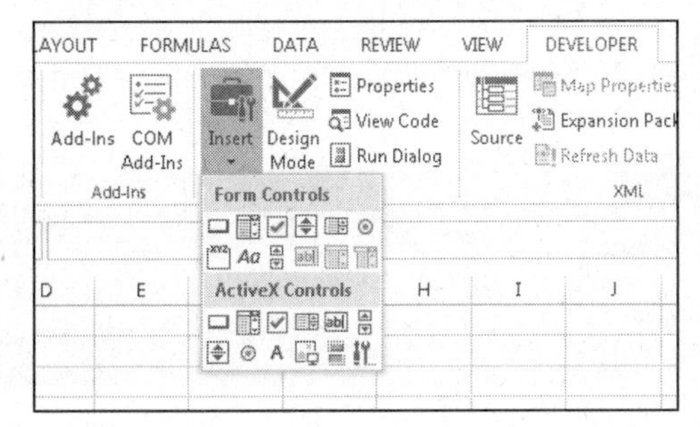

A description of ActiveX controls appears in Table 41.1.

TABLE 41.1 ActiveX Controls

Button	What It Does
Command Button	Inserts a `CommandButton` control (a clickable button).
Combo Box	Inserts a `ComboBox` control (a drop-down list).
Check Box	Inserts a `CheckBox` control (to control Boolean options).
List Box	Inserts a `ListBox` control (to allow the user to select an item from a list).
Text Box	Inserts a `TextBox` control (to allow the user to type text).
Scroll Bar	Inserts a `ScrollBar` control (to specify a value by dragging a bar).
Spin Button	Inserts a `SpinButton` control (to specify a value by clicking up or down).
Option Button	Inserts an `OptionButton` control (to allow a user to select from multiple options).
Label	Inserts a `Label` control (a container for text).
Image	Inserts an `Image` control (to hold an image).
Toggle Button	Inserts a `ToggleButton` control (to control Boolean options).
More Controls	Displays a list of other ActiveX controls that are installed on your system. Not all these controls work with Excel.

Using Controls

Adding ActiveX controls in a worksheet is easy, but you need to learn a few basic facts about how to use them.

Adding a control

To add a control to a worksheet, choose Developer ⇨ Controls ⇨ Insert. From the Insert drop-down list, click the control that you want to use and then drag in the worksheet to create the control. You don't need to be too concerned about the exact size or position because you can modify those properties at any time.

CAUTION

Make sure that you select a control from the ActiveX controls, *not from the Forms controls.* If you insert a Forms control, the instructions in this chapter will not apply. When you choose Developer ⇨ Controls ⇨ Insert, the ActiveX controls appear in the lower half of the list.

About Design mode

When you add a control to a worksheet, Excel goes into Design mode. In this mode, you can adjust the properties of any controls on your worksheet, add or edit macros for the control, or change the control's size or position.

NOTE

When Excel is in Design mode, the Design Mode icon in the Developer ⇨ Controls group appears highlighted. You can click this icon to toggle Design mode on and off.

When Excel is in Design mode, the controls aren't enabled. To test the controls, you must exit Design mode by clicking the Design Mode icon. When you're working with controls, you'll probably need to need to switch in and out of Design mode frequently.

Adjusting properties

Every control that you add has various properties that determine how it looks and behaves. You can adjust these properties only when Excel is in Design mode. When you add a control to a worksheet, Excel enters Design mode automatically. If you need to change a control after you exit Design mode, click the Design Mode icon in the Controls section of the Developer tab.

To change the properties for a control, follow these steps:

1. **Make sure that Excel is in Design mode.**
2. **Click the control to select it.**
3. **If the Properties window isn't visible, click the Properties icon in the Controls section of the Developer tab.** The Properties window appears, as shown in Figure 41.3.
4. **Select the property and make the change.**

FIGURE 41.3

Use the Properties window to adjust the properties of a control — in this case, a `CommandButton` control.

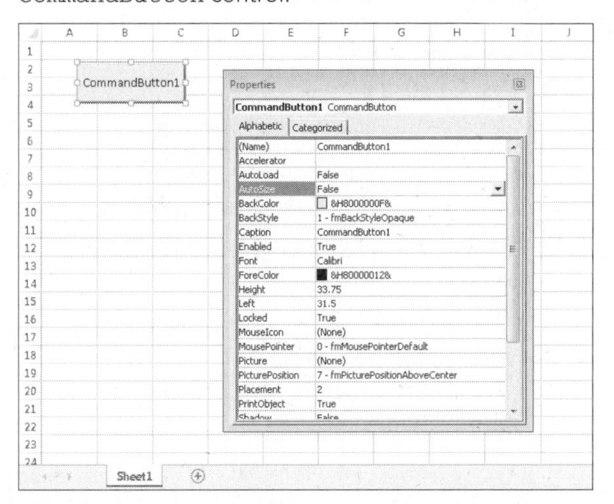

The manner in which you change a property depends upon the property. Some properties display a drop-down list from which you can select from a list of options. Others (such as `Font`) provide a button that, when clicked, displays a dialog box. Other properties require you to type the property value. When you change a property, the change takes effect immediately.

TIP

To find out about a particular property, select the property in the Properties window and press F1.

The Properties window has two tabs. The Alphabetic tab displays the properties in alphabetical order. The Categorized tab displays the properties by category. Both tabs show the same properties; only the order is different.

Common properties

Each control has its own unique set of properties. However, many controls share properties. This section describes some properties that are common to all or many controls, as set forth in Table 41.2.

NOTE

Some ActiveX control properties are required (for example, the `Name` property). In other words, you can't leave the property empty. If a required property is missing, Excel will always tell you by displaying an error message.

TABLE 41.2 Properties Shared by Multiple Controls

Property	Description
`AutoSize`	If `True`, the control resizes itself automatically, based on the text in its caption.
`BackColor`	The background color of the control.
`BackStyle`	The style of the background (either transparent or opaque).
`Caption`	The text that appears on the control.
`LinkedCell`	A worksheet cell that contains the current value of a control.
`ListFillRange`	A worksheet range that contains items displayed in a `ListBox` or `ComboBox` control.
`Value`	The control's value.
`Left` and `Top`	Values that determine the control's position.
`Width` and `Height`	Values that determine the control's width and height.
`Visible`	If `False`, the control is hidden.
`Name`	The name of the control. By default, a control's name is based on the control type. You can change the name to any valid name. However, each control's name must be unique on the worksheet.
`Picture`	Enables you to specify a graphic image to display.

Linking controls to cells

Often, you can use ActiveX controls in a worksheet without using any macros. Many controls have a `LinkedCell` property, which specifies a worksheet cell that is linked to the control.

For example, you may add a `SpinButton` control and specify cell B1 as its `LinkedCell` property. After doing so, cell B1 contains the value of the `SpinButton`, and clicking the `SpinButton` changes the value in cell B1. You can, of course, use the value contained in the linked cell in your formulas.

NOTE

When specifying the `LinkedCell` property in the Properties window, you can't "point" to the linked cell in the worksheet. You must type the cell address or its name (if it has one).

Creating macros for controls

To create a macro for a control, you must use the Visual Basic (VB) Editor. The macros are stored in the code module for the sheet that contains the control. For example, if you place an ActiveX control on Sheet2, the VBA code for that control is stored in the `Sheet2` code module. Each control can have a macro to handle any of its events. For example, a `CommandButton` control can have a macro for its `Click` event, its `DblClick` event, and various other events.

TIP

The easiest way to access the code module for a control is to double-click the control while in Design mode. Excel displays the VB Editor and creates an empty procedure for the control's default event. For example, the default event for a `CheckBox` control is the `Click` event. Figure 41.4 shows the autogenerated code for a control named `CheckBox1`, located on Sheet1.

FIGURE 41.4

Double-clicking a control in Design mode activates the VB Editor and enters an empty event-handler procedure.

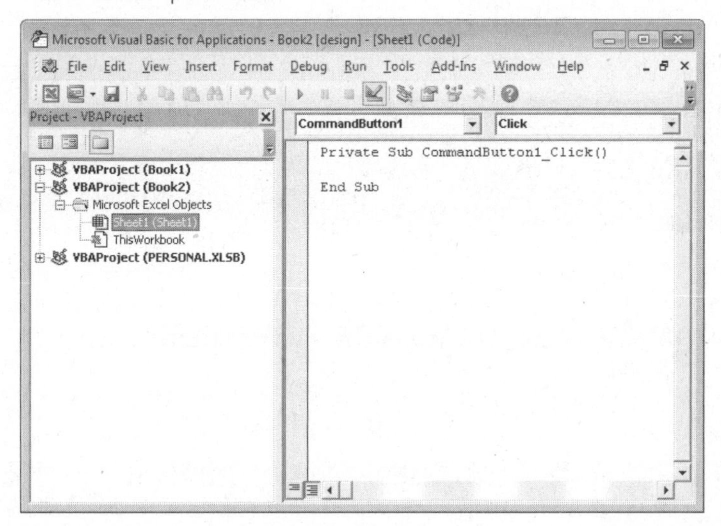

The control's name appears in the upper-left portion of the code window, and the event appears in the upper-right area. If you want to create a macro that executes when a different event occurs, select the event from the list in the upper-right area.

The following steps demonstrate how to insert a `CommandButton` and create a simple macro that displays a message when the button is clicked:

1. **Choose Developer ➪ Controls ➪ Insert.**
2. **Click the CommandButton tool in the ActiveX Controls section.**

3. **Click and drag in the worksheet to create the button.** Excel automatically enters Design mode.
4. **Double-click the button.**

   The VB Editor window is activated, and an empty `Sub` procedure is created.
5. **Enter the following VBA statement before the `End Sub` statement:**

   ```
   MsgBox "Hello, it's " & Time
   ```
6. **Press Alt + F11 to return to Excel.**
7. **(Optional) Adjust any other properties for the CommandButton, using the Properties window.** Choose Developer ➪ Controls ➪ Properties if the Properties window isn't visible.
8. **Click the Design Mode button in the Developer ➪ Controls section to exit design mode.**

After performing the preceding steps, when you click the `CommandButton`, the message box appears and displays the current time.

NOTE

You must enter the VBA code manually. You can't create macros for controls using the VBA macro recorder. However, you can record a macro and then execute it from an event procedure. For example, if you've recorded a macro named `FormatCells`, you can insert `Call FormatCells` as a VBA statement in the event procedure. Or you can copy the recorded code and paste it to your event procedure.

Reviewing the Available ActiveX Controls

The following sections describe the ActiveX controls that are available for use in your worksheets.

ON THE WEB

This book's website contains a file that includes examples of all the ActiveX controls. This file is named `worksheet controls.xlsm`.

CheckBox

A `CheckBox` control is useful for getting a binary choice: yes or no, true or false, on or off, and so on.

The following is a description of the most useful properties of a `CheckBox` control:

- `Accelerator`: A letter that enables the user to change the value of the control by using the keyboard. For example, if the accelerator is A, pressing Alt+A changes the value of the `CheckBox` control. The accelerator letter is underlined in the Caption of the control.
- `LinkedCell`: The worksheet cell that's linked to the `CheckBox`. The cell displays `TRUE` if the control is checked or `FALSE` if the control is not checked.

ComboBox

A `ComboBox` control is similar to a `ListBox` control. A `ComboBox`, however, is a drop-down list, and it displays only one item at a time. Another difference is that, with a `ComboBox`, the user may be allowed to enter a value that doesn't appear in the list of items.

Figure 41.5 shows a `ComboBox` control that uses the range D1:D12 for the `ListFillRange` and cell A1 for the `LinkedCell`.

FIGURE 41.5

A `ComboBox` control.

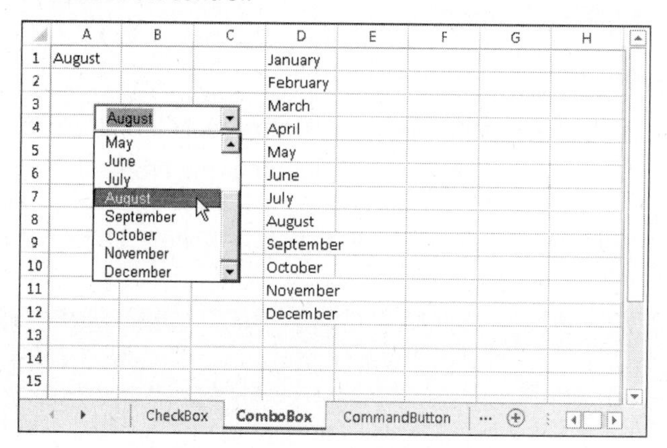

The following is a description of the most useful properties of a `ComboBox` control:

- `BoundColumn`: If the `ListFillRange` contains multiple columns, this property determines which column contains the returned value.
- `ColumnCount`: The number of columns in the list.
- `LinkedCell`: The worksheet cell that displays the selected item.
- `ListFillRange`: The worksheet range that contains the list items.

- `ListRows`: The number of items to display when the list drops down.
- `ListStyle`: Determines the appearance of the list items.
- `Style`: Determines whether the control acts like a drop-down list or a `ComboBox`. A drop-down list doesn't allow the user to enter a new value.

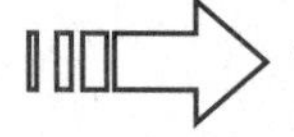

You can also create a drop-down list directly in a cell, by using data validation. See Chapter 26 for details.

CommandButton

A `CommandButton` control is used to execute a macro. When a `CommandButton` is clicked, it executes an event procedure with a name that is made up of the `CommandButton` name, an underscore, and the word *Click*. For example, if a `CommandButton` is named `MyButton`, clicking it executes the macro named `MyButton_Click`. This macro is stored in the code module for the sheet that contains the `CommandButton`.

Image

An `Image` control is used to display an image.

These are the most useful properties of an `Image` control:

- `AutoSize`: If `TRUE`, the `Image` control is resized automatically to fit the image.
- `Picture`: The path to the image file. Click the button in the Properties window, and Excel displays a dialog box so you can locate the image. Or copy the image to the Clipboard, select the `Picture` property in the Properties window, and press Ctrl + V.

TIP

You can also insert an image on a worksheet by choosing Insert ➪ Illustrations ➪ Picture. In fact, using an Image control offers no real advantage.

Label

A `Label` control simply displays text. This control isn't very useful for use on worksheets; a `TextBox` control (described later in this chapter) gives you more versatility.

ListBox

A `ListBox` control presents a list of items, and the user can select an item (or multiple items). It's similar to a `ComboBox`. The main difference is that a `ListBox` displays more than one item at a time.

The following is a description of the most useful properties of a `ListBox` control:

- `BoundColumn`: If the list contains multiple columns, this property determines which column contains the returned value.
- `ColumnCount`: The number of columns in the list.
- `IntegralHeight`: This is `TRUE` if the height of the `ListBox` adjusts automatically to display full lines of text when the list is scrolled vertically. If `FALSE`, the `ListBox` may display partial lines of text when it's scrolled vertically.
- `LinkedCell`: The worksheet cell that displays the selected item.
- `ListFillRange`: The worksheet range that contains the list items.
- `ListStyle`: Determines the appearance of the list items.
- `MultiSelect`: Determines whether the user can select multiple items from the list.

NOTE

If you use a `MultiSelect` `ListBox`, you can't specify a `LinkedCell`; you need to write a macro to determine which items are selected.

OptionButton

`OptionButton` controls are useful when the user needs to select from a small number of items. `OptionButtons` are always used in groups of at least two.

The following is a description of the most useful properties of an `OptionButton` control:

- `Accelerator`: A letter that lets the user select the option by using the keyboard. For example, if the accelerator for an `OptionButton` is C, pressing Alt + C selects the control.
- `GroupName`: A name that identifies an `OptionButton` as being associated with other `OptionButtons` with the same `GroupName` property.
- `LinkedCell`: The worksheet cell that's linked to the `OptionButton`. The cell displays `TRUE` if the control is selected or `FALSE` if the control isn't selected.

NOTE

If your worksheet contains more than one set of `OptionButton` controls, you *must* ensure that each set of `OptionButtons` has a different `GroupName` property. Otherwise, all `OptionButtons` become part of the same set.

ScrollBar

A ScrollBar control is useful for specifying a cell value. Figure 41.6 shows a worksheet with three ScrollBar controls. These ScrollBars are used to change the color in the rectangle shape. The value of the ScrollBars determines the red, green, or blue component of the rectangle's color. This example uses a few simple macros to change the colors.

FIGURE 41.6

This worksheet has three ScrollBar controls.

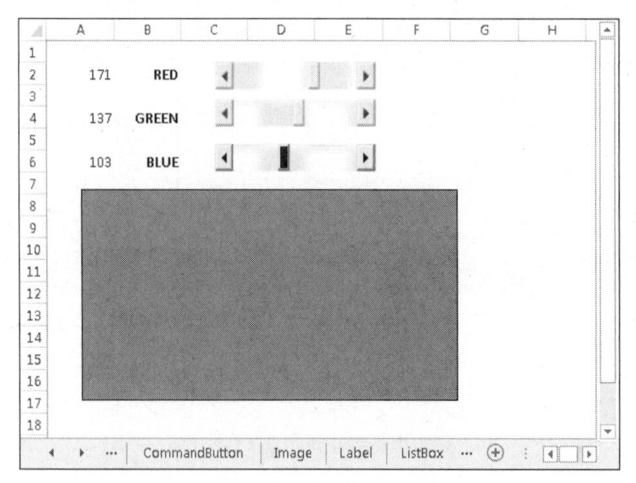

The following is a description of the most useful properties of a ScrollBar control:

- Value: The current value of the control
- Min: The minimum value for the control
- Max: The maximum value for the control
- LinkedCell: The worksheet cell that displays the value of the control
- SmallChange: The amount that the control's value is changed by a click
- LargeChange: The amount that the control's value is changed by clicking either side of the button

The ScrollBar control is most useful for selecting a value that extends across a wide range of possible values.

SpinButton

A `SpinButton` control lets the user select a value by clicking the control, which has two arrows (one to increase the value and the other to decrease the value). A `SpinButton` can display either horizontally or vertically.

The following is a description of the most useful properties of a `SpinButton` control:

- `Value`: The current value of the control.
- `Min`: The minimum value of the control.
- `Max`: The maximum value of the control.
- `LinkedCell`: The worksheet cell that displays the value of the control.
- `SmallChange`: The amount that the control's value is changed by a click. Usually, this property is set to `1`, but you can make it any value.

TextBox

On the surface, a `TextBox` control may not seem useful. After all, it simply contains text — you can usually use worksheet cells to get text input. In fact, `TextBox` controls are useful not so much for input control as for output control. Because a `TextBox` can have scroll bars, you can use a `TextBox` to display a great deal of information in a small area.

Figure 41.7 shows a `TextBox` control that contains Lincoln's *Gettysburg Address.* Notice the vertical scroll bar, displayed using the `ScrollBars` property.

FIGURE 41.7

A `TextBox` control with a vertical scroll bar.

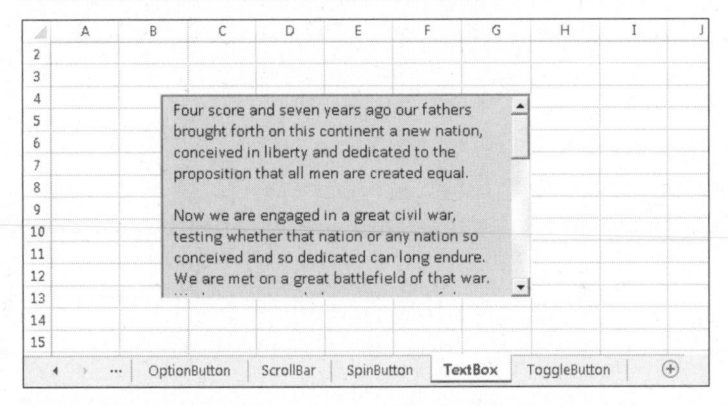

The following is a description of the most useful properties of a `TextBox` control:

- `AutoSize`: Determines whether the control adjusts its size automatically, based on the amount of text.
- `IntegralHeight`: If `TRUE`, the height of the `TextBox` adjusts automatically to display full lines of text when the list is scrolled vertically. If `FALSE`, the `ListBox` may display partial lines of text when it's scrolled vertically.
- `MaxLength`: The maximum number of characters allowed in the `TextBox`. If `0`, no limit exists on the number of characters.
- `MultiLine`: If `TRUE`, the `TextBox` can display more than one line of text.
- `TextAlign`: Determines how the text is aligned in the `TextBox`.
- `WordWrap`: Determines whether the control allows word wrap.
- `ScrollBars`: Determines the type of `ScrollBars` for the control: horizontal, vertical, both, or none.

ToggleButton

A `ToggleButton` control has two states: on and off. Clicking the button toggles between these two states, and the button changes its appearance. Its value is either `TRUE` (pressed) or `FALSE` (not pressed). You can often use a `ToggleButton` in place of a `CheckBox` control.

CHAPTER

42

Working with Excel Events

IN THIS CHAPTER

Understanding events

Using workbook-level events

Working with worksheet events

Using non-object events

In the preceding chapters, I presented a few examples of VBA event-handler procedures. These procedures are the keys to making your Excel applications interactive. This chapter provides an introduction to the concept of Excel events and includes many examples that you can adapt to meet your own needs.

Understanding Events

Excel can monitor a wide variety of events and execute your VBA code when a particular event occurs. This chapter covers the following types of events:

- **Workbook events:** These occur for a particular workbook. Examples include `Open` (the workbook is opened or created), `BeforeSave` (the workbook is about to be saved), and `NewSheet` (a new sheet is added). VBA code for workbook events must be stored in the `ThisWorkbook` code module.
- **Worksheet events:** These occur for a particular worksheet. Examples include `Change` (a cell on the sheet is changed), `SelectionChange` (the cell pointer is moved), and `Calculate` (the worksheet is recalculated). VBA code for worksheet events must be stored in the code module for the worksheet (for example, the module named `Sheet1`).
- **Events not associated with objects:** The final category consists of two useful application-level events: `OnTime` and `OnKey`. These work differently from other events.

Entering Event-Handler VBA Code

Every event-handler procedure must reside in a specific type of code module. Code for workbook-level events is stored in the `ThisWorkbook` code module. Code for worksheet-level events is stored in the code module for the particular sheet (for example, the code module named `Sheet1`).

In addition, every event-handler procedure has a predetermined name. You can declare the procedure by typing it, but a much better approach is to let the VB Editor do it for you, by using the two drop-down controls at the top of the window.

Figure 42.1 shows the code module for the `ThisWorkbook` object. Select this code module by double-clicking it in the Project window. To insert a procedure declaration, select `Workbook` from the objects list in the upper left of the code window. Then select the event from the procedures list in the upper right. When you do, you get a procedure "shell" that contains the procedure declaration line and an `End Sub` statement.

FIGURE 42.1

The best way to create an event procedure is to let the VB Editor do it for you.

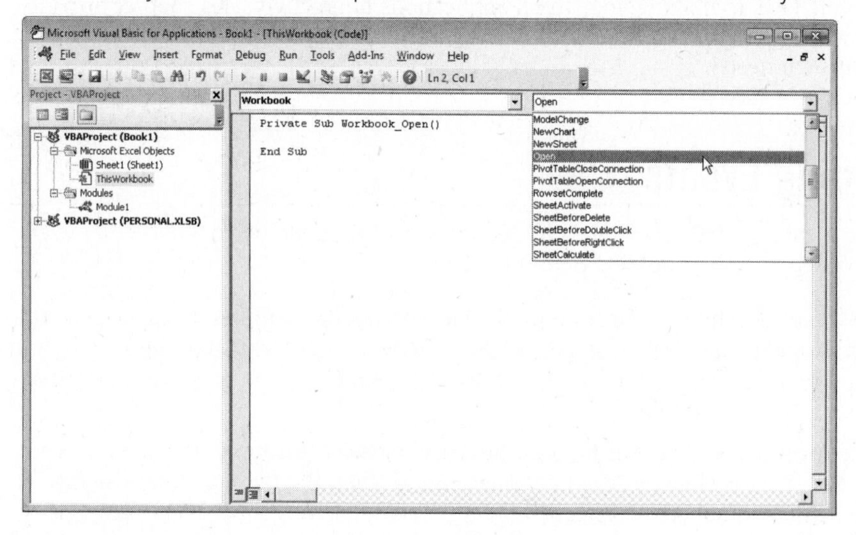

For example, if you select `Workbook` from the objects list and `Open` from the procedures list, the VB Editor inserts the following (empty) procedure:

```
Private Sub Workbook_Open()

End Sub
```

Your event-handler VBA code goes between these two lines.

Some event-handler procedures contain an argument list. For example, you may need to create an event-handler procedure to monitor the `SheetActivate` event for a workbook. (This event is triggered when a user activates a different sheet.) If you use the technique described in the previous section, the VB Editor creates the following procedure:

```
Private Sub Workbook_SheetActivate(ByVal Sh As Object)

End Sub
```

This procedure uses one argument (`Sh`), which represents the activated sheet. In this case, `Sh` is declared as an `Object` data type rather than a `Worksheet` data type because the activated sheet also can be a chart sheet.

Your code can, of course, make use of information passed as an argument. The following example displays the name of the activated sheet by accessing the argument's `Name` property. The argument becomes either a `Worksheet` object or a `Chart` object.

```
Private Sub Workbook_SheetActivate(ByVal Sh As Object)
   MsgBox Sh.Name & " was activated."
End Sub
```

Several event-handler procedures use a `Boolean` argument named `Cancel`. For example, the declaration for a workbook's `BeforePrint` event is

```
Private Sub Workbook_BeforePrint(Cancel As Boolean)
```

The value of `Cancel` passed to the procedure is `FALSE`. However, your code can set `Cancel` to `TRUE`, which cancels the printing. The following example demonstrates this:

```
Private Sub Workbook_BeforePrint(Cancel As Boolean)
   Msg = "Have you loaded the 5164 label stock? "
   Ans = MsgBox(Msg, vbYesNo, "About to print... ")
   If Ans = vbNo Then Cancel = True
End Sub
```

The `Workbook_BeforePrint` procedure executes before the workbook prints. This procedure displays a message box asking the user to verify that the correct paper is loaded. If the user clicks the No button, `Cancel` is set to `TRUE`, and nothing prints.

Here's another procedure that uses the workbook's `BeforePrint` event. This example overcomes a deficiency in Excel's headers and footers: It's not possible to use the contents of a cell for a page header or footer. This simple procedure is triggered when the workbook is printed. It places the contents of cell A1 in the page header.

```
Private Sub Workbook_BeforePrint(Cancel As Boolean)
    ActiveSheet.PageSetup.CenterHeader = Worksheets(1).Range("A1")
End Sub
```

Using Workbook-Level Events

Workbook-level events occur for a particular workbook. Table 42.1 lists the most commonly used workbook events, along with a brief description of each.

TABLE 42.1 Workbook Events

Event	Action That Triggers the Event
`Activate`	The workbook is activated.
`AfterSave`	The workbook was saved.
`BeforeClose`	The workbook is about to be closed.
`BeforePrint`	The workbook (or anything in it) is about to be printed.
`BeforeSave`	The workbook is about to be saved.
`Deactivate`	The workbook is deactivated.
`NewSheet`	A new sheet is created in the workbook.
`Open`	The workbook is opened.
`SheetActivate`	Any sheet in the workbook is activated.
`SheetBeforeDoubleClick`	Any worksheet in the workbook is double-clicked. This event occurs before the default double-click action.
`SheetBeforeRightClick`	Any worksheet in the workbook is right-clicked. This event occurs before the default right-click action.
`SheetChange`	Any worksheet in the workbook is changed by the user.
`SheetDeactivate`	Any sheet in the workbook is deactivated.
`SheetSelectionChange`	The selection on any worksheet in the workbook is changed.
`WindowActivate`	Any window of the workbook is activated.
`WindowDeactivate`	Any workbook window is deactivated.

The remainder of this section presents examples of using workbook-level events.

CAUTION

All the example procedures that follow must be located in the code module for the `ThisWorkbook` object. If you put them into any other type of code module, they won't work.

Using the Open event

One of the most common monitored events is a workbook's `Open` event. This event is triggered when the workbook (or add-in) opens, and executes the `Workbook_Open` procedure. A `Workbook_Open` procedure is very versatile and is often used for the following tasks:

- Displaying welcome messages.
- Opening other workbooks.
- Activating a specific sheet.
- Ensuring that certain conditions are met; for example, a workbook may require that a particular add-in is installed.

CAUTION

There is no guarantee that your `Workbook_Open` procedure will be executed. For example, the user may choose to disable macros. And if the user holds down the Shift key while opening a workbook, the workbook's `Workbook_Open` procedure won't execute.

The following is a simple example of a `Workbook_Open` procedure. It uses the VBA `Weekday` function to determine the day of the week. If it's Friday, a message box appears to remind the user to perform a file backup. If it's not Friday, nothing happens.

```
Private Sub Workbook_Open()
   If Weekday(Now) = 6 Then
      Msg = "Make sure you do your weekly backup!"
      MsgBox Msg, vbInformation
   End If
End Sub
```

The following example performs a number of actions when the workbook is opened. It maximizes the workbook window, activates the sheet named DataEntry, selects the first empty cell in column A, and enters the current date into that cell. If a sheet named DataEntry does not exist, the code generates an error.

```
Private Sub Workbook_Open()
   ActiveWindow.WindowState = xlMaximized
   Worksheets("DataEntry").Activate
   Range("A1").End(xlDown).offset(1,0).Select
   ActiveCell.Value = Date
End Sub
```

Using the SheetActivate event

The following procedure executes whenever the user activates any sheet in the workbook. The code simply selects cell A1. Including the `On Error Resume Next` statement causes the procedure to ignore the error that occurs if the activated sheet is a chart sheet.

```
Private Sub Workbook_SheetActivate(ByVal Sh As Object)
   On Error Resume Next
   Range("A1").Select
End Sub
```

An alternative method to handle the case of a chart sheet is to check the sheet type. Use the `Sh` argument, which is passed to the procedure.

```
Private Sub Workbook_SheetActivate(ByVal Sh As Object)
   If TypeName(Sh) = "Worksheet" Then Range("A1").Select
End Sub
```

Using the NewSheet event

The following procedure executes whenever a new sheet is added to the workbook. The sheet is passed to the procedure as an argument. Because a new sheet can be either a worksheet or a chart sheet, this procedure determines the sheet type. If it's a worksheet, it inserts a date and time stamp in cell A1.

```
Private Sub Workbook_NewSheet(ByVal Sh As Object)
  If TypeName(Sh) = "Worksheet" Then _
    Range("A1") = "Sheet added " & Now()
End Sub
```

Using the BeforeSave event

The `BeforeSave` event occurs before the workbook is actually saved. As you know, choosing File➪Save sometimes brings up the Save As dialog box — for example, when the file has never been saved or was opened in read-only mode.

When the `Workbook_BeforeSave` procedure executes, it receives an argument that enables you to identify whether the Save As dialog box will appear. The following example demonstrates this:

```
Private Sub Workbook_BeforeSave _
 (ByVal SaveAsUI As Boolean, Cancel As Boolean)
    If SaveAsUI Then
       MsgBox "Use the new file-naming convention."
    End If
End Sub
```

When the user attempts to save the workbook, the `Workbook_BeforeSave` procedure executes. If the save operation brings up the Save As dialog box, the `SaveAsUI` variable is `TRUE`. The preceding procedure checks this variable and displays a message only if the Save As dialog box is displayed. In this case, the message is a reminder about how to name the file.

The `BeforeSave` event procedure also has a `Cancel` variable in its argument list. If the procedure sets the `Cancel` argument to `TRUE`, the file is not saved.

Using the BeforeClose event

The `BeforeClose` event occurs before a workbook is closed. This event often is used in conjunction with a `Workbook_Open` event handler. For example, use the `Workbook_Open` procedure to initialize items in your workbook, and use the `Workbook_BeforeClose` procedure to clean up or restore settings to normal before the workbook closes.

If you attempt to close a workbook that hasn't been saved, Excel displays a prompt that asks whether you want to save the workbook before it closes.

CAUTION

A problem can arise from this event. By the time the user sees this message, the `BeforeClose` event has already occurred. This means that the `Workbook_BeforeClose` procedure has already executed.

Working with Worksheet Events

The events for a `Worksheet` object are some of the most useful. As you'll see, monitoring these events can make your applications perform feats that otherwise would be impossible.

Table 42.2 lists the more commonly used worksheet events, with a brief description of each. Remember that these event procedures must be entered into the code module for the sheet. These code modules have default names like Sheet1, Sheet2, and so on.

TABLE 42.2 Worksheet Events

Event	Action that triggers the event
`Activate`	The worksheet is activated.
`BeforeDoubleClick`	The worksheet is double-clicked. This event occurs before the default double-click action.
`BeforeRightClick`	The worksheet is right-clicked. This event occurs before the default right-click action.
`Change`	Cells on the worksheet are changed by the user.
`Deactivate`	The worksheet is deactivated.
`SelectionChange`	The selection on the worksheet is changed.

Using the Change event

A `Change` event is triggered when any cell in the worksheet is changed by the user. A `Change` event is not triggered when a calculation generates a different value for a formula or when an object (such as a chart or a shape) is added to the sheet.

When the `Worksheet_Change` procedure executes, it receives a `Range` object as its `Target` argument. This `Range` object corresponds to the changed cell or range that triggered the event. The following example displays a message box that shows the address of the `Target` range:

```
Private Sub Worksheet_Change(ByVal Target As Excel.Range)
    MsgBox "Range " & Target.Address & " was changed."
End Sub
```

To get a feel for the types of actions that generate the `Change` event for a worksheet, enter the preceding procedure into the code module for a `Worksheet` object. After entering this procedure, activate Excel and, using various techniques, make changes to the worksheet. Every time the `Change` event occurs, a message box displays the address of the range that changed.

Unfortunately, the `Change` event doesn't always work as expected. For example,

- Changing the formatting of a cell does not trigger the `Change` event (as expected), but choosing Home ➪ Editing ➪ Clear ➪ Clear Formats *does*.
- Pressing Delete generates an event even if the cell is empty at the start.
- Cells changed via Excel commands may or may not trigger the `Change` event. For example, sorting and goal-seeking operations do not trigger the `Change` event. However, operations such as Find and Replace, using the AutoSum button, or adding a Totals row to a table *do* trigger the event.
- If your VBA procedure changes a cell, it *does* trigger the `Change` event.

Monitoring a specific range for changes

Although the `Change` event occurs when any cell on the worksheet changes, most of the time, you'll be concerned only with changes that are made to a specific cell or range. When the `Worksheet_Change` event-handler procedure is called, it receives a `Range` object as its argument. This `Range` object corresponds to the cell(s) that changed.

Assume that your worksheet has a range named `InputRange`, and you want your VBA code to monitor changes to this range only. No `Change` event exists for a `Range` object, but you can perform a quick check within the `Worksheet_Change` procedure. The following procedure demonstrates this:

```
Private Sub Worksheet_Change(ByVal Target As Excel.Range)
   Dim VRange As Range
   Set VRange = Range("InputRange")
   If Union(Target, VRange).Address = VRange.Address Then
      Msgbox "The changed cell is in the input range."
   End if
End Sub
```

This example creates a Range object variable named VRange, which represents the worksheet range that you want to monitor for changes. The procedure uses the VBA Union function to determine whether VRange contains the Target range (passed to the procedure in its argument). The Union function returns an object that consists of all the cells in both of its arguments. If the range address is the same as the VRange address, VRange contains Target, and a message box appears. Otherwise, the procedure ends, and nothing happens.

The preceding procedure has a flaw: Target may consist of a single cell or a range. For example, if the user changes more than one cell at a time, Target becomes a multicell range. Therefore, the procedure requires modification to loop through all the cells in Target. The following procedure checks each changed cell and displays a message box if the cell is within the desired range:


```
Private Sub Worksheet_Change(ByVal Target As Excel.Range)
   Set VRange = Range("InputRange")
   For Each cell In Target
     If Union(cell, VRange).Address = VRange.Address Then
        Msgbox "The changed cell is in the input range."
     End if
   Next cell
End Sub
```

On the Web

A workbook with this example is available on this book's website. The file is named monitor a range.xlsm.

Using the SelectionChange event

The following procedure demonstrates a SelectionChange event. It executes whenever the user makes a new selection on the worksheet:

```
Private Sub Worksheet_SelectionChange(ByVal Target _
  As Excel.Range)
     Cells.Interior.ColorIndex = xlNone
     With ActiveCell
         .EntireRow.Interior.ColorIndex = 35
         .EntireColumn.Interior.ColorIndex = 35
     End With
End Sub
```

This procedure shades the row and column of an active cell, making it easy to identify. The first statement removes the background color of all cells. Next, the entire row and column of the active cell is shaded light yellow. Figure 42.2 shows the shading.

On the Web

A workbook with this example is available on this book's website. The file is named selection change event.xlsm.

FIGURE 42.2

Moving the cell cursor causes the active cell's row and column to become shaded.

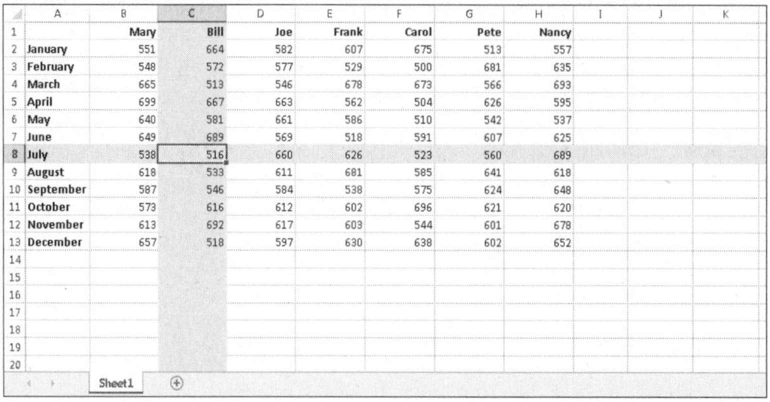

	Mary	Bill	Joe	Frank	Carol	Pete	Nancy
January	551	664	582	607	675	513	557
February	548	572	577	529	500	681	635
March	665	513	546	678	673	566	693
April	699	667	663	562	504	626	595
May	640	581	661	586	510	542	537
June	649	689	569	518	591	607	625
July	538	516	660	626	523	560	689
August	618	533	611	681	585	641	618
September	587	546	584	538	575	624	648
October	573	616	612	602	696	621	620
November	613	692	617	603	544	601	678
December	657	518	597	630	638	602	652

Sheet1

CAUTION

You won't want to use this procedure if your worksheet contains background shading because the macro will erase it. However, if the shading is the result of a style applied to a table, the macro doesn't erase the table's background shading.

Using the BeforeRightClick event

Normally, when the user right-clicks in a worksheet, a shortcut menu appears. If, for some reason, you want to prevent the shortcut menu from appearing, you can trap the `RightClick` event. The following procedure sets the `Cancel` argument to `TRUE`, which cancels the `RightClick` event — and, thus, the shortcut menu. Instead, a message box appears.

```
Private Sub Worksheet_BeforeRightClick _
  (ByVal Target As Excel.Range, Cancel As Boolean)
    Cancel = True
    MsgBox "The shortcut menu is not available."
End Sub
```

Using Non-Object Events

So far, the events discussed in this chapter are associated with an object (`Application`, `Workbook`, `Sheet`, and so on). This section discusses two additional events: `OnTime` and `OnKey`. These events are not associated with an object. Instead, you access them by using methods of the `Application` object.

NOTE
Unlike the other events discussed in this chapter, you use a general VBA module to program the `On` events in this section.

Using the OnTime event

The `OnTime` event occurs at a specified time. The following example demonstrates how to program Excel to beep and then display a message at 3 p.m.:

```
Sub SetAlarm()
  Application.OnTime 0.625, "DisplayAlarm"
End Sub

Sub DisplayAlarm()
  Beep
  MsgBox "Wake up. It's time for your afternoon break!"
End Sub
```


In this example, the `SetAlarm` procedure uses the `OnTime` method of the `Application` object to set up the `OnTime` event. This method takes two arguments: the time (`0.625`, or 3 p.m., in the example) and the procedure to execute when the time occurs (`DisplayAlarm` in the example). In the example, after `SetAlarm` executes, the `DisplayAlarm` procedure is called at 3 p.m., bringing up the message.

Most people find it difficult to think of time in terms of Excel's time numbering system. Therefore, you may want to use the VBA `TimeValue` function to represent the time. `TimeValue` converts a string that looks like a time into a value that Excel can handle. The following statement shows an easier way to program an event for 3 p.m.:

```
Application.OnTime TimeValue("3:00:00 pm"), "DisplayAlarm"
```

If you want to schedule an event that's relative to the current time — for example, 20 minutes from now — you can write an instruction like this:

```
Application.OnTime Now + TimeValue("00:20:00"), "DisplayAlarm"
```

You also can use the `OnTime` method to schedule a procedure on a particular day. Of course, you must keep your computer turned on, and Excel must be running.

Using the OnKey event

While you work, Excel constantly monitors what you type. As a result, you can set up a keystroke or a key combination that — when pressed — executes a particular procedure.

The following example uses the `OnKey` method to set up an `OnKey` event. This event essentially reassigns the PgDn and PgUp keys. After the `Setup_OnKey` procedure executes, pressing PgDn executes the `PgDn_Sub` procedure, and pressing PgUp executes the `PgUp_Sub` procedure. The next effect is that pressing PgDn moves down one row, and pressing PgUp moves up one row.

```
Sub Setup_OnKey()
  Application.OnKey "{PgDn}", "PgDn_Sub"
  Application.OnKey "{PgUp}", "PgUp_Sub"
End Sub

Sub PgDn_Sub()
  On Error Resume Next
  ActiveCell.Offset(1, 0).Activate
End Sub

Sub PgUp_Sub()
  On Error Resume Next
  ActiveCell.Offset(-1, 0).Activate
End Sub
```

Note

The key codes are enclosed in brackets, not parentheses. For a complete list of the keyboard codes, consult VBA Help. Search for OnKey.

Tip

The preceding examples used `On Error Resume Next` to ignore any errors generated. For example, if the active cell is in the first row, trying to move up one row causes an error. Furthermore, if the active sheet is a chart sheet, an error occurs because no such thing as an active cell exists in a chart sheet.

By executing the following procedure, you cancel the `OnKey` events, and the keys return to their normal functions.

```
Sub Cancel_OnKey()
   Application.OnKey "{PgDn}"
   Application.OnKey "{PgUp}"
End Sub
```

Caution

Contrary to what you may expect, using an empty string as the second argument for the `OnKey` method does *not* cancel the `OnKey` event. Instead, it causes Excel to ignore the keystroke and do nothing. For example, the following instruction tells Excel to ignore Alt+F4 (the percent sign represents the Alt key):

```
Application.OnKey "%{F4}", ""
```

CHAPTER 43

VBA Examples

IN THIS CHAPTER

Working with ranges

Working with charts

Modifying properties

Speeding up your VBA code

My philosophy about learning to write Excel macros places heavy emphasis on examples. Often, a well thought-out example communicates a concept much better than a lengthy description of the underlying theory. In this book, space limitations don't allow describing every nuance of VBA, so I prepared many examples. Don't overlook the VBA Help system for specific details. To get help while working in the VB Editor window, press F1. For context-sensitive help, select a VBA keyword, object name, property, or method before you press F1.

This chapter consists of several examples that demonstrate common VBA techniques. You may be able to use some examples directly, but in most cases, you must adapt them to your own needs.

Working with Ranges

Most of what you do in VBA probably involves worksheet ranges. When you work with range objects, keep the following points in mind:

- Your VBA code doesn't need to select a range in order to work with the range.
- If your code *does* select a range, its worksheet must be active.
- The macro recorder doesn't always generate the most efficient code. Often, you can use the recorder to create your macro and then edit the code to make it more efficient.
- I recommend that you use named ranges in your VBA code. For example, a reference such as `Range ("Total")` is better than `Range ("D45")`. In the latter case, you need to modify the macro if you add a row above row 45.
- When you record macros that select ranges, pay close attention to Relative versus Absolute recording mode. The recording mode that you choose can determine whether your macro works correctly.

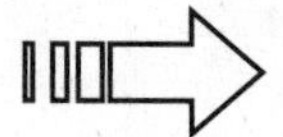

See Chapter 38 for more on recording modes.

- If you create a macro that loops through each cell in the current range selection, be aware that the user can select entire columns or rows. In such a case, you need to create a subset of the selection that consists only of nonblank cells. Or, you can work with cells in the worksheet's used range (by using the `UsedRange` property).
- Be aware that Excel allows you to select multiple ranges in a worksheet. For example, you can select a range, press Ctrl, and then select another range. You can test for this in your macro and take appropriate actions.

The examples in the following sections demonstrate these points.

Copying a range

Copying a range is a frequent activity in macros. When you turn on the macro recorder (using Absolute recording mode) and copy a range from A1:A5 to B1:B5, you get a VBA macro like this:

```
Sub CopyRange()
  Range("A1:A5").Select
  Selection.Copy
  Range("B1").Select
  ActiveSheet.Paste
  Application.CutCopyMode = False
End Sub
```

This macro works, but it's not the most efficient way to copy a range. You can accomplish exactly the same result with the following one-line macro:

```
Sub CopyRange2()
  Range("A1:A5").Copy Range("B1")
End Sub
```

This code takes advantage of the fact that the `Copy` method can use an argument that specifies the destination. Useful information about properties and methods is available in the Help system.

The example demonstrates that the macro recorder doesn't always generate the most efficient code. As you see, you don't have to select an object to work with it. Note that `CopyRange2` doesn't select a range; therefore, the active cell doesn't change when this macro is executed.

Copying a variable-size range

Often, you want to copy a range of cells in which the exact row and column dimensions are unknown.

Figure 43.1 shows a range on a worksheet. This range contains data that is updated weekly. Therefore, the number of rows changes. Because the exact range address is unknown at any given time, writing a macro to copy the range can be challenging.

FIGURE 43.1

This range can consist of any number of rows.

	A	B	C	D	E
1	Week Ending	Calls	Orders		
2	4/5/2013	452	89		
3	4/12/2013	546	102		
4	4/19/2013	587	132		
5	4/26/2013	443	65		
6	5/3/2013	609	156		
7	5/10/2013	592	92		
8	5/17/2013	487	95		
9	5/24/2013	601	105		
10	5/31/2013	515	133		
11	6/7/2013	540	122		
12					

Copying a variable-sized range | Sheet2

The macro that follows demonstrates how to copy this range to Sheet2 (beginning at cell A1). It uses the `CurrentRegion` property, which returns a `Range` object that corresponds to the block of used cells surrounding a particular cell. This is equivalent to choosing Home ➪ Editing ➪ Find & Select ➪ Go To, clicking the Special button, and then selecting the Current Region option.

```
Sub CopyCurrentRegion()
  Range("A1").CurrentRegion.Copy Sheets("Sheet2").Range("A1")
End Sub
```

On the Web

A workbook that contains this macro is available on this book's website. The file is named `range copy.xlsm`.

Selecting to the end of a row or column

You're probably in the habit of using key combinations, such as pressing Ctrl+Shift+→ and Ctrl+Shift+↓, to select from the active cell to the end of a row or column. When you record these actions in Excel (using Relative recording mode), you'll find that the resulting code works as you would expect it to.

The following VBA procedure selects the range that begins at the active cell and extends down to the last cell in the column (or to the first empty cell, whichever comes first).

When the range is selected, you can do whatever you want with it — copy it, move it, format it, and so on.

```
Sub SelectDown()
  Range(ActiveCell, ActiveCell.End(xlDown)).Select
End Sub
```

Notice that the `Range` property has two arguments. These arguments represent the upper-left and lower-right cells in a range.

This example uses the `End` method of the `Range` object, which returns a `Range` object. The `End` method takes one argument, which can be any of the following constants: `xlUp`, `xlDown`, `xlToLeft`, or `xlToRight`.

On the Web

A workbook that contains this macro is available on this book's website. The file is named `select cells.xlsm`.

Selecting a row or column

The macro that follows demonstrates how to select the column of the active cell. It uses the `EntireColumn` property, which returns a range that consists of a column:

```
Sub SelectColumn()
  ActiveCell.EntireColumn.Select
End Sub
```

As you may suspect, an `EntireRow` property also is available, which returns a range that consists of a row.

If you want to perform an operation on all cells in the selected column, you don't need to select the column. For example, when the following procedure is executed, all cells in the row that contains the active cell are made bold:

```
Sub MakeRowBold()
  ActiveCell.EntireRow.Font.Bold = True
End Sub
```

Moving a range

Moving a range consists of cutting it to the Clipboard and then pasting it to another area. If you record your actions while performing a move operation, the macro recorder generates code as follows:

```
Sub MoveRange()
  Range("A1:C6").Select
  Selection.Cut
  Range("A10").Select
  ActiveSheet.Paste
End Sub
```

As demonstrated with copying earlier in this chapter (see "Copying a range"), this method is not the most efficient way to move a range of cells. In fact, you can do it with a single VBA statement, as follows:

```
Sub MoveRange2()
 Range("A1:C6").Cut Range("A10")
End Sub
```

This statement takes advantage of the fact that the `Cut` method can use an argument that specifies the destination.

On the Web

A workbook that contains this macro is available on this book's website. The file is named `range move.xlsm`.

Looping through a range efficiently

Many macros perform an operation on each cell in a range, or they may perform selective actions based on the content of each cell. These operations usually involve a `For-Next` loop that processes each cell in the range.

The following example demonstrates how to loop through all the cells in a range. In this case, the range is the current selection. In this example, `Cell` is a variable name that refers to the cell being processed. (Notice that this variable is declared as a `Range` object.) Within the `For-Next` loop, the single statement evaluates the cell. If the cell is negative, it's converted to a positive value.

```
Sub ProcessCells()
  Dim Cell As Range
  For Each Cell In Selection
    If Cell.Value < 0 Then Cell.Value = Cell.Value * -1
  Next Cell
End Sub
```

The preceding example works, but what if the selection consists of an entire column or an entire range? This is not uncommon because Excel lets you perform operations on entire columns or rows. In this case, though, the macro seems to take forever because it loops through each cell — even those that are blank. What's needed is a way to process only the nonblank cells.

You can accomplish this task by using the `SelectSpecial` method. In the following example, the `SelectSpecial` method is used to create a new object: the subset of the selection that consists of cells with constants (as opposed to formulas). This subset is processed, with the net effect of skipping all blank cells and all formula cells.

```
Sub ProcessCells2()
    Dim ConstantCells As Range
    Dim Cell As Range
```

```
'   Ignore errors
    On Error Resume Next
'   Process the constants
    Set ConstantCells = Selection.SpecialCells(xlConstants, xlNumbers)
    For Each Cell In ConstantCells
       If Cell.Value < 0 Then Cell.Value = Cell.Value * -1
    Next Cell
End Sub
```

The `ProcessCells2` procedure works fast, regardless of what is selected. For example, you can select the range, select all columns in the range, select all rows in the range, or even select the entire worksheet. In all these cases, only the cells that contain constants are processed inside the loop. This procedure is a vast improvement over the `ProcessCells` procedure presented earlier in this section.

Notice that the following statement is used in the procedure:

```
On Error Resume Next
```

This statement causes Excel to ignore any errors that occur and simply to process the next statement. This statement is necessary because the `SpecialCells` method produces an error if no cells qualify and because the numerical comparison will fail if a cell contains an error value. Normal error checking is resumed when the procedure ends. To tell Excel explicitly to return to normal error-checking mode, use the following statement:

```
On Error GoTo 0
```

On the Web

This macro is available on this book's website. The file is named `skip blanks while looping.xlsm`.

Prompting for a cell value

As discussed in Chapter 40, you can take advantage of the VBA `InputBox` function to ask the user to enter a value. Figure 43.2 shows an example.

You can assign this value to a variable and use it in your procedure. Often, however, you want to place the value into a cell. The following procedure demonstrates how to ask the user for a value and place it into cell A1 of the active worksheet, using only one statement:

```
Sub GetValue()
  Range("A1").Value = InputBox("Enter the value for cell A1")
End Sub
```

FIGURE 43.2

Using the VBA `InputBox` function to get a value from the user.

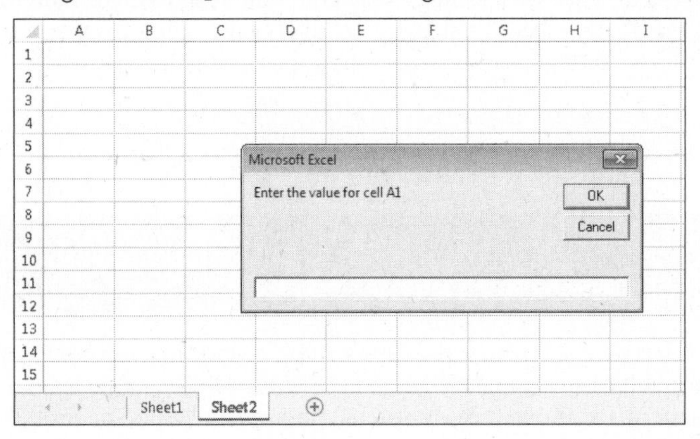

This procedure has a problem: If the user clicks Cancel, the contents of cell A1 are replaced with an empty string. Here's a modified version in which the `InputBox` entry is assigned to a variable named `UserVal`. The code checks this variable and takes action only if the variable is not empty.


```
Sub GetValue()
  UserVal = InputBox("Enter the value for cell A1")
  If UserVal <> "" Then Range("A1").Value = UserVal
End Sub
```

Here's a variation that accepts only a numeric value. If the user enters a non-number, a message box appears and the `GetValue` procedure is executed again.

```
Sub GetValue()
    UserVal = InputBox("Enter the value for cell A1")
    If UserVal = "" Then
        Exit Sub
    Else
        If IsNumeric(UserVal) Then
            Range("A1").Value = UserVal
        Else
            MsgBox "You must enter a number."
            Call GetValue
        End If
    End If
End Sub
```

Determining the type of selection

If your macro is designed to work with a range selection, you need to determine that a range is actually selected. Otherwise, the macro most likely fails. The following procedure identifies the type of object selected:

```
Sub SelectionType()
  MsgBox TypeName(Selection)
End Sub
```

On the Web

A workbook that contains this macro is available on this book's website. The file is named `selection type.xlsm`.

If a cell or a range is selected, the `MsgBox` displays `Range`. If your macro is designed to work only with ranges, you can use an `If` statement to ensure that a range is actually selected. The following is an example that displays a message and exits the procedure if the current selection is not a `Range` object:

```
Sub CheckSelection()
  If TypeName(Selection) <> "Range" Then
    MsgBox "Select a range."
    Exit Sub
  End If
' ... [Other statements go here]
End Sub
```

Another way to approach this task is to define a custom function that returns `TRUE` if the selection (represented by the `sel` argument) is a `Range` object, and `FALSE` otherwise. The following function does just that:

```
Function IsRange(sel) As Boolean
 IsRange = False
 If TypeName(sel) = "Range" Then IsRange = True
End Function
```

Here's a more compact version of the `IsRange` function:

```
Function IsRange(sel) As Boolean
  IsRange = (TypeName(sel) = "Range")
End Function
```

If you enter the `IsRange` function in your module, you can rewrite the `CheckSelection` procedure as follows:

```
Sub CheckSelection()
 If IsRange(Selection) Then
```

```
' ... [Other statements go here]
 Else
  MsgBox "Select a range."
  Exit Sub
 End If
End Sub
```

This approach is efficient if you have many procedures that need to check for a range selection.

Identifying a multiple selection

Excel enables you to make a multiple selection by pressing Ctrl while you select objects or ranges. This method can cause problems with some macros; for example, you can't copy a multiple selection that consists of nonadjacent ranges. The following macro demonstrates how to determine whether the user has made a multiple selection:

```
Sub MultipleSelection()
  If Selection.Areas.Count > 1 Then
    MsgBox "Multiple selections not allowed."
    Exit Sub
  End If
' ... [Other statements go here]
End Sub
```


This example uses the `Areas` method, which returns a collection of all `Range` objects in the selection. The `Count` property returns the number of objects that are in the collection.

The following is a VBA function that returns `TRUE` if the selection is a multiple selection:

```
Function IsMultiple(sel) As Boolean
  IsMultiple = Selection.Areas.Count > 1
End Function
```

Counting selected cells

You can create a macro that works with the selected range of cells. Use the `Count` property of the `Range` object to determine how many cells are contained in a range selection (or any range, for that matter). For example, the following statement displays a message box that contains the number of cells in the current selection:

```
MsgBox Selection.Count
```

CAUTION

With the larger worksheet size introduced in Excel 2007, the `Count` property can generate an error. The `Count` property uses the `Long` data type, so the largest value that it can store is `2,147,483,647`. For example, if the user selects 2,048 complete columns (2,147,483,648 cells), the `Count` property generates an error. Fortunately, Microsoft added a new property — `CountLarge` — which uses the `Double` data type, which can handle values up to `1.79+E^308`.

For more on VBA data types, see Table 43.1.

Bottom line? In the vast majority of situations, the `Count` property will work fine. If there's a chance that you may need to count more cells (such as all cells in a worksheet), use `CountLarge` instead of `Count`.

If the active sheet contains a range named data, the following statement assigns the number of cells in the data range to a variable named `CellCount`:

```
CellCount = Range("data").Count
```

You can also determine how many rows or columns are contained in a range. The following expression calculates the number of columns in the currently selected range:

```
Selection.Columns.Count
```

And, of course, you can also use the `Rows` property to determine the number of rows in a range. The following statement counts the number of rows in a range named data and assigns the number to a variable named `RowCount`:

```
RowCount = Range("data").Rows.Count
```

Working with Workbooks

The examples in this section demonstrate various ways to use VBA to work with workbooks.

Saving all workbooks

The following procedure loops through all workbooks in the `Workbooks` collection and saves each file that has been saved previously:

```
Public Sub SaveAllWorkbooks()
    Dim Book As Workbook
    For Each Book In Workbooks
        If Book.Path <> "" Then Book.Save
    Next Book
End Sub
```

Notice the use of the Path property. If a workbook's Path property is empty, the file has never been saved (it's a new workbook). This procedure ignores such workbooks and saves only the workbooks that have a nonempty Path property.

Saving and closing all workbooks

The following procedure loops through the Workbooks collection. The code saves and closes all workbooks.

```
Sub CloseAllWorkbooks()
    Dim Book As Workbook
    For Each Book In Workbooks
        If Book.Name <> ThisWorkbook.Name Then
            Book.Close savechanges:=True
        End If
    Next Book
    ThisWorkbook.Close savechanges:=True
End Sub
```

The procedure uses an If statement within the For-Next loop to determine whether the workbook is the workbook that contains the code. This is necessary because closing the workbook that contains the procedure would end the code, and subsequent workbooks would not be affected.

Working with Charts

Manipulating charts with VBA can be confusing, mainly because of the large number of objects involved. To get a feel for working with charts, turn on the macro recorder, create a chart, and perform some routine chart editing. You may be surprised by the amount of code that's generated.

When you understand how objects function within in a chart, however, you can create some useful macros. This section presents a few macros that deal with charts. When you write macros that manipulate charts, you need to understand some terminology. An embedded chart on a worksheet is a ChartObject object, and the ChartObject contains the actual Chart object. A chart on a chart sheet, on the other hand, does not have a ChartObject container.

It's often useful to create an object reference to a chart (see "Simplifying object references," later in this chapter). For example, the following statement creates an object variable (MyChart) for the embedded chart named Chart 1 on the active sheet.

```
Dim MyChart As Chart
Set MyChart = ActiveSheet.ChartObjects("Chart 1")
```

The following sections contain examples of macros that work with charts.

On the Web

These macros are available on this book's website. The file is named `chart macros.xlsm`.

Modifying the chart type

The following example changes the chart type of every embedded chart on the active sheet. It makes each chart a clustered column chart by adjusting the `ChartType` property of the `Chart` object. A built-in constant, `xlColumnClustered`, represents a standard column chart.

```
Sub ChartType()
    Dim ChtObj As ChartObject
    For Each ChtObj In ActiveSheet.ChartObjects
        ChtObj.Chart.ChartType = xlColumnClustered
    Next ChtObj
End Sub
```

The preceding example uses a `For-Next` loop to cycle through all the `ChartObject` objects on the active sheet. Within the loop, the chart type is assigned a new value, making it a column chart.

The following macro performs the same function but works on all chart sheets in the active workbook:

```
Sub ChartType2()
    Dim Cht As Chart
    For Each Cht In ActiveWorkbook.Charts
        Cht.ChartType = xlColumnClustered
    Next Cht
End Sub
```

Modifying chart properties

The following example changes the legend font for all charts that are on the active sheet. It uses a `For-Next` loop to process all `ChartObject` objects and uses the `HasLegend` property to ensure that the chart has a legend. The code then adjusts the properties of the `Font` object contained in the `Legend` object:

```
Sub LegendMod()
   Dim ChtObj As ChartObject
   For Each ChtObj In ActiveSheet.ChartObjects
      ChtObj.Chart.HasLegend = True
      With ChtObj.Chart.Legend.Font
         .Name = "Arial"
         .FontStyle = "Bold"
```

```
            .Size = 8
        End With
    Next ChtObj
End Sub
```

Applying chart formatting

This example applies several different formatting types to the specified chart (in this case, Chart 1 on the active sheet):

```
Sub ChartMods()
    With ActiveSheet.ChartObjects("Chart 1").Chart
        .ChartType = xlColumnClustered
        .ChartTitle.Text = "XYZ Corporation"
        .ChartArea.Font.Name = "Arial"
        .ChartArea.Font.FontStyle = "Regular"
        .ChartArea.Font.Size = 9
        .PlotArea.Interior.ColorIndex = 6
        .Axes(xlValue).TickLabels.Font.Bold = True
        .Axes(xlCategory).TickLabels.Font.Bold = True
    End With
End Sub
```

One way to learn about these properties is to record a macro while you apply various changes to a chart.

VBA Speed Tips

VBA is fast, but it's often not fast enough. This section presents programming examples that you can use to help speed your macros.

Turning off screen updating

You've probably noticed that when you execute a macro, you can watch everything that occurs in the macro. Sometimes, this view is instructive, but after you get the macro working properly, it can be annoying and slow things considerably.

Fortunately, you can disable the normal screen updating that occurs when you execute a macro. Insert the following statement to turn off screen updating:

```
Application.ScreenUpdating = False
```

If, at any point during the macro, you want the user to see the results of the macro, use the following statement to turn screen updating back on:

```
Application.ScreenUpdating = True
```

Preventing alert messages

One benefit of using a macro is that you can perform a series of actions automatically. You can start a macro and then get a cup of coffee while Excel does its thing. Some operations cause Excel to display messages that must be attended to, however. For example, if your macro deletes a sheet, you see the message that is shown in the dialog box in Figure 43.3. These types of messages mean that you can't execute your macro unattended.

FIGURE 43.3

You can instruct Excel not to display these types of alerts while a macro is running.

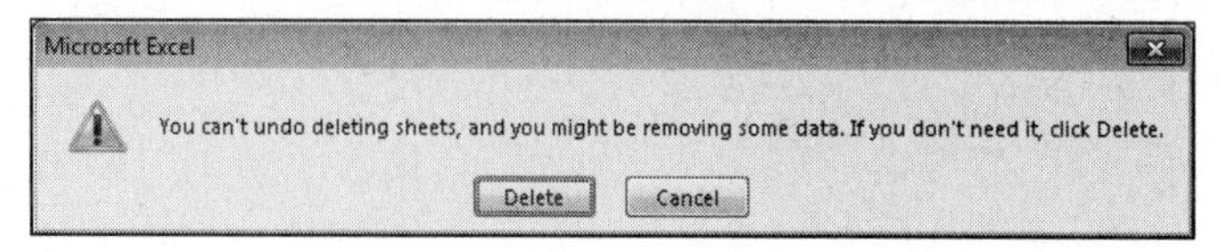

To avoid these alert messages (and automatically choose the default response), insert the following VBA statement:

```
Application.DisplayAlerts = False
```

To turn alerts back on, use this statement:

```
Application.DisplayAlerts = True
```

Simplifying object references

As you may have discovered, references to objects can get very lengthy — especially if your code refers to an object that's not on the active sheet or in the active workbook. For example, a fully qualified reference to a `Range` object may look like this:

```
Workbooks("MyBook.xlsx").Worksheets("Sheet1").Range("IntRate")
```

If your macro uses this range frequently, you may want to use the `Set` command to create an object variable. For example, to assign this `Range` object to an object variable named `Rate`, use the following statement:

```
Set Rate= Workbooks("MyBook.xlsx").Worksheets("Sheet1").Range("IntRate")
```

After this variable is defined, you can use the object variable `Rate` instead of the lengthy reference. For example,

```
Rate.Font.Bold = True
Rate.Value = .0725
```

Besides simplifying your coding, using object variables also speeds your macros quite a bit. I've seen complex macros execute twice as fast after creating object variables.

Declaring variable types

Usually, you don't have to worry about the type of data that's assigned to a variable. Excel handles all these details behind the scenes. For example, if you have a variable named `MyVar`, you can assign a number of any type to it. You can even assign a text string to it later in the procedure.

If you want your procedures to execute as fast as possible, though, you should tell Excel in advance what type of data is going be assigned to each of your variables. Providing this information in your VBA procedure is known as *declaring* a variable's type.

Table 43.1 lists all the data types that are supported by VBA. This table also lists the number of bytes that each type uses and the approximate range of possible values.

TABLE 43.1 VBA Data Types

Data Type	Bytes Used	Approximate Range of Values
`Byte`	1	0 to 255
`Boolean`	2	True or False
`Integer`	2	–32,768 to 32,767
`Long` (long integer)	4	–2,147,483,648 to 2,147,483,647
`Single` (single precision floating point)	4	–3.4E38 to –1.4E–45 for negative values; 1.4E–45 to 4E38 for positive values
`Double` (double precision floating point)	8	–1.7E308 to –4.9E–324 for negative values; 4.9E–324 to .7E308 for positive values
`Currency` (scaled integer)	8	–9.2E14 to 9.2E14
`Decimal`	14	+/–7.9E28 with no decimal point
`Date`	8	January 1, 100 to December 31, 9999
`Object`	4	Any object reference
`String` (variable length)	10 + string length	0 to approximately 2 billion
`String` (fixed length)	Length of string	1 to approximately 65,400
`Variant` (with numbers)	16	Any numeric value up to the range of a `Double`
`Variant` (with characters)	22 + string length	Same range as for variable-length `String`
User-defined (using `Type`)	Number required by elements	Range of each element is the same as the range of its data type

If you don't declare a variable, Excel uses the `Variant` data type. In general, the best technique is to use the data type that uses the smallest number of bytes yet can still handle all the data assigned to it. An exception is when you're performing floating-point calculations. In such a case, it's always best to use the `Double` data type (rather than the `Single` data type) to maintain maximum precision. Another exception involves the `Integer` data type. Although the `Long` data type uses more bytes, it usually results in faster performance.

When VBA works with data, execution speed is a function of the number of bytes that VBA has at its disposal. In other words, the fewer bytes that are used by data, the faster VBA can access and manipulate the data.

To declare a variable, use the `Dim` statement before you use the variable for the first time. For example, to declare the variable `Units` as a `Long` data type, use the following statement:

```
Dim Units as Long
```

To declare the variable `UserName` as a string, use the following statement:

```
Dim UserName as String
```

If you declare a variable within a procedure, the declaration is valid only within that procedure. If you declare a variable outside of any procedures (but before the first procedure), the variable is valid in all procedures in the module.

If you use an object variable (as described in "Simplifying object references," earlier in this chapter), you can declare the variable as the appropriate object data type. The following is an example:

```
Dim Rate as Range
Set Rate = Workbooks("MyBook.xlsx").Worksheets("Sheet1").Range("IntRate")
```

To force yourself to declare all the variables that you use, insert the following statement at the top of your module:

```
Option Explicit
```

If you use this statement, Excel displays an error message if it encounters a variable that hasn't been declared. After you get into the habit of correctly declaring all your variables, you'll find that it helps eliminate errors and makes spotting errors easier.

CHAPTER

44

Creating Custom Excel Add-Ins

IN THIS CHAPTER

Understanding add-ins

Converting a workbook to an add-in

For developers, one of the most useful features in Excel is the capability to create add-ins. This chapter discusses this concept and provides a practical example of creating an add-in.

What Is an Add-In?

Generally speaking, an *add-in* is something that's added to software to give it additional functionality. Excel includes several add-ins, including the Analysis ToolPak and Solver. Ideally, the new features blend in well with the original interface so that they appear to be part of the program.

Excel's approach to add-ins is quite powerful: Any knowledgeable Excel user can create add-ins from workbooks. The type of add-in covered in this chapter is basically a different form of a workbook file. Any Excel workbook can be converted into an add-in, but not every workbook is a good candidate for an add-in.

What distinguishes an add-in form a normal workbook? Add-ins, by default, have an `.xlam` extension. In addition, add-ins are always hidden, so you can't display worksheets or chart sheets that are contained in an add-in. But you can access its VBA procedures and display dialog boxes that are contained on UserForms.

The following are some typical uses for Excel add-ins:

- **Store one or more custom worksheet functions.** When the add-in is loaded, you can use the functions like any built-in worksheet function.
- **Store Excel utilities.** VBA is ideal for creating general-purpose utilities that extend the power of Excel. The Power Utility Pak that I created is an example.
- **Store proprietary macros.** If you don't want end-users to see (or modify) your macros, store the macros in an add-in and protect the VBA project with a password. Users can use the macros, but they can't view or change them unless they knows the password. An additional benefit is that the add-in doesn't display a workbook window, which can be distracting.

As previously noted, Excel ships with several useful add-ins, and you can acquire other add-ins from third-party vendors or online. In addition, Excel includes the tools that enable you to create your own add-ins. I explain this process later in this chapter (see "Creating Add-Ins").

Working with Add-Ins

The best way to work with add-ins is to use the Excel Add-In Manager. To display the Add-In Manager, follow these steps:

1. **Choose File➪Options.** The Excel Options dialog box appears.
2. **Select the Add-Ins category.**
3. **At the bottom of the dialog box, select Excel Add-Ins from the Manage list and then click Go.**

The Add-Ins dialog box, shown in Figure 44.1, appears. The dialog box contains all the add-ins that Excel knows about. The add-ins that are checked are open. You can open and close add-ins from this dialog box by selecting or deselecting the check boxes.

FIGURE 44.1

The Add-Ins dialog box.

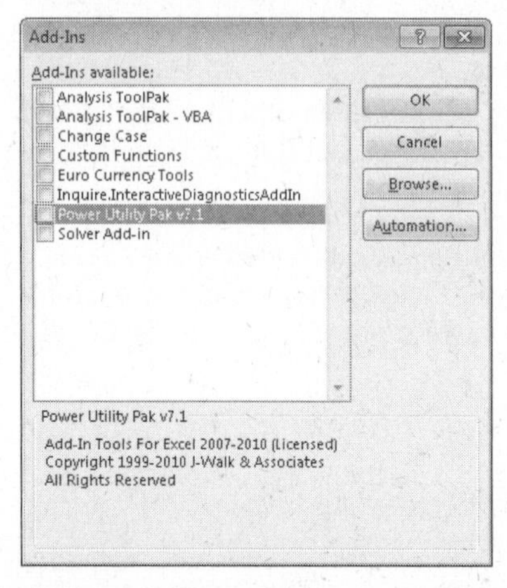

TIP

Pressing Alt+T+I is a much faster way to display the Add-Ins dialog box. Or, if the Developer tab is visible, choose Developer➪Add-Ins➪Add-Ins.

CAUTION

You can also open most add-in files by choosing File ➪ Open. After an add-in is opened, however, you can't choose File ➪ Close to close it. The only way to remove the add-in is to exit and restart Excel or to write a macro to close the add-in. Therefore, you're usually better off opening the add-ins by using the Add-Ins dialog box.

The user interface for some add-ins (including those included with Excel) may be integrated into the Ribbon. For example, when you open the Analysis ToolPak add-in, you access these tools by choosing Data ➪ Analysis ➪ Data Analysis.

NOTE

If you open an add-in created in a version prior to Excel 2007 (an `*.xla` file), any user interface modifications made by the add-in will not appear as they were intended to appear. Instead, you must access the user interface items (menus and toolbars) by choosing Add-Ins ➪ Menu Commands or Add-Ins ➪ Custom Toolbars.

Why Create Add-Ins?

Most Excel users have no need to create add-ins. However, if you develop spreadsheets for others — or if you simply want to get the most out of Excel — you may be interested in pursuing this topic further.

Here are some reasons you may want to convert your Excel workbook application to an add-in:

- **To avoid confusion:** If an end-user loads your application as an add-in, the file isn't visible in a window — and, therefore, is less likely to confuse novice users or get in the way. Unlike a hidden workbook window, an add-in can't be unhidden.
- **To simplify access to worksheet functions:** Custom worksheet functions stored in an add-in don't require the workbook name qualifier. For example, if you have a custom function named `MOVAVG` stored in a workbook named `Newfuncs.xlsm`, you have to use a syntax such as the following to use this function in a different workbook:

  ```
  =NEWFUNC.XLSM!MOVAVG(A1:A50)
  ```

  However, if this function is stored in an add-in file that's open, the syntax is much simpler because you don't need to include the file reference:

  ```
  =MOVAVG(A1:A50)
  ```

- **To provide easier access:** After you identify the location of your add-in, it appears in the Add-Ins dialog box and can display a friendly name and a description of what it does.
- **To permit better loading control:** You can automatically open add-ins when Excel starts, regardless of the directory in which they're stored.

- **To omit prompts when unloading:** When an add-in is closed, the user never sees the `Save Change In` prompt because changes to add-ins aren't saved unless you specifically do so from the VB Editor window.

Creating Add-Ins

Technically, you can convert any workbook to an add-in. Not all workbooks benefit from this conversion, though. In fact, workbooks that consist only of worksheets (that is, not macros or custom dialog boxes) become unusable because add-ins are hidden.

Workbooks that benefit from conversion to an add-in are those with macros. For example, you may have a workbook that consists of general-purpose macros and functions. This type of workbook makes an ideal add-in.

The following steps describe how to create an add-in from a workbook:

1. **Develop your application and make sure that everything works properly.**
2. **(Optional) Add a title and description for your add-in.** Choose File ⇨ Info and click Show All Properties at the bottom of the right panel. Enter a brief descriptive title in the Title field, and then enter a longer description in the Comments field. Although this step isn't required, it makes installing and identifying the add-in easier.
3. **(Optional) Lock the VBA Project.** This step protects the VBA code and UserForms from being viewed. You do this in the VB Editor; choose Tools ⇨ *<Project Name>* Properties (where *<Project Name>* corresponds to your VB Project name). In the dialog box, click the Protection tab and select Lock Project for Viewing. If you like, you can specify a password to prevent others from viewing your code.
4. **Save the workbook as an add-in file by choosing File ⇨ Save As and selecting Excel Add-In (*.xlam) from the Save As Type drop-down list.** By default, Excel saves your add-in in your `AddIns` directory. You can override this location and choose any directory you like.

NOTE

After you save the workbook as an add-in, the original (non-add-in) workbook remains active. If you're going to install the add-in and test it, you should close this file to avoid having two macros with the same name.

After you create the add-in, you need to install it:

1. **Choose File ⇨ Options ⇨ Add-Ins.**
2. **Select Excel Add-Ins from the Manage drop-down list and then click Go.** The Add-Ins dialog box appears.

3. **Click the Browse button to locate the XLAM file that you created, which installs the add-in.** The Add-Ins dialog box uses the descriptive title that you provided in the Properties panel.

> **NOTE**
>
> You can continue to modify the macros and UserForms in the XLAM version of your file. Because the add-in doesn't appear in the Excel window, you save your changes in the VB Editor by choosing File ⇨ Save.

An Add-In Example

This section discusses the steps to create a useful add-in from the `change case.xlsm` workbook that I cover in Chapter 40. This workbook contains a UserForm that displays options that change the text case of selected cells (uppercase, lowercase, or proper case). Figure 44.2 shows the add-in in action.

FIGURE 44.2

This dialog box enables the user to change the case of text in the selected cells.

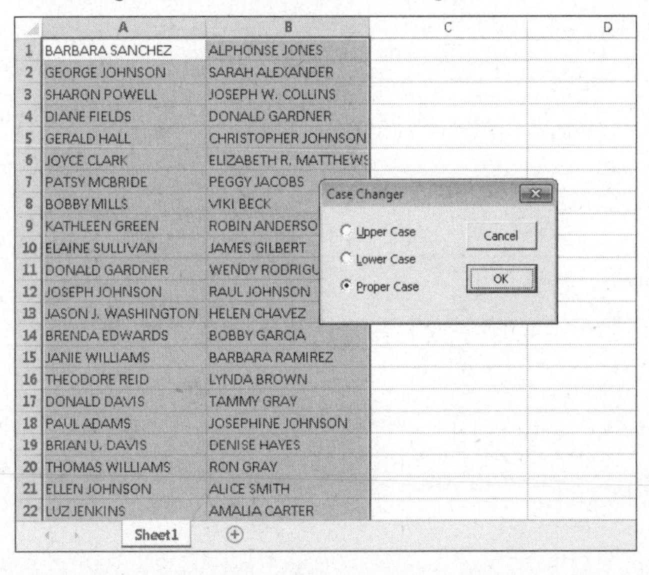

> **ON THE WEB**
>
> This book's website contains the original version of the workbook (`change case.xlsm`), plus a version after it was converted to an add-in (`change case.xlam`). Neither file is locked, so you have full access to the VBA code and UserForm.

This workbook contains one worksheet, which is empty. Although the worksheet is not used, it must be present because every workbook must have at least one sheet.

It also contains one VBA module and one UserForm.

About Module1

The Module1 code module contains one procedure that displays the UserForm. The `ShowChangeCaseUserForm` procedure checks the type of selection. If a range is selected, the dialog box in UserForm1 appears. If anything other than a range is selected, a message box is displayed.

```
Sub ShowChangeCaseUserForm ()
    If TypeName(Selection) = "Range" Then
        UserForm1.Show
    Else
        MsgBox "Select some cells."
    End If
End Sub
```

About the UserForm

Figure 44.3 shows the UserForm1 form, which has five controls: three `OptionButton` controls and two `CommandButton` controls. The controls have descriptive names, and the `Accelerator` property is set so that the controls display an accelerator key (for keyboard users). The option button with the Upper Case caption has its `Value` property set to `TRUE`, which makes it the default option.

FIGURE 44.3

The custom dialog box.

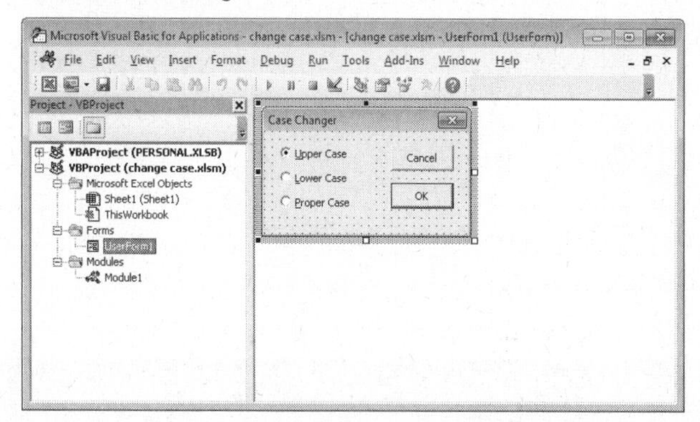

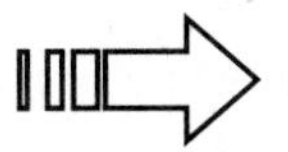

Refer to Chapter 40 for details about how the code works.

Testing the workbook

Before you convert a workbook to an add-in, test it when a different workbook is active to simulate what happens when the workbook is an add-in. Remember that an add-in is never the active workbook, and it never displays any of its worksheets.

To test it, save the XLSM version of the workbook, close it, and then reopen it. With the workbook open, activate a different workbook, select some cells that contain text, and then press Alt + F8 to display the Macros dialog box. Execute the `ShowChangeCaseUserForm` macro and try all the options.

Adding descriptive information

Adding descriptive information is recommended but not necessary. Choose File➪Info and click Show All Properties at the bottom of the right panel (see Figure 44.4). Enter a title for the add-in in the Title field. This text appears in the Add-Ins dialog box. In the Comments field, enter a description. This information appears at the bottom of the Add-Ins dialog box when the add-in is selected.

FIGURE 44.4

Adding descriptive information about your add-in.

Properties ˅

Size	21.9KB
Title	Change Case of Text
Tags	Add a tag
Comments	Changes the case of text in ...
Template	
Status	Add text
Categories	
Subject	
Hyperlink Base	
Company	JWalk & Associates

Creating the user interface for your add-in macro

At this point, the future add-in is missing one key component: a way to execute the macro that displays the UserForm. The easiest solution is to provide a shortcut key that executes the macro. Ctrl + Shift + C is a good key combination. Here's how to do it:

1. **In Excel, press Alt + F8.** The Macro dialog box appears.
2. **In the Macro Name list, select the macro named ShowChangeCaseUserForm.**

3. **Click the Options button.** The Macro Options dialog box appears.
4. **Specify Ctrl + Shift + C as the shortcut key, and click OK.**
5. **Click Cancel to close the Macro dialog box.**

Make sure you save the workbook after making this change.

NOTE

In previous editions of this book, I describe how to write code that adds a new item to the shortcut menu that appears when you right-click a cell or range. That's actually an excellent (and very convenient) way execute the macro. Unfortunately, the new single document interface in Excel 2013 affects the way shortcut menus work. In the past, adding a shortcut menu affected all open workbooks. That's no longer the case. Based on my testing, I conclude that it's no longer feasible to modify a shortcut menu in an add-in.

Protecting the project

In some situations (such as a commercial product), you may want to protect your project so that others can't see the source code. To protect the project, follow these steps:

1. **Activate the VB Editor.**
2. **In the Project window, click the project.**
3. **Choose Tools ➪ <*Project Name*> Properties.** The VB Editor displays its Project Properties dialog box.
4. **Select the Protection tab (as shown in Figure 44.5).**

FIGURE 44.5

The Protection tab of the Project Properties dialog box.

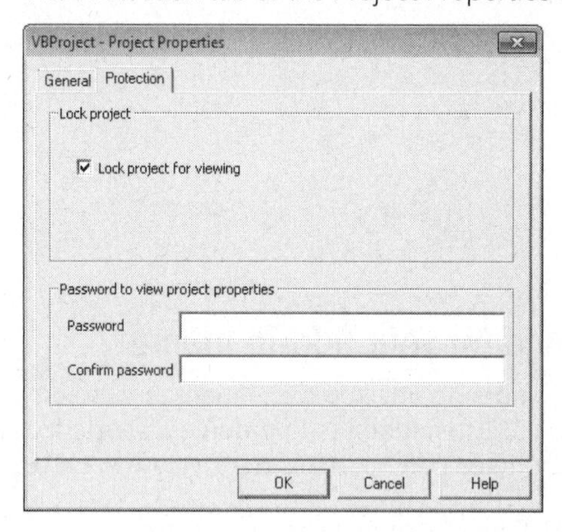

5. **Select the Lock Project for Viewing check box.**
6. **Enter a password (twice) for the project.**
7. **Click OK.**

Creating the add-in

To save the workbook as an add-in, follow these steps:

1. **Switch to the Excel window and activate your workbook.**
2. **Choose File⇨Save As.**
3. **Select Microsoft Excel Add-In (*.xlam) from the Save as Type drop-down list.**
4. **Enter a name for the add-in file, and then click OK.**

   By default, Excel saves the add-in in your `AddIns` directory, but you can choose a different directory if you like.

Installing the add-in

Now it's time to try the add-in. Make sure the XLSM version of the workbook is not open, and then follow these steps:

1. **Choose File⇨Excel Options⇨Add-Ins.**
2. **Select Excel Add-ins from the Manage drop-down list, and click Go.** The Add-Ins dialog box appears.
3. **Click the Browse button and locate and select the change case.xlam add-in that you just created.** The Add-Ins dialog box displays the add-in in its list. Notice that the information that you provided in the Properties panel appears here.
4. **Click OK to close the dialog box and open the add-in.**

When the add-in is installed, you can access it by pressing Ctrl + Shift + C. Another option is to add a new item to your Quick Access toolbar or to the Ribbon.

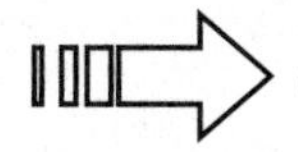

See Chapter 24 for information about customizing Excel's user interface.

Part VII

Appendixes

This part contains two very useful appendixes. Appendix A provides a complete reference of all the worksheet functions. Appendix B covers Excel's shortcut keys.

IN THIS PART

APPENDIX

A

Worksheet Function Reference

This appendix contains a complete list of Excel worksheet functions. The functions are arranged alphabetically by the categories displayed in the Insert Function dialog box.

For more information about a particular function, including its arguments, select the function in the Insert Function dialog box and then click Help on This Function.

For newer functions, the Excel version in which they first appeared is indicated. Knowing when a function first became available is useful if you share your workbooks with people who use an earlier version of Excel.

On the Web

An interactive workbook that contains this information is available on this book's website. The filename is `worksheet functions.xlsx`.

TABLE A.1 Compatibility Category Functions

Function	What It Does
BETADIST	Returns the cumulative beta probability density function.
BETAINV	Returns the inverse of the cumulative beta probability density function.
BINOMDIST	Returns the individual term binomial distribution probability.
CEILING	Rounds a number to the nearest integer or to the nearest multiple of significance.
CHIDIST	Returns the one-tailed probability of the chi-squared distribution.
CHIINV	Returns the inverse of the one-tailed probability of the chi-squared distribution.
CHITEST	Returns the test for independence.
CONFIDENCE	Returns the confidence interval for a population mean.
COVAR	Returns *covariance*, the average of the products of paired deviations.
CRITBINOM	Returns the smallest value for which the cumulative binomial distribution is less than or equal to a criterion value.
EXPONDIST	Returns the exponential distribution.
FDIST	Returns the F probability distribution.
FINV	Returns the inverse of the F probability distribution.

continued

TABLE A.1 *(continued)*

Function	What It Does
FLOOR	Rounds a number down, toward zero.
FTEST	Returns the result of an F-Test.
GAMMADIST	Returns the gamma distribution.
GAMMAINV	Returns the inverse of the gamma cumulative distribution.
HYPGEOMDIST	Returns the hypergeometric distribution.
LOGINV	Returns the inverse of the lognormal distribution.
LOGNORMDIST	Returns the cumulative lognormal distribution.
MODE	Returns the most common value in a data set.
NEGBINOMDIST	Returns the negative binomial distribution.
NORMDIST	Returns the normal cumulative distribution.
NORMINV	Returns the inverse of the normal cumulative distribution.
NORMSDIST	Returns the standard normal cumulative distribution.
NORMSINV	Returns the inverse of the standard normal cumulative distribution.
PERCENTILE	Returns the *k*th percentile of values in a range.
PERCENTRANK	Returns the percentage rank of a value in a data set.
POISSON	Returns the Poisson distribution.
QUARTILE	Returns the quartile of a data set.
RANK	Returns the rank of a number in a list of numbers.
STDEV	Estimates standard deviation based on a sample, ignoring text and logical values.
STDEVP	Calculates standard deviation based on the entire population, ignoring text and logical values.
TDIST	Returns the Student's t-distribution.
TINV	Returns the inverse of the Student's t-distribution.
TTEST	Returns the probability associated with a Student's t-Test.
VAR	Estimates variance based on a sample, ignoring logical values and text.
VARP	Calculates variance based on the entire population, ignoring logical values and text.
WEIBULL	Returns the Weibull distribution.
ZTEST	Returns the two-tailed p-value of a Z-test.

The functions in the Compatibility category all have new versions that were introduced in Excel 2010 or Excel 2013. The new versions are listed in the Statistical or Math & Trigonometry category. The old versions are still available for compatibility.

TABLE A.2 Cube Category Functions

Function	What It Does
CUBEKPIMEMBER*	Returns a key performance indicator name, property, and measure, and displays the name and property in the cell.
CUBEMEMBER*	Returns a member or tuple in a cube hierarchy.
CUBEMEMBERPROPERTY*	Returns the value of a member property in the cube.
CUBERANKEDMEMBER*	Returns the *n*th, or ranked, member in a set.
CUBESET*	Defines a calculated set of members or tuples by sending a set expression to the cube on the server.
CUBESETCOUNT*	Returns the number of items in a set.
CUBEVALUE*	Returns an aggregated value from a cube.

* Indicates a function introduced in Excel 2007.

TABLE A.3 Database Category Functions

Function	What It Does
DAVERAGE	Averages the values in a column of a list or database that match conditions you specify.
DCOUNT	Counts the cells that contain numbers in a column of a list or database that match conditions you specify.
DCOUNTA	Counts the nonblank cells in a column of a list or database that match conditions you specify.
DGET	Extracts a single value from a column of a list or database that matches conditions you specify.
DMAX	Returns the largest number in a column of a list or database that matches conditions you specify.
DMIN	Returns the smallest number in a column of a list or database that matches conditions you specify.
DPRODUCT	Multiplies the values in a column of a list or database that match conditions you specify.
DSTDEV	Estimates the standard deviation of a population based on a sample by using the numbers in a column of a list or database that match conditions you specify.
DSTDEVP	Calculates the standard deviation of a population based on the entire population, using the numbers in a column of a list or database that match conditions you specify.
DSUM	Adds the numbers in a column of a list or database that match conditions you specify.
DVAR	Estimates the variance of a population based on a sample by using the numbers in a column of a list or database that match conditions you specify.
DVARP	Calculates the variance of a population based on the entire population by using the numbers in a column of a list or database that match conditions you specify.

TABLE A.4 Date & Time Category Functions

Function	What It Does
DATE	Returns the serial number of a particular date.
DATEVALUE	Converts a date in the form of text to a serial number.
DAY	Converts a serial number to a day of the month.
DAYS**	Returns the number of days between two dates
DAYS360	Calculates the number of days between two dates, based on a 360-day year.
EDATE	Returns the serial number of the date that is the indicated number of months before or after the start date.
EOMONTH	Returns the serial number of the last day of the month before or after a specified number of months.
HOUR	Converts a serial number to an hour.
ISOWEEKNUM**	Returns the number of the ISO week number of the year for a given date
MINUTE	Converts a serial number to a minute.
MONTH	Converts a serial number to a month.
NETWORKDAYS	Returns the number of whole workdays between two dates.
NETWORKDAYS.INTL*	Returns the number of whole workdays between two dates (international version).
NOW	Returns the serial number of the current date and time.
SECOND	Converts a serial number to a second.
TIME	Returns the serial number of a particular time.
TIMEVALUE	Converts a time in the form of text to a serial number.
TODAY	Returns the serial number of today's date.
WEEKDAY	Converts a serial number to a day of the week.
WEEKNUM	Returns the week number in the year.
WORKDAY	Returns the serial number of the date before or after a specified number of workdays.
WORKDAY.INTL*	Returns the serial number of the date before or after a specified number of workdays (International version).
YEAR	Converts a serial number to a year.
YEARFRAC	Returns the year fraction representing the number of whole days between *start_date* and *end_date*.

* Indicates a function introduced in Excel 2010.

** Indicates a function introduced in Excel 2013.

TABLE A.5 Engineering Category Functions

Function	What It Does
BESSELI	Returns the modified Bessel function In(x).
BESSELJ	Returns the Bessel function Jn(x).
BESSELK	Returns the modified Bessel function Kn(x).
BESSELY	Returns the Bessel function Yn(x).
BIN2DEC	Converts a binary number to decimal.
BIN2HEX	Converts a binary number to hexadecimal.
BIN2OCT	Converts a binary number to octal.
BITAND**	Returns a bitwise AND of two numbers.
BITLSHIFT**	Returns a value number shifted left by shift_amount bits.
BITOR**	Returns a bitwise OR of two numbers.
BITRSHIFT**	Returns a value number shifted right by shift_amount bits.
BITXOR**	Returns a bitwise Exclusive OR of two numbers.
COMPLEX	Converts real and imaginary coefficients into a complex number.
CONVERT	Converts a number from one measurement system to another.
DEC2BIN	Converts a decimal number to binary.
DEC2HEX	Converts a decimal number to hexadecimal.
DEC2OCT	Converts a decimal number to octal.
DELTA	Tests whether two values are equal.
ERF	Returns the error function.
ERF.PRECISE*	Returns the error function.
ERFC	Returns the complementary error function.
ERFC.PRECISE*	Returns the complementary error function.
GESTEP	Tests whether a number is greater than a threshold value.
HEX2BIN	Converts a hexadecimal number to binary.
HEX2DEC	Converts a hexadecimal number to decimal.
HEX2OCT	Converts a hexadecimal number to octal.
IMABS	Returns the absolute value (modulus) of a complex number.
IMAGINARY	Returns the imaginary coefficient of a complex number.
IMARGUMENT	Returns the argument *theta*, an angle expressed in radians.
IMCONJUGATE	Returns the complex conjugate of a complex number.
IMCOS	Returns the cosine of a complex number.
IMCOSH**	Returns the hyperbolic cosine of a complex number.
IMCOT**	Returns the cotangent of a complex number.

continued

TABLE A.5 *(continued)*

Function	What It Does
IMCSC**	Returns the cosecant of a complex number.
IMDIV	Returns the quotient of two complex numbers.
IMEXP	Returns the exponential of a complex number.
IMLN	Returns the natural logarithm of a complex number.
IMLOG10	Returns the base-10 logarithm of a complex number.
IMLOG2	Returns the base-2 logarithm of a complex number.
IMPOWER	Returns a complex number raised to an integer power.
IMPRODUCT	Returns the product of complex numbers.
IMREAL	Returns the real coefficient of a complex number.
IMSEC**	Returns the secant of a complex number
IMSECH**	Returns the hyperbolic secant of a complex number
IMSIN	Returns the sine of a complex number.
IMSINH**	Returns the hyperbolic sine of a complex number.
IMSQRT	Returns the square root of a complex number.
IMSUB	Returns the difference of two complex numbers.
IMSUM	Returns the sum of complex numbers.
IMTAN**	Returns the tangent of a complex number.
OCT2BIN	Converts an octal number to binary.
OCT2DEC	Converts an octal number to decimal.
OCT2HEX	Converts an octal number to hexadecimal.

* Indicates a function introduced in Excel 2010.

** Indicates a function introduced in Excel 2013.

TABLE A.6 Financial Category Functions

Function	What It Does
ACCRINT	Returns the accrued interest for a security that pays periodic interest.
ACCRINTM	Returns the accrued interest for a security that pays interest at maturity.
AMORDEGRC	Returns the depreciation for each accounting period.
AMORLINC	Returns the depreciation for each accounting period. (The depreciation coefficient depends on the life of the assets.)

Function	What It Does
COUPDAYBS	Returns the number of days from the beginning of the coupon period to the settlement date.
COUPDAYS	Returns the number of days in the coupon period that contains the settlement date.
COUPDAYSNC	Returns the number of days from the settlement date to the next coupon date.
COUPNCD	Returns the next coupon date after the settlement date.
COUPNUM	Returns the number of coupons payable between the settlement date and maturity date.
COUPPCD	Returns the previous coupon date before the settlement date.
CUMIPMT	Returns the cumulative interest paid between two periods.
CUMPRINC	Returns the cumulative principal paid on a loan between two periods.
DB	Returns the depreciation of an asset for a specified period, using the fixed declining-balance method.
DDB	Returns the depreciation of an asset for a specified period, using the double declining-balance method or some other method that you specify.
DISC	Returns the discount rate for a security.
DOLLARDE	Converts a dollar price, expressed as a fraction, into a dollar price expressed as a decimal number.
DOLLARFR	Converts a dollar price, expressed as a decimal number, into a dollar price expressed as a fraction.
DURATION	Returns the annual duration of a security with periodic interest payments.
EFFECT	Returns the effective annual interest rate.
FV	Returns the future value of an investment.
FVSCHEDULE	Returns the future value of an initial principal after applying a series of compound interest rates.
INTRATE	Returns the interest rate for a fully invested security.
IPMT	Returns the interest payment for an investment for a given period.
IRR	Returns the internal rate of return for a series of cash flows.
ISPMT	Returns the interest associated with a specific loan payment.
MDURATION	Returns the Macauley modified duration for a security with an assumed par value of $100.
MIRR	Returns the internal rate of return where positive and negative cash flows are financed at different rates.
NOMINAL	Returns the annual nominal interest rate.

continued

TABLE A.6 *(continued)*

Function	What It Does
NPER	Returns the number of periods for an investment.
NPV	Returns the net present value of an investment based on a series of periodic cash flows and a discount rate.
ODDFPRICE	Returns the price per $100 face value of a security with an odd first period.
ODDFYIELD	Returns the yield of a security with an odd first period.
ODDLPRICE	Returns the price per $100 face value of a security with an odd last period.
ODDLYIELD	Returns the yield of a security with an odd last period.
PDURATION*	Returns the number of periods required by an investment to reach a specified value.
PMT	Returns the periodic payment for an annuity.
PPMT	Returns the payment on the principal for an investment for a given period.
PRICE	Returns the price per $100 face value of a security that pays periodic interest.
PRICEDISC	Returns the price per $100 face value of a discounted security.
PRICEMAT	Returns the price per $100 face value of a security that pays interest at maturity.
PV	Returns the present value of an investment.
RATE	Returns the interest rate per period of an annuity.
RECEIVED	Returns the amount received at maturity for a fully invested security.
RRI*	Returns an equivalent interest rate for the growth of an investment.
SLN	Returns the straight-line depreciation of an asset for one period.
SYD	Returns the sum-of-years' digits depreciation of an asset for a specified period.
TBILLEQ	Returns the bond-equivalent yield for a Treasury bill.
TBILLPRICE	Returns the price per $100 face value for a Treasury bill.
TBILLYIELD	Returns the yield for a Treasury bill.
VDB	Returns the depreciation of an asset for a specified or partial period using a double declining-balance method.
XIRR	Returns the internal rate of return for a schedule of cash flows that is not necessarily periodic.
XNPV	Returns the net present value for a schedule of cash flows that is not necessarily periodic.
YIELD	Returns the yield on a security that pays periodic interest.
YIELDDISC	Returns the annual yield for a discounted security, for example, a Treasury bill.
YIELDMAT	Returns the annual yield of a security that pays interest at maturity.

* Indicates a function introduced in Excel 2013.

TABLE A.7 Information Category Functions

Function	What It Does
CELL	Returns information about the formatting, location, or contents of a cell.
ERROR.TYPE	Returns a number corresponding to an error type.
INFO	Returns information about the current operating environment.
ISBLANK	Returns TRUE if the value is blank.
ISERR	Returns TRUE if the value is any error value except #N/A.
ISERROR	Returns TRUE if the value is any error value.
ISEVEN	Returns TRUE if the number is even.
ISFORMULA*	Returns TRUE if there is a reference to a cell that contains a formula.
ISLOGICAL	Returns TRUE if the value is a logical value.
ISNA	Returns TRUE if the value is the #N/A error value.
ISNONTEXT	Returns TRUE if the value is not text.
ISNUMBER	Returns TRUE if the value is a number.
ISODD	Returns TRUE if the number is odd.
ISREF	Returns TRUE if the value is a reference.
ISTEXT	Returns TRUE if the value is text.
N	Returns a value converted to a number.
NA	Returns the error value #N/A.
SHEET*	Returns the sheet number of the referenced sheet.
SHEETS*	Returns the number of sheets in a reference.
TYPE	Returns a number indicating the data type of a value.

* Indicates a function introduced in Excel 2013.

TABLE A.8 Logical Category Functions

Function	What It Does
AND	Returns TRUE if all its arguments are TRUE.
FALSE	Returns the logical value FALSE.
IF	Specifies a logical test to perform.
IFERROR*	Returns a different result if the first argument evaluates to an error.
IFNA**	Returns the value you specify if the expression resolves to #N/A; otherwise, returns the result of the expression.
NOT	Reverses the logic of its argument.

continued

A

TABLE A.8 *(continued)*

Function	What It Does
OR	Returns TRUE if any argument is TRUE.
TRUE	Returns the logical value TRUE.
XOR**	Returns a logical exclusive OR of all arguments

* Indicates a function introduced in Excel 2007.

** Indicates a function introduced in Excel 2013.

TABLE A.9 Lookup & Reference Category Functions

Function	What It Does
ADDRESS	Returns a reference as text to a single cell in a worksheet.
AREAS	Returns the number of areas in a reference.
CHOOSE	Chooses a value from a list of values.
COLUMN	Returns the column number of a reference.
COLUMNS	Returns the number of columns in a reference
FORMULATEXT*	Returns the formula at the given reference as text
GETPIVOTDATA	Returns data stored in a pivot table.
HLOOKUP	Searches for a value in the top row of a table and then returns a value in the same column from a row you specify in the table.
HYPERLINK	Creates a shortcut that opens a document on your hard drive, a server, or the Internet.
INDEX	Uses an index to choose a value from a reference or array.
INDIRECT	Returns a reference indicated by a text value.
LOOKUP	Returns a value from either a one-row or one-column range or from an array.
MATCH	Returns the relative position of an item in an array.
OFFSET	Returns a reference offset from a given reference.
ROW	Returns the row number of a reference.
ROWS	Returns the number of rows in a reference.
RTD	Returns real-time data from a program that supports COM automation.
TRANSPOSE	Returns the transpose of an array.
VLOOKUP	Searches for a value in the leftmost column of a table and then returns a value in the same row from a column you specify in the table.

* Indicates a function introduced in Excel 2013.

TABLE A.10 Math & Trig Category Functions

Function	What It Does
ABS	Returns the absolute value of a number.
ACOS	Returns the arccosine of a number.
ACOSH	Returns the inverse hyperbolic cosine of a number.
ACOT***	Returns the arccotangent of a number
ACOTH***	Returns the hyperbolic arccotangent of a number
AGGREGATE**	Returns an aggregate in a list or database.
ARABIC***	Converts a Roman number to Arabic, as a number.
ASIN	Returns the arcsine of a number.
ASINH	Returns the inverse hyperbolic sine of a number.
ATAN	Returns the arctangent of a number.
ATAN2	Returns the arctangent from *x* and *y* coordinates.
ATANH	Returns the inverse hyperbolic tangent of a number.
BASE***	Converts a number into a text representation with the given radix (base).
CEILING.MATH***	Rounds a number up, to the nearest integer or to the nearest multiple of significance.
COMBIN	Returns the number of combinations for a given number of objects.
COMBINA***	Returns the number of combinations with repetitions for a given number of items.
COS	Returns the cosine of a number.
COSH	Returns the hyperbolic cosine of a number.
COT***	Returns the cotangent of an angle.
COTH***	Returns the hyperbolic cotangent of a number.
CSC***	Returns the cosecant of an angle.
CSCH***	Returns the hyperbolic cosecant of an angle.
DECIMAL***	Converts a text representation of a number in a given base into a decimal number.
DEGREES	Converts radians to degrees.
EVEN	Rounds a number up to the nearest even integer.
EXP	Returns *e* raised to the power of a given number.
FACT	Returns the factorial of a number.
FACTDOUBLE	Returns the double factorial of a number.

continued

A

TABLE A.10 *(continued)*

Function	What It Does
FLOOR.MATH***	Rounds a number down, to the nearest integer or to the nearest multiple of significance.
GCD	Returns the greatest common divisor.
INT	Rounds a number down to the nearest integer.
LCM	Returns the least common multiple.
LN	Returns the natural logarithm of a number.
LOG	Returns the logarithm of a number to a specified base.
LOG10	Returns the base-10 logarithm of a number.
MDETERM	Returns the matrix determinant of an array.
MINVERSE	Returns the matrix inverse of an array.
MMULT	Returns the matrix product of two arrays.
MOD	Returns the remainder from division.
MROUND	Returns a number rounded to the desired multiple.
MULTINOMIAL	Returns the multinomial of a set of numbers.
MUNIT***	Returns the unit matrix or the specified dimension.
ODD	Rounds a number up to the nearest odd integer.
PI	Returns the value of pi.
POWER	Returns the result of a number raised to a power.
PRODUCT	Multiplies its arguments.
QUOTIENT	Returns the integer portion of a division.
RADIANS	Converts degrees to radians.
RAND	Returns a random number between 0 and 1.
RANDBETWEEN	Returns a random number between the numbers that you specify.
ROMAN	Converts an Arabic numeral to Roman, as text.
ROUND	Rounds a number to a specified number of digits.
ROUNDDOWN	Rounds a number down, toward zero.
ROUNDUP	Rounds a number up, away from zero.
SEC***	Returns the secant of an angle.
SECH***	Returns the hyperbolic secant of an angle.
SERIESSUM	Returns the sum of a power series based on the formula.
SIGN	Returns the sign of a number.
SIN	Returns the sine of the given angle.
SINH	Returns the hyperbolic sine of a number.

Function	What It Does
SQRT	Returns a positive square root.
SQRTPI	Returns the square root of pi.
SUBTOTAL	Returns a subtotal in a list or database.
SUM	Adds its arguments.
SUMIF	Adds the cells specified by a given criteria.
SUMIFS*	Adds the cells specified by a multiple criteria.
SUMPRODUCT	Returns the sum of the products of corresponding array components.
SUMSQ	Returns the sum of the squares of the arguments.
SUMX2MY2**	Returns the sum of the difference of squares of corresponding values in two arrays.
SUMX2PY2**	Returns the sum of the sum of squares of corresponding values in two arrays.
SUMXMY2**	Returns the sum of squares of differences of corresponding values in two arrays.
TAN	Returns the tangent of a number.
TANH	Returns the hyperbolic tangent of a number.
TRUNC	Truncates a number (you specify the precision of the truncation).

* Indicates a function introduced in Excel 2007.

** Indicates a function introduced in Excel 2010.

*** Indicates a function introduced in Excel 2013.

TABLE A.11 Statistical Category Functions

Function	What It Does
AVEDEV	Returns the average of the absolute deviations of data points from their mean.
AVERAGE	Returns the average of its arguments.
AVERAGEA	Returns the average of its arguments and includes evaluation of text and logical values.
AVERAGEIF*	Returns the average for the cells specified by a given criterion.
AVERAGEIFS*	Returns the average for the cells specified by multiple criteria.
BETA.DIST**	Returns the beta cumulative distribution function.
BETA.INV**	Returns the inverse of the cumulative distribution function for a specified beta distribution.
BINOM.DIST**	Returns the individual term binomial distribution probability.

continued

A

TABLE A.11 *(continued)*

Function	What It Does
BINOM.DIST.RANGE***	Returns the probability of a trial result using a binomial distribution.
BINOM.INV**	Returns the smallest value for which the cumulative binomial distribution is less than or equal to a criterion value.
CHISQ.DIST**	Returns the chi-square distribution.
CHISQ.DIST.RT**	Returns the right-tailed probability of the chi-squared distribution.
CHISQ.INV**	Returns the inverse of the left-tailed probability of the chi-squared distribution.
CHISQ.INV.RT**	Returns the inverse of the right-tailed probability of the chi-squared distribution.
CHISQ.TEST**	Returns the test for independence.
CONFIDENCE.NORM**	Returns the confidence interval for a population mean.
CONFIDENCE.T**	Returns the confidence interval for a population mean, using a student's t-distribution.
CORREL	Returns the correlation coefficient between two data sets.
COUNT	Counts how many numbers are in the list of arguments.
COUNTA	Counts how many values are in the list of arguments.
COUNTBLANK	Counts the number of blank cells in the argument range.
COUNTIF	Counts the number of cells that meet the criteria you specify in the argument.
COUNTIFS*	Counts the number of cells that meet multiple criteria.
COVARIANCE.P**	Returns covariance, the average of the products of paired deviations.
COVARIANCE.S**	Returns the sample covariance, the average of the products deviations for each data point pair in two data sets.
DEVSQ	Returns the sum of squares of deviations.
EXPON.DIST**	Returns the exponential distribution.
F.DIST**	Returns the F probability distribution.
F.DIST.RT**	Returns the F probability distribution.
F.INV**	Returns the inverse of the F probability distribution.
F.INV.RT**	Returns the inverse of the F probability distribution.
F.TEST**	Returns the result of an F-test.
FISHER	Returns the Fisher transformation.
FISHERINV	Returns the inverse of the Fisher transformation.
FORECAST	Returns a value along a linear trend.

Function	What It Does
FREQUENCY	Returns a frequency distribution as a vertical array.
GAMMA***	Returns the Gamma function value
GAMMA.DIST**	Returns the gamma distribution.
GAMMA.INV**	Returns the inverse of the gamma cumulative distribution.
GAMMALN	Returns the natural logarithm of the gamma function, G(x).
GAMMALN.PRECISE**	Returns the natural logarithm of the gamma function, G(x).
GAUSS***	Returns 0.5 less than the standard normal cumulative distribution.
GEOMEAN	Returns the geometric mean.
GROWTH	Returns values along an exponential trend.
HARMEAN	Returns the harmonic mean.
HYPGEOM.DIST**	Returns the hypergeometric distribution.
INTERCEPT	Returns the intercept of the linear regression line.
KURT	Returns the kurtosis of a data set.
LARGE	Returns the *k*th largest value in a data set.
LINEST	Returns the parameters of a linear trend.
LOGEST	Returns the parameters of an exponential trend.
LOGNORM.DIST**	Returns the cumulative lognormal distribution.
LOGNORM.INV**	Returns the inverse of the lognormal cumulative distribution.
MAX	Returns the maximum value in a list of arguments, ignoring logical values and text.
MAXA	Returns the maximum value in a list of arguments, including logical values and text.
MEDIAN	Returns the median of the given numbers.
MIN	Returns the minimum value in a list of arguments, ignoring logical values and text.
MINA	Returns the minimum value in a list of arguments, including logical values and text.
MODE.MULT**	Returns a vertical array of the most frequently occurring or repetitive values in an array or range of data.
MODE.SNGL**	Returns the most common value in a data set.
NEGBINOM.DIST**	Returns the negative binomial distribution.
NORM.DIST**	Returns the normal cumulative distribution.
NORM.INV**	Returns the inverse of the normal cumulative distribution.
NORM.S.DIST**	Returns the standard normal cumulative distribution.

continued

TABLE A.11 *(continued)*

Function	What It Does
NORM.S.INV**	Returns the inverse of the standard normal cumulative distribution.
PEARSON	Returns the Pearson product moment correlation coefficient.
PERCENTILE.EXC**	Returns the *k*th percentile of values in a range, where *k* is in the range 0 through 1, exclusive.
PERCENTILE.INC**	Returns the *k*th percentile of values in a range.
PERCENTRANK.EXC**	Returns the rank of a value in a data set as a percentage (0 through 1, exclusive) of the data set.
PERCENTRANK.INC**	Returns the percentage rank of a value in a data set.
PERMUT	Returns the number of permutations for a given number of objects.
PERMUTATIONA***	Returns the number of permutations for a given number of objects (with repetitions) that can be selected from the total objects.
PHI***	Returns the value of the density function for a standard normal distribution.
POISSON.DIST**	Returns the Poisson distribution.
PROB	Returns the probability that values in a range are between two limits.
QUARTILE.EXC**	Returns the quartile of the data set, based on percentile values from 0 through 1, exclusive.
QUARTILE.INC**	Returns the quartile of a data set.
RANK.AVG**	Returns the rank of a number in a list of numbers.
RANK.EQ**	Returns the rank of a number in a list of numbers.
RSQ	Returns the square of the Pearson product moment correlation coefficient.
SKEW	Returns the skewness of a distribution.
SKEW.P***	Returns the skewness of a distribution based on a population: a characterization of the degree of asymmetry of a distribution around its mean.
SLOPE	Returns the slope of the linear regression line.
SMALL	Returns the *k*th smallest value in a data set.
STANDARDIZE	Returns a normalized value.
STDEV.P**	Calculates standard deviation based on the entire population.
STDEV.S**	Estimates standard deviation based on a sample.
STDEVA	Estimates standard deviation based on a sample, including text and logical values.
STDEVPA	Calculates standard deviation based on the entire population, including text and logical values.

Function	What It Does
STEYX	Returns the standard error of the predicted *y*-value for each *x* in the regression.
T.DIST	Returns the Percentage Points (probability) for the student T-distribution.
T.DIST.2T**	Returns the Percentage Points (probability) for the Student T-distribution.
T.DIST.RT**	Returns the student's T-distribution.
T.INV**	Returns the t-value of the student's T-distribution as a function of the probability and the degrees of freedom.
T.INV.2T**	Returns the inverse of the student's T-distribution.
T.TEST**	Returns the probability associated with a student's T-test.
TREND	Returns values along a linear trend.
TRIMMEAN	Returns the mean of the interior of a data set.
VAR.P**	Calculates variance based on the entire population.
VAR.S**	Estimates variance based on a sample.
VARA	Estimates variance based on a sample, including logical values and text.
VARPA	Calculates variance based on the entire population, including logical values and text.
WEIBULL.DIST**	Returns the Weibull distribution.
Z.TEST**	Returns the one-tailed probability-value of a Z-test.

* Indicates a function introduced in Excel 2007.

** Indicates a function introduced in Excel 2010.

*** Indicates a function introduced in Excel 2013.

TABLE A.12 Text Category Functions

Function	What It Does
BAHTTEXT	Converts a number to Baht text.
CHAR	Returns the character specified by the code number.
CLEAN	Removes all nonprintable characters from text.
CODE	Returns a numeric code for the first character in a text string.
CONCATENATE	Joins several text items into one text item.
DOLLAR	Converts a number to text, using currency format.

continued

TABLE A.12 *(continued)*

Function	What It Does
EXACT	Checks to see whether two text values are identical.
FIND	Finds one text value within another (case-sensitive).
FIXED	Formats a number as text with a fixed number of decimals.
LEFT	Returns the leftmost characters from a text value.
LEN	Returns the number of characters in a text string.
LOWER	Converts text to lowercase.
MID	Returns a specific number of characters from a text string, starting at the position you specify.
NUMBERVALUE*	Converts text to number in a locale-independent manner.
PROPER	Capitalizes the first letter in each word of a text value.
REPLACE	Replaces characters within text.
REPT	Repeats text a given number of times.
RIGHT	Returns the rightmost characters from a text value.
SEARCH	Finds one text value within another (not case sensitive).
SUBSTITUTE	Substitutes new text for old text in a text string.
T	Returns the text referred to by value.
TEXT	Formats a number and converts it to text.
TRIM	Removes excess spaces from text.
UNICHAR*	Returns the Unicode character that is references by the given numeric value.
UNICODE*	Returns the number (code point) that corresponds to the first character of the text.
UPPER	Converts text to uppercase.
VALUE	Converts a text argument to a number.

* Indicates a function introduced in Excel 2013.

TABLE A.13 Web Category Functions

Function	What It Does
ENCODEURL*	Returns a URL-encoded string.
FILTERXML*	Returns specific data from the XML content by using the specified xpath.
WEBSERVICE*	Returns data from a web service.

* Indicates a function introduced in Excel 2013.

APPENDIX

B

Excel Shortcut Keys

Many users have discovered that using their keyboard can often be much more efficient than using their mouse. This appendix lists the most useful shortcut keys available in Excel. The shortcuts are arranged by context.

The keys listed assume that you're *not* using the Transition Navigation Keys, which are designed to emulate Lotus 1-2-3. You can select the Transition Navigation Keys option of the Advanced tab of the Excel Options dialog box (in the Lotus Compatibility section).

NOTE

On the surface, the Ribbon interface appears to be designed for a mouse. However, you can access nearly all the Ribbon commands by using the keyboard. Press the Alt key, and Excel displays "keytips" next to each command. Just press the key that corresponds to the command you need. For example, the command to toggle worksheet gridlines is View ⇨ Show ⇨ Gridlines. The keyboard equivalent is Alt, followed by WVG. Note that you don't need to keep the Alt key depressed while you type the subsequent letters.

TABLE B.1 Moving through a Worksheet

Key(s)	What It Does
Navigation keys (←, →, ↑, ↓)	Moves left, right, up, or down one cell
Navigation keys* (←, →, ↑, ↓)	Scrolls left, right, up, or down one cell
Home	Moves to the beginning of the row
Home*	Moves to the upper-left cell displayed in the window
End*	Moves to the lower-left cell displayed in the window
PgUp	Moves up one screen
PgDn	Moves down one screen
Ctrl+PgUp	Moves to the previous sheet
Ctrl+PgDn	Moves to the next sheet
Alt+PgUp	Moves one screen to the left
Alt+PgDn	Moves one screen to the right
Ctrl+Home	Moves to the first cell in the worksheet (A1)
Ctrl+End	Moves to the last nonempty cell of the worksheet
Ctrl+navigation key	Moves to the edge of a data block; if the cell is blank, moves to the first nonblank cell

continued

TABLE B.1 *(continued)*

Key(s)	What It Does
Ctrl+Backspace	Scrolls to display the active cell
End, followed by Home	Moves to the last nonempty cell on the worksheet
F5	Prompts for a cell address to go to
F6	Moves to the next pane of a window that has been split
Shift+F6	Moves to the previous pane of a window that has been split
Ctrl+Tab	Moves to the next window
Ctrl+Shift+Tab	Moves to the previous window
Ctrl+F6	Moves to the next window
Ctrl+Shift+F6	Moves to the previous window

* With Scroll Lock on

TABLE B.2 Selecting Cells in the Worksheet

Key(s)	What It Does
Shift+navigation key	Expands the selection in the direction indicated.
Shift+spacebar	Selects the entire row(s) in the selected range.
Ctrl+spacebar	Selects the entire column(s) in the selected range.
Ctrl+Shift+spacebar	Selects the entire worksheet.
Ctrl+Shift+spacebar	If the active cell is within a table, selects the table without the header row and totals row. Pressing Ctrl+Shift+spacebar again selects the complete table. Pressing Ctrl+Shift+spacebar again selects the entire worksheet.
Shift+Home	Expands the selection to the beginning of the current row.
Ctrl+*	If the active cell is within a multicell range, selects the block of data surrounding the active cell.
F8	Extends the selection as you use navigation keys. Press F8 again to return to normal selection mode.
Shift+F8	Adds other nonadjacent cells or ranges to the selection; pressing Shift+F8 again ends Add mode.
F5	Prompts for a range or range name to select.
Ctrl+G	Prompts for a range or range name to select.
Ctrl+A	Selects the entire worksheet.
Ctrl+A	If the active cell is within a table. Selects the table without the header row and totals row. Pressing Ctrl+Shift+spacebar again selects the complete table. Pressing Ctrl+Shift+spacebar again selects the entire worksheet.
Shift+Backspace	Cancels a range selection and selects only the active cell.

TABLE B.3 Moving within a Range Selection

Key(s)	What It Does
Enter	Moves the cell pointer. The direction depends on the setting in the Edit tab of the Options dialog box.
Shift+Enter	Moves the cell pointer up to the preceding cell in the selection.
Tab	Moves the cell pointer right to the next cell in the selection.
Shift+Tab	Moves the cell pointer left to the preceding cell in the selection.
Ctrl+. (period)	Moves the cell pointer to the next corner of the current cell range.
Shift+Backspace	Collapses the cell selection to just the active cell.

TABLE B.4 Editing Keys in the Formula Bar

Key(s)	What It Does
F2	Begins editing the active cell
Navigation keys	Moves the cursor one character in the direction of the arrow
Home	Moves the cursor to the beginning of the line
End	Moves the cursor to the end of the line
Ctrl+→	Moves the cursor one word to the right
Ctrl+←	Moves the cursor one word to the left
F3	Displays the Paste Name dialog box when you're creating a formula
Ctrl+A	Displays the Function Arguments dialog box (after you type a function name in a formula)
Del(ete)	Deletes the character to the right of the cursor
Ctrl+Del(ete)	Deletes all characters from the cursor to the end of the line
Backspace	Deletes the character to the left of the cursor
Esc	Cancels the editing

TABLE B.5 Formatting Keys

Key(s)	What It Does
Ctrl+1	Displays the Format dialog box for the selected object
Ctrl+B	Sets or removes boldface
Ctrl+I	Sets or removes italic
Ctrl+U	Sets or removes underlining

continued

TABLE B.5 *(continued)*

Key(s)	What It Does
Ctrl+5	Sets or removes strikethrough
Ctrl+Shift+~	Applies the general number format
Ctrl+Shift+!	Applies the comma format with two decimal places
Ctrl+Shift+#	Applies the date format (day, month, year)
Ctrl+Shift+@	Applies the time format (hour, minute, a.m./p.m.)
Ctrl+Shift+$	Applies the currency format with two decimal places
Ctrl+Shift+%	Applies the percent format with no decimal places
Ctrl+Shift+&	Applies border to outline
Ctrl+Shift+_	Removes all borders

TABLE B.6 Other Shortcut Keys

Key(s)	What It Does
Ctrl+F1	Toggles the display of the Ribbon
Alt+=	Inserts the AutoSum formula
Alt+Backspace	Undo
Alt+Enter	Starts a new line in the current cell
Ctrl+;	Enters the current date
Ctrl+:	Enters the current time
Ctrl+0 (zero)	Hides columns
Ctrl+6	Cycles among various ways of displaying objects on a worksheet
Ctrl+8	Toggles the display of outline symbols
Ctrl+9	Hides rows
Ctrl+[	Selects direct precedent cells
Ctrl+]	Selects directly dependent cells
Ctrl+C	Equivalent to Home ➪ Clipboard ➪ Copy
Ctrl+D	Equivalent to Home ➪ Editing ➪ Fill ➪ Down
Ctrl+F	Equivalent to Home ➪ Editing ➪ Find & Select ➪ Find
Ctrl+H	Equivalent to Home ➪ Editing ➪ Find & Select ➪ Replace
Ctrl+K	Equivalent to Insert ➪ Links ➪ Hyperlink
Ctrl+N	Creates a new workbook
Ctrl+O	Equivalent to File ➪ Open
Ctrl+P	Equivalent to File ➪ Print

B

Key(s)	What It Does
Ctrl+R	Equivalent to Home ➪ Editing ➪ Fill ➪ Fill Right
Ctrl+T	Equivalent to Insert ➪ Tables ➪ Table
Ctrl+Shift+T	Toggles the Total row in a table
Ctrl+Shift+L	Toggles the AutoFilter controls in a table
Ctrl+S	Equivalent to File ➪ Save
Ctlr+Alt+V	Equivalent to Home ➪ Clipboard ➪ Paste ➪ Paste Special
Ctrl+Shift+(	Unhides rows in the selection
Ctrl+Shift+)	Unhides columns in the selection
Ctrl+Shift+A	Inserts the argument names and parentheses for the function (after you type a valid function name in a formula)
Ctrl+V	Equivalent to Home ➪ Clipboard ➪ Paste
Ctrl+X	Equivalent to Home ➪ Clipboard ➪ Cut
Ctrl+Z	Undo

TABLE B.7 Function Keys

Key(s)	What It Does
F1	Displays Help
Alt+F1	Inserts default chart object that uses the selected range
Alt+Shift+F1	Inserts a new worksheet
F2	Edits the active cell
Shift+F2	Edits a cell comment
Alt+F2	Equivalent to File ➪ Save As
Alt+Shift+F2	Equivalent to File ➪ Save
F3	Pastes a name into a formula
Shift+F3	Pastes a function into a formula
Ctrl+F3	Equivalent to Formulas ➪ Defined Names ➪ Name Manager
Ctrl+Shift+F3	Equivalent to Formulas ➪ Defined Names ➪ Create From Selection
F4	Repeats the last action
Shift+F4	Repeats the last Find (Find Next)
Ctrl+F4	Closes the window
Alt+F4	Equivalent to File ➪ Exit

continued

TABLE B.7 *(continued)*

Key(s)	What It Does
F5	Equivalent to Home ➪ Editing ➪ Find & Select ➪ Go To
Shift+F5	Equivalent to Home ➪ Editing ➪ Find & Select ➪ Find
Ctrl+F5	Restores a minimized or maximized workbook window
Alt+F5	Refreshes active query or pivot table
F6	Moves to the next pane
Shift+F6	Moves to the previous pane
Ctrl+F6	Activates to the next window
Ctrl+Shift+F6	Activates the previous workbook window
F7	Equivalent to Review ➪ Proofing ➪ Spelling
Ctrl+F7	Allows moving the window with the arrow keys
F8	Extends a selection (toggle)
Shift+F8	Adds to the selection (toggle)
Ctrl+F8	Allows resizing the window with the arrow keys
Alt+F8	Equivalent to View ➪ Macros ➪ Macros, or Developer ➪ Code ➪ Macros
F9	Calculates all sheets in all open workbooks
Shift+F9	Calculates the active worksheet
Ctrl+Alt+F9	Global calculation
Ctrl+F9	Minimizes the workbook window
Ctrl+Alt+Shift+F9	Rebuilds all dependencies and recalculates
F10	Displays keytips for the Ribbon
Shift+F10	Displays a shortcut menu for the selected object (equivalent to right-clicking)
Ctrl+F10	Maximizes or restores the workbook window
F11	Creates a chart in a chart sheet
Shift+F11	Inserts a new worksheet
Ctrl+F11	Inserts an Excel 4.0 macro sheet
Alt+F11	Equivalent to Developer ➪ Code ➪ Visual Basic
F12	Equivalent to File ➪ Save
Shift+F12	Equivalent to File ➪ Save As
Ctrl+F12	Equivalent to File ➪ Open
Ctrl+Shift+F12	Equivalent to File ➪ Print

Index

SPECIAL CHARACTERS AND NUMERICS

A

B

C

D

F

G

H

J

K

L

M

N

Q

R

S

T

U

V

W

X

Y

Z